Lecture Notes in Computer Science 666
Edited by G. Goos and J. Hartmanis

J.W. de Bakker W.-P. de Roever
G. Rozenberg (Eds.)

Semantics: Foundations and Applications

REX Workshop
Beekbergen, The Netherlands, June 1-4, 1992
Proceedings

Springer-Verlag
Berlin Heidelberg New York
London Paris Tokyo
Hong Kong Barcelona
Budapest

Series Editors

Gerhard Goos
Universität Karlsruhe
Postfach 69 80
Vincenz-Priessnitz-Straße 1
W-7500 Karlsruhe, FRG

Juris Hartmanis
Cornell University
Department of Computer Science
4130 Upson Hall
Ithaca, NY 14853, USA

Volume Editors

J. W. de Bakker
Centre for Mathematics and Computer Science
P. O. Box 4079, 1009 AB Amsterdam, The Netherlands

W.-P. de Roever
Institute of Computer Science and Practical Mathematics II
Christian-Albrechts-Universität zu Kiel, Preußerstraße 1-9, W-2300 Kiel, FRG

G. Rozenberg
Department of Computer Science, Leiden University
P. O. Box 9512, 2300 RA Leiden, The Netherlands

CR Subject Classification (1991): F.3, D.1-3

ISBN 3-540-56596-5 Springer-Verlag Berlin Heidelberg New York
ISBN 0-387-56596-5 Springer-Verlag New York Berlin Heidelberg

Typesetting: Camera ready by author/editor
45/3140-543210 - Printed on acid-free paper

Preface

The aim of the workshop on 'Semantics - Foundations and Applications' was to bring together researchers working on the semantics of programming languages. Faithfully reflecting the rich variety in present-day semantic research, the program of the workshop included presentations on a wide range of topics situated in the two areas:

Foundations

- comparative domain theory, category theory, information systems,

Applications

- concurrency - process algebras, asynchronous communication, trace nets, action semantics, process refinement, concurrent constraint programming,
- predicate transformers, refinement, weakest preconditions,
- comparative semantics of programming concepts, full abstraction,
- reasoning about programs - total correctness, epistemic logic,
- logic programming,
- functional programming - sequentiality, integration with concurrency,
- applied structured operational semantics,

and several others.

The present volume is based on this meeting which the editors organized June 1-4, 1992, in Conference Centre De Wipselberg, Beekbergen, The Netherlands. The workshop was an activity of the project REX - Research and Education in Concurrent Systems, one of the projects sponsored by the Netherlands NFI (Nationale Faciliteit Informatica) Programme. A short description of the REX project is given below.

The material presented in this volume was prepared by the lecturers (and their coauthors) after the meeting took place - in this way the papers also reflect the discussions that took place during the workshop. The editors moreover invited a few authors to contribute papers not based on work presented during the meeting. We were fortunate to enjoy the cooperation of such an excellent group of lecturers and further participants. We are grateful to all of them for contributing to the success of the event. Special thanks go to Jan Rutten for his help in preparing the scientific program of the workshop.

We gratefully acknowledge the financial support for the workshop from the NFI programme.

The CWI, Amsterdam, was responsible for the technical organization of the meeting. The local organization was in the capable hands of Mieke Bruné and Frans Snijders.

The REX project

The REX - Research and Education in Concurrent Systems - project investigates syntactic, semantic and proof-theoretic aspects of concurrency. In addition, its objectives are the education of young researchers and, in general, the dissemination of scientific results relating to these themes. REX is a collaborative effort of Leiden University (G. Rozenberg), the CWI in Amsterdam (J.W. de Bakker), and the Eindhoven University of Technology (W.P. de Roever), representing the areas of syntax, semantics and proof theory, respectively. The project is supported by the Netherlands National Facility for Informatics (NFI); its duration is approximately six years starting in 1988. The educational activities of REX include regular "concurrency days", consisting of tutorial introductions, presentations of research results, and lecture series of visiting professors. The research activities of the REX project include, more specifically:

a) Three subprojects devoted to the themes: syntax of concurrent systems; comparative semantics, metric transition systems and domain theory; and high-level specification and refinement of real-time distributed systems.
b) Collaboration with visiting professors and post-doctoral researchers.
c) Workshops and Schools. Aiming at a broad coverage of major themes in, or relating to, concurrency, REX has organized the following events:

1988	Linear Time, Branching Time and Partial Order in Logics and Models for Concurrency Proceedings published as Springer Lecture Notes in Computer Science 354
1989	Stepwise Refinement of Distributed Systems - Models, Formalisms, Correctness LNCS 430
1990	Foundations of Object-Oriented Languages LNCS 489
1991	Real-Time: Theory in Practice LNCS 600
1992	Semantics: Foundations and Applications These Proceedings.

The project closes in 1993 with the School/Symposium "A Decade of Concurrency - Reflections and Perspectives", where the accomplishments in the field of concurrency will be surveyed and a look into the future will be attempted as to (un)expected developments.

February 1993

J.W. de Bakker
W.P. de Roever
G. Rozenberg

Table of Contents

Predicate Transformers and Higher Order Logic

R.J.R. Back
Åbo Akademi University, Department ofComputer Science
Lemminkäinengatan 14, SF-20520 Åbo, Finland

J. von Wright
Swedish School of Economics and Business Education
Biblioteksgatan 16, SF-65100 Vasa, Finland

ABSTRACT Predicate transformers are formalized in higher order logic. This gives a basis for mechanized reasoning about total correctness and refinement of programs. The notions of program variables and logical variables are explicated in the formalization. We show how to describe common program constructs, such as assignment statements, sequential and conditional composition, iteration, recursion, blocks and procedures with parameters, are described as predicate transformers in this framework. We also describe some specification oriented constructs, such as assert statements, guards and nondeterministic assignments. The monotonicity of these constructs over the lattice of predicates is proved, as well as the monotonicity of the statement constructors with respect to the refinement ordering on predicate transformers.

Key words Stepwise refinement, weakest preconditions, total correctness, predicate transformers, higher order logic, HOL, semantics of programming languages, state spaces, nondeterminism, procedures

CONTENTS

1 Introduction

1. Statements of a programming language can be given a semantics by associating every statement with a predicate transformer, i.e., a function mapping predicates to predicates. The *weakest precondition* semantics associates a statement with a predicate transformer with the following property: each postcondition is mapped to the weakest precondition that guarantees that the execution of the statement will terminate in a final state that satisfies the postcondition. This semantic interpretation of statements is useful for reasoning about total correctness and refinement of programs and specifications [5, 1].

The proofs used in such reasoning are usually semi-formal, done in the tradition of classical mathematics. This proof method generally works well, but there are situations when a higher level of formality is desirable. For example, reasoning about blocks with local variables is often done without an exact definition of the status of the local variables.

In this paper we show how reasoning in the weakest precondition framework can be given a solid logical foundation by using higher order logic (simple type theory) as a basis. We describe a programming notation that covers basic programming constructs, as well as blocks with local variables, recursion and procedures with parameters. Statements are predicate transformers, defined as terms of higher order logic. This formalization captures the weakest precondition semantics of the corresponding traditional programming notations.

An important property of statements in the weakest precondition calculus is monotonicity. All reasonable statements of a programming notation should denote monotonic predicate transformers. Statement constructors should also be monotonic with respect to the refinement relation on statements [1]. We prove that all the statement constructors introduced here have both these monotonicity properties.

2. One of our main motivations for this work is the desire to mechanize reasoning about programs, using a theorem prover based on simple type theory. One such prover is HOL [6], and we have admittedly been inspired by the HOL logic when we developed this theory. Our aim is to overcome some of the problems encountered in formalizing the theory of imperative languages using theorem provers [7, 6, 4].

The formalization of predicate transformers and refinement calculus as described here has in fact been implemented in HOL as a mechanized theory. The monotonicity results stated here have also all been constructed and checked in HOL.

3. The paper is organized as follows. In the next section, we give a very brief overview of higher order logic. In Section 3 we describe the basic ideas underlying our formalization of predicate transformers. Section 4 shows how to define basic program statements within this framework. Section 5 introduces

some additional constructs, that are found useful in practice, and which can be defined in terms of the basic constructs. Section 6 proves that all the constructs introduced have the required monotonicity properties. Section 7 ends with a few comments and remarks.

2 Higher order logic

1. The logic assumed is a polymorphic higher order logic. We assume that there is a collection of basic types. Every type σ is interpreted as a set (also denoted σ). Examples of basic types are `bool` (the booleans), `num` (the natural numbers) and `int` (the integers). We adopt the convention that constants and type names are written in typewriter font.

We use traditional symbols for logical connectives. The boolean truth values are denoted `F` (falsity) and `T` (truth). The scope of binders ($\forall$, $\exists$ and λ) extends as far to the right as possible.

From the basic types we can form new types by repeatedly applying *type constructors*: we will need only product types $\sigma \times \tau$ and function types $\sigma \to \tau$, defined as usual. For a given type σ, the *predicate type* $\overline{\sigma}$ is defined by

$$\overline{\sigma} \stackrel{\text{def}}{=} \sigma \to \texttt{bool}.$$

This type is so common in our treatment that it is convenient to have it as an abbreviation.

2. The elements of $\overline{\sigma}$ can also be interpreted as sets, by identifying a set with its characteristic function. Thus p is identified with the set

$$\{s \mid p\,s\}$$

Then we can write e.g., $\emptyset$ for `false` and $p \cup q$ for $p \wedge q$. We also have that $v \in p$ is equivalent to $p\,v$. We will use the predicate and the set notation interchangeably, choosing whichever is more convenient for the moment.

We also generalize the set notation in the following way: for arbitrary $q : \alpha \to \beta$ and $p : \alpha \to \texttt{bool}$ the notation

$$\{q\,s \mid s : p\,s\}$$

(the set of all $q\,s$ where s ranges over all values such that $p\,s$ holds) stands for the corresponding characteristic function

$$\lambda s'.\, \exists s.\, p\,s \wedge (s' = q\,s)$$

3. In the HOL system, rigorous proofs are carried out within the framework of a sequent calculus. In order to make proofs shorter, we use an informal calculational proof style in this paper. However, all proofs are easily transformed into formal proofs.

Since the logic is higher-order, we permit quantification and lambda abstraction over arbitrary types. Functions can have arguments of any type. New constants can be introduced by simple definitions. When defining a function f we often write

$$f\,x \stackrel{\text{def}}{=} E$$

rather than the equivalent $f \stackrel{\text{def}}{=} \lambda x.\, E$. Note that in a definition such as (1), all free variables of E must occur free on the left hand side also.

4. We permit type variables α, β and γ in types. A type variable can be instantiated to any type (even to a type containing type variables). This means that we can define *polymorphic constants*. An example of a polymorphic constant is infix equality, with type

$$= : \alpha \to \alpha \to \texttt{bool}$$

(the fact that a term t has type σ is indicated by writing $t : \sigma$).

As another example, the everywhere false predicate is defined by pointwise extension:

$$\texttt{false} \stackrel{\text{def}}{=} (\lambda v : \alpha . \mathrm{F})$$

Note how powerful the definition of a polymorphic constant is: we have one single definition of **false**, but it has many possible instantiations. For example, instantiating the type variable to **int** gives $\texttt{false} : \overline{\texttt{int}}$.

3 Basic domains

1. A predicate on program variables is not the same thing as a boolean formula over program variables. In programming logic, these two things are often identified (or confused). This is the case in, e.g., Hoare logic, where program variables are free variables in formulas. A Hoare triple is written as $P\{S\}Q$, where P and Q are predicates and S is a statement. The Hoare triple

$$x \geq y \, \{x := x + 1\} \, x > y$$

does not identify the program variables are: x and y can be the program variables, or maybe x is the only program variable. In the latter case, we would have to interpret y as a logical variable (unless it happens to be some constant in the underlying domain). There may also be some other program variables, such as z, which happen not to occur in the pre-and postconditions, nor in the statement.

The merit of this approach is that it simplifies the notation and calculations. However, the advantage is often offset by the conceptual confusion that results from interpreting program variables as free variables. A typical case in point is the interpretation of logical variables. Often one assumes that there are two classes of variables, program variables and logical variables, and that different rules apply these two classes.

Below we show that by making the program variables explicit, a simple and precise treatment of program variables and logical variables in programming logics becomes possible. Program variables will correspond to bound variables in this approach, whereas logical variables will be free variables. This explains their different treatment in programming logics.

State spaces

2. A *state space* is a product type

$$\sigma = \sigma_1 \times \ldots \times \sigma_m, \tag{1}$$

where $m \geq 0$. A *state* in this state space is an element $(x_1, \ldots, x_m)$ of type σ. For $m = 0$, we have $\sigma = \texttt{unit}$, the trivial type with only one element.

3. Program variables are used in imperative languages to denote state components. The association of program variables with state components is done by a *declaration*, which we define to be a tuple

$$v = (x_1 : \sigma_1, \ldots, x_m : \sigma_m),$$

$m \geq 0$, of distinct variables x_i with associated types σ_i. The declaration v *declares* the state space $\sigma_v = \sigma_1 \times \ldots \times \sigma_m$, and associates variables names $x_1, \ldots, x_m$ with the state components.

Because higher order logic assumes that each variable in a term is associated with a type, we get declarations for free. The type of a variable may be explicitly indicated in a formula, or, if a type inference mechanism like the one in HOL is used, it can be left implicit in most cases.

4. We permit that the state space $\sigma = \sigma_1 \times \ldots \times \sigma_m$ contains type variables, and thus defines a polymorphic type. Hence, the theory of predicate transformers we describe here is *generic*, it is not bound to a specific choice of the program state space, nor to a specific number of state components.

As a special case, the state space may contain a single component. This means that any type can be instantiated for the state space, i.e., the approach we have taken does not even restrict the interpretation of states to be tuples.

Predicates

5. Let σ be a declaration. A *state predicate* on σ is a function

$$p : \sigma \rightarrow \texttt{bool},$$

or $p : \overline{\sigma}$, using the abbreviation introduced earlier.

Let $P : \texttt{bool}$ be a boolean term. Assume that we want to interpret P as a predicate on the program variables $v = (x_1 : \sigma_1, \ldots, x_m : \sigma_m)$. Then

$$\lambda v.\, P$$

is this state predicate. *Program variables* are thus bound in a predicate, while the free variables in the predicate $\lambda v.\, P$ are the *logical variables*. A state predicate is thus determined by a boolean term $P : \texttt{bool}$ and a declaration v of program variables. The boolean term alone is not sufficient to determine a state predicate.

For instance, if P is $x+y < z+1$ and the program variables are $(x : \texttt{int}, y : \texttt{int})$, this determines the state predicate

$$p \quad = \quad \lambda(x : \texttt{int}, y : \texttt{int}).\, x + y < z + 1.$$

Here z is free, and is thus a logical variable. The predicate p states that the sum of the first and the second state component is less than $z + 1$. The variables x and y are only used as local names for the state components, whereas z is some logical variable whose value is assumed to be determined by the environment. Assuming $z = 3$, the predicate p is true in state $(0, 1)$ but false in state $(2, 2)$.

6. A predicate $P : \texttt{bool}$ with implicit program variables v determines the state predicate $\lambda v.\, P$. In the other direction, any state predicate $p : \overline{\sigma}$ can be described as a predicate with given implicit program variables v: we have by η-reduction that

$$p = \lambda v.\, p v$$

whenever v is a declaration of the state space σ. Here $pv : \texttt{bool}$ is the predicate with implicit program variables v.

Manipulating state predicates

7. In order to express axioms and proof rules in programming logics, we need to manipulate predicates in different ways, such as renaming variables in predicates and substituting terms for free variables. We show below how to do these manipulations on state predicates.

8. Consider first renaming. Assume that $P : \texttt{bool}$ is a predicate with implicit program variables v. We want to rename some of the program variables in P, changing the program variables v to w. The result is the predicate $P[w/v]$ with implicit program variables w.

Making the program variables explicit gives the state predicate $p = \lambda v.\, P$. The meaning of the state predicate does not depend on the way program variables are named. By α-conversion, we are therefore free to rename the program variables in predicates:

$$p = \lambda v.\, P = \lambda w.\, P[w/v].$$

9. Another important operation on predicates is *substitution*. Given a predicate P on implicit program variables v, we want to substitute the terms t for the program variables v. The result is denoted $P[t/v]$ in Hoare logic. When the program variables are explicit, the effect of substitution is achieved with β-reduction. Let again p be the corresponding state predicate. The result of the substitution is the state predicate $\lambda v.\, p t$,

$$\lambda v.\, p t \; = \; \lambda v.(\lambda v.\, P)t \; = \; \lambda v.\, P[t/v]$$

(Application is assumed to bind stronger than lambda-abstraction.)

For example, the result of substituting $x+y$ for x in the predicate $\lambda(x,y).\, x>y$ is denoted by the term:

$$\lambda(x,y).\,(\lambda(x,y).\, x>y)(x+y,y) \;=\; \lambda(x,y).\, x+y>y.$$

We use β-reduction to compute the result. Note how the application to $(x+y,y)$ shows explicitly that no substitution is made for y. Simultaneous substitution is also easily expressed in this way.

10. When program variables are implicit, it is easy to mix predicate expressions over different state spaces. For example, we can write

$$x<y \wedge x=z+1$$

even though originally $x<y$ had state space (x,y) and $x=z+1$ had state space (x,z). Implicitly, we have projected both to the state space (x,y,z).

With state predicates, such a projection must be made explicit. Assume that v and w are declarations with $v \subseteq w$ (i.e., every component in v is also a component in w). If p is a predicate over the state declared by v, then the corresponding predicate over w is

$$\lambda w.\, p\, v$$

Consider as an example the state predicate $\lambda(x,y).\, x<y$. Projecting this on the larger state space (x,y,z) gives us the state predicate

$$\lambda(x,y,z).\,(\lambda(x,y).\, x<y)(x,y) = \lambda(x,y,z).\, x<y.$$

In a similar way, it is sometimes possible to project a predicate expression into a smaller state space (e.g., if we have quantified over or substituted for some variable). If $v \subseteq w$ and if p is a predicate over the state declared by w, such that p is independent of the variables in $u = w - v$ (i.e., that $(\forall u.\, p\, w) = p\, w$), then the corresponding predicate over v is

$$\lambda v.\, p\, w$$

In practice, we know that p is independent of u if no variables in u occur free in the predicate expression corresponding to p.

In fact, the operation $\lambda w.\, p\, v$ is meaningful also in the general case. It may be used to change some program variables to free variables and vice versa. The program variables in $v - w$ become logical variables, while the logical variables in $w - v$ become program variables.

Predicate lattice

11. The usual logical connectives are only defined for truth values, i.e., for boolean terms. We define the logical connectives for state predicates by pointwise extension of the corresponding operations on truth values. Let v be a declaration of state σ. We define the following operations on predicates on σ:

$$\begin{array}{rcl}
\mathtt{false} & \stackrel{\text{def}}{=} & \lambda v.\, \mathrm{F} \\
\mathtt{true} & \stackrel{\text{def}}{=} & \lambda v.\, \mathrm{T} \\
\neg p & \stackrel{\text{def}}{=} & \lambda v.\, \neg p\, v \\
p \wedge q & \stackrel{\text{def}}{=} & \lambda v.\, p\, v \wedge q\, v \\
p \vee q & \stackrel{\text{def}}{=} & \lambda v.\, p\, v \vee q\, v \\
p \Rightarrow q & \stackrel{\text{def}}{=} & \lambda v.\, p\, v \Rightarrow q\, v
\end{array}$$

The type `bool` is a two-element complete boolean lattice, with $\Rightarrow$ as the lattice ordering. We extend this ordering to state predicates, by defining.

$$p \leq q \stackrel{\text{def}}{=} \forall v.\, p\,v \Rightarrow q\,v$$

Note the difference between $\leq$ and $\Rightarrow$: the term $p \leq q$ has type `bool` while the term $p \Rightarrow q$ is a predicate.

The pointwise extension implies that every state predicate type $\overline{\sigma} = \sigma \rightarrow$ `bool` is also a complete boolean lattice, with the ordering $\leq$ on state predicates. The operations $\wedge$, $\vee$ and $\neg$ defined above for state predicates are the lattice meet, join and inverse operators, respectively. `true` is the top element while `false` is the bottom element of the state predicate lattice.

12. We can extend the definition of conjunction and disjunction of predicates to arbitrary conjunctions (meets) and disjunctions (joins) of predicates. If $A : \overline{\sigma} \rightarrow$ `bool` is (the characteristic function for) a set of predicates (i.e.,; $A : \overline{\overline{\sigma}}$), then we define

$$\bigwedge A \stackrel{\text{def}}{=} \lambda v.\, \forall p.\, A\,p \Rightarrow p\,v$$
$$\bigvee A \stackrel{\text{def}}{=} \lambda v.\, \exists p.\, A\,p \wedge p\,v$$

If the set A is given as $A = \{p_i | i \in I\}$, then we write $\bigwedge_{i \in I} p_i$ for $\bigwedge A$ (and similarly for joins). Note that $\bigwedge \emptyset = \texttt{true}$ and $\bigvee \emptyset = \texttt{false}$.

In the special case that $I = \alpha$ for some type α, we have that $A : \alpha \rightarrow \overline{\sigma}$. In that case, we can write the meet and join as

$$(\forall a : \alpha.\, A) = (\lambda v.\, \forall a : \alpha.\, A\,a\,v) \quad \text{and} \quad (\exists a : \alpha.\, A) = (\lambda v.\, \exists a : \alpha.\, A\,a\,v).$$

We do not define any operation corresponding to quantifying over program variables in a predicate. However, it is always possible to make the quantification inside the lambda abstraction of a predicate. Thus, universal quantification over x of the predicate $\lambda v.\, P$ yields the predicate $\lambda v.\, \forall x.\, P$.

State transformations and state relations

13. A *state transformation* is a function $f : \sigma \rightarrow \tau$. An example of a state function is

$$f \;=\; \lambda(x : \texttt{int}, y : \texttt{int}).\, (x + y, x - z).$$

Thus f will transform any state (x, y) to the new state $(x + y, x - z)$. Here z is a logical variable.

A *state relation* (or *nondeterministic state transformation*) is a function $r : \sigma \rightarrow \overline{\tau}$. State relations can also be expressed $r : \overline{\sigma \times \tau}$, but we prefer the first typing, which emphasizes the interpretation of a relation as a function from initial states to sets of final states.

Predicate transformers

14. Let σ and τ be two state spaces. A *predicate transformer* is a function

$$s : \overline{\sigma} \rightarrow \overline{\tau}.$$

Such a function maps predicates on σ to predicates on τ.

15. Operations on predicates are pointwise extended to predicate transformers, in the same way as operations on `bool` were extended to predicates. We define for predicate transformers $s, t : \overline{\sigma} \rightarrow \overline{\tau}$

the operations

$$\begin{array}{rcl}
\texttt{abort} & \stackrel{\text{def}}{=} & \lambda q.\,\texttt{false} \\
\texttt{magic} & \stackrel{\text{def}}{=} & \lambda q.\,\texttt{true} \\
\neg s & \stackrel{\text{def}}{=} & \lambda q.\,\neg(s\,q) \\
s \wedge t & \stackrel{\text{def}}{=} & \lambda q.\,s\,q \wedge t\,q \\
s \vee t & \stackrel{\text{def}}{=} & \lambda q.\,s\,q \vee t\,q \\
s \Rightarrow t & \stackrel{\text{def}}{=} & \lambda q.\,s\,q \Rightarrow t\,q
\end{array}$$

16. If H is (the characteristic function for) a set of predicate transformers (i.e., $H : (\overline{\sigma} \to \overline{\tau}) \to \texttt{bool}$), then we define

$$\begin{array}{rcl}
\bigwedge H & \stackrel{\text{def}}{=} & \lambda p.\,\bigwedge\{s\,p \mid s : s \in H\} \\
\bigvee H & \stackrel{\text{def}}{=} & \lambda p.\,\bigvee\{s\,p \mid s : s \in H\}
\end{array}$$

Both $\bigwedge$ and $\bigvee$ have type $\overline{\overline{\sigma} \to \overline{\tau}} \to \overline{\sigma} \to \overline{\tau}$.

Again, in the special case that H is given as $H : \alpha \to (\overline{\tau} \to \overline{\sigma})$, we can define

$$(\forall a : \alpha.\, H\,a) = (\lambda q.\, \forall a : \alpha.\, H\,a\,q) \quad \textit{and} \quad (\exists a : \alpha.\, H\,a) = (\lambda q.\, \exists a : \alpha.\, H\,a\,q).$$

17. With these definitions $\overline{\sigma} \to \overline{\tau}$ is a complete boolean lattice, for all σ and τ. The partial order induced by the lattice structure is the same as the pointwise extension of the ordering on predicates: for predicate transformers s and s' in $\overline{\sigma} \to \overline{\tau}$, we define

$$s \leq s' \quad \stackrel{\text{def}}{=} \quad (\forall p.\, s\,p \leq s'\,p)$$

This is the refinement ordering introduced in [1].

18. Since predicate transformers are functions, functional composition is also defined for these. For predicate transformers $s : \overline{\sigma} \to \overline{\tau}$ and $t : \overline{\tau} \to \overline{\rho}$, the functional composition $s;t$ has type $\overline{\sigma} \to \overline{\rho}$.

4 Statements as predicate transformers

1. Rather than introducing a separate programming language for the statements we are interested in, we will work directly with predicate transformers. Thus, we will define an algebra of predicate transformers, with constants corresponding to certain basic statements and operations on predicate transformers corresponding to structured statements. Ordinary programming notations, such as skip or $x := 0$ can then be seen as just textual abbreviation for specific predicate transformers.

The reason that we build the theory in this way is two-fold. First, by not fixing a specific programming language, our results will be independent of any particular language. We will define a number of useful operations on predicate transformers that can be used in any combination. There is no need to put all the constructs into a single language. The approach is also open-ended; we may add new operations to the algebra later, at will.

The other reason for this approach is that we can work directly with predicate transformers in higher order logic. Instead of working with two different domains, a syntactic domain of terms and a semantic domain of predicates and predicate transformers, we work directly with the semantics in higher order logic. The syntax of our terms is the syntax of higher order logic, while the semantics of our terms is given by the standard semantics of higher order logic. Hence, there is no need for us to give a separate semantic definition. Moreover, we also do not need to introduce a separate proof theory for statements, the proof theory for higher order logic is sufficient to reason about all aspects of our statements. The new constructs we need are introduced by definitions, so the resulting theory is a conservative extension of the basic theory of higher order logic. This guarantees that our theory is consistent.

This does not, of course, preclude us from proving a number of useful theorems about program statements, which in other approaches would be treated as defining axioms. In our approach, they will be theorems, and proving these theorems corresponds to giving a soundness proof of the axioms in other logics.

Below we define constants that will correspond to a basic set of program statements constructs. These constructs are complete, in the sense that any monotonic predicate transformer can be built out of these constructs. We refer to predicate transformers built as terms with these constructs as *statements*.

Assignment statements

2. The assignment statement is the cornerstone of any imperative programming language. It is also one of the most cumbersome constructs to get right. We define an assignment statement to be an operation of type

$$\mathtt{assign} : (\sigma \to \tau) \to (\overline{\tau} \to \overline{\sigma}),$$

where

$$\mathtt{assign}\, e \stackrel{\text{def}}{=} \lambda q.\lambda v.\, q(e\, v).$$

Thus, an assignment statement takes a state transformer $e : \sigma \to \tau$ and converts it to a predicate transformer in $(\overline{\tau} \to \overline{\sigma})$. Note that the assignment statement may change the state space also, it is not restricted to only change the value of some state components.

3. Let us make things more concrete by an example. Consider the expression

$$\mathrm{wp}(x := x + y, P)$$

in Dijkstra's original notation. Let P be the predicate $x + y < z + 1$ and let the state space be $(x : \mathtt{int}, y : \mathtt{int})$. In our notation, the assignment statement is $\mathtt{assign}(\lambda(x,y).\,(x+y,y))$ and the predicate P is $\lambda(x,y).\, x + y < z + 1$. We calculate the value of the predicate transformer expression using a sequence of beta conversions:

$$\begin{array}{rcl}
\mathrm{wp}(x := x + y, P) & \sim & \mathtt{assign}(\lambda(x,y).\,(x+y,y))(\lambda(x,y).\, x+y<z+1) \\
& = & \lambda(x,y).(\lambda(x,y).\, x+y<z+1)(\lambda(x,y).\,(x+y,y))(x,y) \\
& = & \lambda(x,y).(\lambda(x,y).\, x+y<z+1)(x+y,y) \\
& = & \lambda(x,y).x+y+y<z+1 \\
& = & \lambda(x,y).(x+y<z+1)[x+y/x] \\
& \sim & P[e/x]
\end{array}$$

4. We define the identity statement **skip** as

$$\mathtt{skip} \;=\; \mathtt{assign}(\lambda v.v).$$

By calculation, we have that

$$\begin{array}{ll}
 & \mathtt{skip}\, q \\
= & \{\text{Definition}\} \\
 & \mathtt{assign}(\lambda v.v)\, q \\
= & \{\text{Definition}\}
\end{array}$$

$$\begin{aligned}&\lambda v.\, q((\lambda v.\, v)v)\\ =\;&\{\text{Beta reduction}\}\\ &\lambda v.\, q\, v\\ =\;&\{\text{Eta reduction}\}\\ &q\end{aligned}$$

This shows that $\texttt{skip} = \lambda q.\, q$.

Sequential and conditional composition

5. Sequential and conditional composition are defined as operations on predicate transformers, of the type

$$\begin{aligned}\texttt{seq} &: (\overline{\tau} \to \overline{\sigma}) \times (\overline{\rho} \to \overline{\tau}) \to (\overline{\rho} \to \overline{\sigma})\\ \texttt{cond} &: \overline{\sigma} \to (\overline{\tau} \to \overline{\sigma}) \times (\overline{\tau} \to \overline{\sigma}) \to (\overline{\tau} \to \overline{\sigma})\end{aligned}$$

defined by

$$\begin{aligned}\texttt{seq}\,(s_1, s_2)q &\stackrel{\text{def}}{=} s_1(s_2\, q)\\ \texttt{cond}\, b\,(s_1, s_2)q &\stackrel{\text{def}}{=} (b \wedge s_1\, q) \vee (\neg b \wedge s_2\, q).\end{aligned}$$

6. To make example programs easier to read, we permit the following alternative notation for sequential and conditional composition:

$$\begin{aligned}s_1; s_2 &= \texttt{seq}\,(s_1, s_2)\\ b \to s_1 | s_2 &= \texttt{cond}\, b\,(s_1, s_2)\end{aligned}$$

We can also permit a more traditional syntax for assignments. For example, we could write $x, z := x + y, x$ for the assignment $assign(\lambda(x, y, z).\,(x + y, y, x))$ above. However, for this way of writing (multiple) assignments to be meaningful, the following three conditions must be satisfied:

(i) The initial and final state spaces must be equal,

(ii) the declaration of the state tuple must be obvious from the context, and

(iii) the variable(s) on the left hand side of the assignment symbol must be in the state tuple.

Demonic and angelic nondeterminism

7. We have already defined meet and join operators on predicate transformers. For $s, t : (\overline{\tau} \to \overline{\sigma})$, we interpret

$$s \wedge t : (\overline{\tau} \to \overline{\sigma})$$

as a *demonic choice* between the two alternatives s and t, while

$$s \vee t : (\overline{\tau} \to \overline{\sigma})$$

is interpreted as an *angelic choice* between the two alternatives.

More generally, if S is a set of predicate transformers, we interpret $\bigwedge S$ as demonic choice and $\bigvee S$ as angelic choice between the statements in S. Intuitively, execution of $\bigwedge S$ is guaranteed to terminate in a final state where a given predicate q holds if and only if all of the statements in S do this. Dually, execution of $\bigvee S$ is guaranteed to terminate in a final state where q holds if and only if at least one of the statements in S does this.

8. The bottom of the predicate transformer lattice is

$$\texttt{abort} \stackrel{\text{def}}{=} \bigvee \emptyset$$

By definition, we have that $\texttt{abort}\, q = \texttt{false}$ for all predicates q. As a statement, abort corresponds to the always *nonterminating* program (it does not establish any postcondition).

The top of the predicate transformer lattice is

$$\texttt{magic} \stackrel{\text{def}}{=} \bigwedge \emptyset$$

Again, by definition, we have that $\texttt{magic}\, q = \texttt{true}$ for all predicates q. As a statement, magic corresponds to the *miraculous* program (it will establish any postcondition whatsoever).

Completeness

9. It turns out that the assignment statement, the sequential and conditional composition and the arbitrary meet and join are sufficient to express any monotonic predicate transformer [3]. In other words, any monotonic predicate transformer can be described as a term where only these constructs are employed. The converse also hold, as we will show in Section 6, so the set of statements coincides with the set of monotonic predicate transformers.

This characterization is infinitary in nature, because both meets and joins may contain an infinite number of components, and hence do not qualify as ordinary (finite) programming language constructs. However, this completeness result gives a nice and tight characterization of monotonic predicate transformers.

5 Derived constructs

1. The completeness result states that only the statement constructs defined above are really needed to describe a monotonic predicate transformer. From a practical point of view, we are, however, interested in a larger set of program constructs. Some infinitary constructs can, e.g., be expressed also in a finite way, such as nondeterministic assignments, recursion and iteration. In other cases, we need a convenient way of describing predicate transformers involving more than one state space. Below we define a collection of such useful constructs. We extend the notion of statement to cover also predicate transformers built using the constructs defined below.

Conditional constructs

2. Having permitted the nonterminating statement **abort** and the miraculous statement **magic**, we can introduce conditional nontermination (*assertions*) and conditional miracles (*guards*). We add the constants **assert** and **guard** to our notation:

$$\begin{aligned}\mathbf{assert}\,b &\stackrel{\text{def}}{=} b \rightarrow \mathbf{skip}|\mathbf{abort}\\ \mathbf{guard}\,b &\stackrel{\text{def}}{=} b \rightarrow \mathbf{skip}|\mathbf{magic}\end{aligned}$$

Both these constants have type $\overline{\sigma} \rightarrow (\overline{\sigma} \rightarrow \overline{\sigma})$ (note that since **skip** has type $(\overline{\sigma} \rightarrow \overline{\sigma})$, τ in the type of **cond** must here be σ). From the definitions it follows that

$$\begin{aligned}\mathbf{assert}\,b\,q &= b \wedge q\\ \mathbf{guard}\,b\,q &= b \Rightarrow q\end{aligned}$$

We permit the abbreviations $\{b\}$ and $[b]$ for **assert** b and **guard** b, respectively.

3. Dijkstra's nondeterministic conditional composition can now be introduced by defining a new constant **if**:

$$\mathbf{if}\,(b_1, b_2)\,(s_1, s_2) \stackrel{\text{def}}{=} \{b_1 \vee b_2\}; ([b_1]; s_1 \wedge [b_2]; s_2)$$

We may use the abbreviation **if** $b_1 \rightarrow s_1 \;[]\; b_2 \rightarrow s_2$ **fi** for this construct.

Nondeterministic assignments

4. We may also define statements that change the state space in a nondeterministic way, according to some specified state relation. These statement are useful for specifying computations[1, 2, 8].

Let $r : \sigma \rightarrow \overline{\tau}$ be a state relation. Then r can be viewed as a function from initial states to sets of possible final states. We want to capture the notion of a statement which chooses nondeterministically between these possible final states. Since the choice may be demonic or angelic, we have two forms of the statement. The *demonic assignment statement* is defined by

$$\mathbf{demass}\,r\,q \stackrel{\text{def}}{=} \lambda v.\, \forall v'.\, r\,v\,v' \Rightarrow q\,v',$$

while the *angelic assignment statement* is defined by

$$\texttt{angass}\,r\,q \stackrel{\text{def}}{=} \lambda v.\,\exists v'.\,r\,v\,v' \wedge q\,v'$$

Both constructs have polymorphic type $(\sigma \rightarrow \overline{\tau}) \rightarrow (\overline{\tau} \rightarrow \overline{\sigma})$. (Both these statements can also be defined in terms of the basic constructs of the previous section, but defining them directly gives a somewhat better feeling for their meaning).

5. As an example, consider the state relation $r = \lambda(x,y)(x',y').\,x' > x$, which specifies that the final value of x should be greater than the initial value (we prime the variables in the tuple that corresponds to the final state). The following calculation applies $\texttt{demass}\,r$ to the predicate $q = \lambda(x,y).\,x > 1$:

$$\begin{array}{cl} & \texttt{demass}\,r\,q \\ = & \{\text{Definitions}\} \\ & \lambda(x,y).\,\forall(x',y').\,(\lambda(x,y)(x',y').\,x' > x)(x,y)(x',y') \Rightarrow (\lambda(x,y).\,x > 1)(x',y') \\ = & \{\text{Beta reduction}\} \\ & \lambda(x,y).\,\forall(x',y').\,x' > x \Rightarrow x' > 1 \\ = & \{\text{Arithmetic}\} \\ & \lambda(x,y).\,x \geq 1 \end{array}$$

Hence, to guarantee that $x > 1$ holds in the final state, $x \geq 1$ must hold in the initial state.

6. Similar calculations for the corresponding angelic assignment give

$$\begin{array}{rcl} \texttt{angass}\,r\,(\lambda(x,y).\,x' = x+1) & = & \texttt{true} \\ \texttt{angass}\,r\,(\lambda(x,y).\,x' = x+2) & = & \texttt{true} \end{array}$$

This shows a characteristic feature of angelic nondeterminism. Loosely speaking, it anticipates the postcondition that we want established. Operationally, we can interpret this as parallel execution on a (possible infinite) number of separate identical copies of the state space. The postcondition is established, if one of these executions is guaranteed to establish it.

7. A convenient abbreviation for demonic and angelic assignment statements is as follows. Let $v = u, w$. Then define

$$\begin{array}{rcl} u := u'.Q & \stackrel{\text{def}}{=} & \texttt{demass}(\lambda(u,w)\,(u',w').\,Q \wedge w' = w) \\ u :\approx u'.Q & \stackrel{\text{def}}{=} & \texttt{angass}(\lambda(u,w)\,(u',w').\,Q \wedge w' = w) \end{array}$$

Both statements assign some values u' to u such that condition Q becomes satisfied, leaving w unchanged. In the first case, the choice when there is more than one possible assignment is demonic, in the second case the choice is angelic. Also, in the first case the result is miraculous termination if there is no possible assignment, in the second case the result is abortion. As was the case with the assignment statement, this abbreviation is meaningful only if the naming of the state components is clear from the context.

Blocks and local variables

8. Let $s : (\overline{\sigma \times \tau} \rightarrow \overline{\sigma \times \tau})$ be a predicate transformer. We want the notation $\texttt{block}\,s$ to correspond to a statement which adds *local variables* to the state space, then executes s and finally removes the variables from the state space. For this, we define the constant **block** as follows:

$$\texttt{block}\,s = \texttt{enter};\,s;\,\texttt{exit}$$

where **enter** and **exit** are defined as follows. First, let us define the state relation $\texttt{any} : \tau \rightarrow \overline{\sigma \times \tau}$ and the state transformer $\texttt{drop} : \sigma \times \tau \rightarrow \tau$, by

$$\begin{array}{rcl} \texttt{any}\,u\,(v',u') & = & u = u' \\ \texttt{drop}\,(v,u) & = & u. \end{array}$$

Then, we define **enter** : $\overline{\sigma\times\tau}\rightarrow\overline{\tau}$ and **exit** : $\overline{\tau}\rightarrow\overline{\sigma\times\tau}$ by

$$\begin{aligned}\texttt{enter} &= \texttt{demass any}\\ \texttt{exit} &= \texttt{assign drop}.\end{aligned}$$

Thus, the **enter** statement adds a new state component v without changing the old state component u, choosing the value for the new state component arbitrarily. The **exit** statement simply drops the new state component, without changing the old state component.

The typing of **block** is as follows:

$$\texttt{block} : (\overline{\sigma\times\tau}\rightarrow\overline{\sigma\times\tau})\rightarrow(\overline{\tau}\rightarrow\overline{\tau})$$

Note that the local variables are visible only in the type of **block**. For simplicity, we may permit the outfix notation

$$\|\ \texttt{var}\ u; s\ \|$$

for **block** s, where the local variables are given by the declaration u.The role of u is to determine how the state space of s is divided up into local and global variables.

9. Using the definitions of the constructs involved, we can compute the predicate transformer for the block statement. We then get that

$$\texttt{block}\, s\, q \;=\; \lambda v.\, \forall u.\, s(\lambda(u,v).\, q\, v)(u,v) \tag{2}$$

A more common definition of the block is wp($\|$ var x; S $\|$, Q) = $\forall x$.wp(S, Q), with the side condition that x must not be free in Q. Our definition needs no side condition, due to the type discipline.

Recursion and iteration

10. We may also construct new statements using recursion. In the next section we will show that all the predicate transformers that can be built using operations defined here are in fact monotonic. Since the monotonic predicate transformers of any given type form a complete lattice, we can define an operator μ such that if c is a unary predicate transformer constructor, then $\mu\, c$ is the least fixpoint of c. The definition is as follows:

$$\mu c \;\stackrel{\text{def}}{=}\; \bigwedge\{s \mid c\, s \leq s\}$$

The type of μ is

$$\mu : ((\overline{\tau}\rightarrow\overline{\sigma})\rightarrow(\overline{\tau}\rightarrow\overline{\sigma}))\rightarrow(\overline{\tau}\rightarrow\overline{\sigma})$$

We permit the use of μ as a binder, writing $\mu X.\, H$ for $\mu(\lambda X.\, H)$.

11. We define iteration as a special case of recursion in the usual way. We define a constant **do** by

$$\texttt{do}\, b\, s \;\stackrel{\text{def}}{=}\; \mu X.\, (b\rightarrow s; X \mid \texttt{skip})$$

Straighforward calculations show that

$$\texttt{do}\, b\, s\, q \;=\; \mu x.\, (\neg b\wedge q)\vee(b\wedge s\, x)$$

which corresponds to the usual fixpoint definition of the semantics of iteration. We permit the traditional notation do $b\rightarrow s$ od for do $b\, s$.

A notation for procedures

12. The **let** construct is commonly used as a notational device in the λ-calculus: let $X = s$ in t indicates that X is used inside t as a name for s. We introduce this construct as an abbreviation:

$$\texttt{let}\, X = s\ \texttt{in}\ t \quad \text{stands for} \quad \texttt{apply}((\lambda X.\, t), s) \tag{3}$$

where

$$\texttt{apply}(f, t) = f\, t.$$

We have the typing

$$\texttt{apply} : ((\overline{\tau} \to \overline{\sigma}) \to (\overline{\tau'} \to \overline{\sigma'})) \times (\overline{\tau} \to \overline{\sigma}) \to (\overline{\tau'} \to \overline{\sigma'})$$

when X has predicate transformer type.

Parameterless procedure declarations are directly expressible with the `let` notation:

$$\textbf{procedure}\, X = s; \tag{4}$$
$$t \tag{5}$$

corresponds to $\texttt{let}\, X = s \;\texttt{in}\; t$ when s is a statement.

By β-reduction, we have that $\texttt{let}\, X = s \;\texttt{in}\; t$ is the same as $t[s/X]$, which corresponds to the usual interpretation of a procedure without parameters.

Note that we do not define `let` as a constant. This is because its syntax obscures the fact that its real arguments are the function $\lambda X.t$ and the statement s. However, the rule (3) shows how every `let`-construct is translated into a corresponding `apply`-term, which in turn can be simplified into a straightforward substitution.

Procedures with parameters

13. Consider next procedures with parameters. We want to permit the notation

$$\texttt{let}\, X = \|\; \texttt{val}\;\; x; \texttt{res}\;\; y; s \;\|\; \texttt{in}\; t \tag{6}$$

The declarations x and y indicate how the state space of s is to be partitioned into value parameters, result parameters and global variables. Here s must have type

$$s : \overline{(\sigma \times \sigma' \times \tau} \to \overline{\sigma \times \sigma' \times \tau)}$$

where $x : \sigma$ and $y : \sigma'$.

14. A *call* has the form

$$X\, e\, e'$$

where the terms e and e' have the following types:

$$e : \tau \to \sigma$$
$$e' : \sigma \times \sigma' \times \tau \to \sigma \times \sigma' \times \tau$$

The idea is that e is a state function which shows what value the value parameter is to get before execution of the body s, while e' indicates what is to happen with the result in the result parameter after execution. The example below shows the details of this.

The notation (6) is defined to be equal to the term

$$\texttt{apply}\, (\lambda X.\, t)\, s'$$

where s' is the following term:

$$s' \;=\; \lambda e\, e'.\texttt{block}\, (\texttt{assign}\, (\lambda(x, y, v).\, (e v, y, v))\, ;\, s;\, \texttt{assign}\, e')$$

This term s' is substituted for X in t.

15. The following example shows the intended us of this parameterized procedure construct. We consider a state space declared as $(a : \texttt{int}, b : \texttt{int})$ and a procedure which squares an integer:

$$\begin{aligned}&\texttt{let}\, X = \|\; \texttt{val}\;\; x; \texttt{res}\;\; y; \texttt{assign}\, \lambda(x, y, a, b).(x, x^2, a, b)\; \| \\ &\;\;\texttt{in}\;\; \texttt{assign}(\lambda(a, b).(2, b));\; X(\lambda(a, b).a + 1)(\lambda(x, y, a, b).(x, y, a, y))\end{aligned} \tag{7}$$

In a more conventional notation this would look as follows:

$$\begin{aligned}&\textbf{procedure}\, X(\texttt{val}\;\; x; \texttt{res}\;\; y)\, \textbf{is}\, y := x^2; \\ &\textbf{begin}\, a := 2;\; X(a + 1, b)\, \textbf{end}\end{aligned}$$

The effect is that a is assigned the value 2 and b the value 9. Note that in (7), the first argument in the call of X is

$$\lambda(a, b).\, a + 1$$

which indicates that the value parameter is to get the value $a + 1$ (i.e., the first component of the state plus one). The second argument in the call of X is

$$\lambda(x, y, a, b).\, (x, y, a, y)$$

which indicates that the result y (i.e., the second component in the state) is to be placed in the variable b (i.e., the fourth component in the state, which is the second component of the global state).

16. We can also permit a procedure to have only value parameters or only result parameters, with appropriate adaptions. In case a procedure has neither value nor result parameters, then its definition coincides with the definition of parameterless procedures given previously.

6 Monotonicity

1. A *statement* is a term of type $(\overline{\tau} \to \overline{\sigma})$ that is built using only the specific predicate transformers and predicate transformer constructors introduced in the previous sections: assignment, demonic and angelic assignment, sequential composition, conditional composition, meet and join, blocks, application, and fixpoint construction. A statement may contain free variables, which may also be of predicate transformer type.

In this section we want to show two things:

(i) that every statement is a monotonic predicate transformer, and

(ii) subcomponent replacement in statements is monotonic.

The former expresses the requirement of monotonicity with respect to the ordering on predicates. The latter means that if $s(t)$ is a predicate transformer with predicate transformer t as a component, then $t \leq t' \Rightarrow s(t) \leq s(t')$. This is the basic property needed for program refinement: replacing a component by its refinement gives a refinement of the whole statement.

Preliminary definitions

2. In order to express and prove the monotonicity properties for predicate transformers, it turns out to be convenient to introduce a more flexible notation for subtypes in higher order logic. Subtypes are not directly supported in the logic, but we can introduce notational conventions that mimic the use of subtypes.

Given a type α, a ***subtype*** α' of α denotes some subset $\alpha' = \{x \in \alpha \mid R(x)\}$. Here $R(x)$ is the characteristic predicate that the elements of α must satisfy in order to belong to the subtype. For simplicity, we identify the subtype with its characteristic function, writing α' for both.

3. We would like to use subtypes in our formulas in the same way as we use the ordinary types. This can be done, if we adopt the following conventions for typing:

$x : \alpha'$	is correct when	$x : \alpha$ and $\alpha'(x)$
$x : \alpha' \times \beta'$	is correct when	$x : \alpha \times \beta$ and $\alpha'(\mathtt{fst}\, x) \wedge \beta'(\mathtt{snd}\, x)$
$f : \alpha' \to \beta'$	is correct when	$f : \alpha \to \beta$ and $(\forall x : \alpha'.\beta'(f(x)))$.

These conventions are easily explained by considering types as sets. We have, e.g., that

$$x \in \alpha' \quad = \quad x \in \{y \in \alpha \mid \alpha'(y)\} \quad = \quad x \in \alpha \wedge \alpha'(x).$$

For the functional type, the convention expresses that the function on subtypes must be well defined, in the sense that if the argument is in subtype α', then the value must be an element of subtype β'.

With these conventions we can quantify over subtypes. For example, we have

$$\begin{array}{lll} \forall x : \alpha'. H & \text{stands for} & \forall x : \alpha. (\alpha'(x) \Rightarrow H) \\ \exists f : \alpha' \to \beta'. H & \text{stands for} & \exists f : \alpha \to \beta. (\forall x : \alpha. \alpha'(x) \Rightarrow \beta'(f(x)) \wedge H \end{array}$$

The conventions permit us to use subtypes as if they were ordinary types in our formulas. The difference to ordinary types is that we have to prove explicitly the associated closedness assumptions, since subtypes are only a notational abbreviation.

4. Let α and β be two types with associated partial orderings $\leq_\alpha$ and $\leq_\beta$. A function $f : \alpha \to \beta$ is *monotonic*, if

$$x \leq_\alpha x' \quad \Rightarrow \quad f(x) \leq_\beta f(x'), \tag{8}$$

for each $x, x' : \alpha$. We denote by $\alpha \to_m \beta$ the subtype of all monotonic functions $f : \alpha \to \beta$.

5. The subtype of $(\overline{\tau} \to \overline{\sigma})$ containing all *monotonic predicate transformers* is thus $(\overline{\tau} \to_m \overline{\sigma})$.

6. A *monotonic predicate transformer constructor* (on monotonic predicate transformers) is a function of the form

$$c : (\overline{\tau_1} \to_m \overline{\sigma_1}) \times \ldots \times (\overline{\tau_n} \to_m \overline{\sigma_n}) \to_m (\overline{\tau} \to_m \overline{\sigma}) \tag{9}$$

To prove that a constructor c is of this type, we need to show the following two properties (by the definition of subtypes given in the beginning):

$$\forall s_1, \ldots, s_n. (\bigwedge_{i=1}^{n} s_i \text{ is monotonic }) \;\Rightarrow\; c(s_1, \ldots, s_n) \text{ is monotonic} \tag{10}$$

$$\forall s_1, \ldots, s_n, t_1, \ldots, t_n. (\bigwedge_{i=1}^{n} s_i \leq t_i \;\Rightarrow\; c(s_1, \ldots, s_n) \leq c(t_1, \ldots, t_n) \tag{11}$$

We extend the ordering on predicate transformers pointwise to an ordering on monotonic predicate transformer constructors, by

$$c \leq c' \;\stackrel{\text{def}}{=}\; \forall s_1 : (\overline{\tau_1} \to_m \overline{\sigma_1}), \ldots, s_n : (\overline{\tau_n} \to_m \overline{\sigma_n}).\; c(s_1, \ldots, s_n) \leq c'(s_1, \ldots, s_n)$$

7. The Knaster-Tarski fixpoint theorem tells us that every monotonic predicate transformer on a fixed predicate space has a least fixpoint. The following definition defines a polymorphic fixpoint operator μ:

$$\mu f \;\stackrel{\text{def}}{=}\; \bigwedge \{p \mid f p \leq p\}$$

The type of μ is

$$\mu : (\alpha \to \alpha) \to \alpha$$

From the definition it is straighforward to prove the following two properties provided that f is monotonic:

$$\begin{array}{rcl} f(\mu f) & = & \mu f \\ \forall x. f x \leq x & \Rightarrow & \mu f \leq x \end{array}$$

This shows that μ is in fact the required least fixpoint operator.

Monotonicity of statements

8. Our main result is the following.

THEOREM 1 *Let $s : (\overline{\tau} \to \overline{\sigma})$ be a statement, and let $X_1 : (\overline{\tau_1} \to \overline{\sigma_1}), \ldots, X_n : (\overline{\tau_n} \to \overline{\sigma_n})$ be the free predicate transformer variables in s, $n \geq 0$. Then*

$$\lambda X_1 \ldots X_n. s : (\overline{\tau_1} \to_m \overline{\sigma_1}) \to_m \ldots (\overline{\tau_n} \to_m \overline{\sigma_n}) \to_m (\overline{\tau} \to_m \overline{\sigma}).$$

This expresses formally both requirement (i) and (ii) above, (i) being the special case where there are no free predicate transformer variables.

Proof The theorem is established by the lemmas proved below, as any statement can be built from assignment and the two kinds of nondeterministic assignment using sequential and conditional composition, nondeterministic choice, the block construction, recursion and functional application. Q.E.D

9. The following lemma establishes the monotonicity of assignment statements.

LEMMA 1 $\mathtt{assign}\,e : (\overline{\sigma} \to_m \overline{\tau})$, *for any* $e : \sigma \to \tau$.

Proof

$$
\begin{array}{cl}
 & p \le q \\
= & \{\text{Definition of predicate ordering}\} \\
 & \forall v.\, p\,v \Rightarrow q\,v \\
\Rightarrow & \{\text{Property of universal quantification}\} \\
 & \forall v.\, p(e\,v) \Rightarrow q(e\,v) \\
= & \{\text{Definition of ordering of predicates}\} \\
 & (\lambda v.\, p(e\,v)) \le (\lambda v.\, q(e\,v)) \\
= & \{\text{Definition of } \mathtt{assign}\} \\
 & \mathtt{assign}\,e\,p \le \mathtt{assign}\,e\,q
\end{array}
$$

Q.E.D

Note that we do not have to prove monotonicity of the **skip** statement, since it is defined as an **assign**-statement.

10. The monotonicity of sequential and conditional composition is established by the following lemma.

LEMMA 2 (i) $\mathtt{seq} : (\overline{\tau} \to_m \overline{\sigma}) \times (\overline{\rho} \to_m \overline{\tau}) \to (\overline{\rho} \to_m \overline{\sigma})$.

(ii) $\mathtt{cond}\,b : (\overline{\tau} \to_m \overline{\sigma}) \times (\overline{\tau} \to_m \overline{\sigma}) \to (\overline{\tau} \to_m \overline{\sigma})$, *for any* $b : \overline{\sigma}$.

Proof We only show the proof of (i), as the proof of (ii) is similar.

$$
\begin{array}{cl}
 & p \le q \\
\Rightarrow & \{\text{Assumption that } t \text{ is monotonic}\} \\
 & t\,p \le t\,q \\
\Rightarrow & \{\text{Assumption that } s \text{ is monotonic}\} \\
 & s(t\,p) \le s(t\,q) \\
= & \{\text{Definition of sequential composition}\} \\
 & \mathtt{seq}\,(s,t)\,p \le \mathtt{seq}\,(s,t)\,q
\end{array}
$$

Q.E.D

11. The monotonicity of sequential and conditional composition, viewed as predicate transformer constructors is established by the following lemma.

LEMMA 3 (i) $\mathtt{seq} : (\overline{\tau} \to_m \overline{\sigma}) \times (\overline{\rho} \to_m \overline{\tau}) \to_m (\overline{\rho} \to_m \overline{\sigma})$.

(ii) $\mathtt{cond}\,b : (\overline{\tau} \to_m \overline{\sigma}) \times (\overline{\tau} \to_m \overline{\sigma}) \to_m (\overline{\tau} \to_m \overline{\sigma})$, *for any* $b : \overline{\sigma}$.

Proof Assume that $s \le s'$ and $t \le t'$ and let q be an arbitrary predicate over σ.

Consider first sequential composition. Assume that s, s', t and t are monotonic, with $s \leq s'$ and $t \leq t'$. Starting from the trivial fact that $q \leq q$, we have

$$\begin{array}{ll} & q \leq q \\ \Rightarrow & \{\text{assumptions } t \leq t' \text{ and } s \text{ monotonic}\} \\ & s(t\,q) \leq s(t'\,q) \\ \Rightarrow & \{\text{transitivity of } \leq, \text{ since } s(t'\,q) \leq s'(t'\,q) \text{ by assumption}\} \\ & s(t\,q) \leq s'(t'\,q) \end{array}$$

As q was arbitrarily chosen, this shows that $s; t \leq s'; t'$, as required.
For conditional composition, the proof is trivial. Q.E.D

12. From the theory of lattices it is well known that the monotonic functions form a complete sublattice of any function lattice. This means that the typings

$$\bigwedge : ((\overline{\tau} \rightarrow_m \overline{\sigma}) \rightarrow \texttt{bool}) \rightarrow (\overline{\tau} \rightarrow_m \overline{\sigma})$$
$$\bigvee : ((\overline{\tau} \rightarrow_m \overline{\sigma}) \rightarrow \texttt{bool}) \rightarrow (\overline{\tau} \rightarrow_m \overline{\sigma})$$

are correct. The subcomponent monotonicity property is proved in the following lemma:

LEMMA 4 *Let $S = \{s_i | i \in I\}$ and $T = \{t_i | i \in I\}$ be two sets of predicate transformers in $(\overline{\tau} \rightarrow_m \overline{\sigma})$. If $s_i \leq t_i$ holds for all $i \in I$, then*

$$\bigwedge_{i \in I} s_i \leq \bigwedge_{i \in I} t_i$$
$$\bigvee_{i \in I} s_i \leq \bigvee_{i \in I} t_i$$

Proof Both results follow directly from basic properties of meets and joins in complete lattices. Q.E.D

13. As a matter of fact, $\bigvee$ is also monotonic (and $\bigwedge$ antimonotonic) in the sense that it has type

$$\bigvee : ((\overline{\tau} \rightarrow_m \overline{\sigma}) \rightarrow \texttt{bool}) \rightarrow_m (\overline{\tau} \rightarrow_m \overline{\sigma})$$

since lifting the order on `bool` to sets yields the subset ordering. However, this monotonicity property is quite different from the subcomponent monotonicity property proved above.

Monotonicity of derived constructs

14. The monotonicity of the nondeterministic assignments are established by the following lemma.

LEMMA 5 *(i)* $\texttt{demass}\, r : (\overline{\tau} \rightarrow_m \overline{\sigma})$*, for any* $r : \sigma \rightarrow \tau$*, and*

(ii) $\texttt{angass}\, r : (\overline{\tau} \rightarrow_m \overline{\sigma})$*, for any* $r : \sigma \rightarrow \tau$*.*

Proof Assume that $p \leq q$ holds. Then

$$(\lambda v. \forall v'. r\, v\, v' \Rightarrow p\, v') \;\Rightarrow\; (\lambda v. \forall v'. r\, v\, v' \Rightarrow q\, v')$$

by the monotonicity of the logical operators. By the definition of **demass**, this proves the first case. The proof for **angass** is similar. Q.E.D

15. The following lemma shows that the block construct preserves monotonicity and that `block` is a monotonic constructor.

LEMMA 6 $\texttt{block} : (\overline{\sigma \times \tau} \rightarrow_m \overline{\sigma \times \tau}) \rightarrow_m (\overline{\tau} \rightarrow_m \overline{\tau})$

This result follows directly from the monotonicity of the constructs in terms of which the block construct is defined.

16. For the fixpoint operator, we can prove the following general result:

LEMMA 7 $\mu : ((\overline{\tau} \rightarrow_m \overline{\sigma}) \rightarrow_m (\overline{\tau} \rightarrow_m \overline{\sigma})) \rightarrow_m (\overline{\tau} \rightarrow_m \overline{\sigma})$

Proof First we have to show that if c is a function of type $(\overline{\tau} \rightarrow_m \overline{\sigma}) \rightarrow_m (\overline{\tau} \rightarrow_m \overline{\sigma})$, then μc is in fact monotonic. This is a well-known fact from the theory of function lattices.

Now let c and d both have type $(\overline{\tau} \rightarrow_m \overline{\sigma}) \rightarrow_m (\overline{\tau} \rightarrow_m \overline{\sigma})$. Then

$$\begin{array}{ll} & c \leq d \\ \Rightarrow & \{\text{Definition of partial order}\} \\ & c(\mu d) \leq d(\mu d) \\ \Rightarrow & \{\mu d \text{ is fixpoint of } d\} \\ & c(\mu d) \leq \mu d \\ \Rightarrow & \{\mu c \text{ is least prefixed point of } c\} \\ & \mu c \leq \mu d \end{array}$$

which shows that μ is monotonic. Q.E.D

17. Assume that σ and τ are types with associated partial orders (both written $\leq$). Then application is monotonic for these types.

LEMMA 8 $\texttt{apply} : (\sigma \rightarrow_m \tau) \times \sigma \rightarrow_m \tau$

Proof Let $t, t' : \sigma$ and $f, f' : (\sigma \rightarrow_m \tau)$. Assume that $t \leq t'$ and $f \leq f'$. Then

$$\begin{array}{ll} & f \leq f' \\ \Rightarrow & \{\text{Definition of partial order, instantiation}\} \\ & f\,t \leq f'\,t \\ \Rightarrow & \{\text{Assumption } t \leq t', \text{ monotonicity of } f', \text{ transitivity of } \leq\} \\ & f\,t \leq f'\,t' \end{array}$$

Q.E.D

18. The `let`-construct is monotonic, in the sense that the `apply`-construct that it stands for is monotonic. It immediately follows that procedure calls, which are described by `let`-constructs, are also monotonic.

7 Conclusions

1. We have shown how a programming and specification language based on a weakest precondition-semantics can be formulated in higher order logic. In particular, we showed how statements can be defined as terms in the logic. This means that we can use higher order logic as a logic for reasoning about imperative programs. Our syntax is slightly more complicated than ordinary syntax for simple imperative languages (in particular, this is the case for assignments and procedures with parameters). However, we have shown how more ordinary syntax can be permitted, using suitable abbreviations and conventions.

2. Our work can be used as a basis for mechanical reasoning about programs. Theorem provers based on simple type theory (such as the HOL proof assistant) can be used to formalize the programming notation we have developed. Reasoning about program correctness and refinement can then be carried out within higher order logic without the need for a separate proof theory.

3. Our notation permits predicate statements that map predicates over one state space to predicates over another space. In this paper, we have used this possibility to define special commands to entering and exiting a block with local variables. It can also be used for incorporating data refinement (data reification) into the notation, along the lines described in [3, 9]. This is done by introducing state transformations that transform a state of one (abstract) state space into a state of another (concrete) state space.

References

[1] R. J. R. Back. *Correctness Preserving Program Refinements: Proof Theory and Applications*, volume 131 of *Mathematical Center Tracts*. Mathematical Centre, Amsterdam, 1980.

[2] R. J. R. Back. A calculus of refinements for program derivations. *Acta Informatica*, 25:593–624, 1988.

[3] R. J. R. Back and J. von Wright. Refinement calculus I: Sequential nondeterministic programs. In J. W. deBakker, W. P. deRoever, and G. Rozenberg, editors, *Stepwise Refinement of Distributed Systems*, Lecture Notes in Computer Science, pages 42–66. Springer–Verlag, 1990.

[4] R. J. R. Back and J. von Wright. Refinement concepts formalized in higher order logic. *Formal Aspects of Computing*, 1991.

[5] E. W. Dijkstra. *A Discipline of Programming*. Prentice–Hall International, 1976.

[6] M. J. Gordon. Hol: A proof generating system for higher order logic. In G. Birtwistle and P. Subrahmanyam, editors, *VLSI Specification, Verification and Synthesis*, pages 73–128. Kluwer Academic Publishers, 1988.

[7] I. A. Mason. Hoare's logic in the LF. Technical report 87-32, Laboratory for the Foundations of Computer Science, University of Edinburgh, 1987.

[8] C. C. Morgan. The specification statement. *ACM Transactions on Programming Languages and Systems*, 10(3):403–419, July 1988.

[9] J. von Wright, J. Hekanaho, T. Langbacka, , and P. Luostarinen. Mechanizing some advanced refinement concepts. In L. Claesen and M. Gordon, editors, *Proceedings of the 1992 International Workshop on Higher Order Logic, Theorem Proving and its Applications*, pages 77 – 96. North-Holland, 1992.

Trace Nets

Eric Badouel

Philippe Darondeau

IRISA-INRIA
Campus de Beaulieu, F-35042 Rennes Cedex, France
E-mail : Eric.Badouel@irisa.fr - Philippe.Darondeau@irisa.fr

Abstract Trace Nets are a variant of one-safe Petri Nets, where input and output places may be filled as well as emptied by transitions. Those extended nets have been introduced by the authors for modelling concurrency in a simple format of structural operational specifications, based on permutation of proved transitions. Trace Nets are connected by an adjunction to a particular class of Trace Automata in the sense of Stark, namely the Separated Trace Automata. The adjunction is based on a calculus of 'regions' that differ significantly from the ones devised by Ehrenfeucht and Rozenberg for Elementary Nets, although the axioms of separation are the same.

Keywords Trace Automata, Regions, Trace Nets.

CONTENTS

1 Introduction

Although the operational meanings of concurrent systems are always given in terms of transition systems, few efforts have been spent to characterize the resulting classes of transition systems. The main contributions in that field are De Simone's result characterizing the transition systems realized in Meije (up to strong bisimulation) as the recursively enumerable transition systems [DS84], and Ehrenfeucht and Rozenberg's result characterizing the transition systems realized by elementary nets as the so-called elementary transition systems [ER90]. The present study follows the line of the latter reference, where the stress is on the structure on concurrency and not on computability aspects.

The principle laid down by Ehrenfeucht and Rozenberg for extracting nets from transition systems is to derive places from *regions*, defined as sets of places sharing the property to be entered or exited uniformly by all transitions with identical label. An elementary transition system is a transition system with enough regions for separating states and for separating states from actions they do not enable. An elementary net is a condition-event net in which transitions are disabled by their output conditions. The correspondence between elementary nets and elementary transition systems has been raised to an adjunction by Nielsen, Rozenberg, and Thiagarajan. More precisely, two reflections have been constructed from elementary nets to elementary transition systems [NRT90] and from elementary transition systems to their unfoldings which are equivalent to prime event structures [NRT91]. A similar chain of reflections has been constructed by Winskel, leading from nets to separated *asynchronous transition systems*, therefrom to trace languages, and finally to prime event structures [Win91]. Nets considered by Winskel are like elementary nets except that transitions are not disabled by their output conditions which are also input conditions. And asynchronous transition systems are labelled transition systems where set of labels comes equipped with an independence relation such that every pair of independent and co-initial transitions may be amalgamated to a diamond while every pair of independent and successive actions can be commuted [Bed88].

In the opinion of the authors, asynchronous transition systems are not general enough to give concurrent meanings to structural operational specifications. For instance, the event structure with enabling relation $\emptyset \vdash a$, $\emptyset \vdash b$, $\{a\} \vdash c$, $\{b\} \vdash c$ may be realized in SOS by $f(a, b, c)$ where the operator f allows its first two arguments to move (by a or b) and thereby evolves to a ternary operator that enables all arguments to move independently. When equipped with the independence relation where a, b, and c are pairwise independent, the transition system induced by the above event structure is not an asynchronous transition system, but is a *trace automaton* [Sta89a]. A trace automaton is a labelled transition system equipped with an independence relation on actions, such that every pair of co-initial and independent transitions may be amalgamated to a diamond (whereas two successive and independent actions are not forced to commute). Reversing the situation, we shall therefore search for a class of nets realizing trace automata.

There is no hope to solve the above question without imposing on trace automata a structural constraint, namely that independence of actions reflects diamond situations. Those trace automata are called *canonical*. We have defined a wider concept of regions for canonical trace automata, inducing condition-event nets where transitions are not disabled by their output conditions. The main outcome is that a canonical trace automaton is the realization of a net if and only if it is *separated*, i.e. satisfies Ehrenfeucht and Rozenberg's properties of separation interpreted with our specific definition of regions.

2 Canonical Trace Automata

The first part of the section recalls the definition of trace automata and their relationship to event structures and domains, and suggests on that basis behavioural equivalences for trace automata. The second part of the section studies the so-called *canonical* trace automata (where local confluence determines the relation of independence) and deals incidentally with foldings and unfoldings.

A trace automaton produces words over a *concurrent* alphabet $(A, \|)$, which means that words identical up to permutations of independent actions have to be merged. The domain of configurations of a trace automaton is the language it generates factored out by the equivalence of permutations and ordered by the prefix relation. Trace automata have the same domains of configurations as event structures with binary conflicts, and we indicate how to unfold a trace automaton into an event structure with the same domain. We suggest two notions of behavioural equivalence: trace automata are *weakly equivalent* if they induce the same domain of configurations or the same event structure, and they are *equivalent* if they have the same concurrent alphabet and the same language, or equivalently if they induce identical *labelled* event structures labelled on A.

Our purpose is to supply trace automata with behaviourally equivalent nets, using a calculus of regions inspired from [ER90]. The concept of regions in an automaton relies on labelled transitions and does not account for any relation on actions, hence there is no hope to retrieve the relation of independence from the calculus of regions unless that relation is fully reflected by diamonds in the transition system. We consider therefore the so-called *canonical trace automata* in which the relation of independence is encoded univocally in the transition system. The restriction to canonical trace automata is not too demanding, since we show that a finite trace automaton may always be transformed by finite unfolding into a finite and canonical trace automaton with the same behaviour.

The following is an adaptation from [Sta89a].

Definition 2.1 (Trace Automata) *An automaton* $\mathcal{A} = (A, Q, q_0, T)$ *consists of a* countable *set of actions* A*, a set of states* Q *with initial state* $q_0 \in Q$*, and a transition relation* $T \subset Q \times A \times Q$*. It is* a trace automaton *when the alphabet* A *comes equipped with a symmetric and irreflexive relation* $\| \subset A \times A$*, called the* independence relation*, and the following conditions on transitions* $p \xrightarrow{a} q \in T$ *are satisfied.*

determinism : $p \xrightarrow{a} q$ *and* $p \xrightarrow{a} r \Rightarrow q = r$
commutativity : $(a \| b$ *and* $q \xrightarrow{a} r$ *and* $q \xrightarrow{b} s) \Rightarrow (r \xrightarrow{b} p$ *and* $s \xrightarrow{a} p$ *for some* $p)$

We have dropped the unit transitions $p \xrightarrow{\varepsilon} p$ from Stark's original definition which is not significantly affected. This seems an appropriate place for fixing notations and terminology. In a deterministic transition system $T \subset Q \times A \times Q$, $x \xrightarrow{a}$ is an abbreviation for $\exists y \,.\, x \xrightarrow{a} y$, and $x.a$ denotes the unique y such that $x \xrightarrow{a} y$ when exists. For $q \in Q$ and $u \in A^*$, $q \xrightarrow{u}$ and $q.u$ are defined inductively: $q \xrightarrow{\varepsilon}$ always, with $q.\varepsilon = q$, and $q \xrightarrow{a.u}$ *iff* $q \xrightarrow{a}$ & $q.a \xrightarrow{u}$, with $q.(a.u) = (q.a).u$. The *language* $\mathcal{L}(\mathcal{A})$ induced by an automaton $\mathcal{A}$ is the set of words $\{m \in A^* / \ q_0 \xrightarrow{m}\}$ produced from its initial state. The set of *finite configurations* of a trace automaton $\mathcal{A}$ is the induced language $\mathcal{L}(\mathcal{A})$ factored out by the equivalence of permutations $\sim$ generated by the pairs $(uabv, ubav)$ in $\mathcal{L}(\mathcal{A}) \times \mathcal{L}(\mathcal{A})$ such that $a \| b$ in $\mathcal{A}$. Let $\lesssim \ = (\leq \cup \sim)^*$ be the prefix preorder ($\leq$) modulo permutations. The equivalence of permutations coincides with the equivalence induced by that preorder (i.e. $m \sim n$ iff $m \lesssim n$ and $n \lesssim m$). Thus $(\mathcal{L}(\mathcal{A}) / \sim, \ \lesssim / \sim)$ is an ordered set whose ideal completion is the ***domain of configurations*** of $\mathcal{A}$.

It is worth noting that languages $\mathcal{L}(\mathcal{A})$ defined by trace automata do not always coincide with linearizations of trace languages defined in trace monoids. Let us recall that the trace monoid $M(A, \|)$ induced by a concurrent alphabet $(A, \|)$ is the free monoid A^* factored out by the *congruence* generated by the pairs (ab, ba) such that $a \| b$. That monoid is left-cancellable and it has no divisor of the unit, and so the prefix relation $\sqsubseteq$ is an order on $M(A, \|)$. The domain $\hat{A}$ induced by the concurrent alphabet $(A, \|)$ is the ideal completion of the order $(M(A, \|), \sqsubseteq)$. For $m \in A^*$, let $\mathbf{tr}(m)$ denote the associated trace in $M(A, \|)$, i.e. $\mathbf{tr}(m)$ is the congruence class of m. The relations between trace monoids $M(A, \|)$ and languages $\mathcal{L}(\mathcal{A})$ defined by trace automata on $(A, \|)$ may be described as follows.

Theorem 2.2 (Stark ([Sta89a])) *Let $\mathcal{A}$ be a trace automaton on the concurrent alphabet $(A, \|)$ then $\forall m, n \in \mathcal{L}(\mathcal{A})$: $m \lesssim n$ iff $\mathbf{tr}(m) \sqsubseteq \mathbf{tr}(n)$.*

After that brief survey of the algebraic properties of $\lesssim$, let us review the domain theoretic properties of $\lesssim / \sim$. First, we fix notations and terminology. In an ordered set $(D, \leq)$, a subset X is *compatible* (notation: $X \uparrow$) if it has an upper bound, two elements x and y are *compatible* (notation: $x \uparrow y$) if $\{x, y\}$ is compatible. An element x is *covered* by an element y (notation: $x \longrightarrow\!\!< y$) if $x < y$ and $(x \leq z \leq y \Rightarrow z = x$ or $z = y)$. When $x \longrightarrow\!\!< y$, the interval $[x, y]$ is *prime*. The relation of *projectivity*, noted $\smile$, is the least equivalence on prime intervals such that $(x \longrightarrow\!\!< y) \smile (z \longrightarrow\!\!< t)$ if $x = y \wedge z$ and $t = y \vee z$. The following representation theorem was split in two parts by Stark, who used normal subdomains of domains $\hat{A}$ as mediators between event domains and domains of configurations of trace automata [Sta89a, Sta89b].

Proposition 2.3 *The domains of configurations of trace automata are the finitary Scott domains that satisfy the following three axioms:*

Axiom C: $[\, x \longrightarrow\!\!< y \ \& \ x \longrightarrow\!\!< z \,] \ \& \ [\, y \uparrow z \ \& \ y \neq z \,] \Rightarrow [\, y \longrightarrow\!\!< y \vee z \ \& \ z \longrightarrow\!\!< y \vee z \,]$
Axiom R: $(x \longrightarrow\!\!< y) \smile (x \longrightarrow\!\!< y') \Rightarrow y = y'$
Axiom V: $(x \longrightarrow\!\!< x') \smile (y \longrightarrow\!\!< y') \ \& \ (x \longrightarrow\!\!< x'') \smile (y \longrightarrow\!\!< y'') \ \& \ x' \uparrow x'' \Rightarrow y' \uparrow y''$

For the sake of completeness, we recall that a *Scott domain* is an ω-algebraic and consistently complete partial order, and that it is *finitary* if every element dominates finitely many elements in that partial order.

A PO is *consistenly complete* if every finitely compatible subset has a least upper bound (X is finitely compatible if every finite subset of X is compatible). Consistently complete PO's coincide with coherent CPO's (a PO is coherent if every compatible pair has a least upper bound; a PO is a *CPO* if every directed subset X has a least upper bound). A PO is *algebraic* if, for every element x, the set of finite elements smaller than x is directed and x is its least upper bound (y is finite if, for every directed X with least upper bound $\bigsqcup X$, $y < \bigsqcup X \Rightarrow \exists x \in X \,.\, y \leq x$). A PO is *$\omega$-algebraic* if it is algebraic and has countably many finite elements.

Now Winskel proved in [Win80] that the finitary Scott domains which satisfy the axioms (C), (R) and (V) are exactly the domains of configurations of event structures with binary conflict (whence their name of event domains).

Definition 2.4 (Event Structures and their Configurations)
An event structure *is a triple* $(E, \#, \vdash)$ *where*

1. *E is a* countable *set of* events*;*
2. *# is a binary, symmetric and irreflexive relation on E, called the* conflict *relation;*
3. *let Con be the family of finite and conflict-free subsets of E then* $\vdash$ *is a subset of* $Con \times E$*, called the* enabling *relation, such that*

$$(X \vdash e \;\; and \;\; X \subset Y \in Con) \;\; \Rightarrow \vdash e$$

A labelled event structure *labelled in A is a quadruple* $(E, \#, \vdash, \lambda)$*, where* $(E, \#, \vdash)$ *is an event structure and* $\lambda : E \to A$ *is a* labelling function .

A configuration *is a subset* $X \subset E$ *which is*

1. conflict free*:* $e\#e' \Rightarrow (e \notin X \; or \; e' \notin X)$*,*
2. secured*:* $\forall e \in x \; \exists e_0 \ldots e_n \in x$ *such that* $e_n = e$ *and* $\forall i \leq n \; \{e_0, \ldots e_{i-1}\} \vdash e_i$.

A minor adaptation of Winskel's proof that all event domains are domains of configurations of event structures leads to a straightforward method for constructing directly from a trace automaton an event structure with the same domain of configurations (the reverse construction is obvious). The adaptation consists in the use of concurrent alphabets for handling domains of configurations $(\mathcal{L}(\mathcal{A})/\sim, \lesssim/\sim)$. Namely, the events are the classes of projective prime intervals $[u, ua]$ where $ua \in \mathcal{L}(\mathcal{A})$ and $a \in A$.

A simpler construction in the same spirit was proposed by Bednarczyk for ***asynchronous*** automata and ***prime*** event structures. In [Bed88], the events are the traces $\mathbf{tr}(ua)$ such that $\mathbf{tr}(ua) = \mathbf{tr}(vb) \Rightarrow a = b$. In the case of trace automata, domains of configurations are no longer distributive and several traces satisfying that condition may correspond to the same class of projective prime intervals $[u, ua]$.

The detailed construction of the *unlabelled* event structure $(E, \#, \vdash)$ associated with a trace automaton $\mathcal{A} = (A, \|, Q, q_0, T)$ is as follows. The set of *events* E is the set of pairs $<w, a>$ representing prime intervals $[w, wa]$, i.e. $wa \in \mathcal{L}(\mathcal{A})$ and $a \in A$, factored out by the equivalence of projectivity $\smile$ generated by the conditional axioms $w \sim w' \Rightarrow <w, a> \smile <w', a>$ and $a \| b \Rightarrow <w, a> \smile <wb, a>$. Two events e_1 and e_2 are in conflict ($e_1 \# e_2$) if $e_1 = <w, a>_\smile$ and $e_2 = <w, b>_\smile$ for some pair of non independent letters a and b (not $a \| b$). For $w \in \mathcal{L}(\mathcal{A})$, define inductively $X_w \subset E$ by $X_\varepsilon = \emptyset$ and $X_{w.a} = X_w \cup \{<w, a>_\smile\}$. Let Con be the family of conflict free sets of events. Define $\mid\!\sim \subset (Con \times E)$ by $X_w \mid\!\sim <w, a>_\smile$ for $w.a \in \mathcal{L}(\mathcal{A})$. The enabling relation $\vdash \subset (Con \times E)$ is then given by: $X \vdash e$ iff $\exists w \in \mathcal{L}(\mathcal{A})$ such that $X_w \subset X$ and $X_w \mid\!\sim e$. The *labelled* event structure $(E, \#, \vdash, \lambda)$ associated with $\mathcal{A}$ is constructed in a similar way, with the labelling function $\lambda : E \rightarrow A$ given by $\lambda(<w, a>_\smile) = a$.

Proposition 2.5 *A trace automaton and the associated event structure have the same domain of configurations. Two trace automata with the same domain of configurations induce two isomorphic (unlabelled) event structures.*

The second part of the proposition is clear since our construction is just Winskel's construction rephrased in terms of concurrent alphabets. The proof for the first part of the proposition is a mere repetition of Winskel's proof accounting for that adaptation.

Two variant definitions of the *behaviour* of a trace automaton emerge now from the above construction, depending on whether the concurrent alphabet is observed.

Definition 2.6 (Behaviour of Trace Automata) *The* behaviour *(resp.* weak behaviour*) of a trace automaton is the associated labelled (resp. unlabelled) event structure. Two trace automata are equivalent (resp. weakly equivalent) if they have isomorphic behaviours (resp. weak behaviours).*

A much simpler definition of behaviour, consistent with the above, may be stated for the restricted class of reduced trace automata which we introduce now.

Definition 2.7 (Reduced Trace Automata) *A trace automaton* $(A, \|, Q, q_0, T)$ *is said to be* reduced *when:* (i) *every state is accessible,* (ii) *each action is enabled in some state,* (iii) *each pair of independent actions is enabled in some state.*

Remark 2.8 (Behaviour of Reduced Trace Automata) *The behaviour of a reduced trace automaton determines and is determined by its language and its independence relation.*

The remark follows directly from the construction of the labelled event structure associated with a trace automaton.

Our general purpose is to supply trace automata with equivalent nets, meaning that the trace automaton and the net exhibit the same language and the same relation of independence of actions. For already presented reasons, this is not feasible unless we restrict ourselves to trace automata $(A, \|, Q, q_0, T)$ in which the relation of independence $\|$ may be retrieved from the underlying automaton (A, Q, q_0, T). Let us proceed to the definition of *canonical* trace automata presenting that feature.

Definition 2.9 (Diamond) *In a deterministic transition system $T \subset Q \times A \times Q$, a diamond $\diamond(q, a, b)$ is given by a state $q \in Q$ and a pair of* distinct *actions $a, b \in A$ such that $q \xrightarrow{ab}$, $q \xrightarrow{ba}$ and $q.ab = q.ba$.*

Definition 2.10 (Canonical Trace Automata)
A reduced trace automaton $(A, \|, Q, q_0, T)$ is said to be canonical *if the relation of independence reflects diamond situations, i.e. $a\|b$ as soon as $\diamond(q, a, b)$ for some state q.*

In a canonical trace automaton, the relation of independence is encoded univocally in the transition system and may be retrieved as $a\|b \Leftrightarrow \exists q \in Q\ \diamond(q, a, b)$. In particular a canonical trace automaton satisfies the following property of *uniformity*:

$$[\exists q \in Q\ \diamond(q, a, b)] \Rightarrow [\forall q \in Q\quad q \xrightarrow{a}\ \&\ q \xrightarrow{b} \Rightarrow \diamond(q, a, b)].$$

Remark 2.11 *An automaton (A, Q, q_0, T) satisfying the above condition of uniformity and the conditions (i) and (ii) of Def. 2.7 is the projection of a unique canonical trace automaton, which we also note (A, Q, q_0, T).*

The next proposition shows that the restriction to canonical trace automata is not too demanding.

Proposition 2.12 *Every finite trace automaton has a finite and canonical equivalent.*

Proof: Let $\mathcal{A} = (A, \|, Q, q_0, T)$ be a finite trace automaton. We may assume without loss of generality, that $\mathcal{A}$ is reduced since the construction of the labelled event structure associated with $\mathcal{A}$ depends exclusively on the accessible states, enabled actions, and co-enabled pairs of independent actions. This enables us to benefit from Rem. 2.8 for showing the equivalence between $\mathcal{A}$ and the trace automaton $Can(\mathcal{A}) = (A, \|, Q', q_0', T')$ which we define hereafter. A state $<q, E> \in Q'$ consists of a state $q \in Q$ and of a subset $E \subset A$ of pairwise independent actions. The initial state is $q_0' = <q_0, \emptyset>$ and T' is the set of transitions $<q, E> \xrightarrow{a} <q', E'>$ where $q \xrightarrow{a} q'$ in T and $E' = \{a\} \cup \{b \in E / a\|b\}$ (denoted $= E.a$). Let Q' be the subset of states $<q, E>$ accessible from $<q_0, \emptyset>$ in T'. It follows from our assumptions on $\mathcal{A}$ that $Can(\mathcal{A})$ is reduced. Now, in any diamond situation $\diamond(<q, E>, a, b)$, $E.ab = E.ba$ and $a\|b$ by definition of T'. The trace automaton $Can(\mathcal{A})$ is therefore canonical, and it is clearly finite. Since $\mathcal{A}$ and $Can(\mathcal{A})$ have the same language and the same relation of independence, the proposition follows. ∎

Figure 1 illustrates the 'partial' unfolding of a trace automaton into a canonical trace automaton. In the remaining of the section, we elaborate notions of folding

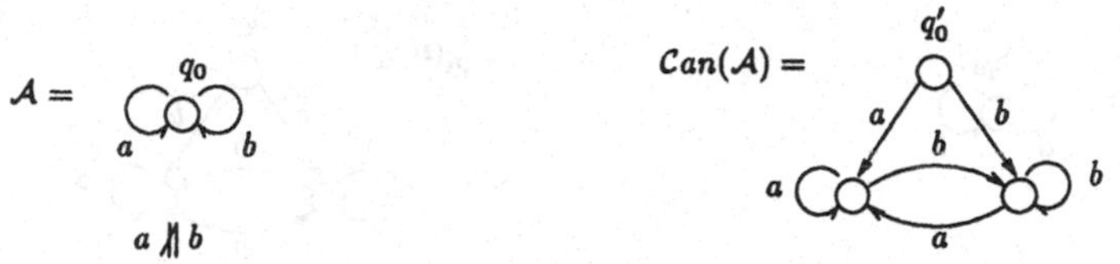

Fig. 1. unfolding a trace automaton into a canonical one

and unfolding for trace automata and we study their effect on behaviours and weak behaviours. In section 4, unfolding will be proved essential for achieving the property of separation of trace automata up to behavioural equivalence (Prop. 4.12).

Definition 2.13 (Unfolding) *Let $\mathcal{A}$ be a trace automaton. The* unfolding *of $\mathcal{A}$ is the canonical trace automaton $\mathcal{U}(\mathcal{A}) = (A', Q', q'_0, T')$ with components as follows:*

1. *Q' is the set of finite configurations $w_\sim$ of $\mathcal{A}$,*
2. *$q'_0 = \varepsilon_\sim$ is the initial configuration,*
3. *A' is the set of events $<w,a>_\smile$ induced by $\mathcal{A}$, and*
4. *T' is the set of transitions $w_\sim \xrightarrow{<w,a>_\smile} wa_\sim$.*

The label preserving unfolding *of $\mathcal{A}$ is the canonical trace automaton $\mathcal{U}'(\mathcal{A}) = (A, Q', q'_0, T)$ where A is the alphabet of $\mathcal{A}$ and T is the set of transitions $w_\sim \xrightarrow{a} wa_\sim$.*

Since the transitions in T or T', resp. the events in A' represent the prime intervals, resp. the classes of projective prime intervals in the domain of configurations of $\mathcal{A}$, one can state the following.

Remark 2.14 *Two trace automata are weakly equivalent iff their unfoldings are isomorphic (i.e. identical up to bijective renamings of states and actions), and they are equivalent iff their label preserving unfoldings are isomorphic.*

Fig. 2 shows two canonical trace automata $\mathcal{A}^{(1)}$, $\mathcal{A}^{(2)}$ and their unfoldings. Notice that $a \parallel^{(1)} b$ while $a \not\parallel^{(2)} b$.

We introduce now a preorder $\mathcal{A} > \mathcal{B}$ on reduced trace automata carrying the intuition that $\mathcal{A}$ is a *partial* unfolding of $\mathcal{B}$.

Definition 2.15 (Folding) *A* folding morphism *$(\eta, \sigma) : \mathcal{A}^{(1)} \rightarrow \mathcal{A}^{(2)}$ between two* reduced *trace automata is a pair of* surjective *mappings $\eta : A^{(1)} \rightarrow A^{(2)}$, $\sigma : Q^{(1)} \rightarrow Q^{(2)}$ between their respective sets of actions and states satisfying the conditions:*

1. *$\sigma(q_0^{(1)}) = q_0^{(2)}$,*
2. *for every $q \in Q^{(1)}$ and $a \in A^{(1)}$, $q \xrightarrow{a} \Rightarrow [\, \sigma(q) \xrightarrow{\eta(a)}$ and $\sigma(q.a) = \sigma(q).\eta(a) \,]$,*
3. *for every $q \in Q^{(1)}$, η restricts to a local bijection between $\{a/q \xrightarrow{a}\}$ and $\{b/\sigma(q) \xrightarrow{b}\}$,*
4. *for every $a, b \in A^{(1)}$, if there exists $q \in Q^{(1)}$ such that $q \xrightarrow{a}$ and $q \xrightarrow{b}$ in $\mathcal{A}^{(1)}$, then $a \parallel^{(1)} b \Leftrightarrow \eta(a) \parallel^{(2)} \eta(b)$.*

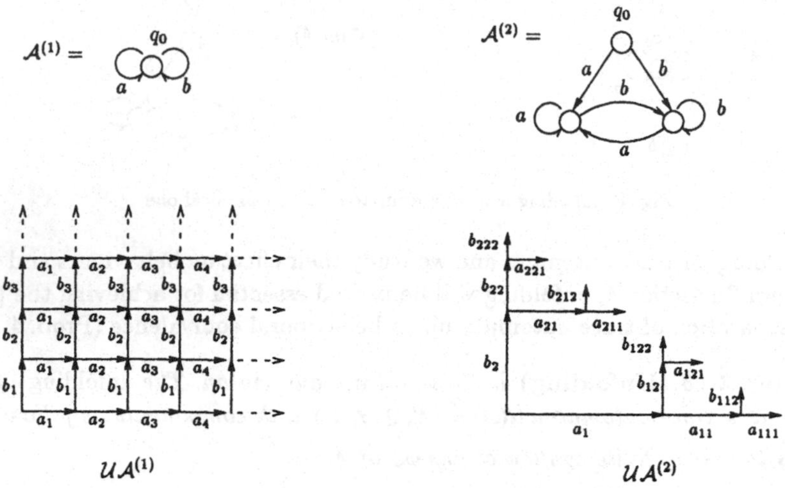

Fig. 2. two canonical trace automata and their unfoldings

When there exists a folding morphism from $\mathcal{A}^{(1)}$ *to* $\mathcal{A}^{(2)}$, $\mathcal{A}^{(2)}$ *is a* folding *of* $\mathcal{A}^{(1)}$, *and* $\mathcal{A}^{(1)}$ *folds to or* is a covering of $\mathcal{A}^{(2)}$ *(notation:* $\mathcal{A}^{(1)} > \mathcal{A}^{(2)}$*).*

Observe that relation $\eta(a)\|^{(2)}\eta(b) \Rightarrow a\|^{(1)}b$ is not asked for in the above definition, while the reverse implication is entailed by (2) and (4). Thus, if we consider the canonical trace automata $\mathcal{A}^{(1)}$ and $\mathcal{A}^{(2)}$ shown in Fig.3, where $a\|^{(2)}b$ but $a_2 \not\|^{(1)} b_1$, the mapping η that erases subscripts from actions and the mapping σ indicated by dashed lines define a folding morphism from $\mathcal{A}^{(1)}$ to $\mathcal{A}^{(2)}$.

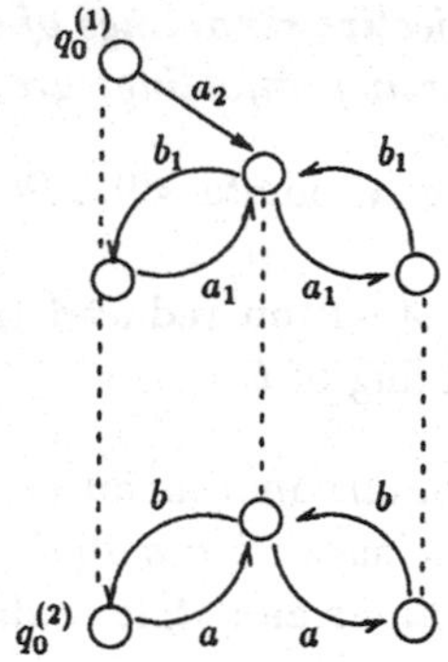

Fig. 3. a folding morphism

We have already encountered several examples of folding morphisms. For instance the pair of mappings sending respectively the configuration $m_\sim$ to the state $<q_0.m, \emptyset.m>$ and the event $<m, a>_\smile$ to the action a is a folding morphism from $\mathcal{U}(\mathcal{A})$

to $Can(\mathcal{A})$, and the mapping sending the state $<q,E>$ to the state q is a folding morphism from $Can(\mathcal{A})$ to $\mathcal{A}$ in the case when $\mathcal{A}$ is reduced. In that case, the composition of the above is a folding morphism $Fold_{\mathcal{A}} : \mathcal{U}(\mathcal{A}) \to \mathcal{A}$, defined by $\sigma(m_{\sim}) = q_0.m$ and $\eta(<m,a>_{\smile}) = a$. For instance, in Fig.2, $Fold_{\mathcal{A}^{(1)}}$ sends a_i to a and b_i to b (for $i \in I\!N$), and $Fold_{\mathcal{A}^{(2)}}$ sends $a_{\alpha 1}$ to a and $b_{\alpha 2}$ to b (for $\alpha \in \{1,2\}^*$).

Owing to the deterministic nature of trace automata, folding morphisms (η,σ) are entirely determined by their relabelling component η, and they are monic due to condition 3 (notice they are also epic since their component η is surjective). In particular, a folding morphism is a folding isomorphism as soon as it has a right or left inverse (in any category, Split Monic $\cap$ Epic = Split Epic $\cap$ Monic = Isomorphisms). If (η,σ) is a folding isomorphism, both η and σ are bijections. Conversely, if both components of a folding morphism (η,σ) are bijections, (η^{-1},σ^{-1}) is a folding morphism, and thus (η,σ) is a folding isomorphism. It should be clear from the third condition in the definition of reduced trace automata that folding isomorphisms are just the same as isomorphisms of reduced trace automata, where $\mathcal{A}$ and $\mathcal{B}$ are isomorphic (notation: $\mathcal{A} \approx \mathcal{B}$) iff they are identical up to bijective renamings of states and actions. Beware of the fact that $\mathcal{A} < \mathcal{B}$ and $\mathcal{B} < \mathcal{A}$ do not imply $\mathcal{A} \approx \mathcal{B}$ (hence folding automorphisms are not always isomorphisms). Nevertheless, $\approx$ coincides with the equivalence induced by $<$ for the restricted class of *finitely branching* trace automata (i.e. such that $\{a/q \xrightarrow{a}\}$ is always finite). In the sequel, a reduced trace automaton $\mathcal{A}$ is said to be *unfolded* iff $Fold_{\mathcal{A}} : \mathcal{U}(\mathcal{A}) \to \mathcal{A}$ is an isomorphism. Clearly, $\mathcal{U}(\mathcal{A})$ is unfolded for every $\mathcal{A}$.

Proposition 2.16 *Unfolded trace automata are a coreflective full subcategory of the category of reduced trace automata and folding morphisms.*

Proof: It is enough to prove that for every reduced trace automaton $\mathcal{A}$, $Fold_{\mathcal{A}} : \mathcal{U}(\mathcal{A}) \to \mathcal{A}$ is a co-universal arrow : it will follow therefrom that $\mathcal{U}$ is a functor, right adjoint to the inclusion functor, with $Fold_{\mathcal{A}}$ as the co-unit of the adjunction. So let $\mathcal{A}^{(1)}$ be an *unfolded* trace automaton, and let $(\eta,\sigma) : \mathcal{A}^{(1)} \to \mathcal{A}^{(2)}$ be a folding morphism. We should construct a folding morphism $(\eta,\sigma)^* : \mathcal{A}^{(1)} \to \mathcal{U}\mathcal{A}^{(2)}$ such that $(\eta,\sigma) = Fold_{\mathcal{A}^{(2)}} \circ (\eta,\sigma)^*$. Such a morphism, if it exists, is unique because folding morphisms are monic. We observe first that the relabelling component η of (η,σ) extends to a bijection between $\mathcal{L}(\mathcal{A}^{(1)})$ and $\mathcal{L}(\mathcal{A}^{(2)})$ (due to condition 3 in Def. 2.15), and more precisely to a bijection $\eta^{\sim}$ between $\mathcal{L}(\mathcal{A}^{(1)})/\sim_{(1)}$ and $\mathcal{L}(\mathcal{A}^{(2)})/\sim_{(2)}$ (due to condition 4 in Def. 2.15). That property does *not* depend on the assumption that $\mathcal{A}^{(1)}$ is unfolded. Second, we observe that η extends to a bijection $\eta^{\smile}$ between the respective sets of events of $\mathcal{U}\mathcal{A}^{(1)}$ and $\mathcal{U}\mathcal{A}^{(2)}$, due to the η-correspondance between the instances of axioms defining the respective equivalences $\smile_{(1)}$ and $\smile_{(2)}$. Indeed, the following relations are satisfied for every pair of intervals $<w,a>,<w',a'>$ in $\mathcal{A}^{(1)}$: (*i*) if $w \sim^{(1)} w'$ and $<\eta w,\eta a> \smile^{(2)} <\eta w',\eta a'>$ then $a = a'$ by condition 4 in Def. 2.15, (*ii*) if $<\eta w,\eta a> \smile^{(2)} <\eta w',\eta a'>$ with $\eta w' = \eta w \cdot b$ and $\eta a \| \eta b$ then $w_{\smile} \uparrow^{(1)} w'_{\smile}$ (whence also $(w)_1 \multimap_1 (w')_1$) and $a = a'$ by conditions 3 and 4 in Def. 2.15.

Let $\mathcal{U}((\eta,\sigma)) = (\eta^{\sim},\eta^{\smile})$, then $\mathcal{U}((\eta,\sigma)) : \mathcal{UA}^{(1)} \rightarrow \mathcal{UA}^{(2)}$ is a folding morphism, with inverse $((\eta^{\sim})^{-1},(\eta^{\smile})^{-1})$. Now clearly, $(\eta,\sigma)\circ Fold_{\mathcal{A}^{(1)}}$ and $Fold_{\mathcal{A}^{(2)}} \circ \mathcal{U}((\eta,\sigma))$ coincide on their relabelling component, hence they are equal, and we are done if we set $(\eta,\sigma)^* = \mathcal{U}((\eta,\sigma)) \circ (Fold_{\mathcal{A}^{(1)}})^{-1}$, which is an isomorphism! ∎

Corollary 2.17 *A reduced trace automaton $\mathcal{A}$ is unfolded iff $\mathcal{A} \approx \mathcal{UA}$.*

Proof: The left to right implication is immediate. So let $(\eta,\sigma) : \mathcal{UA} \rightarrow \mathcal{A}$ be an isomorphism. Since $\mathcal{UA}$ is unfolded, $(\eta,\sigma) = Fold_{\mathcal{A}} \circ (\eta,\sigma)^*$, where $(\eta,\sigma)^*$ is also an isomorphism. Thus $Fold_{\mathcal{A}} = (\eta,\sigma)\circ((\eta,\sigma)^*)^{-1}$ is an isomorphism. ∎

Corollary 2.18 *A reduced trace automaton $\mathcal{A}$ is unfolded iff $\mathcal{A} > \mathcal{UB}$ for some $\mathcal{B}$.*

Proof: Let $(\eta,\sigma) : \mathcal{A} \rightarrow \mathcal{UB}$, then $(\eta',\sigma') = (\eta,\sigma)\circ Fold_{\mathcal{A}}$ is an isomorphism from $\mathcal{UA}$ to $\mathcal{UB}$, since it is equal to the composition $Fold_{\mathcal{UB}} \circ (\eta',\sigma')^*$ of two isomorphisms. Now let $(\eta",\sigma") = (\eta',\sigma')^{-1}\circ(\eta,\sigma)$, then $(\eta",\sigma")\circ Fold_{\mathcal{A}} = 1_{\mathcal{A}}$ and $(\eta,\sigma)\circ Fold_{\mathcal{A}} \circ (\eta",\sigma") = (\eta,\sigma)$, which entails $Fold_{\mathcal{A}} \circ (\eta",\sigma") = 1_{\mathcal{A}}$ since folding morphisms are monic. Hence, $Fold_{\mathcal{A}} : \mathcal{UA} \rightarrow \mathcal{A}$ is an isomorphism. ∎

Corollary 2.19 *A reduced trace automaton $\mathcal{A}$ is unfolded iff $\mathcal{A} \approx \mathcal{UB}$ for some $\mathcal{B}$.*

The above shows that the class of unfolded trace automata is the image of the unfolding operator $\mathcal{U}$ and hence also the image of $\mathcal{U}$ restricted to reduced trace automata. In the case of *finitely branching* reduced trace automata, $\mathcal{U}$ acts in fact as a closure operator w.r.t. preorder $<$ since it is:

1. extensive: $\mathcal{A} < \mathcal{UA}$ (by $Fold_{\mathcal{A}}$) ,
2. increasing: $\mathcal{A} < \mathcal{B} \Rightarrow \mathcal{UA} < \mathcal{UB}$ (by functoriality of $\mathcal{U}$) , and
3. idempotent: $\mathcal{UUA} \approx \mathcal{UA}$ (since $\mathcal{UA}$ is unfolded).

To conclude the section, we state two characterizations of $\mathcal{UA}$. The first characterization is merely a by-product of the proof of Prop. 2.16.

Corollary 2.20 *The unfolding $\mathcal{UA}$ of a reduced trace automaton $\mathcal{A}$ is the unique (up to isomorphism) unfolded trace automaton that folds to $\mathcal{A}$. In particular $\mathcal{B} > \mathcal{A}$ entails $\mathcal{UB} \approx \mathcal{UA}$ for any trace automaton $\mathcal{B}$.*

Corollary 2.21 *The unfolding $\mathcal{UA}$ of a reduced trace automaton $\mathcal{A}$ is the greatest (up to isomorphism) reduced trace automaton that folds to $\mathcal{A}$. In particular, $\mathcal{B} > \mathcal{A} \Rightarrow \mathcal{UA} > \mathcal{B}$ if $\mathcal{B}$ is reduced.*

Proof: $\mathcal{B} > \mathcal{A}$ entails $\mathcal{UB} \approx \mathcal{UA}$ and then $\mathcal{UA} > \mathcal{B}$. Now let $\mathcal{B} > \mathcal{UA}$ then $\mathcal{B} \approx \mathcal{UB}$ since $\mathcal{UA}$ is unfolded, $\mathcal{UB} \approx \mathcal{UUA}$ by the above corollary, and $\mathcal{UUA} \approx \mathcal{UA}$ by idempotence of $\mathcal{U}$, hence $\mathcal{B} \approx \mathcal{UA}$. ∎

3 From Nets to Canonical Trace Automata

In this section we introduce Nets in which the transitions depend on input conditions but may either set or clear their input and output conditions; we show that every net induces a trace automaton with the same behaviour; we express a condition of separation characterizing the nets which may be reconstructed from the associated trace automata.

Before stating our definition of nets, let us fix notations and terminology. For any relation $\nabla \subset A \times B$, let $()^{\nabla} : A \to 2^B$ and ${}^{\nabla}() : B \to 2^A$ be the mappings given by:

$$a \nabla b \quad \text{iff} \quad b \in a^{\nabla} \quad \text{iff} \quad a \in {}^{\nabla}b$$

We say that a family of subsets $X_i \subset A$ is a *partitioning* of A whenever it is pairwise disjoint ($X_i \cap X_j = \emptyset$ for $i \neq j$) and covers the whole of A ($\bigcup_i X_i = A$). A partitioning is like a partition except that some of its components may be empty. Notice that a family $\nabla_i \subset A \times B$ is a partitioning of $A \times B$ iff for all $a \in A$, the family a^{∇_i} is a partitioning of B iff for all $b \in B$ the family ${}^{\nabla_i}b$ is a partitioning of A.

Definition 3.1 (Nets) *A net* $\mathcal{N} = (P, A, \overset{0}{\leftarrow}, \overset{1}{\leftarrow}, \overset{0}{\rightarrow}, \overset{1}{\rightarrow}, \perp, M_0)$ *consists of a set of places P, a set of actions (or events) A, a family of flow relations* $\overset{0}{\leftarrow}, \overset{1}{\leftarrow}, \overset{0}{\rightarrow}, \overset{1}{\rightarrow}, \perp$ *which form a partitioning of $A \times P$, and an initial marking $M_0 \subset P$.*

If $M \subset P$ is a marking and $x \in M$ (respectively $x \notin M$) we say that the place x is *full* (resp. *empty*) for the marking M. x is said to be an *input place* for a if $a \leftarrow x$ where $\leftarrow = \overset{0}{\leftarrow} \cup \overset{1}{\leftarrow}$ and x is said to be an *output place* for a if $a \rightarrow x$ where $\rightarrow = \overset{0}{\rightarrow} \cup \overset{1}{\rightarrow}$. The behaviour of a net is the following: an action a is *enabled* at a marking M (in notation $M \overset{a}{\rightarrow}$) if every input place of a is full for the marking M, thus the input places are the *pre-conditions* for an action to be *fired*. When an action a is fired, the places x such that $a\mathbf{0}x$ (where $\mathbf{0} = \overset{0}{\leftarrow} \cup \overset{0}{\rightarrow}$) are emptied if they were not already empty, and the places x such that $a\mathbf{1}x$ (where $\mathbf{1} = \overset{1}{\leftarrow} \cup \overset{1}{\rightarrow}$) are filled if they were not already full. Therefore, if $\mathcal{M} = 2^P$ is the set of *markings*, the set of transitions $\mathcal{T} \subset \mathcal{M} \times A \times \mathcal{M}$ for the net $\mathcal{N}$ is given by:

$$M \overset{a}{\rightarrow} M' \text{ iff } a^{\leftarrow} \subset M \text{ and } M' = (M \setminus a^{\mathbf{0}}) \cup a^{\mathbf{1}}$$

The *language* $\mathcal{L}(\mathcal{N})$ induced by a net $\mathcal{N}$ with set of actions A is the set of words $\{m \in A^* / q_0 \overset{m}{\rightarrow}\}$; the net $\mathcal{N}$ is *reduced* if $\mathcal{L}(\mathcal{N})$ has projections different from $\emptyset$ and $\{\varepsilon\}$ for every $a \in A$. *All nets considered from now on are reduced.*

Summing up, there are two types of input places for an action a: one type corresponds to pre-conditions that must hold for executing a but which are unaffected by that action (we say that action a *tests* condition x when $a \overset{1}{\leftarrow} x$), whereas the pre-conditions of the other type do no longer hold after a has executed (we say that action a *consumes* resource x when $a \overset{0}{\leftarrow} x$). As regards the ouput places of an action a, they do not condition the firing of a but on the contrary, they are set unconditionally to a fixed value (0 or 1) at each execution of a. The remaining case when $a \perp x$ (read a and x are *orthogonal*) corresponds to conditions which are neither tested nor affected by the action a. A net may be depicted as shown in

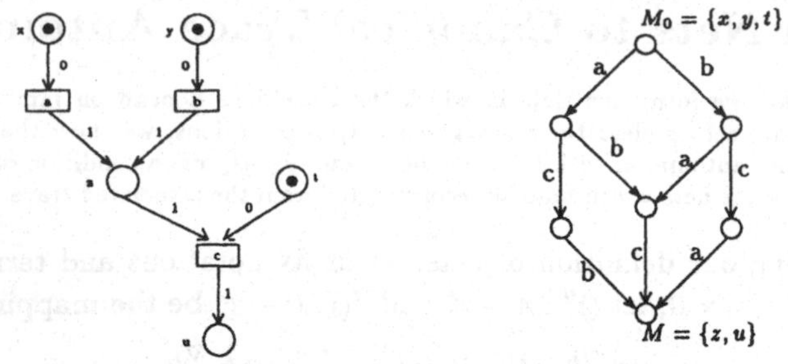

Fig. 4. a net and its transition system

Fig. 4 where an arc is drawn from a place x (depicted by a circle) to an action a (depicted by a box) when x is an input place for a, and conversely an arc is drawn from an action a to each of its ouput places. An arc between a place and an action is labelled according to the value of the place after the execution of the action (empty: 0 or full: 1). A marking M may be represented by putting down one token in each of its places. In Fig. 4 we have represented the transition system associated to the net with initial marking as indicated. In this example, the actions a and b consume their respective resources x and y and each of them turns on the condition z, the action c tests the condition z and thus awaits for a or b (or both) to be performed, and then consumes its resource t and turns on the condition u. Intuitively the actions a and b are compatible, hence they may be performed in parallel, and when for instance a has been fired, the actions b and c may also be performed in parallel. This is reflected in the transition system by the presence of *diamond situations* $\diamond(M, a, b)$. A diamond situation occurs when two actions enabled at a given marking are *independent* according to the following definition.

Definition 3.2 (Behaviour of Nets) *In a net, two distinct actions a and b are said to be* independent *(notation: $a \| b$) when the following hold:*
(i) *they are both enabled at some accessible marking M,*
(ii) $a^{\overset{0}{\leftarrow}} \subset b^{\perp}$ & $a^0 \cap b^1 = \emptyset$, *and symmetrically*
(iii) $b^{\overset{0}{\leftarrow}} \subset a^{\perp}$ & $b^0 \cap a^1 = \emptyset$.
The behaviour *of a net is given by its language plus its independence relation.*

When two actions are structurally independent (conditions *ii* and *iii*), no resource consumed by one is tested or modified by the other, and they do not deliver incompatible values to shared places. Condition *(i)* is not structural but it ensures that all the information about independence is available from the transition system, in the sense that two actions a and b are independent if and only if they occur in a diamond situation:

Proposition 3.3 *Given a net $\mathcal{N}$, let $\|$ be the independence relation stated for $\mathcal{N}$ in Def. 3.2, and let $\mathcal{T}_a \subset \mathcal{M}_a \times A \times \mathcal{M}_a$ be the accessible restriction of the transition system induced by $\mathcal{N}$ (with set of accessible markings $\mathcal{M}_a$), then $na(\mathcal{N}) = (A, \|, \mathcal{M}_a, M_0, \mathcal{T}_a)$ is a canonical trace automaton.*

Proof: We show first that independence *produces* diamond situations:

$$(\forall M \in \mathcal{M}_a)\ [a\|b \text{ and } M \xrightarrow{a} \text{ and } M \xrightarrow{b}] \Rightarrow [M.a \xrightarrow{b} \text{ and } M.b \xrightarrow{a} \text{ and } M.ab = M.ba],$$

second that independence *reflects* diamond situations:

$$(\exists M \in \mathcal{M}_a) \,.\, (M \xrightarrow{ab} \text{ and } M \xrightarrow{ba} \text{ and } M.ab = M.ba) \ \Rightarrow\ a = b \text{ or } a\|b\,.$$

First, assume that $a\|b$ and $\exists M \in \mathcal{M}_a$ such that $M \xrightarrow{a}$ and $M \xrightarrow{b}$. The action b is enabled at M, thus $b^{\leftarrow} \subset M$, and $a\|b$ entails $a^0 \cap b^{\leftarrow} = \emptyset$, thus $b^{\leftarrow} \subset M.a$ and $M.a \xrightarrow{b}$. Symmetrically, $M.b \xrightarrow{a}$. Now we have:

$$\begin{aligned}(M.a).b &= (((M \setminus a^0) \cup a^1) \setminus b^0) \cup b^1) \\ &= (M \setminus (a^0 \cup b^0)) \cup (a^1 \cup b^1) && \text{because } a^1 \cap b^0 = \emptyset \\ &= (M.b).a && \text{by symmetry.}\end{aligned}$$

The proof that independence reflects diamond situations is sketched in Fig. 5 where each slot in an array represents the set of places satisfying the flow relations indicated by its coordinates, e.g. the slot with coordinates $a^{\overset{0}{\leftarrow}}$ and $b^{\overset{1}{\rightarrow}}$ represents the set $a^{\overset{0}{\leftarrow}} \cap b^{\overset{1}{\rightarrow}}$. As indicated, from $M.a \xrightarrow{b}$ we deduce (1) $a^0 \cap b^{\leftarrow} = \emptyset$, from $M.b \xrightarrow{a}$ we deduce (2) $b^0 \cap a^{\leftarrow} = \emptyset$, and the equality $M.ab = M.ba$ finally gives us (3) $a^1 \cap b^0 = b^1 \cap a^0 = \emptyset$. ∎

Corollary 3.4 *A net and the induced (canonical) trace automaton have the same behaviour.*

In the remaining part of the section, we state conditions on nets enabling to retrieve their flow relations from the induced trace automata. Let us observe beforehand the following relations where M and M' range over the set of *accessible* markings of a net, justified by the logical equivalence $M \xrightarrow{a} M' \Leftrightarrow a^{\leftarrow} \subset M \;\&\; M' = (M \setminus a^0) \cup a^1$:

$$\begin{aligned} a \leftarrow x &\Rightarrow (M \xrightarrow{a} M' \Rightarrow x \in M) \\ a1x &\Rightarrow (M \xrightarrow{a} M' \Rightarrow x \in M') \\ a0x &\Rightarrow (M \xrightarrow{a} M' \Rightarrow x \notin M') \\ a{\perp}x &\Rightarrow (M \xrightarrow{a} M' \Rightarrow (x \in M \text{ iff } x \in M')) \end{aligned}$$

A net in which the first three implications may be strengthened to equivalences (as would be the case if M and M' ranged over all markings, accessible or not) is called a *weakly separated* net, which means that its accessible markings are enough for reconstructing its flow relations. A *separated* net is then a weakly separated net in which any two distinct places are distinguished by some accessible marking, containing one but not the other.

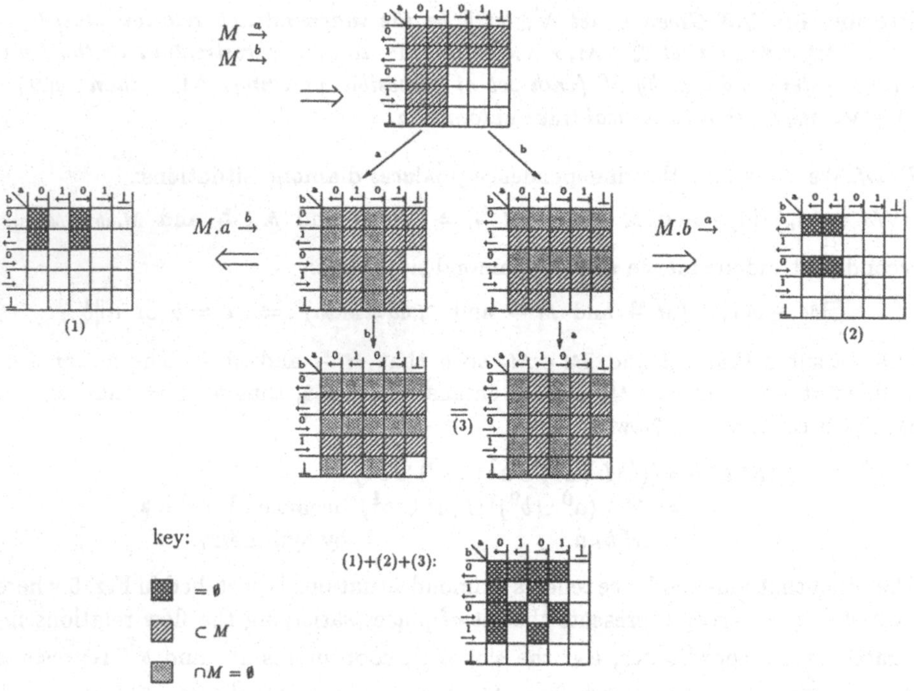

Fig. 5. **reflection of diamond situations**

Definition 3.5 (Separated Nets) *A net* $\mathcal{N}$ *is* weakly separated *when the following conditions are met by its accessible markings:*
(i) $[M \xrightarrow{a} M' \;\Rightarrow x \in M] \Rightarrow a \leftarrow x$,
(ii) $[M \xrightarrow{a} M' \;\Rightarrow x \in M'] \Rightarrow a 1 x$,
(iii) $[M \xrightarrow{a} M' \;\Rightarrow x \notin M'] \Rightarrow a 0 x$.
A weakly separated net is separated *if it satisfies also the condition:*
(iv) $[\forall M (x \in M \Leftrightarrow x' \in M)] \Rightarrow x = x'$.

We shall see (Cor. 4.11) that for every finite net there exists a finite and separated net with the same behaviour.

Proposition 3.6 *In a weakly separated net* $\mathcal{N} = (P, A, \overset{0}{\leftarrow}, \overset{1}{\leftarrow}, \overset{0}{\rightarrow}, \overset{1}{\rightarrow}, \perp, M_0)$ *the flow relations are characterized by the following equivalences where* M *and* M' *range over accessible markings.*

$a \overset{0}{\leftarrow} x$ **iff** $M \xrightarrow{a} M' \Rightarrow x \in M \;\;\&\;\; x \notin M'$

$a \overset{0}{\rightarrow} x$ **iff** $(M \xrightarrow{a} M' \Rightarrow x \notin M') \;\&\; (\exists M \xrightarrow{a} M' \text{ with } x \notin M)$

$a \overset{1}{\leftarrow} x$ **iff** $M \xrightarrow{a} M' \Rightarrow (x \in M \;\;\&\;\; x \in M')$

$a \overset{1}{\rightarrow} x$ **iff** $(M \xrightarrow{a} M' \Rightarrow x \in M') \;\&\; (\exists M \xrightarrow{a} M' \text{ with } x \notin M)$

$a \perp x$ **iff** $[M \xrightarrow{a} M' \Rightarrow (x \in M \text{ iff } x \in M')] \;\&\; (\exists M \xrightarrow{a} M' \text{ with } x \notin M) \;\&\; (\exists M \xrightarrow{a} M' \text{ with } x \in M))$

Proof: The following relations hold clearly for weakly separated nets :

$$a \leftarrow x \Leftrightarrow (M \xrightarrow{a} M' \Rightarrow x \in M)$$
$$a 1 x \Leftrightarrow (M \xrightarrow{a} M' \Rightarrow x \in M')$$
$$a 0 x \Leftrightarrow (M \xrightarrow{a} M' \Rightarrow x \notin M')$$
$$a \perp x \Rightarrow (M \xrightarrow{a} M' \Rightarrow (x \in M \text{ iff } x \in M'))$$

Since $\{1, 0, \perp\}$ is a partitioning of $A \times P$, we draw therefrom:

$$a \perp x \Leftrightarrow [(M \xrightarrow{a} M' \Rightarrow (x \in M \text{ iff } x \in M')) \& (\exists M \xrightarrow{a} M' \text{ with } x \notin M) \& (\exists M \xrightarrow{a} M' \text{ with } x \in M))]$$

The proposition follows, using the fact that $\{\leftarrow, \rightarrow, \perp\}$ is a partitioning of $A \times P$ and the identities $\overset{0}{\leftarrow} = \leftarrow \cap\, 0$, $\overset{1}{\leftarrow} = \leftarrow \cap\, 1$, $\overset{0}{\rightarrow} = \rightarrow \cap\, 0$, and $\overset{1}{\rightarrow} = \rightarrow \cap\, 1$. ∎

Corollary 3.7 *A separated net is a weakly separated net with no redundant places, where x and y are redundant when $x \in M_0 \Leftrightarrow y \in M_0$ and $a \nabla x \Leftrightarrow a \nabla y$ for all $a \in A$ and $\nabla \in \{\overset{0}{\leftarrow}, \overset{0}{\rightarrow}, \overset{1}{\leftarrow}, \overset{1}{\rightarrow}, \perp\}$.*

4 From Canonical Trace Automata to Nets

In the preceding section, we have constructed canonical trace automata $na(\mathcal{N})$ from nets $\mathcal{N}$. In this section, we construct nets $na(\mathcal{A})$ from canonical trace automata $\mathcal{A}$. We express both a necessary condition and a sufficient condition for the equivalence of the behaviours of $\mathcal{A}$ and $an(\mathcal{A})$. Those conditions are exactly the two conditions of separation of Ehrenfeucht and Rozenberg [ER90], although our definition of regions is different. We show that an resp. na produce separated nets resp. trace automata, and that $na \circ an$ resp. $an \circ na$ preserve the transition resp. flow relations when they are applied to weakly separated trace automata resp. nets. And moreover $\mathcal{A}$ and $na(an(\mathcal{A}))$ are isomorphic if, and only if, $\mathcal{A}$ is separated.

According to Prop. 3.6, a weakly separated net $\mathcal{N}$ may always be reconstructed from $na(\mathcal{N})$. In order to extend the construction to all canonical trace automata, we must replace accessible sets of places M by usual states q. By symmetry, usual places are then replaced by sets of states, leading to the following definition of *regions*.

Definition 4.1 (Regions) *Let (A, Q, q_0, T) be a canonical trace automaton, we define the following (disjoint) flow relations on $A \times 2^Q$:*

$a \overset{0}{\leftarrow} x$ **iff** $q \xrightarrow{a} q' \Rightarrow (q \in x \;\;\&\;\; q' \notin x)$

$a \overset{0}{\rightarrow} x$ **iff** $(q \xrightarrow{a} q' \Rightarrow q' \notin x) \;\;\&\;\; (\exists q \xrightarrow{a} q' \text{ with } q \notin x)$

$a \overset{1}{\leftarrow} x$ **iff** $q \xrightarrow{a} q' \Rightarrow (q \in x \;\;\&\;\; q' \in x)$

$a \overset{1}{\rightarrow} x$ **iff** $(q \xrightarrow{a} q' \Rightarrow q' \in x) \;\;\&\;\; (\exists q \xrightarrow{a} q' \text{ with } q \notin x)$

$a \perp x$ **iff** $[q \xrightarrow{a} q' \Rightarrow (q \in x \text{ iff } q' \in x)] \;\&\; (\exists q \xrightarrow{a} q' \text{ with } q \notin x) \;\&\; (\exists q \xrightarrow{a} q' \text{ with } q \in x)$

A set of states $x \subset Q$ is said to be a region *(or place) if $\{\overset{0}{\leftarrow} x, \overset{1}{\leftarrow} x, \overset{0}{\rightarrow} x, \overset{1}{\rightarrow} x, \perp x\}$ is a partitioning of the set of actions A. In that case, the above defined relations restrict to homonymic flow relations on $A \times P$ where P is the set of regions. The net $an(\mathcal{A})$ derived from the canonical trace automaton $\mathcal{A}$ is then defined as $(P, A, \overset{0}{\leftarrow}, \overset{1}{\leftarrow}, \overset{0}{\rightarrow}, \overset{1}{\rightarrow}, \perp, M_0)$ with $M_0 = \{x \in P / \; q_0 \in x\}$.*

Like we did for nets, we define on $A \times 2^Q$ the derived flow relations $\leftarrow = \overset{0}{\leftarrow} \cup \overset{1}{\leftarrow}$, $\rightarrow = \overset{0}{\rightarrow} \cup \overset{1}{\rightarrow}$, $\mathbf{0} = \overset{0}{\leftarrow} \cup \overset{0}{\rightarrow}$,and $\mathbf{1} = \overset{1}{\leftarrow} \cup \overset{1}{\rightarrow}$. The first one and the last two have a clear characterization:

Proposition 4.2 *For any region x the following hold:*

$$\begin{array}{rl} a \leftarrow x & \textbf{iff } q \overset{a}{\rightarrow} q' \Rightarrow q \in x \\ a\mathbf{0}x & \textbf{iff } q \overset{a}{\rightarrow} q' \Rightarrow q' \notin x \\ a\mathbf{1}x & \textbf{iff } q \overset{a}{\rightarrow} q' \Rightarrow q' \in x \end{array}$$

Proof: By the definition of regions, $(a \leftarrow x \ \& \ q \overset{a}{\rightarrow}) \Rightarrow q \in x$. Conversely, assume $\forall q \in Q$ $q \overset{a}{\rightarrow} \Rightarrow q \in x$ but $a \not\leftarrow x$. In that case, there should exist two transitions $q_1 \overset{a}{\rightarrow} q_1'$ and $q_2 \overset{a}{\rightarrow} q_2'$ such that $q_1' \in x$ and $q_2' \notin x$, but this is impossible since we have neither $a \overset{0}{\rightarrow} x$ because $q_1' \in x$, nor $a \overset{1}{\rightarrow} x$ because $q_2' \notin x$, nor $a \perp x$ because $q_2 \overset{a}{\rightarrow} q_2'$ with $q_2 \in x$ and $q_2' \notin x$. The last two equivalences follow directly from the definition of the flow relations and actually hold *for any set* $x \subset Q$. ∎

In order to obtain a simple characterization of regions, let us finally define:

$$a \dagger x \textbf{ iff } q \overset{a}{\rightarrow} q' \Rightarrow (q \in x \textbf{ iff } q' \in x)$$

then x is a region if and only if $A = {}^{\mathbf{0}}x \cup {}^{\mathbf{1}}x \cup {}^{\dagger}x$. Thus $x \subset Q$ is a region if and only if none of the two *excluded patterns* depicted in Fig. 6 occurs for x, more precisely:

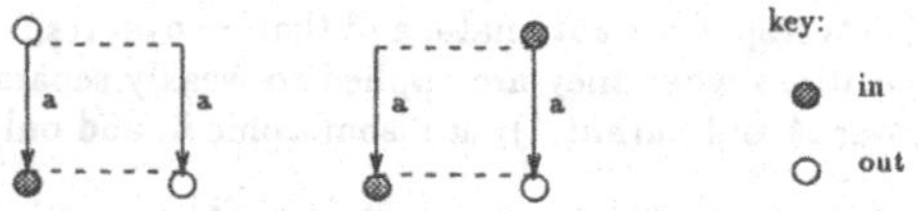

Fig. 6. **excluded patterns for a region**

Remark 4.3 (Excluded patterns) *In a canonical trace automaton, a set of states $x \subset Q$ is a region if and only if the following conditions hold.*

$$(\exists q \overset{a}{\rightarrow} q' \in T \ \textit{with} \ q \notin x \ \& \ q' \in x) \Rightarrow a\mathbf{1}x$$
$$(\exists q \overset{a}{\rightarrow} q' \in T \ \textit{with} \ q \in x \ \& \ q' \notin x) \Rightarrow a\mathbf{0}x$$

The complement $\bar{x} = Q \setminus x$ of a region x is also a region, with ${}^{\mathbf{0}}\bar{x} = {}^{\mathbf{1}}x$, ${}^{\mathbf{1}}\bar{x} = {}^{\mathbf{0}}x$, and ${}^{\dagger}\bar{x} = {}^{\dagger}x$. In Fig. 7 we have represented 8 out of the 14 regions for the transition system associated with the net in Fig. 4. The missing items are the trivial regions (the whole set Q and the empty set) plus four regions obtained by exchanging a and b in the upper half. By adding the flow relations and initial marking indicated in Def. 4.1 and shown in Fig. 7 we recover the original net of Fig. 4 enriched with additional places but with unchanged behaviour (see Fig. 8). We have seen that a net and its associated canonical trace automaton have the same behaviour. The next definition and proposition state a necessary condition and a sufficient condition for the converse.

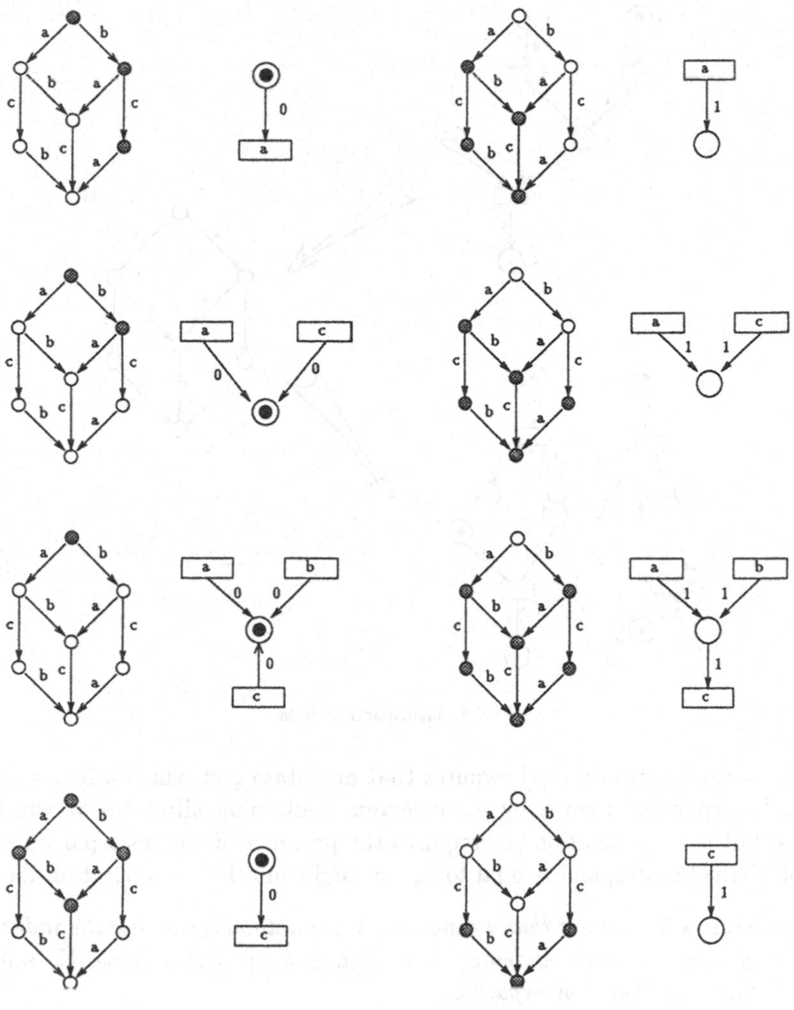

Fig. 7. examples of regions

Definition 4.4 (Separated trace automata) *A canonical trace automaton is* weakly separated *if it satisfies the condition:*
(i) $(\forall x \in P \;\; a \leftarrow x \Rightarrow q \in x) \Rightarrow q \xrightarrow{a}$.
A weakly separated trace automaton is separated *if it satisfies the condition:*
(ii) $(\forall x \in P \;\; q \in x \Leftrightarrow q' \in x) \Rightarrow q = q'$.

In view of Prop. 4.2 weakly separated automata satisfy the following equivalence:

$$q \xrightarrow{a} \quad \text{iff} \quad \forall x \in P \;\; a \leftarrow x \Rightarrow q \in x$$

which means that there are enough regions for retrieving the enabling relation from the flow relations. This condition is the exact counterpart for weak separability of

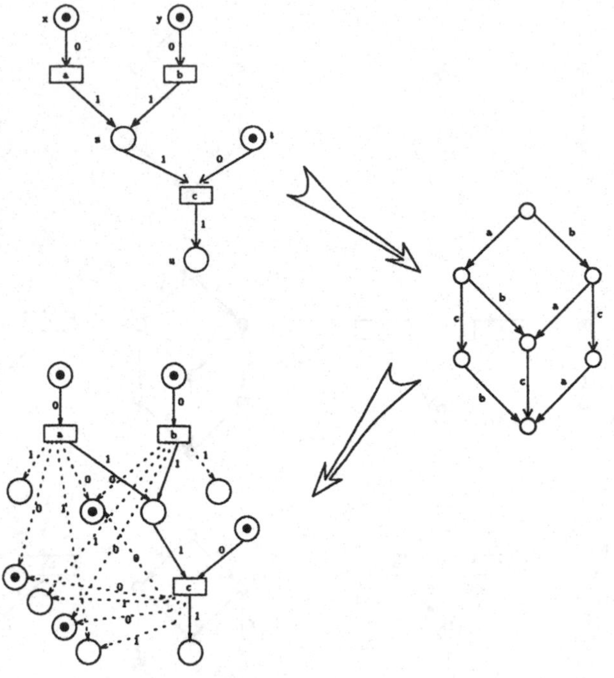

Fig. 8. saturation of nets

nets. Technically, property *(i)* requires that any state q at which a is not enabled should be separated from a by some region, containing all states at which a is enabled but not q. Condition *(ii)* requires the presence of regions separating every pair of distinct states, and is dual to the second condition of separation for nets.

Proposition 4.5 *In order that a canonical trace automaton $\mathcal{A}$ and the induced net $an(\mathcal{A})$ may have the same behaviour, it is* (i) necessary *that $\mathcal{A}$ be weakly separated and* (ii) sufficient *that $\mathcal{A}$ be separated.*

Proof:
(i) Since bisimilarity and equality of languages are the same for *deterministic* transition systems, there suffices to prove that the underlying transition systems of a canonical trace automaton and of the induced net are bisimilar if and only if the trace automaton is weakly separated. For that purpose, we show that $q \xrightarrow{a}$ implies $a^{\leftarrow} \subset q^{\in}$ and $(q.a)^{\in} = q^{\in}.a$. Thus, if $\mathcal{A}$ is weakly separated, $\mathcal{L}(\mathcal{A}) = \mathcal{L}(an(\mathcal{A}))$, as $q \xrightarrow{a} \Rightarrow a^{\leftarrow} \subset q^{\in}$ by definition of $a^{\leftarrow}$ and $a^{\leftarrow} \subset q^{\in} \Rightarrow q \xrightarrow{a}$ by contraposition of the first property of separation; and conversely, $\mathcal{L}(\mathcal{A}) = \mathcal{L}(an(\mathcal{A}))$ entails $a^{\leftarrow} \subset q^{\in} \Rightarrow q \xrightarrow{a}$. So, assuming $q \xrightarrow{a} q'$, let us establish the logical equivalence $q' \in x$ iff $[(q \in x \ \& \ a \notin {}^{0}x)$ or $a \in {}^{1}x]$, where x ranges over the regions of $\mathcal{A}$.

1. $([(q \in x \ \& \ a \notin {}^{0}x)$ or $a \in {}^{1}x] \ \& \ q \xrightarrow{a} q') \Rightarrow q' \in x$:

(a) $(a \in {}^1x \;\&\; q \xrightarrow{a} q') \Rightarrow q' \in x$ by definition of ${}^1x$.
(b) $(q \in x \;\&\; a \notin {}^0x \;\&\; a \notin {}^1x \;\&\; q \xrightarrow{a} q') \Rightarrow q' \in x$ by definition of a region x.

2. $(q' \in x \;\&\; q \xrightarrow{a} q') \Rightarrow [(q \in x \;\&\; a \notin {}^0x)$ or $a \in {}^1x]$:
   (a) $(q' \in x \;\&\; q \xrightarrow{a} q') \;\Rightarrow\; a \notin {}^0x$ by definition of ${}^0x$.
   (b) $(q \notin x \;\&\; q \xrightarrow{a} q' \;\&\; q' \in x) \Rightarrow a \in {}^1x$ by definition of a region x.

(ii) We show that $\mathcal{A}$ and $an(\mathcal{A})$ have the same relation of independence when $\mathcal{A}$ is a separated trace automaton, in which case $\mathcal{A}$ and $an(\mathcal{A})$ have the same behaviour by part *(i)* of the proposition. Let $\mathcal{A}$ be a separated trace automaton. Assume that a and b are independent in $\mathcal{A}$. Since $a\|b$, there exists at least one state q in which both actions are enabled, leading to a diamond situation

$$q \xrightarrow{a} q.a \xrightarrow{b} q' \;\&\; q \xrightarrow{b} q.b \xrightarrow{a} q'$$

Let $x \in a^{\overset{0}{\leftarrow}}$ then $q \in x$, $q.b \in x$, $q.a \notin x$, and $q' \notin x$ by the definition of regions, hence $b \bot x$ since neither $b0x$ (as $q.b \in x$) nor $b1x$ (as $q' \notin x$). Thus, $a^{\overset{0}{\leftarrow}} \subset b^{\bot}$. Now let $x \in a^0$, then $q' \notin x$ by the definition of regions, hence we cannot have $b1x$. Thus $a^0 \cap b^1 = \emptyset$. Moreover, $q^{\in}$ is an *accessible* marking (of $an(\mathcal{A})$) in which both a and b are enabled, because $()^{\in}$ is a (functional) bisimulation between the underlying transition systems of $\mathcal{A}$ and $na(an(\mathcal{A}))$. Hence, independence in $\mathcal{A}$ entails independence in $an(\mathcal{A})$. Conversely, assume a and b are independent in $an(\mathcal{A})$. Since $()^{\in}$ is a (functional) bisimulation, all the accessible markings are of the form $q^{\in}$ for some $q \in Q$. Therefore there exists a state q in which a and b are both enabled. Thanks to relations $q \xrightarrow{a} \Leftrightarrow (q)^{\in} \xrightarrow{a}$ and $(q.a)^{\in} = q^{\in}.a$, and by the second property of separation, the diamond $\diamond(q^{\in}, a, b)$ in $na(an(\mathcal{A}))$ may be "carried" into a corresponding diamond $\diamond(q, a, b)$ in $\mathcal{A}$. Hence a and b are independent in $\mathcal{A}$ since it is canonical.
Summing up, the first condition of separation is necessary and sufficient for the preservation of languages, while the two conditions of separation (plus the condition of reflection of diamonds) ensure that independence is preserved. ∎

The next two propositions, together with Cor. 3.4 and Prop. 4.5, tell the gist of the correspondence between canonical trace automata and nets to those who are not interested in the adjunction constructed in the final section.

Proposition 4.6 *Let $\mathcal{A}$ be a canonical trace automaton.*

1. *For every state q in $\mathcal{A}$, the set $q^{\in} = \{x / q \in x\}$ of the regions containing q is an accessible marking of $an(\mathcal{A})$.*

2. *If $\mathcal{A}$ is a weakly separated trace automaton, then $an(\mathcal{A})$ is a separated net.*

3. *If $\mathcal{A}$ is a weakly separated trace automaton, then all the accessible markings of $an(\mathcal{A})$ are of the form $q^{\in}$, $q \xrightarrow{a} \Leftrightarrow q^{\in} \xrightarrow{a}$, and $(q.a)^{\in} = q^{\in}.a$.*

4. *If $\mathcal{A}$ is a separated trace automaton, then $\mathcal{A}$ is isomorphic to $na(an(\mathcal{A}))$.*

Proof: (1, 3, 4) see the proof of Prop. 4.5. (2) By Prop. 4.2, $an(\mathcal{A})$ is weakly separated. Suppose now that two regions x and y belong exactly to the same markings $q^{\in}$ of $an(\mathcal{A})$, then $q \in x$ iff $q \in y$ and so $x = y$. ∎

Definition 4.7 *For any net $\mathcal{N}$ we define the auxiliary flow relation $\dagger \subset A \times P$ by*

$$a \dagger x \ \textbf{ iff } \ [\forall M \in \mathcal{M}_a \ \ M \xrightarrow{a} M' \Rightarrow (x \in M \ \textit{ iff } \ x \in M')]$$

Hence, $\perp \subset \dagger$ for any net and $a \perp x \Leftrightarrow [a \dagger x$ and $not(a0x)$ and $not(a1x)]$ for any weakly separated net. Whereas the flow relations ∇ in $an(\mathcal{A})$ ($\nabla \in \{\overset{0}{\leftarrow}, \overset{1}{\leftarrow}, \overset{0}{\rightarrow}, \overset{1}{\rightarrow}, \perp\}$) are defined by restriction to regions of the homonymic relations $\nabla \subset A \times 2^Q$ in the automaton $\mathcal{A}$, the auxiliary flow relation $\dagger$ for $an(\mathcal{A})$ is in fact defined as the "dagger" relation in $na(an(\mathcal{A}))$! Nevertheless if $\mathcal{A}$ is separated, it is isomorphic to $na(an(\mathcal{A}))$ and we have therefore the following

Proposition 4.8 *If $\mathcal{A}$ is a separated trace automaton, the flow relation $\dagger \subset A \times P$ of $\mathcal{N} = an(\mathcal{A})$ is the restriction to regions of the corresponding flow relation $\dagger \subset A \times 2^Q$ computed for $\mathcal{A}$.*

Proposition 4.9 *Let $\mathcal{N}$ be a net.*

1. *For every place x in $\mathcal{N}$, the set $x^{\in} = \{M / x \in M\}$ of the accessible markings containing x is a region in $na(\mathcal{N})$.*
2. *$na(\mathcal{N})$ is a separated trace automaton.*
3. *If $\mathcal{N}$ is a weakly separated net then $a \nabla x \Leftrightarrow a \nabla x^{\in}$ for every flow relation $\nabla \in \{\overset{0}{\leftarrow}, \overset{1}{\leftarrow}, \overset{0}{\rightarrow}, \overset{1}{\rightarrow}, \perp\}$.*

Proof: (1) By definition of nets, $M \xrightarrow{a} M' \Rightarrow M' = (M \setminus a^0) \cup a^1$, hence the following relations hold:

$$(M \xrightarrow{a} M' \text{ and } x \notin M \text{ and } x \in M') \Rightarrow a1x$$
$$(M \xrightarrow{a} M' \text{ and } x \in M \text{ and } x \notin M') \Rightarrow a0x$$

Thus the set $x^{\in} = \{M / x \in M\}$ is a region by Rem. 4.3. (2) By definition of nets, $M \xrightarrow{a} \Leftrightarrow a^{\leftarrow} \subset M$, hence $M \overset{a}{\not\rightarrow} \Rightarrow \exists x \in P$ s.t. $a \leftarrow x$ and $x \notin M$. By definition of nets, $a \leftarrow x \Rightarrow (M \xrightarrow{a} \Rightarrow M \in x^{\in})$, hence $a \leftarrow x \Rightarrow a \leftarrow x^{\in}$ by Prop. 4.2. So, if $M \overset{a}{\not\rightarrow}$, there exists a region y (namely $y = x^{\in}$) such that $a \leftarrow y$ and $M \notin y$. $na(\mathcal{N})$ is therefore weakly separated. Now suppose M and M' are two markings such that $M \in y$ iff $M' \in y$ for every region y. Since this holds in particular for $y = x^{\in}$, M and M' contain exactly the same places. $na(\mathcal{N})$ is therefore separated. (3) We have

$a \leftarrow x$ in $\mathcal{N}$ **iff** $M \xrightarrow{a} \Rightarrow x \in M$		by the assumption on $\mathcal{N}$
iff $M \xrightarrow{a} \Rightarrow M \in x^{\in}$		by the definition of $x^{\in}$
iff $a \leftarrow x^{\in}$ in $an(na(\mathcal{N}))$		by Prop. 4.2

The same reasoning applies to $\nabla \in \{0, 1\}$. Now since the flow relations 0, 1 and $\perp$ form a partitioning of $A \times P$, $a \perp x \Leftrightarrow a \perp x^{\in}$ and the expected conclusion follows by the identities $\overset{0}{\leftarrow} = \leftarrow \cap 0$, $\overset{1}{\leftarrow} = \leftarrow \cap 1$, $\overset{0}{\rightarrow} = \rightarrow \cap 0$, and $\overset{1}{\rightarrow} = \rightarrow \cap 1$. ∎

Corollary 4.10 *The canonical trace automata $\mathcal{A}$ and $na(an(\mathcal{A}))$ are isomorphic if, and only if, $\mathcal{A}$ is separated.*

Proof: By Prop. 4.6.4 and Prop. 4.9.2. ∎

Corollary 4.11 *For every net $\mathcal{N}$, there exists a separated net $\overline{\mathcal{N}}$ with the same behaviour. Moreover $\overline{\mathcal{N}}$ is finite if $\mathcal{N}$ is finite.*

Proof: By Cor. 3.4, the net $\mathcal{N}$ and the trace automaton $na(\mathcal{N})$ have the same behaviour; by Prop. 4.9 and Prop. 4.5, $na(\mathcal{N})$ is separated and it has the same behaviour as $an(na(\mathcal{N}))$; by Prop. 4.6, and seeing that $na(\mathcal{N})$ is separated, $an(na(\mathcal{N}))$ is a separated net. ∎

Notice that $an(na(\mathcal{N}))$ is not always the "simplest" separated net equivalent to $\mathcal{N}$. in particular (as illustrated by Fig. 8) it may be the case that $an(na(\mathcal{N})) \neq \mathcal{N}$ even for a separated net $\mathcal{N}$.

In the end of the section, we examine the relationship between unfoldings, foldings and separation. We show that unfolded trace automata are always separated, and we exhibit an unfolded (and hence separated) trace automaton that cannot be folded to any finite *and* separated trace automaton. So, complete unfoldings may be necessary to achieve separation.

Proposition 4.12 *Every unfolded trace automaton is separated.*

Proof: It is enough to prove that every trace automaton in the range of $\mathcal{U}$ is separated. Let $\mathcal{U}(\mathcal{A}) = (A, Q, q_0, T)$. By definition of $\mathcal{U}$, Q is the set of accessible configurations of an event structure with binary conflicts $(A, \sharp, \vdash)$, q_0 is its empty configuration, and $q \xrightarrow{a} q'$ in T if and only if $a \notin q$, a is not in conflict with any event in q, $q \vdash a$, and $q' = q \cup \{a\}$. Given $q \in Q$ and $a \in A$ such that $q \stackrel{a}{\not\rightarrow}$, we should construct a region P separating q from a. We consider first the case when $q' \xrightarrow{a}$ for no $q' \subset q$. Define $below(q) = \{q' \in Q / q' \subseteq q\}$ then $below(q)$ is a region (since $q', q" \subseteq q, q' \xrightarrow{b}, b \in q" \Rightarrow q' \cup \{b\} \subseteq q$), and its complement $P = \overline{below(q)}$ separates q from a. We consider next the case when $a \in q$. Define $after(a) = \{q' \in Q / a \in q'\}$ then $after(a)$ is a region (since $a \notin q', q' \xrightarrow{b}, a \in q'.b \Rightarrow a = b$), and its complement $P = \overline{after(a)}$ separates q from a. We consider finally the case when $a \notin q$ but $q' \xrightarrow{a}$ for some $q' \subset q$ $(q' \neq q)$. Let $q_a = \bigcup\{q' \in Q / q' \subset q \text{ and } q' \xrightarrow{a}\}$ then q_a is a configuration for $\{q' \in Q / q' \subseteq q\}$ is an algebraic lattice, and thus $q_a \xrightarrow{a}$ because $q_a \vdash a$ by monotonicity of $\vdash$ and a does not conflict with any $b \in q'$ such that $q' \xrightarrow{a}$. But $q_a \neq q$ because $q \stackrel{a}{\not\rightarrow}$, and there should exist some event b such that $q_a \xrightarrow{b}$ and $q_a.b \subset q$. By definition of $q_a =$, $q_a.b \stackrel{a}{\not\rightarrow}$, thus necessarily $a \sharp b$. Since $q \in after(b)$, the region $\overline{after(b)}$ separates q from a. Thus, $\mathcal{U}(\mathcal{A})$ is weakly separated. Now let $q \neq q'$ then either $q' \notin below(q)$ or $q \notin below(q')$; let $x = below(q)$ in the first case then x is a region, $q \in x$ and $q' \notin x$; the other case is symmetric. Thus, $\mathcal{U}(\mathcal{A})$ is separated. ∎

Proposition 4.13 *The following relations hold for any folding morphism (η, σ) : $\mathcal{A}^{(1)} \rightarrow \mathcal{A}^{(2)}$ between two canonical trace automata:*

1. *if x is a region in $\mathcal{A}^{(2)}$ then $\sigma^{-1}(x)$ is a region in $\mathcal{A}^{(1)}$,*
2. *if x separates $\sigma(q)$ from $\eta(a)$ in $\mathcal{A}^{(2)}$ then $\sigma^{-1}(x)$ separates q from a in $\mathcal{A}^{(1)}$,*
3. *if $\mathcal{A}^{(2)}$ is weakly separated then $\mathcal{A}^{(1)}$ is weakly separated.*

Proof: Any excluded pattern for $\sigma^{-1}(x)$ should provide by applying σ an identical excluded pattern for x, hence the first assertion follows, the other assertions are immediate consequences. ∎

The reason why only *weak* separation has been considered in statement 3 is the following: as soon as some region x separates $\sigma(q)$ from $\sigma(q')$, the region $\sigma^{-1}(x)$ separates q from q', but how separating q from q' when $\sigma(q) = \sigma(q')$? Fig. 9 exhibits

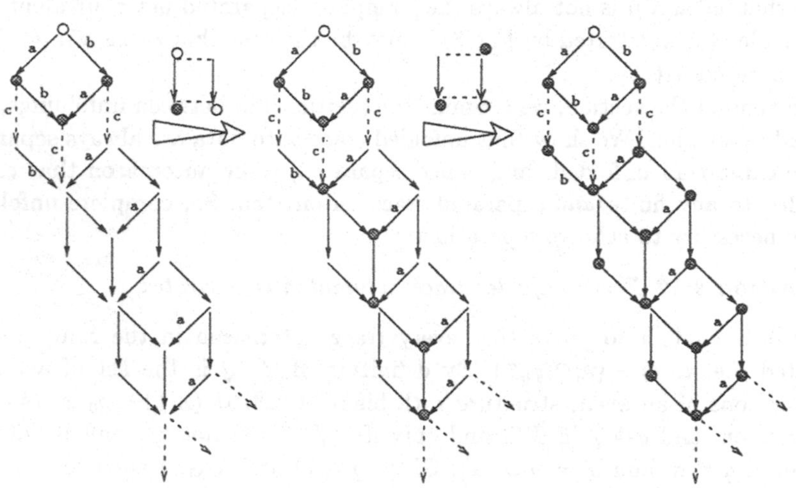

Fig. 9. an unfolded automaton with no finite and separated folding

an infinite trace automaton $\mathcal{A}$, with topmost state chosen as the initial state $q_0 \in Q$, that cannot be folded to any finite and separated trace automaton. Since action c is not enabled at q_0 and $\mathcal{A}$ is unfolded, there exists in $\mathcal{A}$ a region x containing all the sources of c-transitions but not q_0. By the first excluded pattern for regions (see Fig. 6), all the targets of a-transitions are in x. By the second excluded pattern, the membership property $q \in x$ is propagated downwards to all the sources of a-transitions except the initial state, and therefrom to all the remaining states. So, there is a unique region separating the initial state from c, namely the set $Q \backslash \{q_0\}$. Let (η, σ) : $\mathcal{A} \rightarrow \mathcal{B}$ be a folding morphism, and suppose $\mathcal{B}$ is separated. By the definition of folding morphisms $\sigma(q_0) \overset{\eta(c)}{\not\rightarrow}$, and thus by the assumption of separation there exists a region x' separating $\sigma(q_0)$ from $\eta(c)$ in $\mathcal{B}$. By Prop. 4.13, $\sigma^{-1}(x')$ separates q_0 from c, hence necessarily $\sigma^{-1}(x') = Q \backslash \{q_0\}$. As a consequence

$\sigma(q_0) \notin \sigma(Q\backslash\{q_0\})$. A similar conclusion may be expressed for $q_1 = q_0.bc$, and more generally for every state q_i originating a sub-automaton isomorphic to $\mathcal{A}$: for each q_i we get $\sigma(q_i) \notin \sigma(Q_i\backslash\{q_i\})$ where Q_i denotes the subset of states accessible from q_i. Thus all states $\sigma(q_i)$ are different, and the separated trace automaton $\mathcal{B}$ is infinite.

5 An Adjunction between Automata and Nets

Let us recall that $an(\mathcal{A})$ denotes the net obtained by calculating regions in the canonical trace automaton $\mathcal{A}$ while $na(\mathcal{N})$ denotes the canonical trace automaton obtained by calculating accessible configurations in the net $\mathcal{N}$. In this section, we raise the correspondence (an, na) to an adjunction between separated trace automata and nets.

Definition 5.1 (Category of Separated Trace Automata) *A morphism* $(\eta,\sigma): \mathcal{A}^{(1)} \to \mathcal{A}^{(2)}$ *between two separated trace automata is a pair of mappings* $\eta : A^{(1)} \to A^{(2)}$, $\sigma : Q^{(1)} \to Q^{(2)}$ *between their respective sets of actions and states satisfying the following conditions where* $a \in A^{(1)}$ *and* $q \in Q^{(1)}$.

1. $\sigma(q_0^{(1)}) = q_0^{(2)}$,

2. $q \xrightarrow{a} \Rightarrow [\ \sigma(q) \xrightarrow{\eta(a)}$ *and* $\sigma(q.a) = \sigma(q).\eta(a)\ ]$.

Observe that two isomorphic separated trace automata are also equivalent since $\diamond(q,a,b) \Rightarrow \diamond(\sigma(q),\eta(a),\eta(b))$ for any morphism (η,σ).

Definition 5.2 (Category of Nets) *A morphism* $(\eta,\beta): \mathcal{N}^{(1)} \to \mathcal{N}^{(2)}$ *between two nets is a mapping* $\eta : A^{(1)} \to A^{(2)}$ *between sets of actions together with a mapping* $\beta : P^{(2)} \to P^{(1)}$ *in the opposite direction between sets of places, satisfying the following conditions where* $a \in A^{(1)}$, $x \in P^{(2)}$, *and* $\nabla \in \{\leftarrow, 0, 1, \dagger\}$:

1. $\beta^{-1}(M_0^{(1)}) = M_0^{(2)}$,

2. compatibility with the flow relations: $\eta(a)\nabla x \Rightarrow a\nabla\beta(x)$.

Observe that two isomorphic nets are again equivalent. The flow relation $\dagger$, used as a substitute for $\perp$ in the above definition, was introduced in Def. 4.7.

Theorem 5.3 *There is an adjunction* $an \dashv na :$ **Nets** $\to$ **STA** *between the categories of separated trace automata and nets where both functors preserve behaviour.*

In order to facilitate the construction we introduce an intermediate category and split the adjunction in two halves, a reflection and a co-reflection, following the principles recalled below. A functor $F : \mathcal{A} \to \mathcal{B}$ induces an *image* of $\mathcal{A}$ into $\mathcal{B}$, and the comma category $F \downarrow \mathcal{B}$, whose objects (A, f, B) consist of an object in each category together with an arrow $f : FA \to B$ relating them within $\mathcal{B}$, describes how the image of $\mathcal{A}$ approximates $\mathcal{B}$. For instance, if $\mathcal{B}$ is an ordered set viewed as a category and $\mathcal{A}$ is a subset of $\mathcal{B}$, the comma category $F \downarrow \mathcal{B}$ (where F is the inclusion) is the union of all those sets $F \downarrow B = \{A \in \mathcal{A}/\ A \leq B\}$ which approximate the element $B \in \mathcal{B}$ by elements in $\mathcal{A}$. An adjunction situation $F \dashv G : \mathcal{B} \to \mathcal{A}$ is a natural isomorphism $\mathcal{B}(Fa, b) \cong \mathcal{A}(a, Gb)$ expressing that the approximation of $\mathcal{B}$ by $\mathcal{A}$ via F coincides with the approximation of $\mathcal{A}$ by $\mathcal{B}$ via G. Actually, such an adjunction amounts to an isomorphism between the comma categories $\mathcal{A} \downarrow G \cong F \downarrow \mathcal{B}$ which commutes with the projections.

$$\begin{array}{ccc} & \mathcal{A} \downarrow G \cong F \downarrow \mathcal{B} & \\ \swarrow^{\pi_1} & & \searrow^{\pi_2} \\ \mathcal{A} & & \mathcal{B} \end{array}$$

The objects of the intermediate category are *compound objects* (A, f, B) consisting of an object in each category together with a connection $f = (f_\#, f^\#)$ where $f_\# : A \to GB$ in $\mathcal{A}$ and $f^\# : FA \to B$ in $\mathcal{B}$ are adjoint arrows. A morphism between two compound objects $(A^{(1)}, f^{(1)}, B^{(1)})$ and $(A^{(2)}, f^{(2)}, B^{(2)})$ is a pair of arrows between their respective components: $a : A^{(1)} \to A^{(2)}$ in $\mathcal{A}$ and $b : B^{(1)} \to B^{(2)}$ in $\mathcal{B}$ which respects the connections in each compound object, i.e. $Gb \circ f^{(1)}_\# = f^{(2)}_\# \circ a$ or equivalently $b \circ f^{(1)\#} = f^{(2)\#} \circ Fa$. Now the projection $\pi_1 : \mathcal{A} \downarrow G \to \mathcal{A}$ has a right-inverse left-adjoint $\rho_1 : \mathcal{A} \to \mathcal{A} \downarrow G$ which takes an object A of $\mathcal{A}$ to the unit of the adjunction $\eta_A : A \to GFA$ and takes the arrow $f : A \to B$ to the pair (f, Ff). In the same way, the second projection $\pi_2 : F \downarrow \mathcal{B} \to \mathcal{B}$ has a right-inverse right-adjoint $\rho_2 : \mathcal{B} \to F \downarrow \mathcal{B}$ which takes an object B to the co-unit $\epsilon_B : FGB \to B$. And we recover the adjunction $F \dashv G$ as the composite of the adjunctions $\rho_1 \dashv \pi_1$ (a co-reflection) and $\pi_2 \dashv \rho_2$ (a reflection). Here we are going to use a category of compound objects called *trace-nets* which is a little bit simpler than the comma categories $\mathbf{STA} \downarrow na \cong an \downarrow \mathbf{Nets}$ but plays a similar role. We build actually a family of adjunctions indexed by the alphabet of actions: a trace net $(\mathcal{A}, \models, \mathcal{N})$ consists of a separated trace automaton $\mathcal{A}$ and a net $\mathcal{N}$ on the same alphabet, together with a relation $\models$ connecting states and places. The pair of adjoint arrows $(\models_\#, \models^\#)$ connecting the $\mathcal{A}$ and $\mathcal{N}$ components of a trace net may then be retrieved as $(1, {}^{\models}())$ and $(1, ()^{\models})$ letting $q^{\models} = \{x / q \models x\}$ and ${}^{\models}x = \{q / q \models x\}$ (see corollary 5.6). Conditions 1 to 5 in the definition below aim precisely at ensuring that $q^{\models}$ is an accessible configuration of $\mathcal{N}$ and that ${}^{\models}x$ is a region of $\mathcal{A}$.

Definition 5.4 (Trace Nets) *Trace nets are triples* $(\mathcal{A}, \models, \mathcal{N})$ *where* $\mathcal{A} = (A, Q, q_0, T)$ *is a separated trace automaton,* $\mathcal{N} = (P, A, \overset{0}{\leftarrow}, \overset{1}{\leftarrow}, \overset{0}{\rightarrow}, \overset{1}{\rightarrow}, \perp, M_0)$ *is a net on the same alphabet, and* $\models \subset Q \times P$ *is a link between the two structures, satisfying as a whole the following conditions:*

1. $M_0 = q_0{}^{\models}$, *i.e.* $M_0 = \{x \in P / q_0 \models x\}$,
2. $(a \leftarrow x \ \& \ q \xrightarrow{a} q') \Rightarrow q \models x$,
3. $(a 1 x \ \& \ q \xrightarrow{a} q') \Rightarrow q' \models x$,
4. $(a 0 x \ \& \ q \xrightarrow{a} q') \Rightarrow q' \not\models x$, *and*
5. $(a \dagger x \ \& \ q \xrightarrow{a} q') \Rightarrow (q \models x \text{ iff } q' \models x)$.

A morphism between two trace nets is a pair of mappings $\eta : A^{(1)} \to A^{(2)}$, $\sigma : Q^{(1)} \to Q^{(2)}$ *between sets of actions and states together with a mapping* $\beta : P^{(2)} \to P^{(1)}$ *in the opposite direction between sets of places, such that*

1. (η, σ) *is a morphism of separated trace automata,*
2. (η, β) *is a morphism of nets, and*
3. σ *and* β *are adjoint mappings:* $q \models^{(1)} \beta(x) \Leftrightarrow \sigma(q) \models^{(2)} x$.

Proposition 5.5 *A trace net* $(\mathcal{A}, \models, \mathcal{N})$ *satisfies the following properties:*

1. $q \xrightarrow{a} \Rightarrow [\, a^{\leftarrow} \subset q^{\models}$ *and* $(q.a)^{\models} = (q^{\models} \setminus a^{0}) \cup a^{1}]$.
2. *Excluded patterns:*
   (a) $(\exists q \xrightarrow{a} q'$ *with* $q \models x$ *and* $q' \not\models x) \Rightarrow a0x$,
   (b) $(\exists q \xrightarrow{a} q'$ *with* $q \not\models x$ *and* $q' \models x) \Rightarrow a1x$

Proof: (1) The first half of the implication is exactly condition (2) in Def. 5.4. For the second half, we assume $q \xrightarrow{a} q'$ and then establish:

$$q' \models x \;\text{ iff }\; [(q \models x \;\&\; a \notin {}^{0}x) \text{ or } a \in {}^{1}x]$$

showing that q' satisfies x if either x was already satisfied by q and a does not falsify x, or a validates x.

1. $([(q \models x \;\&\; a \notin {}^{0}x) \text{ or } a \in {}^{1}x] \;\&\; q \xrightarrow{a} q') \Rightarrow q' \models x$:
   (a) $(a \in {}^{1}x \;\&\; q \xrightarrow{a} q') \Rightarrow q' \models x$ by condition (4) in Def. 5.4.
   (b) $(q \models x \;\&\; a \notin {}^{0}x \;\&\; a \notin {}^{1}x \;\&\; q \xrightarrow{a} q') \Rightarrow (q \models x \;\&\; a \bot x \;\&\; q \xrightarrow{a} q')$ because $\{0, 1, \bot\}$ is a partitioning of $A \times P$, and since $\bot \subset \dagger$ $q' \models x$ by condition (5) in Def. 5.4.

2. $(q' \models x \;\&\; q \xrightarrow{a} q') \Rightarrow [(q \models x \;\&\; a \notin {}^{0}x) \text{ or } a \in {}^{1}x]$:
   $(q' \models x \;\&\; q \xrightarrow{a} q') \Rightarrow a \notin {}^{0}x$ by condition (4) in Def. 5.4, and $(q' \models x \;\&\; q \xrightarrow{a} q') \Rightarrow (q \models x \text{ or } a \in {}^{1}x)$, because $(q \not\models x \;\&\; q \xrightarrow{a} q' \;\&\; q' \models x)$ entails $a \notin {}^{0}x$ by condition (4) in Def. 5.4 and $a \notin {}^{\dagger}x$ by condition (5) in Def. 5.4, whence necessarily $a \in {}^{1}x$.

(2) Assume $(\exists q \xrightarrow{a} q'$ with $q \models x$ and $q' \not\models x)$ then neither $a1x$ nor $a \dagger x$ by conditions (3) and (5) in Def. 5.4, thus necessarily $a0x$. The argument is similar for the second excluded pattern. ∎

Corollary 5.6 *In a trace net* $(\mathcal{A}, \models, \mathcal{N})$, *if* x *is a place of* $\mathcal{N}$ *then* ${}^{\models}x = \{q / q \models x\}$ *is a region of* $\mathcal{A}$ *and conversely, if* q *is a state of* $\mathcal{A}$ *then* $q^{\models} = \{x / q \models x\}$ *is an accessible marking of* $\mathcal{N}$. *Moreover* $\models^{\#} = (1, {}^{\models}())$ *is a morphism of nets from* $an(\mathcal{A})$ *to* $\mathcal{N}$ *and* $\models_{\#} = (1, ()^{\models})$ *is a morphism of separated trace automata from* $\mathcal{A}$ *to* $na(\mathcal{N})$.

Proof: In view of the excluded patterns of Prop. 5.5 ${}^{\models}x = \{q / q \models x\}$ is a region of $\mathcal{A}$ for any place x of $\mathcal{N}$; in view of Prop. 4.2 and the definition of $\dagger$, the conditions in Def. 5.4 state precisely that $\models^{\#} = (1, {}^{\models}())$ is a morphism of nets from $an(\mathcal{A})$ to $\mathcal{N}$. Thanks to condition 1 in Def. 5.4, part 1 of Prop. 5.5 shows that $q^{\models} = \{x / q \models x\}$

is an accessible marking of $na(\mathcal{N})$ for any state q of $\mathcal{A}$; in view of Prop. 4.2 and the definition of $\dagger$, the remaining conditions in Def. 5.4 show that $\models_{\#} = (1, ()^{\models})$ is a morphism of separated trace automata from $\mathcal{A}$ to $na(\mathcal{N})$. ∎

Now, there exists a pair of projection functors from the category **TrNets** of trace nets to the categories of separated trace automata and nets

$$\textbf{STA} \xleftarrow{\pi_1} \textbf{TrNets} \xrightarrow{\pi_2} \textbf{Nets}$$

that split a trace net to its underlying trace automaton and net, and split a morphism (η, σ, β) to (η, σ) and (η, β). In order to establish theorem (5.3), it suffices to prove that both functors π_1 and π_2 have right-inverses embedding separated trace automata and nets into trace nets and providing adjunction pairs $\rho_1 \dashv \pi_1$ and $\pi_2 \dashv \rho_2$.

Proposition 5.7 *π_1 has a right-inverse left-adjoint.*

Proof: By Prop. 4.8 any separated trace automaton $\mathcal{A} = (A, Q, q_0, T)$ may be extended into a trace net $\rho_1(\mathcal{A}) = (\mathcal{A}, \models, an(\mathcal{A}))$ where $an(\mathcal{A}) = (P, A, \overset{0}{\leftarrow}, \overset{1}{\leftarrow}, \overset{0}{\rightarrow}, \overset{1}{\rightarrow}, \perp, M_0)$, P is the set of regions of $\mathcal{A}$, $\models$ is membership, the flow relations are the restrictions to $A \times P$ of the corresponding relations on $A \times 2^Q$ (see Def. 4.1), and $M_0 = \{x \in P /\ q_0 \models x\}$. In order to show that ρ_1 is left-adjoint to π_1 we have to prove that every morphism $(\eta, \sigma) : \mathcal{A} \to \pi_1(\mathcal{X})$ in **STA** extends in a unique way into a morphism $(\eta, \sigma, \beta) : \rho_1(\mathcal{A}) \to \mathcal{X}$ in **TrNets**. We recall that the functoriality of ρ_1 follows from that universal property. Let $\rho_1(\mathcal{A}) = (\mathcal{A}^{(1)}, \models^{(1)}, \mathcal{N}^{(1)})$ and $\mathcal{X} = (\mathcal{A}^{(2)}, \models^{(2)}, \mathcal{N}^{(2)})$. By condition (3) for morphisms in definition (5.4), $\beta : P^{(2)} \to P^{(1)}$ must be defined as $\beta(x) = \{q \in Q^{(1)} /\ \sigma(q) \models^{(2)} x\}$. The extended morphism (η, σ, β), if it exists, is therefore unique. It remains to verify that for every place $x \in P^{(2)}$, the set $\beta(x) \subset Q^{(1)}$ is a region; and that (η, β) is a morphism of nets. First we prove that $\beta(x)$ is a region: suppose $q_1 \xrightarrow{a} q_1'$ and $q_2 \xrightarrow{a} q_2'$ where $q_1' \in \beta(x)$ and $q_1, q_2' \notin \beta(x)$, then $\sigma(q_1) \xrightarrow{\eta(a)} \sigma(q_1')$ and $\sigma(q_2) \xrightarrow{\eta(a)} \sigma(q_2')$ where $\sigma(q_1') \models^{(2)} x$, $\sigma(q_1) \not\models^{(2)} x$, and $\sigma(q_2') \not\models^{(2)} x$ which by Prop.5.5.2 entails $\eta(a) 1 x$, in contradiction with $\sigma(q_2' \not\models^{(2)} x$ (condition 3 for Trace Nets). The second excluded pattern is treated in the same manner. Now the condition $\beta^{-1}(M_0^{(1)}) = M_0^{(2)}$ is satisfied because the relations $M_0^{(i)} = q_0^{i\models} = \{x \in P^{(i)} /\ q_0^i \models x\}$, $\sigma(q_0^{(1)}) = q_0^{(2)}$, and $q \models \beta(x) \Leftrightarrow \sigma(q) \models x$ entail together:

$$\beta^{-1}(M_0^{(1)}) = \beta^{-1}(q_0^{1\models}) = \{x \in P^{(2)} / q_0^1 \models \beta(x)\} = \{x \in P^{(2)} / q_0^2 = \sigma(q_0^1) \models x\} = M_0^{(2)}$$

There remains just to establish the compatibility with flow relations. In view of Prop. 4.8, this amount to prove

$$\forall a \in A^{(1)}\ \forall x \in P^{(2)}\ \forall \nabla \in \{\leftarrow, 1, 0, \dagger\} \quad \eta(a) \nabla x \Rightarrow a \nabla \beta(x)$$

where the occurrence of ∇ on the right-hand side stands for one of the flow relations $\nabla \subset A^{(1)} \times 2^{Q^{(1)}}$ associated to the separated trace automaton $\mathcal{A}^{(1)}$ (according to Def. 4.1), whereas the occurrence of ∇ on the left-hand side stands for one of the flow relations $\nabla \subset A^{(2)} \times P^{(2)}$ of the net $\mathcal{N}^{(2)}$. We give hereafter the detailed proof for the case $\nabla = \dagger$ (the others cases are similar).

By the definition of relation $\dagger$ (see after Def. 4.1):

$$a \dagger \beta(x) \text{ iff } [q \xrightarrow{a} q' \Rightarrow (q \in \beta(x) \text{ iff } q' \in \beta(x))]$$

By the definition of trace nets (see Def. 5.4):

$$\eta(a) \dagger x \Rightarrow [q \xrightarrow{\eta(a)} q' \Rightarrow (q \models x \text{ iff } q' \models x)]$$

Assume $q \xrightarrow{a} q'$ and $\eta(a) \dagger x$ then $\sigma(q) \xrightarrow{\eta(a)} \sigma(q')$, $\sigma(q) \models x$ iff $\sigma(q') \models x$ and $q \in \beta(x)$ iff $q' \in \beta(x)$, whence finally $a \dagger \beta(x)$ as required. ∎

Proposition 5.8 *π_2 has a right-inverse right-adjoint.*

Proof: Let $\mathcal{N} = (P, A, \overset{0}{\leftarrow}, \overset{1}{\leftarrow}, \overset{0}{\rightarrow}, \overset{1}{\rightarrow}, \perp, M_0)$ be a net, with set of markings $\mathcal{M} = 2^P$ and set of accessible markings $\mathcal{M}_a \subset \mathcal{M}$. We recall that the transitions of $\mathcal{N}$ are given by $M \xrightarrow{a} M'$ iff $a^{\leftarrow} \subset M$ and $M' = (M \setminus a^0) \cup a^1$ and that two distinct actions a and b are said to be independent (written $a \| b$) when *(i)* there exists an accessible marking $M \in \mathcal{M}_a$ at which they are both enabled, *(ii)* $a^{\overset{0}{\leftarrow}} \subset b^{\perp}$ & $a^0 \cap b^1 = \emptyset$, and symmetrically *(iii)* $b^{\overset{0}{\leftarrow}} \subset a^{\perp}$ & $b^0 \cap a^1 = \emptyset$. The net $\mathcal{N}$ may be extended into a trace net $\rho_2(\mathcal{N}) = (na(\mathcal{N}), \models, \mathcal{N})$ where $na(\mathcal{N}) = (A, \|, \mathcal{M}_a, M_0, \mathcal{T}_a)$, $\mathcal{T}_a$ is the set of transitions between accessible markings, and $\models \subset \mathcal{M} \times P$ is reverse membership: $M \models x$ iff $x \in M$. Since $M \xrightarrow{a} M' \Leftrightarrow a^{\leftarrow} \subset M$ and $M' = (M \setminus a^0) \cup a^1$ and by definition of $\dagger$, we have:

$$\begin{aligned} x \in a^{\leftarrow} \ \& \ M \xrightarrow{a} M' &\Rightarrow x \in M \\ x \in a^1 \ \& \ M \xrightarrow{a} M' &\Rightarrow x \in M' \\ x \in a^0 \ \& \ M \xrightarrow{a} M' &\Rightarrow x \notin M', \textit{and} \\ x \in a^{\dagger} \ \& \ M \xrightarrow{a} M' &\Rightarrow x \in M \text{ iff } x \in M' \end{aligned}$$

and thus the triple $(na(\mathcal{N}), \ni, \mathcal{N})$ is actually a trace net.

In order to prove that ρ_2 is right-adjoint to π_2 we must check that every morphism $(\eta, \beta): \pi_2(\mathcal{X}) \to \mathcal{N}$ in **Nets** extends in a unique way into a morphism (η, σ, β): $\mathcal{X} \to \rho_2(\mathcal{N})$ in **TrNets**. Again functoriality of ρ_2 follows from that universal property. Let $\mathcal{X} = (\mathcal{A}^{(1)}, \models^{(1)}, \mathcal{N}^{(1)})$ and $\rho_2(\mathcal{N}) = (\mathcal{A}^{(2)}, \models^{(2)}, \mathcal{N}^{(2)})$. By condition (3) for morphisms in definition (5.4), $\sigma: Q^{(1)} \to Q^{(2)}$ must be defined as $\sigma(q) = \{x \in P^{(2)} / \ q \models^{(1)} \beta(x)\}$. The extended morphism (η, σ, β), if it exists, is therefore unique. It remains to verify that (η, σ) is a morphism between separated trace automata. Let σ be defined as $\sigma(q) = \{x \in P^{(2)} / \ q \models^{(1)} \beta(x)\}$. In order to show that $\sigma: Q^{(1)} \to Q^{(2)}$, i.e. that $\sigma(q)$ is always an accessible marking of $\mathcal{N}^{(2)}$, it suffices to verify that (η, σ) is a morphism of separated trace automata (see Def. 5.1) because every state in $Q^{(1)}$ is accessible from the initial state $q_0^{(1)}$.

First, we prove $\sigma(q_0^{(1)}) = q_0^{(2)}$:

$M_0^{(1)} = \{x \in P^{(1)} / \ q_0^{(1)} \models x\}$ because $\mathcal{X}$ is a trace net, and $q_0^{(2)} = M_0^{(2)} \subset 2^{P^{(2)}}$ by construction of $na(\mathcal{N})$, whence $\beta^{-1}(M_0^{(1)}) = \{y \in P^{(2)} / \ q_0^{(1)} \models \beta(y)\} = \sigma(q_0^{(1)})$ and $\sigma(q_0^{(1)}) = q_0^{(2)}$ by the first condition in Def. 5.2.

Second, we prove that $q \xrightarrow{a}$ *in* $\mathcal{A}^{(1)}$ *entails* $\sigma(q) \xrightarrow{\eta(a)}$ *in* $\mathcal{A}^{(2)} = na(\mathcal{N})$.

In view of the definition of trace nets (Def. 5.4) :

$$q \xrightarrow{a} \;\Rightarrow\; \forall x \in P^{(1)} \;\; a \leftarrow x \Rightarrow q \models x,$$

whereas the firability of $\eta(a)$ at $\sigma(q)$ in the net $\mathcal{N}$ is given by:

$$\sigma(q) \xrightarrow{\eta(a)} \quad \text{iff} \quad \forall y \in P^{(2)} \;\; \eta(a) \leftarrow y \Rightarrow y \in \sigma(q).$$

Assume $q \xrightarrow{a}$ and let $y \in P^{(2)}$. If $\eta(a) \leftarrow y$ then $a \leftarrow \beta(y)$, hence $q \models \beta(y)$ which is equivalent to $y \in \sigma(q)$. This proves $\sigma(q) \xrightarrow{\eta(a)}$ as required.

Third, we prove that $\sigma(q.a) = \sigma(q).\eta(a)$ *if* a *is enabled in* q :

Let us observe the following equivalences :

$$\begin{array}{rlr} x \in \sigma(q.a) & \text{iff } q.a \models \beta(x) & (\text{definition of } \sigma) \\ & \text{iff } (q \models \beta(x) \;\&\; not(a0\beta(x)) \text{ or } a1\beta(x) & ((q.a)^{\models} = (q^{\models} \setminus a^{0}) \cup a^{1}) \\ x \in \sigma(q).\eta(a) & \text{iff } [\sigma(q) \models x \;\&\; not(\eta(a)0x)] \text{ or } \eta(a)1x & (\text{idem}) \end{array}$$

Hence we have to show that $q \xrightarrow{a}$ entails $A \Leftrightarrow B$ with $A \equiv ([q \models \beta(x) \;\&\; not(a0\beta(x))]$ and $a1\beta(x))$ to $B \equiv ([\sigma(q) \models x \;\&\; not(\eta(a)0x)]$ or $\eta(a)1x)$.

1. (B and $q \xrightarrow{a}$) $\Rightarrow A$:
   Since $\eta(a)1x \Rightarrow a1\beta(x)$ it is enough to show that ($x \in \sigma(q)$ and $\eta(a) \perp x$ and $q \xrightarrow{a}$) entails A. Now $x \in \sigma(q) \Leftrightarrow q \models \beta(x)$, $\eta(a) \perp x \Rightarrow \eta(a) \dagger x \Rightarrow a \dagger \beta(x)$, and ($q \models \beta(x)$ and $a \dagger \beta(x)$ and $q \xrightarrow{a}$) $\Rightarrow q.a \models \beta(x) \Rightarrow not(a0\beta(x))$.
2. (A and $q \xrightarrow{a}$) $\Rightarrow B$:
   Since ($q \models \beta(x)$ and $not(a \in {}^{0}\beta(x))$) $\Rightarrow$ ($x \in \sigma(q)$ and $not(\eta(a) \in {}^{0}x)$) it is enough to prove the implication [$a1\beta(x)$ and ($q \not\models \beta(x)$ or $a0\beta(x)$) and $q \xrightarrow{a}$] $\Rightarrow B$. Since $a1\beta(x) \Rightarrow not(a0\beta(x) \Rightarrow not(\eta(a)0x)$, and since $x \in \sigma(q) \Leftrightarrow q \models \beta(x)$, that implication can be restated equivalently as ($a1\beta(x)$ and $q \not\models \beta(x)$ and $q \xrightarrow{a}$) $\Rightarrow \eta(a)1x$. Now, the latter implication is true because its left hand side entails $not(a0\beta(x))$ and $not(a \dagger \beta(x))$, whence $not(\eta(a)0x)$ and $not(\eta(a) \dagger x)$ and therefore $\eta(a)1x$. ∎

The expected adjunction $an \dashv na$: **Nets** $\rightarrow$ **STA** between separated trace automata and nets results from the composition of the elementary adjunctions $\rho_1 \dashv \pi_1$ and $\pi_2 \dashv \rho_2$, i.e. $an = \pi_2 \circ \rho_1$ and $na = \pi_1 \circ \rho_2$. This completes the proof of Theo. 5.3: the preservation of behaviour follows from Cor. 3.4 and Prop. 4.5. ∎

We saw in Prop. 4.6 that

Proposition 5.9 *Any separated trace automaton* $\mathcal{A}$ *is isomorphic to* $na(an(\mathcal{A}))$.

The example of Fig. 8 shows that the dual result for nets does not hold. The best we can state is the following:

Proposition 5.10 *A separated net* $\mathcal{N}$ *is isomorphic to* $an(na(\mathcal{N}))$ *if and only if every region* y *in* $na(\mathcal{N})$ *is the image* $x^{\in}$ *of some place* x *in* $\mathcal{N}$.

Proof: The mapping $()^{\in}$, sending a places x in $\mathcal{N}$ to the set $x^{\in} = \{M / x \in M\}$ of accessible markings containing x, preserves the flow relations $\nabla \in \{\overset{0}{\leftarrow}, \overset{1}{\leftarrow}, \overset{0}{\rightarrow}, \overset{1}{\rightarrow}, \perp\}$ if $\mathcal{N}$ is weakly separated (by Prop. 4.9), and it is moreover separated if $\mathcal{N}$ is separated. Therefore, the co-unit $(1, ()^{\in}) : an(na(\mathcal{N})) \to \mathcal{N}$ is an isomorphism in **Nets** if and only if every region y in $na(\mathcal{N})$ is the image $x^{\in}$ of some place x in $\mathcal{N}$. ∎

A different way to obtain an adjunction between trace automata and a category of nets is to get rid of the assumption of separation on automata, and to supply places with an involution: one obtains in this way an adjunction between the category **CTA** of canonical trace automata and a category **INets** of involutive nets. It is not clear so far whether one can also construct an adjunction between canonical trace automata and (general) nets with an adapted notion of net morphisms. Actually, our present definition of net morphisms is not satisfactory, since the auxiliary flow relation † is defined on the induced transition system, but we don't know how avoiding that drawback unless an involutive operation of "negation" is assumed on places. A possibly related question is the following.

Question 5.11 *Given a separated net $\mathcal{N}$ is it true that every region of $na(\mathcal{N})$ is a boolean combination of regions $x^{\in}$ for places x in $\mathcal{N}$?*

References

[Bed88] BEDNARCZYK, M.A., *Categories of asynchronous systems.* PhD thesis, University of Sussex, report no.1/88 (1988).

[DS84] DE SIMONE, R., *Calculabilité et expressivité dans l'algèbre de processus parallèles Meije.* Thèse de 3eme cycle, Université de Paris VII (1984).

[ER90] EHRENFEUCHT, A., and ROZENBERG, G., *Partial 2-structures;* Part I: *Basic Notions and the Representation Problem,* and Part II: *State Spaces of Concurrent Systems,* Acta Informatica, vol 27 (1990).

[NRT90] NIELSEN, M., ROZENBERG, G., AND THIAGARAJAN, P.S., *Elementary Transition Systems.* DAIMI PB-310 Aarhus (1990).

[NRT91] NIELSEN, M., ROZENBERG, G., AND THIAGARAJAN, P.S., *Transition Systems, Event Structures and Unfoldings.* DAIMI PB-353 Aarhus (1991).

[Sta89a] STARK, E.W., *Connections between a Concrete and an Abstract Model of Concurrent Systems.* 5th Mathematical Foundations of Programming Semantics (1989) 53-79.

[Sta89b] STARK, E.W., *Compositional Relational Semantics for Indeterminate Dataflow Networks.* Summer Conference on Category Theory and Computer Science, LNCS 389 (1989) 52-74.

[Win80] WINSKEL, G., *Events in Computations.* Ph.D thesis, University of Edinburgh, available as a Comp. Sc. report (1980).

[Win91] WINSKEL, G., *Categories of Models for Concurrency.* Advanced School on the Algebraic, Logical, and Categorical Foundations of Concurrency, Gargnano del Garda (1991).

PROVING TOTAL CORRECTNESS OF PROGRAMS IN WEAK SECOND-ORDER LOGIC

Rudolf Berghammer, Birgit Elbl, Ulf Schmerl

Fakultät für Informatik
Universität der Bundeswehr München
Werner-Heisenberg-Weg 39
8014 Neubiberg

ABSTRACT A purely syntactical but nevertheless handy definition of the predicate transformer wp is presented. Weak second-order logic is used to formalize the weakest precondition for an imperative programming language similar to Dijkstra's language of guarded commands. It is demonstrated how to express and prove important properties of wp in this logic. Here a new normal form representation for wp plays an important rôle.

Keywords Imperative programming language, weakest preconditions, weak second-order logic, nondeterminism, guarded commands, normal form theorem.

CONTENTS

0. INTRODUCTION

Based on the axiomatic method of [Hoare 69], in [Dijkstra 75] and [Dijkstra 76] a new approach to reasoning about total correctness of imperative programs has been proposed, which is based on the concept of weakest preconditions. This approach has been carried further by a number of people. In particular, in [Back 81] it is shown how Dijkstra's definition of the predicate transformer wp on sets of states rigorously can be formalized in the infinitary first-order logic $\mathcal{L}_{\omega_1\omega}$ (see e.g., [Karp 64] and [Keisler 71]) as a function mapping a program of Dijkstra's nondeterministic programming language of guarded commands and an infinite formula to an infinite formula. In the same article it is also proved that weakest preconditions can't be expressed in the usual finitary first-order logic if the underlying programming language contains loops.

The first objective here is also to present a rigorous syntactical formalization of weakest preconditions. In contrast to [Back 81], however, we don't use infinitely long formulae but formalize Dijkstra's predicate transformer as a function on finite formulae of a language of weak second-order logic. Also [Tucker Zucker 88] uses weak second-order logic to formalize wp; however, the approach is quite different from ours.

The second objective of the paper is to clarify the rôle of the healthiness conditions assumed to hold for the predicate transformer (see e.g., [Dijkstra 76], Chaps. 4 and 9). These basic properties of predicate transformers are useful when program correctness has to be proved. As they are valid, they *may* be used in a proof, but when considering a formalization of wp and a corresponding deductive system, the question arises whether they are already *derivable*. Of course the answer is "yes" as soon as a complete deductive system is used, but this is unsatisfactory for logics like $\mathcal{L}_{\omega_1\omega}$, because here complete deductive systems necessarily make use of infinite derivations, i.e., they are only semi-formal systems. We show that the healthiness conditions can be derived without infinitary reasoning. To this end, firstly, we introduce an additional property expressing the finiteness of nondeterminacy or the determinacy respectively. From this so-called *normal form* in combination with monotonicity the usual properties can be obtained easily. Compatibility with the quantifiers are also properties we add, for the restriction to propositional connectives seems artificial.

Usually, weakest preconditions are also used as a framework in which to establish the soundness of verification techniques. Therefore, the formalization we were looking for has to be well suited for this purpose, too. To meet this postulate can be regarded as our third objective.

The rest of the article is organized as follows: Section 1 introduces a simple deterministic programming language L_P and gives Dijkstra's predicate transformer in its original formulation as a function wp mapping a program and a set of states onto a set of states. The next Section 2 constitutes the core of the article. In 2.1 we introduce a many-sorted language $\mathcal{L}_V$ of weak second-order logic. In 2.2 we give a syntactical characterization of weakest preconditions over L_P as finitary formulae over $\mathcal{L}_V$ by defining a function wp mapping a program and a finite formula onto a finite formula. For this function we prove by purely syntactical reasoning some basic properties including the above mentioned normal form and Dijkstra's postulates. In this section it is also shown that our finitary syntactical formalization actually coincides with the set-based formulation of Section 1. Section 2.3 generalizes the results of Section 2.2 to Dijkstra's nondeterministic programming language of guarded commands. Some applications are presented in Section 3 in order to demonstrate the adequateness of the formal wp. By their means we want to show again the importance of the normal form theorem. Finally, Section 4 contains some concluding remarks.

1. A SIMPLE PROGRAMMING LANGUAGE

We want to discuss the weakest precondition for imperative programming languages. Offering the typical constructs of this kind of languages, the rather simple L_P introduced in this section will serve as an example. We assume the reader to be familiar with the notions of a signature Σ and a Σ-algebra. Details can be found in [Ehrig Mahr 85], for example.

1.1. SYNTACTICAL DEFINITION

Let $\Sigma = (S, C, F)$ be a signature, where S, C, F are the set of sorts, constant symbols and function symbols respectively. The set S is supposed to contain the two sorts bool and nat for truth values and natural numbers. For every $s \in S$, PV_s denotes a set of names used as the programming variables of sort s and $PV := \bigcup_{s \in S} PV_s$. The set EXP_s of expressions of sort $s \in S$ over Σ and PV is defined as usual. Concerning C, F, PV as well as the sets of symbols to be defined later, we postulate that syntactical objects of different sorts have different names. Now we define the set of L_P-statements:

1.1.1 Definition *The set of statements* STAT *is inductively defined as follows:*

- **skip** $\in$ STAT
- **abort** $\in$ STAT
- *If* $x \in PV_s$ *and* $t \in EXP_s$, *then* $(x := t) \in$ STAT.
- *If* $P_1, P_2 \in$ STAT, *then* $(P_1\ ;\ P_2) \in$ STAT.
- *If* $P_1, P_2 \in$ STAT *and* $b \in EXP_{bool}$, *then* **if** b **then** P_1 **else** P_2 **fi** $\in$ STAT.
- *If* $P \in$ STAT *and* $b \in EXP_{bool}$, *then* **while** b **do** P **od** $\in$ STAT.

Later on we will also discuss a nondeterministic variant of L_P. $STAT^{nondet}$ denotes the set of statements of this variant and is defined similar to STAT except for the conditional statement. This is replaced by

$$\textbf{if } b_1 \textbf{ then } P_1 \mathbin{[\!]} b_2 \textbf{ then } P_2 \mathbin{[\!]} \dots \mathbin{[\!]} b_n \textbf{ then } P_n \textbf{ fi},$$

where $b_1, b_2, \dots, b_n \in EXP_{bool}$ and $P_1, P_2, \dots, P_n \in STAT^{nondet}$. We will use the notation

$$\textbf{if } \mathop{[\!]}_{i=1}^{n} (b_i \textbf{ then } P_i) \textbf{ fi}$$

for this statement.

1.2. WEAKEST PRECONDITION SEMANTICS

A fixed Σ-algebra $\mathcal{A} = ((s^{\mathcal{A}})_{s\in S}, (c^{\mathcal{A}})_{c\in C}, (f^{\mathcal{A}})_{f\in F})$ is used to determine the meaning of the symbols of the signature Σ. The sorts $s \in S$ are interpreted as sets, the function symbols $f \in F$ as total functions. We choose the standard interpretation for the sorts bool and nat and for the symbols which denote the usual operations on them. STATE is the set of value assignments in $\mathcal{A}$ (respecting the sorts, of course), i.e., the set of mappings $v : PV \longrightarrow \bigcup_{s\in S} s^{\mathcal{A}}$ which meet the condition $x \in PV_s$ iff $v(x) \in s^{\mathcal{A}}$. Given an expression $t \in EXP_s$ and an assignment $v \in STATE$, we write $t^{\mathcal{A},v}$ for the value of t according to v. We will omit here a denotational semantic description of L_P using the element $\bot$, complete partial orderings and so on. Instead we present a definition according to the axiomatic approach: Given a program P and predicates M and N, we call P "totally correct with respect to the precondition M and the postcondition N" if the following is true:

> Whenever M holds for an assignment $v \in STATE$, then the program P terminates and N holds for (all) the assignment(s) (possibly) attained by executing P for v.

From the weakest such precondition for any program P and all postconditions N we can tell whether P terminates for a given v, and if termination is guaranteed, we can recover the assignment(s) which results/can result from the execution. Regarding predicates as sets of assignments, we will use a mapping $wp : STAT \times \mathcal{P}(STATE) \longrightarrow \mathcal{P}(STATE)$ (where $\mathcal{P}$ is the powerset-former). This use of weakest precondition is due to Dijkstra [Dijkstra 75, Dijkstra 76]. His axioms and rules yield the following inductive definition of wp for L_P-statements:

1.2.1 Definition *The function* $wp : STAT \times \mathcal{P}(STATE) \longrightarrow \mathcal{P}(STATE)$ *is inductively defined by:*

- $wp(\textbf{skip}, N) := N$
- $wp(\textbf{abort}, N) := \emptyset$
- $wp(x := t, N) := \{v \in STATE : v\{t^{\mathcal{A},v}/x\} \in N\}$
  Here $v\{t^{\mathcal{A},v}/x\}$ *is a notation for the mapping* $w : PV \longrightarrow \bigcup_{s\in S} s^{\mathcal{A}}$ *satisfying the equations* $w(x) = t^{\mathcal{A},v}$ *and* $w(y) = v(y)$ *for all* $y \neq x$.
- $wp(P_1\ ;\ P_2, N) := wp(P_1, wp(P_2, N))$
- $wp(\textbf{if } b \textbf{ then } P_1 \textbf{ else } P_2 \textbf{ fi}, N) := (Mod(b) \cap wp(P_1, N)) \cup (Mod(\neg b) \cap wp(P_2, N))$
- $wp(\textbf{while } b \textbf{ do } P \textbf{ od}, N) := \bigcup_{k=0}^{\infty} M_k$, *where*

$$\begin{aligned} M_0 &:= Mod(\neg b) \cap N \\ M_{k+1} &:= wp(\textbf{if } b \textbf{ then } P \textbf{ else } \textbf{skip } \textbf{fi}, M_k) \\ &= (Mod(b) \cap wp(P, M_k)) \cup (Mod(\neg b) \cap M_k) \end{aligned}$$

Here Mod(b) *and* Mod($\neg b$) *are notations for the set of those assignments* v, *where* $b^{\mathcal{A},v} = \text{tt}$ *or* $b^{\mathcal{A},v} = \text{ff}$ *respectively.*

This definition coincides with the denotational semantics presented, e.g., in the textbook [Loeckx Sieber 84]. For the nondeterministic variant we have to replace the definition of $w\wp$ for the conditional statement by

$$\textbf{if} \mathop{[\!]}_{i=1}^{n} (b_i \textbf{ then } P_i) \textbf{ fi} := (\bigcup_{i=1}^{n} \mathrm{Mod}(b_i)) \cap \bigcap_{i=1}^{n}((\mathrm{Mod}(b_i) \cap w\wp(P_i, N)) \cup \mathrm{Mod}(\neg b_i)).$$

2. A FINITARY DESCRIPTION OF WEAKEST PRECONDITION

First we will define our verification language and demonstrate its adequateness next. The latter includes the formalization of the usual as well as additional properties of wp. We will focus now on the deterministic case, leaving nondeterminism for later consideration.

2.1. A MANY-SORTED LANGUAGE OF WEAK SECOND-ORDER LOGIC

$\mathcal{L}_V$ is a many-sorted language of weak second-order logic. The programming language L_P is defined as a scheme language based on a signature Σ. Similarly $\mathcal{L}_V$ depends on Σ. In order to facilitate reasoning, additional functions and predicates may be introduced.

The sorts of $\mathcal{L}_V$ include the elements of S. For every $s \in$ S, a sort sequ_s is added. The intended meaning of sequ_s is the set of finite sequences over s. As these sequences can be regarded as functions from the natural numbers into the interpretation of s, this language is called second-order. The prefixed "weak" stems from the fact that only *finite* sequences are under discussion.

For every $s \in$ S, there is an infinite set of first-order variables V^1_s, which extends the set of programming variables PV_s of sort s, and an infinite set of second-order variables V^2_s. Let $(C, F, \ldots; |\cdot|, \cdot(\cdot))$ be the set of $\mathcal{L}_V$-symbols, i.e.:

- The constant and function symbols of Σ are $\mathcal{L}_V$-symbols.
- Apart from these arbitrary function and predicate symbols for the sorts in S may occur in $\mathcal{L}_V$.
- To handle the finite sequences, the function symbols $|\cdot|$ and $\cdot(\cdot)$ are contained in $\mathcal{L}_V$ (for any sort sequ_s).

$\mathcal{L}_V$-terms are defined as usual. Infix notation is used for basic operations or subscript notation s_i for $s(i)$ is used when comfortable and unambiguous. The formulae $\mathcal{L}_V$ are built from literals using $\wedge, \vee, \forall, \exists$ (first and second-order). We assume that programming variables do not occur bound in a formula: When quantification is used, we will rename first. **F** and **T** are special 0-ary predicate symbols. Negation and implication can be defined as operations on formulae.

The basis of $\mathcal{L}_V$'s semantics is an extension of the Σ-algebra $\mathcal{A}$ of Section 2.2. Let $\mathcal{A}^+$ be a structure for $\mathcal{L}_V$ and $\mathcal{A}^+|_\Sigma = \mathcal{A}$. Here **F**, **T**, $|\cdot|$ and $\cdot(\cdot)$ have to be interpreted in the obviously intended way, i.e. as truth values false, true and length and access function for sequences. STATE$^+$ denotes the set of assignments in $\mathcal{A}^+$. So STATE$^+$ consists of the mappings

$$v : \bigcup_{s\in S} V^1_s \cup \bigcup_{s\in S} V^2_s \longrightarrow \bigcup_{s\in S} s^{\mathcal{A}} \cup \bigcup_{s\in S} (s^{\mathcal{A}})^*$$

which meet the conditions

$$v(x) \in s^{\mathcal{A}} \Longleftrightarrow x \in V_s^1 \qquad \text{and} \qquad v(x) \in (s^{\mathcal{A}})^* \Longleftrightarrow x \in V_s^2.$$

Here $(s^{\mathcal{A}})^*$ is the set of finite sequences over $s^{\mathcal{A}}$. The value of a term t^v (leaving out the subscript $\mathcal{A}^+$ as we won't consider any other structure) and the satisfaction relation $\mathcal{A}^+ \models \varphi[v]$ (keeping $\mathcal{A}^+$ to stress the dependency on $\mathcal{A}^+$) of a formula φ according to an assignment v are defined as usual. We write $\mathcal{A}^+ \models \varphi$, if $\mathcal{A}^+ \models \varphi[v]$ for every assignment v. For every formula φ we define the set of models:

$$\mathrm{Mod}(\varphi) := \{v \in \mathrm{STATE}^+ : \mathcal{A}^+ \models \varphi[v]\}$$

As the set of $\mathcal{L}_V$-symbols and $\mathcal{A}^+$ are the extensions of Σ and $\mathcal{A}$ respectively, for each $s \in \mathrm{S}$ the elements of EXP_s are $\mathcal{L}_V$-terms and $t^v = t^{\mathcal{A},v}$ for every $t \in \mathrm{EXP}_s$. We confined ourselves to total basic functions in order to get an embedding of the boolean terms. Obviously, for every $b \in \mathrm{EXP}_{\mathrm{bool}}$ there is a propositional formula B satisfying

$$b^v = \mathrm{tt} \Longleftrightarrow \mathcal{A}^+ \models \mathrm{B}[v] \qquad \text{and} \qquad b^v = \mathrm{ff} \Longleftrightarrow \mathcal{A}^+ \not\models \mathrm{B}[v].$$

We will assume such a fixed embedding and write b also for the formula related to b.

In Section 2.2. the mapping $wp : \mathrm{STAT} \times \mathcal{P}(\mathrm{STATE}) \longrightarrow \mathcal{P}(\mathrm{STATE})$ has been defined. Now we added further variables whose values are of no importance for and can not be changed by the program. The extension of wp to a mapping

$$\mathrm{STAT} \times \mathcal{P}(\mathrm{STATE}^+) \longrightarrow \mathcal{P}(\mathrm{STATE}^+)$$

is then straightforward. We will write wp for the latter again. $\mathcal{L}_V$ offers the opportunity to formulate important properties of programs and argue about them. To show this, we will present a formalization of wp in $\mathcal{L}_V$.

2.2. EXPRESSING WEAKEST PRECONDITIONS

In the sequel, we shall formalize the weakest precondition predicate as a finitary formula of the extended language $\mathcal{L}_V$. For that purpose we define, for each program P and each formula φ of $\mathcal{L}_V$, a new formula of $\mathcal{L}_V$ denoted by $\mathrm{wp}(P, \varphi)$. In other words, wp will be a mapping

$$\mathrm{wp} : \text{programs} \times \text{formulae} \longrightarrow \text{formulae}.$$

We then prove that wp has the desired properties of the weakest precondition predicate. These will follow in a purely logical way from the definition of the formula $\mathrm{wp}(P, \varphi)$. Next we show that our formalized wp actually coincides with the (semantically defined) common weakest precondition predicate wp.

2.2.1 Definition *Let* $P \in \mathrm{STAT}$ *and* φ *be a formula of* $\mathcal{L}_V$. *By recursion on* P, *we define a formula* $\mathrm{wp}(P, \varphi)$ *of* $\mathcal{L}_V$ *as follows:*

- $\mathrm{wp}(\mathbf{skip}, \varphi) :\equiv \varphi$
- $\mathrm{wp}(\mathbf{abort}, \varphi) :\equiv \mathbf{F}$
- $\mathrm{wp}(x := t, \varphi) :\equiv \varphi\{t/x\}$ *for* $x \in \mathrm{PV}_s$ *and* $t \in \mathrm{EXP}_s$

- $\mathrm{wp}(P_1\ ;\ P_2, \varphi) :\equiv \mathrm{wp}(P_1, \mathrm{wp}(P_2, \varphi))$
- $\mathrm{wp}(\textbf{if } b \textbf{ then } P_1 \textbf{ else } P_2 \textbf{ fi}, \varphi) :\equiv (b \wedge \mathrm{wp}(P_1, \varphi)) \vee (\neg b \wedge \mathrm{wp}(P_2, \varphi))$
- $\mathrm{wp}(\textbf{while } b \textbf{ do } P \textbf{ od}, \varphi) :\equiv \exists f \mathrm{E}_{b,P,\varphi}(f, \bar{x})$, *where*

$$\begin{aligned} \mathrm{E}_{b,P,\varphi}(f,\bar{x}) :\equiv\ & (\neg b \wedge \varphi)\{f_{|f|-1}/\bar{x}\} \wedge \\ & \forall 0 \leq i < |f|-1[b \wedge \mathrm{wp}(P, \bar{x} = f_{i+1})]\{f_i/\bar{x}\} \wedge \\ & f_0 = \bar{x} \end{aligned}$$

Here $\bar{x}$ is the list of the programming variables contained in the loop.

The meaning of the formula $\mathrm{E}_{b,P,\varphi}(f, \bar{x})$ is as follows: f is a computation sequence consisting of storage states. The length $|f|$ of f corresponds to the number of repetitions of the while-loop (plus 1). The last component of f, i.e. $f_{|f|-1}$, gives the storage which results from the execution of the while-loop, f_0 the storage before entering the loop. The $\forall i$-part of the formula describes the transition of consecutive storage states inside the while-loop.

2.2.2 Example *Consider the following program P:*

$$\begin{aligned} & z := x\ ; \\ & \textbf{while } z \geq y \textbf{ do } z := z - y \textbf{ od} \end{aligned}$$

The program variables of P are x, y, z, which we suppose to be declared of sort integer. Let φ be an arbitrary formula having x, y, z as free variables. We compute $\mathrm{wp}(P, \varphi)$*:*

$$\begin{aligned} \mathrm{wp}(P, \varphi) &\equiv \mathrm{wp}(z := x\ ;\ \textbf{while } z \geq y \textbf{ do } z := z - y \textbf{ od}, \varphi) \\ &\equiv \mathrm{wp}(z := x, \mathrm{wp}(\textbf{while } z \geq y \textbf{ do } z := z - y \textbf{ od}, \varphi)) \\ &\equiv \mathrm{wp}(\textbf{while } z \geq y \textbf{ do } z := z - y \textbf{ od}, \varphi)\{x/z\}, \end{aligned}$$

where

$$\mathrm{wp}(\textbf{while } z \geq y \textbf{ do } z := z - y \textbf{ od}, \varphi) \equiv \exists f \mathrm{E}(f, y, z)$$

and

$$\begin{aligned} \mathrm{E}(f, y, z) \equiv\ & (\neg z \geq y \wedge \varphi)\{f_{|f|-1}/(y, z)\} \wedge \\ & \forall 0 \leq i < |f|-1[z \geq y \wedge \mathrm{wp}(z := z - y, (y, z) = f_{i+1})]\{f_i/(y, z)\} \wedge \\ & f_0 = (y, z) \\ \equiv\ & f^2_{|f|-1} < f^1_{|f|-1} \wedge \varphi\{f^1_{|f|-1}/y, f^2_{|f|-1}/z\} \wedge \\ & \forall 0 \leq i < |f|-1[f^2_i \geq f^1_i \wedge (f^1_i, f^2_i - f^1_i) = (f^1_{i+1}, f^2_{i+1})] \wedge \\ & (f^1_0, f^2_0) = (y, z). \end{aligned}$$

We use f as a variable for sequences of pairs and f^1_i, f^2_i for the two components of the $(i+1)$th element of f. Obviously, these pairs satisfy

$$f_i = (y, z - i * y) \qquad \textit{for all } 0 \leq i \leq |f| - 1,$$

hence f is uniquely determined by y, z. So we obtain

$$\exists f \mathrm{E}(f, y, z) \iff \exists n(z - n * y < y \wedge \forall i < n(z - i * y \geq y) \wedge \varphi\{z - n * y/z\}).$$

If y is not positive, this is equivalent to $z < y \wedge \varphi$. Therefore we get:

$$\begin{aligned} \mathrm{wp}(P, \varphi) \iff\ & (y > 0 \wedge \exists n(x - n * y < y \wedge \forall i < n(x - i * y \geq y) \wedge \varphi\{x - n * y/z\})) \vee \\ & (x < y \leq 0 \wedge \varphi\{x/z\}) \end{aligned}$$

The first part is equivalent to $\varphi\{x \bmod y/z\}$ if x is nonnegative, otherwise it is equivalent to $\varphi\{x/z\}$. Therefore we have:

$$\mathrm{wp}(P,\varphi) \Longleftrightarrow (y>0 \wedge x \geq 0 \wedge \varphi\{x \bmod y/z\}) \vee \\ (x<0 \wedge x<y \wedge \varphi\{x/z\})$$

In particular we found that our program P is totally correct with respect to the postcondition $\varphi \equiv (z = x \bmod y)$ if the precondition $x \geq 0 \wedge y > 0$ is satisfied — provided that $\mathrm{wp}(P,\varphi)$ formalizes $w\wp(P,\mathrm{Mod}(\varphi))$. This will be shown in 2.2.7.

We show now that the formula wp(P,φ) has all the properties we expect.

2.2.3 Theorem *(Monotonicity) If $\mathcal{A}^+ \models \varphi \rightarrow \psi$, then also $\mathcal{A}^+ \models \mathrm{wp}(P,\varphi) \rightarrow \mathrm{wp}(P,\psi)$.*

Proof: We use structural induction on P and consider the following cases:

- **abort**: Trivial.
- **skip**: Trivial.
- $x := t$: If $\mathcal{A}^+ \models \varphi \rightarrow \psi$, then also $\mathcal{A}^+ \models \varphi\{t/x\} \rightarrow \psi\{t/x\}$.
- Q ; R: Suppose $\mathcal{A}^+ \models \varphi \rightarrow \psi$. Then we get $\mathcal{A}^+ \models \mathrm{wp}(R,\varphi) \rightarrow \mathrm{wp}(R,\psi)$ by induction hypothesis for R, hence, by induction hypothesis for Q,

  $$\mathcal{A}^+ \models \mathrm{wp}(Q,\mathrm{wp}(R,\varphi)) \rightarrow \mathrm{wp}(Q,\mathrm{wp}(R,\psi)).$$

  By definition

  $$\mathrm{wp}(Q\ ;\ R,\varphi) \equiv \mathrm{wp}(Q,\mathrm{wp}(R,\varphi)) \quad \text{and} \quad \mathrm{wp}(Q,\mathrm{wp}(R,\psi)) \equiv \mathrm{wp}(Q\ ;\ R,\psi),$$

  so we get the desired result.
- **if** b **then** Q **else** R **fi**: Suppose $\mathcal{A}^+ \models \varphi \rightarrow \psi$. We have

  $$\mathrm{wp}(P,\varphi) \equiv (b \wedge \mathrm{wp}(Q,\varphi)) \vee (\neg b \wedge \mathrm{wp}(R,\varphi)).$$

  By induction hypothesis for Q and R,

  $$\mathcal{A}^+ \models (b \wedge \mathrm{wp}(Q,\varphi)) \vee (\neg b \wedge \mathrm{wp}(R,\varphi)) \rightarrow (b \wedge \mathrm{wp}(Q,\psi)) \vee (\neg b \wedge \mathrm{wp}(R,\psi)),$$

  and the right part is syntactically equal to $\mathrm{wp}(P,\psi)$.
- **while** b **do** Q **od**: Suppose $\mathcal{A}^+ \models \varphi \rightarrow \psi$. Then we get

  $$\begin{aligned} \mathrm{E}_{b,Q,\varphi}(f,\bar{x}) \ \equiv\ & (\neg b \wedge \varphi)\{f_{|f|-1}/\bar{x}\} \wedge \\ & \forall 0 \leq i < |f|-1 [b \wedge \mathrm{wp}(Q, \bar{x} = f_{i+1})]\{f_i/\bar{x}\} \wedge \\ & f_0 = \bar{x} \\ \Longrightarrow\ & (\neg b \wedge \psi)\{f_{|f|-1}/\bar{x}\} \wedge \\ & \forall 0 \leq i < |f|-1 [b \wedge \mathrm{wp}(\mathrm{Q}, \bar{x} = f_{i+1})]\{f_i/\bar{x}\} \wedge \\ & f_0 = \bar{x} \\ \equiv\ & \mathrm{E}_{b,Q,\psi}(f,\bar{x}). \end{aligned}$$

  Therefore we have $\mathcal{A}^+ \models \exists f \mathrm{E}_{b,Q,\varphi}(f,\bar{x}) \rightarrow \exists f \mathrm{E}_{b,Q,\psi}(f,\bar{x})$, so by definition of wp, $\mathcal{A}^+ \models \mathrm{wp}(P,\varphi) \rightarrow \mathrm{wp}(P,\psi)$.

□

Remark: Obviously we have $\mathrm{wp}(P,\varphi)\{t/a\} \equiv \mathrm{wp}(P,\varphi\{t/a\})$ if neither a nor any variable in t occurs in the program P. We will use this fact without further comment.

The next theorem provides something like a "normal form representation" of the formula $\mathrm{wp}(P,\varphi)$. In the case of a deterministic language its statements can also be regarded as laws of determinacy.

2.2.4 Theorem *(Normal form, laws of determinacy) Let P be a program, φ a formula and $\bar{x}$ the list of the variables in P. Then we have:*

(i) $\mathrm{wp}(P,\varphi) \Longleftrightarrow \exists\bar{y}[\mathrm{wp}(P,\bar{x}=\bar{y}) \wedge \varphi\{\bar{y}/\bar{x}\}]$

(ii) The formula $\forall\bar{y}\forall\bar{z}[\mathrm{wp}(P,\bar{x}=\bar{y}) \wedge \mathrm{wp}(P,\bar{x}=\bar{z}) \rightarrow \bar{y}=\bar{z}]$ *holds.*

Remark: The statements (i) and (ii) can be contracted to

$$\mathrm{wp}(P,\varphi) \Longleftrightarrow \exists!\bar{y}[\mathrm{wp}(P,\bar{x}=\bar{y}) \wedge \varphi\{\bar{y}/\bar{x}\}].$$

Proof: We use the notation $\varphi(\bar{x})$ to exhibit the occurrences of the variables $\bar{x}$ in φ and $\varphi(\bar{y})$ to abbreviate subsequent substitution.

(i): We use structural induction on P:

- **abort**: Trivial.
- **skip**: Trivial.
- $x := t$: Let $\bar{x}, x$ be the list of the variables in P. Then we obtain

$$\begin{aligned} \mathrm{wp}(P,\varphi(\bar{x},x)) &\equiv \varphi(\bar{x},x)\{t/x\} \\ &\Longleftrightarrow x\{t/x\} = t \wedge \bar{x}=\bar{x} \wedge \varphi(\bar{x},t) \\ &\Longleftrightarrow \exists\bar{y},y[x\{t/x\} = y \wedge \bar{x}=\bar{y} \wedge \varphi(\bar{y},y)] \\ &\equiv \exists\bar{y},y[\mathrm{wp}(x:=t,(\bar{x},x)=(\bar{y},y)) \wedge \varphi(\bar{y},y)]. \end{aligned}$$

- $Q\ ;\ R$: By induction hypothesis for R we have

$$(1)\ \mathrm{wp}(R,\varphi) \Longleftrightarrow \exists\bar{z}[\mathrm{wp}(R,\bar{x}=\bar{z}) \wedge \varphi(\bar{z})].$$

The induction hypothesis for Q yields the following equivalences:

$$\begin{aligned} &(2) \quad \mathrm{wp}(Q,\mathrm{wp}(R,\varphi)) \Longleftrightarrow \exists\bar{y}[\mathrm{wp}(Q,\bar{x}=\bar{y}) \wedge \mathrm{wp}(R,\varphi)\{\bar{y}/\bar{x}\}] \\ &(3) \quad \mathrm{wp}(Q,\mathrm{wp}(R,\bar{x}=\bar{z})) \Longleftrightarrow \exists\bar{y}[\mathrm{wp}(Q,\bar{x}=\bar{y}) \wedge \mathrm{wp}(R,\bar{x}=\bar{z})\{\bar{y}/\bar{x}\}] \end{aligned}$$

Using (1) and (2) we deduce

$$\begin{aligned} \mathrm{wp}(Q\ ;\ R,\varphi) &\equiv \mathrm{wp}(Q,\mathrm{wp}(R,\varphi)) \\ &\Longleftrightarrow \exists\bar{y}[\mathrm{wp}(Q,\bar{x}=\bar{y}) \wedge \exists\bar{z}(\mathrm{wp}(R,\bar{x}=\bar{z})\{\bar{y}/\bar{x}\} \wedge \varphi(\bar{z}))] \\ &\Longleftrightarrow \exists\bar{z}[\exists\bar{y}(\mathrm{wp}(Q,\bar{x}=\bar{y}) \wedge \mathrm{wp}(R,\bar{x}=\bar{z})\{\bar{y}/\bar{x}\}) \wedge \varphi(\bar{z})]. \end{aligned}$$

By (3) we obtain

$$\begin{aligned} \mathrm{wp}(Q\ ;\ R,\varphi) &\Longleftrightarrow \exists\bar{z}[\mathrm{wp}(Q,\mathrm{wp}(R,\bar{x}=\bar{z})) \wedge \varphi(\bar{z})] \\ &\equiv \exists\bar{z}[\mathrm{wp}(Q\ ;\ R,\bar{x}=\bar{z}) \wedge \varphi(\bar{z})]. \end{aligned}$$

- **if** b **then** Q **else** R **fi**: We use the induction hypothesis for both Q and R and obtain the result as follows:

$$\begin{aligned}
\mathrm{wp}(P,\varphi) &\equiv (b(\bar{x}) \wedge \mathrm{wp}(Q,\varphi(\bar{x}))) \vee (\neg b(\bar{x}) \wedge \mathrm{wp}(R,\varphi(\bar{x})))\\
&\Longleftrightarrow (b(\bar{x}) \wedge \exists \bar{y}[\mathrm{wp}(Q,\bar{x}=\bar{y}) \wedge \varphi(\bar{y})]) \vee\\
&\quad\ (\neg b(\bar{x}) \wedge \exists \bar{y}[\mathrm{wp}(R,\bar{x}=\bar{y}) \wedge \varphi(\bar{y})])\\
&\Longleftrightarrow \exists \bar{y}[((b(\bar{x}) \wedge \mathrm{wp}(Q,\bar{x}=\bar{y})) \vee (\neg b(\bar{x}) \wedge \mathrm{wp}(R,\bar{x}=\bar{y}))) \wedge \varphi(\bar{y})]\\
&\equiv \exists \bar{y}[\mathrm{wp}(P,\bar{x}=\bar{y}) \wedge \varphi(\bar{y})].
\end{aligned}$$

- **while** b **do** Q **od**: This case can be proved without using the induction hypothesis:

$$\begin{aligned}
\mathrm{wp}(P,\varphi(\bar{x})) \ \equiv\ & \exists f[(\neg b(\bar{x}) \wedge \varphi(\bar{x}))\{f_{|f|-1}/\bar{x}\} \wedge\\
& \quad \forall 0 \leq i < |f|-1[b(\bar{x}) \wedge \mathrm{wp}(Q,\bar{x}=f_{i+1})]\{f_i/\bar{x}\} \wedge\\
& \quad f_0 = \bar{x}]\\
\Longleftrightarrow\ & \exists f[(\neg b(\bar{x}) \wedge \bar{x} = f_{|f|-1})\{f_{|f|-1}/\bar{x}\} \wedge\\
& \quad \forall 0 \leq i < |f|-1[b(\bar{x}) \wedge \mathrm{wp}(Q,\bar{x}=f_{i+1})]\{f_i/\bar{x}\} \wedge\\
& \quad f_0 = \bar{x} \wedge \varphi(f_{|f|-1})]\\
\Longleftrightarrow\ & \exists f \exists \bar{y}[(\neg b(\bar{x}) \wedge \bar{x} = \bar{y})\{f_{|f|-1}/\bar{x}\} \wedge\\
& \quad \forall 0 \leq i < |f|-1[b(\bar{x}) \wedge \mathrm{wp}(Q,\bar{x}=f_{i+1})]\{f_i/\bar{x}\} \wedge\\
& \quad f_0 = \bar{x} \wedge \varphi(\bar{y})]\\
\Longleftrightarrow\ & \exists \bar{y} \exists f[\mathrm{E}_{b,Q,\bar{x}=\bar{y}}(f,\bar{x}) \wedge \varphi(\bar{y})]\\
\equiv\ & \exists \bar{y}[\mathrm{wp}(P,\bar{x}=\bar{y}) \wedge \varphi(\bar{y})].
\end{aligned}$$

(ii): We proceed again by structural induction on P:

- **abort**: Trivial.
- **skip**: $\bar{x}=\bar{y} \wedge \bar{x}=\bar{z} \Longrightarrow \bar{y}=\bar{z}$
- $x := t$: $(\bar{x},x) = (\bar{y},y)\{t/x\} \wedge (\bar{x},x) = (\bar{z},z)\{t/x\} \Longrightarrow (\bar{y},y) = (\bar{z},z)$.
- Q ; R: By (i) we have

$$\begin{aligned}
&(1)\quad \mathrm{wp}(Q\ ;\ R,\bar{x}=\bar{y}) \Longleftrightarrow \exists \bar{u}[\mathrm{wp}(Q,\bar{x}=\bar{u}) \wedge \mathrm{wp}(R,\bar{x}=\bar{y})\{\bar{u}/\bar{x}\}]\\
&(2)\quad \mathrm{wp}(Q\ ;\ R,\bar{x}=\bar{z}) \Longleftrightarrow \exists \bar{v}[\mathrm{wp}(Q,\bar{x}=\bar{v}) \wedge \mathrm{wp}(R,\bar{x}=\bar{z})\{\bar{v}/\bar{x}\}].
\end{aligned}$$

By induction hypothesis for Q we have

$$(3)\quad \mathrm{wp}(Q,\bar{x}=\bar{u}) \wedge \mathrm{wp}(Q,\bar{x}=\bar{v}) \Longrightarrow \bar{u}=\bar{v}$$

and by induction hypothesis for R we have

$$\mathrm{wp}(R,\bar{x}=\bar{y}) \wedge \mathrm{wp}(R,\bar{x}=\bar{z}) \Longrightarrow \bar{y}=\bar{z},$$

hence

$$(4)\quad \bar{u}=\bar{v} \wedge \mathrm{wp}(R,\bar{x}=\bar{y})\{\bar{u}/\bar{x}\} \wedge \mathrm{wp}(R,\bar{x}=\bar{z})\{\bar{v}/\bar{x}\} \Longrightarrow \bar{y}=\bar{z}.$$

By combining (3) and (4) we obtain

$$\mathrm{wp}(Q,\bar{x}=\bar{u}) \wedge \mathrm{wp}(R,\bar{x}=\bar{y})\{\bar{u}/\bar{x}\} \wedge \mathrm{wp}(Q,\bar{x}=\bar{v}) \wedge \mathrm{wp}(R,\bar{x}=\bar{z})\{\bar{v}/\bar{x}\} \Longrightarrow \bar{y}=\bar{z}.$$

Now the assertion follows by introducing existential quantifiers on the left and using (1) and (2).

- **if** b **then** Q **else** R **fi**: Assume $\mathrm{wp}(P, \bar{x} = \bar{y})$ and $\mathrm{wp}(P, \bar{x} = \bar{z})$. If $b(\bar{x})$ holds, then we obtain $\mathrm{wp}(Q, \bar{x} = \bar{y})$ and $\mathrm{wp}(Q, \bar{x} = \bar{z})$, hence $\bar{y} = \bar{z}$ by induction hypothesis for Q. Otherwise we obtain $\mathrm{wp}(R, \bar{x} = \bar{y})$ and $\mathrm{wp}(R, \bar{x} = \bar{z})$, so $\bar{y} = \bar{z}$ follows again by induction hypothesis for R.

- **while** b **do** Q **od**: Suppose we have
$$\neg b(f_m) \wedge f_m = \bar{y} \wedge \forall 0 \leq i < m[b(f_i) \wedge \mathrm{wp}(Q, \bar{x} = f_{i+1})]\{f_i/\bar{x}\} \wedge f_0 = \bar{x}$$
and
$$\neg b(g_n) \wedge g_n = \bar{z} \wedge \forall 0 \leq i < n[b(g_i) \wedge \mathrm{wp}(Q, \bar{x} = g_{i+1})]\{g_i/\bar{x}\} \wedge g_0 = \bar{x}.$$
Then trivially, $f_0 = g_0$. By induction on j we further obtain:
$$f_j = g_j \text{ for } j = 0, 1, 2, \ldots$$
So it follows that $m = n$ (if $m < n$ or $n < m$, we have $\neg b(f_m)$ and $b(g_m)$ or $\neg b(g_n)$ and $b(f_n)$, hence a contradiction, since $f_m = g_m$ or $f_n = g_n$ respectively). But then $\bar{y} = f_m = g_n = \bar{z}$. □

The normal form theorem enables us to obtain further properties of wp easily. In the following theorem we will give a first example. Using the normal form of wp in combination with monotonicity we show that wp behaves well on some of the logical operators. For further applictions of the normal form theorem, see the next section.

2.2.5 Theorem *The function* wp *satisfies the following healthiness conditions:*

(i) $\mathrm{wp}(P, \mathbf{F}) \Longleftrightarrow \mathbf{F}$

(ii) $\mathrm{wp}(P, \varphi \wedge \psi) \Longleftrightarrow \mathrm{wp}(P, \varphi) \wedge \mathrm{wp}(P, \psi)$

(iii) $\mathrm{wp}(P, \varphi \vee \psi) \Longleftrightarrow \mathrm{wp}(P, \varphi) \vee \mathrm{wp}(P, \psi)$

(iv) $\mathrm{wp}(P, \forall u\varphi) \Longleftrightarrow \forall u\,\mathrm{wp}(P, \varphi)$

(v) $\mathrm{wp}(P, \exists u\varphi) \Longleftrightarrow \exists u\,\mathrm{wp}(P, \varphi)$

Proof:

(i) By Theorem 2.2.4(i), $\mathrm{wp}(P, \mathbf{F}) \Longleftrightarrow \exists y(\mathrm{wp}(P, \bar{x} = \bar{y}) \wedge \mathbf{F}) \Longleftrightarrow \mathbf{F}$.

(ii) "$\Longrightarrow$": This direction follows immediately by monotonicity.

"$\Longleftarrow$": By Theorem 2.2.4(i) we have
$$\mathrm{wp}(P, \varphi(\bar{x})) \Longrightarrow \exists \bar{y}(\mathrm{wp}(P, \bar{x} = \bar{y}) \wedge \varphi(\bar{y}))$$
and also
$$\mathrm{wp}(P, \psi(\bar{x})) \Longrightarrow \exists \bar{z}(\mathrm{wp}(P, \bar{x} = \bar{z}) \wedge \psi(\bar{z}));$$
by Theorem 2.2.4(ii) we have $\mathrm{wp}(P, \bar{x} = \bar{y}) \wedge \mathrm{wp}(P, \bar{x} = \bar{z}) \rightarrow \bar{y} = \bar{z}$, hence we obtain
$$\exists \bar{y}(\mathrm{wp}(P, \bar{x} = \bar{y}) \wedge \varphi(\bar{y}) \wedge \psi(\bar{y})),$$
which implies $\mathrm{wp}(P, \varphi \wedge \psi)$ by using again Theorem 2.2.4(i).

(iii) By Theorem 2.2.4(i) we obtain

$$\begin{aligned}\mathrm{wp}(P,\varphi\vee\psi) &\Longleftrightarrow \exists\bar{y}[\mathrm{wp}(P,\bar{x}=\bar{y})\wedge(\varphi(\bar{y})\vee\psi(\bar{y}))]\\ &\Longleftrightarrow \exists\bar{y}[\mathrm{wp}(P,\bar{x}=\bar{y})\wedge\varphi(\bar{y})]\vee\exists\bar{y}[\mathrm{wp}(P,\bar{x}=\bar{y})\wedge\psi(\bar{y})]\\ &\Longleftrightarrow \mathrm{wp}(P,\varphi)\vee\mathrm{wp}(P,\psi).\end{aligned}$$

(iv) "$\Longrightarrow$": This direction is also straightforward by monotonicity.

"$\Longleftarrow$": First we note that by Theorem 2.2.4(i)

$$\forall u\mathrm{wp}(P,\varphi(\bar{x},u)) \Longleftrightarrow \forall u\exists\bar{y}[\mathrm{wp}(P,\bar{x}=\bar{y})\wedge\varphi(\bar{y},u)],$$

so we have to show that the quantifiers on the right can be interchanged. By Theorem 2.2.4(ii),

$$\mathrm{wp}(P,\bar{x}=\bar{y})\wedge\mathrm{wp}(P,\bar{x}=\bar{z}) \Longrightarrow \bar{y}=\bar{z}.$$

Using the properties of equality, we obtain

$$\mathrm{wp}(P,\bar{x}=\bar{y})\wedge\varphi(\bar{y},u)\wedge\mathrm{wp}(P,\bar{x}=\bar{z})\wedge\varphi(\bar{z},v) \Longrightarrow \mathrm{wp}(P,\bar{x}=\bar{y})\wedge\varphi(\bar{y},v).$$

Now quantifiers can be introduced on the left in order to obtain the implication

$$\begin{aligned}&\mathrm{wp}(P,\bar{x}=\bar{y})\wedge\varphi(\bar{y},u)\wedge\forall u\exists\bar{y}[\mathrm{wp}(P,\bar{x}=\bar{y})\wedge\varphi(\bar{y},u)]\\ &\qquad\Longrightarrow \mathrm{wp}(P,\bar{x}=\bar{y})\wedge\varphi(\bar{y},v).\end{aligned}$$

Since v occurs freely only on the right, a universal quantifier can be introduced:

$$\begin{aligned}&\mathrm{wp}(P,\bar{x}=\bar{y})\wedge\varphi(\bar{y},u)\wedge\forall u\exists\bar{y}[\mathrm{wp}(P,\bar{x}=\bar{y})\wedge\varphi(\bar{y},u)]\\ &\qquad\Longrightarrow \mathrm{wp}(P,\bar{x}=\bar{y})\wedge\forall u\varphi(\bar{y},u)\end{aligned}$$

Hence, we get

$$\forall u\exists\bar{y}[\mathrm{wp}(P,\bar{x}=\bar{y})\wedge\varphi(\bar{y},u)] \Longrightarrow \exists\bar{y}[\mathrm{wp}(P,\bar{x}=\bar{y})\wedge\forall u\varphi(\bar{y},u)].$$

Now by Theorem 2.2.4(i) the assertion follows.

(v) Here we obtain the desired equivalence

$$\begin{aligned}\mathrm{wp}(P,\exists u\varphi(\bar{x})) &\Longleftrightarrow \exists\bar{y}[\mathrm{wp}(P,\bar{x}=\bar{y})\wedge\exists u\varphi(\bar{y},u)]\\ &\Longleftrightarrow \exists u\exists\bar{y}[\mathrm{wp}(P,\bar{x}=\bar{y})\wedge\varphi(\bar{y},u)]\\ &\Longleftrightarrow \exists u\mathrm{wp}(P,\varphi(\bar{x},u))\end{aligned}$$

by using Theorem 2.2.4(i) twice. □

So the function wp "commutes" with the boolean constant **F** and with the positive logical operators. However, wp does not commute with negation – this can easily be seen as follows: Consider the equivalence

$$\mathrm{wp}(P,\mathbf{F}) \Longleftrightarrow \mathbf{F}.$$

Negating both sides we obtain

$$\neg\mathrm{wp}(P,\mathbf{F}) \Longleftrightarrow \mathbf{T}.$$

Now, if $\neg\text{wp}(P,\varphi) \Longleftrightarrow \text{wp}(P,\neg\varphi)$ were true, we would obtain

$$\text{wp}(P,\mathbf{T}) \Longleftrightarrow \text{wp}(P,\neg\mathbf{F}) \Longleftrightarrow \neg\text{wp}(P,\mathbf{F}) \Longleftrightarrow \mathbf{T},$$

which is a contradiction if P is a nonterminating program. Termination, that means $\text{wp}(P,\mathbf{T})$, indeed describes the gap between $\text{wp}(P,\neg\varphi)$ and $\neg\text{wp}(P,\varphi)$:

2.2.6 Corollary $\text{wp}(P,\neg\varphi) \Longleftrightarrow \text{wp}(P,\mathbf{T}) \wedge \neg\text{wp}(P,\varphi)$

Proof: "$\Longrightarrow$": From $\neg\varphi \rightarrow \mathbf{T}$ and the monotonicity of wp we deduce

$$\text{wp}(P,\neg\varphi) \Longrightarrow \text{wp}(P,\mathbf{T}).$$

From Theorem 2.2.5(ii) and (i) we get

$$\text{wp}(P,\neg\varphi) \wedge \text{wp}(P,\varphi) \Longrightarrow \text{wp}(P,\neg\varphi \wedge \varphi) \Longrightarrow \mathbf{F},$$

which in turn implies $\text{wp}(P,\neg\varphi) \Longrightarrow \neg\text{wp}(P,\varphi)$.

"$\Longleftarrow$": Here we have

$$\begin{aligned}\text{wp}(P,\mathbf{T}) \wedge \neg\text{wp}(P,\varphi) &\Longrightarrow \exists\bar{y}[\text{wp}(P,\bar{x}=\bar{y})] \wedge \forall\bar{y}[\text{wp}(P,\bar{x}=\bar{y}) \rightarrow \neg\varphi(\bar{y})] \\ &\Longrightarrow \exists\bar{y}[\text{wp}(P,\bar{x}=\bar{y}) \wedge \neg\varphi(\bar{y})] \\ &\Longrightarrow \text{wp}(P,\neg\varphi)\end{aligned}$$

using 2.2.4(i) in the first and the third step. □

We will show now that our formula $\text{wp}(P,\varphi)$ exactly describes the semantically defined weakest precondition predicate $\mathit{wp}(P,\text{Mod}(\varphi))$ for arbitrary postconditions that can be expressed by a formula of the language $\mathcal{L}_V$.

2.2.7 Theorem *Let P be a program and φ a $\mathcal{L}_V$-formula. Then:*

$$\text{Mod}(\text{wp}(P,\varphi)) = \mathit{wp}(P,\text{Mod}(\varphi))$$

Proof: By structural induction on P:

- **skip**: $\text{Mod}(\text{wp}(\mathbf{skip},\varphi)) = \text{Mod}(\varphi) = \mathit{wp}(\mathbf{skip},\text{Mod}(\varphi))$
- **abort**: $\text{Mod}(\text{wp}(\mathbf{abort},\varphi)) = \text{Mod}(\mathbf{F}) = \emptyset = \mathit{wp}(\mathbf{abort},\text{Mod}(\varphi))$
- $x := t$: $$\begin{aligned}\text{Mod}(\text{wp}(x:=t,\varphi)) &= \text{Mod}(\varphi\{t/x\}) \\ &= \{v \in \text{STATE}^+ : \mathcal{A}^+ \models \varphi\{t/x\}[v]\} \\ &= \{v \in \text{STATE}^+ : \mathcal{A}^+ \models \varphi[v\{t^v/x\}]\} \\ &= \{v \in \text{STATE}^+ : v\{t^v/x\} \in \text{Mod}(\varphi)\} \\ &= \mathit{wp}(x:=t,\text{Mod}(\varphi))\end{aligned}$$
- Q ; R: Using the induction hypothesis for Q (Step 2) and R (Step 3), we obtain: $$\begin{aligned}\text{Mod}(\text{wp}(Q\ ;\ R,\varphi)) &= \text{Mod}(\text{wp}(Q,\text{wp}(R,\varphi))) \\ &= \mathit{wp}(Q,\text{Mod}(\text{wp}(R,\varphi))) \\ &= \mathit{wp}(Q,\mathit{wp}(R,\text{Mod}(\varphi))) \\ &= \mathit{wp}(Q\ ;\ R,\text{Mod}(\varphi))\end{aligned}$$

- **if** b **then** Q **else** R **fi**: Here we have

$$\begin{aligned}
&\mathrm{Mod}(\mathrm{wp}(\textbf{if } b \textbf{ then } Q \textbf{ else } R \textbf{ fi}, \varphi)) \\
&\quad = \mathrm{Mod}((b \wedge \mathrm{wp}(Q,\varphi)) \vee (\neg b \wedge \mathrm{wp}(R,\varphi))) \\
&\quad = (\mathrm{Mod}(b) \cap \mathrm{Mod}(\mathrm{wp}(Q,\varphi))) \cup (\mathrm{Mod}(\neg b) \cap \mathrm{Mod}(\mathrm{wp}(R,\varphi))) \\
&\quad = (\mathrm{Mod}(b) \cap w\wp(Q, \mathrm{Mod}(\varphi))) \cup (\mathrm{Mod}(\neg b) \cap w\wp(R, \mathrm{Mod}(\varphi))) \\
&\quad = w\wp(\textbf{if } b \textbf{ then } Q \textbf{ else } R \textbf{ fi}, \mathrm{Mod}(\varphi)),
\end{aligned}$$

  where the third step uses the induction hypothesis for Q and R.

- **while** b **do** Q **od**: Let $\bar{x}$ be a sequence containing all the variables in P and

$$\begin{aligned}
\mathrm{E}^k_{b,Q,\varphi}(f,\bar{x}) :\equiv\ & (\neg b \wedge \varphi)\{f_{|f|-1}/\bar{x}\} \wedge \\
& \forall 0 \le i < |f|-1 [b \wedge \mathrm{wp}(Q, \bar{x} = f_{i+1})]\{f_i/\bar{x}\} \wedge \\
& f_0 = \bar{x} \wedge \\
& |f| \le k+1
\end{aligned}$$

  for all numbers $k \in \mathbb{N}$. Then $\mathrm{wp}(\textbf{while } b \textbf{ do } Q \textbf{ od}, \varphi)$ holds iff $\exists f \mathrm{E}^k_{b,Q,\varphi}(f,\bar{x})$ holds for some $k \in \mathbb{N}$. Let

$$\begin{aligned}
M_0 &:= \mathrm{Mod}(\neg b) \cap \mathrm{Mod}(\varphi) \\
M_{k+1} &:= (\mathrm{Mod}(b) \cap w\wp(Q, M_k)) \cup (\mathrm{Mod}(\neg b) \cap M_k)
\end{aligned}$$

  for all $k \in \mathbb{N}$. Then $w\wp(\textbf{while } b \textbf{ do } Q \textbf{ od}, \mathrm{Mod}(\varphi)) = \bigcup_{k=0}^{\infty} M_k$. We will show the equation $\mathrm{Mod}(\exists f \mathrm{E}^k_{b,Q,\varphi}(f,\bar{x})) = M_k$ for all $k \in \mathbb{N}$ by induction on k.

  The induction begin $k = 0$ is rather trivial:

$$\begin{aligned}
& v \in \mathrm{Mod}(\exists f \mathrm{E}^0_{b,Q,\varphi}(f,\bar{x})) \\
\iff\ & \mathcal{A}^+ \models \exists f((\neg b \wedge \varphi)\{f_{|f|-1}/\bar{x}\} \wedge f_0 = \bar{x} \wedge |f| \le 1)[v] \\
\iff\ & \mathcal{A}^+ \models (\neg b \wedge \varphi)[v] \\
\iff\ & v \in M_0
\end{aligned}$$

  For the induction step $k \mapsto k+1$ we prove two inclusions:

  "$\subset$": Let $v \in \mathrm{Mod}(\exists f \mathrm{E}^{k+1}_{b,Q,\varphi}(f,\bar{x}))$. Then there exists a sequence σ such that

$$\mathcal{A}^+ \models \mathrm{E}^{k+1}_{b,Q,\varphi}(f,\bar{x})[v\{\sigma/f\}].$$

  If $|\sigma| \le k+1$, then $v \in \mathrm{Mod}(\exists f \mathrm{E}^k_{b,Q,\varphi}(f,\bar{x})) = M_k$ (by side induction hypothesis). Otherwise we cut off the first element of σ and call the result τ. From the property $\mathcal{A}^+ \models \mathrm{E}^{k+1}_{b,Q,\varphi}(f,\bar{x})[v\{\sigma/f\}]$ we deduce

$$\begin{aligned}
&(1)\quad \mathcal{A}^+ \models \mathrm{E}^k_{b,Q,\varphi}(f,\bar{x})[v\{\tau/f, \sigma_1/\bar{x}\}] \\
&(2)\quad \mathcal{A}^+ \models b \wedge \mathrm{wp}(Q, \bar{x} = f_1)[v\{\sigma/f\}].
\end{aligned}$$

  Applying the induction hypothesis to (1), we conclude $v\{\sigma_1/\bar{x}\} \in M_k$. Since the membership in M_k of an assignment is not affected by changing any but the programming variables, we get $\mathrm{Mod}(\bar{x} = \sigma_1) \subset M_k$. From (2) we deduce

$$\mathcal{A}^+ \models b \wedge \mathrm{wp}(Q, \bar{x} = \sigma_1)[v].$$

So $v \in \mathrm{Mod}(b)$ and application of the principal induction hypothesis for Q yields $v \in w\wp(Q, \mathrm{Mod}(\bar{x} = \sigma_1))$. Therefore $v \in \mathrm{Mod}(b) \cap w\wp(Q, M_k) \subset M_{k+1}$.

"$\supset$": Let $v \in M_{k+1} = (\mathrm{Mod}(b) \cap w\wp(Q, M_k)) \cup (\mathrm{Mod}(\neg b) \cap M_k)$. Then either we have $v \in \mathrm{Mod}(\neg b) \cap M_k$, in which case the induction hypothesis is used to get the inclusion

$$v \in \mathrm{Mod}(\exists f \mathrm{E}^k_{b,Q,\varphi}(f, \bar{x})) \subset \mathrm{Mod}(\exists f \mathrm{E}^{k+1}_{b,Q,\varphi}(f, \bar{x})),$$

or we have $v \in \mathrm{Mod}(b) \cap w\wp(Q, M_k)$, where the subsequent application of the side and principal induction hypothesis yields

$$v \in \mathrm{Mod}(b \wedge \mathrm{wp}(Q, \exists f \mathrm{E}^k_{b,Q,\varphi}(f, \bar{x}))).$$

From the normal form theorem we get

$$\begin{aligned} & b \wedge \mathrm{wp}(Q, \exists f \mathrm{E}^k_{b,Q,\varphi}(f, \bar{x})) \\ & \iff b \wedge \exists \bar{y}(\mathrm{wp}(Q, \bar{x} = \bar{y}) \wedge \exists f \mathrm{E}^k_{b,Q,\varphi}(f, \bar{y})) \\ & \iff \exists \bar{y}(b \wedge \mathrm{wp}(Q, \bar{x} = \bar{y}) \wedge \exists f \mathrm{E}^k_{b,Q,\varphi}(f, \bar{y})). \end{aligned}$$

Therefore, there is a sequence τ and values $\bar{a}$ such that

$$\mathcal{A}^+ \models (b \wedge \mathrm{wp}(Q, \bar{x} = \bar{y}) \wedge \mathrm{E}^k_{b,Q,\varphi}(f, \bar{y}))[v\{\tau/f, \bar{a}/\bar{y}\}].$$

Now prefixing $v(\bar{x})$ to the sequence τ gives another sequence – let us call it σ. Then $\mathcal{A}^+ \models \mathrm{E}^{k+1}_{b,Q,\varphi}(f, \bar{x})[v\{\sigma/f\}]$, hence $v \in \mathrm{Mod}(\exists f \mathrm{E}^{k+1}_{b,Q,\varphi}(f, \bar{x}))$. □

2.3. NONDETERMINISM

Let us finally have a short look on how to formalize the weakest precondition predicate in the case of nondeterministic programs. We consider finite nondeterminism expressed by Dijkstra's guarded commands [Dijkstra 75, Dijkstra 76]:

if b_1 **then** P_1 ▯ b_2 **then** P_2 ▯ ... ▯ b_n **then** P_n **fi**

The operational behaviour of a program of this kind can be described by: One of the subprograms P_i for which the condition b_i holds is carried out, but it is not determined which one if more than one of the b_i's happen to be true. If every condition yields false, the execution results in an error. Consequently, the computation process can no longer be represented by a sequence of storage states. In fact, a finite tree, whose branches represent all possible computations, has to be used. Therefore, the formalization of the weakest precondition has to be modified:

- The verification language is supposed to contain new sorts: finite sets and finite labelled trees with labels in s ($s \in \mathrm{S}$). The nodes themselves can be regarded as natural numbers. Then our access function $\cdot(\cdot)$ takes a tree τ and a natural number i as arguments and gives a result in s if i is a node of τ: We fix 0 as the root and let $\mathrm{n}(\tau)$, $\mathrm{l}(\tau)$, $\mathrm{succ}(\tau, i)$ denote the set of nodes of τ, leaves of τ and successor nodes of i in τ (if $i \in \mathrm{n}(\tau)$) respectively. We will use a predicate symbol $\in$ for the membership relation and a function symbol h for the height of a tree.
- The definition of $\mathrm{wp}(P, \varphi)$, where P is a program in the extended programming language $\mathrm{STAT}^{\mathrm{nondet}}$ and φ a formula of the modified verification language, is as

follows:

$$\text{wp}(\textbf{if } \mathop{[\!]}_{i=1}^{n} (b_i \textbf{ then } P_i) \textbf{ fi}, \varphi) :\equiv \bigvee_{i=1}^{n} b_i \wedge \bigwedge_{i=1}^{n} (b_i \rightarrow \text{wp}(P_i, \varphi))$$

$$\text{wp}(\textbf{while } b \textbf{ do } P \textbf{ od}, \varphi) :\equiv \exists\tau \text{F}_{b,P,\varphi}(\tau, \bar{x}), \text{ where}$$

$$\begin{aligned} \text{F}_{b,P,\varphi}(\tau, \bar{x}) :\equiv\ & \forall i \in \text{l}(\tau)(\neg b \wedge \varphi)\{\tau_i/\bar{x}\} \wedge \\ & \forall i \in \text{n}(\tau)[i \notin \text{l}(\tau) \rightarrow (b \wedge \text{wp}(P, \exists j \in \text{succ}(\tau, i)(\bar{x} = \tau_j)))\{\tau_i/\bar{x}\}] \wedge \\ & \tau_0 = \bar{x}. \end{aligned}$$

For all other programming language constructs the definition of wp remains unchanged.

Now the analogies of the above theorems can be proved. Since these proofs can be carried out using the same techniques as in the deterministic case, we omit them and simply state the theorems:

2.3.1 Theorem *(Monotonicity) If $\varphi \rightarrow \psi$ holds in the standard interpretation for every assignment, then so does* $\text{wp}(\text{P}, \varphi) \rightarrow \text{wp}(\text{P}, \psi)$.

2.3.2 Theorem *(Normal form, finiteness of nondeterminacy) Let P be a program, φ a formula and $\bar{x}$ the list of the variables in P. Then*

(i) $\text{wp}(P, \varphi) \Longleftrightarrow \exists\tau[h(\tau) = 1 \wedge \text{wp}(P, \exists i \in \text{l}(\tau)(\bar{x} = \tau_i)) \wedge \forall i \in \text{l}(\tau)\varphi\{\tau_i/\bar{x}\}]$

(ii) The set of trees τ which satisfy $\text{wp}(P, \exists i \in \text{l}(\tau)(\bar{x} = \tau_i))$ is either empty or contains a least element (wrt. the subtree ordering).

In a less formal way, (i) can be restated as

$$\text{wp}(P, \varphi) \Longleftrightarrow \exists\{\bar{y}_1, \ldots, \bar{y}_m\}[\text{wp}(P, \bar{x} \in \{\bar{y}_1, \ldots, \bar{y}_m\}) \wedge \forall 1 \leq i \leq m\, \varphi(\bar{y}_i)]$$

and, by (ii), if you take m minimal, then $\{\bar{y}_1, \ldots, \bar{y}_m\}$ is unique. Therefore, in the case of a nondeterministic language the statements of the normal form theorem express the finiteness of nondeterminacy.

2.3.3 Theorem *(Healthiness properties)*

(i) $\text{wp}(P, \text{F}) \Longleftrightarrow \text{F}$

(ii) $\text{wp}(P, \varphi \wedge \psi) \Longleftrightarrow \text{wp}(P, \varphi) \wedge \text{wp}(P, \psi)$

(iii) $\text{wp}(P, \forall u\varphi) \Longleftrightarrow \forall u \text{wp}(P, \varphi)$

Compatibility of disjunction and existential quantification are in general not true for nondeterministic programs. Clearly, the easy implications

$$\begin{aligned} \text{wp}(P, \varphi) \vee \text{wp}(P, \psi) &\Longrightarrow \text{wp}(P, \varphi \vee \psi) \\ \exists u \text{wp}(P, \varphi) &\Longrightarrow \text{wp}(P, \exists u\varphi) \end{aligned}$$

remain true, as they follow from monotonicity. The new normal form theorem is not strong enough to maintain the negation property. Intuitively it is clear that, even if termination is ensured, $\text{wp}(P, \neg\varphi)$ and $\neg\text{wp}(P, \varphi)$ need not coincide: The former tells us that $\neg\varphi$ holds after every possible execution of P, while the latter only expresses the existence of a possible execution of P whose result would satisfy $\neg\varphi$. A counter example is found easily:

2.3.4 Example *Let P denote the following program, where x is a variable of sort* nat*:*

$$\textbf{if } \mathbf{T} \textbf{ then } x := 0$$
$$[] \ \mathbf{T} \textbf{ then } x := 1 \textbf{ fi}$$

Then we have $\text{wp}(P, \neg x = 0) \iff \mathbf{F}$ *but also* $\text{wp}(P, \mathbf{T}) \wedge \neg\text{wp}(P, x = 0) \iff \mathbf{T}$.

3. SOME APPLICATIONS

In this section some applications are presented in order to demonstrate the adequateness of our formalization of weakest preconditions. First, we define partial correctness by means of wp and show that the Hoare calculus is sound. Then, we generalize Theorem 11.6 of [Gries 81] ("A theorem concerning a loop, an invariant and a bound function") in the case of the "conventional" **while**-loop and prove its correctness. Some immediate consequences of this generalization are given, too. Both applications show again the importance of the normal form theorem.

3.1. SOUNDNESS OF THE HOARE CALCULUS

Originally, $\mathfrak{wp}$ is a semantic definition closely related to verification. So besides offering a certain strategy — "calculate" the weakest precondition and transform it according to logical rules until you reach the given precondition — it is a good framework for considering *any* verification technique. Therefore we try our formalization first in a proof of the soundness of the Hoare calculus. Having used $\mathfrak{wp}$ for the semantic description, we arrive at the following exact definition of total and partial correctness:

3.1.1 Definition *Let ψ and φ be $\mathcal{L}_V$ formulae. A program P is said to be*

(i) totally correct with respect to ψ and φ *iff for all states $v \in$* STAT

$$\textit{if } \mathcal{A}^+ \models \psi[v], \textit{ then } v \in \mathfrak{wp}(P, \text{Mod}(\varphi)),$$

(ii) partially correct with respect to ψ and φ *iff for all states $v \in$* STAT

$$\textit{if } \mathcal{A}^+ \models \psi[v] \textit{ and } v \in \mathfrak{wp}(P, \text{Mod}(\mathbf{T})), \textit{ then } v \in \mathfrak{wp}(P, \text{Mod}(\varphi)).$$

In this section we consider only deterministic programs. So we can use the results of Section 3.2. The following statements are immediate consequences from 2.2.7 and 2.2.6:

3.1.2 Corollary *A program P is*

(i) totally correct wrt. ψ and φ iff $\mathcal{A}^+ \models \psi \rightarrow \text{wp}(P, \varphi)$,

(ii) partially correct wrt. ψ and φ iff $\mathcal{A}^+ \models \psi \rightarrow \neg\text{wp}(P, \neg\varphi)$.

Let us resume the most important facts about the Hoare calculus (for a more detailed discussion see e.g. [Loeckx Sieber 84]): Triples $\{\psi\}P\{\varphi\}$, where ψ and φ are first-order formulae and P is a program, are called Hoare formulae. The calculus is a tool to derive such formulae. Its axioms and rules are as follows:

1. Axioms:
   - $\{\varphi\}\,\mathbf{skip}\,\{\varphi\}$
   - $\{\psi\}\,\mathbf{abort}\,\{\varphi\}$
   - $\{\varphi\{t/x\}\}\; x := t\,\{\varphi\}$
2. Rules:
   - $\dfrac{\{\psi\}P_1\{\rho\} \qquad \{\rho\}P_2\{\varphi\}}{\{\psi\}\,P_1\ ;\ P_2\,\{\varphi\}}$
   - $\dfrac{\{\psi \wedge b\}P_1\{\varphi\} \qquad \{\psi \wedge \neg b\}P_2\{\varphi\}}{\{\psi\}\,\mathbf{if}\ b\ \mathbf{then}\ P_1\ \mathbf{else}\ P_2\ \mathbf{fi}\,\{\varphi\}}$
   - $\dfrac{\{\psi \wedge b\}P\{\psi\}}{\{\psi\}\,\mathbf{while}\ b\ \mathbf{do}\ P\ \mathbf{od}\,\{\psi \wedge \neg b\}}$
   - $\dfrac{\{\rho\}P\{\theta\}}{\{\psi\}P\{\varphi\}}$ if $\mathcal{A}^+ \models \psi \rightarrow \rho$ and $\mathcal{A}^+ \models \theta \rightarrow \varphi$

A Hoare formula $\{\psi\}P\{\varphi\}$ is meant to express the partial correctness of the program P wrt. ψ and φ. Therefore, the soundness property takes the following form.

3.1.3 Theorem *For arbitrary first-order formulae ψ and φ and every program P we have: If $\{\psi\}P\{\varphi\}$ is derivable in the Hoare calculus, then P is partially correct wrt. ψ and φ.*

Proof: We show by induction on the length of the derivation: If $\{\psi\}P\{\varphi\}$ is derivable, then $\psi \rightarrow \neg\mathrm{wp}(P, \neg\varphi)$ holds. We present the only non-trivial case: Let the Hoare formula be derived by an application of the **while**-rule:

$$\frac{\{\psi \wedge b\}P\{\psi\}}{\{\psi\}\,\mathbf{while}\ b\ \mathbf{do}\ P\ \mathbf{od}\,\{\psi \wedge \neg b\}}$$

We make use of the induction hypothesis to get

$$\psi \wedge b \rightarrow \neg\mathrm{wp}(P, \neg\psi).$$

From this and the normal form theorem we obtain ($\bar{x}$ is the list of variables of the loop)

$$(1) \quad \psi \wedge b \rightarrow \forall \bar{y}(\mathrm{wp}(P, \bar{x} = \bar{y}) \rightarrow \psi\{\bar{y}/\bar{x}\}).$$

By definition we have $\mathrm{wp}(\mathbf{while}\ b\ \mathbf{do}\ P\ \mathbf{od}, \neg\psi \vee b) \equiv \exists f \mathrm{E}(f, \bar{x})$, where

$$\begin{aligned} \mathrm{E}(f, \bar{x}) \equiv\ & (\neg b \wedge (\neg\psi \vee b))\{f_{|f|-1}/\bar{x}\} \wedge \\ & \forall 0 \le i < |f| - 1(b \wedge \mathrm{wp}(P, \bar{x} = f_{i+1}))\{f_i/\bar{x}\} \wedge \\ & f_0 = \bar{x}. \end{aligned}$$

Therefore, the following three formulae are valid:

$$\begin{array}{ll} (2) & \mathrm{E}(f,\bar{x}) \rightarrow \neg\psi\{f_{|f|-1}/\bar{x}\} \\ (3) & \mathrm{E}(f,\bar{x}) \wedge 0 \leq i < |f|-1 \rightarrow b\{f_i/\bar{x}\} \\ (4) & \mathrm{E}(f,\bar{x}) \wedge 0 \leq i < |f|-1 \rightarrow \mathrm{wp}(P, \bar{x} = f_{i+1})\{f_i/\bar{x}\} \end{array}$$

Formulae (1), (3) and (4) imply

$$\mathrm{E}(f,\bar{x}) \wedge 0 \leq i < |f|-1 \rightarrow (\psi\{f_i/\bar{x}\} \rightarrow \psi\{f_{i+1}/\bar{x}\}),$$

hence we obtain

$$\mathrm{E}(f,\bar{x}) \wedge \psi\{f_0/\bar{x}\} \rightarrow \psi\{f_0/\bar{x}\} \wedge \forall 0 \leq i < |f|-1(\psi\{f_i/\bar{x}\} \rightarrow \neg\psi\{f_{i+1}/\bar{x}\}).$$

Using induction it can easily be shown that

$$\mathrm{E}(f,\bar{x}) \wedge \psi\{f_0/\bar{x}\} \rightarrow \psi\{f_{|f|-1}/\bar{x}\}.$$

Observing $\mathrm{E}(f,\bar{x}) \rightarrow f_0 = \bar{x}$, we have $\mathrm{E}(f,\bar{x}) \wedge \psi \rightarrow \psi\{f_{|f|-1}/\bar{x}\}$. Using the validity of formula (2) we conclude $\mathrm{E}(f,\bar{x}) \rightarrow \neg\psi$. Hence we may infer $\exists f \mathrm{E}(f,\bar{x}) \rightarrow \neg\psi$, or equivalently $\psi \rightarrow \neg\exists f \mathrm{E}(f,\bar{x})$. □

3.2. A THEOREM CONCERNING A LOOP, AN INVARIANT AND A BOUND FUNCTION

In contrast to the Hoare calculus $w\!p$ is about *total* correctness. Therefore, we consider next a **while**-rule, which deals also with termination. The starting point is the rule presented in [Gries 81], p.144. This rule uses an integer bound function expressible by a term of the programming language.

In principle integer valued functions together with the usual strict ordering relation $<$ are sufficient — after all we could use the function that gives the number of execution steps. But this may be very inconvenient. For example, consider the program

```
y := x ;
while x > 1 do if    maxprime(x) = 2
               then y := 2 * y ; x := (y + 1) * (x div 2)
               else  x := x div maxprime(x)
               fi
            od ,
```

where x and y are variables of sort nat and maxprime is supposed to be a basic function that computes the greatest prime number which divides its argument. Termination of this program can easily be shown considering the function

$$\mathrm{F} : \mathbb{N} \longrightarrow \omega^2, \qquad \mathrm{F}(x) := \omega * n + m, \text{ where } x = 2^n * m \text{ and } m \text{ is odd.}$$

(Here ω is the first limit ordinal.) Then each transition of the loop strictly lowers the value of the function F. We would like to be free to use any well-founded ordering.

The second restriction that the bound function is expressible by a term of the programming language is a more serious one. Consider the program

$$\textbf{while } \mathrm{odd}(x) \textbf{ do } x := (3 * x + 1) \text{ div } 2 \textbf{ od },$$

where x is again a variable of sort nat. It can easily be shown that a natural bound function for this program is given by the recursive definition

$$t(x) := \begin{cases} 0 & \text{if } x \text{ is even} \\ 1 + t\left(\frac{x-1}{2}\right) & \text{if } x \text{ is odd,} \end{cases}$$

which is usually not available as a term in an imperative programming language.

For the rule we will present in the next theorem, the distinction between the programming and the verification language is useful. We assume the latter to contain a sort wf and a binary relation symbol $\prec$ interpreted as a well-founded ordering. Furthermore we use symbols F for embeddings of the other sets. Their interpretations correspond to the term t above. Then we obtain the following rule:

3.2.1 Theorem *Consider a program* **while** b **do** P **od**. *Suppose furthermore that a weak second-order formula* ψ *satisfies*

$$(1)\quad \psi \wedge b \rightarrow \mathrm{wp}(P, \psi) \qquad (2)\quad \psi \wedge b \rightarrow \mathrm{wp}(P, \mathrm{F}(\bar{x}) \prec \mathrm{F}(\bar{y}))\{\bar{x}/\bar{y}\},$$

where in (2) $\bar{y}$ denotes a list of variables not occuring in the body P of the loop. Then the formula $\psi \rightarrow \mathrm{wp}(\textbf{while } b \textbf{ do } P \textbf{ od}, \psi \wedge \neg b)$ *is valid.*

Proof: Applying the normal form theorem 2.2.4 we can conclude that the following two formulae hold:

$$\begin{array}{ll} (1') & \psi \wedge b \rightarrow \exists \bar{u}[\mathrm{wp}(P, \bar{x} = \bar{u}) \wedge \psi\{\bar{u}/\bar{x}\}] \\ (2') & \psi \wedge b \rightarrow \exists \bar{v}[\mathrm{wp}(P, \bar{x} = \bar{v}) \wedge \mathrm{F}(\bar{v}) \prec \mathrm{F}(\bar{x})] \end{array}$$

Due to the uniqueness of $\bar{u}$ (see 2.2.4) we obtain

$$(*)\quad \psi \wedge b \rightarrow \exists \bar{u}[\mathrm{wp}(P, \bar{x} = \bar{u}) \wedge \mathrm{F}(\bar{u}) \prec \mathrm{F}(\bar{x}) \wedge \psi\{\bar{u}/\bar{x}\}].$$

Now let Φ be the formula $\mathrm{wp}(\textbf{while } b \textbf{ do } P \textbf{ od}, \psi \wedge \neg b)$. The definition of wp yields

$$\Phi\{\bar{u}/\bar{x}\} \wedge b \wedge \mathrm{wp}(P, \bar{x} = \bar{u}) \Longrightarrow \Phi.$$

From this it is easy to obtain the implication

$$\begin{array}{l} b \wedge \psi \wedge \exists \bar{u}[\mathrm{wp}(P, \bar{x} = \bar{u}) \wedge \mathrm{F}(\bar{u}) \prec \mathrm{F}(\bar{x}) \wedge \psi\{\bar{u}/\bar{x}\}] \\ \qquad \Longrightarrow \forall \bar{u}(\mathrm{F}(\bar{u}) \prec \mathrm{F}(\bar{x}) \rightarrow (\psi \rightarrow \Phi)\{\bar{u}/\bar{x}\}) \rightarrow \Phi. \end{array}$$

Using $(*)$, we get, furthermore, the validity of

$$(**)\quad b \rightarrow (\forall \bar{u}(\mathrm{F}(\bar{u}) \prec \mathrm{F}(\bar{x}) \rightarrow (\psi \rightarrow \Phi)\{\bar{u}/\bar{x}\}) \rightarrow (\psi \rightarrow \Phi)).$$

From wp's definition $\neg b \rightarrow (\psi \rightarrow \Phi)$ is immediate. So we have found

$$\neg b \rightarrow (\forall \bar{u}(\mathrm{F}(\bar{u}) \prec \mathrm{F}(\bar{x}) \rightarrow (\psi \rightarrow \Phi)\{\bar{u}/\bar{x}\}) \rightarrow (\psi \rightarrow \Phi)),$$

which combined with $(**)$ implies

$$\forall \bar{x}[\forall \bar{u}(\mathrm{F}(\bar{u}) \prec \mathrm{F}(\bar{x}) \rightarrow (\psi \rightarrow \Phi)\{\bar{u}/\bar{x}\}) \rightarrow (\psi \rightarrow \Phi)].$$

Using induction along the well-founded ordering $\prec$ we get that the formula

$$\psi \rightarrow \mathrm{wp}(\textbf{while } b \textbf{ do } P \textbf{ od}, \psi \wedge \neg b)$$

holds, which is exactly the desired result. □

Having a closer look at the proof of this theorem, we find that the implication

$$\Phi\{\bar{u}/\bar{x}\} \wedge b \wedge \mathrm{wp}(P, \bar{x} = \bar{u}) \Longrightarrow \Phi$$

had been crucial. According to the normal form theorem this implies

$$\neg\Phi \wedge b \wedge \mathrm{wp}(P, \mathbf{T}) \Longrightarrow \mathrm{wp}(P, \neg\Phi).$$

Therefore we can state:

3.2.2 Corollary *If for the program* **while** b **do** P **od** *the formula* $b \rightarrow \mathrm{wp}(P, \mathbf{T})$ *holds, then* $\neg\mathrm{wp}(\textbf{while } b \textbf{ do } P \textbf{ od}, \varphi)$ *is an invariant, i.e. it holds*

$$\neg\mathrm{wp}(\textbf{while } b \textbf{ do } P \textbf{ od}, \varphi) \wedge b \rightarrow \mathrm{wp}(P, \neg\mathrm{wp}(\textbf{while } b \textbf{ do } P \textbf{ od}, \varphi)).$$

Of course this is not the invariant we are looking for when trying to apply the **while**-rule in a correctness proof: Bringing the proof to an end would then include showing that the precondition implies the invariant, i.e. $\psi \rightarrow \neg\mathrm{wp}(\textbf{while } b \textbf{ do } P \textbf{ od}, \varphi)$, which expresses already partial correctness wrt. ψ and φ. This corollary is of a more theoretical nature, but enables us also to derive the following statement from a special instance of the theorem.

3.2.3 Corollary *Consider the program* **while** b **do** P **od**. *Suppose* φ *is a formula that satisfies*

$$(1)\ \neg b \rightarrow \varphi \qquad\qquad (2)\ b \rightarrow \mathrm{wp}(P, \mathrm{F}(\bar{x}) \prec \mathrm{F}(\bar{y}))\{\bar{x}/\bar{y}\}.$$

Then the formula $\mathrm{wp}(\textbf{while } b \textbf{ do } p \textbf{ od}, \varphi)$ *holds.*

Proof: From (2) we conclude $b \rightarrow \mathrm{wp}(P, \mathbf{T})$. Applying 3.2.2 we obtain

$$\neg\mathrm{wp}(\textbf{while } b \textbf{ do } P \textbf{ od}, \neg b) \wedge b \rightarrow \mathrm{wp}(P, \neg\mathrm{wp}(\textbf{while } b \textbf{ do } P \textbf{ od}, \neg b)).$$

Together with (2) we have the prerequisites of Theorem 3.2.1. So we may conclude the validity of the formula

$$\neg\mathrm{wp}(\textbf{while } b \textbf{ do } P \textbf{ od}, \neg b) \rightarrow \mathrm{wp}(\textbf{while } b \textbf{ do } P \textbf{ od}, \neg\mathrm{wp}(\textbf{while } b \textbf{ do } P \textbf{ od}, \neg b) \wedge \neg b),$$

hence the formula $\mathrm{wp}(\textbf{while } b \textbf{ do } P \textbf{ od}, \neg b)$ holds. Now we use (1) and the monotonicity of wp to prove our assertion. □

4. CONCLUSION

In this article we have given a syntactical characterization of weakest preconditions by defining a function wp mapping a program and a formula onto a formula. Like [Tucker Zucker 88] and in contrast to the earlier work on this topic (see e.g., [Back 81]), we have chosen a language of weak second-order logic.

For our function wp we have proved by purely syntactical reasoning some basic properties including a normal form theorem and Dijkstra's postulates. We have also shown that our finitary syntactical formalization actually coincides with the originally set-based formulation and have presented some applications. Here the normal form theorem has turned out to be very helpful. By both the proofs of the basic properties and the applications we have tried to demonstrate that our formalization is a natural and handy one.

Our formalization of weakest preconditions uses finite sequences only in the case of a loop whereas in the above mentioned monograph [Tucker Zucker 88] finite sequences are used for each command. We believe that the use of sequences for each statement makes the formulation of weakest preconditions unnecessary complicated and, hence, more difficult to use in reasoning about program correctness, as compared to our approach.

In [Platek 90] it has been pointed out before that weak second-order logic is useful for reasoning about programs. We believe that also our formalization of weakest preconditions shows that this logic is qualified for further use in the field of program correctness and verification.

5. REFERENCES

[Back 81] Back R.J.R.: Proving total correctness of nondeterministic programs in infinitary logic. Acta Informatica 15, 233-249 (1981)

[Dijkstra 75] Dijkstra E.W.: Guarded commands, nondeterminacy and formal derivation of programs. Comm. ACM 18, 8, 453-457 (1975)

[Dijkstra 76] Dijkstra E.W.: A discipline of programming. Engelwood-Cliffs: Prentice-Hall (1976)

[Ehrig Mahr 85] Ehrig H., Mahr B.: Fundamentals of algebraic specifications 1. Equations and initial semantics. EATCS Monographs in Theoretical Computer Science, Vol. 6, Berlin: Springer (1985)

[Gries 81] Gries D.: The science of programming. Texts and Monographs in Computer Science, New York: Springer (1981)

[Hoare 69] Hoare C.A.R.: An axiomatic basis for computer programming. Comm. ACM 12, 10, 576-583 (1969)

[Karp 64] Karp C.R.: Languages with expressions of infinite length. Amsterdam: North-Holland (1964)

[Keisler 71] Keisler H.J.: Model theory of infinitary logic. Amsterdam: North-Holland (1971)

[Loeckx Sieber 84] Loeckx J., Sieber K.: The foundations of program verification. Stuttgart: Teubner (1984)

[Platek 90] Platek R.A.: Making computers safe for the world: An introduction to proofs of programs. Part I. In: Logic and Computer Science, Lecture Notes in Mathematics 1429, Berlin: Springer (1990)

[Tucker Zucker 88] Tucker J.V., Zucker J.I.: Program correctness over abstract data types with error-state semantics. CWI Monographs 6, Amsterdam: North-Holland (1988)

On Blocks: locality and asynchronous communication (Extended abstract)

F.S. de Boer[1], J.N. Kok[2], C. Palamidessi[3], J.J.M.M. Rutten[4]

[1]Department of Computer Science, Technical University Eindhoven, P.O. Box 513, 5600 MB Eindhoven, The Netherlands

[2]Department of Computer Science, Utrecht University, P.O. Box 80089, 3508 TB Utrecht, The Netherlands

[3]Dipartimento di Informatica, Università di Pisa, Corso Italia, 40, 56125 Pisa, Italy

[4]CWI, Kruislaan 413, 1098 SJ Amsterdam, The Netherlands

Abstract. A general construct for locality in languages based on asynchronous communication is introduced which allows a uniform semantic description of such apparently diverse notions as the introduction of local variables in concurrent imperative languages with shared variables and the hiding of logical variables in concurrent constraint languages.

Keywords: Parallelism, locality, block structure, asynchronous communication.

Contents

0 Introduction

In [dBKPR91], an abstract language ($\mathcal{L}$) is introduced as the basis for a semantic theory for asynchronous communication in concurrent languages. It is built from a set A of atomic actions and three binary operators for sequential composition, nondeterministic choice and parallel composition. An operational semantics for $\mathcal{L}$ is given by first interpreting atomic actions as state transformations (assuming an abstract set of states), and next defining the meaning of composite statements in terms of a labelled transition system in Plotkin's SOS style ([Plo81]). This semantics formally captures the following computational intuition. Statements represent (compositions of) computing agents or processes. These act on a global state (or store)—which can be seen as a data structure common to all processes—by performing atomic actions. Such actions can either query the state, and possibly suspend in case the required information is not present, or update the state by adding or changing information. (A combination of the two aspects in one and the same atomic action is also possible.) The kind of communication that can be established in this way is of an asynchronous nature because such query and update actions are independent in the sense that they can happen at different moments.

Then it is shown that $\mathcal{L}$ actually is a family of languages, the members of which are obtained by making a specific choice for the set A. Each of these members has its own semantics that is obtained as an instance of the semantics for $\mathcal{L}$, by fixing a specific interpretation of the atomic actions.

An example is an imperative language obtained by taking for A the collection of guarded assignments, $A = \{b.x := e \mid x \in Var, b, e \in Exp\}$ (where Var and Exp are given sets of variables and expressions), and for states the usual function from variables to values. The interpretation of $b.x := e$ in a given state σ amounts to first evaluating the Boolean expression b in σ; if this results to true then the outcome of the evaluation of the expression e in σ is assigned to x. If b evaluates to false, however, the whole action suspends.

As a second example, concurrent constraint languages ([Sar89]) can also be obtained as an instance of $\mathcal{L}$. The set of atomic action is defined as the collection of *ask* and *tell* primitives, and states are constraints. The interpretation of these actions follows the standard semantics for constraint languages. (See [dBKPR91] for more examples of instantiations of $\mathcal{L}$.)

As was observed in the concluding section of the above paper, one important notion has not been addressed, namely that of *locality*. Many parallel programming languages, whether their basic communication mechanism is of a synchronous or asynchronous nature, contain some kind of *block* structure for modelling local computations. Examples are the *block* structure in imperative programming (like *let* $x = v$ *in* s), and the *projection* (or hiding) operator (like $\exists X.s$) in constraint programming.

Therefore we shall in this paper extend the abstract language $\mathcal{L}$ with a block construct that generalizes these two examples. We assume given an abstract set of variables $\mathcal{V}ar$, and for every $x \in \mathcal{V}ar$ and $s \in \mathcal{L}$, a statement $\alpha_x(s)$ is introduced, which should be read as 'x is a variable local in the statement s'.

The semantics of the block construct $\alpha_x(s)$ is complicated for two reasons. First it calls for the distinction between a local and and global 'version' of variables, since the same variable x can be used in a block $\alpha_x(s)$ as well as in, e.g., a statement t (a process running) in parallel with $\alpha_x(s)$. Then changes concerning x made by s should not influence the value of the global x occurring in t and vice versa. Secondly, if the statement $\alpha_x(s)$ performs a computation step that only changes the value of x, then this step should be considered as an internal or silent step, and ideally not be visible in the semantics. Thus some kind of abstraction of silent steps (sometimes also called 'stuttering' steps) is needed.

The first problem will be solved by generalizing the idea of [SRP90] of using (a variant of) cylindric algebras (see [HMT71]) to capture the notion of projecting away information. We shall assume the state space to be a partial order structure (not necessarily complete). Further for each variable x a projection function $\exists_x$ from states to states will be defined, satisfying the axioms of a cylindric algebra. These will be used in defining the semantics of $\alpha_x(s)$. In Section 3, it will be shown that for our two main examples (imperative and constraint languages) this yields a very intuitive and understandable semantics. (For the constraint case, the rule for projection given in [SRP90] is found back as a special instance of the general rule for $\mathcal{L}$.)

This approach has at least two considerable advantages over more traditional treatments of blocks: first it does not require the use of explicitly named location variables or stacks; second, it does not require a renaming mechanism for local variables (like the one used in [dBP91]).

The second problem, that of stuttering, can be solved in the operational semantics, which yields sets of sequences of states, by simply omitting the successive occurrence of identical states. For the compositional semantics, which is provided in Section 4, the situation is more difficult. We follow here the same strategy that was applied in [dBKPR91]: statements that behave the same but for some stuttering steps are given the same semantics by saturating both their (initial) semantics with arbitrary stuttering steps. This saturation procedure is very similar to the way in which weak observational congruence ([Mil80]) can be modelled as strong bisimulation by adding certain transition rules (see [BK86] or [vG87]).

The paper ends with the observation that the compositional model is fully abstract with respect to the operational one.

Conclusions and related work

Summarizing: We formalized a general notion of information hiding in parallel languages which involve some notion of a shared state, by means of which processes communicate asynchronously. This notion of information hiding has been characterized semantically in a uniform way, i.e., abstracting from the specific features of the underlying communication mechanism. Thus our approach reveals the common semantic principles underlying such apparently diverse phenomena as the hiding of logical variables in concurrent constraint programming and the introduction of local variables in concurrent imperative languages with shared variables. Furthermore, since hiding of local information gives rise to "finite stuttering", we develop a method for abstraction from silent steps in order to obtain a fully abstract model for information hiding in parallel languages.

To the best of our knowledge, the semantics of block structures has been studied mainly in the context of sequential programming languages (see for instance [dB80, Bro85, HZ91]). Here we have generalized the semantics of the hiding of logical variables in concurrent constraint programming as given in [SRP90]. This paper has been a source of inspiration.

1 Operational semantics

We shall introduce a simple programming language $\mathcal{L}$. The language $\mathcal{L}$ represents an entire family of different languages, parameterized by a set of *atomic actions* and a set of *variables*. These languages have in common that the basic mechanism for interaction is based on querying and updating a shared data structure (the *state*). Each particular choice for the set of actions and variables yields a specific language. Various examples of such instances will be presented below. After having given the syntax of $\mathcal{L}$, a description of an operational semantic model is given.

1.1 The language $\mathcal{L}$

Let $(a \in)A$ and $(x \in)\mathcal{V}ar$ be arbitrary sets, the elements of which are respectively called *atomic* (or *basic*) *actions* and *variables*. (Note that here and in the sequel we use $(z \in)Z$ for introducing at the same time a set Z and a special element z ranging over Z.) We define the set $(s \in)\mathcal{L}$ of statements as follows:

$$s ::= a \in A \mid s_1; s_2 \mid s_1 + s_2 \mid s_1 \parallel s_2 \mid \alpha_x(s), x \in \mathcal{V}ar$$

Moreover, $\mathcal{L}$ contains a special element E, the terminated statement.

An atomic action a can perform one computation step, in which it may change the state of the system. (The set of states will be introduced shortly.) The *sequential* composition $s_1; s_2$ is executed by first performing s_1 and next s_2. The execution of the *nondeterministic* choice $s_1 + s_2$ between the statements s_1 and s_2 amounts to executing either s_1 or s_2. It will be global in the sense that such a choice can be influenced by the activity of the environment. The *parallel* composition $s_1 \parallel s_2$ of s_1 and s_2 is executed by interleaving computation steps from both components. The *block construct* $\alpha_x(s)$ hides the (information about) variable x in statement s. The block construct in $\mathcal{L}$ is an abstraction of block constructs found in, e.g., imperative and constraint languages. We do not include any constructs for recursion for the sake of simplicity.

1.2 The operational model

The operational model will be defined in three stages. First the meaning of atomic actions is given, next a transition system for $\mathcal{L}$ is defined, and finally a notion of observables is derived from the transition system.

Definition 1.1 *Let*

$$(\Sigma, \leq, \{\exists_x : \Sigma \to \Sigma \mid x \in \mathcal{V}ar\})$$

be a set Σ *of abstract states, together with an ordering* $\leq$ *on* Σ *and a set of semantic hiding operators* $\exists_x$, $x \in \mathcal{V}ar$. *We assume that* $\langle \Sigma, \leq \rangle$ *is a partial order with a minimal element* $\perp \in \Sigma$ *and that the semantic hiding operators satisfy, for all* $\sigma, \theta \in \Sigma$,

1. $\exists_x(\sigma) \leq (\sigma)$
2. $\sigma \leq \theta \Rightarrow \exists_x(\sigma) \leq \exists_x(\theta)$
3. $\exists_x(\exists_y(\sigma)) = \exists_y(\exists_x(\sigma))$
4. $\exists_x(\sigma \sqcup \exists_x(\theta)) = \exists_x(\sigma) \sqcup \exists_x(\theta)$, *if these* $\sqcup$ *exist.*

Sometimes we identify Σ with the triple $(\Sigma, \leq, \{\exists_x : \Sigma \rightarrow \Sigma \mid x \in \mathcal{V}ar\})$. The ordering on states is intended to be an information ordering: if $\sigma \leq \theta$ then σ contains less information than θ. The requirements on the semantic hiding operators can be understood as follows: if we hide x in state σ then we get a state with less information then σ; hiding of (information about) x is monotonic; and it does not matter in what order we hide.

The actions of our language will be interpreted as transformations on Σ. Let Σ_δ be defined by $\Sigma \cup \{\delta\}$. In the sequel we shall use σ, θ, ρ as typical elements of Σ (so different from δ), and ψ as typical element of Σ_δ.

Definition 1.2 *An interpretation is a function of type*

$$I : A \rightarrow (\Sigma \rightarrow \Sigma_\delta)$$

An interpretation maps atomic actions to state transformations. If $I(a)(\sigma) = \delta$, the action cannot proceed in the current state σ; its execution is suspended. This need not necessarily lead to a definitive deadlock of the whole system, because some other component of the program may be enabled to take a next step. (See the transition rules below.) Note that the operator plus models global rather than local nondeterminism, since the choice may depend on the state, which is global.

Before giving the semantic model we first introduce the notion of x-pair. It will be used in the definition of the transition system.

Definition 1.3 *Let* $\sigma, \theta \in \Sigma$. *We call* (σ, θ) *an* x*-pair if*

1. $\exists_x(\theta) \leq \sigma$
2. $\exists_x(\sigma) = \sigma$
3. $\sigma \sqcup \theta$ *exists*

Note that $\sigma \sqcup \theta$ does not always exists: Σ is a partial ordering, not necessarily a lattice. We use the notion of x-pair to split a state ρ into two parts such that $\rho = \sigma \sqcup \theta$: the right component θ contains (at least) the information about x and the left component σ does not contain information about x. If we hide the information about x in θ the remaining information should be less than the information in σ.

The following property implies that the first component of x-pairs for a state ρ is uniquely determined.

Lemma 1.4 *If $\langle\sigma,\theta\rangle$ is an x-pair with $\sigma \sqcup \theta = \rho$ then $\sigma = \exists_x(\rho)$.*

Proof.

$$\begin{aligned}\exists_x(\rho) &= \exists_x(\sigma \sqcup \theta)\\ &= \exists_x(\exists_x(\sigma) \sqcup \theta)\\ &= \exists_x(\sigma) \sqcup \exists_x(\theta)\\ &= \sigma \sqcup \exists_x(\theta)\\ &= \sigma\end{aligned}$$

In an x-pair $\langle\sigma,\theta\rangle$ the right component is not uniquely determined: we can add also information about other variables as long as it is not in contradiction with the other component. Another observation is that we can split an arbitrary state σ always by $\sigma = \exists_x(\sigma) \sqcup \sigma$.

Now instantiations of $\mathcal{L}$ are obtained by fixing a specific choice for the following tuple

$$(A, \mathcal{V}ar, \Sigma, I)$$

(the set of atomic actions A, the set of variables $\mathcal{V}ar$, the set of states Σ, and the interpretation function I).

Given such a tuple, we next describe how the semantics of the language $\mathcal{L}$ can be constructed. It is based on a *labelled transition system* $(\mathcal{L}, Label, \rightarrow)$. The set $(\lambda \in)Label$ of labels is defined by $Label = \Sigma \times \Sigma_\delta$. A label represents the state transformation caused by the action that is performed during the transition step.

For the transition system we extend the language $\mathcal{L}$ with a help construct $\alpha_x^\sigma(\cdot)$:

$$s ::= \cdots \mid \alpha_x^\sigma(s), \; x \in \mathcal{V}ar, \; \sigma \in \Sigma$$

Definition 1.5 *The transition relation $\rightarrow \subseteq \mathcal{L} \times Label \times \mathcal{L}$ is defined as the smallest relation satisfying the rules of Table 1.*

The interpretation of a transition step $s \xrightarrow{\langle\sigma,\sigma'\rangle} s'$ is as follows. Under the assumption that the current state is σ, the statement s can perform a computation step, changing the state into σ', and resulting in the statement s'. (Below σ is sometimes called the input state, and σ' the output state.)

Rules R1 through R4, and D1 and D2 are straightforward. Rules D3 and D4 express that in the parallel and nondeterministic composition of two statements, a suspending step $(\langle\sigma,\delta\rangle)$ is only possible if (and only if) both statements can perform such a step.

In rules R5 and D5, the value of x is initialized to the state $\perp$. Note that here the help construct α_x^σ is introduced.

Rule R6 is the most interesting one and surely requires some explanation. In the conclusion of the rule, the input state is decomposed into a part (σ_1) which can be affected by the local computation, and a part (θ) which remains invariant over the local computation. This latter part will contain information about the global variable x. The input state of the local computation then is composed of of σ_1 and the local state θ_1. Finally, the output state of the local computation is decomposed into a global part (σ_2), which is required to be consistent with the invariant θ in the sense that the upper bound

R1 $a \xrightarrow{\langle\sigma,\sigma'\rangle} E$ *if* $I(a)(\sigma)=\sigma'$	D1 $a \xrightarrow{\langle\sigma,\delta\rangle} E$ *if* $I(a)(\sigma)=\delta$
R2 $\dfrac{s \xrightarrow{\langle\sigma,\sigma'\rangle} s'}{s;t \xrightarrow{\langle\sigma,\sigma'\rangle} s';t}$	D2 $\dfrac{s \xrightarrow{\langle\sigma,\delta\rangle} E}{s;t \xrightarrow{\langle\sigma,\delta\rangle} E}$
R3 $\dfrac{s \xrightarrow{\langle\sigma,\sigma'\rangle} s'}{\begin{array}{c} s \parallel t \xrightarrow{\langle\sigma,\sigma'\rangle} s' \parallel t \\ t \parallel s \xrightarrow{\langle\sigma,\sigma'\rangle} t \parallel s' \end{array}}$	D3 $\dfrac{s \xrightarrow{\langle\sigma,\delta\rangle} E \quad t \xrightarrow{\langle\sigma,\delta\rangle} E}{s \parallel t \xrightarrow{\langle\sigma,\delta\rangle} E}$
R4 $\dfrac{s \xrightarrow{\langle\sigma,\sigma'\rangle} s'}{\begin{array}{c} s + t \xrightarrow{\langle\sigma,\sigma'\rangle} s' \\ t + s \xrightarrow{\langle\sigma,\sigma'\rangle} s' \end{array}}$	D4 $\dfrac{s \xrightarrow{\langle\sigma,\delta\rangle} E \quad t \xrightarrow{\langle\sigma,\delta\rangle} E}{s + t \xrightarrow{\langle\sigma,\delta\rangle} E}$
R5 $\dfrac{\alpha_x^{\perp}(s) \xrightarrow{\langle\sigma,\sigma'\rangle} s'}{\alpha_x(s) \xrightarrow{\langle\sigma,\sigma'\rangle} s'}$	D5 $\dfrac{\alpha_x^{\perp}(s) \xrightarrow{\langle\sigma,\delta\rangle} E}{\alpha_x(s) \xrightarrow{\langle\sigma,\delta\rangle} E}$
R6 $\dfrac{s \xrightarrow{\langle\sigma_1\sqcup\theta_1,\sigma_2\sqcup\theta_2\rangle} s'}{\alpha_x^{\theta_1}(s) \xrightarrow{\langle\sigma_1\sqcup\theta,\sigma_2\sqcup\theta\rangle} \alpha_x^{\theta_2}(s')}$	D6 $\dfrac{s \xrightarrow{\langle\sigma\sqcup\theta,\delta\rangle} E}{\alpha_x^{\theta}(s) \xrightarrow{\langle\sigma\sqcup\theta',\delta\rangle} E}$

Table 1: The transition system. If $s' = E$ then read t for $s';t$ in R2, read t for $s' \parallel t$ and $t \parallel s'$ in R3, and read E for $\alpha_x^{\theta_2}(s')$ in R5. All of the pairs $\langle\sigma_1,\theta_1\rangle$, $\langle\sigma_2,\theta_2\rangle$, $\langle\sigma_1,\theta\rangle$, $\langle\sigma_2,\theta\rangle$ in R6, and $\langle\sigma,\theta\rangle$, $\langle\sigma,\theta'\rangle$ in D6 should be x-pairs.

of σ_2 and θ exists, and a local part θ_2 which in general will contain information about the local variable x. This local part θ_2 is stored by means of the help construct: $\alpha_x^{\theta_2}(s)$. Note that this transition rule for blocks allows (in general) several ways of splitting a given input state into an x-pair. Crucial is the splitting of the input state of the conclusion of the rule in a part which can be affected by the local computation and a part which remains invariant over the local computation. The invariance over the local computation of this latter part (θ) of the input state is guaranteed by the fact that it is compatible with the global part (σ_2) of the output state of the local computation: formally, this is expressed by the the existence of the least upper bound, $\sigma_2 \sqcup \theta$.

Based on this transition system, an observational semantics is defined next. It gives for every statement the set of sequences of states corresponding to its (completed) transition sequences.

First we introduce an auxiliary operator. Let $(w \in)\Sigma^+$ be the set of nonempty words over Σ, and let $D = \mathcal{P}(\Sigma^+ \cup \Sigma^+ \cdot \{\delta\})$. Let $\cdot : \Sigma \times D \to D$ be given by

$$\sigma \cdot X = \{\sigma \cdot w \mid w \in X\}$$

Next we give the the definition of $\mathcal{O}$:

Definition 1.6 *The function*

$$\mathcal{O} : \mathcal{L} \to \Sigma \to D$$

is given by $\mathcal{O}[\![E]\!](\sigma) = \{\sigma\}$ *and, for* $s \neq E$,

$$\begin{array}{rcl} \mathcal{O}[\![s]\!](\sigma) & = & \bigcup\{\sigma \cdot \mathcal{O}[\![s']\!](\sigma') \mid s \xrightarrow{\langle\sigma,\sigma'\rangle} s',\ \sigma \neq \sigma'\} \\ & \cup & \bigcup\{\mathcal{O}[\![s']\!](\sigma) \mid s \xrightarrow{\langle\sigma,\sigma\rangle} s'\} \\ & \cup & \{\sigma \cdot \delta \mid s \xrightarrow{\langle\sigma,\delta\rangle} E)\} \end{array}$$

In the definition of $\mathcal{O}$, only *connected* transition sequences are considered (unfolding the definition): the labels of successive transitions have the property that the last element of the first label equals the first element of the second. The second component in the definition of $\mathcal{O}$ shows that a stuttering step (with label $\langle\sigma,\sigma\rangle$) does not yield any visible output. Note that the last element ψ of the sequences in $\mathcal{O}[\![s]\!](\sigma)$ is either a proper state $\sigma' \in \Sigma$, or the deadlock state δ.

The model $\mathcal{O}$ is not compositional for two different reasons, related to the fact that the semantics of our language is *nonuniform* (the meaning of atomic actions depends on the current state), and the fact that deadlock in general is dependent on the choice structure of statements -which is not taken into account by $\mathcal{O}$.

Let us end this section with an example of a simple computation of a block structure.

Example 1.7 Choose

$$A = \{x := 0,\ x := 1,\ x := s(x)\},$$
$$\mathcal{V}ar = \{x\}$$

The states are given by

$$(\{\bot, 0, 1, \ldots\}, \leq, \{\exists_x\})$$

where

$$\sigma \leq \sigma' \equiv (\sigma = \bot \vee \sigma = \sigma')$$

and

$$\exists_x = \lambda\sigma.\ \bot$$

Let $s(x)$ denote the successor of x for $x \in \Sigma - \{\bot\}$. Further let the interpretation I be given by

$$I(x := 0)(\sigma) = 0,\quad I(x := 1)(\sigma) = 1,\quad I(x := s(x))(\sigma) = \begin{cases} \bot & \textit{if } \sigma = \bot \\ s(\sigma) & \textit{otherwise} \end{cases}$$

We show how to derive

$$\mathcal{O}[\![\alpha_x(x := 1; x := s(x))]\!](0) = \{0\}$$

1. $x := 1 \xrightarrow{\langle\bot,1\rangle} E$ (R1)

2. $x := 1; x := s(x) \xrightarrow{\langle\bot,1\rangle} x := s(x)$ (1., R2)

3. $x := 1; x := s(x) \xrightarrow{\langle \bot\sqcup\bot, \bot\sqcup 1\rangle} x := s(x)$ (introduce x-pair)

4. $\alpha_x^{\bot}(x := 1; x := s(x)) \xrightarrow{\langle \bot\sqcup 0, \bot\sqcup 0\rangle} \alpha_x^1(x := s(x))$ (3., R6)

5. $\alpha_x^{\bot}(x := 1; x := s(x)) \xrightarrow{\langle 0,0\rangle} \alpha_x^1(x := s(x))$ (join)

6. $\alpha_x(x := 1; x := s(x)) \xrightarrow{\langle 0,0\rangle} \alpha_x^1(x := s(x))$ (5., R5)

7. $x := s(x) \xrightarrow{\langle 1,2\rangle} E$ (R1)

8. $x := s(x) \xrightarrow{\langle \bot\sqcup 1, \bot\sqcup 2\rangle} E$ (introduce x-pair)

9. $\alpha_x^1(x := s(x)) \xrightarrow{\langle \bot\sqcup 0, \bot\sqcup 0\rangle} E$ (8., R6)

10. $\alpha_x^1(x := s(x)) \xrightarrow{\langle 0,0\rangle} E$ (join)

Combining 6. and 10. we arrive at

$$\alpha_x(x := 1; x := s(x)) \xrightarrow{\langle 0,0\rangle} \alpha_x^1(x := s(x)) \xrightarrow{\langle 0,0\rangle} E$$

and

$$\mathcal{O}[\![\alpha_x(x := 1; x := s(x))]\!](0) = \{0\}$$

The initial value of x (which is 0) is not changed by the statement $\alpha_x(x := 1; x := s(x))$.

2 Two instantiations of L

In this section we present two examples of instantiations of the language $\mathcal{L}$. First we consider an imperative language with local variables, then we treat the case of a concurrent constraint language with hiding of logical variables. Recall that instantiations of $\mathcal{L}$ are obtained by fixing a specific choice for the set A of atomic actions, the set of variables $\mathcal{V}ar$, the collection Σ of states, and the interpretation function I.

2.1 An imperative language

Let A be the set of guarded assignments,

$$A = \{b.x := e \mid x \in Var, b, e \in Exp\}$$

where Var is a set of (programming) variables and Exp is a set of (Boolean) expressions. Assume that the evaluation of expressions is simple in that it does not have side effects and is instantaneous. The execution of a guarded assignment $b.x := e$ starts with the evaluation of the Boolean expression b; if this yields true then the value of e is assigned to x, otherwise the execution of the assigment suspends.

Let the set of states be defined by

$$\Sigma = Var \rightarrow (Val_{\bot})$$

where $Val_\perp$ is a flat cpo of values with bottom element $\perp$. The ordering on states is the pointwise extension of the ordering on the set of values, i.e., $\sigma \leq \sigma'$ iff for all $x \in Var$ $\sigma(x) \leq \sigma'(x)$. The bottom element of Σ, i.e., the state $\lambda x.\perp$, is again denoted by $\perp$. The context will make clear which one is meant.

For the set $\mathcal{V}ar$ we can take the set Var of programming variables. For every $x \in \mathcal{V}ar$, a function $\exists_x : \Sigma \rightarrow \Sigma$ is defined, for any σ, by

$$\begin{aligned} \exists_x(\sigma)(y) &= \sigma(y) \quad \text{if } y \neq x \\ &= \perp \quad\quad \text{otherwise} \end{aligned}$$

It is not difficult to check that these functions $\exists_x$ satisfy the four properties of Definition 2.1.

The interpretation of guarded assignments is given by

$$I(b.x := e)(\sigma)(y) = \begin{cases} \sigma(y) & \text{if } \mathcal{E}(b)(\sigma) \text{ and } y \neq x \\ \mathcal{E}(e)(\sigma) & \text{if } \mathcal{E}(b)(\sigma) \text{ and } y = x \\ \delta & \text{otherwise} \end{cases}$$

(assuming the presence of a function $\mathcal{E}$ for the evaluation of expressions).

The construct $\alpha_x(s)$ is interpreted as the introduction of a new variable x which is local to s. Let us next consider, given the above choice for A, Σ, $\exists_x$ and I the interpretation of the transition rule

$$\frac{s_1 \overset{(\sigma_1 \sqcup \theta_1,\, \sigma_2 \sqcup \theta_2)}{\longrightarrow} s_2}{\alpha_x^{\theta_1}(s_1) \overset{(\sigma_1 \sqcup \theta,\, \sigma_2 \sqcup \theta)}{\longrightarrow} \alpha_x^{\theta_2}(s_2)}$$

where all the pairs $(\sigma_1, \theta_1), (\sigma_2, \theta_2), (\sigma_1, \theta), (\sigma_2, \theta)$ are x-pairs. Note that (σ, θ) being a x-pair implies that $\sigma(x) = \perp$ (since $\exists_x(\sigma) = \sigma$), and that σ and θ agree with respect to all the variables different from x (because $\exists_x(\theta) \leq \sigma$).

The input state of the conclusion of the rule consists of two parts: σ_1, which contains all the information about all the variables different from x, and θ, which contains the information about the *global* variable x. Since the information about the *local* variable x is supposed to be stored in θ_1, the input state of the premise of the rule is the state $\sigma_1 \sqcup \theta_1$, which thus contains the information about the local variable x and the global variables different from x. Also the output state of the premise of the rule consists of a global part σ_2, which contains the information about all the global variables different from x, and a local part θ_2, which contains the information about the local variable x. Finally, the output state of the conclusion of the rule combines the global effects of the computation of s_1 as represented by σ_2, and the information represented by θ about the global variable x which has not been affected.

Note that a canonical way of splitting any state into an x-pair (for any x) can be defined as follows. Let $x \in Var$ and $v \in Val$; the state $(x = v)$ is defined by

$$(x = v)(y) = \begin{cases} \perp & \text{if } x \neq y \\ v & \text{otherwise} \end{cases}$$

Now for any $\sigma \in \Sigma$, the pair $\langle \exists_x(\sigma), (x = \sigma(x)) \rangle$ can be readily seen to be an x-pair. Using this fixed way of splitting states, the above rule looks like

$$\frac{s_1 \overset{\langle \exists_x(\sigma_1) \sqcup (x=v),\, \sigma_2 \rangle}{\longrightarrow} s_2}{\alpha_x^{x=v}(s_1) \overset{\langle \sigma_1,\, \exists_x(\sigma_2) \sqcup (x=\sigma_1(x)) \rangle}{\longrightarrow} \alpha_x^{x=\sigma_2(x)}(s_2)}$$

Note that this way of splitting states is the most economical one: the information in the second component is only about x and not about any other variables. Formally, this can be expressed as follows. If $\langle \exists_x(\sigma), \theta\rangle$ is another x-pair for σ (i.e., $\exists_x(\sigma) \sqcup \theta = \sigma$), then $(x = \sigma(x)) \leq \theta$.

2.2 Concurrent constraint programming

Concurrent constraint programming was proposed by Saraswat in [Sar89]. Constraint programming is based on the notion of computing with systems of partial information. The main feature is that the state is seen as a constraint on the range of values that variables can assume, rather than a function from variables to values (valuation) as in the imperative case. In other words, the state is seen as a (possibly infinite) set of valuations. Constraints are just finite representations of these sets. For instance, a constraint can be a first order formula, like $\{x = f(y)\}$, representing the set $\{\{y = a, x = f(a)\}, \{y = b, x = f(b)\}, \ldots\}$. As discussed in [Sar89, SR89], this notion of state leads naturally to a paradigm for concurrent programming. All processes share a common *store*, i.e., a set of variables and the constraints established on them until that moment. Communication is achieved by adding (telling) some constraint to the store, and by checking (asking) if the store entails (implies) a given constraint. Synchronization is based on a blocking ask: a process waits (suspends) until the store is "strong" enough to entail a certain constraint.

A typical example of a constraint system is a decidable first-order theory, a constraint in this case being simply a first-order formula. Given a set of function symbols and predicate symbols L and a set of logical variables *Var*, let A be defined as the set of ask and tell primitives, i.e.,

$$A = \{ask(\vartheta) \mid \vartheta \in L\} \cup \{tell(\vartheta) \mid \vartheta \in L\}$$

(Here $\vartheta \in L$ means that ϑ is a first-order formula formulated in L using as variables $x \in Var$.) Let the set of states be defined by

$$\Sigma = \{\vartheta : \vartheta \in L\}$$

(For the set $\mathcal{V}ar$ we thus take the set *Var* of logical variables.) Given a decidable first-order theory T in L (i.e., a set of first-order formulas in L) the ordering on states is reversed logical implication: $\vartheta \leq \vartheta'$ iff $T \cup \{\vartheta'\} \vdash \vartheta$. Note that with respect to this ordering, the least upperbound of two states ϑ and ϑ' is given by $\vartheta \wedge \vartheta'$, i.e., the conjunction of ϑ and ϑ'. Hiding a local variable x in a state ϑ then corresponds to existential quantification: $\exists_x(\vartheta) = \exists x.\vartheta$. The interpretation function I is given by

$$I(ask(\vartheta))(\vartheta') = \begin{cases} \vartheta' & \text{if } T \cup \{\vartheta'\} \vdash \vartheta \\ \text{undefined} & \text{otherwise} \end{cases}$$

and

$$I(tell(\vartheta))(\vartheta') = \vartheta \wedge \vartheta'$$

As in the previous example of imperative programming, it is again convenient to fix a canonical way of splitting states into x-pairs. In fact, the trivial way of splitting a state

σ into an x-pair $\langle \exists_x(\sigma), \sigma \rangle$ works well here. The rule for blocks then becomes

$$\frac{s_1 \overset{\langle \exists_x(\sigma_1) \sqcup \theta, \sigma_2 \rangle}{\longrightarrow} s_2}{\alpha_x^{\theta}(s_1) \overset{\langle \sigma_1, \exists_x(\sigma_2) \sqcup \sigma_1 \rangle}{\longrightarrow} \alpha_x^{\sigma_2}(s_2)}$$

which is exactly the rule given in [SRP90]. In a way this scheme of splitting is the least economical: the second component is chosen maximally. Intuitively it is immediately clear that this does not influence the correctness of the semantics, since computations of constraint programs increase the store monotonically. (One might consider different schemes, possibly depending on implementation considerations.)

Let us give an example: consider $s = tell(x = y); ask(x = a)$. We then have that

$$s \overset{\langle true, x=y \rangle}{\longrightarrow} ask(x = a)$$

(Note that $true$ is the bottom element of Σ.) Thus an application of the above transition rule yields:

$$\alpha_x^{true}(s) \overset{\langle true, true \rangle}{\longrightarrow} \alpha_x^{x=y}(ask(x = a))$$

Furthermore, we have

$$ask(x = a) \overset{\langle x=y \wedge y=a, x=y \wedge y=a \rangle}{\longrightarrow} E$$

A second application of the above transition rule then yields:

$$\alpha_x^{x=y}(ask(x = a)) \overset{\langle y=a, y=a \rangle}{\longrightarrow} E$$

This example shows that a local variable in concurrent constraint programming can be exported by equating it with a global variable, or, in other words, by creating aliases.

3 Compositional semantics

Next a compositional characterization will be given of the operational semantics, which itself is not compositional.

3.1 The model

In order to give a compositional semantics for $\mathcal{L}$ that is correct with respect to the operational semantics, and moreover sufficiently abstract in the sense that no more statements get different meanings than 'strictly necessary', it is convenient to first change the transition system specification by adding a number of transition rules that deal with 'stuttering'. Next the definition of the semantics will be based on this extended system. (See [dBKPR91] for an extensive discussion on this matter.)

Definition 3.8 *Let τ be a special element of A, with $I(\tau)(\sigma) = \sigma$, for all $\sigma \in \Sigma$. Let the transition relation*

$$\rightarrow_{ns} \subseteq \mathcal{L} \times Label \times \mathcal{L}$$

be defined as the smallest relation satisfying the rules given in Table 1 and, in addition, the rules in Table 2.

S1	$a \xrightarrow{\langle\sigma,\sigma'\rangle} \tau$	if $I(a)(\sigma)=\sigma'\neq\delta$
S2	$\dfrac{s \xrightarrow{\langle\sigma,\sigma'\rangle} s'}{s \xrightarrow{\langle\sigma,\sigma\rangle} s}$	
S3	$\dfrac{s \xrightarrow{\langle\sigma,\sigma'\rangle} s',\ s' \xrightarrow{\langle\sigma',\sigma'\rangle} s''}{s \xrightarrow{\langle\sigma,\sigma'\rangle} s''}$	
S4	$\dfrac{s \xrightarrow{\langle\sigma,\sigma\rangle} s',\ s' \xrightarrow{\langle\sigma,\sigma'\rangle} s''}{s \xrightarrow{\langle\sigma,\sigma'\rangle} s''}$	
S5	$\dfrac{s \xrightarrow{\langle\sigma,\sigma\rangle} s',\ s' \xrightarrow{\langle\sigma,\delta\rangle} E}{s \xrightarrow{\langle\sigma,\delta\rangle} E}$	

Table 2: Additional rules for stuttering.

Rule S1 and S2 enable statements to make arbitrary (and arbitrarily many) 'stuttering' steps in between their original steps (note that τ can do two kinds of steps: either $\tau \xrightarrow{\langle\sigma,\sigma\rangle} \tau$ or $\tau \xrightarrow{\langle\sigma,\sigma\rangle} E$). These need not be connected to the preceding or the next step. Rules S3, S4 and S5 allow the contraction of two connected successive steps in case one of them is a 'stuttering' step.

The extension of the transition system with the above rules is reminiscent of the way one can model weak observational congruence ([Mil80]) (or rooted tau-bisimulation ([BK86])), as strong bisimulation by adding rules like, for instance,

$$if\ \ s \xrightarrow{\tau} s'\ \ and\ \ s' \xrightarrow{a} s''\ \ then\ \ s \xrightarrow{a} s''$$

(See [BK86, vG87].) The present case is by its non-uniform nature more intricate.

Since the operational semantics abstracts from 'stuttering' and depends on connected sequences only, the definition of $\mathcal{O}$ could equally well have been based on this extended transition system.

The definition of the second semantics for $\mathcal{L}$ is based on the extended transition system and is given in a non-compositional way. Therefore it looks rather operational. Below we shall show, however, that it *is* compositional.

Definition 3.9 *Let* $(X, Y \in)P$ *be defined by*

$$P = \mathcal{P}(Q)$$

$$Q = (\Sigma \times \Sigma)^* \cup (\Sigma \times \Sigma)^* \cdot (\Sigma \times \{\delta\})$$

(The empty sequence is denoted by ϵ.) A model $C : \mathcal{L} \to P$ is defined by $C[\![E]\!] = \{\epsilon\}$, and for all $s \in \mathcal{L}$, $s \neq E$,

$$C[\![s]\!] = \{\langle\sigma_1, \sigma_1'\rangle \cdots \langle\sigma_n, \psi\rangle \mid s \xrightarrow{\langle\sigma_1,\sigma_1'\rangle}_{ns} s_1 \xrightarrow{\langle\sigma_2,\sigma_2'\rangle}_{ns} \cdots \xrightarrow{\langle\sigma_n,\psi\rangle}_{ns} E\}$$

(where $\psi \in \Sigma \cup \{\delta\}$).

Note that the steps considered in the definition of $C[\![s]\!]$ need not be connected: σ_1' is in general different from σ_2, σ_2' different from σ_3, and so on. The intuition behind these gaps is that in between any two such steps (like $\langle\sigma_1, \sigma_1'\rangle$ and $\langle\sigma_2, \sigma_2'\rangle$), the (at this stage unknown) environment may perform a step (changing the state σ_1' to a new, unknown state, σ_2).

The correctness of C follows directly from the fact that the operational semantics depends on connected sequences only. Formally, O and C are related by the following abstraction function β.

Definition 3.10 *Let $\beta : P \to \Sigma \to \mathcal{P}(\Sigma_\delta^+)$ be defined, for $X \in P$ and $\sigma \in \Sigma$, by*

$$\beta(X)(\sigma) = \{r(w) \mid w \in X \ \wedge \ connected_\sigma(w)\}$$

where

$$connected_\sigma(<\sigma_1, \sigma_1'> \cdots, <\sigma_{n-1}, \sigma_{n-1}'><\sigma_n, \psi>) \equiv$$
$$\sigma_1 = \sigma \ \wedge \ \forall 1 \leq i \leq n, \ \sigma_i' = \sigma_{i+1}$$

and

$$r(<\sigma_1, \sigma_2><\sigma_2, \sigma_3> \cdots, <\sigma_{n-1}, \sigma_n><\sigma_n, \psi>) =$$
$$Remove(\sigma_1\sigma_2 \cdots \sigma_n\psi)$$

and where Remove removes all states in a sequence that are identical to their immediate successor. (E.g., $Remove(\sigma_1\sigma_2\sigma_2\sigma_3\sigma_3) = \sigma_1\sigma_2\sigma_3$, supposing that σ_1, σ_2, and σ_3 all are different.)

Lemma 3.11 $O = \beta \circ C$

3.2 Semantic operators

We show that C is compositional by first defining semantic interpretations of the syntactic operators of $\mathcal{L}$. The following help operator will be convenient. It models the 'effect' of the transition rules S1 through S5 above on elements in P.

Definition 3.12 *The operator Close : $P \to P$ is defined as follows. For $X \in P$, the set $Close(X)$ is the smallest set $Y \in P$ such that, for all $\sigma, \sigma' \in \Sigma$ and $w, w_1, w_2 \in Q$,*

1. $X \subseteq Y$
2. *if $w_1 \cdot w_2 \in Y$ and either $w_1 \neq \epsilon$ or $w_2 \neq \langle\sigma, \delta\rangle$ then $w_1 \cdot \langle\sigma, \sigma\rangle \cdot w_2 \in Y$*
3. *if $w_1 \cdot \langle\sigma, \sigma'\rangle \cdot \langle\sigma', \sigma'\rangle \cdot w_2 \in Y$ then $w_1 \cdot \langle\sigma, \sigma'\rangle \cdot w_2 \in Y$*

4. *if* $w_1 \cdot \langle\sigma,\sigma\rangle \cdot \langle\sigma,\sigma'\rangle \cdot w_2 \in Y$ *then* $w_1 \cdot \langle\sigma,\sigma'\rangle \cdot w_2 \in Y$

5. *if* $w \cdot \langle\sigma,\sigma\rangle \cdot \langle\sigma,\delta\rangle \in Y$ *then* $w \cdot \langle\sigma,\delta\rangle \in Y$

The definition of each of the semantic operators is dictated by the rules from the transition system corresponding to it.

Definition 3.13 *For each of the syntactic operators* $;$, $+$, $\|$, α_x *and* α_x^θ, *a semantic interpretation can be defined as follows. We shall only treat the latter three operators, leaving the first two to the reader. So we shall define (using the same symbols again)*

$$\|: P \times P \to P, \quad \alpha_x : P \to P, \quad \alpha_x^\theta : P \to P$$

The following convention will be used below: prefixing a set $X \in P$ *with a pair of states* $\langle\sigma,\sigma'\rangle$ *is defined by*

$$\langle\sigma,\sigma'\rangle \cdot X = \{\langle\sigma,\sigma'\rangle \cdot w \mid w \in X\}$$

For $X \in P$ *put* $\{\epsilon\} \parallel X = X \parallel \{\epsilon\} = X$; *further let* $\alpha_x(\{\epsilon\}) = \alpha_x^\theta(\{\epsilon\}) = \{\epsilon\}$. *For* $X_1, X_2 \in P$ *with* $X_1 \neq \{\epsilon\} \neq X_2$ *and* $X \neq \{\epsilon\}$, *we define*

- $X_1 \parallel X_2 = Close($
  $\bigcup\{\langle\sigma,\sigma'\rangle \cdot (\{w\} \parallel X_2) \mid \langle\sigma,\sigma'\rangle \cdot w \in X_1\}$
  $\cup$
  $\bigcup\{\langle\sigma,\sigma'\rangle \cdot (X_1 \parallel \{w\}) \mid \langle\sigma,\sigma'\rangle \cdot w \in X_2\}$
  $\cup$
  $\{\langle\sigma,\delta\rangle \mid \langle\sigma,\delta\rangle \in X_1 \wedge \langle\sigma,\delta\rangle \in X_2\}$
  $)$

- $\alpha_x(X) = \alpha_x^\perp(X)$

- $\alpha_x^{\theta_1}(X) = Close($
  $\bigcup\{\langle\sigma_1 \sqcup \theta, \sigma_2 \sqcup \theta\rangle \cdot \alpha_x^{\theta_2}(\{w\}) \mid \langle\sigma_1 \sqcup \theta_1, \sigma_2 \sqcup \theta_2\rangle \cdot w \in X,\ \theta \in \Sigma\}$
  $\cup$
  $\{\langle\sigma \sqcup \theta, \delta\rangle \mid \langle\sigma \sqcup \theta_1, \delta\rangle \in X,\ \theta \in \Sigma\}$
  $)$

  where all of the pairs $\langle\sigma_1,\theta\rangle$, $\langle\sigma_2,\theta\rangle$, $\langle\sigma_1,\theta_1\rangle$, $\langle\sigma_2,\theta_2\rangle$, $\langle\sigma,\theta\rangle$ *and* $\langle\sigma,\theta_1\rangle$ *are required to be x-pairs.*

The parallel composition of two sets consists of words that are the result of interleaving a word from the first and a word from the second set, with the proviso that $\langle\sigma,\delta\rangle$ steps are postponed until the end of the interleaving. Moreover the result of the interleaving can only end in such a step if either one of the two words that are interleaved ends successfully (with a step $\langle\sigma',\sigma''\rangle$), or both words end with the same step $\langle\sigma,\delta\rangle$. (In particular, $\{\langle\sigma_1,\delta\rangle\} \parallel \{\langle\sigma_2,\delta\rangle\} = \emptyset$, whenever $\sigma_1 \neq \sigma_2$.) The use of the closure operator *Close* mimics the rules for stuttering, S1 through S5.

The recursive definition of $\alpha_x^{\theta_1}$ above is, again, directly inspired by the transition system. A possibly more intuitive description can be obtained as follows.

Lemma 3.14 *First a definition. A pair of states $\langle\sigma_1, \sigma_2\rangle$ is called x-connected if there exist $\rho_1, \rho_2, \theta \in \Sigma$ such that*

$$\langle\rho_1, \theta\rangle \text{ and } \langle\rho_2, \theta\rangle \text{ are } x\text{-pairs, and}$$

$$\sigma_1 = \rho_1 \sqcup \theta, \quad \sigma_2 = \rho_2 \sqcup \theta$$

The intuition behind this definition is that if two states are x-connected then they contain the same information about (the value of) x.

Now let $X \in P$. Then

$$\alpha_x^{\theta_1}(X) = Close(V_1 \cup V_2)$$

where

$$\begin{aligned} V_1 \;=\; & \{\langle\exists_x(\sigma_1) \sqcup \rho_1, \exists_x(\sigma_1') \sqcup \rho_1\rangle \cdots \langle\exists_x(\sigma_n) \sqcup \rho_n, \exists_x(\sigma_n') \sqcup \rho_n\rangle \mid \\ & \rho_i \in \Sigma, \text{ for } 1 \le i \le n, \text{ and } \langle\sigma_1, \sigma_1'\rangle\langle\sigma_2, \sigma_2'\rangle \cdots \langle\sigma_n, \sigma_n'\rangle \in X \\ & \text{such that, for all } 1 \le i \le n-1,\ \langle\sigma_i', \sigma_{i+1}\rangle \text{ is } x\text{-connected}\} \end{aligned}$$

and

$$V_2 = \{\langle\sigma \sqcup \theta, \delta\rangle \mid \langle\sigma \sqcup \theta_1, \delta\rangle \in X,\ \theta \in \Sigma\}$$

and where all of the above pairs of states that are connected by a $\sqcup$ symbol, are x-pairs.

Ignoring the above application of *Close* and assuming for explanatory reasons that V_2 is empty, this characterization of the set $\alpha_x^{\theta_1}(X)$ shows that it can be constructed in three steps: first all x-connected sequences in X are selected. These correspond with computations in which the environment does not change the value of the local variable x—its value can change only in the steps of X itself, e.g., the value of x in σ_1 may be different from the value of x in σ_1'.

Secondly, the information about (the value of) the local variable x in such a sequence is discarded by means of an application of $\exists_x$ to all the states occurring in it. Thus sequences

$$\langle\exists_x(\sigma_1), \exists_x(\sigma_1')\rangle \cdots \langle\exists_x(\sigma_n), \exists_x(\sigma_n')\rangle$$

are obtained.

Finally, arbitrary assumptions on (the value of) x are made in any of the pairs of this sequence. That is, each of the pairs $\langle\exists_x(\sigma_i), \exists_x(\sigma_i')\rangle$ is changed into a pair $\langle\exists_x(\sigma_i) \sqcup \rho_i, \exists_x(\sigma_i') \sqcup \rho_i\rangle$, where ρ_i is an arbitrary state containing the new information on x, such that both $\langle\exists_x(\sigma_i), \rho_i\rangle$ and $\langle\exists_x(\sigma_i'), \rho_i\rangle$ are x-pairs. This ensures that only information on x is added (and not, e.g., on any other variables), since $\exists_x(\rho_i) \le \sigma_i$ and $\exists_x(\rho_i) \le \sigma_i'$ by the definition of x-pair. Also note that the same ρ_i is added to both sides of the pair $\langle\exists_x(\sigma_i), \exists_x(\sigma_i')\rangle$. This corresponds to the fact that the information about x is now to be considered global, and hence cannot change during any of the steps of $\alpha_x^{\theta_1}(X)$. (Of course it *can* change in between such steps: the states ρ_i and ρ_j need not be the same for $1 \le i \ne j \le n$.)

The most important result of the section is stated next.

Theorem 3.15 *The following equalities hold, for every $s, t \in \mathcal{L}$:*

$$\begin{aligned} C[\![s;t]\!] &= C[\![s]\!]; C[\![t]\!] \\ C[\![s+t]\!] &= C[\![s]\!] + C[\![t]\!] \\ C[\![s \parallel t]\!] &= C[\![s]\!] \parallel C[\![t]\!] \\ C[\![\alpha_x(s)]\!] &= \alpha_x(C[\![s]\!]) \\ C[\![\alpha_x^\theta(s)]\!] &= \alpha_x^\theta(C[\![s]\!]) \end{aligned}$$

The proof of this theorem is fairly easy because of the fact that the definitions of the semantic operators all reflect in a direct way the structure of the rules of the transition system. An important step in the proof is the observation that the additional transition rules S1 and S2, S3, S4, and S5 correspond to the clauses 1, 2, 3, and 4 in the definition of the operator *Close*, respectively.

We end this section with the observation that for two classes of interpretation functions, the model C is fully abstract with respect to O. (Recall that both models depend on (a specific choice for) I.) In [dBKPR91], the notions of *complete* and *monotonic* interpretations are introduced. They are intended as generalizations of the two example interpretations we saw in the previous section, for an imperative and a constraint language, respectively. Without repeating these definitions here, and without a proof, we state the following theorem.

Theorem 3.16 *For interpretations I that are either complete or monotonic the model C is fully abstract with respect to O.*

This result can be summarized by saying that the extension of $\mathcal{L}$ with the block construct $\alpha_x(s)$ does not disturb the full abstractness property of C as it was obtained in [dBKPR91] for $\mathcal{L}$ without blocks.

References

[BK86] J.A. Bergstra and J.W. Klop. A complete inference system for regular processes with silent moves. In F.R. Drake and J.K. Truss, editors, *Proceedings Logic Colloquium 1986*, pages 21–81, Hull, 1986. North-Holland.

[Bro85] S.D. Brookes. A fully abstract semantics for an ALGOL-like language with sharing. Technical report, Carnegie-Mellon University, Pittsburgh, 1985.

[dB80] J.W. de Bakker. *Mathematical theory of program correctness.* Prentice-Hall International, 1980.

[dBKPR91] F.S. de Boer, J.N. Kok, C. Palamidessi, and J.J.M.M. Rutten. The failure of failures in a paradigm for asynchronous communication. In J.C.M. Baeten and J.F. Groote, editors, *Proceedings of CONCUR'91*, volume 527 of *Lecture Notes in Computer Science*, pages 111–126. Springer-Verlag, 1991.

[dBP91] F.S. de Boer and C. Palamidessi. A fully abstract model for concurrent constraint programming. In S. Abramsky and T.S.E. Maibaum, editors, *Proceedings of TAPSOFT/CAAP 1991*, volume 493 of *Lecture Notes in Computer Science*, pages 296–319. Springer-Verlag, 1991.

[HMT71] L. Henkin, J.D. Monk, and A. Tarski. *Cylindric algebras (Part 1)*. North Holland Publishing company, 1971.

[HZ91] H.K. Hung and J.I. Zucker. Semantics of pointers, referencing and dereferencing with intensional logic. In *Proceedings of Logic in Computer Science 1991*, page ?? IEEE Computer Society Press, 1991.

[Mil80] R. Milner. *A Calculus of Communicating Systems*, volume 92 of *Lecture Notes in Computer Science*. Springer-Verlag, New York, 1980.

[Plo81] G.D. Plotkin. A structural approach to operational semantics. Technical Report DAIMI FN-19, Aarhus University, Computer Science Department, 1981.

[Sar89] V.A. Saraswat. *Concurrent Constraint Programming Languages*. PhD thesis, Carnegie-Mellon University, January 1989. Published by The MIT Press, U.S.A., 1990.

[SR89] V.A. Saraswat and M. Rinard. Concurrent constraint programming. In *Proc. of the 17th ACM Symposium on Principles of Programming Languages*, pages 232–245, New York, 1989. ACM.

[SRP90] V.A. Saraswat, M. Rinard, and P. Panangaden. A fully abstract semantics for concurrent constraint programming. In *Proc. of the 18th ACM Symposium on Principles of Programming Languages*, New York, 1990. ACM.

[vG87] R.J. van Glabbeek. Bounded nondeterminism and the approximation induction principle in process algebra. In F.J. Brandenburg, G. Vidal-Naquet, and M. Wirsing, editors, *Proceedings STACS 1987*, volume 247 of *Lecture Notes in Computer Science*, pages 336–??? Springer-Verlag, 1987.

Semantics, Orderings and Recursion in the Weakest Precondition Calculus

Marcello Bonsangue*
CWI,
P.O. Box 4079, 1009 AB Amsterdam, The Netherlands.
Email: marcello@cwi.nl.

Joost N. Kok
Utrecht University, Department of Computer Science,
P.O. Box 80.089, 3508 TB Utrecht, The Netherlands.
Email: joost@cs.ruu.nl.

ABSTRACT An extension of Dijkstra's guarded command language is studied, including sequential composition, demonic choice and a backtrack operator. To guide the intuition about this language we give an operational semantic that relates the initial states with possible outcome of the computations. Next we consider three orderings on this language: a refinement ordering defined by Back, a new deadlock ordering, and an approximation ordering of Nelson. The deadlock ordering is in between the two other orderings. All operators are monotonic in Nelson's ordering, but backtracking is not monotonic in Back's ordering and sequential composition is not monotonic for the deadlock ordering. At first sight recursion can only be added using Nelson's ordering. By extending the fixed point theory we show that, under certain circumstances, least fixed points for non monotonic functions can be obtained by iteration from the least element. This permits us the addition of recursion even using Back's ordering or the deadlock ordering. Furthermore, we give a semantic characterization of the three orderings above by extending the well known duality theory between predicate transformers and Smyth's powerdomain.

Keywords weakest preconditions, predicate transformers, refinement, deadlock, backtracking, recursion, fixed points, fixed point transformations, Smyth powerdomain, Egli-Milner powerdomain.

CONTENTS

*The research of this author was supported by a grant of the Universita' degli Studi di Milano, Italy.

1 Introduction

The weakest precondition calculus of Dijkstra identifies statements in the guarded command language with weakest precondition predicate transformers (see [Dij76]). The language was extended to use it as a vehicle for program refinement. Specification constructs were added and a refinement ordering was defined. This approach was introduced in [Bac78, Bac80] and is suited for refinement (see [BvW90, Bac90] and also [MRG88, Mor87]). The refinement ordering can be used to add recursion to the language, but not in a fully compositional way. For example, for each set of guards there is a different conditional command.

Recursion was added in a fully compositional way by Nelson in [Nel87]: the guarded command language was embedded in a language with sequential composition, demonic choice and a backtrack operator in which the operators can be used freely. An ordering is given for which the operators are all monotonic. This ordering is an approximation ordering of the kind used in denotational semantics and does not seem to be suited for refinement. It is defined with the additional notion of weakest liberal preconditions.

Our starting point is the language of [Nel87]. In this language we also have a form of infinite behaviour (a loop construct) and atomic actions that can deadlock (to initiate backtracking). Then we consider three orderings; besides the orderings of Back and Nelson we define a new ordering in between. It is called deadlock ordering because it preserves deadlocks as can be seen from the semantic characterization of the deadlock ordering. In terms of refinement: a normal (non-miraculous) terminating statement is not refined by a miracle in the deadlock ordering.

Only Nelson's ordering is monotonic with respect to all three operators, while the backtrack operator is not monotonic with respect to Back's ordering and the sequential composition is not monotonic for the deadlock ordering. At first sight only Nelson's ordering seems to be suited to add recursion to the full language. But the fact that for Nelson's ordering all the operators are monotonic implies that also recursion can be added with the other two orderings.

In order to show this we extend the fixed point theory. It is well known that a monotone and continuous function from a complete partial order to itself has least fixed point that can be obtained by iteration from the least element. This result was extended at first by Hitchcock and Park [HP72] showing that for a function from a complete partial order to itself is enough to be monotone in order to have a lest fixed point. Then Apt and Ploktin [AP86] have shown that the least fixed point property can be transferred, via a commutative diagram, to monotone functions from a partial order to itself. Finally, in [BK92] we show that the least fixed point property can be transferred, via a commutative diagram, also to functions (even non monotone) from a partial order to itself. Here we give a theorem that uses only part of the results given in [BK92], but this theorem is enough to imply that for both Back's and the deadlock ordering the standard operator associated to a declaration of recursive procedures has a least fixed point that can be obtained by iteration from the least element. It also gives the correct result because it is related to the least fixed point with respect to Nelson's ordering.

Moreover we provide a semantic characterization of the three orderings based on a semantic model for the language that relates initial states to possible outcomes of the computation. We start from the duality theory connecting the discrete version of the Smyth powerdomain [Smy78] and the Dijkstra's predicate transformers [Wan77, Plo79, Smy83, Bes83, AP86]. The presence of a backtrack operator in our language justifies the introduction of two different versions of the Smyth powerdomain in which a constant representing the deadlock is added in two different way. We extend the duality theory described above to these two versions of the Smyth powerdomain giving in this way a semantic characterization for the Back and the deadlock orderings. A similar result is also proved for the Egli-Milner powerdomain showing its relationship with the Nelson's predicate transformers.

For reason of space, almost all the proofs are omitted; they can be found in [BK92].

2 Language and Semantics

We first introduce the language. We use the notation $(d \in)Dom$ to introduce the domain *Dom* and a typical element d of this domain. Function application is denoted by . and associates to the left, that is $f.g.x = (f.g).x$.

Let $(v \in)\, Var$ be a set of variables, let $(t \in)IExp$ be a set of integer expressions, and let $(b \in)BExp$ be a set of boolean expressions. Then the set $(S \in)Stat$ is defined by

$$S \;::=\; v := t \mid b \rightarrow \mid loop \mid S_1; S_2 \mid S_1 \Box S_2 \mid S_1 \Diamond S_2.$$

This language has three operators: the sequential composition ; , the demonic choice $\Box$, and the backtrack operator $\Diamond$.

The backtrack operator backtracks to its second component if its first component deadlocks. The only atomic action that can deadlock is $b \rightarrow$: it deadlocks in a state in which the boolean expression b does not evaluate to true. A form of infinite behaviour (the *loop*-statement) is added to the language to distinguish different orderings on the language. A similar language is studied in [Nel87]: the only difference is that we have split actions as in [Hes89] in the sense that we consider as atomic actions both the assignment actions $v := t$ and the test actions $b \rightarrow$.

Dijkstra's guarded command language [Dij76] can be seen as a subset of this language, except for the **do** – **od**-construct which will be handled when we add recursion. For example, the conditional command **if** $b_1 \rightarrow S_1 \Box b_2 \rightarrow S_2$ **fi** can be expressed by the statement $(b_1 \rightarrow\, ;\, S_1 \Box b_2 \rightarrow\, ;\, S_2)\Diamond loop \in Stat$. More general derived statements are $skip = \mathbf{true} \rightarrow$, $abort = loop$, $magic = \mathbf{false} \rightarrow$, and **if** S **fi** $= S \Diamond loop$.

Next we give an operational semantic model that relates initial states with possible outcomes of the computation. A state is a function that yields an integer for each variable in $(v \in)$ *Var*, thus the set of states $(\sigma \in)\Sigma$ is given by $\Sigma = Var \rightarrow N$. Also, we assume that we can consider integer expressions t as functions that given a state σ yield an integer $t.\sigma$. The same applies to boolean expressions b.

We introduce a set of extended statements $(m \in)\overline{Stat}$ to treat backtracking in a transition system:

$$m ::= S \mid m_1 \Delta (m_2, \sigma)$$

where $S \in Stat$ and $\sigma \in \Sigma$. After the next definition we give some more explanation.

Definition 2.1 *Let* $Conf = (\overline{Stat} \cup \{E\}) \times (\Sigma \cup \{\delta\})$ *be a set of configurations, and define a transition relation* $\longrightarrow \subseteq Conf \times Conf$ *to be the least relation satisfying the following axioms and rules:*

$$\langle v := t, \sigma\rangle \longrightarrow \langle E, \sigma[t.\sigma/v]\rangle$$

$$\langle b \rightarrow, \sigma\rangle \longrightarrow \langle E, \delta\rangle \text{ if not } b.\sigma \qquad \langle b \rightarrow, \sigma\rangle \longrightarrow \langle E, \sigma\rangle \text{ if } b.\sigma$$

$$\langle loop, \sigma\rangle \longrightarrow \langle loop, \sigma\rangle$$

$$\frac{\langle m_1, \sigma\rangle \longrightarrow \langle E, \delta\rangle}{\langle m_1;\, m_2, \sigma\rangle \longrightarrow \langle E, \delta\rangle} \qquad \frac{\langle m_1, \sigma\rangle \longrightarrow \langle m_1' | E, \sigma'\rangle}{\langle m_1;\, m_2, \sigma\rangle \longrightarrow \langle m_1';\, m_2 | m_2, \sigma'\rangle}$$

$$\frac{\langle m_1, \sigma\rangle \longrightarrow \langle E, \delta\rangle \wedge \langle m_2, \sigma\rangle \longrightarrow \langle E, \delta\rangle}{\langle m_1 \Box m_2, \sigma\rangle \longrightarrow \langle E, \delta\rangle}$$

$$\frac{\langle m_1, \sigma\rangle \longrightarrow \langle m_1' | E, c'\rangle}{\langle m_1 \Box m_2, \sigma\rangle \longrightarrow \langle m_1' | E, \sigma'\rangle} \qquad \frac{\langle m_1, \sigma\rangle \longrightarrow \langle m_1' | E, \sigma'\rangle}{\langle m_2 \Box m_1, \sigma\rangle \longrightarrow \langle m_1' | E, \sigma'\rangle}$$

$$\frac{\langle m_1, \sigma\rangle \longrightarrow \langle E, \delta\rangle \wedge \langle m_2, \sigma\rangle \longrightarrow \langle E, \delta\rangle}{\langle m_1 \Diamond m_2, \sigma\rangle \longrightarrow \langle E, \delta\rangle}$$

$$\frac{\langle m_1, \sigma\rangle \longrightarrow \langle E, \delta\rangle \wedge \langle m_2, \sigma\rangle \longrightarrow \langle m_2' | E, \sigma'\rangle}{\langle m_1 \Diamond m_2, \sigma\rangle \longrightarrow \langle m_2' | E, \sigma'\rangle} \qquad \frac{\langle m_1, \sigma\rangle \longrightarrow \langle m_1' | E, \sigma'\rangle}{\langle m_1 \Diamond m_2, \sigma\rangle \longrightarrow \langle m_1' \Delta (m_2, \sigma) | E, \sigma'\rangle}$$

$$\frac{\langle m_1, \sigma\rangle \longrightarrow \langle E, \delta\rangle \wedge \langle m_2, \sigma'\rangle \longrightarrow \langle E, \delta\rangle}{\langle m_1 \Delta (m_2, \sigma'), \sigma\rangle \longrightarrow \langle E, \delta\rangle}$$

$$\frac{\langle m_1, \sigma\rangle \longrightarrow \langle E, \delta\rangle \wedge \langle m_2, \sigma'\rangle \longrightarrow \langle m_2' | E, \sigma''\rangle}{\langle m_1 \Delta (m_2, \sigma'), \sigma\rangle \longrightarrow \langle m_2' | E, \sigma''\rangle} \qquad \frac{\langle m_1, \sigma\rangle \longrightarrow \langle m_1' | E, \sigma'\rangle}{\langle m_1 \Delta (m_2, \sigma''), \sigma\rangle \longrightarrow \langle m_1' \Delta (m_2, \sigma'') | E, \sigma'\rangle}$$

In the definition above $\sigma[t.\sigma/v]$ denotes the state

$$(\sigma[t.\sigma/v]).v' = \begin{cases} t.\sigma & \text{if } v = v' \\ \sigma.v & \text{otherwise.} \end{cases}$$

Furthermore $\langle m_1 | E, \sigma\rangle$ is an abbreviation for the two alternative configurations $\langle m_1, \sigma\rangle$ and $\langle E, \sigma\rangle$. Intuitively, $\langle m_1, \sigma\rangle \longrightarrow \langle m_1', \sigma'\rangle$ states that one step of execution of the statement m_1 in the state σ leads to a state σ' with m_1' being the remainder of m_1 to be executed.

Definition 2.2 *We say that m can diverge from* σ, *denoted by* $(m, \sigma) \uparrow$, *if there exists an infinite sequence of configuration* c_i *such that*

$$(\forall i \geq 0 \ : \ c_i \longrightarrow c_{i+1})$$

where $c_0 = \langle m, \sigma \rangle$. *Furthermore, by* $c_0 \longrightarrow^* c_n'$ *we denote that there exists a finite sequence of configuration* c_i *such that*

$$c_0 \longrightarrow c_1 \longrightarrow \cdots \longrightarrow c_{n-1} \longrightarrow c_n'$$

For each statement in *Stat* we can now define its operational semantics:

Definition 2.3 *Let the function* $Op : Stat \rightarrow (\Sigma \rightarrow \mathcal{P}.\Sigma \cup \Sigma_\perp)$[1] *defined by:*

$$Op.S.\sigma = \begin{cases} \Sigma_\perp & \textit{if } (S, \sigma) \uparrow \\ \{\sigma' | \langle S, \sigma \rangle \longrightarrow^* \langle E, \sigma' \rangle\ \} & \textit{otherwise} \end{cases}$$

The definition of the function *Op* explains why $\Box$ is called demonic choice: if there is the possibility of infinite behaviour (*S* can diverge) then it will be chosen. Next we discuss the backtrack operator $\Diamond$. If we execute the statement $S_1 \Diamond S_2$ in a state σ then we look if we can do a step from S_1 (that possibly changes σ say in σ') and we remember the starting state σ changing $\Diamond$ in Δ. If this computation deadlocks at a later stage, then we still have the alternative S_2 left reinstalling the state σ.

As a second step we define the weakest precondition semantics and relate it to the model *Op*. Let $\mathbf{B} = \{tt, ff\}$ be the boolean set and $(P, Q \in) Pred = \Sigma \rightarrow \mathbf{B}$ be predicates.

Definition 2.4 *(weakest preconditions) Let* $wp \ : \ Stat \rightarrow (Pred \rightarrow Pred)$ *be defined as follows:*

$$\begin{array}{ll} wp.b \rightarrow .Q = b \Rightarrow Q & wp.S_1;\ S_2.Q = wp.S_1.(wp.S_2.Q) \\ wp.v := t.Q = Q[t/v] & wp.S_1 \Box S_2.Q = wp.S_1.Q \wedge wp.S_2.Q \\ wp.loop.Q = \mathbf{false} & wp.S_1 \Diamond S_2.Q = wp.S_1.Q \wedge (wp.S_1.\mathbf{false} \Rightarrow wp.S_2.Q). \end{array}$$

In this definition $Q[t/v]$ denotes syntactic substitution in Q of t for v. It is not difficult to prove that for any statement S the predicate transformer $wp.S$ is monotonic with respect to $\Rightarrow$: we have that if $P \Rightarrow Q$ then $wp.S.P \Rightarrow wp.S.Q$.

The following theorem relates the weakest precondition semantics with the operational semantics in the same way as in [Bak80]; at first generalize predicates P from Σ to $(\mathcal{P}.\Sigma \cup \Sigma_\perp)$ by $P.\perp = \mathbf{false}$ and $P.X = (\forall \sigma \in X : P.\sigma)$.

Theorem 2.5 $\qquad wp.S.P = \{\sigma | P.(Op.S.\sigma)\}$

Notice that this means $Op.S_1 = Op.S_2$ if and only if $(\forall P \ : \ wp.S_1.P = wp.S_2.P)$.

[1] $\Sigma_\perp$ denotes the set $\Sigma \cup \{\perp\}$

3 Orderings

In this section we introduce three relations on *Stat*; they are pre-orders, but using Theorem 2.5 they are partial orders when we identify statements with the same operational semantics. We start by two orderings that can be defined by means of weakest preconditions. The first ordering $\sqsubseteq_B$ was proposed by Back [Bac78, Bac80] and is suited for refinement (see [Bac90] and also [Mor87, MRG88]). The second ordering $\sqsubseteq_D$ is a new ordering which preserves deadlocks (as we show below when we give a semantic characterization of the two orderings).

Definition 3.1 *Let $\sqsubseteq_B, \sqsubseteq_D$ be two orderings on Stat defined as follows:*

$$S_1 \sqsubseteq_B S_2 \text{ if } (\forall Q : wp.S_1.Q \Rightarrow wp.S_2.Q),$$

$$S_1 \sqsubseteq_D S_2 \text{ if } wp.S_1.\mathbf{false} \Rightarrow wp.S_2.\mathbf{false} \land$$

$$(\forall Q : (wp.S_1.Q \land \neg wp.S_1.\mathbf{false}) \Rightarrow (wp.S_2.Q \land \neg wp.S_2.\mathbf{false})).$$

For the third ordering we need the additional notion of weakest liberal precondition.

Definition 3.2 *(weakest liberal preconditions) Let $wlp : Stat \rightarrow (Pred \rightarrow Pred)$ be defined by*

$$\begin{array}{ll} wlp.b \rightarrow .Q = b \Rightarrow Q & wlp.S_1; S_2.Q = wlp.S_1.(wlp.S_2.Q) \\ wlp.v := t.Q = Q[t/v] & wlp.S_1 \Box S_2.Q = wlp.S_1.Q \land wlp.S_2.Q \\ wlp.loop.Q = \mathbf{true} & wlp.S_1 \Diamond S_2.Q = wlp.S_1.Q \land (wp.S_1.\mathbf{false} \Rightarrow wlp.S_2.Q). \end{array}$$

Note that the weakest liberal precondition differs from the weakest precondition only in the definition of $wlp.loop$ and $wlp.S_1 \Diamond S_2$. The next lemma relates wp and wlp:

Lemma 3.3 $(\forall S, Q : wp.S.Q \Leftrightarrow (wp.S.\mathbf{true} \land wlp.S.Q))$.

Since wp is monotone with respect to the $\Rightarrow$ order, we have by the precedent lemma $(\forall S, Q : wp.S.Q \Rightarrow wlp.S.Q)$. We give a third ordering which was introduced by Nelson in [Nel87].

Definition 3.4 $\quad S_1 \sqsubseteq_N S_2$ *if* $(\forall Q : wp.S_1.Q \Rightarrow wp.S_2.Q \land wlp.S_2.Q \Rightarrow wlp.S_1.Q)$.

The three orderings can be related as follows:

Theorem 3.5 $\quad \sqsubseteq_N \underset{\neq}{\subset} \sqsubseteq_D \underset{\neq}{\subset} \sqsubseteq_B$

Proof We only show the inequalities. They follow from

$$v := 1 \sqsubseteq_B (\textbf{false} \rightarrow) \quad \text{but} \quad v := 1 \not\sqsubseteq_D (\textbf{false} \rightarrow)$$
$$(v := 1 \Box v := 2) \sqsubseteq_D v := 2 \quad \text{but} \quad (v := 1 \Box v := 2) \not\sqsubseteq_N v := 2.$$

□

We have the following problems with monotonicity of the orderings $\sqsubseteq_B$ and $\sqsubseteq_D$:

1. $(\textbf{true} \rightarrow) \sqsubseteq_B (\textbf{false} \rightarrow)$

   but

   $$(\textbf{true} \rightarrow) \Diamond v := 1 \not\sqsubseteq_B (\textbf{false} \rightarrow) \Diamond v := 1$$

2. $(v := 1 \Box v := 2) \sqsubseteq_D v := 2$

   but

   $$(v := 1 \Box v := 2); (v = 1 \rightarrow) \not\sqsubseteq_D v := 2; (v = 1 \rightarrow).$$

Theorem 3.6 *We have for all statements $S_1, S_2, S_1', S_2' \in Stat$:*

$$S_1 \sqsubseteq_B S_2 \wedge S_1' \sqsubseteq_B S_2' \Rightarrow (\forall op \in \{;, \Box\} : S_1 op S_1' \sqsubseteq_B S_2 op S_2')$$

$$S_1 \sqsubseteq_D S_2 \wedge S_1' \sqsubseteq_D S_2' \Rightarrow (\forall op \in \{\Box, \Diamond\} : S_1 op S_1' \sqsubseteq_D S_2 op S_2')$$

$$S_1 \sqsubseteq_N S_2 \wedge S_1' \sqsubseteq_N S_2' \Rightarrow (\forall op \in \{;, \Box, \Diamond\} : S_1 op S_1' \sqsubseteq_N S_2 op S_2')$$

Proof For $\sqsubseteq_N$ we refer to [Nel87], for $\sqsubseteq_D$ to [BK92] and for $\sqsubseteq_B$ to [BvW90]. □

4 Order Theory

In this section we provide the mathematical basis for the next section. We give some general results on fixed points and we show that under particular conditions they can be obtained (even by iteration) also for non-monotonic functions. Moreover, we give relationships between discrete powerdomains and predicate transformers, following the ideas of [Wan77],[Plo79], [Bes83], [AP86] and [Smy83].

Let P a partial order and A a nonempty subset of P. Then A is said to be *directed* if every finite subset of A has an upper bound. P is a *complete partial order* (cpo) if there exist a least element $\perp$ and every directed subset A of P has least upper bound (lub) $\bigsqcup A$.

For example, for any set X, the *flat* complete partial order $X_\perp$ is the set $X \cup \{\perp\}$ ordered by $x \sqsubseteq y \Leftrightarrow x = \perp$ or $x = y$.

Let P, Q be two partial orders. A function $f : P \rightarrow Q$ is *monotone* if for all $x, y \in P$ with $x \sqsubseteq_P y$ we have $f.x \sqsubseteq_Q f.y$. Moreover, f is *continuous* if for each directed subset A of P with least upper bound $\bigsqcup A$ we have $f.(\bigsqcup A) = \bigsqcup(f.A)$; f is *strict* if and only if

$f.\perp_P = \perp_Q$. If f is continuous then it is monotone, and if f is onto and monotone then it is also strict. Let $g : P \to P$, we denote by $\mu.g$ the least fixed point of g, that is, $g.\mu.g = \mu.g$ and for every other $x \in P$ such that $g.x = x$ then $\mu.g \sqsubseteq x$.

Let P, Q be two partial orders. Then $P \times Q$ is the cartesian product ordered coordinatewise and $P \to Q$ is the function space ordered pointwise. Moreover, if $f^{-1}.y$ exist for $y \in Q$ and $f : P \to Q$ then the partial order determined by $f^{-1}.y$ is the partial order that has for elements $x \in f^{-1}.y \subseteq P$ ordered as in P, that is, for each $x_1, x_2 \in f^{-1}.y$, $x_1 \sqsubseteq x_2 \Leftrightarrow x_1 \sqsubseteq_P x_2$.

4.1 Fixed Points

For any partial order P, function $f : P \to P$ and ordinal λ, define $f^{<\lambda>} \in P$ by

$$f^{<\lambda>} = f.\bigsqcup_{k<\lambda} f^{<k>}.$$

Of course $f^{<\lambda>}$ need not to exist, since $\bigsqcup_{k<\lambda} f^{<k>}$ need not to exist. Note that $f^{<0>} = f.\perp$ when the least element $\perp$ of P exists. If $f^{<\lambda>}$ does not exist , then for any $\lambda' \geq \lambda$ $f^{<\lambda'>}$ does not exist, and if f is monotone then $f^{<\lambda>}$ is monotone in λ. We say $(f^{<\lambda>})_\lambda$ stabilizes at k if whenever $\lambda \geq k$ then $f^{<\lambda>} = f^{<k>}$; the closure ordinal is the least ordinal k by which the sequence stabilizes. If f is monotone then $f^{<k>}$ is the least (pre-)fixed point of f since $f.f^{<k>} = f^{<k+1>}$ and $f.a \sqsubseteq a$ implies $f^{<\lambda>} \sqsubseteq a$ for all λ. If P is a complete partial order and f is monotone then of course $f^{<\lambda>}$ always exists and moreover, $(f^{<\lambda>})_\lambda$ stabilizes [HP72]. If additionally f is continuous then it has closure ordinal $\leq \omega$.

The following theorem, that can be found in [AP86], shows that under certain circumstances $g^{<\lambda>}$ always exists and stabilizes for a monotone function $g : Q \to Q$ even if Q is not a complete partial order:

Theorem 4.1 *Let $(P, \sqsubseteq_P)$ and $(Q, \sqsubseteq_Q)$ be two partial orders, and $f : P \to P$, $g : Q \to Q$ be two monotone functions and $h : P \to Q$ be a strict and continuous function such that the following diagram commutes:*

$$\begin{array}{ccc} P & \xrightarrow{f} & P \\ {\scriptstyle h}\downarrow & * & \downarrow{\scriptstyle h} \\ Q & \xrightarrow[g]{} & Q \end{array}$$

Then if $f^{<\lambda>}$ exists so does $g^{<\lambda>}$, and indeed $g^{<\lambda>} = h.f^{<\lambda>}$. In particular if $\mu.f$ exists (being an $f^{<\lambda>}$) then so does $\mu.g$ and $\mu.g = h.\mu.f$.

We can even drop the condit.on of g to be monotone provided that h satisfies some extra conditions (in [BK92] even a more general theorem is proved but this is not needed here):

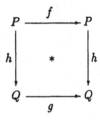

Theorem 4.2 *Let* $(P, \sqsubseteq_P)$ *and* $(Q, \sqsubseteq_Q)$ *be two partial orders, and* $f : P \rightarrow P$ *be a monotone function,* $g : Q \rightarrow Q$ *be a function and* $h : P \rightarrow Q$ *be an onto and monotone function such that for all* $y \in Q$ *the partial order* $h^{-1}.y$ *has a top element and the following diagram commutes:*

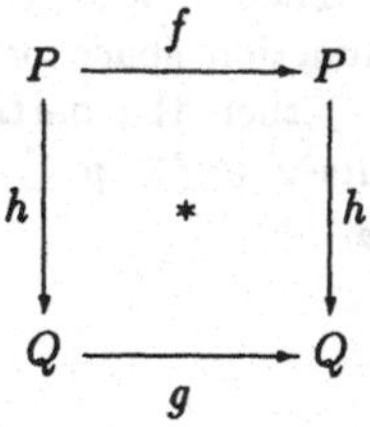

Then if $\mu.f$ *exists so does* $\mu.g$*, and indeed* $\mu.g = h.\mu.f$*. Moreover, if* h *is also continuous then for each ordinal* λ *if* $f^{<\lambda>}$ *exists so does* $g^{<\lambda>}$*, and* $g^{<\lambda>} = h.f^{<\lambda>}$*.*

Proof The proof contains part of the proof of the Theorem 4.1 [AP86]: assume $\mu.f$ exists, then $\mu.f = f^{<\alpha>}$ for some ordinal α. We have:

$$h.f^{<\alpha>} = h.f^{<\alpha+1>} = h.f.f^{<\alpha>} = g.h.f^{<\alpha>}.$$

So $h.f^{<\alpha>}$ is a fixed point of g. Now it remains to prove that $h.f^{<\alpha>} = \mu.g$. Let $y \in Q$ such that $g.y = y$ and let $a \in P$ be the top element of the partial order generated by $h^{-1}.y$.

First we prove $f.a \sqsubseteq a$, indeed, $f.a \in h^{-1}.y$ because

$$h.f.a = g.h.a = g.y = y$$

and as a is the top element of $h^{-1}.y$ we obtain $f.a \sqsubseteq a$.

As second step we prove by transfinite induction $f^{<\lambda>} \sqsubseteq a$ for each ordinal λ:

$\lambda = 0)$ $f^{<0>} = \perp \sqsubseteq a$

$\lambda > 0)$ { induction hypothesis }

$$(\forall k < \lambda \ : \ f^{<k>} \sqsubseteq a)$$

$\Rightarrow$ { definition of $\bigsqcup$ }

$$\bigsqcup_{k<\lambda} f^{<k>} \sqsubseteq a$$

$\Rightarrow$ { f is monotone }

$$f.\bigsqcup_{k<\lambda} f^{<k>} \sqsubseteq f.a$$

$\Rightarrow$ { definition of $f^{<\lambda>}$ }

$$f^{<\lambda>} \sqsubseteq f.a$$

$\Rightarrow$ { $f.a \sqsubseteq a$ }

$$f^{<\lambda>} \sqsubseteq a$$

Hence also $f^{<\alpha>} \sqsubseteq a$ and by monotonicity of h:

$$h.f^{<\alpha>} \sqsubseteq h.a = y$$

Therefore $h.f^{<\alpha>} = h.\mu.f$ is the least fixed point of g.

Suppose now $f^{<\lambda>}$ exists for some ordinal λ, and let h be continuous. Thus it is also monotone and hence it is also strict as it is onto. The fact that $h.f^{<\lambda>} = g^{<\lambda>}$ follows the line of the proof of the Theorem 4.1 (see [AP86]). □

Note that even if $g : Q \to Q$ is not monotone and Q is not a complete partial order, the theorem above ensures the existence of a least fixed point for g that can be obtained by iteration, since g^{λ} exists for all ordinals λ.

4.2 Predicate Transformers and Discrete Powerdomains

Let Σ be a nonempty set of states, fixed for the rest of this section, and assume, in order to avoid degenerate cases, its cardinality be greater than 1. Recall that a predicate is a function from states to the boolean set $\mathbf{B} = \{tt, ff\}$. With every predicate $P \in Pred$ we can associate the set $\{\sigma |\ P.\sigma = tt\} \subseteq \Sigma$ while with every set A we can associate the function in *Pred*, $P(A) = \lambda\sigma \in \Sigma.(\text{if } \sigma \in A \text{ then } tt \text{ else } ff)$. If A is a subset of Σ then $A = \{\sigma |\ P(A).\sigma = tt\}$ and conversely, if P is a predicate then $P = P(\{\sigma |\ P.\sigma = tt\})$.

A predicate transformer π is a function in $Pred \to Pred$ which satisfies some properties. There are different definitions of predicate transformers in the literature that differ in the sets of properties. Next we give a list of possible requirements on the function space $Pred \to Pred$ that are used in various definitions of predicate transformers:

1. Σ is countable,
2. $\pi.\mathbf{false} = \mathbf{false}$ *(exclusion of miracles)*,
3. π is monotone with respect to the $\Rightarrow$ order,
4. π is continuous with respect to the $\Rightarrow$ order,
5. $\pi.(P \wedge Q) = \pi.P \wedge \pi.Q$ for all $P, Q \in Pred$ *(finite multiplicativity)*,
6. $\pi. \bigwedge_{n \in N} P_n = \bigwedge_{n \in N} \pi.P_n$ where N is the set of natural number and $P_n \in Pred$ for all $n \in N$ *(countable multiplicativity)*,

7. $\pi.\bigwedge_{i\in I} P_i = \bigwedge_{i\in I} \pi.P_i$ where I is an index set of the same cardinality as Σ and $P_i \in Pred$ for all $i \in I$ *(Σ-multiplicativity)*,

8. $\pi.\bigwedge_{i\in I} P_i = \bigwedge_{i\in I} \pi.P_i$ where $I \neq \emptyset$ is an index set and $P_i \in Pred$ for all $i \in I$ *(multiplicativity)*.

In [Dij76] a predicate transformer $\pi \in Pred \rightarrow Pred$ satisfies the properties 1. - 5.; in [Wan77, Plo79] it satisfies the properties 1., 2., 4. and 5.; in [Bes83] the properties 1., 2. and 8.; in [AP86] the properties 1., 2. and 6.; and finally in [BvW90] only the property 3.. A predicate transformer can also satisfy property 7. and we choose this property for defining the predicate transformers that we will use in the rest of the section:

Definition 4.3 *A predicate transformer is any function $\pi \in PTran = Pred \rightarrow Pred$ which satisfies the Σ-multiplicativity law.*

Predicate transformers as defined above are stable functions [Plo81], as is shown in the following lemma that is a slight generalization of the stability lemma in [AP86]:

Lemma 4.4 *Let $\pi \in PTran$ and let $\sigma \in \Sigma$ such that $\pi.\mathbf{true}.\sigma$. Then there is a set $min(\pi,\sigma) \subseteq \Sigma$ such that*

$$(\forall Q \ : \ \pi.Q.\sigma \Leftrightarrow min(\pi,\sigma) \subseteq \{\sigma' | Q.\sigma'\}).$$

Next we show some of the relationships among the properties enumerated above:

Lemma 4.5 *Let Σ be a countable set of states. We have:*

$$(4. \wedge 5.) \Rightarrow 6. \Leftrightarrow 7. \Leftrightarrow 8. \Rightarrow 3.$$

Note that if Σ is uncountable we have 8. $\Leftrightarrow$ 7. $\Rightarrow$ 6. $\Rightarrow$ 3.

The previous lemma shows that predicate transformers as defined in [Dij76] are exactly the same predicate transformers in the sense of [Wan77, Plo79], and these are predicate transformers as defined in [Bes83]. The predicate transformers as defined in [Bes83] are the same predicate transformers defined in [AP86] and these predicate transformers are also predicate transformers in the sense of our definition 4.3. Finally predicate transformers in the sense of our definition 4.3 are also predicate transformers in the sense of [BvW90].

Thus our definition 4.3 generalizes the definitions of [Wan77, Plo79, Bes83, AP86] and we will generalize some of their results. As far as we know similar results do not hold for the definition of predicate transformers of [BvW90]. We will generalize the relationship between the Smyth powerdomain and the predicate transformers [Wan77, Plo79, Bes83, AP86, Smy83] to two our new versions of the Smyth powerdomains. Moreover, we will introduce a relationship between the Egli-Milner powerdomain and pair of predicate transformers like is done in [Nel87]. The following commuting diagram summarizes all the relationships between predicate transformers and discrete powerdomains that we will define in the next three subsections:

$$
\begin{array}{ccc}
PTran_N & \xrightarrow[\eta]{\cong} & ETran^{\emptyset} = (\Sigma \longrightarrow \mathcal{E}^{\emptyset}.\Sigma_\perp) \\
\Big\downarrow {\scriptstyle \downarrow_1} & * & \Big\downarrow {\scriptstyle e_\Sigma \,.\_} \\
PTran_D & \xrightarrow[\gamma]{\cong} & STran^{\delta} = (\Sigma \longrightarrow \mathcal{S}^{\delta}.\Sigma_\perp) \\
\Big\downarrow {\scriptstyle id_{PTran}} & * & \Big\downarrow {\scriptstyle d_\Sigma \,.\_} \\
PTran_B & \xrightarrow[\omega]{\cong} & STran^{\emptyset} = (\Sigma \longrightarrow \mathcal{S}^{\emptyset}.\Sigma_\perp)
\end{array}
$$

Egli-Milner powerdomain with empty set

Definition 4.6 *Let $X_\perp$ be a flat domain. Then the Egli-Milner powerdomain with empty set of $X_\perp$, denoted by $\mathcal{E}^{\emptyset}.X_\perp$, is the partial order with elements all the subset of $X_\perp$ ordered as follows:*

$$A \sqsubseteq B \;\Leftrightarrow\; (\perp \notin A \;\wedge\; A = B) \;\vee\; (\perp \in A \;\wedge\; A \backslash \{\perp\} \subseteq B).$$

Note that this differs from the usual definition of the Egli-Milner powerdomain because we add the empty set. It is added by means of a smash product following the ideas of [HP79, MM79, Abr91], in fact we have for all $A \subseteq X_\perp$:

$$(A \sqsubseteq \emptyset \;\Leftrightarrow\; A = \{\perp\} \;\vee\; A = \emptyset) \text{ and also } (\emptyset \sqsubseteq A \Leftrightarrow A = \emptyset).$$

The partial order $\mathcal{E}^{\emptyset}.X_\perp$ is also complete, as $\{\perp\}$ is the least element and if $\mathcal{F} \subseteq \mathcal{E}^{\emptyset}.X_\perp$ is a directed family then $\bigsqcup \mathcal{F} = (\bigcup \mathcal{F} \backslash \{\perp\}) \cup \{\perp \mid (\forall A \in \mathcal{F} : \perp \in A)\}$.

A meaning of a statement will be a function in the *Egli-Milner State-Transformers*, denoted by $ETran^{\emptyset}$, that is, the complete partial order $\Sigma \rightarrow \mathcal{E}^{\emptyset}.\Sigma_\perp$, ordered pointwise. Elements of $\mathcal{E}^{\emptyset}.\Sigma_\perp$ denote resulting computations. Non-terminating computation are represented by the element $\perp$ in the set of all the possible computations. The empty set is interpreted as a deadlock. The Egli-Milner State-Transformers are in the following relation with the predicate transformers (as noted by [Nel87]):

Definition 4.7 *Define the Nelson's predicate transformers $PTran_N$ to be the set of all the functions $\pi \in Pred \rightarrow Pred \times Pred$ such that:*

1. $\downarrow_1 .\pi \in PTran$ *and* $\downarrow_2 .\pi \in PTran$
2. $(\forall Q \in Pred : \downarrow_1 .\pi.\mathbf{true} \wedge \downarrow_2 .\pi.Q \Leftrightarrow \downarrow_1 .\pi_1.Q)$
3. $\downarrow_2 .\pi.\mathbf{true} = \mathbf{true}$

where $\downarrow_i$ denotes a projection operator on the i-th component of the codomain of a function. The functions are ordered as follows

$$\pi \sqsubseteq_{PN} \hat{\pi} \text{ if } (\forall Q \ : \downarrow_1 .\pi.Q \Rightarrow \downarrow_1 .\hat{\pi}.Q \wedge \ \downarrow_2 .\hat{\pi}.Q \Rightarrow \downarrow_2 .\pi.Q).$$

By definition of Nelson's predicate transformers we have that $\downarrow_1$: $PTran_N \rightarrow PTran$ is onto, since for each $\pi_1 \in PTran$ the function $\pi : Pred \rightarrow Pred \times Pred$ defined by $\pi.Q = (\pi_1.Q, \pi_2.Q)$ is in $PTran_N$, where

$$\pi_2.Q = \begin{cases} \textbf{true} & \text{if } Q = \textbf{true} \\ \pi_1.Q & \text{otherwise} \end{cases}$$

for all $Q \in Pred$.

For any statement S the pair $(wp.S, wlp.S)$ defined in the definitions 2.4 and 3.2 is a Nelson's predicate transformer and the order $\sqsubseteq_{PN}$ is the lifting of $\sqsubseteq_N$ to $PTran_N$.

Now we can show the relationship between the Egli-Milner powerdomain and the Nelson Predicate Transformers: define the function $\eta : ETran^{\emptyset} \rightarrow PTran_N$, for $m \in ETran^{\emptyset}$ and $P \in Pred$, by

$$\eta.m.P = (\{\sigma | P.m.\sigma\}, \{\sigma | P.(m.\sigma \backslash \{\bot\})\}).$$

Lemma 4.8 *Let $m \in ETran^{\emptyset}$. Then the function $\eta.m \in PTran_N$.*

Lemma 4.9 *The function η is monotone.*

The function η has an inverse. Define the function $\eta^{-1} : PTran_N \rightarrow ETran^{\emptyset}$, for $\pi \in PTran_N$ and $\sigma \in \Sigma$, by:

$$\eta^{-1}.\pi.\sigma = \begin{cases} min(\downarrow_2 .\pi, \sigma) & \text{if } \downarrow_1 .\pi.\textbf{true}.\sigma \\ min(\downarrow_2 .\pi, \sigma) \cup \{\bot\} & \text{otherwise.} \end{cases}$$

Lemma 4.10 *The function η^{-1} is monotone.*

Finally we have:

Theorem 4.11 *The function $\eta : ETran^{\emptyset} \rightarrow PTran_N$ is an isomorphism of partial orders with inverse η^{-1}.*

Smyth powerdomain with deadlock

Definition 4.12 *Let $X_\bot$ be a flat domain. Then the Smyth's powerdomain with deadlock of $X_\bot$, is defined as the partial order*

$$\mathcal{S}^{\delta}.X_\bot = \{A | \ A \subseteq X \ \wedge \ A \neq \emptyset\} \cup \{X_\bot\} \cup \{\delta\}$$

where $A \sqsubseteq B \Leftrightarrow (A = X_\bot) \vee (A = \delta \ \wedge \ B = \delta) \vee (A \supseteq B)$.

This definition differs from the original definition of the Smyth powerdomain [Smy78] because we add an extra element δ (interpreted as deadlock) that is comparable only with itself and the bottom. This makes that in general $\mathcal{S}^{\delta}.X_{\perp}$ is not a complete partial order, in fact consider in $\mathcal{S}^{\delta}.N_{\perp}$ the following directed set which has no upper bound:

$$N \sqsubseteq N\backslash\{0\} \sqsubseteq N\backslash\{0,1\} \sqsubseteq ..., \qquad \text{(this example appears also in [AP86]).}$$

The Egli-Milner powerdomain with empty set and Smith powerdomain with deadlock are related by the function $e_X : \mathcal{E}^{\emptyset}.X_{\perp} \rightarrow \mathcal{S}^{\delta}.X_{\perp}$ defined by

$$e_X.A = \begin{cases} A & \text{if } \perp \notin A \wedge A \neq \emptyset \\ \delta & \text{if } A = \emptyset \\ X_{\perp} & \text{otherwise} \end{cases}$$

as it is shown in the following lemma:

Lemma 4.13 *The function $e_X : \mathcal{E}^{\emptyset}.X_{\perp} \rightarrow \mathcal{S}^{\delta}.X_{\perp}$ is onto, continuous, and for each $B \in \mathcal{S}^{\delta}.X_{\perp}$ the partial order $e_X^{-1}.B$ has a top element.*

We will use this lemma in the next section in order to apply theorem 4.2.

The *Smyth State-Transformers respecting deadlock*, are all the functions $\Sigma \rightarrow \mathcal{S}^{\delta}.\Sigma_{\perp}$, ordered pointwise. We denote this partial order $STran^{\delta}$. Elements of $\mathcal{S}^{\delta}.\Sigma_{\perp}$ denote resulting computations. All the computations that are possibly non terminating are identified with the element $\{\Sigma_{\perp}\}$.

Next we show how $STran^{\delta}$ is related to the predicate transformers. Take $PTran_D$ as the set of predicate transformers $PTran$ ordered as follows

$$\begin{aligned} \pi \sqsubseteq_{PD} \hat{\pi} \text{ if } & \pi.\mathbf{false} \Rightarrow \hat{\pi}.\mathbf{false} \wedge \\ & \wedge (\forall Q : (\pi.Q \wedge \neg\pi.\mathbf{false}) \Rightarrow (\hat{\pi}.Q \wedge \neg\hat{\pi}.\mathbf{false})). \end{aligned}$$

The order $\sqsubseteq_{PD}$ is the lifting of $\sqsubseteq_D$ to $PTran$.

Define for $m \in STran^{\delta}$ and $Q \in Pred$ the function $\gamma : STran^{\delta} \rightarrow PTran_D$ by

$$\gamma.m.Q = \{\sigma | Q.m.\sigma\} \cup \{\sigma | m.\sigma = \delta\}$$

Define for $\pi \in PTran_D$ and $\sigma \in \Sigma$ the function $\gamma^{-1} : PTran_D \rightarrow STran^{\delta}$ by:

$$\gamma^{-1}.\pi.\sigma = \begin{cases} min(\pi, \sigma) & \text{if } \pi.\mathbf{true}.\sigma \wedge \neg\pi.\mathbf{false}.\sigma \\ \delta & \text{if } \pi.\mathbf{false}.\sigma \\ \Sigma_{\perp} & \text{otherwise.} \end{cases}$$

Also in this case we have an order-isomorphism:

Theorem 4.14 *The function $\gamma : STran^{\delta} \rightarrow PTran_D$ is an isomorphism of partial orders with inverse γ^{-1}.*

Smyth powerdomain with empty set

Definition 4.15 *Let $X_\perp$ be a flat domain. Then the Smyth powerdomain of $X_\perp$ (with empty set), is defined as the partial order*

$$\mathcal{S}^\emptyset.X_\perp = \{A|\ A \subseteq X\} \cup \{X_\perp\}$$

ordered by the superset order, that is, $A \sqsubseteq B \Leftrightarrow A \supseteq B$.

This definition differs from the original definition of the Smyth's powerdomain [Smy78] because we add the empty set as a top element, as suggested in [Plo79].

The partial order $\mathcal{S}^\emptyset.X_\perp$ is also complete, $\{X_\perp\}$ is the least element and if $\mathcal{F} \subseteq \mathcal{S}^\emptyset.X_\perp$ is a directed family then $\bigcap \mathcal{F}$ is its least upper bound. Moreover, it is also closed under arbitrary union and intersection.

The *Smyth State-Transformers domain*, denoted by $STran^\emptyset$, is the complete partial order $\Sigma \rightarrow \mathcal{S}^\emptyset.\Sigma_\perp$, ordered pointwise. Elements of $\mathcal{S}^\emptyset.\Sigma_\perp$ denote resulting computations. All the computations that are possibly non terminating are identified with the element $\{\Sigma_\perp\}$; the empty set is interpreted as a deadlock.

Also the Egli-Milner powerdomain with empty set and Smith powerdomain with empty set are related by the function $d_X : \mathcal{E}^\emptyset.X_\perp \rightarrow \mathcal{S}^\emptyset.X_\perp$ defined by

$$d_X.A = \begin{cases} A & \text{if } \perp \notin A \\ X_\perp & \text{otherwise} \end{cases}$$

as is shown in the following lemma:

Lemma 4.16 *The function $d_X : \mathcal{E}^\emptyset.X_\perp \rightarrow \mathcal{S}^\emptyset.X_\perp$ is onto, continuous, and for each $B \in \mathcal{S}^\emptyset.X_\perp$ the partial order $d_X^{-1}.B$ has a top element.*

We will also use this lemma in the next section in order to apply theorem 4.2.

Next we show the relationship between Smyth state transformers and predicate transformers. Take $PTran_B$ to be the set of predicate transformers $PTran$ ordered pointwise as follows

$$\pi \sqsubseteq_{PB} \hat{\pi} \text{ if } (\forall Q\ :\ \pi.Q \Rightarrow \hat{\pi}.Q).$$

Note that the order $\sqsubseteq_{PB}$ is just the lifting of $\sqsubseteq_B$ to $PTran$.

Define for $m \in STran^\emptyset$ and $Q \in Pred$ the function $\omega : STran^\emptyset \rightarrow PTran_B$ by

$$\omega.m.Q = \{\sigma | Q.m.\sigma\}$$

If $m.\sigma = \Sigma_\perp$ then $\omega.m.Q.\sigma = ff$ for all the predicate Q, because $Q.\perp = ff$.

Define for $\pi \in PTran_B$ and $\sigma \in \Sigma$ the function $\omega^{-1} : PTran_B \rightarrow STran^\emptyset$ by:

$$\omega^{-1}.\pi.\sigma = \begin{cases} min(\pi, \sigma) & \text{if } \pi.\mathbf{true}.\sigma \\ \Sigma_\perp & \text{otherwise.} \end{cases}$$

It is the inverse of ω, indeed we have:

Theorem 4.17 *The function $\omega : STran^{\bullet} \to PTran_B$ is an isomorphism of partial orders with inverse ω^{-1}.*

5 Recursion

In this section we add recursion to the language. Let $(x \in)PVar$ be a nonempty set of procedure variables. We remove *loop* from and add procedure variables to the set of statements *Stat*: it is now given by

$$S ::= x \mid v := t \mid b \to \mid S_1; S_2 \mid S_1 \Box S_2 \mid S_1 \Diamond S_2.$$

For the semantics we introduce the set of environments $Env = (PVar \to PTran)$, that is, an environment gives a predicate transformer for each procedure variable.

Next we give the extension of *wp* and *wlp* as defined in definition 2.4 and definition 3.2 to the new set of statements:

Definition 5.1 *(Extension of wp and wlp) Let $wp : Stat \to (Env \to PTran)$ for $\xi \in Env$ be defined by*

$$\begin{array}{ll} wp.b \to .\xi.Q = b \Rightarrow Q & wp.S_1; S_2.\xi.Q = wp.S_1.\xi.(wp.S_2.\xi.Q) \\ wp.x.\xi.Q = \xi.x.Q & wp.S_1 \Box S_2.\xi.Q = wp.S_1.\xi.Q \wedge wp.S_2.\xi.Q \\ wp.v := t.\xi.Q = Q[t/v] & wp.S_1 \Diamond S_2.\xi.Q = wp.S_1.\xi.Q \wedge (wp.S_1.\xi.\mathbf{false} \Rightarrow wp.S_2.\xi.Q) \end{array}$$

and let $wlp : Stat \to (Env \to PTran)$ be extended in similar way.

Take a fixed declaration $d \in Decl : Pvar \to Stat$. Sometimes we denote $d.x = S$ by $x \Leftarrow S$. A declaration assigns to each procedure variable a statement, possibly containing procedure variables. The idea is to associate with a declaration an environment by means of a fixed point construction.

First we show how familiar constructions can be defined in a declaration: the do-loop **do** S **od** can be defined by $x \Leftarrow (S; x)\Diamond(\mathbf{true} \to)$ and *loop* by $x \Leftarrow x$.

Define $\phi : Decl \to (Env \to Env)$ for $\xi \in Env$ by

$$\phi.d.\xi.x = wp.(d.x).\xi.$$

We would like to show that $(\phi.d)$ has a (least) fixed point (for any declaration d) that can be obtained by iteration, such that we can take this fixed point as the meaning of the declaration.

In order to do this we lift *Env* to the partial orders $(Env_B, \sqsubseteq_{EB}), (Env_D, \sqsubseteq_{ED})$ and $(Env_N, \sqsubseteq_{EN})$ defined, respectively, by

- $Env_B = (PVar \to PTran_B)$ and $\xi_1 \sqsubseteq_{EB} \xi_2$ *if* $(\forall x \in PVar : \xi_1.x \sqsubseteq_{PB} \xi_2.x)$
- $Env_D = (PVar \to PTran_D)$ and $\xi_1 \sqsubseteq_{ED} \xi_2$ *if* $(\forall x \in PVar : \xi_1.x \sqsubseteq_{PD} \xi_2.x)$
- $Env_N = (PVar \to PTran_N)$ and $\xi_1 \sqsubseteq_{EN} \xi_2$ *if* $(\forall x \in PVar : \xi_1.x \sqsubseteq_{PN} \xi_2.x)$.

Theorem 5.2 *$(Env_N, \sqsubseteq_{EN})$ is a complete partial ordering.*

Lift the definition above of ϕ to $\phi_k : Decl \rightarrow (Env_k \rightarrow Env_k)$, for $k \in \{B, D, N\}$ and $\xi_k \in Env_k$, by

$$\phi_k.d.\xi_k.x = \begin{cases} wp.(d.x).\xi_k & \text{if } k \in \{B, D\} \\ (wp.(d.x).\downarrow_1 .\xi_k, wlp.(d.x).\downarrow_2 .\xi_k) & \text{if } k = N. \end{cases}$$

The main problem is that fcr a fixed declaration d the functions $(\phi_B.d)$ and $(\phi_D.d)$ are in general not monotone (adapt the examples at the end of section 3).
However, define two functions $h_{NB} : Env_N \rightarrow Env_B$ and $h_{ND} : Env_N \rightarrow Env_D$ by:

$$(\forall \xi \in Env_N \ : \ h_{NB}.\xi = h_{ND}.\xi = \downarrow_1 .\xi).$$

Using the results of the previous section, we have that both h_{NB} and h_{ND} are onto, continuous and for every $\xi \in Env_B$ there is a top element in $h_{NB}^{-1}.\xi$, and similarly for every $\xi \in Env_D$ there is a top element in $h_{ND}^{-1}.\xi$.
Hence we can apply the theorem 4.2:

Theorem 5.3 *The function $(\phi_k.d)$ defined above has for a fixed declaration d a least fixed point $\mu.(\phi_k.d)$ both with respect to $\sqsubseteq_{EB}$, $\sqsubseteq_{ED}$ and $\sqsubseteq_{EN}$ that can be obtained by iteration as follows: define $\xi^{<0>}$ the environment such that for all x and Q*

$$\xi^{<0>}.x.Q = \textbf{false}$$

and define for each ordinal $\lambda > 0$

$$\xi^{<\lambda>} = \phi_k.d. \bigsqcup_{\alpha<\lambda} \xi^{<\alpha>},$$

then there is an ordinal $\hat{\lambda}$ such that $\mu.(\phi_k.d) = \xi^{<\hat{\lambda}>}$.

Finally we can give the following three weakest precondition semantics:

Definition 5.4 *Let $S \in Stat$, $d \in Decl$ and $k \in \{B, D, N\}$. We define the following three weakest precondition semantics $\mathcal{W}_k : Stat \rightarrow (Decl \rightarrow PTran_k)$ by:*

- $\mathcal{W}_B.S.d = wp.S.(\mu.(\phi_B.d))$
- $\mathcal{W}_D.S.d = wp.S.(\mu.(\phi_D.d))$
- $\mathcal{W}_N.S.d = (wp.S.\downarrow_1 .(\mu.(\phi_N.d)), wlp.S.\downarrow_2 .(\mu.(\phi_N.d)))$.

Acknowledgements

We like to acknowledge all the members of the Amsterdam Concurrency Group especially Jaco de Bakker, Franck van Breugel, Jan Rutten, and Daniele Turi, for discussions and suggestions about the contents of this paper. Thanks also to Ralph Back, Manfred Broy, Lambert Meertens, Doaitse Swierstra, Kaisa Sere, Rob Udink, Hans Zantema, and Prakash Panaganden.

References

[Abr91] S. Abramsky. A domain equation for bisimulation. *Information and Computation*, 92:161–218, 1991.

[AP86] K. R. Apt and G. Plotkin. Countable nondeterminism and random assignment. *Journal of the ACM*, 33(4):724–767, October 1986.

[Bac78] R.-J.R. Back. *On the correctness of Refinement Steps in Program Development.* PhD thesis, Department of Computer Science, University of Helsinki, 1978. Report A-1978-4.

[Bac80] R.-J.R. Back. *Correctness Preserving Program Refinements: Proof Theory and Applications*, volume 131 of *Mathematical Centre Tracts.* Mathematical Centre, Amsterdam, 1980.

[Bac90] R.-J.R. Back. Refinement calculus, part ii: Parallel and reactive programs. In J.W. de Bakker, W.-P. de Roever, and G. Rozenberg, editors, *Stepwise Refinement of Distributed Systems: Models, Formalisms, Correctness*, number 430 in Lecture Notes in Computer Science, pages 67–93, 1990.

[Bak80] J. W. de Bakker. *Mathematical Theory of Program Corretness.* Prentice-Hall, 1980.

[Bes83] E. Best. Relational semantic of concurrent programs (with some applications). In D. Bjorner, editor, *Proc. of the IFIP Working Conference on on Formal Description of Programming Concepts - II*, pages 431–452, Garmisch-Partenkirchen, FRG, 1983. North-Holland Publishing Company.

[BK92] M. M. Bonsangue and J. N. Kok. Semantics, orderings and recursion in the weakest precondition calculus. Technical report, Centre for Mathematics and Computer Science, Amsterdam, 1992. To appear.

[BvW90] R.-J.R. Back and J. von Wright. Refinement calculus, part i: Sequential nondeterministic programs. In J.W. de Bakker, W.-P. de Roever, and G. Rozenberg, editors, *Stepwise Refinement of Distributed Systems: Models, Formalisms, Correctness*, number 430 in Lecture Notes in Computer Science, pages 42–66, 1990.

[Dij76] E.W. Dijkstra. *A Discipline of Programming.* Prentice-Hall, 1976.

[Hes89] W.H. Hesselink. Predicate transformer semantics of general recursion. *Acta Informatica*, 26:309–332, 1989.

[HP72] P. Hitchcock and D. Park. Induction rules and termination proofs. In *International Conference on Automata, Languages and Programming*, 1972.

[HP79] M. Hennessy and G. D. Plotkin. Full abstraction for a simple parallel programming language. In J. Becvar, editor, *Proc. 8th Int'l Symp. on Mathematical Foundations on Computer Science*, volume 74 of *Lecture Notes in Computer Science*, pages 108–120. Springer-Verlag, Berlin, 1979.

[MM79] G. Milne and R. Milner. Concurrent processes and their syntax. *J. ACM*, 26, 2:302–321, 1979.

[Mor87] J. Morris. A theoretical basis for stepwise refinement and the programming calculus. *Science of Computer Programming*, 9:287–306, 1987.

[MRG88] C.C. Morgan, K.A. Robinson, and P.H.B. Gardiner. On the refinement calculus. Technical Report PRG–70, Programming Research Group, 1988.

[Nel87] G. Nelson. A generalization of Dijkstra's calculus. Technical Report 16, Digital Systems Research Center, 1987.

[Plo79] G. D. Plotkin. Dijkstra's predicate transformer and Smyth's powerdomain. In *Proceedings of the Winter School on Abstract Software Specification*, volume 86 of *Lecture Notes in Computer Science*, pages 527–553. Springer-Verlag, Berlin, 1979.

[Plo81] G.D. Plotkin. Post-graduate lecture notes in advanced domain theory (incorporating the "Pisa Notes"). Department of Computer Science, Univ. of Edinburgh, 1981.

[Smy78] M.B. Smyth. Power domains. *J. Comput. Syst. Sci.*, 16,1:23–36, 1978.

[Smy83] M.B. Smyth. Power domains and predicate transformers: A topological view. In *Proceeding of ICALP '83 (Barcelona)*, volume 154 of *Lecture Notes in Computer Science*, pages 662–675. Springer-Verlag, Berlin, 1983.

[Wan77] M. Wand. A characterisation of weakest preconditions. *J. Comput. Syst. Sci.*, 15:209–212, 1977.

A Categorical Model for Logic Programs: Indexed Monoidal Categories

Andrea Corradini

Università di Pisa
Dipartimento di Informatica
Corso Italia 40
I - 56125, Pisa, Italy
andrea@di.unipi.it

Andrea Asperti

INRIA - Rocquencourt
Domaine de Voluceau
Le Chesnay FRANCE
asperti@margaux.inria.fr

ABSTRACT: We propose a simple notion of model for Logic Programs based on indexed monoidal categories. On the one hand our proposal is consistent with well-known techniques for providing a categorical semantics for logical systems. On the other hand, it allows us to keep the effectiveness of the Horn Clause Logic fragment of first order logic. This is shown by providing an effective construction of the initial model of a program, obtained through the application of a general methodology aimed at defining a categorical semantics for structured transition systems. Thus the declarative view (as logical theory) and the operational view (as structured transition system) of a logic program are reconciled in a highly formal framework, which provides interesting hints to possible generalizations of the logic programming paradigm.

Keywords: Category Theory, Logic Programming, Categorical Logic, Structured Transition Systems, Model Theory.

CONTENTS

0 Introduction

In this work we present a simple notion of model for (negation-free, cut-free) Logic Programs [Ll87] based on indexed monoidal categories. Since the works of Seely on Hyperdoctrines and First Order Logic [Se77, Se83], indexed categories have proved to be a main tool for the categorical semantics of logical systems. From this respect, we do not claim any originality for our model definition: Horn Clause Logic is just a small subset of first order (intuitionistic) logic, and any model of the latter is a model of the former as well.

Anyway, and apart from the intrinsic complexity of the categorical notion of models proposed in literature for full logical systems, it is a common practice of theoretical research to maintain assumptions to a minimum, in order to exploit the real significance of the involved syntactical notions. As a matter of fact, the "predicates" and the "connectives" in Logic Programming have an obviously looser meaning than in a full logical system (how it is also reflected in the various "operational" interpretations proposed in the literature). Note for instance that we do not have to cope, in the operational semantics of Logic Programs (regarded here as a fragment of the intuitionistic calculus of sequents), with weakening, contraction and exchange operations, justifying the fact that the tupling of predicates in the body are more faithfully described by a monoidal (non commutative) operation than by a cartesian product. Our work goes indeed in the direction of providing a deeper investigation of logical connectives starting from their operational properties, and independently from any assumptions on their "intended" semantics.

The models we propose are categorical structures that provide a faithful interpretation for all the components of a logic program and of its computations, namely for the logical connectives (i.e., conjunction and implication), for atomic formulas, for Horn clauses, and for entire refutations as well. We shall introduce our definition of models in an incremental manner, considering first the propositional case: this allow us to focus first on the interpretation of logical connectives and derivations. A propositional program can be regarded simply as a logic program without terms, that is, where all predicates have rank 0: each predicate can be considered as a propositional variable. As a consequence, the resolution step is greatly simplified, since the unification phase reduces to an equality test. For a given propositional program (i.e., a collection of propositional Horn clauses) a model will be defined as a (strict) monoidal category C together with two functions stating how the propositional variables and the clauses are interpreted as objects and arrows of C, respectively. The monoidal bifunctor of C provides the interpretation for the conjunction, while the implication (in the restricted form in which it appears in such programs) is modelled by the arrows of C. The definition of a suitable notion of morphism between models allows us to associate every propositional program P with a category of model, **Mod**(P).

In the case of full logic programs, one has to provide an interpretation also for terms, formulas, substitutions, and related notions. Using standard categorical techniques, we propose to take as interpretation of terms any model of the functional signature of the program, in the spirit of Lawvere's algebraic theories. This means that we do not restrict ourselves to the standard Herbrand interpretation: more flexible interpretations of terms (like the 'constraint systems' considered in Constraint Logic Programming [JL87]) can be accommodated in our framework as well. Next we interpret formulas and clauses as objects and arrows, respectively, of suitable monoidal categories (like in the propositional case), but this time indexed by the interpretation of terms. The resulting notion of model is an *indexed monoidal category* (i.e., an indexed category where all the fibres are monoidal categories), together with functions stating how predicate symbols and clauses are interpreted as objects and arrows, respectively, of a suitable fibre. Also in this case, a category of models is associated with each logic program.

On the one hand, our proposal for logic program models perfectly agrees with the categorical semantics of first order logic ([Se83]), since a Hyperdoctrine is certainly an indexed monoidal category as well, regarding the categorical product in the fibres as the monoidal bifunctor. On the other hand, we show that this definition is also fully consistent with a quite different (much operational in flavour) categorical description of logic programs. Such a description is the result of the application to logic programming of a general methodology, presented in [Co90, CM92], conceived to provide a categorical semantics for a large class of formalisms.

The methodology (which generalizes the algebraic description of Petri Nets proposed in [MM90]) considers as a general model of computation transition systems [Ke76] that have an (essentially) algebraic structure *both* on states and transitions, namely *structured transition systems* (while for example in Plotkin's Structured Operational Semantics approach [Pl81] just the algebraic structure of states is put in evidence).

As pointed out in [Co90], often a computational system (in our case a logic program) is endowed with a natural notion of states and transitions, where the states have a richer structure than the transitions: therefore programs can be regarded as 'structured graphs'. For example, a logic program has a set of clauses as 'transitions', while the 'states' are goals, i.e., tuples of atomic formulas. Although they include states and transitions, such programs cannot be considered, as they are, as true transition systems. In fact, while in the case of transition systems a transition t: u → v can be applied only to state u, usually a more permissive *matching rule* is either implicitly or explicitly associated with such programs, stating when and how a transition can be applied to a state, and which the resulting new state is. For example, in the case of logic programs, when applying a clause to a goal a unification step can be performed. Although such programs are not transition systems, often it is the case that a structured transition system can be defined, which, incorporating the matching rule into the structure of transitions, is able to model faithfully the operational behaviour of the original program. This will be called the *induced transition system* of the program. In many cases the induced transition system can be generated automatically from the program it simulates via a free construction that lifts the algebraic structure of states to transitions.

The fundamental advantage of considering transition systems with an algebraic structure on both states and transitions is that often the same structure can be extended automatically and consistently to the set of computations of the system, through an effective free construction which generalizes the well-known generation of the free category of a graph. Thus every program can be associated (through this two steps construction) with a *structured* category (its *free model*) whose arrows are not simple sequences of elementary transitions, but are instead *abstract* computations, equipped with an algebraic structure. In the case of (propositional) logic programs, we will show that the resulting free model is a category having equivalence classes of derivations as arrows.

The steps of the methodology just summarized are formalized in pure categorical terms as left adjoint functors between suitable categories of programs, of transition systems, and of models. The *theory of sketches* [BW85] has been used as a handy tool to prove the existence of the needed adjunctions. A direct consequence of the clean categorical formulation of the methodology is that the semantic functor which associates each program with its free model enjoys interesting properties of compositionality, which are the consequence of very general categorical results (shortly, since it is a left adjoint functor, it preserves all colimits). For example, it is compositional w.r.t. various 'generalised' notions of union of programs, including the disjoint union, and the union of programs w.r.t. a common subset of predicate symbols. This fact suggests that also the semantics of the so-called Open Logic Programs [BGLM92] can be handled in our framework.

The consistency of the approach just described with the above sketched definition of the category of models of a program is proved by showing that the free model of a (propositional) program P is actually the initial object of **Mod**(P). Thus the interpretation of a program as a transition system, and the resulting 'operational' semantics as category of computations is perfectly reconciled with the declarative definition of model based on simple model-theoretic considerations.

This effort of algebraic formalization of the "operational" semantics of Logic Programs, already interesting by itself from the purely theoretical point of view, also has a practical relevance. As a matter of fact, the unstructured, "flat" nature of Horn Clause Logic, has always created problems of readability, reliability, and software development. Many recent research on typing systems, and on first or higher order extensions of Horn Clause Logic [NM88, NM90] mostly go in the direction of providing logic programming with more restrictive compile time constraints and/or with some kind of structured control operations. These extensions of logic programming are not easily captured by the traditional set-theoretic interpretation, and arise the need of more powerful semantical tools. Moreover, even more than these kinds of "intrinsic" reliability of the logic programming software, what is really lacking is a general algebraic (hopefully, logical) framework inside which to develop formal correctness proofs relatively to given specifications (that is, a good programming environment for logic programming). This logical framework goes obviously beyond the expressive power of logic programming itself, since, for instance, one would be interested to prove, for a given program, specifications involving complex dependencies of quantifiers, and not just existential goals. Moreover, one could be interested to prove specifications with respect to the so called "intended" model of the program, that is the initial model, that can be naturally captured by a second order quantification over predicates. This suggests the relevance of regarding logic programming as a subset of more powerful logical systems, and more generally, of a "reconciliation" between logic programming and others different and richer perspectives of Logic in Computer Science.

Our point is that such a possible and desirable reconciliation between logic programming and more powerful constructive logics should start from a semantical point of view. As a matter of fact, the current, standard semantics of logic programming and higher order intuitionistic calculi are quite distant. The former is largely set-theoretic, while it is well known that no set-theoretic semantics is possible for higher order λ-calculi [Re84]. Moreover, while from the point of view of the categorical semantics of intuitionistic logical systems much work has been devoted to provide an interpretation for proofs, this is not the case for logic programming, for which only the derivability relation among formulas is usually considered of interest. The semantics for logic programs that we propose is an attempt to fill in this gap: on the one hand it is close to the standard categorical approaches to (intuitionistic) logical systems (providing an interpretation for the proofs as well); on the other hand it saves the effectiveness and the operational intuition of this small fragment of first order logic.

The paper is organized as follows. In Section 1 we recall the basic definitions about logic programs and propositional logic programs. Section 2 introduces some relevant definitions and results of Category Theory, mainly related to the theory of sketches. Most of these notions will be used in the formal definition of the methodology for the categorical semantics of structured transition systems, presented in Section 3. The original contribution starts in Section 4, where we consider the categorical semantics of propositional programs, which is the first step towards an analogous semantics for full logic programs. First we propose a definition of model for propositional programs based on simple model-theoretic considerations; then we provide an effective semantics through the application of the methodology of Section 3 to propositional programs. Finally, we show the consistency of the two approaches, because the methodology generates exactly the initial model of a program. The same outline is followed for full logic programs in Section 5, where we also discuss various standard models of logic programs that fall in our general definition. In Section 6 we summarizes the main results and give some hints for the future development of this work. In order to make the paper as self-contained as possible, some very basic categorical definitions are shortly listed in an appendix.

1 Logic Programming: basic notions

We introduce here the basic definitions concerning the syntax and the semantics of pure logic programs (i.e., cut-free, negation-free). The definitions essentially follow [Ll87], but some of them are suitably adapted to fit better into our categorical approach.

1.1 Definition *(terms, formulas, substitutions, Herbrand universe and base)*

Let Σ be a ranked set of function symbols ($\Sigma = \cup_n \Sigma_n$), and let Π be a ranked set of predicate symbols ($\Pi = \cup_n \Pi_n$). The pair (Σ, Π) is called a *logic program signature*, and is a special kind of two-sorted signature, since the sort of predicates cannot appear in the arity of any operator.

Let $X_n \triangleq \langle x_1, \ldots, x_n \rangle$ be a *canonical tuple* of distinct variables, uniquely determined by its length; a *term (over X_n)* is an element of $T_\Sigma(X_n)$, that is, an element of the free Σ-algebra generated by X_n. Notice that we consider terms (and below also formulas and substitutions) over *tuples* (instead of *sets*) of variables. The set of all *ground* terms (i.e., terms without variables) is called the *Herbrand universe* of (Σ, Π).

If p is a predicate symbol, $p \in \Pi_n$, and $t_1, \ldots, t_n$ are terms over X_n, then $p(t_1, \ldots, t_n)$ is an *atomic formula over* X_n. The set of atomic formulas over X_n (and over the signature (Σ, Π)) will be denoted by $F_{\Sigma,\Pi}(X_m)$ A *(conjunctive) formula* is simply a tuple of atomic formulas, i.e., an element of $F_{\Sigma,\Pi}(X_m)^*$. The set of all ground, atomic formulas is called the *Herbrand base* for (Σ, Π).

If X_n and X_m are canonical tuples of variables, a *substitution from X_n to X_m* is a function $\sigma: X_n \rightarrow T_\Sigma(X_m)$, also represented as $\langle x_1/\sigma(x_1), \ldots, x_n/\sigma(x_n) \rangle$. Since the names of the variables are inessential (they are individuated by the position in the tuple), σ can also be written as $\langle \sigma(x_1), \ldots, \sigma(x_n) \rangle$; thus a substitution is simply a tuple of terms.

If t is a term (formula) over X_n and σ is a substitution from X_n to X_m, the *application of σ to t*, written $t \circ \sigma$, is the term (formula) over X_m obtained by simultaneously substituting in t all the occurrences of the variables in X_n with their image through σ. The term (formula) $t \circ \sigma$ is also called an *instantiation* of t.

Finally, if σ is a substitution from X_n to X_m, and σ' is a substitution from X_m to X_i, its *composition* is the substitution $\sigma \circ \sigma'$ from X_n to X_i, defined as $\sigma \circ \sigma' \triangleq \langle \sigma(x_1) \circ \sigma', \ldots, \sigma(x_n) \circ \sigma' \rangle$. Given two substitutions σ and σ', σ is said to be *more general* than σ' if there exists a substitution θ such that $\sigma \circ \theta = \sigma'$. ♦

1.2 Definition *(definite clauses, goals and logic programs)*

A *definite clause* c is an expression of the form

$$H :- B_1, \ldots, B_n \qquad (n \geq 0)$$

where ':-' means logic implication (from right to left), ',' means logical conjunction, H is an atomic formula called the *head* of c, and $\langle B_1, \ldots, B_n\rangle$, the *body*, is a formula.

A *goal* G is an expression of the form

$$:- G_1, \ldots, G_m \qquad (m \geq 0)$$

where $\langle G_1, \ldots, G_m\rangle$ is a formula. Each G_i $(1 \leq i \leq m)$ is an *atomic (sub-)goal* of G. If m = 0, then G is called the *empty goal*. A *logic program P (over (Σ, Π))* is a finite set of definite clauses such that all the function and predicate symbols appearing in P are contained in Σ and Π, respectively. ♦

A logic program is associated with three different but equivalent semantics: the operational, the model-theoretic, and the fixpoint semantics. We shortly recall some definitions related to the operational and to the model-theoretic semantics, referring to [Ll87] for the other notions.

In the operational reading of a logic program, the *resolution rule* states how to transform a goal into another, by unifying an atomic subgoal with the head of a clause, and then by substituting it with the corresponding body. The operational semantics is then defined as the set of all (ground) atomic formulas which can be transformed into the empty goal through a sequence of resolution steps.

1.3 Definition *(unification, resolution steps, refutations, operational semantics)*

Two atomic formulas A and B *unify* if there exists a substitution θ such that $A \circ \theta = B \circ \theta$. In this case θ is called a *unifier* of A and B. The set of unifiers of any two atomic formulas is either empty, or it has a most general element (up to variable renaming) called the *most general unifier* (*mgu*).

Given a clause $c \equiv H :- B_1, \ldots, B_n$ and a goal $G \equiv :- G_1, \ldots, G_m$, a *(SLD-)resolution step* involves the selection of an atomic goal G_i and the construction of the most general unifier (if any) θ of H and G_i. The result of such a step is the new goal $G' \equiv :- (G_1, \ldots, G_{i-1}, B_1, \ldots, B_n, G_{i+1}, \ldots, G_m) \circ \theta$, called the *resolvent* of G and c. In this case we say that *G' is derived from G and c using θ*, and we write $G \Rightarrow_{c,\theta} G'$.

Given a logic program $P = \{c_i\}_{i \in I}$, a *(SLD-)derivation* of a goal G in P is a (finite or infinite) sequence $G_0 = G, G_1, \ldots$ of goals, a sequence $c_1, c_2, \ldots$ of (variants of)[1] clauses of P, and a sequence $\theta_1, \theta_2, \ldots$ of mgu's such that each G_{i+1} is derived from G_i and c_{i+1} using θ_{i+1}. Moreover a *(SLD-)refutation* of G is a finite derivation of G such that the last goal is the empty goal '□'. If $G \Rightarrow_{c_1,\theta_1} G_1 \Rightarrow_{c_2,\theta_2} \cdots \Rightarrow_{c_n,\theta_n} G_n = \Box$, the substitution $\theta = (\theta_1 \circ \ldots \circ \theta_n)|_{Var(G)}$ (i.e., the restriction of $\theta_1 \circ \ldots \circ \theta_n$ to the variables of G) is called a *computed answer substitution* for G, and we write $G \overset{\theta}{\Rightarrow}{}^* \Box$. An *unrestricted (SLD-)refutation* of G is almost like a refutation, but the unifiers $\theta_1, \theta_2, \ldots, \theta_n$ are not required to be most general. Every instantiation of a computed answer substitution for G is called a *correct answer substitution* for G.

The *operational semantics* of a program P is defined as its *success set* SS_P, i.e., the set of all ground atomic goals for which a refutation exists:

$$SS_P = \{G \in B_P \mid G \Rightarrow^* \Box\}. \ ♦$$

It is worth stressing that although a comma appearing in a goal means conjunction (from a logical point of view), it has a much looser meaning in the operational semantics. In fact, since in the operational reading of

---

[1] We always suppose that the variables of a clause are suitably renamed to avoid clashes with the variables of the goal.

a program the unique inference rule that can be applied to a goal is the resolution, the comma does not enjoy the algebraic properties of the logical conjunction that are described (e.g., in natural deduction) by the rules of exchange, contraction, and weakening. This observation will motivate the choice of interpreting the comma simply as a monoidal operation, without requiring additional properties like commutativity, absorption, or existence of projections, which corresponds to the rules just mentioned.

As hinted in the Introduction, a *propositional program* is simply a logic program without terms, and can be defined easily by imposing some constraints on the corresponding logic program signature. We introduce propositional programs explicitly because they allow us to introduce the categorical semantics of logic programs in a stepwise manner, focusing first (in Section 4, where propositional programs are considered) on the interpretation of logical connectives and of derivations, and then (in Section 5) on the interpretation of terms, substitutions, and related notions.

1.4 Definition *(propositional programs and their semantics)*

A logic program P over (Σ, Π) is called a *propositional program* if $\Pi_i = \emptyset$ for all $1 \leq i < \omega$. In this case the signature of terms Σ is inessential, and we say that P is a propositional program over the set of *propositional variables* Π_0. As a consequence an atomic formula is just a propositional variable, and all the notions introduced in Definitions 1.1 to 1.3 specialize to their simpler propositional variant. For example, given a propositional clause $c \equiv H :\text{-}\ B_1, \ldots, B_n$ and a propositional goal $G \equiv :\text{-}\ G_1, \ldots, G_m$, a *propositional resolution step* can be applied to G if $H = G_i$ for some $i \leq m$, yielding the new propositional goal $G' \equiv :\text{-}\ G_1, \ldots, G_{i-1}, B_1, \ldots, B_n, G_{i+1}, \ldots, G_m$. Notice that unification reduces to an equality test in the propositional case. ♦

The operational reading of (propositional) logic programs is the starting point for applying to them the methodology sketched in the Introduction, as we will see in Sections 4 and 5. We introduce shortly some notions related to the model-theoretic semantics of a program.

1.5 Definition *(model-theoretic semantics of logic programs)*

Let $P = \{C_i : H_i :\text{-}\ B_{i1}, \ldots, B_{n_i}\}_{i \leq k}$ be a logic program. A *Herbrand interpretation* is a subset of the Herbrand base. A *Herbrand model M for P* is a Herbrand interpretation where all clauses of P are 'true', i.e., for all ground substitution θ, if $B_{ij} \circ \theta \in M$ for all $1 \leq j \leq n_i$, then also $H_i \circ \theta \in M$. Actually, the notion of *model* in mathematical logic [Sh67] is much more general, but since logic programs include just definite clauses, it is possible to prove that if a program has a model, then it has a Herbrand model. Moreover, for definite clauses it also holds that Herbrand models are closed under intersection: therefore there exists a *least Herbrand model*, which is defined as the *model-theoretic semantics* of a logic program. ♦

2 Categorical background

In this section we remind the main definitions and results of Category Theory used along the paper. In order to make the paper as self-contained as possible, other very basic categorical definitions are summarized in the Appendix. We point to standard references for all the missing or incomplete definitions and results, e.g., to [BW85, BW90] for sketches and to [ML71, AL91] for the rest. Many topics of this section are developed in depth in [Co90].

2.1 Sketches

The theory of sketches has been introduced [BE73] as an extension of the *algebraic theories* of Lawvere [La63]. The basic motivation of these works was to provide a categorical notion for mathematical theories (like rings, groups, etc.), where the *theory* is represented by a suitable category#, while their *models* are functors# based on that category. Then a morphism between models becomes a natural transformation.# The use of sketches allows one to represent a theory as a graph (with some additional information), instead of as a category, therefore in a way closer to the mathematical intuition.

For the following presentation we refer to [BW85]. We recall just the basic definitions and some results about the categories of models of sketches, which will be useful in the rest of the paper. A sketch is basically a graph, equipped with some diagrams# and cones#, which play an important role in the definition of models. We are interested mainly in *left exact* sketches, i.e., sketches where all the cones are over finite diagrams.

2.1 Definition *(sketches, morphisms of sketches, models)*

A *sketch* is a triple $S = \langle R, D, C\rangle$, where $R = \langle R_0, R_1, \partial_0, \partial_1, U\rangle$ is a reflexive graph, D is a class of diagrams in R, and C is a class of cones in R. Each cone in C goes from some node in R_0 to some diagram in R, not necessarily to a diagram in D. A *sketch morphism* $h: \langle R, D, C\rangle \to \langle R', D', C'\rangle$ is a reflexive graph morphism $h: R \to R'$ such that the image of every diagram in D is a diagram in D', and similarly for cones.

A *finite product (FP-) sketch* is a sketch where all cones are discrete; i.e., there are no arrows between two distinct nodes of the base. A *left exact (LE-) sketch* is a sketch where all cones are over finite diagrams. Clearly, every FP-sketch is also a LE-sketch.

If C is a category, the *underlying sketch* of C is $US_C = \langle R_C, D_C, C_C\rangle$, where R_C is the underlying reflexive graph# of C, D_C is the class of all the commutative diagrams in C, and C_C is the collection of all its limit cones#. A *model* M for a sketch S in a category C is a sketch morphism from S to the underlying sketch of C, $M: S \to US_C$. It follows that a model forces all the diagrams of a sketch to commute in C, and maps all the cones of the sketch to limit cones of C. The models for a sketch $S = \langle R, D, C\rangle$ in C form a category, where arrows are 'natural transformations#'. That is, if $F, G: S \to S_C$ are models for S in C, then a morphism $\tau: F \dashrightarrow G$ is a family of arrows in C, $\{\tau_a \mid a \in R_0\}$ such that

- for each node a of R, $\tau_a \in C(F(a), G(a))$
- for each $f: a \to b$ in R, $F(f) ; \tau_b = \tau_a ; G(f)$.

The category of models for S in **Set** will be denoted by **Mod(S)**, and that of models for S in a category C by $\mathbf{Mod}_C(S)$. In the following, by *models* for a sketch we intend *models in Set*, unless differently specified. ♦

In the rest of the paper, when talking about a model for a sketch S in a category C we will always assume that C is cartesian if S is a FP-sketch, and that C is finite complete if S is left-exact.

All categorical notions marked with a '#' at the first occurrence in the paper are shortly defined in the Appendix.

Many categories of algebras (like rings, groups, monoids, etc.) can be characterized as the category of models of a suitable FP-sketch, while LE-sketches can be used to characterize other well known categories, like **Cat** (the category of all small categories)#, **PreOrd** (the category of preorders), **CCat** (the category of cartesian categories with chosen products, and with functors preserving products 'on the nose'), **CCCat** (the category of cartesian closed categories), and many others. The categories of models of LE-sketches are often called *essentially algebraic*.

As an example of sketch, let us consider the simple case of a one-sorted signature $\Sigma = \{\Sigma_n\}_{n<\omega}$, i.e., a family of sets of *operator symbols* indexed by their arity. Then the sketch for Σ, denoted S_Σ, includes:

- one node, say 's', denoting the unique sort of Σ;
- for each operator symbol $f \in \Sigma_n$, a node 's^n', an arc $f: s^n \rightarrow s$, and a cone# with vertex# s^n and with the discrete diagram $\{s, \ldots, s\}$ (n times) as base#.

By the definition of models, this cone forces each model of S_Σ to interpret 's^n' as the product# $s \times \ldots \times s$, n times. Obviously, we can equivalently take natural numbers as the nodes of the sketch, letting $n \equiv s^n$: we will use this presentation in the following.

A model A of S_Σ in **Set** is exactly a Σ-algebra: in fact by the above definitions it consists of a set 1_A (the *carrier*, which is the image of the node '1' through A), together with one total function $f_A: n_A = 1_A \times \ldots \times 1_A \rightarrow 1_A$ for each operator $f \in \Sigma_n$. Moreover, a morphism of models $F: A \rightarrow B$ in **Mod**(S_Σ) is exactly a Σ-homomorphism, i.e., a function $\{F_1: 1_A \rightarrow 1_B\}$ which preserve the operators in the expected way. That is, the categories **Mod**(S_Σ) and Σ-**Alg** are isomorphic.

The original intuition by Lawvere of considering a mathematical theory as a category and a model as a functor based on that category can be reconciled easily with the use of sketches. In fact, a fundamental result (reported for example in [BW85]) states that for every (FP- or LE-) sketch S there exists a *generic model* $\mathcal{T}(S)$, i.e., a category such that the models for S in **C** are in bijective correspondence with the functors (which preserve certain limits) from $\mathcal{T}(S)$ to **C**. We shortly present the structure and some properties of the generic model of a signature Σ, denoted by CC_Σ, which is a cartesian category 'freely generated' by the sketch S_Σ (this construction is due to Lawvere [La63]).

Category CC_Σ has the natural numbers as objects: 0 is the terminal object#, and the categorical product# is just addition. The arrows of CC_Σ are freely generated from the arc of the sketch (i.e., one arrow $f: n \rightarrow 1$ for each $f \in \Sigma_n$), identities, projections# and arrows to the terminal object, and are closed under pairing and composition, satisfying the axioms for cartesian categories. It can be shown that the arrows of CC_Σ from m to 1 are in one-to-one correspondence with the terms over $X_m = \langle x_1, \ldots, x_m \rangle$ (see Definition 1.1). In one direction, function $[\_]_m: T_\Sigma(X_m) \rightarrow CC_\Sigma(m, 1)$ is defined as

- $[x_i]_m = \pi_i: m \rightarrow 1$, if $x_i \in \{x_1, \ldots, x_m\}$, where π_i is i-th projection of $m = 1 \times \ldots \times 1$
- $[f(t_1, \ldots, t_n)]_m = f \circ \langle [t_1]_m, \ldots, [t_n]_m \rangle: m \rightarrow 1$, if $f \in \Sigma_n$.

Moreover, tuples of terms can be regarded as substitutions (as described in Definition 1.1), and arrow composition models substitution composition in a faithful way [AM89]. Thus the generic model of a signature includes not only a representation of the sort and of the operators, but also of the substitutions together with a rich collection of basic operations: every model of S_Σ in a category **C** (which by the defining property of the generic model CC_Σ is essentially a cartesian functor# $M: CC_\Sigma \rightarrow C$) will provide a specific interpretation for all that stuff in **C**.

2.2 Categories of internal structures

When considering the category of models of a sketch in a category different from **Set**, sometimes one encounters well-known structures. As an example, the category of models of S_{Mon} (the sketch of monoids) in **Cat**, $\mathbf{Mod_{Cat}}(S_{Mon})$, is exactly the category of *strict monoidal categories.*# In order to use a uniform terminology and to simplify the notation, we adopt the following conventions.

2.2 Definition *(categories of internal structure)*

Let S_C be a LE-sketch and $C = \mathbf{Mod}(S_C)$, and suppose that the objects of C are called 'C-structures'. If **D** is a finite complete category, we will call the objects of $\mathbf{Mod_D}(S_C)$ *internal C-structures of D*, and we will denote $\mathbf{Mod_D}(S_C)$ also by **C(D)**. ♦

Thus, for example, an *internal monoid of Cat* is just a strict monoidal category, and $\mathbf{Mod_{Cat}}(S_{Mon})$ will be abbreviated to **Mon(Cat)**.

In the rest of the paper we will consider various categories of internal structures, like categories of *internal graphs* (**Graph(_)**) and of *internal reflexive graphs* (**RGraph(_)**), which will be used to model structured transition systems. An internal graph of C, G ∈ **Graph(C)**, is a model in C of the sketch for graphs, i.e., of the diagram containing two nodes and two parallel arcs between them. More explicitly, G is a tuple G = $\langle c_0, c_1, \partial_0, \partial_1 \rangle$ where c_0 and c_1 are objects of C and $\partial_0, \partial_1 : c_1 \to c_0$ are arrows of C. If C = **Set**, c_1 can be interpreted as the set of arcs of G, c_0 is the set of nodes, and ∂_0 and ∂_1 are two functions associating each arc with its source and with its target, respectively. Internal graph morphisms are defined in the expected way. Similarly, an internal *reflexive* graph of C is a tuple R = $\langle c_0, c_1, \partial_0, \partial_1, id \rangle$, where the first four components are as for graphs, and $id: c_0 \to c_1$ is an arrow. It is required that $\partial_0 \circ id = \partial_1 \circ id = id_{c_0}$.

It is well known that there exists a forgetful functor U: **RGraph** → **Graph** (which forgets the identities), and that U has a left adjoint functor R: **Graph** → **RGraph**, which adds a new identity arc to each node of its argument graph. The following easy result is a first application of a general scheme that will be exploited further in this section, i.e., that if the universe category C has 'sufficiently nice properties', then the categories of internal structures of C can be related essentially as the corresponding categories of structures in **Set**. A proof can be found in [Co90].

2.3 Proposition *(from internal graphs to internal reflexive graphs)*

If C is a category with binary coproducts, then the obvious forgetful functor U_C: **RGraph(C)** → **Graph(C)** has a free adjoint R_C: **Graph(C)** → **RGraph(C)**. ♦

The next nice property of essentially algebraic categories will be exploited various times.

2.4 Proposition *(internalization commutes)*

Let C and **D** be essentially algebraic categories. Then the categories **C(D)** and **D(C)** are equivalent.

Proof outline. In [Gr89] it is defined a tensor product '⊗' in the category of sketches such that Mod(S ⊗ S') ≃ $\mathbf{Mod_{Mod(S')}}(S)$. Thus if C = $\mathbf{Mod}(S_C)$ and D = $\mathbf{Mod}(S_D)$, we have

$$\mathbf{C(D)} \equiv \mathbf{Mod_{Mod(S_D)}}(S_C) \simeq \mathbf{Mod}(S_C \otimes S_D) \approx \mathbf{Mod}(S_D \otimes S_C) \simeq \mathbf{Mod_{Mod(S_C)}}(S_D) \equiv \mathbf{D(C)} \ \blacklozenge$$

As an example, it follows that a strict monoidal category can also be regarded as an *internal category of Mon*, i.e., as an object of **Cat(Mon)**. For a proof of the next important result we refer to [BW85], Section 4.4.

2.5 Theorem *(a property of sketch morphisms)*

Let f: S → S' be a morphism of LE-sketches. Then f induces a functor f*: Mod(S') → Mod(S) which has a left adjoint $f_\#$. ♦

This result suggests a very handy technique for proving the existence of an adjunction between two categories, if both are essentially algebraic. Indeed, it suffices to find a sketch morphism between the generating sketches: this induces a functor, almost always obvious, which has a left adjoint. The next theorem exploits this technique to prove an important result which, as we will see, plays a central role in the methodology described below in Section 3. It states that the well-known construction of the free category generated by a (possibly reflexive) graph can be performed 'internally' to any essentially algebraic category C: such a construction associates each internal (reflexive) graph of C with its free internal category.

2.6 Theorem *(from internal reflexive graphs to internal categories)*

If C is the category of models in **Set** of a left-exact sketch, then the forgetful functor **Cat(C)** → **RGraph(C)** has a free adjoint C_C: **RGraph(C)** → **Cat(C)**.

Proof outline. Let C = Mod(S_C). Both **Cat** and **RGraph** are essentially algebraic categories, and there is an obvious sketch inclusion morphism $S_{RGraph} \to S_{Cat}$ which induces a similar morphism f: $S_C \otimes S_{RGraph} \to S_C \otimes S_{Cat}$ (where ⊗ is the tensor product defined in [Gr89]). Thus by Theorem 2.5 there exists a functor f*: Mod($S_C \otimes S_{Cat}$) → Mod($S_C \otimes S_{RGraph}$) with left adjoint $f_\#$: Mod($S_C \otimes S_{RGraph}$) → Mod($S_C \otimes S_{Cat}$). The statement follows by observing that Mod($S_C \otimes S_{Cat}$) ≃ **Cat(C)** and Mod($S_C \otimes S_{RGraph}$) ≃ **RGraph(C)**, and by checking that f* is the expected forgetful functor. ♦

A stronger version of the last theorem has been proved in [Co90], where the universe category C is required to have suitable limits and colimits. The free internal category is then characterized in an effective way as the least fixpoint of a ω-continuous endofunctor on a suitable category of diagrams, which, by the Knaster-Tarski theorem, is the (co)limit of a ω-chain of partial approximations. That proof provides a deep insight into the actual structure of the free internal category generated by an internal reflexive graph, but it is not presented here for the sake of brevity.

In order to be able to apply in the widest and simplest possible way the results introduced in this section, we will use the following observation which states that the topos of presheaves on a category E can be regarded as an essentially algebraic category.

2.7 Observation *(categories of functors as categories of models of sketches)*

Let E be a category, and [E^{op} → **Set**] be the category of contravariant functors from E to **Set**, with natural transformations as arrows (also known as the topos of *presheaves* on E). Then [E^{op} → **Set**] is essentially algebraic. In fact, it is exactly the category of models of the sketch including the underlying reflexive graph of E^{op} as graph, all the commutative diagrams of E^{op} as diagrams, and no cone at all. ♦

Combining the last observation with Proposition 2.4, we get easily a nice result relating indexed categories and presheaves (cf. [AM92]).

2.8 Fact *(indexed categories are internal categories in the topos of presheaves)*

Let E be a category. A functor C: $E^{op} \to$ **Cat** is called an ***indexed category***. By Observation 2.7 and Proposition 2.4 we have that $[E^{op} \to \mathbf{Cat}] \approx \mathbf{Cat}([E^{op} \to \mathbf{Set}])$. Thus C can be regarded equivalently as an internal category of the topos of presheaves on E. ♦

2.3 Heterogeneous graphs

The notion of internal graph introduced in the last section provides a good formalization for the concept of structured transition systems, for which we will assume an *identical* structure for states and transitions. However, it is not flexible enough to represent programs, which, as suggested in the Introduction, usually have a richer structure on states than on transitions. Therefore we introduce the notion of *heterogeneous graphs*, i.e. graphs where the collections of arcs and of nodes can be objects of distinct categories.

2.9 Definition *(heterogeneous graphs)*

Let **C** and **B** be two categories, such that a forgetful functor U: **C** → **B** exists. Then the category of *heterogeneous graphs with arcs in B and nodes in C*, denoted **Graph(B, C)**, is the comma category ($\Delta_B \downarrow \Delta_B \circ U$), where Δ_B: **B** → **B** × **B** is the diagonal functor. More explicitly, G = ‹c, b, ∂_0, ∂_1› is a heterogeneous graph if c ∈ |**C**|, b ∈ |**B**|, and ∂_0, ∂_1: b → U[c] are arrows of **B**. A ***heterogeneous graph morphism*** f: ‹c, b, ∂_0, ∂_1› → ‹c', b', ∂'_0, ∂'_1› is a pair ‹f_0, f_1› where f_1: b → b' is an arrow of **B**, f_0: c → c' is an arrow of **C**, and such that $f_1;\partial'_0 = \partial_0;U[f_0]$ and $f_1;\partial'_1 = \partial_1;U[f_0]$. ♦

Practically a heterogeneous graph ‹c, b, ∂_0, ∂_1› ∈ |**Graph(B, C)**| can be considered as an internal graph ‹U[c], b, ∂_0, ∂_1› ∈ |**Graph(B)**|, but the morphisms are required to preserve the richer structure of nodes. The following result ([CM92]) shows that if the forgetful functor U: **C** → **B** has a free adjoint, then one can safely enrich the structure of the arcs of a heterogeneous graph in order to get an internal graph of the more structured category.

2.10 Proposition *(enriching the arcs of a heterogeneous graph)*

If the forgetful functor U: **C** → **B** has a free adjoint F: **B** → **C**, then the obvious forgetful functor U': **Graph(C)** → **Graph(B, C)** induced by U (which forgets just the structure of arcs) has a free adjoint F': **Graph(B, C)** → **Graph(C)**. ♦

3 A methodology for a categorical semantics for structured transition system

In this section we present the formal definition of the methodology first proposed in [Co90], which, as anticipated in the Introduction, allows one to define a categorical semantics for a wide class of rule-based formalisms. The methodology is inspired to and generalizes the algebraic description of Place/Transitions Petri Nets proposed in [MM90]. It individuates suitable categories for three different levels of description of a formalism, and relates these categories with free adjoint functors. The first level consists of *programs*, which are regarded as heterogeneous graphs, whose structure of states and transitions depends on the particular formalism. The second category includes *structured transition systems*, i.e., internal reflexive graphs, which can be obtained from the programs by 'lifting' the richer structure of states to the transitions in a free way. Finally, the third category includes the *models*, that is internal categories: the natural generalization of the construction of the free category of a graph allows us to associate each structured transition system with its free model of computations. The generality of the methodology derives from the fact that all the definitions and results are parametric with respect to the structure of states and transitions, which are objects of suitable categories. For the application of the methodology it is sufficient to require that the category of states is essentially algebraic: in this case we can apply the results of Section 2 to prove the existence of the required free functors. The following definition provides a precise outline for the methodology.

3.1 Definition *(guidelines for the methodology)*

Suppose that we have a class of 'programs' **Prog**. The following steps define a methodology which defines the categories of programs, of transition systems and of models, together with a functor which associates in an effective way a program with its free model.

1) Determine the 'natural' structure of the states and of the transitions of programs in **Prog**, and what the morphisms among systems in **Prog** are, in order to regard **Prog** as a category. This category has the form **Graph(B, C)**, i.e., it is a category of heterogeneous graphs with states in **C** and transitions in **B**. Since **C** is more structured than **B**, there exists a forgetful functor $U: C \to B$. To be able to apply the next steps, one has to look for its free adjoint $F: B \to C$.

2) Define a category of *transition systems* which model the dynamic behaviour of the programs of Prog. This category usually has the form **RGraph(C)**, i.e., it is the category of reflexive internal graphs having both transitions and states in **C**. If **C** has binary coproducts, by Propositions 2.3 and 2.10 the forgetful functor U: **RGraph(C)** → **Graph(B,C)** has a free adjoint TS_C: **Graph(B,C)** → **RGraph(C)**, which associates with a system its *induced transition system*.

3) Define a category of *models* for transition systems. This category usually has the form **Cat(C)**, i.e., it includes internal categories of **C**. If **C** satisfies the hypotheses of Theorem 2.6, the forgetful functor **Cat(C)** → **RGraph(C)** has a free adjoint C_C, which associates with each transition system its *free model*.

♦

The methodology has been applied to Place/Transition Petri Nets (yielding to constructions equivalent to the ones proposed in [MM90]), to Phrase Structured Grammars (for which the free model results to be the *syntax category* [Be75]), and to Logic Programs, but using a representation of programs completely different from the one proposed here. Besides of [Co90], partial results concerning the definition of the methodology and its applications can be found in [CM90a, CM90b, CM92].

The outline of Definition 3.1 will be faithfully applied in Section 4.2 to propositional programs, and in Section 5.3 to full logic programs.

4 A categorical semantics for Propositional Programs

The main goal of this section is the definition of a categorical semantics for propositional programs, introduced in Definition 1.4. As stressed in various places, the restriction to propositional programs allows us to concentrate on the interpretation of the logical connectives and of the derivations (and refutations), postponing to the next section the handling of terms, substitutions and related notions.

In Section 4.1 we propose a notion of model for propositional programs, based on elementary model-theoretic considerations. The models are equipped with a suitable notion of morphism, giving rise to the definition of the category of models associated with a given propositional program. In Section 4.2 we show how to generate the free model of a program through the application of the methodology presented in Section 3. We also show the consistency between the two approaches, proving that the free model of a program is initial in the category of its models.

We recall that a propositional program is essentially a logic program where the atomic formulas are zeradic predicates, also called propositional variables. In the rest of this section we will refer to notions like goals, resolution steps, refutations, etc., meaning their propositional variant.

4.1 Models of Propositional Programs

What a categorical model for a propositional program should be? We will try to keep our requirements as simple and intuitive as possible, while guaranteeing the greatest level of generality. Any reasonable model for a definite program P over a set of propositional variables V should provide an interpretation for

- the elements of V
- the logical connectives that appear in the clauses, i.e., conjunction and implication
- the clauses of P, i.e., the implications they represent must hold in the model
- the computations of P, i.e., its derivations (sequences of resolution steps).

By the observation after Definition 1.3 about the weaker properties that the logical conjunction enjoys in the operational reading of programs, an interpretation for the propositional variables and conjunction can be simply a set with a monoidal operation. Moreover, since the implication always appear at the top level of a formula (that is implications cannot be nested) it suffices to interpret it with an arrow of a category, with no closure requirements. For what concerns computations, the categorical structure provides the transitivity of implications, but we also need to interpret resolution steps. This can be obtained in a natural way by extending the binary operation to arrows, and by exploiting the identities provided by the categorical structure. For example, if

$$A_1, \ldots, A_n \Rightarrow_c A_1, \ldots, A_{i-1}, B_1, \ldots, B_m, A_{i+1}, \ldots, A_n$$

is a resolution step from goal $A_1, \ldots, A_n$ using clause ($c \equiv A_i$:- $B_1, \ldots, B_m$), it can be interpreted faithfully by the arrow (in the opposite direction)

$$id_{A_1} \cdot \ldots \cdot id_{A_{i-1}} \cdot c \cdot id_{A_{i+1}} \cdot \ldots \cdot id_{A_n} : A_1 \cdot \ldots \cdot A_{i-1} \cdot B_1 \cdot \ldots \cdot B_m \cdot A_{i+1} \cdot \ldots \cdot A_n \rightarrow A_1 \cdot \ldots \cdot A_n$$

where each propositional variable stays for its own interpretation. These considerations yield to the individuation of ***monoidal categories*** as natural models for propositional programs.[2]

4.1 Definition *(models for propositional programs)*

Let V be a set of propositional variables, and $P = \{c_i\}$ be a propositional program on V. A ***model for P*** is a triple (M, [_], [[_]]), where

---

[2] It must be stressed that if we consider conjunction as non commutative then a propositional program can be considered as a context-free grammar over the vocabulary V with no terminal symbols. Thus the application of our methodology to context-free grammars, presented in detail in [CM92], produces essentially the same structures and results as those presented in this section.

- **M** is a strict monoidal category#. We denote by '·' the associated bifunctor.[3]
- [_]: V → |M| is a function mapping each propositional variable to an object of M, its interpretation.
- [_]: P → M_{mor} is a function mapping each clause of P to an arrow of M, such that if (c ≡ A :- B_1, ..., B_m) is in P, then [c]: [B_1]· ...·[B_m] → [A]. ♦

The collection of models of a propositional program can be equipped easily with a categorical structure: an arrow between two models is simply a monoidal functor# which preserves the interpretations of propositional variables and clauses.

4.2 Definition *(the category of models of a program)*

Let P be a propositional program over V. A *morphism of models for P* F: (M, [_], [_]) → (M', [_]', [_]') is a monoidal functor F = (F_0, F_1): M → M' such that

- F_0 ∘ [_] = [_]', and
- F_1 ∘ [_] = [_]'

The category of models for P is denoted by Mod(P). ♦

4.2 Construction of the free model

We apply here the methodology introduced in Section 3 to propositional programs. First, we have to individuate the 'natural' structure for the states and the transitions of propositional programs, in order to regard them as objects of a category. The states of a programs are simply strings of propositional variables, thus the obvious algebraic structure for the collection of states is a monoid, i.e., an object of category Mon. As a consequence Mon plays the role of category C of Definition 3.1. On the other hand, a program is a *set* of clauses; thus we take Set as the category of structures of transitions (i.e., the category called B in Definition 3.1). Since there is an obvious free adjunction between Set and Mon, we can define the category of propositional programs as **PropProg ≡ Graph(Set, Mon)**, i.e., the category of heterogeneous graphs having a set of arcs and a monoid of nodes. This corresponds to the first step of Definition 3.1.

Next we have to consider the structured transition systems which are able to model the dynamic behaviour of propositional programs. More explicitly, we require that the transitions of the structured transition system induced by a program are able to model the (propositional) resolution steps. By the informal considerations in the previous section, this can be obtained by adding idle transitions for each state, and introducing a monoidal operation on transitions as well, which represents the parallel composition of (possibly idle) transitions. These requirements imply that a structured transition system for a propositional program must be a reflexive graph with a monoidal structure both on nodes and on arcs, or, in other words, an internal reflexive graph of Mon, i.e., an object of RGraph(Mon).

Since category **Mon** has binary coproducts, the free functor TS_{Mon}: **Graph(Set, Mon)** → **RGraph(Mon)** is guaranteed to exist: it associates with each program its induced transition system, having the same states and the free monoid generated by its clauses and idle transitions as arcs. This completes the second step of the methodology.

---

[3] From now on, unless differently specified, by *monoidal category* we mean *strict monoidal category*.

Since the dynamic behaviour of propositional programs is modelled by suitable internal graphs, it is natural to consider as their models the corresponding internal categories of **Mon**, i.e., categories where the arrows represent (abstract) computations of a program, and are closed under a monoidal operation which extends the parallel operation to transitions. Thus the category of models for propositional programs can be defined as **Cat(Mon)**. Moreover, since **Mon** is essentially algebraic, the free functor C_{Mon}: **RGraph(Mon)** $\rightarrow$ **Cat(Mon)** exists. Combining this functor with the generation of the induced transition system, we get the functor $Mod \equiv C_{Mon} \circ TS_{Mon}$: **PropProg** $\rightarrow$ **Cat(Mon)** which maps each program to its free model. This completes the application of the methodology to propositional programs.

Notice that, since **Cat(Mon)** $\approx$ **Mon(Cat)** by Proposition 2.4, the last definition of model for propositional programs (based on more operational considerations) is consistent with the one of Definition 4.1, based instead on model-theoretic arguments. The complete agreement between these two definitions of models is confirmed by the next result.

4.3 Proposition *(the free model of P is initial in Mod(P))*

Let P be a logic program over V, regarded as an object of category **PropProg**. That is, $P = \langle V^*, \{c_i\}, \partial_0, \partial_1 \rangle$, with $c: A_1 \cdot \ldots \cdot A_n \rightarrow H$ for each $(c \equiv H \text{ :- } A_1, \ldots, A_n) \in P$. Moreover, let $\eta_P = (\eta_{P_0}, \eta_{P_1})$: $P \rightarrow Mod(P)$ be the component on P of the unit of the free adjunction **Cat(Mon)**$(Mod(\_), \_) \equiv$ **PropProg**$(\_, U(\_))$. Then $(Mod(P), \eta_{P_0} \circ \eta_V, \eta_{P_1})$ is initial in **Mod(P)**, where $\eta_V: V \rightarrow V^*$ is the obvious inclusion.

Proof. A model $(M, [\_], [\![\_]\!])$ for P can be regarded as an arrow $([\_]^*, [\![\_]\!]): P \rightarrow U(M)$ in category **PropProg** and viceversa, the correspondence being a bijection. The statement follows by the properties of adjunctions, since $\langle \eta_P, Mod(P) \rangle$ is initial in the comma category $(P \downarrow U)$. ♦

By the definition of models, the initial model gives an interpretation not only to the clauses, but also to the computations of a program, i.e., to sequences of resolution steps. Furthermore, since the arrows are closed under the monoidal operation, also *parallel derivations* (i.e., where more than one propositional variable of a goal can be rewritten in a single step) are meaningful. The next result gives a precise characterization of some arrows of the initial model.

4.4 Proposition *(arrows from the unit to a goal are (most parallel) refutations)*

Let $G \in V^*$ be a goal, and P be a program over V. Then the arrows of $Mod(P)$ from the unit ε (representing the empty goal) to G are in one-to-one correspondence with the ***most parallel refutations*** for G, i.e., to the sequences of the form

$$G \overset{c_{11},\ldots,c_{1n}}{\Rrightarrow} G_1 \ \ldots \ G_{k-1} \overset{c_{k1},\ldots,c_{km}}{\Rrightarrow} \varepsilon$$

where at step i all the propositional variables of goal G_{i-1} are rewritten by some clause in P.[4]

Proof outline. Since the initial model $Mod(P)$ is generated freely from P, every arrow of $Mod(P)$ is composed of clauses of P, identities, and the associative (non commutative) operators ';' and '·', satisfying the interchange axiom for monoidal categories:

---

[4] The same result can be proved for context free grammars, by exploiting the correspondence with propositional programs stressed in Footnote 2. As shown in [CM92], the free model of a context-free grammar is a strict monoidal category whose arrows are isomorphic to the derivation trees of the grammar. This category is well known in literature as the ***syntax category*** of the grammar [Be75].

$(f ; g) \cdot (h ; k) = (f \cdot h) ; (g \cdot k)$.

By applying repeatedly this axiom to an arrow $f: \varepsilon \rightarrow G$, we can reduce it to the form $f_1; \ldots; f_k$, with each f_i including no ;'s. Then by exploiting the structure of definite clauses we can eliminate all the identities, by shifting the clauses towards the right. The resulting arrow is a sequence of parallel compositions of clauses, and corresponds one-to-one with a most parallel refutation for G. ♦

As the last result stresses, unlike the classical semantics of logic programs, in the initial model of a program also the proofs (i.e., the refutations) have a suitable representation as arrows, in agreement with the categorical semantics of intuitionistic logical systems. Interestingly enough, not all sequential refutations are represented by distinct arrows: because of the algebraic (monoidal) structure of the models, two refutations that differ only for the order in which two clauses are applied to two unrelated propositional variables are interpreted in the model by the same arrow.

5 From Propositional Programs to Logic Programs

Passing from propositional programs to logic programs, the new ingredients for which we have to provide an interpretation are terms, substitutions, and atomic formulas built over a logic program signature (Σ, Π), together with all the related notions. In Section 5.1 we propose our notion of model for logic programs, which combines successfully the interpretation of logical connectives seen in Section 4 for propositional programs with the standard categorical techniques for the interpretation of the terms over a given signature, briefly summarized in Section 2.1. Section 5.2 is devoted to the presentation of some examples of models for logic programs: among other things we will show that the classical set-theoretic models can be obtained easily by constraining in a suitable way our general definition. Finally, in Section 5.3 we present the construction of the free model of a logic program through the application of the methodology of Section 3, and we shortly summarize some results analogous to those presented for the propositional case.

5.1 Models for Logic Programs

In Section 4.1 we proposed monoidal categories as a suitable model for propositional programs, showing that all the basic components of such a program and of its computations have an interpretation in a monoidal category. In the case of full logic programs (i.e., programs over an arbitrary signature) we go a step farther, and propose to consider a logic program as a *collection of propositional programs*, suitably correlated.

In fact, if we fix a set X of variables and force a program P to use only variables of X without instantiating them, then the logic program behaves exactly like a propositional program (say P_X) over a set of propositional variables containing all the atomic formulas with at most variables in X. Thus a model for a logic program should include one monoidal category (say M_X) for each finite set of variables. If Y is another set of variables, how are related P_X and P_Y? Clearly, if $\sigma: X \rightarrow T_\Sigma(Y)$ is a substitution mapping each variable of X to a term over Y, then applying σ to any 'item' of P_X (be it an atomic formula, a clause, or an entire computation) we should obtain a corresponding 'item' of P_Y. Thus every substitution σ: $X \rightarrow T_\Sigma(Y)$ should induce a monoidal functor $\sigma^*: M_X \rightarrow M_Y$.

It follows that a reasonable definition of model for a logic program is a family of monoidal categories indexed by sets of variables, and related by functors indexed by substitutions. This is the basic idea which lies behind the following definitions, although the demand for generality suggests us to consider also non set-theoretic models for the signature of terms.

As customary in mathematical logic, we will first introduce the notion of *interpretation* of a logic program, and then we will define a *model* as an interpretation which satisfies the clauses of the program. As a matter of fact, the definition of interpretation only depends on a logic program signature (Definition 1.1), and is the same for all the programs over the same signature. The relationship between Herbrand interpretations, Herbrand models and our definitions will be considered in Section 5.2.

First at all we introduce the following Convention, which allows us to regard the collection of predicate symbols Π and also every logic program P as functors. This will be helpful in the categorical definitions below.

5.1 Convention ***(set of predicates and logic programs as functors)***

Let Π be a ranked set of predicate symbols, $\Pi = \cup_n \Pi_n$. In the rest of the paper, Π will be considered as a functor $\Pi: \mathcal{N} \to \mathbf{Set}$ (where $\mathcal{N}$ is the discrete category of natural numbers), associating with each natural number n the set of predicates of rank n: thus $\Pi(n) = \Pi_n$.

Similarly, we regard a logic program P as a functor $P: \mathcal{N} \to \mathbf{Set}$, associating with each natural number n the set P_n containing the clauses of P with exactly n variables. ♦

In the definition of interpretation of a logic program signature (Σ, Π) we will refer to the free cartesian category generated by signature Σ, CC_Σ, whose structure has been shortly described in Section 2.1. It is worth recalling that the objects of CC_Σ are simply natural numbers, and therefore there exists an inclusion functor $in_{\mathcal{N}}: \mathcal{N} \to CC_\Sigma{}^{op}$ (we consider below the dual category# of CC_Σ for technical reasons). In the next definition we not only introduce the interpretations, but we also give them a categorical structure by defining a suitable notion of morphism.

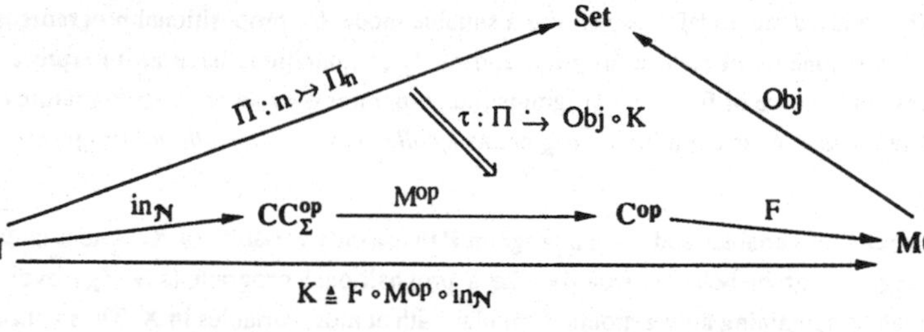

Figure 1 *An interpretation of a logic program signature (Σ, Π)*

5.2 Definition ***(the category of interpretations of a logic program signature)***

An *interpretation* for a logic program signature (Σ, Π) is a triple $I = (M, F, \tau)$ where:

- $M = CC_\Sigma \to C$ is a model for Σ, i.e., a cartesian functor (cf. Section 2.1.).
- F is a functor $F: C^{op} \to \mathbf{MCat}$.[5]

---

[5] From now on, we denote by MCat the category of strict monoidal categories.

Let $K \triangleq F \circ M^{op} \circ in_{\mathcal{N}}: \mathcal{N} \to \mathbf{MCat}$ be the composite functor depicted in Figure 1, where $in_{\mathcal{N}}$, F, and M are as above. Moreover let Obj: **MCat** $\to$ **Set** be the functor that maps every (small) strict monoidal category to the set of its objects. Then $\tau: \Pi \dot{\to} Obj \circ K$ is a natural transformation, where Π is the functor introduced in Convention 5.1.

If $I = (M, F, \tau)$ and $I' = (M', F', \tau')$ are two interpretations for (Σ, Π), a *morphism of interpretations* $\phi: I \to I'$ is natural transformation $\phi: F \circ M^{op} \dot{\to} F' \circ M'^{op}$, such that $\tau ; (Obj \circ \phi \circ in) = \tau'$, where '$\circ$' and ';' denote the horizontal and the vertical composition of natural transformations, respectively. **Int**(Σ, Π) is the category having interpretations for (Σ, Π) as objects, and morphisms of interpretations as arrows. ♦

Let $I = (M, F, \tau)$ be an interpretation for (Σ, Π). Spelling out the definition of natural transformation, τ has one component τ_m for each natural number $m \in \mathcal{N}$, which is a function $\tau_m: \Pi(m) \to Obj \circ K(m)$ providing an interpretation for each predicate symbol of rank m as an object of the monoidal category K(m). Given a canonical tuple of m variables $X_m = \langle x_1, \ldots, x_m \rangle$, we can extend τ_m to a function $⟪\_⟫_m$ which interprets every tuple of atomic formulas over X_m as an object of K(m). Function $⟪\_⟫_m: F_{\Sigma,\Pi}(X_m)^* \to Obj \circ K(m)$ is defined as follows, exploiting the interpretation function $[\_]_m$ of terms over X_m as arrows of CC_Σ introduced in Section 2.1:

- $⟪p(t_1, \ldots, t_n)⟫_m = F(M(\langle [t_1]_m, \ldots, [t_n]_m \rangle)^{op})(\tau_n(p)) \in Obj \circ K(m)$, if $p \in \Pi_n$;
- $⟪A_1, \ldots, A_n⟫_m = ⟪A_1⟫_m \cdot \ldots \cdot ⟪A_n⟫_m$ where '$\cdot$' is the monoidal operation in K(m).

The interpretation of formulas with m variables over (Σ, Π) as objects of the monoidal category K(m) is what we need to define the models of a logic program: they are interpretations that satisfy the clauses of the program, in the sense that for each clause with m variables there is an arrow in the category K(m) from the object that interprets the body of the clause to the object that interprets its head.

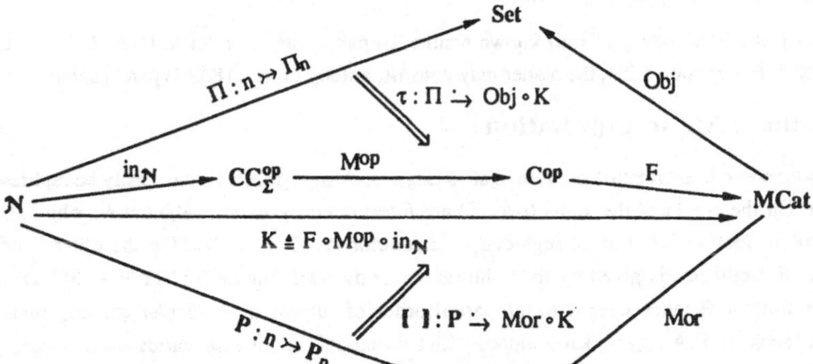

Figure 2 *A model of a logic program P over signature (Σ, Π)*

5.3 Definition *(the category of models of a logic program)*

Let **P** be a logic program over the logic program signature (Σ, Π) (**P** is regarded as a functor as in Convention 5.1). A *model* for **P** is a pair $\mathcal{M} = (I, ⟦\_⟧)$ where

- $I = (M, F, \tau)$ is an interpretation for (Σ, Π)

- Let Mor: **MCat** $\rightarrow$ **Set** be the functor that maps every (small) strict monoidal category to the set of its arrows. Then $[\![\_]\!]$: P $\dashrightarrow$ Mor $\circ$ K is a natural transformation, as depicted in Figure 2. For each n $\in$ $\mathcal{N}$, the component $[\![\_]\!]_n$: $P_n \rightarrow$ Mor(K(n)) of $[\![\_]\!]$ provides the interpretation for the clauses with n variables of P as arrows of the fibre K(n). Such an interpretation must be consistent with the head and the body of the clause: therefore we require that if ($c \equiv H$:- $A_1, \ldots, A_m$) $\in P_n$, then $[\![c]\!]_n$: $\langle\!\langle A_1, \ldots, A_m \rangle\!\rangle_n \rightarrow \langle\!\langle H \rangle\!\rangle_n$.

If $\mathcal{M}$ = (I, $[\![\_]\!]$) and $\mathcal{M}'$ = (I', $[\![\_]\!]'$) are two models for P, a *morphism of models* ϕ: $\mathcal{M} \rightarrow \mathcal{M}'$ is a morphism of interpretations ϕ: I $\rightarrow$ I' such that the interpretation of clauses is preserved, i.e.,

$$[\![\_]\!]' = [\![\_]\!] ; (\mathrm{Mor} \circ \phi \circ in_{\mathcal{N}}).$$

Mod(P) is the category having models for P as objects, and morphisms of models as arrows. ♦

In summary, a model for a logic program P is an indexed monoidal category# F: $C^{op} \rightarrow$ **MCat** where the base is a model of the term signature Σ, equipped with two natural transformations providing the interpretations for the predicates and for the clauses of P.

5.2 Examples of models

In this section we present some possible models of a logic program, concentrating mainly on the part of the interpretation of predicates, i.e., on the functor F: $C^{op} \rightarrow$ **MCat**. Category C should be understood as the universe for terms. The objects of C are possible carriers (domains) of the functional signature Σ, and its morphisms provide a meaning for the operations of Σ. Note that, fixed an interpretation for the term signature M: $CC_\Sigma \rightarrow C$, only the behaviour of F on the subcategory M(CC_Σ) of C would be of interest. Anyway, in the perspective of considering C as a universe for terms, F should provide a general setting for interpreting predicates over every carrier in C, i.e., every possible domain of the interpretation, independently from a chosen M: $CC_\Sigma \rightarrow C$.

This section is just a brief survey of well-known results. In particular, we refer to [MR77, Go79, LS86] for Section 5.2.2. For Section 5.2.3, the reader may consult, among others, [KW71] and [Se84].

5.2.1 Set-theoretic interpretation

The usual set-theoretic interpretation of Horn Clause Logic and logic programs can easily be rephrased in our approach. On the one hand the terms (over Σ) are interpreted by some Σ-algebra A, which, by the considerations in Section 2.1, can be regarded as a functor A: $CC_\Sigma \rightarrow$ **Set**. On the other hand, the interpretation of predicates is given by the contravariant powerset functor $\mathcal{P}$: $\mathbf{Set}^{op} \rightarrow$ **MCat**. More precisely, the functor $\mathcal{P}$ takes a set A to the partial order of subsets of A, ($\mathcal{P}$(A), $\subseteq$), regarded as a category. The category ($\mathcal{P}$(A), $\subseteq$) is then equipped with a monoidal (in this case, cartesian) structure, given by the operation of intersection. A is the monoidal identity in ($\mathcal{P}$(A), $\subseteq$). Given a function f: B $\rightarrow$ A, $\mathcal{P}$(f): $\mathcal{P}$(A) $\rightarrow \mathcal{P}$(B) is defined by taking the inverse image of subsets of A along f. That is, if A' $\subseteq$ A, $\mathcal{P}(f)(A') = f^{-1}(A') \subseteq B$. Note that $\mathcal{P}$(f)(A) = B, and $\mathcal{P}(f)(A' \cap A'') = f^{-1}(A' \cap A'') = f^{-1}(A') \cap f^{-1}(A'') = \mathcal{P}(f)(A') \cap \mathcal{P}(f)(A'')$, proving that $\mathcal{P}$(f) is indeed a monoidal functor.

Therefore the usual set-theoretic interpretation of a predicate symbol p $\in \Pi_n$ as a subset of D^n, is consistent with ours, because for a set-theoretic interpretation (A, $\mathcal{P}$, τ) of (Σ, Π) we require that τ_n(p) is an object in $\mathcal{P}(D^n)$. Suppose now to have an atomic formula $\Phi = p(t_1,\ldots,t_n)$ with free variables in $\langle x_1, \ldots, x_m \rangle$, and let $\sigma = \langle [t_1]_m, \ldots, [t_n]_m \rangle$: $D^m \rightarrow D^n$. The usual set-theoretic interpretation of Φ is the subset of tuples of elements $\langle d_1, \ldots, d_m \rangle \in D^m$, such that $\sigma(d_1, \ldots, d_m) \in \tau_n(p)$. But this is exactly the inverse image of $\tau_n(p)$ along σ, that is, $\mathcal{P}(\sigma)(\tau_n(p))$. In particular, note that Φ is true w.r.t a given interpretation, if and only if $\mathcal{P}(\sigma)(\tau_n(p)) = D^m$.

Given two formulas Φ and Γ with variables in $\langle x_1, \ldots, x_m \rangle$, the interpretation of the conjunction $\Phi \wedge \Gamma$, $⟦\Phi \wedge \Gamma⟧_m$, is just the intersection of the interpretations of Φ and Γ. But we have just chosen intersection as monoidal operation in $(\mathcal{P}(D^m), \subseteq)$, that keeps the consistency between the two interpretations. Finally, a clause $c \equiv H \text{:- } B_1, \ldots, B_n$ with variables in $\langle x_1, \ldots, x_m \rangle$ holds true in a given set-theoretic interpretation, if and only if the interpretation of H is contained in the interpretation of $B_1, \ldots, B_n$. Still, since we have inclusions as morphisms in $(\mathcal{P}(D^m), \subseteq)$, this is equivalent to require the existence of a (necessarily unique) morphism $[c]_m$ from $⟦B_1, \ldots, B_n⟧_m$ to $⟦H⟧_m$.

The Herbrand interpretations and the Herbrand models of a logic program (Definition 1.5) play a relevant role in the classic model-theoretic semantics of logic programs. They can be regarded easily as interpretations and models in our sense, respectively, just constraining the choice of the functors M and F (see Definition 5.2). As expected, the interpretation of predicates must be given by the functor $\mathcal{P}$ just introduced, for the simple reason that Herbrand models are set-theoretic. On the other hand, the terms have to be interpreted in an initial Σ-algebra, accordingly to the definition of Herbrand universe. If T_Σ: $CC_\Sigma \rightarrow$ Set is the functor mapping object '1' of CC_Σ to the initial Σ-algebra (i.e., the term algebra over Σ), then we have that:

- The interpretations of a logic program P over (Σ, Π) of the form $(T_\Sigma, \mathcal{P}, \tau)$ (as in Definition 5.2) are one-to-one with the Herbrand interpretations of P.
- The models of a logic program P over (Σ, Π) of the form $((T_\Sigma, \mathcal{P}, \tau), [\_])$ (as in Definition 5.3) are one-to-one with the Herbrand models of P.

5.2.2 Topos semantics (a)

The set-theoretic semantics of first order logic can be generalized to arbitrary topoi. Formally, a topos is a cartesian closed category with finite limits and subobject classifier. A topos can be considered roughly as a constructive universe of sets and functions; in particular, in an arbitrary topos E it is still possible to define typical set-theoretic notions like subsets and powersets. The correspondent of a subset of a set Z in Topos Theory is a so-called *subobject* of an object Z of E, that is an object X of E and a mono $m \in E[X, Z]$. Subobjects with isomorphic domain are identified (thus, formally, a subobject is an equivalence class of monos up to isomorphism of their sources). Given two subobjects of Z, $m \in E[X, Z]$ and $n \in E[Y, Z]$, we say that $m \subseteq n$ iff there exists an arrow $f \in E[X, Y]$ such that $n \circ f = m$. If such an f exists, it is easy to prove that it is unique, and that it is itself a monic. As a consequence, the collection of subobjects of a fixed object Z is a partial order. This is true in an arbitrary category; the relevant property pertaining to topoi is that these partial orders are in fact Heyting algebras. In particular, the operation of intersection of two subobjects $m \in E[X, Z]$ and $n \in E[Y, Z]$ is given by their pullback, i.e., by their cartesian product local to the slice category E/Z.

The powerset function of the previous example, can then be replaced by a functor **Sub**: $E^{op} \rightarrow$ **MCat** mapping an object A to the collection of its subobjects **Sub**(A). Given an arrow f: A $\rightarrow$ B, **Sub**(f): **Sub**(B) $\rightarrow$ **Sub**(A) is defined by taking the pullback along f of subobjects of B (it is a basic property of Category Theory that pulling back a mono along any morphism gives again a mono). Thus **Sub**(f) is the pulling back functor f^*: E/B $\rightarrow$ E/A, restricted to the monos in E/B (note also that the partial order category

(**Sub**(A), $\subseteq$) is equivalent to the full subcategory of monos in **E**/A). In every category with finite limits, the pullback functor f^*: **E**/B $\rightarrow$ **E**/A has a left adjoint Σ_f: **E**/A $\rightarrow$ **E**/B, that is defined (on objects) as $\Sigma_f(g) = f \circ g$. Since every functor with a left adjoint preserves limits, f^*: **E**/B $\rightarrow$ **E**/A preserves the (local) terminal object and (local) products. Regarding the cartesian structure of (**Sub**(A), $\subseteq$) as monoidal, we have so proved that **Sub**(f) is indeed a monoidal (in fact, cartesian) functor from (**Sub**(B), $\subseteq$) to (**Sub**(A), $\subseteq$).

5.2.3 Topos semantics (b)

In both the previous examples, the monoidal category of each fibre is actually a partial order. This is satisfactory from the point of view of classical semantics, where we are only interested in modelling the notion of provability among formulas. Anyway we could be interested to have a finer vision of the inference process, that leads to provide a non-trivial interpretation for derivations. This is the aim of the so-called 'Heyting semantics' of proofs. The main idea is that a given formula is interpreted as the collection of its proofs. This is achieved in topos theory simply by dropping the requirement that formulas should be monos. Then, the interpretation runs as in the previous case, by replacing the category of subobjects of D^m with the comma category **E**/D^m. In a topos **E**, every comma category is still a topos; in particular, it is cartesian, so we can interpret conjunction via products. From our point of view, the previous interpretation is modelled by taking the contravariant functor **E**/_: **E** $\rightarrow$ **MCat**, mapping every object A to **E**/A (i.e. to the monoidal category underlying the cartesian structure of **E**/A).

The relation between the two topos-theoretic interpretations a) and b) is given by the fact that, for any object A, the inclusion functor i_A: **Sub**(A)$\rightarrow$**E**/A has a left adjoint σ_A (that preserves products). In other words, **Sub**(A) is a reflective subcategory of **E**/A. The proof of this fact relies on one of the main properties of topoi, namely that every arrow f: X $\rightarrow$ A has a unique (up to isomorphisms) epi-mono factorization (see [KW71] for more details).

5.3 Construction of the free model

Let us come back to the methodology of Section 3. In this section we show briefly how it can be applied to logic programs, yielding results very similar to the ones presented for propositional programs. It is interesting to notice that, in spite of the much more complex categorical structure, a logic program can still be regarded as a heterogeneous graph, and its initial model is again obtained as a free internal category in a suitable universe. We introduce the various categories we need, following step by step the methodology introduced in Section 3.

The category $\mathbf{LPStates}_\Sigma$ (corresponding to category **C** of Definition 3.1) of the structures of states for logic programs over a fixed functional signature Σ is $[\mathbf{CC}_\Sigma{}^{op} \rightarrow \mathbf{Mon}]$, i.e., the category of contravariant functors from $\mathbf{CC}_\Sigma$ to **Mon**, with natural transformations as arrows. Intuitively, if $S \in \mathbf{LPStates}_\Sigma$, each monoid S(n) has to be interpreted as a collection of tuples of atomic formulas over at most n variables. The monoidal operation means tupling, while if σ: n $\rightarrow$ m is an arrow of $\mathbf{CC}_\Sigma$, its image through S, S(σ): S(m) $\rightarrow$ S(n), maps each formula with at most m variables to a formula with at most n variables obtained by applying substitution σ to it.

The 'transitions' of a logic program are simply its clauses, i.e., a family of sets indexed by natural numbers, where the set over n includes all clauses with exactly n distinct variables. Thus a possible collection of clauses is simply a functor T: $\mathcal{N} \rightarrow$ **Set**, where, as usual, the set of natural numbers $\mathcal{N}$ is regarded as a discrete category. An arrow from T to T' is a natural transformation $\rho: T \dot{\rightarrow} T'$. Thus the category of structures for transitions of logic programs is $[\mathcal{N} \rightarrow \mathbf{Set}]$: we denote it by **LPTrans** (this corresponds to the category named **B** in Definition 3.1). The following proposition gives us the free adjunction that we need to complete steps 1 and 2 of the methodology.

5.4 Proposition

There is a forgetful functor U: $\mathbf{LPStates}_\Sigma \rightarrow \mathbf{LPTrans}$, with free adjoint F: $\mathbf{LPTrans} \rightarrow \mathbf{LPStates}_\Sigma$.

Proof. If $S: CC_\Sigma{}^{op} \rightarrow \mathbf{Mon}$ is an object of $\mathbf{LPStates}_\Sigma$, $U(S): \mathcal{N} \rightarrow \mathbf{Set}$ is obtained by forgetting the arrows of CC_Σ and the monoidal structure of each S(n). On the other hand, we define F as the composition $F \equiv F'' \circ F'$, with $F': [\mathcal{N} \rightarrow \mathbf{Set}] \rightarrow [CC_\Sigma{}^{op} \rightarrow \mathbf{Set}]$ and $F'': [CC_\Sigma{}^{op} \rightarrow \mathbf{Set}] \rightarrow [CC_\Sigma{}^{op} \rightarrow \mathbf{Mon}]$ given as follows.

F" is the free adjoint to the obvious forgetful functor $U'': [CC_\Sigma{}^{op} \rightarrow \mathbf{Mon}] \rightarrow [CC_\Sigma{}^{op} \rightarrow \mathbf{Set}]$, which can be proved to exists with the same techniques used in the proof of Theorem 2.6, thanks to Proposition 2.4 and Observation 2.7. For F', if $G: \mathcal{N} \rightarrow \mathbf{Set}$, define

- $F'(G)(n) = \{A\sigma \mid A \in G(m), \text{ and } \sigma: n \rightarrow m \text{ in } CC_\Sigma\}$ for each object n of CC_Σ
- $F'(G)(\tau)(A\sigma) = A(\sigma \circ \tau) \in F'(G)(m)$ for each arrow $\tau: m \rightarrow n$ of CC_Σ

It can be shown easily that F' is the left adjoint to $U': [CC_\Sigma{}^{op} \rightarrow \mathbf{Set}] \rightarrow [\mathcal{N} \rightarrow \mathbf{Set}]$. ♦

The existence of the forgetful functor U: $\mathbf{LPStates}_\Sigma \rightarrow \mathbf{LPTrans}$ allows us to complete the first step of Definition 3.1, and to define the category of logic programs over a fixed signature of function symbols Σ, $\mathbf{LogProg}_\Sigma$, as the category of heterogeneous graphs $\mathbf{Graph}(\mathbf{LPTrans}, \mathbf{LPStates}_\Sigma)$.

Given a logic program **P** over signature (Σ, Π), how can we represent it as an object of category $\mathbf{LogProg}_\Sigma$, i.e., as a heterogeneous graph? Quite obviously, if **P** and Π are regarded as functors from $\mathcal{N}$ to Set as in Convention 5.1, then the program is represented by the tuple $\langle F(\Pi), \mathbf{P}, \partial_0, \partial_1 \rangle$, where:

- The collection of states of the graph is given by functor $F(\Pi): CC_\Sigma{}^{op} \rightarrow \mathbf{Mon} \in |\mathbf{LPStates}_\Sigma|$, i.e., the functor freely generated by $\Pi: \mathcal{N} \rightarrow \mathbf{Set}$. In fact, $F(\Pi)$ provides a 'free' interpretations for the formulas over the signature (Σ, Π).
- The collection of transitions is given simply by functor $\mathbf{P}: \mathcal{N} \rightarrow \mathbf{Set} \in |\mathbf{LPTrans}|$.
- By Definition 2.9, ∂_0 and ∂_1 must be two arrows of **LPTrans** (i.e., two natural transformations) ∂_0, $\partial_1: \mathbf{P} \dot{\rightarrow} U(F(\Pi))$. They must map each clause of **P** to the interpretation of its body and of its head, respectively: therefore for each $m \in \mathcal{N}$, their component on m is uniquely determined by the condition: if $(c \equiv H :- A_1, \ldots, A_n) \in \mathbf{P}_m$, then $(\partial_0)_m(c) = ⟪A_1, \ldots, A_n⟫_m$ and $(\partial_1)_m(c) = ⟪H⟫_m$, where $⟪\_⟫_m$ is the interpretation of formulas over m variables presented in Section 5.1.

The left adjoint F: $\mathbf{LPTrans} \rightarrow \mathbf{LPStates}_\Sigma$ (together with the existence of binary coproducts in $\mathbf{LPStates}_\Sigma$) allows us to prove the existence of a free adjoint TS: $\mathbf{Graph}(\mathbf{LPTrans}, \mathbf{LPStates}_\Sigma) \rightarrow \mathbf{RGraph}(\mathbf{LPStates}_\Sigma)$, which maps every logic program to its induced transition system. Finally, by the third step of the methodology, the category of models for logic programs over Σ is automatically individuated as $\mathbf{Cat}(\mathbf{LPStates}_\Sigma)$, i.e., the category of internal categories of $[CC_\Sigma{}^{op} \rightarrow \mathbf{Mon}]$. Furthermore, the free functor C: $\mathbf{RGraph}(\mathbf{LPStates}_\Sigma) \rightarrow \mathbf{Cat}(\mathbf{LPStates}_\Sigma)$ exists thanks to Theorem 2.6, because $[CC_\Sigma^{op} \rightarrow \mathbf{Mon}]$ is essentially algebraic by Observation 2.7. We will denote by *Mod*: $\mathbf{LogProg}_\Sigma \rightarrow \mathbf{Cat}(\mathbf{LPStates}_\Sigma)$ the composite functor $C \circ TS$.

As in the propositional case, the notion of model for logic programs produced by the application of the methodology is perfectly consistent with the definition of model given in Section 5.1, and based of elementary model-theoretic considerations. In fact, by Proposition 2.4 we have:

$$\mathbf{Cat(LPStates_\Sigma)} \equiv \mathbf{Cat([CC_\Sigma{}^{op} \to Mon])} \approx \mathbf{[CC_\Sigma{}^{op} \to Cat(Mon)]} \approx \mathbf{[CC_\Sigma{}^{op} \to MCat]}$$

As expected, a result analogous to Proposition 4.3 holds for logic programs as well.

5.5 Proposition *(the free model of P is initial in Mod(P))*

Let P be a logic program over (Σ, Π), regarded as an object of category $\mathbf{LogProg_\Sigma}$ as described above, and let $\eta_P = (\eta_{P_0}, \eta_{P_1})$: $P \to U'(Mod(P))$ be the component on P of the unit of the free adjunction $\mathbf{Cat(LPStates_\Sigma)}(Mod(\_), \_) \cong \mathbf{LogProg_\Sigma}(\_, U'(\_))$. Then $((Id, Mod(P), U(\eta_{P_0}) \circ \eta_\pi), \eta_{P_1})$ is initial in Mod(P), where Id is the identity of $CC_\Sigma{}^{op}$ and η_π: $\Pi \dashrightarrow U(F(\Pi))$: $\mathcal{N} \to \mathbf{Set}$ is the obvious inclusion.

Proof. As for Proposition 4.3, the statement follows from the observation that the models for P are in bijective correspondence with the arrows in $\mathbf{LogProg_\Sigma}$ from P to U'(M), where M is an object of $\mathbf{Cat(LPStates_\Sigma)}$. ♦

As in the propositional case, we have a correspondence between the refutations of a program P and the arrows of its free model *Mod*(P). We omit here the proofs and give the definitions just in an informal way.

5.6 Proposition *(refutations as arrows of the fibres of Mod(P))*

Let P be a logic program, G be a goal, and $G \overset{\theta}{\Rightarrow}{}^* \Box$ be a (possibly unrestricted) refutation of G in P with computed (possibly correct) answer substitution θ (see Definition 1.3). Moreover, let n be the total number of variables which are not instantiated by that refutation. Then there exists an arrow of the monoidal category *Mod*(P)(n) having as source the unit ε, and as target $⟪G \circ \theta⟫_n$, i.e., the representation of goal $G \circ \theta$. ♦

Not all (unrestricted) refutations (with at most n uninstantiated variables) are represented by distinct arrows of *Mod*(P)(n). For example, two refutations differing just for the order in which two clauses are applied to independent atomic goals are represented by the same arrow, which also represents a 'parallel' refutation where the two clauses are applied concurrently. Moreover, if two unrestricted refutations differ just for the ordering in which some instantiations are performed, then they are equivalent. In the same spirit of Proposition 4.4 for the propositional case, the arrows of each fibre of *Mod*(P) can be put in one-to-one correspondence with equivalence classes of (possibly unrestricted, possibly parallel) refutations, for which a canonical representative exists. A similar result, but in a different formal framework, has been presented in [CM92].

5.7 Theorem *(arrows in the fibres of the free model are most parallel, unrestricted refutations)*

Let G be a goal with variables, and θ be a substitution. Then the arrows of *Mod*(P)(n) from the unit ε to $⟪G \circ \theta⟫_n$ are in one-to-one correspondence with most parallel, most instantiated unrestricted refutations of $G \circ \theta$, with at most n uninstantiated variables. ♦

6 Conclusions and future work

In this paper we presented a simple, although highly formalized approach to the semantics of logic programs based on indexed monoidal categories. Our approach seems to provide a comfortable setting inside which either syntactical extensions of Logic Programming, or interesting refinements of the semantics can be studied. In particular, the separated treatment of the functional and of the logical aspects of a program allows one to consider extensions of the paradigm along either of these two aspects separately.

For example, the functional signature of a program could be interpreted in an algebra including infinite terms as well, where unification without occur-check (as in PROLOG II [Co82]) may have a natural interpretation. Or the interpretation of terms could be extended in order to include functional terms as well, by postulating some closure property for the category which interprets the terms. Or also, one could provide a uniform semantics to Constraint Logic Programming [JL87] in our setting, simply by showing that a 'constraint system' is a suitable model of the term signature.

On the other hand, by taking monoidal *closed* categories (instead of just monoidal) in the fibres, one might give semantics to linear (or intuitionistic) implication. This could provide an interesting framework inside which to develop the semantics of generalizations of logic programming in the direction of the higher-order features of λ-Prolog [NM88, NM90]. All these extensions are topics for future research.

A different aspect of our proposal that should be investigated more in depth is the compositionality of the construction of the free model of a program. Since this construction is defined as a left adjoint functor *Mod* from the category of logic programs to the category of models, by general properties of left adjoint functors it preserves all colimits. It would be interesting to study which kind of (non-trivial) operations on logic programs can be defined as colimit constructions in the category of programs. An example of such an operation is the composition of *open logic programs* [BGLM92], which are programs where a specific subset of the predicate symbols is considered as 'partially defined': their definition can be extended or refined by another program. It should be reasonably easy to model this form of composition as a pushout in the category of logic programs: in this case the construction of the free model is automatically compositional w.r.t. this operation.

Finally, it must be stressed that there is an aspect of our semantical approach that is not completely satisfactory. In fact, by incorporating the matching rule (i.e., the unification) into the structure of transitions (i.e., by generating the structured transition system induced by the program), we loose some interesting information about the operational behaviour of the program, namely when and how the variables of a goal are instantiated during a refutation. In fact, since all the computations have a fixed number of variables which cannot be instantiated, this is equivalent to say that all the variables of the goal are instantiated once and for all before the beginning of the refutation.

Actually, we would like to have a sort of *generalized composition* for handling unification dynamically. Our proposal of using indexed categories seems to be quite promising from this respect. Let $F: C^{op} \to MCat$, and suppose to have two arrows $\sigma: A \to D$ and $\tau: A \to E$ in the base category C. Then we can say that two arrows in different fibres $f \in F(D)_{mor}$ and $g \in F(E)_{mor}$ are *(σ, τ)-composable* if and only if $F(\sigma)(f)$ and $F(\tau)(g)$ are composable in F(A). Intuitively, we can 'instantiate' the two arrows through $F(\sigma)$ and $F(\tau)$, respectively, in order to reduce them to the same fibre, where they can be composed using the local composition. Of course, it would be interesting to turn this operation of composition into a natural transformation between two suitable functors, and we are actually working in this direction (note that this approach does not rely on the existence of mgu's, which would guarantee nice additional properties for this generalized composition operation).

7 References

[AL91] A. Asperti, G.Longo, *Categories, Types and Structures, an Introduction to Category Theory for the Working Computer Scientist*, Foundations of Computing Series (MIT Press, Cambridge, MA, 1991).

[AM89] A. Asperti, S. Martini, *Projections instead of variables, A category theoretic interpretation of logic programs*, Proc. 6th Int. Conf. on Logic Programming, MIT Press, 1989, pp. 337-352.

[AM92] A. Asperti, S. Martini, *Categorical Models of Polymorphism*, Information and Computation, **99** (1), 1992, pp. 1-79.

[BE73] A. Bastiani, C. Ehresmann, *Categories of sketched structures*, Cahiers de Topologie et Géometrie Différentielle, **13**, 1973, pp. 1-105.

[Be75] D.B. Benson, *The Basic Algebraic Structures in Categories of Derivations*, Information and Control, **28** (1), 1975, pp. 1-29.

[BGLM92] A. Bossi, M. Gabbrielli, G. Levi, and M. C. Meo, *Contributions to the Semantics of Open Logic Programs*, in Proceedings of the International Conference on Fifth Generation Computer Systems 1992, pp. 570-580.

[BW85] M. Barr, C. Wells, *Toposes, Triples and Theories*, Grundlehren der mathematischen Wissenschaften 278, Springer Verlag, 1985.

[BW90] M. Barr, C. Wells, *Category Theory for Computing Science*, Prentice Hall, 1990.

[CM90a] A. Corradini, U. Montanari, *Towards a Process Semantics in the Logic Programming Style*, in Proc. 7th Symposium on Theoretical Aspects of Computer Science (STACS '90), LNCS 415, 1990, pp. 95-108.

[CM90b] A. Corradini, U. Montanari, *An Algebraic Semantics of Logic Programs as Structured Transition Systems*, in Proc. of the North American Conference on Logic Programming (NACLP '90), MIT Press, 1990.

[CM92] A. Corradini, U. Montanari, *An Algebraic Semantics for Structured Transition Systems and its Application to Logic Programs*, Theoretical Computer Science, **103**, 1992, pp. 51-106.

[Co82] A. Colmerauer, *PROLOG II - Reference Manual and Theoretical Model*, Internal Report, Groupe Intelligence Artificielle, Université Aix-Marseille II, October 1982.

[Co90] A. Corradini, *An Algebraic Semantics for Transition Systems and Logic Programming*, Ph.D. Thesis TD-8/90, Dipartimento di Informatica, Università di Pisa, March '90.

[Go79] R. Goldblatt, *Topoi. The Categorical Analysis of Logic*, Studies in Logic and the Foundations of Mathematics, 98, North-Holland, Amsterdam. 1979.

[Gr89] J. W. Gray, *The Category of Sketches as a Model for Algebraic Semantics*, Contemporary Mathematics, **92**, 1989, pp. 109-135.

[JL87] Jaffar, J., Lassez, J.-L., *Constraint Logic Programming*, Proc. 12th ACM Symp. on Principles of Programming Languages, pp. 111-119, 1987.

[Ke76] R. Keller, *Formal Verification of Parallel Programs*, Com. ACM, 7, 1976, pp. 371-384.

[KW71] A. Kock, G.C. Wraith, *Elementary Toposes*, Aarhus Universitet, Matematisk Institut, Lecture Notes 30, September 1971.

[La63] F. W. Lawvere, *Functorial semantics of algebraic theories*, Proc. National Academy of Sciences, U.S.A., 50, 1963, pp. 869-872. Summary of Ph.D. Thesis, Columbia University.

[Ll87] J.W. Lloyd, *Foundations of Logic Programming*, Springer Verlag, 1984, (2nd Edition 1987).

[LS86] J. Lambek, P.J. Scott, *Introduction to Higher-Order Categorical Logic*, Cambridge University Press. 1986.

[ML71] S. Mac Lane, *Categories for the Working Mathematician*, Springer Verlag, New York, 1971.

[MM90] J. Meseguer, U. Montanari, *Petri Nets are Monoids*, Information and Computation, 88 (2), 1990, 105-155.

[MR77] M. Makkai, G.E. Reyes, *First Order Categorical Logic*, Lecture Notes in Mathematics 611, 1977.

[NM88] G. Nadathur, D. Miller, *An overview of λProlog*, Proc. of the Fifth Int. Conf. on Logic Programming, MIT Press, 1988, pp. 810-827.

[NM90] G. Nadathur, D. Miller, *Higher-Order Horn Clauses*, Journal of the ACM, 37 (4), 1990, pp. 777-814.

[P181] G. Plotkin, *A Structural Approach to Operational Semantics*, Technical Report DAIMI FN-19, Aarhus University, Department of Computer Science, Aarhus, 1981.

[Re84] J. Reynolds, *Polymorphism is not set-theoretic*, Symposium on Semantics of Data Types; Khan, MacQueen, Plotkin eds., LNCS 173, Springer-Verlag, 1984.

[Sh67] Shoenfield, J.R., *Mathematical logic*. Addison-Wesley Publishing Company, Reading, Massachusetts, 1967.

[Se77] R.A.G. Seely, *Hyperdoctrines and Natural Deduction*, Ph.D. Thesis, University of Cambridge, 1977.

[Se83] R.A.G. Seely, *Hyperdoctrines, Natural Deduction and the Beck Condition*, Zeitschrift für Math. Logik Grundlagen der Math., 29, 1983, pp. 505-542.

[Se84] R.A.G. Seely, *Locally cartesian closed categories and type theories*, Math. Proc. Camb. Phil. Soc. 95, 1984, pp. 33-48.

Appendix: A summary of basic definitions of Category Theory

A *(small) category* C is a tuple $C = \langle O, A, \partial_0, \partial_1, id, \circ \rangle$ where O is a set of *objects*, A is a set of *arrows*, $\partial_0, \partial_1: A \to O$ are functions associating to each arrow its *source* and its *target* object, respectively (we write $f: u \to v$ if $\partial_0(f) = u$ and $\partial_1(f) = v$), $id: O \to A$ maps each objects to its *identity arrow*, and $\_\circ\_ : A \times A \to A$ is a partial function of *composition* of arrows, such that $f \circ g$ is defined iff $\partial_0(f) = \partial_1(g)$. Moreover, the following axioms must be satisfied: (1) $\partial_0(id(u)) = u = \partial_1(id(u))$; (2) $(f \circ g) \circ h = f \circ (g \circ h)$; (3) $f \circ id(u) = f = id(v) \circ f$, if $f{:}u \to v$.

Let $C = \langle O, A, \partial_0, \partial_1, id, \circ \rangle$ be a category. Then its *dual category* is $C^{op} = \langle O, A, \partial_1, \partial_0, id, \circ' \rangle$, where $f \circ' g = g \circ f$. The *underlying graph* and the *underlying reflexive graph* of C are $\langle O, A, \partial_0, \partial_1 \rangle$ and $\langle O, A, \partial_0, \partial_1, id \rangle$, respectively.

Given two categories $C = \langle O, A, \partial_0, \partial_1, id, \circ \rangle$ and $C' = \langle O', A', \partial'_0, \partial'_1, id', \circ' \rangle$, a *functor* $F: C \to C'$ is a pair of functions $\langle F_O: O \to O', F_A: A \to A' \rangle$ such that $F_O(\partial_i(f)) = \partial'_i(F_A(f))$ for $i = 0, 1$, $F_A(id(u)) = id'(F_O(u))$, and $F_A(f \circ g) = F_A(f) \circ' F_A(g)$. The category having all small categories as objects and functors as arrows is denoted by Cat.

If C and C' are as above and $F, G: C \to C'$ are two functors, then a *natural transformation* $\tau: F \to; G$ is a family of arrows of C' $\{\tau_u \mid u \in O\}$ indexed by the objects of C, such that for every arrow $f: u \to v$ in C, $\tau_v \circ F_A(f) = G_A(f) \circ \tau_u$. The same definition applies if C is a graph, and F, G are graph morphisms to the underlying graph of C'.

A *strict monoidal category* M is a triple ‹C, ε, ⊗›, where C is a category, ⊗: C × C → C is an associative bifunctor (i.e., a pair of monoidal operations ‹$\otimes_O$, $\otimes_A$› defined on objects and arrows, respectively, which preserve the categorical structure), and ε is an object of C which is the unit for $\otimes_O$ and such that id(ε) is the unit for $\otimes_A$. A *monoidal category* is defined similarly, but the bifunctor is required to be associative (and ε is the unit) just up to a natural isomorphism (this makes the definition a bit more complex, see [ML71]). A *monoidal functor* is a functor between two monoidal categories which commutes with the associated bifunctors. The category of (small) monoidal categories and monoidal functors is denoted by **MCat**.

A *cartesian category* is a monoidal category ‹C, 1, ×› equipped with *projections* (i.e., arrows $\pi_{u,v}$: u×v → u and $\pi'_{u,v}$: u×v → v for each pair of objects u and v of C), such that for each pair of arrows ‹f: w → u, g: w → v› there exists a unique arrow denoted ‹f,g›: w → u×v satisfying $\pi_{u,v}$∘‹f, g› = f and $\pi'_{u,v}$∘‹f, g› = g. Moreover, **1** is a *terminal object* (i.e., there exists exactly one arrows from every object of C to **1**), and × is called the *(categorical) product*. A *cartesian functor* is a functor between cartesian categories which preserves the product, the terminal object and the projections (up to a natural isomorphisms).

A *diagram* in a category C is just a sub-graph of the underlying graph of C. A *cone* in C with an object u as *vertex* and a diagram D as *base* is a family of arrows of C from u to all the objects in D, such that all the resulting triangles commute. A cone in C with base D and vertex u is a *limit cone* if for each other cone with the same base and vertex v there exists a unique arrow from v to u such that all the resulting triangles commute.

An *indexed category* is a functor F: C^{op} → **Cat**. Thus F maps each object u of C to a small category F(u), and each arrow f: u → v of C to a functor F(f): F(v) → F(u). An *indexed monoidal category* is a functor M: C^{op} → **MCat**, associating to each object and arrow of C a monoidal category and a monoidal functor, respectively.

A categorical view of process refinement

P. Degano[1,2]
R. Gorrieri[3]
G. Rosolini[2]

[1] Dipartimento di Informatica
Corso Italia 40
56100 Pisa, Italy

[2] Dipartimento di Matematica
via D'Azeglio 85A
43100 Parma, Italy

[3] Dipartimento di Matematica
Porta S. Donato 5
40127 Bologna, Italy

ABSTRACT: **A very general notion of refinement of event structures is presented that refines both the events and the relations of causality and conflict. It is based on a purely semantic construction based on sections of a functor between domain-like categories. The present construction is compared to others in the literature.**

Keywords: ***Hierarchical specifications, concurrent programs, categories, true concurrency, event structures.***

Contents

Introduction

The idea of considering modular representations of concurrent processes has the obvious intention of reducing the complexity of specific programs. Indeed refinement of concurrent processes has already appeared in the literature, cf. [8]. There are now two main lines of approach to set up a discipline for the specification, the design and the verification of concurrent processes: one takes the algebraic, linguistic point of view where a new operator of *action refinement* is added to the usual operators of Process Description Languages, *e.g.* extensions of CCS-like languages as in [1, 10, 9, 15], enrichment of event structures and causal trees as in [6, 18, 19]. The other considers processes as collections of (guarded) actions with no additional structure, and actions are freely transformed into more detailed processes, *e.g.* refinement of action systems [4, 2], communication closed layers [12, 13, 17], and concurrent database transactions [3].

A first synthesis of the approaches mentioned above is in [14] where the collections of actions are endowed with an algebraic structure by means of a process description language. Essentially its (linear time, truly concurrent) denotational semantics maps a process to a set of partial orderings of events. These represent process activities, and they are partially ordered by relative *causality*. The language has also a non-standard operator of sequentialization and the semantics of sequentialization between two actions states that (part of) the refinement of the second action may occur before the execution of the first is completed.

The present paper continues the investigation on those lines, starting with branching time, truly concurrent models for Process Description Languages—the event structures of [20]. A set of *events* comes equipped with two binary relations of *causality* (an order usually denoted as $\leq$) and of *conflict* (an irreflexive symmetric relation persistent w.r.t. the order, usually written as $\sharp$). The intuition is that when $\alpha \sharp \beta$ at most one of the two can occur in the same execution, and that two events are concurrent if they are neither in the causal relation nor in conflict. On these structures we propose a notion of refinement where an event structure $\mathcal{E}'$ is substituted for an event α of another structure $\mathcal{E}$. It is more liberal than similar proposals as in [6, 18, 9], in that we allow also the relations of causality and conflict that involve α to be refined.

It is worth noting that, while the operations of refinement presented in [1, 6, 10, 9, 18, 15] preserve, in some algebraic sense, the two basic relations, the notion presented in this paper does not distribute in general over $\leq$ or $\sharp$. In fact it is a more general construction than the others; but the basic construction from category theory involved in building the semantic domains is rather simple, and we believe it deserves further attention.

The basic construction considers the data of a refinement as a domain D (of configurations of an event structure) and a functor $F: D \to \mathsf{Dom}$ from the order category D into some category of domains (to be specified later). The values of F on the elements (= objects) of D are the replacement domains and the values of F on arrows $x \leq y$ in D describe how to refine the relations of causality and conflict. With these data one can consider a fibration $\sum F \to D$; the category of sections turns out to be a poset, actually a domain under mild assumption on F.

The construction proposed in the paper implements a purely semantic notion of refinement. As mentioned above, it is a conservative extension of analogous proposals in [6, 9, 18], as these notions correspond to the case when the relations of causality and conflict are preserved under refinement (in a sense specified in section 3). Beside the notion proposed in [14] is a particular case of that presented here when the event structure is *deterministic*, *i.e.* $\# = \emptyset$.

We have completely neglected here the issue of defining a process description language apt to express the power of the broad notion of refinement we suggest. A straightforward definition of the denotational semantics should be easy, but a definition of an operation semantics appears to be much more difficult.

1 Domains and event structures

This section is a brief survey of the basic notions about Scott domains and event structures which will be used in the sequel. It can safely be skipped by an acquainted reader; for more details see [20].

A poset $(P, \leq)$—or simply P discarding mention of the order relation—is a *Scott domain* (often simply a *domain*) if

(i) sups of directed subsets always exist in P, (complete)

(ii) sups of bounded subsets always exist in P, (consistent)

(iii) every element is the sup of the finite elements below it, (algebraic)

where we recall that an element $e \in P$ is *finite* (or *compact*) when

$$\text{if } e \leq \bigvee D \text{ and } D \text{ is directed, then } e \leq x \text{ for some } x \in D.$$

One can see that, under (i), condition (ii) can be requested only for doublets: if two elements have a common upper bound, or shortly they are *compatible*, then they have a least upper bound. Moreover the sup of two finite elements, if it exists, is again finite, thus the sup in (iii) is always directed.

A map $f: D \to D'$ between Scott domains is *continuous* if it preserves sups of directed subsets. One can thus say that the continuous function between Scott domains is completely determined by its values on the finite elements of D as

$$f(x) = \bigvee\{f(e) : e \leq x, e \text{ finite}\}.$$

The category **Dom** has Scott domains as objects and continuous functions between them as arrows. We shall be using a subcategory of **Dom** consisting of those maps that preserve finiteness and binary sups, and will denote it as $\mathbf{Dom}_r$. Note that a map in $\mathbf{Dom}_r$ preserves all existing sups, and is therefore strict.

It will be useful for the sequel to notice that every poset P gives rise to a category where the objects are the elements of the poset and there is exactly one arrow from x to y if $x \leq y$. A monotone map between posets corresponds precisely to a functor between the posetal categories. In particular, a domain can be seen as a category.

The other concept we recall from the literature is that of an event structure, cf. [20]. They form a well-studied semantics for true concurrency in the general branching-time approach. An *event structure* $\mathcal{E} = (E, \leq, \#)$ consists of a poset $(E, \leq)$ and an irreflexive relation $\#$ of *conflict* which is disjoint from $\leq$ and such that

(i) $\{e' : e' \leq e\}$ is finite for every $e \in E$, (finitely preceded)

(ii) if $e \# e' \leq e''$, then $e \# e''$, for every $e, e', e'' \in E$. (hereditary)

One usually calls *events* the elements of the event structure $\mathcal{E}$ and says that two events are *concurrent* if they are not related in either relation.

Finally a subset $X \subset E$ is a *configuration* when it satisfies the following conditions:

- if whenever $e \leq e' \in X$, then also $e \in X$, (left closed)
- if $(X \times X) \cap \sharp = \emptyset$. (conflict-free)

$\mathrm{Conf}(\mathcal{E})$ denotes the set of configurations of $\mathcal{E}$. When ordered by inclusion, $\mathrm{Conf}(\mathcal{E})$ is a Scott domain. It also has sups of subsets whose elements are pairwise bounded (such a domain is said to be *coherent*).

Moreover, since a *principal* configuration $e^{\downarrow} = \{e' : e' \leq e\}$ is contained in another configuration X if and only if $e \in X$, every configuration is the union (= sup in $\mathrm{Conf}(\mathcal{E})$) of the principal configurations contained in it. The principal configurations $e^{\downarrow}$ are the *prime* elements of the domain $\mathrm{Conf}(\mathcal{E})$, where an element of a poset is (*completely*) *prime* when for any subset S which has a least upper bound

$$\text{if } e \leq \bigvee S, \text{ then } e \leq x \text{ for some } x \in S.$$

A domain where every element is the sup of the prime elements below it is said *prime algebraic.*

Finally a finite element in the domain $\mathrm{Conf}(\mathcal{E})$ has only finitely many elements below it. A domain with this property is said *finitary.*

We are now in a position to state the representation theorem for event structures, cf. [16].

1.1 Theorem *If $\mathcal{E}$ is an event structure, then* $\mathrm{Conf}(\mathcal{E})$ *is a finitary, coherent, prime algebraic Scott domain. Moreover any domain D which is finitary, coherent, prime algebraic is of the form* $\mathrm{Conf}(\mathcal{E})$ *for some event structure $\mathcal{E}$.*

The event structure $\mathcal{E}$ mentioned in the statement above is built on the set of prime elements of D, with the induced order and with the conflict relation defined by

$$p \,\sharp\, q \text{ if } \nexists x \in D. p \leq x \text{ and } q \leq x.$$

2 The category-theoretic construction

The construction we intend to use is not new in domain theory, a particular instance of it appeared in [5] and was used to explain the properties of the category of domains which provide a model of polymorphism. We refer the reader to that paper for more information about it.

2.1 Definition Let C and D be small categories (= category with a *set* of objects). A functor $P: \mathsf{D} \to \mathsf{C}$ is a *refinement* if it satisfies the following properties:

(i) for every object c in C, its inverse image category

$$P^{-1}(c) = \{f : x \to y \mid P(f) = \mathrm{id}_c\} \subset \mathsf{D}$$

is a Scott domain,

(ii) for every object c in C, the joins computed in $P^{-1}(c)$ are colimits in D,

(iii) for every finite element e and every $f: e \to x$ in D there is a map $g: e \to e'$ such that

$$P(f) = P(g), \qquad P(e' \to x) = \mathrm{id}_{Px}, \qquad f = e \xrightarrow{g} e' \to x$$

and e' is least in $P^{-1}(P(x))$ with these properties.

The following is obvious, but necessary.

2.2 Proposition *Suppose $P: \mathsf{D} \to \mathsf{C}$ and $P': \mathsf{E} \to \mathsf{D}$ are refinements, and suppose moreover that E is posetal with directed joins, and P preserves them. Then their composite $P \circ P': \mathsf{E} \to \mathsf{C}$ is a refinement.*

We say that a functor $\sigma: \mathsf{C} \to \mathsf{D}$ is a *section of P* if

$$P \circ \sigma = \mathrm{id}_{\mathsf{C}}.$$

Let $\prod P$ be the poset on the set of sections of P with the pointwise order. Note that $\prod P$ has sups of directed subsets which are computed pointwise.

2.3 Theorem *Suppose $P: \mathsf{D} \to \mathsf{C}$ is a refinement functor and satisfies the following* finiteness *condition*

(i) *for every c, x in C the hom-set $\mathsf{C}(x, c)$ is finite,*

If the poset $\prod P$ has a bottom element, then it is a Scott domain.

The main intuition about the construction and the theorem we shall peruse in the paper is the following. Take an event structure as the base category C. Construct the category D over C by putting over each event c in C the domain of configurations of the event structure which we intend to substitute for the given event c in C. The maps connecting events from one structure to another are put in according to the specifications one is after.

A very particular instance is when C is the posetal category of finite elements of a domain D and D is the poset $\mathsf{C} \times E$ where E is another domain. Take the first projection as the functor $P: \mathsf{D} \to \mathsf{C}$. Then $\prod P$ is (isomorphic to) the continuous function space $[D \to E]$.

The leading instance of 2.3 is that constructed from a functor $F: \mathsf{C} \to \mathbf{Dom}$ into the category of Scott domains and continuous maps. From this build the *fibration* $\sum F$ associated with F: the objects are pairs $\langle c, x \rangle$ where c is an object in C and $x \in Fc$. A map $\langle f, k \rangle: \langle c, x \rangle \to \langle c', x' \rangle$ where $f: c \to c'$ in C and $k: Ff(x) \leq x'$ denotes the order in $F(c')$. The set $\sum F$ is ordered pointwise, thus has pointwise sups of directed subsets, but in general one cannot expect that $\sum F$ be a domain. There is an obvious projection functor $P_F: \sum F \to \mathsf{C}$. By definition P_F satisfies condition 2.1(i). As for condition 2.1(ii), this is equivalent to assuming that Ff preserve finite elements for every arrow F in C. Condition 2.1(iii) is ensured by requiring that the maps Ff preserve existing finite joins, in other words the functor is defined as $F: \mathsf{C} \to \mathbf{Dom}_r$.

2.4 Remark A way to justify the assumptions on F is to consider it as an ordered presheaf (on C^{op}). One sees that the required continuity for the restriction maps need not entail that, as an object of the topos $\mathcal{S}et^{\mathsf{C}}$, it has directed joins. In fact, one can only reduce consideration to the *finite* elements of the poset. Then one can generate a domain from these as usual: the result would be the presheaf of *local* sections. At each point c in

C one should consider directed joins of finite elements which have appeared up to c, but also directed joins which may increase as one moves on from c. The following statements can be read as describing properties of F inside the topos of presheaves.

2.5 Corollary *Suppose* C *is a category with finite hom-sets,* $F: \mathsf{C} \to \mathsf{Dom}_r$ *is a functor such that for every arrow* f *in* C *the function* $F(f)$ *takes finite elements to finite elements. Let* $P_F: \sum F \to \mathsf{C}$ *be the functor constructed above. Then the poset* $\prod P_F$ *is a domain.*

The particular case we are interested in is when the category C is a poset. A list of statements about domains constructed using the operator $\prod$ follows. We shall pursue a possible intuition about them in the next sections. In the posetal case we can extend the previous theorem to prime algebraic domains under some obvious added hypotheses.

2.6 Theorem *Suppose* $P: \mathsf{D} \to \mathsf{C}$ *is such that*

(i) *the category* C *is posetal,*

(ii) *for every object* c *in* C*, its inverse image category*

$$P^{-1}(c) = \{f: x \to y \mid P(f) = \mathrm{id}_c\} \subset \mathsf{D}$$

is a prime algebraic domain,

(iii) *for every object* c *in* C*, the joins computed in* $P^{-1}(c)$ *are colimits in* D*,*

(iv) *for every prime element* p *and every* $f: p \to x$ *in* D *there is a map* $g: p \to p'$ *such that* $P(f) = P(g)$ *and* $p' \to x$ *in* $P^{-1}(P(x))$ *and* p' *is least with these properties.*

If the domain of sections $\prod P$ *has a bottom element, then it is prime algebraic.*

As a corollary of this we obtain a result similar to 2.5. Let PDom_r be the full subcategory of Dom_r on the prime algebraic domains.

2.7 Corollary *Suppose* C *is a posetal category,* $F: \mathsf{C} \to \mathsf{PDom}_r$ *is a such that for every arrow* f *in* C *the function* $F(f)$ *takes prime elements to prime elements. Let* $P_F: \sum F \to \mathsf{C}$ *be the projection functor of the fibration associated to* F*. Then the domain* $\prod P_F$ *is prime algebraic.*

Although we shall not use it we state also a result about meet- preserving sections.

2.8 Proposition *Suppose* $P: \mathsf{D} \to \mathsf{C}$ *is a refinement and that* C *is a poset with finite meets and all the domains* $P^{-1}(c)$ *have meets which distribute over finite joins. Then the subset of* $\prod P$ *which consists of those sections* σ *such that*

$$\sigma(c \wedge d) = \sigma c \wedge \sigma d, \qquad c, d \in \mathsf{C}$$

is a Scott domain.

Finally, it is useful for our presentation purposes to describe source categories D in succinct terms. It is clear that 2.5 is a very particular case of 2.3. In particular, we want to describe a generalisation of 2.5 where the connecting morphisms $F(d \leq d'): Fd \to Fd'$ are merely continuous relations R which determine continuous functions when corestricted to downward segments, *i.e.* satisfying the following

1. if $x\,R\,x'$, $y\,R\,y'$, $x \leq y$ and x' and y' are compatible, then $x' \leq y'$,
2. if $\{x_i : i \in I\}$ is directed, $x_i\ R\ x'_i$, for every $i \in I$, and the x'_i's are pairwise compatible, then $\bigvee_i x_i\ R\ \bigvee_i x'_i$.

3. if $x\ R\ x'$, $y\ R\ y'$, x and y are compatible, and x' and y' are compatible, then $(x \sqcup y)\ R\ (x' \sqcup y')$,
4. if $x\ R\ x'$ and x is finite, then x' is finite.

Note that if $x\ R\ x'$ and $x\ R\ y'$, then x' and y' are either equal or not compatible. The category of domains and continuous relations form a category Rel_r.

One defines the category $\sum R$ in much a similar way as before: given a functor $R\colon \mathsf{C} \to \mathsf{Rel}_r$ (whose action on arrows we will denote as R_f), the objects of $\sum R$ are pairs $\langle c, x\rangle$ where c is an object in C and $x \in Fc$. A map $f\colon \langle c, x\rangle \to \langle c', x'\rangle$ is a map $f\colon c \to c'$ in C such that there is a (necessarily unique) $x"$ with

$$x\ R_f\ x" \leq x'.$$

The projection functor $P_R\colon \sum R \to \mathsf{C}$ is defined as before.

2.9 Theorem *Given a functor $R\colon \mathsf{C} \to \mathsf{Rel}_r$, the poset $\prod P_R$ is a Scott domain. Moreover, in case the category C is posetal, and the relations R_f always relate prime elements to prime elements, then the domain $\prod P_R$ is prime algebraic.*

3 Event refinement as a functor

We apply the results of the previous section to obtain a semantic operation of refinement. The event structure E to be refined takes the place of the category C: the events are the objects of C and the causal relation determines the arrows. The relation of conflict deserves particular care, and for the sake of simplicity we shall look first at conflict-free event structures, then move to the general case.The refinement is represented by a functor F defined on C taking values in an appropriate category of domains (of configurations). The resulting domain $\prod P_F$ is the domain of configurations of the refined event structure. We shall present a few examples which will illustrate the semantic action of refinement.

3.1 Example Given an event structure $(E, \leq, \sharp)$, consider the category C to be the opposite of the posetal category on E. So the objects are the events of $\mathcal{E}$ and there is an arrow $x \to y$ exactly when $y \leq x$. The functor T takes constantly value $2 = \{\bot, \top\} = \mathrm{Conf}(1)$ on objects and id_2 on arrows. The domain of sections of $\sum T$ is then all the downward closed subsets of E. If $\sharp = \emptyset$, then it trivially is the domain of configurations of the event structure $\mathcal{E}$.

3.2 Example (preserving causality) Consider the event structure $\mathcal{E}$ with events $\{\alpha, \beta, \gamma\}$ and the event structure $\mathcal{B}$ with events $\{\zeta, \rho, \tau\}$ ordered as follows

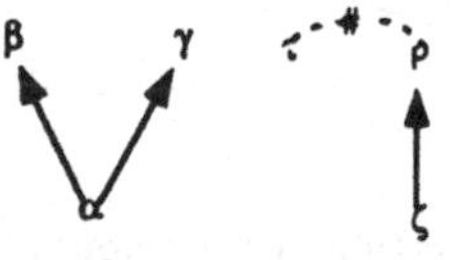

where $\tau \ \sharp\ \rho$. The event β will be replaced by $\mathcal{B}$ *preserving the causal relation* in the sense that *every* event in $\mathcal{B}$ needs to await α to be activated. Again let the base category C be the opposite of the posetal category on E, and the functor F acts on objects by sending any event x not to be refined to the domain of configuration on the trivial event structure

Conf($\{x\}$) $\cong$ 2, and the only event to be refined β to the domain of configurations Conf($\mathcal{B}$) of the event structure $\mathcal{B}$. The functor then acts obviously on all arrows of C but for $\beta \rightarrow \alpha$:

$$\begin{array}{rccl} F(\beta \geq \alpha)\colon & \mathrm{Conf}(\mathcal{B}) & \longrightarrow & \mathrm{Conf}(\{\alpha\}) \\ & \bot & \longmapsto & \bot = \emptyset \\ & \{\tau\} & \longmapsto & \top = \{\alpha\} \\ & \{\zeta\} & \longmapsto & \top \\ & \{\tau,\zeta\} & \longmapsto & \top \\ & \{\zeta,\rho\} & \longmapsto & \top. \end{array}$$

Note that the requirements F must satisfy in order to verify the hypotheses of 2.5 force all the lines of the definition of the function $F(\beta \geq \alpha)$ but the second and the third. A pictorial representation of the action of the functor is given below

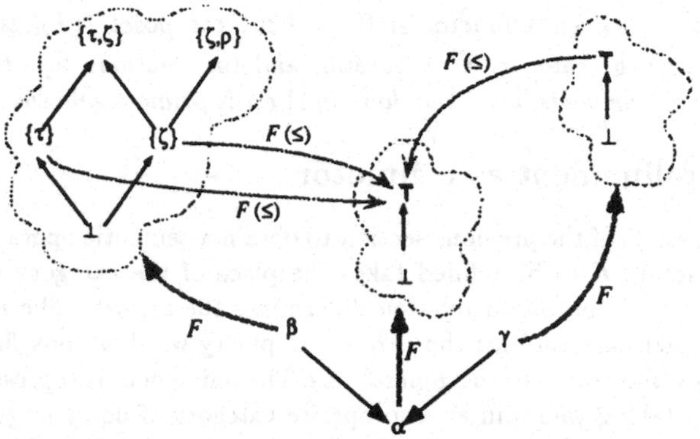

The domain $\prod P_F$ obtained from it is drawn below with its the prime elements marked, and the event structure related to it via the representation theorem 1.1 is on the right-hand side.

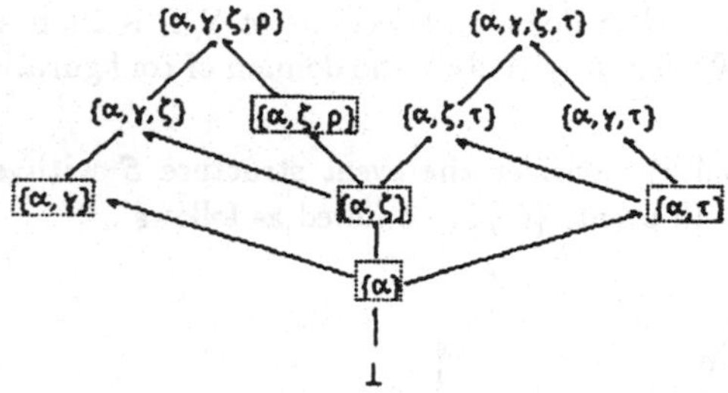

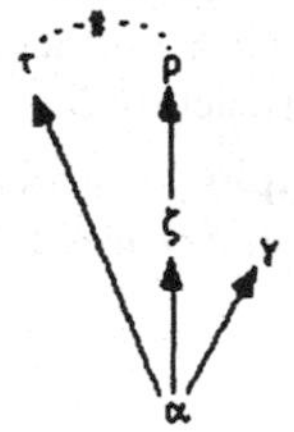

In the picture we have denoted a section by listing only the elements of those configurations which are not $\bot$. More precisely, the section σ is denoted by listing the elements of all the configurations X such that $\sigma(x) = \langle x, X\rangle \neq \bot$ as x varies in $\mathcal{E}$ (we tacitly assume that the event structures involved have disjoint sets of events).

3.3 Example Consider again $\mathcal{E}$ and $\mathcal{B}$ as in 3.2, with $\mathcal{B}$ substituting in for β, but a different functor F' with

$$\begin{array}{rccc} F'(\beta \geq \alpha): & \mathrm{Conf}(\mathcal{B}) & \longrightarrow & \mathrm{Conf}(\{\alpha\}) \\ & \{\tau\} & \longmapsto & \bot \\ & \{\zeta\} & \longmapsto & \top \end{array}$$

(we have discarded the inessential information about F' this time). The domain of sections $\prod P_{F'}$ is shown below with the event structure represented by it on the side:

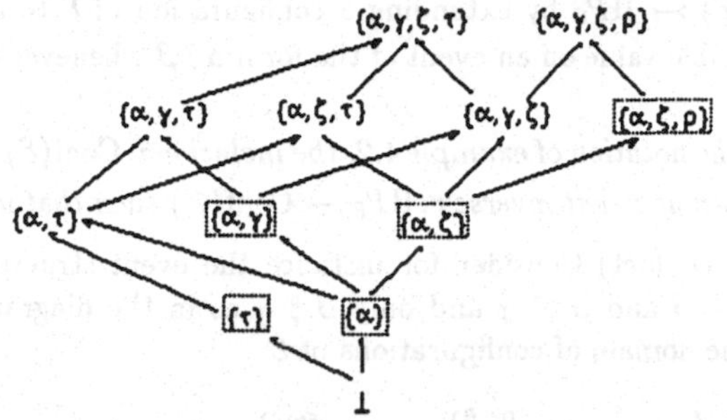

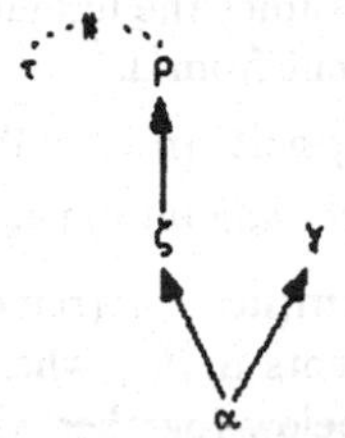

The next example is an application of 2.9. The particular choice of the functor originates a *deadlock* as an event that was enabled to fire before the refinement is no longer enabled after it.

3.4 Example (originating a deadlock) Take the event structure $\mathcal{E}$ of the previous examples: we shall refine event α using an event structure $\mathcal{A}$ of *pure conflict*: $\mathcal{A}$ consists of two events $\{\eta, \mu\}$ related only in $\#$. The functor R takes β and γ to 2 and takes α to $\mathrm{Conf}(\mathcal{A})$. Its non-trivial action on arrows is defined as follows (denoting a relation in the form of a multi-valued function)

$$\begin{array}{rccc} R(\beta \geq \alpha): & \mathrm{Conf}(\{\beta\}) & \longrightarrow & \mathrm{Conf}(\mathcal{A}) \\ & \{\beta\} & \longmapsto & \{\eta\} \\ R(\beta \geq \alpha): & \mathrm{Conf}(\{\gamma\}) & \longrightarrow & \mathrm{Conf}(\mathcal{A}) \\ & \{\gamma\} & \longmapsto & \{\eta\}, \{\mu\}. \end{array}$$

The domain of configurations $\prod P_R$ is the following

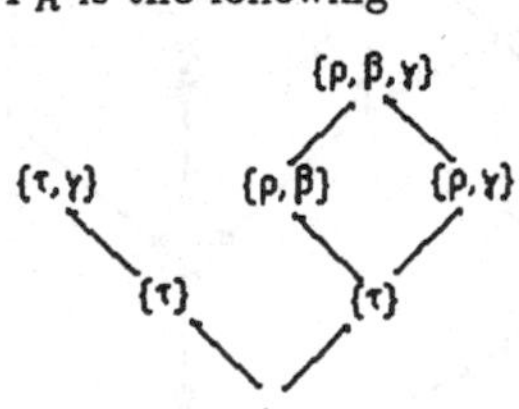

As $\{\beta\}$ is not connected to $\{\mu\}$, the assignment

$$\begin{array}{ccc} \alpha & \mapsto & \langle \alpha, \{\mu\} \rangle \\ \beta & \mapsto & \langle \beta, \{\beta\} \rangle \\ \gamma & \mapsto & \langle \gamma, \emptyset \rangle \end{array}$$

is *not* a section of P_R: one may say that the occurrence of μ prevents β to occur originating a deadlock. Note that this fact is reflected by the absence of the set $\{\mu, \beta\}$ in the domain.

The situation of deadlock just exemplified shows that our definition of refinement is broader than other proposed in the literature, *e.g.* [6, 19] which introduce a notion of refinement of configurations which may be described in our setting roughly as follows. A refinement of a configuration X is obtained by replacing each event α by a non-empty configuration of $F(\alpha)$; events which depend on α may occur only when a maximal configuration of $F(\alpha)$ occurs. A basic property of these proposals is that the domain of configurations of a refined event structure and the domain of the refined configurations are the same. Say that the refinement is *lively* if this is the case.

In the last example 3.4, this does not happen because the refinement of the configuration $\{\alpha, \beta\}$ of E according to [6, 19] would yield $\{\eta, \beta\}$ and also $\{\mu, \beta\}$. In section 5 we shall give conditions on the refinement functor to guarantee liveliness.

Finally, note that the notion of refinement in [14] can be treated in our framework. This acts on posets of events, *i.e.* on conflict-free structures, and does not preserve the order. Whenever an event in a poset P is replaced by a poset Q, also an additional relation is defined specifying which events in P are connected to which events of Q. It is clear that the relation can be rendered by the action on arrows of the refinement functors.

4 Refinement in the general case

An event structure with conflicts can be represented by a conflict-free event structure with a suitable refinement. For each pair of conflicting events a new *choice* event $\alpha ? \beta$ is added to the structure, it causes α and β and inherits their their causes, cf. [11]. The conflict relation is left empty on the new structure. Each choice event is refined by a flat two-point domain: the event structure of pure conflict on $\{\alpha, \beta\}$, see example 3.4. Formally,

4.1 Definition Given an event structure $\mathcal{E}$ let

$$\mathcal{E}_{\sharp} = (E \cup \{\{\alpha, \beta\} : \alpha \sharp \beta \in E\}, \leq_{\sharp}, \emptyset),$$

where $\leq_{\sharp}$ is the smallest order extending $\leq$ on E such that

- $\{\alpha, \beta\} \leq_{\sharp} \alpha$ and $\{\alpha, \beta\} \leq_{\sharp} \beta$,
- $\gamma \leq_{\sharp} \{\alpha, \beta\}$ if $\gamma \leq \alpha$ and $\gamma \leq \beta$.

We shall use an infix notation $\alpha ? \beta$ in place of $\{\alpha, \beta\}$.

Note that, in a sense, $\mathcal{E}_{\sharp}$ is the free completion of $\mathcal{E}$ with all infs of pairs of elements in $\sharp$.

The parallel example to 3.1 is to take the opposite category of $E_{\sharp}$ as a base and the functor F which takes value 2 on the events in $\mathcal{E}$ and is valued at $\mathcal{B}$ on the events in $E_{\sharp} - E$. More specifically,

4.2 Example Given an event structure $\mathcal{E}$, consider the associated conflict-free event structure $\mathcal{E}_{\sharp}$, and let C be the opposite category of $E_{\sharp}$. Let the functor F be defined as follows

- $F(\alpha) = \mathrm{Conf}(\{\alpha\})$, for $\alpha \in E$,
- $F(\alpha ? \beta) = \mathrm{Conf}(C_{\alpha ? \beta})$, for $\alpha \sharp \beta$ in E where $C_{\alpha ? \beta}$ is the event structure with $\alpha \sharp \beta$.

The non-trivial refinement functions are defined as $F(\alpha \geq_{\sharp} \alpha ? \beta) = \mathrm{Conf}(\{\alpha\} \hookrightarrow \mathcal{C}_{\alpha ? \beta})$, or to put it less dramatically

$$\begin{array}{rrcl} F(\alpha \geq_{\sharp} \alpha ? \beta): & \mathrm{Conf}(\{\alpha\}) & \longrightarrow & \mathrm{Conf}(\mathcal{C}_{\alpha ? \beta}) \\ & \{\alpha\} & \longmapsto & \{\alpha\} \\ F(\alpha ? \beta \geq_{\sharp} \gamma): & \mathrm{Conf}(\mathcal{C}_{\alpha ? \beta}) & \longrightarrow & \mathrm{Conf}(\{\gamma\}) \\ & \{\alpha\} & \longmapsto & \{\gamma\} \\ & \{\beta\} & \longmapsto & \{\gamma\} \end{array}$$

It should be clear that $\mathrm{Conf}(\mathcal{E}) \rightarrowtail \Pi P_F$ by extending a configuration of $\mathcal{E}$ to a section which assumes the unique possible value on an event of the form $\alpha ? \beta$ whenever this may be different from $\perp$.

4.3 Proposition *With the notation of example 4.2, the inclusion* $i: \mathrm{Conf}(\mathcal{E}) \rightarrowtail \Pi P_F$ *has a right adjoint* r, i.e. a *continuous left inverse* $r: \Pi P_F \to \mathrm{Conf}(E)$ *such that* $\mathrm{id} \leq i \circ r$.

4.4 Example (removing conflict) Consider for instance the event structure $\mathcal{E}$ on three events α, β, γ where $\alpha \leq \beta$ and $\alpha \leq \gamma$ and only $\beta \sharp \gamma$ as in the diagram which appear below together with the domain of configurations of $\mathcal{E}$.

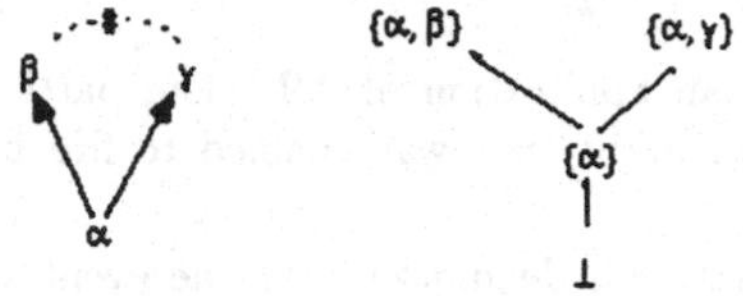

The functor of trivial refinement is represented as follows

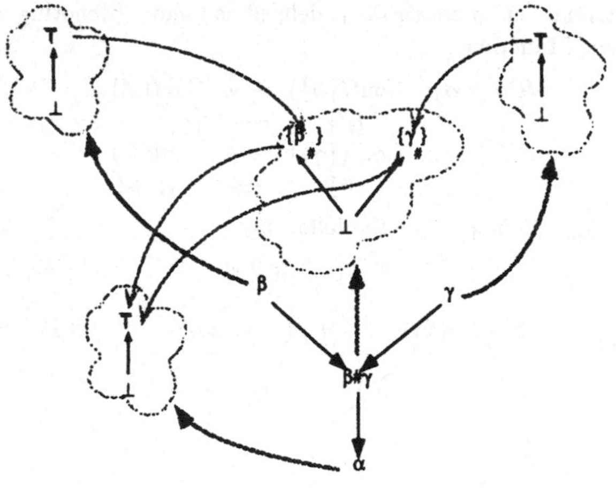

and the sections are the following

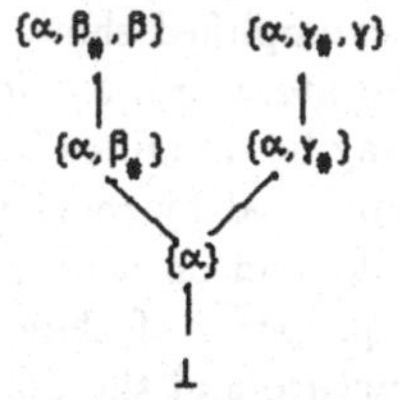

where we have added a subscript ♯ for the configurations of the C's. For instance, the assignment

$$\begin{array}{rcl} \alpha & \longmapsto & \langle \alpha, \{\alpha\} \rangle \\ \alpha ? \beta & \longmapsto & \langle \alpha ? \beta, \{\gamma_\sharp\} \rangle \\ \beta & \longmapsto & \langle \beta, \{\beta\} \rangle \\ \gamma & \longmapsto & \langle \gamma, \emptyset \rangle \end{array}$$

is *not* a section because there is no relation from $\{\beta\}$ to $\{\gamma_\sharp\}$.

It is worthwhile noticing that the right adjoint $r: \Pi P_F \to \mathrm{Conf}(\mathcal{E})$ acts exactly by "erasing the index ♯".

The next two examples instantiate the Π construction in three significant cases: one refining only the relation of conflict, another refining both relations, another more preserving the relation of conflict and refining that of causality.

4.5 Example (refining conflict) Consider the event structure $\mathcal{E}$ of example 4.4, and let C be the opposite category of E. Consider a functor $R: \mathsf{C} \to \mathsf{Rel}_r$ as in 2.9 sketched below

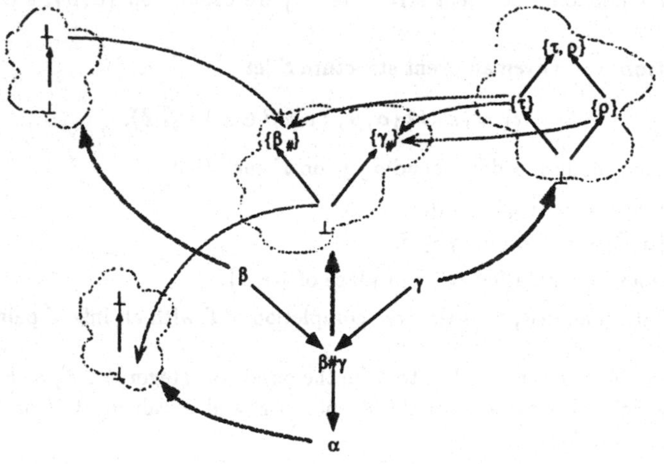

Note that $R(\gamma \geq_\sharp \beta ? \gamma)$ relates $\{\tau\}$ to both $\beta_\sharp$ and to $\gamma_\sharp$, thus neither $\beta_\sharp$ nor $\gamma_\sharp$ prevent to occur τ. Note also that causality is preserved as $\{\tau\}$ and $\{\rho\}$ are related to the maximal elements of $C_{\{\beta,\gamma\}}$.

4.6 Example Consider the same event structure $\mathcal{E}$ of the previous example 4.5, but the functor $R': \mathsf{C} \to \mathsf{Rel}_r$ is the following

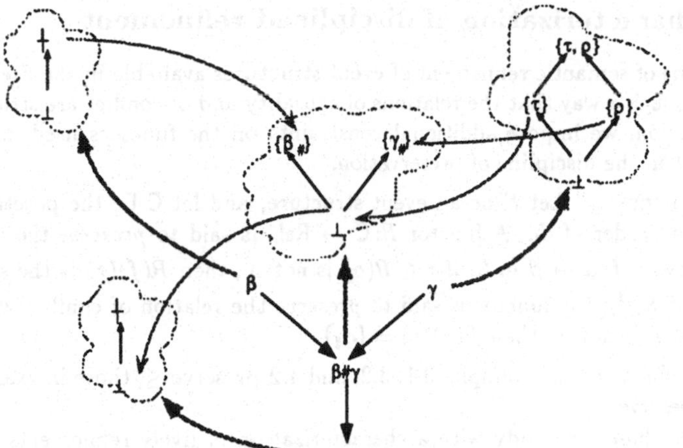

which differs from the other in that $R'(\gamma \geq_{\|} \beta ? \gamma)$ relates $\{\tau\}$ only to $\emptyset$. In this case the assignment defined by the singleton $\{\tau\}$ is a section, and part of the structure that replaces γ becomes concurrent with α and no longer in conflict with β.

4.7 Example Again take the structure $\mathcal{E}$ of example 4.5, and a functor $R''\colon \mathsf{C} \to \mathsf{Rel}_r$ which is presented as

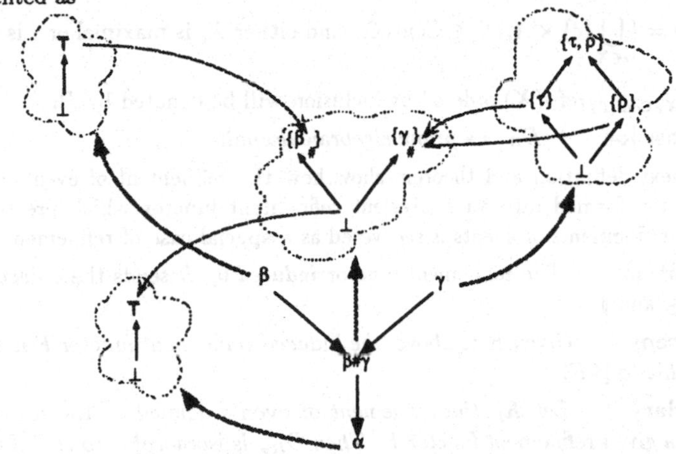

It is easy to see that $\{\beta\}$ is a section, but that $\{\alpha, \beta, \gamma_{\|}\}$ is not. The conflict relation has been preserved, and the relation of causality has been grossly refined.

At the time of writing we still have cases in which we are unable to refine causality more finely and to leave the relation of conflict unchanged. Also we are still working on finer category-theoretical methods to manage directly the conflict relation. We hope to bring our ideas to the fore and to present them in a subsequent paper.

Finally, recall from 2.2 that refinements can be composed in order to obtain more complex structures.

5 A characterization of disciplined refinement

The notions of semantic refinement of event structures available in the literature are disciplined in such a way that the relations of causality and of conflict are strictly preserved. In this section, we impose additional constraints on the functors used in refinement in order to fit in the discipline of preservation.

5.1 Definition Let $\mathcal{E}$ be an event structure, and let C be the posetal category on the opposite order of $\mathcal{E}_{\sharp}$. A functor $R: \mathsf{C} \to \mathsf{Rel}_r$ is said to *preserve* the causal relation when for every $f: \alpha \to \beta$ in C, if $\tau \in R(\alpha)$ is not $\perp$, then $R(f)(\tau)$ is the set of maximal elements of $R(\beta)$; the functor is said to *preserve* the relation of conflict whenever $\alpha \sharp \beta$ and $\tau \in R(\alpha)$ is not $\perp$, then $R(f)(\tau) = \{\alpha_{\sharp}\}$.

The refinements in examples 3.1, 3.2, and 4.2 preserve $\leq$, those in examples 3.3, 3.4, and 4.5 preserve $\sharp$.

We conclude our study with a characterization of lively refinements which we discussed briefly at the end of section 3. The following definition introduces the notion of refinement of domains of configurations, cf. [6, 19]. First some notation: for a fixed event structure $\mathcal{E}$ let $(R_\epsilon)_{\epsilon \in E}$ be a family of disjoint prime event structures, representing the *refinements of the events* of [6, 19].

5.2 Definition Let $X \subset E$ be a configuration. The *refinement of X under R* is the set

$$\mathrm{ref}_R(X) = \{\bigcup_{\epsilon \in X} \{\epsilon\} \times X_\epsilon | X_\epsilon \in \mathrm{Conf}(\mathcal{L}_\epsilon) \text{ and either } X_\epsilon \text{ is maximal or } \epsilon \text{ is maximal}\}.$$

The set $\bigcup_{X \in \mathrm{Conf}(\mathcal{L})} \mathrm{ref}_R(X)$ ordered by inclusion will be denoted by D_R.

5.3 Proposition *D_R is a prime algebraic domain.*

The next definition and theorem show how the refinement of events of [6, 19] can be easily transformed into an equivalent refinement functor which preserve $\leq$ and $\sharp$. Therefore, refinements of events is recovered as a special case of refinement functors.

5.4 Definition The refinement functor *induced* by R sends the object ϵ to L_ϵ, and preserves $\leq$ and $\sharp$.

5.5 Theorem *Given R as above, the induced refinement functor F is such that D_R is isomorphic to $\prod F$.*

5.6 Corollary *Let R_F the refinement of events defined as the restriction to the objects of a given refinement functor F. Then D_{R_F} is isomorphic to $\prod F$ if and only if F preserve $\leq$ and $\sharp$.*

Now the notion of lively refinement, intuitively introduced after example 3.4 can be made precise: it coincides with $\leq$- and $\sharp$-preserving refinement functors. Recall that the notions of refinement of event structures of [6, 18, 19] are such that the domain of configurations of a refined event structure and the domain of the refined configurations are the same. Besides them, any other refinement with such a property can be captured by the construction presented in this paper, due to 5.6.

Acknowledgements

The authors would like to acknowledge the useful discussions with T. Coquand, Ph. Darondeau and G. Winskel. Pierpaolo Degano was partially supported by C.N.R. project "Progetto Finalizzato Sistemi Informatici e Calcolo Parallelo" and by project MASK SC1 - CT92 - 00776, founded by the C.E.C. Roberto Gorrieri was partially supported by C.N.R. project "Ambienti di sviluppo e architetture per la realizzazione di sistemi di elaborazione distribuiti". Pino Rosolini was partially supported by ESPRIT project no. 6811. The three authors were also partially supported by M.U.R.S.T. 40%.

References

[1] L. Aceto and M. Hennessy. Towards Action-Refinement in Process Algebras. In A. Meyer, editor, **Proc. 4th Symposium in Logic in Computer Science**, pages 138–145, Asilomar. I.E.E.E. Computer Society, 1989.

[2] R. Back. A Calculus of refinements for program derivations. *Acta Informatica*, 25, 1988.

[3] P. Bernstein, V. Hadzilacos, and N. Goodman. **Concurrency Control and Recovery in Database Systems.** Addison-Wesley, 1987.

[4] K. Chandy and J. Misra. **Parallel Program Design: A Foundation.** Addison-Wesley, 1988.

[5] T. Coquand, C. Gunter, and G. Winskel. Domain theoretic models of polymorphism. *Inform. and Comput.*, 81:123–167, 1989.

[6] P. Darondeau and P. Degano. Event Structures, Causal Trees, and Refinements. In **Proc. 15th Symp. on Mathematical Foundations of Computer Science**, *Lectures Notes in Computer Science* vol. 452, 1990. To appear in Theo. Comp. Sci.

[7] J. de Bakker, W. de Roever, and G. Rozenberg, editors. **Proc. REX School/Workshop on Linear Time, Branching Time and Partial Order in Logics and Models for Concurrency**, *Lectures Notes in Computer Science* vol. 354. Springer-Verlag, 1989.

[8] J. de Bakker, W. de Roever, and G. Rozenberg, editors. **Stepwise Refinement of Distributed Systems: Models, Formalism, Correctness**, *Lectures Notes in Computer Science* vol. 430. Springer-Verlag, 1990.

[9] P. Degano and R. Gorrieri. An Operational Definition of Action Refinement. submitted for publication.

[10] P. Degano and R. Gorrieri. Atomic Refinement for Process Description Languages. In A. Tarlecki, editor, **Proc. 16th Symp. on Mathematical Foundations of Computer Science**, *Lectures Notes in Computer Science* vol. 520, pages 121–130. Springer-Verlag, 1991. Extended abstract, complete version in Technical Report 17-91, Hewlett-Packard Pisa Science Center, January 1991.

[11] P. Degano, R. D. Nicola, and U. Montanari. Partial Ordering Descriptions and Observations of Nondeterministic Concurrent Processes. In de Bakker et al. [7], pages 438–466.

[12] T. Elrda and N. Francez. Decomposition of Distributed Programs into Communication Closed Layers. *Science of Computer Programming*, 2, 1982.

[13] R. Gallager, P. Humblet, and P. Spira. A Distributed Algorithm for Minimum-Weight Spanning Trees. *ACM TOPLAS*, pages 5-1, 1983.

[14] W. Janssen, M. Poel, and J. Zwiers. Action Systems and Action Refinement in the Development of Parallel Systems. In **Proc. CONCUR'91**, *Lectures Notes in Computer Science* vol. 527, pages 298-316. Springer-Verlag, 1991.

[15] M. Nielsen, U. Engberg, and K. Larsen. Fully Abstract Models for a Process Language with Refinement. In de Bakker et al. [7], pages 523-548.

[16] M. Nielsen, G. Plotkin, and G. Winskel. Petri Nets, Event Structures and Domains, part I. *Theo. Comp. Sci.*, 13(1):85-108, 1981.

[17] F. Stomp and W. de Roever. Designing Distributed Algorithms by means of Formal Sequentially Phased Reasoning. In J.-C. Bermond and M. Raynal, editors, **Proc. 3rd Int. Workshop on Distributed Algorithms**, *Lectures Notes in Computer Science* vol. 392, pages 242-253. Springer-Verlag, 1990.

[18] R. van Glabbeek and U. Goltz. Equivalence Notions for Concurrent Systems and Refinement of Actions. In **Proc. 14th Symp. on Mathematical Foundations of Computer Science**, *Lectures Notes in Computer Science* vol. 379, pages 237-248. Springer-Verlag, 1989.

[19] R. van Glabbeek and U. Goltz. Refinement of Action in Causality Based Models. In de Bakker et al. [8].

[20] G. Winskel. Event Structures. In **Petri Nets: Applications and Relationships to Other Models of Concurrency, Advances in Petri Nets 1986, Part II**, *Lectures Notes in Computer Science* vol. 255, pages 325-392. Springer-Verlag, 1987.

Compact Metric Information Systems

(Extended Abstract)

Abbas Edalat
Michael B. Smyth

Department of Computing
Imperial College of Science, Technology and Medicine
180 Queen's Gate
London SW7 2BZ, UK.

Abstract

We present information systems for compact metric spaces using the notions of diameter and strong inclusion of open sets. It is shown that the category of compact metric information systems and metric approximable mappings, dual to the category of compact metric spaces and non-expansive maps, is a partially complete I-category in which canonical solution of domain equations can be found by taking the union (least upper bound) of certain Cauchy chains. For the class of contracting functors, the domain equation has a unique solution. We present such a class which includes the product, the co-product and the hyperspace functor (with Hausdorff metric).

Keywords: metric information systems, strong inclusion, Stone duality, I-category, domain equations, Cauchy chains, contracting functors, unique fixed point.

Contents

0 Introduction

An information system, following Scott [Sco82], may be taken to be a primitive logic with which to represent, or specify, the elements of a domain of computation. The use of information systems enables many domain constructions, notably recursion (solution of recursive domain equations), to be described in a simple and concrete fashion. Many classes of domains have been described by means of variations on Scott's scheme. Indeed, various precursors of [Sco82] may be understood as embodying an information system approach, taken in a sufficiently loose sense (e.g. [BC81, Smy77]).

In this context, a *domain* is required to be (at least) a countably-based continuous (d)cpo. An information system is (at least) a countable set of *propositions* or *tokens*, together with an entailment relation. The description of a domain D by an information system I then incorporates the idea that an element of D may be specified by a *consistent theory*, or filter, of I. In the other direction, an information system for a domain D can (in general) be abstracted from D by choosing certain convenient subsets of D to be the *propositions* (tokens), with entailment given by inclusion, and with additional structure as appropriate.

Stated in this generality, the situation is reminiscent of Stone duality (a point to which we return below), and one may well ask why the technique should be available only for *domains* in the strict sense. Indeed, there does not appear to be any intrinsic reason for restricting its application to domains as cpo's; by varying the means of description slightly, other classes of spaces can be captured. *Metric spaces* are quite widely employed in place of cpo's as semantic domains. In this paper, we begin to address the problem of devising information systems for metric spaces.

The description of metric spaces by tokens will not be exactly the same as in the case of domains. It is natural to expect that a notion of *Cauchy* filter will be required; of course this requires that metric structure be built into the information systems, say as a *diameter* defined on tokens. This is reminiscent of recent work on metric *locales* (or frames) by B. Banaschewski and A. Pultr; see especially [BP89]. An information system is more "primitive" than a locale. Thus, for the tokens of an information system for a (separable) metric space M, we may choose, in some convenient way, a countable *base* of the topology of M. This will be more amenable to constructivist treatment than the (in general, uncountable) locale corresponding to M. From an information system we may obtain the locale via a construction by *ideals*, and the space via a construction by *filters*. (Only the latter of these is considered in this paper.) Our main aim in the present work, of which this paper is the first step, is to show that the principal domain (or type) constructions can be carried out conveniently at the level of information systems.

Following metric locale theory, we use *diameter* of tokens as the metric primitive. This choice is, perhaps, in conflict with the idea of an information system as a primitive "logic": diameter is not easily regarded as a logical notion. Interestingly, however, diameter is interdefinable with a notion of *strong inclusion*, denoted $<_\epsilon$, which has a more "logical" appearance: the idea is that for open sets a and b the relation $a <_\epsilon b$ holds provided that the ϵ-neighbourhood of a is contained in b. Strong inclusion is a more flexible concept than diameter: it can be used very effectively in studying *quasi-metric* (or quasi-uniform) spaces, where a suitable notion of diameter is not available, cf. [Smy92]. In the present work we find it convenient to work with both strong inclusion and diameter.

In this paper we present information systems for *compact* metric spaces (which are the most significant for computational purposes), leaving the general case for later consideration. We construct the category of compact metric information systems and metric approximable mappings and show that it is dual to the category of compact metric spaces and non-expansive maps. We then show that, using a slight generalisation of the notion of a *complete I-category*, the general method of solving domain equations presented in [ES91] works in the category of metric information systems as well for the appropriate class of *contracting* endofunctors. We show that any contracting endofunctor gives rise to a unique fixed point, which is obtained by taking the union (least upper bound) of the *Cauchy chain* of the iterates of the functor on the initial object. This provides (at least for compact spaces) an alternative to the "spatial" treatment of De Bakker and Zucker [dBZ82], America and Rutten [AR88] and that of Majster-Cederbaum and Zetzsche [MCZ91]. We then consider particular type constructors including the product, the coproduct and the hyperspace (with Hausdorff metric) in the setting of information systems.

1 Stone duality for compact metric spaces

Suppose a compact metric space X with a countable base is given. Since the diameter of X is finite, we can assume by a simple rescaling of the metric that the diameter of X is at most one. This assumption will be most convenient when we define the co-product of two such spaces. We want to represent X by the basic open sets and their diameters. For this, we use

(i) the countable distributive lattice $(A, \leq, \vee, \wedge, \perp, \top)$ of open sets generated by the given base containing the empty set $\perp$ and the whole space $\top$,

(ii) the diameters of these open sets, given by a map $d : A \to [0,1]$ (where $[0,1]$ is the unit interval), and

(iii) the *strong inclusion* relation $<$ between the open sets, with $a < b$ if and only if the closure of a is contained in b, which in view of compactness of X is equivalent to saying that there is an ϵ-neighbourhood of a which is contained in b.

All in all, we have a structure $I(X) = (A, \leq, <, \vee, \wedge, \perp, \top, d)$, associated with X. We will now axiomatise our construction. In order to simplify the presentation of various constructors, notably the Hausdorff power functor, it is convenient to work with pre-ordered sets rather than lattices.

A *compact metric information system* is a tuple $\mathbf{A} = (A, \leq, <, \vee, \wedge, \perp, \top, d)$, where $(A, \leq)$ is a countable pre-order, $<$ is a binary relation, $\vee$ and $\wedge$ are binary operators, $\perp$ and $\top$ are constants (i.e. they are elements of A) and $d : A \to [0,1]$ is a mapping called the *diameter* mapping. The pre-ordered structure $(A, \leq, \vee, \wedge, \perp, \top)$ satisfies the following basic axioms:

- $a \leq a \vee b \qquad b \leq a \vee b \qquad a \leq c \,\&\, b \leq c \Rightarrow a \vee b \leq c$
- $a \wedge b \leq a \qquad a \wedge b \leq b \qquad c \leq a \,\&\, c \leq b \Rightarrow c \leq a \wedge b$
- $a \wedge (b \vee c) \leq (a \wedge b) \vee (a \wedge c)$
- $\perp \leq a \qquad a \leq \top \qquad (\{\perp, \top\}, \vee, \wedge)$ is a two element lattice.

We denote by $=$ the equivalence induced by the preorder $\leq$, i.e. $a = a'$ iff $a \leq a'$ & $a' \leq a$. The above axioms imply that the Lindenbaum algebra $(A_{/=}, \leq_{/=}, \vee_{/=}, \wedge_{/=}, \perp_{/=}, \top_{/=})$ is a distributive lattice with top and bottom. We further require the following axioms:

O(i) $d(\perp) = 0 \qquad\qquad a \leq b \Rightarrow d(a) \leq d(b)$

O(ii) $a \wedge b \neq \perp \Rightarrow d(a \vee b) \leq d(a) + d(b)$

O(iii) for all $a \in A$, all $\epsilon > 0$ and all $\gamma < d(a)$, there exist $b, c \in A$ such that $b \leq a$, $c \leq a$, $d(b), d(c) < \epsilon$ and $\gamma < d(b \vee c)$

O(iv) $a < b$ iff $\exists \epsilon > 0 \forall c \in A\, [d(c) < \epsilon, c \wedge a \neq \perp \Rightarrow c \leq b]$

O(v) $\downarrow a \subseteq \downarrow b \Rightarrow a \leq b$ (where $\downarrow c = \{c' \mid c' < c\}$)

O(vi) for all $a \in A$ and all $\epsilon > 0$, there exists a finite set of tokens $\{a_i \mid 1 \leq i \leq n\}$ such that $d(a_i) < \epsilon$, $a_i \wedge a \neq \perp$ $(1 \leq i \leq n)$ and $a < \bigvee_i a_i$.

We can axiomatise ultrametric spaces, where the triangular inequality on the metric r takes the stronger form $r(x,y) \leq \max\{r(x,z), r(y,z)\}$, by replacing $d(a) + d(b)$ in O(ii) with $\max\{d(a), d(b)\}$.

We immediately deduce the following.

Proposition 1.1 *For any compact metric space X with a given countable base, the structure $I(X)$ is a compact metric information system.*

Conversely, we will see shortly that any compact metric information system represents a compact metric space. Broadly speaking, the significance of the axioms is as follows. Axioms O(i)-(iii) are the very basic conditions on the diameter mapping d, which also appear in [BP89]. Axiom O(ii) ensures the triangular inequality of the metric and O(iii) implies that the diameter of an open set a^* induced by the token a is in fact the same as $d(a)$. Axiom O(iv) gives the meaning of the strong inclusion $<$ in terms of the diameters of tokens. O(v) ensures that the frame generated by the information system is spatial, or, in other words, the order relation between the tokens $a \in A$ coincides with the order relation between the open sets a^* induced by them. Finally, O(vi) ensures that the metric space represented by the information system is compact.

If $a < b$, we sometimes write $a <_\epsilon b$, where $\epsilon > 0$ is given by O(iv). Clearly such ϵ is not unique, in fact $a <_\epsilon b$ implies $a <_{\epsilon'} b$ for all $\epsilon' < \epsilon$. The strong inclusion has some basic properties which are summed up in the following.

Proposition 1.2 *The relation $<$ satisfies:*

(i) $\bot < \bot$ $\qquad$ $\top < \top$

(ii) $a < b < c \Rightarrow a < c$ $\qquad$ $a < c \Rightarrow \exists b.\, a < b < c$

(iii) $a < b \Rightarrow a \leq b$

(iv) $a \leq b < c \Rightarrow a < c$ $\qquad$ $a < b \leq c \Rightarrow a < c$

(v) $a < b, a < c \Rightarrow a < b \wedge c$

(vi) $a < b, c < b \Rightarrow a \vee c < b$.

We also have the following useful result which gives the diameter of tokens in terms of the strong inclusion $<_\epsilon$.

Proposition 1.3

$$d(c) < \epsilon \text{ iff } \forall a, b.\, [a \wedge c \neq \bot \;\&\; a <_\epsilon b \;\Rightarrow\; c \leq b]$$

Note that axiom O(iv) defines the strong inclusion in terms of diameter.

Suppose $\mathbf{A} = (A, \leq, <, \vee, \wedge, \bot, \top, d)$ is a compact metric information system. A filter of $\mathbf{A}$ is a non-empty subset $x \subseteq A$ which is upward closed and meet closed (i.e. $a \in x, a \leq a' \Rightarrow a' \in x$ and $a, b \in x \Rightarrow a \wedge b \in x$). It is a *round* filter if whenever $a \in x$ there exists $a' \in x$ with $a' < a$. A filter is Cauchy if it contains tokens of arbitrarily small diameter. We denote the set of round Cauchy filters of $\mathbf{A}$ by $S(\mathbf{A})$. Given two points x and y in $S(\mathbf{A})$, we define the distance between them by

$$\rho(x, y) = \inf\{d(a) \mid a \in x \cap y\}.$$

Proposition 1.4 *ρ is a metric on $S(\mathbf{A})$.*

We note here that if we had dispensed with the strong inclusion $<$ and worked with the simpler structure $(A, \leq, \vee, \wedge, \perp, \top, d)$, we could have defined points by taking Cauchy filters. But we would have then only obtained a pseudometric, i.e. $\rho(x,y) = 0 \Rightarrow x = y$ would no longer hold in general. For example, consider the real interval $[-1,1]$ with the usual metric and take as basic open sets all open intervals with rational end points. Then the two Cauchy filters generated by the sets $\{(p,0) \mid p < 0\}$ and $\{(0,q) \mid 0 < q\}$ are distinct but have zero distance from each other.

We will now define a base of topology on $S(\mathbf{A})$. For $a \in A$, let $a^* \subseteq S(\mathbf{A})$ be given by $a^* = \{x \mid a \in x\}$. Then we have:

Proposition 1.5 *$a \leq b$ iff $a^* \subseteq b^*$.*

It then follows that the set $\{a^* \mid a \in A\}$, ordered by inclusion, is a lattice isomorphic with $(A_{/=}, \leq_{/=}, \vee_{/=}, \wedge_{/=}, \perp_{/=}, \top_{/=})$, and so it gives a base of a topology τ on $S(\mathbf{A})$.

Proposition 1.6 *The ρ-metric topology and the τ-topology on $S(\mathbf{A})$ coincide.*

Let $a \in A$. Then the open set a^* has a diameter, diam(a^*), with respect to the metric ρ.

Proposition 1.7 *$diam(a^*) = d(a)$*

Therefore, $S(\mathbf{A})$ is a metric space having basic open sets a^* with diameter $d(a)$. It remains to show:

Proposition 1.8 *$S(\mathbf{A})$ is compact.*

Proof Let $X = S(\mathbf{A}) = \top^*$. Suppose $X = \bigcup_{k \geq 1} a_k^*$ where a_k's are increasing and assume $\top \neq a_k$ for any $k \geq 1$. For each $k \geq 1$, there is a finite set B_k of tokens with diameter at most $1/2^k$ whose join is $\top$. Without loss of generality, assume that B_{k+1} refines B_k for all $k \geq 1$. We now construct a finitary branching tree, whose k^{th} level consists of tokens b in B_k with $b \not\leq a_k$. Since the descendents of such a b cannot all be below a_{k+1}, we have an infinite finitary branching tree. Therefore, by König's lemma, there is an infinite branch in the tree, i.e. a decreasing sequence

$$b_1 \geq b_2 \cdots b_k \geq b_{k+1} \cdots$$

with $d(b_k) \leq 1/2^k$ and $b_k \not\leq a_k$ for all $k \geq 1$.

Now, we construct a round Cauchy filter generated by a decreasing sequence

$$c_1 \geq c_2 \geq c_3 \geq \cdots$$

with $d(c_k) \leq 1/2^{k-1}$, $c_{k+1} < c_k$ and $b_k < c_k$. Given a finite set C of tokens, for convenience we denote the join of all tokens in C by $\bigvee C$. We let $c_1 = \bigvee C_1$, where C_1 is a finite set of tokens of diameter at most $1/2^2$ with $b_1 < \bigvee C_1$. Then $d(c_1) \leq d(b_1) + 2 \times 1/2^2 \leq 1/2 + 1/2 = 1$. Suppose c_k has been chosen with $b_k < c_k$ and $d(c_k) \leq 1/2^{k-1}$. We have $b_{k+1} \leq b_k < c_k$ which implies $b_{k+1} < c_k$. Suppose $b_{k+1} <_\epsilon c_k$. Let $b_{k+1} < \bigvee C_{k+1}$, where C_{k+1} is a finite set of tokens of diameter at most $\min(\epsilon/2, 1/2^{k+2})$. Put $c_{k+1} = \bigvee C_{k+1}$. Then

$$d(c_{k+1}) \leq d(b_{k+1}) + 1/2^{k+1} \leq 1/2^k$$

and we have $b_{k+1} < c_{k+1} < c_k$ as required. The point $x \in X$ represented by the round Cauchy filter generated by c_k's does not belong to any a_k^*'s since $b_k \neq a_k$ and $b_k < c_k$ together imply $c_k \nleq a_k$ for all $k \geq 1$. But this contradicts the assumption that $X = \bigcup_{k \geq 1} a_k^*$. Hence, X is compact. □

We now define morphisms between compact metric information systems, which will correspond to non-expansive maps between the corresponding metric spaces in the opposite direction. A *metric approximable mapping* $R: A \to B$ between compact metric information systems **A** and **B** is a relation $R \subseteq A \times B$ satisfying:

M(i) $\bot R \bot$ $\qquad\qquad$ $\top R \top$

M(ii) $a \geq a' R b' \geq b \Rightarrow aRb$

M(iii) $aRb \Rightarrow \exists a'. a > a' Rb$ $\qquad\qquad$ $aRb \Rightarrow \exists b'. aRb' > b$

M(iv) $aRb, a'Rb \Rightarrow (a \wedge a')Rb$ $\qquad\qquad$ $aRb, aRb' \Rightarrow aR(b \vee b')$

M(v) $\forall \epsilon > 0, d(b) < \epsilon, \exists a. [d(a) < \epsilon \;\&\; aRb]$.

For any compact metric information system $\mathbf{A} = (A, \leq, <, \vee, \wedge, \bot, \top, d)$, we have:

Proposition 1.9 *The strong inclusion relation $>$ is the identity morphism on* **A**.

The two propositions which follow justify the axioms for morphisms. Let $f: Y \to X$ be a non-expansive map of compact metric spaces. Define $I(f): I(X) \to I(Y)$ by $aI(f)b$ iff $\overline{b^*} \subseteq f^{-1}(a^*)$, i.e. iff the closure of b^* is contained in the inverse image of a^*. Then we can deduce:

Proposition 1.10 *$I(f)$ is a metric approximable mapping.*

Conversely, given a metric approximable mapping $R : A \to B$, we define a mapping $S(R) : S(B) \to S(A)$ by $S(R)(y) = \{a \mid \exists b \in y.\, aRb\}$. It is easy to show that $S(R)(y)$ is in fact a round Cauchy filter, i.e. the mapping is well-defined. Moreover, we have:

Proposition 1.11 *$S(R)$ is a non-expansive map.*

We have now provided enough motivation to define the category **CM-ISys**, of compact metric information systems and metric approximable mappings. We assume that all compact metric information systems have the same tokens $\top$ and $\bot$. Composition of morphisms is obtained by composing relations in the usual way. Denoting the category of compact metric spaces (with a given countable base) and non-expansive maps by **CM-Sp**, it is easy to check that we have the two functors

$$I : \mathbf{CM\text{-}Sp} \longrightarrow \mathbf{CM\text{-}ISys}^{op} \qquad S : \mathbf{CM\text{-}ISys}^{op} \longrightarrow \mathbf{CM\text{-}Sp}$$

which we have already defined on objects and morphisms.

Theorem 1.12 *The functors I and S induce an equivalence between* **CM-Sp** *and* **CM-ISys**^{op}.

Proof If (Y, r) is a compact metric space with a given countable base, then the mapping $\eta_Y : Y \to S(I(Y))$, where $\eta_Y(y)$ is the round Cauchy filter of the basic open sets generated by the point y, is easily seen to be a metric embedding. Furthermore, any round Cauchy filter of basic open sets gives rise to a unique point of Y: Construct a shrinking sequence $\langle a_i \rangle_{i \geq 0}$ of the elements of the filter with $d(a_i) \leq 1/2^i$ and choose a point $x_i \in a_i$ for each $i \geq 0$. Then the Cauchy sequence $\langle x_i \rangle_{i \geq 0}$ in the compact space Y has a limit y which is contained in all elements of the filter. If y' is any other point with $r(y, y') > \epsilon$, say, then the filter has an element with diameter less than ϵ which contains y and hence not y'. Therefore, the intersection of all elements of a round Cauchy filter is a singleton. Moreover, it is easy to see that distinct round Cauchy filters give rise to distinct points. We conclude that η_Y has an inverse and is therefore an isometry. If we are given a non-expansive mapping $f : Y \to S(\mathbf{A})$, where $\mathbf{A}$ is a metric information system, then the metric approximable mapping $R : A \to I(Y)$ defined by aRb iff $\overline{b} \subseteq f^{-1}(a^*)$ is the unique morphism which makes the diagram

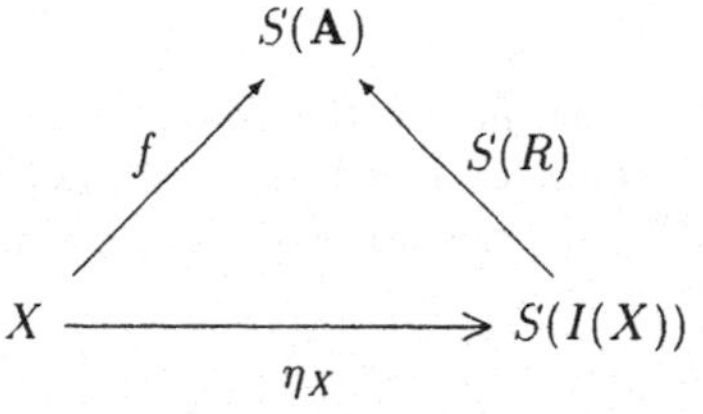

commute. Therefore, the functors I and S form an adjunction with unit η, which is a natural isomorphism. On the other hand, if $\mathbf{A}$ is a compact metric information system, we know by Proposition 1.5 that the order structures in $\mathbf{A}$ and in $I(S(\mathbf{A}))$ are isomorphic via $a \rightarrow a^*$, and by Proposition 1 we know that the diameters of a and a^* are the same. It then follows that the co-unit of adjunction $\epsilon : I(S(\mathbf{A})) \rightarrow \mathbf{A}$, whose component at $\mathbf{A}$ is induced by the approximable mapping $T = \epsilon_{\mathbf{A}} : \mathbf{A} \rightarrow I(S(\mathbf{A}))$, defined by aTb^* iff $b < a$, is a natural isomorphism. □

Finally in this section we determine the approximable mappings which correspond to surjective maps. We say that a metric approximable map $R : A \rightarrow B$ is *injective* if $R(a_1) = R(a_2) \Rightarrow a_1 = a_2$, where $R(a) = \{b \mid aRb\}$. We then obtain:

Proposition 1.13 *R is injective iff S(R) is surjective.*

2 Partially complete I-categories

In this section, we first recall from [ES91, ES92] the definition of an I-category and then show that there is an initial algebra theorem for I-categories which are only partially complete, in the sense that only a certain class of chains of objects and morphisms have least upper bounds.

An *I-category* $(P, \mathrm{Inc}, \sqsubseteq, \Delta)$ consists of

- a category P with a partial order $\sqsubseteq^{A,B}$ on each homset $\hom(A, B)$,
- a subclass $\mathrm{Inc} \subseteq \mathrm{Mor}$, called the *inclusion morphisms* of P, such that in each hom-set, $\hom(A, B)$, there is at most one inclusion morphism which we denote by $\mathrm{in}(A, B)$ or $A \rightarrowtail B$,
- a distinguished object $\Delta \in \mathrm{Obj}$,

satisfying the following two axioms:

Axiom 1 (i) *The class of objects Obj and the inclusion morphisms Inc form a partial order represented as a category.*

(ii) *$in(\Delta, A)$ exists, for all $A \in Obj$ and $in(\Delta, A) \sqsubseteq f$ for all morphisms $f \in \hom(\Delta, A)$.*

(iii) *$f; in(A, B) \sqsubseteq g; in(A, B) \Rightarrow f \sqsubseteq g$, for all $f, g \in Mor$, $in(A, B) \in Inc$, such that the compositions are defined.*

Axiom 2 *Composition of morphisms is monotone with respect to the partial order on hom-sets, i.e.*

$$f_1 \sqsubseteq f_2 \;\&\; g_1 \sqsubseteq g_2 \;\Rightarrow\; f_1; g_1 \sqsubseteq f_2; g_2$$

whenever the compositions are defined.

The partial orders $\trianglelefteq$ on Obj_P and $\trianglelefteq^m$ on Mor_P of an I-category $(P, \mathrm{Inc}, \sqsubseteq, \Delta)$ are defined as follows:

- $A \trianglelefteq B$ if $\mathrm{in}(A, B)$ exists;
- $f \trianglelefteq^m g$ if

  (i) $\mathrm{dom}(f) \trianglelefteq \mathrm{dom}(g)$,
  (ii) $\mathrm{cod}(f) \trianglelefteq \mathrm{cod}(g)$,
  (iii) $f; \mathrm{in}(\mathrm{cod}(f), \mathrm{cod}(g)) \sqsubseteq \mathrm{in}(\mathrm{dom}(f), \mathrm{dom}(g)); g$.

Note that $f \trianglelefteq^m g$ iff the diagram

$$\begin{array}{ccc} \mathrm{dom}(g) & \xrightarrow{g} & \mathrm{cod}(g) \\ \uparrow & \sqsupseteq & \uparrow \\ \mathrm{dom}(f) & \xrightarrow{f} & \mathrm{cod}(f) \end{array}$$

weakly commutes. In the present paper, we will deal with I-categories whose hom-sets are discretely ordered. This means that the above diagram will commute in the usual sense, Δ will be an initial object and all morphisms $f : A \to B$ will be *strict* i.e. $\mathrm{in}(\Delta, A); f = \mathrm{in}(\Delta, B)$.

Let P be an I-category with a distinguished class of $\trianglelefteq$-chains of objects, called *admissible* chains, which include all eventually constant chains. We say that a $\trianglelefteq^m$-chain of morphisms in P is admissible if the corresponding $\trianglelefteq$-chains of domains and codomains are admissible. A *partially complete I-category* is an I-category with a class of admissible chains which satisfy the following completeness axioms:

Axiom 3 Every admissible chain of morphisms has a lub.

Axiom 4 The lub of any admissible chain of inclusion morphisms is an inclusion morphism.

Axiom 5 If $\langle f_i \rangle_{i \geq 0}$ and $\langle g_i \rangle_{i \geq 0}$ are two admissible chains of element-wise composable morphisms, then $\bigsqcup_i (f_i; g_i) = (\bigsqcup_i f_i); (\bigsqcup_i g_i)$.

All the basic results for complete I-categories have their counterparts for partially complete I-categories which are stated in terms of admissible chains.

Lemma 2.1 *The lub of any admissible chain of objects in a partially complete I-category P is a colimit of the chain in P. It is also a colimit of the chain in the subcategory of strict morphisms P^s.*

A standard (i.e. inclusion preserving) endofunctor of a partially complete I-category is called *admissible* if the chain

$$\Delta \rightarrowtail F(\Delta) \rightarrowtail F^2(\Delta) \rightarrowtail \cdots$$

is admissible. It is called *continuous* if it maps admissible chains of morphisms to admissible chains preserving their lubs.

Theorem 2.2 *An admissible continuous endofunctor F on a partially complete I-category P has an initial algebra in P^s, which is given by $(D, Id(D))$ with $D = \bigsqcup_i F^i(\Delta)$ and has the property that for any strict $k : F(E) \to E$, there exists a unique strict $h : D \to E$ making the following diagram commute:*

$$\begin{array}{ccc} D & = & F(D) \\ {\scriptstyle h}\downarrow & & \downarrow{\scriptstyle F(h)} \\ E & \xleftarrow{\;k\;} & F(E) \end{array}$$

3 CM-ISys as an I-category

We will see in this section that **CM-ISys** is in fact an I-category. The hom-sets are discretely ordered and the distinguished object Δ has only the two elements $\top$ and $\bot$ with $d(\top) = d(\bot) = 0$ representing the open subsets of the one element set.

Let $\mathbf{A} = (A, \leq_A, <_A, \vee_A, \wedge_A, \bot, \top, d_A)$ and $\mathbf{B} = (B, \leq_B, <_B, \vee_B, \wedge_B, \bot, \top, d_B)$ be compact metric information systems. Recall that $\bot$ and $\top$ are assumed to be the same constants in all compact metric information systems.

Definition 3.1 We say $\mathbf{A}$ is a subsystem of $\mathbf{B}$, written $\mathbf{A} \trianglelefteq \mathbf{B}$, if

(i) $(A, \leq_A, <_A, \vee_A, \wedge_A, \bot, \top)$ is a substructure of $(B, \leq_B, <_B, \vee_B, \wedge_B, \bot, \top)$, i.e.

- $A \subseteq B$.
- The relations $\leq_A$ and $<_A$ and the operations $\vee_A$ and $\wedge_A$ are respectively the restrictions of $\leq_B$, $<_B$, $\vee_B$ and $\wedge_B$ to A.

(ii) $\forall a \in A \forall b \in B \forall \epsilon > 0 \exists a' \in A.\ [d_B(b) < \epsilon, a >_B b \Rightarrow d_A(a') < \epsilon \mathbin{\&} a >_A a' >_B b]$.

The condition (i) above says that $(A, \leq_A, <_A, \vee_A, \wedge_A, \bot, \top)$ is a substructure of $(B, \leq_B, <_B, \vee_B, \wedge_B, \bot, \top)$ in the usual sense of the word, whereas (ii) is basically a condition on the metrics, which in particular implies:

Proposition 3.2 *If $\mathbf{A} \trianglelefteq \mathbf{B}$ then $d_A(a) \leq d_B(a)$ for all $a \in A$.*

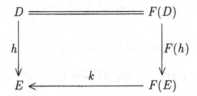

When $\mathbf{A} \trianglelefteq \mathbf{B}$, it can be easily verified that $>_A; >_B = >_B \cap (A \times B)$ is a metric approximable mapping from $\mathbf{A}$ to $\mathbf{B}$, which we take as the inclusion morphism $\mathrm{in}(\mathbf{A}, \mathbf{B})$. Clearly $\mathrm{in}(\mathbf{A}, \mathbf{A}) = >_A$ is the identity morphism, and

$$\mathrm{in}(\mathbf{A}, \mathbf{B}); \mathrm{in}(\mathbf{B}, \mathbf{C}) \ = >_A; >_B; >_B; >_C = >_A; >_C = \ \mathrm{in}(\mathbf{A}, \mathbf{C})$$

as can be easily checked. Furthermore if $\mathbf{A} \trianglelefteq \mathbf{B}$ and $\mathbf{B} \trianglelefteq \mathbf{A}$, it follows by the above proposition that $\mathbf{A} = \mathbf{B}$. We also have $\Delta \trianglelefteq \mathbf{A}$ for all objects $\mathbf{A}$.

It follows by axiom O(v) that inclusion morphisms are injective. We now determine the surjective non-expansive map corresponding to the inclusion morphism $i = \mathrm{in}(\mathbf{A}, \mathbf{B})$. Using the definition of S, and putting $Y = S(\mathbf{B})$ and $X = S(\mathbf{A})$, we get the map $f = S(i) : Y \to X$ with $f(y) = \{a \mid \exists b \in B.\ a >_B b\} \ = \ y \cap A$ as can be easily checked. It now follows that $f^{-1}(a_X^*) = a_Y^*$. We also obtain the following:

Proposition 3.3 *Suppose* $\mathbf{A} \trianglelefteq \mathbf{B}$ *and* $a \in A$. *Then*

$$d_B(a) = sup\, \{d_B(b) \mid b \in B, a >_B b\}.$$

3.1 Cauchy chains

We will now define a class of admissible chains in **CM-ISys**. For this, we need a measure of how much a morphism expands the diameters of tokens, which in turn is an indication of the amount the corresponding non-expansive map contracts distances between points.

Definition 3.4 The *expansion index* of a metric approximable mapping $R : A \to B$ is the number $\delta(R) = \sup\, \{d_B(b) - d_A(a) \mid aRb\}$.

Let $S(A) = (X, \rho_X)$, $S(B) = (Y, \rho_Y)$ and $S(R) = f : Y \to X$. Then we have:

Proposition 3.5

$$\delta(R) = sup\, \{diam_X(f^{-1}(O)) - diam_Y(O) \mid O \ open\ in\ Y\} \ =$$

$$sup\, \{\rho_Y(y, y') - \rho_X(f(y), f(y')) \mid y, y' \in Y\}$$

Corollary 3.6 (i) *The expansion index is non-negative.*

(ii) *If R is an injective morphism (corresponding to a surjective map), then $\delta(R) = 0$ iff R is an isomorphism.*

(iii) *If R is an isomorphism, we have $\delta(R; R') = \delta(R')$ and $\delta(R''; R) = \delta(R'')$ for all morphisms R' and R'' which compose respectively from right and left with R.*

(iv) $\delta(R_1; R_2) \leq \delta(R_1) + \delta(R_2)$.

As regards inclusion morphisms, the expansion index takes a simple form as follows.

Proposition 3.7 *Let $i = in(\mathbf{A}, \mathbf{B})$. Then,*

(i) $\delta(i) = sup\{d_B(a) - d_A(a) \mid a \in A\}$.

(ii) *If $\delta(i) = 0$ then $\mathbf{A} = \mathbf{B}$.*

Suppose T is a chain of compact metric information systems $\mathbf{A_0} \trianglelefteq \mathbf{A_1} \trianglelefteq \mathbf{A_2} \trianglelefteq \cdots$. Let δ_{ij}, for $j \geq i \geq 0$, be the expansion index of $\text{in}(A_i, A_j)$. We say that T is a *Cauchy chain* if for all $\epsilon > 0$ there exists an integer N such that $\delta_{ij} < \epsilon$ for $j \geq i \geq N$. Since the expansion index of an identity morphism is zero, an eventually constant chain is always Cauchy.

For a Cauchy chain $\langle \mathbf{A_i} \rangle_{i \geq 0}$, with $\mathbf{A_i} = (A_i, \leq_i, <_i, \vee_i, \wedge_i, \perp, \top, d_i)$, define

$$\bigcup_i \mathbf{A_i} = (\bigcup_i A_i, \bigcup_i \leq_i, \bigcup_i <_i, \bigcup_i \vee_i, \bigcup_i \wedge_i, \perp, \top, \text{sup}_i d_i).$$

Proposition 3.8 (i) *The structure $\bigcup_i \mathbf{A_i}$ is a compact metric information system and is the lub of the Cauchy chain $\langle \mathbf{A_i} \rangle_{i \geq 0}$.*

(ii) $\delta_i = \delta(in(\mathbf{A_i}, \bigcup_j \mathbf{A_j})) \to 0$ *as $i \to \infty$.*

Suppose now $R_i : \mathbf{A_i} \to \mathbf{B_i}$, $i \geq 0$ is a chain of morphisms such that $\langle \mathbf{A_i} \rangle_{i \geq 0}$ and $\langle \mathbf{B_i} \rangle_{i \geq 0}$ are both Cauchy chains.

Proposition 3.9 (i) *The relation $\bigcup_i R_i : \bigcup_i \mathbf{A_i} \to \bigcup_i \mathbf{B_i}$ is a metric approximable mapping and is the lub of the chain $\langle R_i \rangle_{i \geq 0}$.*

(ii) *$\bigcup_i R_i$ is injective if R_i is injective for all $i \geq 0$.*

All together we have shown the following.

Theorem 3.10 *The category* **CM-ISys**, *with the class of Cauchy chains as the admissible chains, is a partially complete I-category.*

We therefore have an initial algebra theorem in **CM-ISys** for all admissible functors.

4 Standard functors on metric information systems

In this section we will present some standard functors on compact metric information systems.

4.1 Contractions

For each $s > 0$, there is a functor ID^s on **CM-ISys** which simply rescales all diameters by s. In more detail, given an object $\mathbf{A} = (A, \leq, <, \vee, \wedge, \perp, \top, d)$, the object $\mathrm{ID}^s(\mathbf{A})$, more simply written as $\mathbf{A}^s$, is given by $(A, \leq, <, \vee, \wedge, \perp, \top, d^s)$, where $d^s(a) = sd(a)$ for all $a \in A$; and for a morphism $R : \mathbf{A} \to \mathbf{B}$ we put $\mathrm{ID}^s(R) = R$. It is trivial to see that ID^s is a standard endofunctor. If $s < 1$, we say that ID^s is a *contraction* with *contraction coefficient* s. Clearly ID^1 is just the identity functor.

4.2 Product

The product of two metric information systems corresponds in the dual category to the co-product of the metric spaces. Given compact metric information systems $\mathbf{A}$ and $\mathbf{B}$, their product is defined by $\mathbf{A} \times \mathbf{B} = (|\mathbf{A} \times \mathbf{B}|, \leq, <, \vee, \wedge, \perp, \top, d)$, where

(i) $|\mathbf{A} \times \mathbf{B}|$ is the set of pairs (a, b), $a \in A$ and $b \in B$, with $(\perp, \perp) = \perp$ and $(\top, \top) = \top$,

(ii) the relations $\leq$ and $<$ and the operations $\vee$ and $\wedge$ are defined componentwise, e.g. $(a, b) \leq (a', b')$ iff $a \leq_A a'$ and $b \leq_B b'$,

(iii)

$$\begin{aligned} d(a,b) &= d_A(a) && \text{if } b = \perp \\ &= d_B(b) && \text{if } a = \perp \\ &= 1 && \text{otherwise} \end{aligned}$$

Given morphisms $R : \mathbf{A} \to \mathbf{A}'$ and $T : \mathbf{B} \to \mathbf{B}'$, the morphism $R \times T : \mathbf{A} \times \mathbf{B} \to \mathbf{A}' \times \mathbf{B}'$ is defined by $(a, b)(R \times T)(a', b')$ iff aRa' and bTb'.

4.3 Co-product

The co-product of metric information systems corresponds to the product of metric spaces. The co-product of metric information systems $\mathbf{A}$ and $\mathbf{B}$ is defined by $\mathbf{A} + \mathbf{B} = (|\mathbf{A} + \mathbf{B}|, \leq, <, \vee, \wedge, \perp, \top, d)$, where

(i) $|\mathbf{A} + \mathbf{B}|$ is the set of pairs (a, b), $a \in A$ and $b \in B$, with $(a, \perp) = (\perp, b) = \perp$ for all $a \in A$ and $b \in B$, and $(\top, \top) = \top$,

(ii) the relations $\leq$ and $<$ and the operation $\wedge$ are defined componentwise,

(iii) $(a, b) \leq \bigvee_{i \in I}(a_i, b_i)$ iff $a \leq \bigvee_{i \in I} a_i$ and $b \leq \bigvee_{i \in I} b_i$,

(iv) $d(a, b) = \max\{d_A(a), d_B(b\}$ $\quad (a, b \neq \perp) \qquad d(a, \perp) = d(\perp, b) = 0$

For morphisms $R : \mathbf{A} \to \mathbf{A}'$ and $T : \mathbf{B} \to \mathbf{B}'$, the morphism $R + T : \mathbf{A} + \mathbf{B} \to \mathbf{A}' + \mathbf{B}'$ is defined by $(a, b)(R + T)(a', b')$ iff aRb and bTb'.

4.4 Power system

For any metric space (X, r), we can define a new metric space $(\mathcal{H}(X), r_H)$, called the *Hausdorff* construction, whose points are the closed non-empty subsets of X and the *Hausdorff distance* r_H is defined by

$$r_H(A,B) = \max\{\sup_{x\in A} r(x,B), \sup_{y\in B} r(y,A)\}$$

where $r(x,C) = \inf_{c\in C}\{r(x,c)\}$. Equivalently, $r_H(A,B)$ is the infimum of numbers r such that A is contained in the r-neighbourhood of B and B is contained in the r-neighbourhood of A.

We will now outline how we can capture this construction for our compact metric information systems. The idea is that a base for the topology of $(\mathcal{H}(X), r_H)$, where (X, r) is now assumed to be compact, can be given as follows. Consider any non-empty finite collection $a_I = \{a_i \mid i \in I\}$ of open sets of X. Then the basic open set a_I represented by this collection is the set of all closed (hence compact) sets of X which are contained in the union of a_i's and intersect each of them, i.e. $a_I \subseteq \mathcal{H}(X)$ with $C \in a_I$ iff $C \subseteq \bigcup_i a_i$ and $C \cap a_i \neq \emptyset$, for all $i \in I$. Given that we are working with compact spaces, this choice of tokens agrees with the Hausdorff metric topology (see for example [Mic51]. Furthermore, we obtain the same topology if we choose the a_i's from any base of X. We will axiomatise this construction below.

Let $\mathbf{A}$ be a compact metric information system. Then the power system $\mathcal{P}(\mathbf{A}) = (\mathcal{P}(A), \leq, <, \vee, \wedge, \perp, \top, d)$ is defined as follows. $\mathcal{P}(A)$ is generated by finite non-empty collections $a_I = \{a_i \in A \mid i \in I\}$, where I is a finite indexing set, with $\top = \{\top\}$ and $\perp = \{a_I\}$ iff $\exists a \in a_I\ [a = \perp]$. More specifically, it consists of finite joins $a_{I_1} \vee a_{I_2} \vee \ldots \vee a_{I_n}$ of such collections. For clarity, we will always use a_i, a_j, a_k etc. for elements of A and finite joins of a_I, a_J, a_K etc. for elements of $\mathcal{P}(A)$. It then becomes clear from the context whether the relations $\leq$ and $<$, the operations $\vee$ and $\wedge$ and the mapping d are those of $\mathbf{A}$ or of $\mathcal{P}(\mathbf{A})$. The structure in $\mathcal{P}(\mathbf{A})$ is then defined as follows.

(i) The relation $\leq$ is generated by the following conditions:

- $a_I \leq a_J$ (for $a_I \neq \perp$) iff $\bigvee_{i\in I} a_i \leq \bigvee_{j\in J} a_j$ and $\forall j \in J \exists i \in I\ [a_i \leq a_j]$.

  To determine when $a_I \leq (a_{I_1} \vee a_{I_2} \ldots \vee a_{I_n})$ holds, we proceed as follows. Put $I' = I_1 \cup I_2 \cup \ldots \cup I_n$. Assume $\bigvee_{i\in I} a_i \leq \bigvee_{i\in I'} a_i$. Then, each $a \in a_I$ can be expressed as a finite join $a = a_1 \vee a_2 \vee \ldots \vee a_m$ where each a_k $(1 \leq k \leq m)$ is an *atom* of the token a wrt $a_{I_1}, a_{I_2}, \ldots a_{I_n}$, i.e. each a_k is a meet of elements of the set $\{a_i \mid i \in I'\}$ and it is indecomposable, i.e. it cannot be expressed as the the join of two such (non-trivial) elements. A *subtoken* of a_I wrt $a_{I_1}, a_{I_2}, \ldots a_{I_n}$ is a set of atoms of a's $(a \in a_I)$ which has at least one atom of each $a \in a_I$. Clearly, each such subtoken b_J of a_I satisfies $b_J \leq a_I$. We then have the following condition:

- $a_I \leq (a_{I_1} \vee a_{I_2} \ldots \vee a_{I_n})$ (for $a_I \neq \perp$) iff $\bigvee_{i\in I} a_i \leq \bigvee_{i\in I'} a_i$ and for each subtoken b_J of a_I wrt a_{I_t}'s, there exists t $(1 \leq t \leq n)$ with $b_J \leq a_{I_t}$.

(ii) The relation $<_\epsilon$ is defined precisely as the definition of $\leq$ given above in (i) with $\leq$ replaced everywhere by $<_\epsilon$.

(iii) $a_I \wedge a_J = \{a_i \wedge a_j \mid i \in I, j \in J, a_i \wedge a_j \neq \bot\}$.

(iv) d is defined using $<_\epsilon$ as in Proposition 1.3, i.e. by $d(a_I) \leq \epsilon$ iff for all a_J and a_K with $a_J \wedge a_I \neq \bot$ and $a_J <_\epsilon a_K$ we have $a_I \leq a_K$.

Given a morphism $R : \mathbf{A} \to \mathbf{B}$, the metric approximable mapping $\mathcal{P}(R) : \mathcal{P}(A) \to \mathcal{P}(B)$ is generated by the following conditions:

- $a_I \mathcal{P}(R) b_J$ iff $(\bigvee_{i\in I} a_i) R (\bigvee_{j\in J} b_j)$ and for all $i \in I$ there exists $j \in J$ such that $a_i R b_j$.
- $(a_{I_1} \vee a_{I_2} \ldots \vee a_{I_n}) \mathcal{P}(R)\, b_J$ holds iff for each $b \in b_J$ there is a decomposition $b = b_1 \vee b_2 \vee \ldots \vee b_m$ into subelements such that for each subtoken $c_K \leq b_J$ consisting of subelements of b's ($b \in b_J$), there is a t ($1 \leq t \leq n$) such that $a_{I_t} \mathcal{P}(R) c_K$.

5 Unique fixed point of contracting functors

A suitable class of admissible functors are provided by contracting functors.

Definition 5.1 A standard endofunctor F of **CM-ISys** is *contracting* if there exists a number s with $0 \leq s < 1$ such that for all morphisms R we have $\delta(F(R)) \leq s\delta(R)$. We call s a *contractivity factor* for F.

Proposition 5.2 (i) *A contracting endofunctor F is admissible, i.e. the chain*

$$\Delta \trianglelefteq F(\Delta) \trianglelefteq F^2(\Delta) \trianglelefteq \cdots$$

is Cauchy.

(ii) *A contracting functor is continuous.*

Using Theorem 2.2, we can therefore deduce the initial algebra theorem for compact metric information systems.

Theorem 5.3 *Any contracting endofunctor on* **CM-ISys** *has an initial algebra.*

This gives us a canonical fixed point solution to domain equations for contracting functors. Moreover, we can show that this fixed point is essentially unique.

Theorem 5.4 *Any contracting endofunctor on* **CM-ISys** *has a unique fixed object up to isomorphism.*

Proof Let F be a contracting endofunctor. Then the initial algebra is given by $(D, \mathrm{Id}(D))$ where $D = \bigcup_i F^i(\Delta)$. Suppose E is any other fixed point with isomorphism $k : F(E) \to E$. The initial algebra theorem provides us with a unique morphism h, given by $h = \bigcup_i g_i$ with $g_0 = \mathrm{in}(\Delta, E)$ and $g_{i+1} = F(g_i); k$, such that

$$\begin{array}{ccc} D & = & F(D) \\ {\scriptstyle h}\downarrow & & \downarrow{\scriptstyle F(h)} \\ E & \xleftarrow{\;k\;} & F(E) \end{array}$$

commutes. We will now show that h is an isomorphism. By Corollary 3.6(iii), we have $0 \leq \delta(h) = \delta(F(h); k) = \delta(F(h)) \leq s\delta(h)$, where $0 \leq s < 1$ is a contractivity factor for F. We conclude that $\delta(h) = 0$. Next we claim that, for each $i \geq 0$, $g_i = \mathrm{in}(F^i(\Delta), F^i(E)); t_i$ where t_i is an isomorphism. For $i = 0$ this is evident. Suppose now that the claim holds for i. Then

$$g_{i+1} = F(g_i); k = \mathrm{in}(F^{i+1}(\Delta), F^{i+1}(E)); F(t_i); k = \mathrm{in}(F^{i+1}(\Delta), F^{i+1}(E)); t_{i+1}$$

where $t_{i+1} = F(t_i); k$ is an isomorphism. Since inclusion morphisms are injective, it follows that g_i is injective for all $i \geq 0$. By Proposition 3.9(ii), we deduce that $h = \bigcup_i g_i$ is also injective. By Corollary 3.6(i), it now follows that h is an isomorphism. □

6 A class of contracting functors

We will give below a class of contracting endofunctors. Our presentation is similar in spirit to that in [AR88]. A class of standard functors *Stnd* is defined by BNF notation as follows:

$$F ::= F_{\mathbf{A}} \mid \mathrm{ID}^{\epsilon} \mid \mathcal{P}(F) \mid F_1 \times F_2 \mid F_1 + F_2 \mid F_1 \circ F_2$$

where for any metric information system $\mathbf{A}$, $F_{\mathbf{A}}$ is the constant functor with value $\mathbf{A}$. For $F \in \mathit{Stnd}$, the contraction index $c(F)$ is defined recursively by:

(i) $c(F_{\mathbf{A}}) = 0$.

(ii) $c(\mathrm{ID}^{\epsilon}) = \epsilon$.

(iii) $c(\mathcal{P}(F)) = c(F)$.

(iv) $c(F_1 \times F_2) = \max\{c(F_1), c(F_2)\}$.

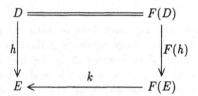

(v) $c(F_1 + F_2) = \max\{c(F_1), c(F_2)\}$.

(vi) $c(F_1 \circ F_2) = c(F_1) \times c(F_2)$.

Proposition 6.1 *For all functors $F \in Stnd$, we have $\delta(F(R)) \leq c(F)\delta(R)$.*

Corollary 6.2 *Any functor $F \in Stnd$ with $c(F) < 1$ is contracting.*

It follows by Theorem 5.4 that any such functor with $c(F) < 1$ has a unique fixed point. This enables us to solve many interesting domain equations in **CM-ISys**. One such equation is $\mathbf{A} \cong \mathbf{2} \times \mathcal{P}(\mathbf{A}^{\frac{1}{2}})$ where $\mathbf{2}$ is the metric information system of the one point space. Its solution gives a metric and topological representation of non-well founded sets, in the same way that the corresponding spatial equatqion $X \cong 1 + \mathcal{P}_H(X^{\frac{1}{2}})$ (where 1 is a one point space and $X^{\frac{1}{2}}$ is X with its metric halved), considered by Abramsky [Abr88], leads to a description of these sets. Here, we will content ourselves with solving another interesting equation.

Example 6.3 Consider the domain equation $\mathbf{A} \cong F(\mathbf{A}) = B + \mathbf{A}^{\frac{1}{2}}$, where $\mathbf{B} = (\{\bot, \top, 0, 1\}, \leq, <, \vee, \wedge, \bot, \top, d)$ is the four element metric structure representing the two point metric space of diameter 1; that is to say:

(i) $0 \vee 1 = \top$ $\qquad\qquad$ $0 \wedge 1 = \bot$.

(ii) $d_B(0) = d_B(1) = 0$ $\qquad\qquad$ $d_B(\top) = 1$.

The functor $F = F_{\mathbf{B}} + \mathrm{ID}^{\frac{1}{2}}$ has contraction index $c(F) = \max\{0, \frac{1}{2}\} = \frac{1}{2}$ and is therefore contracting. It has up to isomorphism a unique fixed point given by $\bigcup_{i \geq 0} \mathbf{A_i}$ where $\mathbf{A_i} = F^i(\Delta)$. We give below explicitly the first few terms and the general term in the approximating chain $\langle \mathbf{A_i} \rangle_{i \geq 0}$. Let d_i denote the diameter map for $\mathbf{A_i}$. For convenience, we will drop all brackets in the denotation of tokens of co-products, for example $01\top$ represents the token $(0, (1, \top))$.

- $A_0 = \{\bot, \top\}$ $\qquad\qquad$ $d_0(\top) = 0$.
- $A_1 = |\mathbf{B} + \Delta^{\frac{1}{2}}| = \{\bot, \top, 0\top, 1\top\}$.
  $d_1(\top) = \max\{d_B(\top), d_0(\top)/2\} = 1$ $\qquad$ $d_1(0\top) = \max\{d_B(0), d_0(\top)/2\} = 0$
  $d_1(1\top) = \max\{d_B(1), d_0(\top)/2\} = 0$.
- $A_2 = |\mathbf{B} + \mathbf{A_1}^{\frac{1}{2}}| = \{\bot, \top, 0\top, 1\top, \top 0\top, \top 1\top, 00\top, 01\top, 10\top, 11\top\}$
  $d_2(\top) = \max\{d_B(\top), d_1(\top)/2\} = 1$ $\qquad$ $d_2(0\top) = \max\{d_B(0), d_1(\top)/2\} = 1/2$
  $d_2(1\top) = 1/2$ $\qquad$ $d_2(\top 0\top) = d_2(\top 1\top) = 1$
  $d_2(00\top) = d_2(01\top) = d_2(10\top) = d_2(11\top) = 0$

- $A_i = \{\bot\} \cup \{k\top \mid k \text{ is a string of } 0,\ 1 \text{ or } \top \text{ of length at most } i\} \quad (1 \le i)$

$$d_i(k\top) = 1/2^n \quad n < i$$
$$= 0 \quad n = i$$

where $0 \le n \le i$ is the position of the first occurrence of $\top$ in $k\top$.

The lub $\mathbf{A} = \bigcup_{i \ge 0} \mathbf{A_i}$ therefore consists of $\bot$ and tokens of the form $k\top$ for all finite strings k of 0, 1 and $\top$. Moreover, the diameter map d of $\mathbf{A}$ is given by $d(k\top) = \sup\{d_i(k\top) \mid k\top \in A_i\} = 1/2^n$, where $n \ge 0$ is the position of the first $\top$ in $k\top$. Clearly A represents the base of the product topology on the Cantor space $C = \{0,1\}^\omega$. The token $k\top$ represents the basic open set with a finite number of 0 or 1 fixed co-ordinates. For example, $0\top 1\top$ is the set of all points of the Cantor space with 0 as 0th co-ordinate and 1 as 2nd co-ordinate. Moreover, the diameter of each token is equal to the diameter of the corresponding open set induced by the standard metric ρ on C defined by $\rho(x,y) = 1/2^n$ where n is the least integer such that $x_n \ne y_n$. All in all we have $S(\mathbf{A}) \cong (C, \rho)$.

7 Future work

A slight blemish of the preceding work is that the subsystem relation $\trianglelefteq$ (Definition 3.1) involves the rather technical condition 3.1(ii) which is alien to the usual notion of substructure relation. In fact this flaw can be overcome if one uses as a primitive (in place of strong inclusion) the strong *covering* relation $\vdash_\epsilon$, where $a \vdash_\epsilon \Gamma$, with a a token and Γ a set of tokens, means in effect that the ϵ-neighbourhood of each point in a is contained in one of tokens in Γ. In view of compactness Γ can be assumed to be finite here. This idea will be developed on another occasion.

Another topic reserved for later treatment is that of the function space constructor. There is an initial difficulty here in describing the tokens of the function space. These need to provide a base for the topology, which in view of compactness may be described either as the compact-open or as the point-open topology. To handle this we have to admit into our information systems a second *sort* of tokens, representing either (basic) *compact sets* or (a dense set of) *points*.

The restriction to compact spaces may be justified by appeal to the intended applications of the work (for example, *bounded* nondeterminism); more fundamentally, however, the finitary character of information systems, as usually understood, requires such restriction. If we are willing to admit, say an infinitary covering relation into the basic apparatus, it may be possible to treat general (complete) metric spaces by adapting the methods of this paper. The *locally compact* (metric) spaces form the largest class of spaces which one expects to be able to present by means of finitary information systems; a suitable extension of the methods of this paper should suffice to handle these.

Acknowledgement. This work has been supported by the SERC grant "Foundational Structures for Computer Science".

References

[Abr88] S. Abramsky. A Cooks tour of the finitary non-well founded sets (abstract). *EATCS Bulletin*, 36:233–234, 1988.

[AR88] P. America and J. Rutten. Solving reflexive domain equations in a category of complete metric spaces. In *3rd workshop on mathematical foundations of programming language semantics*, volume 298 of *Lecture Notes in Computer Science*, pages 254–288. Springer Verlag, 1988.

[BC81] G. Berry and P.-L. Curien. Sequential algorithms on concrete data structures. Technical report, Report of Ecole Nationale Superieure des Mines de Paris, Centre de Mathematiques Appliquées, Sophia Antipolis, 1981.

[BP89] B. Banaschewski and A. Pultr. Cauchy points of metric locales. *Can. J. Math.*, 41:830–854, 1989.

[dBZ82] J. W. de Bakker and J. Zucker. Processes and the denotational semantics of concurrency. *Information and Control*, 54:70–120, 1982.

[ES91] A. Edalat and M. B. Smyth. Categories of information systems. In D. H. Pitt, P. L. Curien, S. Abramsky, A. M. Pitts, A. Poigne, and D. E. Rydeheard, editors, *Category theory in computer science*, pages 37–52. Springer-Verlag, 1991.

[ES92] A. Edalat and M. B. Smyth. I-categories as a framework for solving domain equations. *Theoretical Computer Science*, 1992. to appear.

[MCZ91] M. E. Majster-Cederbaum and F. Zetzsche. Towards a foundation for semantics in complete metric spaces. *Information and Computation*, 90:217–243, 1991.

[Mic51] E. Michael. Topologies on spaces of subsets. *Trans. Amer. Math. Soc.*, 71:152–82, 1951.

[Sco82] D. S. Scott. Domains for denotational semantics. In M. Nielson and E. M. Schmidt, editors, *Automata, Languages and Programming: Proceedings 1982*. Springer-Verlag, Berlin, 1982. Lecture Notes in Computer Science **140**.

[Smy77] M. B. Smyth. Effectively given domains. *Theoretical Computer Science*, 5:257–274, 1977.

[Smy92] M. B. Smyth. Completeness of quasi-uniform and syntopological spaces. *Journal of London Mathematical Society*, 1992. to appear.

Asynchronous rendez-vous in distributed logic programming

A. Eliëns & E.P. de Vink

Vrije Universiteit, Department of Mathematics and Computer Science

De Boelelaan 1081, 1081 HV Amsterdam The Netherlands

email: eliens@cs.vu.nl vink@cs.vu.nl

Abstract

In this paper the semantics of the communication mechanism of the distributed logic programming language DLP is studied. DLP combines logic programming with object oriented features and parallelism. For an abstract subset of DLP both an operational and denotational semantics is given. The language DLP supports active objects, method call by rendez-vous and moreover (distributed) backtracking over the results of such a rendez-vous. To enable further exploitation of parallelism, the rendez-vous provided is asynchronous. A distinction is made between the creation of a process for evaluating the method call on the one hand, and the request for an answer on the other hand. To model this communication mechanism (syntactic) resumptions are employed. The notion of a resumption explains the backtracking taking place in the asynchronous rendez-vous. In addition, resumptions facilitate the systematic comparison of the operational and denotational semantics presented.

Keywords: ***concurrency, metric semantics, distributed logic programming, continuations***

Contents

1 Introduction

Distributed logic programming is the result of combining logic programming with object oriented features and parallelism. In this paper we will study the semantics of the distributed logic programming language DLP [Eliëns, 1992]. In particular we will pay attention to the communication mechanism of DLP, that supports an asynchronous rendez-vous with distributed backtracking over the resulting answers.

In previous work ([Eliëns, 1991b] and [Eliëns and de Vink, 1992]) we have studied the semantics of the synchronous rendez-vous with backtracking. This paper extends our previous work by providing a solution that enables to maintain search-completeness when backtracking over the results of an asynchronous call.

DLP is a language for distributed logic programming. It extends Prolog with constructs for parallel object oriented programming. From a programming point of view it supports explicit parallelism through active multi-threaded objects. Its distinguishing feature is a backtrackable rendez-vous that allows (distributed) backtracking over the solutions resulting from a method call. The communication primitives of DLP in fact allow to employ what one may call an asynchronous rendez-vous, in which the request for the result of a method call is postponed until the evaluation of an arbitrary intermittent goal has succeeded. This feature enables the programmer himself to define and-parallelism, and restricted variants thereof, in a convenient way. However, in the implementation and subsequently in the semantic description, record has to be kept of the answers resulting from a method call, in order to preserve completeness.

As examples of languages combining logic programming, object oriented programming and parallelism we mention Vulcan, an object oriented extension of Concurrent Prolog [Kahn et al, 1986] and Polka, an object oriented extension of Parlog [Davison, 1989]. A serious drawback of these two languages is that backtracking over multiple answers is not allowed, which may be directly attributed to their heritage to respectively Concurrent Prolog and Parlog. As another example we mention MultiLog, a multitasking object oriented extension of Prolog that may be used for prototyping embedded systems. MultiLog does not support backtracking over the answers to a method call, since its designers, taking Ada as a starting point, did not conceive of such backtracking as a necessary feature. The absence of backtracking is particularly felt in applications that rely on search, which is in general true for knowledge based systems. (A parallel logic programming language that does support backtracking over the results of a communication is Delta Prolog [Pereira and Nasr, 1984]. However Delta Prolog lacks any object oriented features and supports a communication mechanism that is less powerful method call by rendez-vous. For non-concurrent examples of extending Prolog with object oriented features we refer to [Zaniolo, 1984] or [Yokoi, 1986].)

A prototype of DLP has been implemented in a variant of the language introduced in [America, 1987] and is described in [Eliëns, 1992]. In [Eliëns, 1991b] the implementation of a distributed medical expert system is described, illustrating the distribution of control over multiple active objects using DLP.

Semantics In this paper we will focus mainly on the behavioral aspects of DLP. Following the "logic programming without logic" approach (cf. [de Bakker, 1991]) we will propose an abstract, uninterpreted language $\mathcal{B}$ that will serve as a vehicle for an examination of the asynchronous rendez-vous as present in DLP. The strategy of analyzing the control flow of a skeletal language first, before given an account of the full programming language under consideration has been shown profitable in, e.g., [Kok, 1988] and [de Bruin and de Vink, 1989]. Since the semantics for (the core of) Prolog including the cut operator, and therefore of individual DLP objects, has been extensively studied in [Jones and Mycroft, 1984], [de Vink, 1990] and [de Bakker, 1991], attention is given primarily to the creation of processes and the flow of control during communication. Complementary to the approach followed here one could stress the logical aspects of DLP by studying a declarative semantics as done, e.g., for contextual logic programming in [Monteiro and Porto, 1988].

The language $\mathcal{B}$ that we introduce in order to study the semantics of DLP includes as primitives actions (that result in updating a substitution or may fail), recursive procedure call, a construct for creating (active) objects and three communication primitives: method calls, a statement that allows an object to state its willingness to accept a method call and a statement by which the caller can request for the results of a rendez-vous.

Answer continuations The asynchronous nature of the rendez-vous lies in the explicit distinction between method call and the request for the results thereof. The idea is that the caller may use the time needed to evaluate the method call by doing something useful, like evaluating some goal. The decoupling of call and answer-request may lead to ***search incompleteness***. Combining all the solutions of the intermediate goals with the solutions resulting from the evaluation of the method call requires extra precautions. The solution that we will propose to solve this problem is to record the solutions generated by the object in response to the method call.

Semantically, this led us to consider what we call ***answer continuations*** in addition to the kind of continuations that we use to model backtracking and the safety aspects of our communication mechanism. A somewhat uncommon feature of our approach is to regard ***answers as actions***. This allows us to treat the results of a rendez-vous by means of (syntactic) resumptions, which are statements executed by the caller to effect the results of a rendez-vous. We think that this approach drastically reduces the requirements we have to impose on our semantic domain since (in opposition to e.g. [America et al, 1989]) we do not need a domain equation of the form $\mathbb{P} \cong \mathbb{P} \rightarrow A \times \mathbb{P}$ where the process domain $\mathbb{P}$ occurs on the left-hand side of a function arrow.

Syntactic resumptions come in three flavors. Evaluating the action that represents an answer may result either in updating a substition (when a new answer is generated), in failure (when no new answers can be produced) or in a choice between the answers already generated. In the latter case the resumption is a (compound) disjunctive goal that allows to backtrack over the actions generated previously as answers to the call. This will only occur when there are finitely many solutions for a method call.

Metric spaces The development of the semantics of $\mathcal{B}$ takes place in a metrical setting. The use of metric topology for the formulation of denotational semantics of programming languages has been advocated over the years by De Bakker and co-workers. See, e.g., [de Bakker and Zucker, 1982], [de Bakker et al, 1988], [America et al, 1989], [de Boer et al, 1990]. Here, following the method proposed in [Kok and Rutten, 1990], not only the denotational semantics but also the operational semantics, and moreover, the equivalence of the operational and (a projection of) the denotational semantics is established through the help of higher order contractions that have, according to Banach's theorem, unique fixed points on complete metric spaces.

2 DLP – a language for distributed logic programming

The DLP language is an extension of Prolog with *objects* and *special forms* for dealing with non-logical variables, object creation, and engaging in a rendez-vous. Objects in DLP are module-like entities with private non-logical (instance) variables and methods that have access to these variables in a protected way. Methods are defined by clauses that are written as Prolog clauses; these clauses may however contain as goals the special forms mentioned. We will treat here a subset covering the special forms listed below. An important restriction of this subset of DLP is that *accept* goals may occur only in the constructor process.

The special forms include:

- $v := t$ – to assign (the value of) the term t to the non-logical variable v
- $O = new(c(t))$ – to create a new (active) instance of the object c and start the constructor process evaluating the goal $c(t)$, O thereafter refers to the newly created object
- $Q = O!m(t)$ – to request a rendez-vous with the object to which O refers, Q will thereafter refer to the process created for evaluating the method call $m(t)$
- $Q?$ – to collect the answers resulting from the goal evaluated by the process to which Q refers,
- $accept(m_1, ..., m_n)$ – to state the willingness to accept methods $m_1, ..., m_n$

When assigning a term t to a non-logical variable, all non-logical variables in the term are first replaced by their values. The same applies when unifying two terms.

In particular we will concentrate on the issues of object creation and the communication occurring in a rendez-vous. Instances of objects are created by using the special form

$O = new(c(t))$ that results in binding O to the newly created instance of object c. When creating the object the constructor process evaluating the goal $c(t)$ is started for it. An asynchronous rendez-vous is initiated by a request of the form $Q = O!m(t)$, with O bound to an object. When the request is accepted the logical variable Q will become bound to a pointer to the process created to evaluate the goal $m(t)$. A resumption request of the form $Q?$, where Q must be bound to a process, is used to collect the results of a rendez-vous. For a rendez-vous to take place the object must state its willingness to answer a method call by an accept statement of the form $accept(m_1, ..., m_n)$.

DLP is a distributed language in the sense that it supports processes, communication between processes and is able to handle failure arising in a communication. C.f. [Bal et al, 1989]. The distinguishing feature of DLP, compared with other approaches at combining logic programming with object oriented features and parallelism, is the possible occurrence of distributed backtracking in a rendez-vous. In the absence of distributed backtracking an object could have been identified with a process, since an object would then be either executing its own activity or evaluating a method call. Backtracking however requires to keep administration of what part of the search space has been explored. A notion of processes, separate from objects, is thus motivated by the need to keep record of this information; processes are created for each method call to enable backtracking over the answers. The language DLP also supports inheritance. However, since inheritance is statically implemented by copying the code of the inherited objects, we need not consider this issue when characterizing the dynamic behavior of objects.

2.1 The execution model: objects, processes and backtracking

An execution model for DLP must give an account of the behavior of objects and processes and must explain how process creation and communication interact with backtracking. Before giving a formal account in section 3 and 4 of process creation and communication in the presence of backtracking we will briefly discuss each of these notions.

Objects serve as a means for modularization and provide protection for (local) data. Non-logical variables may be used to store the data encapsulated by an object. The clauses defined for an object act as methods, in that they have exclusive access to these data.

An object declaration in DLP contains the names of the non-logical variables of (instances of) the object and a definition of both the constructor clauses and method clauses. The clauses are written in standard Prolog format, but may contain as goals the special forms listed previously. A clause is considered a constructor clause when the predicate name of the head of the clause is identical to the name of the declared object. A method for an object is defined by all clauses having that method name as the predicate name of their head.

When a new object is created, by a goal of the form $O = new(c(t))$, then this newly created object contains a copy of the non-logical variables of the declared object and also (conceptually) a copy of all its clauses. We will consider only active objects, that is objects with own activity arising from evaluating the constructor for that object. Since inheritance is effected by copying the non-logical variables and clauses from the inherited objects, then for giving a semantic characterization of the interpretation of DLP programs it suffices to look at DLP without inheritance.

Processes are created on the occasion of creating a new object, and when requesting a rendez-vous. When a new object is created, the constructor process, defined by clauses for the predicate with the name of the object, is started. When a rendez-vous is requested by a method call, a process is started for evaluating the method call. Creating a new process for evaluating such a goal is necessitated by our approach to distributed backtracking. Both the constructor process and the processes started for evaluating a goal by an object are said to refer to that object.

Distributed backtracking may occur when multiple answer substitutions result from evaluating a method call. As an example, a method call to the object declared below may generate an indefinite number of solutions.

nat

```
obj nat {
number(0).
number(s(X)) :- number(X).
}
```

The constructor clause for the object states that any call to *num* will be accepted.

Evaluating the goal

:- O=new(nat()), Q=O!number(X), Q?, write(X), fail.

results in printing all natural numbers, eventually. The process created for evaluating *num(X)* backtracks each time that backtracking over *Q*? is tried due to the occurrence of *fail* in the goal.

In the example above, multiple processes could safely be active for the object simultaneously. However, in the presence of non-logical variables, protection is needed from concurrently changing the value of a such a variable, by disallowing method calls to be simultaneously active. DLP supports mutual exclusion between method calls to the extent that any state change due to an assignment to a non-logical variable may safely occur before the first answer. For backtracking over the remaining answers, the state may be fixed in a non-logical variable in order to avoid interference from other method calls. We thus allow multiple processes refering to a single object to backtrack concurrently over answer substitutions generated in a rendez-vous, since by a decision of design, we do not wish to exclude other processes from having a method call evaluated by that object, any longer than until the first answer substitution or failure has been delivered.

Related to the issue of mutual exclusion is the question whether in backtracking any assignment made to non-logical variables must be undone. Again, as a matter of design, we have decided that assignments to non-logical variables are permanent. Non-logical variables were introduced for storing persistent data, shared by all processes refering to an object. We observe moreover that restoring a state may be programmed, using additional non-logical variables. From the point of view of a semantic description, neither choice seems to present any serious difficulties.

An example As an another example, consider the object declaration for a travel agency.

agency

```
object agency {
var cities = [amsterdam, paris, london].
agency() :-  run().
run() :-  accept(destination,add), run().
destination(X) :-  member(X,cities).
add(X) :-  append([X],cities,R), cities :=  R.
}
```

An agency may be asked for a destination. The destinations an agency offers are contained in a list of cities. The non-logical variable *cities* storing this list is initialized to contain as possible destinations *amsterdam*, *paris* and *london*.

Creating a new agency, and subsequently asking it for a destination is done as in the following goal.

```
O = new(agency()),
Q = O!destination(Y),
Q?
...
```

When evaluating the first component of this goal the logical variable O will become bound to the newly created *agency* that offers as destinations *amsterdam*, *paris* and *london*. Immediately thereafter the method call $Q = O!destination(Y)$ will be evaluated, but the call will not be accepted until the accept statement expressing the willingness of the agency referred to by O to accept a call is reached. The evaluation of the method call will result (when requesting for an answer by the goal Q?) in binding Y to *amsterdam* and when backtracking occurs, subsequently to *paris* and *london*. Then the call will fail. Backtracking over the statement $Q = O!new(agency())$ is not possible. This call will simply fail.

The own activity of the travel agency consists of stating its willingness to accept any method call for *destination* and *add*. (The travel agency must be an active object to ensure that the non-logical variable *cities* will not be updated during the request for a *destination*.)

2.2 The asynchronous rendez-vous mechanism

The rendez-vous presented consists of two parts, the creation of a process to evaluate a method call and the request for an answer. For creation of the evaluating process, the special statement

- $Q = O!m(t)$

is used to request the object to which O refers to create a process to evaluate the goal $m(t)$. The variable Q thereafter refers to that process. For the request of the result we have introduced the resumption request

- $Q?$

that asks the process, referred to by Q, for an (other) answer.

Informal semantics A call of the form $Q = O!m(t)$ may be regarded as an asynchronous method call, since receiving the answers requires an explicit request of the form $Q?$. The variable Q is bound to a pointer to the process evaluating $m(t)$. The method call $m(t)$ be explicitly accepted by an accept goal of the object to which O refers. We call the goal $Q?$ a *resumption request*, since it delivers a resumption containing the answer substitutions that result from the call. Evaluating the resumption enables the possible variable bindings of these answers to take effect in the current context.

The decomposition of a method call in the request of evaluation and the request of a result allows the programmer to achieve extra parallelism, since the newly created process runs independently of the invoking process, which does not have to wait for an answer. Such overlapping of processes is expressed by a goal of the form

$$Q = O!G, A, Q?$$

Between the creation of the process evaluating the goal G and stating the resumption request to collect the answers to G, the invoking process can perform any action whatsoever.

The asynchronous rendez-vous preserves completeness in coupling the solutions produced by evaluating G with the bindings resulting from the evaluation of A. When backtracking occurs each alternative binding resulting from the evaluation of A must be coupled with all possible solutions of G. However, if G has infinitely many solutions, A will never be tried for producing alternative bindings.

And-parallelism The decomposition of the rendez-vous allows the programmer to define and-parallelism in a rather straightforward way, as

```
A&B :-  Q = self! B, A, Q?.
```

where *self* refers to the object evaluating the goal *A&B*. Such goals may however occur only in passive objects, since only passive objects allow internal concurrency.

An advantage of this approach is that the programmer may restrict the cases where parallel evaluation occurs by imposing extra conditions (cf. [DeGroot, 1984]) as in

```
A&B :-  ground(B),!, Q = self! B, A, Q?.
A&B :-  A, B.
```

where splitting of a new process is allowed only when B is ground. Note that the cut in the first clause is used to avoid unwanted backtracking over the second solution of A&B.

2.3 Search completeness

Coupling the solutions of an intermediate goal with the solutions generated by a method call requires some extra precautions. We will illustrate the possible pitfalls with an example.

Suppose that we have an object *c* that contains some information, for instance a list of items satisfying some constraint.

constraints

```
object c {
c() :-  accept(a), c().
a(1).
a(3).
}
```

Now suppose that we have also clauses enumerating candidate solutions. For example these clauses may be as depicted below.

clauses

```
b(1).
b(2).
b(3).
```

These clauses and constraints may be used to test each constraint against a candidate solution. Moreover, as the following goal illustrates, part of this work may be done in parallel. Let the goal be as follows (comments are given after the %-sign):

```
?-
  O = new(c()),        % creates an instance of c
  Q = O!a(X),          % creates a process to evaluate a(X)
  b(Y),                % in the meantime we may evaluate b
  Q?,                  % requests answer for a
  write(r(X,Y)),       % write the result r(X,Y)
  fail.                % backtracks to generate all solutions
```

When evaluating this goal, backtracking will occur for the resumption request *Q*?, so initially the output will be

r(1,1) r(3,1)

Thereafter, there will be no more answers so the result of evaluating *Q*? will be failure. Now the goal *b*(*Y*) will be tried for further solutions. However, when trying *Q*? for an answer, we have a problem since all solutions for the goal $a(X)$ have already been generated. One option is to re-evaluate $a(X)$. However, this seems a waste of computing resources and moreover this might be dangerous due to possible side-effects. The solution we have adopted is to store the answers when they are for the first time produced for a method call. These answers may be re-produced to allow backtracking over the answers that have been given when a new solution is produced for the intermediate goal. For our example, the output will then become:

r(1,1) r(3,1) r(1,2) r(3,2) r(1,3) r(3,3)

combining all the answers of $a(X)$ with all the answers of $b(Y)$.

2.4 Resumptions

So-called resumptions are used to implement the backtracking behavior of the rendezvous. A *resumption* is an ordinary Prolog goal that must be executed by the caller of a method to effect the bindings produced by evaluating the call.

Let us briefly explain the role played by the resumptions. In order to deliver the proper resumption, the process evaluating the method call can be thought of as having an attribute

- *goal* – for storing the initial goal

that is used to create a resumption when the process is asked for an answer. In addition, we use two attributes to store the resulting answers.

- *result* – to store the most recent answer,
- *solutions* – which contains all the answers that have been produced.

What resumption is returned depends on the state, i.e., the values of the logical and non-logical variables, of the process evaluating the method call and the contents of the *result* attribute. Assuming that we have an appropriate translation of the values of the attributes *goal*, *result* and *solutions* to Prolog terms, resumptions may take the following form:

- *goal* = *result* – the unifying resumption, that is delivered when the *result* is not empty (the process may continue to compute other solutions);
- *fail* – the failing resumption, that is delivered when there are no more new solutions; and
- *member*(*goal*, *solutions*) – the backtracking resumption, that is delivered when the process has sent all the solutions it can compute.

The failing resumption, when executed by the process requesting an answer, results in failure, evidently. Both the unifying and the backtracking resumption bind the variables occurring in *goal* to their instantiations in respectively *result* and *solutions*. The latter resumption, moreover, backtracks over all solutions generated. Backtracking resumptions may be delivered when goals occur in between a call and a resumption request.

To enable the calling process to backtrack repeatedly over the generated solutions, the evaluation process created to answer the method call stores the last solution found (in the variable *result*) as well as all the solutions produced thus far (in the variable *solutions*). As long as new solutions are produced the evaluation process returns the last solution stored in *result* to the calling process. When no more solutions can be generated and the calling process asks for another solution then the resumption request $Q?$ initially fails. If the resumption request immediately follows the method call as is the case with a synchronous method call, this is the end of the story. However, when the calling process successfully backtracks over a goal in between the method call and the resumption request, as may be the case for goals of the form

?- Q = O!m(t), B, Q?,...

then calling the resumption request *Q*? will result in trying all the solutions generated. These solutions will be handed over to the calling process by a *backtracking resumption*. This is only possible (and necessary), of course, when the number of solutions is finite.

3 The metric approach

In the next section we will introduce the language $\mathcal{B}$ that reflects in an abstract way the functionality of DLP.

The behavior of the abstract language $\mathcal{B}$ will be modeled, denotationally, using tools from metric topology. In short the approach is as follows: The processes that will serve as denotations of programs are taken from a process domain, a complete metric space that is given by reflexive domain equation. The semantical definitions then are given systems of equations that implicitly specify a contracting mapping on a complete metric space. As by Banach's theorem such a mapping has a unique fixed point the resulting operators or models are well-defined.

The use of contractions to characterize a variety of models has been advocated in [Kok and Rutten, 1990], and has moreover proven its usefulness in verifying the equality of operational and denotational semantics. See [de Bakker, 1991], [Jacquet and Monteiro, 1990], [Rutten, 1990], [America and Rutten, 1991], [van Breugel, 1991] for several applications in imperative, logical, object oriented and real-time programming languages. See also [de Bakker and Meyer, 1988], [de Bakker, 1989], [de Bakker and de Vink, 1991], for some more introductory overviews of the method for the several programming paradigms. In short, when we succeed in proving that both the operational semantics and the denotational semantics are a fixed point of a higher order contraction, then by the uniqueness of fixed points they are equal.

In somewhat more detail, when we have, say, a language $\mathcal{L}$ we may specify a (labeled) transition system describing the possible computation steps of a program in $\mathcal{L}$. With $\mathbb{R}$ a set containing the possible results, for instance sets of strings of action labels, we may define an operational semantics $\mathcal{O}[\![\cdot]\!] : \mathcal{L} \rightarrow \mathbb{R}$ as the fixed point of a higher order contracting mapping $\Psi : (\mathcal{L} \rightarrow \mathbb{R}) \rightarrow (\mathcal{L} \rightarrow \mathbb{R})$, collecting all possible computation sequences. Next we define $\mathcal{D}[\![\cdot]\!] : \mathcal{L} \rightarrow \mathbb{P}$ for a domain $\mathbb{P}$. Now taking a projection $\pi : \mathbb{P} \rightarrow \mathbb{R}$, mapping elements from $\mathbb{P}$ to $\mathbb{R}$, we must show that $\pi \circ \mathcal{D}$, the composition of π and $\mathcal{D}[\![\cdot]\!]$ is a fixed point of the mapping Ψ, and by the uniqueness of fixed points for contractions we are done. This technique has been used here for structuring the equivalence proof, following [de Bakker, 1991].

4 Operational semantics

The abstract language $\mathcal{B}$ includes actions, recursive procedure calls, and has primitives that support object creation and the asynchronous rendez-vous. These primitives reflect the functionality of similar primitives in DLP.

4.1 Syntax

We assume a set of actions *Act*, with typical elements a. As primitive actions we assume the actions *fail* included in *Act*. We have method variables $m \in Meth$, that act as procedure variables. Further we introduce a set of (names for) method processes *MProc*, with typical elements $\hat{\alpha}$ and $\hat{\beta}$, and assume to have also a set of (names for) object or constructor process *OProc*, with typical elements $\underline{\alpha}$ and $\underline{\beta}$. Since method processes will refer to an object process, for each element $\hat{\alpha}$ in *MProc*, we state that there is an object name $\underline{\hat{\alpha}}$ in *OProc*.

Further we need (asynchronous) method calls of the form $\hat{\alpha}!m$, accept statements of the form $[m_1, ..., m_k]$ and resumption requests of the form $\hat{\alpha}?$.

We define extensions $e \in Ext$ by

$$e ::= new(\underline{\alpha}) \mid \hat{\alpha}!m \mid [m_1, ..., m_k] \mid \hat{\alpha}?$$

and define *goals* $G \in Goal$ by

$$G ::= a \mid m \mid G_1; G_2 \mid G_1 \Box G_2 \mid e$$

A *declaration* D is of the form

$$D \in Decl = (Meth \to Goal) \times (OProc \to Goal)$$

For a clause $m \leftarrow G$ we use $D(m)$ to denote G and for an object name $\underline{\alpha}$ we use $D(\underline{\alpha})$ to denote the constructor of $\underline{\alpha}$.

A *program* is a tuple

$$< D \mid G >$$

We assume that the goal G and the goals occurring as the body of a clause satisfy guardedness restrictions, which informally means that recursion is always preceded by some action. More precisely, we define *guarded* goals $g \in GGoal$ and *strictly guarded* goals $s \in SGGoal$ by

$$g ::= s \mid g_1; g_2 \mid g_1 \Box g_2 \mid new(g)$$

$$s ::= a \mid \hat{\alpha}!m \mid [m_1, ..., m_k] \mid \hat{\alpha}? \mid s; G \mid s_1 \Box s_2$$

and demand that $D(m) \in GGoal$ for each method variable m.

In order to treat process creation and method call properly in the (half) uniform setting of the language $\mathcal{B}$, we lay the burden of providing fresh process names in the constructs $new(\alpha)$ and $\hat{\beta}?$ on the shoulders of the programmer. Alternatively, global counters could be introduced, that keep track of the process names all ready used. To our opinion this aspect is of minor importance and would obscure the semantical modelling. However, it should be noted that, as a consequence of the treatment here, in the correctness proof for the denotational model in the next section we have to make assumptions on the algebraic properties of the semantical operators (which can straightforwardly be proven in a setting with a explicit naming mechanism).

4.2 Observable behavior

The successful evaluation of a goal results in a substitution that binds the variables of the goal to a value. When a goal has multiple solutions there are correspondingly many substitutions.

A substitution is a function from logical variables to terms with finite support.. Substitutions are extended to terms in a straightforward way. We assume a set of substitutions Σ with elements σ, θ. The substitution σ_{id} is the empty substitution that acts as the identity function on terms. We will use Σ_δ to denote the set Σ with the ***impossible substitution*** δ added. For characterizing the behavior of a program we use a set of labels Λ with typical elements ℓ. The actual labels employed will be described when introducing the transition rules in section 4.6.

As the result domain for characterizing the behavior of a program we take

$$\mathbb{R} = \mathcal{P}nc(\Lambda_\delta^\infty)$$

the non-empty closed powerset of finite and infinite strings over Λ, possibly ending with δ.

In order to compare the operational and denotational semantics we need to endow the domain of the operational semantics with a metric structure. One may argue that such restrictions on $\mathbb{R}$ (to non-empty and closed subsets of Λ_δ^∞) are not needed for an operational model. The alternative of using plain sets, however, is possible too. In that case the definition of the operational semantics, where the metric structure of $\mathbb{R}$ is essential, would be replaced by a result capturing a fixed point characterization.

Processes We use a set processes (or more adequately process names) *Proc*. We already distinguished between object processes (*OProc*) and method processes (*MProc*). We have that *Proc* = *OProc* ∪ *MProc*. An object process corresponds to the constructor process of an object. Method processes are used to carry out the evaluation of a method call. We use α and β to denote elements of *Proc*.

4.3 Communication by rendez-vous

A rendez-vous is decomposed in a method call of the form $\hat{\beta}!m$ and a request for the answers resulting from evaluating m, of the form $\hat{\beta}?$. A method call $\hat{\beta}!m$ is considered to be addressed to the object $\underline{\hat{\beta}}$. The caller is assumed to provide the process name $\hat{\beta}$ for the process that is created to evaluate m.

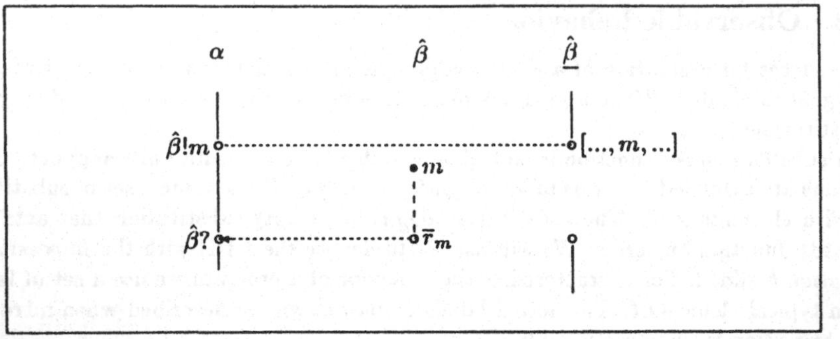

We have pictured a typical rendez-vous above. As soon as the call $\hat{\beta}!m$ is accepted, due to the occurrence of $[..., m, ...]$ in $\underline{\hat{\beta}}$, process α can continue. The process $\hat{\beta}$, which refers to the object $\underline{\hat{\beta}}$, starts evaluating the goal m. The object process $\underline{\hat{\beta}}$ itself is then suspended. When arrived at the request $\hat{\beta}?$ process α must wait until process $\hat{\beta}$ has computed an answer. When the first answer is computed it is sent to α. The process $\underline{\hat{\beta}}$ may then proceed with the evaluation of its constructor. The process $\hat{\beta}$ continues computing alternative answers.

4.4 Resumptions

To specify how the results of a rendez-vous are transferred between the process evaluating the method call and the caller we introduce so-called *resumptions*.

First, however, we introduce an auxiliary syntactic class *Res* with elements R that we define as

$$R ::= \sigma \mid \delta \mid \varepsilon$$

that are used to prepare the actual resumptions. We call the elements of *Res pre-resumptions*. A pre-resumption R represents the information that is sent to the process that requests a resumption. Three cases must be distinguished. Either the answer is (equivalent to) a substitution (that binds the variables in a call to some value), or the answer represents failure (when no more solutions can be generated), or, finally, the answer consists of the disjunction of all previously generated answers.

Answer continuations The answers that are generated in response to a method call are stored in a so-called *answer continuation*.

We introduce the set *ACont* of answer continuations with typical elements A that we define as

$$A ::= fail \mid A \,\square\, a_\sigma$$

When no answer has been generated the answer continuation will be *fail*. For each answer that is produced the answer continuation is the disjunctive goal that consists of the previous answer continuation and the action a_σ that represents the effect of the substitution σ.[1]

Evaluation The actual resumption is computed by the function $eval : Req \times Res \times ACont \rightarrow Goal$, that takes a resumption request, a pre-resumption and an answer continuation to deliver the proper resumption goal. *Req* is the set of resumption requests; its elements are of the form $\hat{\alpha}?$. The function *eval* is defined by the equations

$$eval(\hat{\beta}?, \sigma, A) = a_\sigma \Box \hat{\beta}?$$

$$eval(\hat{\beta}?, \delta, A) = fail$$

$$eval(\hat{\beta}?, \varepsilon, A) = A$$

As follows from our previous discussion, when the pre-resumption is an ordinary substitution σ (that is when a new answer has been produced) the caller is allowed to backtrack over alternative solutions. In that case the resumption is a disjunctive goal containing a resumption request as an alternative to the action a_σ representing the answer substitution σ.

The counterpart of the function *eval* is the function $\overline{eval} : Req \times Res \times ACont \rightarrow ACont$ that determines how to modify the answer continuation for the process to which the request for a resumption is addressed. (Here, the argument $\hat{\beta}?$ is in fact redundant, but included to stress the symmetry between *eval* and $\overline{eval}$.) The function $\overline{eval}$ is defined by the equations

$$\overline{eval}(\hat{\beta}?, \sigma, A) = A \Box a_\sigma$$

$$\overline{eval}(\hat{\beta}?, \delta, A) = A$$

$$\overline{eval}(\hat{\beta}?, \varepsilon, A) = A$$

Evidently, when the pre-resumption is an ordinary substitution σ, the action a_σ corresponding to that substitution must be stored in disjunction with the previous answer continuation to deliver the new answer continuation.

4.5 Continuations

To model the actual computation we employ, respectively, (syntactic) success continuations S, (syntactic) failure continuations F (which may be considered as stacks of success continuations), answer continuations A (that are used to store the solutions generated for a method call) and process continuations P (that are used to model the mutual exclusion protocol of DLP).

Success continuations $S \in SCont$ are defined as

$$S ::= \surd \mid G : S$$

A success continuation represents the part of the program that must be executed to find a solution and corresponds to the sequential evaluation of a goal (without backtracking).

[1]For example, the substitution $\{X_1/t_1, ..., X_n/t_n\}$ is represented by the unification goal $(X_1, ..., X_n) = (t_1, ..., t_n)$.

Failure continuations $F \in FCont$ are defined as

$$F ::= \Delta \mid E \mid R : F \mid [S,\sigma] : F$$

Failure continuations may be regarded as stacks of success continuations. We use two bottom elements for this stack, namely Δ and E to distinguish respectively between the situation that there are no further solutions and the situation that an answer continuation must be returned.

A failure continuation of the form $[S,\sigma] : F$ occurs in the course of evaluating a goal. Whenever (for a method process) the failure continuation becomes $[\surd,\sigma] : F$ or Δ it will be replaced by a continuation of the form $\sigma : F$ or $\delta : E$ to enable the process to communicate with the process that initially invoked the goal.

Answer continuations $A \in ACont$ have been defined as

$$A ::= fail \mid A \Box a_\sigma$$

Recall that answer continuations are goals that are sent to the calling process only after all solutions for the method call have been found and sent to the caller.

Process continuations $P \in PCont$ are defined as

$$P ::= \Xi \mid < \alpha, F, A >: P$$

Process continuations are used to model the mutual exclusion protocol of DLP. It is guaranteed that during the rendez-vous no other method call will be accepted until the first answer to the call has been delivered. When accepting a method call, the accepting (object) process is blocked by the process evaluating the call. After delivering the first result the blocked process is released and may continue its computation in parallel with the process evaluating the call.

4.6 Transition system

The transition system T which is defined with respect to a declaration D, is embodied in the transition schemes below. For configurations of T we use $\Gamma \in Conf = \mathcal{P}_{nf}(PCont)$ are non-empty and finite sets of syntactic process continuations. As sets of labels ℓ in Λ we will employ

$$\ell ::= \langle\alpha,\sigma\rangle \mid \langle\alpha,\delta\rangle \mid \langle\alpha,\surd,\alpha\rangle \mid \langle\alpha,\Delta\rangle \mid [\alpha,\hat{\beta}!m,\underline{\hat{\beta}}] \mid [\alpha,R,A,\hat{\beta}]$$

The formats $\langle\alpha,\sigma\rangle$, $\langle\alpha,\delta\rangle$ represent *local* success and failure. The formats $\langle\alpha,\surd,\alpha\rangle$, $\langle\alpha,\Delta\rangle$ represent *global* failure. The formats $[\alpha,\hat{\beta}!m,\underline{\hat{\beta}}]$, $[\alpha,R,A,\hat{\beta}]$ represent inter-process communication, viz. acceptance of a method call and delivery of a result on request.

To give meaning to the actions we assume to have an abstract interpretation function $I : Act \rightarrow \Sigma \rightarrow \Sigma_\delta$ defining for each action whether it is successful (and what subsequently is the update of the substitution) or fails.

B

$$\{\ldots,\langle\alpha,[a:S,\sigma]:F,A\rangle:P,\ldots\} \xrightarrow{\langle\alpha,\theta\rangle}_D \{\ldots,\langle\alpha,[S,\theta]:F\rangle:P,\ldots\} \text{ if } I(a)(\sigma)=\theta$$

Act_1

$$\{\ldots,\langle\alpha,[a:S,\sigma]:F,A\rangle:P,\ldots\}\xrightarrow{\langle\alpha,\delta\rangle}_D\{\ldots,\langle\alpha,F,A\rangle:P,\ldots\}\text{ if }I(a)(\sigma)=\delta \qquad \mathit{Act}_2$$

$$\frac{\{\ldots,\langle\alpha,[D(m):S,\sigma]:F,A\rangle:P,\ldots\}\xrightarrow{\ell}_D\Gamma}{\{\ldots,\langle\alpha,[m:S,\sigma]:F,A\rangle:P,\ldots\}\xrightarrow{\ell}_D\Gamma} \qquad \mathit{Rec}$$

$$\frac{\{\ldots,\langle\alpha,[G_1:(G_2:S),\sigma]:F,A\rangle:P,\ldots\}\xrightarrow{\ell}_D\Gamma}{\{\ldots,\langle\alpha,[(G_1;G_2):S,\sigma]:F,A\rangle:P,\ldots\}\xrightarrow{\ell}_D\Gamma} \qquad \mathit{Seq}$$

$$\frac{\{\ldots,\langle\alpha,[G_1:S,\sigma]:[G_2:S,\sigma]:F,A\rangle:P,\ldots\}\xrightarrow{\ell}_D\Gamma}{\{\ldots,\langle\alpha,[(G_1\,\Box\,G_2):S,\sigma]:F,A\rangle:P,\ldots\}\xrightarrow{\ell}_D\Gamma} \qquad \mathit{Alt}$$

$$\frac{\{\ldots,\langle\alpha,[S,\sigma]:F,A\rangle:P,<\underline{\beta},[D(\underline{\beta}):\surd,\sigma_{id}]:\Delta,\mathit{fail}\rangle:\Xi,\ldots\}\xrightarrow{\ell}_D\Gamma}{\{\ldots,\langle\alpha,[\mathit{new}(\beta):S,\sigma]:F,A\rangle:P,\ldots\}\xrightarrow{\ell}_D\Gamma} \qquad \mathit{New}$$

$$\begin{array}{l}\{\ldots,\langle\alpha,[\beta!m:S_1,\sigma_1]:F_1,A_1\rangle:P_1, \qquad \mathit{Method}\\ \quad\langle\hat{\underline{\beta}},[\,[\ldots,m,\ldots]:S_2,\sigma_2]:F_2,A_2\rangle:P_2,\ldots\}\\ \xrightarrow{[\alpha,\hat{\beta}!m,\hat{\beta}]}_D\{\ldots,\langle\alpha,[S_1,\sigma_1],F_1,A_1\rangle:P_1,\\ \qquad\qquad\langle\hat{\beta},[D(m):\surd,\sigma_1]:\Delta,\mathit{fail}\rangle:\langle\hat{\underline{\beta}},[S_2,\sigma_2]:F_2,A_2\rangle:P_2,\ldots\}\end{array}$$

$$\begin{array}{l}\{\ldots,\langle\alpha,[\hat{\beta}?:S,\sigma]:F_1,A_1\rangle:P_1,\langle\hat{\beta},R:F_2,A_2\rangle:P_2,\ldots\} \qquad \mathit{Result}\\ \xrightarrow{[\alpha,R,A_2,\hat{\beta}]}_D\{\ldots,\langle\alpha,[\mathit{eval}(\hat{\beta}?,R,A_2):S,\sigma]:F\rangle:P_1,\\ \qquad\qquad\langle\beta,F_2,\overline{\mathit{eval}(\hat{\beta}?,R,A_2)}\rangle:\Xi,\\ \qquad\qquad P_2,\ldots\}\end{array}$$

$$\{\ldots,\langle\underline{\alpha},[\surd,\sigma]:F,A\rangle:P,\ldots\}\xrightarrow{\langle\underline{\alpha},\surd,\sigma\rangle}_D\{\ldots,<\underline{\alpha},F,A\rangle:P,\ldots\} \qquad \mathit{Tick}_1$$

$$\frac{\{\ldots,\langle\hat{\alpha},\sigma:F,A\rangle:P,\ldots\}\xrightarrow{\ell}_D\Gamma}{\{\ldots,\langle\hat{\alpha},[\surd,\sigma]:F,A\rangle:P,\ldots\}\xrightarrow{\ell}_D\Gamma} \qquad \mathit{Tick}_2$$

$$\{\ldots,\langle\underline{\alpha},\Delta,A\rangle:P,\ldots\}\xrightarrow{(\alpha,\surd,\sigma)}_D\{\ldots,\Xi,\ldots\}\qquad \textit{Delta}_1$$

$$\frac{\{\ldots,\langle\hat{\alpha},\delta:E,A\rangle:P,\ldots\}\xrightarrow{\ell}_D\Gamma}{\{\ldots,\langle\hat{\alpha},\Delta,A\rangle:P,\ldots\}\xrightarrow{\ell}_D\Gamma}\qquad \textit{Delta}_2$$

$$\frac{\{\ldots,\langle\alpha,\epsilon:E,A\rangle:P,\ldots\}\xrightarrow{\ell}_D\Gamma}{\{\ldots,\langle\alpha,E,A\rangle:P,\ldots\}\xrightarrow{\ell}_D\Gamma}\qquad \textit{Epsilon}$$

The suggestive notation employed above indicates, of course, that other process continuations in the configurations remain unaffected and are the same for the premise and conclusion of a rule.

Explanation The treatment of actions and recursion is straightforward. A sequential composition $G_1; G_2$ amounts to an update of the success continuation, whereas an alternative composition $G_1 \square G$ amounts to an update of the failure continuation. Executing a new construct *new*($\underline{\beta}$) adds a new object process $\underline{\beta}$ to the configuration with as constructor the goal $D(\hat{\beta})$.

Entrance of the rendez-vous is issued by the synchronization of a method call $\hat{\beta}!m$ and an accept statement $[\ldots, m, \ldots]$ of the addressed object process $\underline{\hat{\beta}}$. The calling process continues, while the called process is blocked by the evaluation of $D(m)$. Here the transition is labelled with the communication $[\alpha, \hat{\beta}, \underline{\hat{\beta}}]$ expressing the call of α for m using $\hat{\beta}$ to $\underline{\hat{\beta}}$. Communication of the result of a method is dealt with by the resumption mechanism. If α requests $\hat{\beta}$ for an answer, while $\hat{\beta}$ is ready to deliver a result in mode R (possibly using A), the resumption *eval*($\hat{\beta}?, R, A$) is passed to α. The method process $\hat{\beta}$ continues, after adjusting the answer continuation, exploring new answers or remains stand-by (in case $F_2 \equiv E$). Since a (possibly first) answer is delivered the process continuation P_2 is put in parallel with the ones for α and $\hat{\beta}$.

For the pre-resumption $\surd$ and Δ we have to distinguish between the cases for object processes and method processes. For an object process $\surd$ (Δ) means global success (failure) and a corresponding label is delivered. For a method process, however, it means that a new answer to a method call is found (change of $[\surd, \sigma]$ to σ), respectively, that the alternatives for the call are exhausted (change of Δ to $\delta : E$). In the latter case, the process will furtheron be ready to communicate the answer already found and stored in the answer continuation. (In this case there is no need to distinguish between object and method processes.)

Operational semantics The operational semantics $\mathcal{O} : \mathcal{B} \to \mathbb{R}$ for $\mathcal{B}$ is based on the transition system. The words of labels of the transition sequences constitute the meaning of a *configuration*. If a configuration (not equal to $\{E\}$ which is terminating) does not permit a transition the meaning $\{\delta\}$, denoting deadlock, is delivered, since this situation can only arise in the presence of unsuccessful communication. We will employ, in modelling this, the notation $\bigcup_\delta \{ X_\alpha \mid \alpha \in I \}$ which represents $\bigcup \{ X_\alpha \mid \alpha \in I \}$ if I is non-empty and $\{\delta\}$ otherwise.

More precisely, we put

$$\mathcal{O}[\![< D \mid G >]\!] = \mathcal{O}_D[\![\langle \alpha_{rt}, G; \surd, \sigma_{id}] : \Delta \rangle : \Xi]\!]$$

where $\mathcal{O}_D$ is the fixed point of the contraction $\Phi_D : (Conf \to \mathbb{R}) \to (Conf \to \mathbb{R})$ given by

$$\Phi_D(\mathcal{O})(\{\Xi\}) = \{\epsilon\}$$

$$\Phi_D(\mathcal{O})(\Gamma) = \bigcup_\delta \{ \ell \cdot \mathcal{O}(\overline{\Gamma}) \mid \Gamma \xrightarrow{\ell}_D \overline{\Gamma} \}$$

5 Denotational semantics

We will present a continuation semantics for the language $\mathcal{B}$ based on a branching time process domain. The protocol of mutual exclusion is handled using the merge and a so-called grafting operator. Finally, the soundness of the denotational semantics with respect to the operational model of the previous section is shown.

5.1 Semantical domain and operators

The denotational model for $\mathcal{B}$ will employ the semantical domain $\mathbb{P}$ given by the domain equation

$$\mathbb{P} = \{\Xi\} \cup \mathcal{P}^*(Step \times \mathbb{P}) \cup Acc \times (MProc \to \mathbb{P}) \cup Req' \times (Res \times ACont \to \mathbb{P})$$

with

$$\zeta \in Step = \Lambda \cup \{ [\alpha, \hat{\beta}!m], [\hat{\beta}, R, A] \mid \alpha \in Proc, \hat{\beta} \in MProc \}$$

$$Acc = \{ [\underline{\alpha}, m] \mid \underline{\alpha} \in OProc, m \in Meth \}$$

$$Req' = \{ [\alpha, \hat{\beta}?] \mid \alpha \in Proc, \hat{\beta}? \in Req \}$$

The powerset operator $\mathcal{P}^*(\cdot)$ indicates that only compact sets should be included.

Step consists of the labels in Λ (of the form $\langle \alpha, \sigma \rangle$, $\langle \alpha, \delta \rangle$, $\langle \alpha, \surd, \sigma \rangle$, $\langle \alpha, \Delta \rangle$, and $[\alpha, \hat{\beta}!m, \hat{\beta}]$, $[\alpha, R, A, \hat{\beta}]$) and labels of the form $\langle \alpha, \hat{\beta}!m]$ and $[\hat{\beta}, R, A]$. The latter two represent communication *intentions*: $[\alpha, \hat{\beta}!m]$ expresses that process α wants to have method m executed (by method process $\hat{\beta}$ belonging to object $\underline{\hat{\beta}}$), $[\hat{\beta}, R, A]$ expresses that method process $\hat{\beta}$ is willing to transfer the result embodied by R, A.

An element of *Acc*, $[\underline{\alpha}, m]$ say, indicates that object process $\underline{\alpha}$ wants to accept a method call for m. It depends on the process name for the evaluating process (taken from *MProc*) how, or rather with which name $\underline{\alpha}$ proceeds. This explains the function space arrow in $Acc \times (MProc \to \mathbb{P})$. Similarly, an element $[\alpha, \hat{\beta}?]$ of Req' indicates that process α requests method process $\hat{\beta}$ for an answer. It will be dependent on the actual R,A-pair $\hat{\beta}$ conveys, how α can continue. Therefore we have parametrized the remainder of α over $Res \times ACont$ in the component $Req' \times (Res \times ACont \to \mathbb{P})$ of the domain equation.

We will reserve in the sequel ϕ to range over $MProc \to \mathbb{P}$ and ψ to range over $Res \times ACont \to \mathbb{P}$. The pairs in $Step \times \mathbb{P}$, $Acc \times (MProc \to \mathbb{P})$ and $Req' \times (Res \times ACont \to \mathbb{P})$ will be denoted by an infix dot notation

$$\zeta \cdot p,\ [\underline{\alpha}, m] \cdot \phi \text{ and } [\alpha, \hat{\beta}?] \cdot \psi$$

or alternatively by surrounding angle brackets

$$\langle \zeta, p \rangle,\ \langle [\underline{\alpha}, m], \phi \rangle \text{ and } \langle [\alpha, \hat{\beta}?], \psi \rangle$$

Semantical Operators For the modelling of the new-construct and the protocol of mutual exclusion (as discussed in section 2) we will use the semantical operators merge $\|$ and grafting $\rhd_\alpha$ (with $\alpha \in Proc$).

In the interleaving approach adopted in this paper the merge is a combination of a left merge, a right merge and a communication merge. The synchronization between $[\underline{\alpha}, \hat{\beta}!m]$ with $[\underline{\hat{\beta}}, m]$ or $[\alpha, \hat{\beta}?]$ with $[\hat{\beta}, R, A]$ results in a step $[\alpha, \hat{\beta}!m, \underline{\hat{\beta}}]$ or $[\alpha, R, A, \hat{\beta}]$ together with the passing of the process name $\hat{\beta}$ or the pre-resumption/answer continuation pair R,A.

The grafting operation $\rhd_\alpha$ is used to mimic blocking of the activity of an (object) process. The own activity of the object is resumed *after* the first answer of α, signaled by the communication intention $[\alpha, R, A]$, has been set ready to communicate.

The merge $\| : \mathbb{P} \times \mathbb{P} \to \mathbb{P}$ is defined by

$$p \,\|\, \Xi = \Xi \,\|\, p = p$$

$$p \,\|\, q = p \,\lfloor\!\lfloor\, q \cup q \,\lfloor\!\lfloor\, p \cup p \mid q$$

where

$$\begin{aligned} p \,\lfloor\!\lfloor\, q = \;& \{ \langle \zeta, (p' \,\|\, q) \rangle \mid \zeta \cdot p' \in p \} \\ & \cup \{ \langle [\underline{\alpha}, m], (\lambda \hat{\beta}.\phi(\hat{\beta}) \,\|\, q) \rangle \mid [\underline{\alpha}, m] \cdot \phi \in p \} \\ & \cup \{ \langle [\alpha, \hat{\beta}?], (\lambda RA.\psi(R, A) \,\|\, q) \rangle \mid [\alpha, \hat{\beta}?] \cdot \psi \in p \} \end{aligned}$$

and

$$\begin{aligned} p \mid q = \;& \{ \langle [\alpha, \hat{\beta}!m, \underline{\hat{\beta}}], (r \,\|\, \phi(\hat{\beta})) \rangle \mid [\alpha, \hat{\beta}!m] \cdot r \in p, [\underline{\hat{\beta}}, m] \in q \text{ or symm.} \} \\ & \cup \{ \langle [\alpha, R, A, \hat{\beta}], (\psi(R, A) \,\|\, r) \rangle \mid [\alpha, \hat{\beta}?] \cdot \psi \in p, [\hat{\beta}, R, A] \cdot r \in q \text{ or symm.} \} \end{aligned}$$

For a process $\alpha \in Proc$ the grafting operator $\rhd_\alpha : \mathbb{P} \times \mathbb{P} \to \mathbb{P}$ is given by

$$\Xi \rhd_\alpha p = p,\ p \rhd_\alpha \Xi = \Xi$$

$$\begin{aligned} p \rhd_\alpha q = \;& \{ \langle \zeta, (p \rhd_\alpha r) \rangle \mid \zeta \cdot r \in q, \zeta \neq [\alpha, R, A] \} \\ & \cup \{ \langle [\alpha, R, A], (p \,\|\, r) \rangle \mid [\alpha, R, A] \cdot r \in q \} \\ & \cup \{ \langle [\underline{\beta}, m], (\lambda \hat{\gamma}.p \rhd_\alpha \phi(\hat{\gamma})) \rangle \mid [\underline{\beta}, m] \cdot \phi \in q \} \\ & \cup \{ \langle [\beta, \hat{\gamma}?], (\lambda RA.p \rhd_\alpha \psi(R, A)) \rangle \mid [\beta, \hat{\gamma}?] \cdot \psi \in q \} \end{aligned}$$

5.2 Denotational Semantics

The semantic mappings $[\![\cdot]\!]_D$ (dependent on the declaration D) on which we will base the denotational semantics for $\mathcal{B}$ employs semantical counterparts of the syntactic success and failure continuations. We let $FCont'$, ranged over by F, denote the set of (semantic) failure continuations and $SCont'$, ranged over by S, denote the set of (semantic) success continuations. These sets are given by

$$FCont' = ACont \to Proc \to \mathbb{P}$$

$$SCont' = FCont' \to ACont \to Proc \to \Sigma \to \mathbb{P}$$

We distinguish in $FCont'$ the empty failure continuation F_0 defined by

$$F_0(A)(\underline{\alpha}) = \{ \langle \underline{\alpha}, \Delta \rangle \cdot \Xi \}$$

$$F_0(A)(\hat{\alpha}) = \{ [\hat{\alpha}, \delta, A] \cdot [\hat{\alpha}, \epsilon, A]^{\omega} \}$$

representing that basically failure for an object process is global failure ($\langle \alpha, \Delta \rangle$) followed by termination(Ξ), and for a method process, delivery of a failure pre-resumption δ followed by the willingness to communicate the results stored in the answer continuation A, ad infinitum .

In $SCont'$ we have the special element S_0, the empty success continuation given by

$$S_0(F)(A)(\underline{\alpha})(\sigma) = \{ \langle \underline{\alpha}, \surd, \sigma \rangle \cdot FA\underline{\alpha} \}$$

$$S_0(F)(A)(\hat{\alpha})(\sigma) = \{ [\hat{\alpha}, \sigma, A] \cdot F\bar{A}\hat{\alpha}$$

where $\bar{A} = \overline{eval}(\hat{\alpha}?, \sigma, A) = A \,\square\, a_{\sigma}$, representing that basically success for an object process means global success ($\langle \underline{\alpha}, \surd, \sigma \rangle$) followed by the meaning of the alternatives stored in the failure continuation, and for a method process, a new answer pre-resumption ($[\hat{\alpha}, \sigma, A]$) followed by the unexploited alternatives to the initialing method call, but with the answer continuation A updated with the new result coded in a_{σ}.

The denotational semantics uses the auxiliary mappings $[\![\cdot]\!]_D$ which take several types of continuations, a process name and a substitution as their arguments. The meaning of a program then is the outcome of applying this map $[\![\cdot]\!]_D$ with the standard initial parameters, viz. S_0, F_0, **fail**, $\underline{\alpha}_{rt}$ and σ_{id}.

For $D \in Decl$, the function $[\![\cdot]\!]_D : Goal \to SCont' \to FCont' \to ACont \to Proc \to Subst \to \mathbb{P}$ is given by

$\mathcal{D}$

(i) $[a]_D SFA\alpha\sigma = \{<\alpha,\theta>\cdot SFA\alpha\theta\}$ if $I(a)(\sigma) = \theta$
$\{<\alpha,\delta>\cdot FA\alpha\}$ if $I(a)(\sigma) = \delta$

(ii) $[x]_D SFA\alpha\sigma = [D(x)]_D SFA\alpha\sigma$

(iii) $[G_1; G_2]_D SFA\alpha\sigma = [G_1]_D([G_2]_D S)FA\alpha\sigma$

(iv) $[G_1 \square G_2]_{DSFA}\alpha\sigma = [G_1]_D S(\lambda\tilde{A}\tilde{\alpha}.[[G2]]_D SF\tilde{A}\tilde{\alpha}\sigma)A\alpha\sigma$

(v) $[new(\underline{\beta})]_D SFA\alpha\sigma = (SFA\alpha\sigma) \parallel ([D(\underline{\beta})]_D S_0 F_0 \, \mathbf{fail} \, \underline{\beta} \, \sigma_{id})$

(vi) $[\hat{\beta}!m]_D SFA\alpha\sigma = \{[\alpha, \hat{\beta}!m]\cdot SFA\alpha\sigma\}$

(vii) $[[m_1, ..., m_k]]_D SFA\alpha\sigma = \{[\alpha, m_i]\cdot\phi_i : 1 \le i \le k, \alpha \in MProc\}$
with $\phi_i = \lambda\hat{\beta}.SFA\alpha\sigma \rhd_\beta [D(m_i)]_D S_0 F_0 \mathbf{fail}\hat{\beta}\sigma_{id}$

(viii) $[\hat{\beta}?]_D SFA\alpha\sigma = \{[\alpha, \beta?]\cdot\psi\}$
with $\psi = \lambda\overline{R}.\lambda\overline{A}.[eval(\hat{\beta}?, \overline{R}, \overline{A})]_D SFA\alpha\sigma$

The denotational semantics $\mathcal{D} : \mathcal{B} \rightarrow \mathbb{P}$ for $\mathcal{B}$ can now be given by

$$\mathcal{D}(<D, G>) = [G]_D S_0 F_0 \, \mathbf{fail} \, \underline{\alpha}_{rt} \sigma_{id}$$

5.3 Correctness of the denotational model

The relationship between the operational semantics of section 4 and the denotational semantics just presented can be expressed as

$$\mathcal{O} = abs \circ \mathcal{D}$$

for a suitable abstraction operator *abs* which transforms a denotation in $\mathbb{P}$ into a set of words from $\mathcal{P}(\Lambda_\delta^\infty)$. In order to show this correctness of the denotational model we use the proof method proposed by Kok and Rutten [Kok and Rutten, 1990] as applied fruitfully in the context of DLP in the previous paper [Eliëns and de Vink, 1992].

The strategy is as follows: First we extend the auxiliary map $[\cdot]_D$ to a function $[\cdot]_\Gamma$ acting on configurations. Second, we check, using an appropriate inductive argument that (with respect to some fixed declaration D) the composition $abs \circ [\cdot]_\Gamma$ is a fixed point of the higher order transformation Φ_D which characterizes $\mathcal{O}_D$. Third, we conclude from the uniqueness of Φ_D's fixed point that $abs \circ [\cdot]_\Gamma$ and $\mathcal{O}_D$ coincide, from which the desired relationship immediately follows.

Abstraction The abstraction operator $abs : \mathbb{P} \rightarrow \mathbb{R}$ is defined by

$$abs(\Xi) = \{\epsilon\}$$

$abs(p) = \bigcup_\delta\{abs(x) \mid x \in p\}$ for $p \neq \Xi$

where

$abs(\ell \cdot p) = \ell \cdot abs(p)$ if $\zeta \in \Lambda$

$abs(\zeta \cdot p) = \emptyset$ if $\zeta \notin \Lambda$

$abs([\underline{\alpha}, m] \cdot \phi) = \emptyset$

$abs([\alpha, \hat{\beta}?] \cdot \psi) = \emptyset$

The abstraction operator *abs* delivers, given a process p, the singleton set $\{\epsilon\}$ if p is the terminating process Ξ, the abstractions of all its branches $\langle \ell, q\rangle$, where ℓ is a label in Λ (hence not of the additional forms $[\alpha, \hat{\beta}!m]$, $[\underline{\alpha}, m]$, $[\alpha, \hat{\beta}?]$ and $[\hat{\beta}, R, A]$ since these represent single sided communication intentions only) or the abstraction operator delivers the singleton set $\{\delta\}$ in case p does not perform any (semantic) ℓ-step. In the latter case the process deadlocks.

Extended semantic mappings We next extend the semantical map $[\![\cdot]\!]_D$ to a meaning function $[\![\cdot]\!]_\Gamma$ which acts on configurations, i.e. non-empty, finite sets of process continuations. We will show for this $[\![\cdot]\!]_\Gamma$ that it is related via the abstraction operator to the transition system based $\mathcal{O}_D$.

The mapping $[\![\cdot]\!]_\Gamma : Conf \rightarrow \mathbb{P}$ is given by

$$[\![\{P_1, \ldots, P_k\}]\!]_\Gamma = [\![P_1]\!]_P \parallel \cdots \parallel [\![P_k]\!]_P$$

The mapping $[\![\cdot]\!]_P : PCont \rightarrow \mathbb{P}$ is given by

$$[\![\Xi]\!]_P = \Xi$$

$$[\![< \alpha, F, A >: P]\!]_P = [\![P]\!]_P \rhd_\alpha [\![F]\!]_F A\alpha$$

The mapping $[\![\cdot]\!]_F : FCont \rightarrow ACont \rightarrow Proc \rightarrow \mathbb{P}$ is given by

$$[\![\Delta]\!]_F A\alpha = \{\langle \alpha, \Delta\rangle \cdot \Xi\} \text{ if } \alpha \in OProc$$

$$\{[\alpha, \delta, A] \cdot [\![E]\!]_F A\alpha\} \text{ if } \alpha \in MProc$$

$$[\![E]\!]_F A\alpha = \{[\alpha, \epsilon, A]^\omega\}$$

$$[\![R : F]\!]_F A\alpha = \{[\alpha, R, A] \cdot [\![F]\!]_F \overline{A}\alpha\} \text{ where } \overline{A} = \overline{eval}(\sigma, R, A)$$

$$[\![[S, \sigma] : F]\!]_F A\alpha = [\![S]\!]_S [\![F]\!]_F A\alpha\sigma$$

The mapping $[\![\cdot]\!]_S : SCont \rightarrow FCont' \rightarrow ACont \rightarrow Proc \rightarrow Subst \rightarrow \mathbb{P}$ is given by

$$[\![\surd]\!]_S FA\alpha\sigma = \{\langle \alpha.\surd, \sigma\rangle \cdot FA\alpha\} \text{ if } \alpha \in OProc$$

$$\{[\alpha, \sigma, A] \cdot \overline{FA\alpha}\} \text{ if } \alpha \in MProc \text{ with } \overline{A} = \overline{eval}(\sigma, A)$$

$$[\![G : S]\!]_S FA\alpha\sigma = [\![G]\!]_D [\![S]\!]_S FA\alpha\sigma$$

Roughly speaking, the proof of $\Phi_D(abs \circ [\![\cdot]\!]_\Gamma) = abs \circ [\![\cdot]\!]_\Gamma$ goes by induction on the height of the derivations of the transitions of a configuration. To make this explicit we introduce the following weight function.

For $D \in Decl$ the mapping *wgt* is given by

$$wgt(\{P_1, \ldots, P_k\}) = wgt(P_1) + \cdots + wgt(P_k)$$

$$wgt(\Xi) = 0, \; wgt(<\alpha, F, A>: P) = wgt(F)$$

$$wgt(\Delta) = wgt(\mathrm{E}) = 1, \; wgt([S,\sigma] : F) = wgt(S), \; wgt(R : F) = 0$$

$$wgt(\surd) = 1, \; wgt(a : S) = wgt(\hat{\alpha}!m : S) = wgt([m_1, \ldots, m_k] : S) = wgt(\hat{\alpha}? : S) = 0\,,$$
$$wgt(x : S) = wgt(D(x) : S) + 1$$

$$wgt((G_1; G_2) : S) = wgt(G_1 : \surd) + 1 \text{ if } G_1 \in SGGoal$$

$$wgt((G_1; G_2) : S) = wgt(G_1 : \surd) + wgt(G_2 : S) + 1 \text{ if } G_1 \notin SGGoal$$

$$wgt((G_1 \Box G_2) : S) = wgt(G_1 : S) + 1, \; wgt(new(\underline{\alpha}) : S) = wgt(S) + wgt(D(\underline{\alpha}) : \surd) + 1$$

Note the distinction for the sequential composition $G_1; G_2$ into a case where G_1 is strictly guarded and a case where G_1 is not. (See section 4.1 for the definition of strictly guarded.) The desired property of the weight function is

$$wgt(\text{ LHS premise }) < wgt(\text{ LHS conclusion })$$

for all transition schemes from section 4. (The proof of this fact is based on the observations $wgt(s : S) = wgt(s : \surd)$ and $wgt(G : S) \leq wgt(G : \surd) + wgt(S)$.)

In the proof below we have ocassion to express for two configurations Γ, Γ' that a transition based on a successful communication has taken place between a process in Γ and a process in Γ'. More precisely, we write

$$\Gamma, \Gamma' \overset{\ell}{\leadsto}_D \overline{\Gamma} \iff P, P' \overset{\ell}{\longrightarrow}_D \overline{\Gamma}', \text{ with } \ell = [\alpha, R, A, \hat{\beta}] \text{ or } [\alpha, \hat{\beta}!m, \underline{\beta}],$$
$$\text{and } \overline{\Gamma} = \Gamma \backslash P \cup \Gamma' \backslash P' \cup \overline{\Gamma}'$$

We are now ready for the main lemma of this section.

Lemma 5.1

1. $abs([\![\Gamma]\!]_\Gamma) = abs(\{<\ell, [\![\overline{\Gamma}]\!]_\Gamma> \mid \Gamma \overset{\ell}{\longrightarrow}_D \overline{\Gamma}\})$

2. $abs([\![\Gamma]\!]_\Gamma \mid [\![\Gamma']\!]_\Gamma) = abs(\{<\ell, [\![\overline{\Gamma}]\!]_\Gamma> \mid \Gamma, \Gamma' \overset{\ell}{\leadsto}_D \overline{\Gamma}\})$

Proof: Simultaneous proof of 1. and 2. by induction on $wgt(\Gamma)$ and $wgt(\Gamma')$. We exhibit a few typical cases.

Case $\Gamma = \{<\alpha, [G_1; G_2 : S, \sigma] : F, A>: P\}$:

$$abs([\![\Gamma]\!]_\Gamma)$$
$$= abs([\![P]\!]_P \rhd_\alpha [\![G_1; G_2]\!]_D [\![S]\!]_S [\![F]\!]_F A \alpha \sigma) \qquad (\text{definition } [\![\cdot]\!]_\Gamma)$$

$= abs(\llbracket P\rrbracket_P \rhd_\alpha \llbracket G_1\rrbracket_D(\llbracket G_2\rrbracket_D\llbracket S\rrbracket_S)\llbracket F\rrbracket_F A\alpha\sigma)$ (definition $\llbracket\cdot\rrbracket_D$)

$= abs(\llbracket\{<\alpha,[G_1:(G_2:S),\sigma]:F,A>:P\}\rrbracket_\Gamma)$ (definition $\llbracket\cdot\rrbracket_\Gamma$, $\llbracket G_2\rrbracket_D\llbracket S\rrbracket_S = \llbracket G_2:S\rrbracket_S$)

$= abs(\{<\ell,\llbracket\bar{\Gamma}\rrbracket_\Gamma>\mid <\alpha,[G_1:(G_2:S),\sigma]:F,A>:P \xrightarrow{\ell}_D \bar{\Gamma}'\})$
(induction hypothesis)

$= abs(\{<\ell,\llbracket\bar{\Gamma}\rrbracket_\Gamma \mid \Gamma \xrightarrow{\ell}_D \bar{\Gamma}'\})$ (rule (*Seq*))

$abs(\llbracket\Gamma\rrbracket_\Gamma \mid \llbracket\Gamma'\rrbracket_\Gamma)$

$= abs(\llbracket\{<\alpha,[G_1:(G_2:S),\sigma]:F,A>:P\}\rrbracket_\Gamma \mid \llbracket\Gamma'\rrbracket_\Gamma)$ (as above)

$= abs(\{<\ell,\llbracket\bar{\Gamma}\rrbracket_\Gamma>\mid \{<\alpha,[G_1{:}(G_2{:}S),\sigma]{:}F,A>{:}P\},\Gamma' \overset{\ell}{\leadsto}_D \bar{\Gamma}\})$
(induction hypothesis)

$= abs(\{<\ell,\llbracket\bar{\Gamma}\rrbracket_\Gamma>\mid \Gamma,\Gamma' \overset{\ell}{\leadsto}_D \bar{\Gamma}\})$ (rule (*Seq*))

Case $\Gamma = \{<\alpha,[new(\beta):S,\sigma]:F,A>:P\}$. Let $D(\underline{\beta}) = G$:

$abs(\llbracket\Gamma\rrbracket_\Gamma)$

$= abs(\llbracket P\rrbracket_P \rhd_\alpha \llbracket new(\underline{\beta})\rrbracket_D\llbracket S\rrbracket_S\llbracket F\rrbracket_F A\alpha\sigma)$

$= abs(\llbracket P\rrbracket_P \rhd_\alpha (\llbracket S\rrbracket_S\llbracket F\rrbracket_F A\alpha\sigma \parallel \llbracket G\rrbracket_D S_0 F_0 \mathbf{fail}\underline{\beta}\sigma_{id}))$

$= abs(\llbracket<\alpha,[S,\sigma]:F,A>:P\rrbracket_P \parallel \llbracket<\underline{\beta},[G:\surd,\sigma_{id}]:\Delta,\mathbf{fail}>:\Xi\rrbracket_P)$
(modulo assumption on process names)

$= abs(\llbracket\{<\alpha,[S,\sigma]:F,A>:P,<\underline{\beta},[G:\surd,\sigma_{id}]:\Delta,\mathbf{fail}>:\Xi\}\rrbracket_\Gamma)$

$= abs(\{<\ell,\llbracket\bar{\Gamma}\rrbracket_\Gamma>\mid$
$\{<\alpha,[S,\sigma]{:}F,A>{:}P,<\underline{\beta},[G{:}\surd,\sigma_{id}]{:}\Delta,\mathbf{fail}>{:}\Xi\} \xrightarrow{\ell}_D \bar{\Gamma}\})$
(induction hypothesis)

$= abs(\{<\ell,\llbracket\bar{\Gamma}\rrbracket_\Gamma>\mid \Gamma \xrightarrow{\ell}_D \bar{\Gamma}\})$ (rule (*New*))

$abs(\llbracket\Gamma\rrbracket_\Gamma \mid \llbracket\Gamma'\rrbracket_\Gamma)$

$= abs(\llbracket\{<\alpha.[S,\sigma]:F.A>:P,<\underline{\beta},[G:\surd,\sigma_{id}]:\Delta,A>:\Xi\}\rrbracket_\Gamma \mid \llbracket\Gamma'\rrbracket_\Gamma)$
(as above)

$$= abs(\{ <\ell, [\![\bar\Gamma]\!]_\Gamma> \mid \{ <\alpha,[S,\sigma]:F,A>:P, <\underline{\beta},[G:\surd,\sigma_{id}]:\Delta,\mathbf{fail}>:\Xi \}, \Gamma' \overset{\ell}{\leadsto}_D \bar\Gamma \})$$ (induction hypothesis)

$$= abs(\{ < \ell, [\![\bar\Gamma]\!]_\Gamma > \mid \Gamma, \Gamma' \overset{\ell}{\leadsto}_D \bar\Gamma \})$$ (rule (*New*))

Case $\Gamma = \{ \alpha, [\hat\beta!m:S,\sigma]:F, A > :P \}, \Gamma' = \{ < \underline{\beta}, [\ldots,m,\ldots]:S',\sigma']:F',A' > :P' \}$:

$$abs([\![\Gamma]\!]_\Gamma)$$

$$= abs([\![P]\!]_P \rhd_\alpha [\![\hat\beta!m]\!]_D [\![S]\!]_S [\![F]\!]_F A\alpha\sigma)$$ (definition $[\![\cdot]\!]_\Gamma$)

$$= abs(\{ < [\alpha,\hat\beta!m], [\![P]\!]_P \rhd_\alpha [\![S]\!]_S [\![F]\!]_F A\alpha\sigma > \})$$ (definition $[\![\cdot]\!]_D$, $\rhd_\alpha$)

$$= abs(\emptyset)$$ (definition *abs*)

$$= abs(\{ < \ell, [\![\bar\Gamma]\!]_\Gamma > \mid \Gamma \overset{\ell}{\longrightarrow}_D \bar\Gamma \})$$

$$abs([\![\Gamma]\!]_\Gamma \mid [\![\Gamma']\!]_\Gamma)$$

$$= abs(\{ < [\alpha,\hat\beta!m], [\![P]\!]_P \rhd_\alpha [\![S]\!]_S [\![F]\!]_F A\alpha\sigma > \} \mid$$
$$\{ < [\underline{\beta}, m_i], \lambda\hat\gamma.([\![P']\!]_P \rhd_{\underline{\beta}} [\![S']\!]_S [\![F]\!]_F A'\underline{\beta})$$
$$\rhd_{\hat\gamma} [\![G_i]\!]_D S_0 F_0\, \mathbf{fail}\, \hat\gamma\, \sigma_{id} > \mid 1 \le i \le k \})$$
($D(m_i) = G_i$, assumption on process names)

$$= abs(< \{ [\alpha,\hat\beta!m,\underline{\beta}], [\![< \alpha,[S,\sigma] : F, A >: P]\!]_P \|$$
$$[\![< \underline{\beta},[S',\sigma'] : F',A' >: P']\!] \rhd_{\hat\beta} [\![< \hat\beta,[D(m) : \surd,\sigma_{id}] : \Delta >:$$
$$\Xi]\!]_P > \})$$
($m = m_i$ for some i)

$$= abs(\{ < [\alpha,\hat\beta!m,\underline{\beta}],$$
$$[\![\{ < \alpha,[S,\sigma]:F,A > :P, < \hat\beta,[G:\surd,\sigma_{id}]:\Delta,\mathbf{fail} > : < \underline{\beta},[S',\sigma']:F',A' >$$
$$:P' \}]\!]_\Gamma > \})$$

$$= abs(\{ < \ell, [\![\bar\Gamma]\!]_\Gamma > \mid \Gamma, \Gamma' \overset{\ell}{\leadsto}_D \bar\Gamma \})$$ (definition $\overset{\ell}{\leadsto}_D$)

Case $\Gamma = \Gamma_1 \cup \Gamma_2$, ($\Gamma_1, \Gamma_2$ disjoint of $wgt > 0$):

$$abs([\![\Gamma]\!]_\Gamma)$$

$$= abs([\![\Gamma_1]\!]_\Gamma \,\|\, [\![\Gamma_2]\!]_\Gamma)$$

$$= abs([\![\Gamma_1]\!]_\Gamma \,\lfloor\!\lfloor\, [\![\Gamma_2]\!]_\Gamma) \cup abs([\![\Gamma_2]\!]_\Gamma \,\lfloor\!\lfloor\, [\![\Gamma_1]\!]_\Gamma) \cup abs([\![\Gamma_1]\!]_\Gamma \mid [\![\Gamma_2]\!]_\Gamma)$$

$$= abs(\{<\ell,[\![\bar\Gamma_1]\!]_\Gamma>|\,\Gamma_1 \xrightarrow{\ell}_D \bar\Gamma_1\} \mathbin{\lfloor\!\lfloor} [\![\Gamma_2]\!]_\Gamma \cup \{<\ell,[\![\bar\Gamma_2]\!]_\Gamma>|\,\Gamma_2 \xrightarrow{\ell}_D \bar\Gamma_2\} \mathbin{\lfloor\!\lfloor} [\![\Gamma_1]\!]_\Gamma \cup$$
$$\{<\ell,[\![\bar\Gamma]\!]_\Gamma>|\,\Gamma_1,\Gamma_2 \overset{\ell}{\leadsto}_D \bar\Gamma\}) \qquad \text{(induction hypothesis, properties } abs\text{)}$$
$$= abs(\{<\ell,[\![\bar\Gamma_1 \cup \Gamma_2]\!]>|\,\Gamma_1 \xrightarrow{\ell}_D \bar\Gamma_1\} \cup \{<\ell,[\![\Gamma_1 \cup \bar\Gamma_2]\!]>|\,\Gamma_2 \xrightarrow{\ell}_D \bar\Gamma_2\} \cup$$
$$\{<\ell,[\![\bar\Gamma]\!]_\Gamma>|\,\Gamma_1,\Gamma_2 \overset{\ell}{\leadsto}_D \bar\Gamma\})$$
$$= abs(\{<\ell,[\![\bar\Gamma]\!]_\Gamma>|\,\Gamma \xrightarrow{\ell}_D \bar\Gamma\}) \qquad \text{(properties of the transition system)}$$

$$abs([\![\Gamma]\!]_\Gamma \mid [\![\Gamma']\!]_\Gamma)$$
$$= abs(([\![\Gamma_1]\!]_\Gamma \parallel [\![\Gamma_2]\!]_\Gamma) \mid [\![\Gamma']\!]_\Gamma)$$
$$= abs(([\![\Gamma_1]\!]_\Gamma \mid [\![\Gamma']\!]_\Gamma) \mathbin{\lfloor\!\lfloor} [\![\Gamma_2]\!]_\Gamma \cup ([\![\Gamma_2]\!]_\Gamma \mid [\![\Gamma']\!]_\Gamma) \mathbin{\lfloor\!\lfloor} [\![\Gamma_1]\!]_\Gamma) \qquad \text{(property } \parallel\text{)}$$
$$= abs(\{<\ell,[\![\bar\Gamma_1]\!]_\Gamma>|\,\Gamma_1,\Gamma' \overset{\ell}{\leadsto}_D \bar\Gamma_1\} \mathbin{\lfloor\!\lfloor} [\![\Gamma_2]\!]_\Gamma \cup$$
$$\{<\ell,[\![\bar\Gamma_2]\!]_\Gamma>|\,\Gamma_2,\Gamma' \overset{\ell}{\leadsto}_D \bar\Gamma_2\} \mathbin{\lfloor\!\lfloor} [\![\Gamma_1]\!]_\Gamma) \qquad \text{(induction hypothesis)}$$
$$= abs(\{<\ell,[\![\bar\Gamma]\!]_\Gamma>|\,\Gamma,\Gamma' \overset{\ell}{\leadsto}_D \bar\Gamma\}) \qquad \text{(property } \leadsto_D\text{)}$$

The correctness of the denotational model now follows from the lemma and the fixed point characterization of the operational semantics.

Theorem 5.2 $\mathcal{O} = abs \circ \mathcal{D}$.

Proof: $abs \circ [\![\cdot]\!]_\Gamma$ is a fixed point of Φ_D: For $\Gamma \neq \{\Xi\}$: $\Phi(abs \circ [\![\cdot]\!]_\Gamma)(\Gamma) = \bigcup_\delta\{\ell \cdot abs([\![\bar\Gamma]\!]_\Gamma) \mid \Gamma \xrightarrow{\ell}_D \bar\Gamma\} = abs(\{<\ell,[\![\bar\Gamma]\!]_\Gamma>|\,\Gamma \xrightarrow{\ell}_D \bar\Gamma\} = (abs \circ [\![\cdot]\!]_\Gamma)(\Gamma)$ by the lemma. Hence $\mathcal{O}_D = abs \circ [\![\cdot]\!]_\Gamma$. Therefore $\mathcal{O}[\![< D,G >]\!] = \mathcal{O}_D(\{<\alpha_{rt},[G{:}\surd,\sigma_{id}]{:}\Delta,\mathbf{fail}>:\Xi\})$ $= abs([\![\{<\alpha_{rt},[G{:}\surd,\sigma_{id}]{:}\Delta,\mathbf{fail}>:\Xi\}]\!]_\Gamma) =$ $abs([\![G]\!]_D S_0 F_0\,\mathbf{fail}\,\alpha_{rt}\sigma_{id}) = abs(\mathcal{D}[\![< D,G >]\!])$. I.e. $\mathcal{O} = abs \circ \mathcal{D}$.

6 Concluding remarks

The innovating feature of the distributed logic programming language DLP is its support for backtracking over the results of an asynchronous rendez-vous. This phenomenon has been given, in the context, of a derived language a precise meaning by an operational and denotational semantics. The two models are related using a method proposed by Kok and Rutten.

Our semantics still has a number of shortcomings. In order to give a semantic characterization of the mechanism needed to support asynchronous communication, while preserving completeness in combining the results of the rendez-vous with the results of

an intermittent goal, we have coded the computed answers of a method call in the uninterpreted language $\mathcal{B}$. We plan for further research to give a more dynamical semantics for $\mathcal{B}$ using an abstract notion of state where this coding can be avoided.

Also, at the moment, we are not able to express a definition of and-parallelism directly, since we do not have a semantic counterpart of the expression *self*. However we expect to overcome this in a non-uniform setting. Giving a similar treatment of a non-uniform variant of $\mathcal{B}$ along the lines of the present paper will provide a case-study in comparing operational and denotational semantics using metric topology.

References

[America, 1987] P. AMERICA, *POOL-T: a parallel object oriented language,* in: [Yonezawa and Tokoro, 1987]

[America and de Bakker, 1988] P. AMERICA AND J.W. DE BAKKER, *Designing equivalent models for process creation,* Theoretical Computer Science, 60 (2) (1988) pp. 109-176

[America et al, 1989] P. AMERICA, J.W. DE BAKKER, J.N. KOK AND J.J.M.M. RUTTEN, *Denotational semantics of a Parallel Object Oriented Language,* Information and Computation, 83 (2) (1989) pp. 152-205

[America and Rutten, 1989a] P. AMERICA AND J.J.M.M. RUTTEN, *A parallel object-oriented language: design and foundations,* Joint Ph.D. thesis, Vrije Universiteit Amsterdam (1989)

[America and Rutten, 1989b] P. AMERICA AND J.J.M.M. RUTTEN, *Solving reflexive domain equations in a category of complete metric spaces,* Journal of Computer and System Sciences, 39 (1989) pp. 343-375

[America and Rutten, 1991] P. AMERICA AND J.J.M.M. RUTTEN, *A layered semantics for a parallel object-oriented language,* in: Foundations of Object-Oriented Languages, J.W. de Bakker, W.P. de Roever and G. Rozenberg (eds.), Lecture Notes in Computer Science 489, Springer (1991) pp. 91-123

[de Bakker et al, 1986] J.W. DE BAKKER, J.N. KOK, J.-J.CH. MEYER, E.-R. OLDEROG AND J.I. ZUCKER, *Contrasting themes in the semantics of imperative concurrency,* in: Current Trends in Concurrency: Overviews and Tutorials, J.W. de Bakker, W.P. de Roever and G. Rozenberg (eds.), Lecture Notes in Computer Science 224, Springer (1986) pp. 51-121

[de Bakker et al, 1988] J.W. DE BAKKER, J.-J.CH. MEYER, E.-R. OLDEROG AND J.I. ZUCKER, *Transition systems, metric spaces and ready sets in the semantics of uniform concurrency,* Journal of Computer and System Sciences 36 (1988), 158-224

[de Boer et al, 1990] F.S. DE BOER, J.N. KOK, C. PALAMIDESSI, J.J.M.M. RUTTEN, *From failure to success: Comparing a denotational and a declarative semantics for Horn Clause Logic,* in: Proc. International BCS-FACS Workshop on Semantics for Concurrency, M.Z. Kwiatkowska, M.W. Shields and R.M. Thomas (eds.), Workshops in Computing. Springer (1990), pp. 38-60

[Bal et al, 1989] H. BAL, J. STEINER AND A. TANENBAUM, *Programming languages for distributed systems,* ACM Computing Surveys, 21 (3) (1989) pp. 262-322

[de Bakker, 1989] J.W. DE BAKKER, *Designing concurrency semantics,* in: Proc. 11th World Computer Congress, G.X. Ritter (ed.), North Holland (1989) pp. 591-598

[de Bakker and Meyer, 1988] J.W. DE BAKKER AND J.-J.CH. MEYER, *Metric semantics for concurrency,* BIT 28 (1988) pp. 504-529

[de Bakker and de Vink, 1991] J.W. DE BAKKER AND E.P. DE VINK, *CCS for OO and LP,* in: Proc. Theory and Practice of Software Development '91, Vol. 2, S. Abramsky and T.S.E. Maibaum (eds.), Lecture Notes in Computer Science 494, Springer (1991) pp. 1-28

[de Bakker and Zucker, 1982] J.W. DE BAKKER AND J.I. ZUCKER, *Processes and the denotational semantics of concurrency,* Information and Control 54 (1982) pp. 70-120

[de Bakker, 1991] J.W. DE BAKKER, *Comparative semantics for flow of control in logic programming without logic,* Information and Computation 91 (1991) pp. 123-179

[van Breugel, 1991] F. VAN BREUGEL, *Comparative semantics for a real-time programming language with integration,* in: Proc. Theory and Practice of Software Development '91 S. Abramsky and T.S.E. Maibaum (eds.) vol. 1, Lecture Notes in Computer Science 493, Springer (1991) pp 397-411

[de Bruin and de Vink, 1989] A. DE BRUIN, E.P. DE VINK, *Continuation semantics for PROLOG with cut,* in: Proc. Theory and Practice of Software Development '89, Vol I, J. Diaz and F. Orejas (eds.), Lecture Notes in Computer Science 351, Springer (1989) pp. 178-192

[Davison, 1989] A. DAVISON, *Polka: A Parlog object oriented language,* Ph.D. thesis, Dept. of Computing, Imperial College, London (1989)

[DeGroot, 1984] D. DEGROOT, *Restricted and-parallelism,* in: Proc. Future Generation Computer Systems, ICOT (1984) pp. 471-478

[Eliëns, 1989] A. ELIËNS, *Extending Prolog to a Parallel Object Oriented Language,* Proc. IFIP W.G. 10.3 Working Conference on Decentralized Systems (1989) Lyon

[Eliëns, 1991] A. ELIËNS, *Distributed Logic Programming for Artificial Intelligence,* AI Communications Vol. 4 No. 1, 1991, pp. 11-21

[Eliëns and de Vink, 1991] A. ELIËNS AND E.P. DE VINK, *Asynchronous rendez-vous in the presence of backtracking,* ISLP'91 Workshop on Asynchronous Communication, november 1991, San Diego

[Eliëns, 1992] A. ELIËNS, *DLP - A language for Distributed Logic Programming,* Wiley (1992)

[Jones and Mycroft, 1984] N. JONES AND A. MYCROFT, *Stepwise development of operational and denotational semantics for Prolog,* in: Proc. Int. Symp. on Logic Programming, Atlantic City (1984) pp. 281-288

[Jacquet and Monteiro, 1990] J.-M. JACQUET & L. MONTEIRO, *Comparative Semantics for a Parallel Contextual Programming Language,* in: Proc. North-American Logic Programming Conf., S. Debray and M. Hermenegildo (eds.), MIT Press (1990) pp. 195-214,

[Karam, 1988] G.M. KARAM, *Prototyping Concurrent systems with Multilog,* Technical Report Dept. of Systems and Computer Engineering Carleton University (1988)

[Kahn et al, 1986] K. KAHN, E. TRIBBLE, M. MILLAR, D. BOBROW, *Objects in concurrent logic programming languages,* OOPSLA 86, N. Meyrowitz (ed.), SIGPLAN Notices Vol. 21, No. 11, 1986 pp. 242-257

[Kok, 1988] J.N. KOK, *A compositional semantics for Concurrent Prolog,* in: Proc. 5th Annual Symp. on Theoretical Aspects of Computer Science, Bordeaux, February 1988, R. Cori and M. Wirsing (eds.), Lecture Notes in Computer Science 294, Springer (1988) pp. 373-388

[Kok and Rutten, 1988] J. KOK AND J. RUTTEN, *Contractions in comparing concurrency semantics,* in: Proc. Automata, Languages and Programming, T. Lepisto and A. Salomaa (eds.), Lecture Notes in Computer Science 317, Springer (1988) pp. 317-332

[Monteiro and Porto, 1988] L. MONTEIRO AND A. PORTO, *Contextual Logic Programming,* Report UNL-50/88, University Lisboa (1988)

[Pereira and Nasr, 1984] L.M. PEREIRA AND R. NASR, *Delta Prolog: A distributed logic programming language,* in: Proc. FGCS, ICOT (1984) pp. 283-231

[Rutten, 1990] J.J.M.M. RUTTEN, *Semantic correctness for a parallel object-oriented language,* SIAM Journal on Computing 19, 1990, pp. 341-383

[de Vink, 1990] E.P. DE VINK, *Comparative semantics for Prolog with cut,* Science of Computer Programming 13 (1990). pp. 237-264

[Yokoi, 1986] S. YOKOI, *A Prolog based object oriented language SPOOL and its compiler,* in: Proc. Logic Programming 86, Tokyo, E. Wada (ed.), Lecture Notes in Computer Science 264, Springer (1986) pp. 116-125

[Zaniolo, 1984] C. ZANIOLO, *Object oriented programming in Prolog,* in: Proc. Int. Symp. on Logic Programming, Atlantic City, IEEE (1984) pp. 265-270

New Semantic Tools for Logic Programming

Maurizio Gabbrielli Giorgio Levi

Dipartimento di Informatica, Università di Pisa
Corso Italia 40, 56125 Pisa, Italy
e_mail: {gabbri,levi}@di.unipi.it

Maurizio Martelli

Dipartimento di Informatica e Scienze dell'Informazione
Università di Genova
Viale Benedetto XV 3, 16132 Genoa, Italy
e_mail: martelli@cisi.unige.it

ABSTRACT The paper is a general overview of our approach to the semantics of logic programs. We introduce new notions and modify the classical semantics, i.e. we use new *tools* to model those logic programs aspects which really capture their operational semantics, and are therefore useful for defining program equivalences and for semantics-based program analysis. The approach leads to the introduction of extended interpretations which are more expressive than Herbrand interpretations. The semantics in terms of extended interpretations can be obtained as a result of both an operational and a fixpoint construction. It can also be characterized from the model-theoretic viewpoint, by defining a set of extended models which contains standard Herbrand models. The original construction for positive programs is shown to be applicable to other classes of logic programs, such as *constraint logic programs*, *open programs* and *general programs*. Different extensions are also shown capable to handle higher order constructs such as those used to compute sets of solutions.

Keywords: logic programming, operational semantics, declarative semantics.

Contents

0. Introduction

In Knowledge Representation (KR) there has been a long debate on the role of Logic: first order predicate calculus (PC) is a general and convenient KR language, vs. PC does not capture many kinds of knowledge (dynamic, procedural,...). The matter is a complex one, but, in any case, the issue was badly formulated because of considering PC only. The important point is to have a KR language suited for the problem to represent (i.e. with the right expressiveness) and with a well founded semantics. Many researches on different kind of logics (modal, non-monotonic,...) and on various ways of structuring knowledge and their languages (hybrid systems,...) have given valid contributions to shift the debate to a more interesting point.

Logic Programming (LP) can be considered a possible answer to the problem of incorporating also procedural knowledge into the picture. However, pure LP was very soon recognized inadequate and various proposals, from negation as failure to specific meta, second-order or theory modification constructs, became part of the LP languages.

From the semantics point of view, one of the strong points of LP, namely the equivalence of a model theoretic, fixpoint and operational characterization of successful ground atoms (i.e. the possibility to have a logically based declarative semantics) didn't develop at the same pace, with the exception of the modeling of negation.

Even worse, inside the LP community, it started a debate quite similar to the above mentioned one: the standard semantics is all what we need, vs. the important point is to have a clear operational semantics. Again, this is a badly formulated dichotomy: the correct answer is to enrich the semantics of LP, taking into account various observable properties, new constructs and possible extensions, while maintaining as much as possible the good aspects of the standard LP semantics (i.e., the declarative characterizations).

0.1. Why a new semantics

According to a popular view on logic programming, the problem of the semantics (of definite Horn clauses) was solved once and for all by logicians before logic programming was even born. Namely, the only three important concepts are the *program* itself, the *intended interpretation* (declarative semantics) and the *theorem prover* (operational semantics). The program is a logic theory. The declarative semantics formalizes the application the program is trying to capture. It is an interpretation in the conventional logic sense and a model of the program. Finally, the theorem prover is a proof procedure which must be sound (and complete) with respect to the declarative semantics. Is that really *all there is to it*?

The above view is appealing but too simple minded to capture the difference between theorem proving and programming. In fact, it applies to any formal system for which there exists a sound and complete theorem prover. Theorem proving becomes logic programming, when we restrict the class of theories (for example, to definite Horn clauses), so as to obtain a declarative semantics (a unique representative model) and a proof procedure (possibly non-deterministic goal rewriting) similar to the denotational and the operational semantics of conventional programming languages. This is exactly what van Emden and Kowalski did in their seminal paper [78], where the proof procedure was SLD-resolution and the representative model was the least Herbrand model. According to [78], *the* semantics is a mathematical object which is defined in model-theoretic terms and which can be *computed* by a top-down construction (the success set) and by a bottom-up construction (the least fixpoint of the immediate consequences operator). Is the above classical and elegant result a satisfactory solution?

The answer can be found if we first consider a different and more basic question. What a semantics is used for? The first *application* of any semantics is to help understanding the meaning of programs. Other useful applications include areas such as program transformation and program analysis (for instance, abstract interpretation). One can argue that tens of thousands of logic programmers were really helped by the declarative understanding of their programs. One can also argue that semantics-based program transformation and analysis do require deeper results and more elaborate theories, but still only using basically the above mentioned simple and straightforward semantics. The above arguments can become more technical only if we understand which is the basic semantic property of such formal activities as program transformation and analysis. The answer coming from computer science is *program equivalence*, i.e. program understanding is based on our ability to detect when two programs cannot be distinguished by looking at their behaviors.

Defining an equivalence on logic programs $\approx$ and a formal semantics $\mathcal{S}(P)$ are two strongly related tasks. A semantics $\mathcal{S}(P)$ is *correct* wrt $\approx$, if $\mathcal{S}(P_1) = \mathcal{S}(P_2)$ implies $P_1 \approx P_2$. $\mathcal{S}(P)$ is *fully abstract* wrt $\approx$, if the converse holds, i.e. if $P_1 \approx P_2$ implies $\mathcal{S}(P_1) = \mathcal{S}(P_2)$. While full abstraction is known to be a desirable property for any semantics, correctness is a must. The question on the adequacy of the van Emden and Kowalski's semantics can then be rephrased as follows. Is that semantics correct wrt a "natural" notion of program equivalence? And this in turn raises the problem of choosing a satisfactory notion of program equivalence.

0.2. Program equivalences and observables

Equivalences can be defined by using logical arguments only. For example, one can use model-theoretic properties, such as the set of models, the set of logical consequences or the least Herbrand model, and proof-theoretic properties, such as the set of derivable atoms. However, this would lead us nowhere, since the equivalence we need *must* be based on the operational behavior and on what we can observe from a computation. In other words, we have to learn more from computer science than from mathematical logic! From a computer science viewpoint, once we have a formalization of program execution, we have a choice for the equivalence. One important aspect of the formalization, in addition to the inference rules which specify how derivations are made, is the concept of ***observable***, i.e. the property we observe in a computation. In logic programs we can be interested in different observable properties such as successful derivations, finite failures, computed answer substitutions, partial computed answer substitutions, finite sets of solutions, etc. A given choice of the observable X induces an ***observational equivalence*** $\approx_X$ on programs. Namely $P_1 \approx_X P_2$ iff P_1 and P_2 are observationally indistinguishable according to X. For example, if the observable s denotes ***successful derivations***, $P_1 \approx_s P_2$ iff for any goal G, G is refutable in P_1 iff it is refutable in P_2. If the observable c denotes ***computed answer substitutions***, $P_1 \approx_c P_2$ iff for any goal G, G has the same (up to renaming) computed answers in P_1 and in P_2.

Since the observable is the property which allows us to distinguish programs and is also the property we want to preserve in program transformations, the most natural choice in the case of logic programs is ***computed answer substitutions***, which are exactly the result of a logic program execution. Other less abstract observables, such as partial computed answers and call patterns, might be useful in some applications, for example in semantics-based analysis and transformation. However, a more abstract observable like ***successful derivations*** would fail in capturing the essence of logic programming, even if it is the most adequate to the case of first order theorem proving, where there is nothing to be returned as result of the computation.

We can now note that, as first shown in [33, 34], ***the van Emden and Kowalski's semantics is not correct wrt to the observational equivalence based on computed answer substitutions***, while it is correct wrt the one based on successful derivations (a corollary of the completeness theorem). Namely, there exist programs which have the same least Herbrand model, yet compute different answer substitutions. When trying to understand the meaning of programs, when analyzing and transforming programs, this semantics cannot be taken as the reference semantics. This is the reason why the need for a different formal semantics, correct wrt answer substitutions, was recognized by many authors, giving rise to several new definitions (see, for example, [37, 80, 27, 33, 46]). The need for better semantics was also recognized in the case of semantics-based abstract interpretation [7, 67, 55, 9, 21] and transformation [54, 12], where, as already mentioned, less abstract observables (such as partial computed answers or call patterns) have sometimes to be modeled.

0.3. LP extensions

The same problem was even earlier recognized in relation to some ***extensions*** of pure logic programming. In fact the weakness of the traditional semantics is even more serious when trying to model the behavior of extensions such as constraint logic programs or concurrent logic programs, where the observables play a more important role. For example, finding definitions modeling the observable behavior was, from the very beginning, the aim of most of the research on the semantics of concurrent logic languages (see, for example, [61, 44, 38, 75, 23, 24, 41]). This was primarily motivated by the fact that these languages closely resemble traditional (concurrent) languages, whose semantics usually model observables such as traces of input-output interactions, deadlocks, etc. However, one additional motivation was the fact that the "logical" declarative reading doesn't help the understanding of programs. Something similar took place in the case of Constraint Logic Programming. In fact, even if the aim was not finding a semantics modeling the observable behavior, most of the constructions proposed by Jaffar and Lassez [50] are different from the van Emden and Kowalski construction (i.e. they are not $\Re$-models) and one of the proposed semantics was later proved [39] to correctly model the ***answer constraint*** observable.

The same problems occur with less radical extensions of logic programs such as the addition of new constructs to Prolog-like languages, e.g. metaprogramming, built-in's, ***set-of***, etc. For example, to characterize constructs such as ***set-of***, we need a notion of observable that corresponds to the finite sets of solutions.

In a typical logic programming system, given a program P and a goal G, the proof procedure tries to refute the goal, returning the solution (computed answer substitution), related to a successful computation for G. Generally the proof procedure can generate more than one computation for the same goal, so we have to consider derivation trees.

Suppose that we would like to obtain *all solutions* of a goal G, in one step, then the system should look for all success branches of the tree for G and collect the corresponding solutions. This is useful especially in data base oriented application where users are interested in getting many informations in few steps. In case of SLD-resolution [1], this procedure is feasible only in two cases:

- the SLD-tree for P and G is finitely failed;

- the SLD-tree for P and G is finite and with a success branch (has finite success).

This means that if we want to characterize the set of all solutions of a goal, we must restrict ourselves to goals that have a global termination property. Unfortunately the classical fix-point semantics based on the T_P operator captures an existential termination property of the atoms, i.e. it distinguishes atoms which have or not a successful computation. In order to distinguish between finite success and infinite success, it is necessary to introduce new objects in the language that keep track of infinite computations. With this introduction it is possible to give a characterization of the semantics of particular cases of the predicate *setof* existing in Prolog.

In addition to the problem of modeling observational equivalences, there exists a very important property which does not hold in the traditional least Herbrand model semantics, i.e. ***compositionality***. Compositionality has to do with a (syntactic) program composition operator $\circ$, and holds when the semantics of the compound construct $C_1 \circ C_2$ is defined by (semantically) composing the semantics of the constituents C_1 and C_2. "Compositional is beautiful" is the motto that denotational semantics has taught to computer scientists. In the case of logic programs, we could be concerned with AND-composition (of atoms in a goal or in a clause body) or with OR-composition, i.e. composition of (sets of) clauses. However, the construct which raises a compositionality problem is the *union* of clauses. The related property is sometimes called *OR-compositionality*. People got interested in OR-compositional semantics [57, 71, 65, 45] both for theoretical and for practical (i.e. the definition of semantics for modular versions of logic programs) purposes.

When also composition of programs is taken into account, for a given observable property we obtain different equivalences depending on which kind of program composition we consider. Given an observable X and a program composition operator $\circ$, the induced equivalence $\approx_{(\circ,X)}$ is defined as follows. $P_1 \approx_{(\circ,X)} P_2$ iff for any program Q, $P_1 \circ Q \approx_X P_2 \circ Q$, (i.e. iff P_1 and P_2 are observationally indistinguishable under any possible context allowed by the composition operator). Thus if the observable is successful derivations, we find out that OR-compositionality can also be understood in logical terms. In fact, the set of all the models is OR-compositional [64] (and correct wrt successful derivations), while the least Herbrand model is not even OR-compositional. The only OR-compositional semantics correct wrt computed answers are described in [46, 15, 14], while all the other OR-compositional semantics [57, 71, 65, 64, 45] are only correct wrt successful refutations.

0.4. Our approach

Over the last few years we have developed a general approach to the semantics [40], whose aim was modeling the observable behaviors (possibly in a compositional way) for a variety of logic languages, ranging from positive logic programs [33, 34, 35, 60, 15, 14], to general logic programs [77, 42, 72, 68], LP extensions [25, 69], constraint logic programs [39, 17] and concurrent constraint programs [38]. Our approach is based on the idea of choosing (equivalence classes of) sets of clauses as semantic domains. Our denotations are then defined by *syntactic* objects, as in the case of Herbrand interpretations. Denotations (that we sometimes call π-interpretations) are not interpretations in the conventional mathematical logic sense, even if they have some model-theoretic properties. Note also that π-interpretations used in [33, 34, 35], which are sets of possibly non-ground atoms, are indeed interpretations (they were called *canonical realizations* in [73, 56]).

As in the case of the traditional van Emden and Kowalski semantics, our denotations can be computed both by a top-down construction (a success set) and by a bottom-up construction (the least fixpoint of suitable continuous immediate consequence operators on π-interpretations). It is worth noting that our aim is not defining a new (artificial and futile) notion of model. We are simply unhappy with the traditional declarative semantics, because it characterizes the logical properties only and we look for new notions of program denotation useful from the programming (or computer science) point of view. A satisfactory solution even to the simple case of positive logic programs is needed to gain a better understanding of more practical languages, such as real Prolog [5] and its purely declarative counterparts. A partial solution was the s-semantics [33, 34], which was the first (non-compositional) semantics correct wrt computed answers and which used sets of unit clauses as semantic domain.

As already mentioned, our aim was similar to the one of many other authors, who, either from the theory or from the application viewpoint, contributed to the idea that a different semantics was needed. Among them, we need to mention Gaifman and Shapiro, who first introduced the idea of using as semantic domain sets of non-unit clauses to achieve OR-compositionality [45] and then defined an OR-compositional version of the s-semantics [46]. The style of the definitions in [45, 46] is proof-theoretic. A denotation similar to the one in [46] is the Ω-semantics [15, 14], which is the real compositional generalization of the s-semantics and is defined both by a success set and by a fixpoint construction.

0.5. Plan of the paper

The paper will overview some of the most important results obtained along this line of research during the past years. Namely, the possibility to have richer notions of models (with variables and characterizing computed answer substitutions) and the corresponding fixpoint and operational semantics.

In the next section we will describe the general approach. In section 2. we will consider positive logic programs [33, 34, 35], where π-interpretations are sets of possibly non-ground atoms. The approach allows to define several π-models corresponding to various operational semantics notions, such as ***the set of refutable atoms together with their computed answer substitutions.*** These non-ground π-models can be obtained as least fixpoints of suitable continuous immediate consequences operators. In section 3. the construction is generalized [39] to *constraint logic programs (CLP)* [49]. π-interpretations are now sets of *constrained atoms* (i.e. CLP unit clauses), which represent possibly infinite sets of "domain" atoms. We show that the theory developed for positive logic programs extends very naturally to CLP. In particular, there exists an immediate consequences operator whose least fixpoint is a non-minimal π-model corresponding to the *computed answer constraint semantics.* Section 4. is related to *open programs* [15], where π-interpretations are sets of *conditional atoms* (i.e. clauses such that all the atoms in the body are open). Each π-interpretation represents a set of Herbrand interpretations that could be obtained by composing the open program with a definition for the open predicates. π-interpretations of open programs are introduced to obtain a unique representative model, computable as the least fixpoint of a suitable continuous operator, in cases where no such a representative exists in the set of Herbrand models. In section 5. we first discuss how to handle finite failures in case of non ground atoms. This allows to obtain a symmetric characterization of success and failure, and shows a possible extension, the NAI rule [72], to handle negative information. We then consider the extension of the s-semantics to the case of *general logic programs.* In this case, π-interpretations are sets of *conditional constrained atoms* (i.e. clauses such that all the atoms in the body are either constraints or negative literals) [42]. We obtain an incremental fixpoint semantics, consisting of several steps providing a semantics to increasingly more expressive classes of programs. Finally, as an example of other possible tools to be used in semantic construction, in section 6. we will show how to treat sets of solutions. This approach is different from the idea of treating sets of solutions by extending first order languages with the capability of managing sets (with set constructors as operators of the language) as shown in [52, 28]; we look for SLD-tree's properties and then we try to apply them to the semantics of the predicate *setof*. The results obtained about termination are very interesting and could represent another way to solve the problem of global termination of programs as treated in [3, 4].

In the conclusion we will mention some other applications of our approach that could not fit into this paper. They span from modeling metaprograms constructs with the use of interesting proposals such as Hilog [79], to modeling of inheritance, to important LP extensions such as concurrent constraint LP.

1. The general approach

We show our construction in a language independent way by considering three separate steps, which roughly correspond to the three standard semantics of logic programs [78, 62, 1]. The first step is related to the operational semantics and leads to the definition of the structure of π-interpretations. The second step is concerned with the fixpoint semantics. The third and final step is concerned with the definition of π-models.

1.1. Preliminaries

The reader is assumed to be familiar with the terminology of and the basic results in the semantics of logic programs [62, 1]. Let the signature S consist of a set C of *data constructors*, a finite set P of *predicate symbols*, a denumerable set V of *variable symbols*. All the definitions in the following will assume a given signature S. Let T be the set of terms built on C and V. Variable-free terms are called *ground*. The notation $\tilde{t}$ will be used to denote a tuple of terms. A substitution is a mapping $\vartheta : V \rightarrow T$ such that the set $D(\vartheta) = \{X \mid \vartheta(X) \neq X\}$ (*domain* of ϑ) is finite. If $W \subset V$, we denote by $\vartheta_{|W}$ the *restriction* of ϑ to the variables in W, i.e. $\vartheta_{|W}(Y) = Y$ for $Y \notin W$. Moreover if E is any expression, we use the abbreviation $\vartheta_{|E}$ to denote $\vartheta_{|Var(E)}$. ε denotes the empty substitution. The *composition* $\vartheta\sigma$ of the substitutions ϑ and σ is defined as the functional composition. A *renaming* is a substitution ρ for which there exists the inverse ρ^{-1} such that $\rho\rho^{-1} = \rho^{-1}\rho = \varepsilon$. The pre-ordering $\leq$ (more general than) on substitutions is such that $\vartheta \leq \sigma$ iff there exists ϑ' such that $\vartheta\vartheta' = \sigma$. The result of the application of the substitution ϑ to a term t is an *instance* of t denoted by $t\vartheta$. We define $t \leq t'$ (t is more general than t') iff there exists ϑ such that $t\vartheta = t'$. A substitution ϑ is *grounding* for t if $t\vartheta$ is ground. The relation $\leq$ is a preorder. $\approx$ denotes the associated equivalence relation (*variance*). A substitution ϑ is a *unifier* of terms t and t' if $t\vartheta \equiv t'\vartheta$. The *most general unifier* of t_1 and t_2 is denoted by $mgu(t_1, t_2)$. All the above definitions can be extended to other syntactic expressions in the obvious way.

A *literal* L is an object of the form $p(t_1, \ldots, t_n)$ (*atom*) or $\neg p(t_1, \ldots, t_n)$ (*negative literal*), where $p \in P$, $t_1, \ldots, t_n \in T$ and "$\neg$" denotes negation. A *clause* is a formula of the form $H : -L_1, \ldots, L_n$ with $n \geq 0$, where H (the *head*) is an atom and $L_1, \ldots, L_n$ (the *body*) are literals. ": −" and "," denote logic implication and conjunction respectively, and all variables are universally quantified. A *definite clause* is a clause whose body contains atoms only. If the body is empty the clause is a *unit clause*. A *general program* is a finite set of clauses $P = \{C_1, \ldots, C_n\}$. A *positive program* is a finite set of definite clauses. A *general (positive) goal* is a formula $L_1, \ldots, L_m$, where each L_i is a literal (atom).

A *Herbrand interpretation* I for a program P is a subset of the *Herbrand base* B (the set of all ground atoms). The intersection $M(P)$ of all the Herbrand models of a positive program P is a model (least Herbrand model). $M(P)$ is also the least fixpoint $T_P \uparrow \omega$ of a continuous transformation T_P (*immediate consequences operator*) on Herbrand interpretations. The *ordinal powers* of a generic monotonic operator T_P on a complete lattice $(D, \leq)$ with bottom $\perp$ are defined as usual, namely $T_P \uparrow 0 = \bot$, $T_P \uparrow (\alpha+1) = T_P(T_P \uparrow \alpha)$ for α successor ordinal and $T_P \uparrow \alpha = lub(\{T_P \uparrow \beta \mid \beta < \alpha\})$ if α is a limit ordinal. If G is a positive goal. $G \overset{\vartheta}{\leadsto}_{P,R} B_1,\ldots,B_n$ denotes an SLD-derivation of $B_1,\ldots,B_n$ from the goal G in the program P which uses the selection rule R and such that ϑ is the composition of the mgu's used in the derivation. $G \overset{\vartheta}{\longmapsto}_P \Box$ denotes the SLD-refutation of G in the program P with computed answer substitution ϑ. A computed answer substitution is always restricted to the variables occurring in G.

1.2. Observable properties and π-interpretations

The operational semantics is usually given by means of a set of inference rules which specify how derivations are made, and by defining a proper notion of observable. Consider for example positive logic programs with no composition and computed answer substitutions as observable. The operational semantics can be defined as follows

$$\mathcal{O}'(P) = \{\langle p(t_1,\ldots,t_n),\vartheta\rangle \mid p(t_1,\ldots,t_n) \overset{\vartheta}{\longmapsto}_P \Box\}$$

An equivalent operational semantics can be defined as

$$\mathcal{O}(P) = \{p(X_1,\ldots,X_n)\vartheta \mid p(X_1,\ldots,X_n) \overset{\vartheta}{\longmapsto}_P \Box\}$$

where the denotation of a program is a set of non-ground atoms, which can be viewed as a possibly infinite program. This is just an instance of a more general property of denotations within our approach. Namely denotations are possibly infinite programs and semantic domains are made of syntactic objects. The amount of syntax which is needed in the semantic domains depends on the observable and on the composition. For example, in $\mathcal{O}(P)$, the syntactic construct of variables is added to the Herbrand domain. When considering also OR-composition, non-ground unit clauses are not sufficient any longer and more general clauses are needed (see section 4.). Note that the approach is feasible only if the language syntax is powerful enough to express its own semantics. Since we have syntactic objects in the semantic domain, we need an equivalence relation in order to abstract from irrelevant syntactic differences. In the above considered example, this relation is variance. If the equivalence is accurate enough the semantics is fully abstract.

Herbrand interpretations are generalized in our setting by π-interpretations which are possibly infinite sets of equivalence classes of clauses from the semantic domain. The operational semantics of a program P is then a π-interpretation I, which has the following property. P and I are observationally equivalent with respect to any goal G. This is the property which allows us to state that our semantics does indeed capture the observable behavior.

1.3. Fixpoint semantics and unfolding

The aim of the second phase is the definition of a fixpoint semantics equivalent to the previously defined operational semantics. This can be achieved by the following steps.

- The set of π-interpretations is organized in a lattice $(\mathfrak{I}, \sqsubseteq)$ based on a suitable partial order relation $\sqsubseteq$, which in most cases is set inclusion.
- An immediate consequence operator T_P^π is defined and proved monotonic and continuous on $(\mathfrak{I}, \sqsubseteq)$. This allows the definition of the fixpoint semantics $\mathcal{F}(P)$ for P as $\mathcal{F}(P) = T_P^\pi \uparrow \omega$.
- The fixpoint semantics $\mathcal{F}(P)$ is proved equivalent to the operational semantics. If this equivalence holds, the immediate consequences operator T_P^π models the observable properties and may be useful for bottom-up program analysis.

Concise and elegant equivalence proofs can be obtained by introducing the intermediate notion of ***unfolding semantics*** $\mathcal{U}(P)$ [58, 59]. Unfolding is a well known program transformation rule [76] which allows to replace procedure calls by procedure definitions. The unfolding of the clauses of program P using the procedure definitions in program I is denoted by $unf_P(I)$.

The unfolding and the operational semantics are strongly related, since they are based on the same inference rule (applied to clauses and goals respectively). The unfolding semantics $\mathcal{U}(P)$ is obtained as the limit of the unfolding process. If the unfolding rule preserves the observable properties, $\mathcal{U}(P)$ is equivalent to the operational semantics $\mathcal{O}(P)$ which is a π-interpretation and therefore a program. This shows that the statement "the language syntax is powerful enough to express its own semantics" can be rephrased as "the language is closed under unfolding".

On the other side, the unfolding operator unf_P is strongly related to the immediate consequence operator T_P^π. For example, in many cases given a π-interpretation I, the relation $T_P^\pi(I) = unf_P(I)$ holds. The proof of equivalence between $\mathcal{U}(P)$ and $\mathcal{F}(P)$ can be based on such a relation. In particular the equivalence immediately holds for those immediate consequences operators which are ***compatible with*** the unfolding rule [26]. The above relations suggest a methodology to obtain the immediate consequences operator by first defining the unfolding operator, which is easier to define because of its strong relation to the operational semantics.

1.4. Model-theoretic semantics

The operational and fixpoint semantics of a program P define a π-interpretation I_P, which can be viewed as a syntactic notation for a set of Herbrand interpretations. $\mathcal{H}(I_P)$ denotes the set of all the Herbrand interpretations represented by I_P. For instance, in positive logic programs, the operational semantics $\mathcal{O}(P)$ is a set of non-ground atoms and $\mathcal{H}(\mathcal{O}(P))$ is the set containing the least Herbrand model of $\mathcal{O}(P)$. In general, our aim is finding a notion of π-model such that $\mathcal{O}(P)$ (and $\mathcal{F}(P)$) are π-models and every Herbrand model is a π-model. This can be obtained by the following definition.

Definition 1.1 *Given a program P and a π – interpretation I, I is a* π-model of P *iff P is true in all the Herbrand interpretations in $\mathcal{H}(I)$.*

As we will show in the following, the model intersection property does not hold in general for π-models. This is due to the fact that set inclusion does not adequately correspond to the intended meaning of π-interpretations. Namely the information of a π-interpretation I_1 may be contained in I_2 without I_1 being a subset of I_2. In general, we look for a partial order $\preceq$ modeling the meaning of π-interpretations, such that $(\Im, \preceq)$ is a complete lattice and the greatest lower bound of a set of π-models is a π-model. According to the last property there exists a least π-model, which, as we will see in the following, is the least Herbrand model. It is worth noting that the most expressive π-model $\mathcal{O}(P)$ is a non-minimal π-model.

The model-theoretic construction is possible only if π-interpretations can be viewed as representations of Herbrand interpretations. π-interpretations of concurrent constraint languages do not exhibit this property.

2. Positive logic programs

In this section we consider a non-compositional semantics for positive programs. Compositions will be considered in section 4.

2.1. π-interpretations

The first observable we consider is the *computed answer substitution* for which the induced program equivalence $\simeq$ is the following.

Definition 2.1 *Let P_1, P_2 be positive programs. $P_1 \simeq P_2$ if for every positive goal G, $G \stackrel{\vartheta}{\longmapsto}_{P_1} \Box$ iff $G \stackrel{\vartheta'}{\longmapsto}_{P_2} \Box$ and $\vartheta = (\vartheta'\rho)_{|G}$. where ρ is a renaming.*

The above observable is captured by the following operational semantics.

Definition 2.2 (Computed answer substitutions semantics)*[33] Let P be a positive program.*

$$\mathcal{O}(P) = \{A \mid \exists X_1,\ldots,X_n \textit{ distinct variables in } V, \exists\vartheta, \\ p(X_1,\ldots,X_n) \stackrel{\vartheta}{\longmapsto}_P \Box \textit{ and } A = p(X_1,\ldots,X_n)\vartheta \ \}$$

To model $\mathcal{O}(P)$ the usual Herbrand base has to be extended to the set of all the (possibly non-ground) atoms modulo variance.

Definition 2.3 *Let $\mathcal{B}$ be the quotient set of all the atoms w.r.t. variance. A π-interpretation is any subset of $\mathcal{B}$.*

In the following $\mathcal{O}(P)$ will then be formally considered as a subset of $\mathcal{B}$. Moreover, we will denote the equivalence class of an atom A by A itself. Non-ground interpretations have also been used in different semantic frameworks [20. 37, 27, 45]. The following theorem shows that $\mathcal{O}$ actually models computed answer substitutions.

Theorem 2.4 *[33, 34] Let P be a positive program and $G = G_1,\ldots,G_n$ be a positive goal. Then $G \stackrel{\vartheta}{\longmapsto}_P \Box$ iff there exist (renamed apart) atoms $A_1,\ldots,A_n \in \mathcal{O}(P)$ such that $\vartheta = (\gamma\rho)_{|G}$ where $\gamma = mgu((A_1,\ldots,A_n),(G_1,\ldots,G_n))_{|G}$ and ρ is a renaming.*

The $\mathcal{O}(P)$ semantics is fully abstract, since the following theorem holds.

Theorem 2.5 *[33, 34] Let P_1, P_2 be positive programs. $P_1 \simeq P_2$ iff $\mathcal{O}(P_1) = \mathcal{O}(P_2)$.*

Since logic programs compute answer substitutions, the equivalence $\simeq$ is the correct equivalence notion to be chosen from the programming language viewpoint. Other observable properties (and therefore different operational semantics) can be defined. A *partial computed answer substitutions semantics* is defined in [32] and is extended in [43] to consider also the selection rule. We will consider here the *ground success set* and the *atomic logical consequences semantics* [20] formally defined as follows.

Definition 2.6 *[35] Let P be a positive program.*
(ground success set) $\mathcal{O}_1(P) = \{A \mid A$ *is ground and* $A \stackrel{\epsilon}{\longmapsto}_P \Box\}$
(atomic logical consequences semantics) $\mathcal{O}_2(P) = \{A \mid A \stackrel{\epsilon}{\longmapsto}_P \Box\}$

Note that the semantic domain of $\mathcal{O}_1(P)$ is the usual Herbrand base, i.e. the set of all the ground atoms. The following example shows that the three semantics are different. Indeed, if we denote by $\equiv_i$ the program equivalence induced by $\mathcal{O}_i$, $i = 1, 2$, the following (strict) inclusion holds $\simeq \subseteq \equiv_2 \subseteq \equiv_1$, i.e. $\simeq$ is finer than $\equiv_2$, and $\equiv_2$ is finer than $\equiv_1$.

Example 2.7 *Consider the program P on the signature S, defined by $C = \{a\backslash 0, f\backslash 1\}$.*

$$P = \{\ p(f(a)).\\ p(X).\\ q(a).\quad \}$$

$$\begin{array}{lllllllll} \mathcal{O}(P) & = & \{ & q(a). & p(X). & & p(f(a)) & & \} \\ \mathcal{O}_1(P) & = & \{ & q(a). & & p(a). & p(f(a)). & p(f(f(a))). \ \ldots & \} \\ \mathcal{O}_2(P) & = & \{ & q(a). & p(X). & p(a). \ p(f(X)). & p(f(a)). \ p(f(f(X))). & p(f(f(a))). \ \ldots & \} \end{array}$$

In this section we will consider the $\mathcal{O}(P)$ semantics only, since it corresponds to the most natural observable property for logic programs. In section 5, we will use $\mathcal{O}_2(P)$ which is useful when dealing with failure.

2.2. Fixpoint semantics

We will now introduce an immediate consequences operator T_P^π on π-interpretations whose least fixpoint will be shown to be equivalent to the computed answer substitutions semantics $\mathcal{O}(P)$.

Lemma 2.8 *The set of all π-interpretations $(\Im, \subseteq)$ is a complete lattice.*

Definition 2.9 *[33] Let P be a positive program and I be a π-interpretation.*

$$T_P^\pi(I) = \{A \in \mathcal{B} \mid \exists C = A' : -B_1, \ldots, B_n \in P, \exists\, B'_1, \ldots, B'_n \text{ variants of atoms in } I \text{ and renamed apart, } \exists \vartheta = mgu((B_1, \ldots, B_n), (B'_1, \ldots, B'_n)) \text{ and } A = A'\vartheta \quad \}$$

Note that T_P^π is different from the standard T_P operator [78] in that it derives instances of the clause heads by *unifying* the clause bodies with atoms in the current π-interpretation, rather than by taking all the possible ground instances. In other words T_P^π defines a bottom-up inference based on the same rule (unification) which is used by top-down SLD resolution. The following theorem allows to define a fixpoint semantics for positive logic programs.

Theorem 2.10 *[33] The T_P^π operator is continuous on $(\Im, \subseteq)$. Then there exists a least fixpoint $T_P^\pi \uparrow \omega$ of T_P^π.*

Definition 2.11 *[33] The fixpoint semantics of a positive program P is defined as $\mathcal{F}(P) = T_P^\pi \uparrow \omega$.*

The equivalence between $\mathcal{F}(P)$ and $\mathcal{O}(P)$ is proved by introducing the unfolding semantics.

Definition 2.12 *Let P and Q be positive programs. Then the unfolding of P w.r.t. Q is defined as*

$$unf_P(Q) = \{(A : -\tilde{L}_1, \ldots, \tilde{L}_n)\vartheta \mid \exists A : -B_1, \ldots, B_n \in P, \exists B'_i : -\tilde{L}_i \in Q, \text{ renamed apart for } i = 1, \ldots, n, \text{ s.t. } \vartheta = mgu((B_1, \ldots, B_n), (B'_1, \ldots, B'_n))\}$$

The unfolding rule can be applied to any atom in a clause and preserves the operational semantics. i.e. the language is closed under unfolding. Therefore it is possible to define the immediate consequences operator in terms of the unfolding rule. Such a relation allows to prove in a natural way the equivalence between the operational (top-down) and the fixpoint (bottom-up) semantics, by introducing the intermediate notion of "unfolding semantics". The following theorem 2.16 was proved in [59]. An alternative proof is given in [26] by using lemma 2.15. A direct proof of $\mathcal{F}(P) = \mathcal{O}(P)$ was first given in [33].

Definition 2.13 *[59, 26] Let P be a positive program. Then we define the collection of programs*

$$P_1 = unf_P(P)$$
$$P_i = unf_{P_{i-1}}(P)$$

and the collection of π-interpretations $I_i(P) = \{A \mid A \in \mathcal{B} \text{ and } A \in P_i\}$. The unfolding semantics $\mathcal{U}(P)$ of the program P is defined as

$$\mathcal{U}(P) = \bigcup_{i=1,2,\ldots} I_i(P).$$

Theorem 2.14 (equivalence between unfolding and operational semantics)*[59, 26] Let P be a positive program. Then $\mathcal{U}(P) = \mathcal{O}(P)$.*

Lemma 2.15 *[26] Let P, Q be positive programs. Then T_P^π is compatible with $unf_P(Q)$, i.e. $T^\pi_{unf_P(Q)}(\emptyset) = T_P^\pi(T_Q^\pi(\emptyset))$.*

Since T_P^π is compatible with the unfolding rule and by definition of the unfolding rule, $T_P^\pi(I) = unf_P(I)$ and $T \uparrow i = T_{P_i}^\pi(\emptyset) = unf_{P_i}(\emptyset)$. Therefore,

Theorem 2.16 (equivalence between fixpoint and operational semantics)*[59, 26] Let P be a positive program. Then $\mathcal{F}(P) = \mathcal{U}(P) = \mathcal{O}(P)$.*

Theorem 2.16 shows that $\mathcal{F}(P)$ is the fully abstract semantics w.r.t. computed answer substitutions.

2.3. Model-theoretic semantics

In order to define π-models according to definition 1.1 we have to specify the function $\mathcal{H}$ from π-interpretations to sets of Herbrand interpretations.

Definition 2.17 *[35] Let I be a π-interpretation. Then $\mathcal{H}(I) = \{M(I)\}$ where $M(I)$ is the least Herbrand model of I or, equivalently, the set of ground instances of atoms in I.*

Proposition 2.18 *[35] Let P be a program. Then every Herbrand model of P is a π-model of P. Moreover $\mathcal{O}(P), \mathcal{O}_1(P), \mathcal{O}_2(P)$ are π-models of P.*

The program P of example 2.7 shows that the model intersection property does not hold any longer. In fact, $\mathcal{O}(P) \cap \mathcal{O}_1(P) = \{q(a), p(f(a))\}$ which is not a π-model of P. This is not surprising, since set theoretic operations do not adequately model the operations on non-ground atoms, which stand for all their ground instances. The following proposition gives a more adequate partial order relation on π-interpretations.

Proposition 2.19 *[35] Let I_1, I_2 be π-interpretations. Let $\preceq$ be defined as follows*

- *$I_1 \leq I_2$ iff $\forall A_1 \in I_1, \exists A_2 \in I_2$ such that $A_2 \leq A_1$.*
- *$I_1 \preceq I_2$ iff $(I_1 \leq I_2)$ and $(I_2 \leq I_1$ implies $I_1 \subseteq I_2)$.*

Then the relation $\preceq$ is an ordering.

The intuitive meaning of the above defined relations is the following. $I_1 \leq I_2$ means that every atom verified by I_1 is also verified by I_2 (I_2 contains more *positive information*). $I_1 \preceq I_2$ means that either I_2 strictly contains more positive information than I_1 or (if the amount of positive information is the same), that I_1 expresses it by less elements than I_2 (I_2 is more redundant).

Theorem 2.20 *[35] $(\Im, \preceq)$ is a complete lattice. $\mathcal{B}$ is the top element and $\emptyset$ is the bottom element.*

The following proposition generalizes the model intersection property of Herbrand models.

Proposition 2.21 *[35] Let M be a set of π-models of P. Then $glb(M)$ is a π-model of P. Moreover, the least π-model $\mathcal{M}(P) = glb(\{I \in \Im \mid I$ is a π-model of $P\})$ is the least Herbrand model.*

In conclusion, with the new semantic domain $\Im$ and the new notion of π-model, the least Herbrand model is still the least model. This model is completely satisfactory if one is concerned with the logical aspect of logic programs. However, if computed answer substitutions are taken into account, we have to consider the non-minimal π-model $\mathcal{O}(P)$.

3. Constraint logic programs

The *Constraint Logic Programming* paradigm has been proposed by Jaffar and Lassez [50, 49] in order to integrate a generic computational mechanism based on constraints with the logic programming framework. The benefits of such an integration are several. From a pragmatic point of view, CLP(X) (CLP for short) allows to use a specific constraint domain X and a related constraint solver within the declarative paradigm of logic programming. From the theoretical viewpoint, CLP provides a unified view of several extensions to pure logic programming which preserves the unique semantic properties of logic programs. Moreover, since the computation is performed over X, CLP programs have an "algebraic" semantics [50] defined on the algebraic structure of X. Let us introduce an informal description of the language. A formal definition can be found in [50]. A *CLP program* is a set of clauses of the form $H : -c\Box B_1, \ldots, B_n$ where the B_i's are standard atoms and c (the *constraint*) is a conjunction of atoms interpreted over an algebraic structure $\Re$. A constraint c is *solvable* iff there exists a substitution θ (*solution*) mapping variables to elements of the domain of $\Re$, such that $c\theta$ is true in $\Re$. A CLP derivation step of a goal $c\Box A_1, \ldots, A_n$ in a program P results in a goal of the form $\tilde{c}\Box \tilde{B}_1, \ldots, \tilde{B}_n$, if there exist n (renamed apart) clauses in P, $H_i : -c_i\Box \tilde{B}_i, i = 1, \ldots, n$, such that $\tilde{c} = c \wedge c_1 \wedge \ldots \wedge c_n \wedge A_1 = H_1 \wedge \ldots \wedge A_n = H_n$ is solvable. A successful *derivation* of a goal G (denoted by $G \overset{\Re}{\longmapsto}_P (c\Box)$) is a finite sequence of goals such that every goal is obtained from the previous one by means of a derivation step and the last goal has the form $(c\Box)$ where c is the *answer constraint*. The *$\Re$-base* is the set of all the "domain instances" $p(\tilde{d})$, where $\tilde{d}$ is a tuple of elements of the domain of $\Re$. An *$\Re$-interpretation* is any subset of the $\Re$-base. An *$\Re$-model* of P is an *$\Re$-interpretation* I such that all the clauses of P are true in I.

3.1. The answer constraint semantics

The observable we consider is the *computed answer constraint* for which the induced program equivalence $\simeq$ is the following.

Definition 3.1 *Let P_1, P_2 be CLP programs. $P_1 \simeq P_2$ if for every goal G, $G \overset{\Re}{\longmapsto}_{P_1} (c\Box)$ iff $G \overset{\Re}{\longmapsto}_{P_2} (c'\Box)$ and c, c' have the same solutions restricted to the variables of G.*

Definition 3.2 (Computed answer constraint semantics)*[39] Let P be a CLP program.*

$$\mathcal{O}(P) = \{c\Box p(\tilde{X}) \mid true\Box p(\tilde{X}) \overset{\Re}{\longmapsto}_P (c\Box) \}.$$

The semantic domain of $\mathcal{O}(P)$ is then set of *constrained atoms* modulo a suitable equivalence $\approx$. A constrained atom is essentially a unit clause where we allow an infinite conjunction of constraints in the body. Such an assumption is necessary to obtain, as a particular case of π-model, the usual $\Re$-models defined in [50] and hence to obtain proposition 3.12. However note that the $\mathcal{O}(P)$ semantics contains only constrained atoms with finite sets of constraints. The following is the formal definition.

Definition 3.3 *[50] A constrained atom is an object $c\Box p(\tilde{X})$ where c is a (possibly infinite) set of constraints. The set of "domain instances" $[c\Box p(\tilde{X})]$ of a constrained atom $c\Box p(\tilde{X})$ is defined as $\{p(\tilde{X})\theta \mid \theta$ is a solution of $c\}$. If S is a set of constrained atoms, then $[S] = \bigcup_{A \in S}[A]$.*

Definition 3.4 *[39] Let A be the set of the constrained atoms for program P. The preorder $\leq$ on A is the following. $c_1\Box p(\tilde{X}) \leq c_2\Box p(\tilde{X})$ iff $[c_1\Box p(\tilde{X})] \subseteq [c_2\Box p(\tilde{X})]$. The equivalence induced by $\leq$ on the set of constrained atoms is denoted by $\approx$.*

Definition 3.5 *[39] Let $\mathcal{B}$ be the quotient set of all the constrained atoms w.r.t. $\approx$. A π-interpretation is any subset of $\mathcal{B}$.*

As usual, $\mathcal{O}(P)$ will be considered as a π-interpretation and the equivalence class of a constrained atom $c\Box p(\tilde{X})$ will be denoted by $c\Box p(\tilde{X})$ itself. The following theorem shows that $\mathcal{O}(P)$ actually models computed answer constraints.

Theorem 3.6 *[39] Let P be a CLP program and* $G = c_0\Box A_1, \ldots, A_n$ *be any goal. Then* $G \overset{\Re}{\longmapsto}_P (c_{ans}\Box)$ *iff there exist n (renamed apart) constrained atoms* $c_i\Box B_i \in \mathcal{O}(P)$, $i = 1, \ldots n$, *such that* $(c_0 \wedge c_1 \wedge \ldots \wedge c_n \wedge A_1 = B_1 \wedge \ldots \wedge A_n = B_n)$ *and* c_{ans} *have the same solutions restricted to the variables in G.*

Also in this case full abstractness holds. Note also that semantics similar to $\mathcal{O}_1(P)$ and $\mathcal{O}_2(P)$ can be defined [50, 39]. $\mathcal{O}_1(P)$ is the semantics originally defined for CLP [49] and is the CLP counterpart of the ground success set. Its semantic domain is the $\Re$-base. We give now the definition of the immediate consequences operator, the equivalence theorem and the definition of π-model. All the other definitions and results are similar to those in section 2.

Definition 3.7 *[39] Let P be a CLP program and I be a π-interpretation.*

$$
\begin{aligned}
T_P^{\pi}(I) = \{\ & c\Box p(\tilde{X}) \in \mathcal{B}\ | \\
& \exists \text{ a renamed clause } p(\tilde{t}) : -c_0\Box p_1(\tilde{t}_1), \ldots, p_n(\tilde{t}_n) \text{ in } P, \\
& \exists\ c_i\Box p_i(\tilde{X}_i) \in I, 1 \le i \le n \text{ which share no variables}, \\
& c = c_0 \wedge \tilde{X}_i = \tilde{t}_1 \wedge \ldots \wedge \tilde{X}_n = \tilde{t}_n \wedge c_1 \wedge \ldots \wedge c_n \wedge \tilde{X} = \tilde{t} \\
& \text{is solvable and finite} \qquad \}.
\end{aligned}
$$

Definition 3.8 *[39] The fixpoint semantics of a CLP program P is defined as* $\mathcal{F}(P) = T_P^{\pi} \uparrow \omega$ *(since* T_P^{π} *is continuous on* $(\Im, \subseteq)$*).*

Theorem 3.9 (equivalence between the fixpoint and the operational semantics)*[39] Let P be a CLP program. Then* $\mathcal{F}(P) = \mathcal{O}(P)$.

Definition 3.10 *[13] Let I be a π-interpretation. Then* $\mathcal{H}(I) = \{[I]\}$ *(or, equivalently, the set containing the least $\Re$-model of I).*

Proposition 3.11 *[39] Let P be a CLP program. Then every $\Re$-model of P is a π-model of P. Moreover* $\mathcal{O}(P)$ *is a π-model of P.*

Also in the CLP case we need a partial order on π-interpretations to restore the π-model intersection property. The definition of the partial order and the related results are exactly the same of section 2. and lead to the following proposition.

Proposition 3.12 *[39] Let* **M** *be a set of π-models of program P. Then* $glb(\mathbf{M})$ *is a π-model of P. Moreover, the least π-model* $\mathcal{M}(P) = glb(\{I \in \Im \mid I \text{ is a } \pi\text{-model of } P\})$ *is the least $\Re$-model of P.*

A π-interpretation in both the positive logic programs and the CLP case represents one Herbrand or $\Re$-model only, since non-ground atoms and constrained atoms represent (possibly infinite) sets of ground atoms and domain instances respectively. The π-model is different from its least Herbrand model or $\Re$-model, in that it models exactly the observable property. In section 4. we will consider open logic programs, where a notion of composition is introduced. This will show another property of π-interpretations. Namely, the syntax introduced in the semantic domain may have the purpose of representing a (possibly infinite) set of Herbrand models.

4. Open programs

The semantics defined in section 2. is compositional w.r.t. the AND operator. We consider here OR-compositionality, i.e. composition w.r.t. to union of programs. An *Ω-open program* [15] P is a positive program in which the predicate symbols belonging to the set Ω are considered partially defined in P. P can be composed with other programs which may further specify the predicates in Ω. Such a composition is denoted by $\cup_\Omega$. Formally, given a set of predicate symbols Ω, if $Pred(P_1) \cap Pred(P_2) \subseteq \Omega$ then $Pred(P_1) \cup_\Omega Pred(P_2) = Pred(P_1) \cup Pred(P_2)$, otherwise $Pred(P_1) \cup_\Omega Pred(P_2)$ is undefined. The semantics of open programs must be compositional wrt $\cup_\Omega$, i.e. the semantics of $P_1 \cup_\Omega P_2$ must be derivable from the semantics of P_1 and P_2. Note that if Ω contains all predicate symbols then $\cup_\Omega$ is the same as standard union.

4.1. Computed answer substitution semantics for Ω-open programs

Definition 4.1 *Let P_1, P_2 be Ω-open programs. $P_1 \simeq_\Omega P_2$ if for every positive goal G and for every program Q such that, for $i = 1, 2$, $P_i \cup_\Omega Q$ is defined, $G \overset{\vartheta}{\longmapsto}_{P_1 \cup_\Omega Q} \Box$ iff $G \overset{\vartheta'}{\longmapsto}_{P_2 \cup_\Omega Q} \Box$ and $\vartheta = (\vartheta' \rho)_{|G}$, where ρ is a renaming.*

The above observational equivalence is captured by the following operational semantics. In the following we denote by Id_Ω the set of clauses $\{p(\tilde{X}) : -p(\tilde{X}) \mid p \in \Omega\}$ where Ω is a set of predicate symbols.

Definition 4.2 (Ω-compositional computed answer substitutions semantics)*[13] Let P be a positive program, Ω be a set of predicate symbols and let R be a fair selection rule. Then we define*

$$\begin{aligned} \mathcal{O}_\Omega(P) = \{A : -B_1, \ldots, B_n \mid\ & \exists X_1, \ldots, X_n \text{ distinct variables in } V, \exists \text{ a derivation} \\ & p(X_1, \ldots, X_n) \overset{\gamma}{\leadsto}_{P,R} D_1, \ldots, D_m \overset{\vartheta}{\leadsto}_{P \cup Id_\Omega, R} B_1, \ldots, B_n, \\ & A = p(X_1, \ldots, X_n)\gamma\vartheta \\ & \text{and } Pred(B_1, \ldots, B_n) \subseteq \Omega\} \end{aligned}$$

$\mathcal{O}_\Omega(P)$ is a set of *resultants* [63] obtained from goals of the form $p(\tilde{X})$ in P and is essentially the result of the partial evaluation of P, where derivations terminate at open predicates (i.e. predicates in Ω). The set of clauses Id_Ω in the previous definition is used to delay the evaluation of open atoms. This is a trick which allows to obtain, by using a fixed fair selection rule R, all the derivations $p(X_1, \ldots, X_k) \overset{\vartheta}{\leadsto}_{P,R'} B_1, \ldots, B_n$ which use any selection rule R' for $Pred(B_1, \ldots, B_n) \subseteq \Omega$. Therefore the previous definition is independent from the fair selection rule considered.

The semantic domain $\mathcal{C}_\Omega$ for the semantics $\mathcal{O}_\Omega(P)$ is the set of clauses whose body predicates are all in Ω (*conditional atoms*) modulo the following equivalence $\approx$.

Definition 4.3 *Let $c_1 = A_1 : -B_1, \ldots, B_n$ and $c_2 = A_2 : -D_1, \ldots, D_n$. Then $c_1 \approx c_2$ iff $\exists$ a renaming ρ such that $A_1 \equiv A_2\rho$ and $\{^+ B_1, \ldots, B_n\}^+ = \{^+ D_1\rho, \ldots, D_n\rho\}^+$ where $\{^+\ \}^+$ denotes a multiset.*

Definition 4.4 *A π-interpretation for an Ω-open program P is any subset of $\mathcal{C}_\Omega$.*

$\mathcal{O}_\Omega(P)$ is then a π-interpretation for Ω-open programs. Note that we have to consider bodies of clauses as multisets (instead than sets) to ensure the correctness of the semantics wrt the equivalence $\simeq_\Omega$. For example, for $c_1 = p(X) : -p(X)$ and $c_2 = p(X) : -p(X), p(X)$, $c_1 \not\simeq_\Omega c_2$. Indeed c_1 and c_2 produce different answers for the goal $p(X)$ when composed with the set of facts $Q = \{p(f(a, y)), p(f(y, b))\}$, since only in $\{c_2\} \cup Q$ we can obtain the answer $x/f(a, b)$.

Example 4.5 *Consider the following Ω-open program P, where $\Omega = \{p\}$.*

$$P = \{\ q(X) : -p(X)\quad r(b) : -p(b)\quad p(a)\ \}$$

Then $\mathcal{O}_\Omega(P) = \{q(X) : -p(X),\ r(b) : -p(b),\ p(a),\ q(a)\}$.

The functional semantics in [57] is compositional when considering the success set as observable. The corresponding equivalence is logical equivalence [64]. A compositional semantics in terms of clauses, which does not model answer substitutions, has been considered in [45]. A compositional semantics modeling answer substitutions has been given in [46]. However, the semantics is not expressed as a set of clauses, is more complex than $\mathcal{O}_\Omega(P)$ and is then less suitable for semantics based program analysis. The following results shows that $\mathcal{O}_\Omega$ is compositional wrt $\cup_\Omega$ and actually models computed answer substitutions in a compositional way.

Theorem 4.6 *[13] Let P, P_1, P_2 be programs and let us assume that $Pred(P_1) \cap Pred(P_2) \subseteq \Omega$. Then the following facts hold*

- $\mathcal{O}_\Omega(\mathcal{O}_\Omega(P_1) \cup_\Omega \mathcal{O}_\Omega(P_2)) = \mathcal{O}_\Omega(P_1 \cup_\Omega P_2)$,
- $P \cong_\Omega \mathcal{O}_\Omega(P)$.

As usual $\mathcal{O}_\Omega(P)$ can be characterized as the least fixpoint of an immediate consequences operator. We can simply define such an operator in terms of the unfolding rule. Note that we consider as usual a π-interpretation also as a set of (renamed apart) syntactic clauses. Moreover, as previously discussed, operators such as unf_P are considerd also as operators on $\mathcal{C}_\Omega$. These "semantic" versions are well defined since clauses are always renamed apart.

Definition 4.7 *[15]* Let P be an Ω-open program and let $I \subseteq \mathcal{C}_\Omega$. Then we define

$$T^\pi_{P,\Omega}(I) = unf_P(I \cup Id_\Omega).$$

Definition 4.8 *[15] The fixpoint semantics of an Ω-open program P is defined as $\mathcal{F}(P) = T^\pi_{P,\Omega} \uparrow \omega$ (since $T^\pi_{P,\Omega}$ is continuous on $(\Im, \subseteq)$).*

Theorem 4.9 (equivalence between the fixpoint and the operational semantics)*[13] Let P be an Ω-open program. Then $\mathcal{F}(P) = \mathcal{O}_\Omega(P)$.*

As already mentioned, in the case of Ω-open programs, a π-interpretation I represents the set of the least Herbrand models of all the programs which can be obtained by closing the program I with a suitable set of ground atoms defining the open predicates.

Definition 4.10 *[13] Let I be a π-interpretation for an Ω-open program. Then $\mathcal{H}(I) = \{M(I \cup_\Omega J)\}$ where $M(I)$ denotes the least Herbrand model of I and J is any set of ground atoms $p(\tilde{t})$ such that $p \in \Omega$ and $p(\tilde{t})$ is an instance of an atom in I.*

If we consider the program P of example 4.5 on the signature S, defined by $C = \{a\backslash 0, b\backslash 0\}$, then $\mathcal{H}(\mathcal{O}_\Omega(P)) = \{\{p(a), q(a)\}, \{p(a), q(a), p(b), r(b), q(b)\}\}$.

Proposition 4.11 *[13] Let P be an Ω-open program. The following statements hold*

- *every Herbrand model of P is a π-model of P.*
- *$\mathcal{O}_\Omega(P)$ is a π-model of P.*

Also in the open program case we need a partial order on π-interpretations to restore the π-model intersection property. The definition of the partial order and the related results are exactly the same of section 2. and lead to the following proposition.

Proposition 4.12 *[13] Let* **M** *be a set of π-models of an Ω-open program P. Then glb(***M***) is a π-model of P. Moreover, the least π-model $\mathcal{M}(P) = glb(\{I \in \Im \mid I$ is a π-model of $P\})$ is the least Herbrand model of P.*

Let us finally discuss some interesting properties of the π-interpretation $\mathcal{O}_\Omega(P)$.

- It is the syntactic device which allows to obtain a unique representation for a possibly infinite set of Herbrand models when a unique representative Herbrand model does not exist. A similar device was used in [29, 53, 42] to characterize logic programs with negation.
- A related use of syntactic objects as interpretations, even if restricted to the ground case only, can be found in *generalized Horn programs* [36] and in *disjunctive logic programs* [70] (where π-models are called *model states*).
- This framework is strongly related to *abduction* [30]. If Ω is the set of abducible predicates, the abductive consequences of any goal G can be found by executing G in $\mathcal{O}_\Omega(P)$.
- The delayed evaluation of open predicates which is typical of $\mathcal{O}_\Omega(P)$ can easily be generalized to other logic languages, to achieve compositionality w.r.t the union of programs. In particular this matches quite naturally the semantics of CLP previously shown, and that one for concurrent constraint programs given in [38, 41].

5. The treatment of negation and general logic programs

5.1. Finite Failure

The first step necessary to model with our approach negative information is to look at the problem of characterizing finitely failed atoms and goals. In the literature, the set of finitely failed atoms is well characterized (operationally and declaratively), only in the ground case. In [60] we studied the set of (possibly non ground) finitely failed atoms.

Let us first recall the basic operational characterizations of atoms which have a successful and a finitely failed computation. In the classical approach [62, 1] the following sets have been studied and characterized.

- The (ground) success set:

$$\begin{aligned} SS &= \{A \mid A \text{ is ground and } \leftarrow A \overset{\epsilon}{\longmapsto}_P \Box\} && (1)\\ &= \{A \mid A \text{ is ground and } P \models A\} && (2)\\ &= M \text{ (the least Herbrand model)} \\ &= T_P \uparrow \omega \end{aligned}$$

- The (ground) finite failure set:

$$\begin{aligned} FF &= \{A \mid A \text{ is ground and } \leftarrow A \text{ has a finitely failed SLD-tree}\} && (3)\\ &= \mathbf{B} \backslash T_P \downarrow \omega && (4) \end{aligned}$$

In [34] another set has been considered, the atomic consequences set (called ACS), proved equivalent to the set of those atoms having a successful computation with an empty computed answer substitution:

$$ACS = \mathcal{O}_2(P) = \{A \mid P \models A\}$$

The set of non-ground atoms which have a finitely failed computation is not the counterpart of the set ACS. In fact the atomic consequences are (implicitly) universally quantified, whereas in the case of finitely failed atoms it is the negation of their existential closure which is seen as a consequence of the program. Thus a larger set of successful atoms has to be considered; those which have a successful computation with whatever computed answer substitution (the atoms whose existential closure is a consequence of the program). The operational concepts that we characterize are the following.

- The non-ground success set: $NGSS = \{A \mid \exists \vartheta \leftarrow A \overset{\vartheta}{\longmapsto} \Box\}$
- The non-ground finite failure set: $NGFF = \{A \mid \leftarrow A$ has a finitely failed SLD-tree$\}$

To see what happens in our new semantics, let us introduce the following operators on subsets I of $\mathcal{B}$

- $Down(I) = \{A \mid \exists A' \in I\ [A \leq A']\}$
- $Up(I) = \{A \mid \exists A' \in I\ [A' \leq A]\}$

To study negative information the most useful approach is a simpler π-interpretation which corresponds to the c-approach in [34]. The interpretations on this domain are those subsets I of $\mathcal{B}$ that are *upward closed*, i.e., $I = Up(I)$. The set $\mathcal{I}_v$ of interpretations, ordered by set inclusion, is a complete lattice. $\mathcal{B}$ is the supremum. On this structure, the extended immediate consequence operator T_v, defined by

$$T_v(I) = \{H\vartheta \mid H \leftarrow \tilde{B} \in P, \tilde{B}\vartheta \in I\}$$

is continuous. Again, there exist the least and the greatest fixpoints of T_v, $lfp(T_v)$ and $gfp(T_v)$, and

$$T_v \uparrow \omega = lfp(T_v) \subseteq gfp(T_v) \subseteq T_v \downarrow \omega$$

hold.

We recall the basic results, that extend the ones listed in (2), i.e. the model-theoretic and fixpoint characterization of the atomic consequence set ACS

$$\begin{aligned} ACS &= \{A \mid P \models A\} & (5)\\ &= M_v \text{ (the least Herbrand model with variables)} \\ &= T_v \uparrow \omega \end{aligned}$$

Let us first consider the relation between the non-ground success set $NGSS$ and the transformation T_v.

Theorem 5.1 *[60]*

$$NGSS = Down(ACS) = Down(lfp(T_v))$$

Note that $NGSS$ is also equal to $Down(SS)$ and $Down(lfp(T))$. A model-theoretic characterization of $NGSS$ is $\{A \mid P \models \exists A\}$, i.e., the set of atoms whose existential quantification is a logical consequence of the program.

Corollary 5.2 *[60]*

$$NGSS = Down(lfp(T_v)) = Down(\bigcup_{n\geq 0} T_v\uparrow n) = \bigcup_{n\geq 0} Down(T_v\uparrow n)$$

We present now our construction which allows to characterize *NGFF*.

Definition 5.3

- *For every* $n \geq 0$ *define* $I_n = Down(T\downarrow n)$.
- $I_\omega = \bigcap_{n\geq 0} I_n$.

The relation between I_ω (and therefore *NGFF*) and T_v follows immediately.

Corollary 5.4 *[60]* $NGFF = \mathcal{B}\backslash I_\omega = \mathcal{B}\backslash \bigcap_{n\geq 0} Down(T_v\downarrow n)$

Example 5.5 *Let us give an example of this result using the following program*

$$\{\ q(a) \leftarrow p(x) \quad p(f(x)) \leftarrow p(x)\ \} \tag{6}$$

$$T_v\downarrow 1 = \{p(f^n(a)), p(f^n(x)), q(a) \mid n \geq 1\}$$

$$Down(T_v\downarrow 1) = T_v\downarrow 1 \bigcup \{p(x), q(x)\}$$

$$T_v\downarrow k = \{p(f^n(a)), p(f^n(x)), q(a) \mid n \geq k\}$$

$$Down(T_v\downarrow k) = T_v\downarrow k \bigcup \{p(f^n(x)), q(x) \mid n < k\}$$

$$T_v\downarrow \omega = \{q(a)\}$$

$$\bigcap_{n\geq 0} Down(T_v\downarrow n) = \{p(f^n(x)), q(a), q(x) \mid n \geq 0\}$$

$$NGFF = \{p(f^n(a)), q(f^{n+1}(a)), q(f^{n+1}(x)) \mid n \geq 0\}$$

A first symmetry can be noted looking at corollaries 5.2 and 5.4. *NGSS* is characterized as the union of an infinite chain whose elements are obtainable using $T_v\uparrow n$, while *NGFF* is the complement of a set characterized as the intersection of an infinite chain whose elements are obtainable using $T_v\downarrow n$.

Moreover, in [60] the usual notions of Herbrand Universe, Base and Interpretations were extended to complete ones, thus allowing the representation of infinite computations. In this extended setting the immediate consequence operator is downward continuous, and therefore its greatest fixpoint is reachable in ω steps. This result allows to symmetrically characterize the above introduced sets also from the point of view of the fixpoint semantics. In fact, the set of successful non-ground atoms is obtained as the least fixpoint of this transformation, while the set of the finitely failed ones is given by the complement of its greatest fixpoint.

5.2. The NAI-rule

This is only the first step towards an extension of our approach to general goals and programs.

Let's first note that, to infer $\exists\neg A$, we cannot use the NAF-rule. In fact, if $\leftarrow A$ finitely fails, the NAF-rule infers $\forall\neg A$, and otherwise no conclusion is drawn. Let's now observe that if all derivations for $\leftarrow A$ either fail or instantiate some of the variables of A, then $\forall A$ is not a logical consequence of $Comp(P)$. Therefore it is consistent to assume $\neg\forall A$, namely $\exists\neg A$. We will see how to enlarge the reference theory ($Comp(P)$) in order to validly infer $\exists\neg A$. From an operational point of view, such a rule to infer $\exists\neg A$ can be justified by observing the following. If every branch of the SLD-tree for the goal $\leftarrow A$ either fails or instantiates some of the variables of A, then for a grounding substitution η instantiating all variables to distinct fresh constants, the SLD-tree for $\leftarrow A\eta$ finitely fails. Then, by the correctness of NAF (for ground atoms), we can deduce $\neg A\eta$, and therefore $\exists\neg A$. Consequently, the intended reference theory can be obtained by extending $Comp(P)$ by an infinity of new constant symbols. We denote this new theory by $Comp_L(P)$. Based on this concept of "finite instantiation" we define a new negation rule which we call *Negation As Instantiation* (NAI) and an operational semantics for negation: the *FFI* set, i.e. the Failure by Finite Instantiation set, corresponding to the set of atoms whose existentially quantified negation can be inferred.

Notably enough, the introduction of the NAI-rule followed directly from the observation that *NGFF* is not obtained directly as the complement of $T_v \downarrow \omega$. It turned out that this notion was exactly the *FFI* set, thus leading to a nice analogy with the standard semantics.

$$\begin{aligned} FFI &= \{A \mid \text{there is a finitely instantiating SLD-tree for } P \cup \{\leftarrow A\}\} \\ &= \{A \mid Comp_L(P) \models \neg\forall A\} \\ &= \mathcal{B} \setminus T_v \downarrow \omega. \end{aligned}$$

Therefore *FFI* is the negative counterpart of *ACS*.

The NAI-rule can be used with general programs. SLD-resolution must be extended by adding the NAI-rule as the only rule to solve (existentially closed) negative literals, and we called it SLDNI-resolution.

The SLDNI-resolution was shown in [72] correct w.r.t. $Comp_L(P)$, i. e. the failure of all attempts to refute a query Q by our interpreter implies that the formula $\exists\neg Q$ is true in every model of $Comp_L(P)$. Concerning the completeness. SLDNI-resolution does not present the problem of floundering, but still the existence of non-terminating computations are an obstacle to completeness, as in the case of SLDNF-resolution.

Like SLDNF-resolution, SLDNI-resolution cannot bind variables in negative subgoals. However, it can deal with negative literals without requiring them to be ground. To solve the problem of getting bindings for negative literals some other proposals are needed such as intentional negation [10] or constructive negation [19]. Our extension is in between these forms of negation and the NAF rule, with the advantage that the implemetation of the NAI rule is simple and can be obtained by a small modification of the NAF rule.

5.3. General programs

The extension of our approach to general programs is a complex one. During this study we encountered a first difficulty, namely some problems with the operational semantics of SLDNF-resolution. In [68] we first showed the inadequacy of the operational semantics for Negation as Failure given in [62], and then we defined a new notion of SLDNF-tree which solves the problems of the previous definition.

In this section we give an informal description, mainly through examples, of an attempt of this extension [42]. The resulting construction has several similarities with the previously described cases (syntactic objects used as interpretations, fixpoints), but one relevant difference. Namely, there is no operational semantics and therefore we are not concerned with observational equivalences. As a matter of fact, as is the case for most declarative semantics of negation, our semantics tries to model the abstract intended meaning of the program and can be viewed as the ideal semantics to be approximated by effective operational semantics.

Our construction is incremental, i.e. it consists of several sequential steps characterizing increasingly more expressive classes of programs. It was inspired by the intuitionistic reading of logic programs with negation given in [16, 17] and by the non-ground semantics in [77]. At each intermediate step we obtain a unique representative semantics, where some program fragments (the non-positive, the non-stratified and the non-call-consistent fragments, respectively) are left uninterpreted.

We will show the first two steps of our construction. Let us first discuss the structure of π-interpretations, which are sets of *conditional constrained atoms*, i.e. clauses such that all the atoms in the body are constraints or negative literals. Constraints are sets of equalities and inequalities on the Herbrand universe (local variables in inequalities are universally quantified). An inequality $\forall(r \neq s)$ is satisfiable if r and s cannot be unified by binding universally quantified variables only. Constraints are introduced [77] in order to represent non-unifiability of atoms in the style of constructive negation [19]. On the other hand, negative literals occurring in the π-interpretation generated at step i are those literals which cannot be evaluated according to the semantics of step i and are similar to open atoms in section 4. The equivalence relation on conditional constrained atoms is a combination of the relations defined for constrained and conditional atoms. We will consider here the first two steps only.

In the first step the positive fragment of the program is considered and negative atoms are completely ignored. The result of step one is the least fixpoint of an immediate consequence operator, which is exactly the same defined for open programs where every $\neg p$ is considered as a new open predicate. Let us consider an example.

Example 5.6 *Let P be the following general program.*

$$
\begin{aligned}
P = \{\ & p(X) :- q(Y,X), \neg r(Y,X) \\
& r(Y,X) :- s(X) \\
& q(a,Y) \\
& s(g(Y)) \\
& p_1(f(f(X))) :- \neg q_1(f(X)) \\
& q_1(X) :- \neg p_1(f(X)) \quad \}
\end{aligned}
$$

The least fixpoint $\mathcal{F}_1(P)$ of the first step operator is $\mathcal{F}_1(P)= \{p(X) :- \neg r(a,X), q(a,X), r(X,g(Y)), s(g(X)), p_1(f(f(X))) :- \neg q_1(f(X)), q_1(X) :- \neg p_1(f(X))\}$.

The first step can equivalently be defined by an operational semantics which can be viewed as an SLDNF resolution in which negative literals are delayed. The resulting π-interpretation allows to characterize answer substitutions and can be useful to investigate interesting properties, such as *floundering*. Thus, for instance, the program Q: $\{r(b), q(a,Y), p(X) :- q(X,Y), \neg r(X)\}$ is not allowed. However, the analysis of $\mathcal{F}_1(Q) = \{r(b), q(a,Y), p(a) :- \neg r(a)\}$ shows that Q is floundering free.

Our first step is strongly related to other constructions. In particular, the case where constrained conditional interpretations contain ground clauses only has been considered by [16, 17, 29]. Our non-ground operator has also been proposed in [53] as a first step in the transformation of general logic programs into positive constraint logic programs.

The second step interprets the stratified component according to the constructive rule for negation as failure given in [19], which allows to deal with variables in negative literals. A semantics for stratified programs [2] extending the non-ground semantics for positive programs and which is based on constructive negation has been given in [77]. The same result can be obtained by our second step, which however deals with the whole class of general logic programs. The result of the step consists of the least fixpoint of a transformation on π-interpretations which essentially, given a π-interpretation I, replace a literal $\neg B$ in the body of a clause $c \in I$ by a constraint which represents the non-unifiability of B with all the heads of the clauses in I.

The result of step 2 $\mathcal{F}_2(\mathcal{F}_1(P))$ applied to the program P of example 5.6 is the following π-interpretation.
$\mathcal{F}_2(\mathcal{F}_1(P)) = \{p(X) : -\forall Y.X \neq g(Y),\ q(a,X),\ r(X,g(Y)),\ s(g(X)),$
$p_1(f(f(X))) : -\neg q_1(f(X)),\ q_1(X) : -\forall Y.X \neq f(Y),\ q_1(f(X)) : -\neg p_1(f(f(X)))\}.$
Note that the negation in the stratified component has been completely evaluated (and replaced by constraints), while the non-stratified negation is still there in some clausesof $\mathcal{F}_2(\mathcal{F}_1(P))$. Further steps are needed to deal with the call-consistent fragment and then with unrestricted negation.

6. Sets of solutions

In this section we will consider some characteristics needed to model the semantics of a predicate like *setof* (see [25] for more details). The first step has to do with the termination of all SLD-derivations for a given goal.

6.1. The ground case

We start considering only ground atomic goals, and try to figure out if a given goal has a finite tree (succesful or failed). The basic idea is to extend the Herbrand base with special atoms that we call ***uncertain***, represented preceded by a question mark (e.g. $?A$ if A is an atom). Intuitively with $?A$ we indicate that A could have an infinite branch of computation. In the following with P we indicate a definite program.

Definition 6.1 *[25] The hypothetical Herbrand base and the extended Herbrand base are respectively*

$$?B = \{?A \mid A \in B\}. B_E = B \cup ?B.$$

An hypothetical Interpretation is any subset of B_E.

So interpretations can contain uncertain atoms, i.e., $I = \{p(a), ?p(a), \ldots\}$. Before introducing the extended T_P operator, let us consider the following example:

Example 6.2 *Consider the following program P:*

$$P = \{p(a),\ \ p(X) \leftarrow p(X)\}$$

Consider the standar operator T_P and the relative chain $T_P \uparrow i$:

$$T_P \uparrow 0 = \{p(a)\}$$

$$T_P \uparrow 1 = \{p(a)\} \cup \{p(a)\} = \{p(a)\} = T_P \uparrow i, i \geq 0.$$

In the i_th step, $i \geq 0$, we derive $p(a)$ from the fact in P but also from the clause $p(X) \leftarrow p(X)$ and the fact $p(a)$ applying *modus ponens*. What we would like to obtain is to distinguish the two types of '$p(a)$'; the uncertain atoms will help us. We then define the following operator on the extended Herbrand base.

Definition 6.3 *[25] Let P be a definite program, I an hypothetical interpretation.*

$$\begin{aligned} T_P^{hyp}(I) = \{A \in B_E \mid\ & \exists C \leftarrow B_1, \ldots, B_n \in P \\ & \alpha \text{ grounding substitution} \\ & B'_1\alpha, \ldots, B'_n\alpha \in I \text{ where} \\ & B'_j = B_j \text{ or } ?B_j \\ & A = ?C\alpha \text{ if } \exists k : B'_k = ?B_k \\ & A = C\alpha \text{ otherwise } \} \end{aligned}$$

We introduce now a suitable ordering and hence a lattice structure on extended intepretations in order to obtain a chain (as the result of iterated applications of previous operator) which is adequate to model the previously discussed intuitive meaning of $?A$. The limit of such a chain, i.e. the result of ω applications of T_P^{ug}, will be used in the following to give a declarative characterization of termination properties for ground goals in the program P. Note that, according to the meaning of $?A$, the bottom element of the lattice contains all the annotated atoms $?A$. An uncertain atom $?A$ disappears in the result of the iteration $T_P^{ug} \uparrow i$ when we are sure that there exists no derivations of length $\geq i$.

Definition 6.4 *Extractors: given a set D of atoms (not necessarily ground)*

$$Certain(D) = \{A \mid A \in D \cap B\}. Uncertain(D) = \{A \mid A \in D \cap ?B\}.$$

Definition 6.5 *Given* $I_1, I_2 \subseteq B_E$, *the relation* $\ll$ *is*

$$I_1 \ll I_2 \text{ iff } Certain(I_1) \subseteq Certain(I_2) \text{ and } Uncertain(I_1) \supseteq Uncertain(I_2).$$

Let HYP-INT be the set of hypotethical interpretations.

Proposition 6.6 *[25] (HYP-INT,$\ll$) is a complete lattice, where the top is B and the bottom is $?B$.*

Note that if $\mathcal{I}$ is a set of hypothetical interpretations, then according to the previous definition its least upper bound coincides with $\bigcup_{I \in \mathcal{I}} Certain(I) \cup \bigcap_{I \in \mathcal{I}} Uncertain(I)$. Moreover note that according to the general definition of the ordinal powers $\uparrow$ (see the preliminaries), $T_P^{ug} \uparrow 0 = ?B$ while for the ω step we have

$$T_P^{ug} \uparrow \omega = (\bigcup_{i=0}^{\omega} Certain(T_P^{ug} \uparrow i) \cup (\bigcap_{i=0}^{\omega} Uncertain(T_P^{ug} \uparrow i)).$$

The following proposition shows that by iterated applications of $T_P^{ug} \uparrow 0$ we obtain a chain wrt $\ll$.

Proposition 6.7 *[25] Let P be a definite program, then*

$$T_P^{ug} \uparrow i \ll T_P^{ug} \uparrow i+1, i \geq 0.$$

Example 6.8 *Let P be the following program*

$$P = \{\ p(a)$$
$$t(a)$$
$$p(X) \leftarrow t(X), q(X)$$
$$s(X) \leftarrow s(X)$$
$$t(X) \leftarrow t(X) \quad \}$$

Then

$$T_P^{ug} \uparrow 0 = \{?p(a), ?t(a), ?s(a), ?q(a)\}$$

$$T_P^{ug} \uparrow 1 = \{?t(a), t(a), ?s(a), ?p(a), p(a)\}$$

$$T_P^{ug} \uparrow 2 = \{?t(a), t(a), ?s(a), p(a)\} = T_P^{ug} \uparrow \omega.$$

From the previous example we can see that $t(a)$ has only an infinite SLD-tree of success, $s(a)$ has only an infinite branch of computation without success, $p(a)$ has finite success tree and $q(a)$ has a finite failure tree. The atoms contained in $T_P^{ug} \uparrow i$ correspond to the ones in $T_P \uparrow i$, modulo "?", but in $T_P^{ug} \uparrow i$ we operate a stronger distinction.

Now we can show the main result of this subsection:

Theorem 6.9 *[25] Finite success*
Let P be a program. A a ground atom then:

(1) $A \in T_P^{ug} \uparrow \omega$ *and* $?A \notin T_P^{ug} \uparrow \omega$ *iff* $P \cup \{\leftarrow A\}$ *has an SLD-tree of finite success;*

(2) $A \notin T_P^{ug} \uparrow \omega$ *and* $?A \notin T_P^{ug} \uparrow \omega$ *iff* $P \cup \{\leftarrow A\}$ *has an SLD-tree of finite failure;*

(3) $A \in T_P^{ug} \uparrow \omega$ *and* $?A \in T_P^{ug} \uparrow \omega$ *iff every SLD-tree for* $P \cup \{\leftarrow A\}$ *is successful but with at least an infinite branch;*

(4) $A \notin T_P^{ug} \uparrow \omega$ *and* $?A \in T_P^{ug} \uparrow \omega$ *iff every SLD-tree for* $P \cup \{\leftarrow A\}$ *has no success branches but at least an infinite branch.*

6.2. The non-ground case

Previous results can be extended to non ground atoms, using extended π-interpretations.

Definition 6.10 *[25] Non ground extended Herbrand base*
$?\mathcal{B} = \{?A \mid A \in \mathcal{B}\}$. *non ground hypothetical H. base,*
$\mathcal{B}_E = \mathcal{B} \cup ?\mathcal{B}$.
A non-ground hypothetical interpretation is any subset of $\mathcal{B}_E$.

The relation $\ll$ can be straightforwardly extended to the non-ground case by considering $I_1, I_2 \subseteq \mathcal{B}_E$. We denote by NG-HYP-INT be the set af all non ground hypothetical interpretations for a program. Also for the non-ground case we can prove that (NG-HYP-INT,$\ll$) is a complete lattice, where the top is $\mathcal{B}$ and the bottom is $?\mathcal{B}$.

As we did in the ground case, we can now define an extension of the immediate consequence operator which handles uncertain atoms.

Definition 6.11 *[25] Let P be a definite program. I an hypothetical interpretation.*

$$
\begin{aligned}
T_P^u(I) = \{A \in \mathcal{B}_E \mid\ & \exists C \leftarrow B_1, \ldots, B_n \in P \\
& A_1, \ldots, A_n \in I \\
& \vartheta = mgu((B_1, \ldots, B_n), (A'_1, \ldots, A'_n)) \text{ where} \\
& A'_j = D_j \ \text{ if } A_j = ?D_j, \\
& A'_j = A_j \ \text{ otherwise.} \\
& \text{Moreover for any } \gamma \\
& A = ?C\vartheta\gamma \ \text{ if } \exists\, j : A_j = ?D_j \\
& A = C\vartheta \ \text{ otherwise } \}
\end{aligned}
$$

According to the $\ll$ ordering, also for the T_P^u operator we have $T_P^u \uparrow 0 = ?\mathcal{B}$ and $T_P^u \uparrow \omega = (\bigcup_{i=0}^{\omega} Certain(T_P^u \uparrow i)) \cup (\bigcap_{i=0}^{\omega} Uncertain(T_P^u \uparrow i))$.

Note that, for the *certain* atoms, the operator T_P^u behaves exactly as the standard operator T_P^{π}, so if $\mathcal{F}(P)$ is the π-model of a program P which characterizes the computed answer substitutions:

$$\mathcal{F}(P) = \bigcup_{i \geq 0} Certain(T_P^u \uparrow i).$$

Let us define some convenient notation.

Definition 6.12 *Let P be a definite program. Then*

$$Heads(P) = \{C \mid C \leftarrow B_1, \ldots, B_n \in P \text{ with } n > 0\}$$

The main relation with the unfolding semantics $\mathcal{U}(P)$, as defined in section 2.2., is that the instances of uncertain atoms contained in i-th step of the approximation chain are exactly the instances of the heads of non-unit clause of P.

Theorem 6.13 *[25] Let P be a definite program. Then*

$Up(Uncertain(T^u_P \uparrow i)) = Up(Heads(P_{i-1}))$ *modulo the annotation with "?"* $, i \geq 1$.

$Certain(T^u_P \uparrow i) = I_{i-1}(P), i \geq 1$.

With the previous relation, we have then:

Theorem 6.14 *[25] Let P be a definite program and A be a non ground atom. Then there exists i such that A unifies only with certain atoms* $B_1, \ldots, B_n \in T^u_P \uparrow i$, *with mgu respectively* $\theta_1, \ldots, \theta_n$, *iff* $P \cup \{\leftarrow A\}$ *has an SLD-tree of finite success with computed answer substitution* $\theta_1, \ldots, \theta_n$.

In fact if A unifies with $B_1, \ldots, B_n$, certain atoms, then for the properties of the *s*-semantics, the corresponding *mgu*'s are its computed answer substitutions, moreover by the relation between unfolding and the operator T^u_P, since A does not unify with uncertain atoms, then it does not unify with any head of clause in P_{i-1}, and thus it has a finite tree in P_i and as a consequence also in P and viceversa.

As in the ground case we can formulate a proposition about the ω step of T^u_P, that uses the results on non ground finitely failed atoms (NGFF), shown in section 5.1. We must define a new set E to obtain the following proposition.

$$E = (\bigcup_{i=0}^{\infty} Certain(T^u_P \uparrow i)) \cup (\bigcap_{i=0}^{\infty} Down(Uncertain(T^u_P \uparrow i))).$$

Proposition 6.15 *[25] Let P a definite program, A a non ground atom,*

- *A unifies with* $A_1, \ldots, A_n$ *in E with mgu's respectively* $\theta_1, \ldots, \theta_n$ *and* $?A \notin E$ *iff the goal* $\leftarrow A$ *has a finitely successful SLD-tree with c.a.s.* $\theta_1, \ldots, \theta_n$.

- *A unifies with* $A_1, \ldots, A_n \in E$ *and* $?A \in E$ *iff the goal* $\leftarrow A$ *has no finitely successful SLD-trees.*

- *A does not unify with certain atoms and* $?A \notin E$ *iff* $\leftarrow A$ *has a finitely failed SLD-tree.*

- *A does not unify with certain atoms and* $?A \in E$ *iff* $\leftarrow A$ *has not finitely failed SLD-tree.*

Intuitively, through the relation between unfolding and T^u_P, we can deduce that when $?A$ appears in the ω step of T^u_P then in every unfolding step there is a clause that unifies with A, so A cannot have a finite tree (successful or failed). We can now apply this to the *setof* semantics.

6.3. A restricted case of Setof

Let us apply the precedent results to a restricted predicate *setof* with a less general behaviour, than the *setof* of Prolog. Let us enrich our language with the predicate *setof* of arity three, where the first argument is a term, the second argument an atom and the third a variable or a list.

The goal $\leftarrow setof(t, A, L)$ has success iff the goal $\leftarrow A$, has an SLD-tree of finite success with computed answer substitutions $\theta_1, \ldots, \theta_n$ and L unifies with the list obtained ordering lexicographically $t\theta_1, \ldots, t\theta_n$. Note that if the goal $\leftarrow A$ has a finitely failed SLD-tree then the goal $\leftarrow setof(t, A, L)$ has success if L unifies with the empty list [].

In order to capture the meaning of a goal with *setof*, we can use a bottom-up approach based on the transformation T^u_P shown in section 6.2.

Let us consider the approximation chain for T^u_P; we have seen that in every step we can deduce the non ground atoms with a finite tree (of failure or success), so we can extend the idea to setof atoms.

Definition 6.16 *[25] Sets contained in i-th step*
Let P be a program,

$$SETOF_i = \{\ setof(t, A, [s_1, \ldots, s_n]) \mid S \ \ atom,\ t\ \ term \quad A_1, \ldots, A_m \ \ are\ all\ the\ certain\ atoms \in T_P^u \uparrow i \quad s.t.\ \ \varrho_i = mgu(A, A_i) \quad with\ \ [s_1, \ldots, s_n] = ord(t\varrho_1, \ldots, t\varrho_m) \quad and\ moreover\ \neg\exists\ ?C \in T_P^u \uparrow i\ \ s.t.\ \ A\ \ unifiable\ with\ C\ \}.$$

$$CERTAIN_i = Certain(T_P^u \uparrow i).$$

Now we can define the semantics of a program with setof goals.

Definition 6.17 *[25] Bottom-Up semantics*
Let P be a definite program then the bottom-up semantics is defined as:

$$\mathcal{F}_{setof}(P) = \bigcup_{i=1}^{\infty} CERTAIN_i \cup SETOF_i.$$

Example 6.18 *Let P be as follows:*

$$P = \{\ p(X) \leftarrow q(X), t(X,Y) \quad t(X,Y) \leftarrow p(Y), f(X,Y) \quad f(X,Y) \leftarrow g(X) \quad g(a) \quad p(b) \quad q(a)\ \}$$

Then:

$$T_P^u \uparrow 1 = \{g(a), p(b), q(a), ?p(\_), ?t(\_,\_), ?f(\_,\_)\}$$

$$T_P^u \uparrow 2 = \{g(a), p(b), q(a), f(a,Y), ?p(a), ?t(\_,\_)\}$$

$$T_P^u \uparrow 3 = \{g(a), p(b), q(a), f(a,Y), t(a,b), ?t(a,a),\}$$

$$T_P^u \uparrow 4 = \{g(a), p(b), q(a), f(a,Y), t(a,b), p(a), ?p(a), ?t(a,a)\}$$

$$T_P^u \uparrow 5 = \{g(a), p(b), q(a), f(a,Y), t(a,b), p(a), t(a,a), ?p(a), ?t(a,a)\}$$

$$T_P^u \uparrow 5 = T_P^u \uparrow \omega$$

$$\mathcal{F}_{setof}(P) = \{g(a), p(b), q(a), f(a,Y), t(a,b), p(a), t(a,a), setof(X, g(X), [a]), setof(X, q(X), [a]), \ldots\}.$$

7. Conclusions

In this paper we have briefly reviewed the main results of our approach to the semantics of logic programs. This semantic framework has already several applications and can be extended in other directions. Let us briefly discuss here some of the most interesting.

- Program analyses based on our semantic framewok have been recently developed [8, 6, 21, 48]. In particular, our framework allows good bottom-up analysis, since the "non-ground" T_P^S operator describes exactly the program computation. Previous attempts of defining bottom-up abstract interpretation failed on non-trivial applications because they were based on immediate consequences operators which did not contain enough information on the program behavior [66, 67]. Moreover, the compositional semantics we have shown allows to define modular abstract interperation, and hence to obtain semantic tools for the analysis of real software. It may happen that in a system under developement, not all the pieces of the program are available for analysis at some point, but we might want to do some analysis in any case. Moreover often real programs are too big to be examinated as a whole. Clearly a semantics compositional wrt program union can help to solve these problems. A first use of the $\mathcal{O}_\Omega(P)$ semantics for modular analysis in in [22].
- Suitable semantics which use (suitable instances of) π-denotations can be used to model non-standard observables. For example correct (in some cases fully abstract) semantics for partial answers and call patterns are given in [31, 43]. [43] defines also an extension of the compositional semantics which takes into account the selection rule and which allows to correctly model those observables which depend on it.
- Modified versions of the compositional semantics $\mathcal{O}_\Omega(P)$ allow to obtain semantics compositional wrt various composition operators. A semantics compositional wrt a generalized inheritance operator is obtained in [11]. Static and dynamic extension/overriding mechanisms can be expressed using the generalized operator. Since the semantic domains are (equivalence classes of) clauses, [11] shows a uniform treatment of static and dynamic inheritance, which in other compositional semantics [18] require different semantic objects (the least Herbrand model and the immediate consequences operator, respectively) to coexist. Moreover, the semantics in [11] is the first compositional semantics of units and inheritance which correctly models computed answer substitutions. This semantics could be used to develop a modular analysis for programs which are structured by using inheritance mechanisms, according to the usual object-oriented style.
- The approach outlined in the paper has been applied, in [69], to typical metaprogramming techniques, thus obtaining a declarative semantics which encompass various proposals present in the literature and give a uniform characterization of these techniques. The following metapredicates were taken into account: $call(X)$, $X = .. [p, t_1, \ldots, t_n]$, $var(X)$, $nonvar(X)$, $t_1 = t_2$, $t_1 == t_2$, $t_1 = / = t_2$.

  This reault has been obtained combining our approach with some ideas taken from Hilog (HIgher order LOGic programming [79]). Hilog is a language with a higher order syntax and a first order semantic whose main characteristics are: that there is no distinction between functional and predicative symbols (these symbols are named *parameter symbols*) and consequently atoms and terms coincide; and that a parameter symbol has not a fixed arity, thus the functor of a term can be any term.
- The semantics of concurrent constraint languages (cc) was considered by several authors [44, 75, 23, 24, 74], following either the operational or the denotational approach. A semantics which is an instance of our general approach has been given in [38, 41]. This is possible because the syntax of *cc*, since contains the + operator and allows to express sequences of

ask and *tell* constraints, is closed under unfolding. π-interpretations in this case are sets of *reactive behaviors*, which are essentially clauses without procedure calls and without parallel compositions. The set of π-interpretations has a complete lattice structure based on a suitable ordering on reactive behaviors. The semantics can then be characterized also in this case as the least fixpoint of an immediate consequences operator. Such a fixpoint characterization is shown to be equivalent to the operational one, given via a transition system in the usual way.

Acknowledgements. This paper is based on the results of joint work with Roberto Barbuti, Annalisa Bossi, Giorgio Delzanno, Alessandra di Pierro, Moreno Falaschi, Roberto Giacobazzi, Paolo Mancarella, Maria Chiara Meo, Alessandro Messora, Catuscia Palamidessi, Chiara Tricomi and Daniele Turi. We would like to express deep gratitude to all of them.

References

[1] K. R. Apt. Introduction to Logic Programming. In J. van Leeuwen, editor, *Handbook of Theoretical Computer Science*, volume B: Formal Models and Semantics. Elsevier. Amsterdam and The MIT Press, Cambridge, 1990.

[2] K. R. Apt, H. Blair, and A. Walker. Towards a Theory of Declarative Knowledge. In J. Minker, editor, *Foundations of Deductive Databases and Logic Programming*, pages 89–148. Morgan Kaufmann, Los Altos, Ca., 1988.

[3] K. R. Apt and D. Pedreschi. Studies in Pure Prolog: Termination. In J. W. Lloyd, editor, *Computational Logic*, pages 150–176. Springer-Verlag, Berlin, 1990.

[4] K. R. Apt and D. Pedreschi. Proving Termination of General Prolog Programs. In T. Ito and A.R. Meyer, editors, *Proc. of Int. Conf. on Theoretical Aspects of Computer Software*, volume 526 of *Lecture Notes in Computer Science*. pages 265–289. Springer-Verlag, Berlin, 1991.

[5] R. Barbuti, M. Codish, R. Giacobazzi, and G. Levi. Modelling Prolog Control. In *Proc. Nineteenth Annual ACM Symp. on Principles of Programming Languages*, pages 95–104. ACM Press, 1992.

[6] R. Barbuti and R. Giacobazzi. A Bottom-up Polymorphic Type Inference in Logic Programming. Technical Report TR 27/89, Dipartimento di Informatica, Università di Pisa, 1989. To appear in *Science of Computer Programming*.

[7] R. Barbuti, R. Giacobazzi, and G. Levi. A Declarative Abstract Semantics for Logic Programs. In A. Bertoni, C. Böhm, and P. Miglioli. editors, *Proc. of the Third Italian Conference on Theoretical Computer Science*, pages 84–96. World Scientific. 1989.

[8] R. Barbuti, R. Giacobazzi, and G. Levi. A Declarative Approach to Abstract Interpretation of Logic Programs. Technical Report TR 20/89. Dipartimento di Informatica. Università di Pisa. 1989.

[9] R. Barbuti, R. Giacobazzi, and G. Levi. A General Framework for Semantics-based Bottom-up Abstract Interpretation of Logic Programs. Technical Report TR 12/91, Dipartimento di Informatica, Università di Pisa, 1991. To appear in *ACM Transactions on Programming Languages and Systems*.

[10] R. Barbuti, P.Mancarella. D. Pedreschi, and F. Turini. A transformational approach to negation in logic programming. *Journal of Logic Programming*. 8:201–228. 1990.

[11] A. Bossi, M. Bugliesi. M. Gabbrielli. G. Levi, and M. C. Meo. Differential logic programming. In *Proc. Twentieth Annual ACM Symp. on Principles of Programming Languages*. ACM Press, 1993.

[12] A. Bossi and N. Cocco. Basic transformation operations for logic programs which preserve computed answer substitutions. *Journal of Logic Programming*. 1991. To appear.

[13] A. Bossi, M. Gabbrielli, G. Levi. and M. C. Meo. Contributions to the Semantics of Open Logic Programs. Technical Report TR 17/91. Dipartimento di Informatica. Università di Pisa, 1991.

[14] A. Bossi, M. Gabbrielli, G. Levi, and M. C. Meo. Contributions to the Semantics of Open Logic Programs. In *Proceedings of the International Conference on Fifth Generation Computer Systems 1992*, pages 570–580, 1992.

[15] A. Bossi and M. Menegus. Una Semantica Composizionale per Programmi Logici Aperti. In P. Asirelli, editor, *Proc. Sixth Italian Conference on Logic Programming*, pages 95–109, 1991.

[16] F. Bry. Logic Programming as Constructivism: A Formalization and its Application to Databases. In *Proc. Eighth ACM Symp. on Principles of Database Systems*, 1989.

[17] F. Bry. Negation in Logic Programming: A Formalization in Constructive Logic. In *Proc. First Workshop on Information Systems and Artificial Intelligence*, Ulm, West Germany, 1990.

[18] M. Bugliesi. A Declarative View of Inheritance in Logic Programming. In *Proc. 3rd Workshop on Extensions of Logic Programming*, pages 141–143, 1992.

[19] D. Chan. Constructive Negation Based on the Completed Database. In R. A. Kowalski and K. A. Bowen, editors, *Proc. Fifth Int'l Conf. on Logic Programming*, pages 111–125. The MIT Press, Cambridge, Mass., 1988.

[20] K. L. Clark. Predicate logic as a computational formalism. Res. Report DOC 79/59, Imperial College, Dept. of Computing. London. 1979.

[21] M. Codish, D. Dams. and E. Yardeni. Bottom-up Abstract Interpretation of Logic Programs. Technical report, Dept. of Computer Science. The Weizmann Institute. Rehovot, 1990. To appear in *Theoretical Computer Science*.

[22] M. Codish, S. K. Debray. and R. Giacobazzi. Compositional Analysis of Modular Logic Programs. In *Proc. Twentieth Annual ACM Symp. on Principles of Programming Languages*. ACM Press, 1993.

[23] F. S. de Boer and C. Palamidessi. Concurrent logic languages: Asynchronism and language comparison. In S. Debray and M. Hermenegildo, editors, *Proc. North American Conf. on Logic Programming'90*, pages 99–114. The MIT Press. Cambridge. Mass., 1990.

[24] F. S. de Boer and C. Palamidessi. On the asynchronous nature of communication in concurrent logic languages: A fully abstract model based on sequences. In J.C.M. Baeten and J.W. Klop, editors, *Proc. of Concur 90*. volume 458 of *Lecture Notes in Computer Science*, pages 175–194. Springer-Verlag, Berlin, 1990.

[25] G. Delzanno and M. Martelli. S-semantica per modellare insiemi di soluzioni. In S. Costantini, editor, *Proc. Seventh Italian Conference on Logic Programming*, 1992.

[26] F. Denis and J.-P. Delahaye. Unfolding. Procedural and Fixpoint Semantics of Logic Programs. In C. Choffrut and M. Jantzen, editors. *STACS 91*. volume 480 of *Lecture Notes in Computer Science*, pages 511–522. Springer-Verlag. Berlin. 1991.

[27] P. Deransart and G. Ferrand. Programmation en logique avec negation: presentation formelle. Technical Report No. 87/3. Lab. d'Informatique. Département de Mathématiques et d'Informatique, Université d'Orléans. 1987.

[28] A. Dovier, E. G. Omodeo. E. Pontelli. and G. Rossi. A Logic Programming Language with Finite Sets. In *GULP '91: Atti del Sesto Convegno sulla Programmazione Logica*, pages 241–255, 1991.

[29] Phan Minh Dung and K. Kanchanasut. A Fixpoint Approach to Declarative Semantics of Logic Programs. In E. Lusk and R. Overbeek. editors. *Proc. North American Conf. on Logic Programming'89*, pages 604–625. The MIT Press. Cambridge. Mass.. 1989.

[30] K. Eshghi and R. A. Kowalski. Abduction compared with Negation by Failure. In G. Levi and M. Martelli. editors. *Proc. Sixth Int'l Conf. on Logic Programming*. pages 234–254. The MIT Press, Cambridge. Mass.. 1989.

[31] M. Falaschi and G. Levi. Finite failures and partial computations in concurrent logic languages. In R. A. Kowalski and K. A. Bowen, editors, *Proc. Int'l Conf. on Fifth Generation Computer Systems*, pages 364–373. Institute for New Generation Computer Technology, Tokyo, 1988. versione estesa in [32].

[32] M. Falaschi and G. Levi. Finite failures and partial computations in concurrent logic languages. *Theoretical Computer Science*, 75:45–66, 1990.

[33] M. Falaschi, G. Levi, M. Martelli, and C. Palamidessi. A new Declarative Semantics for Logic Languages. In R. A. Kowalski and K. A. Bowen, editors, *Proc. Fifth Int'l Conf. on Logic Programming*, pages 993–1005. The MIT Press, Cambridge, Mass., 1988.

[34] M. Falaschi, G. Levi, M. Martelli, and C. Palamidessi. Declarative Modeling of the Operational Behavior of Logic Languages. *Theoretical Computer Science*, 69(3):289–318, 1989.

[35] M. Falaschi, G. Levi, M. Martelli, and C. Palamidessi. A Model-Theoretic Reconstruction of the Operational Semantics of Logic Programs. Technical Report TR 32/89, Dipartimento di Informatica, Università di Pisa, 1989. To appear in *Information and Computation*.

[36] M. Falaschi, G. Levi, and C. Palamidessi. A Synchronization Logic: Axiomatics and Formal Semantics of Generalized Horn Clauses. *Information and Control*, 60(1):36–69, 1984.

[37] G. Ferrand. A reconstruction of Logic Programming with Negation. Technical Report No. 86/5, Lab. d'Informatique, Département de Mathématiques et d'Informatique, Université d'Orléans, 1986.

[38] M. Gabbrielli and G. Levi. Unfolding and Fixpoint Semantics of Concurrent Constraint Programs. In H. Kirchner and W. Wechler, editors, *Proc. Second Int'l Conf. on Algebraic and Logic Programming*, volume 463 of *Lecture Notes in Computer Science*, pages 204–216. Springer-Verlag, Berlin, 1990.

[39] M. Gabbrielli and G. Levi. Modeling Answer Constraints in Constraint Logic Programs. In K. Furukawa, editor, *Proc. Eighth Int'l Conf. on Logic Programming*, pages 238– 252. The MIT Press, Cambridge, Mass., 1991.

[40] M. Gabbrielli and G. Levi. On the Semantics of Logic Programs. In J. Leach Albert, B. Monien, and M. Rodriguez-Artalejo, editors, *Automata, Languages and Programming, 18th International Colloquium*, volume 510 of *Lecture Notes in Computer Science*, pages 1–19. Springer-Verlag, Berlin, 1991.

[41] M. Gabbrielli and G. Levi. Unfolding and Fixpoint Semantics of Concurrent Constraint Programs. Technical Report TR 2/91, Dipartimento di Informatica, Università di Pisa, 1991. To appear in *Theoretical Computer Science*.

[42] M. Gabbrielli, G. Levi, and D. Turi. A Two Steps Semantics for Logic Programs with Negation. In A. Voronkov, editor, *Proceedings of the Int'l Conf. on Logic Programming and Automated Reasoning*, volume 624 of *Lecture Notes in Artificial Intelligence*, pages 297–308. Springer-Verlag, Berlin, 1992.

[43] M. Gabbrielli and M. C. Meo. Fixpoint Semantics for Partial Computed Answer Substitutions and Call Patterns. In H. Kirchner and G. Levi, editors, *Algebraic and Logic Programming, Proceedings of the Third International Conference*, volume 632 of *Lecture Notes in Computer Science*, pages 84–99. Springer-Verlag, Berlin, 1992.

[44] H. Gaifman, M. J. Maher, and E. Y. Shapiro. Reactive Behavior Semantics for Concurrent Constraint Logic Programs. In E. Lusk and R. Overbeek, editors, *Proc. North American Conf. on Logic Programming'89*, pages 553–572. The MIT Press, Cambridge, Mass., 1989.

[45] H. Gaifman and E. Shapiro. Fully abstract compositional semantics for logic programs. In *Proc. Sixteenth Annual ACM Symp. on Principles of Programming Languages*, pages 134–142. ACM, 1989.

[46] H. Gaifman and E. Shapiro. Proof theory and semantics of logic programs. In *Proc. Fourth IEEE Symp. on Logic In Computer Science*, pages 50–62. IEEE Computer Society Press, 1989.

[47] R. Giacobazzi, S. Debray, and G. Levi. A Generalized Semantics for Constraint Logic Programs. In *Proceedings of the International Conference on Fifth Generation Computer Systems 1992*, pages 581–591, 1992.

[48] R. Giacobazzi and L. Ricci. Pipeline Optimizations in AND-Parallelism by Abstract Interpretation. In D. H. D. Warren and P. Szeredi, editors, *Proc. Seventh Int'l Conf. on Logic Programming*, pages 291–305. The MIT Press, Cambridge, Mass., 1990.

[49] J. Jaffar and J.-L. Lassez. Constraint Logic Programming. In *Proc. Fourteenth Annual ACM Symp. on Principles of Programming Languages*, pages 111–119. ACM, 1987.

[50] J. Jaffar and J.-L. Lassez. Constraint Logic Programming. Technical report, Department of Computer Science, Monash University, June 1986.

[51] J. Jaffar, J.-L. Lassez, and M. J. Maher. PROLOG-II an n instance of the logic programming language scheme. In M. Wirsing, editor, *Formal Descriptions of Programming Concepts*. North-Holland, 1986.

[52] B. Jayaraman and D. A. Plaisted. Programming with Equations, Subsets and Relations. In E. Lusk and R. Overbeek, editors, *Proc. North American Conf. on Logic Programming'89*, pages 1051–1068. The MIT Press, Cambridge, Mass., 1989.

[53] K. Kanchanasut and P. Stuckey. Eliminating Negation from Normal Logic Programs. In H. Kirchner and W. Wechler, editors, *Proc. Second Int'l Conf. on Algebraic and Logic Programming*, volume 463 of *Lecture Notes in Computer Science*, pages 217–231. Springer-Verlag, Berlin, 1990.

[54] T. Kawamura and T. Kanamori. Preservation of Stronger Equivalence in Unfold/Fold Logic Programming Transformation. In *Proc. Int'l Conf. on Fifth Generation Computer Systems*, pages 413–422. Institute for New Generation Computer Technology, Tokyo, 1988.

[55] R. Kemp and G. Ringwood. An Algebraic Framework for the Abstract Interpretation of Logic Programs. In S. Debray and M. Hermenegildo, editors, *Proc. North American Conf. on Logic Programming'90*, pages 506–520. The MIT Press, Cambridge, Mass., 1990.

[56] G. Kreisel and J. L. Krivine. *Elements of Mathematical Logic (Model Theory)*. North-Holland, Amsterdam, 1967.

[57] J.-L. Lassez and M. J. Maher. Closures and Fairness in the Semantics of Programming Logic. *Theoretical Computer Science*, 29:167–184, 1984.

[58] G. Levi. Models, Unfolding Rules and Fixpoint Semantics. In R. A. Kowalski and K. A. Bowen, editors, *Proc. Fifth Int'l Conf. on Logic Programming*, pages 1649–1665. The MIT Press, Cambridge, Mass., 1988.

[59] G. Levi and P. Mancarella. The Unfolding Semantics of Logic Programs. Technical Report TR-13/88, Dipartimento di Informatica, Università di Pisa, 1988.

[60] G. Levi, M. Martelli, and C. Palamidessi. Failure and success made symmetric. In S. Debray and M. Hermenegildo, editors, *Proc. North American Conf. on Logic Programming'90*, pages 3–22. The MIT Press, Cambridge, Mass., 1990.

[61] G. Levi and C. Palamidessi. An approach to the declarative semantics of synchronization in logic languages. In J.-L. Lassez, editor, *Proc. Fourth Int'l Conf. on Logic Programming*, pages 877–893. The MIT Press, Cambridge, Mass., 1987.

[62] J. W. Lloyd. *Foundations of Logic Programming*. Springer-Verlag, Berlin, 1987. Second edition.

[63] J. W. Lloyd and J. C. Shepherdson. Partial Evaluation in Logic Programming. *Journal of Logic Programming*, 11:217–242, 1991.

[64] M. J. Maher. Equivalences of Logic Programs. In J. Minker, editor, *Foundations of Deductive Databases and Logic Programming*, pages 627–658. Morgan Kaufmann, Los Altos, Ca., 1988.

[65] P. Mancarella and D. Pedreschi. An Algebra of Logic Programs. In R. A. Kowalski and K. A. Bowen, editors, *Proc. Fifth Int'l Conf. on Logic Programming*, pages 1006–1023. The MIT Press, Cambridge, Mass., 1988.

[66] K. Marriott and H. Søndergaard. Bottom-up Abstract Interpretation of Logic Programs. In R. A. Kowalski and K. A. Bowen, editors, *Proc. Fifth Int'l Conf. on Logic Programming*, pages 733–748. The MIT Press, Cambridge, Mass., 1988.

[67] K. Marriott and H. Søndergaard. Semantics-based Dataflow Analysis of Logic Programs. In G. Ritter, editor, *Information Processing 89*. North-Holland, 1989.

[68] M. Martelli and C. Tricomi. An Effective Operational Semantics for General Logic Program. In S. Costantini, editor, *Proc. Seventh Italian Conference on Logic Programming*, pages 171–185, 1992.

[69] A. Messora and M. Martelli. Semantica Dichiarativa di Predicati Meta-Logici in Programmazione Logica. In S. Costantini, editor, *Proc. Seventh Italian Conference on Logic Programming*, pages 155–170, 1992.

[70] J. Minker and A. Rajasekar. A Fixpoint Semantics for Disjunctive Logic Programs. *Journal of Logic Programming*, 9:45–74, 1990.

[71] R. A. O'Keefe. Towards an Algebra for Constructing Logic Programs. In *Proc. IEEE Symp. on Logic Programming*, pages 152–160, 1985.

[72] A. Di Pierro, M. Martelli, and C. Palamidessi. Negation as Instantiation: a new rule for the treatment of negation in Logic Programming. In K. Furukawa, editor, *Proc. Eighth Int'l Conf. on Logic Programming*. The MIT Press, Cambridge, Mass., 1991.

[73] H. Rasiowa and R. Sikorski. *The Mathematics of Metamathematics*. North-Holland, Amsterdam, 1963.

[74] V. A. Saraswat, M. Rinard, and P. Panangaden. Semantic foundation of concurrent constraint programming. In *Proc. Eighteenth Annual ACM Symp. on Principles of Programming Languages*. ACM, 1991.

[75] V.A. Saraswat and M. Rinard. Concurrent constraint programming. In *Proc. of the Seventeenth ACM Symposium on Principles of Programming Languages*, pages 232–245. ACM, New York, 1990.

[76] H. Tamaki and T. Sato. Unfold/Fold Transformations of Logic Programs. In Sten-Åke Tärnlund, editor, *Proc. Second Int'l Conf. on Logic Programming*, pages 127–139, 1984.

[77] D. Turi. Extending S-Models to Logic Programs with Negation. In K. Furukawa, editor, *Proc. Eighth Int'l Conf. on Logic Programming*, pages 397–411. The MIT Press, Cambridge, Mass., 1991.

[78] M. H. van Emden and R. A. Kowalski. The semantics of predicate logic as a programming language. *Journal of the ACM*, 23(4):733–742, 1976.

[79] D. Warren and M. Kifer. Hilog : A Foundation for Higher-Order Logic Programming. In E. Lusk and R. Overbeek, editors, *Proc. North American Conf. on Logic Programming'89*, page 1090=1114. The MIT Press, Cambridge, Mass., 1989.

[80] S. Yamasaki, M. Yoshida, and S. Doshita. A fixpoint semantics of Horn Sentences based on Substitution Sets. *Theoretical Computer Science*, 51:309–324, 1987.

Temporal Preconditions of Recursive Procedures

Wim H. Hesselink   Ronald Reinds

Rijksuniversiteit Groningen, Department of Computing Science
P.O. Box 800, 9700 AV Groningen, The Netherlands
Email: wim@cs.rug.nl

ABSTRACT. The meaning of an imperative program is defined to be the precondition of the executions as a function of proposed behaviour. In the case of Dijkstra's weakest precondition, the proposed behaviour is termination in a state with a given postcondition. For the temporal predicate transformers of Lukkien, the proposed behaviour is specified in terms of predicates on the intermediate states. For example, for a command c and predicates p, q and r, the predicate $wto.p.q.c.r$ is the precondition such that, for every execution sequence of c, a state in which p holds is eventually followed by a state in which q holds or by termination in a state in which r holds.

We present these precondition functions for a language with operators for sequential composition, unbounded demonic choice and recursive procedures. Recursion is interpreted by means of extreme fixpoints. The treatment of "eventually" is a straightforward generalization of the ordinary *wp*-calculus. For the treatment of "leads-to", the new concept of accumulator turns out to be useful. The proofs of Lukkien's healthiness laws lead to insights in fixpoint induction. Some of the laws require the recursion to be guarded. It is shown that unfolding of the declaration preserves the semantics.

Keywords: weakest precondition, recursive procedure, leads-to, eventually, healthiness law, guarded recursion, unfolding.

CONTENTS

0. Introduction

The most effective methods for the verification or design of correct sequential programs are extensions of the Floyd-Hoare method of inductive assertions, possibly reworked to some kind of refinement calculus. The semantic basis of these methods is the state of the system or rather the set of predicates on the state. For terminating programs, attention is drawn first to the postcondition, which indeed seems to capture the task the program has to perform, but it has been known for at least two decades that the real issue is the relation between precondition and postcondition. For many interesting sequential programs, however, termination cannot be checked syntactically. Therefore, even when we are only interested in terminating programs, the semantics cannot be expressed in the postcondition only, but needs at least a precondition that guarantees termination. This is one of the reasons for the development of the weakest precondition semantics. An asset of equal importance is that the weakest precondition semantics allows and encourages a calculational style of reasoning: the precondition of an assignment can be calculated directly from the postcondition.

Many useful programs have a specification in terms of the states that may be reached during the execution, independent of the question of termination. For such programs temporal logic has been created, but it seems that temporal logic has too much expressive power to be helpful for a calculational method of design. It is therefore that we are interested in a version of weakest precondition semantics that covers some important temporal aspects, without aiming at the full power of temporal logic.

The ideas we want to discuss go back to Morris [Mo2] and Lukkien [Lu], [LS]. Morris only allows procedures with tail-recursion and Lukkien restricts to the repetition. Since a semantic formalism should be able to deal with all of the language, we prefer to develop the formalism directly for (mutually) recursive procedures and unbounded choice. This preference is based on the belief that the stress to cope with these powerful constructs can force us to make the formalism as elegant as it can possibly be. It is a long range activity, for we are aiming at elegant algebraic laws and not yet at methods for verification and design.

In [H1], Chapter 14, an extension of Morris' approach is treated in which the intermediate states considered are those where a procedure is called. Here the intermediate states are those where simple commands are executed. This is closer to Lukkien's approach.

Some notations are introduced in Section 1. In Section 2, we introduce six temporal semantic functions, give some examples and discuss their behaviour with respect to sequential composition and demonic choice. In Section 3, we describe the syntax to be used and we develop a fixpoint formalism. This formalism is used first to define *wp* and *wlp* for recursive procedures. In Section 4, the same formalism is used to construct the functions for "eventually": *wev* and *wlev*. In Section 5, we prove the classical healthiness laws for *wev* and *wlev*: the universal conjunctivity of $wlev.p.c$ for predicates p and commands c, and the termination law

$$wev.p.c.r \;=\; wev.p.c.true \wedge wlev.p.c.r \;.$$

Section 6 contains the introduction of the functions for "leads-to": *wto* and *wlto*. Here we also prove some monotonicity properties, conjunctivity and a termination law for leads–to.

In Section 7, we treat the temporal healthiness laws, that can be characterized as "ever leads–to ever" and the transitivity law for "leads-to". The laws of [LS] are strengthened slightly. In Section 8, we treat two laws that are only valid if the recursion is guarded. In Section 9 we prove that unfolding of the declaration does not change the temporal semantics. Some conclusions are drawn in Section 10.

1. Notations

Function application is denoted by means of the infix operator ".", which binds to the left. In this way, currying is allowed. For example, $wto.p.q.c.r = (((wto.p).q).c).r$. For sets X and Y, the set of functions from X to Y is denoted by $X \to Y$ and also by Y^X. The operator "$\to$" binds to the right, so that

$$X \to Y \to Z \quad = \quad X \to (Y \to Z) \ .$$

If U is a subset of X and $f \in X \to Y$, then $f|U$ is the restriction to U, which is an element of $U \to Y$.

2. Six semantic functions

The relevant semantic functions are Dijkstra's functions *wp* and *wlp* and four functions introduced by Lukkien. These functions have the following signatures

$$wp, wlp \in \quad Cmd \to \mathbb{P} \to \mathbb{P} \ ,$$
$$wev, wlev \in \mathbb{P} \to Cmd \to \mathbb{P} \to \mathbb{P} \ ,$$
$$wto, wlto \in \mathbb{P} \to \mathbb{P} \to Cmd \to \mathbb{P} \to \mathbb{P} \ ,$$

where $\mathbb{P}$ is the set of predicates on the state space and *Cmd* is the set of commands (the operator $\to$ binds to the right). The intended interpretation is as follows. For a command c and predicates p, q and r, we interpret

(0) $wp.c.r$: the precondition of termination in r
$wlp.c.r$: the precondition of conditional termination in r ,
$wev.p.c.r$: the precondition of ever p or termination in r ,
$wlev.p.c.r$: the precondition of ever p or conditional termination in r ,
$wto.p.q.c.r$: the precondition such that, if ever p, then subsequently ever q or termination in r ,
$wlto.p.q.c.r$: the precondition such that, if ever p, then subsequently ever q or conditional termination in r .

Here, termination in r means that every execution of command c terminates in a state where predicate r holds; conditional termination in r means that every terminating execution of c terminates in a state where r holds. Ever p means that, for every execution of c, predicate p holds in some of the intermediate states, including the initial state, but excluding the final state (Lukkien includes the final state, but in this way the system is somewhat cleaner). For us, the term "subsequently" excludes simultaneously.

Actually, Lukkien writes $wev.c.p.r$ and $wto.c.p.q.r$ instead of our $wev.p.c.r$ and $wto.p.q.c.r$. We have moved the arguments p and q to the left because of the independent interest of the functions $wev.p$ and $wto.p.q$.

Example. Let i be an integer program variable. Consider the repetition

$$L \;=\; \textbf{while } \mathrm{i} \neq 7 \textbf{ do } \mathrm{i} := \mathrm{i}+1 \textbf{ od} \,.$$

Command L terminates if and only if $\mathrm{i} \leq 7$ initially. If L terminates, then $\mathrm{i} = 7$. This implies

$$\begin{aligned} wp.L.(\mathrm{i}=7) &= (\mathrm{i} \leq 7)\,, \\ wlp.L.(\mathrm{i}=7) &= true\,, \\ wp.L.(\mathrm{i} \neq 7) &= false\,, \\ wlp.L.(\mathrm{i} \neq 7) &= (\mathrm{i} > 7)\,. \end{aligned}$$

For the temporal functions, operational arguments can be used to show

$$\begin{aligned} wev.(\mathrm{i}=4).L.false &= (\mathrm{i} \leq 4)\,, \\ wlev.(\mathrm{i}=4).L.false &= (\mathrm{i} \leq 4 \;\vee\; \mathrm{i} > 7)\,, \\ wto.(\mathrm{i}=9).(\mathrm{i}=1).L.false &= (\mathrm{i} \leq 7 \;\vee\; \mathrm{i} > 9)\,, \\ wlto.(\mathrm{i}=9).(\mathrm{i}=1).L.false &= true\,. \end{aligned}$$

The next cases are more delicate, since they use that the final state does not count as an intermediate state. Let $c = (\mathrm{i} := \mathrm{i}+1)$. Then

$$\begin{aligned} wev.(\mathrm{i}=3).(c;c).false &= (\mathrm{i}=3 \;\vee\; \mathrm{i}=2)\,, \\ wto.(\mathrm{i}=2).(\mathrm{i}=3).(c;c).false &= (\mathrm{i} \neq 1)\,. \end{aligned}$$

A final test of a loop is regarded as a simple command. Therefore, the state in which a final test is performed counts as an intermediate state. For the repetition L, this implies

$$\begin{aligned} wev.(\mathrm{i}=7).L.false &= (\mathrm{i} \leq 7)\,, \\ wto.true.(\mathrm{i}=7).L.false &= false\,. \end{aligned}$$

(End of example)

At first sight, one may wonder why Lukkien's functions need the argument r. Compositionality is the reason for this. In fact, consider a sequential composition $(c;d)$. It is easy to see that the precondition such that ever p holds during execution of $(c;d)$, is that p holds ever during c or that c terminates in a state such that p holds ever during d. Therefore, if we only want to express ever p for $(c;d)$, we need the function *wev*. Conversely, function *wev* can be used to express the precondition for ever p: just take $r = false$. We come back to this at the end of this section.

The six functions are supposed to satisfy the following rules for the sequential composition:

(1)
$$\begin{aligned} & wp.(c;d).r = wp.c.(wp.d.r)\,, \\ & wlp.(c;d).r = wlp.c.(wlp.d.r)\,, \\ & wev.p.(c;d).r = wev.p.c.(wev.p.d.r)\,, \\ & wlev.p.(c;d).r = wlev.p.c.(wlev.p.d.r)\,, \\ & wto.p.q.(c;d).r = wto.p.q.c.(wev.q.d.r) \wedge wlp.c.(wto.p.q.d.r)\,, \\ & wlto.p.q.(c;d).r = wlto.p.q.c.(wlev.q.d.r) \wedge wlp.c.(wlto.p.q.d.r)\,. \end{aligned}$$

The rules for *wp* and *wlp* go back to Dijkstra [Di]. The other four rules are due to Lukkien [Lu]. The plausibility of the rules for *wev* and *wlev* is seen in the same way as above. The reader may try and convince himself of the other rules. Lukkien proves the rules in an operational semantics based on sequences of states.

Let a function $w \in Cmd \rightarrow \mathbb{P} \rightarrow \mathbb{P}$ be called *multiplicative* if and only if $w.(c;d).r = w.c.(w.d.r)$ for all commands c and d and all predicates r, or equivalently, if

(2) $w.(c;d) = w.c \circ w.d$ for all $c, d \in Cmd$.
The leading four formulae of (1) express that the functions *wp*, *wlp*, *wev.p* and *wlev.p* are multiplicative.

Our second program operator is the operator to form the *demonic choice* $([\!]\, i \in I :: c.i)$ of a family of commands $c.i$ with $i \in I$. So, unlike the classical treatments of nondeterminacy, [Bak] Chapter 7 and [Di], we allow unbounded demonic choice. The semantic treatment is similar to the one used in [H1] and goes back to [DS]. The syntax is more liberal than in [H1]. The demonic choice of two commands c and d is denoted by $c\, [\!]\, d$. We give the infix operator "$[\!]$" a lower priority than ";".

A function $w \in Cmd \to \mathbb{P} \to \mathbb{P}$ is said to *respect demonic choice* if and only if
(3) $w.([\!]\, i \in I :: c.i).r = (\forall\, i \in I :: w.(c.i).r)$
for every family of commands $(i \in I :: c.i)$ and every predicate r. We shall construct the functions *wp*, *wlp*, *wev.p*, *wlev.p*, *wto.p.q* and *wlto.p.q* in such a way that they satisfy (1) and respect demonic choice.

Remark. Coming back to the necessity of the argument r in Lukkien's functions, one may propose a function $wv \in Cmd \to \mathbb{P} \to \mathbb{P}$ with the interpretation
$wv.c.p$: the precondition that ever p ,
and then expect the composition rule
$$wv.(c;d) \;=\; wv.c.p \vee wp.c.(wv.d.p)\ .$$
This, however, does not work. For example, if i is a program variable and $p = (\mathrm{i} = 5)$ and
$$c \;=\; (\mathrm{i} := \mathrm{i}+1\ ;\ \mathrm{i} := \mathrm{i}+1\ [\!]\ skip)\ ,$$
$$d \;=\; (\mathrm{i} := \mathrm{i}+1\ ;\ skip)\ ,$$
then the interpretation gives that $wv.(c;d).p$ is implied by $\mathrm{i} = 4$, but $wv.c.p = (\mathrm{i} = 5)$ and $wp.c.(wv.d.p) = \mathit{false}$.

3. Syntax and semantics (*wp* and *wlp*)

We first discuss the syntax to be used. Let A be a set of symbols, to be called *elementary commands*. Starting from A, we define the class *Cmd* of command expressions inductively by the clauses

- $A \subseteq Cmd$,
- if $c, d \in Cmd$ then $(c;d) \in Cmd$,
- if $(i \in I :: c.i)$ is a family in *Cmd* then $([\!]\, i :: c.i) \in Cmd$.

We assume that the set of commands A is the disjoint union of two sets S and H, which may be infinite. The elements of S are called simple commands. Their semantics are supposed to be given. The elements of H are called procedure names. Every procedure $h \in H$ is supposed to be equipped with a body $\mathbf{body}.h \in Cmd$.

We assume that *wp* and *wlp* are given for the simple commands $s \in S$ and that the set S contains the usual assignments and also so-called guards. For a predicate $b \in \mathbb{P}$, the *guard* $?b \in S$ is given by
(4) $wp.(?b).r = (\neg b \vee r)$,
$wlp.(?b).r = (\neg b \vee r)$.
It is wellknown that the conditional choice can be expressed by

$$\textbf{if } b \textbf{ then } c \textbf{ else } d \textbf{ fi} \quad = \quad (?b \,;\, c \,[\!]\, ?\neg b \,;\, d) .$$

In relational semantics, the guard $?b$ corresponds to the relation $[\![?b]\!]$ given by

$$(x, y) \in [\![?b]\!] \quad \equiv \quad (x = y \wedge b.x) .$$

Recursive procedures are introduced as follows. The function $\mathbf{body} \in H \rightarrow Cmd$ that, for every procedure h, determines its body is called the *declaration.* A function $w \in Cmd \rightarrow \mathbb{P} \rightarrow \mathbb{P}$ is said to *respect the declaration* if and only if

(5) $\quad w.h = w.(\mathbf{body}.h) \quad$ for every $h \in H$.

We propose to construct the functions *wp*, *wlp*, *wev.p*, *wlev.p*, *wto.p.q* and *wlto.p.q* in such a way that they respect the declaration.

Formula (5) suggests to define the meaning of recursive procedures as an extreme fixpoint by means of the Theorem of Knaster–Tarski. Therefore, we introduce an order on the sets of predicates and predicate transformers. The *strength* order on predicates is defined by

$$p \leq q \quad \equiv \quad (\forall\, y :: p.y \;\Rightarrow\; q.y) ,$$

where y ranges over the state space. So, $p \leq q$ means that p implies q for all states. Accordingly, a function $f \in \mathbb{P} \rightarrow \mathbb{P}$ is called *monotone* if and only if $p \leq q$ implies $f.p \leq f.q$. We write MT to denote the set of monotone functions $\mathbb{P} \rightarrow \mathbb{P}$. If X is an ordered set and Y is an arbitrary set, the induced order on $Y \rightarrow X$ is defined by $f \leq g \equiv (\forall\, y \in Y :: f.y \leq g.y)$. The above order on $\mathbb{P}$ is a special case. The order on $\mathbb{P}$ induces an order on $\mathbb{P} \rightarrow \mathbb{P}$ and hence on its subset MT, and the various sets of the form $MT^Y = (Y \rightarrow MT)$.

It is wellknown that $\mathbb{P}$ and MT with these orders are complete lattices. The infimum or greatest lower bound ($\sqcap$) of a family of predicates $p.i$ with $i \in I$ is denoted $(\inf i :: p.i)$; it is the universal quantification $(\forall\, i :: p.i)$. Similarly, the supremum or least upper bound $(\sup i :: p.i)$ is the existential quantification $(\exists\, i :: p.i)$. The infimum of a family of predicate transformers $f.i$ with $i \in I$ is the predicate transformer given (argumentwise) by $(\inf i :: f.i).p = (\inf i :: f.i.p)$ for every predicate p. Similarly for the supremum.

Recall that the well-known theorem of Knaster–Tarski asserts that, for any complete lattice W, a monotone function $D \in W \rightarrow W$ has a least fixpoint and a greatest fixpoint. It is not hard to prove that, if D and D' are monotone functions with least fixpoints x and x', then $D \leq D'$ implies $x \leq x'$ (similarly for greatest fixpoints).

It is our aim to *construct* the six semantic functions in such a way that, among other things,

$$\begin{aligned} wp, wlp &\in \quad Cmd \rightarrow MT , \\ wev, wlev &\in \mathbb{P} \rightarrow Cmd \rightarrow MT , \\ wto, wlto &\in \mathbb{P} \rightarrow \mathbb{P} \rightarrow Cmd \rightarrow MT . \end{aligned}$$

Recall that the first four functions must be multiplicative (2), and that they all must respect demonic choice (3).

The construction method is fairly standard, compare [H1]. Let us define a function $w \in Cmd \rightarrow MT$ to be a *homomorphism* if and only if it is multiplicative and respects demonic choice. By induction over the structure of *Cmd*, one can easily prove that, for every function $v \in A \rightarrow MT$, there is precisely one homomorphism w with restriction $(w|A) = v$. This function is called the (homomorphic) extension $v^{\odot} = w$ of v. Moreover, the function $v \mapsto v^{\odot}$ is monotone: if $v \leq w$ then $v^{\odot} \leq w^{\odot}$. The proof of this fact is an easy case of structural induction and makes use of $v \in MT^A$.

Let a function $u \in MT^S$ be given, which is to be interpreted as providing the meaning of the simple commands. We now want to extend u to a homomorphism that respects the declaration. For any $x \in MT^H$ we write (u, x) to denote the function in $A \to MT$ with restrictions u on S and x on H. Function (u, x) induces a unique homomorphism $(u, x)^{\odot} \in Cmd \to MT$. This homomorphism $(u, x)^{\odot}$ respects the declaration if and only if $(u, x)^{\odot}.h = (u, x)^{\odot}.(\mathbf{body}.h)$ for all $h \in H$, or equivalently if

(6) $\quad x = D.u.x$

where $D.u$ is the function given by $D.u.x = (u, x)^{\odot} \circ \mathbf{body}$. Function $D.u \in MT^H \to MT^H$ is easily seen to be monotone. By the theorem of Knaster–Tarski, the function $D.u$ has a least fixpoint $\mu_H.u$ and a greatest fixpoint $\nu_H.u$. These fixpoints are two solutions of equation (6). It follows that

$$\mu.u = (u, \mu_H.u)^{\odot} \in Cmd \to MT ,$$
$$\nu.u = (u, \nu_H.u)^{\odot} \in Cmd \to MT$$

are two homomorphisms that extend function u and respect the declaration. One can prove that, if $u \leq u'$ in MT^S, then $\mu.u \leq \mu.u'$ and $\nu.u \leq \nu.u'$.

We assume that *wp.s* and *wlp.s* are known elements of MT for all commands $s \in S$. Then *wp* and *wlp* are defined as the homomorphisms

(7) $\quad wp = \mu.(wp|S)$ and $wlp = \nu.(wlp|S)$.

If all simple commands terminate, then $(wp|S) = (wlp|S)$. Nevertheless, *wp* and *wlp* need not be equal.

Example. Let procedure *loop* have the declaration $\mathbf{body}.loop = loop$. In this case, fixpoint equation (6) reduces, for every $u \in MT^S$, to the trivial equation $x.loop = x.loop$. So the least fixpoint is identically false and the greatest fixpoint is identically true, i.e.,

(8) $\quad \mu.u.loop.r = false \quad , \quad \nu.u.loop.r = true$

for all u and r. In particular, $wp.loop.r = false$ and $wlp.loop.r = true$.

4. The construction of *wev* and *wlev*

Since *wev.p* is supposed to be a homomorphism that respects the declaration and since *wev.false* should be equal to *wp*, definition (7) suggests the definition

(9) $\quad wev.p = \mu.(wvs.p)$

where $wvs.p \in MT^S$ is still to be determined. Since *wvs.p* is the restriction $wev.p|S$, we need to know the intermediate states of executions of simple commands. It seems natural to regard a simple command s as atomic. So every execution of s has no other intermediate states than the initial state and the final state. The set of intermediate states of an execution of $(c; d)$ should be the union of the sets of intermediate states of the executions of c and d. Therefore, either the initial or the final state or both must be regarded as intermediate. For reasons of simplicity, we prefer to regard the initial state as intermediate and the final one not. This leads to the definitions

(10) $\quad wvs.p.s.r = p \vee wp.s.r \quad$ for $p, r \in \mathbb{P}$ and $s \in S$.

In order to see the operational meaning, we use the guards introduced in formula (4). In fact, formula (10) is equivalent to

(11) $wvs.p.s = wp.(?\neg p\ ;\ s)$ for all $p \in \mathbb{P}$ and $s \in S$.
Therefore, $wev.p$ is the function wp modified by prefixing all simple commands with the guard $?\neg p$. This justifies interpretation (0) provided that we interpret intermediate state as "prestate of a simple command of the (repeated) unfolding".

The construction of $wlev$ is completely analogous to wev, but now we take the greatest fixpoint. So we define
(12) $wlev.p = \nu.(wlvs.p)$
where $wlvs.p \in S \rightarrow MT$ is given by
(13) $wlvs.p.s = wlp.(?\neg p\ ;\ s)$.

The operational interpretations of the predicate transformers usually suggest certain properties that are often called healthiness laws. Since we do not provide a formal operational semantics, the proof of such a property can only be based on the formal semantics as defined. In some cases this is easy. In other cases it requires unexpected properties of fixpoints.

The first such property is that wp and wlp are special cases of the new semantic functions wev and $wlev$. In fact, by straightforward arguments one can obtain

(14) **Theorem.** (a) $wp = wev.false$ and $wlp = wlev.false$.
(b) If $p \leq q$ then $wev.p \leq wev.q$ and $wlev.p \leq wlev.q$.

Proof. Part (a) follows from the definitions. In part (b) one uses that $\mu.u$ and $\nu.u$ are monotone in u and that $wvs.p$ and $wlvs.p$ are monotone in p. (End of proof)

The results (a) and (b) are the laws E1', E1 and E4', E4 of [LS].

Since the new semantic functions are finer than the old ones, program transformations valid for wp and wlp need not be valid for wev and $wlev$. For example, the command $c = (\mathtt{i} := 0\ ;\ \mathtt{i} := 1)$ cannot be replaced by $d = (\mathtt{i} := 1)$, since

$$wev.(\mathtt{i}=0).c.(\mathtt{i}=2) \quad = \quad true\ ,$$
$$wev.(\mathtt{i}=0).d.(\mathtt{i}=2) \quad = \quad (\mathtt{i}=0)\ .$$

On the other hand, many program transformations are still valid. For example, since $wev.p$ and $wlev.p$ are homomorphisms that respect the declaration, we still have the following equivalences, which of course should hold for implementable commands:

$$(c;d);e \cong c;(d;e)\ ,$$
$$h \cong body.h\ ,$$
$$(\,[\!]\, i \in I :: c.i); s \cong (\,[\!]\, i \in I :: c.i; s)\ .$$

Remarks. (a) According to (8) and (9), we have $wev.p.loop.r = false$ instead of $wev.p.loop.r = p$, as might be expected from (0). In particular, $wev.true.loop.r = false$ instead of $true$. The point is that no simple command is ever reached in the repeated unfoldings of $loop$. If one wants to preclude such surprises, one can require that the declaration only contains guarded recursion. We come back to this in Section 8.

(b) Lukkien (cf. [Lu] or [LS]) only considers the repetition, which is a special case of guarded recursion. He regards both initial and final states as intermediate. This choice corresponds to replacing (10) and (11) by

$$wvs.p.s.r = p \vee wp.s.(p \vee r)\ ,$$
$$wvs.p.s = wp.(?\neg p\ ;\ s\ ;\ ?\neg p)\ .$$

We prefer our version, since in actual correctness proofs the greater complexity of *wvs* for the simple commands is highly discouraging.

(c) It is possible to extend the language with an operator for the angelic choice $(\Diamond i \in I :: c.i)$ of a family of commands $c.i$ with $i \in I$. A function $w \in Cmd \to \mathbb{P} \to \mathbb{P}$ is said to *respect angelic choice* if and only if

$$w.(\Diamond i \in I :: c.i).r = (\exists i \in I :: w.(c.i).r)$$

for every family of commands $(i \in I :: c.i)$ and every predicate r. We then include respect of angelic choice in the definition of homomorphism. The theory developed thus far goes through completely.

Angelic choice has been proposed for specification purposes, cf. [BW], [Mrg], [MG], [Mo1]. It can be equipped with a kind of game-theoretic semantics, cf. [H2]. We here abstain from angelic choice, because we want to use conjunctivity properties incompatible with it.

5. Classical healthiness laws

Since *wev* and *wlev* are constructed by means of μ and ν, the functions *wev.p* and *wlev.p* are homomorphisms and hence have the properties described in (1) and (3). The informal description of *wev* and *wlev* suggests some other properties. These are called healthiness laws. In this section we treat the healthiness laws E2 and E3 of [LS], which are direct generalizations of Dijkstra's healthiness laws for *wp* and *wlp*, cf. [Di] or [DS].

We first postulate these laws for the weakest (liberal) preconditions of the simple commands only. We then use the general theory to extend the laws to *wev* and *wlev* for all commands.

Many of the proofs are based on the following version of the theorem of Knaster-Tarski (cf. [H1] Section 4.2):

(15) **Principle of fixpoint induction.** Let W be a complete lattice and let $D \in W \to W$ be a monotone function. Let $X \subseteq W$ be D–invariant, i.e., such that $D.x \in X$ for all $x \in X$.
(a) If X is sup–closed (that is, $(\sup U) \in X$ for every $U \subseteq X$), then the least fixpoint of D is an element of X.
(b) If X is inf–closed (that is, $(\inf U) \in X$ for every $U \subseteq X$), then the greatest fixpoint of D is an element of X.

A wellknown rule states that total correctness is equivalent to the conjunction of termination and partial correctness. This is formalized in the postulate that, for all $s \in S$ and $r \in \mathbb{P}$,

(16) $\quad wp.s.r = wp.s.true \wedge wlp.s.r$.

This rule is called the termination law.

A function $f \in \mathbb{P} \to \mathbb{P}$ is called *universally conjunctive* if and only if

$$f.(\forall i :: r.i) = (\forall i :: f.(r.i))$$

for every family of predicates $r.i$. We write MU to denote the set of universally conjunctive functions $f \in \mathbb{P} \to \mathbb{P}$. It is wellknown and easy to prove that $MU \subseteq MT$.

The second postulate is

(17) $\quad wlp.s \in MU \quad$ for every $s \in S$.

We first extend the universal conjunctivity of *wlp* to all commands. More generally, we prove Lukkien's law E2 (cf. [LS]) that *wlev.p.c* is universally conjunctive for all commands *c* and all predicates. For the clarity of the proof, it is useful to start with a more general result.

(18) **Theorem.** Let $u \in S \rightarrow MU$. Then $(\nu.u).c \in MU$ for every $c \in Cmd$.

Proof. The set MU^H may be regarded as a subset of MT^H. Let $x \in MU^H$. We claim that $(u, x)^{\odot}.c \in MU$ for every $c \in Cmd$. This is proved by induction over the structure of command *c*. For $c \in S$, it follows from the assumption on *u*. For $c \in H$, it follows from $x \in MU^H$. If *c* and *d* both satisfy the claim, then $(c; d)$ also satisfies the claim since the composition of universally conjunctive functions is universally conjunctive. Since an arbitrary conjunction of universally conjunctive functions is universally conjunctive, the set of commands that satisfy the claim is closed under demonic choice. It follows that this set equals *Cmd*.

The claim implies that $(u, x)^{\odot} \circ \mathbf{body} \in MU^H$ holds for every function $x \in MU^H$. In other words, the set MU^H is *D*-invariant for the function $D.u \in MT^H \rightarrow MT^H$ of (6). Again using that a conjunction of universally conjunctive functions is universally conjunctive, we see that MU^H is inf-closed. Therefore, the principle of fixpoint induction (15) implies that the greatest fixpoint $\nu_H.u$ is element of MU^H. Again using the claim, we get that $\nu.u = (u, \nu_H.u)^{\odot}$ has values in MU. (End of proof)

(19) **Theorem.** (a) Function *wlp.c* is universally conjunctive for every $c \in Cmd$.
(b) Function *wlev.p.c* is universally conjunctive for every $p \in \mathbb{P}$ and $c \in Cmd$.

Proof. (a) This follows from (17) and (18).

(b) By Theorem (18) is suffices to show that $wlvs.p \in S \rightarrow MU$. This is proved by observing that, for every $s \in S$ and every family $(i :: r.i)$

$$\begin{array}{cl} & wlvs.s.(\forall\, i :: r.i) \\ = & \{(13)\} \\ & p \vee wlp.s.(\forall\, i :: r.i) \\ = & \{(17) \text{ and distributivity}\} \\ & (\forall\, i :: p \vee wlp.(r.i)) \\ = & \{(13)\} \\ & (\forall\, i :: wlvs.p.(r.i)) \;. \end{array}$$

(End of proof)

Since *wlp.c* is universally conjunctive, rule (16) is easily seen to be equivalent to

(20) $\quad wlp.s.q \wedge wp.s.r \;=\; wp.s.(q \wedge r) \quad$ for all $q, r \in \mathbb{P}$.

So, we know that (20) holds for all $s \in S$ and we shall prove the validity of (20) for all $c \in Cmd$. Again we anticipate wider application. In fact, we shall prove the rule with *wlp* and *wp* replaced by *wlev.p* and *wev.p*, i.e., rule E3 of [LS]. We begin with a general lemma.

(21) **Lemma.** Let v and w be homomorphisms. The class of commands K given by

$$c \in K \quad \equiv \quad (\forall\, q, r \in \mathbb{P} :: v.c.q \wedge w.c.r = w.c.(q \wedge r))$$

is closed under sequential composition and demonic choice.

Proof. For c, $d \in K$ and q, $r \in \mathbb{P}$, we observe

$$\begin{array}{ll} & v.(c;d).q \wedge w.(c;d).r \\ = & \{\text{homomorphisms}\} \\ & v.c.(v.d.q) \quad \wedge \quad w.c.(w.d.r) \\ = & \{c \in K\} \\ & w.c.(v.d.q \wedge w.d.r) \\ = & \{d \in K\} \\ & w.c.(w.d.(q \wedge r)) \\ = & \{\text{homomorphism}\} \\ & w.(c;d).(q \wedge r)\ . \end{array}$$

The case of demonic choice is more easy. (End of proof)

(22) **Theorem.** Let $u \in MT^S$. Let v be a homomorphism that respects the declaration. Assume that $v.s.q \wedge u.s.r = u.s.(q \wedge r)$ for all $s \in S$ and q, $r \in \mathbb{P}$. Then, for all $c \in Cmd$ and q, $r \in \mathbb{P}$,

$$v.c.q \quad \wedge \quad \mu.u.c.r \quad = \quad \mu.u.c.(q \wedge r)\ .$$

Proof. We use fixpoint induction (15). Let X be the subset of MT^H given by

$$x \in X \quad \equiv \quad (\forall\, h \in H, q, r \in \mathbb{P} :: v.h.q \wedge x.h.r = x.h.(q \wedge r))\ .$$

Consider $x \in X$. We claim that, for every $c \in Cmd$,

$$(\forall\, q, r \in \mathbb{P} :: v.c.q \wedge (u,x)^{\odot}.c.r = (u,x)^{\odot}.c.(q \wedge r))\ .$$

By assumption, the claim holds for all $c \in S$. By definition of X, it holds for all $c \in H$. Lemma (21) therefore implies the claim for all $c \in Cmd$.

For $x \in X$ we observe

$$\begin{array}{ll} & (u,x)^{\odot} \circ \mathbf{body} \in X \\ \equiv & \{\text{definition } X\} \\ & (\forall\, h, q, r :: v.h.q \wedge (u,x)^{\odot}.(\mathbf{body}.h).r = (u,x)^{\odot}.(\mathbf{body}.h).(q \wedge r)) \\ \Leftarrow & \{v.h = v.(\mathbf{body}.h)\ ;\ \text{use } c := \mathbf{body}.h\} \\ & (\forall\, c, q, r :: v.c.q \wedge (u,x)^{\odot}.c.r = (u,x)^{\odot}.c.(q \wedge r)) \\ \Leftarrow & \{\text{claim}\} \\ & \text{true}\ . \end{array}$$

This proves that X is invariant under function $D.u$ of (6).

The set X is sup–closed, since for every subset Y of X and every $h \in H$ and all q, $r \in \mathbb{P}$,

$$\begin{array}{ll} & v.h.q \quad \wedge \quad (\sup y \in Y :: y).h.r \\ = & \{\text{definition supremum}\} \\ & v.h.q \quad \wedge \quad (\exists\, y \in Y :: y.h.r) \\ = & \{\text{calculus}\} \\ & (\exists\, y \in Y :: v.h.q \quad \wedge \quad y.h.r) \\ = & \{Y \subseteq X\} \\ & (\exists\, y \in Y :: y.h.(q \wedge r)) \\ = & \{\text{definition supremum}\} \end{array}$$

$(\sup y \in Y :: y).h.(q \wedge r)$.

By the standard argument, we get $\mu_H.u \in X$. From this, the assertion follows by means of the claim with $x = \mu_H.u$. (End of proof)

(23) **Theorem.** For all $c \in Cmd$ and all p, q, $r \in \mathbb{P}$:

$$wlev.p.c.q \ \wedge \ wev.p.c.r \ = \ wev.p.c.(q \wedge r) \ ,$$
$$wlp.c.q \ \wedge \ wp.c.r \ = \ wp.c.(q \wedge r) \ .$$

Proof. We use Theorem (22) with $v = wlev.p$ and $u = wvs.p$. In order to get the first formula, it remains to verify that, for all $s \in S$ and q, $r \in \mathbb{P}$,

$$\begin{array}{ll} & wlev.p.s.q \ \wedge \ wvs.p.s.r \\ = & \{(12), (13), (10)\} \\ & (p \vee wlp.s.q) \ \wedge \ (p \vee wp.s.r) \\ = & \{\text{calculus and } (20)\} \\ & p \vee wp.s.(q \wedge r) \\ = & \{(10)\} \\ & wvs.p.s.(q \wedge r) \ . \end{array}$$

The second formula follows from the first one by taking $p = false$. (End of proof)

Remark. The first formula of (23) with $q := r$ implies $wev \leq wlev$. Usually, the formulae of (23) are stated only for $r := true$. In that case, however, the proof is more difficult, especially the analogue of Lemma (21). Compare [H1] Section 4.6, for example. (End of remark)

For completeness and future reference, we mention law E6 of [LS], the proof of which is a completely standard variation of the proof of (19)(b):

(24) **Theorem.** $p \leq wlev.p.c.r$ for every $c \in Cmd$ and p, $r \in \mathbb{P}$.

6. The construction of *wto* and *wlto*

We now turn to the predicate transformers *wto* and *wlto*, which are introduced by Lukkien to capture the leads–to relation of Unity, cf. [CM]. We make a small modification that leads to shorter formulae and more expressiveness. Since the equations in (1) for *wto* and *wlto* are complicated, we apply abstraction.

Let $w \in Cmd \rightarrow MT$ be a homomorphism. A function $g \in Cmd \rightarrow MT$ is called a *w–accumulator* if and only if it respects demonic choice and satisfies, for all c, $d \in Cmd$ and $r \in \mathbb{P}$,

(25) $\quad g.(c;d).r \ = \ g.c.(w.d.r) \ \wedge \ wlp.c.(g.d.r)$.

Using that *wlp* is conjunctive, one can easily verify that every accumulator respects the associativity of the sequential composition: $g.((c;d);e) = g.(c;(d;e))$ for all c, d, $e \in Cmd$.

By induction over the structure of *Cmd*, we see that, for every function $v \in A \rightarrow MT$, there is precisely one w–accumulator $g \in Cmd \rightarrow MT$ with restriction $(g|A) = v$. This extension is denoted $w^+.v = g$.

We now turn to the interpretation of recursive procedures. Let the meaning of the simple commands be given by a function $u \in S \rightarrow MT$. For any function $x \in MT^H$, we have a combined function $(u, x) \in A \rightarrow MT$ and hence a w–accumulator $w^+.(u, x) \in Cmd \rightarrow MT$. This accumulator respects the declaration if and only if

$$w^+.(u, x).h = w^+.(u, x).(\mathbf{body}.h) \quad \text{for all } h \in H,$$

or equivalently if $x = E.w.u.x$, where function E is given by

(26) $\quad E.w.u.x = w^+.(u, x) \circ \mathbf{body}$.

The function $E.w.u \in MT^H \rightarrow MT^H$ is monotone. As Lukkien has argued, the functions *wto* and *wlto* are greatest fixpoints. Therefore, we here define $\tau_H.w.u$ to be the greatest fixpoint of $E.w.u$ in MT^H and

$$\tau.w.u = w^+.(u, \tau_H.w.u) \in Cmd \rightarrow MT \ .$$

By construction, this function $\tau.w.u$ is the greatest w–accumulator that respects the declaration and restricts to $u \in S \rightarrow MT$.

Comparison of (25) with (1) shows that *wto* should be a *wev*.q–accumulator. Furthermore, *wto* is expected to respect the declaration. It remains to choose the restriction of *wto* to the simple commands. Recall that we decided that the initial state is the only intermediate state of a simple command. We therefore conclude that the initial state has no subsequent intermediate states. This suggests

$$wto.p.q.s.r = \neg p \vee wp.s.r$$

for $s \in S$ and p, q, $r \in \mathbb{P}$. So we have $wto.p.q|S = wvs.(\neg p)$. In this way, we arrive at the following definitions

(27) $\quad wto.p.q \ = \ \tau.(wev.q).(wvs.(\neg p))$,

$\quad\quad\ \ wlto.p.q \ = \ \tau.(wlev.q).(wlvs.(\neg p))$.

So, the word "subsequently" in (0) is interpreted in the strict sense.

Remark. Lukkien regards both initial and final state as intermediate and he uses subsequent in the weak sense that allows simultaneity. If we write wto_L to denote Lukkien's function *wto*, then wto_L can be expressed in our function *wto* by

$$wto_L.c.p.q.r \ = \ wto.(p \wedge \neg q).q.c.(q \vee r) \ \wedge \ wlp.c.(\neg p \vee q \vee r) \ .$$

Our function is more expressive: it cannot be expressed in Lukkien's functions. The main reason for our modification, however, is that in actual correctness proofs Lukkien's *wto* for a simple command s has a prohibitive complexity: it is given by

$$wto_L.s.p.q.r \ = \ (\neg p \vee q \vee wp.s.(q \vee r)) \ \wedge \ wlp.s.(\neg p \vee q \vee r) \ .$$

(End of remark)

The first result is a kind of monotony (compare law T4 of [LS]):

(28) **Theorem.** (a) $wto.p.q \leq wlto.p.q$ for all p and $q \in \mathbb{P}$.
(b) If $p \geq p'$ and $q \leq q'$, then $wto.p.q \ \leq \ wto.p'.q'$ and $wlto.p.q \ \leq \ wlto.p'.q'$.
(c) For all p and $q \in \mathbb{P}$: $wp \leq wto.p.q$ and $wlp \leq wlto.p.q$.

Proof. It is easy to see that $\tau.w.u$ is monotone in both u and w. Now part (a) follows from $wev.q \leq wlev.q$ and $wvs.(\neg p) \leq wlvs.(\neg p)$. Part (b) also follows since $wev.q$ and $wlev.q$ are monotone in q and $wvs.(\neg p)$ and $wlvs.(\neg p)$ are anti–monotone in p.

(c) It remains to verify $wp \leq wto.true.false$ and $wlp \leq wlto.true.false$. Since $wev.false = wp$ and $wvs.(\neg true) = (wp|S)$, the first formula follows from the observation that *wp* is a *wp*–accumulator. The liberal formula is proved in the same way. (End of proof)

The next result is law T2 of [LS], the proof of which is a completely standard variation of the proof of (19).

(29) **Theorem.** Function *wlto.p.q.c* is universally conjunctive for all $c \in Cmd$ and p, $q \in \mathbb{P}$.

A more difficult result is the termination law for leads–to (law T3 of [LS]):

(30) **Theorem.** For all commands $c \in Cmd$ and all predicates p, q, r and m,
$$wlto.p.q.c.r \;\wedge\; wto.p.q.c.m \;=\; wto.p.q.c.(r \wedge m)\ .$$

Law T3 of [LS] gives formula (30) only for $m := true$. We state the stronger version (30) not because of its greater strength but because it is easier to prove.

The assertion strongly resembles Theorem (23). So, its proof may rely on (23) or it may look like the proof of (23). An essential difference, however, is that *wto* is defined as a greatest fixpoint, whereas the function *wev* in (23) is a least fixpoint. We therefore use induction on the righthand term. By accident we found that it is convenient to replace the equality by "$\leq$". In other words, we first treat:

(31) **Theorem.** Let v and w be homomorphisms such that, for all $c \in Cmd$ and r, $m \in \mathbb{P}$,
$$v.c.r \;\wedge\; w.c.m \;\leq\; w.c.(r \wedge m)\ .$$
Let g be a v–accumulator and let k be a w–accumulator. Let g and k respect the declaration. Let $u \in MT^S$ be such that, for all $s \in S$ and r, $m \in \mathbb{P}$,
$$g.s.r \;\wedge\; k.s.m \;\leq\; u.s.(r \wedge m)\ .$$
Then, for all $c \in Cmd$ and r, $m \in \mathbb{P}$,
$$g.c.r \;\wedge\; k.c.m \;\leq\; \tau.w.u.c.(r \wedge m)\ .$$

Proof. Let X be the subset of MT^H given by
$$x \in X \;\equiv\; (\forall\, h \in H, r, m \in \mathbb{P} :: \; g.h.r \;\wedge\; k.h.m \;\leq\; x.h.(r \wedge m))\ .$$
Let $x \in X$. Write $y = w^+.(u, x)$. We claim that, for all $c \in Cmd$ and r, $m \in \mathbb{P}$,
$$g.c.r \;\wedge\; k.c.m \;\leq\; y.c.(r \wedge m)\ .$$
As usual, this is proved by induction over *Cmd*. Since $(y|S) = u$ and $(y|H) = x$, the base case follows from the assumption on u and the definition of X. For the sequential composition the induction step is taken in
$$\begin{array}{ll}
 & g.(c;d).r \;\wedge\; k.(c;d).m \\
= & \{g \text{ and } k \text{ are accumulators}\} \\
 & g.c.(v.d.r) \;\wedge\; wlp.c.(g.d.r) \;\wedge\; k.c.(w.d.m) \;\wedge\; wlp.c.(k.d.m) \\
\leq & \{\text{induction hypothesis and (19)}\} \\
 & y.c.(v.d.r \wedge w.d.m) \;\wedge\; wlp.c.(g.d.r \wedge k.d.m) \\
\leq & \{\text{assumption on } v \text{ and } w\text{; induction hypothesis}\} \\
 & y.c.(w.d.(r \wedge m)) \;\wedge\; wlp.c.(y.d.(r \wedge m)) \\
= & \{y \text{ is a } w\text{–accumulator}\}
\end{array}$$

$y.(c;d).(r \wedge m)$.

The induction step for the demonic choice is easy. Since g and k respect the declaration, it follows that X is invariant under function $E.w.u$ of (26). It is easy to see that X is inf–closed. Therefore, $\tau_H.w.u \in X$. Now the assertion follows by application of the claim to $\tau_H.w.u$. (End of proof)

Proof of Theorem (30). We use Theorem (31) with

$$v = wlev.q \quad , \quad w = wev.q \; ,$$
$$g = wlto.p.q \quad , \quad k = wto.p.q \quad , \quad u = wvs.(\neg p) \; .$$

The first condition of (31) is contained in Theorem (23). The second one follows from

$$wlvs.(\neg p).s.r \;\; \wedge \;\; wvs.(\neg p).s.m \;\; = \;\; wvs.(\neg p).s.(r \wedge m) \; .$$

This has been verified in the proof of (23). Therefore, Theorem (31) yields (30) with "=" replaced by "≤". The other inequality of (30) follows from monotony and (28)(a). (End of proof)

Remark. In view of Theorem (23), one could have expected, instead of (30), the inequality

$$wev.q.c.r \;\; \wedge \;\; wto.p.q.c.m \;\; \leq \;\; wto.p.q.c.(r \wedge m) \; .$$

In general, however, this inequality is not valid. For example, let i be an integer program variable. Let $c =$ (i := 0 ; i := 1) and $q =$ (i = 2) and $p =$ (i = 0) and $r =$ (i = 0) and $m = true$. Then the lefthand predicate is q and the righthand one is *false*.

7. Temporal healthiness laws

In this section we investigate the healthiness laws related to progress during execution. The results of [LS] are strengthened in two ways. We have a minor strengthening that also holds for the functions of [LS] and a major strengthening due to our strict interpretation of the word "subsequently" in (0).

The property "p leads to q" means that if ever p then subsequently ever q. It follows that, if ever p and p leads to q, then ever q. We thus get the laws of [LS]:

T8: $\quad wlev.p.c.r \;\; \wedge \;\; wlto.p.q.c.r \;\; \leq \;\; wlev.q.c.r$,

T8': $\quad wev.p.c.r \;\; \wedge \;\; wto.p.q.c.r \;\; \leq \;\; wev.q.c.r$.

Once proved, these laws would show that *wlto* and *wto* are strong enough to imply properties of "ever". One may therefore regard these laws as justifications of the definitions of *wto* and *wlto* as the greatest (i.e., weakest) solutions of their fixpoint equations.

In these laws the leftmost conjunct can be weakened. In fact, the assumption ever p can be replaced by ever $p \vee q$. This is the minor strengthening of the laws. The major strengthening is the observation that in T8 the second conjunct can be weakened as well. In fact, for *wlto*, the condition p leads to q can be replaced by p leads to $p \vee q$. For, if p then does not lead to q, it leads to nontermination. These arguments suggest the following versions for the rules "ever leads to ever":

Theorem. For all $c \in Cmd$ and all p, q, $r \in \mathbb{P}$:

(32) $\quad wev.(p \vee q).c.r \;\; \wedge \;\; wto.p.q.c.r \;\; \leq \;\; wev.q.c.r$,

(33) $\quad wlev.(p \vee q).c.r \;\; \wedge \;\; wlto.p.(p \vee q).c.r \;\; \leq \;\; wlev.q.c.r$.

A more careful examination of the operational arguments for the major step reveals that $wlto.p.(p \vee q)$ should be equal to $wlto.p.q$. We prove this in (36) as a consequence of (33).

Let us now turn to the formal proofs. When we have to prove a result like (32), the first problem is that there are three fixpoints involved. We therefore notice that *wev* is defined by means of a least fixpoint and *wto* by means of a greatest fixpoint. Fixpoint induction usually allows to prove that a least fixpoint is smaller than something and that a greatest fixpoint is greater than something. Therefore, formula (32) is proved by means of fixpoint point induction in the term $wev.(p \vee q)$. So we first prove the following abstract result.

(34) **Theorem.** Let w be a homomorphism and let g be a w–accumulator. Assume that both w and g respect the declaration. Let $u \in MT^S$ be such that, for all $s \in S$ and m, $r \in \mathbb{P}$,

$$u.s.r \;\wedge\; g.s.r \;\leq\; w.s.r \text{ and}$$
$$wlp.s.m \;\wedge\; u.s.r \;\leq\; u.s.(m \wedge r) \;.$$

Then, for all $c \in Cmd$ and $r \in \mathbb{P}$,

$$\mu.u.c.r \;\wedge\; g.c.r \;\leq\; w.c.r \;.$$

Proof. Let X be the subset of MT^H given by

$$x \in X \;\equiv$$
$$(\forall\, h \in H, m, r \in \mathbb{P} :: wlp.h.m \wedge x.h.r \leq x.h.(m \wedge r))$$
$$\wedge \;\; (\forall\, h \in H, r \in \mathbb{P} :: x.h.r \wedge g.h.r \leq w.h.r) \;.$$

Let $x \in X$. Write $v = (u, x)^{\odot}$. We claim that, for all $c \in Cmd$,

$$(\forall\, m, r \in \mathbb{P} :: wlp.c.m \wedge v.c.r \leq v.c.(m \wedge r))$$
$$\wedge \;\; (\forall\, r \in \mathbb{P} :: v.c.r \wedge g.c.r \leq w.c.r) \;.$$

This is proved by induction on c. The assumptions imply the claim for all $c \in S$. For $c \in H$, the claim follows from $x \in X$. Now the first conjunct of the claim follows from a variation of Lemma (21). With respect to the second conjunct, the induction step for the sequential composition is taken in:

$$
\begin{array}{ll}
 & v.(c;d).r \;\wedge\; g.(c;d).r \\
= & \{v \text{ homomorphism and } (25)\} \\
 & v.c.(v.d.r) \;\wedge\; g.c.(w.d.r) \;\wedge\; wlp.c.(g.d.r) \\
\leq & \{\text{first conjunct of the claim}\} \\
 & v.c.(v.d.r \wedge g.d.r) \;\wedge\; g.c.(w.d.r) \\
\leq & \{\text{induction hypothesis on } d, \text{ monotony of } v\} \\
 & v.c.(w.d.r) \;\wedge\; g.c.(w.d.r) \\
\leq & \{\text{induction hypothesis on } c\} \\
 & w.c.(w.d.r) \\
= & \{w \text{ homomorphism}\} \\
 & w.(c;d).r \;.
\end{array}
$$

Demonic choice is easily treated. This proves the claim.

Since g, w and *wlp* all respect the declaration, it follows that X is invariant under the function $D.u$ of (6). It is easy to verify that X is sup–closed. By (15)(a), this implies that $\mu_H.u \in X$. The assertion follows by applying the claim to $\mu_H.u$. (End of proof)

Proof of formula (32). We apply Theorem (34) with the instantiations

$$u = wvs.(p \vee q) \quad , \quad g = wto.p.q \quad , \quad w = wev.q \,.$$

Indeed, w is a homomorphism and g is a w–accumulator and w and g respect the declaration. It remains to verify that, for all $s \in S$ and $m, r \in \mathbb{P}$,

$$\begin{array}{l} wvs.(p \vee q).s.r \;\wedge\; wto.p.q.s.r \;\leq\; wev.q.s.r \\ \equiv \{(10), (27)\} \\ (p \vee q \vee wp.s.r) \;\wedge\; (\neg p \vee wp.s.r) \;\leq\; q \vee wp.s.r \\ \equiv \{\text{calculus}\} \\ \text{true} \end{array}$$

and also

$$\begin{array}{l} wlp.s.m \;\wedge\; wvs.(p \vee q).s.r \;\leq\; wvs.(p \vee q).s.(m \wedge r) \\ \equiv \{(10)\} \\ wlp.s.m \;\wedge\; (p \vee q \vee wp.s.r) \;\leq\; p \vee q \vee wp.s.(m \wedge r) \\ \Leftarrow \{\text{calculus}\} \\ wlp.s.m \;\wedge\; wp.s.r \;\leq\; wp.s.(m \wedge r) \\ \equiv \{(20)\} \\ \text{true}\,. \end{array}$$

(End of proof of (32))

We turn to the proof of formula (33). Since fixpoint induction usually yields that the greatest fixpoint is greater than something, we take the righthand term as a candidate for the induction. This leads to the following abstract result.

(35) **Theorem.** Let v be a homomorphism and let g be a v–accumulator. Assume that v and g respect the declaration and that, for all $c \in Cmd$ and $m, r \in \mathbb{P}$,

$$\begin{array}{l} wlp.c.m \;\wedge\; v.c.r \;\leq\; v.c.(m \wedge r)\,, \\ wlp.c.m \;\wedge\; g.c.r \;\leq\; g.c.(m \wedge r)\,. \end{array}$$

Let $u \in MT^S$ be such that, for all $s \in S$ and $r \in \mathbb{P}$,

$$v.s.r \;\wedge\; g.s.r \;\leq\; u.s.r\,.$$

Then, for all $c \in Cmd$ and $r \in \mathbb{P}$,

$$v.c.r \;\wedge\; g.c.r \;\leq\; \nu.u.c.r\,.$$

Proof. We use fixpoint induction with the subset X of MT^H given by

$$x \in X \;\equiv\; (\forall\, h \in H, r \in \mathbb{P} :: v.h.r \wedge g.h.r \leq x.h.r)\,.$$

Let $x \in X$. We claim that, for all $c \in Cmd$,

$$(\forall\, r \in \mathbb{P} :: v.c.r \wedge g.c.r \leq (u, x)^{\odot}.c.r)\,.$$

This is proved by induction on c. For $c \in S$ it follows from the assumption on u. For $c \in H$ it follows from $x \in X$. The induction step for the sequential composition is taken in

$$\begin{array}{l} v.(c;d).r \;\wedge\; g.(c;d).r \\ = \{v \text{ is a homomorphism, } g \text{ is a } v\text{–accumulator}\} \\ v.c.(v.d.r) \;\wedge\; g.c.(v.d.r) \;\wedge\; wlp.c.(g.d.r) \\ \leq \{\text{assumptions on } v \text{ and } g\} \\ v.c.(v.d.r \wedge g.d.r) \;\wedge\; g.c.(v.d.r \wedge g.d.r) \\ \leq \{\text{induction hypothesis on } c\} \\ (u, x)^{\odot}.c.(v.d.r \wedge g.d.r) \end{array}$$

$$\begin{array}{ll} \leq & \{\text{induction hypothesis on } d, \text{ monotony of } (u,x)^{\odot}\} \\ & (u,x)^{\odot}.c.((u,x)^{\odot}.d.r) \\ = & \{\text{homomorphism}\} \\ & (u,x)^{\odot}.(c;d).r\ . \end{array}$$

The case of demonic choice is straightforward. This proves the claim. Since v and g respect the declaration, it follows that X is invariant under the function $D.u$. It is easy to verify that X is inf–closed. This implies that $\nu_H.u \in X$. The assertion follows from application of the claim to $x = \nu_H.u \in X$. (End of proof)

Proof of formula (33). We apply Theorem (35) with the instantiations

$$v = wlev.(p \vee q) \quad , \quad g = wlto.p.(p \vee q) \quad , \quad u = wlvs.q\ .$$

Indeed, v is a homomorphism and g is a v–accumulator and v and g respect the declaration. It remains to verify the three conditions of (35). The first one is proved by observing that, for all $c \in Cmd$,

$$\begin{array}{ll} & wlp.c.m \ \wedge \ wlev.(p \vee q).c.r \\ \leq & \{(14)\} \\ & wlev.(p \vee q).c.m \ \wedge \ wlev.(p \vee q).c.r \\ = & \{(19)\} \\ & wlev.(p \vee q).c.(m \wedge r)\ . \end{array}$$

The second condition of (35) follows in the same way from (28) and (29). The third condition is verified by observing that, for $s \in S$,

$$\begin{array}{ll} & wlev.(p \vee q).s.r \ \wedge \ wlto.p.(p \vee q).s.r \\ = & \{(12),\ (13),\ (27)\} \\ & (p \vee q \vee wlp.s.r) \ \wedge \ (\neg p \vee wlp.s.r) \\ \leq & \{\text{calculus}\} \\ & q \vee wlp.s.r \\ = & \{(13)\} \\ & wlvs.q.s.r\ . \end{array}$$

(End of proof of (33))

Remark. Taking $q = false$ in (33) and using (14) and (28), we get

$$wlev.p.c.r \ \wedge \ wlto.p.p.c.r \ = \ wlp.c.r\ .$$

Combined with (24), this yields $wlto.true.true = wlp$. (End of remark)

As announced above, our strict interpretation of the term "subsequently" in (0) leads to a new healthiness law:

(36) **Theorem.** $wlto.p.(p \vee q) = wlto.p.q$ for all $p, q \in \mathbb{P}$.

Proof. For commands $c, d \in Cmd$ and predicate r, we observe

$$\begin{array}{ll} & wlto.p.(p \vee q).(c;d).r \\ = & \{\text{accumulator}\} \\ & wlto.p.(p \vee q).c.(wlev.(p \vee q).d.r) \ \wedge \ wlp.c.(wlto.p.(p \vee q).d.r) \\ \leq & \{(28)(c) \text{ and } (29)\} \\ & wlto.p.(p \vee q).c.(wlev.(p \vee q).d.r \ \wedge \ wlto.p.(p \vee q).d.r) \\ & \wedge \ wlp.c.(wlto.p.(p \vee q).d.r) \end{array}$$

$\leq$ {(33)}

$wlto.p.(p \vee q).c.(wlev.q.d.r) \quad \wedge \quad wlp.c.(wlto.p.(p \vee q).d.r)$.

The reverse inequality is easily obtained. It follows that

$wlto.p.(p \vee q).(c;d).r$

$= \quad wlto.p.(p \vee q).c.(wlev.q.d.r) \quad \wedge \quad wlp.c.(wlto.p.(p \vee q).d.r)$.

Moreover, the function $wlto.p.(p \vee q)$ respects demonic choice. This proves that it is an accumulator for $wlev.q$. Since it respects the declaration and restricts to $wlvs.(\neg p)$ on the set S, and since $wlto.p.q$ is the greatest accumulator of that kind, it follows that, for all $c \in Cmd$ and $r \in \mathbb{P}$,

$wlto.p.(p \vee q).c.r \quad \leq \quad wlto.p.q.c.r$.

The other inequality follows from (28). (End of proof)

Remark. Using (28), one can easily show that (36) is equivalent to the assertion that $wlto.p.q = wlto.p.(\neg p \wedge q)$ for all p and q.

The analogues of (33) and (36) for wev and wto are not valid. In fact, for h with **body**.$h = (skip; h)$ and $p = true$ and $q = false$, we have

$wev.(p \vee q).h.r \quad \wedge \quad wto.p.(p \vee q).h.r \quad = \quad true$,

$wev.q.h.r \quad = \quad wto.p.q.h.r \quad = \quad false$.

(End of remark)

If p leads to q and q leads to r then p leads to r. This is expressed by the laws T9' and T9 of [LS]. Just as with T8' and T8, these laws can be strengthened slightly:

(37) **Theorem.** For all commands $c \in Cmd$ and all predicates p, q, r and m,

$wto.p.(q \vee r).c.m \quad \wedge \quad wto.q.r.c.m \quad \leq \quad wto.p.r.c.m$,

$wlto.p.(q \vee r).c.m \quad \wedge \quad wlto.q.r.c.m \quad \leq \quad wlto.p.r.c.m$.

Since wto and $wlto$ are defined as greatest fixpoints, we apply fixpoint induction on the righthand terms. Function $g = wto.p.(q \vee r)$ is an accumulator for the homomorphism $v = wev.(q \vee r)$ and function $k = wto.q.r$ is an accumulator for $w = wev.r$. So we may expect something like the following abstract version where the remaining conditions are generated by the proof.

(38) **Theorem.** Let v and w be homomorphisms. Let g be a v–accumulator and let k be a w–accumulator. Let g and k respect the declaration. Assume that, for all $c \in Cmd$ and r, $m \in \mathbb{P}$,

$wlp.c.r \quad \wedge \quad g.c.m \quad \leq \quad g.c.(r \wedge m)$,

$v.c.m \quad \wedge \quad k.c.m \quad \leq \quad w.c.m$.

Let $u \in MT^S$ be a function such that, for all $s \in S$ and $m \in \mathbb{P}$,

$g.s.m \quad \wedge \quad k.s.m \quad \leq \quad u.s.m$.

Then $g.c.m \quad \wedge \quad k.c.m \quad \leq \quad \tau.w.u.c.m$ for all $c \in Cmd$ and $m \in \mathbb{P}$.

Proof. As usual, we form the subset X of MT^H given by

$x \in X \quad \equiv \quad (\forall\, h \in H, m \in \mathbb{P} :: g.h.m \wedge k.h.m \leq x.h.m)$.

Let $x \in X$. We claim that, for all $c \in Cmd$,

$(\forall\, m \in \mathbb{P} :: g.c.m \wedge k.c.m \leq w^+.(u, x).c.m)$.

For $c \in S$ and $c \in H$ the claim follows from the assumptions. The induction step for the sequential composition is taken in

$$\begin{array}{ll} & g.(c;d).m \ \wedge \ k.(c;d).m \\ = & \{\text{accumulators}\} \\ & g.c.(v.d.m) \ \wedge \ wlp.c.(g.d.m) \ \wedge \ k.c.(w.d.m) \ \wedge \ wlp.c.(k.d.m) \\ \leq & \{\text{assumption on } g \text{ and } (19)\} \\ & g.c.(v.d.m \wedge k.d.m) \ \wedge \ k.c.(w.d.m) \ \wedge \ wlp.c.(g.d.m \wedge k.d.m) \\ \leq & \{\text{assumption on } v,\ k \text{ and } w\} \\ & g.c.(w.d.m) \ \wedge \ k.c.(w.d.m) \ \wedge \ wlp.c.(g.d.m \wedge k.d.m) \\ \leq & \{\text{induction hypothesis}\} \\ & w^{+}.(u,x).c.(w.d.m) \ \wedge \ wlp.c.(w^{+}.(u,x).d.m) \\ = & \{\text{accumulator}\} \\ & w^{+}.(u,x).(c;d).m \ . \end{array}$$

For demonic choice it is easy. This proves the claim. Since g and k respect the declaration, the claim implies that X is invariant under function $E.w.u$ of (26). It is clear that X is inf–closed. This proves that $\tau_H.w.u \in X$. Using the claim with $x = \tau_H.w.u \in X$, we get the assertion. (End of proof)

Remark. It may be instructive to compare the theorems (38) and (31). They have the same same flavour, but there are also big differences. (End of remark)

Proof of Theorem (37). The first formula of Theorem (37) follows from (38) by the instantiations

$$v = wev.(q \vee r) \ , \quad w = wev.r \ ,$$
$$g = wto.p.(q \vee r) \ , \quad k = wto.q.r \ , \quad u = wvs.(\neg p) \ .$$

The first condition of (38) follows from Theorem (30) combined with (28). The second one is formula (32). The condition on u is trivial. The liberal version is proved in the same way (use (29)). (End of proof)

8. Guarded commands

We now come back to remark (a) at the end of Section 4. The problem there was that some recursive procedures never lead to execution of a simple command. We do not want to forbid such procedures, but in this section we describe the behaviour of our formalism if such procedures are avoided. We therefore introduce a class of commands that are in a certain sense guarded by simple commands.

Let *Grd* be the class of commands defined inductively by the clauses

- if $s \in S$ then $s \in Grd$,
- if $c \in Grd$ and $d \in Cmd$ then $(c;d) \in Grd$,
- if $h \in H$ has $\mathbf{body}.h \in Grd$ then $h \in Grd$,
- if $c.i \in Grd$ for all i then $([\!]\, i :: c.i) \in Grd$.

It is clear that procedure *loop* declared by **body**.*loop* = *loop* does not belong to *Grd*. There are two cases where elements of *Grd* behave "better" than arbitrary commands. These cases correspond to the laws E6' and T1' of [LS]:

(39) **Theorem.** (a) If $c \in Grd$ then $p \leq wev.p.c.r$ for all $p, r \in \mathbb{P}$.
(b) If $c \in Grd$ then $wto.true.false.c = wp.c$.

Proof. (a) This is proved by induction over *Grd*. In fact, let T be the set of commands c with $p \leq wev.p.c.r$ for all $p, r \in \mathbb{P}$. For $s \in S$ we have $s \in T$ since $wev.p.s.r = p \vee wp.s.r$. If $c \in T$ and $d \in Cmd$, then $(c; d) \in T$ since

$$\begin{array}{cl} & p \leq wev.p.(c;d).r \\ \equiv & p \leq wev.p.c.(wev.p.d.r) \\ \Leftarrow & c \in T \end{array}$$

For $h \in H$ with $\mathbf{body}.h \in T$, we have $h \in T$ since $wev.p.h = wev.p.(\mathbf{body}.h)$. If $c.i \in T$ for all i then $([\!]\, i :: c.i) \in T$ since $wev.p$ respects demonic choice. This proves $Grd \subseteq T$.

(b) Write $g = wto.true.false$. By definition (27), the restriction of g to S equals $wvs.(\neg true) = wp$ and function g is an accumulator for the homomorphism $wev.false = wp$. Now a straightforward induction (similar to part (a)) on the structure of *Grd* yields $g.c \leq wp.c$ for all $c \in Grd$. The other inequality follows from (28). (End of proof)

Remark. Procedure *loop* with $\mathbf{body}.loop = loop$ satisfies

$$wev.true.loop.r = false \quad \text{and}$$
$$wto.true.false.loop.r = true \qquad \text{for all } r \in \mathbb{P} \text{ .}$$

Therefore, in both parts of (39), the condition $c \in Grd$ cannot be omitted.

9. Unfolding the declaration

Up to this point we assumed a given declaration $\mathbf{body} \in H \rightarrow Cmd$. Different declarations, however, may lead to the same semantics. Since our semantics are finer than the usual semantics of preconditions and postconditions, standard techniques of program transformation have to be reconsidered. In this section we treat a program transformation rule inspired by the behaviour of contextfree grammars. It may be that the rule is considered obvious or wellknown, but, even for ordinary weakest precondition semantics, we do not have a reference for it. The formulation of the rule is due to Albert Thijs.

Since there are different declarations to consider, we use symbols φ and ψ to range over declarations $H \rightarrow Cmd$. Declaration φ will be called an unfolding of declaration ψ if, for every procedure name h, the body $\psi.h$ can be obtained from the body $\varphi.h$ by (repeatedly) replacing some recursive calls h' by their bodies $\varphi.h'$. Since the bodies may contain infinite choices a more careful definition is asked for.

Example. Let i be an integer program variable. For $n \in \mathbb{N}$, let $g.n$ be a simple command. Consider $h \in H$ and $E \in Cmd$ given by

$$E \;=\; (?(\mathrm{i} = 0) \;[\!]\; ([\!]\, n : n > 0 : ?(\mathrm{i} = n) \,;\, g.n \,;\, h)) \text{ .}$$

Let $E_0 = h$ and let E_{m+1} be obtained from E_m by substituting E for h in E_m. Now we compare the two declarations

$$\begin{array}{lcl} \varphi.h & = & E \text{ ,} \\ \psi.h & = & (?(\mathrm{i} = 0) \;[\!]\; ([\!]\, n : n > 0 : ?(\mathrm{i} = n) \,;\, g.n \,;\, E_n)) \text{ .} \end{array}$$

In our opinion, it is not obvious that the declarations φ and ψ provide procedure h with the same semantics. Actually, it is not even clear that φ may be regarded as an unfolding of ψ according to the above description. Yet it is not hard to show that φ is an unfolding of ψ according to the definition given below. Consequently, Theorem (40) below implies that φ and ψ provide h with the same meaning. (End of example)

We use the auxiliary concept of admissible preorders. Recall that a *preorder* is a binary relation that is reflexive and transitive. Let a preorder $\triangleleft$ on *Cmd* be called *admissible* if and only if sequential composition and demonic choice are both monotone with respect to $\triangleleft$, in the sense that
(a) $c \triangleleft c' \wedge d \triangleleft d' \;\Rightarrow\; c;d \triangleleft c';d'$ for all c, c', d, $d' \in Cmd$,
(b) $(\forall\, i :: c.i \triangleleft d.i) \;\Rightarrow\; ([\!]\, i :: c.i) \triangleleft ([\!]\, i :: d.i)$ for every pair of families $(i :: c.i)$ and $(i :: d.i)$ where the index i ranges over the same set.

Let $\varphi \in H \rightarrow Cmd$ be a declaration. The *rewrite preorder* $\triangleleft_\varphi$ on *Cmd* is such that $c \triangleleft_\varphi d$ expresses that command d can be obtained from c by replacing some procedure names h in c by their bodies $\varphi.h$. Relation $\triangleleft_\varphi$ is formally defined as the least admissible preorder that satisfies $h \triangleleft_\varphi \varphi.h$ for all $h \in H$. Declaration φ is called an *unfolding* of a declaration $\psi \in H \rightarrow Cmd$ if and only if $\varphi.h \triangleleft_\varphi \psi.h$ for all $h \in H$.

(40) **Rule of unfolding.** Let φ be an unfolding of ψ. Then ψ and φ induce the same semantics.

In order to prove this rule we need to consider the dependence of *wp*, *wlp*, *wev*, *wlev*, *wto*, *wlto* upon the declaration. Up to now this dependence was kept implicit. Now that the declaration is variable, we use wp_φ (etc.) to denote *wp* (etc.) as induced by declaration φ. The first four cases of rule (40) are contained in:

(41) **Theorem.** Let φ be an unfolding of ψ. Then $wp_\varphi = wp_\psi$ and $wlp_\varphi = wlp_\psi$ and $wev_\varphi = wev_\psi$ and $wlev_\varphi = wlev_\psi$.

Proof. Since *wp* and *wlp* are instances of *wev* and *wlev*, we need only consider the latter two cases. We use the definitions of the Sections 2 and 3. Restricted to simple commands the functions wev_φ and wev_ψ are both equal to *wvs*, and $wlev_\varphi$ and $wlev_\psi$ are both equal to *wlvs*. The extension operator $\odot$ is also independent of the declaration. It therefore suffices to prove that the functions have equal restrictions to the set H. Since these restrictions are defined as extreme fixpoints, it suffices to prove the next, more general, result.

(42) **Theorem.** Let $u \in MT^S$ be given. Let φ be an unfolding of declaration ψ. Let F, $F' \in MT^H \rightarrow MT^H$ be given by

$$F.x = (u,x)^\odot \circ \varphi \quad , \quad F'.x = (u,x)^\odot \circ \psi \ .$$

Then F and F' have the same least fixpoint in MT^H and the same greatest fixpoint.

Proof. We first prove that

$$x \leq F.x \;\Rightarrow\; F.x \leq F'.x \quad \text{for every } x \in MT^H .$$

In fact, for given $x \in MT^H$, let relation $\triangleleft$ on *Cmd* given by

$$c \triangleleft d \;\equiv\; (u,x)^\odot.c \leq (u,x)^\odot.d \ .$$

Since $(u,x)^\odot$ is a homomorphism, relation $\triangleleft$ is an admissible preorder. If $x \leq F.x$, then $h \triangleleft \varphi.h$ for all $h \in H$. Therefore, the definition of $\triangleleft_\varphi$ implies that $\triangleleft_\varphi \subseteq \triangleleft$. Since φ is an unfolding of ψ, it follows that $\varphi.h \lhd \psi.h$ for all $h \in H$. By the definition of $\lhd$, this is equivalent to $F.x \leq F'.x$.

By a completely analogous argument, we also obtain that

$$x \geq F.x \quad \Rightarrow \quad F.x \geq F'.x \quad \text{for every } x \in MT^H .$$

Now the result follows from the next lemma. (End of proof)

(43) **Lemma.** Let $(W, \leq)$ be a complete lattice. Let F, $F' \in W \to W$ be monotone functions such that, for all $x \in W$,

$$x \leq F.x \quad \Rightarrow \quad F.x \leq F'.x \ ,$$
$$x \geq F.x \quad \Rightarrow \quad F.x \geq F'.x \ .$$

Then F and F' have the same least fixpoint and the same greatest fixpoint.

Proof. Let y and y' be the least fixpoints of F and F', respectively. Since y is a fixpoint of F, the assumption implies $y = F.y = F'.y$. Therefore, y is a fixpoint of F' and hence $y' \leq y$. We use fixpoint induction to prove that $y \leq y'$. Let X be the subset of W given by

$$x \in X \quad \equiv \quad x \leq F.x \quad \wedge \quad x \leq y' \ .$$

The set X is invariant under F because of

$$\begin{array}{ll} & F.x \leq F.(F.x) \quad \wedge \quad F.x \leq y' \\ \Leftarrow & \{y' \text{ is a fixpoint of } F'\} \\ & F.x \leq F.(F.x) \quad \wedge \quad F.x \leq F'.x \quad \wedge \quad F'.x \leq F'.y' \\ \Leftarrow & \{\text{monotony and assumption}\} \\ & x \leq F.x \quad \wedge \quad x \leq y' \ . \end{array}$$

An easy verification shows that the set X is sup-closed. It follows that the least fixpoint y of F is an element of X. This proves $y \leq y'$ and, hence, $y = y'$. The case of greatest fixpoints is completely analogous. (End of proof)

The second half of rule (40) is contained in:

(44) **Theorem.** Let φ be an unfolding of ψ. Then $wto_\varphi = wto_\psi$ and $wlto_\varphi = wlto_\psi$.

Proof. We need to analyse how the construction of Section 6 depends on the declaration. The first observation is that Theorem (41) yields $wlp_\varphi = wlp_\psi$, so that the concept of w-accumulator is independent of the choice. It follows that, for a given homomorphism w, the function w^+ is independent of the choice. Using the definitions of Section 6 and, again, Theorem (41), we get that it remains to prove

(45) **Theorem.** Let φ be an unfolding of declaration ψ. Let function $u \in MT^S$ be given. Let $w \in Cmd \to MT$ be a homomorphism. Assume that w and wlp respect declaration φ. Let $F, F' \in MT^H \to MT^H$ be given by

$$F.x = w^+.(u,x) \circ \varphi \quad , \quad F'.x = w^+.(u,x) \circ \psi \ .$$

Then F and F' have the same greatest fixpoint.

Proof. It suffices to prove the conditions of Lemma (43). For given $x \in MT^H$, let relation $\lhd$ on Cmd given by

$$\begin{array}{l} c \lhd d \quad \equiv \\ w^+.(u,x).c \leq w^+.(u,x).d \quad \wedge \quad w.c \leq w.d \quad \wedge \quad wlp.c \leq wlp.d \ . \end{array}$$

Using that w and *wlp* are homomorphisms and that $w^+.(u, x)$ is a w–accumulator, one can prove that relation $\lhd$ is an admissible preorder. If $x \leq F.x$, then $h \lhd \varphi.h$ for all $h \in H$ (here we use that w and *wlp* respect declaration φ). Now, the definition of $\lhd_\varphi$ implies that $\lhd_\varphi \subseteq \lhd$. Since φ is an unfolding of ψ, it follows that $\varphi.h \lhd \psi.h$ for all $h \in H$. By the definition of $\lhd$, this implies that $F.x \leq F'.x$. The other condition of (43) is proved in the same way. (End of proof of (45) and (44))

10. Concluding remarks

By writing *w(l)ev.p.c.r*, instead of *w(l)ev.c.p.r* as in [LS], we are able to treat the functions *w(l)ev.p* as immediate generalizations of *w(l)p*. A second simplification with respect to [LS] is the decision to use abstract simple commands. Since the structure of *Cmd* is simpler than in [LS], all cases of structural induction are simpler. Since we exclude the final state from the intermediate states, the simple functions *wvs* and *wlvs* of (11) and (13) can be used as basic constructors. In this way many proofs become simpler. We pay the price that *skip* is no longer the unit for the sequential composition.

The construction and analysis of the functions *w(l)to* is greatly simplified by the introduction of accumulators. The need to establish so many healthiness laws has yielded the following observation: fixpoint induction usually serves to prove that a least fixpoint is less than something or that a greatest fixpoint is greater than something. This observation may guide the choice when there are several candidates for fixpoint induction.

In our view the more general setting yields a better understanding of the proofs of the healthiness laws of [LS] and [Lu]. Because of our stricter interpretation of the notions "intermediate" and "subsequent", we do not get the laws E5, T1, T5 and T6' of [LS]. The laws E6' and T1' are only valid for guarded recursion. We have chosen not to treat the laws T7 and T7'. The extension of these laws to our setting is fairly straightforward.

Finally it is proved that the extended semantics is not influenced by unfolding the declaration of the recursive procedures. This is as it should be, but the proof is less obvious than might be expected.

References

[BW] R.J.R. Back, J. von Wright: Refinement calculus, Part I: Sequential Nondeterministic Programs. In: J.W. de Bakker, W.-P. de Roever, G. Rozenberg (eds.): Stepwise Refinement of Distributed Systems. Lecture Notes in Computer Science 430 (Springer, Berlin, 1990) pp. 42–66.

[Bak] J.W. de Bakker: Mathematical theory of program correctness. Prentice–Hall, 1980.

[CM] K.M. Chandy, J. Misra [1988]: Parallel Program Design, A Foundation (Addison-Wesley, 1988).

[Di] E.W. Dijkstra: A discipline of programming. Prentice–Hall 1976.

[DS] E.W. Dijkstra, C.S. Scholten: Predicate calculus and program semantics. Springer V. 1990.

[Hl] W.H. Hesselink: Programs, Recursion and Unbounded Choice, predicate transformation semantics and transformation rules. Cambridge University Press 1992.

[H2] W.H. Hesselink: Nondeterminacy and recursion via stacks and queues. Computing Science Notes Groningen CS 9109.

[Lu] J.J. Lukkien: Parallel Program Design and Generalized Weakest Preconditions. Thesis, Groningen, 1991.

[LS] J.J. Lukkien, J.L.A. van de Snepscheut: Weakest preconditions for progress. Formal Aspects of Computing **4** (1992) 195–236.

[Mrg] C. Morgan: Programming from Specifications. Prentice Hall, 1990.

[MG] C. Morgan, P.H.B. Gardiner: Data refinement by calculation. Acta Informatica **27** (1990) 481–503.

[Mo1] J.M. Morris: A theoretical basis for stepwise refinement and the programming calculus. Science of Comp. Programming 9 (1987) 287–306.

[Mo2] J.M. Morris: Temporal predicate transformers and fair termination. Acta Informatica **27** (1990) 287–313.

Towards an Epistemic Approach to Reasoning about Concurrent Programs

W. van der Hoek [*]
University of Nijmegen
Toernooiveld 1
6525 ED Nijmegen
The Netherlands

M. van Hulst
University of Nijmegen
Toernooiveld 1
6525 ED Nijmegen
The Netherlands

J.-J.Ch. Meyer [†]
University of Nijmegen
Toernooiveld 1
6525 ED Nijmegen
The Netherlands

October 16, 1992

Abstract

We show how epistemic logic may be used to reason about concurrent programs. Starting out from Halpern & Moses' interpretation of knowledge in the context of distributed systems, where they use the interleaving model, we extend this to a setting where also truly concurrent computations can be modelled, viz. posets of action labels. Moreover, and more importantly, we prepare grounds for the verification of concurrent programs. We focus on a variant of the well-known 1978-version of Hoare's Concurrent Sequential Processes (CSP) to see how the details work out for a concrete and simple language.

keywords: logics of knowledge, semantics of concurrency, verification of distributed programs, Communicating Sequential Processes

---

[*] also at the Free University of Amsterdam

[†] idem

Contents

0 Introduction

In [HM85] Halpern and Moses presented a framework to reason about distributed processes based on the notion of knowledge. They showed that a modal logic of knowledge (epistemic logic) may be employed fruitfully to reason about the behaviour of networks of processors in which communication protocols take care of the flow of messages between the processors. They were able to prove a number of fundamental results regarding the kind of knowledge that is or is not reachable in such networks ([HM90]). Moreover, using epistemic logic it appeared to be possible to prove the correctness of some well-known protocols such as the alternating bit protocol ([HZ87]).

The question we address in this paper is whether epistemic logic is useful as well in the verification and specification of parallel or concurrent programs. To get a feel for the idea of using epistemic notions (i.e., notions pertaining to knowledge) consider a command $P_i?x$, expressing a request for a value from process i to be stored in the variable x. Restricting ourselves to synchronous communication, of course such a command will only be executed successfully when it is used in a process j, if process i - that is executed in parallel with j - is willing to send a value to process j, and execution of process i will be suspended until this happens. Possibly it will never happen, and then the process i will fail to be executed. But suppose that a successful transmission of a value takes place from the process i to the process j. Then it is not known a priori to the process j which value it will receive to store in x (possibly apart from some information regarding the type of the variable x, e.g. integers), since this depends entirely on process i! The process j must consider possible all values that are allowed by the type of x.

In the 'classical' (Hoare logic-based) proof system for CSP ([AFdR80]) this local uncertainty or rather ignorance is represented by an axiom $\{p\}P_i?x\{q\}$, meaning that if p holds before execution of the command $P_i?x$, then q holds after execution (provided that the execution is successful), for arbitrary p and q. In effect this means that it is left completely open what happens after execution of $P_i?x$! The approach of Apt et al. corrects this arbitrariness by enforcing a co-operation test between the local proofs of the correctness of the (sequential) processes involved. So, the idea amounts to give (guess) correctness proofs of the sequential processes, after which these proofs are checked on global consistency by the co-operation test.

In the approach we propose in this paper we shall directly use notions of knowledge to express the uncertainty in cases as above. More in particular, we employ modal operators K_i to express that something is known to process i. We believe that in proceeding in this way we obtain a natural form of compositionality in the verification of concurrent programs, since thus the language is enriched with pointers to the local processes, which may be used to speak only of the facts that are known locally to some process in isolation. This knowledge may later be combined to reason about a composite process, e.g. the request for receiving a message and the matching request for sending one in parallel. In fact, in 'standard' proof systems for the correctness of nondeterministic programs often a notion of knowledge is left implicit. In our approach this is made explicit by the employment of epistemic operators.

To get an idea of our approach, we focus again on the command $P_i?x$ occurring in the process j. Although it is not known to j what is the value of x after its execution, which we may now express by a formula $\forall\alpha\neg K_j(x = \alpha)$, we *do* know that if the execution has been successfully completed it is the case that x has some value in the domain of the variable x and that this value has been sent from process i to the process j. This may be expressed by the formula $K_j(\exists\alpha[x = \alpha \wedge send(\alpha, i, j)])$. In fact, as we shall see we even know some more, viz. concerning the locations of the commands of sending and receiving, respectively, in the processes i and j. We shall postpone the discussion of this to the formal treatment in the sequel.

This paper should be viewed as a first step towards correctness systems based on epistemic logic. Our choice to consider CSP is a first test how things work out in a concrete and simple setting. We envisage to investigate extensions of our framework in at least three directions:

1. examine how to obtain complete systems, preferably using what is known for epistemic logic.
2. consider more complex programming languages, such as e.g. (subsets of) POOL ([Ame89]) in order to see the practical use of epistemic notions in the context of more advanced programming languages, particularly object-oriented ones. These objects act as natural agents to which epistemic operators may refer.
3. consider extensions of the logic with more expressive power, such as the incorporation of temporal operators. This may also be interesting in itself for devising a logic to reason about truly concurrent processes.

1 Epistemic Logic

In this section we discuss the framework of epistemic logic that we will use in this paper.

In subsection 1.1 we introduce the language of epistemic logic. Then, in subsection 1.2 we give the semantics of this language using Kripke models. In subsection 2.3 we introduce the notion of a view formalizing a notion of observability. Views give rise to kinds of knowledge that we use in this paper.

1.1 Language of Epistemic Assertions

We start out by defining our language of epistemic assertions. For the moment, we assume to have a set VAR of variables $x, y, \ldots, x_1, x_2, \ldots$, together with a set CON of constants $a, b, c_1, c_2, \ldots, 0, 1, 2, \ldots$ and a set FUN of function symbols $f, g, +, *, \ldots$. The set TERM of term expressions is built from variables, constants and function symbols in an obvious way. We will not be specific about the arity of functions, if not necessary. Interpreting constants as 0-ary functions, we may assume that CON $\subset$ FUN. In the sequel, we will not always specify the lexical ingredients that together form the expressions that will denote our terms.

Then, we assume a set PRED of primitive predicates to be given. We will denote typical elements of PRED with P, Q, S etc. and we always assume '=' to be in PRED. As with function symbols, for predicate symbols, we will explicitly mention their arity only if necessary. Interpreting propositions as 0-ary predicates, we assume that the set PROP of propositions is a subset of PRED. We will use p, q and s as typical variables over PROP. After we have given the language of expressions over the semantical domain of states, typical examples of the expressions we will use include assertions like $x_1 = 5$ or $\exists\alpha \in \mathbb{Z}(x_1 = 3\alpha^2)$. The set At(PRED,VAR,FUN), or At for short, with typical element P, is the set of assertions over the set of terms:

$$\mathsf{At} = \{Q(t_1, \ldots, t_n) \mid Q \text{ is an n-ary predicate in PRED}, t_j \in \mathsf{TERM}, j \leq n\}.$$

Since we want to model the knowledge of a set of $Processes = \{1, \ldots, n\}$, we add a set of modal (here: *knowledge-*) operators $\{K_1, \ldots, K_n\}$ to our language. Moreover, we also need to denote the knowledge of any *group* of agents $G \subset Processes$. So, our set of operators will be $\mathsf{O} = \{K_i, K_G \mid i \in Processes,\ G \in 2^{Processes}\}$. In the sequel, if we write K_i or K_j, indices i and j will range over the set *Processes*, while writing K_G presupposes G to range over $2^{Processes}$. Now our language L(At,O) is the smallest set containing At which is closed under both infix attachment of $\wedge, \vee, \rightarrow$, and $\leftrightarrow$, and prefix placing of the logical connective $\neg$, the quantifiers $\exists$ and $\forall$ and operators K_i, $K_G \in \mathsf{O}$. We will denote L(At,O) by Assn. Thus, an *epistemic formula* $\varphi \in$ Assn is given by:

$$\varphi :: P \mid \varphi_1 \wedge \varphi_2 \mid \varphi_1 \rightarrow \varphi_2 \mid \varphi_1 \vee \varphi_2 \mid \varphi_1 \leftrightarrow \varphi_2 \mid \neg\varphi_1 \mid \forall x\varphi_1 \mid \exists x\varphi_1 \mid K_i\varphi_1 \mid K_G\varphi_1$$

A formula that does not contain modal operators is called *objective*.

1.2 Interpretation: Frames, Models, Sets

Our epistemic assertions $\varphi \in$ Assn are interpreted on *Kripke models*.

Definition 1.1 Let the multi modal language L, based on some fixed sets CON, VAR, FUN (which together constitute a set TERM of term-expressions) and PRED be given. Then, a *first-order Kripke model* $\mathcal{M}$ for L is a tuple $< [D, I_{\mathsf{FUN}}], W, \pi, R_1, \ldots, R_n >$, where

- The tuple $[D, I_{\mathsf{FUN}}]$ is called the *domain component* of $\mathcal{M}$ and consists of:
  1. non-empty set D, the *domain* of $\mathcal{M}$;
  2. I_{FUN} which gives for each m-ary function symbol f_m a function $I_{\mathsf{FUN}}(f_m)$: $D^m \rightarrow D$. In particular, it assigns an element $d \in D$ to each $c \in$ CON. Mostly, we will identify a function $I_{\mathsf{FUN}}(f)$ on D with its symbol f;
- W is a non-empty set, the set of *worlds*;

- π is a function, yielding, for each world $s \in W$, an interpretation $\pi(s)(Q) \subset D^m$, for each m-ary predicate symbol $Q \in \mathsf{PRED}$, if $m \geq 1$. Moreover, it gives an interpretation $\pi(s)(x) \in D$ for $x \in \mathsf{VAR}$ assigning values to variables, and an interpretation $\pi(s)(p) \in \{\mathbf{true}, \mathbf{false}\}$ of $p \in \mathsf{PROP}$, for each $s \in W$. With respect to PROP, π is also called a ***truth assignment*** to the propositional part of L;
- $R_i \subseteq W \times W$ is a relation on W, called an ***accessibility relation***, $i \leq n$

Given a function π, $\pi_{[d/x]}$ denotes the assignment that 'acts like π', except that it assigns the value d to x; now, the value of a term t, $val(\mathcal{M}, s)(t)$ given any $s \in \mathcal{M} = \langle [D, I_{\mathsf{FUN}}], W, \pi, R_1, \ldots, R_n \rangle$, is defined as:

1. $val(\mathcal{M}, s)(x) = \pi(s)(x)$, for all $x \in \mathsf{VAR}$;
2. $val(\mathcal{M}, s)(f(t_1, \ldots, t_n)) = (I_{\mathsf{FUN}}(f))(val(\mathcal{M}, s)(t_1), \ldots, val(\mathcal{M}, s)(t_n))$, for all $f \in \mathsf{FUN}, t_i \in \mathsf{TERM}$;

Finally, we are ready to give the truth definition of $\varphi \in \mathsf{L}$ at s in $\mathcal{M}$ (written $(\mathcal{M}, s) \models \varphi$):

1. $(\mathcal{M}, s) \models p$ iff $\pi(s)(p) = \mathbf{true}$
2. $(\mathcal{M}, s) \models P_n(t_1, \ldots, t_n)$ iff $(val(\mathcal{M}, s)(t_1), \ldots, val(\mathcal{M}, s)(t_n)) \in \pi(s)(P_n)$ $(n \geq 1)$
3. $(\mathcal{M}, s) \models \psi \wedge \chi$ iff $(\mathcal{M}, s) \models \psi$ and $(\mathcal{M}, s) \models \chi$
4. $(\mathcal{M}, s) \models \neg\psi$ iff not $(\mathcal{M}, s) \models \psi$
5. $(\mathcal{M}, s) \models \forall x \psi$ iff for all $d \in D$, $(\mathcal{M}', s) \models \psi$ where $\mathcal{M}' = \mathcal{M}$ except for $\pi' = \pi_{[d/x]}$
6. $(\mathcal{M}, s) \models K_i\psi$ iff for all v for which $R_i sv$, $(\mathcal{M}, v) \models \psi$
7. $(\mathcal{M}, s) \models K_G\psi$ iff for all v for which $R_k sv$ is true for all $k \in G$, $(\mathcal{M}, v) \models \psi$

We say that an operator that is defined like K_i for R_i, (i.e. truth of any $K_i\psi$ in s depends on the truth of ψ in *all* of the R_i-accessible worlds from s) is a ***necessity operator*** for R_i. Note that, for any $G = \{g_1, \ldots, g_r\} (r \leq n)$ the operator K_G is the necessity operator for $R_{g_1} \cap \ldots \cap R_{g_r}$. In a standard way, we define $\exists = \neg\forall\neg$. In a similar fashion, for any modal operator K_i, we define $M_i = \neg K_i \neg$. M_i is called the ***possibility operator*** for R_i. We then say that φ is ***satisfiable*** if φ is true at some world w in some model $\mathcal{M}$. Formula φ is ***true in model*** $\mathcal{M}$ ($\mathcal{M} \models \varphi$) if $(\mathcal{M}, s) \models \varphi$ for all worlds s of $\mathcal{M}$, and, finally, φ is ***valid*** ($\models \varphi$) if it is true in all models. For any class $\mathcal{C}$ of models, we write $\models_{\mathcal{C}} \varphi$ if φ is true in all models in $\mathcal{C}$. The class of all Kripke models is denoted with $\mathcal{K}$, and the class of models in which the accessibility relations are all ***equivalence relations*** is denoted denoted with $\mathcal{S}5_n$. Some of the results we want to mention are independent from the domain component in $\mathcal{M}$. In that case, we just denote the Kripke model with $\langle W, \pi, R_1, \ldots, R_m \rangle$.

A few words about the interpretation of $K_i\varphi$ are in order here. We may think of the set of worlds as a set of possible global states of the system during some execution. The accessibility relation R_i may be interpreted as follows: R_iuv holds if the agent (the *process*) considers v to be a possible alternative, given the world u (or given the agent's information 'in' u). Putting it differently, the relation R_i may be considered to be some kind of 'epistemic compatibility relation' between the worlds in the model. Or, putting it still somewhat differently: R_i holds between s and t if the world t is a possible 'extension' of agent i's information about s. For instance, if the agent knows that his local variable x has the value 4, then he will only consider those worlds as possible alternatives in which this is the case, and, conversely, if he considers (given his view) two worlds as possible alternatives that do not agree on the value of x, then he does not exactly know this value.

It will be clear, that, under this interpretation of R_i, it seems natural to take this relation to be an equivalence: given agent i's information about s, the agent will consider s to be a possible alternative (i.e., R_i is *reflexive*); if agent i finds world u to be a possible extension of his information about some world t which, on its turn, is held to be a reasonable alternative for some world s then u will be considered a possible extension s, given the agent's information about s (i.e., R_i is *transitive*); finally, if the agent finds t to be epistemically compatible with s, then this will also be the other way around (i.e., R_i will also be *symmetric*).

We do not claim that these are the only possible and reasonable properties one can impose on the accessibility relation. It are these very properties of the accessibility relations that effectuate (via a notion of *correspondence*, cf. Example 1.7 of Section 1.3) that the modal operators K_i obtain their knowledge-like behaviour, of which we will list some vital examples in Theorem 1.2. From this correspondence between properties of the accessibility relations on one hand, and valid modal formulas on the other hand, it follows from the remark at the beginning of this paragraph, that the epistemic properties that follow from our semantical choices, are not beyond discussion. In fact, (the propositional part of) the system we propose here was already suggested in the sixties by Hintikka (cf. [Hin62]). From then, its popularity and usefulness in the fields of AI and computer science has only increased (cf. [HM85, Hin62, HM88, MHV91a, MHV91b] for a more detailed presentation of the formal system and some motivation for it).

Theorem 1.2

1. *The following holds for both* $\mathcal{X} = \mathcal{K}$ *and* $\mathcal{X} = S5_n$*:*
   R0 $\models_{\mathcal{X}} \varphi, \models_{\mathcal{X}} \varphi \rightarrow \psi \Rightarrow \models_{\mathcal{X}} \psi$
   R1 $\models_{\mathcal{X}} \varphi \Rightarrow \models_{\mathcal{X}} K_i\varphi$

2. *The following are valid in* $\mathcal{K}$ *(and hence in* $S5_n$*):*
   A0 $\models_{\mathcal{K}} \varphi$*, for any propositional tautology* φ
   A1 $\models_{\mathcal{K}} K_i(\varphi \rightarrow \psi) \rightarrow (K_i\varphi \rightarrow K_i\psi)$
   A2 $\models_{\mathcal{K}} \forall x(K_i\varphi) \rightarrow K_i(\forall x\varphi)$

3. The following are valid in $S5_n$:

A3 $\models_{S5_n} K_i\varphi \rightarrow \varphi$

A4 $\models_{S5_n} K_i\varphi \rightarrow K_iK_i\varphi$

A5 $\models_{S5_n} \neg K_i\varphi \rightarrow K_i\neg K_i\varphi$

4. Let $G = \{g_1, \ldots g_k\} \subset$ Processes. Then:

R3 $\models_{S5_n} K_{g_1}(\varphi_0 \rightarrow \varphi_1) \wedge \ldots \wedge K_{g_k}(\varphi_{k-1} \rightarrow \varphi_k) \Rightarrow \models_{S5_n} K_G(\varphi_0 \rightarrow \varphi_k)$

A6 $\models_{S5_n} K_{g_h}\varphi \rightarrow K_G\varphi, (h \leq k)$

A7 $\models_{S5_n} K_G\varphi \rightarrow \varphi$

A8 $\models_{S5_n} K_G\varphi \rightarrow K_GK_G\varphi$

A9 $\models_{S5_n} \neg K_G\varphi \rightarrow K_G\neg K_G\varphi$

The items 1 and 2 of theorem 1.2 state properties of validity of Kripke models in general. As far as our operators K_i are concerned, they imply that valid formulas are known (R1); that knowledge distributes over the implication (A1) and that if something is known for all objects in the domain, then it is known that all objects satisfy that something (A2). We have to accept all those properties in a modal setting (although in [FH88, HK90, HM88] one can find some proposals to intervent these sources of *logical omniscience*), except for A2, which we could easily modify in our set-up. Note that this property is implied by the fact that we have the same domain in each world s, together with the same interpretation of predicates in them. For our purposes, this is a very realistic assumption (cf. section 2); the reader who is interested in a general discussion on this topic, is referred to [Gam91].

Then, Theorem 1.2.3 is about the particular models for our epistemic language. In particular, Theorem 1.2.3 guarantees that we have the following properties for our logic of knowledge: knowledge is assumed to be *veridical* (A3), i.e. one cannot know false assertions; the agents have *positive introspection* (A4), i.e. one knows what one knows; as well as *negative introspection* (A5): one knows what one does not know.

The knowledge operator K_G describes a kind of knowledge that is *implicitly* available in a group of agents: it was indeed called implicit knowledge in [HM85, HM92] but later on also the term *Distributed Knowledge* was used for it (cf. [FHV88, Hoe90]). It is not the knowledge of all the agents in the group G, but the knowledge that would be obtained if the agents would somehow 'put their knowledge together'. Note that this group knowledge very much behaves like that of the particular agents (A7-A9); that the knowledge of one of the agents of G is sufficient for the knowledge of G (A6) and that the group's knowledge can increase if each of the agent's 'knows one sufficient lemma' (R2).

In fact, if we interpret the properties of Theorem 2.4.1 as rules for a logic $S5_n$, and the formulas of Theorem 2.4.3 as axioms for $S5_n$, the resulting logic is a complete axiomatization of validity in $S5_n$. For an overview of this logic, we refer to [HM85] or [MHV91a, MHV91b] where a completeness proof is presented for the logic without the operator K_G. Although adding this operator K_G and its proper axioms to the logic in the first instance corresponds to a much richer class of models with respect to which the logic is complete, in [FHV88, HM92] it is shown that in the second instance this logic is complete as well with respect to the class of models presented above, in which the accessibility relation associated with the operator K_G is the intersection of the accessibility relations R_i associated with the operators K_i for $i \in G$.

In [MHV91a, MHV91b] it is also explained how the valid formulas mentioned in 1.2.3 are connected with the properties we imposed on R_i. We will shortly return to this topic in subsection 1.3.

We end this subsection by mentioning one more property of $S5_n$-validity, which we recall from [Hoe90].

Definition 1.3 A formula with occurrences of K_i s called an *epistemic formula*. A formula φ is *i-doxastic sequenced* if there are ψ, operators $X_1, \dots X_n \in \{K_i, \neg K_i\}$ and $n > 0$ such that $\varphi = X_1 X_2 \dots X_n \psi$. We will not always mention reference to agent i.

Theorem 1.4 ([Hoe90]). *For any i-doxastic sequenced φ, we have:*
$\models_{S5_n} (K_i\varphi \leftrightarrow \varphi)$.

Theorem 1.4 implies that in $S5_n$ i-doxastic sequenced formulas are known by agent i iff they are true. As a corollary, we immediately have that the formulas of definition 1.3 can be reduced to a formula with *at most one main epistemic operator*, provided that all epistemic operators have the same subscript. It implies that our epistemic logic is 'optimally manageable': all sequences of operators and $\neg$'s can be rewritten to a sequence with at most one operator. So, under the assumption that validity in $S5_n$ models our common-sense notion of knowledge, in every-day-life we never need to use complicated 'epistemic phrases' like 'I know, that I don't know that I know ...".

Corollary 1.5 *Let i be given, $1 \le i \le n$. Let $X \in \{K_i, \neg\}$ and let $\overline{X}$ be a sequence of X's. Let φ be any formula in* L. *Then* $\models_{S5_n} \overline{X}K_i\varphi \leftrightarrow (\neg)K_i\varphi$, *where the '$\neg$' is present if the number of '$\neg$'-s in $\overline{X}$ is odd.*

Note that this corollary does not give us any method to simplify complicated sentences in which operators of several agents do occur. In fact, this can be shown to be impossible, even in simple cases. For instance, in the case of 2 agents, it is easily seen that K_1K_2p does not simplify to any of $(\neg)K_1p, (\neg)K_2p$.

1.3 Lexical Views

In subsection 1.2 we already hinted at the connection between several valid knowledge formulas on the one hand, and imposing special properties on the accessibility relations on the other hand. Before we give an example, recall that for the moment we will discard from the 'domain component' in the representation of $S5_n$ models. Let us demonstrate our point with the property $A2$, $K_i\varphi \rightarrow \varphi$. This formula is not valid on all Kripke models, as is demonstrated by the model $\mathcal{M}_1 = < W, \pi_1, R_1 >$ with $W = \{w, v\}$; $R_1 = \{(w,v),(v,w)\}$; $\pi_1(w)(p) =$ **false** and $\pi_1(v)(p) =$ **true**. Then we have $(\mathcal{M}, w) \models K_1p \wedge \neg p$. As is easily verified, reflexivity of R_1 would be *sufficient* to guarantee $\mathcal{M} \models K_1\varphi \rightarrow \varphi$.

On the other hand, reflexivity is not *necessary* to achieve this: let $\mathcal{M}_2$ be $< W, \pi_2, R_1 >$, with $\pi_2(w) = \pi_2(v)$. Then, although $\mathcal{M}_2$ is not reflexive, we have $\mathcal{M}_2 \models K\varphi \rightarrow \varphi$. Note that $K_1\varphi \rightarrow \varphi$ is valid on $\mathcal{M}_2$ due to a specific choice of the valuation π_2. This motivates a shift from Kripke *models* to Kripke *frames*:

Definition 1.6 A *Kripke frame* $\mathcal{F} = < W, R_1, \ldots, R_n >$ consists of a set W and n binary relations R_i on it. We stipulate:
1 $(\mathcal{F}, w) \models \varphi$ if $(< \mathcal{F}, \pi >, w) \models \varphi$ for all valuations π on $\mathcal{F}$.
2 $\mathcal{F} \models \varphi$ if $(\mathcal{F}, w) \models \varphi$ for all $w \in W$.

We say that the model $\mathcal{M} = < W, \pi, R_1, \ldots, R_n >$ is based on the frame $\mathcal{F} = < W, R_1, \ldots, R_n >$.

Now we can establish the following sufficient and necessary condition for veridicality:

Example 1.7 We have the following correspondence between modal formulas and first-order properties of frames:

$$\mathcal{F} \models K_i\varphi \rightarrow \varphi \text{ iff } R_i \text{ of } \mathcal{F} \text{ is reflexive}$$

A property as stated in Example 1.7, that so nicely ties up a modal formula with a first order property (of a binary relation on a frame) is called a *correspondence* property. For more about correspondence theory for modal logic in general, we refer to [Ben83] and for epistemic formulas in particular, to [Hoe90].

In this way, a Kripke model M $= < W, \pi, R_1, \ldots, R_n >$ may be considered as being obtained by adding a specification π of truth of propositional atoms to worlds in the structure (frame) $< W, R_1, \ldots, R_n >$. Once we have identified w with $\pi(w)$, this world has become a ***situation***: it gives a complete description of a state of affairs. However, for our purposes, it will appear also to be worthwhile to proceed the other way around and consider these situations as basic entities in our model, on which we then impose a binary relation, of which we will take care to be an equivalence.

Definition 1.8 A *Kripke set* $S = < W, \pi >$ is a set of worlds along with a valuation function. It gives rise to Kripke models in an obvious way. In particular, let $\mathsf{P}_i \subseteq \mathsf{At}$. We say that in $\mathcal{M} = < W, \pi, R_1, \ldots, R_n >$, R_i is *lexically-view-based on* P_i if it holds that

$$R_iwv \text{ iff for all } P \in \mathsf{P}_i, \pi(w)(P) = \pi(v)(P).$$

In general, we may add binary relations $R_1, \ldots, R_n$ for several $\mathsf{P}_1, \ldots \mathsf{P}_n \subseteq \mathsf{At}$. We say that $\mathcal{M} = < W, \pi, R_1, \ldots R_n >$ is *view based* if $\forall i \exists \mathsf{P}_i [R_i$ is lexically-view-based on $\mathsf{P}_i]$. We say that $\mathcal{M} = < W, \pi, R_1, \ldots R_n >$ is *uniformly view based* if $\mathcal{M}$ is view based, and $\mathsf{P}_1 = \mathsf{P}_2 \ldots = \mathsf{P}_n$. Finally, we denote the class of models that are view based on $\mathsf{P}_1, \mathsf{P}_2 \ldots = \mathsf{P}_n$ by $\mathcal{VB}(\mathsf{P}_1, \mathsf{P}_2 \ldots, \mathsf{P}_n)$.

Remark 1.9 *Let* $\mathcal{M} = < W, \pi, R_1, \ldots, R_n >$ *be a view-based model. Then it follows from definition 1.8 that* R_i *is an equivalence relation.*

Definition 1.10 Let $\mathcal{M} = < W, \pi, R_1, \ldots, R_n >$ be a model in which R_i is lexically view based on P_i. Then, we define the *lexical view* of i as

$$v_i((\mathcal{M}, s)) = \{t \mid R_i(s, t)\}$$

Recall from Definition 1.1 that φ is known to process i in world w iff φ is true in all worlds v that are R_i-accessible from w. In a view-based model, all such worlds v agree with w about a set P_i of atoms. This seems reasonable: an agent who is aware of some atomic facts P_i will, given a world w, only consider those worlds to be possible that are 'P_i-compatible' with w. Our notion of *lexical view* is very close to that of *view* as defined in [HM91]. Our view is defined in terms of the logical language, whereas the notion of view as defined in [HM91] is a semantical notion. In the presentation, it is possible for two worlds u and v to have the same view, without having any means in the logical language to express this. In section 2 we shall return to the notion of view in the context of distributed computing.

The knowledge of a process about the truth of some atoms is inherited by its knowledge about formulas that are made out of those atoms. We will make this presupposition more explicit now.

Theorem 1.11 *Let R in $\mathcal{M} = < W, \pi, R >$ be view-based on $\mathsf{P}_0 \subseteq \mathsf{At}$ and $w, v \in W$. Then:*
i *Rwv iff for all $\varphi \in \mathsf{L}(\mathsf{P}_0, \{K\})$: $(\mathcal{M}, w) \models \varphi \Leftrightarrow (\mathcal{M}, v) \models \varphi$*
ii *for all $\varphi \in \mathsf{L}(\mathsf{P}_0, \{K\})$: $[(\mathcal{M}, w) \models \varphi$ iff $(\mathcal{M}, w) \models K\varphi]$.*

proof Clearly, ii follows from i. So we only prove item i:

$\Leftarrow$: if w and v agree on all formulas of $\mathsf{L}(\mathsf{P}_0, \{K\})$, they also agree on all formulas of $\mathsf{L}(\mathsf{P}_0)$, and, since R is view-based on $\mathsf{L}(\mathsf{P}_0)$ we have Rwv.

$\Rightarrow$: this is proven using induction on φ: if φ is atomic, the claim immediately follows from the fact that R is view based on P_0. The interesting case left is $\varphi = K\psi$. Let π' be the restriction of π to P_0. Suppose Rwv, i.e. $\pi'(w) = \pi'(v)$. If $(\mathcal{M}, w) \models K\psi$ then ψ is true in all worlds u for which $\pi'(w) = \pi'(u)$. Suppose Rvs, i.e. $\pi'(v) = \pi'(s)$. Combining the assertions about π' we get $\pi'(w) = \pi'(s)$, so that ψ must be true in s, and hence $(\mathcal{M}, v) \models K\psi$. Conversely, suppose $(\mathcal{M}, v) \models K\psi$ and Rwv, i.e. $\pi'(w) = \pi'(v)$. Let s be a world for which Rws: $\pi'(w) = \pi'(s)$. Then $\pi'(v) = \pi'(s)$, so Rvs, and $(\mathcal{M}, s) \models \psi$. We conclude that $(\mathcal{M}, w) \models K\psi$.

Note that Theorem 1.11 need not be true for arbitrary formulas $\varphi \in \mathsf{L}$, but only for the subset induced by P_0.

As to finding a complete *axiomatization* of a logic $S5_n(\mathsf{P}_1, \ldots \mathsf{P}_n)$, which should give us a calculus of the valid formulas, given that the view of agent i is based on P_i, it seems clear that we need the axioms

B_i: $\varphi \to K_i\varphi$, for all $\varphi \in \mathsf{Assn}$.

However, it seems that one also needs to put some additional constraints on the class of models in order to be able to prove completeness. Since for the moment, we are mainly concerned with a semantical description of knowledge in a distributed environment, we will not go into those technical problems here.

2 Epistemic Logic and Distributed Programs

2.1 A General Model of Distributed Programs

We consider a collection $p_1, ..., p_n$ of processes which run in parallel and may communicate with each other. Assume a program for the system, in which all actions are uniquely labeled. A possible execution of the system is described by a pair $\langle \sigma, h \rangle$, where σ is a valuation of the program variables, and h is a history, which is a poset consisting of the labels of all actions taking place plus some order on them, the causality relation. Formally, a history h is a poset $(H, <)$.

In this paper, we will not expand on notions concerning poset concatenation and the like; the interested reader is referred to [BRR89] and [MdV89]. As an exception though, we would like to mention the operation of restriction of a poset to a process: $h \restriction i$ denotes the restriction of history h to i-actions, i.e. it is formed by leaving out all non-i actions and adapting the ordering $<$ accordingly.

2.2 Knowledge in Concurrent Programs

In this subsection we will apply the general framework of section 1 to the special case of concurrent programs. To this end we must interpret the ingredients of the general epistemic framework, viz. Kripke models and views. The set of states of Kripke models for concurrent programs is now chosen to be a set of so-called *points*, which is a notion similar to that of Halpern & Moses [HM90]. A point is a pair $\langle \sigma, h \rangle$, where σ is a global state and h is a history. A poset represents a snapshot of a computation performed by the program. The state gives information about the values of variables and the presence/absence of deadlock, and as such it can be viewed as a *world* in the sense of section 1 together with the truth assignment associated with it, i.e. a *situation* in the sense of section 1.

Regarding views: in this context views are induced by some observation criterion on points. The idea is that for some agent some points (computations) are indistinguishable due to a limited "view" on the process as a whole: generally it is the case that only some local entities (such as private variables) can be "seen" by the agent. This may be expressed by some equivalence relation R_i which identifies points (for the agent i). Moreover, these relations may be based on a natural set of atoms $\mathsf{P}_i \subseteq \mathsf{AT}$ that are "known to the agent". In this case we really have a lexical view as in section 1.

Example 2.1 In order to illustrate the notion of view in the context of distributed programs, let us consider the notion of local state knowledge of [HM91]. Two points r and s are i-accessible to each other if the contents of all the local variables of process i are the same in r and s. (This does not guarantee that now there 'is' some knowledge about these variables in r: the language may be too weak to express this.) In our set-up, we would simply define $\mathsf{P}_1 = \{x_1 = \alpha, x_2 = \alpha \mid \alpha \in \mathbb{Z}\}$. Therefore, in the sequel, we will also use the term 'view' if we mean 'lexical view'. Once we have defined our language of value- and history expressions, we can give other interesting examples of views. Here we can mention two extreme cases that were mentioned in [HM91]. The first is called 'Constant Knowledge' in [HM91] and we can obtain this by putting $\mathsf{P}_i = \emptyset$. This has as an effect that $R_i = W \times W$, so that only facts can be known that are true 'everywhere'. This is of course a very weak form of knowledge, which is knowledge about truths in the domain given. The other extreme case is called 'Point Knowledge' in [HM91] and (under the assumption that the language is sufficiently expressive) we obtain it by putting P_i = At, the complete set of atoms. It is easily seen that by choosing our view this way, we can model the (unrealistic) situation in which knowledge (of agent i) and truth do collapse. Note that these two kinds of knowledge are both based on a uniformly view based model.

3 Case Study: A CSP-like Language

3.1 Syntax

We will first give the syntax of our language, which is a variant of CSP ([Hoa78]). It resembles the syntax used in [FLP84] but with two differences: firstly, all commands are labeled, and secondly, we do not have a repetitive command. The labeling of commands is due to the fact that we want to end up with a denotational domain consisting of sets of posets of action labels, and the omission of a repetitive command is because in this first approach, we would like to keep the semantic domain as simple as possible (e.g. no continuity required).

Firstly, we define a *basic command* (we will be using a BNF-like notation):

$$s :: skip \mid y := t \mid P_i!t \mid P_i?y$$

where skip is the null command, y:=t denotes an assignment, $P_i!t$ denotes 'output to process i the value of the expression t', and $P_i?y$ denotes 'input a value from process i and store it in y'. Typically, basic commands will be denoted by s.

Furthermore, a *guard* g is a sequence of at most two elements: b, b;c or c, where b is a boolean expression and c is a basic communication command ($P_i!t$ or $P_i?y$). Missing boolean parts are equivalent to **true**.

A *elementary statement* S is given by

$$S :: S_1; S_2 \mid l : s \mid [l_1 : g_1 \rightarrow S_1 [] ... [] l_n : g_n \rightarrow S_n]$$

which respectively stand for sequential composition, labeled basic command and guarded selection;

A *program PR* is given by

$$PR :: [P_1 :: S_1 \parallel \cdots \parallel P_n :: S_n]$$

which denotes parallel composition of processes, where a process is an elementary statement, labeled with an -indexed- capital P (P_i on its own is called a *process-id*). In the view semantics to be defined in 3.3 we are only interested in processes. We impose the restriction that within each program, labels are unique. Furthermore, given a program PR (statement S), we define $Var(PR)$ ($Var(S)$) to be the set of variables occurring in PR (S). For any two processes $P_i :: S_i, P_j :: S_j$ it holds that $Var(S_i) \cap Var(S_j) = \emptyset$, stating that different processes have disjoint sets of variables.

3.2 The Semantical Domain

Let in the following PR be a program. We define $\overline{\Sigma}$ with typical element $\overline{\sigma}$ to be the set of valuations of $Var(PR)$. Furthermore, we define $Exp = \{\rho^i_j?, \rho^i_j! | P_i, P_j$ are process-id's and P_i appears in S, and $E = \{e(A) | A \subseteq Exp\}$. The elements of E will describe states in which deadlock has occurred. In particular, $\rho^i_j?$ will denote the fact that process i is waiting to receive a message from process j, whereas $\rho^i_j!$ describes the situation in which process i is waiting to output a message to processor j. In the semantics to be defined, we need a function $Dual : Exp \rightarrow Exp$ which is defined by $Dual(\rho^i_j?) = \rho^j_i!$ and $Dual(\rho^i_j!) = \rho^j_i?$ which delivers the 'matching' deadlock. As it will appear, it is impossible for an element of Exp and its dual to be in A at the same time for some element $e(A) \in E$ in the semantics of a statement, because this would denote a deadlock situation in which at least two processors are waiting on each other for a matching handshake!
Now we can define our set S of generalized states with typical element σ:

$$S = \overline{\Sigma} \times E$$

Note the difference between a (generalised) state σ and a valuation $\overline{\sigma}$: $\overline{\sigma}$ gives a valuation of the program variables only, while σ provides additional information about deadlocks.

Next we define the set of program labels:

$\Lambda =$

$\{l | l$ appears in $PR\}$
$\cup \{\langle \alpha, i_l, j \rangle | i, j$ are process-id's, $l : P_j!t$ appears in process $i\}$
$\cup \{\langle \alpha, i, j_l \rangle | i, j$ are process-id's, $l : P_i?y$ appears in process $j\}$
$\cup \{\langle \alpha, i_l, j_{l'} \rangle | i, j$ are process-id's, $l : P_j!t$ appears in process i,
$l' : P_i!y$ appears in process j $\}$

Thus, there are two possible formats for labels, with as intended meaning that a 'simple' label l reflects some internal action, whereas a 'triple-' label describes a communication, or an attempt at a communication.

We will need a predicate *match* which indicates whether two labels are matching or not: $match : \Lambda \times \Lambda \rightarrow \{\mathbf{true}, \mathbf{false}\}$ is defined by

$$match(\langle \alpha_1, i_l, j \rangle, \langle \alpha_2, i', j'_{l'} \rangle) = [\alpha_1 = \alpha_2 \wedge i = i' \wedge j = j']$$

So, two labels are matching if they agree on the sender, receiver and the value of a communication.

On matching labels we also define $unite : \Lambda \times \Lambda \rightarrow \Lambda$ by

$$unite(\langle \alpha, i_l, j \rangle, \langle \alpha, i, j_{l'} \rangle) = \langle \alpha, i_l, j_{l'} \rangle$$

Finally, we define the set of histories $\mathcal{H}$, with typical element h, as the set of posets $(H, <)$ over Λ.

Our semantical domain consists of sets of pairs $\langle (\overline{\sigma}, e(A)), h \rangle \in \mathcal{S} \times \mathcal{H}$, where the first component of the pair is a pair consisting of a proper state and an expectation set. In case we are not interested in the inner structure of the state component we write σ for $(\overline{\sigma}, e(A))$. Note that, in contrast to [FLP84], we allow combinations of proper states and expectation sets; this is motivated by the view that while a program is held up in a deadlock, still some information about the processed values may be gained. The second component describes the history via which the state in the first component was reached. We sometimes abuse notation and write $l \in h$ when we mean $l \in H$, where $h = (H, <)$. We will use the dot "$\cdot$" to denote the concatenation operation between histories. Furthermore, when h is a poset with only one element, we may use that element as denotation for h, and ϵ denotes the empty history.

3.3 View Semantics for Processes

In this section we will provide the semantic clauses assigning views to processes. The semantical operator is typed as follows:

$$[\![\cdot]\!]_v : P_i :: S_i \times \wp(\mathcal{S} \times \mathcal{H}) \rightarrow \wp(\mathcal{S} \times \mathcal{H})$$

It is defined pointwise, as in [FLP84], which means we only have to define $[\![S]\!]_v(\langle \sigma, h \rangle)$, for all pairs. Once this is done, we derive the semantics for sets as follows: $[\![S]\!]_v(V) =$

$\bigcup_{\langle\sigma,h\rangle\in V}\{[S]_v(\langle\sigma,h\rangle\}$. In the sequel, we will inductively define the semantics of a process $P_i :: S_i$, for all possible S_i; we omit the label P_i, as it is obvious from the context.

Before we continue with the clauses, there is one general clause concerned with deadlock that holds for al statements. It states that after the process in question has deadlocked, nothing more can happen to the current point $\langle\sigma,h\rangle$, i.e. deadlock is inherited by all statements:

$$(\rho^i_j? \in A \vee \rho^i_j! \in A) \Rightarrow \forall S_i[[S_i]_v(\langle(\overline{\sigma},e(A)),h\rangle = \langle(\overline{\sigma},e(A)),h\rangle]$$

For the skip statement and the assignment statement, the semantics is simple: the valuation function stays the same, while the history is augmented with the label of the statement. Note that $h \cdot l$ is a poset concatenation.

•$[l : skip]_v(\langle\sigma,h\rangle) = \{\langle\sigma,h\cdot l\rangle\}$

Define t_σ to be $\sigma(t)$, the value of t in σ.

•$[l : y := t]_v(\langle\sigma,h\rangle) = \{\langle\sigma[t_\sigma/y],h\cdot l\rangle\}$

In the semantics of the output-statement we consider two cases: one in which the communication fails, which causes the state to be augmented with the appropriate expectation set, and one in which the communication is established, yielding the corresponding state/history pair.

•$[l : P_j!t]_v(\langle\sigma,h\rangle) = \{\langle(\overline{\sigma},e(\{\rho^i_j!\}),h\rangle,\langle\sigma,h\cdot\langle t_\sigma,i_l,j\rangle\rangle\}$

With respect to the failure of the communication, the output-statement is treated like the input-statement; however, in the case of successful communication, all possible pairs which describe a matching output-statement are included:

•$[l : P_j?y]_v(\langle\sigma,h\rangle) = \{\langle(\overline{\sigma},e(\{\rho^i_j?\})),h\rangle\} \cup \{\langle\sigma[\alpha/y],h\cdot\langle\alpha,j,i_l\rangle\rangle \mid \alpha\in\mathcal{D}\}$

Now we need some more definitions before we can continue with the semantics of the guarded command. We will stick close to the notation which is used in [FLP84], to facilitate comparison.

Let in the following $g_1,...,g_n$ be a set of guards $b_i;c_i$, where either part can be empty. Then we define

$$L_\sigma = \{i \mid \sigma(b_i) = \mathbf{true}\}$$

(note that for empty boolean parts b_i the condition always holds)

We will also need the notion of a function, which delivers the successful communication result set given some communication statement (it will be useful to define this function on the empty statement, ϵ also):

Definition 3.1 *The function Suc is defined by*

$$Suc[l : P_j!t](\langle\sigma,h\rangle) = \{\langle\sigma,h\cdot\langle t_\sigma,i_l,j\rangle\rangle\}$$

$Suc[l : P_j?y](\langle\sigma, h\rangle) = \{\langle\sigma[\alpha/y], h \cdot \langle\alpha, j, i_l\rangle\rangle \mid \alpha \in D\}$
$Suc[\epsilon](\langle\sigma, h\rangle) = \{\langle\sigma, h\rangle\}$

Now we can give the semantic clause for the guarded statement:

$\bullet[[l_1 : g_1 \rightarrow S_1 [] \cdots [] l_n : g_n \rightarrow S_n]]_v(\langle\sigma, h\rangle) = \bigcup_{i \in L_\sigma} [S_i]_v(Suc[l_i; c_i](\langle\sigma, h\rangle))$
$\cup(IF[\forall j \in L_\sigma, c_j \neq \epsilon] THEN \langle(\sigma, e(\{c_j^i | j \in L_\sigma\}), h\rangle ELSE \emptyset)$

So, the semantics of a nondeterministic statement is obtained by considering all possible outcomes of the statement, i.e. all branches that can be taken given the current state. Only if there is no true guard with an empty communication part, deadlock is possible. Finally, the clause for sequential composition:

$\bullet[S_1; S_2]_v(\langle\sigma, h\rangle) = [S_2]_v([S_1]_v(\langle\sigma, h\rangle))$

Next, we define the important notion of *choice function*. This function models an actual choice made nondeterministically. When we switch to the epistemic setting we need such an actual state as the current world/situation in which we evaluate epistemic frames.

Definition 3.2 *Suppose some choice function f_c which chooses an arbitrary pair $\langle\sigma_c, h_c\rangle$ from a given set in $\wp(\mathcal{S} \times \mathcal{H})$.*

3.4 Semantics of Programs

Now that we have defined the view-semantics of individual processes, we are able to define the semantics of a statement *given some Kripke model and point*, possibly composed of several processes. Our domain will be a pair consisting of a Kripke structure $\mathcal{M} = (\mathcal{S} \times \mathcal{H}, \pi, V_1, ..., V_n)$ and a pair $\langle\sigma, h\rangle$, where the set V_i represents the view of processor i. The pair $\langle\sigma, h\rangle$ fulfils the role of current world in the Kripke semantics of statements and assertions. Once this is done, we can supply our language with a semantics by simply defining the starting Kripke model and point. From now on, $\mathcal{K}$ will denote the special class of Kripke models as described in this section.

Definition 3.3 *(semantics of statements)* Let $\mathcal{M} = (\mathcal{S} \times \mathcal{H}, \pi, V_1, ..., V_n)$, then

$$[\cdot] : PR \times \mathcal{K} \times (\mathcal{S} \times \mathcal{H}) \rightarrow \mathcal{K} \times (\mathcal{S} \times \mathcal{H})$$

is defined by

$\bullet[P_i :: S_i](\mathcal{M}, \langle\sigma, h\rangle) = (\mathcal{M}', \langle\sigma', h'\rangle)$, where

$\mathcal{M}' = (\mathcal{S} \times \mathcal{H}, \pi, V_1, ...V_i', ..., V_n)$,
$V_i' = [S_i]_v(V_i)$, and
$\langle\sigma', h'\rangle = f_c(V_i')$

Now, in preparation of the definition of the remaining case, let $\mathcal{M} = (S \times \mathcal{H}, \pi, V_1, ..., V_n)$. For any i we define $POS[P_i : S_i](\mathcal{M}, \langle\sigma, h\rangle) = V_i'$, where $V_i' = [\![S_i]\!]_v(V_i)$. Intuitively, for a statement S, $POS[S](\mathcal{M}, \langle\sigma, h\rangle)$ describes the set of possible worlds (points) after execution of S, according to the processes involved in S. How this definition can be (inductively) extended to parallel statements, in which the set is obtained by taking what is nearly the intersection of the sets of worlds in $POS(S_i)$ for the individual S_i's is shown in the last clause:

•$[\![P_1 :: S_1 \parallel \cdots \parallel P_n :: S_n]\!](\mathcal{M}, \langle\sigma, h\rangle) = (\mathcal{M}', \langle\sigma', h'\rangle)$, where

$\mathcal{M}' = (S \times \mathcal{H}, \pi, V_1', ..., V_n')$,
$V_i' = [\![S_i]\!]_v(V_i)$, and
$\langle\sigma', h'\rangle = f_c(POS[P_1 : S_1 \parallel \cdots \parallel P_n : S_n](\mathcal{M}, \langle\sigma, h\rangle))$, where
$POS[P_1 : S_1 \parallel \cdots \parallel P_n : S_n](\mathcal{M}, \langle\sigma, h\rangle) =$
$POS[P_1 : S_1 \parallel \cdots \parallel P_{n-1} : S_{n-1}](\mathcal{M}, \langle\sigma, \epsilon\rangle)||_{h\{1,...,n-1\}\{n\}}POS[P_n : S_n](\mathcal{M}, \langle\sigma, \epsilon\rangle) =$
$POS[P_1 : S_1 \parallel \cdots \parallel P_{n-1} : S_{n-1}](\mathcal{M}, \langle\sigma, \epsilon\rangle)||_{h\{1,...,n-1\}\{n\}}[\![S_i]\!]_v(V_i')$,
and $||_{hG_1G_2}$ is defined as
$V||_{hG_1G_2}W = \{\langle\sigma_1, h_1\rangle||'_{hG_1G_2}\langle\sigma_2, h_2\rangle \mid \langle\sigma_1, h_1\rangle \in V, \langle\sigma_2, h_2\rangle \in W\}$,

where $||'_{hG_1G_2}$ is defined as follows:

$\langle(\overline{\sigma}_1, e(A_1)), h_1\rangle||'_{hG_1G_2}\langle(\overline{\sigma}_2, e(A_2)), h_2\rangle = \{\langle(\overline{\sigma}_1, e(A_1)) *_{G_1G_2} (\overline{\sigma}_2, e(A_2)), h \cdot h^c\rangle \mid A_1 \cap Dual(A_2) = \emptyset \wedge h^c \in Syn_{G_1G_2}(h_1, h_2)\}$

Define $C_{G_1G_2}(h_1) = \{\langle\alpha, i_l, j\rangle \in h_1 \mid i \in G_1, j \in G_2\} \cup \{\langle\alpha, j, i_l\rangle \in h_1 \mid i \in G_1, j \in G_2\}$, and

$C_{G_1G_2}(h_2) = \{\langle\alpha, i, j_l\rangle \in h_1 \mid i \in G_1, j \in G_2\} \cup \{\langle\alpha, j_l, i\rangle \in h_1 \mid i \in G_1, j \in G_2\}$

Now we define $h^c \in Syn_{G_1G_2}(h_1, h_2)$ iff

$h_1 = (H_1, <_1), h_2 = (H_2, <_2)$ and there exists a bijection

$f : C_{G_1G_2}(h_1) \to C_{G_1G_2}(h_2)$ such that

$$\begin{aligned} &\forall l, l' \in C_{G_1G_2}(h_1)[match(l, f(l)) \wedge l < l' \Rightarrow f(l) \not> f(l')] \\ &\wedge h^c = (H^c, <^c)\text{where} \\ H^c = (((H_1 \cup H_2) \setminus C_{G_1G_2}(h_1)) &\setminus C_{G_1G_2}(h_2)) \cup \{unite(l, f(l)) | l \in C_{G_1G_2}(h_1)\} \text{ and} \\ &<^c = TClos((<_1 \cup <_2 |H^c) \\ &\cup\{(unite(l, f(l)), k) \mid l < k\} \\ &\cup\{(k, unite(l, f(l))) \mid k < l\} \\ &\cup\{(unite(l, f^{-1}(l)), k) \mid l <' k\} \\ &\cup\{(k, unite(l, f(l))) \mid k <' l\}). \end{aligned}$$

Lastly, we define $*_{G_1G_2}$. The intuition behind this operator is that it combines the information available on the variables of the groups G_1 and G_2, while the new set of deadlocks is the union of the former two:

for any $(\overline{\sigma}_1, e(A_1))$ and $(\overline{\sigma}_2, e(A_2)) \in \mathcal{S} \times \mathcal{H}$, we define $(\overline{\sigma}, e(A)) = (\overline{\sigma}_1, e(A_1)) *_{G_1G_2} (\overline{\sigma}_2, e(A_2))$, where $A = A_1 \cup A_2$ and for all x_i it holds that

$$\overline{\sigma}(x_i) = \overline{\sigma}_1(x_i) \text{ if } i \in G_1$$
$$\overline{\sigma}(x_i) = \overline{\sigma}_2(x_i) \text{ if } i \notin G_1$$

Remark 3.4 The operator $||_{hG_1G_2}$ on sets, defined in terms of the operator $||'_{hG_1G_2}$ on points is conceptually close to the intersection operator on sets. The point operator combines two points in that the matching histories are actually 'melted' together; in the case the histories do not match, nothing is delivered. Furthermore, for example $C_{G_1G_2}(h1)$ is the set consisting of exactly those triple labels from h_1 that should match a triple label in h_2. Once these special labels are identified, the unification of h_1 and h_2 can be obtained by a bijection.

Finally, we are ready to define the semantics of any program $[P_1 :: S_1 || ... || P_n :: S_n]$ by providing the initial Kripke model and world. As to the initial world, all variables are set to zero, and the history is empty (ϵ). As to the model, process i considers possible all worlds in which its own variables have the initial value (i.e. zero) and the restriction of the history to i is the empty history ϵ.

Definition 3.5 Let $\sigma_0 = (\overline{\sigma}_0, e(\emptyset))$, where for all variables x_i holds that $\overline{\sigma}_0(x_i) = 0$. Define for all $j \leq n$: $V_j^0 = \{\langle \sigma, h \rangle \mid \sigma(x_i) = 0 \text{ for all } x_i \in Var(S_j) \wedge h \restriction j = \epsilon\}$. Then, the *initial Kripke model* is defined by

$$\mathcal{M}_0 = (\mathcal{S} \times \mathcal{H}, \pi, V_1^0, ..., V_n^0)$$

Definition 3.6 Now, for any program PR we define

$$[\![PR]\!] = [\![PR]\!](\mathcal{M}_0, \langle \sigma_0, \epsilon \rangle)$$

Note that the above results in a non-interleaved semantics for our language in contrast to the semantics which was obtained in [FLP84].

The semantics of programs as given above in terms of models $\mathcal{M} = (\mathcal{S} \times \mathcal{H}, \pi, V_1, ..., V_n)$, in which views V_i are modified can also be put in terms of the regular notion of Kripke models of type $(\mathcal{S} \times \mathcal{H}, \pi, R_1, ..., R_n)$ in which the accessibility relations R_i are modified, as follows. In the above semantics it is stated how a point $\langle \sigma, h \rangle$ together with its view V_i is transformed by the execution of a statement. This view V_i is, in fact, the R_i-equivalence class of the point $\langle \sigma, h \rangle$. Thus, the above semantics determine how points together with their R_i-equivalence classes are modified by the performance of statements. By varying the points over the whole of $\mathcal{S} \times \mathcal{H}$ we obtain how all equivalence classes and hence the relation R_i is transformed. So, we can also give a semantics in terms of the transformation of Kripke models $(\mathcal{S} \times \mathcal{H}, \pi, R_1, ..., R_n)$. (Note that, by the pointwise definition of the transformation of views (or sets of points in general), points that are R_i-equivalent, i.e. are in the same view V_i, transform to points that are R_i-equivalent again.) By viewing the semantics above as transformers of regular Kripke models we can apply the general theory of the previous subsections to this special case. In particular, we have that the parallel execution of matching communication commands, which is defined above as an intersection of views, can be treated as an intersection of accessibility relations on (regular) Kripke models. This will enable us to connect the parallel execution of commands to the notion of distributed knowledge, as we shall do below.

3.5 Syntax of Assertions

In this section, we define our language of assertions. Firstly we define two classes of expressions, the class *expr* of ordinary expressions and the class *hexpr* of history expressions:

$$e :: x_i \mid \alpha \mid val(he[l]) \mid z \mid e_1 + e_2 \mid ...$$

thus, expressions consist of a variable, a value, a value derived from a history expression (this is done by looking up in he an entry $< \alpha, i_k, j_{k'} >$ where $l = k$ or $l = k'$), a logical variable, and expressions built up from other expressions by means of several operators which we will not deal with in detail.

$$he :: l(\in \Lambda) \mid hist \mid he_1 \cdot he_2 \mid he \restriction i$$

which denote simple label, current history, concatenation of histories and projection of a history expression on process i respectively.

Now our class Assn of assertions is defined as follows:

$$\varphi :: e_1 = e_2 \mid he_1 = he_2 \mid \neg\varphi \mid \varphi_1 \wedge \varphi_2 \mid \exists z[\varphi] \mid K_i\varphi \mid K_G\varphi \mid \delta_i \mid \delta_G \mid send(\alpha, i_l, j_{l'})$$

Most assertions are obvious; as to the last three, δ_i and δ_G are assertions expressing the fact that process i, respectively group G has deadlocked, while $send(\alpha, i_l, j_{l'})$ asserts that the value α has been sent by process i to process j via the concerned labels l and l' (note the correspondence with the program label $(\alpha, i_l, j_{l'})$). As is the case with program labels, one of the labels l, l' may be absent expressing that the sender's/receiver's label is not known.

3.6 Semantics of Assertions

Firstly, we need two valuation functions that assign a meaning to expressions and history expressions in a point. Suppose a set $(\gamma \in)\Gamma$ of environments, giving meaning to the free logical variables of an expression.

Definition 3.7 *The valuation function $\mathcal{V} : expr \times \Gamma \times (\Sigma \times H) \rightarrow Val$ is defined as follows:*

$$\begin{aligned}
&\mathcal{V}(x_i)(\gamma)(\langle\sigma,h\rangle) = \sigma(x_i)\\
&\mathcal{V}(\alpha)(\gamma)(\langle\sigma,h\rangle) = \alpha\\
&\mathcal{V}(\gamma)(val(he[l]))(\langle\sigma,h\rangle) = \alpha \quad \text{if} \langle\alpha, i_k, j_{k'}\rangle \in \mathcal{V}_h(\gamma)(he)(\langle\sigma,h\rangle) \wedge l \in \{k,k'\}\\
&\qquad\qquad \textit{undefined otherwise}\\
&\mathcal{V}(z)(\gamma)(\langle\sigma,h\rangle) = \gamma(z)\\
&\mathcal{V}(e_1+e_2)(\gamma)(\langle\sigma,h\rangle) = \mathcal{V}(e_1)(\gamma)(\langle\sigma,h\rangle) + \mathcal{V}(e_2)(\gamma)(\langle\sigma,h\rangle)\\
&\vdots
\end{aligned}$$

The valuation function $\mathcal{V}_h : hexpr \times (\Sigma \times H) \rightarrow H$ is defined as follows:

$$\begin{aligned}
&\mathcal{V}_h(l)(\langle\sigma,h\rangle) = l\\
&\mathcal{V}_h(hist)(\langle\sigma,h\rangle) = h\\
&\mathcal{V}_h(he_1 \cdot he_2)(\langle\sigma,h\rangle) = \mathcal{V}_h(he_1)(\langle\sigma,h\rangle) \cdot \mathcal{V}_h(he_2)(\langle\sigma,h\rangle)\\
&\mathcal{V}_h(he \restriction i)(\langle\sigma,h\rangle) = \mathcal{V}_h(he)(\langle\sigma,h\rangle) \restriction i
\end{aligned}$$

Now we can define the interpretation function on assertions:

Definition 3.8 *The function $\mathcal{T}$: $\mathsf{Assn} \times \Gamma \times \mathcal{K} \times (\mathcal{S} \times \mathcal{H}) \rightarrow \{\mathbf{true}, \mathbf{false}\}$ is defined as follows:*

$$\begin{aligned}
&\mathcal{T}(e_1 = e_2)(\gamma)(\mathcal{M},\langle\sigma,h\rangle) = \mathcal{V}(e_1)(\gamma)(\langle\sigma,h\rangle) = \mathcal{V}(e_1)(\gamma)(\langle\sigma,h\rangle)\\
&\mathcal{T}(he_1 = he_2)(\gamma)(\mathcal{M},\langle\sigma,h\rangle) = \mathcal{V}_h(he_1)(\langle\sigma,h\rangle) = \mathcal{V}_h(he_1)(\langle\sigma,h\rangle)\\
&\mathcal{T}(\neg\varphi)(\gamma)(\mathcal{M},\langle\sigma,h\rangle) = \text{not } \mathcal{T}(\varphi)(\gamma)(\mathcal{M},\langle\sigma,h\rangle)\\
&\mathcal{T}(\varphi_1 \wedge \varphi_2)(\gamma)(\mathcal{M},\langle\sigma,h\rangle) = \mathcal{T}(\varphi_1)(\gamma)(\mathcal{M},\langle\sigma,h\rangle)\text{and } \mathcal{T}(\varphi_2)(\gamma)(\mathcal{M},\langle\sigma,h\rangle)\\
&\mathcal{T}(\exists z[\varphi])(\gamma)(\mathcal{M},\langle\sigma,h\rangle) = \text{there exists } \alpha \text{ such that } \mathcal{T}(\varphi)(\gamma[\alpha/z])(\mathcal{M},\langle\sigma,h\rangle)\\
&\mathcal{T}(K_i\varphi)(\gamma)(\mathcal{M},\langle\sigma,h\rangle) = \forall\langle\sigma',h'\rangle \in V_i[\mathcal{T}(\varphi)(\gamma)(\mathcal{M},\langle\sigma',h'\rangle)]\\
&\mathcal{T}(K_G\varphi)(\gamma)(\mathcal{M},\langle\sigma,h\rangle) = \forall\langle\sigma',h'\rangle \in \textstyle\bigcap_{j\in G} CC(V_j)[\mathcal{T}(\varphi)(\gamma)(\mathcal{M},\langle\sigma,h\rangle)]\\
&\mathcal{T}(\delta_i)(\gamma)(\mathcal{M},\langle\sigma,h\rangle) = \exists j[\rho_j^i? \in A \vee \rho_j^i! \in A] \text{ where } \sigma = (\overline{\sigma}, e(A))\\
&\mathcal{T}(\delta_G)(\gamma)(\mathcal{M},\langle\sigma,h\rangle) = \forall j \in G[\mathcal{T}(\delta_j)(\gamma)(\mathcal{M},\langle\sigma,h\rangle)]\\
&\mathcal{T}(send(t,i_l,j_m))(\gamma)(\mathcal{M},\langle\sigma,h\rangle) = \langle t_\sigma, i_l, j_m\rangle \in h\\
&\mathcal{T}(send(t,i,j_m))(\gamma)(\mathcal{M},\langle\sigma,h\rangle) = \langle t_\sigma, i, j_m\rangle \in h \vee \exists l[\langle t_\sigma, i_l, j_m\rangle \in h]\\
&\mathcal{T}(send(t,i_l,j))(\gamma)(\mathcal{M},\langle\sigma,h\rangle) = \langle t_\sigma, i_l, j\rangle \in h \vee \exists m[\langle t_\sigma, i_l, j_m\rangle \in h]
\end{aligned}$$

where the chaotic closure *operator CC is defined as follows:*

$CC'' : \Lambda \rightarrow \wp(\Lambda)$
$CC''(\langle\alpha, i_l, j\rangle) = \{\langle\alpha, i_l, j_m\rangle \mid m$ *is a (simple) program label from procees j* $\}$
$CC''(\langle\alpha, j, i_l\rangle) = \{\langle\alpha, j_m, i_l\rangle \mid m$ *is a (simple) program label from process i* $\}$

$CC' : \mathcal{S} \times \mathcal{H} \rightarrow \wp(\mathcal{S} \times \mathcal{H})$
$CC'(\langle\sigma,h\rangle) = \{\langle\sigma,h'\rangle \mid h'$ *is h where all labels of the form $\langle\alpha, i_l, j\rangle$ and $\langle\alpha, j, i_l\rangle$ respectively are replaced by an element from $CC''(\langle\alpha, i_l, j\rangle)$ and $CC''(\langle\alpha, j, i_l\rangle)$ respectively* $\}$

$CC : \wp(\mathcal{S} \times \mathcal{H}) \rightarrow \wp(\mathcal{S} \times \mathcal{H})$
$CC(V) = \bigcup_{\langle\sigma,h\rangle \in V} CC'(\langle\sigma,h\rangle)$

Remark 3.9 Note that there are three possible kinds of send, reflecting the possibilities of either label missing.

3.7 Reasoning about Programs

Definition 3.10 *For all closed* φ *we define*

$$(\mathcal{M}, \langle\sigma,h\rangle) \models \varphi \Leftrightarrow \mathcal{T}(\varphi)(\mathcal{M}, \langle\sigma,h\rangle)$$

Definition 3.11

$$\models \{\varphi\}S\{\psi\} \Leftrightarrow \forall(\mathcal{M},\langle\sigma,h\rangle)[(\mathcal{M},\langle\sigma,h\rangle) \models \varphi \Rightarrow [S](\mathcal{M},\langle\sigma,h\rangle) \models \psi]$$

Now we will state and prove some rules which are valid and can be used to establish among others a proof rule concerning communication.

The first rule states that knowledge of one of the subprocesses implies knowledge of the component process:

$$K_i\varphi \rightarrow K_G\varphi \quad (i \in G)$$

(Note that this is A6 of theorem 2.4(4))

Theorem 3.12 *For arbitrary* $\langle\sigma,h\rangle)$, *let* $[P_i :: S_i](\mathcal{M},\langle\sigma,h\rangle) = (\mathcal{M}',\langle\sigma',h'\rangle)$, *and let* $[P_i :: S_i \| P_j :: S_j](\mathcal{M},\langle\sigma,h\rangle) = (\mathcal{M}'',\langle\sigma'',h''\rangle)$. *Then,* $\langle\sigma',h'\rangle$ *and* $\langle\sigma'',h''\rangle$ *are i-view-equivalent.*

proof Trivial, see definitions.

Hence, we have a rule expressing persistence of local knowledge:

$$\frac{\{p\}P_i :: S_i\{K_i\varphi\}}{\{p\}P_1 :: S_1\|P_2 :: S_2\{K_i\varphi\}}(i = 1,2)$$

proof Assume $\models \{p\}P_i :: S_i\{K_i\varphi\}$. Then $\forall(\mathcal{M},\langle\sigma,h\rangle)[(\mathcal{M},\langle\sigma,h\rangle) \models p \Rightarrow [P_i :: S_i](\mathcal{M},\langle\sigma,h\rangle) \models K_i\varphi]$, hence by theorem 4.1 $\forall(\mathcal{M},\langle\sigma,h\rangle)[(\mathcal{M},\langle\sigma,h\rangle) \models p \Rightarrow [P_1 :: S_1\|P_2 :: S_2](\mathcal{M},\langle\sigma,h\rangle) \models K_i\varphi]$ which is equivalent to $\{p\}P_1 :: S_1\|P_2 :: S_2\{K_i\varphi\}$

Next, we have two rules concerning processes in isolation:

$$\{\textbf{true}\}P_i :: l : P_j?x\{K_i(\neg\delta_i \rightarrow \exists\alpha[x = \alpha \wedge send(\alpha, j, i_l)])\}$$

$$\{\textbf{true}\}P_j :: m : P_i!t\{K_j(\neg\delta_j \rightarrow send(t, j_m, i))\}$$

The first rule expresses that after the statement P_i, process i knows that if it does not deadlock, it has received a certain value.

The second rule expresses that after P_j, process j knows that if it does not deadlock, the value of term t has been sent to process i.

Furthermore, we have a rule expressing that after the execution of a matching communication statement starting from a state in which neither i nor j is in deadlock, it is group knowledge of the processes i and j that deadlock is not at hand, and by consequence, a some value has been sent:

$$\{\neg\delta_i \wedge \neg\delta_j\}P_i :: l : P_j?x \| P_j :: m : P_i!t\{K_{\{i,j\}}(\neg\delta_i \wedge \neg\delta_j \wedge \exists\beta[send(\beta, j_m, i_l)])\} \quad (*)$$

Now we are able to combine these last two rules with the first, as follows (we use the abbreviations $\varphi = (\exists\alpha[x = \alpha \wedge send(\alpha, j, i_l)])$ and $\psi = (send(t, j_m, i))$):

$$\{\neg\delta_i \wedge \neg\delta_j\}P_i :: l : P_j?x \| P_j :: m : P_i!t\{(K_i(\neg\delta_i \rightarrow \varphi)) \wedge (K_j(\neg\delta_j \rightarrow \psi))\}$$

$\Longrightarrow$

$$\{\neg\delta_i \wedge \neg\delta_j\}P_i :: l : P_j?x \| P_j :: m : P_i!t\{K_{\{i,j\}}((\neg\delta_i \rightarrow \varphi) \wedge (\neg\delta_j \rightarrow \psi))\}$$

$\Longrightarrow$

$$\{\neg\delta_i \wedge \neg\delta_j\}P_i :: l : P_j?x \| P_j :: m : P_i!t\{K_{\{i,j\}}((\neg\delta_i \wedge \neg\delta_j) \rightarrow (\varphi \wedge \psi))\}$$

$\Longrightarrow$ (using the fact that $K_{\{i,j\}}(\neg\delta_i \wedge \neg\delta_j)$)

$$\{\neg\delta_i \wedge \neg\delta_j\}P_i :: l : P_j?x \| P_j :: m : P_i!t\{K_{\{i,j\}}(\varphi \wedge \psi)\}$$

$\Longrightarrow$ (see below)

$$\{\neg\delta_i \wedge \neg\delta_j\}P_i :: l : P_j?x \| P_j :: m : P_i!t\{K_{\{i,j\}}(x = t)\}$$

The last step is justified by using three natural constraints, viz. the constraint of uniqueness of message, sender and receiver.

As to the first, this can be formalized as follows:

$$send(\alpha, i_l, j_m) \wedge send(\beta, i_l, j_m) \Rightarrow \alpha = \beta$$

Uniqueness of sender is described by

$$send(\alpha, i_x, j_m) \wedge send(\beta, i_y, j_m) \Rightarrow x = y$$

The constraint of uniqueness of receiver (no broadcast) is captured by

$$send(\alpha, i_l, j_x) \wedge send(\beta, i_l, j_y) \Rightarrow x = y$$

Finally, we give the derivation which justifies the last step. We have φ, ψ and(*):

$\exists\alpha[x = \alpha \wedge send(\alpha, j, i_l)]$ (1)

$send(t, j_m, i)$ (2)

$\exists\beta[send(\beta, j_m, i_l)]$ (3)

By uniqueness of sender, (1) and (3) we have

$\exists\alpha[x = \alpha \wedge send(\alpha, j_m, i_l)]$ (4)

By uniqueness of receiver, (2) and (3) we have

$send(t, j_m, i_l)$ (5)

We then can conclude by uniqueness of message, (4) and (5)

$\alpha = t$, and hence $x = t$

Thus we have proven $(\varphi \wedge \psi) \rightarrow x = t$. Now we use the following valid rule of epistemic logic:

$$((K_G\varphi) \wedge (\varphi \rightarrow \psi)) \rightarrow K_G\psi$$

which is a variant of $A1$ from item 2 from theorem 1.2, to derive from $K_{\{i,j\}}(\varphi \wedge \psi)$ that $K_{\{i,j\}}(x = t)$

Because, according to section 3.4 the semantics of a program $[P_i :: S_i || P_j :: S_j]$ is the intersection of the semantics of the individual processes (disregarding deadlock), $K_{\{i,j\}}\varphi$ is related to the semantics of $[P_i :: S_i || P_j :: S_j]$ because it is defined as the modal operator based on the relation which is the intersection of the individual relations on which K_i and K_j are based.

4 Conclusion

Knowledge seems to be a natural notion when reasoning about parallel programs. In the literature references to epistemic notions, such as "process i knows formula φ", are mostly implicit or at best used in the informal explanations of formal definitions.

In this paper we have made a first attempt to make the use of epistemic notions explicit by introducing modal operators K_i and K_G into the language with an epistemic interpretation. First we considered the notion of knowledge in a concurrent environment more in general, and then we focused on the case study of reasoning about CSP-like programs. This choice must be viewed as a kind of test case of how epistemic notions work out in a concrete and relatively simple setting. We plan to investigate more involved and interesting settings as well, such as object-oriented languages, which seem to fit the idea of objects as agents rather well. Also, the issue of a complete calculus, even for the simple CSP case, has yet to be addressed.

Besides, looking at more interesting programming languages also the incorporation of more expressive assertion languages (e.g. involving temporal operators, cf. [LMRT90]) may be of interest. A further interesting issue is that of compositionality and modularity of verification methods. We feel that the introduction of epistemic notions involve a natural kind of compositionality in the sense that the operators K_i and K_G seem to provide means to introduce assertions known only to the local processes (or groups of processes). We intend to compare this with recent advanced (non-epistemic) compositional methods of program verification [Zwi88].

References

[AFdR80] K.R. Apt, N. Francez, and W.P. de Roever. A proof system for communicating sequential processes. *ACM-TOPLAS*, 2(3), 1980.

[Ame89] P.H.M. America. Issues in the design of a parallel object-oriented language. *Formal Aspects of Computing*, 1(4), 1989.

[Ben83] J.F.A.K. van Benthem. *Modal Logic and Classical Logic*. Bibliopolis, Naples, 1983.

[BRR89] J.W. de Bakker, W.-P. de Roever, and G. Rozenberg, editors. *Linear Time, Branching Time and Partial Order in Logics and Models for Concurrency*. Springer-Verlag, 1989. LNCS 354.

[FH88] R.F. Fagin and J.Y. Halpern. Belief, awareness, and limited reasoning. *Artificial Intelligence*, 34:39–76, 1988.

[FHV88] R. Fagin, J.Y. Halpern, and M.Y. Vardi. What can machines know? on the properties of knowledge in distributed systems. Research Report RJ 6250, IBM, 1988. to appear in JACM.

[FLP84] N. Francez, D. Lehmann, and A. Pnueli. A linear-history semantics for languages for distributed programming. *Theoretical Computer Science*, 32:25–46, 1984.

[Gam91] L.T.F. Gamut. *Logic, Language and Meaning*, volume II, Intensional Logic and Logical Grammar. Univerity of Chicago Press, Chicago, 1991.

[Hin62] J. Hintikka. *Knowledge and Belief.* Cornell University Press, Ithaca, NY, 1962.

[HK90] Z. Huang and K. Kwast. Awareness, negation and logical omniscience. In J. van Eijck, editor, *Logics in AI*, number 478 in Lecture Notes in Artificial Intelligence, pages 282–301. Springer, 1990.

[HM85] J.Y. Halpern and Y.O. Moses. A guide to the modal logics of knowledge and belief. In *Proceedings IJCAI-85*, pages 480–490, Los Angeles, CA, 1985.

[HM88] W. van der Hoek and J.-J.Ch. Meyer. Possible logics for belief. Technical Report IR-170, Free University of Amsterdam, 1988. to appear in Logique et Analyse.

[HM90] J.Y. Halpern and Y.O. Moses. Knowledge and common knowledge in a distributed environment. *Journal of the ACM*, 37(3):549–587, 1990.

[HM91] M. van Hulst and J.-J.Ch. Meyer. A taxonomy of knowledge in distribitud systems. Technical Report 91-23, Nijmegen University, The Netherlands, 1991. to appear in Proc of Comp Sc. in the Netherlands, 1992.

[HM92] W. van der Hoek and J.-J.Ch. Meyer. Making some issues of implicit knowledge explicit. *The International Jounal of Foundations of Computer Science*, 3(2):193–223, 1992.

[Hoa78] C.A.R. Hoare. Communicating sequential processes. *Communications of the ACM*, 21(8):666–677, 1978.

[Hoe90] W. van der Hoek. Systems for knowledge and beliefs. In J. van Eijck, editor, *Logics in AI*, number 478 in Lecture Notes in Artificial Intelligence, pages 267–281. Springer, 1990. extended version to appear in the Journal of Logic and Computation.

[HZ87] J.Y. Halpern and L.D. Zuck. A little knowledge goes a long way: Simple knowledge-based derivations and correctness proofs for a family of protocols. In *Proc. of 6th PODC*, pages 269–280, 1987.

[LMRT90] K. Lodaya, M. Mukund, R Ramanujam, and P. S. Thiagarajan. Models and logics for true concurrency. Technical Report TCS-90-3, SPIC Science Foundation, september 1990.

[MdV89] J.-J.Ch. Meyer and E.P. de Vink. Pomset semantics for "true" concurrency with synchronization and recursion. In *Proc. MFCS'89*, number 379 in LNCS, 1989.

[MHV91a] J.-J.Ch. Meyer, W. van der Hoek, and G.A.W. Vreeswijk. Epistemic logic for computer science: A tutorial. *EATCS bulletin*, 44:242–270, 1991. (part I).

[MHV91b] J.-J.Ch. Meyer, W. van der Hoek, and G.A.W. Vreeswijk. Epistemic logic for computer science: A tutorial. *EATCS bulletin*, 45:256–287, 1991. (part II).

[Zwi88] J. Zwiers. *Compositionality, Concurrency and Partial Correctness.* PhD thesis, Technical University Eindhoven, 1988.

A Fully Abstract Model for a Nonuniform Concurrent Language with Parameterization and Locality

Eiichi Horita
NTT Software Laboratories,
3-9-11 Midori-Cho, Musashino-Shi, Tokyo 180, Japan

ABSTRACT. Full abstraction of a denotational model w.r.t. operational ones for a concurrent language $\mathcal{L}$ is investigated. The language is *nonuniform* in that the meaning of atomic statements generally depends on the current state; it has *parameterization* with *channel-* and *value-parameters* and *locality* in the form of *local variables* and *local channels*, in addition to more conventional constructs: *value assignments* to variables, *parallel composition* with CSP/CCS-like communication, *nondeterministic choice*, and *recursion*. First two operational models $\mathcal{O}_L$ and $\mathcal{O}_L^*$ for $\mathcal{L}$ are introduced in terms of a Plotkin-style transition system. Both models are *linear* in that they map each statement to the set of its possible execution paths of a certain kind; the second model $\mathcal{O}_L^*$ is more abstract than the first one in that $\mathcal{O}_L^*$ ignores states while $\mathcal{O}_L$ involves them. Then a denotational model $\mathcal{D}$ is defined compositionally using interpreted operations of the language, with meanings of recursive programs as fixed points in an appropriate complete metric space. The the *full abstraction* of $\mathcal{D}$ w.r.t. $\mathcal{O}_L$ and $\mathcal{O}_L^*$ is established. That is, it is shown for $\mathcal{O} = \mathcal{O}_L, \mathcal{O}_L^*$ that $\mathcal{D}$ is most abstract of those models $\mathcal{C}$ which are compositional and more distinctive than $\mathcal{O}$.

Keywords: domain equations, metric spaces, concurrency, imperative languages, denotational semantics, operational semantics, correctness, full abstraction, linear time, branching time, parameterization, local variables, local channels.

CONTENTS

0 Introduction

We investigate full abstraction of a denotational model w.r.t. operational ones for a concurrent language $\mathcal{L}$. The language is *nonuniform* in that the meaning of atomic statements generally depends on the current state; it has *parameterization* with *channel-* and *value-parameters* and *locality* in the form of *local variables* and *local channels*, in addition to more conventional constructs *value assignments to variables*, *parallel composition with CSP/CCS-like communication*, *nondeterministic choice*, and *recursion*.

First, two operational models $\mathcal{O}_L$ and $\mathcal{O}_L^*$ for $\mathcal{L}$ are introduced in terms of a Plotkin-style transition system ([Plo 81]). Both models are *linear* in that they map each statement to the set of its possible execution paths of a certain kind; the second model $\mathcal{O}_L^*$ is more abstract than the first one in that $\mathcal{O}_L^*$ ignores states while $\mathcal{O}_L$ involves them. Then, a denotational model $\mathcal{D}$ is defined as an extension of the model $\mathcal{D}'$ defined in [HBR 90] for a sublanguage $\mathcal{L}'$ (of $\mathcal{L}$) without parameterization and locality.

In [HBR 90]), the authors defined the model $\mathcal{D}'$ compositionally using interpreted operations of the language, with meanings of recursive programs as fixed points in an appropriate complete metric space, and established the full abstraction of $\mathcal{D}'$ w.r.t. $\mathcal{O}_L$. (The work [HBR 90], in turn, was inspired by earlier ones [BKO 88] and [Rut 89] treating a similar full abstraction problem for a uniform concurrent language.) The present paper extends this result to the language $\mathcal{L}$ with parameterization and locality. Namely, the model $\mathcal{D}$ for $\mathcal{L}$ is defined as an extension of $\mathcal{D}'$ so that the extended model $\mathcal{D}$ is still fully abstract w.r.t. $\mathcal{O}_L$. From this, the full abstraction of $\mathcal{D}$ w.r.t. $\mathcal{O}_L^*$ is also obtained. (The *full abstraction problem* for programming languages was first raised by Milner in [Mil 73]; in general, a model $\tilde{\mathcal{D}}$ for a language $\tilde{\mathcal{L}}$ is called *fully abstract* w.r.t. another model $\tilde{\mathcal{O}}$ if $\tilde{\mathcal{D}}$ is most abstract of those models $\mathcal{C}$ which are *compositional* and more distinctive than $\tilde{\mathcal{O}}$.)

Several mathematical preliminaries are given in § 1; the main body of the present paper consists of §§ 2 to 6.

In § 2 we introduce the language $\mathcal{L}$, which is the result of extending the language $\mathcal{L}'$ treated in [HBR 90] so as to include parameterization and locality. A major motive for the extension is our desire to enhance the *expressive power* of $\mathcal{L}'$ from the viewpoint of *software development*, rather than from that of computability, preserving the desirable properties of its semantics such as *full abstraction*. The new features are important from the viewpoint of *software development*: Parameterization is useful in describing *abstract* programs which can be instantiated with particular parameters suitable for a particular situation; locality is useful in *modular* development of software, where the interaction between two modules should be minimized.

There are two directions for extending a *pure language* like pure CCS so as to include value-passing: One is to define an *applicative language* based on the pure language introducing *parameterization*; the other is to define a *nonuniform language* introducing *individual variables* and *value assignment* to the variables. In many of the literature, only one of these directions is adopted; e.g., the former is adopted in [HI 90], and the latter in [HBR 90]. From a practical point of view, however, both directions are useful; actually many of practical languages, such as Ada, C, and Common Lisp, have both *individual variables* and *parameterization*. We design our language $\mathcal{L}$ so as to include both features. The language $\mathcal{L}$ is obtained by extending a base language, a subset of pure CCS, in the above two directions, in two stages: First, the base language is extended to a *nonuniform* language, which is the one treated in [HBR 90]; then the resulting nonuniform language is extended to an *applicative nonuniform* language, which we name $\mathcal{L}$.

In § 3, three operational models $\mathcal{O}_L$, $\mathcal{O}_L^*$, and $\mathcal{O}_F$ for $\mathcal{L}$ are introduced in terms of a Plotkin-style transition system ([Plo 81]). The first two models $\mathcal{O}_L$ and $\mathcal{O}_L^*$ are *linear* in the sense explained above; the third model $\mathcal{O}_F$ is a variant of the *failures model* which was first introduced in [BHR 84]. The last model is shown, in the following sections, to be equivalent to the denotational model $\mathcal{D}$.

In § 4, the denotational model $\mathcal{D}$ is defined compositionally using semantic operations which are interpretations of the syntactic constructs of $\mathcal{L}$, with meanings of recursive programs as fixed points in an appropriate complete metric space.

Then, in § 5, the semantic equivalence between $\mathcal{O}_F$ and $\mathcal{D}$ is established, by showing that $\mathcal{O}_F$ is compositional w.r.t. all semantic operations of $\mathcal{L}$. From a technical point of view, the *compositionality result* is the *key* of the present paper; from this the semantic equivalence follows immediately, and the full abstraction results in § 6 follows from this equivalence and the corresponding results in [HBR 90] and [Hor 92a].

Finally in § 7, we give some remarks on related work and directions for future study.

The Appendices include two mathematical definitions and description examples in $\mathcal{L}$.

1 Mathematical Preliminaries

As mathematical domains for our operational and denotational models, we will use *complete metric spaces* composed of (sets of) *sequences*. In this section, we present several standard notions on complete metric spaces and domains of (sets of) sequences.

First, we assume the notions of *metric space*, *ultra-metric space*, *complete metric space*, *continuous function*, *closed set*, *contraction*, *nonexpansive mapping*, and *isometry* to be known. The fact that *a contraction from a complete metric space to itself has a unique fixed point*, known as Banach's Theorem, is conveniently used. (For the notions and fact above, the reader might consult [Dug 66] or [Eng 77].)

Throughout the present paper, the phrase "let $(x, y, \ldots \in)$ X be $\cdots$" is used for introducing a set X ranged over by typical elements $x, y, \ldots$; in addition, we use the following notation:

Notation 1 (*Sets and Functions*) Let X, Y be sets. **(1)** The usual λ-notation is used for denoting functions: For a variable x, and an expression $E(x)$, the expression $(\lambda x \in X.\ E(x))$ denotes the function which maps $x \in X$ to $E(x)$. We sometimes write $(E(x))_{x \in X}$ for $(\lambda x \in X.\ E(x))$. **(2)** The cardinality of X is denoted by $\sharp(X)$. The set of *nonempty* subsets and the set of *finite* subsets of X are denoted by $\wp_+(X)$ and $\wp_f(X)$, respectively. The set of functions (resp. partial functions) from X to Y is denoted by $(X \to Y)$ or by Y^X (resp. by $(X \hookrightarrow Y)$). The set of natural numbers is denoted by ω, and each number $n \in \omega$ is identified with the set $\{i \in \omega : 0 \leq i < n\}$ as usual in set theory. For $n \in \omega$, let $\bar{n} = \{m \in \omega : 1 \leq m \leq n\}$. For $f \in (X \to Y)$ and a set Z, let $f \restriction Z$ denote the *restriction* of f to Z, i.e., let $f \restriction Z = (\lambda x \in \mathrm{dom}(f) \cap Z.\ f(x))$. **(3)** Let M be a metric space. We denote by $\wp_{cl}(M)$ (resp. by $\wp_{nc}(M)$) the set of *closed* subsets (resp. *nonempty closed* subsets) of M. For $N \subseteq M$, the *closure* of N is denoted by N^{cls}. ∎

Notation 2 (*Sequences*) Let A be a set. **(1)** The empty sequence is denoted by ϵ. The sequence consisting of $a_0, \ldots, a_{n-1} \in A$ is denoted by $(a_0, \ldots, a_{n-1})$. **(2)** The set of finite sequences of elements of A is denoted by $A^{<\omega}$, and let $A^+ = A^{<\omega} \setminus \{\epsilon\}$. The set of finite or infinite (with length ω) of sequences of elements of A is denoted by $A^{\leq\omega}$. For $a \in A$, we sometimes write simply a instead of (a) to denote the sequence consisting only of a. **(3)** Each sequence $w \in A^{\leq\omega}$ is regarded as a function whose domain is a member of $\omega \cup \{\omega\}$. Thus the length of w is $\text{dom}(w)$; referring to its length as $\text{lgt}(w)$, one has $w = (w(i))_{i\in\text{lgt}(w)} = (\lambda i \in \text{lgt}(w).\ w(i))$, and $\text{ran}(w) = \{w(i)\}_{i\in\text{lgt}(w)}$. **(4)** For $w_1 \in A^{<\omega}$, $w_2 \in A^{\leq\omega}$, let $w_1 \cdot w_2$ denote the *concatenation* of w_1 and w_2. Also for $p_1 \subseteq A^{<\omega}$, $p_2 \subseteq A^{\leq\omega}$, let $p_1 \cdot p_2 = \{w_1 \cdot w_2 : w_1 \in p_1 \wedge w_2 \in p_2\}$. **(5)** For $n \in \omega$ and a sequence $w \in A^{\leq\omega}$, we call $w\restriction n$ the *truncation* of w at level n. For a set of sequences $p \subseteq A^{\leq\omega}$, let $p\restriction n = \{w\restriction n : w \in p\}$. **(6)** For $p \in \wp(A^{\leq\omega})$, and $w \in A^{<\omega}$, let $p[w] = \{w' \in A^{\leq\omega} : w \cdot w' \in p\}$. **(7)** An ordered *pair* $\langle a_0, a_1\rangle$ and a *triple* $\langle a_0, a_1, a_2\rangle$ $(= \langle a_0, \langle a_1, a_2\rangle\rangle)$ are distinguished from, but treated as sequences $(a_i)_{i\in n}$ with n being 2 and 3, respectively; for $n = 2, 3$ and $i \in n$, we sometimes write $\langle a_i\rangle_{i\in n}$ to denote $\langle a_0, \ldots, a_{n-1}\rangle$, and the i-th component of $t = \langle a_i\rangle_{i\in n}$ is denoted by $\pi_i^n(t)$. ∎

Notation 3 Let X, Y be sets. **(1)** For $n \in \omega$, we denote by $X^{\langle n\rangle}$ the set of sequences consisting of n distinct elements of X. **(2)** For $n \in \omega$, $\vec{x} \in X^{\langle n\rangle}$, $\vec{y} \in Y^{\langle n\rangle}$, we denote by $\vec{y}/\vec{x}$ the mapping $\{\langle\vec{x}(i), \vec{y}(i)\rangle : i \in n\}$. In particular, for $x \in X$ and $y \in Y$, $y/x = \{\langle x, y\rangle\}$. **(3)** For $f, g \in (X \hookrightarrow Y)$, we denote by $f[g]$ the result of overlaying f with g, i.e., $f[g] = (f\restriction(\text{dom}(f) \setminus \text{dom}(g))) \cup g$. ∎

We use the following operations on metric spaces. (In our definition the distance between two elements of a metric space is always bounded by 1.)

Definition 1 (*Operations on Metric Spaces*) Let $\langle M, d\rangle, \langle M_1, d_1\rangle, \ldots, \langle M_n, d_n\rangle$ be metric spaces. **(1)** Let $M_1 \uplus \cdots \uplus M_n$ denote the *disjoint union* of $M_1, \ldots, M_n$, which can be defined as $\bigcup_{j\in\bar{n}}[\{j\} \times M_j]$. A metric d_U on $M_1 \uplus \cdots \uplus M_n$ is defined as follows: For $\langle i, x\rangle, \langle j, y\rangle \in M_1 \uplus \cdots \uplus M_n$, $d_U(\langle i, x\rangle, \langle j, y\rangle) = d_i(x, y)$ if $i = j$; otherwise $d_U(\langle i, x\rangle, \langle j, y\rangle) = 1$. **(2)** A metric d_P on the Cartesian product $M_1 \times \cdots \times M_n$ is defined as follows: For $\langle x_1, \ldots, x_n\rangle, \langle y_1, \ldots, y_n\rangle \in M_1 \times \cdots \times M_n$, $d_P(\langle x_1, \ldots, x_n\rangle, \langle y_1, \ldots, y_n\rangle) = \max_{j\in\bar{n}}[d_j(x_j, y_j)]$. **(3)** A metric d_H on $\wp_{cl}(M)$, called the *Hausdorff distance*, is defined as follows: For $X, Y \in \wp_{cl}(M)$, $d_H(X, Y) = \max\{\sup_{x\in X}[d_*(x, Y)], \sup_{y\in Y}[d_*(y, X)]\}$, where $d_*(x, Z) = \inf_{z\in Z}[d(x, z)]$ for $Z \subseteq M$, $x \in X$. (We use the convention that $\sup\emptyset = 0$ and $\inf\emptyset = 1$.) The space $\wp_{nc}(M)$ is supplied with a metric by taking the restriction of d_H to it. ∎

2 A Nonuniform Concurrent Language $\mathcal{L}$

In this section, a nonuniform concurrent language $\mathcal{L}$ is introduced. It is an extension of the language $\mathcal{L}'$ treated in [HBR 90]. The language $\mathcal{L}'$ has value assignments to individual variables, parallel composition with CSP/CCS-like communication, nondeterministic choice, and recursion. In addition to these constructs, $\mathcal{L}$ has *parameterization* with *channel-* and *value-parameters*, and *locality* in the form of *local variables* and *local channels*.

As a preliminary to the definition of $\mathcal{L}$, *value expressions* and *channel expressions* are defined with several related notions by:

Definition 2 (*Value Expressions and Channel Expressions*)

(1) First, the following sets are assumed to be given: **(i)** An infinite set $(\mathbf{c} \in)$ **Chan** of *channels*, **(ii)** A set $(v \in)$ **V** of values, **(iii)** A set $(x \in)$ IVar of *individual variables.* It is also assumed that **V** contains a distinguished element **nil** standing for the logical value *false*.[1] Further, we assume that **Chan** is partitioned into two disjoint sets $\mathbf{Chan}_0$ and $\mathbf{Chan}_1$ with $\mathbf{Chan}_1$ being infinite. (This assumption is made for convenience in semantic interpretation in §§ 3, 4 of local channels.) We fix an enumeration $(\mathbf{c}_n)_{n\in\omega}$ of $\mathbf{Chan}_1$ with $\mathbf{Chan}_1 = \{\mathbf{c}_n : n \in \omega\}$ and $\mathbf{c}_i \neq \mathbf{c}_j$ for distinct indexes i, j.

(2) Let $(\xi \in)$ $\mathcal{X}_\mathcal{V}$ and $(\eta \in)$ $\mathcal{X}_\mathcal{C}$ be the set of *value variables* and the set of *channel variables*, respectively. For $i \geq 1$, let us use variables $\vec{\eta}^{(i)}$ and $\vec{\xi}^{(i)}$ ranging over $(\mathcal{X}_\mathcal{V})^{(i)}$ and $(\mathcal{X}_\mathcal{V})^{(i)}$, respectively.
Note that elements of $\mathcal{X}_\mathcal{V}$ have very different nature from that of *individual variables* $x \in$ IVar. Individual variables are used to store values, while elments of $\mathcal{X}_\mathcal{V}$ are used as parameters, e.g., as ξ in "$(\lambda\xi.\ E)$".

(3) We assume a signature $\mathbf{Sig}_0 = \langle\{\mathcal{V},\mathcal{C}\}, \mathbf{Fun}_0\rangle$ in the sense of many-sorted algebra to be given, where $\mathcal{V}$ and $\mathcal{C}$ are sorts of *value expressions* and *channels expressions* respectively, and $\mathbf{Fun}_0$ is a set of function symbols, which is equipped with a mapping $\mathrm{type}_0(\cdot)$ assigning a type $(\in \{\mathcal{V},\mathcal{C}\}^{<\omega} \times \{\mathcal{V},\mathcal{C}\})$ to each function symbol. It is convenient, for later purposes, to postulate that $v \in \mathbf{Fun}_0$ and $x \in \mathbf{Fun}_0$ with $\mathrm{type}(v) = \mathrm{type}(x) = \langle\epsilon, \mathcal{V}\rangle$ for every $v \in \mathbf{V}$ and $x \in$ IVar, and $\mathbf{c} \in \mathbf{Fun}_0$ with $\mathrm{type}(v) = \langle\epsilon, \mathcal{C}\rangle$ for every $\mathbf{c} \in \mathbf{Chan}$. Moreover, we assume, for convenience in the definition of semantic models in §§ 3 and 4, that there is no function symbol (in $\mathbf{Fun}_0$) which has $\mathcal{C}$ as one of its argument types. Let $(E \in)$ $\tilde{\mathcal{E}}_\mathcal{V}$ and $(G \in)$ $\tilde{\mathcal{E}}_\mathcal{C}$ be the sets of terms generated by $\mathbf{Sig}_0$, $\mathcal{X}_\mathcal{V}$, $\mathcal{X}_\mathcal{C}$ of sort $\mathcal{V}$ and $\mathcal{C}$, respectively. Let $(e \in)$ $\mathcal{E}_\mathcal{V} = \{E \in \tilde{\mathcal{E}}_\mathcal{V} : \mathrm{FV}(E) = \emptyset\}$, where $\mathrm{FV}(E)$ is the set of elements of $\mathcal{X}_\mathcal{V} \cup \mathcal{X}_\mathcal{C}$ contained in E. Likewise, let $(g \in)$ $\mathcal{E}_\mathcal{C} = \{G \in \tilde{\mathcal{E}}_\mathcal{C} : \mathrm{FV}(G) = \emptyset\}$. We use variables $\vec{e}^{(i)}$ (resp. $\vec{g}^{(i)}$) ranging over $(\mathcal{E}_\mathcal{V})^i$ (resp. $(\mathcal{E}_\mathcal{C})^i$) for each $i \in \omega$. (One has $\mathbf{V}, \mathrm{IVar} \subseteq \mathcal{E}_\mathcal{V}$ and $\mathbf{Chan} \subseteq \mathcal{E}_\mathcal{C}$, because $\mathbf{V}, \mathrm{IVar} \subseteq \mathbf{Fun}_0$ and $\mathbf{Chan} \subseteq \mathbf{Fun}_0$.)

(4) Let the set Σ of *states* be defined by: $(\sigma \in)\ \Sigma = (\mathrm{IVar} \to \mathbf{V})$. For each $e \in \mathcal{E}_\mathcal{V}$ (resp. $g \in \mathcal{E}_\mathcal{C}$), an *evaluation function* $[\![e]\!](\cdot) : \Sigma \to \mathbf{V}$ (resp. $[\![g]\!](\cdot) : \Sigma \to \mathbf{Chan}$) is assumed to be given. We assume for each function symbol $F \in \mathbf{Fun}_0$ with $\mathrm{type}_0(F) \in \{\mathcal{V},\mathcal{C}\}^+ \times \{\mathcal{C}\}$ that $\mathrm{ran}([\![F(\cdots)]\!]) \subseteq \mathbf{Chan}_0$, for convenience in semantic interpretation of local channels.) ∎

By means of the sets $\tilde{\mathcal{E}}_\mathcal{V}$ and $\tilde{\mathcal{E}}_\mathcal{C}$, the language $\mathcal{L}$ is defined by:

Definition 3 (*Language $\mathcal{L}$*)

(1) First, let $(X^{(0,0)} \in)$ $\mathcal{X}_\mathcal{P}^{(0,0)}$ be the set of statement variables, and $(X^{(i,j)} \in)$ $\mathcal{X}_\mathcal{P}^{(i,j)}$ the set of *parameterized statement variables* with i channel-parameters and j value-

---

[1]It is possible to introduce *Boolean* expressions, instead of introducing the value **nil** to define conditional statements. The present approach of introducing **nil**, as in Lisp and the language C, is adopted for simplifying the semantic definitions in § 4.

parameters for $(i,j) \neq (0,0)$. In the sequel, we sometimes omit the superscript $^{(0,0)}$, and write X (resp. $\mathcal{X}_{\mathcal{P}}$) for $X^{(0,0)}$ (resp. $\mathcal{X}_{\mathcal{P}}^{(0,0)}$) for brevity. Also let $(Z \in)$ $\mathcal{X}_{\mathcal{P}}^{*} = \bigcup\{\mathcal{X}_{\mathcal{P}}^{(i,j)} : (i,j) \in \omega^2\}$.

(2) First, the language $(S \in)$ $\tilde{\mathcal{L}}$ *without guardedness condition* is defined simultaneously with the sets of *parameterized statements* $(S^{(i,j)} \in)$ $\tilde{\mathcal{L}}^{(i,j)}$ $((i,j) \neq (0,0))$ as follows:

(i)
$$S ::= X \,|\, \mathbf{0} \,|\, (\mathbf{asg}(x,E);S) \,|\, (\mathbf{out}(H,E);S) \,|\, (\mathbf{in}(H,x);S) \,|\, (\mathbf{in}'(H);S^{(0,1)}) \,|\, (S_1 + S_2) \,|\, (S_1 \parallel S_2) \,|\, \partial_C(S) \,|\, \mathbf{if}(E,S_1,S_2) \,|\, \mathbf{let}(x,E,S) \,|\, \mathbf{LC}(S^{(1,0)}) \,|\, (\mu X.\ S) \,|\, S^{(i,j)}(\vec{H}^{(i)} \cdot \vec{E}^{(j)}),$$

where X and x range over $\mathcal{X}_{\mathcal{P}}$ and IVar, respectively; H and E range over $\tilde{\mathcal{E}}_C$ and $\tilde{\mathcal{E}}_V$, respectively; $\vec{H}^{(i)}$ and $\vec{E}^{(j)}$ range over $(\tilde{\mathcal{E}}_C)^i$ and $(\tilde{\mathcal{E}}_V)^j$, respectively; C ranges over $\wp(\mathbf{Chan})$.

Each construct above has the following intuitive meaning: **(a)** The constant $\mathbf{0}$ represents *inaction*; **(b)** $(\mathbf{asg}(x,E);S)$ represents an assignment $\mathbf{asg}(x,E)$ followed by S; **(c)** $(\mathbf{out}(H,E);S)$ represents an *output* of a value E to a channel H followed by S; **(d)** $(\mathbf{in}(H,x);S)$ represents an *input* (from a channel H) followed by S with the input value assigned to x; **(e)** $(\mathbf{in}'(H);S^{(0,1)})$ also represents an *input* (from a channel H) followed by the application of $S^{(0,1)}$ to the input value; **(f)** the operators $+$, $\parallel$, and $\partial_C(\cdot)$ represent *alternative choice*, *parallel composition*, and *action restriction*, respectively; **(g)** $\mathbf{if}(\cdot,\cdot,\cdot)$ is the usual conditional construct; **(h)** $\mathbf{let}(x,E,S)$ is a statement with a *local variable* x whose initial value is E; **(i)** $\mathbf{LC}(S^{(1,0)})$ is a statement with a *local channel*; **(j)** $(\mu X.\ S)$ represents a recursive statement, which intuitively stands for a solution to the equation $X = S$; **(k)** $S^{(i,j)}(\vec{H}^{(i)} \cdot \vec{E}^{(j)})$ is the *application* of a parameterized statement $S^{(i,j)}$ to actual arguments $\vec{H}^{(i)} \cdot \vec{E}^{(j)}$.

(ii) For each $(i,j) \neq (0,0)$,
$$S^{(i,j)} ::= X^{(i,j)} \,|\, (\lambda\vec{\eta}^{(i)} \cdot \vec{\xi}^{(j)}.\ S) \,|\, (\mu X^{(i,j)}.\ S^{(i,j)}),$$
where $X^{(i,j)}$ ranges over $\mathcal{X}_{\mathcal{P}}^{(i,j)}$, and we put $\vec{\eta}^{(0)} = \vec{\xi}^{(0)} = \epsilon$.

For notational convenience, let us set $\tilde{\mathcal{L}}^{(0,0)} = \tilde{\mathcal{L}}$, and let us use the variable $S^{(0,0)}$ ranging over $\tilde{\mathcal{L}}^{(0,0)}$; let $(\mathbf{S} \in)$ $\tilde{\mathcal{L}}^{*} = \bigcup\{\tilde{\mathcal{L}}^{(i,j)} : (i,j) \in \omega^2\}$.

(3) The constructs "$(\lambda\vec{\eta}^{(i)}.\vec{\xi}^{(j)}.\ \cdots)$", "$(\mu X.\ \cdots)$", "$(\mu X^{(i,j)}.\ \cdots)$" have the usual binding property. Let $(\zeta \in)$ $\mathcal{X}$ be the set of all variables, i.e., let $\mathcal{X} = \mathcal{X}_V \cup \mathcal{X}_C \cup \mathcal{X}_{\mathcal{P}}^{*}$. For $\mathbf{S} \in \tilde{\mathcal{L}}^{*}$, let FV($\mathbf{S}$) be the set of free variables in $\mathbf{S}$, i.e., the set of elements of $\mathcal{X}$ having a free occurrence in $\mathbf{S}$. For $(i,j) \in \omega^2$, the language $\mathcal{L}^{(i,j)}$ is defined to be the set of $\mathbf{S} \in \tilde{\mathcal{L}}^{(i,j)}$ satisfying the following *guardedness* condition:

For each subexpression $(\mu Z.\ \mathbf{S}')$ *of* $\mathbf{S}$*, each free occurrence of* Z *in* $\mathbf{S}'$ *occurs in a subexpression of* $\mathbf{S}'$ *of the form* $(\mathbf{asg}(x,E);\mathbf{S}'')$, $(\mathbf{out}(H,E);\mathbf{S}'')$, $(\mathbf{in}(H,x);\mathbf{S}'')$, *or* $(\mathbf{in}'(H);\mathbf{S}'')$. (1)

Let $\mathcal{L} = \mathcal{L}^{(0,0)}$, and $\mathcal{L}^{*} = \bigcup\{\mathcal{L}^{(i,j)} : (i,j) \in \omega^2\}$. (See the Appendix A for an inductive formulation of the guardedness condition and a more formal definition of $\mathcal{L}^{(i,j)}$ for $(i,j) \in \omega^2$.)

(4) For $\mathcal{Y} \subseteq \mathcal{X}$ and $\mathcal{L}' \subseteq \tilde{\mathcal{L}}^{*}$, let $\mathcal{L}'[\mathcal{Y}] = \{S \in \mathcal{L}' : \mathrm{FV}(S) \subseteq \mathcal{Y}\}$. We use the variable $s^{(i,j)}$ ranging over $\mathcal{L}^{(i,j)}[\emptyset]$ $((i,j) \in \omega^2)$, and the variable $\mathbf{s}$ (resp. s) ranging over $\mathcal{L}^{*}[\emptyset]$ (resp. $\mathcal{L}[\emptyset]$). ∎

For description examples in $\mathcal{L}$, see the Appendix C.

We also characterize the language $\mathcal{L}$ in another way: Along the lines of the standard typed λ-calculus (cf. [Mit 90]), we characterize $\tilde{\mathcal{L}}^{(i,j)}$ as the set of terms (of type (i,j)) generated by a *signature* **Sig** as follows ($(i,j) \in \omega^2$):

Definition 4 (*Signature* **Sig**) The signature **Sig** is defined by: $\mathbf{Sig} = \langle\{\mathcal{C}, \mathcal{V}, \mathcal{P}\}, \mathbf{Fun}\rangle$, where $\mathcal{C}$, $\mathcal{V}$, and $\mathcal{P}$ are the *base types* of *channels expressions*, *value expressions*, and *statements*, respectively, and **Fun** is a set function symbols which is equipped with a mapping type$(\cdot)$ assigning a type to each function symbol. The types $\mathcal{C}$, $\mathcal{V}$, and $\mathcal{P}$ correspond to the semantic domains $(h \in)$ $\mathbf{H}$, $(f \in)$ $\mathbf{F}$, and $(p \in)$ $\mathbf{P}$, respectively, where $\mathbf{H} = (\Sigma \to \mathbf{Chan})$, $\mathbf{F} = (\Sigma \to \mathbf{V})$, and $\mathbf{P}$ is the semantic domain for statements to be defined below. For $(i,j) \in \omega^2$, let $(p^{(i,j)} \in)$ $\mathbf{P}^{(i,j)} = (\mathbf{Chan}^i \cdot \mathbf{V}^j \to \mathbf{P})$. We identify $\mathbf{P}^{(0,0)}$ with $\mathbf{P}$, and let $(\mathrm{p} \in)$ $\mathbf{P}^* = \bigcup\{\mathbf{P}^{(i,j)} : (i,j) \in \omega^2\}$.

The set of types of **Sig** is $\{\mathcal{C}, \mathcal{V}\} \cup \{\mathcal{P}^{(i,j)} : (i,j) \in \omega^2\}$, where we identify $\mathcal{P}^{(i,j)}$ with $\mathcal{P}$ and $\mathcal{P}^{(i,j)}$ corresponds to the semantic domain $\mathbf{P}^{(i,j)}$ ($(i,j) \in \omega^2$). The type $\mathcal{P}^{(0,0)}$ is identified with $\mathcal{P}$. It is assumed that for each $F \in \mathbf{Fun}$, type$(F) = \langle \mathcal{C}^i \cdot \mathcal{V}^j \cdot \mathcal{P}^k \cdot (\mathcal{P}^{(0,1)})^\ell \cdot (\mathcal{P}^{(1,0)})^m, \mathcal{P}\rangle$ with $i,j,k,\ell,m \in \omega$. For $i,j,k,\ell,m \in \omega$, let

$$\mathbf{Fun}^{(i,j,k,\ell,m)} = \mathrm{type}^{-1}[\{\langle \mathcal{C}^i \cdot \mathcal{V}^j \cdot \mathcal{P}^k \cdot (\mathcal{P}^{(0,1)})^\ell \cdot (\mathcal{P}^{(1,0)})^m, \mathcal{P}\rangle\}].$$

We define **Fun** as follows: $\mathbf{Fun}^{(0,0,0,0,0)} = \{\mathbf{0}\}$; $\mathbf{Fun}^{(0,1,1,0,0)} = \{(\mathbf{asg}(x,\cdot);\cdot) : x \in \mathrm{IVar}\} \cup \{\mathbf{let}(x,\cdot,\cdot) : x \in \mathrm{IVar}\}$; $\mathbf{Fun}^{(1,1,1,0,0)} = \{(\mathbf{out}(\cdot,\cdot);\cdot)\}$; $\mathbf{Fun}^{(1,0,1,0,0)} = \{(\mathbf{in}(\cdot,x);\cdot) : x \in \mathcal{X}_{\mathcal{V}}\}$; $\mathbf{Fun}^{(0,0,1,0,0)} = \{\partial_C(\cdot) : C \subseteq \wp(\mathbf{Chan})\}$; $\mathbf{Fun}^{(1,0,0,1,0)} = \{(\mathbf{in}'(\cdot);\cdot)\}$; $\mathbf{Fun}^{(0,0,0,0,1)} = \{\mathbf{LC}(\cdot)\}$; $\mathbf{Fun}^{(0,0,2,0,0)} = \{+, \|\}$; $\mathbf{Fun}^{(0,1,2,0,0)} = \{\mathbf{if}(\cdot,\cdot,\cdot)\}$; $\mathbf{Fun}^{(i,j,k,\ell,m)} = \emptyset$ for the other indexes (i,j,k,ℓ,m). ∎

Having defined **Sig**, it is easy to check that the sets $\tilde{\mathcal{L}}^{(i,j)}$ can be characterized as the set of terms of type $\mathcal{P}^{(i,j)}$ generated by **Sig**, $\mathcal{X}$, $\tilde{\mathcal{E}}_{\mathcal{C}}$, and $\tilde{\mathcal{E}}_{\mathcal{V}}$ ($(i,j) \in \omega^2$). Thus the syntax of $\tilde{\mathcal{L}}^*$ fits into the framework of the typed λ-calculus. On the other hand, the semantics for it does not quite fit into the calculus because of its *nonuniform* nature, as we will see in the following two sections (see, e.g., Lemma 7 (5)).

Notation 4 The function type$(\cdot)$ is extended so that it is defined on $\tilde{\mathcal{E}}_{\mathcal{C}} \cup \tilde{\mathcal{E}}_{\mathcal{V}} \cup \tilde{\mathcal{L}}^*$ as usual. For $\phi \in (\mathcal{X} \hookrightarrow \tilde{\mathcal{E}}_{\mathcal{C}} \cup \tilde{\mathcal{E}}_{\mathcal{V}} \cup \tilde{\mathcal{L}}^*)$, we say ϕ respects the type iff $\forall \zeta \in \mathrm{dom}(\phi)[\ \mathrm{type}(\phi(\zeta)) = \mathrm{type}(\zeta)\ ]$. For $\mathbf{S} \in \tilde{\mathcal{L}}^*$ and a type respecting mapping $\phi \in (\mathcal{X} \hookrightarrow \tilde{\mathcal{L}}^*)$, we denote by $\mathbf{S}[\phi]$ the result of simultaneously replacing all free occurrences of ζ by $\phi(\zeta)$ $(\zeta \in \mathrm{dom}(\phi))$. ∎

3 Operational Models $\mathcal{O}_{\mathrm{L}}$, $\mathcal{O}^*_{\mathrm{L}}$, $\mathcal{O}_{\mathrm{F}}$ for $\mathcal{L}$

In this section, three operational models $\mathcal{O}_{\mathrm{L}}$, $\mathcal{O}^*_{\mathrm{L}}$, and $\mathcal{O}_{\mathrm{F}}$ for $\mathcal{L}$ are introduced in terms of a Plotkin-style transition system ([Plo 81]). The first two models $\mathcal{O}_{\mathrm{L}}$ and $\mathcal{O}^*_{\mathrm{L}}$ are *linear* in that both of them map each statement to the set of its possible execution paths of a certain kind; the second model $\mathcal{O}^*_{\mathrm{L}}$ is more abstract than the first one in that $\mathcal{O}^*_{\mathrm{L}}$ ignores states while $\mathcal{O}_{\mathrm{L}}$ involves them. The third model $\mathcal{O}_{\mathrm{F}}$ is a variant of the *failures model* which was first introduced in [BHR 84]. The last model is shown, in § 5, to be equivalent to a denotational model $\mathcal{D}_{\mathrm{F}}$ defined in § 4.

Definition 5 (*Actions and States*)

(1) For $C \subseteq \mathbf{Chan}$, let $C! = \{\mathbf{c}! : \mathbf{c} \in C\}$, $C? = \{\mathbf{c}? : \mathbf{c} \in C\}$, and $C!? = C! \cup C?$. Let $(\gamma \in)$ **C**, the set of *communication sorts*, be defined by: $\mathbf{C} = \mathbf{Chan}!?$. For $\gamma \in \mathbf{C}$, let $\bar{\gamma} = \mathbf{c}?$ if $\gamma = \mathbf{c}!$ for some $\mathbf{c} \in \mathbf{Chan}$; otherwise $\gamma = \mathbf{c}?$ for some $\mathbf{c} \in \mathbf{Chan}$, and let $\bar{\gamma} = \mathbf{c}!$. For $\Gamma \subseteq \mathbf{C}$, let $\bar{\Gamma} = \{\bar{\gamma} : \gamma \in \Gamma\}$.

(2) The set of *actions*, $(a \in)$ **A**, is given by $\mathbf{A} = (\mathbf{C} \times \mathbf{V}) \cup \{\tau\}$. In the sequel, let us use the variable c ranging over $\mathbf{C} \times \mathbf{V}$, the set of *communication actions*. For $c = \langle \gamma, v \rangle \in \mathbf{C} \times \mathbf{V}$, let $\bar{c} = \langle \bar{\gamma}, v \rangle$.

(3) Let $(A \in)$ **ASort**, the set of *action sorts*, be defined by: $\mathbf{ASort} = \mathbf{C} \cup \{\tau\}$.

(4) The function sort : $\mathbf{A} \to \mathbf{ASort}$ is defined as follows: For $a \in \mathbf{A}$,

$$\mathrm{sort}(a) = \begin{cases} \gamma & \text{if } \exists\gamma, \exists v[\, a = \langle \gamma, v \rangle \,], \\ a & \text{otherwise.} \end{cases}$$

(5) For $\gamma \in \mathbf{C}$, let $\mathrm{chan}(\gamma)$ be the unique $\mathbf{c} \in \mathbf{Chan}$ such that $\gamma = \mathbf{c}!$ or $\gamma = \mathbf{c}?$. ∎

As a preliminary to the definition of *transition relations*, the notion of *syntactic sort* is defined by:

Definition 6 (*Syntactical Sort*) For $\mathbf{S} \in \tilde{\mathcal{L}}^*$, the *syntactic sort* of **S**, written $\mathcal{S}(\mathbf{S})$, is the set of function symbols of sort $\mathcal{C}$ occurring in **S**. Formally, it is defined by induction on the structure of **S** as follows: (i) If $\mathbf{S} \in \mathcal{X}^*_{\mathcal{P}}$ or $\mathbf{S} \equiv \mathbf{0}$, then $\mathcal{S}(\mathbf{S}) = \emptyset$. (ii) If $\mathbf{S} \equiv (\mathbf{asg}(x, E); \mathbf{S}')$, $\mathbf{S} \equiv \mathbf{let}(x, E, \mathbf{S}')$, $\mathbf{S} \equiv \mathbf{LC}(\mathbf{S}')$, $\mathbf{S} \equiv (\mu Z.\ \mathbf{S}')$, $\mathbf{S} \equiv \mathbf{S}'(\vec{H} \cdot \vec{E})$, or $\mathbf{S} \equiv (\lambda\vec{\eta} \cdot \vec{\xi}.\ \mathbf{S}')$, then $\mathcal{S}(\mathbf{S}) = \mathcal{S}(\mathbf{S}')$. (iii) If $\mathbf{S} \equiv \partial_C(\mathbf{S}')$, then $\mathcal{S}(\mathbf{S}) = \mathcal{S}(\mathbf{S}') \setminus C$. (iv) If $\mathbf{S} \equiv (\mathbf{S}_1 + \mathbf{S}_2)$, $\mathbf{S} \equiv (\mathbf{S}_1 \parallel \mathbf{S}_2)$, $\mathbf{S} \equiv \mathbf{if}(E, \mathbf{S}_1, \mathbf{S}_2)$, then $\mathcal{S}(\mathbf{S}) = \mathcal{S}(\mathbf{S}_1) \cup \mathcal{S}(\mathbf{S}_2)$. (v) If $\mathbf{S} \equiv (\mathbf{out}(G, E); \mathbf{S}')$, $\mathbf{S} \equiv (\mathbf{in}(G, x); \mathbf{S}')$, or $\mathbf{S} \equiv (\mathbf{in}'(G); \mathbf{S}')$, then $\mathcal{S}(\mathbf{S}) = \mathcal{S}(\mathbf{S}') \cup \mathcal{S}(G)$. ∎

By definition, $\mathcal{S}(\mathbf{S})$ is finite for every $\mathbf{S} \in \tilde{\mathcal{L}}^*$.

Let us define the transition relations $\xrightarrow{a} \subseteq (\mathcal{L}[\emptyset] \times \Sigma) \times (\mathcal{L}[\emptyset] \times \Sigma)$ $(a \in \mathbf{A})$. For $s_1, s_2 \in \mathcal{L}[\emptyset]$, $\sigma_1, \sigma_2 \in \Sigma$, and $a \in \mathbf{A}$, we write $\langle s_1, \sigma_1 \rangle \xrightarrow{a} \langle s_2, \sigma_2 \rangle$ for $\langle \langle s_1, \sigma_1 \rangle, \langle s_2, \sigma_2 \rangle \rangle \in \xrightarrow{a}$, as usual. Whenever $\langle s, \sigma \rangle \xrightarrow{a} \langle s', \sigma' \rangle$, we call $\langle a, \langle s', \sigma' \rangle \rangle$ (resp. $\langle s', \sigma' \rangle$) an *immediate derivative* (resp. an immediate a-derivative) of $\langle s, \sigma \rangle$ as in [Mil 89]. For $\mathbf{c}!, \mathbf{c}? \in \mathbf{C}$ and $v \in \mathbf{V}$, we sometimes write $\mathbf{c}!v$ and $\mathbf{c}?v$ for $\langle \mathbf{c}!, v \rangle$ and $\langle \mathbf{c}?, v \rangle$, respectively.

Definition 7 (*Transition Relations* $\xrightarrow{a}$)

(1) $$\langle (\mathbf{asg}(x, e); s), \sigma \rangle \xrightarrow{\tau} \langle s, \sigma[[\![e]\!](\sigma)/x] \rangle.$$

(2) $$\langle (\mathbf{out}(g, e); s), \sigma \rangle \xrightarrow{\langle [\![g]\!](\sigma)!, [\![e]\!](\sigma) \rangle} \langle s, \sigma \rangle.$$

(3) For every $v \in \mathbf{V}$,

$$\langle (\mathbf{in}(g, x); s), \sigma \rangle \xrightarrow{\langle [\![g]\!](\sigma)?, v \rangle} \langle s, \sigma[v/x] \rangle,$$

where for the notation $\sigma[v/x]$ see Notation 3.

(4) For every $v \in \mathbf{V}$,

$$\langle (\mathbf{in}'(g); s^{(0,1)}), \sigma \rangle \xrightarrow{\langle [\![g]\!](\sigma)?, v \rangle} \langle s^{(0,1)}(v), \sigma \rangle.$$

(5)

$$\frac{\langle s_1, \sigma \rangle \xrightarrow{a} \langle s, \sigma' \rangle}{\begin{array}{c} \langle s_1 + s_2, \sigma \rangle \xrightarrow{a} \langle s, \sigma' \rangle \\ \langle s_2 + s_1, \sigma \rangle \xrightarrow{a} \langle s, \sigma' \rangle \end{array}}.$$

(6.1)

$$\frac{\langle s_1,\sigma\rangle \xrightarrow{a} \langle s,\sigma'\rangle}{\begin{array}{c}\langle s_1 \parallel s_2,\sigma\rangle \xrightarrow{a} \langle s \parallel s_2,\sigma'\rangle \\ \langle s_2 \parallel s_1,\sigma\rangle \xrightarrow{a} \langle s_2 \parallel s,\sigma'\rangle\end{array}}.$$

(6.2) For every $\mathbf{c} \in \mathbf{Chan}$, $v \in \mathbf{V}$,

$$\frac{\langle s_1,\sigma\rangle \xrightarrow{\mathbf{c}!v} \langle s_1',\sigma\rangle,\ \langle s_2,\sigma\rangle \xrightarrow{\mathbf{c}?v} \langle s_2',\sigma'\rangle}{\begin{array}{c}\langle s_1 \parallel s_2,\sigma\rangle \xrightarrow{\tau} \langle s_1' \parallel s_2',\sigma'\rangle \\ \langle s_2 \parallel s_1,\sigma\rangle \xrightarrow{\tau} \langle s_2' \parallel s_1',\sigma'\rangle\end{array}}.$$

(7) For every $C \in \wp(\mathbf{Chan})$, $a \in \mathbf{A} \setminus (C!? \times \mathbf{V})$,

$$\frac{s \xrightarrow{a} s'}{\partial_C(s) \xrightarrow{a} \partial_C(s')}.$$

(8.1)

$$\frac{\langle s_1,\sigma\rangle \xrightarrow{a} \langle s,\sigma'\rangle}{\langle \mathbf{if}(e,s_1,s_2),\sigma\rangle \xrightarrow{a} \langle s,\sigma'\rangle}\ (\llbracket e\rrbracket(\sigma) \neq \mathbf{nil}).$$

(8.2)

$$\frac{\langle s_2,\sigma\rangle \xrightarrow{a} \langle s,\sigma'\rangle}{\langle \mathbf{if}(e,s_1,s_2),\sigma\rangle \xrightarrow{a} \langle s,\sigma'\rangle}\ (\llbracket e\rrbracket(\sigma) = \mathbf{nil}).$$

(9)

$$\frac{\langle s,\sigma[\llbracket e\rrbracket(\sigma)/x]\rangle \xrightarrow{a} \langle s',\sigma'\rangle}{\langle \mathbf{let}(x,e,s),\sigma\rangle \xrightarrow{a} \langle \mathbf{let}(x,\sigma'(x),s'),\sigma'[\sigma(x)/x]\rangle}.$$

Intuitively, this rule is explained as follows: To infer the immediate derivatives of the configuration $\langle \mathbf{let}(x,e,s),\sigma\rangle$, we first need to find the immediate derivatives of the configuration $\langle s,\sigma[\llbracket e\rrbracket(\sigma)/x]\rangle$, because in $\langle \mathbf{let}(x,e,s),\sigma\rangle$ the statement s acts as if it is in the state $\sigma[\llbracket e\rrbracket(\sigma)/x]$ which is the same as σ except that it binds x to the value $\llbracket e\rrbracket(\sigma)$ of e in σ, forgetting the current value $\sigma(x)$ for a moment for later restoration. From $\langle s,\sigma[\llbracket e\rrbracket(\sigma)/x]\rangle \xrightarrow{a} \langle s',\sigma'\rangle$, it is inferred that the configuration $\langle \mathbf{let}(x,e,s),\sigma\rangle$ has an immediate a-derivative $\langle \mathbf{let}(x,\sigma'(x),s'),\sigma'[\sigma(x)/x]\rangle$, where the statement $\mathbf{let}(x,\sigma'(x),s')$ is obtained from s' by putting it in the $\mathbf{let}(\cdots)$ construct *locally* binding x to $\sigma'(x)$, and the state $\sigma'[\sigma(x)/x]$ is obtained from σ' by restoring the original value $\sigma(x)$ of x; the restoration is applied, because in $\mathbf{let}(x,e,s)$, the variable x is *localized*, and so, the (global) value of x never changes whatever action the statement $\mathbf{let}(x,e,s)$ may perform. (See § 7 for related work on the semantics of local variables.)

(10)

$$\frac{\langle \partial_{\{\mathbf{c}_m\}}(s^{(1,0)}(\mathbf{c}_m)),\sigma\rangle \xrightarrow{a} s'}{\langle \mathbf{LC}(s^{(1,0)}),\sigma\rangle \xrightarrow{a} s'},\quad \text{where } m = \min\{n \in \omega : \mathbf{c}_n \notin \mathcal{S}(s^{(1,0)})\}.$$

Note that $\{n \in \omega : \mathbf{c}_n \notin \mathcal{S}(s^{(1,0)})\}$ is nonempty since $\mathcal{S}(s^{(1,0)})$ is finite by definition. (See Remark 1 below for the motivation for this rule.)

(11.1) The following rule is called the *recursion rule*:

$$\frac{\langle S[(\mu X.\ S)/X], \sigma\rangle \xrightarrow{a} \langle s', \sigma'\rangle}{\langle(\mu X.\ S), \sigma\rangle \xrightarrow{a} \langle s', \sigma'\rangle}.$$

(11.2) The following rules are called the *parameterized recursion rule*:

$$\frac{\langle S^{(i,j)}[(\mu X^{(i,j)}.\ S^{(i,j)})/X^{(i,j)}](\vec{g}^{(i)} \cdot \vec{e}^{(j)}), \sigma\rangle \xrightarrow{a} \langle s', \sigma'\rangle}{\langle(\mu X^{(i,j)}.\ S^{(i,j)})(\vec{g}^{(i)} \cdot \vec{e}^{(j)}), \sigma\rangle \xrightarrow{a} \langle s', \sigma'\rangle} \quad ((i,j) \neq (0,0)).$$

(12) The following rule is called the λ*-rule*: For every $(i,j) \neq (0,0)$,

$$\frac{\langle S[(\vec{g}^{(i)}[\![\sigma]\!] \cdot \vec{e}^{(j)}[\![\sigma]\!])/(\vec{\eta}^{(i)} \cdot \vec{\xi}^{(j)})], \sigma\rangle \xrightarrow{a} \langle s', \sigma'\rangle}{\langle(\lambda\vec{\eta}^{(i)} \cdot \vec{\xi}^{(j)}.\ S)(\vec{g}^{(i)} \cdot \vec{e}^{(j)}), \sigma\rangle \xrightarrow{a} \langle s', \sigma'\rangle},$$

where $[\![\vec{g}^{(i)}]\!] = ([\![\vec{g}^{(i)}(k)]\!])_{k\in i}$ and $[\![\vec{e}^{(j)}]\!](\sigma) = ([\![\vec{e}^{(j)}(k)]\!](\sigma))_{k\in j}$. ∎

Remark 1 The present treatment of local channels is very similar to Milner's treatment of auxiliary channels introduced for defining *the linking combinator* '$\frown$' (cf. [Mil 89] § 3.3). This combinator is defined by: $s_1 \frown s_2 = \partial_{\{\mathbf{c}\}}(s_1[\mathbf{c}/\mathbf{c}'] \parallel s_1[\mathbf{c}/\mathbf{c}''])$, where $\mathbf{c}'$ and $\mathbf{c}''$ are predefined channels for output and input, respectively, $\mathbf{c}$ is an auxiliary channel which is fresh, i.e., chosen so that $\mathbf{c} \in \mathcal{S}(s_1) \cup \mathcal{S}(s_2)$, and $[\mathbf{c}/\mathbf{c}']$ is the *renaming operator* which replaces $\mathbf{c}'$ by $\mathbf{c}$. Strictly speaking, however, the combinator '$\frown$' is not defined in the calculus, i.e., there are not a term S and variables X_1, X_2 such that $s_1 \frown s_2 \equiv S[(s_1, s_2)/(X_1, X_2)]$ for all s_1, s_2. In our language, $\mathbf{LC}(\cdot)$ is a predefined function symbol, for which a transition rule in Definition 7 (10) is prescribed in terms of an auxiliary channel $\mathbf{c}_m$ which is fresh. See Example 3 in the Appendix C for a description example using $\mathbf{LC}(\cdot)$. ∎

By the above definition and the guardedness condition in Definition 3, we have the following lemma stating several useful properties of the transition system $\langle\mathcal{L}[\emptyset], \mathbf{A}, \{\xrightarrow{a}: a \in \mathbf{A}\}\rangle$.

Lemma 1 *For every $s \in \mathcal{L}[\emptyset]$ and $\sigma \in \Sigma$, the following hold:* **(1)** *The transition system is* image-finite *in that for every $a \in \mathbf{A}$, the* image set *$\{\langle s', \sigma'\rangle : \langle s, \sigma\rangle \xrightarrow{a} \langle s', \sigma'\rangle\}$ is finite.* **(2)** sort[act(s, σ)] *is finite.* **(3)** *For very $\mathbf{c} \in$ **Chan**, the set $\{v \in \mathbf{V} : \langle \mathbf{c}!, v\rangle \in \mathrm{act}(s, \sigma)\}$ is finite.* ∎

By Definition 7, we have the following lemma which states that immediate derivatives of a configuration of the form $\langle S(\vec{g} \cdot \vec{e}), \sigma\rangle$ are the same as those of $\langle S([\![\vec{g}]\!](\sigma) \cdot [\![\vec{e}]\!](\sigma)), \sigma\rangle$.

Lemma 2 *Let $(i,j) \neq (0,0)$, $\mathbf{S} \in \mathcal{L}^{(i,j)}[\emptyset]$, $\vec{g} \in (\mathcal{E}_\mathrm{C})^i$, and $\vec{e} \in (\mathcal{E}_\mathrm{V})^j$. Then, for every $\sigma, \sigma' \in \Sigma$, $a \in \mathbf{A}$, $s' \in \mathcal{L}[\emptyset]$, $\langle \mathbf{S}(\vec{g} \cdot \vec{e}), \sigma\rangle \xrightarrow{a} \langle s', \sigma'\rangle$ iff $\langle \mathbf{S}([\![\vec{g}]\!](\sigma) \cdot [\![\vec{e}]\!])(\sigma), \sigma\rangle \xrightarrow{a} \langle s', \sigma'\rangle$.* ∎

In terms of the transition relations $\xrightarrow{a}$ $(a \in \mathbf{A})$ three operational models $\mathcal{O}_\mathrm{L}$, $\mathcal{O}_\mathrm{L}^*$, and $\mathcal{O}^\mathrm{F}$ are defined. The first two models $\mathcal{O}_\mathrm{L}$ and $\mathcal{O}_\mathrm{L}^*$ are *linear*, and the third one $\mathcal{O}_\mathrm{F}$ is a variant of the *failures model.*

First, $\mathcal{O}_\mathrm{L}$ is defined by:

Definition 8 (*Operational Model $\mathcal{O}_\mathrm{L}$ for $\mathcal{L}[\emptyset]$*)

(1) Let act : $\mathcal{L}[\emptyset] \times \Sigma \to \wp(\mathbf{A})$ be defined by:

$$\mathrm{act}(s, \sigma) = \{a \in \mathbf{A} : \exists\langle s', \sigma'\rangle \in \mathcal{L}[\emptyset] \times \Sigma[\ \langle s, \sigma\rangle \xrightarrow{a} \langle s', \sigma'\rangle\ ]\}.$$

(2) The function $\mathcal{O}_L : \mathcal{L}[\emptyset] \to (\Sigma \to \wp_{nc}((\mathbf{A} \times \Sigma)^{\leq \omega}))$ is defined as follows: Let $s \in \mathcal{L}[\emptyset]$ and $\sigma \in \Sigma$. For $\chi \in (\mathbf{A} \times \Sigma)^{\leq \omega}$, we put $\chi \in \mathcal{O}_L[\![s]\!](\sigma)$ iff one of the following conditions is satisfied:

$$\exists (\langle s_i, \sigma_i \rangle)_{i \in \omega}, \exists (a_i)_{i \in \omega}[\ \chi = (\langle a_i, \sigma_{i+1} \rangle)_{i \in \omega} \wedge \langle s_0, \sigma_0 \rangle = \langle s, \sigma \rangle \tag{2}$$
$$\wedge \forall i \in \omega[\ \langle s_i, \sigma_i \rangle \xrightarrow{a_i} \langle s_{i+1}, \sigma_{i+1} \rangle\ ]],$$

$$\exists n \in \omega, \exists (\langle s_i, \sigma_i \rangle)_{i \in (n+1)}, \exists (a_i)_{i \in n}[\ \chi = (\langle a_i, \sigma_{i+1} \rangle)_{i \in n} \wedge \langle s_0, \sigma_0 \rangle = \langle s, \sigma \rangle \tag{3}$$
$$\wedge \forall i \in n[\ \langle s_i, \sigma_i \rangle \xrightarrow{a_i} \langle s_{i+1}, \sigma_{i+1} \rangle\ ] \wedge \tau \notin \mathrm{act}(s_n, \sigma_n)\ ]. \blacksquare$$

The second model $\mathcal{O}_L^*$ is defined from $\mathcal{O}_L$ by ignoring states involved in $\mathcal{O}_L$.

Definition 9 (*Operational Model $\mathcal{O}_L^*$ for $\mathcal{L}[\emptyset]$*)   First, a function $\beta^* : (\mathbf{A} \times \Sigma)^{\leq \omega} \to \mathbf{A}^{\leq \omega}$ is defined as follows: For every $(\langle a_i, \sigma_i \rangle)_{i \in \nu} \in (\mathbf{A} \times \Sigma)^{\leq \omega}$ ($\nu \in \omega \cup \{\omega\}$), let $\beta^*((\langle a_i, \sigma_i \rangle)_{i \in \nu}) = (a_i)_{i \in \nu}$. Then, $\mathcal{O}_L^* : \mathcal{L}[\emptyset] \to (\Sigma \to \wp_{nc}(\mathbf{A}^{\leq \omega}))$ is defined as follows: For $s \in \mathcal{L}[\emptyset]$ and $\sigma \in \Sigma$, $\mathcal{O}_L^*[\![s]\!](\sigma) = \beta^*[\mathcal{O}_L^*[\![s]\!](\sigma)]. \blacksquare$

The last model $\mathcal{O}_F$ is a variant of the *failures model* which was first introduced in [BHR 84]; for this model, two alternative definitions, i.e., an *operational* and *denotational* ones are given. First, the operational definition is given by:

Definition 10 (*Failures Model $\mathcal{O}_F$ for $\mathcal{L}[\emptyset]$*)

(1) Let $\mathbf{Q} = (\Sigma \times \mathbf{A} \times \Sigma)^{\omega} \cup ((\Sigma \times \mathbf{A} \times \Sigma)^{< \omega} \cdot (\Sigma \times \wp(\mathbf{C}))^1..$ A metric $d_{\mathbf{Q}}$ on $\mathbf{Q}$ is defined in terms of *truncations* by:

$$d_{\mathbf{Q}}(q_1, q_2) = \begin{cases} (1/2)^m \text{ with } m = \min\{n \in \omega : q_1 \!\restriction\! (n+1) \neq q_2 \!\restriction\! (n+1)\} \\ \qquad \text{if } \exists n \in \omega[\ q_1 \!\restriction\! n \neq q_2 \!\restriction\! n\ ], \\ 0 \qquad \text{otherwise.} \end{cases}$$

(2) The mapping $\mathcal{O}_F : \mathcal{L}[\emptyset] \to \wp(\mathbf{Q})$ is defined as follows: Let $s \in \mathcal{L}[\emptyset]$. For $q \in \mathbf{Q}$, we put $q \in \mathcal{O}_F[\![s]\!]$ iff one of the following propositions (4) and (5) holds:

$$\exists (s_i)_{i \in \omega}, \exists (\sigma_i)_{i \in \omega}, \exists (\sigma_i')_{i \in \omega}, \exists (a_i)_{i \in \omega}[\ q = (\langle \sigma_i, a_i, \sigma_i' \rangle)_{i \in \omega} \wedge s_0 = s \tag{4}$$
$$\wedge \forall i \in \omega[\ \langle s_i, \sigma_i \rangle \xrightarrow{a_i} \langle s_{i+1}, \sigma_i' \rangle\ ]],$$

$$\exists n \in \omega, \exists (s_i)_{i \in (n+1)}, \exists (\sigma_i)_{i \in (n+1)}, \exists (\sigma_i')_{i \in n}, \exists (a_i)_{i \in n}, \exists \Gamma \in \wp(\mathbf{C})[\tag{5}$$
$$q = (\langle \sigma_i, a_i, \sigma_i' \rangle)_{i \in n} \cdot (\langle \sigma_n, \Gamma \rangle) \wedge s_0 \equiv s$$
$$\wedge \forall i \in n[\ \langle s_i, \sigma_i \rangle \xrightarrow{a_i} \langle s_{i+1}, \sigma_i' \rangle\ ]$$
$$\wedge \tau \notin \mathrm{act}(s_n, \sigma_n) \wedge \Gamma \cap \mathrm{act}(s_n, \sigma_n) = \emptyset\ ]. \blacksquare$$

The model $\mathcal{O}_F$ can also be characterized as the fixed-point of a higher-order function. This characterization will be of use when establishing the semantic equivalence between $\mathcal{O}_F$ and the denotational model $\mathcal{D}_F$ to be presented in § 4. As a preliminary to the characterization we define the domain of processes by:

Definition 11 (*Domain $\mathbf{P}$ of Processes*)   Let $p \in \wp_{nc}(\mathbf{Q}_1)$. **(1)** We say p is *uniformly nonempty* iff $\forall r \in (\Sigma \times \mathbf{A} \times \Sigma)^{< \omega}[\ p[r] \neq \emptyset \Rightarrow \forall \sigma \in \Sigma[\ p[r]\langle \sigma \rangle \neq \emptyset\ ]]$. **(2)** For $\sigma \in \Sigma$, let $\mathrm{act}(p, \sigma) = \{a \in \mathbf{A} : \exists \sigma'[\ p[(\langle \sigma, a, \sigma' \rangle)] \neq \emptyset\ ]\}$. We say p is *upward closed w.r.t disabled actions* iff $\forall r \in (\Sigma \times \mathbf{A} \times \Sigma)^{< \omega}, \forall \sigma, \forall \Gamma[\ r \cdot (\langle \sigma, \Gamma \rangle) \in p \Rightarrow r \cdot (\langle \sigma, (\Gamma \cup (\mathbf{C} \setminus \mathrm{act}(p[r], \sigma)))\rangle) \in p\ ]$. **(3)** Let $\mathbf{P} = \{p \in \wp_{cl}(\mathbf{Q}) : p$ is uniformly nonempty and upward closed w.r.t. disabled actions$\}$. The space $\langle \mathbf{P}, d_{\mathbf{P}} \rangle$

is a complete ultra-metric space with $d_{\mathbf{P}}$ being the *Hausdorff distance* (on **P**) induced from $d_{\mathbf{Q}}$. Also for each $(i,j) \in \omega^2$, let $\mathbf{P}^{(i,j)} = (\mathbf{Chan}^i \times \mathbf{V}^j \rightarrow \mathbf{P})$. ∎

Remark 2 **(1)** The domain **P** can also be constructed, along the lines of [BZ 82] and [AR 89], as the unique solution of an appropriate domain equation in the category of complete metric spaces; such a construction may provide an insight into the nature of the domain and its connections with other domains (see [HBR 90] for such a construction of **P**).

(2) The second restriction, *upward closedness w.r.t. disabled actions*, is missing in [HBR 90], but some restriction of this kind is necessary for ensuring the nonemptiness of the parallel composition (to be defined in Definition 13) of two processes. This fact was suggested by Franck van Breugel. Note that the restriction is analogous to the one named (P5) in [BHR 84] § 2. ∎

Now we have the following characterization of $\mathcal{O}_{\mathrm{F}}$:

Lemma 3 (*Fixed-Point Formulation of Failures Model $\mathcal{O}_{\mathrm{F}}$ for $\mathcal{L}$*)

(1) $\forall s \in \mathcal{L}[\emptyset][\ \mathcal{O}_{\mathrm{F}}[\![s]\!] \in \mathbf{P}\ ]$.

(2) *Let* $\mathbf{M}_{\mathcal{O}} = (\mathcal{L}[\emptyset] \rightarrow \mathbf{P})$, *and let* $\Phi_{\mathrm{F}} : \mathbf{M}_{\mathcal{O}} \rightarrow \mathbf{M}_{\mathcal{O}}$ *be defined as follows: For* $F \in \mathbf{M}_{\mathcal{O}}$ *and* $s \in \mathcal{L}[\emptyset]$,

$$\begin{aligned}\Phi_{\mathrm{F}}(F)[\![s]\!] = \{(\langle\sigma,\Gamma\rangle) \in (\Sigma \times \wp(\mathbf{C}))^1 : \tau \notin \mathrm{act}(s,\sigma) \wedge \Gamma \cap \mathrm{act}(s,\sigma) = \emptyset\} \\ \cup \bigcup\{ (\langle\sigma,a,\sigma'\rangle) \cdot F[\![s']\!] : \sigma,\sigma' \in \Sigma \wedge a \in \mathbf{A} \wedge s' \in \mathcal{L}[\emptyset] \\ \wedge \langle s,\sigma\rangle \xrightarrow{a} \langle s',\sigma'\rangle\}.\end{aligned} \tag{6}$$

Then, Φ_{F} *is a contraction from* $\mathbf{M}_{\mathcal{O}}$ *to itself.*

(3) $\mathcal{O}_{\mathrm{F}} = \mathrm{fix}(\Phi_{\mathrm{F}})$, *i.e.,*

$$\begin{aligned}\mathcal{O}_{\mathrm{F}}[\![s]\!] = \{(\langle\sigma,\Gamma\rangle) \in (\Sigma \times \wp(\mathbf{C}))^1 : \tau \notin \mathrm{act}(s,\sigma) \wedge \Gamma \cap \mathrm{act}(s,\sigma) = \emptyset\} \\ \cup \bigcup\{(\langle\sigma,a,\sigma'\rangle) \cdot \mathcal{O}_{\mathrm{F}}[\![s']\!] : \sigma,\sigma' \in \Sigma \wedge a \in \mathbf{A} \wedge s' \in \mathcal{L}[\emptyset] \\ \wedge \langle s,\sigma\rangle \xrightarrow{a} \langle s',\sigma'\rangle\}.\end{aligned} \tag{7}$$ ∎

Proof. **Part (1).** The claim follows immediately from the definition of $\mathcal{O}_{\mathrm{F}}$. **Part (2).** By Lemma 1 (1), it is straightforward to check the right-hand side of (6) is an element of **P**; thus $\Psi_{\mathrm{F}} : \mathbf{M}_{\mathcal{O}} \rightarrow \mathbf{M}_{\mathcal{O}}$. The contractivity of Ψ_{F} follows immediately from its definition. **Part (3).** One has (7) by the definition of $\mathcal{O}_{\mathrm{F}}$. It follows from this and Part (1), that $\mathcal{O}_{\mathrm{F}} = \mathrm{fix}(\Phi_{\mathrm{F}})$. ∎

From Definition 10 and Lemma 2, the following lemma follows immediately.

Lemma 4 *Let* $(i,j) \neq (0,0)$, $\mathrm{s} \in \mathcal{L}^{(i,j)}[\emptyset]$, $\vec{g} \in (\mathcal{E}_{\mathrm{C}})^i$, *and* $\vec{e} \in (\mathcal{E}_{\mathrm{V}})^j$. *Then,*

$$\mathcal{O}_{\mathrm{F}}[\![\mathrm{s}(\vec{g}\cdot\vec{e})]\!] = \bigcup_{\sigma\in\Sigma} [\mathcal{O}_{\mathrm{F}}[\![\mathrm{s}([\![\vec{g}]\!](\sigma)\cdot[\![\vec{e}]\!](\sigma))]\!](\sigma)].$$ ∎

We define two *abstraction functions* $\mathcal{A}_{\mathrm{L}}$ and $\mathcal{A}_{\mathrm{L}}^*$ which relate $\mathcal{O}_{\mathrm{L}}$ and $\mathcal{O}_{\mathrm{L}}^*$ with $\mathcal{O}_{\mathrm{F}}$, respectively.

Definition 12 (*Abstraction Functions* $\mathcal{A}_{\mathrm{L}}$, $\mathcal{A}_{\mathrm{L}}^*$) Two functions $\mathcal{A}_{\mathrm{L}} : \wp(\mathbf{Q}) \rightarrow (\Sigma \rightarrow \wp((\Sigma \times \mathbf{A})^{\leq\omega}))$ and $\mathcal{A}_{\mathrm{L}}^* : \wp(\mathbf{Q}) \rightarrow (\Sigma \rightarrow \wp(\mathbf{A}^{\leq\omega}))$ are defined as follows:

(1) For $p \in \mathbf{P}$, $\sigma \in \Sigma$, we define $\mathcal{A}_{\mathrm{L}}(p)(\sigma)$ from connected paths in p whose initial state is σ as follows:

$$\mathcal{A}_{\rm L}(p)(\sigma) = \{\chi : \exists (a_i)_{i\in\omega} \in \mathbf{A}^\omega, \exists(\sigma_i)_{i\in\omega} \in \Sigma^\omega[\\ \chi = (\langle a_i, \sigma_{i+1}\rangle)_{i\in\omega} \wedge \sigma_0 = \sigma \wedge (\langle \sigma_i, a_i, \sigma_{i+1}\rangle)_{i\in\omega} \in p\,]\} \cup \\ \{\chi : \exists n \in \omega, \exists(a_i)_{i\in n} \in \mathbf{A}^n, \exists(\sigma_i)_{i\in(n+1)} \in \Sigma^{n+1}, \exists \Gamma \in \wp(\mathbf{C})[\\ \chi = (\langle a_i, \sigma_{i+1}\rangle)_{i\in n} \wedge \sigma_0 = \sigma \wedge (\langle \sigma_i, a_i, \sigma_{i+1}\rangle)_{i\in n} \cdot (\langle \sigma_n, \Gamma\rangle) \in p\,]\}.$$

(2) From $\mathcal{A}_{\rm L}$ and β^* (defined in Definition 9), we define $\mathcal{A}^*_{\rm L}$ as follows: For $p \in \mathbf{P}$ and $\sigma \in \Sigma$, $\mathcal{A}^*_{\rm L}(p)(\sigma) = \beta^*[\mathcal{A}_{\rm L}(p)(\sigma)]$. ▮

Having defined $\mathcal{A}_{\rm L}$ and $\mathcal{A}^*_{\rm L}$, the following lemma follows immediately from the definitions of $\mathcal{O}_{\rm L}$, $\mathcal{O}^*_{\rm L}$, and $\mathcal{O}_{\rm F}$.

Lemma 5 (*Correctness of $\mathcal{O}_{\rm F}$ w.r.t. $\mathcal{O}_{\rm L}$ and $\mathcal{O}^*_{\rm L}$*)
(1) $\mathcal{O}_{\rm L} = \mathcal{A}_{\rm L} \circ \mathcal{O}_{\rm F}$. **(2)** $\mathcal{O}^*_{\rm L} = \mathcal{A}^*_{\rm L} \circ \mathcal{O}_{\rm F}$. ▮

4 A Denotational Model $\mathcal{D}$ for $\mathcal{L}$

In this section, we define a denotational model $\mathcal{D}$ compositionally using interpreted operations of the language $\mathcal{L}$, with meanings of recursive programs as fixed points in the complete metric space $\mathbf{P}$; it turns out that $\mathcal{D}$ is equal to the failures model $\mathcal{O}_{\rm F}$, as stated earlier. The model $\mathcal{D}$ is a *conservative extension* of the model $\mathcal{D}'$ presented in [HBR 90], for a sublanguage $\mathcal{L}'$ of $\mathcal{L}$: That is, in $\mathcal{D}$, the semantic operations corresponding to the syntactic constructs in $\mathcal{L}'$ are the same as those in $\mathcal{D}'$, and $\mathcal{D}[\![s]\!] = \mathcal{D}'[\![s]\!]$ for $s \in \mathcal{L}'$.

As a basis for the definition of $\mathcal{D}$, we will define an *interpretation* $\mathcal{I}$ which maps each syntactic operator introduced in Definition 4 to a corresponding semantic operation on $\mathbf{P}$. First, for all the syntactic operators except $\partial_C(\cdot)$, $\mathbf{let}(x,\cdot,\cdot)$, and $\mathbf{LC}(\cdot)$, the corresponding semantic operations are defined as in Definition 21 of [HBR 90] by:

Definition 13 (*Semantic Operations*)

(1) The semantic interpretation $\tilde{\mathbf{0}}$ of $\mathbf{0}$ is defined by: $\tilde{\mathbf{0}} = (\Sigma \times \wp(\mathbf{C}))^1$.

(2) For each $x \in$ IVar, the semantic operation $\mathrm{asg}_x : \mathbf{F} \times \mathbf{P} \to \mathbf{P}$ corresponding to the construct $(\mathbf{asg}(x,\cdot);\cdot)$ is defined as follows: For $f \in \mathbf{F}$ and $p \in \mathbf{P}$,

$$\mathrm{asg}_x(f,p) = \bigcup\{(\langle \sigma, \tau, \sigma[f(\sigma)/x]\rangle) \cdot p : \sigma \in \Sigma\}.$$

(3) The semantic operation out : $\mathbf{H} \times \mathbf{F} \times \mathbf{P} \to \mathbf{P}$ corresponding to the construct $(\mathbf{out}(\cdot,\cdot);\cdot)$ is defined as follows: For $h \in \mathbf{H}$, $f \in \mathbf{F}$, and $p \in \mathbf{P}$,

$$\mathrm{out}(h,f,p) = \bigcup\{(\langle \sigma, \langle h(\sigma)!, f(\sigma)\rangle, \sigma\rangle) \cdot p : \sigma \in \Sigma\} \\ \cup\{(\langle \sigma, \Gamma\rangle) : \sigma \in \Sigma \wedge \Gamma \subseteq \mathbf{C} \setminus \{h(\sigma)!\}\}.$$

(4) For each $x \in$ IVar, the semantic operation $\mathrm{in}_x : \mathbf{H} \times \mathbf{P} \to \mathbf{P}$ corresponding to the construct $(\mathbf{in}(\cdot, x);\cdot)$ is defined as follows: For $h \in \mathbf{H}$ and $p \in \mathbf{P}$,

$$\mathrm{in}_x(h,p) = \bigcup\{(\langle \sigma, \langle h(\sigma)?, v\rangle, \sigma[v/x]\rangle) \cdot p : \sigma \in \Sigma \wedge v \in \mathbf{V}\} \\ \cup\{(\langle \sigma, \Gamma\rangle) : \sigma \in \Sigma \wedge \Gamma \subseteq \mathbf{C} \setminus \{h(\sigma)?\}\}.$$

(5) The semantic operation $\mathrm{in}' : \mathbf{H} \times \mathbf{P}^{(0,1)} \to \mathbf{P}$ corresponding to the construct $(\mathbf{in}'(\cdot);\cdot)$ is defined as follows: For $h \in \mathbf{H}$ and $\mathbf{p} \in \mathbf{P}^{(0,1)}$,

$$\mathrm{in}'(h,\mathbf{p}) = \bigcup\{(\langle\sigma,\langle h(\sigma)?,v\rangle,\sigma\rangle)\cdot\mathbf{p}(v) : \sigma\in\Sigma\wedge v\in\mathbf{V}\} \cup\{(\langle\sigma,\Gamma\rangle) : \sigma\in\Sigma\wedge\Gamma\subseteq\mathbf{C}\setminus\{h(\sigma)?\}\}.$$

(6) The semantic operation $\tilde{+} : \mathbf{P}\times\mathbf{P}\to\mathbf{P}$ corresponding $+$ is defined as follows: For $p\in\mathbf{P}$, $p\cap((\Sigma\times\mathbf{A}\times\Sigma)\times\mathbf{Q}_2)$ is called the *action part* of p and denoted by p^+. For $p_1,p_2\in\mathbf{P}$, $p_1\tilde{+}p_2$ is defined by: $p_1\tilde{+}p_2 = p_1^+\cup p_2^+\cup((\Sigma\times\wp(\mathbf{C}))^1\cap p_1\cap p_2)$.

(7) We have the unique operation $\tilde{\|} : \mathbf{P}\times\mathbf{P}\to\mathbf{P}$ satisfying the following equation (for the existence and uniqueness of such an operation see Definition 8 (5) of [HBR 90]): For $p_1,p_2\in\mathbf{P}$,

$$p_1\,\tilde{\|}\,p_2 = (p_1 \,⫫\, p_2)\cup(p_2 \,⫫\, p_1)\cup(p_1 \lfloor p_2)\cup(p_2\lfloor p_1)\cup(p_1 \,\#\, p_2),$$

where $p_1 \,⫫\, p_2 = \bigcup\{\langle\sigma,a,\sigma'\rangle\cdot(p_1[\langle\sigma,a,\sigma'\rangle]\,\tilde{\|}\,p_2) : p_1[\langle\sigma,a,\sigma'\rangle]\neq\emptyset\}$,

$$p_1\lfloor p_2 = (\bigcup\{\,(\langle\sigma,\tau,\sigma'\rangle)\cdot(p_1[\langle\sigma,c!v,\sigma\rangle]\,\tilde{\|}\,p_2[\langle\sigma,c?v,\sigma'\rangle]) : p_1[\langle\sigma,c!v,\sigma\rangle]\neq\emptyset\wedge p_2[\langle\sigma,c?v,\sigma'\rangle]\neq\emptyset\,\})^{\mathrm{cls}}, \quad (8)$$

$$p_1\,\#\,p_2 = \{\,(\langle\sigma,\Gamma\rangle) : \exists(\langle\sigma,\Gamma_1\rangle)\in p_1,\exists(\langle\sigma,\Gamma_2\rangle)\in p_2[\,(\mathbf{C}\setminus\Gamma_1)\cap\overline{(\mathbf{C}\setminus\Gamma_2)}=\emptyset\wedge\Gamma\subseteq\Gamma_1\cap\Gamma_2\,]\}.$$

(8) For $q\in\mathbf{Q}\cup(\Sigma\times\mathbf{A}\times\Sigma)^+$, let istate$(q)=\sigma$ if $\exists a,\sigma'[\,q=(\langle\sigma,a,\sigma'\rangle)\cdot q'\,]$; otherwise $\exists\Gamma[\,q=(\langle\sigma'',\Gamma\rangle)\,]$ and let istate$_2(q)=\sigma''$. Also for $p\in\mathbf{P}$, $\sigma\in\Sigma$, let $p\langle\sigma\rangle=\{q\in p : \mathrm{istate}(q)=\sigma\}$. The semantic operation $\tilde{\mathrm{if}} : \mathbf{F}\times\mathbf{P}\times\mathbf{P}\to\mathbf{P}$ is defined as follows: For $f\in\mathbf{F}$, $p_1,p_2\in\mathbf{P}$,

$$\tilde{\mathrm{if}}(f,p_1,p_2) = \bigcup\{p_1\langle\sigma\rangle : \sigma\in\Sigma\wedge f(\sigma)\neq\mathbf{nil}\} \cup\bigcup\{p_2\langle\sigma\rangle : \sigma\in\Sigma\wedge f(\sigma)=\mathbf{nil}\}.\ \blacksquare$$

A semantic operation $\tilde{\partial}_C(\cdot)$ corresponding to the construct $\partial_C(\cdot)$ is defined by:

Definition 14 (*Semantic Operation $\tilde{\partial}_C$ Corresponding to ∂_C*) The operation $\tilde{\partial}_C(\cdot) : \mathbf{P}\to\mathbf{P}$ is defined as follows: For $p\in\mathbf{P}$,

$$\begin{aligned}&\tilde{\partial}_C(p) = \\ &\{(\langle\sigma_i,a_i,\sigma_i'\rangle)_{i\in\omega}\in(\Sigma\times\mathbf{A}\times\Sigma)^\omega\cap p : \forall i\in\omega[\ \mathrm{sort}(a_i)\notin C!?\ ]\} \\ &\cup\{q : \exists n\in\omega,\exists(a_i)_{i\in n}\in\mathbf{A}^n,\exists(\sigma_i)_{i\in(n+1)}\in\Sigma^{n+1},\exists(\sigma_i')_{i\in(n+1)}\in\Sigma^n,\exists\Gamma\in\wp(\mathbf{C})[\\ &\quad q=(\langle\sigma_i,a_i,\sigma_i'\rangle)_{i\in n}\cdot(\langle\sigma_n,\Gamma\rangle)\wedge\forall i\in n[\ \mathrm{sort}(a_i)\notin C!?\ ] \\ &\quad\wedge(\langle\sigma_i,a_i,\sigma_i'\rangle)_{i\in n}\cdot(\langle\sigma_n,\Gamma\setminus C!?\rangle)\in p\ ]\}.\ \blacksquare\end{aligned}$$

A semantic operation corresponding to the construct $\mathbf{let}(\cdot,\cdot,\cdot)$ is defined by:

Definition 15 (*Semantic Operation* let_x *corresponding to* $\mathbf{let}_x$) Let $x\in\mathrm{IVar}$. First, we define an auxiliary function $\mathrm{let}_x^0 : \mathbf{F}\times\mathbf{P}\to\mathbf{P}$ as folows: For every $\langle f,p\rangle\in\mathbf{F}\times\mathbf{P}$, $\mathrm{let}_x^0(f,p)=\{(\langle\sigma,\Gamma\rangle)\in(\Sigma\times\wp(\mathbf{C}))^1 : (\langle\sigma[f(\sigma)/x],\Gamma\rangle)\in p\}$.

By means of let_x^0, the operation $\mathrm{let}_x : \mathbf{F}\times\mathbf{P}\to\mathbf{P}$ is defined recursively as follows: For every $\langle f,p\rangle\in\mathbf{F}\times\mathbf{P}$,

$$\mathrm{let}_x(f,p) = \mathrm{let}_x^0(f,p)\cup(\bigcup\{(\langle\sigma,a,\sigma'[\sigma(x)/x]\rangle)\cdot\mathrm{let}_x(\sigma'(x),p[(\langle\sigma[f(\sigma)/x],a,\sigma'\rangle)]) : p[(\langle\sigma[f(\sigma)/x],a,\sigma'\rangle)]\neq\emptyset\})^{\mathrm{cls}}. \quad (9)$$

Formally, let_x is defined as the fixed-point of a higher-order contraction as follows: First let $\mathbf{M}_\ell = (\mathbf{F} \times \mathbf{P}) \to \mathbf{P}$, and let us define $\Phi_\ell : \mathbf{M}_\ell \to \mathbf{M}_\ell$ as follows: For $F \in \mathbf{M}_\ell$, and $\langle f, p \rangle \in \mathbf{F} \times \mathbf{P}$,

$$\begin{aligned}\Phi_\ell(F)(f,p) = \; & \text{let}_x^0(f,p) \\ & \cup (\bigcup \{ (\langle \sigma, a, \sigma'[\sigma(x)/x] \rangle) \cdot F(\sigma'(x), p[(\langle \sigma[f(\sigma)/x], a, \sigma' \rangle)]) : \\ & \quad p[(\langle \sigma[f(\sigma)/x], a, \sigma' \rangle)] \neq \emptyset \})^{\text{cls}}.\end{aligned}$$

It is easy to verify that Φ_ℓ is a contraction from $\mathbf{M}_\ell$ to itself. Let $\text{let}_x = \text{fix}(\Phi_\ell)$. Then one has (9) by definition. For later use, let us put

$$\begin{aligned}\text{let}_x^+(f,p) = (\bigcup \{ (\langle \sigma, a, \sigma'[\sigma(x)/x] \rangle) \cdot \text{let}_x(\sigma'(x), p[(\langle \sigma[f(\sigma)/x], a, \sigma' \rangle)]) : \\ p[(\langle \sigma[f(\sigma)/x], a, \sigma' \rangle)] \neq \emptyset \})^{\text{cls}},\end{aligned} \tag{10}$$

obtaining $\text{let}_x(f,p) = \text{let}_x^0(f,p) \cup \text{let}_x^+(f,p)$ by definition. ∎

The following example illustrates how the elements of $\text{let}_x(e,p)$ are obtained from those of p:

Example 1 Let $x \in \text{IVar}$ and q be a finite element of $\mathbf{Q}$ of the form $(\langle \sigma_i, a_i, \sigma_i' \rangle)_{i \in n} \cdot (\langle \sigma_n, \Gamma \rangle)$, or $(\langle \sigma_i, a_i, \sigma_i' \rangle)_{i \in \omega}$. We say q is *x-stabilized* iff $\forall i \in \text{lgt}(q)[\, i+1 < \text{lgt}(q) \Rightarrow \sigma_i(x) = \sigma_i' \,]$; also we say q is x-connected iff $\forall i \in \text{lgt}(q)[\, i+1 < \text{lgt}(q) \Rightarrow \sigma_i'(x) = \sigma_{i+1} \,]$.

Let $v \in \mathbf{V}$ and $p \in \mathbf{P}$. It follows immediately from the definition of let_x that all elements of $\text{let}_x(p)$ are x-stabilized. Elements of $\text{let}_x(p)$ are obtained from those elements of p' that are x-connected, i.e., for finite elements of $\text{let}_x(p)$ we have (11) below for every $n > 1$, and for its infinite elements we have (12):

$$\begin{aligned}& (\langle \sigma_i, a_i, \sigma_i'[v_i/x] \rangle)_{i \in n} \cdot (\langle \sigma_n, \Gamma \rangle) \in \text{let}_x(v,p) \\ \Leftrightarrow \; & (\langle \sigma_i[v_i'/x], a_i, \sigma_i' \rangle)_{i \in n} \cdot (\langle \sigma_n[v_n'/x], \Gamma \rangle) \in p,\end{aligned} \tag{11}$$

$$(\langle \sigma_i, a_i, \sigma_i'[v_i/x] \rangle)_{i \in \omega} \in \text{let}_x(v,p) \Leftrightarrow (\langle \sigma_i[v_i'/x], a_i, \sigma_i' \rangle)_{i \in \omega} \in p, \tag{12}$$

where $v_i = \sigma_i(x)$, $v_i' = \sigma_{i-1}'(x)$ for $i > 0$, and $v_0' = v$. Note that the sequences $(\langle \sigma_i, a_i, \sigma_i'[v_i/x] \rangle)_{i \in n} \cdot (\langle \sigma_n, \Gamma \rangle)$ and $(\langle \sigma_i, a_i, \sigma_i'[v_i/x] \rangle)_{i \in \omega}$ (resp. $(\langle \sigma_i[v_i'/x], a_i, \sigma_i' \rangle)_{i \in n} \cdot (\langle \sigma_n[v_n'/x], \Gamma \rangle)$ and $(\langle \sigma_i[v_i'/x], a_i, \sigma_i' \rangle)_{i \in \omega}$) are x-stabilized (resp. x-connected). Here we show only (11) for $n = 1$ below (a proof that (11) holds for every $n > 0$ and a proof of (12) can be obtained by induction in a similar fashion).

$$\begin{aligned}& (\langle \sigma_0, a_0, \sigma_0'[v_0/x] \rangle, \langle \sigma_1, \Gamma \rangle) \in \text{let}_x(v,p) \\ \Leftrightarrow \; & p[(\langle \sigma_0[v_0'/x], a_0, \sigma_0' \rangle)] \neq \emptyset \wedge (\langle \sigma_1, \Gamma \rangle) \in \text{let}_x(v_1', p[(\langle \sigma_0[v_0'/x], a_0, \sigma_0' \rangle)]) \\ \Leftrightarrow \; & p[(\langle \sigma_0[v_0'/x], a_0, \sigma_0' \rangle)] \neq \emptyset \wedge (\langle \sigma_1[v_1'/x], \Gamma \rangle) \in p[(\langle \sigma_0[v_0'/x], a_0, \sigma_0' \rangle)] \\ \Leftrightarrow \; & (\langle \sigma_0[v_0'/x], a_0, \sigma_0' \rangle, \langle \sigma_1[v_1'/x], \Gamma \rangle) \in p. \; \blacksquare\end{aligned}$$

As a preliminary to the definition of a semantic operation LC corresponding the construct $\mathbf{LC}(\cdot)$, we introduce the following semantic operation which *renames* channels in processes:

Definition 16 (*Renaming Operation*) Let $\phi : \mathbf{Chan} \to \mathbf{Chan}$. First, we define $\tilde{\phi} : \mathbf{A} \to \mathbf{A}$ as follows: For $a \in \mathbf{A}$,

$$\tilde{\phi}(a) = \begin{cases} \langle \phi(\mathbf{c})!, v \rangle & \text{if } a = \langle \mathbf{c}!, v \rangle, \\ \langle \phi(\mathbf{c})?, v \rangle & \text{if } a = \langle \mathbf{c}?, v \rangle, \\ a & \text{otherwise.} \end{cases}$$

By means of $\tilde{\phi}$, a *renaming operation* $\tilde{\Theta}_f : \mathbf{P} \to \mathbf{P}$ is defined as follows: For $p \in \mathbf{P}$,

$$\begin{aligned} &\tilde{\Theta}_\phi(p) = \\ &\{q \in \mathbf{Q} : \exists(\langle \sigma_i, a_i, \sigma_i' \rangle)_{i\in\omega} \in (\Sigma \times \mathbf{A} \times \Sigma)^\omega \cap p[\, q = (\langle \sigma_i, \tilde{\phi}(a_i), \sigma_i' \rangle)_{i\in\omega} \,]\} \\ &\cup\{q \in \mathbf{Q} : \exists n \in \omega, \exists(\langle \sigma_i, \tilde{\phi}(a_i), \sigma_i' \rangle)_{i\in n} \in (\Sigma \times \mathbf{A} \times \Sigma)^n, \exists\langle \sigma, \Gamma \rangle \in \Sigma \times \wp(\mathbf{C})[\\ &\quad (\langle \sigma_i, a_i, \sigma_i' \rangle)_{i\in n} \cdot (\langle \sigma, \tilde{\phi}^{-1}[\Gamma] \rangle) \in p \wedge q = (\langle \sigma_i, \tilde{\phi}(a_i), \sigma_i' \rangle)_{i\in n} \cdot (\langle \sigma, \Gamma \rangle) \,]\}. \blacksquare \end{aligned}$$

By means of the renaming operation $\tilde{\Theta}_\phi$, a semantic operation corresponding to the construct $\mathbf{LC}(\cdot)$ is defined by:

Definition 17 (*Semantic Operation* LC($\cdot$) *Corresponding to* $\mathbf{LC}(\cdot)$)

(1) For $p \in \mathbf{P}$, the *semantic sort* of p, written $\tilde{\mathcal{S}}(p)$, is defined by:

$$\begin{aligned} \tilde{\mathcal{S}}(p) = \; &\{\mathbf{c} \in \mathbf{Chan} : \exists w_1 \in (\Sigma \times \mathbf{A} \times \Sigma)^{<\omega}, \exists\langle \sigma, a, \sigma' \rangle \in \Sigma \times \mathbf{A} \times \Sigma[\\ &\quad a \neq \tau \wedge \mathbf{c} = \mathrm{chan}(\mathrm{sort}(a)) \wedge p[w_1 \cdot (\langle \sigma, a, \sigma' \rangle)] \neq \emptyset \,]\}. \end{aligned}$$

(2) For $\mathbf{c}, \mathbf{c}'$, let $[\mathbf{c}'/\mathbf{c}]$ be the mapping from **Chan** to **Chan** such that $[\mathbf{c}'/\mathbf{c}](\mathbf{c}) = \mathbf{c}'$ and $[\mathbf{c}'/\mathbf{c}](\mathbf{c}'') = \mathbf{c}''$ for every $\mathbf{c}'' \in \mathbf{Chan} \setminus \{\mathbf{c}\}$. The operation $\mathrm{LC} : \mathbf{P}^{(1,0)} \to \mathbf{P}$ is defined as follows: Let $\mathbf{p} \in \mathbf{P}^{(1,0)}$. If there exists $C \in \wp_f(\mathbf{Chan_1})$ such that

$$\forall \mathbf{c}, \mathbf{c}' \in (\mathbf{Chan_1} \setminus C)[\, \tilde{\Theta}_{[\mathbf{c}'/\mathbf{c}]}(\mathbf{p}(\mathbf{c})) = \mathbf{p}(\mathbf{c}') \wedge (\mathbf{c} \neq \mathbf{c}' \Rightarrow \mathbf{c}' \notin \tilde{\mathcal{S}}(\mathbf{p}(\mathbf{c}))) \,],$$

then let $\mathrm{LC}(\mathbf{p}) = \tilde{\partial}_{\{\mathbf{c}_m\}}(\mathbf{p}(\mathbf{c}_m))$, where

$$\begin{aligned} m = \min\{i \in \omega : \exists C \in \wp_f(\mathbf{Chan_1})[\, \mathbf{c}_i \notin C \wedge \forall \mathbf{c}, \mathbf{c}' \in (\mathbf{Chan_1} \setminus C)[\\ \tilde{\Theta}_{[\mathbf{c}'/\mathbf{c}]}(\mathbf{p}(\mathbf{c})) = \mathbf{p}(\mathbf{c}') \wedge (\mathbf{c} \neq \mathbf{c}' \Rightarrow \mathbf{c}' \notin \tilde{\mathcal{S}}(\mathbf{p}(\mathbf{c}))) \,]]\}. \end{aligned}$$

Otherwise, let $\mathrm{LC}(\mathbf{p}) = \tilde{\mathbf{0}}$. ∎

Let $\mathcal{I}$ be an *interpretation* of **Sig**, a mapping which maps each syntactic operator to its corresponding semantic operation:

Definition 18 (*Interpretation* $\mathcal{I}$ *for* **Sig**) Representing a mapping as a set of pairs as usual, we define $\mathcal{I}$ by:

$$\begin{aligned} \mathcal{I} = \; &\{\langle \mathbf{0}, \tilde{\mathbf{0}} \rangle, \langle (\mathbf{out}(\cdot,\cdot);\cdot), \mathrm{out} \rangle, \langle (\mathbf{in}(\cdot);\cdot), \mathrm{in} \rangle, \langle (\mathbf{in}'(\cdot);\cdot), \mathrm{in}' \rangle\} \\ &\cup\{\langle \mathbf{LC}(\cdot), \mathrm{LC} \rangle, \langle +, \tilde{+} \rangle, \langle \|, \tilde{\|} \rangle, \langle \mathbf{if}(\cdot,\cdot,\cdot), \tilde{\mathrm{if}} \rangle\} \\ &\cup\{\langle (\mathbf{asg}(x,\cdot);\cdot), \mathrm{asg}_x \rangle : x \in \mathrm{IVar}\} \cup \{\langle \mathbf{let}(x,\cdot,\cdot), \mathrm{let}_x \rangle : x \in \mathrm{IVar}\} \\ &\cup\{\langle (\mathbf{in}_x(\cdot);\cdot), \mathrm{in}_x \rangle : x \in \mathrm{IVar}\} \cup \{\langle \partial_C(\cdot), \tilde{\partial}_C(\cdot) \rangle : C \in \wp(\mathbf{Chan})\}. \blacksquare \end{aligned}$$

The semantic operations in $\mathcal{I}$ have the following useful metric properties, which are to be employed in the definition of the denotational model $\mathcal{D}$:

Lemma 6 (*Metric Properties of Semantic Operations*)

(1) Let $(i,j,k,l,m) \in \omega^5$, $F \in \mathbf{Fun}^{(i,j,k,l,m)}$, $\vec{h} \in \mathbf{H}^i$, $\vec{f} \in \mathbf{F}^i$. Then, the mapping

$$(\lambda\langle \vec{p}_1, \vec{\mathbf{p}}, \vec{\mathbf{p}}' \rangle \in \mathbf{P}^k \times (\mathbf{P}^{(0,1)})^\ell \times (\mathbf{P}^{(1,0)})^m.\ \mathcal{I}(F)(\vec{h} \cdot \vec{f} \cdot \vec{p}_1 \cdot \vec{\mathbf{p}} \cdot \vec{\mathbf{p}}'))$$

is a nonexpansive mapping from $\mathbf{P}^k \times (\mathbf{P}^{(0,1)})^\ell \times (\mathbf{P}^{(1,0)})^m$ to $\mathbf{P}$.

(2) For $x \in$ IVar, $f \in \mathbf{F}$, $h \in \mathbf{H}$, the three mappings $(\lambda p \in \mathbf{P}.\ \mathrm{asg}_x(f,p))$, $(\lambda p \in \mathbf{P}.\ \mathrm{out}(h,f,p))$, and $(\lambda p \in \mathbf{P}.\ \mathrm{in}(h,p))$ are a contraction from $\mathbf{P}$ to $\mathbf{P}$ with coefficient 1/2.

(3) Fore every $h \in \mathbf{H}$, $f \in \mathbf{F}$, $(\lambda \mathbf{p} \in \mathbf{P}^{(0,1)}.\ \mathrm{in}'(h,\mathbf{p}))$ is a contraction from $\mathbf{P}^{(0,1)}$ to $\mathbf{P}$ with coefficient 1/2. ▮

In terms of the interpretation $\mathcal{I}$, the denotational model $\mathcal{D}$ is defined compositionally, with meanings of recursive programs as fixed points in the complete metric space $\mathbf{P}$. For the definition of $\mathcal{D}$, a few preliminary definitions are needed.

Definition 19 (*Semantic and Syntactic Valuations*)

(1) For $\mathbf{S} \in \tilde{\mathcal{L}}^*$, let us denote by $\deg(\mathbf{S})$ the depth of nesting of function symbols (including constant symbols), μ-recursions, function applications, and λ-abstractions in $\mathbf{S}$.

(2) For $\rho \in (\mathcal{X}^*_{\mathcal{P}} \to \mathbf{P}^*)$, we say ρ respects the type iff for each $Z \in \mathcal{X}^*_{\mathcal{P}}$ the type of $\rho(Z)$ is the same as that of Z. Let SeVal $= \{\rho \in (\mathcal{X}^*_{\mathcal{P}} \to \mathbf{P}^*) : \rho$ respects the type$\}$.
For $\theta \in (\mathcal{X}^*_{\mathcal{P}} \hookrightarrow \mathcal{L}^*[\emptyset])$, we say θ respects the type iff for each $Z \in \mathrm{dom}(\theta)$ the type of $\theta(Z)$ is the same as that of Z. Let SyVal $= \{\theta \in (\mathcal{X}^*_{\mathcal{P}} \hookrightarrow \mathcal{L}^*[\emptyset]) :$ θ respects the type$\}$.

(3) For $\mathbf{S} \in \mathcal{L}^*[\mathcal{X}^*_{\mathcal{P}}]$ and $\theta \in$ SyVal, let $\mathbf{S}[\theta]$ denote the result of simultaneously replacing all the free occurrences of $Z \in \mathrm{dom}(\theta)$ by $\theta(Z)$. ▮

For $\mathbf{S} \in \mathcal{L}^*[\mathcal{X}^*_{\mathcal{P}}]$, and $\rho \in$ SeVal, we can define $\mathcal{D}[\![\mathbf{S}]\!](\rho)$, *the meaning of* $\mathbf{S}$ *in* $\mathcal{D}$ *under the evaluation* ρ, so that the conditions in the next lemma are satisfied. Moreover, it can be shown that there is a unique mapping $\mathcal{D} : \mathcal{L}^*[\mathcal{X}^*_{\mathcal{P}}] \to (\mathrm{SeVal} \to \mathbf{P}^*)$ satisfying the conditions. (See the Appendix B for the definition of $\mathcal{D}$.)

Lemma 7 (*Characterization of Denotational Model* $\mathcal{D}$)

(1) *For* $\mathbf{S} \in \mathcal{X}^*_{\mathcal{P}}$, *one has* $\mathcal{D}[\![\mathbf{S}]\!](\rho) = \rho(\mathbf{S})$.

(2) *For* $\mathbf{S} \equiv F(\vec{g}\cdot\vec{e}\cdot\vec{S}\cdot\vec{T}\cdot\vec{U})$ *with* $F \in \mathbf{Fun}^{(i,j,k,\ell,m)}$ *and* $\vec{g} \in (\mathcal{E}_C)^i$, $\vec{e} \in (\mathcal{E}_V)^j$, $\vec{S} \in \mathcal{L}^k$, $\vec{T} \in (\mathcal{L}^{(0,1)})^\ell$, $\vec{U} \in (\mathcal{L}^{(1,0)})^m$, *one has*

$$\mathcal{D}[\![\mathbf{S}]\!](\rho) = \mathcal{I}(F)([\![\vec{g}]\!], [\![\vec{e}]\!], \mathcal{D}[\![\vec{S}]\!](\rho)\cdot\mathcal{D}[\![\vec{T}]\!](\rho)\cdot\mathcal{D}[\![\vec{U}]\!](\rho)).$$

(3) *For* $\mathbf{S} \equiv (\lambda\vec{\eta}\cdot\vec{\xi}.\ \mathbf{S}')$, *with* $\mathrm{lgt}(\vec{\eta}) = i$ *and* $\mathrm{lgt}(\vec{\xi}) = j$, *one has*

$$\mathcal{D}[\![\mathbf{S}]\!](\rho) = (\lambda\vec{\mathbf{c}}\cdot\vec{v} \in \mathbf{Chan}^i\cdot\mathbf{V}^j.\ \mathcal{D}[\![\mathbf{S}'[(\vec{\mathbf{c}}\cdot\vec{v})/(\vec{\eta}\cdot\vec{\xi})]]\!](\rho)).$$

(4) *For* $\mathbf{S} \equiv (\mu X^{(i,j)}.\ S^{(i,j)})$ *with* $(i,j) \in \omega^2$, *the mapping* $(\lambda\mathbf{p} \in \mathbf{P}^{(i,j)}.\ \mathcal{D}[\![S^{(i,j)}]\!](\rho[\mathbf{p}/X^{(i,j)}]))$ *is a contraction from* $\mathbf{P}^{(i,j)}$ *to itself (for the notation* $\rho[\mathbf{p}^{(i,j)}/X^{(i,j)}]$ *see Notation 3), and*

$$\mathcal{D}[\![\mathbf{S}]\!](\rho) = \mathrm{fix}(\lambda\mathbf{p} \in \mathbf{P}^{(i,j)}.\ \mathcal{D}[\![(S^{(i,j)})]\!](\rho[\mathbf{p}/X^{(i,j)}])).$$

By definition, the following holds for every $\mathbf{p} \in \mathbf{P}^{(i,j)}$:

$$\mathbf{p} = \mathcal{D}[\![(\mu X^{(i,j)}.\ S^{(i,j)})]\!](\rho) \Leftrightarrow \mathbf{p} = \mathcal{D}[\![(S^{(i,j)})]\!](\rho[\mathbf{p}/X^{(i,j)}]). \tag{13}$$

(5) *The interpretation of function application is* nonuniform *in the following sense: For* $\mathbf{S} \equiv S^{(i,j)}(\vec{g}^{(i)}\cdot\vec{e}^{(j)})$,

$$\mathcal{D}[\![\mathbf{S}]\!](\rho) = \bigcup_{\sigma\in\Sigma} [\mathcal{D}[\![S^{(i,j)}]\!](\rho)([\![\vec{g}^{(i)}]\!](\sigma) \cdot [\![\vec{e}^{(j)}]\!](\sigma))\langle\sigma\rangle]. \blacksquare$$

From the definition of $\mathcal{D}$, we immediately have the following proposition stating that the value $\mathcal{D}[\![\mathbf{S}]\!](\rho)$ does not depend on $\rho(Z)$ for $Z \notin \mathrm{FV}(\mathbf{S})$:

Proposition 1 *Let* $\mathbf{S} \in \mathcal{L}^*$. *Then for every* $\rho_1, \rho_2 \in$ SeVal *such that* $\rho_1 \restriction \mathrm{FV}(\mathbf{S}) = \rho_2 \restriction \mathrm{FV}(\mathbf{S})$, *one has* $\mathcal{D}[\![\mathbf{S}]\!](\rho_1) = \mathcal{D}[\![\mathbf{S}]\!](\rho_2)$. ∎

Thus, for $\mathrm{s} \in \mathcal{L}^*[\emptyset]$, the value $\mathcal{D}[\![\mathrm{s}]\!](\rho)$ does not depend on the choice of ρ; we denote the value by $\mathcal{D}[\![\mathrm{s}]\!]$.

The model $\mathcal{D}$ is *compositional* in the following sense:

Lemma 8 (*Compositionality of* $\mathcal{D}$) *Let* $\mathbf{S} \in \mathcal{L}^*[\mathcal{X}^*_{\mathcal{P}}]$, $(i,j) \in \omega^2$, $Z \in \mathcal{X}^{(i,j)}$, $\mathrm{s} \in \mathcal{L}^{(i,j)}[\emptyset]$, *and* $\rho \in$ SeVal. *Then* $\mathcal{D}[\![(\mathbf{S}[\mathrm{s}/Z])]\!](\rho) = \mathcal{D}[\![\mathbf{S}]\!](\rho[\mathcal{D}[\![\mathrm{s}]\!](\rho)/Z])$. ∎

5 Semantic Equivalence between $\mathcal{O}_{\mathrm{F}}$ and $\mathcal{D}$

In this section, we establish the semantic equivalence between $\mathcal{O}_{\mathrm{F}}$ and $\mathcal{D}$, from which the correctness of $\mathcal{D}$ w.r.t. $\mathcal{O}_{\mathrm{L}}$ and $\mathcal{O}^*_{\mathrm{L}}$ follows immediately.

First, it is shown that $\mathcal{O}_{\mathrm{F}}$ is compositional w.r.t. all operators in **Sig**:

Lemma 9 (*Compositionality of* $\mathcal{O}_{\mathrm{F}}$) *For every* $i, j, k, \ell, m \in \omega$, *and* $F \in \mathbf{Fun}^{(i,j,k,\ell,m)}$, *one has the following: For every* $\vec{h} \in (\mathbf{E}_C)^i$, $\vec{e} \in (\mathcal{E}_V)^j$, $\vec{s} \in \mathcal{L}^k$, $\vec{t} \in (\mathcal{L}^{(0,1)})^\ell$, $\vec{u} \in (\mathcal{L}^{(1,0)})^m$,

$$\mathcal{O}_{\mathrm{F}}[\![F(\vec{h} \cdot \vec{e} \cdot \vec{s} \cdot \vec{t} \cdot \vec{u})]\!] = \mathcal{I}(F)([\![\vec{h}\ ]\!] \cdot [\![\vec{e}\ ]\!] \cdot \mathcal{O}_{\mathrm{F}}[\![\vec{s}\ ]\!] \cdot \mathcal{O}_{\mathrm{F}}[\![\vec{t}\ ]\!] \cdot \mathcal{O}_{\mathrm{F}}[\![\vec{u}\ ]\!]). \blacksquare \quad (14)$$

We will prove the claim (14) for $F \equiv \mathbf{let}(x, \cdot, \cdot)$ and for $F = \mathbf{LC}(\cdot)$; for the other operators except $\partial_C(\cdot)$, the claim has been established in Lemma 19 in [HBR 90]; for $\partial_C(\cdot)$ (14) can be established in a similar fashion to the proof of Lemma 19 in [HBR 90].

As preliminaries to the proof, we present four lemmas (all of them can be proved easily and their proof is omitted). The first two state useful properties of the operation $\mathrm{let}_x(\cdot)$; we will employ them for establishing (14) for $F \equiv \mathbf{let}(x, \cdot, \cdot)$.

Lemma 10 (*Distributivity of* let_x) *For* $x \in$ IVar *and* $f \in \mathbf{F}$, *the operation* $\mathrm{let}_x(f, \cdot)$ *is* distributive *in that* $\forall p_1, p_2 \in \mathbf{P}[\ \mathrm{let}_x(f, p_1 \cup p_2) = \mathrm{let}_x(f, p_1) \cup \mathrm{let}_x(f, p_2)\ ]$. ∎

Lemma 11 *Let us say* $p \in \mathbf{P}$ *is image-finite iff for every* $r \in (\Sigma \times \mathbf{A} \times \Sigma)^{<\omega}$,

$$p[r] \neq \emptyset \Rightarrow \forall \sigma \in \Sigma, \forall a \in \mathbf{A}[\ \{\sigma' \in \Sigma : p[r][(\langle\sigma, a, \sigma'\rangle)] \neq \emptyset\} \textit{ is finite }].$$

(1) *For every* $s \in \mathcal{L}[\emptyset]$, $\mathcal{O}_{\mathrm{F}}[\![s]\!]$ *is image-finite.*
(2) *For image-finite* $p \in \mathbf{P}$, *we can omit taking closure in (10).* ∎

Next, the following two lemmas are used for establishing (14) for $F = \mathbf{LC}(\cdot)$.

Lemma 12 *Let* $\mathrm{s} \in \mathcal{L}^{(1,0)}$, *and let* $\mathbf{c}, \mathbf{c}' \in$ **Chan** *such that* $\mathbf{c}, \mathbf{c}' \notin \mathcal{S}(\mathrm{s})$ *and* $\mathbf{c} \neq \mathbf{c}'$. *Then,* $\mathbf{c}' \notin \tilde{S}(\mathcal{O}_{\mathrm{F}}[\![\mathrm{s}(\mathbf{c})]\!])$ *and* $\tilde{\Theta}_{[\mathbf{c}'/\mathbf{c}]}(\mathcal{O}_{\mathrm{F}}[\![\mathrm{s}(\mathbf{c})]\!]) = \mathcal{O}_{\mathrm{F}}[\![\mathrm{s}(\mathbf{c}')]\!]$. ∎

Lemma 13 *Let* $p \in \mathbf{P}$, $\mathbf{c}, \mathbf{c}' \in$ **Chan** *such that* $\mathbf{c}' \notin \tilde{S}(p)$. *Then,* $\tilde{\partial}_{\{\mathbf{c}'\}}(\tilde{\Theta}_{[\mathbf{c}'/\mathbf{c}]}(p)) = \tilde{\partial}_{\{\mathbf{c}\}}(p)$. ∎

For notational convenience, we extend the domain of $\mathcal{O}_{\mathrm{F}}$ by:

Definition 20 **(1)** For $(i,j) \neq (0,0)$, $\mathbf{s} \in \mathcal{L}^{(i,j)}$, let

$$\mathcal{O}_{\mathrm{F}}[\![\mathbf{s}]\!] = (\lambda \vec{c} \cdot \vec{v} \in \mathbf{Chan}^i \cdot \mathbf{V}^j.\ \mathcal{O}_{\mathrm{F}}[\![\mathbf{s}(\vec{c} \cdot \vec{v})]\!]).$$

(2) For $\in \omega$, $\vec{\mathbf{s}} \in (\mathcal{L}^*)^n$, let $\mathcal{O}_{\mathrm{F}}[\![\vec{\mathbf{s}}]\!] = (\mathcal{O}_{\mathrm{F}}[\![\vec{\mathbf{s}}(i)]\!])_{i \in n}$.
(3) For $\theta \in$ SyVal, let $\mathcal{O}_{\mathrm{F}}[\![\theta]\!] = (\mathcal{O}_{\mathrm{F}}[\![\theta(Z)]\!])_{Z \in \mathrm{dom}(\theta)}$. ∎

Proof of Lemma 9. **Part 1.** First, we will prove (14) for $F \equiv \mathbf{let}(x,\cdot,\cdot)$. That is, we will prove the following for every $x \in$ IVar, $e \in \mathcal{E}_V$, and $s \in \mathcal{L}[\emptyset]$:

$$\mathcal{O}_{\mathrm{F}}[\![\mathbf{let}(x,e,s)]\!] = \mathrm{let}_x([\![e]\!], \mathcal{O}_{\mathrm{F}}[\![s]\!]). \tag{15}$$

Fix $x \in$ IVar, and let $\mathbf{K} = (\mathcal{L} \times \mathcal{E}_V \to \mathbf{P})$. Let us define $F, G \in \mathbf{K}$ as follows: For $\langle e,s \rangle \in \mathcal{L} \times \mathcal{E}_V$, $F(e,s) = \mathcal{O}_{\mathrm{F}}[\![\mathbf{let}(x,e,s)]\!]$, and $G(e,s) = \mathrm{let}_x([\![e]\!], \mathcal{O}_{\mathrm{F}}[\![s]\!])$. Let us show that $F = G$, which is a reformulation of (15), by showing that both F and G are the fixed-point of a higher-order contraction $\mathcal{K} : \mathbf{K} \to \mathbf{K}$ defined as follows: For $K \in \mathbf{K}$, and $\langle e,s \rangle \in \mathcal{E}_V \times \mathcal{L}$,

$$\begin{aligned}
&\mathcal{K}(K)(e,s) = \\
&\{\, (\langle \sigma, \Gamma \rangle) \in (\Sigma \times \wp(\mathbf{C}))^1 : \tau \notin \mathrm{act}(s, \sigma[[\![e]\!](\sigma)/x]) \\
&\quad \wedge \mathrm{act}(s, \sigma[[\![e]\!](\sigma)/x]) \cap \Gamma = \emptyset \} \\
&\cup \bigcup \{ (\langle \sigma, a, \sigma'[\sigma(x)/x] \rangle) \cdot K(s', \sigma'(x)) : \sigma, \sigma' \in \Sigma \wedge a \in \mathbf{A} \wedge s' \in \mathcal{L} \\
&\qquad \wedge \langle s, \sigma[[\![e]\!](\sigma)/x] \rangle \xrightarrow{a} \langle s', \sigma' \rangle \}.
\end{aligned}$$

It is easy to verify that $\mathcal{K}$ is a contraction from $\mathbf{K}$ to itself. Also it follows from the definition of $\mathcal{O}_{\mathrm{F}}$ that $F = \mathcal{K}(F)$, i.e. $F = \mathrm{fix}(\mathcal{K})$. Let us show $G = \mathcal{K}(G)$. For $\langle e,s \rangle \in \mathcal{E}_V \times \mathcal{L}$, it follows from the definition of let_x that

$$G(e,s) = \mathrm{let}_x([\![e]\!], \mathcal{O}_{\mathrm{F}}[\![s]\!]) = \mathrm{let}^0_x([\![e]\!], \mathcal{O}_{\mathrm{F}}[\![s]\!]) \cup \mathrm{let}^+_x([\![e]\!], \mathcal{O}_{\mathrm{F}}[\![s]\!]).$$

Further it follows from the definition of let^0_x that

$$\begin{aligned}
\mathrm{let}^0_x([\![e]\!], \mathcal{O}_{\mathrm{F}}[\![s]\!]) = \{\, (\langle \sigma, \Gamma \rangle)(\Sigma \times \wp(\mathbf{C}))^1 : \tau \notin \mathrm{act}(s, \sigma[[\![e]\!](\sigma)/x]) \\
\wedge \mathrm{act}(s, \sigma[[\![e]\!](\sigma)/x]) \cap \Gamma = \emptyset \}.
\end{aligned} \tag{16}$$

Also one has

$$\begin{aligned}
&\mathrm{let}^+_x([\![e]\!], \mathcal{O}_{\mathrm{F}}[\![s]\!]) \\
&= \bigcup \{\, (\langle \sigma, a, \sigma'[\sigma(x)/x] \rangle) \cdot \mathrm{let}_x(\sigma'(x), (\mathcal{O}_{\mathrm{F}}[\![s]\!])[(\langle \sigma[[\![e]\!](\sigma)/x], a, \sigma' \rangle)]) : \\
&\qquad (\mathcal{O}_{\mathrm{F}}[\![s]\!])[(\langle \sigma[[\![e]\!](\sigma)/x], a, \sigma' \rangle)] \neq \emptyset \}
\end{aligned}$$

(by the definition of let_x, where taking closure of the term $\bigcup\{\cdots\}$ can be omitted by Lemma 11 (2))

$$\begin{aligned}
&= \bigcup \{\, (\langle \sigma, a, \sigma'[\sigma(x)/x] \rangle) \cdot \mathrm{let}_x(\sigma'(x), \bigcup \{ \mathcal{O}_{\mathrm{F}}[\![s']\!] : \langle s, \sigma[[\![e]\!](\sigma)/x] \rangle \xrightarrow{a} \langle s', \sigma' \rangle \}) : \\
&\qquad \exists s' [\, \langle s, \sigma[[\![e]\!](\sigma)/x] \rangle \xrightarrow{a} \langle s', \sigma' \rangle \,] \}
\end{aligned}$$

(by the definition of $\mathcal{O}_{\mathrm{F}}$)

$$\begin{aligned}
&= \bigcup \{ \bigcup \{ (\langle \sigma, a, \sigma'[\sigma(x)/x] \rangle) \cdot \mathrm{let}_x(\sigma'(x), \mathcal{O}_{\mathrm{F}}[\![s']\!]) : \langle s, \sigma[[\![e]\!](\sigma)/x] \rangle \xrightarrow{a} \langle s', \sigma' \rangle \} : \\
&\qquad \exists s' [\, \langle s, \sigma[[\![e]\!](\sigma)/x] \rangle \xrightarrow{a} \langle s', \sigma' \rangle \,] \}
\end{aligned}$$

(by Lemma 10)

$$= \bigcup\{(\langle\sigma, a, \sigma'[\sigma(x)/x]\rangle) \cdot \mathrm{let}_x(\sigma'(x), \mathcal{O}_{\mathrm{F}}[\![s']\!]) : \langle s, \sigma[[\![e]\!](\sigma)/x]\rangle \xrightarrow{a} \langle s', \sigma'\rangle\}$$
$$= \bigcup\{(\langle\sigma, a, \sigma'[\sigma(x)/x]\rangle) \cdot G(\sigma'(x), s') : \langle s, \sigma[[\![e]\!](\sigma)/x]\rangle \xrightarrow{a} \langle s', \sigma'\rangle\}.$$

By this and (16), one has $G(e,s) = \mathrm{let}_x([\![e]\!], s) = \mathcal{K}(G)(e,s)$. Since e and s are arbitrary, one has $G = \mathcal{K}(G)$, i.e., $G = \mathrm{fix}(\mathcal{K})$. Thus, one has the desired result.
Part 2. Next, let us prove (14) for $F \equiv \mathbf{LF}(\cdot)$. That is, we will prove that the following holds for every $\mathbf{s} \in \mathcal{L}^{(1,0)}$: $(*)$: $\mathcal{O}_{\mathrm{F}}[\![\mathbf{LC}(\mathbf{s})]\!] = \mathrm{LC}(\mathcal{O}_{\mathrm{F}}[\![\mathbf{s}]\!])$. Let $\mathbf{s} \in \mathcal{L}^{(1,0)}$, and set $\mathbf{p} = \mathcal{O}_{\mathrm{F}}[\![\mathbf{s}]\!]$. First, one has $(\dagger)$: $\mathcal{O}_{\mathrm{F}}[\![\mathbf{LC}(\mathbf{s})]\!] = \mathcal{O}_{\mathrm{F}}[\![\partial_{\{\mathbf{c}_m\}}(\mathbf{s}(\mathbf{c}_m))]\!]$ with $m = \min\{i \in \omega : \mathbf{c}_i \notin \mathcal{S}(\mathbf{s})\}$, since the only rule by which one can derive transitions of $\langle \mathbf{s}, \sigma\rangle$ is Rule (10) in Definition 7. Next one has, by Lemma 12,

$$\forall \mathbf{c}, \mathbf{c}' \in (\mathbf{Chan}_1 \setminus \tilde{\mathcal{S}}(\mathbf{p}))[\ \tilde{\Theta}_{[\mathbf{c}'/\mathbf{c}]}(\mathbf{p}(\mathbf{c})) = \mathbf{p}(\mathbf{c}') \wedge (\mathbf{c} \neq \mathbf{c}' \Rightarrow \mathbf{c}' \notin \tilde{\mathcal{S}}(\mathbf{p}(\mathbf{c})))\ ].$$

Thus, by Definition 17, one has $(\ddagger)$: $\mathrm{LC}(\mathbf{p}) = \tilde{\partial}_{\{\mathbf{c}_n\}}(\mathbf{p}(\mathbf{c}_n))$ with

$$\begin{aligned} n = \min\{i \in \omega : \exists C \in \wp_{\mathrm{f}}(\mathbf{Chan}_1)[\ \mathbf{c}_i \notin C \wedge \forall \mathbf{c}, \mathbf{c}' \in (\mathbf{Chan}_1 \setminus C)[\\ \tilde{\Theta}_{[\mathbf{c}'/\mathbf{c}]}(\mathbf{p}(\mathbf{c})) = \mathbf{p}(\mathbf{c}') \wedge (\mathbf{c} \neq \mathbf{c}' \Rightarrow \mathbf{c}' \notin \tilde{\mathcal{S}}(\mathbf{p}(\mathbf{c}))) \wedge\ ]\}. \end{aligned} \tag{17}$$

By $(\dagger)$ and $(\ddagger)$, it is sufficient to show $(**)$: $\mathcal{O}_{\mathrm{F}}[\![\partial_{\{\mathbf{c}_m\}}(\mathbf{s}(\mathbf{c}_m))]\!] = \tilde{\partial}_{\{\mathbf{c}_n\}}(\mathbf{p}(\mathbf{c}_n))$, in order to show $(*)$. Let us prove $(**)$.

By (17), there is $C \in \wp_{\mathrm{f}}(\mathbf{Chan}_1)$ such that

$$\mathbf{c}_n \notin C \wedge \forall \mathbf{c}, \mathbf{c}' \in (\mathbf{Chan}_1 \setminus C)[\ \tilde{\Theta}_{[\mathbf{c}'/\mathbf{c}]}(\mathbf{p}(\mathbf{c})) = \mathbf{p}(\mathbf{c}') \wedge (\mathbf{c} \neq \mathbf{c}' \Rightarrow \mathbf{c}' \notin \tilde{\mathcal{S}}(\mathbf{p}(\mathbf{c})))\ ].$$

Let us fix such C. Then fixing $\mathbf{c} \in (\mathbf{Chan}_1 \setminus (\mathcal{S}(\mathbf{s}) \cup C))$, one has

$$\begin{aligned} &\mathcal{O}_{\mathrm{F}}[\![\partial_{\{\mathbf{c}_m\}}(\mathbf{s}(\mathbf{c}_m))]\!] = \tilde{\partial}_{\{\mathbf{c}_m\}}(\mathcal{O}_{\mathrm{F}}[\![\mathbf{s}(\mathbf{c}_m)]\!]) \\ &= \tilde{\partial}_{\{\mathbf{c}_m\}}(\tilde{\Theta}_{[\mathbf{c}_m/\mathbf{c}]}(\mathcal{O}_{\mathrm{F}}[\![\mathbf{s}(\mathbf{c})]\!])) \quad \text{(by Lemma 12)} \\ &= \tilde{\partial}_{\{\mathbf{c}\}}(\mathcal{O}_{\mathrm{F}}[\![\mathbf{s}(\mathbf{c})]\!]) \quad \text{(by Lemma 13).} \end{aligned} \tag{18}$$

Also one has

$$\begin{aligned} &\tilde{\partial}_{\{\mathbf{c}_n\}}(\mathbf{p}(\mathbf{c}_n)) = \tilde{\partial}_{\{\mathbf{c}_n\}}(\tilde{\Theta}_{[\mathbf{c}_n/\mathbf{c}]}(\mathbf{p}(\mathbf{c}))) \quad \text{(by Lemma 12)} \\ &= \tilde{\partial}_{\{\mathbf{c}\}}(\mathbf{p}(\mathbf{c})) \quad \text{(by Lemma 13)} \quad = \tilde{\partial}_{\{\mathbf{c}\}}(\mathcal{O}_{\mathrm{F}}[\![\mathbf{s}(\mathbf{c})]\!]). \end{aligned} \tag{19}$$

By (18) and (19), one has the desired result $(**)$. ■

By means of the compositionality of $\mathcal{O}_{\mathrm{F}}$ w.r.t. the constructs in **Sig** (Lemma 9), one has the equivalence between $\mathcal{O}_{\mathrm{F}}$ and $\mathcal{D}$:

Lemma 14 (*Semantic Equivalence between $\mathcal{O}_{\mathrm{F}}$ and $\mathcal{D}$*)

(1) *For* $\mathbf{S} \in \mathcal{L}^*[\mathcal{X}^*_{\mathcal{P}}]$, $\rho \in \mathrm{SeVal}$, *and* $\theta \in \mathrm{SyVal}$ *with* $\mathrm{FV}(\mathbf{S}) \subseteq \mathrm{dom}(\theta)$, *one has*

$$\mathcal{O}_{\mathrm{F}}[\![\mathbf{S}[\theta]]\!] = \mathcal{D}[\![\mathbf{S}]\!](\rho[\mathcal{O}_{\mathrm{F}}[\![\theta]\!]]). \tag{20}$$

(2) *For* $\mathbf{s} \in \mathcal{L}^*[\emptyset]$, $\mathcal{O}_{\mathrm{F}}[\![\mathbf{s}]\!] = \mathcal{D}[\![\mathbf{s}]\!]$. ■

Proof. Let us prove the claim (20) by induction on $\deg(\mathbf{S})$.
Induction Base. Suppose $\deg(\mathbf{S}) = 0$, i.e., $\mathbf{S} \in \mathcal{X}^*_{\mathcal{P}}$. Then, $\mathcal{O}_{\mathrm{F}}[\![\mathbf{S}[\theta]]\!] = \mathcal{O}_{\mathrm{F}}[\![\theta(\mathbf{S})]\!] = \mathcal{D}[\![\mathbf{S}]\!](\mathcal{O}_{\mathrm{F}}[\![\theta]\!])$.
Induction Step. Let $n > 0$, and assume the claim (20) has been proved for $\mathbf{S}$ with $\deg(\mathbf{S}) < n$. Fix $\mathbf{S} \in \mathcal{L}^*[\mathcal{X}^*_{\mathcal{P}}]$ such that $\deg(\mathbf{S}) = n$. Let us show (20) for S. We distinguish four cases according to the form of S.

Case 1. Suppose $\mathbf{S} \equiv F(\vec{g}\cdot\vec{e}\cdot\vec{S}\cdot\vec{T}\cdot\vec{U})$ with $F \in \mathbf{Fun}^{(i,j,k,\ell,m)}$ and $\vec{g} \in (\mathcal{E}_C)^i$, $\vec{e} \in (\mathcal{E}_V)^j$, $\vec{S} \in (\mathcal{L}[\mathcal{X}_{\mathcal{P}}^*])^k$, $\vec{T} \in (\mathcal{L}^{(0,1)}[\mathcal{X}_{\mathcal{P}}^*])^\ell$, $\vec{U} \in (\mathcal{L}^{(1,0)}[\mathcal{X}_{\mathcal{P}}^*])^m$. Then,

$$\begin{aligned}
&\mathcal{O}_{\mathrm{F}}[\![\mathbf{S}[\theta]]\!](\rho) = \mathcal{I}(F)([\![\vec{g}]\!]\cdot[\![\vec{e}]\!]\cdot\mathcal{O}_{\mathrm{F}}[\![\vec{S}[\theta]]\!](\rho)\cdot\mathcal{O}_{\mathrm{F}}[\![\vec{T}[\theta]]\!](\rho)\cdot\mathcal{O}_{\mathrm{F}}[\![\vec{U}[\theta]]\!](\rho))\\
&= \mathcal{I}(F)([\![\vec{g}]\!]\cdot[\![\vec{e}]\!]\cdot\mathcal{D}[\![\vec{S}]\!](\rho[\mathcal{O}_{\mathrm{F}}[\![\theta]\!]])\cdot\mathcal{D}[\![\vec{T}]\!](\rho[\mathcal{O}_{\mathrm{F}}[\![\theta]\!]])\cdot\mathcal{D}[\![\vec{U}]\!](\rho[\mathcal{O}_{\mathrm{F}}[\![\theta]\!]]))\\
&\quad\text{(by the induction hypothesis)}\\
&= \mathcal{D}[\![S]\!](\mathcal{O}_{\mathrm{F}}[\![\theta]\!]).
\end{aligned}$$

Case 2. Suppose $\mathbf{S} \equiv (\lambda\vec{\eta}\cdot\vec{\xi}.\ \mathbf{S}')$. Then,

$$\begin{aligned}
&\mathcal{O}_{\mathrm{F}}[\![\mathbf{S}[\theta]]\!] = \mathcal{O}_{\mathrm{F}}[\![(\lambda\vec{\eta}\cdot\vec{\xi}.\ \mathbf{S}'[\theta])]\!] = (\lambda\vec{c}\cdot\vec{v}.\ \mathcal{O}_{\mathrm{F}}[\![(\mathbf{S}'[\theta])[(\vec{c}\cdot\vec{v})/(\vec{\eta}\cdot\vec{\xi})]]\!])\\
&= (\lambda\vec{c}\cdot\vec{v}.\ \mathcal{O}_{\mathrm{F}}[\![(\mathbf{S}'[(\vec{c}\cdot\vec{v})/(\vec{\eta}\cdot\vec{\xi})])[\theta]]\!])\quad\text{(by the definition of } \mathcal{O}_{\mathrm{F}})\\
&= (\lambda\vec{c}\cdot\vec{v}.\ \mathcal{D}[\![\mathbf{S}'[(\vec{c}\cdot\vec{v})/(\vec{\eta}\cdot\vec{\xi})]]\!](\rho[\mathcal{O}_{\mathrm{F}}[\![\theta]\!]]))\quad\text{(by the induction hypothesis)}\\
&= \mathcal{D}[\![(\lambda\vec{\eta}\cdot\vec{\xi}.\ \mathbf{S}')]\!](\rho[\mathcal{O}_{\mathrm{F}}[\![\theta]\!]])\quad\text{(by the definition of } \mathcal{D})\\
&= \mathcal{D}[\![\mathbf{S}]\!](\rho[\mathcal{O}_{\mathrm{F}}[\![\theta]\!]]).
\end{aligned}$$

Case 3. Suppose $\mathbf{S} \equiv (\mu Z.\ \mathbf{S}')$. Then,

$$\begin{aligned}
&\mathcal{O}_{\mathrm{F}}[\![\mathbf{S}[\theta]]\!] = \mathcal{O}_{\mathrm{F}}[\![(\mu Z.\ (\mathbf{S}')[\theta])]\!] = \mathcal{O}_{\mathrm{F}}[\![(\mathbf{S}'[\theta])[\mathbf{S}[\theta]/Z]]\!]\\
&= \mathcal{O}_{\mathrm{F}}[\![\mathbf{S}'[\theta[\mathbf{S}[\theta]/Z]]]\!]\quad\text{(for the notation } \theta[\mathbf{S}[\theta]/Z] \text{ see Notation 3)}\\
&= \mathcal{D}[\![\mathbf{S}']\!](\rho[\mathcal{O}_{\mathrm{F}}[\![\hat{\theta}\cup\langle Z,\mathbf{S}[\theta]\rangle]\!]])\quad\text{(by the induction hypothesis)}\\
&= \mathcal{D}[\![\mathbf{S}']\!](\rho[\mathcal{O}_{\mathrm{F}}[\![\theta]\!]][\mathcal{O}_{\mathrm{F}}[\![\mathbf{S}[\theta]]\!]/Z]).
\end{aligned}$$

Thus, $\mathcal{O}_{\mathrm{F}}[\![\mathbf{S}[\theta]]\!] = \mathcal{D}[\![\mathbf{S}']\!](\rho[\mathcal{O}_{\mathrm{F}}[\![\theta]\!]][\mathcal{O}_{\mathrm{F}}[\![\mathbf{S}[\theta]]\!]/Z])$. By this and (13), one has

$$\mathcal{O}_{\mathrm{F}}[\![\mathbf{S}[\theta]]\!] = \mathcal{D}[\![(\mu Z.\ \mathbf{S}')]\!](\rho[\mathcal{O}_{\mathrm{F}}[\![\theta]\!]]) = \mathcal{D}[\![\mathbf{S}]\!](\rho[\mathcal{O}_{\mathrm{F}}[\![\theta]\!]]).$$

Case 4. Suppose $\mathbf{S} \equiv \mathbf{S}'(\vec{g}\cdot\vec{e})$. Then,

$$\begin{aligned}
&\mathcal{O}_{\mathrm{F}}\llbracket\mathbf{S}[\theta]\rrbracket = \mathcal{O}_{\mathrm{F}}\llbracket\mathbf{S}'[\theta](\vec{g}\cdot\vec{e})\rrbracket = \bigcup_{\sigma\in\Sigma}[\mathcal{O}_{\mathrm{F}}\llbracket\mathbf{S}'[\theta](\llbracket\vec{g}\rrbracket(\sigma)\cdot\llbracket\vec{e}\rrbracket(\sigma))\rrbracket\langle\sigma\rangle]\quad\text{(by Lemma 4)}\\
&= \bigcup_{\sigma\in\Sigma}[\mathcal{O}_{\mathrm{F}}[\![\mathbf{S}'[\theta]]\!]([\![\vec{g}]\!](\sigma)\cdot[\![\vec{e}]\!](\sigma))\langle\sigma\rangle]\quad\text{(by Definition 20 (1))}\\
&= \bigcup_{\sigma\in\Sigma}[\mathcal{D}[\![\mathbf{S}']\!](\rho[\mathcal{O}_{\mathrm{F}}[\![\theta]\!]])([\![\vec{g}]\!](\sigma)\cdot[\![\vec{e}]\!](\sigma))\langle\sigma\rangle]\quad\text{(by the induction hypothesis)}\\
&= \mathcal{D}[\![\mathbf{S}'(\vec{g}\cdot\vec{e})]\!](\rho[\mathcal{O}_{\mathrm{F}}[\![\theta]\!]]).\quad\text{(by Lemma lem:deno-model (5))}
\end{aligned}$$

Thus, one has the desired result. ■

From the above lemma and Lemma 5, the following lemma follows immediately:

Corollary 1 (*Correctness of $\mathcal{D}$ w.r.t. $\mathcal{O}_{\mathrm{L}}$ and $\mathcal{O}_{\mathrm{L}}^*$*)
(1) $\forall s \in \mathcal{L}[\emptyset][\ \mathcal{O}_{\mathrm{L}}[\![s]\!] = \mathcal{A}_{\mathrm{L}}(\mathcal{D}[\![s]\!])\ ]$. **(2)** $\forall s \in \mathcal{L}[\emptyset][\ \mathcal{O}_{\mathrm{L}}^*[\![s]\!] = \mathcal{A}_{\mathrm{L}}^*(\mathcal{D}[\![s]\!])\ ]$. ■

6 Full Abstraction of $\mathcal{D}$ w.r.t. $\mathcal{O}_{\mathrm{L}}$ and $\mathcal{O}_{\mathrm{L}}^*$

Having established the compositionality of $\mathcal{D}$ (Lemma 8) and its correctness w.r.t. $\mathcal{O}_{\mathrm{L}}$ and $\mathcal{O}_{\mathrm{L}}^*$ (Corollary 1), the full abstraction of $\mathcal{D}$ w.r.t. $\mathcal{O}_{\mathrm{L}}$ and $\mathcal{O}_{\mathrm{L}}^*$ follows immediately from the full abstraction results in [HBR 90] and [Hor 92a]:

Theorem 1 (*Full Abstraction of $\mathcal{D}$ w.r.t. $\mathcal{O}_L$ and $\mathcal{O}^*_L$*) *If* **V** *is infinite, then the following hold:*

(1) *For every $s_1, s_2 \in \mathcal{L}[\emptyset]$,*

$$\begin{array}{l}\mathcal{D}[\![s_1]\!] = \mathcal{D}[\![s_2]\!] \Leftrightarrow \\ \forall X \in \mathcal{X}_\mathcal{P}, \forall S \in \mathcal{L}[\{X\}][\ \mathcal{O}_L[\![S[s_1/X]]\!] = \mathcal{O}_L[\![S[s_2/X]]\!]\ ].\end{array} \tag{21}$$

(2) *For every $s_1, s_2 \in \mathcal{L}[\emptyset]$,*

$$\begin{array}{l}\mathcal{D}[\![s_1]\!] = \mathcal{D}[\![s_2]\!] \Leftrightarrow \\ \forall X \in \mathcal{X}_\mathcal{P}, \forall S \in \mathcal{L}[\{X\}][\ \mathcal{O}^*_L[\![S[s_1/X]]\!] = \mathcal{O}^*_L[\![S[s_2/X]]\!]\ ].\ \blacksquare\end{array} \tag{22}$$

In order to prove the above theorem, we employ the following two lemmas, which have been established in [HBR 90] and [Hor 92a], respectively.

Lemma 15 *If* **V** *is infinite, then*

$$\forall p_1, p_2 \in \mathbf{P}[\ p_1 \neq p_2 \Rightarrow \exists \tilde{s} \in \mathcal{L}[\ \mathcal{A}_L(p_1 \tilde{\|} \mathcal{D}[\![\tilde{s}]\!]) \neq \mathcal{A}_L(p_2 \tilde{\|} \mathcal{D}[\![\tilde{s}]\!])\ ].\ \blacksquare$$

Proof. See Theorem 2 of [HBR 90]. ■

Lemma 16 *If* **V** *is infinite, then*

$$\forall s_1, s_2 \in \mathcal{L}[\ \mathcal{O}_L[\![s_1]\!] \neq \mathcal{O}_L[\![s_2]\!] \Rightarrow \exists \tilde{s} \in \mathcal{L}[\ \mathcal{O}^*_L[\![s_1 \| \tilde{s}]\!] \neq \mathcal{O}^*_L[\![s_2 \| \tilde{s}]\!]\ ]].\ \blacksquare$$

Proof. See Lemma 3 of [Hor 92a]. There, the proof is given for a sublanguage of $\mathcal{L}$. However, it is straightforward to verify that the same argument applies to the language $\mathcal{L}$. ■

Proof of Theorem 1. Part (1). Let $s_1, s_2 \in \mathcal{L}[\emptyset]$. The $\Rightarrow$-part of (21) follows from Lemma 8 and Corollary 1 (1) as follows: Suppose $\mathcal{D}[\![s_1]\!] = \mathcal{D}[\![s_2]\!]$, let $X \in \mathcal{X}_\mathcal{P}$, $S \in \mathcal{L}[\{X\}]$, and let ρ be an arbitrary element of SeVal. Then

$$\begin{array}{l}\mathcal{O}_F[\![S[s_1/X]]\!] = \mathcal{A}_L(\mathcal{D}[\![S[s_1/X]]\!]) \quad \text{(by Corollary 1 (1))} \\ = \mathcal{A}_L(\mathcal{D}[\![S]\!](\rho[\mathcal{D}[\![s_1]\!]/X])) \quad \text{(by Lemma 8)} \\ = \mathcal{A}_L(\mathcal{D}[\![S]\!](\rho[\mathcal{D}[\![s_2]\!]/X])) \quad (\text{since } \mathcal{D}[\![s_1]\!] = \mathcal{D}[\![s_2]\!]) \\ = \mathcal{A}_L(\mathcal{D}[\![S[s_2/X]]\!]) = \mathcal{O}_F[\![S[s_2/X]]\!].\end{array}$$

The $\Leftarrow$-part of (21) follows from Lemma 15 as follows: Let us show the contrapositive. Suppose $\mathcal{D}[\![s_1]\!] \neq \mathcal{D}[\![s_1]\!]$. Then, by Lemma 15, there is $\tilde{s} \in \mathcal{L}[\emptyset]$ such that

$$\mathcal{O}_L[\![s_1 \| \tilde{s}]\!] = \mathcal{A}_L(\mathcal{D}[\![s_1]\!] \tilde{\|} \mathcal{D}[\![s]\!]) \neq \mathcal{A}_L(\mathcal{D}[\![s_2]\!] \tilde{\|} \mathcal{D}[\![s]\!]) = \mathcal{O}_L[\![s_2 \| \tilde{s}]\!].$$

Thus, putting $S \equiv (X \| \tilde{s})$, one has $\mathcal{O}_F[\![S[s_1/X]]\!] \neq \mathcal{O}_F[\![S[s_2/X]]\!]$. Summing up one has the contrapositive of the $\Leftarrow$-part of (21).

Part (2). Let $s_1, s_2 \in \mathcal{L}[\emptyset]$. The $\Rightarrow$-part of (21) follows from Lemma 8 and Corollary 1 (2) as in Part (1). The $\Leftarrow$-part of (22) follows from Lemma 15 and Lemma 16 as follows: Suppose $\mathcal{D}[\![s_1]\!] \neq \mathcal{D}[\![s_1]\!]$. Then, by Lemma 15, there is $\tilde{s} \in \mathcal{L}[\emptyset]$ such that $\mathcal{O}_L[\![s_1 \| \tilde{s}]\!] \neq \mathcal{O}_L[\![s_2 \| \tilde{s}]\!]$. Also by Lemma 16, there is $\tilde{s}' \in \mathcal{L}$ such that $\mathcal{O}^*_L[\![(s_1 \| \tilde{s}) \| \tilde{s}']\!] \neq \mathcal{O}^*_L[\![(s_2 \| \tilde{s}) \| \tilde{s}']\!]$. Thus, putting $S \equiv ((X \| \tilde{s}) \| \tilde{s}')$, one has $\mathcal{O}_F[\![S[s_1/X]]\!] \neq \mathcal{O}_F[\![S[s_2/X]]\!]$. ■

7 Concluding Remarks

We conclude this paper with some remarks about related work and directions for future study.

We have shown how the simple nonuniform concurrent language presented in [HBR 90] can be extended so as to incorporate parameterization and locality (local variables and local channels), with the full abstraction result obtained in [HBR 90] being preserved.

Our treatment of parameterization paper is standard except that the interpretation of function application is *nonuniform* in the sense of Lemma 7 (5). Our treatment of local channels is very similar to Milner's treatment of auxiliary channels introduced for defining *the linking combinator* '$\frown$' (see Remark 1 in § 3). There are several approaches to the semantics of local variables. Our treatment of them is similar to that in [BKPR92] which treats more general setting with a state space including states with partial information. The treatment in [BKPR92], in turn, is based on the idea of [SRP 90] of using cylindric algebras (see [HMT 71]) to capture the notion of projecting away information. For other approaches to the problem of giving semantics to local variables especially those using categorical methods, we refer the reader to an expository article [OT 92]

There are two directions for extending the reported results. One is to investigate fully abstract models for extended languages such as ones including real-time constructs. The other is to investigate fully abstract models for the same language $\mathcal{L}$, but w.r.t. more abstract operational models, e.g, linear models which are *weak* in that it ignores internal steps denoted by τ. Such models which are fully abstract w.r.t. weak linear models have been proposed for *uniform* concurrent languages (cf., e.g., [DH 83], [Hen 85], [Hen 88], [HI 90], [Hor 92]); a similar problem for *nonuniform* concurrent languages is an interesting topic for future study.

Acknowledgments. The author would like to thank Jaco de Bakker, Prakash Panangaden, Jan Rutten, and Franck van Breugel for useful discussions and comments. He would also like to thank his colleagues at NTT Software Laboratories, especially Haruhisa Ichikawa, for their helpful comments and encouragement.

Appendix A Formal Definition of Language $\mathcal{L}$

In this appendix $\mathcal{L}$ is defined formally along the lines of of the definition of a simple language $\mathcal{L}_0$ in [KR 90] § 1.1. For each $n \in \omega$, we define $\mathcal{L}^{(i,j)}(n)$ and $\mathcal{G}_Z^{(i,j)}(n)$ for $(i,j) \in \omega^2$ and $Z \in \mathcal{X}_\mathcal{P}^*$ simultaneously, by induction on n as follows:

Definition 21 (*Definition of Language $\mathcal{L}$*)

(1) For each $(i,j) \in \omega^2$ and $Z \in \mathcal{X}_\mathcal{P}^*$, let $\mathcal{L}^{(i,j)}(0) = \emptyset$, and $\mathcal{G}_Z^{(i,j)}(0) = \emptyset$.

(2) Let $n \in \omega$. In terms of $\mathcal{L}^{(i,j)}(n)$ and $\mathcal{G}_Z^{(i,j)}(n)$ for $(i,j) \in \omega^2$ and $Z \in \mathcal{X}_\mathcal{P}^*$, we define $\mathcal{L}^{(i,j)}(n+1)$ as follows: First let

$$\begin{aligned}&\mathcal{L}^{(0,0)}(n+1) = \\ &\mathcal{X}_\mathcal{P}^{(0,0)} \cup \bigcup \{\, \{ F(\vec{H} \cdot \vec{E} \cdot \vec{S} \cdot \vec{T} \cdot \vec{U}) : F \in \mathbf{Fun}^{(i,j,k,\ell,m)} \wedge \vec{H} \in (\tilde{\mathcal{E}}_C)^i \wedge \vec{E} \in (\tilde{\mathcal{E}}_V)^j \\ &\qquad \wedge \vec{S} \in (\mathcal{L}^{(0,0)}(n))^k \wedge \vec{T} \in (\mathcal{L}^{(0,1)}(n))^\ell \wedge \vec{U} \in (\mathcal{L}^{(1,0)}(n))^m \} : \\ &\quad (i,j,k,\ell,m) \in \omega^5 \}\end{aligned}$$

$$\cup\bigcup\{\{\mathbf{S}(\vec{H}\cdot\vec{E}) : \mathbf{S}\in\mathcal{L}^{(i,j)}(n) \wedge \vec{H}\in(\tilde{\mathcal{E}}_C)^i \wedge \vec{E}\in(\tilde{\mathcal{E}}_V)^j\} : (i,j)\neq(0,0)\}$$
$$\cup\{(\mu X : S).\ X\in\mathcal{X}_{\mathcal{P}} \wedge S\in\mathcal{G}_X(n)\};$$

then for $(i,j)\neq(0,0)$ let

$$\mathcal{L}^{(i,j)}(n+1) =$$
$$\mathcal{X}_{\mathcal{P}}^{(i,j)} \cup\bigcup\{\{(\lambda\vec{\eta}\cdot\vec{\xi}.\ \mathbf{S}) : \vec{\eta}\in(\mathcal{X}_C)^{(i)} \wedge \vec{\xi}\in(\mathcal{X}_V)^{(j)} \wedge \mathbf{S}\in\mathcal{L}^{(0,0)}(n)\} : (i,j)\in\omega^2\}$$
$$\cup\{(\mu Z.\ \mathbf{S}) : Z\in\mathcal{X}^{(i,j)} \wedge \mathbf{S}\in\mathcal{G}_Z^{(i,j)}(n)\}.$$

Also for each $Z\in\mathcal{X}_{\mathcal{P}}^*$, we define $\mathcal{G}_Z^{(i,j)}(n+1)$ as follows: First let

$$\mathcal{G}_Z^{(0,0)}(n+1) ::=$$
$$(\mathcal{X}^{(0,0)}\setminus\{Z\})\cup\{(\mathbf{asg}(x,E);S) : x\in\text{IVar} \wedge S\in\mathcal{L}^{(0,0)}(n)\}$$
$$\cup\{(\mathbf{out}(H,E);S) : H\in\tilde{\mathcal{E}}_C \wedge E\in\tilde{\mathcal{E}}_V \wedge S\in\mathcal{L}^{(0,0)}(n)\}$$
$$\cup\{(\mathbf{in}(H,x);S) : x\in\text{IVar} \wedge H\in\tilde{\mathcal{E}}_C \wedge S\in\mathcal{L}^{(0,0)}(n)\}$$
$$\cup\{(\mathbf{in}'(G);\mathbf{S}) : H\in\tilde{\mathcal{E}}_C \wedge \mathbf{S}\in\mathcal{L}^{(0,1)}(n)\}$$
$$\cup\bigcup\{\{F(\vec{H}\cdot\vec{E}\cdot\vec{S}\cdot\vec{T}\cdot\vec{U}) : F\in\mathbf{Fun}^{(i,j,k,\ell,m)} \wedge \vec{H}\in(\tilde{\mathcal{E}}_C)^i \wedge \vec{E}\in(\tilde{\mathcal{E}}_V)^j$$
$$\wedge\vec{S}\in(\mathcal{G}_Z(n))^k \wedge \vec{T}\in(\mathcal{G}_Z^{(0,1)}(n))^\ell \wedge \vec{U}\in(\mathcal{G}_Z^{(1,0)}(n))^m\} :$$
$$(i,j,k,\ell,m)\in\omega^5\}$$
$$\cup\bigcup\{\{\mathbf{S}(\vec{H}\cdot\vec{E}) : \mathbf{S}\in\mathcal{G}_Z^{(i,j)}(n) \wedge \vec{H}\in(\tilde{\mathcal{E}}_C)^i \wedge \vec{E}\in(\tilde{\mathcal{E}}_V)^j\} : (i,j)\neq(0,0)\}$$
$$\cup\{(\mu Z'.\ \mathbf{S}) : Z'\in\mathcal{X}_{\mathcal{P}}^{(i,j)} \wedge \mathbf{S}\in\mathcal{G}_Z^{(i,j)}(n) \wedge \mathcal{G}_{Z'}^{(i,j)}(n)\};$$

then for $(i,j)\neq(0,0)$ let

$$\mathcal{G}_Z^{(i,j)}(n+1) ::=$$
$$(\mathcal{X}_{\mathcal{P}}^{(i,j)}\setminus\{Z\})\cup\{(\lambda\vec{\eta}\cdot\vec{\xi}.\ \mathbf{S}) : \vec{\eta}\in(\mathcal{X}_C)^{(i)} \wedge \vec{\xi}\in(\mathcal{X}_V)^{(i)} \wedge \mathbf{S}\in\mathcal{G}_Z^{(0,0)}\}$$
$$\cup\{(\mu Z'.\ \mathbf{S}) : Z'\in(\mathcal{X}_{\mathcal{P}})^{(i,j)} \wedge \mathbf{S}\in\mathcal{G}_{Z'}^{(0,0)}(n)\cap\mathcal{G}_Z^{(i,j)}(n)\}.$$

It can be shown immediately by induction on n that

$$\forall n\in\omega, \forall(i,j)\in\omega^2, \forall Z\in\mathcal{X}_{\mathcal{P}}^*[\ \mathcal{G}_Z^{(i,j)}(n)\subseteq\mathcal{L}^{(i,j)}(n)$$
$$\wedge\,\mathcal{G}_Z^{(i,j)}(n)\subseteq\mathcal{G}_Z^{(i,j)}(n+1) \wedge \mathcal{L}^{(i,j)}(n)\subseteq\mathcal{L}^{(i,j)}(n+1)\ ].$$

(3) For each $n\in\omega$ and $Z\in\mathcal{X}_{\mathcal{P}}^*$, let $\mathcal{L}^*(n) = \bigcup\{\mathcal{L}^{(i,j)}(n) : (i,j)\in\omega^2\}$, and $\mathcal{G}_Z^*(n) = \bigcup\{\mathcal{G}_Z^{(i,j)}(n) : (i,j)\in\omega^2\}$. Also for each $(i,j)\in\omega^2$, let $\mathcal{L}^{(i,j)} = \bigcup\{\mathcal{L}^{(i,j)}(n) : n\in\omega\}$. ∎

Appendix B Definition of Denotational Model $\mathcal{D}$

For each $n\in\omega$, $\mathbf{S}\in\mathcal{L}^*(n)[\mathcal{X}_{\mathcal{P}}^*]$, and $\rho\in$ SeVal, we will define $\mathcal{D}[\![\mathbf{S}]\!](\rho)$, by induction on n. In other words, we will define for each $n\in\omega$, a family of mappings $(\lambda\mathbf{S}\in\mathcal{L}^*(n)[\mathcal{X}_{\mathcal{P}}^*].\ (\lambda\rho\in$ SeVal. $\mathcal{D}[\![\mathbf{S}]\!](\rho)))$ by induction on n. We will define this family so that the following two conditions are satisfied for every $n\in\omega$:

$$\forall(i,j)\in\omega^2, \forall\mathbf{S}\in\mathcal{L}^{(i,j)}(n)[\mathcal{X}_{\mathcal{P}}^*][$$
$$(\lambda\rho\in\text{SeVal}.\ \mathcal{D}[\![\mathbf{S}]\!](\rho)) \text{ is a nonexpansive mapping from SeVal to } \mathbf{P}^{(i,j)}\ ], \tag{23}$$

$$\forall (k,\ell),(i,j) \in \omega^2, \forall Z \in \mathcal{X}_{\mathcal{P}}^{(k,\ell)}, \forall \mathbf{S} \in \mathcal{G}_Z^{(i,j)}(n)[\mathcal{X}_{\mathcal{P}}^*], \forall \rho \in \text{SeVal}[\ (\lambda \mathbf{p} \in \mathbf{P}^{(k,\ell)}.\ \mathcal{D}[\![\mathbf{S}]\!](\rho[\mathbf{p}/Z])) \text{ is a contraction from } \mathbf{P}^{(k,\ell)} \text{ to } \mathbf{P}^{(i,j)} \text{ with coefficient } (1/2).\ ] \quad (24)$$

Step 1. For $n = 0$, we simply define $(\lambda \mathbf{S} \in \mathcal{L}^*(0)[\mathcal{X}_{\mathcal{P}}^*].\ (\lambda \rho \in \text{SeVal}.\ \mathcal{D}[\![\mathbf{S}]\!](\rho)))$ to be the empty mapping, since $\mathcal{L}^*(0)[\mathcal{X}_{\mathcal{P}}^*] = \emptyset$.
Step 2. Let $n \in \omega$ and assume that

For $\mathbf{S} \in \mathcal{L}^*(n)[\mathcal{X}_{\mathcal{P}}^*]$ and $\rho \in$ SeVal, $\mathcal{D}[\![\mathbf{S}]\!](\rho)$ has been defined so that the conditions (23) and (24) are satisfied. (25)

Step 2.1. First, let us define $\mathcal{D}[\![\mathbf{S}]\!](\rho)$ for $(i,j) \in \omega^2$, $\mathbf{S} \in \mathcal{L}^{(i,j)}(n+1)[\mathcal{X}_{\mathcal{P}}^*]$ and $\rho \in$ SeVal. Fix $(i,j) \in \omega^2$. We distinguish two cases according to whether or not $(i,j) = (0,0)$.
Case 1. Suppose $(i,j) = (0,0)$. We distinguish several cases according to the form of $\mathbf{S}$.
Subcase 1.1. Suppose $\mathbf{S} \in \mathcal{X}_{\mathcal{P}}$. Then let $\mathcal{D}[\![\mathbf{S}]\!](\rho) = \rho(\mathbf{S})$. Obviously the mapping $(\lambda \rho \in \text{SeVal}.\ \mathcal{D}[\![\mathbf{S}]\!](\rho)) = (\lambda \rho \in \mathbf{P}^1.\ \rho(\mathbf{S}))$ is nonexpansive.
Subcase 1.2. Suppose $\mathbf{S} \equiv F(\vec{h} \cdot \vec{e} \cdot \vec{S} \cdot \vec{T} \cdot \vec{U})$ for some (i',j',k',ℓ',m'), $F \in \mathbf{Fun}^{(i',j',k',\ell',m')}$, $\vec{g} \in (\mathcal{E}_C)^{i'}$, $\vec{e} \in (\mathcal{E}_V)^{j'}$, $\vec{S} \in (\mathcal{L}^{(0,0)}(n)[\mathcal{X}_{\mathcal{P}}^*])^{k'}$, $\vec{T} \in (\mathcal{L}^{(0,1)}(n)[\mathcal{X}_{\mathcal{P}}^*])^{\ell'}$, $\vec{U} \in (\mathcal{L}^{(1,0)}(n)[\mathcal{X}_{\mathcal{P}}^*])^{m'}$. Then let $\mathcal{D}[\![\mathbf{S}]\!](\rho) = \mathcal{I}(F)([\![\vec{g}]\!] \cdot [\![\mathbf{e}]\!] \cdot \mathcal{D}[\![\vec{S}]\!](\rho) \cdot \mathcal{D}[\![\vec{T}]\!](\rho) \cdot \mathcal{D}[\![\vec{U}]\!](\rho))$, where $\mathcal{D}[\![\vec{S}]\!](\rho) = (\mathcal{D}[\![\vec{S}(i)]\!](\rho))_{i \in k'}$, and $\mathcal{D}[\![\vec{T}]\!](\rho)$, $\mathcal{D}[\![\vec{U}]\!](\rho)$ are defined in a similar fashion. In this subcase also, the mapping $(\lambda \rho \in \text{SeVal}.\ \mathcal{D}[\![\mathbf{S}]\!](\rho))$ is nonexpansive, by the induction hypothesis (25) stating that (23) holds and Lemma 6 (1).
Subcase 1.3. Suppose $\mathbf{S} \equiv \mathbf{S}'(\vec{g} \cdot \vec{e})$ for some $(i',j') \in \omega^2$, $\mathbf{S}' \in \mathcal{L}^{(i',j')}(n)[\mathcal{X}_{\mathcal{P}}^*]$ $\vec{g} \in (\mathcal{E}_C)^{i'}$, $\vec{e} \in (\mathcal{E}_V)^{j'}$. Then let

$$\mathcal{D}[\![\mathbf{S}]\!](\rho) = \bigcup_{\sigma \in \Sigma} [\mathcal{D}[\![\mathbf{S}']\!](\rho)([\![\vec{g}]\!](\sigma) \cdot [\![\vec{e}]\!](\sigma))\langle\sigma\rangle].$$

It follows immediately from the induction hypothesis (25) stating that (23) holds and the definition of the metric on $\mathbf{P}^{(i',j')}$ that the mapping $(\lambda \rho \in \text{SeVal}.\ \mathcal{D}[\![\mathbf{S}]\!](\rho))$ is nonexpansive.
Subcase 1.4. Suppose $\mathbf{S} \equiv (\mu X.\ \mathbf{S}')$ with $\mathbf{S}' \in \mathcal{G}_X(n)[\mathcal{X}_{\mathcal{P}}^*]$. For $\rho \in$ SeVal, let $\varphi(\rho) = (\lambda p \in \mathbf{P}.\ \mathcal{D}[\![\mathbf{S}']\!](\rho[p/X]))$. By the induction hypothesis (25) stating that (24) holds, the mapping $\varphi(\rho)$ is a contraction from $\mathbf{P}$ to itself with coefficient (1/2). We define $\mathcal{D}[\![\mathbf{S}]\!](\rho) = \text{fix}(\varphi(\rho))$.

It can shown that the mapping $(\lambda \rho \in \text{SeVal}.\ \mathcal{D}[\![\mathbf{S}]\!](\rho))$ is nonexpansive as follows: Let p_0 be an arbitrary element of $\mathbf{P}$. Then, by Banach's Theorem,

$$\mathcal{D}[\![\mathbf{S}]\!](\rho) = \text{fix}(\varphi(\rho)) = \lim_{n \to \infty} [(\varphi(\rho))^n(p_0)],$$

where $(\varphi(\rho))^n$ is the n-th iteration of $\varphi(\rho)$. Let $\rho_1, \rho_1 \in$ SeVal. Then, by induction, it can be shown immediately that

$$\forall n \in \omega[\ d((\varphi(\rho_1))^n(p_0), (\varphi(\rho_2))^n(p_0)) \leq d(\rho_1, \rho_2)\ ].$$

Thus, one has

$$d(\mathcal{D}[\![\mathbf{S}]\!](\rho_1), \mathcal{D}[\![\mathbf{S}]\!](\rho_2)) = \lim_{n \to \infty} [d((\varphi(\rho_1))^n(p_0), (\varphi(\rho_2))^n(p_0))] \leq d(\rho_1, \rho_2).$$

Hence, the mapping $(\lambda \rho \in \text{SeVal}.\ \mathcal{D}[\![\mathbf{S}]\!](\rho))$ is nonexpansive.
Case 2. Suppose $(i,j) \neq (0,0)$. In this case also, we distinguish several cases according to the form of $\mathbf{S}$.

Subase 2.1. Suppose $\mathbf{S} \in \mathcal{X}_{\mathcal{P}}^{(i,j)}$ (resp. $\mathbf{S} \equiv (\mu Z.\ \mathbf{S}')$ for some $\mathbf{S}'$). Then, we can define $\mathcal{D}[\![\mathbf{S}]\!](\rho)$ for $\rho \in \text{SeVal}$, and show that $(\lambda\rho \in \text{SeVal}.\ \mathcal{D}[\![\mathbf{S}]\!](\rho))$ is nonexpansive, in a similar fashion to Subcase 1.1 (resp. to Subcase 1.3) above.
Subcase 2.2. Suppose $\mathbf{S} \equiv (\lambda\vec{\eta}\cdot\vec{\xi}.\ \mathbf{S}')$ with $\vec{\eta} \in (\mathcal{X}_C)^{(i)}$, $\vec{\xi} \in (\mathcal{X}_V)^{(j)}$, $\mathbf{S}' \in \mathcal{L}^{(0,0)}(n)[\mathcal{X}_{\mathcal{P}}^{*}]$. Then let

$$\mathcal{D}[\![\mathbf{S}]\!](\rho) = (\lambda\vec{\mathbf{c}}\cdot\vec{v} \in \mathbf{Chan}^{i}\cdot\mathbf{V}^{j}.\ \mathcal{D}[\![\mathbf{S}'[(\vec{\mathbf{c}}\cdot\vec{v})/(\vec{\eta}\cdot\vec{\eta})]]\!](\rho)).$$

By the induction hypothesis (25) stating that (23) holds and the definition of the metric on $\mathbf{P}^{(i,j)}$, one has

$$\forall\rho_1,\rho_2 \in \text{SeVal}[\ d(\mathcal{D}[\![\mathbf{S}]\!](\rho_1),\mathcal{D}[\![\mathbf{S}]\!](\rho_2)) \leq d(\rho_1,\rho_2)\ ].$$

Namely, the mapping $(\lambda\rho \in \text{SeVal}.\ \mathcal{D}[\![\mathbf{S}]\!](\rho))$ is nonexpansive.
Step 2.2. Having defined $\mathcal{D}[\![\mathbf{S}]\!](\rho)$ for $\mathbf{S} \in \mathcal{L}^{(i,j)}(n+1)[\mathcal{X}_{\mathcal{P}}^{*}]$ and $\rho \in \text{SeVal}$, let us show the following holds for every $(k,\ell),(i,j) \in \omega^2$, $Z \in \mathcal{X}_{\mathcal{P}}^{(k,\ell)}$, $\mathbf{S} \in \mathcal{G}_Z^{(i,j)}(n+1)[\mathcal{X}_{\mathcal{P}}^{*}]$, and $\rho \in \text{SeVal}$:

$(\lambda\mathbf{p} \in \mathbf{P}^{(k,\ell)}.\ \mathcal{D}[\![\mathbf{S}]\!](\rho[\mathbf{p}/Z])$ is a contraction from $\mathbf{P}^{(k,\ell)}$ to $\mathbf{P}^{(i,j)}$ with coefficient $(1/2)$. (26)

Fix $(k,\ell),(i,j) \in \omega^2$, $Z \in \mathcal{X}_{\mathcal{P}}^{(k,\ell)}$, $\mathbf{S} \in \mathcal{G}_Z^{(i,j)}(n+1)[\mathcal{X}_{\mathcal{P}}^{*}]$, and $\rho \in \text{SeVal}$. We distinguish two cases according to whether or not $(i,j) = (0,0)$.
Case 1. Suppose $(i,j) = (0,0)$. Again, we distinguish several cases according to the form of $\mathbf{S}$.
Subcase 1.1. Suppose $\mathbf{S} \in (\mathcal{X}_{\mathcal{P}}^{(0,0)} \setminus \{Z\})$. Then,

$$\forall\mathbf{p} \in \mathbf{P}^{(k,\ell)}[\ \mathcal{D}[\![\mathbf{S}]\!](\rho[\mathbf{p}/Z]) = \rho(\mathbf{S})\ ].$$

Thus, the mapping $(\lambda\mathbf{p} \in \mathbf{P}^{(k,\ell)}.\ \mathcal{D}[\![\mathbf{S}]\!](\rho[\mathbf{p}/Z]))$ is a constant mapping, and hence, a contraction from $\mathbf{P}^{(k,\ell)}$ to $\mathbf{P}^{(i,j)}$. Thus, one has (26).
Subcase 1.2. Suppose one of the following holds:

(i) $\mathbf{S} \equiv (\mathbf{asg}(x,e);S')$ with $x \in \text{IVar}$, $S' \in \mathcal{L}^{(0,0)}(n)$,

(ii) $\mathbf{S} \equiv (\mathbf{out}(h,e);S')$ with $h \in \mathcal{E}_C$, $e \in \mathcal{E}_V$, $S' \in \mathcal{L}^{(0,0)}(n)$,

(iii) $\mathbf{S} \equiv (\mathbf{in}(h,x);S')$ with $h \in \mathcal{E}_C$, $x \in \text{IVar}$, $S' \in \mathcal{L}^{(0,0)}(n)$,

(ivf) $\mathbf{S} \equiv (\mathbf{in}'(h);\mathbf{S}')$ with $h \in \mathcal{E}_C$, $\mathbf{S}' \in \mathcal{L}^{(0,1)}(n)$.

We consider the case **(i)**; in the other cases, the same conclusion is obtained in a similar fashion. For every $\mathbf{p} \in \mathbf{P}^{(k,\ell)}$,

$$\mathcal{D}[\![\mathbf{S}]\!](\rho[\mathbf{p}/Z]) = \text{asg}_x(\mathcal{D}[\![S']\!](\rho[\mathbf{p}/Z])).$$

Thus, $(\lambda\mathbf{p} \in \mathbf{P}^{(k,\ell)}.\ \mathcal{D}[\![\mathbf{S}]\!](\rho[\mathbf{p}/Z]))$ is a contraction with coefficient $(1/2)$, since asg_x is a contraction with coefficient $(1/2)$, and $(\lambda\mathbf{p} \in \mathbf{P}^{(k,\ell)}.\ \mathcal{D}[\![S']\!](\rho[\mathbf{p}/Z]))$ is nonexpansive.
Subcase 1.3. Suppose $\mathbf{S} \equiv F(\vec{h}\cdot\vec{e}\cdot\vec{S}\cdot\vec{T}\cdot\vec{U})$ with $F \in \mathbf{Fun}^{(i',j',k',\ell',m')}$, $\vec{h} \in (\mathcal{E}_C)^{i'}$, $\vec{e} \in (\mathcal{E}_V)^{j'}$, $\vec{S} \in (\mathcal{G}_Z(n)[\mathcal{X}_{\mathcal{P}}^{*}])^{k'}$, $\vec{T} \in (\mathcal{G}_Z^{(0,1)[\mathcal{X}_{\mathcal{P}}^{*}]}(n))^{\ell'}$, $\vec{U} \in (\mathcal{G}_Z^{(1,0)}(n)[\mathcal{X}_{\mathcal{P}}^{*}])^{m'}$. Then, one has the desired conclusion that $(\lambda\mathbf{p} \in \mathbf{P}^{(\ell,m)}.\ \mathcal{D}[\![\mathbf{S}]\!](\rho[\mathbf{p}/Z]))$ is a contraction with coefficient $(1/2)$, by the induction hypothesis (25) stating that (24) holds and the fact the semantic operation $\mathcal{I}(F)$ is nonexpansive (cf. Lemma 6 (1)).

Subcase 1.4. Suppose $\mathbf{S} \equiv \mathbf{S}'(\vec{h} \cdot \vec{e})$ with $(i', j') \neq (0,0)$, $\mathbf{S}' \in \mathcal{G}_Z^{(i',j')}(n)[\mathcal{X}_{\mathcal{P}}^*]$, $\vec{h} \in (\mathcal{E}_C)^i$, $\vec{e} \in (\mathcal{E}_V)^i$. Then, for every $\rho' \in \mathrm{SeVal}$,

$$\mathcal{D}[\![\mathbf{S}]\!](\rho') = \bigcup_{\sigma \in \Sigma} [\mathcal{D}[\![\mathbf{S}']\!](\rho')([\![\vec{h}]\!](\sigma) \cdot [\![\vec{e}]\!](\sigma))\langle\sigma\rangle].$$

Thus, the desired result that $(\lambda \mathbf{p} \in \mathbf{P}^{(k,\ell)}.\ \mathcal{D}[\![\mathbf{S}]\!](\rho[\mathbf{p}/Z]))$ is a contraction with coefficient $(1/2)$ follows from the induction hypothesis (25) stating that (24) holds and the definition of the metric on the function space $\mathbf{P}^{(i,j)}$.

Subcase 1.5. Suppose $\mathbf{S} \equiv (\mu Z'.\ \mathbf{S}')$ with $\mathbf{S}' \in \mathcal{G}_Z^{(0,0)}(n)[\mathcal{X}_{\mathcal{P}}^*]$. Thus, by Definition 21 (2), one has $\mathbf{S}' \in \mathcal{G}_Z^{(0,0)}(n)[\mathcal{X}_{\mathcal{P}}^*] \cap \mathcal{G}_{Z'}^{(0,0)}(n)[\mathcal{X}_{\mathcal{P}}^*]$. For every $\rho' \in \mathrm{SeVal}$,

$$\mathcal{D}[\![\mathbf{S}]\!](\rho') = \mathrm{fix}(\varphi(\rho')), = \lim_{n\to\infty} [(\varphi(\rho))^{(n)}(p_0)],$$

where $\varphi(\rho') = (\lambda p' \in \mathbf{P}.\ \mathcal{D}[\![\mathbf{S}']\!](\rho[p'/Z']))$, and p_0 is an arbitrary element of $\mathbf{P}$, and $(\varphi(\rho))^{(n)}$ is the n-th interation of $\varphi(\rho)$. For $\mathbf{p}_1, \mathbf{p}_2 \in \mathbf{P}^{(k,\ell)}$, it can be shown that for every $n \in \omega$ the following holds:

$$d((\varphi(\rho[\mathbf{p}_1/Z]))^{(n)}(p_0), (\varphi(\rho[\mathbf{p}_2/Z]))^{(n)}(p_0)) \leq (1/2) \cdot d(\mathbf{p}_1, \mathbf{p}_2), \tag{27}$$

by induction on n using the induction hypothesis (25) stating that (24) holds and the fact that d_P is a *ultra-metric* as follows: For $n = 0$, (27) holds obviously. Fix $k' \in \omega$, and assume (27) holds for $n = k'$. Let us show (27) for $n = k' + 1$. One has

$$\begin{aligned}
& d((\varphi(\rho[\mathbf{p}_1/Z]))^{(k'+1)}(p_0), (\varphi(\rho[\mathbf{p}_2/Z]))^{(k'+1)}(p_0)) \\
& = d(\varphi(\rho[\mathbf{p}_1/Z])((\varphi(\rho[\mathbf{p}_1/Z]))^{k'}(p_0)), \varphi(\rho[\mathbf{p}_2/Z])((\varphi(\rho[\mathbf{p}_2/Z]))^{k'}(p_0))) \\
& = d(\mathcal{D}[\![\mathbf{S}']\!](\rho[\mathbf{p}_1/Z][(\varphi(\rho[\mathbf{p}_1/Z]))^{k'}(p_0)/Z']), \mathcal{D}[\![\mathbf{S}']\!](\rho[\mathbf{p}_2/Z][(\varphi(\rho[\mathbf{p}_2/Z]))^{k'}(p_0)/Z'])), \\
& \leq \max\{ d(\mathcal{D}[\![\mathbf{S}']\!](\rho[\mathbf{p}_1/Z][(\varphi(\rho[\mathbf{p}_1/Z]))^{k'}(p_0)/Z']), \\
& \qquad \mathcal{D}[\![\mathbf{S}']\!](\rho[\mathbf{p}_1/Z][(\varphi(\rho[\mathbf{p}_2/Z]))^{k'}(p_0)/Z'])), \\
& \qquad d(\mathcal{D}[\![\mathbf{S}']\!](\rho[\mathbf{p}_1/Z][(\varphi(\rho[\mathbf{p}_2/Z]))^{k'}(p_0)/Z']), \\
& \qquad \mathcal{D}[\![\mathbf{S}']\!](\rho[\mathbf{p}_2/Z][(\varphi(\rho[\mathbf{p}_2/Z]))^{k'}(p_0)/Z']))\} \\
& \quad \text{(since } d \text{ is an ultra-metric)} \\
& \leq \max\{(1/4) \cdot d(\mathbf{p}_1, \mathbf{p}_2), (1/2) \cdot (\mathbf{p}_1, \mathbf{p}_2)\} \\
& \quad \text{(by the induction hypothesis (25) stating that (24) holds)} \\
& \leq (1/2) \cdot d(\mathbf{p}_1, \mathbf{p}_2).
\end{aligned}$$

Thus (27) holds for $n = k' + 1$. Thus, one has

$$\begin{aligned}
& d(\mathcal{D}[\![\mathbf{S}]\!](\rho[\mathbf{p}_1/Z]), \mathcal{D}[\![\mathbf{S}]\!](\rho[\mathbf{p}_2/Z])) \\
& = d(\lim_{n\to\infty}[(\varphi(\rho[\mathbf{p}_1/Z]))^{(n)}(p_0)], \lim_{n\to\infty}[(\varphi(\rho[\mathbf{p}_2/Z]))^{(n)}(p_0)]) \\
& \leq (1/2) \cdot d(\mathbf{p}_1, \mathbf{p}_2).
\end{aligned}$$

Since $\mathbf{p}_1, \mathbf{p}_2$ have been chosen arbitrarily, one has the desired conclusion that $(\lambda \mathbf{p} \in \mathbf{P}^{(k,\ell)}.\ \mathcal{D}[\![\mathbf{S}]\!](\rho[\mathbf{p}/Z]))$ is a contraction with coefficient $(1/2)$.

Case 2. Suppose $(i, j) \neq (0,0)$. Then, one of the following holds: **(i)** $\mathbf{S} \in \mathcal{X}^{(i,j)}$, **(ii)** $\mathbf{S} \equiv (\lambda \vec{\eta} \cdot \vec{\xi}.\ \mathbf{S}')$, **(iii)** $\mathbf{S} \equiv (\mu Z'.\ \mathbf{S}')$. We consider the case (ii) here; for the other cases (i) and (iii) the same conclusion is obtained as in Subcase 1.1 and Subcase 1.5 above.

By the definition of $\mathcal{D}[\![\mathbf{S}]\!](\rho)$, one has the following for $\mathbf{p} \in \mathbf{P}^{(i,j)}$:

$$\mathcal{D}[\![\mathbf{S}]\!](\rho[\mathbf{p}/Z]) = (\lambda \vec{c} \cdot \vec{v} \in \mathbf{Chan}^i \cdot \mathbf{V}^j.\ \mathcal{D}[\![(\mathbf{S}'[(\vec{c} \cdot \vec{v})/(\vec{\eta} \cdot \vec{\xi})])]\!](\rho[\mathbf{p}/Z])).$$

Thus by the induction hypothesis (25) stating that (24) holds, one has the following for $\mathbf{p}_1, \mathbf{p}_2 \in \mathbf{P}^{(k,\ell)}$, $\langle \vec{\mathbf{c}}, \vec{v} \rangle \in \mathbf{Chan}^i \times \mathbf{V}^j$:

$$d(\mathcal{D}[\![(\mathbf{S}'[(\vec{\mathbf{c}} \cdot \vec{v})/(\vec{\eta} \cdot \vec{\xi})])]\!](\rho[\mathbf{p}_1/Z]), \mathcal{D}[\![(\mathbf{S}'[(\vec{\mathbf{c}} \cdot \vec{v})/(\vec{\eta} \cdot \vec{\xi})])]\!](\rho[\mathbf{p}_2/Z])) \\ \leq (1/2) \cdot d(\mathbf{p}_1, \mathbf{p}_2).$$

Thus, one has, $d(\mathcal{D}[\![\mathbf{S}]\!](\rho[\mathbf{p}_1/Z]), \mathcal{D}[\![\mathbf{S}]\!](\rho[\mathbf{p}_2/Z])) \leq (1/2) \cdot d(\mathbf{p}_1, \mathbf{pf}2)$. Since p_1, p_2 have been chosen arbitrarily, one has the desired conclusion that $(\lambda \mathbf{p} \in \text{SeVal}.\ \mathcal{D}[\![\mathbf{S}]\!](\rho[\mathbf{p}/Z]))$ is a contraction with coefficient (1/2). ∎

Appendix C Description Examples in $\mathcal{L}$

In this appendix, two description examples in $\mathcal{L}$ are given.

Example 2 In Figure 1, we give a description in $\mathcal{L}$ of the sever of a typical server-client system supporting an indefinite number of clients.

In the description, the following constructs in $\mathbf{Fun}_0$ are assumed to be predefined: **(a)** a constant **c** of type $\mathcal{C}$ used when clients request the service, **(b)** a constant 'client-indexes' of type $\mathcal{V}$ representing a predefined set of possible client indexes, **(c)** a constant 'sorry' of type $\mathcal{V}$ indicating that all the client indexes are being used, **(d)** a constant 'exit' of type $\mathcal{V}$, **(e)** a function symbol 'service-chan' of type $\langle(\mathcal{V}), \mathcal{C}\rangle$, **(f)** a function symbol 'update' of type $\langle \mathcal{V}^3, \mathcal{V}\rangle$ such that $\text{update}(f, n, i) = f[n/i]$ for $f \in (\text{client-ids} \to \omega)$, $n \in \omega$, $i \in$ client-ids, where 'client-ids' is a predefined set of identifiers of clients, **(g)** a function symbol 'bill' of type $\langle \mathcal{V}^2, \mathcal{V}\rangle$ such that $[\![\text{bill}(f, i)]\!] = f(i)$ for $f \in (\text{client-ids} \to \omega)$ and $i \in$ client-ids.

We use three individual variables x_0, x_1, x_2 as *local* variables, and another individual variable x_3 as a *global* variable: **(h)** The variable x_0 stores the set of client indexes being used; **(i)** the variable x_1 stores the *client index* of the current session; **(j)** the variable x_2 stores the *bill* of the current session; **(k)** the variable x_3 stores the list of bills of all the clients.

Firstly, the server initialize the variable x_0 to $\emptyset$ (line 1); then the body in lines 2–20 runs as follows: **(1)** The server receive a service request from a client through the channel **c** with the passed value, the identifier of the client, bound to ξ (lines 3–4). **(2)** If the all the possible client-indexes are being used, i.e., if client-indexes $\setminus x_0 = \emptyset$, then the server output a message 'sorry' (line 6); otherwise the block in lines 7–20 is executed.

The block runs as follows: **(3)** The variable x_1 is set to the client-index of the current session (line 7). **(4)** The index is sent to the client through **c**, thereby the client knows which service channel is used in the session (line 8). **(5)** The value of x_0 is updated so as to include the value of x_1 (line 9).

The rest of the block is the parallel composition of the original server, which can receive new service requests, and a subprocess (in lines 11–20) managing the current session. The subprocess runs as follows: First, x_2 is initialized to account(x_3, ξ) (line 11). The rest of the subprocess is the iteration of the service transaction (in lines 12–20), which runs as follows: **(6)** The subprocess receive a query through the channel 'service-channel(x_1)' with the passed value (the query) is bound to ξ_1 (lines 13–14). **(7)** When the passed value is 'exit', the subprocess informs the bill of the session of the client, updates the values of x_3 and x_0, and then terminates (lines 16–18). Otherwise the subprocess retrieve the

Figure 1: Description of a Server

1. $\mathbf{let}(x_0, \emptyset,$
2. $\quad(\mu X_0.$
3. $\quad\quad\mathbf{in}'(\mathbf{c});$
4. $\quad\quad\quad(\lambda\xi.$
5. $\quad\quad\quad\quad\mathbf{if}(\text{clients-indexes} \setminus x_0 = \emptyset,$
6. $\quad\quad\quad\quad\quad\mathbf{out}(\mathbf{c}, \text{`sorry'}); \mathbf{0},$
7. $\quad\quad\quad\quad\quad\mathbf{let}(x_1, \min(\text{clients-indexes} \setminus x_0),$
8. $\quad\quad\quad\quad\quad\quad\mathbf{out}(\mathbf{c}, x_1);$
9. $\quad\quad\quad\quad\quad\quad\mathbf{asg}(x_0, x_0 \cup \{x_1\});$
10. $\quad\quad\quad\quad\quad\quad(X_0 \parallel$
11. $\quad\quad\quad\quad\quad\quad\quad\mathbf{let}(x_2, \text{account}(x_3, \xi),$
12. $\quad\quad\quad\quad\quad\quad\quad\quad(\mu X_1.$
13. $\quad\quad\quad\quad\quad\quad\quad\quad\quad\mathbf{in}'(\text{service-chan}(x_1));$
14. $\quad\quad\quad\quad\quad\quad\quad\quad\quad\quad(\lambda\xi_1.$
15. $\quad\quad\quad\quad\quad\quad\quad\quad\quad\quad\quad\mathbf{if}(\xi_1 = \text{`exit'},$
16. $\quad\quad\quad\quad\quad\quad\quad\quad\quad\quad\quad\quad(\mathbf{out}(\text{service-chan}(x_1), x_2);$
17. $\quad\quad\quad\quad\quad\quad\quad\quad\quad\quad\quad\quad\quad\mathbf{asg}(x_3, \text{update}(x_3, \text{bill}(x_3, \xi) + x_2, \xi));$
18. $\quad\quad\quad\quad\quad\quad\quad\quad\quad\quad\quad\quad\quad\mathbf{asg}(x_0, x_0 \setminus \{x_1\}); \mathbf{0}\ ),$
19. $\quad\quad\quad\quad\quad\quad\quad\quad\quad\quad\quad\quad(\mathbf{out}(\text{service-chan}(x_1), \text{retrieve}(\xi_1));$
20. $\quad\quad\quad\quad\quad\quad\quad\quad\quad\quad\quad\quad\quad\mathbf{asg}(x_2, x_2 + 1); X_1\ ))))))))))).$ ∎

answer to the query ξ_1, and sends it to the client (line 19); then it increase the value of x_2 by 1, and iterates the transaction (line 20). ∎

Example 3 Let us name the following parameterized statement **fact**:

$$(\mu X^{(1,1)}.$$
$$(\lambda(\eta, \xi).\ \mathbf{if}(\xi = 0, (\mathbf{out}(\eta, 1); \mathbf{0}),$$
$$\mathbf{LC}(\lambda\eta'.\ X^{(1,1)}(\eta', \xi - 1) \parallel (\mathbf{in}'(\eta'); (\lambda\eta'.\ \mathbf{out}(\eta, \eta \cdot \eta'); \mathbf{0}))\ )))).$$

For $\mathbf{c} \in \mathbf{Chan}$, $n \geq 0$, the statement $\mathbf{fact}(\mathbf{c}, n)$ computes $n!$ and outputs it through $\mathbf{c}$, creating n processes which operate concurrently. ∎

References

[AR 89] P. America and J.J.M.M. Rutten (1989), Solving reflexive domain equations in a category of complete metric spaces, *Journal of Computer and System Sciences, Vol. 39, No. 3*, pp. 343–375.

[BZ 82] J.W. de Bakker and J.I. Zucker (1982), Processes and the denotational semantics of concurrency, *Information and Control Vol. 54*, pp. 70–120.

[BKO 88] J.A. Bergstra, J.W. Klop, and E.-R. Olderog (1988), Readies and failures in the algebra of communicating processes, *SIAM J. of Computing Vol. 17, No. 6*, pp. 1134–1177.

[BKPR92] F.S. de Boer, J.N. Kok, C. Palamidesi, and J.J.M.M. Rutten (1992), *On blocks: locality and asynchronous communication (extended abstract)*, to appear as a CWI Report, Amsterdam.

[BHR 84] S.D. Brookes, C.A.R. Hoare, and A.W. Roscoe (1984), A theory of communicating sequential processes, *Journal of the Association for Computing Machinery, Vol. 31*, pp. 560–599.

[DH 83] R. De Nicola and M. Hennessy (1983), Testing equivalence and processes, *Theoretical Computer Science, Vol. 34*, pp. 83–133.

[Dug 66] J. Dugundji (1966), *Topology*, Allyn and Bacon, Boston.

[Eng 77] R. Engelking (1977), *General topology*, Polish Scientific Publishers.

[HMT 71] L. Henkin, J.D. Monk, and A. Tarski (1971), *Cylindric Algebras (Part 1)*, North-Holland.

[Hen 85] M. Hennessy (1985), Acceptance trees, *Journal of the Association for Computing Machinery, Vol. 32*, pp. 896–928.

[Hen 88] M. Hennessy (1988), *Algebraic theory of processes*, MIT Press.

[HI 90] M. Hennessy and A. Ingólfsdóttir (1990), A theory of communicating processes with value-passing, in *Proceedings 17th ICALP, Warwick University, Lecture Notes in Computer Science, Vol.443*, pp. 209–219, Springer.

[Hor 92] E. Horita (1992), Fully abstract models for communicating processes with respect to weak linear semantics with divergence, *IEICE Transactions on Information and Systems Vol. E75-D, No. 1*, pp. 64–77.

[Hor 92a] E. Horita (1992), *Full abstraction of metric semantics for imperative concurrency with communication*, to appear as a CWI Report, Amsterdam.

[Hor 92b] E. Horita (1992), *Full abstraction of metric semantics for communicating processes with value-passing*, to appear as a CWI Report, Amsterdam.

[HBR 90] E. Horita, J.W. de Bakker, and J.J.M.M. Rutten (1990), *Fully abstract denotational models for nonuniform concurrent languages, CWI Report CS-R9027*, Amsterdam.

[KR 90] J.N. Kok and J.J.M.M. Rutten (1990), Contractions in comparing concurrency semantics, in *Theoretical Computer Science, Vol. 76*, pp. 179–222.

[Mil 73] R. Milner (1973), Processes: a mathematical model of computing agents, in *Proceedings of Logic Colloquium 73* (H.E. Rose, J.C. Shepherdson, eds.), pp. 157–173, North-Holland.

[Mil 89] R. Milner (1989), *Communication and concurrency*, Prentice Hall International.

[Mit 90] J.C. Mitchell (1990), Type systems for programming languages, in *Handbook of Theoretical Computer Science, Vol. B, Formal Models and Semantics* (J.V. Leeuwen, ed.), pp. 365–458, The MIT Press/Elsevier.

[OT 92] P.W. O'Hearn and R.D. Tennent (1992), *Semantics of local variables*, LFCS Report ECS-LFCS-92-192, Department of Computer Science, University of Edinburgh.

[Plo 81] G.D. Plotkin (1981), *A structured approach to operational semantics*, Report DAIMI FN-19, Computer Science Department, Aarhus University.

[Rut 89] J.J.M.M. Rutten (1989), Correctness and full abstraction of metric semantics for concurrency, in *Linear Time, Branching Time and Partial Order in Logics and Models for Concurrency* (J.W. de Bakker, W.P. de Roever, G. Rozenberg, eds.), *Lecture Notes in Computer Science Vol. 354*, pp. 628–658, Springer.

[SRP 90] V.A. Saraswat, M. Rinard, and P. Panangaden, Semantic foundation of concurrent constraint programming (preliminary report), In *Prod. of the eighteenth ACM Symposium on Principles of Programming Languages*, pp. 333–352, ACM.

SPCF: Its Model, Calculus, and Computational Power (Preliminary Version)

Ramarao Kanneganti, Robert Cartwright, Matthias Felleisen*
Department of Computer Science
Rice University
Houston, TX 77005

Abstract

SPCF is an idealized sequential programming language, based on Plotkin's language PCF, that permits programmers and programs to observe the evaluation order of procedures. In this paper, we construct a fully abstract model of SPCF using a new mathematical framework suitable for defining fully abstract models of sequential functional languages. Then, we develop an extended typed λ-calculus to specify the operational semantics of SPCF and show that the calculus is complete for the constant-free sub-language. Finally, we prove that SPCF is ***computationally complete***: it can express all the computable (recursively enumerable) elements in its fully abstract model.

1 SPCF: Observing Sequentiality

Most contemporary programming languages, *e.g.*, Scheme, Pascal, Fortran, C, and ML, are "sequential", that is, they impose a serial order on the evaluation of parts of programs. Unfortunately, the familiar mathematical models for sequential languages based on continuous functions do not capture this property. They make artificial distinctions between phrases with the same sequential behavior, preventing the familiar models from being ***fully abstract***. Milner [19] and Plotkin [22] recognized this problem nearly twenty years ago and identified the construction of sequential denotational language models as an important research problem.

Early work in the search for "sequential models" focused on the typed λ-calculus with constants for arithmetic and recursion (PCF) [32, 19, 22, 17, 3, 4, 6, 11, 20]. While this strategy avoids many arbitrary language design decisions and simplifies the investigation, it also eliminates programming facilities that are essential for understanding the sequential behavior of programs. The missing facilities include error values, which permit a programmer to observe the order of evaluation among sub-expressions, and constructs for non-local transfer of control, which permit a program to detect and exploit the evaluation order of procedures.

Cartwright and Felleisen [9] recently observed that the addition of error values and control constructs to the idealized programming language PCF facilitated the construction of a natural, fully abstract denotational model. Most importantly, the same construction is applicable to variations of PCF with call-by-value parameter-passing and with constants for observing the

*The authors were supported in part by NSF grants CCR 89-17022 and CCR 91-22518.

behavior of higher-order expressions as long as these languages include error values and appropriate control constructs. Instead of continuous functions, the Cartwright-Felleisen model uses *decision trees* to assign meaning to procedures. In a subsequent paper, Curien [12] showed that the decision tree model is an extension of the sequential algorithm model [4, 11], and that the set of observably sequential domains and functions form a Cartesian-closed category.

In this paper, we continue the investigation of SPCF, Cartwright and Felleisen's extension of PCF. First, we reconstruct the model using simpler, more abstract methods based on Winskel's [33] idea of a prime basis (also compare Kahn and Plokin's technical report on concrete domains Second, we show that the extended language corresponds to a simple extension of the typed λ-calculus and prove that the constant-free fragment of the calculus is complete. Finally, we prove that SPCF is computationally complete, that is, it can express all computable (recursively enumerable) elements of the model, including those of higher-order function domains.

2 From PCF to SPCF

PCF is an extension of the simply typed λ-calculus. In addition to the usual λ-calculus constructs, it provides a family of fixpoint operators and a set of constant symbols for performing arithmetic (non-negative numerals, a successor, a predecessor, and a zero recognizer). SPCF enriches PCF in two ways. First, it adds error values to the data domain so that the behavior of a program reveals when functions are *misapplied* to arguments, *e.g.*, an attempt to subtract from zero or to divide by zero. Second, SPCF includes a family of control constructs for escaping from the evaluation of a phrase. In PCF, both of these capabilities are missing. Programs that misapply functions merely diverge. PCF does not include any non-local control constructs, so programs cannot escape from pending computations.

Syntax:

$$
\begin{aligned}
M &::= c \mid x \mid (\lambda x.M) \mid (M\ M)\\
c &::= \ulcorner n \urcorner \mid \mathsf{error}_1 \mid \mathsf{error}_2 \mid \mathsf{add1} \mid \mathsf{sub1} \mid \mathsf{if0} \mid \mathsf{Y}^\tau \mid \mathsf{call/cdc}\\
x &::= x^\tau \mid y^\tau \mid \ldots
\end{aligned}
$$

Types:

$$\sigma, \tau ::= o \mid (\tau \rightarrow \sigma)$$

Type Checking:

$$\frac{A, x^\tau \vdash M : \tau'}{A \vdash \lambda x^\tau.M : \tau \rightarrow \tau'} \qquad \frac{A \vdash M : \tau' \rightarrow \tau; \quad A \vdash M' : \tau'}{A \vdash (M M') : \tau}$$

$A \vdash x^\tau : \tau$ if $x^\tau \in A$	$A \vdash \ulcorner n \urcorner : o$ for all n	$A \vdash \mathsf{Y}^\tau : (\tau \rightarrow \tau) \rightarrow \tau$
$A \vdash \mathsf{add1} : o \rightarrow o$	$A \vdash \mathsf{sub1} : o \rightarrow o$	$A \vdash \mathsf{if0} : o \rightarrow o \rightarrow o \rightarrow o$
$A \vdash \mathsf{call/cdc} : ((o \rightarrow o) \rightarrow o) \rightarrow o$	$A \vdash \mathsf{error}_1 : o$	$A \vdash \mathsf{error}_2 : o$

FIGURE 1: SPCF: Syntax

The first part of Figure 1 defines the set of syntactically well-formed SPCF phrases. An SPCF phrase M is either a constant (i.e., a numeral $\ulcorner n \urcorner$, $n \geq 0$, one of two error constants, error_1 and error_2, or a functional constant), a typed variable x^τ, a λ-abstraction, or an application. We call an application of the form (call/cdc $\lambda x.M$) a call/cdc-*application*; the variable x is called a *downward continuation (variable)*.

As usual, λ-abstraction is the only binding form in this language: $\lambda x.M$ binds x in M. A variable that is not bound by some surrounding λ-abstraction is *free*. We identify phrases that are equal up to renaming bound variables, *e.g.*, $\lambda x.x \equiv \lambda y.y$. We use the standard syntactic conventions of the λ-calculus for writing SPCF phrases, e.g., $\lambda xyz.M$ is short for $\lambda x.(\lambda y.(\lambda z.M))$. In the remainder of the paper, we will use the symbol $\mathcal{V}$ to denote the set of SPCF variable names.

A typed SPCF phrase is an untyped phrase that conforms to the typing rules of SPCF given in Figure 1. The set of SPCF types consists of a single ground type (o), denoting the observable set of non-negative integers, and an infinite collection of finitely generated procedure types ($\sigma \rightarrow \tau$). In conformance with the usual convention, the type expression $\tau \rightarrow \sigma \rightarrow \nu$ abbreviates $\tau \rightarrow (\sigma \rightarrow \nu)$. The typing rules for SPCF are similar to those of the simply typed λ-calculus, but in SPCF every well-typed phrase M has a unique type τ. In the typing rules given in Figure 1, the only interesting clauses are the ones on the last line, which handle the additional constructs of SPCF. Λ^τ is the sub-language of SPCF that is built without constants.

Functional and Syntactic Extensions. When we write SPCF programs, we freely use functions and syntactic abbreviations that are easily definable in the language. Specifically, we will assume that the names + and − denote some addition and subtraction functions. When we use these names, the evaluation order of the arguments for these functions is unimportant. We will also use the following syntactic abbreviations:

$$\begin{aligned}
\Omega &\stackrel{df}{=} \mathsf{Y}(\lambda x.x) \\
\textbf{let } x = M \textbf{ in } N &\stackrel{df}{=} ((\lambda x\,.\,N)\,M) \\
\textbf{let* } x = M \ \ldots \textbf{ in } N &\stackrel{df}{=} ((\lambda x\,.\,\textbf{let*} \ \ldots \textbf{ in } N)\,M) \\
\textbf{let* } x = M \textbf{ in } N &\stackrel{df}{=} ((\lambda x\,.\,N)\,M) \\
\textbf{letrec } L = M \textbf{ in } (L\ N) &\stackrel{df}{=} \mathsf{Y}\,(\lambda L\,.\,M)\,N
\end{aligned}$$

and some occasional syntactic extensions that are self-explanatory. ∎

The meaning of the PCF sub-language of SPCF is the usual one, *i.e.*, numerals and functional constants have their expected behavior, λ-abstractions are call-by-name procedures, and juxtaposition is function application. The meaning of the SPCF primitives not present in PCF is easy to describe informally; Section 3 contains a denotational, Section 4 an operational description.

The **error** constants, $\mathbf{error}_1$ and $\mathbf{error}_2$, generate special "error" values that are propagated according to the usual by-need evaluation order in call-by-name programs. If an SPCF procedure uses an argument and the by-need evaluation of the argument generates an error value e, the procedure returns the value e. On the other hand, if the procedure ignores an argument, the meaning of the argument—even if it generates an error—is irrelevant because by-need evaluation never evaluates the argument.

SPCF's call/cdc procedure of type $(o \rightarrow o) \rightarrow o$ is similar to Scheme's call/cc procedure. It applies its argument to the current continuation, but unlike full-fledged call/cc-style continuations, call/cdc-continuations can be used at most once.[1] Specifically, its type prevents call/cdc from returning the continuation or a procedure invoking the continuation.

[1]Operationally speaking, the continuation can only be used to erase portions of the control stack in a *downward* fashion.

To illustrate the use of **error** elements and **call/cdc** for observing the sequentiality of procedures, consider the following two definitions of a binary addition procedure in SPCF:

$$\begin{aligned} +_l &= \mathsf{Y}(\lambda f.(\lambda xy.\,\mathsf{if0}\; x\; y\; (\mathbf{add1}\; (f\; (\mathbf{sub1}\; x)\; y)))) \\ +_r &= \mathsf{Y}(\lambda f.(\lambda xy.\,\mathsf{if0}\; y\; x\; (\mathbf{add1}\; (f\; x\; (\mathbf{sub1}\; y))))) \end{aligned}$$

The first version $+_l$ recurs on the first argument (x); the second version recurs on the second argument (y). In contrast to PCF where the two procedures are observationally indistinguishable, SPCF provides several ways to distinguish these procedures. To begin with, the two procedures could be applied to error-generating arguments: (f $\mathbf{error}_1$ $\mathbf{error}_2$). When f is replaced by $+_l$ the resulting program will produce $\mathbf{error}_1$, otherwise, when f is replaced by $+_r$, the result will be $\mathbf{error}_2$. While these observations are accessible to the user of the program, the program itself cannot exploit them. A program can find out which addition procedure is used by applying the following procedure:

$$\mathit{Distinguish} = \lambda f.(\mathsf{call/cdc}(\lambda t.(f\; (t\; \ulcorner 0 \urcorner)\; (t\; \ulcorner 1 \urcorner)))).$$

On the input $+_l$, it yields $\ulcorner 0 \urcorner$; on the input $+_r$, it yields $\ulcorner 1 \urcorner$.

Because SPCF can determine which schedule a procedure uses to evaluate its arguments, the denotations of these procedures are *observably sequential* functions, a sub-domain of the continuous functions. In the next section, we describe the construction of a model for SPCF and discuss its important properties.

Constructs for non-local control: catch versus call/cdc. The original version of SPCF [9] used a family of **catch** procedures instead of **call/cdc**. The **catch** family includes a control operator $\mathbf{catch}^\tau$ of type $\tau \to o$ for every type τ. The decision tree representing $\mathbf{catch}^\tau$ depends only on the number k of inputs in type

$$\tau = \tau_1 \to \ldots \to \tau_k \to o\,.$$

The two constructs, **catch** and **call/cdc**, are interdefinable. Given **call/cdc**, it is trivial to define the $\mathbf{catch}^\tau$ procedure for each type τ by the equations

$$\begin{aligned} \mathbf{catch}_0 &= \lambda x\,.\,x \\ \mathbf{catch}_k &= \lambda f\,.\,\mathsf{call/cdc}(\lambda t.(+\; \ulcorner k \urcorner\; (f\; (t\; \ulcorner 0 \urcorner) \ldots (t\; \ulcorner k-1 \urcorner)))) \end{aligned}$$

where the subscript k indicates the number of inputs in type τ.

Conversely, given the family **catch** procedures, the function **call/cdc** is defined by the equation follows:

$$\begin{aligned} \mathsf{call/cdc} \;=\; & \lambda f.\mathbf{letrec}\; L = \lambda v.\mathbf{let}\; \mathit{test}_v = \lambda xy.(f(\lambda a\,.\,\mathsf{if0}\; (-\; a\; v)\; x\; y))) \\ & \qquad\qquad\qquad\quad \mathbf{in}\;\mathbf{let}\; \mathit{root} = (\mathbf{catch}\; \mathit{test}_v) \\ & \qquad\qquad\qquad\qquad \mathbf{in}\; (\mathsf{if0}\; \mathit{root}\; a\; (\mathsf{if0}\; (\mathbf{sub1}\; \mathit{root})\; (L\; (\mathbf{add1}\; v))\; (-\; \mathit{root}\; \ulcorner 2 \urcorner))) \\ & \quad \mathbf{in}\; (L\; \ulcorner 0 \urcorner) \end{aligned}$$

The **call/cdc** procedure repeatedly explores its argument f until it finds the value $\ulcorner n \urcorner$ that f first passes to its argument (the continuation), which it returns as the answer. If f does not call its argument, **call/cdc** returns f's result. ∎

3 The Observably Sequential Type Frame

To define the semantics for SPCF we need

1. a collection *Dom* of *domains*, one for each type τ;
2. a meaning function $\mathcal{T} : Types \rightarrow Dom$ to assign meaning to type expressions;
3. a meaning function $\mathcal{C} : Const_\tau \rightarrow \mathcal{T}[\![\tau]\!]$ to assign meaning to constants of type τ in the domain $\mathcal{T}[\![\tau]\!]$; and
4. a meaning function $\mathcal{M} : Terms_\tau \rightarrow Env \rightarrow \mathcal{T}[\![\tau]\!]$ to assign meaning to terms of type τ in the domain for τ.

To describe the error values and control operators of SPCF, we must build domains with a topological structure that reflects the observably sequential behavior of computations. This section describes how to construct these domains, which are called *observably sequential domains* (or *OS*-domains). It also shows how to use these domains to build a denotational model for SPCF.

3.1 *OS*-Domains

A *Scott domain* $(D, \sqsubseteq)$ is the ideal completion of a *Scott basis* $(E, \leq)$. A *Scott basis* $(E, \leq)$ is a partial order closed under least upper bounds for bounded subsets. The *finite elements* of of the domain are the principal ideals generated by the elements of the Scott basis E. Given Scott domains A and B, the set $A \rightarrow_c B$ of *continuous* functions forms a Scott domain under the pointwise ordering: $f \sqsubseteq g \Leftrightarrow \forall x \in A : f(x) \sqsubseteq_B g(x)$.

OS-domains are Scott domains that satisfy certain topological constraints and include a sufficient number of error (generating) elements. To specify the topological constraints, we need to identify a restricted set of finite elements called the *prime basis*. In fact, the simplest way to describe an *OS*-domain is to start with a prime basis and construct the domain by a process similar to ideal completion.

A prime basis is a partial order partitioned into *conflict* sets of pairwise unbounded elements. To account for the behavior of *errors*, we need to ensure that the prime basis is *error-rich*. To formalize the definition of a prime basis, we need to define the *precedes* relation $\prec$ and the *unique predecessor property*.

Definition 3.1. (*Unique Predecessor Property*) Recall that in a partial order $(P, \leq)$, an element p *immediately precedes* an element q (written $p \prec q$) iff (i) $p < q$ and (ii) $p \leq r < q$ implies that $r = p$. An element p such that $p \prec q$ is called a *predecessor* of q. The partial order $(P, \leq)$ has the *unique predecessor property* if every element $p \in P$ has at most one predecessor. ∎

Given the preceding definition, we can succinctly define the notion of a prime-basis as follows.

Definition 3.2. ((*Error-rich*) *Prime Basis*) A triple $(P, \leq, C)$ is a *prime basis* iff

[PO] $(P, \leq)$ is a countable partial order;

[UP] $(P, \leq)$ satisfies the unique predecessor property;

[C] the set $C = \{Q_1, Q_2, \ldots\}$ of *conflict* sets (or C-sets) is a partitioning of P such that $p, q \in C_i$ implies that p and q have the same set of predecessors;

[F] only a finite number of elements in P approximate each element of P.

A prime basis $(P, \leq, C)$ is *error-rich* iff

[E] each C-set $Q \in C$ has two designated *maximal* elements $\mathbf{error}_1^Q$, $\mathbf{error}_2^Q$.

We refer to C-sets by capital letters such as Q, R and S; we refer to elements of C-sets by the letters q, r, and s. We will augment these names by prime (′) superscripts and integer subscripts. The designated error elements play an essential role in the definition of *observably sequential functions* given in Section 3.2. ∎

An observably sequential domain (OS-domain) is the "prime-closure" of an error-rich prime basis.

Definition 3.3. (*Prime-Domain, OS-domain*) A *prime-domain* is a partial order $(D, \sqsubseteq)$ generated from a prime basis $(P, \leq, C)$ where

- the elements of D are *downward-closed* subsets of P:

$$I \in D \Leftrightarrow I \subseteq P \text{ and } \forall x \in I, y \in P: \text{ if } y \leq x \text{ then } y \in I;$$

- the elements of D do not contain conflicting primes:

$$\forall I \in D, Q \in C\ x, y \in I: \{x, y\} \not\subseteq Q;$$

and

- the relation $\sqsubseteq$ is the subset ordering $\subseteq$ on D.

The domain generated by the prime basis $(P, \leq, C)$ is denoted $\mathbf{D}(P, \leq, C)$. If the prime basis $(P, \leq, C)$ is error-rich, then the prime-domain $\mathbf{D}(P, \leq, C)$ is an OS-domain. We refer to domain elements in an OS-domain by the letters d and e (with primes and indices). ∎

It is easy to show that every prime-domain $(D, \sqsubseteq)$ is a Scott domain; the finite sets of primes in D are the finite elements. As is customary in denotational semantics, we will identify all Scott domains that are order-isomorphic, eliminating the distinction between a prime basis B and the corresponding finite elements in the domain $\mathbf{D}(B)$.

Given an arbitrary Scott domain S, it is easy to determine whether S is a prime-domain. First, we identify the set P of *prime* elements of S, the (finite) elements other than $\bot$ that are not least upper bounds of sets of other elements. Second, we confirm that the prime elements form a prime basis $(P, \leq, C)$ where C is the partitioning of P determined by the relation

$$p \sim q \quad \Leftrightarrow \quad p = q \text{ or } \{p, q\} \text{ is unbounded and } p \text{ and } q \text{ have the same predecessors in } S.$$

Finally, we must verify that the "prime-closure" of $(P, \leq, C)$ is order-isomorphic to the original domain.

If S is a prime-domain with designated error elements, then it is an OS-domain iff the prime basis is error-rich, *i.e.*, exactly two maximal elements in each C-set are designated as error elements (property [E]).

Most domains encountered in the literature are either prime domains or domains that are *weakly generated* by their prime elements. In the latter case, every element of the domain is the least upper bound of the set of primes that approximate it, but the primes do not necessarily form a prime basis.

Consider the following simple examples.

1. The flat domain $\mathbf{T}_\bot$ of truth values $\{\mathbf{tt}, \mathbf{ff}\}$ is a prime-domain; the truth values $\{\mathbf{tt}, \mathbf{ff}\}$ are the prime elements.

2. The flat domain $\mathbf{N}_\bot$ of natural numbers is a prime-domain; every number is a prime element.

3. The continuous function space $\mathbf{T}_\bot \rightarrow_c \mathbf{T}_\bot$ is not a prime-domain, but it is weakly generated by its prime elements, which are the "one-step" functions:

$$(d \Rightarrow e)(x) \stackrel{df}{=} \begin{cases} e & \text{if } d \sqsubseteq x \\ \bot & \text{otherwise} \end{cases}$$

   where $d \in \mathbf{T}_\bot$, $e \in \mathbf{T}$. $\mathbf{T}_\bot \rightarrow \mathbf{T}_\bot$ is not a prime-domain, because it violates property [C].

4. The continuous function space $\mathbf{N}_\bot \rightarrow_c \mathbf{N}_\bot$ is not a prime-domain, but it is weakly generated by its prime elements, which are the "one-step" functions:

$$(d \Rightarrow e)(x) \stackrel{df}{=} \begin{cases} e & \text{if } d \sqsubseteq x \\ \bot & \text{otherwise} \end{cases}$$

   where $d \in \mathbf{N}_\bot$, $e \in \mathbf{N}$. $\mathbf{N}_\bot \rightarrow \mathbf{N}_\bot$ is not a prime-domain, because it violates both property [F] and property [C]. The prime element $(\bot\Rightarrow 1)$ has infinitely many prime elements $(n \Rightarrow 1)$ $(n \in \mathbf{N})$ below it.

In the sequel, we will use "one-step" functions as parts of prime functions over OS-domains. As we saw in the examples above, the prime elements of non-trivial continuous function spaces do not form a prime basis, because they fail property [C]. They also fail property [F] if the input space is infinite.

A simple example of an observably sequential domain (a prime-domain with designated error elements) is $\mathbf{N}_\bot^E$, the flat domain of natural numbers plus two error elements, error_1 and error_2. It is generated by the prime basis $(\mathbf{N}^E, =, C)$ where

$$\begin{aligned} \mathbf{N}^E &= \mathbf{N} \cup \{\mathsf{error}_1, \mathsf{error}_2\} \\ C &= \{\{n\} \mid n \in \mathbf{N}^E\} \end{aligned}$$

We will use this domain later to assign meaning to the SPCF type o.

A more interesting example of observably sequential domain is the domain of functions generated by error-rich prime basis is $(P_{os}, \leq_{os}, C_{os})$ where P_{os} consists of three disjoint subsets of continuous functions from $\mathbf{N}_\bot^E$ to $\mathbf{N}_\bot^E$:

Constant primes generate outputs independent of their inputs. Since a function of this form ignores its inputs, it never returns an error value unless its constant output is an error value. For every $e \in \mathbf{N}^E$, there exists one constant prime:

$$g_e = (\bot\Rightarrow e).$$

In SPCF, the procedure $\lambda x.\ulcorner 5 \urcorner$ denotes the prime g_5.

Strict one-step primes output designated elements if their inputs contain enough information. If the input is an error value error_i, a strict one-step prime returns error_i. For every pair $d \in \mathbf{N}, e \in \mathbf{N}^E$, there is a strict, one-step prime:

$$f_{d,e} = (d \Rightarrow e) \sqcup (\mathsf{error}_1 \Rightarrow \mathsf{error}_1) \sqcup (\mathsf{error}_2 \Rightarrow \mathsf{error}_2).$$

In SPCF, the procedure $\lambda x.(\text{if0}\ (=\ x\ \ulcorner d \urcorner)\ \ulcorner e \urcorner\ \Omega)$ denotes the strict one-step prime $f_{d,e}$ for $d, e \in \mathbb{N}$.

The diverging prime s inspects its inputs and then diverges. If the input is an error value e, the function s returns e:

$$s = (\bot \Rightarrow \bot) \sqcup (\text{error}_1 \Rightarrow \text{error}_1) \sqcup (\text{error}_2 \Rightarrow \text{error}_2).$$

In SPCF, the procedure $\lambda x.\text{if0}\ x\ \Omega\ \Omega$ denotes the diverging prime function.

In summary, $P_{os} = \{g_e, f_{d,e}, s \mid d \in \mathbb{N}, e \in \mathbb{N}^E\}$. The approximation ordering on P_{os} is the usual pointwise approximation ordering on functions. The conflict partitioning for P_{os} is:

$$C = \{B, C_k \mid k \in \mathbb{N}\}$$

where

$$\begin{aligned} B &\stackrel{df}{=} \{s, g_e \mid e \in \mathbb{N}_\bot^E\} \\ C_k &\stackrel{df}{=} \{f_{k,e} \mid e \in \mathbb{N}_\bot^E\} \end{aligned}$$

The designated error elements in B and C are g_{error_i} and f_{error_i}, respectively.

Technically, each element in the prime domain $\mathbf{D}(P_{os}, \leq_{os}, C_{os})$ is a set of functions rather than a function. However, we can identify each such set of functions with its least upper bound under the usual pointwise ordering on functions. Since every function in P_{os} is continuous, these bounding functions are also continuous.

A simple example is the set $\{s, f_{k,k} \mid k \in \mathbb{N}\} \in \mathbf{D}(P_{os}, \leq_{os}, C_{os})$, which has the identity function as its least upper bound. Similarly, the set $\{s, f_{k,k+1} \mid k \in \mathbb{N}\}$ corresponds to the successor function.

The domain $\mathbf{D}(P_{os}, \leq_{os}, C_{os})$ is a simple example of an *observably sequential* function space. To describe the topological structure of an arbitrary observably sequential function space, we need to introduce the concepts of "coverage", "direction", and "distance".

Definition 3.4. (*Coverage, Direction, Distance*) Let $(P, \leq, C)$ be a prime basis. A C-set Q *covers* a *prime element* $p \in P$ (written $p \prec Q$) iff there is a $q \in Q$ such that $p \prec q$ (implying that $p \prec r$ for all $r \in Q$). A C-set Q *covers* an *element* a in $\mathbf{D}(P, \leq, C)$ (written $a \prec Q$) iff there exists a prime $p \in a$ such that

$$(Q \cap a = \emptyset) \text{ and } (p \prec Q).$$

We say that Q *covers* a.

The *direction* relation is the transitive generalization of the *coverage* relation between primes and C-sets. More precisely, a prime element p has *direction* Q, where $Q \in C$ iff $\exists q \in Q : p \leq q$. We extend this notion to a relation on C-sets by saying that a C-set R is in the direction Q if there is a prime in R in the direction Q.

In conformance with the notation $p \leq Q$, we write $p \leq Q$ when $p \leq q \in Q$.

If p and q are primes in a prime-domain D such that $p \leq q$, the *distance from* p *to* q is the cardinality of the set of all the primes that approximate q, but not p. We extend this notion to C-sets by defining the distance between C-sets Q and R as the distance between any two primes $q \in Q$ and $r \in R$ such that $q \leq r$. ∎

A C-set Q covers a finite element a iff for any element $q \in Q$, $\{q\} \cup a$ is an element of the domain and $a \prec \{q\} \cup a$. Hence, the elements of a C-set Q covering a are mutually exclusive bits of information that can be incrementally added to the set of information a. In general, a finite element a may be covered by several different C-sets.

In the observably sequential domain generated by $(P_{os}, \leq_{os}, C_{os})$, the C-set B does not cover any prime elements. On the other hand, C_k covers the element s.

3.2 *OS*-Function Spaces

The *OS*-functions between two *OS*-domains A and B are a subset of continuous functions $A \rightarrow B$. Like their operational counterparts in SPCF, observably sequential functions propagate error values returned by *inspected* inputs. Since inputs are inspected only when they are "needed", we must formalize the concept of "need" to understand the semantics of error propagation. The notion of a sequentiality index [4, 17] captures the informal idea of "need" in a general context. The following definition adapts this notion to *OS*-domains.

Definition 3.5. (*Sequentiality Index*) Let $\mathbf{D}_1(P_1, \leq_1, C_1), \mathbf{D}_2(P_2, \leq_2, C_2)$ be *OS*-domains. For a continuous function $f : D_1 \rightarrow_c D_2$, a ***sequentiality index*** for finite input $a \in D_1$ and output C-set Q_2 covering $f(a)$ is a C-set R_1 covering a such that for all $x \sqsupset a$, $(f(x) \cap Q_2) \neq \emptyset$ implies $(x \cap R_1) \neq \emptyset$. ∎

The presence of the error elements in the domain force a function to indicate which C-set above a is explored first. If R_1 is a sequentiality index of f at a and Q_2, then f determines which element $r \in R_1$ approximates f's input $x \sqsupset a$ when it generates the output prime in Q_2. If f propagates errors, then it must generate the output prime $\mathsf{error}_i^{Q_2}$ if r is $\mathsf{error}_i^{R_1}$. Such a function implicitly has its evaluation strategy embedded in its graph, and hence it is called observably sequential function or *OS*-function for short.

Definition 3.6. (*Observably Sequential Function*) Let D_1 and D_2 be *OS*-domains, generated from the bases $(P_1, \leq_1, C_1)$ and $(P_2, \leq_2, C_2)$, respectively. A continuous function $f : D_1 \rightarrow_c D_2$ is an *OS*-function iff it is

sequential: for every pair (a, Q_2), where Q_2 covers $f(a)$, there is a sequentiality index R_1 if $q \in f(x)$ for some $q \in Q_2$ and $x \sqsupset a$; and

error sensitive: if R is the sequentiality index of f for the input a and the output C-set Q, $\mathsf{error}_1^Q \in (f(a \cup \mathsf{error}_1^R))$ and $\mathsf{error}_2^Q \in f(a \cup \mathsf{error}_2^R)$.

We use $D_1 \rightarrow_{os} D_2$ to denote the set of the *OS*-functions between two *OS*-domains D_1, D_2. ∎

An *OS*-function $f : D_1 \rightarrow_{os} D_2$ has at most one sequentiality index for a given finite input $a \in D_1$ and C-set Q_2 covering $f(a)$ [10]. This property is a direct consequence of the fact that f propagates errors. Therefore, for *OS*-functions, it makes sense to introduce the function si where $si_f(a, Q)$ is the sequentiality index of f for a and Q.

A simple example of an *OS*-function space is $\mathbf{D}(P_{os}, \leq_{os}, C_{os})$ defined in the previous subsection. It is isomorphic to the function space $\mathsf{N}_\perp^E \rightarrow_{os} \mathsf{N}_\perp^E$. We will prove that the *OS*-functions between two *OS*-domains form an *OS*-domain under the usual pointwise approximation ordering.

The following lemma reduces the observable sequentiality of an arbitrary function in $D_1 \rightarrow_c D_2$ to the observable sequentiality of its finite approximations:

Lemma 3.7 *A function $f : D_1 \rightarrow_c D_2$ is observably sequential iff every finite approximation $g \sqsubseteq f$ in $D_1 \rightarrow_c D_2$ is observably sequential.*

Proof. The lemma is an immediate consequence of the definitions of observable sequentiality and the approximation ordering on $D_1 \rightarrow_c D_2$. ∎

To prove that $D_1 \rightarrow_{os} D_2$ is an OS-domain, we need to identify a prime basis for the space, specifically, the set of primes and the conflict sets.

Definition 3.8. (*Prime Basis for $\rightarrow_{os}$*) Let $D_i(P_i, \leq_i, C_i$ be OS-domains, for $i = 1, 2$. The partial order $(P_\rightarrow, \leq_\rightarrow)$ consists of special functions in $D_1 \rightarrow_{os} D_2$ that map finite elements of D_1 to prime elements of D_2. There are two disjoint subsets of primes:

1. **Output Primes:** an OS-function $f : D_1 \rightarrow_{os} D_2$ is an *output* prime function iff there exists a finite element $a \in D_1$ and a prime $p \in P_2$ such that f is a minimal function in $D_1 \rightarrow_{os} D_2$ satisfying the constraint $f(a) = p$ and $\forall a' \subset a \; f(a') \subset f(a)$. The function f has the C-set *label* $\langle a, Q_2, F' \rangle$ where $Q_2 \in C_2$ is the C-set containing p and $F' = \{g \in D_1 \rightarrow_{os} D_2 \,|\, g \subseteq f\}$.

2. **Schedule Primes:** an OS-function $f : D_1 \rightarrow_{os} D_2$ is a *schedule prime* iff there exists a finite element $a \in D_1$, a C-set $R_1 \in C_1$ where $a \prec R_1$, and a C-set $Q_2 \in C_2$ such that f is a minimal function with the property $f(a \sqcup \mathsf{error}_i^{R_1}) = \mathsf{error}_i^{Q_2}$ and $f(a) \subset \mathsf{error}_1^{Q_2}$. The function f has the C-set *label* $\langle a, Q_2, F' \rangle$ where $F' = \{g \in D_1 \rightarrow_{os} D_2 \,|\, g \subseteq f\}$.

$C_\rightarrow$ is the partitioning of $P_\rightarrow$ determined by the equivalence relation $\sim$ on $P_\rightarrow$ where

$$p \sim q \Leftrightarrow \text{ the C-set } \textit{label} \text{ of } p = \text{ the C-set } \textit{label} \text{ of } p.$$

The two designated error elements of a C-set with label $\langle a, Q, F' \rangle$ are $F' \cup \{(a, \mathsf{error}_1^Q)\}$ and $F' \cup \{(a, \mathsf{error}_2^Q)\}$. ∎

It is easy to show that $(P_\rightarrow, \leq, C_\rightarrow)$ forms a prime basis.

Lemma 3.9 *$(P_\rightarrow, \leq_\rightarrow, C_\rightarrow)$ is an error-rich prime basis.*

Proof Sketch. We prove that $(P_\rightarrow, \leq_\rightarrow, C_\rightarrow)$ satisfies each of the properties of a prime basis. The verification of the conditions **[PO]**, **[UP]**, and **[C]** is straightforward. Also, each C-set has two maximal primes designated as error_1 and error_2. Finally, as to [**[F]**], let $\langle a, Q_2, F' \rangle$ be the C-set label of p. The function p needs to perform only a finite number of "actions" looking for each prime in a in the input and generating each prime approximating Q_2 in the output. Since each action corresponds to a prime function, the prime functions approximating p are equal to the number of actions, that is, number of primes in a plus the number of primes approximating Q_2. Hence, the property **[F]** holds for the prime functions. ∎

In the sample OS-function space $\mathbf{N}_\perp^E \rightarrow_{os} \mathbf{N}_\perp^E$ given in Section 3.1, the output primes are $\{g_e, f_{d,e} \,|\, d \in \mathbf{N}, e \in \mathbf{N}^E\}$ and the sole schedule prime is s. The output primes approximating a function determine what output the function produces for a given input. But this information does not completely describe the behavior of the function; it leaves open the possibility that a function could explore several different sequentiality indices simultaneously, permitting an output prime to be generated by either of two consistent pieces of information. To avoid this ambiguity, schedule primes uniquely determine the sequentiality index of a function. Specifically, the schedule prime determined by F', a, R_1, and Q_2 has the unique sequentiality index R_1 at a and Q_2; the set F' is the chain of approximations.

Theorem 3.10 *Let* $\mathsf{D}(P_1, \leq_1, C_1)$ *and* $\mathsf{D}(P_2, \leq_2, C_2)$ *be OS-domains. Then, the function space* $\mathsf{D}(P_1, \leq_1, C_1) \rightarrow_{os} \mathsf{D}(P_2, \leq_2, C_2)$ *is isomorphic to the domain* $\mathsf{D}(P_\rightarrow, \leq_\rightarrow, C_\rightarrow)$. *Each set of functions* $d \in \mathsf{D}(P_\rightarrow, \leq_\rightarrow, C_\rightarrow)$ *is identified with its least upper bound in* $\mathsf{D}(P_1, \leq_1, C_1) \rightarrow_c \mathsf{D}(P_2, \leq_2, C_2)$.

Proof Sketch. The proof has two parts. First, we prove that any function generated from the prime basis $(P_\rightarrow, \leq_\rightarrow, C_\rightarrow)$ is observably sequential. Second, we prove that any OS-function is the least upper bound of all its prime approximations in $P_\rightarrow$. These two facts imply that $(P_\rightarrow, \leq_\rightarrow, C_\rightarrow)$ generates the OS-function domain $D_1 \rightarrow_{os} D_2$.

Claim 1: *The least upper bound in* $D_1 \rightarrow_c D_2$ *of a non-conflicting, downward-closed subset* $S \subseteq P_\rightarrow$ *is observably sequential.*

By Lemma 3.7, the proof of **Claim 1** reduces to proving that every bounded pair of finite OS-functions in $D_1 \rightarrow_c D_2$ has a least upper bound in $D_1 \rightarrow_c D_2$.

Let f and g be two OS-functions in $P_\rightarrow$ with least upper bound h in $D_1 \rightarrow_c D_2$. Let (a, Q_2) be a pair where Q_2 covers $h(a)$. If $h(x) \cap Q_2 \neq \emptyset$ and $x \supset a$, we need to show that h has a unique sequentiality index R_1 at (a, Q_2). We also need to show that $\mathsf{error}_i^{Q_2} \in h(a \sqcup \mathsf{error}_i^{R_1})$ for $i = 1, 2$.

Let $R_f = si_f(a, Q_2)$ and $R_g = si_g(a, Q_2)$. Either $R_f = R_g$ or only one of them exists. If $R_f \neq R_g$, then f and g can not be bounded above by any continuous function. If neither R_f nor R_g exists, then for all x, $h(x) \not\supset h(a)$.

Without loss of generality, assume that R_f is defined. Clearly, $R_f = si_h(a, Q_2)$ because $h(a \sqcup \mathsf{error}_1^{R_f}) \supseteq f(a \sqcup \mathsf{error}_i^{R_f})$. Since f is observably sequential, $\mathsf{error}_i^{Q_2} \in h(a \sqcup \mathsf{error}_1^{R_f})$. ∎$_1$

Claim 2: *Any OS-function is the least upper bound of its prime approximations.*

Let the set $S_f = \{p \in P_\rightarrow \mid p \sqsubseteq f\}$. We will show that

$$\forall x \in D_1 : f(x) = \bigsqcup \{p(x) \mid p \in S_f\}.$$

Set $z = \bigsqcup S_f(x)$. It is clear that $z \subseteq f(x)$. To prove the inclusion in the opposite direction, we observe that if $z \subset f(x)$, there must be a prime element q in $f(x)$ that is absent in z. Without loss of generality, we assume that x is a minimal element that has q in $f(x)$. Therefore x is a finite element in D_1. We will define a prime function g in S_f such that $g(x) = q$, contradicting the fact that $q \in f(x) \setminus z$.

If x does not have errors, we must define an output prime g such that $g(x) = q$. We can construct such an output prime $g \in S_f$ as follows:

$$\begin{array}{rcll} g(y) & = & f(y) \sqcap g(x) & \text{if } y \subseteq x \\ g(y \sqcup \mathsf{error}_i^{R_1}) & = & g(y) \sqcup \mathsf{error}_i^{Q_2} & \text{if } y \subset x, R_1 \text{ covers } y, Q_2 \leq q, \\ & & & \text{and } \mathsf{error}_i^{Q_2} \in f(y \sqcup \mathsf{error}_i^{R_1}) \end{array}$$

If x has an error_i^R, then $g(x)$ must be error_i^Q. In this case, we must define a schedule prime g with final step $si_g(a, Q) = R$ where $a = x \setminus \{\mathsf{error}_i^R\}$. We can construct such a scheme prime $g \in S_f$ as follows:

$$\begin{array}{rcll} g(a \sqcup \mathsf{error}_i^R) & = & \mathsf{error}_i^Q & \\ g(y) & = & f(y) \sqcap \mathsf{error}_1^Q & \text{if } y \subseteq a \\ g(y \sqcup \mathsf{error}_i^{R_1}) & = & g(y) \sqcup \mathsf{error}_i^{Q_2} & \text{if } y \subseteq a, R_1 \text{ covers } y, Q_2 \leq \mathsf{error}_1^Q, \\ & & & \text{and } \mathsf{error}_i^{Q_2} \in f(y \sqcup \mathsf{error}_i^{R_1}). \end{array}$$

Hence, $z \supseteq f(x)$, implying that **Claim 2** and thus the entire theorem are true. ∎

3.3 Semantics of SPCF

Using the framework of OS-domains, we can define a fully abstract "environment" model [18] for SPCF. The model is called the *Observably Sequential Type Frame*; its formal definition is given in Figure 2. The model maps each type τ to an OS-domain $\mathcal{T}[\![\tau]\!]$. The ground type (o) is interpreted as the flat domain of natural numbers with error values ($\mathsf{N}_\bot^E$), which is clearly a prime domain. The function types are domains of observably sequential function between appropriate spaces. An *environment* ρ is an observably sequential function mapping the flat OS-domain $\mathcal{V}_\bot^E = \mathcal{V} \cup \mathsf{E}_\bot$ of SPCF variable names to the union *Dom* of all domains $\mathcal{T}[\![\tau]\!]$ that respects the types of variable names: for all $x^\tau \in \mathcal{V}$, $\rho(x^\tau) \in \mathcal{T}[\![\tau]\!]$. It is easy to prove that the set of environments forms an OS-domain $\mathcal{E}$ under the pointwise approximation ordering. The function $\mathcal{C}$ maps constants of type τ to denotations in $\mathcal{T}[\![\tau]\!]$. Finally, if M is of type τ, the meaning function $\mathcal{M}$ assigns M the denotation $\mathcal{M}[\![M]\!] \in \mathcal{E} \to \mathcal{T}[\![\tau]\!]$.

The notation used in the definition follows the standard conventions in the literature. In particular, for a closed term M, we simply write $\mathcal{M}[\![M]\!]$ to denote the meaning of the term M—instead of $\mathcal{M}[\![M]\!]\rho$—because the environment ρ is irrelevant. By the same token, we write $\mathcal{M}[\![M]\!]$ to denote the meaning of an SPCF program M, since it is closed term of type o.

Figure 2 asserts that for any environment $\rho \in \mathcal{E}$ and a term M of type τ in SPCF, the meaning $\mathcal{M}[\![M]\!]\rho \in \mathcal{T}[\![\tau]\!]$. To prove this fact, we rely on standard techniques from Meyer [18] and Curien [11, 12]. In either case, the proof is laborious but uninteresting; the only interesting cases rely on the fact that OS-functions are closed under composition and λ-abstraction, which can be interpreted as a combinator [11, 7]. Following Curien's path shows that the set of OS-domains and OS-functions form a cartesian closed category.

Given a meaning function for SPCF, we can formulate the observational congruence relation ($\simeq_{SPCF}$). This relation captures the *behavioral* equivalences among terms and provides a mathematical justification for many compiler optimizations. It equates two terms precisely when an observer cannot tell the difference between these terms in arbitrary program contexts.

Definition 3.11. (*Observational Equivalence*) Let M and N be two SPCF terms of type τ. Then, M and N are observationally equivalent if for all contexts C^τ (programs with holes in places of terms of type τ) such that $C[M]$ and $C[N]$ are programs,

$$\mathcal{M}[\![C[M]]\!] = \mathcal{M}[\![C[N]]\!].$$

We write $M \simeq_{SPCF} N$ if M and N are observationally equivalent. ∎

The important property of the OS-domains model of SPCF is that two terms map to the same denotation (for all environments) if and precisely if they are observationally equivalent.

Theorem 3.12 *Let M and N be two SPCF terms of type τ. Then,*

$$M \simeq_{SPCF} N \text{ if and only if } \mathcal{M}[\![M]\!]\rho = \mathcal{M}[\![N]\!]\rho \text{ for all } \rho.$$

The original proof of this theorem for a concrete model of SPCF based on trees is due to Cartwright and Felleisen [9]. For the OS-domains model, the theorem follows from Theorem 5.8 in Section 5.

Domains

$$\begin{aligned}
\mathcal{T}[\![o]\!] &= \mathsf{N}_\bot^E \\
\mathcal{T}[\![\sigma \to \tau]\!] &= [\mathcal{T}[\![\sigma]\!] \to_{os} \mathcal{T}[\![\tau]\!]] \\
\mathcal{V}_\bot^E &= \mathcal{V} \cup \mathsf{E}_\bot \\
\mathcal{E} &= \{f \in \mathcal{V}_\bot^E \to_{os} \bigcup_\tau \mathcal{T}[\![\tau]\!] \mid f(x^\tau) \in \mathcal{T}[\![\tau]\!]\}
\end{aligned}$$

where

$$\begin{aligned}
\mathsf{N}_\bot^E &\stackrel{df}{=} \mathsf{N} \cup \mathsf{E}_\bot \\
\mathsf{E}_\bot &\stackrel{df}{=} \{\bot, \mathsf{error}_1, \mathsf{error}_2\}
\end{aligned}$$

Semantic functions

$$\begin{aligned}
\mathcal{C} &: \mathit{Constants}_\tau \to \mathcal{T}[\![\tau]\!] \\
\mathcal{C}[\![\ulcorner n \urcorner]\!] &= n \\
\mathcal{C}[\![\mathsf{error}_i]\!] &= \mathsf{error}_i \\
\mathcal{C}[\![\mathsf{add1}]\!] &= \{(\bot,\bot), (\mathsf{error}_i, \mathsf{error}_i), (l, l+1) \mid l \in \mathsf{N}\} \\
\mathcal{C}[\![\mathsf{sub1}]\!] &= \{(\bot,\bot), (\mathsf{error}_i, \mathsf{error}_i), (0,\bot), (l+1, l) \mid l \in \mathsf{N}\} \\
\mathcal{C}[\![\mathsf{if0}]\!] &= \{(\bot, l, m, \bot), (\mathsf{error}_i, l, m, \mathsf{error}_i), (0, l, m, l), (k+1, l, m, m) \mid l, m, k \in \mathsf{N}\} \\
\mathcal{C}[\![\mathsf{Y}]\!] &= \underline{\lambda} f^{(\sigma\to\tau)\to(\sigma\to\tau)}.\bigsqcup_{n=0}^{\infty} f^n(\bot^{(\sigma\to\tau)}) \\
\mathcal{C}[\![\mathsf{call/cdc}]\!](f) &= \begin{cases} n & ((\bot,\bot),n) \in f, ((\mathsf{error}_i,\mathsf{error}_i),n) \in f, \text{ or } ((n,\mathsf{error}_i),\mathsf{error}_i) \in f \\ \mathsf{error}_i & ((\bot,\bot),\mathsf{error}_i) \in f \end{cases}
\end{aligned}$$

$$\begin{aligned}
\mathcal{M} &: \mathit{Terms}_\tau \to_{os} \mathcal{E} \to_{os} \mathcal{T}[\![\tau]\!] \\
\mathcal{M}[\![b]\!]\rho &= \mathcal{C}[\![b]\!] \\
\mathcal{M}[\![x]\!]\rho &= \rho[\![x]\!] \\
\mathcal{M}[\![\lambda x.M]\!]\rho &= (\underline{\lambda} v.\mathcal{M}[\![M]\!]\rho[x/v]) \\
\mathcal{M}[\![(M\ N)]\!]\rho &= \mathcal{M}[\![M]\!]\rho(\mathcal{M}[\![N]\!]\rho)
\end{aligned}$$

FIGURE 2: The semantics of SPCF

SPCF is more expressive than PCF. While SPCF is a conservative extension of PCF in the sense that it preserves the meanings of all proper PCF programs, its control operators add expressive power to PCF. More precisely, PCF cannot *simulate* SPCF's new features via "functions" or "macros": There is no syntactically homomorphic translation from SPCF to PCF that maps programs and sub-expressions that are already in PCF syntax to themselves. By Felleisen's theorem on expressiveness [13:Thm 3.14], this claim reduces to showing that the theory of observational equivalence for SPCF is not a superset of the theory of observational equivalence for PCF.

Based on the explanation of the possibilities of observing sequentiality at the end of Section 2, it is easy to prove that some of PCF's observational equalities no longer hold in SPCF. Consider the equation:

$$(\lambda f.(f +_l)) \simeq_{PCF} (\lambda f.(f +_r))$$

In SPCF, we can use either error values or call/cdc to distinguish these functions. Both of the contexts

$$C_1 = ([\ \ ]\ (\lambda + .(+\ \mathsf{error}_1\ \mathsf{error}_2)))$$

and

$$C_2 = ([\ \ ]\ \mathit{Distinguish})$$

distinguish these functions. And hence, $(\lambda f.(f\ +_l)) \not\simeq_{SPCF} (\lambda f.(f\ +_r))$ as predicated. ∎

4 An SPCF Calculus

The λ-calculus for SPCF is an extension of the calculus for PCF [22]. The second part of Figure 3 contains the axioms of the PCF calculus: (β), (Y), and the axioms for PCF constants in the left-hand column. The SPCF calculus adds the four new axioms in the right-hand column of the second part of the same figure. Two axioms capture the behavior of each of the two error values, one that of a return and one that of an escape from a call/cdc-application.

Evaluation Contexts:

$$\begin{array}{rcl} E & ::= & [\ ] \mid (c^1\ E) \mid (c^3\ E\ M\ M) \mid (\mathsf{call/cdc}\ (\lambda x.E)) \\ c^1 & ::= & \mathsf{add1} \mid \mathsf{sub1} \mid \mathsf{call/cdc} \\ c^3 & ::= & \mathsf{if0} \end{array}$$

Axioms:

$$\begin{array}{rcll} (\lambda_n x.M)\ M' & = & M[x/M'] & (\beta) \\ \mathsf{Y}\ M & = & M\ (\mathsf{Y}\ M) & (\mathsf{Y}) \end{array}$$

$$\begin{array}{rcll} (\mathsf{add1}\ \ulcorner n \urcorner) & = & \ulcorner n+1 \urcorner & (\mathsf{add1}) \\ (\mathsf{sub1}\ \ulcorner n+1 \urcorner) & = & \ulcorner n \urcorner & (\mathsf{sub1}) \\ (\mathsf{if0}\ \ulcorner 0 \urcorner\ M\ N) & = & M & (\mathsf{if0}_0) \\ (\mathsf{if0}\ \ulcorner n+1 \urcorner\ M\ N) & = & N & (\mathsf{if0}_1) \end{array} \qquad \begin{array}{rcll} E[\mathsf{error}_1] & = & \mathsf{error}_1 & (\mathsf{error}_1) \\ E[\mathsf{error}_2] & = & \mathsf{error}_2 & (\mathsf{error}_2) \\ \mathsf{call/cdc}(\lambda f.\ulcorner n \urcorner) & = & \ulcorner n \urcorner & (\mathsf{return}) \\ \mathsf{call/cdc}(\lambda f.E[f\ \ulcorner n \urcorner]) & = & \ulcorner n \urcorner & (\mathsf{catch}) \\ & & \text{if } f \text{ is not captured by } E & \end{array}$$

Semantics: $eval_{SPCF}(M) = \ulcorner m \urcorner$ if and only if $M = \ulcorner m \urcorner$

FIGURE 3: SPCF: Calculus and Semantics

The formalization of the additional axioms relies on the concept of an *evaluation context* [14, 15]. An evaluation context is a phrase with a hole at a position of ground type: see the first part of Figure 3. Filling the hole with a phrase yields a complete phrase. The process of filling a hole may capture free variables that are bound as downward continuation variables in nested call/cdc-application.

The crucial property of the notion of evaluation context is that every phrase of ground type, is either a numeral, a variable, or has a unique decomposition into an evaluation context and a redex. The hole of the evaluation context specifies the position of the unique sub-phrase that *must* be evaluated in order to be able to evaluate the complete phrase. A *redex* R_E, relative to an evaluation context E, is either one of the following applications: (**add1** $\ulcorner n \urcorner$), (**sub1** $\ulcorner n \urcorner$), (**if0** $\ulcorner n \urcorner$ M N), or (**call/cdc** $(\lambda x.\ulcorner n \urcorner)$); or it is an **error** value; or it is an application of an E-bound variable (f), a downward continuation, to a numeral: (f $\ulcorner n \urcorner$).

Lemma 4.1 (Unique Decomposition) *If M is an expression of ground type, then it is either a numeral, a variable, or there exists a* unique *evaluation context E and a redex R_E such that $M \equiv E[R_E]$.*

Proof Sketch. The proof is a simple induction on the structure of terms. ∎

If the hole of an evaluation context contains an **error**, the evaluation context is useless: it will never affect the evaluation of the program. If the hole contains the application of a downward continuation to a numeral ($\ulcorner n \urcorner$), the evaluation continues by eliminating the evaluation context and by returning $\ulcorner n \urcorner$ as the result of the (binding) **call/cdc**-application.

Given the SPCF calculus, the operational semantics of SPCF is specifed in the conventional fashion. A program, *i.e.*, a closed SPCF phrase of type o, evaluates to a numeral, if the SPCF calculus proves the equivalence between the two. To prove that this definition determines an evaluation *function*, we need to establish a Church-Rosser Theorem.

Theorem 4.2 (Consistency) *$eval_{SPCF}$ is a function.*

Proof Sketch. Let $\rightarrow_s$ denote the reduction system, based on reading the SPCF axioms from left to right. Then, it is easy to see that the theorem is implied by a Church-Rosser theorem for the reduction system. We already know that the PCF calculus is Church-Rosser. Based on the Unique Decomposition Lemma, we can easily prove that the reductions **error**$_1$, **error**$_2$ and **catch**, **return** satisfy the diamond property. Finally, the three reduction relations commute with each other, which by the Hindley-Rosen Lemma [1:3.3.5] proves that the complete system ($\rightarrow_s$) is Church-Rosser. (Also compare the proof of the Church-Rosser Theorem for the λ_v-C-calculus [14].) ∎

Given two distinct functions for determining a result for a program, it is natural to ask whether the functions are the same. The following theorem shows that the operational and the denotational semantics are indeed in complete agreement.

Theorem 4.3 (Adequacy) *For all SPCF programs M, $eval_{SPCF}(M) = \ulcorner m \urcorner$ iff $[\![M]\!] = m$.*

Proof Sketch. Curien [12] proved an adequacy theorem for SPCF with **catch** and for a *concrete* denotational model. As mentioned above, his concrete domains are isomorphic to our abstract domains. Hence, our denotational meaning functions agree. Furthermore, it is easy to show that Curien's calculus proves the same equations between programs that our calculus proves. Thus, our operational evaluators agree, too. ∎

Beyond its rôle in defining an operational semantics, a calculus is also a simple logic for reasoning about observational congruences. By the Adequacy Theorem, the axioms are clearly sound with respect to observational equivalence. The more interesting question, however, concerns the extent to which these axioms are *complete*. Since SPCF can clearly define all partial recursive functions on the natural numbers, the calculus cannot be an axiomatization for the entire theory. But, given the related results for λ-calculus-based languages, we can ask whether it is possible to axiomatize SPCF's observational congruence relation for certain sub-languages of SPCF.

The completeness question for the pure typed λ-calculus was first addressed by H. Friedman [16]. He proved that equality for the language Λ^{τ} in the full type hierachy is completely characterized by the $\lambda\beta\eta$ calculus where (η) is the equational characterization of extensionality for Λ^τ:

$$(\lambda x.(M\ x)) \;=\; x \text{ if } x \text{ is not free in M} \qquad (\eta)$$

Plotkin [21] and Statman [23, 30, 31] later strengthened Friedman's theorem by proving that $\lambda\beta\eta$ is also complete for the continuous type frame. Statman's 1-Section Theorem also provides a general proof method for determining whether $\lambda\beta\eta$ is a complete axiomatization of equality for arbitrary extensional models of the simply typed λ-calculus. It follows from this latter theorem that we can completely axiomatize observational equality for the sub-language Λ^τ of SPCF.

Theorem 4.4 (Completeness for Λ^τ) *If $M, N \in \Lambda^\tau$, then*

$$\beta\eta \vdash M = N \textit{ iff } [\![M]\!] = [\![N]\!] \textit{ iff } M \simeq_{SPCF} N.$$

Proof Sketch. To prove the completeness of the $\lambda\beta\eta$ calculus for an extensional model according to Statman's 1-Section Theorem [30, 31, 23], we need to prove that there is a faithful embedding of the free algebra of binary trees over a single constant into the first-order portion of the model.

Recall the definition of the free binary tree algebra. It contains all finite terms over the signature $\{C^0, F^2\}$, i.e., it is the language generated by the production

$$T \rightarrow C \mid (F\ T\ T).$$

A faithful embedding of this algebra into a model requires an extension of the meaning function for constants, $\mathcal{C}$, that maps C to a natural number, $c \in \mathbf{N}$, and F to a pairing function,

$$p : \mathbf{N}^E_\bot \rightarrow_{os} \mathbf{N}^E_\bot \rightarrow_{os} \mathbf{N}^E_\bot,$$

such that $t_1 = t_2$ if and only if $\mathcal{M}[\![t_1]\!] = \mathcal{M}[\![t_2]\!]$.

For our purposes, we can take $c = 0$ and

$$p = \begin{cases} 2^x \cdot 3^y & \text{if } x, y \in \mathbf{N} \\ x & \text{if } x \in \mathbf{E}_\bot \\ y & \text{if } x \in \mathbf{N}, y \in \mathbf{E}_\bot \end{cases}$$

It is straightforward to show that an extension of $\mathcal{C}$ for C^0, F^2 based on c and p is faithful. ∎

In an upcoming paper, Riecke and Subrahmanyam [24] prove an extension of Statman's 1-Section Theorem to mixtures of Λ^τ and first-order algebras. Based on their central theorem [24:Thm. 11], it is possible to extend the above theorem to Λ^τ plus **add1** and the numerals. As to further extensions with first-order constants, their results show that the addition of **sub1**[2] or **if0** based on their algebraic axioms does *not* yield a complete calculus.

A more interesting question with respect to SPCF's constants is whether the operational axioms for **call/cdc** completely capture its observable behavior. Unfortunately, this is not the case. Consider the following equation:[3]

$$(\lambda x^{o\rightarrow o}.(\mathsf{call/cdc}\ (\lambda y^{o\rightarrow o}.(x\ (x\ (y\ z)))))) \;=\; (\lambda x^{o\rightarrow o}.(\mathsf{call/cdc}\ (\lambda y^{o\rightarrow o}.(x\ (y\ z))))) \qquad (\dagger)$$

[2]The problem with sub1 is due to the specification that PCF's sub1 diverges when applied to $\ulcorner 0 \urcorner$. Setting $(\mathsf{sub1}\ulcorner 0 \urcorner) = \mathsf{error}_1$ also does not solve the problem because the presence of error values in the ground domain violates another antecedent of the Riecke-Subrahmanyam meta-theorem [Riecke: private communication, 15 October 1992].

[3]The idea for this equation is due to John Gateley.

It is easy to prove by a simple case analysis that the model validates this equation. If either of the two procedures is applied to a constant procedure f, the result is that of f. Otherwise, if they are applied to a strict procedure g, then they will both attempt to evaluate the sub-expression $(y\ z)$, which will cause them to return the value of z. Thus, the two procedures denote the same functions, and the equation holds in our model. The SPCF calculus, on the other hand, cannot prove the equation (†) because the two terms are in normal form and the underlying reduction system $(\rightarrow_s)$ is CR.

The counter-example reveals that the calculus cannot reason about the strictness behavior of variables. We conjecture that only an extension of the calculus to a sequent-style theory for case-based reasoning can completely axiomatize the equation that govern call/cdc's behavior.

5 The Computational Power of SPCF

Given a model $\mathcal{M}$ for a language L, it is natural to ask whether the language L can express all the ***computable*** elements in the model. More precisely, the question is whether every recursively enumerable element $d \in \mathcal{T}[\![\tau]\!]$ is definable by a term M of type τ in $\mathcal{L}$, *i.e.*, $\mathcal{M}[\![M]\!] = d$. When this property holds, we say that L is ***computationally complete*** for $\mathcal{M}$. Plotkin [22:Section 5][4] proved that PCF is not computationally complete for the familiar continuous function model. The continuous function model contains "parallel deterministic" functions that PCF *cannot* express. Two well-known independent examples are the parallel conditional function (pif0) and the parallel *exists* function ($\exists$). The pif0 function is similar to if0, but it returns the least upper bound of the two alternatives if the test argument diverges. The function $\exists$ tests whether its argument, a function from $\mathbf{N}_\perp$ to itself, produces tt (0 in our simplified version of PCF) for any input or whether it always returns ff.

In contrast to PCF and PCF+pif0, SPCF does not need any extensions to be computationally complete. For any computable element in its natural model, there is a term that denotes this element. Given this fact, it is easy to show that the natural model of SPCF is fully abstract.

This section sketches a proof of the computational completeness of SPCF. The first subsection defines a generalization of Turing computability suitable for OS-domains. The second subsection applies this definition to SPCF and presents an algorithm for constructing an SPCF term that denotes a given domain element definable by a partial recursive function. This algorithm shows that SPCF is computationally complete for its OS-domains model.

5.1 Computability in Observably Sequential Domains

Computability over Scott domains is a generalization of the familiar notion of Turing computability over natural numbers. A computation over a Scott domain produces a recursively enumerable set of finite approximations whose least upper bound is the "answer" produced by the computation. In a computation over a Scott domain D, every finite element is represented by a distinct natural number. The specific choice of representation is determined by the *presentation* of the domain [27]; the presentation assigns a distinct integer code to each finite element and specifies the ordering relationship between any two finite elements.

[4] Also compare Sazonov's paper [25] on the expressibility of PCF. He proved that PCF can only express the sequential functions of its continuous function model, and conjectured that adding parallel-or and parallel-exists would make PCF a computationally complete language. His discovery of parallel-or and parallel-exists was independent of Plotkin's, but both operators were discussed in early manuscripts of D. Scott [Plotkin, Sazonov, & Scott: private communication, July 1992].

5.1.1 Domain Presentations

When a Scott domain is an OS-domain, every finite approximation is the least upper bound of its prime approximations. Consequently, a *presentation* only needs to assign integer codes to the prime elements of an OS-domain. Given such a presentation, it is easy to generate unique codes for all finite elements using a standard pairing function.

We formalize the concept of a presentation of an OS-domain as follows:

Definition 5.1. (OS-*domain Presentation*) A *presentation* of an OS-domain D with prime-basis $(P, \leq, C)$ is a quadruple of functions $\langle \mathbf{E}, \mathbf{c}, \mathbf{pr}, \mathbf{err} \rangle$:

- a one-to-one function $\mathbf{E} : P \rightarrow \mathbb{N}$, such that $p \leq_P q \Rightarrow \mathbf{E}(p) \leq_{\mathbb{N}} \mathbf{E}(q)$ that maps the elements of P into their codes in the index set in $\mathbb{N}$. By convention, we extend $\mathbf{E}$ to $\perp$ by defining $\mathbf{E}(\perp) \stackrel{df}{=} 0$. Let $\mathcal{I}$ be the range of the function $\mathbf{E}$.
- a function $\mathbf{c} : \mathcal{I} \rightarrow \mathbb{N}$ such that $\forall i, j > 0 : \mathbf{c}(i) = \mathbf{c}(j)$ iff $p_i, p_j \in Q$ for $Q \in C$; by convention, we define $\mathbf{c}(0) \stackrel{df}{=} 0$. Let the range of the function $\mathbf{c}$ be $\mathcal{S}$.
- a predecessor function $\mathbf{pr} : \mathcal{I} \rightarrow \mathcal{I}$ such that $\mathbf{pr}(i) = j$ iff $p_j \prec p_i$. If there is no predecessor for an element p_i, we define $\mathbf{pr}(i) \stackrel{df}{=} 0$. Similarly, we define $\mathbf{pr}(0) \stackrel{df}{=} 0$.
- a function $\mathbf{err} : \mathcal{I} \rightarrow \{0, 1, 2\}$ such that

$$\mathbf{err}(k) = \begin{cases} i & p_k = \mathsf{error}_i^Q \\ 0 & \text{otherwise}. \end{cases}$$

The presentation is *effective* iff the functions $\mathbf{c}$, $\mathbf{pr}$, $\mathbf{err}$ are partial recursive functions mapping $\mathbb{N}$ into $\mathbb{N}$. The function $\mathbf{E}$ is called a *prime enumerator* for D. ∎

The prime enumerator $\mathbf{E}$ maps each prime element to a unique index in $\mathbb{N}$. Hence, $\mathbf{E}$ determines an enumeration of prime elements $p_{i_1}, p_{i_2}, \ldots$ where $\mathbf{E}(p_{i_j}) = i_j$. For the sake of convenience, we require that the indexing determined by $\mathbf{E}$ be topologically sorted, which makes 0 the end-of-list marker.

The remaining three components of a presentation—$\mathbf{c}$, $\mathbf{pr}$, and $\mathbf{err}$—specify how prime elements are partitioned in C-sets, what prime element precedes each C-set, and which prime elements are errors. The function $\mathbf{c}$ implicitly assigns a unique code number in $\mathcal{S} \subseteq \mathbb{N}$ to each C-set in the prime-basis. We refer to the C-set with index m as C_m. As usual, we remove the ambiguity by superscripting the C-sets with the domain whenever needed. This indexing scheme for C-sets determines the following partial order on $\mathcal{S}$, which we will use later in this section.

Definition 5.2. ($\leq'$) Let $m, m' \in \mathbb{N}$ be in the range of the function $\mathbf{c}$. Then $m' \leq' m$ iff for all $q \in C_m$ there exists $p \in C_{m'}$ such that $p \leq q$. ∎

5.1.2 Encoding Finite Elements

Since finite elements are least upper bounds of finite sets of primes, it is easy to generate codes for the finite elements of $\mathbf{D}$ given $\mathbf{E}$. The index of a finite element d is the integer code representing the finite set S_d of prime indices of primes below d. To make this encoding unique, we represent S_d as a sorted list of prime indices terminated by the *end-of-list* marker 0 and use a standard bijective pairing function to encode this list as an integer.

Definition 5.3. (*Index of finite element*) In the *OS*-domain with prime enumerator $\mathbf{E}$, the finite element $a = \sqcup\{p_{k_1}, p_{k_2}, \ldots, p_{k_n}\}$ where $k_1 > k_2 > \ldots > k_n$ has the *index*

$$\langle k_1, \langle k_2, \ldots, \langle k_n, 0\rangle \ldots\rangle\rangle$$

where $\langle\cdot,\cdot\rangle : \mathbb{N} \times \mathbb{N} \to \mathbb{N}$ is the standard pairing function defined by

$$\langle i, j\rangle = \frac{(i+j)*(i+j+1)}{2} + i .$$

We denote the finite element with index I by a_I. We superscript the element by the domain it belongs to, if there is ambiguity.
Note: Each prime element has two indices: one as a prime element and another as a finite element. ∎

The encoding described above is unique for every n-tuple of positive numbers $\langle k_1, k_2, \ldots, k_n\rangle$. Since the pairing function, the projection functions, and the sorting function over the encoded tuples are recursive, they can be expressed in SPCF as $\langle\cdot,\cdot\rangle$, **1st**, **2nd**, and **sort** respectively.

5.1.3 Computable Elements

We have now finally developed all of the machinery required to define the *computable* elements of an *OS*-domain. Informally, an element d of an effectively presented *OS*-domain D is computable iff there exists a partial recursive function that "represents" the element. The following definition makes this notion precise.

Definition 5.4. (*Computable Element (OS Domains)*) Let D be an *OS*-domain with the effective presentation $\langle \mathbf{E}, \mathbf{c}, \mathbf{pr}, \mathbf{err}\rangle$ where $\mathcal{I}$ denotes the range of $\mathbf{E}$ and $\mathcal{S}$ denotes the range of $\mathbf{c}$. An element d of an *OS*-domain D is *computable* iff the function $f_d : \mathcal{S} \multimap \mathcal{I}$ defined by

$$f_d(m) = \begin{cases} k & \text{if } \mathbf{c}(k) = m \text{ and } p_k \sqsubseteq d \\ \text{undefined} & \text{otherwise} \end{cases}$$

is a partial recursive function over $\mathbb{N}$. We call the function f_d the *characteristic function* of d. ∎

5.1.4 A Comparison with Classical Domain Theory

The standard definition of computability for Scott domains is similar to our definition of computability for *OS*-domains. The only difference is that our definition exploits the additional topological structure of *OS*-domains. It is easy to show that an element d of an *OS*-domain D with effective presentation $\mathbf{E}$ is computable iff it is computable in the isomorphic Scott domain with the corresponding effective presentation.

Definition 5.5. (*Scott Presentation*) A *presentation* δ_s of a Scott domain D with basis $(B, \leq)$ is a triple $\langle \mathbf{E}_s, \mathbf{lub}, \mathbf{con}\rangle$ consisting of:

- a one-to-one onto function $\mathbf{E}_s : B \to \mathcal{I} \subseteq \mathbb{N}$, such that $\mathbf{E}_s(\perp) = 0$; $\mathbf{E}_s$ maps the elements of B into their codes in the index set $\mathcal{I} \subseteq \mathbb{N}$.
- a ternary predicate $\mathbf{lub} \subseteq \mathcal{I} \times \mathcal{I} \times \mathcal{I}$ such that

$$\mathbf{lub}(x, y, z) \Leftrightarrow b_x \sqcup b_y = b_z$$

  where $b_x = E^{-1}(x), b_y = E^{-1}(y)$, and $b_z = E^{-1}(z)$;

- a binary predicate **con** $\subseteq \mathcal{I} \times \mathcal{I}$ such that

$$\mathbf{con}(x, y) \Leftrightarrow \exists z \in B : x \sqsubseteq z \text{ and } y \sqsubseteq z\,.$$

The function $\mathbf{E}_s$ is called the *enumerator* for D. The presentation δ_s is *effective* iff the relations **lub** and **con** are recursive. ∎

Given an effective presentation δ for an OS-domain D, it is easy to generate the effective presentation δ_s for D viewed as a Scott domain.

We will show that d is a computable element an OS-domain D with effective presentation δ iff d is a computable element in the isomorphic Scott domain with effective presentation δ_s.

Definition 5.6. (*Computable Element (Scott Domains)*) Let D be a Scott domain with the enumerator $\mathbf{E}_s$, and let $\mathcal{I} = range(\mathbf{E}_s)$. An element d of the domain D is computable iff there is a partial recursive predicate g_d over $\mathcal{I}$ such that

$$g_d(i) = \begin{cases} \mathbf{tt} & \text{iff } a_i \sqsubseteq d \\ \text{undefined} & \text{otherwise} \end{cases}$$

We call g_d the (*Scott*) *characteristic function* for d. ∎

In an OS-domain D, the two definitions of computability coincide.

Lemma 5.7 *Let D be an* OS*-domain with effective presentation δ and let δ_s be the effective Scott for the isomorphic Scott domain D_s. An element $d_s \in D_s$ has a* Scott-characteristic function g_d *iff the corresponding element in $d \in D$ has a characteristic function f_d.*

Proof Sketch. ($\Leftarrow$) Given f_d we can define the corresponding Scott-characteristic function g_d as follows. Since

$$g_d(I) = \mathbf{tt} \Leftrightarrow g_d(k) = \mathbf{tt}\ \forall k : a_k \sqsubseteq a_I \text{ and } a_k \text{ is prime}$$

it suffices to define g_d on k such that a_k is prime. The function g_d is defined on *prime elements* a_k by the rule

$$g_d(k) = \mathbf{tt} \quad \Leftrightarrow \quad \forall j : p_j \sqsubseteq a_k : [f_d(\mathbf{c}(j)) = j]\,.$$

where the index k is the encoding of the tuple $\langle k_1, \ldots, k_n\rangle$. The set of prime indices $\{j \mid p_j \sqsubseteq a_k\}$ is simply $\{j_1, j_2, \ldots, j_n\}$ where $\langle j_1, \langle j_2, \ldots, \langle j_n, 0\rangle \ldots\rangle\rangle = k$. Hence, $g_d(k)$ is computable for k such that a_k is prime.

Conversely, given g_d, we can define f_d as follows. Given any prime index $k_1 \in \mathcal{I}$, Let $a_{\langle k_1, \ldots, k_n\rangle} = p_{k_1}$ and let $m = \mathbf{c}(k_1)$, the code of the C-set containing p_{k_1}. Then,

$$f_d(m) = k_1 \Leftrightarrow g_d(\langle k_1, \ldots, k_n\rangle) = \mathbf{tt}.$$

Since only one element of the C-set with index m can approximate d, $f_d(m)$ can be calculated by finding element a_k in C-set C_m such that $g_d(k)$ is true. If such an element exists, a dovetailing search will eventually find it. ∎

5.2 Computability in SPCF

To apply the preceding general framework to SPCF, we need to define an effective presentation δ^τ for each of the domains $\mathcal{T}[\![t]\!]$ of the SPCF model. We proceed by induction on the structure of the type t.

Conventions. In this subsection, the letters I, J range over indices of *finite* elements, i, j, k, l over indices of prime elements, and m, n over the indices of C-sets. A C-set in the domain $\mathcal{T}[\![\tau]\!]$ is called a c^τ-set. ∎

The design of an enumerator $\mathbf{E}^o : \mathbf{N}_\perp^E \to \mathbf{N}$ for the base domain is straightforward:

$$\begin{aligned} \mathbf{E}^o(\perp) &= 0 \\ \mathbf{E}^o(\mathsf{error}_1) &= 1 \\ \mathbf{E}^o(\mathsf{error}_2) &= 2 \\ \mathbf{E}^o(x) &= x+3 \qquad (x \in \mathbf{N}) \end{aligned}$$

It is easy to confirm that the enumerator $\mathbf{E}^o$ is topologically sorted. Moreover, it is effective because the functions $\mathbf{c}^o$, $\mathbf{pr}^o$, and $\mathbf{err}^o$ are definable as primitive recursive functions:

$$\begin{aligned} \mathbf{c}^o(0) &= 0 \\ \mathbf{c}^o(x+1) &= 1 \\ \mathbf{pr}^o(x) &= 0 \end{aligned} \qquad \mathbf{err}^o(x) = \begin{cases} x & \text{if } x = 1 \text{ or } x = 2 \\ 0 & \text{otherwise} \end{cases}$$

The definition of the enumerator $\mathbf{E}^{\sigma\to\tau} : \mathcal{T}[\![\sigma \to \tau]\!] \to \mathbf{N}$ and corresponding functions $\mathbf{c}^{\sigma\to\tau}$, $\mathbf{pr}^{\sigma\to\tau}$, and $\mathbf{err}^{\sigma\to\tau}$ for higher types $\sigma \to \tau$ proceeds by sub-induction on the structure of prime functions using the prime approximation ordering. First, set $\mathbf{E}^{\sigma\to\tau}(\perp_{\sigma\to\tau}) = 0$. Next, let f be a prime function with predecessor f', *i.e.*, $f' \prec f$, and let l be the index of f'. Then,

$$\mathbf{E}^{\sigma\to\tau}(f) = \begin{cases} \langle\langle \mathsf{O}, I, k\rangle, l\rangle & \text{if } f \text{ is an output prime, determined by } f', a_I, \text{ and } p_k \\ \langle\langle \mathsf{S}, \langle I, m\rangle, n\rangle, l\rangle & \text{if } f \text{ is a schedule prime with } si_f(a_I, C_m) = C_n \end{cases}$$

where the tags O (for output prime) and S (for schedule prime) stand for 0 and 1, respectively. The functions $\mathbf{c}^{\sigma\to\tau}$, $\mathbf{pr}^{\sigma\to\tau}$ and $\mathbf{err}^{\sigma\to\tau}$ are defined as follows:

$$\begin{aligned} \mathbf{c}^{\sigma\to\tau}(\langle\langle \mathsf{O}, I, k\rangle, l\rangle) &= \langle\langle I, \mathbf{c}^\tau(k)\rangle, l\rangle \\ \mathbf{c}^{\sigma\to\tau}(\langle\langle \mathsf{S}, \langle I, m\rangle, n\rangle, l\rangle) &= \langle\langle I, m\rangle, l\rangle \\ \mathbf{pr}^{\sigma\to\tau}(\langle\langle \cdots\rangle, l\rangle) &= l \end{aligned} \qquad \begin{aligned} \mathbf{err}^{\sigma\to\tau}(\langle\langle \mathsf{O}, I, k\rangle, l\rangle) &= \mathbf{err}^\tau(k) \\ \mathbf{err}^{\sigma\to\tau}(\langle\langle \mathsf{S}, \langle I, m\rangle, n\rangle, l\rangle) &= 0 \end{aligned}$$

Since $\langle 0, 0\rangle = 0$, $\mathbf{c}(0) = 0$ and $\mathbf{pr}(0) = 0$ as required. It is straightforward to verify that these functions are legitimate, *i.e.*, follow the conditions of an effective presentation.

Given the preceding definition of computability in the SPCF model, we can now state and prove the central claim of this section: *SPCF is a computationally complete language for its obserably sequential model.*

Theorem 5.8 *Let τ be an SPCF type. For every computable element $d \in \mathcal{T}[\![\tau]\!]$ there exists a closed SPCF term M such that $\mathcal{M}[\![M]\!] = d$.*

Proof Sketch. Let d be a computable element with characteristic function f_d. Since SPCF is a conservative (upward-compatible) extension of PCF, which can express all recursive functions in $\mathbf{N} \rightharpoonup \mathbf{N}$, SPCF contains a term N_d that computes the function in $f_d^\dagger$ corresponding to f_d. More precisely, $f_d^\dagger : \mathbf{N}_\bot^E \rightarrow_{os} \mathbf{N}_\bot^E$ satisfies the conditions:

$$\begin{aligned} f_d^\dagger(x) &= x \text{ iff } x \in \mathbf{E}_\bot \\ f_d^\dagger(m) &= n \text{ iff } f_d(m) = n \\ f_d^\dagger(m) &= \bot \text{ if } f_d(m) \text{ is undefined.} \end{aligned}$$

We call $f_d^\dagger$ the SPCF-characteristic function for d.

By the same argument, the functions **c**, **pr**, and **err** from any effective domain presentation have SPCF counterparts **C**, **Pr**, and **Err** corresponding to **c**, **pr**, and **err**.

To prove the theorem, all we have to do is construct an SPCF function Decode^τ that maps $f_d^\dagger$ to the corresponding element d. Unfortunately, the obvious approach to writing Decode^τ fails for higher types τ because it requires writing an inverse function Encode^τ, which maps an element d to the corresponding SPCF characteristic function $f_d^\dagger$. The latter function cannot be written in SPCF because *it is not observably sequential.* The function Encode^τ recognizes and discards rather than propagates error elements.

We can circumvent this problem by introducing an alternate functional representation for elements of D. Given an element $d \in D$, the *OS-characteristic* function f_d^* is defined in terms of the the characteristic function f_d for d as follows:

$$\begin{aligned} f_d^*(x) &= x && \text{for } x \in \mathbf{E}_\bot \\ f_d^*(m) &= k && \text{iff } f_d(m) = k \text{ and } \mathbf{err}(k) = 0 \\ f_d^*(m) &= \mathsf{error}_i && \text{iff } \exists\, m' \leq' m : \mathbf{err}(f_d(m')) = i \text{ for } i > 0 \\ f_d^*(m) &= \bot && \text{otherwise.} \end{aligned}$$

Figure 4 contains the code of a procedure **convert** that converts a characteristic function $f_d^\dagger$ to a *OS*-characteristic function f_d^*, *i.e.*, (**convert** N_d) denotes f_d^*. Given an index m for a C-set, (**convert** f), the code for the *OS*-characteristic function, works as follows. It visits all C-sets that approximate m, starting at the lowest possible one, and checks whether f maps the current C-set index to an error-generating prime. If so, it generates the correct error value; if not, it outputs the prime index (f m). The correctness of the function depends on correctness of the auxiliary function *NextCset* that gives unique n for a given m' and m such that $m' \prec' n \leq' m$. The correctness of the function *NextCset* can easily be verified by studying the encoding of the C-sets.

In contrast to Encode^τ, the function encode^τ mapping an element $d \in D$ to f_d^* is definable in SPCF. Similarly, the function decode^τ mapping a *OS*-characteristic function f_d^* to the corresponding element $d \in D$ is definable in SPCF. If we construct a procedure decode^τ, the proof of the theorem is complete, because

$$\mathcal{M}[\![(\mathsf{decode}^\tau\ (\mathsf{convert}\ x))]\!] = \mathcal{M}[\![(\mathsf{Decode}^\tau\ x)]\!]\,.$$

The function **decode** relies on the function **encode**; both these functions are simultaneously constructed inductively. The construction of the code for decode^τ and encode^τ proceeds by induction on the type τ. At each stage in the construction, we will assume the following induction hypothesis for smaller types, which simply states that **encode** and **decode** satisfy their specifications.

$$
\begin{array}{ll}
\text{convert}^{\tau} & = \lambda f.\lambda m. \\
& \quad \textbf{letrec } z{=}\lambda m'.\ \textbf{let } v{=}(f\ m') \\
& \quad\quad\quad \textbf{in } (\text{ifO}\ (\mathit{generr}^{\tau}\ v) \\
& \quad\quad\quad\quad (\text{ifO}\ \ (=\ m'\ m)\ v \\
& \quad\quad\quad\quad\quad (z\ (\mathit{NextCset}\ m'\ m))) \\
& \quad\quad\quad\quad \Omega) \\
& \quad \textbf{in } (z\ (\mathit{InitCset}^{\tau}\ m))
\end{array}
$$

$$
\begin{array}{ll}
\mathit{generr}^{\tau} & = \lambda v.\ \textbf{let } \mathit{errnum}{=}(\mathbf{Err}^{\tau}\ v) \\
& \quad \textbf{in } (\text{ifO}\ \ (\textbf{sub1}\ \mathit{errnum})\ \text{error}_1\ (\text{ifO}\ (\textbf{sub1}^2\ \mathit{errnum})\ \text{error}_2\ \ulcorner 0 \urcorner))
\end{array}
$$

Comment The function ($NextCset\ m'\ m$) calculates the unique n such that $m' \prec' n \leq' m$.

$$
\begin{array}{l}
\mathit{NextCset}^{\tau} = \lambda m', m.(\text{ifO}\ \ (=\ \ (\mathbf{C}^{\tau}\ (\textsf{2nd}\ m))\ m') \\
\quad\quad\quad\quad m \\
\quad\quad\quad\quad (\mathit{NextCset}^{\tau}\ m'\ (\mathbf{C}^{\tau}\ (\textsf{2nd}\ m))))
\end{array}
$$

$$
\mathit{InitCset}^{\tau} = (\mathit{NextCset}^{\tau}\ \ulcorner 0 \urcorner)
$$

FIGURE 4: The Function convert

Induction Hypothesis: For every type τ:

1. There is an SPCF function **decode**$^{\tau}$, which decodes a *OS*-characteristic function f_d^* into the data object d, *i.e.*,
$$\mathcal{M}[\![\mathbf{decode}^{\tau}]\!](f_d^*) = d\,.$$

2. There is an SPCF function **encode**$^{\tau}$, which encodes a data object $e \in \mathcal{T}[\![\tau]\!]$ as its *OS*-characteristic function f_e^*, *i.e.*,
$$\mathcal{M}[\![\mathbf{encode}^{\tau}]\!](e) = f_e^*\,.$$

Consequently, we must show that the induction hypothesis holds for the constructed functions **decode**$^{\tau}$ and **encode**$^{\tau}$.

The definition of the functions **decode**^{o} and **encode**^{o} for the base type o is straightforward:

$$
\begin{array}{rcl}
\mathbf{decode}^{o} & = & \lambda f_d^*.(f_d^*\ 1) \\
\mathbf{encode}^{o} & = & \lambda x.\lambda n.(\text{ifO}\ n\ \ulcorner 0 \urcorner\ (\text{ifO}\ (\mathbf{sub1}\ n)\ (+\ \ulcorner 3 \urcorner\ x)\ \Omega))
\end{array}
$$

The induction hypothesis obviously holds for type o.

Assume that the induction hypothesis holds for the types σ and τ, implying that we can use the functions **decode**$^{\sigma}$, **encode**$^{\sigma}$, **decode**$^{\tau}$, and **encode**$^{\tau}$ in the construction of the functions **decode**$^{\sigma\to\tau}$ and **encode**$^{\sigma\to\tau}$. The function **decode**$^{\sigma\to\tau}$ is shown in Figure 5. It accepts an *OS*-characteristic function f_d^* and some argument e for the function d. It relies on the function **encode**$^{\sigma}$ to encode e as its *OS*-characteristic function f_e^*. In the body of **decode**$^{\sigma\to\tau}$, the auxiliary function *Apply* takes the arguments f_d^* and f_e^* constructs the *OS*-characteristic function $f_{d(e)}^*$ for $d(e)$. Then **decode**$^{\sigma\to\tau}$ decodes the *OS*-characteristic function $f_{d(e)}^*$ to produce the data object $d(e)$.

```
decode^{σ→τ}  = λf*_d.λe^σ.(decode^τ (Apply^τ f*_d (encode^σ e)))

Apply^τ       = λf*_d, f*_e.λm.
        letrec z = λl.(let final = (1st l)
                         in (if0 (= O (1st final))
                                 (let ⟨I, k⟩ = (2nd final)
                                   in (if0 (= m (C^τ k))
                                           k
                                           (let* n_τ = (NextCset^τ (C^τ k) m)
                                                   l = (f*_d ⟨⟨I, n⟩, l⟩)
                                              in (z l))))
                                 (let* ⟨⟨I, m'⟩, n⟩ = (2nd final)
                                        I' = (sort ⟨(f*_e n), I⟩)
                                        l = (f*_d ⟨⟨I', m'⟩, l⟩)
                                   in (z l))))
        in (z ⌜0⌝)
```

FIGURE 5: The Function *decode*

To prove that $\mathbf{decode}^{\sigma\to\tau}$ satisfies the induction hypothesis, we observe that by the extensionality of $\mathcal{T}[\![\sigma \to \tau]\!]$

$$\mathcal{M}[\![\mathbf{decode}^{\sigma\to\tau}]\!](f_d^*) = d$$

iff for all finite elements $e \in \mathcal{T}[\![\sigma]\!]$,

$$(\mathcal{M}[\![\mathbf{decode}^{\sigma\to\tau}]\!](f_d^*))(e) = d(e).$$

By the definition of $\mathbf{decode}^{\sigma\to\tau}$, the preceding line reduces to showing

$$\mathcal{M}[\![(\mathbf{decode}^{\tau}(Apply\ F_d\ (\mathbf{encode}^{\sigma}\ E)))]\!] = d(e)$$

where the terms F_d and E have the denotations f_d^* and e respectively. The term E exists by the induction hypothesis. If we assume $\mathcal{M}[\![Apply]\!](f_d^*)(f_e^*) = f_{d(e)}^*$ for all d and e, then the proof obligation reduces to

$$\mathcal{M}[\![\mathbf{decode}^{\tau}]\!](f_{d(e)}^*) = d(e),$$

which holds by the induction hypothesis. Thus, we have reduced the claim about the correctness of **decode** function to a specific lemma about the function *Apply*.

Lemma 5.9 *Let f_d^*, f_e^* be the OS-characteristic functions for $d \in \mathcal{T}[\![\sigma \to \tau]\!]$ and $e \in \mathcal{T}[\![s]\!]$, respectively. Then,*

$$\mathcal{M}[\![Apply]\!](f_d^*)(f_e^*) = f_{d(e)}^*.$$

Proof Sketch. Let h denote $\mathcal{M}[\![Apply]\!](f_d^*)(f_e^*)$. The lemma holds if h is the *OS*-characteristic function for $d(e)$, *i.e.*

$$\forall\, m, i:\ h(m) = i \Leftrightarrow p_i \in d(e) \text{ and } \mathbf{c}^{\tau}(i) = m\,.$$

We show that $h(m)$ gives the correct result by analyzing the three possible cases:

$f^*_{d(e)}(m) = j$. We must show that $h(m) = j$. First, we observe that for any $d \in \mathcal{T}[\![\sigma \to \tau]\!]$, and $e \in \mathcal{T}[\![\sigma]\!]$, $p_j \in d(e)$ iff there exists a least prime $q_* \in d$ such that $q_*(e) = p_j$. Otherwise, d would not have a unique sequentiality index at each point during its exploration of e in the direction $\mathbf{c}^\tau(j)$.

By simple rewriting rules $h(m) = z(0)$ and q_0 approximates q_*. By the following claim, $z(0) = j$, proving the required result for this case.

Claim: $z(l) = j$ if q_l approximates q_*.

We prove the claim by induction on the distance (see Definition 3.4) from q_l to q_*.

Base Case: If the distance is 0 then q_l must be equal to q_*. Then, by simple rewriting rules, the function z generates j.

Inductive Case: The next approximation to q_* is constructed from current approximation l as follows:

- If l is the index of an output prime $\langle\langle \mathsf{O}, I, k\rangle, l'\rangle$, the function d has two options:
  - it can output a prime $p_{k'}$ in the C-set m' immediately above p_k in the direction C^τ_m without further examining the input e; or
  - it can examine the input e above a_I to help determine which prime to output in the C-set m'.

  In either case, the next element above l in d in the direction of q_* must be in the C-set $\langle\langle I, m'\rangle, l\rangle$. Therefore the index of the next approximation to q_* is $f^*_d(\langle\langle I, m'\rangle, l\rangle)$.
- If l is a schedule prime $\langle\langle \mathsf{S}, \langle I, m'\rangle, n\rangle, l'\rangle$, then if $\mathsf{error}_i^{C_n} \in e$ we must have $\mathsf{error}_i^{m'} \in d(e)$. In other words, the function d has to explore the C-set n in the input e where C_n covers a_I. Since q_* exists, this exploration yields a better approximation $a_{I'} = a_I \sqcup r_i$ to the input e where $r_i \in e$ and $\mathbf{c}^\sigma(i) = n$. Therefore, the next prime immediately above l in the direction of q_* (if it exists) is a prime in the C-set $\langle\langle I', m'\rangle, l\rangle$.

Therefore the next approximation decreases the distance from q_* by 1. By the induction hypothesis, z applied to this better approximation gives j as the result.

$f^*_{d(e)}(m) = \mathsf{error}_i$. Let m' be the C-set approximating m and $\mathsf{error}_i^{C_{m'}} \in d(e)$. Then q_* be the maximum prime in d such that $q_*(e) \prec C_{m'}$.

By rewriting the code, $h(m) = z(0)$. Since q_0 approximates q_*, the following claim gives $h(m) = \mathsf{error}_i$.

Claim: If q_l approximates q_* then $z(l) = \mathsf{error}_i$.

The proof of the claim proceeds by induction on the distance from q_l to q_*.

Base Case: If $q_l = q_*$, then the function h has two choices depending on q_l. If it is an output prime, it will generate an error without looking for further input. If it is a schedule prime, it will generate an error while looking at an error in the input e. In either case the corresponding error value error_i is generated.

Inductive Case: As in the preceding case, each time z reduces the distance between q_* and q_l by 1. Therefore, by the induction hypothesis, $z(l) = \mathsf{error}_i$.

$f^*_{d(e)}(m) = \bot$. There are two possibilities:

- $\exists p_{j'} \in d(e) \cap C^\tau_{m'}$ such that $m' \leq' m$ and $p_{j'}$ is not in the direction C^τ_m. In other words, there is a conflicting prime along the direction C^τ_m.

- $\exists p_{j'} \in d(e)$ such that $p_{j'} \notin C^{\tau}_{m}$ and it is the maximum prime in the direction C^{τ}_{m}.

In either case, divergence of the function $h(m)$ can be proved by an analysis of the behavior of z as in the preceding cases.

Thus, in each of the above cases, $h(m)$ returns the same result as $f^*_{d(e)}$. That is, h is the *OS*-characteristic function for $d(e)$. Hence, we proved the claim $\mathcal{M}[\![Apply]\!](f^*_d)(f^*_e) = f^*_{d(e)}$. ∎5.10

The remaining obligation in the proof of Theorem 5.8 is to show that the family of functions **encode**$^{\sigma\rightarrow\tau}$ satisfy the condition specified in the induction hypothesis. The definition of the functions **encode**$^{\sigma\rightarrow\tau}$ is given in Figure 6.

For the moment, let us assume that the auxiliary function *chk* satisfies its specification: $chk(g, m) = f^*_g(m)$ if $\exists p_k \in g : p_k \prec C^{\sigma\rightarrow\tau}_m$. We can prove that **encode**$^{\sigma\rightarrow\tau}$ returns f^*_g for a data object $g \in \mathcal{T}[\![\sigma \rightarrow \tau]\!]$ as follows.

First, we observe that *InitCset* is an auxiliary function that returns the index of first C-set above 0 that approximates the given input. If the input is 0 it returns 0. Therefore the result of *InitCset*(m) always approximates m and there is no non-zero C-set that approximates the *InitCset*(m).

Set $h = \mathcal{M}[\![\mathbf{encode}]\!](g)$. The function **encode** satisfies the induction hypothesis if $h = f^*_g$. We prove this equality by analyzing the possible results of $f^*_d(m)$:

$f^*_g(m) \in \mathbf{N}$: Therefore, we must prove that $h(m) = f^*_g(m)$. By simple rewriting rules, $h(m) = z(InitCset(m))$. If we prove the following claim, we have the result that $h(m) = f^*_g(m)$ since $InitCset(m) \leq' m$.

Claim: If $m' \leq' m$, then $z(m') = f^*_g(m)$.

The proof of the claim is by induction on the distance between the C-sets (see Definition 3.4) $C_{m'}$ and C_m.

Base Case: If the distance is 0 then $m' = m$. Since $\exists p_k \in g : p_k \prec C_{m'}$, the function $chk(g, m)$ returns $f^*_g(m)$ by Lemma 5.10. Therefore, $z(m') = f^*_g(m)$.

Inductive Case: By the assumption that $f^*_g(m) \in \mathbf{N}$, the function $chk(g, m')$ returns a prime in the direction C_m. Therefore, z is recursively invoked with $NextCset(m', m)$, the index of the C-set one step closer to m. By induction hypothesis and simple rewriting, $z(m') = z(NextCset(m', m)) = f^*_g(m)$.

$f^*_g(m) = \mathbf{error}_i$: We must prove that $h(m)$ also generates the error element $\mathbf{error}_i$, for $i = 1, 2$. As in the preceding case, $h(m) = z(InitCset(m))$.

Since $f^*_g(m) = \mathbf{error}_i$ there must be a least $n \leq' m$ where $f^*_g(n) = \mathbf{error}_i$. Since $InitCset(m) \leq' n$, we can prove the required result for this case by proving the following claim.

Claim: If $m' \leq' n$, then $z(m') = \mathbf{error}_i$.

Proof of the claim proceeds by induction on the distance between m' and n. It is similar to the preceding case.

$f^*_g(m) = \perp$: We must prove that $h(m) = \perp$. Then only of the statements is true:

- There is a p_k in g such that and p_k is not in the direction C_m and $p_k \in C_n$ where $n \leq' m$.
- There is a p_k in g such that p_k is the maximum prime in the direction C_m. Let C_n be the C-set covering p_k. It is easy to see $n \leq' m$.

```
encode^{σ→τ}   = λg.λm.
                    letrec z=λm'.(if0 (= m' m) (chk^{σ→τ} g m)
                                      (if0 (<?^τ (chk^{σ→τ} g m') m)
                                           (z (NextCset^{σ→τ} m' m))
                                           Ω))
                      in (z (InitCset m))

chk^{σ→τ}      = λg,m. (let ⟨⟨I,n⟩,j⟩ = m
                         in call/cdc(λt.(let* f*_{a'} = (Extend^σ I n j t)
                                              a'      = (decode^σ f*_{a'})
                                              l       = ((encode^τ (g a')) n)
                                         in ⟨⟨O,I,l⟩,j⟩)))

Extend^σ       = λI,n,j,t.λm'.(if0 (InElt^σ I m')
                                   ((GenFun^σ I) m')
                                   (t ⟨⟨S,⟨i,n⟩,(Direction^σ I m')⟩ j⟩)))
```

Comment (*GenFun I*) generates $f^*_{a_I}$.

```
GenFun^σ       = λI.λm. (letrec z=λI.(if0 (= (C^σ (1st I)) m)
                                          (1st I)
                                          (z (2nd I)))
                          in (z I))
```

Comment (*Direction I m*) = *n* where a_I is covered by C_n and $n \leq' m$.

```
Direction^σ    = λI,m.(if0 I
                           (InitCset m)
                           (if0 (<?^σ (1st I) m)
                                (NextCset^σ (C^σ (1st I)) m)
                                (Direction^σ (2nd I) m)))
```

Comment (*InElt I m*) = ⌜0⌝ iff $p_k \in a_I$ and $c(k) = m$; otherwise ⌜1⌝.

```
InElt^σ        = λI,m.(if0 m ⌜0⌝
                          (if0 I ⌜1⌝
                               (if0 (= (C^σ (1st I)) m)
                                    ⌜0⌝
                                    (InElt^σ (2nd I) m))))
```

Comment (<? *k m*) = ⌜0⌝ iff $p_k < C_m$; otherwise ⌜1⌝.

```
<?^τ           = λk,m.(if0 m ⌜1⌝
                          (if0 (= k (2nd m))
                               ⌜0⌝
                               (<?^τ k (C^τ (2nd m)))))
```

FIGURE 6: The Function *encode*

In either case, the claim that $m' \leq' n$ implies $z(m') = \perp$ can be proved by induction on the distance from m' and n. Therefore $h(m) = z(InitCset(m)) = \bot$.

Therefore, $f_g^*(m) = h(m)$ for all valid values of m, implying that **encode** satisfies its specification. Hence, we have reduced the proof of Theorem 5.8 to the proof of the following lemma.

Lemma 5.10 *Let $g \in \mathcal{T}[\![\sigma \to \tau]\!]$ and m be the C-set code in the domain $\mathcal{T}[\![\sigma \to \tau]\!]$. If there is a $p_k \in g$ such that p_k is covered by $C_m^{\sigma\to\tau}$, then $chk(g,m) = f_g^*(m)$.*

Proof Sketch. Let g and m be the inputs to the function chk and let $m = \langle I, n, j\rangle$. Then $p_j \in \mathcal{T}[\![\sigma \to \tau]\!]$ approximates g by assumption. In addition, by the definition of our coding scheme, C_n covers $p_j(a_I)$.

We first observe that chk, with the help of *Extend*, generates a *OS*-characteristic function $f_{a'}^*$. This function agrees with $f_{a_I}^*$ on the queries m' such that $\mathbf{c}^\sigma(j) = m$ and $p_j \in a_I$; but, if the function $f_{a'}^*$ is explored beyond a_I, it "throws" an index back to chk, which returns this index as the final result.

The specifications for the auxiliary functions *GenFun*, *Direction*, *InElt* and <? is given in the comments. It is straightforward to verify that the functions follow the specifications by the induction on encodings of the primes and C-sets.

Now we analyze the four possible cases of $f_g^*(m)$:

$f_g^*(m) = \bot$: In this case, we must show that $chk(g,m) = \bot$. Since $m = \langle I, n, j\rangle$, we know that $f_g^*(m)$ is $\bot$ iff $g(a_I) \cap C_n^\tau$ is empty. In other words, there is no prime element in the C-set C_n^τ at the output of $g(a_I)$. Therefore, by the induction hypothesis of **encode**, $\mathbf{encode}^\tau(g(a_I))(n)$ should diverge. Since $a_I = a'$ for all the queries within a_I, the function chk diverges on the given inputs g and m.

$f_g^*(m) = \mathbf{error}_i$: Just as in the preceding case, $g(a_I)$ should have an error prime, $\mathbf{error}_i^{C_n}$. By the induction hypothesis of **encode**, $\mathbf{encode}^\tau(g(a_I))(n)$ returns $\mathbf{error}_i$; therefore the result of the function chk is $\mathbf{error}_i$.

$f_g^*(m) = \langle\langle \mathsf{O}, I, l\rangle, j\rangle$: In that case, $g(a_I)$ should have the prime element p_l at the C-set C_n^τ. By the induction hypothesis of **encode**, $\mathbf{encode}^\tau(g(a_I))(n) = l$. Therefore, the function chk returns the index $\langle\langle \mathsf{O}, I, l\rangle, j\rangle$. Notice that by the assumption that $p_k \prec C_m^{\sigma\to\tau}$ is in g, all of the input a_I is necessary for generating the output at the C-set C_n^τ, which means that the index of the output prime is correct.

$f_g^*(m) = \langle\langle \mathsf{S}, \langle I, n\rangle, n'\rangle, j\rangle$: Therefore, $\mathbf{error}_i^{C_n} \in g(a \sqcup \mathbf{error}_i^{C_{n'}})$. That means, the function g checks the input at the C-set $C_{n'}^\sigma$ to generate the output at the C-set C_n^τ. When the function $f_{a'}^*$ is queried for the input at the C-set $C_{n'}^\sigma$ it throws the index $\langle\langle \mathsf{S}, \langle I, n\rangle, n'\rangle, j\rangle$, which is returned by the function chk.

Therefore, in all possible cases, the function $chk(g,m)$ returns $f_g^*(m)$ assuming that the prime covered by m is in g. ∎5.11

This also finishes the sketch of the theorem's proof. ∎

Acknowledgments. We are grateful to Albert Meyer for raising the completeness question of the $\lambda\beta\eta$ calculus addressed in Section 4 and to John Gateley and Jon Riecke for discussions about the material in that section. Discussions with Pierre-Louis Curien improved our understanding of the sequential model and brought the Kahn-Plotkin-Winskel material to our attention.

References

1. BARENDREGT, H.P. *The Lambda Calculus: Its Syntax and Semantics.* Revised Edition. Studies in Logic and the Foundations of Mathematics 103. North-Holland, Amsterdam, 1984.
2. BERRY, G. Séquentialité de l'evaluation formelle des λ-expressions. In *Proc. 3rd International Colloquium on Programming,* 1978.
3. BERRY, G. *Modèles complètement adéquats et stables des lambda-calculus typé.* Ph.D. dissertation, Université Paris VII, 1979.
4. BERRY, G. AND P-L. CURIEN. Sequential algorithms on concrete data structures. *Theor. Comput. Sci.* **20**, 1982, 265–321.
5. BERRY, G. AND P-L. CURIEN. Theory and practice of sequential algorithms: the kernel of the applicative language cds. In *Algebraic Methods in Semantics,* edited by J. Reynolds and M.Nivat. Cambridge University Press. London, 1985, 35–88.
6. BERRY, G., P-L. CURIEN, AND P.-P. LÉVY. Full-abstraction of sequential languages: the state of the art. In *Algebraic Methods in Semantics,* edited by J. Reynolds and M.Nivat. Cambridge University Press. London, 1985, 89–131.
7. CARTWRIGHT, R. Lambda: The ultimate combinator. *Artificial Intelligence and Mathematical Theory of Computation: Papers in Honor of John McCarthy.* Edited by Vladimir Lifschitz (ed.), Academic Press, 1991, 27–46.
8. CARTWRIGHT, R. AND A. DEMERS. The topology of program termination. In *Proc. Symposium on Logic in Computer Science,* 1988, 296–308.
9. CARTWRIGHT, R.S. AND M. FELLEISEN. Observable sequentiality and full abstraction. Technical Report 91-167. Rice University Department of Computer Science, 1991. Preliminary version: In *Proc. 19th ACM Symposium on Principles of Programming Languages,* 1992, 328–342.
10. CARTWRIGHT, R.S., CURIEN, P.-L., AND M. FELLEISEN. Fully abstract models of observably sequential languages. Forthcoming, December 1992.
11. CURIEN, P-L. *Categorical Combinators, Sequential Algorithms, and Functional Programming.* Research Notes in Theoretical Computer Science. Pitman, London. 1986. Birkhäuser, Revised Edition, to appear.
12. CURIEN, P.-L.. Observable algorithms on concrete data structures. In *Proc 7th Symposium on Logic in Computer Science,* 1992, to appear.
13. FELLEISEN, M. On the expressive power of programming languages. *Science of Computer Programming* **17**, 1991, 35–75. Preliminary version in: *Proc. 3rd European Symposium on Programming.* Neil Jones, Ed. Lecture Notes in Computer Science, 432. Springer Verlag, Berlin, 1990, 134–151.
14. FELLEISEN, M. AND R. HIEB. The revised report on the syntactic theories of sequential control and state. Technical Report 100, Rice University, June 1989. *Theor. Comput. Sci.* **102**, 1992.
15. FELLEISEN, M., D.P. FRIEDMAN, E. KOHLBECKER, AND B. DUBA. A syntactic theory of sequential control. *Theor. Comput. Sci.* **52**(3), 1987, 205–237. Preliminary version in: *Proc. Symposium on Logic in Computer Science,* 1986, 131–141.
16. FRIEDMAN, H. Equality between functionals. In *Logic Colloquium'73,* Rohit Parikh (Ed.), Lecture Notes in Mathematics 453, Springer Verlag, Berlin, 1973, 22–37.

17. KAHN, G. AND G. PLOTKIN. Structures des donnés concrètes (Domaines Concrètes). IRIA Report 336. 1978.

18. MEYER, A.R. What is a model of the λ-calculus? *Inf. and Control* **52**, 1982, 87–122.

19. MILNER, R. Fully abstract models of typed λ-calculi. *Theor. Comput. Sci.* **4**, 1977, 1–22.

20. MULMULEY, K. *Full Abstraction and Semantic Equivalences.* Ph.D. dissertation, Carnegie Mellon University, 1985. MIT Press, Cambridge, Massachusetts, 1986.

21. PLOTKIN, G. Notes on completeness of the full continuous type hierarchy. Unpublished manuscript, MIT, December 1982.

22. PLOTKIN, G.D. LCF considered as a programming language. *Theor. Comput. Sci.* **5**, 1977, 223–255.

23. RIECKE, J. Statman's 1-section theorem. Tech. Rpt. MS-CIS-92-03. Uinversity of Pennsylvania. 1992.

24. RIECKE, J. AND R. SUBRAHMANYAM. Algebraic reasoning and completeness in typed languages. In *Proc. 20th ACM Symposium on Principles of Programming Languages*, 1992, to appear.

25. SAZONOV, V.Y. Expressibility of functions in D.Scott's LCF language. *Algebra i Logika* **15**(3), 1976, 308–330.

26. SCOTT, D. S. Domains for denotational semantics. In *Proc. International Conference on on Automata, Languages, and Programming*, Lecture Notes in Mathematics 140, Springer-Verlag, Berlin, 1982, ??–??.

27. SCOTT, D.S. Data types as lattices. *SIAM J. Comput.* **5**(3), 1976, 522–587.

28. SCOTT, D.S. *Lectures on a Mathematical Theory of Computation.* Techn. Monograph PRG-19, Oxford University Computing Laboratory, Programming Research Group, 1981.

29. SITARAM, D. AND M. FELLEISEN. Reasoning with continuations II: Full abstraction for models of control. In *Proc. 1990 ACM Conference on Lisp and Functional Programming*, 1990, 161–175.

30. STATMAN, R. Equality between functionals revisited. In L.A. Harrinton, et al (Eds), *Harvey Friedman's Research on the Foundations of Mathematics.* Studies in Logic. North-Holland, 1985, 331–338.

31. STATMAN, R. Completeness, invariance, and lambda-definability. *Journal of Symbolic Logic* **47**, 1982, 17–26.

32. VUILLEMIN, J. Proof techniques for recursive programs. IRIA Report. 1973.

33. WINSKEL, G. *Events in Computations.* Ph.D. dissertation, University of Edinburgh, 1980.

INFINITE BEHAVIOUR AND FAIRNESS IN CONCURRENT CONSTRAINT PROGRAMMING

Marta Kwiatkowska*

Department of Mathematics and Computer Science†
University of Leicester
Leicester LE1 7RH
and
Department of Computing‡
Imperial College
180 Queens Gate
London SW7 2BZ

Abstract

In concurrent constraint programming, *divergence* (*i.e.* an infinite computation) and *failure* are often identified. This is undesirable when modelling systems in which infinite behaviour arises naturally. This paper sets out a framework for an axiomatic and denotational view of concurrent constraint programming, and considers the relationship of both views as an instance of Stone duality. We propose a construction of a constraint system which allows both finite and infinite constraints. Subsequently, we provide semantic, topological definitions of safety, liveness and fairness properties in a given constraint system. The process language considered is parametrized by the constraint system. It allows the actions *ask* and *tell*, the prefix operator $\rightarrow$, the (angelic) non-deterministic choice operator $\oplus$, the procedure call $p(X)$, and the concurrency operator $\|$.

Keywords: concurrent constraint programming, liveness, fairness, semantic properties.

---

*This paper was partly written when the author was Visiting Professor at CWI, Amsterdam, sponsored by the Netherlands Organisation for Scientific Research (NWO).

†Permanent address.

‡Institution visited for the duration of the Nuffield Science Research Fellowship.

Contents

1 INTRODUCTION

Concurrent constraint programming (18, 19, 4, 8) is an approach rooted in constraint logic programming and concurrent logic programming. The basic paradigm is that a number of agents, which are executed concurrently, communicate via a common store. The store is not viewed as a mapping of variables to their contents, but as a "constraint", that is, partial information about what the variables may contain. Agents communicate through the (indivisible) *ask* and *tell* actions. The action *ask(c)*, where c is a constraint, succeeds if the store contains enough information to entail c; otherwise, it will be blocked until such time. The action *tell(c)* results in a new store, which is a conjunction of the old store and the constraint c. Depending on the choice of remaining operators (*e.g.* guards, concurrency, non-determinism), we can obtain concurrent asynchronous languages of varying power.

This paper is concerned with the foundations of a semantic framework for such languages, which would allow to formalise the notion:

$$P \models \phi \tag{1}$$

i.e. "P satisfies ϕ", where P is a syntactic description of a program (*i.e.* a (well-formed) term in a concurrent constraint programming language), and ϕ is a syntactic description of a formula (*i.e.* a specification written in some logic). Note that the two syntaxes are not necessarily the same, and there is no reason why they should be; while P will be defined in a transition-system based language and given meaning as a point in some denotational domain, ϕ will be defined in some axiomatic, deductive system.

We shall employ the concept of *Stone duality*, the significance of which to computer science was first recognised by Abramsky (2). Stone duality refers to a categorical correspondence (in fact, it is a duality of categories) between logical, axiomatic systems and their topological models. The first instance of this duality was pointed out by Stone, and it concerned Boolean algebras. Stone sought a representation of every Boolean algebra as a field of sets, in which *the operations of meet, join and complement are represented by set-theoretic intersection, union and complement.* Apart from Boolean algebras, a number of logical systems have been considered to date; for more information see (9). The duality ensures that the program logic and the denotational semantics are in perfect synchrony (not only soundness and completeness in the usual sense, but also that each determines the other up to isomorphism). We are thus provided with two different perspectives: the "localic" (axiomatic) and "spatial" (model-theoretic). In the spatial side of the duality, points (programs) are viewed as primary objects, and properties are constructed from open sets of points; this is the usual denotational view, where $P \in \phi$ (P is a point, ϕ an open set) is used to model $P \models \phi$. The "localic" side views properties as primary, and constructs points (programs) as theories (prime filters or, dually, ideals) of properties; this is a logical view, where $\phi \in P$ (ϕ is a property, P a filter) is used to model $P \models \phi$.

The ultimate aim of the research initiated in this paper is to provide a framework for expressing and reasoning about a large class of program properties including *infinitary* properties, that is, properties that cannot be detected in finite time. This class includes *e.g. liveness* and *fairness* properties (15, 13, 5, 11), such as "guaranteed response", "weak fairness" and "strong fairness". One characteristic feature of these properties is that one has to consider infinite computations, as well as the finite ones. Unfortunately, in concurrent constraint programming infinite computations are often treated as *divergence*, and are identified with *failure*. This is unsatisfactory if the so called *reactive systems*, *e.g.* operating systems, dataflow networks, are to be modelled correctly. In such systems, the possibility of infinite behaviour arises naturally, and is often desirable. Thus, the identification of infinite computations with failure is no longer acceptable.

The outline of the paper is as follows. We begin with a deductive, finitely axiomatizable system E of constraints, the purpose of which is to express constraints syntactically and reason about them. We then construct a constraint system $\mathcal{C}(E)$ as a model of E, and consider the issue of Stone duality of E and $\mathcal{C}(E)$. Through the localic side of the Stone duality, E can be shown isomorphic to a sub-algebra of a topology on $\mathcal{C}(E)$. This allows us to interpret each syntactic constraint ϕ as *a subset* $[\![\phi]\!]$ of $\mathcal{C}(E)$.

At the other end of spectrum, we consider a process language parametrized by the constraint system $\mathcal{C}$. The language allows: actions *tell*(c) for $c \in \mathcal{K}(C)$, guards *ask*$(c) \rightarrow A$, concurrency operator $\|$, angelic non-determinism operator $\oplus$, hiding operator $\exists X.A$ and procedure call $p(X)$. Following the approach of (19, 8), which defines denotations of processes as certain closure operators on $\mathcal{C}$, we can identify a denotation $[\![P]\!]$ of a term P in this language as *a subset* of $\mathcal{C}$. Finally, we take advantage of the representations of formulae and processes as subsets of $\mathcal{C}$ and the notion $P \models \phi$ by $[\![P]\!] \subseteq [\![\phi]\!]$.

Following the work of Smyth (21) and Abramsky (2), we identify *finite observations* in $\mathcal{C}$ with (a subfamily of) the *open sets*, and construct more general *semantic* properties, *e.g.* safety, liveness and fairness, from these. We also exemplify these notions using some well-known properties. Although we are not yet capable of expressing the above classes of properties *syntactically* as formulae of E as finite axiomatizability does not suffice for this purpose, we briefly suggest possible extensions to the theory.

2 SAFETY, LIVENESS AND FAIRNESS

The classification of program properties into safety and liveness is due to Lamport (14). He justified the distinction on the grounds of employing two different methods when verifying that a given program P satisfies a property ϕ. In order to verify properties such as mutual exclusion (no two processes should be in their critical section at the same time) it is sufficient to use induction. On the other hand, properties such as termination require the well-founded set method. Informally, a *safety* property is one which states that

Nothing bad happens.

whereas a liveness property states that

Something good happens.

Thus, in mutual exclusion the "bad" thing is (at least) two processes being in their critical sections at the same time, while in termination the "good" thing is that the program reaches its final state. While safety properties must *avoid* the bad things, liveness properties must *guarantee* the good things. A more detailed classification based on the syntactic representation in temporal logic appeared in (15).

The class of liveness properties includes two quite different types of properties: those which can be detected at finite time (termination being such), and those which cannot. An example of the latter class is "guaranteed response" (every request will eventually be granted), since no finite examination of a computation can determine that every occurrence of a request action is followed by a granting action.

Fairness properties constitute a large class of infinitary properties, typically viewed as a a subclass of liveness properties. There are many definitions of fairness properties, see *e.g.* (5, 10, 12). What they all have in common is that they restrict the set of potential computations of a system by disallowing those infinite computations which indefinitely delay some system component. Depending on the choice of a component (*e.g.* a process, non-deterministic guard or state), one can obtain fairness properties of different *granularity*, which can be further varied in terms of *strength* (*e.g.* weak, strong fairness). In state-transition system models, fairness properties usually take the form of an implication, see *e.g.* a typical formulation of "strong process fairness":

$\forall P$, *P process. P enabled infinitely often* $\Rightarrow$ *P taken infinitely often.*

In denotational semantics, where the notion of "being enabled in a state" is not readily definable, other formulations of fairness have to be used. A typical notion applicable in such contexts is *fairmerge* (16), which for strings can be defined as an interleaving merge of string languages in such a way that the whole of each string is taken. For example,

$$fm(0^\omega, 1^\omega) = (0^+1^+)^\omega + (1^+0^+)^\omega \tag{2}$$

which excludes strings such as 0^ω, 1^n0^ω, and is clearly an infinitary property in the sense explained above.

Fairness is known to affect liveness properties (even the finitary ones), in the sense that the correctness of the program with respect to some property cannot be proved *unless* the infinite computations of the program are restricted to just the fair ones. Thus, the issue of fairness cannot be easily ignored.

On the other hand, fairness is regarded as a confused and difficult subject: it requires the addition of infinite computations, causes discontinuity of semantic functions (16), and is sensitive to the particular features of the semantic model such as confusion (10).

3 MATHEMATICAL PRELIMINARIES

We shall assume some knowledge of lattice theory and topology. For the benefit of those readers who are not familiar with these subjects, we give a brief summary of basic definitions and facts. For more information consult (6, 7, 3, 9).

3.1 Lattices

A *join-semilattice* is a poset $(A, \leq)$ in which every pair of elements $a, b \in A$ has a join $a \vee b$, and which has the least element 0. Dually, we can define a *meet-semilattice* as a poset $(A, \leq)$ in which every pair of elements $a, b \in A$ has a meet $a \wedge b$, and which has the greatest element 1.

A *semilattice homomorphism* is a map f which preserves the distinguished element 0 (*i.e.* $f(0) = 0$) and the operation $\vee$ (*i.e.* $f(a \vee b) = f(a) \vee f(b)$). Every semilattice homomorphism is necessarily monotone (*i.e.* it satisfies $a \leq b \Rightarrow f(a) \leq f(b)$), but a monotone map between semilattices need not be a homomorphism.

A *lattice* is a poset $(A, \leq)$ in which every finite subset has a join and a meet. Equivalently, a lattice is a structure $(A, \vee, \wedge, 0, 1)$ such that: A is a set, 0 and 1 are the distinguished elements, $\vee$ (resp. $\wedge$) is associative, commutative and idempotent and has 0 (resp. 1) as unit element, and the absorptive laws ($a \vee (a \wedge b) = a$, $a \wedge (a \vee b) = a$) are satisfied. A lattice A is *distributive* iff the distributive law $a \wedge (b \vee c) = (a \wedge b) \vee (a \wedge c)$ is satisfied. The dual of this law can be deduced by applying the absorptive laws. A is *complete* iff every subset has a join and a meet.

In any lattice, an element x satisfying $x \wedge a = 0$ and $x \vee a = 1$ is called a *complement* of a. It can be shown that in a distributive lattice complements are unique if they exist. A *Boolean algebra* is a distributive lattice A equipped with an additional operation $\neg : A \longrightarrow A$ such that $\neg a$ is a complement of a.

A lattice is said to be a *Heyting algebra* if, for each pair of elements (a, b), there exists an element $(a \rightarrow b)$ such that $c \leq (a \rightarrow b)$ iff $c \wedge a \leq b$[1]. It can be shown that a Heyting algebra is distributive. In fact, it satisfies the infinite distributive law:

$$a \wedge \bigvee S \quad = \quad \bigvee \{a \wedge s \mid s \in S\}$$

Furthermore, a complete lattice is a Heyting algebra iff it satisfies the infinite distributive law (9). Also, a Heyting algebra A is a Boolean algebra iff $\neg\neg a = a$ for all $a \in A$.

An element p of a complete Heyting algebra is *prime* if $S \subseteq A$, S finite, and $\wedge S \leq p$, then $s \leq p$ some $s \in S$. An element p is *coprime* iff it is prime with respect to the opposite ordering.

Example 3.1 *Let X be a set, then the set $F(X)$ of cofinite subsest of X is a meet-semilattice, and the powerset $\wp(X)$ is a complete lattice, with $\leq$ interpreted as inclusion, and the operations $\vee$ and $\wedge$ interpreted as union and intersection.*

3.2 Ideals and Filters

A subset S of a join-semilattice is *directed* iff it is non-empty, and every pair of elements of S has an upper bound in S. A subset I of a join-semilattice A is said to be an *ideal* if it is a lower set (*i.e.* $a \in I$ and $b \leq a$ imply $b \in I$) such that $0 \in I$, and $a \in I, b \in I$ imply $a \vee b \in I$. The set of all ideals of the join-semilattice A is denoted $\mathcal{I}(A)$.

For any $a \in A$, the subset $\downarrow a = \{b \in A \mid b \leq a\}$ is the smallest ideal of A containing a, and is often called the *principal ideal* generated by a.

The notion dual to that of an ideal is a filter. A subset F of a meet-semilattice A is said to be a *filter* if it is an upper set such that $1 \in F$, and $a \in F, b \in F$ imply $a \wedge b \in F$.

Let I be an ideal of a lattice A. I is said to be a *prime ideal* iff the complement of I in A is a filter, or, equivalently, $1 \notin I$ and $a \wedge b \in I$ implies either $a \in I$ or $b \in I$. This definition is also equivalent to I being the *kernel*, that is $f^{-1}(0)$, of a lattice homomorphism $f : A \rightarrow \mathbf{2}$, where $\mathbf{2}$ denotes the two-element lattice. The dual (and a complement) of a prime ideal is a *prime filter*. Likewise, a prime filter can be characterized as the dual kernel $f^{-1}(1)$ of a lattice homomorphism $f : A \rightarrow \mathbf{2}$.

Let A be a complete Heyting algebra. A subset F of A is said to be a *completely prime filter* iff $1 \in F$; $a \in F, b \in F$ imply $a \wedge b \in F$; F is an upper set; and $\bigvee S \in F$ iff $\exists a \in S. a \in F$. Every completely prime filter F can be identified with $f^{-1}(1)$ for $f : A \longrightarrow \mathbf{2}$ a frame homomorphism.

[1] In a Boolean algebra, the operation $\neg$ can be recovered from the binary operation $\rightarrow$ since $\neg a = (a \rightarrow 0)$. In a general Heyting algebra, this is the *definition* of $\neg$.

3.3 Algebraic Lattices and Closure Operators

Let A be a complete lattice. An element $a \in A$ is called *compact* (or *finite*) iff, for every directed set $S \subseteq A$ with $\bigvee S \geq a$, there exists $s \in S$ with $s \geq a$. The set of all compact elements of A is denoted $\mathcal{K}(A)$. A is *algebraic* iff every element in A is expressible as the join of compact elements of A.

The following results are now considered standard. The isomorphism is given by $b \mapsto \downarrow b$ (*i.e.* an element maps onto the principal ideal determined by it, and $I \mapsto \bigvee I$ (*i.e.* an ideal maps onto its join).

Lemma 3.2 (Johnstone (9)) *Let $(A, \leq)$ be a join-semilattice.*

1. *The ideal completion $(\mathcal{I}(A), \subseteq)$ is a complete algebraic lattice.*
2. *$(\mathcal{K}(\mathcal{I}(A)), \subseteq)$ is isomorphic to $(A, \leq)$.*

Lemma 3.3 (Vickers (22)) *The ideal completion $(\mathcal{I}(A), \subseteq)$ of a distributive lattice A is a complete Heyting algebra.*

Let $(A, \leq)$ be a partial order. A *closure operator* on A is a map $f : A \longrightarrow A$ which is: extensive (*i.e.* $\forall c.c \leq f(c)$), idempotent (*i.e.* $\forall c.f(f(c)) = f(c)$), and monotone (*i.e.* $\forall c, d.c \leq d \Rightarrow f(c) \leq f(d)$). A *kernel operator* on A is a map $f : A \longrightarrow A$ which is idempotent, monotone and satisfies $\forall c.f(c) \leq c$.

Example 3.4 *Let X be a topological space, then the function c mapping $Y \subseteq X$ to its closure is a closure operator, and the function k mapping $Y \subseteq X$ to its interior is a kernel operator. The image of c are the closed sets $\Gamma(X)$ and of k are the open sets $\Omega(X)$.*

3.4 Topological Spaces and Locales

A *topology* on the set X is a family of subsets $\Omega(X)$ (called *open sets*) which contains X and $\emptyset$, and is closed under finite intersections and arbitrary union. A *topological space* is a pair $(X, \Omega(X))$, where X is a set and $\Omega(X)$ is a topology on X.

A topological space is *Hausdorff* (or $\mathcal{T}_2$) iff for each pair of points $x \neq y$ there exist two open sets G, H such that

$$x \in G, y \in H, G \cap H = \emptyset. \qquad (3)$$

A topological space is called $\mathcal{T}_1$ iff for each pair of points $x \neq y$ there exists an open set G such that $x \in G$ and $y \notin G$. A topological space is called $\mathcal{T}_0$ iff for each pair of distinct points there exists an open set which contains one of the points and does not contain the other one. A topology is *compact* iff every open cover contains a finite subcover.

A set $Y \subseteq X$ is *closed* iff its complement $\overline{Y}$ is open. The family of all closed sets of the space X will be denoted $\Gamma(X)$. A set $Y \subseteq X$ is *clopen* iff it is both closed and open. A G_δ*-set* is a countable (*i.e.* finite or infinite) intersection of open sets. An F_σ*-set* is a countable (*i.e.* finite or infinite) union of closed sets. A set $Y \subseteq X$ is *dense* iff its complement contains no non-empty open set.

A family $\mathcal{B}$ of open sets is called a *base* iff each open set can be represented as the union of elements of a subfamily of $\mathcal{B}$. A family $\mathcal{S}$ of open sets is called a *subbase* iff the family of all finite intersections of elements of $\mathcal{S}$ is a base of the space.

Let $(A, \leq)$ be a complete partial order. The *Scott topology* on A consists of all sets U such that U is upward-closed (*i.e.* $x \in U \wedge x \leq y \Rightarrow y \in U$) and, for every directed set $M \subseteq A$, if $\bigsqcup M \in U$ then some element of M is in U. The Scott-open subsets of a cpo A will be denoted $\sigma\Omega(A)$, and the Scott-closed by $\sigma\Gamma(A)$. It is easy to see that a set is Scott-closed iff it is a lower set closed under directed joins. The closure of a singleton set $\{x\}$ in the Scott topology is $\downarrow x$.

In an algebraic lattice, the basis of the Scott topology is the family of sets $\uparrow x$ for $x \in \mathcal{K}(A)$, together with the empty set. A subset U of A is *Scott-compact* iff any cover of U with compact elements, *i.e.* a set $V \subseteq \mathcal{K}(A)$ such that $U \subseteq \uparrow V$, contains a finite subset $F \subseteq U$ which is also a cover. The Scott-compact subsets are closed under finite union and intersection. A subset U of A is *Scott compact-open*[2] (notation $\mathcal{K}\Omega(A)$) iff there exists a finite subset $F \subseteq \mathcal{K}(U)$ such that $U = \uparrow F$.

A topological space X is *coherent* if the compact-open subsets $\mathcal{K}\Omega(X)$ form a basis closed under finite intersections, *i.e.* for which $\mathcal{K}\Omega(X)$ is a distributive sublattice of $\Omega(X)$.

Given a topological space X, the lattice $\Omega(X)$ of open subsets is complete and satisfies the infinite distributive law:

$$a \wedge (\bigvee S) = \bigvee \{a \wedge s \mid s \in S\}$$

and hence it is a complete Heyting algebra. However, the natural morphisms on Heyting algebras are maps preserving finite meets and arbitrary joins, and not necessarily the continuous maps used as morphisms for topological spaces.

Given $f : X \longrightarrow Y$ continuous, then $f^{-1}(U)$ is open, and thus f^{-1} can be viewed as a map $\Omega(Y) \longrightarrow \Omega(X)$, which clearly preserves finite meets and infinite joins. We shall sometimes distinguish between the category of *frames*, which are complete Heyting algebras with morphisms preserving finite meets and infinite joins, and the category of *locales*, which is the opposite of the category of frames (the morphisms on locales are

[2]This coincides with the usual definition of compactness in terms of existence of a finite subcover for every open cover.

referred to as continuous maps). The functor from topological spaces to locales sends the space X to $\Omega(X)$ and a continuous map $f : X \to Y$ to the function $f^{-1} : \Omega(Y) \longrightarrow \Omega(X)$. We adopt the convention that if $f : A \to B$ is a continuous map of locales, we write $f^* : B \to A$ for the corresponding frame homomorphism.

Lemma 3.5 (Johnstone (9)) *A locale is coherent iff it is isomorphic to the locale of ideals of a distributive lattice.*

3.5 Stone Duality

The importance of *Stone duality* in computer science (9) was first recognised by Abramsky (1, 2); it provides, in the words of the author, "a mechanical way of finding the right logic for the denotational semantics". The original Stone theorem established a precise correspondence between Boolean algebras and topological spaces (so called *Stone spaces*[3]), where

> ***operations of conjunction, disjunction and complement correspond to the set-theoretic operations of intersection, union and complement.***

Stone observed that, for any topological space S, the lattice $ClopS$ of the clopen subsets is a Boolean algebra. He also constructed for an arbitrary Boolean algebra B a topological space $SpecB$. The construction is as follows: points are Boolean algebra homomorphisms $f : B \longrightarrow \mathbf{2}$ where $\mathbf{2} = \{0,1\}$ is a two-element lattice. Each such f can be identified with the inverse image $f^{-1}(1) \subseteq B$, which is a prime filter. This allows to define the topology by

$$U_a \quad = \quad \{x \in SpecB \mid a \in x\}$$

for $a \in B$. Furthermore, there are isomorphisms:

$$\begin{array}{ll} B \cong ClopSpecB & b \mapsto \{x \in SpecB \mid b \in x\} \\ S \cong SpecClopS & x \mapsto \{U \in ClopS \mid s \in U\} \end{array}$$

which can be expressed as a duality of categories:

$$\mathrm{Bool}^{\mathrm{op}} \quad \cong \quad \mathrm{Stone}.$$

A variety of Stone-duality-type theorems have been proposed to date (9), typically identifying a category of axiomatic systems with a dual of a category of certain topological spaces. The duality that is of interest to us in this paper is between distributive lattices and coherent spaces. Let A be a distributive lattice. The space $SpecA$ (*prime spectrum*) is the set of prime filters over A with the topology generated by:

$$U_a \quad = \quad \{x \in SpecA \mid a \in x\}$$

[3]Hausdorff and coherent spaces; see (9) for alternative characterizations.

for $a \in A$. On the other hand, the *points* $Pt\mathcal{I}(A)$ of $\mathcal{I}(A)$ are the completely prime filters over $\mathcal{I}(A)$ ($\mathcal{I}(A)$ is a complete Heyting algebra) with the topology given by the basis:

$$U_a = \{x \in Pt\,\mathcal{I}(A) \mid a \in x\}.$$

Theorem 3.6 (Johnstone (9))

1. *If A is a distributive lattice then $Spec A \cong Pt\mathcal{I}(A)$*

2. *The duality theorem for distributive lattices is:*

$$\mathrm{DLat}^{\mathrm{op}} \cong \mathrm{CohLoc} \cong \mathrm{CohSp}$$

where CohSp *is the category of coherent $\mathcal{T}_0$-spaces with continuous maps which preserve compact-open subsets under inverse image, and* CohLoc *is the image of* DLat *through the functor $\mathcal{I}$ (ideal completion).*

As observed in (2), the significance of this theorem is that finitary syntax (specifically finite disjunctions) suffices. This is because the duality allows to recover the original lattice from its prime spectrum by taking the set $\mathcal{K}\Omega(X)$ of the compact-open subsets; the latter can be identified with finite disjunctions of compact elements. More precisely, there are isomorphisms (A a distributive lattice, X coherent topological space):

$$A \cong \mathcal{K}\Omega(Spec A) \quad a \mapsto \{x \in Spec A \mid a \in x\}$$
$$X \cong Spec\mathcal{K}\Omega(X) \quad x \mapsto \{U \in \mathcal{K}\Omega(X) \mid x \in U\}$$

Theorem 3.7 (Abramsky (2)) *Let A be a countable distributive lattice. Say that $a \in A$ is* coprime *if $a \sqsubseteq \sqcup_{i=1}^{n} b_i$ implies $a \sqsubseteq b_i$ some $1 \leq i \leq n$. Then $Spec A$ is a coherent algebraic domain in its Scott topology iff 1 is coprime, and every element $a \in A$ is expressible as a finite join $\sqcup_{i=1}^{n} b_i$ for b_i coprime.*

The isomorphism should be understood as isomorphism of ordered spaces, where the order is the *specialization* order defined for the space X by:

$$x \leq y \iff \forall O \in \Omega(X). x \in O \Rightarrow y \in O$$

(this is equivalent to stating that $x \leq y$ iff x is contained in the closure of y). The significance of the theorem is due to the fact that the specialization order on the Scott topology (of an algebraic cpo) coincides with the original order, and hence Scott domains can be viewed either as topological spaces or partial orders.

Stone-duality-type theorems allow two different perspectives: the *localic* side (a formal system with axioms and rules), and the *spatial* side (a model), each being determined by the other up to isomorphism. In computer science, where models correspond to denotational semantics and axiomatic systems define program logics, this "provides the right framework for understanding the relationship between denotational semantics and program logics" (2).

4 CONSTRAINT SYSTEMS

4.1 Elementary Constraint Systems

We introduce a notion of a pre-constraint system, which is an axiomatic system involving a set A of propositions and an entailment preorder $\vdash$. We assume A is a countable set of terms built from *atomic* propositions ϕ and constants tt and ff by means of binary operations such as conjunction $\wedge$ and disjunction $\vee$.

Definition 4.1 *An* elementary pre-constraint system *is a tuple* $E = \langle A, \vdash, tt, ff, \wedge, \vee \rangle$ *such that:*

1. *A is a countable set of tokens (propositions) over syntax:*

$$A \ ::== \ tt \mid ff \mid \phi \mid \phi \wedge \phi \mid \phi \vee \phi$$

2. $\vdash \subseteq A \times A$ *is an entailment relation (preorder);*

3. $\wedge : A \times A \to A$ *and* $\vee : A \times A \to A$ *are binary conjunction and disjunction operations;*

4. ff *is coprime;*

5. *if* ϕ *is coprime and* $\bigwedge_{i \in I} \psi_i \vdash \phi$ *(I finite index set) then* $\psi_i \vdash \phi$ *for some* $i \in I$*;*

6. *every* ϕ *is expressible as* $\wedge_{i=1}^{n} \psi_i$ *with* ψ_i *coprime;*

subject to the set of axioms shown in Table 1 being satisfied.

By $\phi \vdash \psi$, where $\phi, \psi \in A$, we mean ϕ implies ψ (ϕ "is larger than" ψ). The entailment relation is a preorder, rather than a partial order, so that account is taken of different syntactic forms of logical formulae. The conjunction $\phi \wedge \psi$ of two tokens ϕ and ψ is "larger than" both ϕ and ψ with respect to the entailment order $\vdash$, and thus it behaves like the join operation. The equivalence relation $\approx$ is a congruence.

The *Lindenbaum algebra* of an elementary pre-constraint system $E = \langle A, \vdash, tt, ff, \wedge, \vee \rangle$ is defined to be the quotient structure:

$$\mathcal{LA}(E) \ = \ \langle A/_{\approx}, \vdash/_{\approx}, [tt], [ff], \wedge/_{\approx}, \vee/_{\approx} \rangle$$

where $\vdash/_{\approx}$, $\wedge/_{\approx}$ and $\vee/_{\approx}$ are the induced partial order, meet and join on the $\approx$-quotient of A defined by:

1. $[\phi] \vdash/_{\approx} [\psi]$ iff $\phi \vdash \psi$;

Table 1: Axioms for elementary pre-constraint systems.

(RF)	$\phi \vdash \phi$	(TR)	$\dfrac{\phi \vdash \psi, \psi \vdash \theta}{\phi \vdash \theta}$
($\approx$-I)	$\dfrac{\phi \vdash \psi, \psi \vdash \phi}{\phi \approx \psi}$	($\approx$-E)	$\dfrac{\phi \approx \psi}{\phi \vdash \psi, \psi \vdash \phi}$
(tt-I)	$\phi \vdash tt$	(ff-E)	$ff \vdash \phi$
($\wedge$-I)	$\dfrac{\phi \vdash \psi, \phi \vdash \theta}{\phi \vdash \psi \wedge \theta}$		
($\wedge$-E-L)	$\phi \wedge \psi \vdash \phi$	($\wedge$-E-R)	$\phi \wedge \psi \vdash \psi$
($\vee$-I)	$\dfrac{\phi \vdash \theta, \psi \vdash \theta}{\phi \vee \psi \vdash \theta}$		
($\vee$-E-L)	$\phi \vdash \phi \vee \psi$	($\vee$-E-R)	$\psi \vdash \phi \vee \psi$
($\wedge$-DST)	$\phi \wedge (\psi \vee \theta) \vdash (\phi \wedge \psi) \vee (\phi \wedge \theta)$		

2. $[\phi] \wedge/_{\approx} [\psi] = [\phi \wedge \psi]$.
3. $[\phi] \vee/_{\approx} [\psi] = [\phi \vee \psi]$.

That $\wedge/_{\approx}$ and $\vee/_{\approx}$ are well-defined follows from the fact that $\approx$ is a congruence wrt $\wedge$ and $\vee$.

Definition 4.2 *The Lindenbaum algebra $\mathcal{LA}(E) = \langle A/_{\approx}, \sqsubseteq, [tt], [ff], \sqcup, \sqcap \rangle$ of some elementary pre-constraint system E will be called an* elementary constraint system.

Note that we have introduced new symbols: $\sqsubseteq$ will denote $\vdash/_{\approx}$, while $\sqcup$ and $\sqcap$ will denote $\wedge/_{\approx}$ and $\vee/_{\approx}$ respectively. Also, if it is clear from the context, we shall shall often omit square brackets when referring to elements of an elementary constraint system, *i.e.* we shall use ϕ instead of the $\approx$-equivalence class $[\phi]$.

Observe that the Lindenbaum algebra $\mathcal{LA}(E)$ has the structure of a (coherent algebraic) distributive lattice[4] with two distinguished elements (0 identified with $[tt]$ and 1 with $[ff]$), $[\phi] \sqcup [\psi]$ interpreted as $[\phi \wedge \psi]$, and $[\phi] \sqcap [\psi]$ interpreted as $[\phi \vee \psi]$. Note that coprimes

[4] In concurrent constraint programming, a semilattice structure with tt, ff and $\wedge$ often suffices. It is possible to give Stone duality for semilattices, see *e.g.* (20), but we shall not consider this case. We should point out, however, that distributivity plays an important part in duality.

are essential as demonstrated by Theorem 3.7. It is also possible to axiomatize the notion of coprimeness in the style of (2).

Note also that $\mathcal{LA}(E)$ is not, in general, complete - only *finite* sets of tokens are guaranteed to have joins. Before we explain how to allow joins of infinite sets of tokens, let us consider some examples of elementary pre-constraint systems, which we have simplified by omitting disjunction.

Example 4.3 (First-order constraint system) *Let Var be a non-empty set of variables $x, y, z, \ldots$. Let Σ be a (many sorted) first-order alphabet (function symbols $f, g, \ldots$, predicate symbols and their signature). Let Φ be a non-empty subset of (Var, Σ)-formulae closed under conjunction, and let $\vdash$ to be interpreted as the usual implication. Then*

$$E_M = \langle \Phi \cup \{tt, ff\}, \vdash, tt, ff, \wedge \rangle$$

is an elementary pre-constraint system.

Example 4.4 (Mutual exclusion) *Let c_1, c_2 denote variable names in some concurrent programming language, t and f the truth and falsity constants in this language. Consider the set A_M of terms of the form:*

$$A_M = \{c_1 = t, c_1 = f, c_2 = t, c_2 = f, tt, ff\}$$

and the elementary pre-constraint system:

$$E_M = \langle A_M^{\wedge}, \vdash, tt, ff, \wedge \rangle$$

where $\vdash$ and $\wedge$ are the usual implication and conjunction, and $A_M^{\wedge}$ denotes the set A_M closed under finite conjunctions. If $c_1 = t$ denotes that the process number 1 is in its critical section, and similarly, $c_2 = t$ denotes that the process number 2 is in its critical section, then:

1. $c_1 = t \wedge c_2 = f$ *denotes that only the process number 1 is in its critical section;*
2. $c_1 = t \wedge c_1 = f$ *entails ff (failure);*
3. $c_1 = t \wedge c_2 = t$ *denotes the situation in which the* mutual exclusion *protocol is violated as both processes are in their critical sections.*

Example 4.5 (Infinitely Often) *Let e_1, e_2 denote variable names in some concurrent programming language, and $n \in \mathbf{N}$ denotes a natural number constant. Consider the set A of terms of the form:*

$$A_I = \{e_1 \geq n \mid n \in \mathbf{N}\} \cup \{e_2 \geq n \mid n \in \mathbf{N}\} \cup \{tt, ff\}$$

and the elementary pre-constraint system:

$$E_I = \langle A_I^{\wedge}, \vdash, tt, ff, \wedge \rangle$$

where $\vdash$ *and* $\wedge$ *are the usual implication and conjunction. If* $e_1 \geq n$ *denotes that the process number* 1 *has entered its critical section* at least n *times, and similarly for the process number* 2*, then:*

1. $e_1 \geq 1$ *denotes that the process number* 1 *has entered its critical section at least once;*

2. $c_1 \geq 1 \wedge c_2 \geq 2$ *denotes that both processes have entered their critical section at least once.*

Observe that we cannot correctly express the property that the process number 1 *has entered its critical section* infinitely often, *since*

$$\bigsqcup\{e_1 \geq n \mid n \in \mathbf{N}\} = ff$$

and thus this property is identified with failure.

Example 4.6 (Lists) *Let* A_L *be the set of terms* $\{t = t'\} \cup \{tt, ff\}$*, where* t, t' *are terms denoting lists built following the syntax rules below:*

t	::==	$\mathbf{0}$	*list terminator*
	|	x	*list variable*
	|	ax	*list consisting of a followed by x*
	|	bx	*list consisting of b followed by x*

and $=$ *is the usual equality. Consider the elementary pre-constraint system*

$$E_L = \langle A_L^{\wedge}, \vdash, tt, ff, \wedge \rangle$$

where $\vdash$ *and* $\wedge$ *are the usual implication and conjunction. Then*

1. $x_1 = ax_2 \wedge x_2 = bx_3 \wedge x_3 = \mathbf{0}$ *denotes the list* $ab\mathbf{0}$*;*

2. $x_1 = ax_2 \wedge x_2 = ax_3 \wedge \ldots \wedge x_{n+1} = \mathbf{0}$ *denotes the list* $a^n\mathbf{0}$*.*

Observe that we cannot correctly express infinite *lists such as* a^ω *(a repeated infinitely often), since the join of the infinite set:*

$$\{x_1 = ax_2 \wedge x_2 = ax_3 \wedge \ldots \wedge x_n = ax_{n+1} \wedge \ldots\} \quad (4)$$

will be ff.

4.2 Adding Infinite Constraints

Let $E = \langle A, \vdash, tt, ff, \wedge, \vee \rangle$ be an elementary pre-constraint system. E is a *formal*, deductive system, where the entailment relation $\vdash$ is a preorder. We shall require a *semantic* model $\mathcal{C}(E) = \langle C, \sqsubseteq \rangle$ for E, where $\sqsubseteq$ is a partial order. Thus, we shall require a function:

$$\kappa(\cdot) : A \longrightarrow \mathcal{K}(C) \tag{5}$$

where $\mathcal{K}(C)$ are the compact elements of $\mathcal{C}(E)$. But what should the domain $\mathcal{C}(E)$ look like? One would expect to be able to prove, at least, soundness and completeness theorems. One way of constructing such a model is by taking the ideal completion (see Section 3.1 for basic definitions and facts) of the (Lindenbaum algebra) of E. We therefore adopt the following definition.

Define the interpretation $\kappa(\cdot) : A \longrightarrow \mathcal{K}(C)$ by:

$$\kappa(\phi) \;=\; \downarrow[\phi]$$

i.e. $\kappa(\cdot)$ assigns to each ϕ the principal ideal of the Lindenbaum algebra $\mathcal{LA}(E)$ determined by ϕ[5]. The ordering on $\mathcal{K}(C)$ is by subset inclusion.

Definition 4.7 *Let $E = \langle A, \vdash, tt, ff, \wedge, \vee \rangle$ be an elementary pre-constraint system. A* constraint system *$\mathcal{C}(E) = \langle C, \sqsubseteq \rangle$ determined by E is the ideal completion*

$$\langle \mathcal{I}(\mathcal{LA}(E)), \subseteq \rangle$$

of the Lindenbaum algebra of E. $\mathcal{C} = \langle C, \sqsubseteq \rangle$ is said to be a constraint system *iff it is the ideal completion of some elementary constraint system.*

We adopt the following notation convention. Elements of C will be referred to as *constraints*, and will be denoted by letters c, d, etc., or, where confusion does not arise, by their syntactic representation $\phi \in A$. For example, tt will be used to denote the principal ideal $\{tt\}$ determined by the proposition tt.

We shall now motivate the choice of ideals for the construction of a constraint system. Suppose I is an ideal in $\mathcal{LA}(E)$, then it is also an $\vdash$-ideal in E, and hence by definition:

1. I must contain tt;
2. if $\phi \in I$ and $\phi \vdash \psi$ then ψ must also be in I;
3. if $\phi, \psi \in I$ then $\phi \wedge \psi$ must be in I.

[5] Strictly speaking, the mapping is $\phi \mapsto [\phi] \mapsto \downarrow[\phi]$, where $\phi \mapsto [\phi]$ is the canonical valuation. The usual inductive definition of $\kappa(\cdot)$ has been replaced with the direct definition because it can be shown that if atomic formulae are mapped onto their canonical valuation, then so are all the formulae.

Thus, I constitutes a *deductively closed theory* in E.

The following result is immediate from the construction.

Proposition 4.8

1. *$\langle C, \sqsubseteq \rangle$ is an algebraic lattice.*

2. *The Lindenbaum algebra $\langle \mathcal{LA}(E), \sqsubseteq \rangle$ is isomorphic to $\langle \mathcal{K}(C), \sqsubseteq \rangle$ via the isomorphism $[\phi] \mapsto \downarrow[\phi]$.*

Proof: Direct from Lemma 3.2. □

The importance of the above theorem lies in the fact that concurrent constraint systems are freely constructed from elementary constraint systems. In other words, there is just enough (*i.e.* no more, no less) structure in $\langle C, \sqsubseteq \rangle$. The isomorphism between the Lindenbaum algebra of an elementary pre-constraint system and the compact elements states that each point of the constraint system C is uniquely determined by a theory in E.

Furthermore, we can show that the constraint system $\langle C, \sqsubseteq \rangle$ admits join and meet operations, which can be characterized as follows. Note that, although the join of two constraints exists, it does not coincide with their set-theoretic union.

Proposition 4.9

1. *For $c, d \in C$, $c \sqcap d$ is their intersection.*

2. *For $c, d \in C$, $c \sqcup d$ is their union closed under finite joins.*

Proof:

1. Assume c, d respectively denote ideals $I, J \in \mathcal{I}(\mathcal{LA}(E))$. It is easy to see that $I \cap J$ is also an ideal (it is a lower set and $a, b \in I \cap J$ implies $a \sqcup b \in I \cap J$). Since for any ideal $I' \subseteq I, J$ we have $I' \subseteq I \cap J$, it follows that $I \cap J$ is the largest such ideal, and hence the meet of I and J.

2. Assume c, d respectively denote ideals $I, J \in \mathcal{I}(\mathcal{LA}(E))$. Then it is easy to see that $(I \cup J)^{\sqcup}$, *i.e.* the set $I \cup J$ closed under finite joins, is an ideal. Take any $I' \supseteq I, J$, then $I' \supseteq I \cup J$, and hence $I' = I'^{\sqcup} \supseteq (I \cup J)^{\sqcup}$ as required.

□

We can now show the following result.

Theorem 4.10 (Soundness and completeness) *For all $\phi, \psi \in A$:*

$$\phi \vdash \psi \iff \kappa(\phi) \sqsupseteq \kappa(\psi).$$

Proof:

1. We verify that axioms are satisfied. (TR), (RF), ($\approx$-I) and ($\approx$-E) follow by transitivity, reflexivity and antisymmetry of $\subseteq$. (tt-I) holds since $\kappa(tt) = \downarrow[tt] = \{tt\} \subseteq \downarrow[\phi]$ for all ϕ. Likewise, (tt-E) holds since $\kappa(f\!f) = \downarrow[f\!f] = A/_{\approx} \supseteq \downarrow[\phi]$ for all ϕ. We have $\kappa(\phi \wedge \psi) = \downarrow[\phi \wedge \psi] = \downarrow([\phi] \sqcup [\psi]) = \downarrow[\phi] \cap \downarrow[\phi] = \kappa(\phi) \sqcup \kappa(\psi)$, so $\kappa(\phi) \sqsupseteq \kappa(\psi)$ and $\kappa(\phi) \sqsupseteq \kappa(\theta)$ iff $\kappa(\phi) \sqsupseteq \kappa(\psi) \sqcup \kappa(\theta) = \kappa(\psi \wedge \theta)$, and the $\wedge$ axioms follow. The case of $\vee$ is similar. Finally, distributivity axiom follows from distributivity of the underlying lattice.
2. Suppose $\kappa(\phi) \sqsupseteq \kappa(\psi)$. Then by definition $\downarrow[\phi] \supseteq \downarrow[\psi]$, which implies $\phi \vdash \psi$.

□

Notice that the soundness and completeness theorem makes use of the order inherent in the lattice $\mathcal{C}(E)$, rather than an appropriate set-theoretic operation (*i.e.* containment) as required by Stone duality. Also note the order reversal. This reversal can be understood on the grounds of the Scott topology of $\mathcal{C}(E)$. Recall that the Scott topology (of an algebraic cpo) is determined by the basis $\{\uparrow b \mid b \in \mathcal{K}(C)\}$. It is easy to see that for any poset:

$$c \sqsubseteq d \iff \uparrow c \subseteq \uparrow d \tag{6}$$

and hence we can reformulate soundness as follows.

Corollary 4.11 (Soundness wrt Scott topology) *For all $\phi, \psi \in A$:*

$$\phi \vdash \psi \Rightarrow \uparrow\kappa(\phi) \subseteq \uparrow\kappa(\psi)$$

Moreover, we have the following results. The definability theorem states that every compact semantic constraint can be expressed as a formula in E. Although this does not, in general, hold for an arbitrary semantic constraint, we can characterize such a constraint as the join of the compact constraints below it. In other words, each constraint c is the join of all the (equivalence classes of) formulae in E which are below c.

Theorem 4.12 (Definability) $\forall c \in \mathcal{K}(C), \exists \phi \in A.\kappa(\phi) = c.$

Proof: Direct from Lemma 3.2. □

Theorem 4.13 (Approximation) $\forall d \in C.d = \bigsqcup\{c \in \mathcal{LA}(E) \mid c \sqsubseteq d\}.$

Proof: Direct from Lemma 3.2 since $\mathcal{LA}(E)$ is isomorphic with the compact elements of the algebraic lattice $\mathcal{C}(E)$. □

Once again, the above theorem makes use of the inherent order in the lattice C, whereas one would expect conjunction to be interpreted in terms of a set-theoretic intersection, as required by Stone duality. As in the case of the entailment - containment correspondence, we can show that this view can be understood on the grounds of the Scott topology. Note that for any poset we have:

$$\uparrow(b \sqcup c) = \uparrow b \cap \uparrow c \tag{7}$$

whenever $b \sqcup c$ is defined, so the following can be shown.

Corollary 4.14 (Approximation wrt Scott topology)

$$\forall d \in C.\uparrow d \;=\; \bigcap\{\uparrow c \mid c \sqsubseteq d\}.$$

Observe that the approximation theorem only guarantees that each constraint c in a concurrent constraint system $\langle C, \sqsubseteq\rangle$ can be approximated as a join of (a possibly infinite) set of (equivalence classes of) formulae of A. It does not, however, guarantee that *every* constraint $c \in C$ can be syntactically expressed as a formula in A.

The remaining question is to find a complete model for E, in which the operations of $\wedge$ and $\vee$ have been replaced by the set-theoretic intersection and union. We can utilize Stone duality for this purpose, thus interpreting formulae as the compact-open subsets of $Spec\mathcal{LA}(E)$. Recall that the space $Spec\mathcal{LA}(E)$, the prime filters over $\mathcal{LA}(E)$ with inclusion of filters as the specialization ordering, is isomorphic to the points (completely prime filters) of the ideal completion of E (Theorem 3.6), which allows us to identify $Spec\mathcal{LA}(E)$ with $Pt\,\mathcal{C}(E)$. Since *ff* is coprime, and every element of the lattice $\mathcal{LA}(E)$ is expressible as $\sqcup_{i=1}^{n}\psi_i$ for ψ_i coprime, there are enough coprimes, and hence $Spec\mathcal{LA}(E)$ is a coherent domain in its Scott topology. It follows (Theorem 3.7) that the usual topology on $Spec\mathcal{LA}(E)$ coincides with the Scott topology $\sigma\Omega Spec\mathcal{LA}(E)$.

This leads us to the following definition. Note that the basic open sets of the Scott topology $\sigma\Omega Spec\mathcal{LA}(E)$ have the form:

$$\uparrow_{Spec\mathcal{LA}(E)}(\uparrow_{\mathcal{LA}(E)}(\phi))$$

for $\phi \in \mathcal{LA}(E)$ coprime, *i.e.* they are upper-closed sets of prime filters over $\mathcal{LA}(E)$.

Let $E = \langle A, \vdash, tt, ff, \wedge, \vee \rangle$ be a pre-constraint system, and let $\mathcal{C}(E) = \langle C, \sqsubseteq \rangle$ be the constraint system determined by E. Define an interpretation map:

$$[\![\cdot]\!] : A \longrightarrow \mathcal{K}\Omega(Spec\mathcal{LA}(E))$$

by

$$\begin{array}{rcl} [\![ff]\!] & = & \emptyset \\ [\![tt]\!] & = & Spec\mathcal{LA}(E) \\ [\![\phi]\!] & = & \uparrow_{Spec\mathcal{LA}(E)}(\uparrow_{\mathcal{LA}(E)}[\phi]) \quad \phi \text{ coprime} \\ [\![\phi \wedge \psi]\!] & = & [\![\phi]\!] \cap [\![\psi]\!] \\ [\![\phi \vee \psi]\!] & = & [\![\phi]\!] \cup [\![\psi]\!] \end{array}$$

This is the localic side of Stone duality.

Theorem 4.15 (Stone duality) *Let $E = \langle A, \vdash, tt, ff, \wedge, \vee \rangle$ be a pre-constraint system, $\mathcal{C}(E) = \langle C, \sqsubseteq \rangle$ be the constraint system determined by E. Then:*

$$\mathcal{LA}(E) \;\cong\; \mathcal{K}\Omega(Spec\mathcal{LA}(E)).$$

Proof: First observe that from coherence the Scott-compact opens form a distributive lattice under the converse of inclusion, with $\emptyset$ acting as 1 and $Spec\mathcal{LA}(E) = \uparrow tt$ as 0. Thus, $\langle \mathcal{K}\Omega(Spec\mathcal{LA}(E)), \supseteq, Spec\mathcal{LA}(E), \emptyset, \cap, \cup \rangle$ is an elementary constraint system.

It remains to show that $[\![\cdot]\!]$ is a bijection preserving the distinguished elements and the lattice operations. It is easy to see that $[\![\cdot]\!]$ is injective and preserves the distinguished elements and both operations. That $[\![\cdot]\!]$ is surjective follows from the fact that every compact-open in $Spec\mathcal{LA}(E)$ (which is coherent algebraic) has a unique, irredundant, and finite coprime decomposition (see (22)). □

As a consequence, we obtain the following correspondence between entailment of formulae and inclusion of the interpreted constraints.

Corollary 4.16 $\forall \phi, \psi \in A. \phi \vdash \psi$ *iff* $[\![\phi]\!] \subseteq [\![\psi]\!]$.

Example 4.17 (Mutual Exclusion and Infinitely Often) *Consider the elementary pre-constraint system:*

$$E = \langle (A_M \cup A_I)^\wedge, \vdash, tt, ff, \wedge \rangle \tag{8}$$

where A_M is the set of formulae introduced in Example 4.4, and A_I is the set of formulae from Example 4.5. The following shows a part of the constraint system determined by E:

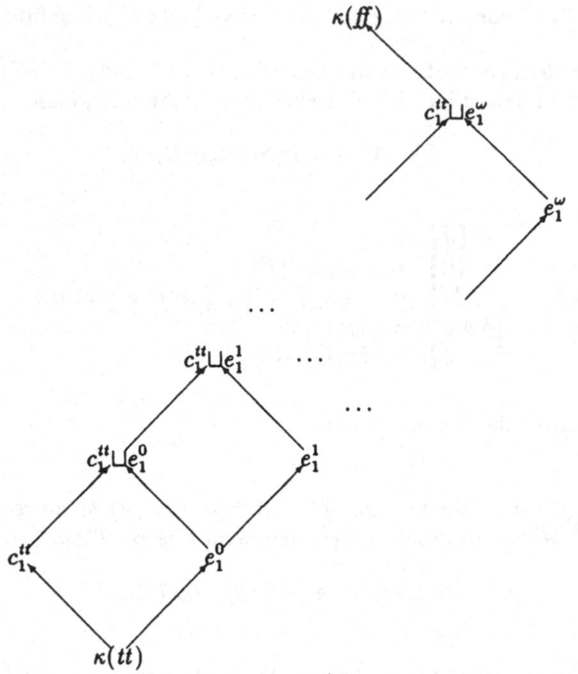

where c_1^{tt} *denotes* $\kappa(c_1 = tt)$, e_1^0 *denotes* $\kappa(e_1 = 0)$, $c_1^{tt} \sqcup e_1^0$ *denotes* $\kappa(c_1 = tt \wedge e_1 = 0)$, *etc. Note that* $c_1^{tt} \wedge e_1^{\omega}$ *and* e_1^{ω} *are* not *compact, while* $\kappa(ff)$ *is.*

4.3 Cylindric Constraint Systems

As many programming languages come equipped with a notion of hiding information within a module from the rest of the program, we shall introduce a kind of a constraint system which supports *hiding operators*. Our definition follows the approach of (19).

Definition 4.18 *A* cylindric pre-constraint system *is a tuple* $E = \langle A, Var, \vdash, tt, ff, \wedge, \vee \rangle$ *such that*

1. *A is a set of propositions over syntax:*

$$A \ ::== \ tt \mid ff \mid \phi \mid \phi \wedge \phi \mid \phi \vee \phi \mid \exists X.\phi$$

2. *Var is an infinite set of variables,*

3. $\langle A, \vdash, tt, ff, \wedge, \vee \rangle$ *is an elementary pre-constraint system*

subject to the set of axioms shown in Table 2.

Table 2: Additional axioms for cylindric pre-constraint systems.

(∃-I)	$\phi \vdash \exists X.\phi$	(∃-⊢)	$\dfrac{\phi \vdash \psi}{\exists X.\phi \vdash \exists X.\psi}$
(∃-∧)	$\exists X.(\phi \wedge \exists X.\psi) \approx \exists X.\phi \wedge \exists X.\psi$	(∃-COM)	$\exists X.(\exists Y.\phi) \approx \exists Y.(\exists X.\phi)$

Definition 4.19 *Let $E = \langle A, Var, \vdash, tt, ff, \wedge\rangle$ be a cylindric pre-constraint system. A* cylindric constraint system $\mathcal{C}(E) = \langle C, \sqsubseteq\rangle$ *determined by E is the ideal completion*

$$\langle \mathcal{I}(\mathcal{LA}(E)), \subseteq\rangle$$

of the Lindenbaum algebra of E.

As observed in (19), cylindric pre-constraint systems determine constraint systems $\langle C, \sqsubseteq\rangle$ which are equipped with a family $\{\exists_X \mid X \in Var\}$ of operators $\exists_X : C \longrightarrow C$, which map a formula ϕ onto its existential closure $\exists X.\phi$.

Proposition 4.20 *Let $E = \langle A, Var, \vdash, tt, ff, \wedge, \vee\rangle$ be a cylindric pre-constraint system. Define $\exists^0_X : \mathcal{K}(C) \longrightarrow \mathcal{K}(C)$ by:*

$$\exists^0_X(\phi) \quad = \quad \exists X.\phi$$

Then $\exists^0_X$ is monotone, and $\exists_X$, the continuous extension of $\exists^0_X$ to C, is a kernel operator.

Proof: We have $\phi \vdash \psi$ implies $\exists X.\phi \vdash \exists X.\psi$ from axiom (∃-⊢), and hence $\exists^0_X(\phi) \sqsupseteq \exists^0_X(\psi)$.

Since $\exists^0_X$ is monotone on compact elements, its continuous extension $\exists_X$ to C exists and is unique. We show $\exists_X$ is idempotent. $\phi \vdash \exists X.\phi$ implies $\exists X.\phi \vdash \exists X.(\exists X.\phi)$ from axiom (∃-⊢), and hence $\exists_X(\phi) \sqsupseteq \exists_X(\exists_X(\phi))$. The other direction follows similarly. Finally, since $\phi \vdash \exists X.\phi$ we have $\phi \sqsupseteq \exists_X(\phi)$. □

Another important kind of constraint systems are those with the "diagonal formulae" due to Tarski. These are terms of the form $X = Y$, where $X, Y \in Var$. They have been found useful when dealing with variable substitution, which in turn is used for parameter passing to and from procedures (19). Given a formula ϕ, the formula $\phi[Y/X]$, for $X, Y \in Var$, denotes ϕ with all the (free) occurrences of the variable X replaced with Y. Using existential quantification, $\phi[Y/X]$ can be modelled as $\exists X.(X = Y) \wedge \phi$. This leads us to the following definition.

Table 3: Additional axioms for diagonal pre-constraint systems.

($X = X$-I)	$\phi \vdash X = X$	(Z-I)	$X = Y \approx \exists Z.(X = Y \wedge Y = Z)$
($X = Y$-E)	$X = Y \wedge \exists X.(\phi \wedge X = Y) \vdash \phi$		

Definition 4.21 *A* diagonal pre-constraint system *is a tuple* $E = \langle A, Var, \vdash, tt, ff, \wedge, \vee\rangle$ *such that*

1. *A is a set of propositions over syntax:*

$$A \ ::== \ tt \mid ff \mid \phi \mid \phi \wedge \phi \mid \exists X.\phi \mid X = Y$$

2. *$(X, Y \in)$ Var is an infinite set of variables,*

3. *$\langle A, \vdash, tt, ff, \wedge, \vee\rangle$ is a cylindric pre-constraint system,*

subject to the set of axioms shown in Table 3.

Definition 4.22 *Let* $E = \langle A, Var, \vdash, tt, ff, \wedge, \vee\rangle$ *be a diagonal pre-constraint system. A* diagonal constraint system $\mathcal{C}(E) = \langle C, \sqsubseteq\rangle$ *determined by E is the ideal completion*

$$\langle \mathcal{I}(\mathcal{LA}(E)), \subseteq\rangle$$

of the Lindenbaum algebra of E.

We shall denote the semantic constraints corresponding to propositions of the form $X = Y$ by d_{XY}.

Unless otherwise stated, we shall assume that E denotes a cylindric, diagonal pre-constraint system.

5 CONSTRAINTS, FINITE OBSERVATIONS, AND PROPERTIES

Let $\mathcal{C}(E)$ be a constraint system. Define a *semantic property* Ψ to be any subset of C. This is an extensional, non-constructive view; note that we are not requiring at this stage that each property be expressed as a formula in E. By definition, a semantic property may contain any combination of compact elements contained in $\mathcal{K}(C)$, and the non-compact elements $C \setminus \mathcal{K}(C)$. We shall find that this is rather general, and thus will aim to restrict the approach later by allowing some "basic" properties and certain constructions from them.

It would be convenient to distinguish between properties that are detectable in finite time (so called "finitary") from those which cannot be detected at finite time ("infinitary"). One possible distinction would be by identifying subsets of $\mathcal{K}(C)$ with finitary properties, and subsets of $C \setminus \mathcal{K}(C)$ with infinitary ones (see *e.g.* (15)). This may be justified by the fact that, by definition of compactness, each compact element is the supremum of a finite chain of elements, and thus can be reached in a finite number of "computation steps", where a computation step corresponds to moving up to the next element in the chain. On the other hand, a non-compact element is a supremum of an infinite chain, and hence cannot be reached by a finite number of computation steps. However, we shall find that allowing infinite (*i.e.* non-compact) elements in finitary properties, and compact elements in infinitary properties is advantageous. Therefore, we define a semantic property $\Psi \subseteq C$ to be *finitary* iff:

$$c \in \Psi \cap (C \setminus \mathcal{K}(C)) \iff \exists c' \in (\Psi \cap \mathcal{K}(C)).c' \sqsubseteq c$$

Otherwise, the property Ψ is *infinitary*.

The intuition behind the above definition is as follows. A finitary property is one which may contain infinite elements *only* if some compact element below is also in the property. Thus, a finitary property can always be decided in finite time[6] (in the sense of semi-decidability). On the other hand, given an infinitary property, it is possible that it will not be detected in finite time. We shall find that properties like "mutual exclusion" or "termination" will be finitary, while fairness will not.

Example 5.1 *Consider the constraint system shown in Example 4.17. Then* $\downarrow(c_1^{tt} \wedge e_1^0)$, $\uparrow(c_1^{tt} \wedge e_1^0)$, $\{\kappa(f\!f)\}$ *are finitary,* $\uparrow c_1^{tt} \wedge e_1^{\omega}$ *is infinitary.*

Recall that safety properties state that "nothing bad will happen", while liveness that "something good will happen". It seems that we need to state what each such "thing" is, and also define what it means for each "thing" to be "good" or "bad". Following (21), observations must correspond to open sets in some topology over C. But which topology?

It is natural to require that a single "thing" must be detectable in finite time, and hence be (a subset of C) determined by an element of $\mathcal{K}(C)$. For $c \in \mathcal{K}(C)$ call such subset U_c a *basic observation* of c. If $d \sqsupseteq c$, then we would like d to belong to U_c; this guarantees that to observe something above c (*i.e.* stronger than c in the sense of the entailment relation), it is sufficient to observe c. It is easy to see that for $c \in \mathcal{K}(C)$ we can now define a basic observation U_c to be $\uparrow c$. Note that to observe c *and* to observe

[6] We are assuming that satisfaction corresponds to containment.

d means to be inside $U_c \cap U_d = U_{s \sqcup d}$, and hence basic observations should be closed under (finite) intersections.

Ideally, we would like to be able to observe collections of "things", in the sense that to observe $\{c, d\}$ means to observe either c or d. Thus, we would expect $U_{\{c,d\}} = U_c \cup U_d$. This immediately gives rise to an identification of observations with a topology (the Scott topology) on C. The problem is whether we should restrict the size of collections of "things" in any way - should they be finite, countable or arbitrary sets of compact elements? Since we would like observations to be syntactically expressible as formulae of E, and our axiomatization permits only finitely expressible constraints, which are moreover identified with the compact open subsets, we propose the following definition.

Definition 5.2 *Define a* finite observation *in the constraint system* $\mathcal{C}(E) = \langle C, \sqsubseteq \rangle$ *to be a Scott-compact open subset of* C.

Thus finite observations are closed under finite intersection and finite union. Moreover, by Stone duality, each finite observation has a syntactic form. Note that this definition does not allow arbitrary open sets as finite observations. This is not to say that open sets, which are finitary, are not observable - they are, in the sense of semi-decidability, but what concerns us here is both *observability* and *finiteness* of syntactic definition, and, in particular, finite disjunctions. However, we should point out that such a restriction may be considered too strong, and arbitrary, or at least countable, collections of "things" may be allowed (13).

As discussed earlier, we have We remark that, in the light of Stone duality, perhaps we should have identified finite observations with the Scott-compact open subsets $U \in \mathcal{K}\Omega(Pt\mathcal{C}(E))$. However, since we are working with coherent algebraic locales, any such U is an intersection of a $U' \in \mathcal{K}\Omega(\mathcal{C}(E))$ with $Pt, \mathcal{C}(E)$, so we can work with the Scott topology of $\mathcal{C}(E)$.

6 PROCESS LANGUGAGE

6.1 Operational Semantics

We now introduce a concurrent constraint language $\mathcal{L}$ with angelic non-determinism, similar to the language introduced in (8). The language is interpreted over the disjunctive, cylindric and diagonal constraint system $\langle C, \sqsubseteq \rangle$, and is given by the following syntax:

$$A ::== tell(c) \mid ask(c) \rightarrow A \mid A \oplus A \mid A \parallel A \mid \exists X.A \mid p(Y)$$

where $c \in \mathcal{K}(C)$. Each such c will denote the state of the store at some *finite* time, and we shall often use constraints to describe such finite stores. As we allow infinite constraints $c \in C$, we may also refer to *infinite* stores not reachable in finite time.

For $c \in \mathcal{K}(C)$, *tell*(c) denotes the action which conjoins the constraint c to the current store. The guard *ask*$(c) \rightarrow A$ denotes the action, which will behave as the agent A if run in the store which entails d with $d \vdash c$; otherwise, the process will be suspended until such condition holds. $A \oplus A$ denotes angelic non-determinism, in the sense of (8); a choice will be made between the two agents, and the other agent will be discarded[7]. $A \parallel A$ will cause the agent to decompose into two concurrent subagents, which can proceed autonomously. $\exists X.A$ will be used for information hiding. $p(Y)$ denotes procedure call, where $Y \in Var$ is the actual parameter. It is straightforward to generalize procedure calls to vectors $\vec{X}$ of variables. To avoid having to use environments, we shall assume a fixed set W of procedure declarations of the form $p(X)$: $-A \in W$, $X \in Var$ (X is fixed).

Operational semantics is given in the form of a transition system. The transition system is of the form $\langle Conf, \longrightarrow \rangle$, where $Conf$ is the set of *configurations*, that is pairs consisting of a process and a constraint $c \in \mathcal{K}(C)$. $(P, c) \longrightarrow (P', c')$ means that the agent P when initiated in the store c will upgrade the store to c' and subsequently behave like P'. The transition rules are shown in Table 4. As usual, the transition relation $\longrightarrow$ is defined to be the smallest relation satisfying the axioms. The rules are based on the language (8), with the exception of the procedure call, which has been simplified. The reader should note that, to aid hiding, transition relation has been extended to agents of the form $\exists X.(d, A)$, where d denotes an internal store holding information about X which is hidden outside $\exists X.(d, A)$. An agent of the form $\exists X.A$ evolves into the agent $\exists X.(d, B)$, with d storing the information about the hidden X for b to use.

Unlike the treatment of (4), we shall not distinguish between *successful* and *deadlocking* termination.

6.2 Computations and Observations

Let P be a process (term) in the language $\mathcal{L}$ interpreted over the constraint system $\langle C, \sqsubseteq \rangle$. An *execution sequence of P from $c \in \mathcal{K}(C)$* is a finite or infinite sequence of pairs from $\mathcal{L} \times \mathcal{K}(C)$ of the form:

$$\langle P_1, c_1 \rangle \langle P_2, c_2 \rangle \cdots \langle P_i, c_i \rangle \cdots$$

such that $\forall i$:

- $P_1 = P, c_1 = c$
- $\langle P_i, c_i \rangle \longrightarrow \langle P_{i+1}, c_{i+1} \rangle$

We shall sometimes write execution sequences as:

$$P_1 \stackrel{\langle c_1, c_2 \rangle}{\longrightarrow} P_2 \stackrel{\langle c_2, c_3 \rangle}{\longrightarrow} \cdots P_i \stackrel{\langle c_i, c_{i+1} \rangle}{\longrightarrow} \cdots$$

[7]The reader should note that this is *not* demonic non-determinism, as will be made clear later.

Table 4: Transition rules for $\mathcal{L}$

T1	$\langle tell(d), c\rangle \longrightarrow \langle tell(tt), c \sqcup d\rangle$	if $c \neq tt$
T2	$\langle ask(d) \rightarrow A, c\rangle \longrightarrow \langle A, c\rangle$	if $d \vdash c$
T3	$\langle p(Y), c\rangle \longrightarrow \langle \exists Y.(tell(X = Y) \parallel A), c\rangle$	if $p(X)\colon -A \in W$
T4	$\dfrac{\langle A, \exists_X c\rangle \longrightarrow \langle B, d\rangle}{\langle \exists X.A, c\rangle \longrightarrow \langle \exists X.(d, B), c \sqcup \exists_X d\rangle}$	
T5	$\dfrac{\langle A, d \sqcup \exists_X c\rangle \longrightarrow \langle B, d'\rangle}{\langle \exists X.(d, A), c\rangle \longrightarrow \langle \exists X.(d', B), c \sqcup \exists_X d'\rangle}$	
T6	$\dfrac{\langle A, c\rangle \longrightarrow \langle A', c'\rangle}{\begin{array}{c}\langle A \parallel B, c\rangle \longrightarrow \langle A' \parallel B, c'\rangle \\ \langle B \parallel A, c\rangle \longrightarrow \langle B \parallel A', c'\rangle\end{array}}$	
T7	$\dfrac{\langle A, c\rangle \longrightarrow \langle A', c'\rangle}{\begin{array}{c}\langle A \oplus B, c\rangle \longrightarrow \langle A', c'\rangle \\ \langle B \oplus A, c\rangle \longrightarrow \langle A, c'\rangle\end{array}}$	

If an execution sequence s is finite of length n and there is no d such that $\langle P_n, c_n\rangle \longrightarrow \langle P', d\rangle$ then s is called *terminating*; otherwise, it is *non-terminating*.

Define an execution sequence s to be *weakly fair* iff no subagent remains enabled continuously from some point on. s is *strongly fair* iff no subagent remains enabled infinitely often. Note that, since a subagent enabled infinitely often implies it must be enabled continuously from some point on, strong and weak fairness coincide. This does not hold in general, but here it is a result of the calculus having a restricted form of non-determinism[8].

The set of all execution sequences of P from c will be denoted $S(P, c)$, and the fair ones $FS(P, c)$.

In the previous section we have identified finite observations with the Scott-compact open subsets $U \in \mathcal{K}\Omega(\mathcal{C}(E))$. Given U Scott compact-open, there must exist a finite subset $F \subseteq \mathcal{K}(C)$ such that $U = \uparrow F$.

Definition 6.1 *A constraint (store) $c \in C$ is said to* satisfy *an observation U (notation $c \models U$) iff $c \in U$.*

Note that this means that $c \sqsupseteq d$ for some $d \in Min(F)$.

Definition 6.2 *For a process P and a constraint $c \in \mathcal{K}(C)$, the* observations of P at c, *denoted $Obs(P)(c)$ are:*

$$Obs(P)(c) \quad = \quad \left\{U \in \mathcal{K}\Omega(\mathcal{C}(E)) \mid \forall s = \langle P_i, c_i\rangle_{i\in\omega} \in FS(P, c), \exists k. c_k \in U\right\}$$

A failed computation is one that leads to a store that satisfies ff. As $ff \in U$ for any $U \in \mathcal{K}\Omega(\mathcal{C}(E))$ (by $\uparrow$-closure), it follows that an inconsistent store (*i.e.* a store satisfying the constraint ff) will satisfy all finite observations. However, note that the observation $\{ff\} \in \mathcal{K}\Omega(\mathcal{C}(E))$ is satisfied by a program P only if all (fair) computations lead to failure; hence, failure can be distinguished from a non-failing computation. Also, failed computations do not matter (in the sense of not being observable) as long as there exist non-failing computations. This explains the nature of *angelic non-determinism* as discussed in (8) – we can think of it as allowing *all* the non-deterministic sub-agents to proceed, and then discarding those which lead to a failure.

Note that, unlike the treatment of (4), we cannot distinguish between deadlocked and non-deadlocked computations.

---

[8]We do not admit a mechanism for synchronization between *tell*()/*ask*() actions to be refused, but an extension is possible, see *e.g.* (4).

6.3 Denotational Semantics

As the language $\mathcal{L}$ is non-deterministic, we shall require a suitable *powerdomain* construction over the given constraint system $\mathcal{C}(E)$ to allow for situations in which a number of possible results is produced by a non-deterministic process. For example, the process

$$ask(X = 1) \rightarrow tell(Y = 1) \oplus ask(X = 1) \rightarrow tell(Y = 2)$$

when initiated in a store satisfying the constraint $X = 1$, will *either* lead to the store satisfying $X = 1 \wedge Y = 1$ *or* to the store satisfying $X = 1 \wedge Y = 2$. We shall thus require a *set* of constraints to model the result of a non-deterministic process.

One such construction is the *Smyth* (or *upper*) powerdomain, which, as shown in (8), allows to reduce the representation of a process to a *set* of constraints, instead of a subset of a set of sets of constraints. We shall briefly explain the construction here (the reader is referred to (7) for more details). Given a constraint system $\mathcal{C} = \langle C, \sqsubseteq \rangle$, which is an algebraic lattice with a countable set $\mathcal{K}(C)$ of compact elements, and hence also an ω-algebraic cpo, we can define the *Smyth preorder* $\preceq \subseteq \wp_f^{ne}(\mathcal{K}(C)) \times \wp_f^{ne}(\mathcal{K}(C))$ on finite sets of compact elements by

$$u \preceq v \iff \forall c \in u, \exists d \in v . c \sqsupseteq d.$$

Note that this order identifies all subsets containing *tt*. For the remaining subsets, the fewer constraints in the set, the higher it is in the ordering. Now define the *Smyth powerdomain* $(\mathcal{P}_u(\mathcal{C}), \sqsubseteq)$ as the ideal completion of $(\wp_f^{ne}(\mathcal{K}(C)), \preceq)$, *i.e.*

$$(\mathcal{I}(\wp_f^{ne}(\mathcal{K}(C))), \subseteq).$$

An alternative representation for the Smyth powerdomain (up to isomorphism) is as the family of all non-empty $\uparrow$-closed Scott-compact subsets of the constraint system $\mathcal{C}$ ordered by superset (17).

It can be shown that, for a constraint system $\mathcal{C} = \langle C, \sqsubseteq \rangle$, the Smyth powerdomain $\mathcal{P}_u(\mathcal{C})$ is also a constraint system (*i.e.* it is an algebraic lattice, possibly satisfying additional properties depending on the underlying constraint system). Moreover, the Smyth powerdomain is closed under set-theoretic union (*i.e.* for any $u, v \in \mathcal{P}_u(\mathcal{C})$, $u \cup v \in \mathcal{P}_u(\mathcal{C})$), and there exists a "singleton" mapping $\{\!|\cdot|\!\} : \mathcal{C} \longrightarrow \mathcal{P}_u(\mathcal{C})$, defined by $\{\!|c|\!\} = \uparrow c$ for $c \in C$. The supremum $\bigsqcup_{i \in \omega} x_i$ for an increasing chain $x_1 \supseteq x_2 \cdots$ is $\bigcap_{i \in \omega} x_i$.

Following (8), we identify deterministic processes with continuous closure operators on $\mathcal{C}$, and non-deterministic ones with linear, continuous closure operators on $\mathcal{P}_u(\mathcal{C})$. Such closure operators can be represented by sets of fixed-points, *i.e.* $\{c \in \mathcal{C} \mid f(c) = c\}$ for $f : \mathcal{C} \longrightarrow \mathcal{C}$ a closure operator. For linear closure operators $f : \mathcal{P}_u(\mathcal{C}) \longrightarrow \mathcal{P}_u(\mathcal{C})$ on the Smyth powerdomain, we can use the set of singleton fixed-points, *i.e.* elements $c \in \mathcal{C}$ such that $f(\{\!|c|\!\}) = c$.

Theorem 6.3 (8) *Let $C(E)$ be a constraint system. $S \subseteq C(E)$ is the set of singleton fixed-points of a linear closure operator $f : \mathcal{P}_u(C(E)) \longrightarrow \mathcal{P}_u(C(E))$ iff it is Scott-compact. f is the linear extension of $\lambda x.(\uparrow x \cap S)$. Moreover, f is continuous iff for all chains $(c_i)_{i\in\omega}$, $S \cap \uparrow(\bigsqcup_{i\in\omega} c_i) = \bigcap_{i\in\omega}(S \cap \uparrow c_i)$.*

Given the set S_f of singleton fixed-points, the linear closure operator can be recovered through the equation $f(x) = \uparrow(x \cap S_f)$. ***From now on, we shall identify linear closure operators on the Smyth powerdomain of $C(E)$ with the Scott-compact subsets of $C(E)$.***

The following are semantic equations, compositional in style, defining inductively the sets of singleton fixed-points of a process. The process *tell*(c) is a fuction of x which returns $\{\!|c|\!\}\sqcup x$. The process *ask*$(c) \rightarrow A$ behaves like a function of x, which tests if x is above $\{\!|c|\!\}$ returning the result of A on c if that is the case, and $\{\!|x|\!\}$ otherwise. The parallel and choice operators correspond to intersection and union of the sets of fixed-points respectively. The hiding operator $\exists X.A$ is a kernel operator (behaves like a projection); the result of $\exists X.A$ on c should be $c\sqcup\exists_X(A(\exists_X c))$ (here $c\sqcup X$ means $\{c\sqcup x \mid x \in X\}$).

$$
\begin{aligned}
[\![tell(c)]\!] &= \uparrow c \\
[\![ask(c) \rightarrow A]\!] &= \overline{\uparrow c} \cup [\![A]\!] \\
[\![A \parallel B]\!] &= [\![A]\!] \cap [\![B]\!] \\
[\![A \oplus B]\!] &= [\![A]\!] \cup [\![B]\!] \\
[\![\exists X.A]\!] &= \exists_X^{-1}(\exists_X([\![A]\!])) \\
[\![p(Y)]\!] &= \exists_Y(\uparrow d_{XY} \cap [\![A]\!]) \quad \text{if } p(Y)\colon -A \in W
\end{aligned}
$$

Proposition 6.4

1. *If $\exists_X$ preserves Scott-compactness under inverse image then the set of fixed-points of a possibly infinite process is Scott compact.*

2. *If $\exists_X$ preserves Scott-compact opens then the set of fixed-points of a finite process is Lawson clopen.*

3. *If $\exists_X$ preserves Scott-compact opens then the set of fixed-points of a possibly infinite process is Lawson closed.*

Proof: By induction. Observe that $\uparrow c, \overline{\uparrow c}$ are Scott open and closed respectively, and hence Lawson subbasic open and Lawson clopen. Continuous functions preserve Scott compactness; also, Scott open and closed sets are preserved under inverse image. The open closed and clopen sets are closed under finite union and intersection. An infinite process is a result of recursive procedure calls; through unwindings these can be reduced inductively to countable intersections of finite processes of the form:

$$
\begin{aligned}
[\![p^0(Y)]\!] &= \uparrow tt \\
[\![p^{k+1}(Y)]\!] &= \exists_Y(\uparrow d_{XY} \cap \exists_Y(\uparrow d_{XY} \cap [\![p^k(Y)]\!])).
\end{aligned}
$$

In an algebraic lattice, countable intersections of Scott compact sets (Lawson closed) are compact (Lawson closed) respectively. □

It is interesting that the interpretation of *ask*() gives rise to a subset which is neither Scott-open nor Scott-closed (but it is Lawson clopen). Since the clopen subsets form a Boolean algebra, this would mean that we are extracting classical logic from the constraint system. It would be interesting to find out if a suitable (intuitionistic) interpretation could be found in the Scott topology.

6.4 Observables, Properties and Satisfacton

Given a process $P \in \mathcal{L}$ define the *observables* function $\mathcal{O} : \mathcal{L} \times \mathcal{K}(C) \to \mathcal{P}(C)$ as follows.

Definition 6.5 *For a process P and a constraint $c \in \mathcal{K}(C)$, the* observables of P at c, *denoted $\mathcal{O}(P)(c)$, is the linear continuous extension of:*

$$\mathcal{O}(P)(c) \quad = \quad \bigcap \{U \mid U \in Obs(P)(c)\}$$

to $\mathcal{P}_{\mathrm{u}}(\mathcal{C}(E))$.

Note that $\mathcal{O}(P)$ is monotone, *i.e.* $c \sqsubseteq d$ implies $\mathcal{O}(P)(c) \subseteq \mathcal{O}(P)(d)$, so the continuous extension exists.

A process P initiated in the store c *satisfies* the observation U (notation $P \models U$) iff $\mathcal{O}(P)(c) \subseteq U$. Given an arbitrary property $\Psi \subseteq C$, we say P satisfies Ψ iff

$$\forall c \in \mathcal{K}(C). \mathcal{O}(P)(c) \subseteq \Psi$$

This means that $\bigcup_{c \in \mathcal{K}(C)} \mathcal{O}(P)(c)$ (disjunction on all possible inputs) must be included in Ψ.

It can be shown that operational semantics (the observables) and the denotational semantics agree (as functions).

Theorem 6.6 (8) $\mathcal{O}(P) = [\![P]\!]$.

7 SEMANTIC PROPERTIES

Given a language $\mathcal{L}$ interpreted over a constraint system $\langle C, \sqsubseteq \rangle$, processes written in this language "compute" subsets of C (the *observables*). This is formally stated in terms of a function $\mathcal{O} : \mathcal{L} \times \mathcal{K}(C) \to \mathcal{P}_{\mathrm{u}}(C)$. Recall that each (well-formed) process expression determines some subset $\mathcal{O}(P)(c)$ of C. In Section 6.3 we shall give a more specific definition of the observables function, and also characterize those subsets of C which correspond to the process expressions.

The aim of this section is to describe the subsets of C which correspond to *safety*, *liveness* and *fairness* properties in the intuitive sense explained in Section 2.

7.1 Safety Properties

Intuitively, a safety property states that nothing bad must happen. The "thing" must be observable, and hence there must exist a corresponding finite observation $U \subseteq C$. It must also be "bad", that is, the process is prohibited from ever entering the set U, or, in other words, must remain entirely within the set-theoretic complement of the open set U.

Definition 7.1 *$S \subseteq C$ is a* safety property *iff S is a Scott closed set.*

Note that this means that S is a safety property iff there exists a (countable) family of finite observations $\{U_i \subseteq \mathcal{K}\Omega(C) \mid i \in \omega\}$ such that for all $c \in C$, $c \in S$ iff $\forall i \in \omega.\ c \not\models U_i$. The countability restriction is sufficient because we have an ω-algebraic lattice.

The following statement says: (1) a safety property contains those, and only those, constraints which do not entail the "bad" thing; (2) if ϕ is safe, then so are all formulae entailed by it; (3) "once lost, a safety property is never regained"; and (4) safety is inaccessible through directed sups.

Proposition 7.2 *Let S be a safety property.*

1. *$\phi \in S$ iff $\phi \not\vdash \psi$ some $\psi \in C$*

2. *If $\phi \in S$ and $\phi \vdash \psi$ then $\psi \in S$.*

3. *If $\phi \notin S$ then $\forall \psi \in C. \psi \vdash \phi$ we have $\psi \notin S$.*

4. *If $D \subseteq S$ then $\bigsqcup D \in S$.*

Proof: Direct from definitions. □

Example 7.3 *In Example 4.4, $c_1 = t \wedge c_2 = t$ is "bad", so $A_M^{\wedge} \setminus \{\uparrow(c_1 = t \wedge c_2 = t)\}$ is the corresponding safety property.*

Proposition 7.4 *The class of all safety properties over the constraint system $\mathcal{C}(E)$ is closed under finite unions and countable intersections.*

The following statement is an often repeated intuitive property of safety, which allows to deduce that a safety property holds for some system if it can be proved (inductively) that it holds for every finite computation.

Proposition 7.5 *Let S be a safety property in the constraint system $\mathcal{C}(E)$, P a closed term in $\mathcal{L}$. Then P satisfies S iff $\mathcal{O}(P)(c) \cap \mathcal{K}(C) \subseteq S$ for all $c \in \mathcal{K}(C)$.*

Proof:

1. ($\Rightarrow$) P satisfies S iff $\forall c \in \mathcal{K}(C).\mathcal{O}(P)(c) \subseteq S$, which certainly implies $\mathcal{O}(P)(c) \cap \mathcal{K}(C) \subseteq S$.

2. ($\Leftarrow$) Suppose for all $c \in \mathcal{K}(C)$, $\mathcal{O}(P)(c) \cap \mathcal{K}(C) \subseteq S$ then $Cl(\mathcal{O}(P)(c) \cap \mathcal{K}(C)) \subseteq Cl(S) = S$ where $Cl(\cdot)$ denotes Scott closure, and so $\mathcal{O}(P)(c) \cap \mathcal{K}(C) \subseteq S$ (because Scott closure is prefix closure and closure under directed sups).

□

7.2 Liveness Properties

On the other hand, a liveness property requires that something "good" happens. It is often the case that countable families of such good things are necessary, just consider the property "infinitely often a". Each "good" thing ϕ must be observable, and therefore there must exist a family $\{U_i \mid i \in \mathbf{N}\}$ of observations such that $\phi \models U_i$ for all i. This motivates the following:

Definition 7.6 *$L \subseteq C$ is a* finitary liveness *property iff L is a Scott open set. $L \subseteq C$ is an* infinitary liveness *property iff L is a Scott G_δ.*

Unlike safety, liveness properties may be infinitary. Note that for every finitary liveness property there exists a (countable) family of finite observations $\{U_i \subseteq \mathcal{K}\Omega(C) \mid i \in \omega\}$ such that for all $c \in C$, $c \in L$ iff $\exists i \in \omega \,.\, c \models U_i$. On the other hand, for an infinitary property there exists a countable family of finitary liveness properties $\{L_i \mid i \in \omega\}$ such that for all $c \in C$, $c \in L$ iff $\forall i \in \omega \,.\, c \models L_i$.

Finitary liveness can be useful to model properties such as *odd*(n) where $n \in \omega$ in the flat domain (we either observe $\uparrow 1$, or $\uparrow 3$, etc).

Example 7.7 *In Example 4.17, for a process to enter its critical section is a "good" thing, and the set* $\uparrow(e_1 \geq 1)$ *is therefore a (finitary) liveness property stating "process no 1 entered its critical section at least once". An infinitary liveness property ("process no 1 has entered its critical section infinitely often") is* $\bigcap_{i \in \omega} \uparrow(e_1 \geq i)$.

The following statement says: (1) if ϕ is "good', then so are all formulae which entail it ("once gained, never lost"); (2) every finitary liveness property must be determined at finite time; and (3) safety is a notion dual to finitary liveness.

Proposition 7.8 *Let L be a liveness property.*

1. *If* $\phi \in L$ *and* $\psi \vdash \phi$ *then* $\psi \in L$.

2. *If L is finitary then* $\forall \psi \in L, \exists \phi \in \mathcal{K}(C)$ *such that* $\psi \vdash \phi$*;*

3. *Every safety property is a complement of a finitary liveness property, and vice-versa.*

Proof: Direct from definitions. □

Proposition 7.9 *The class of all finitary liveness properties over the constraint system* $\mathcal{C}(E)$ *is closed under countable unions and finite intersections. The class of all liveness properties is closed under finite intersections and unions.*

7.3 Fairness Properties

Fairness properties are viewed either as a subclass of liveness. We define a fairness property to be a subset of the maximal elements of $\mathcal{C}(E) \setminus \{ff\}$ (maximal after ff has been removed). However, not every such subset corresponds to fairness in the intuitive sense – only those subsets whose $\downarrow$-closure includes *all* the compact elements $\mathcal{K}(C)$ are. This is to guarantee that: (1) every terminating computation is fair; (2) every finite computation has some fair computation above it.

Definition 7.10 $F \subseteq Max(C \setminus \{ff\})$ *is a* fairness *property iff F is a Scott* G_δ *set dense in* $C \setminus \{ff\}$.

Example 7.11 *In Example 4.6, the set of lists which contain a finite number of b and an infinite number of a is not a fairness property (because the list* b^{n+1} *does not have a fair computation above), while the set of lists containing an infinite number of both a and b is a fairness property.*

We have the following statement directly from definition.

Proposition 7.12 *Let F be a fairness property. Then for all $\psi \in \mathcal{K}(C)$ there exists $\phi \in F$ such that $\phi \vdash \psi$.*

Proof: By maximality and density. □

8 CONCLUSION AND FURTHER WORK

We have set out a basic framework for an axiomatic presentation of constraint systems, derived their semantic model, interpreted a process language in it, and characterized certain properties semantically.

Note that not all semantic properties can be expressed syntactically – only a subclass of finitary liveness corresponding to the Scott-compact opens is. The restriction to the compact-opens is a consequence of Stone duality, and is rather severe. We should point out, however, that the compact-opens are simply "building blocks", from which the more general properties can be built. We have shown how these "building blocks" can be composed semantically; what seems to be needed is a suitable syntax. As already suggested in (2), we would need least and greatest fixpoints as modalities of formulae, interpreted as $\bigsqcup_{i \in \omega} \phi_i$ and $\bigsqcap_{i \in \omega} \phi_i$. We are currently investigating a version of Stone duality for a formal system allowing fixpoint operators. The reason we have not considered it in this paper is that finite axiomatization is no longer sufficient. We would require an enhancement of the theory with suitable modalities and an axiomatization in terms of schemas. Finally, an investigation of the correspondence between the constructed concurrent constraint system and the extended elementary constraint system would have to be carried out.

It should be mentioned that we have considered a distributive lattice structure, partly because distributivity is essential to Stone duality. One can work with semilattices, which are more common in concurrent constraint programming, by suitably extending them. We have not included implication – complete Heyting algebras admit implication, but unfortunately implication does not preserve compactness, and it is not preserved by morphisms. A further point worth investigating is the relationship between implication and guards.

9 ACKNOWLEDGEMENTS

The author would like to acknowledge the AP1 group at CWI, especially Jaco de Bakker, Jan Rutten, Katuscia Palamidessi, Frank de Boer and Jeroen Warmerdam for a stimulating environment. Paul Taylor's diagrams package was used to produce the figures in this paper.

References

[1] S. Abramsky. Domain theory in logical form. In *Proceedings, Annual Symposium on Logic in Computer Science*, pages 47–53. IEEE CS, 1987.

[2] S. Abramsky. Domain theory in logical form. *Annals of Pure and Applied Logic*, 51:1–77, 1991.

[3] B. Davey and H. Priestley. *Introduction to Lattices and Order.* Cambridge University Press, 1990.

[4] F. de Boer and C. Palamidessi. A fully abstract model for concurrent constraint programming. In S. Abramsky and T. Maibaum, editors, *Proc. of TAPSOFT/CAAP*, volume 493 of *Lecture Notes in Computer Science*, pages 296–319. Springer-Verlag, 1991.

[5] N. Francez. *Fairness.* Springer-Verlag, 1986.

[6] G. Gierz, K. Hofmann, K. Keimel, J. Lawson, M. Mislove, and D. Scott. *A Compendium of Continuous Lattices.* Springer-Verlag, 1980.

[7] C. Gunter and D. Scott. Semantic domains. In J. van Leeuwen, editor, *Handbook of Theoretical Computer Science.* Elsevier Science Publishers, 1990.

[8] R. Jagadeesan, V. A. Saraswat, and V. Shanbogue. Angelic non-determinism in concurrent constraint programming. Technical report, System Sciences Laboratory, Xerox PARC, 1991.

[9] P. T. Johnstone. *Stone Spaces.* Cambridge University Press, 1982.

[10] M. Z. Kwiatkowska. Event fairness and non-interleaving concurrency. *Formal Aspects of Computing*, 1(3):213–228, 1989.

[11] M. Z. Kwiatkowska. Survey of fairness notions. *Information and Software Technology*, 31(7):371–386, 1989.

[12] M. Z. Kwiatkowska. Defining process fairness for non-interleaving concurrency. In K. Nori and Veni-Madhavan, editors, *Foundations of Software Technology and Theoretical Computer Science*, volume 472 of *Lecture Notes in Computer Science*, pages 286–300. Springer-Verlag, 1990.

[13] M. Z. Kwiatkowska. On topological characterization of behavioural properties. In G. Reed, A. Roscoe, and R. Wachter, editors, *Topology and Category Theory in Computer Science*, pages 153–177. Oxford University Press, 1991.

[14] L. Lamport. Proving the correctness of multiprocess programs. *IEEE Transactions on Software Engineering*, SE-3(2):125–143, 1977.

[15] Z. Manna and A. Pnueli. A hierarchy of temporal properties. In *Proceedings, 9th ACM Symposium on Principles of Distributed Computing*, pages 377–408. ACM Press, 1990.

[16] D. Park. Concurrency and automata on infinite sequences. In P. Deussen, editor, *Theoretical Computer Science*, volume 104 of *Lecture Notes in Computer Science*, pages 167–183. Springer-Verlag, 1981.

[17] G. D. Plotkin. Post-graduate lecture notes in advanced domain theory. Incorporating the "Pisa Notes", 1981.

[18] V. Saraswat and M. Rinard. Concurrent constraint programming. In *Proc. of the seventeenth ACM Symposium on Principles of Programming Languages*, pages 232–245. ACM, New York, 1990.

[19] V. Saraswat, M. Rinard, and P. Panangaden. A fully abstract semantics for concurrent constraint programming. In *Proc. of the eighteenth ACM Symposium on Principles of Programming Languages.* ACM, New York, 1991.

[20] H. Simmons. Frames: the point-free approach to topology. Lecture notes for a Logic for IT course, 1989.

[21] M. B. Smyth. Powerdomains and predicate transformers: A topological view. In *Automata, Languages and Programming*, volume 154 of *Lecture Notes in Computer Science.* Springer, 1983.

[22] S. Vickers. *Topology via Logic*, volume 5 of *Cambridge Tracts in Theoretical Computer Science.* Cambridge University Press, 1989.

Full Abstraction and Unnested Recursion

Michael W. Mislove*
Department of Mathematics
Tulane University
New Orleans, LA 70118

and

Frank J. Oles
Mathematical Sciences Department
IBM T.J. Watson Research Center
Yorktown Heights, NY 10598

Abstract We begin with the assumption that we are given a basic programming language L without identifiers (i.e., variables), which is, nonetheless, fairly expressive. We also assume L has been provided with both an operational semantics and a denotational semantics. Furthermore, the denotational semantics is adequate and fully abstract with respect to the operational semantics. After clarifying exactly what these assumptions entail,

1. we discuss what it means to extend L algebraically to a language $L[X]$ by the addition of identifiers,
2. we discuss the semantics of $L[X]$ in the context of possibly self-referential environments (i.e., systems of recursive definitions of the identifiers), and
3. we show that extremely mild topological assumptions about the operational model ensure that adequacy and full abstraction of the denotational semantics of $L[X]$ with respect to its operational semantics follow automatically from the corresponding results for L.

Essentially, we will assume that the operational model is a Hausdorff space, and the operational process of unwinding a recursive program converges to its operational meaning. Some work has been done on the issues we are confronting, but from the standpoint of fair unwindings of recursive constructs. That work indicates that full abstraction results are not generally to be expected in all situations. Our goal, however, is to establish that full abstraction results are indeed available in a very general setting.

Keywords Full abstraction, adequacy, algebraic semantics, homomorphism, algebraic poset.

*Work partially supported by the Office of Naval Research

Contents

0 Introduction

If L is a programming language without variables, then an important question is whether it is possible to extend a semantic model for L to one for the extended language $L[X]$ which includes identifiers (i.e., variables) and, implicitly, recursive constructs. Indeed, it has become increasingly popular in research on ***uniform languages*** – ones whose syntax is given in terms of uninterpreted atomic actions, to focus on a possible denotational model for the ***basic language*** – the one without variables or identifiers. Most researchers believe it is a simple matter to build a model supporting the extended language which includes recursive constructs once a model in a suitable cartesian closed category for the basic language is described. In this paper, we confront this question and discuss precisely (1) what it means to extend the basic language to one including variables and recursion, (2) what is meant by an ***adequate*** and a ***fully abstract*** semantics for the basic language and the extended language, and (3) how, under mild conditions on the operational and denotational models for the basic language, adequacy and full abstraction for the models of the extended language can be guaranteed if these properties are satisfied by the models for the basic language.

Previous work in this area has provided negative results for the case that one wants to treat recursive constructs involving nondeterministic choice in a "fair" manner. For example, in the program $\mu x.(a; x+b; x)$, a fair operational semantics would discard those infinite execution sequences in which from some point onwards only one branch is chosen. It is shown in [AP86] that there are example languages such that there is no denotational semantics that is fully abstract with respect to a given fair operational semantics. The results in [BKO88] also address related issues.

In this paper we also are concerned with the issue of full abstraction, but we do not pursue fair semantic models for recursive constructs. Instead we content ourselves with results which allow one to build a fully abstract model for a language including recursive constructs from one for the language without variables, but with no special assumptions of how recursive constructs are unwound. In the process of establishing our results, we make precise definitions of adequacy and full abstraction in general settings, and we show how universal algebra provides an elegant setting in which to frame our results.

Our presentation assumes we are dealing with algebraic posets as the denotational models for the languages we consider. Thus, the results have wide applicability, including all models with which we are familiar that are algebraic cpo's. In particular, the results here indicate how identifiers and guarded recursion can be added to the language studied in [MiO92a] and [MiO92b]. All the proofs apply to denotational models that are algebraic bounded complete sup-semilattices, so the results also apply to the language studied in [MaO92], which is esssentially the same as the language given in [Oles87]. Complete ultra-metric spaces have been often used as denotational models of programming languages; we believe that the results and proofs presented here can readily be modified to apply to such models, with a dense denotable set of meanings playing the role of the compact elements in an algebraic poset.

The organization of the paper is as follows. In the next section we state the central problem in mathematical terms. This includes defining precisely how we view the language $L[X]$ with variables, given a basic language L without variables, what we expect in the way of an operational model for L, and how to extend it to one for $L[X]$. Section 2 then discusses how to extend a denotational model for L to one for $L[X]$. The third section looks at the operational implications of our topological assumptions about the operational model. The final two sections then discuss the adequacy and the full abstraction questions for the denotational model for $L[X]$.

1 The Problem

It is advantageous to present programming languages as algebras, both for reasons of elegance and to take advantage of the well-developed concepts of universal algebra in technical arguments. For simplicity, we assume we are given a basic language L which is presented as an Ω-algebra for a one-sorted (as opposed to a many-sorted) signature Ω. There is no need to make any assumption about exactly what operators are in Ω. There does not appear to be any obstacle to extend the results here to the many-sorted case. We will *not* assume that L is an initial or free Ω-algebra. In particular, as is often the case, L may be an Ω-algebra satisfying some set of equations. This added generality means that the proofs are somewhat more elaborate than might be anticipated.

If O is the set of *observations* we can make of programs in L, then the *operational semantics* of L is some fixed *behavior function* $\mathcal{B}_L: L \to O$. Typically the behavior function is defined using some sort of transition system or rewriting system, but where it comes from isn't the issue here. On the other hand, the set D of *denotational meanings* for L is an Ω-algebra, and the *denotational semantics* of L is a function $\mathcal{M}_L: L \to D$. The idea that the denotational semantics be compositional is captured by requiring $\mathcal{M}_L$ to be a homomorphism. We will assume that $\mathcal{M}_L$ is *adequate* with respect to $\mathcal{B}_L$, i.e., if two terms of L are denotationally equal according to $\mathcal{M}_L$, then they are observationally equal according to $\mathcal{B}_L$.

To handle recursive definitions eventually, D should be a poset with a minimum element, $\perp$, and D should be a continuous Ω-algebra in the sense that the interpretations of the operators in Ω should be Scott continuous (i.e., preserve sup's of directed sets when they exist). It is *not* necessary to assume that D is a cpo. To ensure that L is sufficiently expressive, we require that D be an algebraic poset (i.e., the compact elements below an element $d \in D$ form a directed set whose supremum is d) and that $K(D)$, the set of compact elements of D, be a subset of the image of $\mathcal{M}_L$. Since $\perp$ is a compact element of D, there exists $b_L \in L$ such that $\mathcal{M}_L b_L = \perp$; this program b_L is what we refer to as the *undefined program*. For more on algebraic posets, see [M91], [MiO92a], and [MiO92b].

We would like the various spaces of continuous functions constructed from D to again be algebraic posets. The most elegant way to do this is to assume that D is an object in a Cartesian closed category of algebraic posets, with Scott continuous maps as morphisms, such that D^S (ordered pointwise) is in the category for any set S. The category of algebraic complete lattices, the category of SFP-objects, the category of Scott domains, and the category of algebraic bounded complete sup-semilattices are all examples of such a category. The last-mentioned category is not a category of cpo's.

Next, we will establish some notation. Let S be a set and let A be an Ω-algebra. The identity homomorphism on A will be denoted $1_A: A \to A$. Let $T_\Omega[S]$ be a free Ω-algebra generated by S. For notational simplicity, we assume that the function $S \to T_\Omega[S]$ that is the unit of the adjunction is actually an inclusion map $S \hookrightarrow T_\Omega[S]$. Just as in the construction of rings of polynomials, S can be added freely to any Ω-algebra A by letting the polynomial algebra $A[S]$ be a coproduct of A and $T_\Omega[S]$. A proof of the existence of coproducts of Ω-algebras and some applications of coprducts to the theory of programming languages can be found in [W90]. Without loss of generality, we assume A is a subalgebra of $A[S]$ and the coproduct injection $A \to A[S]$ is the inclusion $A \hookrightarrow A[S]$. As long as $A \cap S = \emptyset$, which we always tacitly assume whenever it is convenient, we can arrange matters so that the restriction of the coproduct injection $T_\Omega[S] \to A[S]$ to S is the inclusion map $S \hookrightarrow A[S]$. It is easy to see that the polynomial algebra $A[S]$ satisfies the following universal mapping property: for each Ω-algebra B, each homomorphism $\alpha: A \to B$, and each function $f: S \to B$, there exists a unique homomorphism $\alpha[f]: A[S] \to B$ such that the diagram

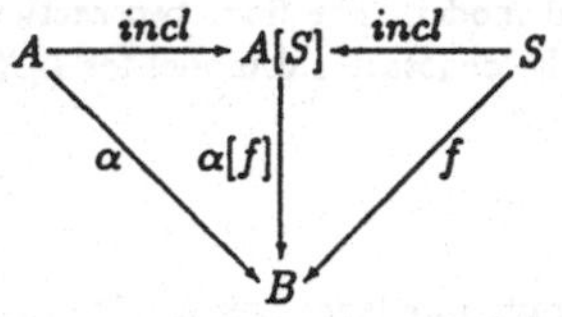

commutes.

Additionally, we assume that $\mathcal{M}_L$ is fully abstract with respect to $\mathcal{B}_L$. The definition of full abstraction requires the concept of a *context*, i.e., "a program with a hole in it." To be precise about it (and we do indeed need to be precise about it, as the proof of Proposition 5.1 shows), the Ω-algebra of contexts is nothing more than the algebra of polynomials $L[*]$ ($= L[\{*\}]$) in one indeterminate $*$. Let $l \in L$. The universal mapping property for polynomial algebras gives a unique homomorphism $1_L[* \mapsto l]: L[*] \to L$ such that

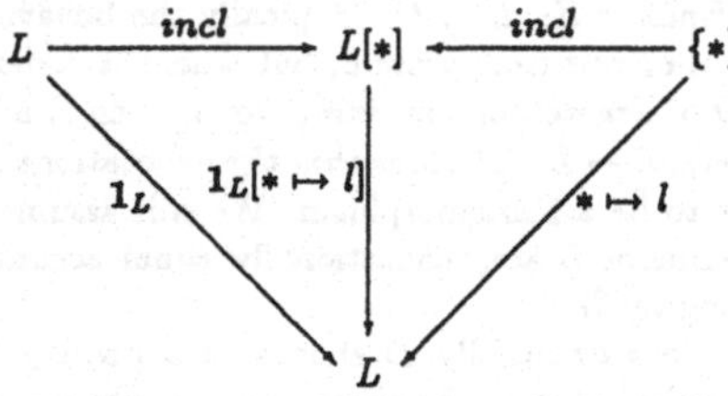

commutes. Substitution of $l \in L$ for $*$ in a context $C \in L[*]$ is usually written $C[l]$ and is defined to be $C[l] = 1_L[* \mapsto l]C$. Thus, we say $\mathcal{M}_L$ is *fully abstract* with respect to $\mathcal{B}_L$ if, for all $l, l' \in L$ such that $\mathcal{M}_L l \neq \mathcal{M}_L l'$, there exists some context $C \in L[*]$ such that $\mathcal{B}_L(C[l]) \neq \mathcal{B}_L(C[l'])$.

Let X be a set of identifiers such that $L \cap X = \emptyset$. The polynomial algebra $L[X]$ is what we get when we extend L by adding the identifiers in X.

Terms in $L[X]$ cannot in general be assigned meanings in either O or D without an environment that provides meanings for the identifiers. The set of *simple syntactic environments* is defined to be $E = L^X$, the set of all functions from X to L. The set of *recursive syntactic environments* is $E[X] = L[X]^X$. The set of *semantic environments* is the algebraic poset D^X of all functions from X to D, ordered pointwise.

There is a straighforward extension of the operational semantics $\mathcal{B}_L: L \to O$ to an operational semantics $\mathcal{B}': L[X] \times E \to O$, which can be derived as follows. Given a simple syntactic environment $e: X \to L$, the universal property of $L[X]$ means there is a unique homomorphism $1_L[e]: L[X] \to L$ such the diagram

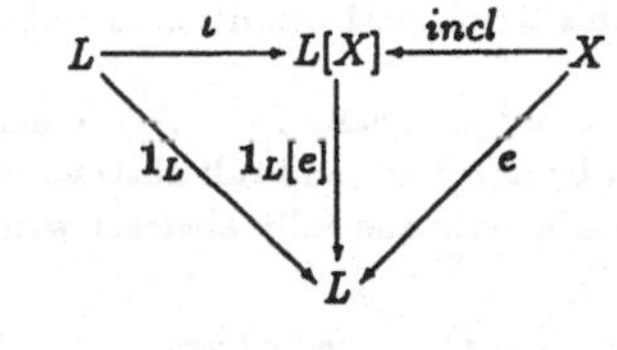

commutes, where $\iota: L \to L[X]$ be the inclusion homomorphism. Thus, $1_L[e]$ evaluates a polynomial in $L[X]$ with the values specified by $e \in E$. So, we can define the mapping $\mathcal{B}': L[X] \times E \to O$ by $\mathcal{B}'\langle p, e\rangle = \mathcal{B}_L(1_L[e]p)$. An alternative characterization of $\mathcal{B}'$ will be given in Proposition 3.2. It might be tempting to assume that there is also a straightforward extension of the operational semantics $\mathcal{B}_L: L \to O$ to a function from $L[X] \times E[X]$ to O, but this does not seem to be always possible, especially in languages supporting nondeterministic choice, where only so-called *guarded recursion* is operationally tractable. For example, see [BW90]. Thus, we will assume that there is a set $E'[X] \subseteq E[X]$ of acceptable recursive definitions such that the image of the injection $e \mapsto \iota \circ e: E \to E[X]$ is a subset of $E'[X]$, and there is an operational semantics

$$\mathcal{B}_{L[X]}: L[X] \times E'[X] \to O.$$

A discussion of the precise sense in which $\mathcal{B}_{L[X]}$ must be related to $\mathcal{B}_L$ is the subject of the rest of this section.

When we extend L to the language $L[X]$ that supports recursion, we want to say that the operational semantics of a recursive program is obtained by unwinding the recursion and is consistent with the operational semantics of L. Thus, we want to be able to assert that, for every recursive program p with a given recursive syntactic environment $g \in E'[X]$, there is a sequence of elements of L whose succesive operational meanings look increasingly like, i.e., *converges to*, the operational semantics of $\langle p, g\rangle$. Just to be able to say this, we make the mild assumption that O is a topological space in which convergent nets have unique limit points, i.e., O is a *Hausdorff space*.

Actually, a program $p \in L[X]$ can be unwound in a step-by-step way in the context of an arbitrary recursive syntactic environment $r \in E[X]$. This can be accomplished by using the unique homomorphism $\iota[r]: L[X] \to L[X]$ that makes

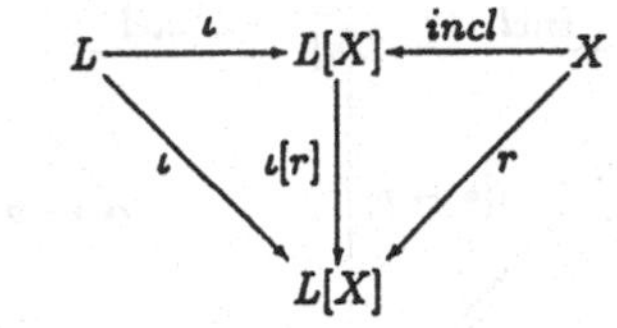

a commutative diagram. Then one step of recursive unwinding is accomplished by evaluating $\iota[r]p$, two steps by evaluating $\iota[r](\iota[r]p)$, and so on.

Let $b_E: X \to L$ be the simple syntactic environment which assigns the undefined program b_L to every $x \in X$. Then the evaluation of $1_L[b_E]p$ replaces each occurrence of every identifier in $p \in L[X]$ by the undefined program b_L. Hence, to obtain a sequence of elements of L that succesively operationally resemble p more and more in the context of a recursive syntactic environment r, take the sequence

$$1_L[b_E]p,\ 1_L[b_E](\iota[r]p),\ 1_L[b_E]((\iota[r])^2p),\ \cdots,\ 1_L[b_E]((\iota[r])^np),\ \cdots.$$

We can now state the precise topological condition that must relate $\mathcal{B}_L$ and $\mathcal{B}_{L[X]}$ in order to capture the intuition that operational semantics of a recursive program be determined by the gradual unwinding of the recursive definitions provided by its environment: for all $p \in L[X]$ and $g \in E'[X]$,

$$\mathcal{B}_{L[X]}\langle p, g\rangle = \lim_{n\to\infty} \mathcal{B}_L(1_L[b_E]((\iota[g])^n p)).$$

We will see in Theorem 3.4 that this topological condition is sufficient to imply that $\mathcal{B}_{L[X]}$ agrees with $\mathcal{B}'$ on $L[X] \times E$.

The problem is then to generate automatically from $\mathcal{M}_L$ a denotational semantics $\mathcal{M}_{L[X]}$ for $L[X]$, to say clearly what is meant by adequacy and full abstraction, and finally to prove that the dervived denotational semantics is adequate and fully abstract with respect to $\mathcal{B}_{L[X]}$.

2 Denotational Semantics of $L[X]$

Let $[D^X \to D]$ be the collection of *Scott continuous* maps from the algebraic poset of semantic environments to D, ordered pointwise. Since D is a continuous Ω-algebra, $[D^X \to D]$ is also a continuous Ω-algebra, with operations defined pointwise. By ignoring the semantic environment, it is easy to get a continuous homomorphism $\kappa_D\colon D \to [D^X \to D]$ given by $\kappa_D dh = d$, where $d \in D$ and $h \in D^X$. Let $v_D\colon X \to [D^X \to D]$ be the evaluation function $v_D xh = hx$, where $x \in X$ and $h \in D^X$. Although there is an obvious difficulty in assigning terms in $L[X]$ denotational meanings in D, there is no problem in making $[D^X \to D]$ the target of a semantic homomorphism by letting

$$\mathcal{M}_{L[X]}\colon L[X] \to [D^X \to D]$$

be the unique homomorphism that makes

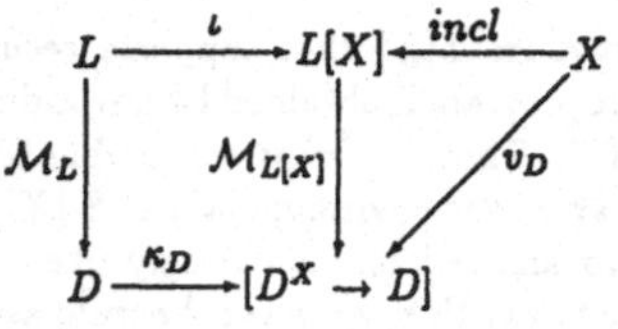

a commutative diagram.

Again using the universal mapping property for $L[*]$, substitution of $p \in L[X]$ for $*$ in a context $C \in L[*]$ is defined to be $C[p] = \iota[* \mapsto p]C$.

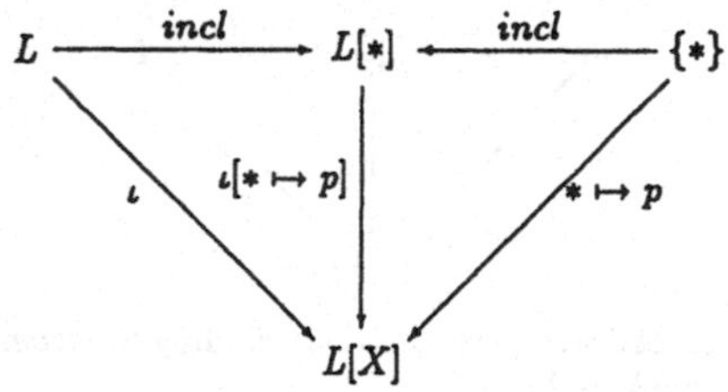

Now we can formulate the definitions of adequacy and full abstraction for $L[X]$ by varying the corresponding definitions L to take syntactic environments into account.

Definition

1. $\mathcal{M}_{L[X]}$ is *adequate* with respect to $\mathcal{B}_{L[X]}$ if, for all $p, p' \in L[X]$, $\mathcal{M}_{L[X]}p = \mathcal{M}_{L[X]}p'$ implies that, for all $g \in E'[X]$, $\mathcal{B}_{L[X]}\langle p, g\rangle = \mathcal{B}_{L[X]}\langle p', g\rangle$.

2. $\mathcal{M}_{L[X]}$ is *fully abstract* with respect to $\mathcal{B}_{L[X]}$ if, for all $p, p' \in L[X]$, $\mathcal{M}_{L[X]}p \neq \mathcal{M}_{L[X]}p'$ implies that there exist $C \in L[*]$ and $g \in E'[X]$ such that $\mathcal{B}_{L[X]}\langle C[p], g\rangle \neq \mathcal{B}_{L[X]}\langle C[p'], g\rangle$.

3 Operational Semantics of $L[X]$

Suppose S, U, and V are sets. If $f: S \to V^U$, then by $\overline{f}: S \times U \to V$ we mean the uncurried version of f given by $\overline{f}\langle s, u\rangle = fsu$. If $g: S \to V$, then $g^U: S^U \to V^U$ is just composition with g: $g^U h = g \circ h$, for all $h: U \to S$.

The first order of business in this section will be to prove Proposition 3.2, an alternative characterization of the natural operational semantics $\mathcal{B}': L[X] \times E \to O$ of $L[X]$ in the context of simple syntactic environments.

The set L^E is naturally an Ω-algebra in which the operations are defined pointwise. The function $\kappa_L: L \to L^E$ that assigns to each element of L the corresponding constant function (so that $\kappa_L le = l$) is then a homomorphism. By combining κ_L with the function $v_L: X \to L^E$ that looks up the value assigned to an identifier by an environment (so that $v_L xe = ex$), we get a unique homomorphism $\sigma: L[X] \to L^E$ such that

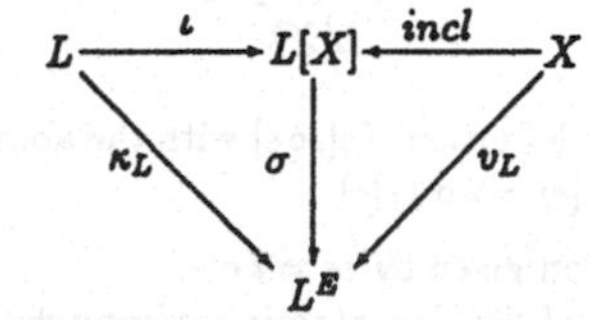

commutes.

Our first lemma will be used repeatedly.

Lemma 3.1 *For all $p \in L[X]$ and $e \in E$,*

$$\sigma pe = 1_L[e]p.$$

Proof Let $\sigma': E \to L^{L[X]}$ be defined by reversing the arguments of σ: $\sigma' ep = \sigma pe$. We claim that, for every $e \in E$, $\sigma' e: L[X] \to L$ is a homomorphism. To see this, suppose ω is an n-ary operator and $p_1, \ldots, p_n \in L[X]$. Then

$$\begin{aligned} \sigma' e(\omega_{L[X]}\langle p_1, \ldots, p_n\rangle) &= \sigma(\omega_{L[X]}\langle p_1, \ldots, p_n\rangle)e \\ &= \omega_{L^E}\langle \sigma p_1, \ldots, \sigma p_n\rangle e \\ &= \omega_L\langle \sigma p_1 e, \ldots, \sigma p_n e\rangle \\ &= \omega_L\langle \sigma' e p_1, \ldots, \sigma' e p_n\rangle. \end{aligned}$$

Next we check that $\sigma' e$ satisfies the universal mapping property that defines $1_L[e]$. For $l \in L$, we have $\sigma' el = \sigma le = \kappa_L le = l$. For $x \in X$, $\sigma' ex = \sigma xe = v_L xe = ex$. Thus, $\sigma' e = 1_L[e]$, from which the lemma follows immediately. □

Proposition 3.2 $\mathcal{B}' = \mathcal{B}_L \circ \overline{\sigma}$.

Proof Suppose $p \in L[X]$ and $e \in E$. Then $\mathcal{B}'\langle p, e\rangle = \mathcal{B}_L(1_L[e]p) = \mathcal{B}_L(\sigma pe) = (\mathcal{B}_L \circ \overline{\sigma})\langle p, e\rangle$. □

The next lemma says that, after performing a recursive unwinding using a simple syntactic substitution, a second unwinding has no effect (for the intuitive reason that there are no occurrences of identifiers left after the first unwinding).

Lemma 3.3 *Suppose $r \in E[X]$ and $e \in E$. Then $\iota[r] \circ \iota[\iota \circ e] = \iota \circ 1_L[e]$.*

Proof Consider the commutative diagram

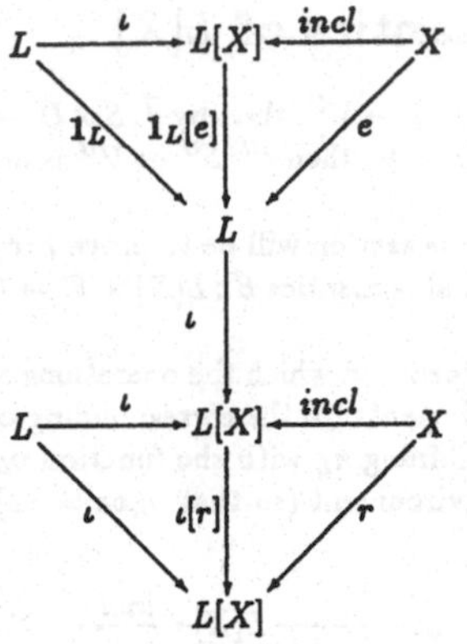

It is clear from a comparison of the definition of $\iota[\iota \circ e]$ with the above diagram that $\iota[\iota \circ e] = \iota \circ 1_L[e]$. Hence, $\iota[r] \circ \iota[\iota \circ e] = (\iota[r] \circ \iota) \circ 1_L[e] = \iota \circ 1_L[e]$. □

Let $\epsilon: E \to E'[X]$ be the injection given by $\epsilon e = \iota \circ e$.

To relate $\mathcal{B}_{L[X]}$ to $\mathcal{B}_L$ in the case of simple syntactic environments, we have the following theorem.

Theorem 3.4 *The diagram*

$$
\begin{array}{ccc}
L[X] \times E & \xrightarrow{\ 1_{L[X]} \times \epsilon\ } & L[X] \times E'[X] \\
\bar{\sigma} \downarrow & & \downarrow \mathcal{B}_{L[X]} \\
L & \xrightarrow{\ \mathcal{B}_L\ } & O
\end{array}
$$

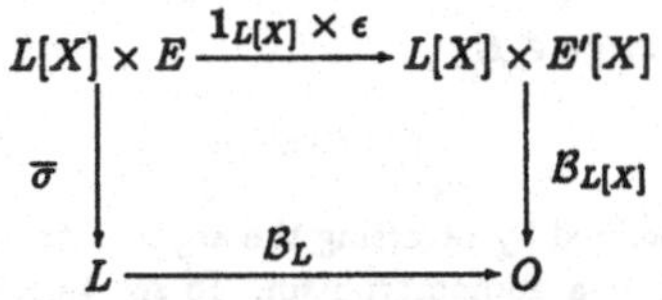

commutes.

Proof Let $p \in L[X]$ and $e: X \to L$. By Lemmas 3.1 and 3.3, and the fact that $1_L[b_E] \circ \iota = 1_L$, we have

$$\mathcal{B}_{L[X]}\langle p, \iota \circ e\rangle = \lim_{n \to \infty} \mathcal{B}_L(1_L[b_E]((\iota[\iota \circ e])^n p)) = \mathcal{B}_L(1_L[b_E]((\iota \circ 1_L[e])p)) = \mathcal{B}_L(1_L[e]p) = \mathcal{B}_L(\bar{\sigma}\langle p, e\rangle).$$

□

4 Adequacy

By defining operations pointwise, we see that D^X and D^E are continuous Ω-algebras. Clearly, the homomorphism $\mathcal{M}_L: L \to D$ induces homomorphisms $\mathcal{M}_L^X: E = L^X \to D^X$ and $\mathcal{M}_L^E: L^E \to D^E$.

Let

$$Ap: [D^X \to D] \times D^X \to D$$

be functional application: $Ap\langle m, h\rangle = mh$, for $m \in [D^X \to D]$ and $h \in D^X$.

The various functions that enter into the proof that $\mathcal{M}_{L[X]}$ is adequate and fully abstract with respect to $\mathcal{B}_{L[X]}$ are shown in the diagram

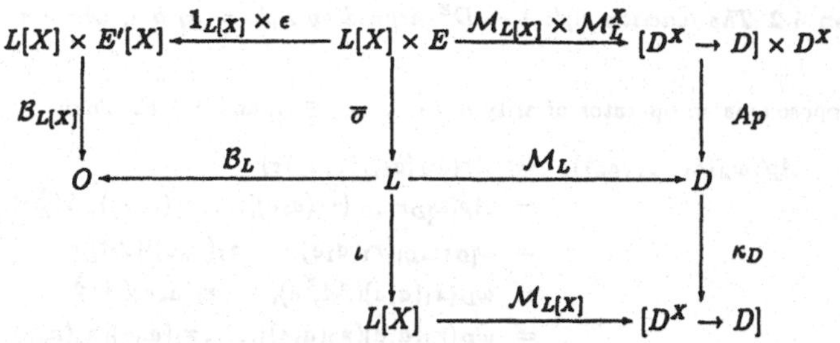

We already know two of the squares are commutative. In this section we will show the other square also commutes, which turns out to be the main result needed to prove adequacy.

Let

$$\pi_1\colon ([D^X \to D] \times D^X) \to [D^X \to D]$$

and

$$\pi_2\colon ([D^X \to D] \times D^X) \to D^X$$

be the projections onto the two factors in the product. The key to proving that the remaining square commutes is the introduction of the Ω-algebra

$$A = \{a \in (([D^X \to D] \times D^X)^E \mid \pi_2 \circ a = \mathcal{M}_L^X\},$$

in which the homomorphism $\mathcal{M}_L^X$ plays a central role. Let ω be an operator of arity n. The interpretion of the n-ary operation ω_A on A is defined by

$$\omega_A\langle a_1, \cdots, a_n\rangle e = \langle \omega_{[D^X \to D]}\langle \pi_1(a_1 e), \cdots, \pi_1(a_n e)\rangle, \mathcal{M}_L^X e\rangle,$$

where $a_1, \cdots, a_n \in A$ and $e \in E$.

Proposition 4.1 *Let the function $\mathcal{H}\colon L[X] \to A$ be defined by $\mathcal{H}pe = \langle \mathcal{M}_{L[X]}p, \mathcal{M}_L^X e\rangle$, where $p \in L[X]$ and $e \in E$. Then $\mathcal{H}$ is a homomorphism.*

Proof Let ω be an operator of arity n, $p_1, \ldots, p_n \in L[X]$, and $e \in E$. We then have the following computation:

$$\begin{aligned} \mathcal{H}(\omega_{L[X]}\langle p_1, \ldots, p_n\rangle)e &= \langle \mathcal{M}_{L[X]}(\omega_{L[X]}\langle p_1, \ldots, p_n\rangle), \mathcal{M}_L^X e\rangle \\ &= \langle \omega_{[D^X \to D]}\langle \mathcal{M}_{L[X]}p_1, \ldots, \mathcal{M}_{L[X]}p_n\rangle, \mathcal{M}_L^X e\rangle \\ &= \langle \omega_{[D^X \to D]}\langle \pi_1(\mathcal{H}p_1 e), \ldots, \pi_1(\mathcal{H}p_n e)\rangle, \mathcal{M}_L^X e\rangle \\ &= \omega_A\langle \mathcal{H}p_1, \ldots, \mathcal{H}p_n\rangle e. \end{aligned}$$

□

Let $\mathcal{Q}\colon L[X] \to ([D^X \to D] \times D^X)^E$ be defined by the commutative diagram

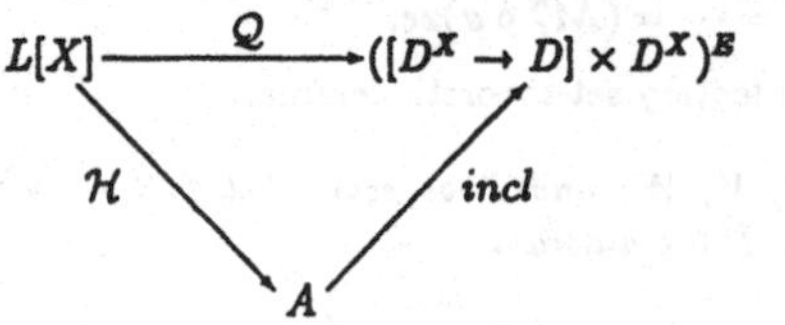

There does not seem to be any way to make $([D^X \to D] \times D^X)^E$ into an Ω-algebra so that A becomes a subalgebra. In a similar vein, the next proposition is a bit surprising because the application function

$$Ap\colon [D^X \to D] \times D^X \to D$$

does not appear to be a homomorphism.

Proposition 4.2 *The function $Ap': A \to D^E$ defined by $Ap'a = Ap \circ a$, where $a \in A$, is a homomorphism.*

Proof Suppose ω is an operator of arity n, $a_1, \ldots, a_n \in A$, and $e \in E$. Then

$$\begin{aligned}
Ap'(\omega_A\langle a_1,\ldots,a_n\rangle)e &= Ap(\omega_A\langle a_1,\ldots,a_n\rangle e)\\
&= Ap\langle \omega_{[D^X \to D]}\langle \pi_1(a_1e),\ldots,\pi_1(a_ne)\rangle, \mathcal{M}_L^X e\rangle\\
&= \omega_{[D^X \to D]}\langle \pi_1(a_1e),\ldots,\pi_1(a_ne)\rangle(\mathcal{M}_L^X e)\\
&= \omega_D\langle \pi_1(a_1e)(\mathcal{M}_L^X e),\ldots,\pi_1(a_ne)(\mathcal{M}_L^X e)\rangle\\
&= \omega_D\langle \pi_1(a_1e)(\pi_2(a_1e)),\ldots,\pi_1(a_ne)(\pi_2(a_ne))\rangle\\
&= \omega_D\langle Ap(a_1e),\ldots,Ap(a_ne)\rangle\\
&= \omega_D\langle Ap'a_1e,\ldots,Ap'a_ne\rangle\\
&= \omega_{D^E}\langle Ap'a_1,\ldots,Ap'a_n\rangle e.
\end{aligned}$$

□

Note that $Ap' \neq Ap^E$ because these two functions have different codomains.

Proposition 4.3 *The diagram*

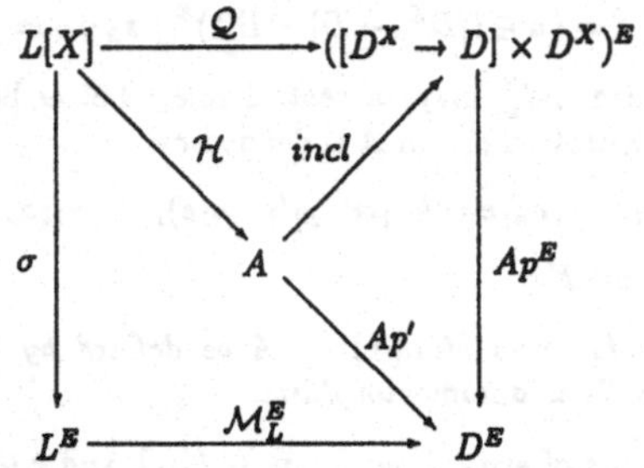

commutes.

Proof The commutativity of the two triangles is clear.

To prove that the two homomorphisms $Ap' \circ \mathcal{H}$ and $\mathcal{M}_L^E \circ \sigma$ are equal, we will appeal to the universal mapping property for $L[X]$. Thus, we need only to show they agree on both L and X. Suppose $l \in L$. Then, for all $e \in E$, $(Ap' \circ \mathcal{H})le = Ap'(\mathcal{H}l)e = (Ap \circ (\mathcal{H}l))e = Ap(\mathcal{H}le) = Ap\langle \mathcal{M}_{L[X]}l, \mathcal{M}_L^X e\rangle = \mathcal{M}_{L[X]}l(\mathcal{M}_L^X e) = (\kappa_D \circ \mathcal{M}_L)l(\mathcal{M}_L^X e) = \kappa_D(\mathcal{M}_L l)(\mathcal{M}_L^X e) = \mathcal{M}_L l = \mathcal{M}_L(\kappa_L le) = \mathcal{M}_L(\sigma le) = (\mathcal{M}_L \circ (\sigma l))e = \mathcal{M}_L^E(\sigma l)e = (\mathcal{M}_L^E \circ \sigma)le$. Suppose $x \in X$. Then, for all $e \in E$, $(Ap' \circ \mathcal{H})xe = \cdots = \mathcal{M}_{L[X]}x(\mathcal{M}_L^X e) = v_D x(\mathcal{M}_L^X e) = \mathcal{M}_L^X ex = (\mathcal{M}_L \circ e)x = \mathcal{M}_L(ex) = \mathcal{M}_L(v_L xe) = \mathcal{M}_L(\sigma xe) = \cdots = (\mathcal{M}_L^E \circ \sigma)xe$. □

We will need an elementary set-theoretic lemma.

Lemma 4.4 *Let S, U, V, W, and Z be sets. Let $f: S \to V^U$, $g: S \to W^U$, $h: V \to Z$, and $k: W \to Z$ be functions. If the diagram*

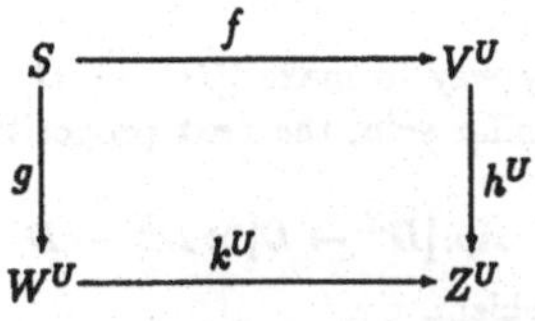

commutes, then the diagram

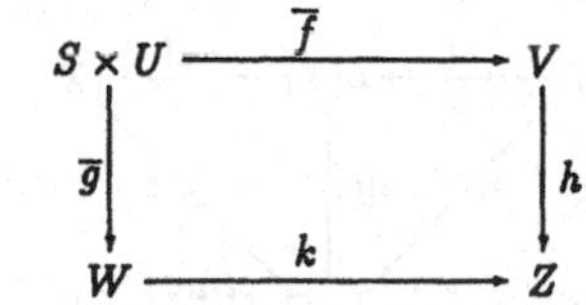

also commutes.

Proof Let $s \in S$ and $u \in U$. Then $(h \circ \overline{f})\langle s,u\rangle = h(\overline{f}\langle s,u\rangle) = h(fsu) = (h \circ (fs))u = h^U(fs)u = (h^U \circ f)su = (k^U \circ g)su = \cdots = (k \circ \overline{g})\langle s,u\rangle$. □

Theorem 4.5 *The diagram*

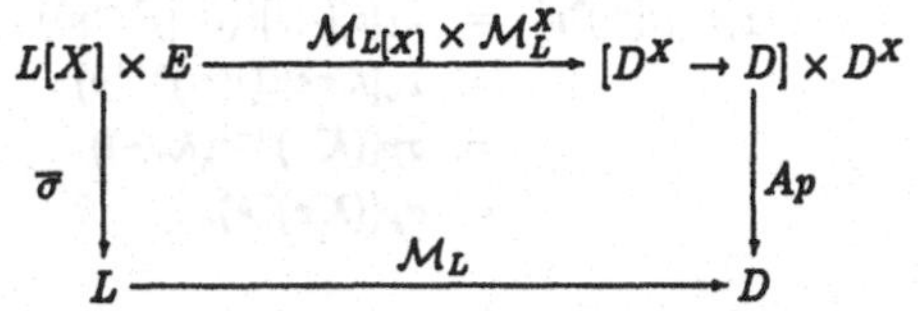

commutes.

Proof The theorem follows by using Proposition 4.3 and Lemma 4.4 in combination with the observation that $\overline{Q} = \mathcal{M}_{L[X]} \times \mathcal{M}_L^X$. □

The commutative diagram

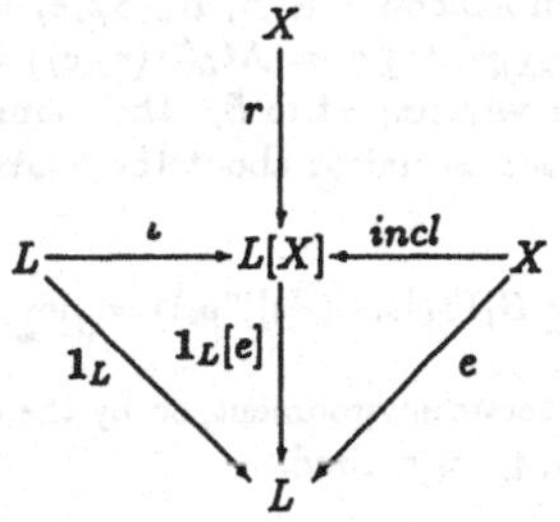

shows that each recursive syntactic environment determines a transformation of simple syntactic environments via the function $\mathcal{K}: E[X] \to E^E$ defined by $\mathcal{K}re = 1_L[e] \circ r$, for all $r \in E[X]$ and $e \in E$. Intuitively, $\mathcal{K}re$ gives the result of substituting in r the values associated to identifiers by e. Recall that $b_E: X \to L$ is the simple syntactic environment which assigns the undefined program b_L to every $x \in X$. Thus, a sequence of simple syntactic environments that intuitively become progressively more like the the recursive syntactic environment r is

$$b_E,\ \mathcal{K}rb_E,\ \mathcal{K}r(\mathcal{K}rb_E),\ \cdots,\ (\mathcal{K}r)^n b_E,\ \cdots .$$

Proposition 4.6 *Let n be a nonnegative integer. For all $e \in E$, $r \in E[X]$, and $p \in L[X]$,*

$$1_L[e]((\iota[r])^n p) = \sigma p((\mathcal{K}r)^n e).$$

Proof We proceed by induction on n. The base case $n = 0$ is covered by Lemma 3.1.

So suppose that $n \geq 1$. From the commutative diagram

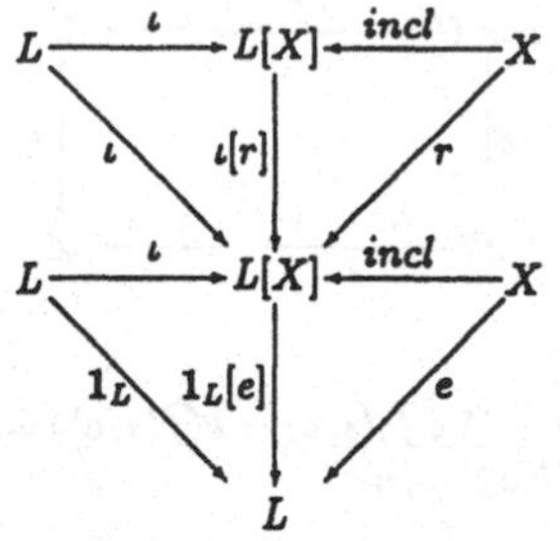

we can read off that $1_L[e] \circ \iota[r] = 1_L[1_L[e] \circ r] = 1_L[\mathcal{K}re]$. Hence, by the induction hypothesis,

$$\begin{aligned} 1_L[e]((\iota[r])^n p) &= 1_L[e](\iota[r]((\iota[r])^{n-1}p)) \\ &= 1_L[\mathcal{K}re]((\iota[r])^{n-1}p) \\ &= \sigma p((\mathcal{K}r)^{n-1}(\mathcal{K}re)) \\ &= \sigma p((\mathcal{K}r)^n e). \end{aligned}$$

□

We now come to the main theorem of this section.

Theorem 4.7 *The denotational semantics* $\mathcal{M}_{L[X]}: L[X] \to [D^X \to D]$ *is adequate with respect to the operational semantics* $\mathcal{B}_{L[X]}: L[X] \times E'[X] \to O$.

Proof Suppose p_1 and p_2 are programs in $L[X]$ such that $\mathcal{M}_{L[X]}p_1 = \mathcal{M}_{L[X]}p_2$. We claim that, for all simple syntactic environments $e \in E$, $\mathcal{B}_L(\sigma p_1 e) = \mathcal{B}_L(\sigma p_2 e)$. By Theorem 4.5, for each i, $\mathcal{M}_{L[X]}p_i(\mathcal{M}_L^X e) = Ap\langle \mathcal{M}_{L[X]}p_i, \mathcal{M}_L^X e\rangle = \mathcal{M}_L(\overline{\sigma}\langle p_i, e\rangle) = \mathcal{M}_L(\sigma p_i e)$. Hence, $\mathcal{M}_L(\sigma p_1 e) = \mathcal{M}_L(\sigma p_2 e)$. Since $\mathcal{M}_L$ is adequate with respect to $\mathcal{B}_L$, the claim follows.

Suppose $g \in E'[X]$. By our basic assumtion about the relationship between $\mathcal{B}_{L[X]}$ and $\mathcal{B}_L$, and by Proposition 4.6,

$$\mathcal{B}_{L[X]}\langle p_i, g\rangle = \lim_{n\to\infty} \mathcal{B}_L(1_L[b_E]((\iota[g])^n p_i)) = \lim_{n\to\infty} \mathcal{B}_L(\sigma p_i((\mathcal{K}g)^n b_E)).$$

Note that $(\mathcal{K}g)^n b_E$ is a simple syntactic environment, so by the claim established in the preceeding paragraph, $\mathcal{B}_{L[X]}\langle p_1, g\rangle = \mathcal{B}_{L[X]}\langle p_2, g\rangle$, as desired. □

5 Full Abstraction

Given the groundwork we laid in the course of our proof of adequacy, it turns out to be fairly easy to prove full abstraction. This is where the assumption that all the compact elements of D are denotable by elements of L plays a crucial role. To get adequacy, we only needed that $\bot$ be denotable.

Before giving the full abstraction proof, we need to prove a proposition describing how contexts interact with substitutions.

Proposition 5.1 *For all contexts* $C \in L[*]$, *all* $p \in L[X]$, *and all simple syntactic environments* $e \in E$,

$$C[\sigma pe] = \sigma(C[p])e.$$

Proof Note that $C[\sigma pe] = 1_L[* \mapsto \sigma pe]C$. By Lemma 3.1,

$$\sigma(C[p])e = 1_L[e](C[p]) = 1_L[e](\iota[* \mapsto p]C).$$

Thus, what we really want to show is that $1_L[* \mapsto \sigma pe] = 1_L[e] \circ \iota[* \mapsto p]$. By considering the commutative diagram

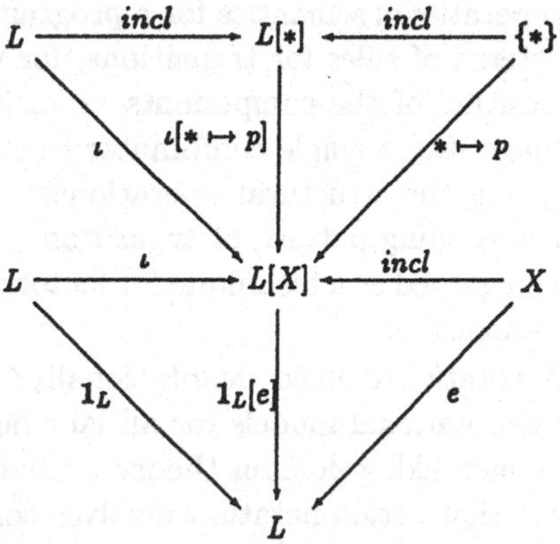

it is easy, using Lemma 3.1, to see that the homomorphism $1_L[e] \circ \iota[* \mapsto p]$ satisfies the universal mapping property that defines $1_L[* \mapsto \sigma pe]$, so the desired equality follows. □

Theorem 5.2 *The denotational semantics $\mathcal{M}_{L[X]}: L[X] \to [D^X \to D]$ is fully abstract with respect to the operational semantics $\mathcal{B}_{L[X]}: L[X] \times E'[X] \to O$.*

Proof Suppose p_1 and p_2 are elements of $L[X]$ such that the continuous functions $\mathcal{M}_{L[X]}p_1$ and $\mathcal{M}_{L[X]}p_2$ are *not* equal. Since D^X is an algebraic poset, there is a compact element $h \in D^X$ such that $\mathcal{M}_{L[X]}p_1 h \neq \mathcal{M}_{L[X]}p_2 h$. For each $x \in X$, hx is a compact element of D. Since all compact elements of D are denotable by programs in L, there exists a simple syntactic environment $e \in E$ satisfying the equation $\mathcal{M}_L(ex) = hx$, i.e., such that $h = \mathcal{M}_L \circ e = \mathcal{M}_L^X e$. Hence, $\mathcal{M}_{L[X]}p_1(\mathcal{M}_L^X e) \neq \mathcal{M}_{L[X]}p_2(\mathcal{M}_L^X e)$. By Theorem 4.5, $\mathcal{M}_L(\sigma p_1 e) \neq \mathcal{M}_L(\sigma p_2 e)$. Because of our assumption that $\mathcal{M}_L$ is fully abstract with respect to $\mathcal{B}_L$, there exists a context $C \in L[*]$ such that $\mathcal{B}_L(C[\sigma p_1 e]) \neq \mathcal{B}_L(C[\sigma p_2 e])$. From Proposition 5.1 and Theorem 3.4, we see that, for each i, $\mathcal{B}_L(C[\sigma p_i e]) = \mathcal{B}_L(\sigma C[p_i]e) = \mathcal{B}_{L[X]}\langle C[p_i], \iota \circ e\rangle$. Thus, $\mathcal{B}_{L[X]}\langle C[p_1], \iota \circ e\rangle \neq \mathcal{B}_{L[X]}\langle C[p_2], \iota \circ e\rangle$, which proves the theorem. □

References

[AP86] Apt. K. and G. D. Plotkin, *Countable nondeterminism and random assignment*, JACM 34 (1986), pp.724-767.

[BW90] Baeten, J.C.M. and W.P. Weijland, *Process Algebra*, Cambridge University Press (Cambridge, England) (1990).

[BK90] Bergstra, J.A., and J.W. Klop, *An Introduction to Process Algebra* in: Applications of Process Algebra, J.C.M. Baeten (Ed.). Cambridge University Press (Cambridge, England) (1990), pp. 1-21.

[BKO88] Bergstra, J.A., J.W. Klop and E. R. Olderog, *Readies and failures in the algebra of communicating processes* SIAM Journal of Computing 17 (1988), pp. 1134-1177.

[MaO92] Machlin, R.S. and F.J. Oles, *Non-well-founded fully abstract semantics for concurrency*, in preparation.

[M91] Mislove, M.W., *Algebraic posets, algebraic cpo's, and models of concurrency*, *Proceedings of the Oxford Symposium on Topology* (1991).

[MiO92a] Mislove, M. W. and F. J. Oles, *A simple language supporting angelic nondeterminism and parallel composition*, Lecture Notes in Computer Science 598 (1992), pp. 77-101.

[MiO92b] Mislove, M. W. and F. J. Oles, *A topological algebra for angelic nondeterminism*, submitted for publication.

[Oles87] Oles, F. J., *Semantics for concurrency without powerdomains*, *Proceedings of the 14th ACM Symposium on the Principles of Programming Languages*, ACM Press (1987) pp. 211-222.

[W90] Wagner, E.G., *Algebras, polynomials, and programs*, Theoretical Computer Science 70 (1990) pp. 3-34.

ON THE ACTION SEMANTICS OF CONCURRENT PROGRAMMING LANGUAGES

Peter D. Mosses

Computer Science Department, Aarhus University
Ny Munkegade Bldg. 540, DK–8000 Aarhus C, Denmark

ABSTRACT Action semantics is a framework for semantic description of programming languages. In this framework, actions are semantic entities, used to represent the potential behaviour of programs—also the contributions that parts of programs make to such behaviour. The notation for expressing actions, called action notation, is combinator-based. It is used in much the same way that lambda-notation is used in denotational semantics. However, the essence of action notation is operational, rather than mathematical, and its meaning is formally defined by a structural operational semantics together with a bisimulation equivalence.

This paper briefly motivates action semantics, and explains the basic concepts. It then illustrates the use of the framework by giving an action semantic description of a small example language. This language includes a simple form of concurrency: tasks that may synchronize by means of rendezvous. The paper also discusses the operational semantics of action notation, focusing on the primitive actions that represent asynchronous message transmission and process initiation.

Keywords semantics, action semantics, action notation, concurrency, synchronization, asynchrony, distributed processing.

CONTENTS

0. INTRODUCTION

Action semantics is a recently-developed framework for formal semantics [12, 14]. It combines formality with many good pragmatic features. Regarding comprehensibility and accessibility, for instance, action semantic descriptions compete with informal language descriptions. Action semantic descriptions scale up smoothly from small example languages to full-blown practical languages. The addition of new constructs to a described language does not require reformulation of the already-given description. An action semantic description of one language can make widespread reuse of that of another, related language. All these pragmatic features are highly desirable. Action semantics is, however, so far the *only* semantic framework that enjoys them! See [12] for a comprehensive exposition of action semantics, with demonstration of its claimed pragmatic qualities.

Action semantics is *compositional*, like denotational semantics [10]. The main difference between action semantics and denotational semantics concerns the universe of semantic entities: action semantics uses entities called *actions*, rather than the higher-order functions used with denotational semantics. Actions are inherently more operational than functions: when *performed*, actions process information *gradually*.

Primitive actions, and the various ways of combining actions, correspond to fundamental concepts of information processing. Action semantics provides a particular notation for expressing actions. The symbols of action notation are suggestive words, rather than cryptic signs, which makes it possible to get a broad impression of an action semantic description from a superficial reading, even without previous experience of action semantics. The action *combinators*, a notable feature of action notation, obey desirable algebraic laws that can be used for (simple) reasoning about semantic equivalence. We shall consider the basic concepts of action performance in Section 1.

The main aim of this paper is to illustrate the action semantics of concurrent programming languages. In Section 2 we shall describe a simple example language having *task* declarations. Tasks may *synchronize* by means of rendezvous, arranged by matching entry call and accept statements. The action semantic description of this language shows how the standard primitive actions for *asynchronous* message transmission can be used to explicate synchronization. The intended interpretation of all the action notation used in the description will be explained (albeit briefly) when we first meet it.

The formal definition of action notation [12, Appendices B and C] consists of a structural operational semantics [13, 5, 1], together with a bisimulation equivalence. In Section 3 we shall consider the configurations that arise in this operational semantics, paying particular attention to aspects supporting message passing and concurrent action performance. We shall also discuss how the asynchrony of message transmission and action performance is related to the

straightforward *distributed* implementation of concurrent processing.

It is worth pointing out that the structural operational semantics of action notation induces an operational semantics for all languages described using action semantics. However, the induced semantics is not really structural in the usual sense, since configurations involve action terms rather than program syntax. Note that a structural operational semantics for a programming language usually involves repetitious patterns of rules for transitions, for instance determining a sequential order of execution of the components of various phrases; an action semantics for the language uses a single combinator to express the fundamental concept of sequencing, and the structural operational semantics of the combinator specifies the corresponding pattern of transitions, once and for all. Thus action semantics can be regarded as a technique for factorization of a conventional structural operational semantics.

Why isn't action notation defined denotationally? That would have the advantage of inducing denotational models for all languages with action semantic descriptions, as well as making domain theory available for reasoning about actions. The difficulty is that action notation involves concepts, such as concurrency and unbounded nondeterminism, whose available denotational models are not only very intricate but also not fully abstract with respect to the intended operational semantics of actions. Such a denotational 'model' would not satisfy all the desired algebraic laws. However, action notation could be exploited as auxiliary notation in a conventional denotational semantics [11].

On the other hand, although our combination of structural operational semantics and bisimulation does verify the essential algebraic laws, this does not provide a sufficiently strong action theory for reasoning about nontrivial program equivalence. It is currently unclear how to develop a stronger action theory, to avoid the need for direct and tedious reasoning at the operational level. In Section 4 we shall consider some possible directions for future research.

Readers are assumed to be familiar with the general ideas of denotational and structural operational semantics.

1. BASIC CONCEPTS

Just as the lambda-notation is used in denotational semantics for specifying functions, so our action notation is used in action semantics for specifying *actions*. Action notation includes also notation for *data* and for auxiliary entities called *yielders*.

Actions are essentially dynamic, *computational* entities. The *performance* of an action directly represents information processing behaviour and reflects the gradual, step-wise nature of computation. Items of data are, in contrast, essentially static, *mathematical* entities, representing pieces of information, e.g.,

particular numbers. (Of course actions are 'mathematical' too, in the sense that they are abstract, formally-defined entities, analogous to abstract machines defined in automata theory.) A yielder represents an *unevaluated* item of data, whose value depends on the *current information*, i.e., the previously-computed and input values that are available to the performance of the enclosing action. For example, a yielder might always evaluate to the datum currently stored in a particular cell, which could change during the performance of an action.

1.1. ACTIONS

A performance of an action, which may be part of an enclosing action, either:

- *completes*, corresponding to normal termination (the performance of the enclosing action proceeds normally); or
- *escapes*, corresponding to exceptional termination (parts of the enclosing action are skipped until the escape is trapped); or
- *fails*, corresponding to abandoning the performance of an action (the enclosing action performs an alternative action, if there is one, otherwise it fails too); or
- *diverges*, corresponding to nontermination (the enclosing action diverges).

Actions can be used to represent the semantics of programs: action performances correspond to possible program behaviours. Furthermore, actions can represent the (perhaps indirect) contribution that *parts* of programs, such as statements and expressions, make to the semantics of entire programs.

An action may be nondeterministic, having different possible performances for the same initial information. Nondeterminism represents implementation-dependence, where the behaviour of a program (or the contribution of a part of it) may vary between different implementations—or even between different instants of time on the same implementation. Note that nondeterminism does not imply actual randomness: an implementation of a nondeterministic behaviour may be absolutely deterministic.

The information processed by action performance may be classified according to how far it tends to be propagated, as follows:

- *transient*: tuples of data, corresponding to intermediate results;
- *scoped*: bindings of tokens to data, corresponding to symbol tables;
- *stable*: data stored in cells, corresponding to the values assigned to variables;
- *permanent*: data communicated between distributed actions that are performed by separate *agents*.

Transient information is made available to an action for immediate use. Scoped information, in contrast, may generally be referred to throughout an entire action, although it may also be hidden temporarily. Stable information can be changed, but not hidden, in the action, and it persists until explicitly destroyed. Permanent information cannot even be changed, merely augmented.

When an action is performed, transient information is given only on completion or escape, and scoped information is produced only on completion. In contrast, changes to stable information and extensions to permanent information are made *during* action performance, and are unaffected by subsequent divergence, failure, or escape.

The different kinds of information give rise to so-called *facets* of actions, focusing on the processing of at most one kind of information at a time:

- the *basic* facet, processing independently of information (control flows);
- the *functional* facet, processing transient information (actions are *given* and *give* data);
- the *declarative* facet, processing scoped information (actions *receive* and *produce* bindings);
- the *imperative* facet, processing stable information (actions *reserve* and *unreserve* cells of storage, and *change* the data stored in cells); and
- the *communicative* facet, processing permanent information (actions *send* messages, *receive* messages in buffers, and offer *contracts* to *agents*).

These facets of actions are independent. For instance, changing the data stored in a cell—or even unreserving the cell—does not affect any bindings. There are, however, some *directive* actions, which process a mixture of scoped and stable information, so as to provide finite representations of self-referential bindings. There are also some *hybrid* primitive actions and combinators, which involve more than one kind of information at once, such as an action that both reserves a cell of storage and gives it as transient data. In this paper, for simplicity, we ignore the directive facet of actions; we also ignore escapes (exceptional termination).

The notation for specifying actions consists of action *primitives*, which may involve yielders, and action *combinators*, which operate on one or two *subactions*. Action notation provides also some notation for specifying *sorts* of actions.

1.2. YIELDERS

Yielders are entities that can be *evaluated* to yield data during action performance. The data yielded may depend on the current information, i.e., the given transients, the received bindings, and the current state of the storage. In fact action notation provides primitive yielders that evaluate to compound data (tuples, maps, lists) representing entire slices of the current information, such as the current state of storage. Evaluation cannot affect the current information.

Compound yielders can be formed by the application of data operations to yielders. The data yielded by evaluating a compound yielder are the result of applying the operation to the data yielded by evaluating the operands. For instance, one can form the sum of two number yielders. Items of data are a special case of data yielders, and always yield themselves when evaluated.

1.3. DATA

The information processed by actions consists of items of *data*, organized in structures that give access to the individual items. Data can include various familiar mathematical entities, such as truth-values, numbers, characters, strings, lists, sets, and maps. It can also include entities such as tokens and cells, used for accessing other items. Actions themselves are not data, but they can be incorporated in so-called *abstractions*, which are data, and subsequently *enacted* back into actions. (Abstraction and enaction are a special case of so-called *reification* and *reflection*.) New kinds of data can be introduced *ad hoc*, for representing special pieces of information.

2. AN ILLUSTRATIVE EXAMPLE

Now that we have introduced the main concepts underlying action notation, let us take a walk through an illustrative action semantic description of a concurrent programming language, briefly indicating the intended interpretation of the notation that it uses as we go along. For a summary of the entire standard action notation, see [12, Appendix D].

The language described here is a small-scale, 'ideal' programming language. Syntactically, it is a sublanguage of ADA (and of the language described in [12, Appendix A]), and the specified semantics is quite close to that indicated in the ADA Reference Manual.

The modular structure of our illustrative action semantic description is formally specified as follows.

Abstract Syntax

Semantic Functions

(needs: Abstract Syntax, Semantic Entities.)

Semantic Entities

Sorts	**(needs: Values, Variables, Tasks.)**
Values	**(needs: Numbers.)**
Variables	**(needs: Values, Types.)**
Types	**.**
Numbers	**.**
Tasks	**.**
Required Bindings	**(needs: Types, Numbers.)**

The action semantic description consists of three main modules, concerned with specifying abstract syntax, semantic functions, and semantic entities. Here, let us not worry about the formal details of modularization, and concentrate on the bodies of the modules.

2.1. ABSTRACT SYNTAX

The grammar-like specification given in this subsection consists mainly of a set of (numbered) equations. Ignoring the double brackets ⟦ ... ⟧, the equations have the same form as *productions* in a particular variant of BNF grammar. Terminal symbols are written as quoted strings of characters, such as "(" and "or". Nonterminal symbols are written as unquoted words, such as Expression, and we adopt the convention that they generally start with a capital letter, to avoid confusing them with symbols for semantic functions and entities, which we write using lower case letters. There is a precise formal interpretation of a grammar as an algebraic specification of sorts of trees [12, Chapter 3]. Here, it is enough to know that occurrences of ⟦ ... ⟧ indicate the construction of nodes of trees. (In denotational semantics such brackets merely separate abstract syntax from semantic notation, and cannot be nested.)

grammar:

(1) Identifier = ⟦ letter (letter | digit)* ⟧ .

(2) Literal = ⟦ digit⁺ ⟧ .

The standard nonterminals digit and letter are always implicitly available in our grammars, for convenience when specifying the lexical syntax of identifiers and numerals. The terminal symbols that they generate are single characters, rather than strings of characters. (A string is simply a node whose branches are all characters.)

The equations above involve so-called *regular expressions*. In our notation, a regular expression is either a single symbol, or it consists of a *sequence* $\langle R_1 \ldots R_n \rangle$, a grouped set of *alternatives* $(R_1 \mid \ldots \mid R_n)$, an *optional* part $R^?$, an *optional repeatable* part R^*, or an *obligatory repeatable* part R^+.

(3) Expression = Literal | Identifier | ⟦ "(" Expression ")" ⟧ |
⟦ Unary-Operator Expression ⟧ |
⟦ Expression Binary-Operator Expression ⟧ .

Note that literals and identifiers are *special cases* (formally, *subsorts*) of expressions, rather than merely occurring as components of expressions.

We make no attempt to distinguish syntactically between expressions according to the sort of entity to which they evaluate: truth-values or numbers. Such distinctions between expressions would not simplify the semantic description at all, and they would in any case be context-dependent.

(4) Unary-Operator = "+" | "−" | "not" .

(5) Binary-Operator = "+" | "−" | "*" | "/" | "mod" |
"=" | "<" | "and" | "or" .

(6) Statement = ⟦ "null" ";" ⟧ | ⟦ Identifier ":=" Expression ";" ⟧ |
⟦ "if" Expression "then" Statement$^+$
"else" Statement$^+$ "end" "if" ";" ⟧ |
⟦ "while" Expression "loop" Statement$^+$ "end" "loop" ";" ⟧ |
⟦ "declare" Block ";" ⟧ | ⟦ Identifier "." Identifier ";" ⟧ |
⟦ "accept" Identifier ⟨ "do" Statement$^+$ "end" ⟩$^?$ ";" ⟧ .

The statement ⟦ I_1 "." I_2 ⟧ here is a call on the entry I_2 of task I_1, to be matched by an accept statement for I_2 in the body declared for I_1.

(7) Block = ⟦ Declaration* "begin" Statement$^+$ "end" ⟧ .

A block is essentially a statement with some local declarations. Following ADA, blocks can occur directly in ordinary statement sequences.

(8) Declaration = ⟦ Identifier ":" "constant" Identifier ":=" Expression ";" ⟧ |
⟦ Identifier ":" Identifier ":=" Expression ";" ⟧ |
⟦ "task" Identifier "is" Entry$^+$ "end" ";" ⟧ |
⟦ "task" "body" Identifier "is" Block ";" ⟧ .

(9) Entry = ⟦ "entry" Identifier ";" ⟧ .

Task entries are supposed to be declared before the corresponding task bodies, although we cannot insist on this in our context-free grammar. We retain the entries of a task head only for the sake of familiarity, as they are irrelevant to our dynamic semantics of tasks.

(10) Program = ⟦ Block "." ⟧ .

closed.

That concludes the specification of the abstract syntax of our illustrative language.

2.2. SEMANTIC FUNCTIONS

In action semantics, we specify *semantic functions* by *semantic equations*, much as in denotational semantics. Each equation defines the semantics of a particular sort of phrase in terms of the semantics of its components, if any, using constants and operations for constructing semantic entities. The required compositionality of semantic functions is generally apparent from the semantic equations.

A semantic function always takes a single, syntactic argument and gives a semantic entity as result. It is usual to specify the *functionality* of each semantic function. For instance,

evaluate _ :: Expression → action [giving a value]

asserts that for every abstract syntax tree E for an expression, the semantic entity evaluate E is an action which, when performed, gives a value. The actual definition of evaluate E by the semantic equations is then required to be consistent with this. Formally, action [giving a value] is a term denoting a sort of actions, as specified in [12, Appendix B].

The right hand sides of the semantic equations involve the standard notation for actions and data provided by action semantics, together with any further notation introduced for special semantic entities. It must be emphasized that all the notation is *absolutely formal*! The fact that it is possible to read it informally—and reasonably fluently—does not preclude reading it formally as well. The grouping of the symbols might not be completely obvious to those who have not seen action notation before, but it is in fact unambiguous. The following hints about the general form of action notation may be helpful.

The standard symbols used in action notation are ordinary English *words*. In fact action notation mimics natural language: terms standing for actions form imperative verb phrases involving conjunctions and adverbs, e.g., check it and then escape, whereas terms standing for data and yielders form noun phrases, e.g., the items of the given list. Definite and indefinite articles can be exploited appropriately, e.g., choose a cell then reserve the given cell. (This feature of action notation is reminiscent of Apple's HyperCard scripting language HyperTalk [2], and of Cobol.)

These simple principles for choice of symbols provide a surprisingly grammatical fragment of English, allowing specifications of actions to be made fluently readable—without sacrificing formality at all! To specify grouping unambiguously, we may use parentheses, but for large-scale grouping it is less obtrusive to use indentation, which we emphasize by vertical rules, as illustrated in the semantic equations given later. Moreover, let infix operation symbols always associate to the left, with weaker precedence than prefix symbols (which in turn have weaker precedence than postfix symbols).

Compared to other formalisms, such as the so-called *λ-notation*, action notation may appear to lack conciseness: each symbol generally consists of several letters, rather than a single sign. But the comparison should also take into account that each action combinator usually corresponds to a complex pattern of applications and abstractions in λ-notation. For instance, (under the simplifying assumption of determinism!) the action term A_1 **then** A_2 might correspond to something like $\lambda\varepsilon_1.\lambda\rho.\lambda\kappa.A_1\varepsilon_1\rho(\lambda\varepsilon_2.A_2\varepsilon_2\rho\kappa)$. In any case, the increased length of each symbol seems to be far outweighed by its increased perspicuity. It would also be rather misleading to use familiar mathematical signs to express actions, whose essence is unashamedly computational. For some applications, however, such as formal reasoning about program equivalence on the basis of their action semantics, optimal conciseness may be highly desirable, and it would then be appropriate to allow abbreviations for our verbose symbols. Note that the *essence* of action notation lies in the standard collection of primitives and combinators with their intended operational interpretation, rather than in the standard verbose symbols themselves.

The informal appearance and suggestive words of action notation should encourage programmers to read it, at first, rather casually, in the same way that they might read reference manuals. Having thus gained a broad impression of the intended actions, they may go on to read the specification more carefully, paying attention to the details. A more cryptic notation might discourage programmers from reading it altogether.

The intended interpretation of the standard notation for actions is specified operationally, once and for all, in [12, Appendix C]. All that one has to do before using action notation is to specify the information that is to be processed by actions, which may vary significantly according to the programming language being described. This may involve *extending* data notation with further sorts of data, and *specializing* standard sorts, using sort equations. Furthermore, it may be convenient to introduce formal *abbreviations* for commonly-occurring, conceptually-significant patterns of notation. Extensions, specializations, and abbreviations are all specified *algebraically*, as illustrated in Section 2.3.

Now let us begin to define the semantic functions for our illustrative language. We first declare the symbols used for the semantic functions.

introduces: the value of _ , evaluate _ ,
the unary-operation-result of _ , the binary-operation-result of _ ,
execute _ , elaborate _ , synchronize _ , run _ .

The place-holder _ indicates argument positions in operation symbols. For semantic function symbols, we keep to prefix notation, but otherwise we exploit infix and more generally, 'mixfix' notation.

For simplicity, let identifiers be their own semantics. They are included in the sort token, which is specified in Section 2.3.1 to be a subsort of strings.

• the value of _ :: Literal → number .

The sort number is specified in Section 2.3.5.

(1) the value of ⟦ d:digit$^+$ ⟧ = integer-number of decimal ⟦ d ⟧ .

The operation decimal _ is a standard data operation on strings. We could define a corresponding semantic function, but it wouldn't be very exciting, so we take this short-cut. The use of ⟦ ... ⟧ in the right hand side of the semantic equation above is atypical; it is needed because decimal _ expects its argument to be a string, not a tuple of characters.

The unbounded natural number returned by decimal ⟦ d ⟧ is mapped either to a bounded number, or to nothing (which is included in every sort of data and can be used to represent error values) by the operation integer-number of _ , specified in Section 2.3.5.

• evaluate _ :: Expression → action
 [giving a value]
 [using current bindings | current storage] .

The sort action [giving a value] includes those actions which, whenever performed, complete giving an individual of sort value as transient data; the performance must never give any other sort of transient data, produce any bindings, escape, or diverge. However, failure is *always* an implicit possibility (because actions that refer to current information generally fail when performed with no information available).

Similarly, action [using ...] includes actions that refer at most to the indicated kinds of information.

(2) evaluate L:Literal = give the value of L .

The primitive action give Y completes, giving the data yielded by evaluating the yielder Y.

(3) evaluate I:Identifier =
 give the entity bound to I then
 | give the given value or
 | give the value assigned to the given variable .

The functional action combination A_1 then A_2 represents ordinary functional composition of A_1 and A_2: the transients given to the whole action are propagated only to A_1, the transients given by A_1 on completion are given only to A_2, and only the transients given by A_2 are given by the whole action. Regarding control flow, A_1 then A_2 specifies normal left-to-right sequencing.

The primitive action give Y fails when Y yields nothing. In the above equation, Y is the yielder the entity bound to T, which refers to the current binding for the particular token T, provided that there is one; otherwise it yields nothing, causing the giving action to fail.

The yielder given Y yields all the data given to its evaluation, provided that this is of the data sort Y. For instance the given value (where 'the' is optional) yields a single individual of sort value, if such is given. Otherwise it yields nothing, and give the given value fails. This causes the alternative currently being performed to be abandoned and, if possible, some other alternative to be performed instead, i.e., *back-tracking*.

The action A_1 or A_2 represents implementation-dependent choice between alternative actions, although here A_1, A_2 are such that one or the other of them is always bound to fail, so the choice is actually deterministic.

The special yielder the value assigned to Y, specified in Section 2.3.3, refers to the current storage for the particular variable yielded by Y, analogously to the entity bound to T. If I is currently bound to an entity that is neither a value nor a variable (e.g., a task) both alternatives fail, causing their combination to fail as well.

The special data sorts entity, value, and variable are specified in Section 2.3.

(4) evaluate ⟦ "(" E:Expression ")" ⟧ = evaluate E .

(5) evaluate ⟦ O:Unary-Operator E:Expression ⟧ =
  evaluate E then give the unary-operation-result of O .

(6) evaluate ⟦ E_1:Expression O:Binary-Operator E_2:Expression ⟧ =
  (evaluate E_1 and evaluate E_2)
  then give the binary-operation-result of O .

The action A_1 and A_2 represents implementation-dependent order of performance of the indivisible subactions of A_1, A_2. When these subactions cannot 'interfere' with each other, as here, it indicates that their order of performance is simply irrelevant. Left-to-right order of evaluation can be specified by using the combinator A_1 and then A_2 instead of A_1 and A_2 above. In both cases, the values given by the subactions get *tupled*, and subsequently passed on by the combinator A_1 then A_2.

The evaluation of an expression may give any individual of sort value. We leave it to the semantics of operators, specified below, to insist on individuals of particular sorts—numbers, for instance. For simplicity, we do not bother with precise error messages in case the given operands are *not* of the right sort for a particular operator: we merely let the application of the corresponding operation yield nothing, so that the action which gives it must fail. In any case, errors arising due to wrong sorts of operands are statically detectable in most languages, and should therefore be the concern of a static semantic description, not of the dynamic semantics that we are developing here.

Note that we would *not* have to modify the above equation at all if we were to extend the example language so that expression evaluation could have 'side-effects', such as changing stored values or communicating. This is in marked contrast to the situation in denotational semantics.

- the unary-operation-result of _ :: Unary-Operator → yielder
  [of value] [using given value] .

The notation for sorts of yielders is analogous to that for sorts of actions.

(7) the unary-operation-result of "+" = the given number .

(8) the unary-operation-result of "−" = the negation of the given number .

(9) the unary-operation-result of "not" = not the given truth-value .

Numerical operations such as negation _ and absolute _ are specified in Section 2.3.5. The truth-values are the usual ones from our standard data notation, equipped with various logical operations, such as not _ .

- the binary-operation-result of _ :: Binary-Operator → yielder
  [of value] [using given value^2] .

(10) the binary-operation-result of "+" =
the sum of (the given number#1, the given number#2) .

The yielder given $Y\#n$ yields the n'th individual component of a given tuple, for $n > 0$, provided that this component is of sort Y.

(11) the binary-operation-result of "−" =
the difference of (the given number#1, the given number#2) .

(12) the binary-operation-result of "*" =
the product of (the given number#1, the given number#2) .

(13) the binary-operation-result of "/" =
the quotient of (the given number#1, the given number#2) .

(14) the binary-operation-result of "mod" =
the modulo of (the given number#1, the given number#2) .

(15) the binary-operation-result of "=" =
the given value#1 is the given value#2 .

(16) the binary-operation-result of "<" =
the given number#1 is less than the given number#2 .

(17) the binary-operation-result of "and" =
both of (the given truth-value#1, the given truth-value#2) .

(18) the binary-operation-result of "or" =
either of (the given truth-value#1, the given truth-value#2) .

So much for the action semantics of expressions. Now for statements.

- execute _ :: Statement+ → action
  [completing | diverging | storing | communicating]
  [using current bindings | current storage | current buffer] .

(19) execute ⟨ S_1:Statement S_2:Statement+ ⟩ = execute S_1 and then execute S_2 .

The basic action combination A_1 and then A_2 combines the actions A_1, A_2 into a compound action that represents their normal, left-to-right sequencing, performing A_2 only when A_1 completes.

(20) execute ⟦ "null" ";" ⟧ = complete .

The primitive action complete is the unit for A_1 and then A_2.

(21) execute ⟦ I:Identifier ":=" E:Expression ";" ⟧ =
    | give the variable bound to I and
    | evaluate E
    then assign the given value#2 to the given variable#1 .

The special action assign Y_1 to Y_2 is specified in Section 2.3.3.

(22) execute ⟦ "if" E:Expression "then" S_1:Statement+
        "else" S_2:Statement+ "end" "if" ";" ⟧ =
    evaluate E then
    | | check the given truth-value and then execute S_1
    | or
    | | check not the given truth-value and then execute S_2 .

The action check Y requires Y to yield a truth-value; it completes when the value is true, otherwise it fails. It is used for guarding alternatives. Here, the compound action (check Y and then A_1) or (check not Y and then A_2) expresses a deterministic choice between A_1 and A_2, depending on the condition Y. The transients given to the combination A_1 or A_2 are passed on to both its subactions; similarly for the action A_1 and A_2, and for A_1 and then A_2.

(23) execute ⟦ "while" E:Expression "loop" S:Statement+ "end" "loop" ";" ⟧ =
    unfolding
    | evaluate E then
    | | | check the given truth-value and then execute S and then unfold
    | | or
    | | | check not the given truth-value .

The action combination unfolding A performs A but whenever it reaches the dummy action unfold, it performs A instead. It is mostly used in the semantics of iterative constructs, with unfold occurring exactly once in A, but it can also be used with several occurrences of unfold.

(24) execute ⟦ "declare" B:Block ";" ⟧ = execute B .

(25) execute ⟦ I_1:Identifier "." I_2:Identifier ";" ⟧ =
give the agent bound to I_1 then
| send a message [to the given agent] [containing entry of I_2] and then
| receive a message [from the given agent] [containing the done-signal] .

Task declarations bind task identifiers to agents, as specified later. They do not bind entry identifiers to anything at all, treating them literally as labels.

The primitive action send Y, where Y yields a *sort* of message, initiates the transmission of a message. The usual form of Y is message [to Y_1] [containing Y_2], where Y_1 yields an individual *agent* and Y_2 yields individual data. The sort yielded by Y is implicitly restricted to messages from the performing agent and this should determine an individual message.

The action receive Y waits indefinitely for a message of the sort specified by Y to arrive, removes it from the buffer, and gives it.

The notation for entries and signals that are contained in the messages is specified in Section 2.3.

(26) execute ⟦ "accept" I:Identifier "end" ";" ⟧ =
receive a message [from any agent] [containing entry of I] then
send a message [to the sender of the given message]
[containing the done-signal] .

Synchronization is ensured by the entry call statement action waiting for the done-signal before completing. Our action semantics is merely expressing the usual informal explanation of the basic notion of a rendezvous in ADA. Extended rendezvous is just as straightforward:

(27) execute ⟦ "accept" I:Identifier "do" S:Statement$^+$ "end" ";" ⟧ =
receive a message [from any agent] [containing entry of I] then
| execute S and then
| send a message [to the sender of the given message]
| [containing the done-signal] .

For simplicity, we do not include selection between alternative accept statements in the language described here. The action semantics of such constructs is given in [12, Chapter 17].

Although Block is not a subsort of Statement, let us overload the semantic function execute _ by extending it to blocks:

- execute _ :: Block → action
  [completing | diverging | storing | communicating]
  [using current bindings | current storage | current buffer] .

(28) execute ⟦ "begin" S:Statement$^+$ "end" ⟧ = execute S .

(29) execute ⟦ D:Declaration$^+$ "begin" S:Statement$^+$ "end" ⟧ =
furthermore elaborate D hence
| synchronize D and then
| execute S .

The action furthermore A produces the same bindings as A, together with any received bindings that A doesn't override. In other words, it overlays the received bindings with those produced by A.

The combination A_1 hence A_2 lets the bindings produced by A_1 be received by A_2, which limits their scope—unless they get reproduced by A_2. It is analogous to functional composition. The compound combination furthermore A_1 hence A_2 (recall that prefixes have higher precedence than infixes!) corresponds to ordinary block structure, with A_1 being the block head and A_2 the block body: nonlocal bindings, received by the combination, are also received by A_2 unless they are overridden by the local bindings produced by A_1.

The action synchronize D above is concerned with task initialization, considered later. Now for declarations.

- elaborate _ :: Declaration$^+$ → action
  [binding | diverging | storing | communicating]
  [using current bindings | current storage | current buffer] .

(30) elaborate ⟨ D_1:Declaration D_2:Declaration$^+$ ⟩ =
elaborate D_1 before elaborate D_2 .

The action A_1 before A_2 represents sequencing of declarations. Like furthermore A_1 hence A_2, it lets A_2 receive bindings from A_1, together with any bindings received by the whole action that are not thereby overridden. The combination produces all the bindings produced by A_2, as well as any produced by A_1 that are not overridden by A_2. Thus A_2 may rebind a token that was bound by A_1. Note that the bindings received by the combination are not reproduced at all, unless one of A_1, A_2 explicitly reproduces them.

The use of the combinator A_1 before A_2 in the semantics of declaration sequences allows later declarations to refer to the bindings produced by earlier declarations—but not the other way round. Mutually-recursive task declarations are considered later.

(31) elaborate ⟦ I_1:Identifier ":" "constant" I_2:Identifier ":=" E:Expression ";" ⟧ =
evaluate E then bind I_1 to the given value .

The declarative action bind T to Y produces the binding of the token T to the bindable data yielded by Y. It does *not* reproduce any of the received bindings!

(32) elaborate ⟦ I_1:Identifier ":" I_2:Identifier ":=" E:Expression ";" ⟧ =
| allocate a variable for the type bound to I_2 and
| evaluate E
then
| bind I_1 to the given variable#1 and
| assign the given value#2 to the given variable#1 .

The action allocate d for Y is special notation, specified in Section 2.3.3. As we only deal with simple variables in this simple example, allocate a variable for Y merely chooses, reserves, and gives a single storage cell.

The basic and functional combinators, such as A_1 and A_2, all pass the *received* bindings to their subactions without further ado—analogously to the way A_1 and A_2 passes all the given data to both A_1 and A_2. They are similarly unbiased when it comes to combining the bindings produced by their subactions: they produce the *disjoint union* of the bindings, providing this is defined, otherwise they simply fail. Here, one or the other of the combined actions never produces any bindings at all, so failure cannot arise.

(33) elaborate ⟦ "task" I:Identifier "is" E:Entry$^+$ "end" ";" ⟧ =
offer a contract [to any agent]
[containing abstraction of the initial task-action] and then
| receive a message [containing an agent] then
| bind I to the task yielded by the contents of the given message .

The primitive action offer Y, where Y yields a sort of contract, initiates the arrangement of a contract with another agent. The usual form of Y is a contract [to any agent] [containing abstraction of A], where A is the action to be performed according to the contract.

The action initial task-action is defined in Section 2.3.6.

(34) elaborate ⟦ "task" "body" I:Identifier "is" B:Block ";" ⟧ =
send a message [to the agent bound to I]
[containing task of the closure of abstraction of execute B] .

The use of closure above ensures static bindings: the execution of the block B when the task is initiated receives the same bindings as the declaration. These may include bindings to other tasks: a system of communicating tasks can be set up by first declaring all the task entries, then all the bodies. They may also include bindings to variables; but attempts to assign to these variables, or to inspect their values, always fail, because the cells referred to are not local to the agent performing the action. It is currently a bit complicated to describe the action semantics of distributed tasks that have access to shared variables—the task that declares a variable has to act as a *server* for assignments and inspections—so we let our illustrative language deviate from ADA in this respect. We shall return to this matter in Section 3.

- synchronize _ :: Declaration⁺ → action
  [completing | diverging | communicating]
  [using current bindings | current buffer] .

The action synchronize D is used to delay the execution of the statements of a block until all the tasks declared locally in the block have been started.

(35) synchronize ⟨ D_1:Declaration D_2:Declaration⁺ ⟩ =
synchronize D_1 and synchronize D_2 .

(36) synchronize ⟦ "task" "body" I:Identifier "is" B:Block ";" ⟧ =
receive a message [from the agent bound to I]
[containing the begin-signal] .

(37) D: ⟦ Identifier ":" "constant"? Identifier ":=" Expression ";" ⟧ |
⟦ "task" Identifier "is" Entry⁺ "end" ";" ⟧ ⇒
synchronize D = complete .

The above conditional equation corresponds to several ordinary semantic equations.

Finally, we specify the action semantics of entire programs.

- run _ :: Program → action
  [completing | diverging | storing | communicating]
  [using current storage | current buffer] .

(38) run ⟦ B:Block "." ⟧ =
produce required-bindings hence
| execute B and then
| send a message [to the user-agent] [containing the terminated-signal] .

The primitive action produce Y produces a binding for each token mapped to a bindable value by the map yielded by Y. See Section 2.3.7 for the definition of the bindings of required identifiers in our illustrative language.

The termination message sent above insists that the user should be able to notice when the program has terminated.

Some evidence of the good pragmatic qualities (modifiability, extensibility, comprehensibility) of action semantic descriptions may be observed in the semantic equations given above. In particular, notice how the *polymorphism* of the action combinators makes the well-formedness of the action terms independent of whether or not subactions might change storage, refer to bindings, communicate, etc.: our semantic equations would not need any significant modifications when adding, say, function calls with side-effects to expressions.

2.3. SEMANTIC ENTITIES

To complete our semantic description of the illustrative language, we have to specify the notation that is used in the semantic equations for expressing semantic entities. Most of the notation used here has a fairly obvious interpretation, so rather few comments are provided.

includes: [12]/Action Notation.

2.3.1. SORTS

introduces: entity .

- entity = value | variable | type | task (*disjoint*) .
- datum = entity | message | entry | □ .
- token = string of (letter, (letter | digit)*) .
- bindable = entity .
- storable = value .
- sendable = agent | task | entry | signal | □ .

All the sorts specified above have a standard usage in action notation, except for entity. Although our sort equations look a bit like the so-called domain equations used in denotational semantics, their formal interpretation is quite different. We use the same symbol _ | _ for *sort union* as we used for combining alternatives in grammars. Thinking of sorts of data as *sets* we may regard _ | _ as ordinary set union; it is associative, commutative, and idempotent. The use of □ above formally expresses an inclusion, leaving open what other sorts might be included in datum and sendable.

2.3.2. VALUES

introduces: value .

includes: [12]/Data Notation/Instant/Distinction (value *for* s , _ is _).

- value = truth-value | number (*disjoint*) .

2.3.3. VARIABLES

introduces: variable , assign _ to _ , the _ assigned to _ , allocate _ for _ .

- assign _ to _ :: yielder [of value], yielder [of variable] → action [storing] .
- the _ assigned to _ :: value, yielder [of variable] → yielder [of value] .
- allocate _ for _ :: variable, yielder [of type] →
  action [giving a variable | storing] .

(1) variable = cell .

(2) assign (Y_1:yielder [of value]) to (Y_2:yielder [of variable]) =
store the storable yielded by Y_1 in the cell yielded by Y_2 .

(3) the ($v \leq$value) assigned to (Y:yielder [of variable]) =
the (v & storable) stored in the cell yielded by Y .

(4) allocate ($v \leq$variable) for (Y:yielder [of type]) =
allocate a cell .

The sort cell has a standard usage in action notation, corresponding to 'locations' in denotational semantics. For simplicity here, we do not bother to distinguish between cells for storing different sorts of values, so the type entities are quite redundant. In a more realistic example, the specification of variable allocation and assignment can become quite complex.

The standard action store Y_1 in Y_2 changes the data stored in the cell yielded by Y_2 to the storable data yielded by Y_1. The cell concerned must have been previously reserved, using reserve Y, otherwise the storing action fails. The standard yielder the d stored in Y evaluates to the data of sort d currently stored in the cell yielded by Y.

The standard notation allocate a cell abbreviates the following hybrid action:

```
indivisibly
| choose a cell [not in the mapped-set of the current storage] then
| | reserve the given cell and give it .
```

2.3.4. Types

introduces: type , boolean-type , integer-type .

- type = boolean-type | integer-type (*individual*) .

2.3.5. NUMBERS

introduces: number , min-integer , max-integer , integer-number of _ ,
negation _ , sum _ , difference _ , product _ ,
quotient _ , modulo _ .

- min-integer , max-integer : integer .
- integer-number of _ :: integer → number (*partial*) .
- negation _ :: number → number (*partial*) .
- sum _ , difference _ , product _ , quotient _ ::
number^2 → number (*partial*) .
- modulo _ :: number^2 → number (*partial*) .
- _ is _ , _ is less than _ :: number, number → truth-value (*total*) .

(1) i : integer [min min-integer] [max max-integer] $\Rightarrow$
integer-number of i : number .

(2) i : integer [min successor max-integer] $\Rightarrow$ integer-number of i = nothing .

(3) i : integer [max predecessor min-integer] $\Rightarrow$ integer-number of i = nothing .

(4) integer-number of i : number $\Rightarrow$
negation integer-number of i = integer-number of negation i .

(5) integer-number of i_1 : number ; integer-number of i_2 : number $\Rightarrow$

(1) sum (integer-number of i_1, integer-number of i_2) =
integer-number of sum (i_1, i_2) ;

(2) difference (integer-number of i_1, integer-number of i_2) =
integer-number of difference (i_1, i_2) ;

(3) product (integer-number of i_1, integer-number of i_2) =
integer-number of product (i_1, i_2) ;

(4) quotient (integer-number of i_1, integer-number of i_2) =
integer-number of integer-quotient (i_1, i_2) ;

(5) modulo (integer-number of i_1, integer-number of i_2) =
integer-number of integer-modulo (i_1, i_2) .

(6) integer-number of i_1 : integer-number ; integer-number of i_2 : integer-number $\Rightarrow$

(1) integer-number of i_1 is integer-number of i_2 = i_1 is i_2 ;

(2) integer-number of i_1 is less than integer-number of i_2 = i_1 is less than i_2 .

The specification of integer arithmetic uses loosely-specified bounds on integers. It extends the standard arithmetic operations from standard integers to the sort number in a uniform way: the result is nothing when it would have been out of bounds.

2.3.6. TASKS

introduces: task , task of _ , task-abstraction _ , initial task-action , signal , begin-signal , done-signal , terminated-signal , entry , entry of _ .

- task of _ :: abstraction → task (*total*) .
- task-abstraction _ :: task → abstraction (*total*) .
- signal = begin-signal | done-signal | terminated-signal (*individual*) .
- initial task-action : action .
- entry of _ :: token → entry (*total*) .

(1) t = task of a ⇒ task-abstraction t:task = a .

(2) initial task-action =

```
  | send a message [to the contracting-agent]
  |      [containing the performing-agent]
  | and then
  | receive a message [from the contracting-agent] [containing a task]
 then
  | send a message [to the contracting-agent] [containing the begin-signal]
  | and then
  | enact the task-abstraction of the task yielded by
  |      the contents of the given message .
```

(3) entry of k_1:token is entry of k_2:token = k_1 is k_2 .

The action enact Y performs the action incorporated in the abstraction yielded by Y. The use of closure _ on an abstraction ensures that the incorporated action receives whatever bindings were current when the closure was evaluated.

2.3.7. REQUIRED BINDINGS

introduces: required-bindings .

- required-bindings : map [token to value | type] .

(1) required-bindings =

```
    disjoint-union of ( map of "TRUE" to true,
                        map of "FALSE" to false,
                        map of "BOOLEAN" to boolean-type,
                        map of "MININT" to integer-number min-integer,
                        map of "MAXINT" to integer-number max-integer,
                        map of "INTEGER" to integer-type ) .
```

3. FOUNDATIONS

Now that we have seen the use of action notation in the semantic description of a simple concurrent programming language, let us consider the operational semantics of action notation. We shall pay particular attention to communicative actions, i.e., actions for sending and receiving messages and for offering contracts.

The operational semantics of action notation [12, Appendix C] uses a variant of structural operational semantics [13, 5, 1] to define a transition system. Sequences of transitions correspond to performances of actions, representing program behaviour. The transition system is the basis for defining action equivalence; see [12, Section C.4].

Here we shall consider mainly what *configurations* arise in the operational semantics of action notation. Once one has seen that, it should be fairly easy to imagine how particular primitive actions and combinators determine transitions between configurations.

To start with, suppose that a single agent is performing an action in isolation, without any message transmission. The relevant components of the current configuration are just the (abstract) syntax of the rest of the action being performed, together with the current transient data, bindings, and storage. Actually, due to the interleaving of steps in the performance of the combination A_1 and A_2, various subactions may have different current transients and bindings at the same time, and it is easiest to keep track of this by inserting transients and bindings directly in the abstract syntax tree of the action. On the other hand, an agent only has one current storage, which is best kept separate from the syntax tree.

Next, let the action being performed involve the sending and receipt of messages. The current configuration should now record what messages have been sent (at least since the previous configuration) and the messages that have been received but not yet removed, i.e., the current buffer. We may imagine the single agent making transitions between such local configurations. Between transitions, any messages to be sent get dispatched, and fresh messages may be inserted in the buffer. Transitions may inspect and remove messages from the buffer, but not add any new ones.

Finally, consider a (conceptually) *distributed* collection of concurrent agents, each performing its own action by making transitions between local configurations as described above. Now the only messages that get inserted in the buffer of a particular agent are supposed to be those messages that have been sent to that agent by other agents in the system; moreover, all messages that get sent are supposed to arrive, sooner or later. A global configuration of the system of agents is essentially a map from the agents to their local configurations; this can be represented as a set of local configurations, provided the identity of the performing agent is a component of each local configuration.

We are not to make any assumptions at all about the relative processing speeds of different agents—not even that they are stable.[1] Thus it would *not* be appropriate for a global transition to consist a local transition for *each* agent in the system. Nor would it be satisfactory for each global transition to consist of local transitions for an arbitrary subset of the agents, for then some particular agent might never be included, whereas all action performances are supposed to proceed concurrently.

The simplest way to represent arbitrary relative processing speed while ensuring that all agents eventually make transitions (until there is nothing more

[1]However, we exclude the possibility that one agent can make infinitely many transitions while another agent makes only one!

of their actions to perform, of course) seems to be the following: associate an arbitrary finite *delay* with each local transition when it is made; then let each global transition reduce all the delays by one unit, and make new local transitions for all agents whose transition delay has become zero. (It is convenient, but not essential, to let delays be positive integers.)

Similarly we may represent the time-consuming nature of physical message transmission by attaching arbitrary finite delays to messages when they are sent, only inserting them in the buffer of the receiving agent when the delay has been reduced to zero.

This technique is analogous to the way that one can represent *fairness* in terms of unbounded nondeterministic choice. The nondeterminism that arises is enormous; in many cases it is also irrelevant, in the sense that the overall message-passing and termination behaviour of a system of agents may be independent of the particular delays chosen for local transitions and message transmissions. The appeal of our operational semantics lies in the directness with which it represents the arbitrary processing speeds of agents.

Notice that each local transition involved in a global transition is determined exclusively by the corresponding local configuration—not by some global property of the entire set of local configurations. This suggests that a distributed implementation of multi-agent action performance could be obtained straightforwardly from implementations of single-agent performances. Models for concurrency based on *synchronous* communication, such as CCS [7, 8, 9] and CSP (with output guards) [3, 4], can be surprisingly difficult to implement on a distributed system—without introducing centralistic arbiters, that is.

The above considerations have not addressed the question of how a system of agents gets initialized, with the identities of particular agents known to other agents so as to permit direct communication between them. In fact it is sufficient to start from a single active agent, the so-called user-agent, all other agents being initially inactive. An active agent can offer a *contract* that incorporates an action; some inactive agent can accept the contract, whereupon it starts performing the incorporated action. As illustrated in Section 2, one can make the incorporated action report back the identity of its performing agent to its contracting agent (i.e., the sender of its contract) and then wait for a message containing an abstraction to be enacted. By offering several such contracts, binding tokens to the reported agent identities, and forming closures from the abstractions subsequently sent, each agent involved acquires knowledge of the other agents' identities, so that direct communication between them is possible.

Contracts get arbitrary finite delays, just as messages do. In [12] the agent that accepts a contract is chosen from those inactive when the delay on the contract becomes zero. But this involves some global knowledge. To eradicate this remaining trace of synchrony, one could let a contract be offered to each agent in some arbitrary order, with a new delay each time the agent is found to be active, until an inactive agent is found—if ever!

Note that agents correspond more to process activation identities than to processors, and cannot be re-contracted: once active, they remain active. This avoids confusion about what to do with messages where the target agent gets re-contracted between the sending and receipt of the message.

Message buffers are supposed to be unbounded. If they were bounded, messages that arrived when the target buffer happened to be full would presumably disappear, whereas with the present semantics of action notation, all messages are assumed to arrive safely. Incidentally, to prevent confusion between messages with identical contents sent between the same two agents, each message gets a local serial number, whose latest value is a component of the local configuration of the agent sending the message.

As mentioned in Section 2, each agent has its own local storage, which cannot directly be allocated, updated, or inspected by other agents. Shared storage, which would be needed for the action semantics of tasks in full ADA (and which is also convenient for describing *threads*) can be represented by introducing an auxiliary 'server' agent, contracted to wait for messages from 'client' agents instructing it how to act on its own local storage. Although this representation of shared storage corresponds quite well to conventional computer architecture, it is desirable to provide direct support for the concept of shared storage. It now seems possible to achieve this by a very minor extension to action notation, where the corresponding changes to the operational semantics of action notation do not invalidate the established laws of action equivalence. This extension is joint work with Martín Musicante, and we hope to report on it in detail in the near future.

4. CONCLUSION

We have looked at an action semantic description of a simple programming language that includes constructs for synchronization between concurrent tasks. The presence of concurrency does not affect the description of the other constructs at all—in sharp contrast to the situation with conventional denotational descriptions, where the domains of higher-order functions used to model concurrency and nondeterminism are radically different from those normally used to model sequential computation.

The action semantics of an ordinary rendezvous between tasks is easily expressed by a simple pattern of asynchronous message passing. It is much more complicated to give an action semantics for languages like CCS and CSP, where commitment to one synchronization possibility between two processes can exclude other possibilities—also between other processes. When processes are represented by agents, one is forced to explicate *how* a commitment made by one agent gets communicated to the other agents. But perhaps this difficulty merely reflects the fact that CCS and CSP are abstract specification languages, rather than realistic programming languages for *distributed* processing, where communication delays can be significant.

Further experiments with the action semantic description of concurrent programming languages are needed, to test the adequacy of the communicative part of action notation. We have already discussed the desirability of extending action notation with direct support for shared storage. Other features that are not so easy to represent directly in the current notation include interrupts and time-outs; some preliminary investigations addressing these topics were reported in [6].

Finally, it remains to develop a decent *theory* for reasoning about equivalence between communicative actions. The current theory of action notation [12, Appendix B] is quite weak, and doesn't provide any useful equivalences between systems of communicating agents.

The author welcomes collaboration on all aspects of the development of action semantics. The Internet address for e-mail is pdmosses@daimi.aau.dk.

Acknowledgments David Watt collaborated on the development of action notation. The work reported here has been partially funded by the Danish Science Research Council project DART (5.21.08.03).

References

[1] E. Astesiano. Inductive and operational semantics. In E. J. Neuhold and M. Paul, editors, *Formal Description of Programming Concepts*, IFIP State-of-the-Art Report, pages 51–136. Springer-Verlag, 1991.

[2] D. Goodman. *The Complete HyperCard Handbook*. Bantam, 1987.

[3] C. A. R. Hoare. Communicating sequential processes. *Commun. ACM*, 21:666–677, 1978.

[4] C. A. R. Hoare. *Communicating Sequential Processes*. Prentice-Hall, 1985.

[5] G. Kahn. Natural semantics. In *STACS'87, Proc. Symp. on Theoretical Aspects of Computer Science*, number 247 in Lecture Notes in Computer Science. Springer-Verlag, 1987.

[6] P. Krishnan and P. D. Mosses. Specifying asynchronous transfer of control. In *RTFT'92, Proc. Symp. on Formal Techniques in Real-Time and Fault-Tolerant Systems, Delft*, number 571 in Lecture Notes in Computer Science. Springer-Verlag, 1992.

[7] R. Milner. *A Calculus of Communicating Systems*. Number 92 in Lecture Notes in Computer Science. Springer-Verlag, 1980.

[8] R. Milner. *Communication and Concurrency*. Prentice-Hall, 1989.

[9] R. Milner. Operational and algebraic semantics of concurrent processes. In J. van Leeuwen, A. Meyer, M. Nivat, M. Paterson, and D. Perrin, editors, *Handbook of Theoretical Computer Science*, volume B, chapter 19. Elsevier Science Publishers, Amsterdam; and MIT Press, 1990.

[10] P. D. Mosses. Denotational semantics. In J. van Leeuwen, A. Meyer, M. Nivat, M. Paterson, and D. Perrin, editors, *Handbook of Theoretical Computer Science*, volume B, chapter 11. Elsevier Science Publishers, Amsterdam; and MIT Press, 1990.

[11] P. D. Mosses. A practical introduction to denotational semantics. In E. J. Neuhold and M. Paul, editors, *Formal Description of Programming Concepts*, IFIP State-of-the-Art Report, pages 1–49. Springer-Verlag, 1991.

[12] P. D. Mosses. *Action Semantics*. Number 26 in Cambridge Tracts in Theoretical Computer Science. Cambridge University Press, 1992.

[13] G. D. Plotkin. A structural approach to operational semantics. Lecture Notes DAIMI FN–19, Computer Science Dept., Aarhus University, 1981. Now available only from University of Edinburgh.

[14] D. A. Watt. *Programming Language Syntax and Semantics*. Prentice-Hall, 1991.

LAYERED PREDICATES

Flemming Nielson
Computer Science Department, Aarhus University, Bldg. 540
Ny Munkegade, DK-8000 Aarhus C, Denmark

Hanne Riis Nielson
Computer Science Department, Aarhus University, Bldg. 540
Ny Munkegade, DK-8000 Aarhus C, Denmark

Abstract: We review the concept of logical relations and how they interact with structural induction; furthermore we give examples of their use, and of particular interest is the combination with the PER-idea (partial equivalence relations). This is then generalized to Kripke-logical relations; the major application is to show that in combination with the PER-idea this solves the problem of establishing a substitution property in a manner conducive to structural induction. Finally we introduce the concept of Kripke-layered predicates; this allows a modular definition of predicates and supports a methodology of "proofs in stages" where each stage focuses on only one aspect and thus is more manageable. All of these techniques have been tested and refined in "realistic applications" that have been documented elsewhere.

Keywords: logical relations, partial equivalence relations, Kripke-logical relations, layered predicates, Kripke-layered predicates, substitution properties, well-structured proofs, denotational semantics, correctness of code generation, proof principles.

Contents:

0 Introduction

It is common mathematical practice to structure the development of a theory into a series of definitions and a series of facts, lemmas, propositions and theorems. Each definition introduces some concept, predicate or relation. Each fact, lemma, proposition and theorem presents insights of increasing importance and, at least in principle, increasing difficulty of proof. By structuring the main insight into a number of definitions and theorems, the latter structured into a number of lemmas etc., the claim is that each step in the overall development becomes more amenable, easier to conduct and check, and easier to adopt to analogous settings. By combining all the theorems one then obtains the insight desired about the aggregation of concepts introduced.

Well-structured and amenable proofs are of no less importance in computer science than in mathematics. Perhaps they are more important here because the structures studied are often much "bulkier" than in mathematics. As an example consider a realistic programming language with its massive amount of syntax and syntactic categories; any interesting claim about such a language is likely to be at least as "bulky" as the syntax of the language since every syntactic category must participate in the formulation of the claim and each syntactic construct in the proof. Machine implementations of automatic and semi-automatic proof systems have been devised to help in dealing with such "bulky" proofs but they all need some amount of guidance, e.g. in the form of proof tactics, and some require human interaction to solve subgoals beyond the power of the machine. Thus the need for well-structured proofs is of no less importance for automatic proofs than for manual proofs.

The main problem in adapting the techniques of mathematics to computer science is that most structures in computer science have some higher-order or recursive aspects. Examples include the meaning of procedures, the context free syntax of programming languages, domain equations, and type systems. Here even the definition of the predicates may require some ingenuity and the use of special techniques. As we shall see one such technique is that of logical relations where the predicate is defined to hold on a function if and only if the predicate is preserved across function calls: if the predicate holds of the argument it must also hold of the result. The difficulty now is that preservation of an aggregation of predicates (or a strong predicate) does not imply the preservation of each individual predicate (or of a weaker predicate). The reason is that the strong predicate may be preserved simply because it holds for no arguments and that the weak predicate may fail to be preserved because it holds for no results; we shall study concrete examples in Examples 3.1 and 3.2.

The solution is to be more careful in the aggregation of predicates and to this end a notion of layered predicates is developed. To conduct this development we first give an overview of logical relations and partial equivalence relations and we give examples suggesting that these notions are unavoidable. We next consider Kripke-logical relations and we give an extended example suggesting that this notion is unavoidable for establishing a substitution property. Finally the notion of layered predicates is developed.

Throughout the presentation we aim at avoiding complex examples; however extensive applications of the development may be found in [10, Chapter 6] and in [9] in the context of proving the correctness of code generation. Indeed the present work is a synthesis of the ideas developed there and we aim at presenting the (often rather implicit) ideas in an application-independent setting. This allows to study the techniques on their own and will make it easier to apply them to other tasks. Of particular interest would be the use of these techniques as a tool in structuring computer-based proofs. Also more general and more mathematical (e.g. categorical) formulations would be an avenue for further research.

1 Logical Relations

Our example language throughout this paper will be a monotyped λ-calculus. Its types t, expressions e, variables v and constants c are given by

$$\begin{aligned} t &::= \texttt{num} \mid \texttt{bool} \mid \texttt{charlist} \mid t \to t \\ e &::= \lambda v : t.e \mid e\, e \mid v \mid c \\ v &::= x \mid y \mid z \mid f \mid g \mid \cdots \\ c &::= * \mid + \mid - \mid \ldots \end{aligned}$$

Here **num**, **bool** and **charlist** are base types and $t_1 \to t_2$ denotes the type of functions from t_1 to t_2. It is merely for simplicity of presentation that sum types, product types and recursive types have not been included. Expressions include λ-abstraction, function application, and the use of variables and constants. We leave the exact nature of variables and constants unspecified and we shall use infix rather than prefix notation for constants.

Example 1.1 To make our examples appear a bit more realistic we shall impose a module structure upon the language. It consists of specifications and implementations. An example specification is

```
spec  sum1:  num → num
with  sum1 maps nonnegative integers to nonnegative integers
      /* sum1 x = 1 +...+ x */
```

Here the first line gives the functionality of the function **sum1**. The third line states our intention with the function but this is merely a comment and of no semantic consequence. The second line states a property of **sum1** that any acceptable implementation must satisfy. Part of our work is to formalize the informal wording of that property but the more difficult part (in general) is to do it in a way that lends itself to proofs by structural induction (on the syntax of implementations). An example implementation then is

$$\texttt{impl sum1} = \lambda \texttt{x}.\frac{\texttt{x*x}}{2} + \frac{\texttt{x}}{2}$$

Here we take some liberty in the use of the infix notation. We shall shortly return to the proof that the implementation satisfies its specification. □

This language is subject to the usual rules for well-formedness. It is worthwhile to write this out in detail. The judgements are of the form

$$tenv \vdash e : t$$

saying that in the type environment *tenv* the expression e has type t. As usual a type environment is a finite list of pairs of variables and types and we write $tenv(v) = t$ whenever (v, t) is the rightmost pair in *tenv* of form (v, t') for some t'. The central portions of the inference system are given by

$$\frac{tenv, (v,t) \vdash e : t'}{tenv \vdash \lambda v : t.\, e : t \to t'}$$

$$\frac{tenv \vdash e_1 : t \rightarrow t' \quad tenv \vdash e_2 : t}{tenv \vdash e_1\, e_2 : t'}$$

$$tenv \vdash v : t \qquad \text{if } tenv(v) = t$$

$$tenv \vdash c : t \qquad \text{if } TYPE(c) = t$$

For constants we have assumed a global assignment *TYPE* of types to the constants much like the type environment but we shall leave the details implicit. Expressions are uniquely typed; this means that if an expression has two types, as in $tenv \vdash e : t_1$ and $tenv \vdash e : t_2$, then they are equal, i.e. $t_1 = t_2$, but it does not guarantee the existence of a type for all expressions (e.g. the application `1 2`). In examples we shall allow to dispense with the types after λ-abstracted variables. The empty type environment is written ( ).

The semantics of types and expressions is usually parametrized on an interpretation $\mathcal{I}$ of the meaning of base types and constants. An example interpretation is the standard interpretation **S** that has

S(`num`)	=	NUM	(the flat domain of *rational* numbers)
S(`bool`)	=	BOOL	(the flat domain of booleans)
S(`charlist`)	=	CHARLIST	(the flat domain of lists of characters)

The semantics $\mathcal{I}[\![t]\!]$ of a type t is then given by

$$\begin{aligned}
\mathcal{I}[\![\texttt{num}]\!] &= \mathcal{I}(\texttt{num}) \\
\mathcal{I}[\![\texttt{bool}]\!] &= \mathcal{I}(\texttt{bool}) \\
\mathcal{I}[\![\texttt{charlist}]\!] &= \mathcal{I}(\texttt{charlist}) \\
\mathcal{I}[\![t_1 \rightarrow t_2]\!] &= [\mathcal{I}(t_1) \rightarrow \mathcal{I}(t_2)]
\end{aligned}$$

where the arrow constructs the set of total functions and the square brackets extract those that are continuous. It is helpful also to define the semantics $\mathcal{I}[\![tenv]\!]$ of a type environment *tenv* . Here we simply set

$$\mathcal{I}[\![(v_1, t_1), \ldots, (v_n, t_n)]\!] = \mathcal{I}[\![t_1]\!] \times \ldots \times \mathcal{I}[\![t_n]\!]$$

where the righthand side is the n-ary cartesian product ordered componentwise (and the one-point domain if $n = 0$). Corresponding to the notation $tenv(v) = t$ we define the associated projection function

$$\pi_v^{tenv} : \mathcal{I}[\![tenv]\!] \rightarrow \mathcal{I}[\![t]\!]$$

but we shall not use space for the tedious details of the formal definition. Turning to expressions we define the semantics $\mathcal{I}[\![e]\!]_{tenv} \in \mathcal{I}[\![tenv]\!] \rightarrow \mathcal{I}[\![t']\!]$ of a well-formed expression e, i.e. $tenv \vdash e : t'$, as follows

$$\begin{aligned}
\mathcal{I}[\![\lambda v : t.\ e]\!]_{tenv} &= \lambda(w_1, \ldots, w_n).\ \lambda w.\ \mathcal{I}[\![e]\!]_{tenv,(v,t)}(w_1, \ldots, w_n, w) \\
\mathcal{I}[\![e_1\ e_2]\!]_{tenv} &= \lambda(w_1, \ldots, w_n).\ \mathcal{I}[\![e_1]\!]_{tenv}(w_1, \ldots, w_n)(\mathcal{I}[\![e_2]\!]_{tenv}(w_1, \ldots, w_n)) \\
\mathcal{I}[\![v]\!]_{tenv} &= \pi_v^{tenv} \\
\mathcal{I}[\![c]\!]_{tenv} &= \lambda(w_1, \ldots, w_n).\ \mathcal{I}(c)
\end{aligned}$$

where the interpretation specifies the meaning $\mathcal{I}(c) \in \mathcal{I}[\![TYPE(c)]\!]$ of constants. We shall not go further into the behaviour of the standard interpretation **S** at this stage.

A predicate over a domain (or set) D is a total function from D to the set $\{true, false\}$ of truth values. We shall write $D \to \{true, false\}$ for the set of predicates over D. An m-ary relation over $D_1, \ldots, D_m$ is simply a predicate over the cartesian product $D_1 \times \ldots \times D_m$ and henceforth we shall regard the words predicate and relation as interchangable.

Definition 1.2 An *indexed relation* R over interpretations $\mathcal{I}_1, \ldots, \mathcal{I}_m$ is a collection of m-ary relations $R_t : \mathcal{I}_1[\![t]\!] \times \ldots \times \mathcal{I}_m[\![t]\!] \to \{true, false\}$ one for each type t. It is a *logical relation* iff

$$R_{t_1 \to t_2}(f_1, \ldots, f_m) \equiv \forall (w_1, \ldots, w_m) : \quad \begin{array}{c} R_{t_1}(w_1, \ldots, w_m) \\ \Downarrow \\ R_{t_2}(f_1(w_1), \ldots, f_m(w_m)) \end{array}$$

holds for all types t_1 and t_2. □

Clearly a logical relation is uniquely determined by its effect on the base types. To avoid excessive use of brackets we write $e \models R[t]$ for $R_t(\mathcal{I}_1[\![e]\!]_{()}(\,), \ldots, \mathcal{I}_m[\![e]\!]_{()}(\,))$ whenever R is an indexed relation.

We shall next consider some examples of the use of logical relations. These will be grouped into three groups corresponding to increasing complexity of formulation. The first group is concerned with logical relations over one interpretation only.

Example 1.3 Returning to the `sum1` example our first task is to formalize the interface condition:

```
sum1 maps nonnegative integers to nonnegative integers
```

We may define a logical relation *NONNEG* over **S** as follows:

$$\begin{array}{lll} NONNEG_{\texttt{num}}(w) & \equiv & w \geq 0 \\ NONNEG_{\texttt{bool}}(w) & \equiv & true \\ NONNEG_{\texttt{charlist}}(w) & \equiv & true \end{array}$$

The definition of $NONNEG_{\texttt{bool}}$ and $NONNEG_{\texttt{charlist}}$ may seem arbitrary but they will be instances of a general pattern that will emerge later. In a similar way we may define a logical relation *INT* as follows:

$$\begin{array}{lll} INT_{\texttt{num}}(w) & \equiv & w \in \{\ldots, -2, -1, 0, 1, 2, \ldots\} \\ INT_{\texttt{bool}}(w) & \equiv & true \\ INT_{\texttt{charlist}}(w) & \equiv & true \end{array}$$

Given logical relations R' (e.g. *NONNEG*) and R'' (e.g. *INT*) we may define a logical relation $R' \wedge R''$ by

$$\begin{array}{lcl}(R' \wedge R'')_{\mathtt{num}}(w) & \equiv & R'_{\mathtt{num}}(w) \wedge R''_{\mathtt{num}}(w) \\ (R' \wedge R'')_{\mathtt{bool}}(w) & \equiv & R'_{\mathtt{bool}}(w) \wedge R''_{\mathtt{bool}}(w) \\ (R' \wedge R'')_{\mathtt{charlist}}(w) & \equiv & R'_{\mathtt{charlist}}(w) \wedge R''_{\mathtt{charlist}}(w)\end{array}$$

It is very important to point out, as was already hinted at in the Introduction, that in general $(R' \wedge R'')_t(w)$ will be different from $R'_t(w) \wedge R''_t(w)$; we shall study concrete examples in Examples 3.1 and 3.2. Turning to the logical relation *NONNEG* ∧ *INT* we see that

$$\mathtt{sum1} \models (\mathit{NONNEG} \wedge \mathit{INT})[\mathtt{num} \rightarrow \mathtt{num}]$$

is the desired reformulation of the interface condition.

A direct proof would proceed by assuming that x is a nonnegative integer and would then show that also $\frac{\mathtt{x*x}}{2} + \frac{\mathtt{x}}{2}$ is. This is not simply a structural induction because for odd x also $\mathtt{x*x}$ and x will be odd; but luckily $\mathtt{x*x+x}$ is even so that $\frac{\mathtt{x*x}}{2} + \frac{\mathtt{x}}{2}$ is an integer. The details of this proof are of no interest to us, however.

A more well-structured proof might split the combined proof about the relation *NONNEG*∧ *INT* into separate proofs about *NONNEG* and *INT*. Clearly one can show

$$\begin{array}{lcl}\mathtt{sum1} & \models & \mathit{NONNEG}[\mathtt{num} \rightarrow \mathtt{num}] \\ \mathtt{sum1} & \models & \mathit{INT}[\mathtt{num} \rightarrow \mathtt{num}]\end{array}$$

by the same methods of reasoning that we sketched above. From this we would like to infer

$$\mathtt{sum1} \models (\mathit{NONNEG} \wedge \mathit{INT})[\mathtt{num} \rightarrow \mathtt{num}]$$

We may do so if we have available to us a proof rule

$$\frac{e \models R'[t] \quad e \models R''[t]}{e \models (R' \wedge R'')[t]} \quad \text{if } t \ldots$$

but this does not hold for all types t; as was claimed above, the reason is that there are likely to be types t' such that $(R' \wedge R'')_{t'}(w)$ differs from $R'_{t'}(w) \wedge R''_{t'}(w)$. However, the proof rule is available to us for $t = \mathtt{num} \rightarrow \mathtt{num}$ (as well as $t = \mathtt{num}$) and the proof carries through. □

Example 1.4 For an example of a somewhat different flavour, and to prepare for the development of the next sections, consider the following module:

```
spec  badge:  charlist→ charlist
with  badge only involves 7 bit ASCII characters
impl  badge = λx. if #x ≤ 17
                  then "Professor" ++ x
                  else "Prof." ++ x
```

Here # gives the length of a list and ++ concatenates two lists. (In the standard semantics these functions will be strict in each argument.) The purpose of the module is to construct a conference badge but taking into account that some names are long and that badges have fixed sizes. Additionally the badge printer only correctly deals with 7 bit ASCII characters.

To formalize the interface condition we define a logical relation *LOWASCII* by

$$
\begin{aligned}
LOWASCII_{\texttt{num}}(w) &\equiv \textit{true}\\
LOWASCII_{\texttt{bool}}(w) &\equiv \textit{true}\\
LOWASCII_{\texttt{charlist}}(w) &\equiv \text{all characters in } w \text{ have ASCII value}\\
&\ \text{at most 127 (or } w = \bot)
\end{aligned}
$$

(We shall not bother to be more formal about the formulation of $LOWASCII_{\texttt{charlist}}$.) This follows the pattern of the previous example. Then

$$\texttt{badge} \models LOWASCII[\texttt{charlist} \to \texttt{charlist}]$$

presents the desired formalization. Clearly if applied to a name that contains an offending character (like the Danish æ, ø and å) so will the result but at least no such characters will be introduced by **badge** provided that none are present in the argument. □

The second group of examples is concerned with logical relations over a sequence of pairwise distinct interpretations.

Example 1.5 Strictness analysis aims at determining when functions need to evaluate their arguments. It is based upon the 2-point domain

2 = 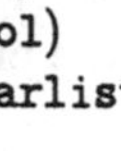

An interpretation **I** for a simple version of strictness analysis is obtained by specifying

$$
\begin{aligned}
\mathbf{I}(\texttt{num}) &= \mathbf{2}\\
\mathbf{I}(\texttt{bool}) &= \mathbf{2}\\
\mathbf{I}(\texttt{charlist}) &= \mathbf{2}
\end{aligned}
$$

Concerning constants we shall give two examples. If

$$\mathbf{S}(*) = \lambda w_1.\ \lambda w_2.\ \begin{cases} \bot & \text{if } w_1 = \bot \vee w_2 = \bot \\ w_1 \times w_2 & \text{otherwise} \end{cases}$$

it is natural to set

$$\mathbf{I}(*) = \lambda w_1.\ \lambda w_2.\ w_1 \sqcap w_2$$

where $\sqcap$ denotes binary meet, i.e. $0 \sqcap 0 = 0 \sqcap 1 = 1 \sqcap 0 = 0$ and $1 \sqcap 1 = 1$. Similarly, if

$$\mathbf{S}(\texttt{if}) = \lambda w_1.\ \lambda w_2.\ \lambda w_3.\ \begin{cases} \bot & \text{if } w_1 = \bot \\ w_2 & \text{if } w_1 = \mathit{true} \\ w_3 & \text{if } w_1 = \mathit{false} \end{cases}$$

then it is natural to set

$$\mathbf{I}(\texttt{if}) = \lambda w_1.\ \lambda w_2.\ \lambda w_3.\ \begin{cases} \bot & \text{if } w_1 = \bot \\ w_2 \sqcup w_3 & \text{otherwise} \end{cases}$$

where $\sqcup$ denotes binary join.

To express the correctness of the strictness analysis we define a logical relation *COR* over the interpretations **S** and **I**. It is given by

$$\begin{aligned} \mathit{COR}_{\mathbf{num}}(w^1, w^2) &\equiv (w^2 = \bot \Rightarrow w^1 = \bot) \\ \mathit{COR}_{\mathbf{bool}}(w^1, w^2) &\equiv (w^2 = \bot \Rightarrow w^1 = \bot) \\ \mathit{COR}_{\mathbf{charlist}}(w^1, w^2) &\equiv (w^2 = \bot \Rightarrow w^1 = \bot) \end{aligned}$$

It is then quite standard to prove the correctness of `*` and `if`, but we shall dispense with the details. □

The third group of examples is concerned with logical relations over a sequence of interpretations that are not necessarily pairwise distinct.

Example 1.6 The need for more than one appearance of the same interpretation arises when we want to relate values rather than just express properties about them. To be more specific let us consider the following module:

```
spec sq : num → num
with sq is independent of the sign of the argument
impl sq = λx. x * x
```

It is not difficult to be more formal about the interface condition. Some possibilities are

$$\texttt{sq} = \texttt{sq} \circ \mathit{abs}$$
$$\texttt{sq} = \texttt{sq} \circ \mathit{neg}$$
$$\forall x^1, x^2 : \mathit{abs}(x^1) = \mathit{abs}(x^2) \Rightarrow \texttt{sq}(x^1) = \texttt{sq}(x^2) \qquad \text{(a)}$$

where *abs* is the function that gives the absolute value and *neg* is the function that multiplies by (-1).

However, these formulations do not immediately lend themselves to proof by structural induction. As we shall see below this will be the case if we can use the framework of logical relations. Our first approach will be to consider

$$\forall x^1, x^2 : abs(x^1) = abs(x^2) \Rightarrow abs(\mathtt{sq}(x^1)) = abs(\mathtt{sq}(x^2)) \qquad \text{(b)}$$

We may define a logical relation SQ over interpretations $\mathbf{S}$, $\mathbf{S}$ by

$$\begin{aligned} SQ_{\mathbf{num}}(w^1, w^2) &\equiv abs(w^1) = abs(w^2) \\ SQ_{\mathtt{bool}}(w^1, w^2) &\equiv w^1 = w^2 \\ SQ_{\mathtt{charlist}}(w^1, w^2) &\equiv w^1 = w^2 \end{aligned}$$

and clearly (b) is then equivalent to

$$\mathtt{sq} \models SQ[\mathbf{num} \rightarrow \mathbf{num}]$$

Since **sq** always yields a nonnegative result this is equivalent to (a) as well.

To capture (a) directly we may proceed as follows. Rather than having the base type **num** we shall have several distinct versions; for the present purposes $\mathbf{num}_{abs}$ and $\mathbf{num}_{id}$ suffice. These will be interpreted in the same way in all interpretations but their presence allows us to give the following modified definition of the logical relation SQ over $\mathbf{S}$, $\mathbf{S}$:

$$\begin{aligned} SQ_{\mathbf{num}_{abs}}(w^1, w^2) &\equiv abs(w^1) = abs(w^2) \\ SQ_{\mathbf{num}_{id}}(w^1, w^2) &\equiv w^1 = w^2 \\ SQ_{\mathtt{bool}}(w^1, w^2) &\equiv w^1 = w^2 \\ SQ_{\mathtt{charlist}}(w^1, w^2) &\equiv w^1 = w^2 \end{aligned}$$

Then the condition

$$\mathtt{sq} \models SQ[\mathbf{num}_{abs} \rightarrow \mathbf{num}_{id}]$$

is equivalent to the desired interface condition (a).

For any base type t, i.e. $t \in \{\mathbf{num}_{abs}, \mathbf{num}_{id}, \mathtt{bool}, \mathtt{charlist}\}$, each SQ_t is an equivalence relation over $\mathbf{S}[\![t]\!]$, i.e. SQ_t is a reflexive, transitive and symmetric relation. But is it more advantageous to exploit only the weaker fact that each such SQ_t is a *partial equivalence relation* (abbreviated PER); this just means that for a base type t each SQ_t is a (not necessarily reflexive) transitive and symmetric relation. Then one can show by structural induction over all types t that SQ_t is a partial equivalence relation over $\mathbf{S}[\![t]\!]$, i.e. we do not need to restrict our attention to base types only. (This would not be the case if we had studied equivalence relations.)

So our approach is essentially that of [1]. A notational difference is that our formulation is close to that of the *faithfulness* relation studied in [8]. This means that the formulation would be useful also for analyses carried out by means of non-standard type inference. The use of binary relations over the same domain, e.g. in the form of partial equivalence relations, rather than just unary predicates seems to be necessary for validating a number of analyses. Examples include binding time analysis [2] and liveness analysis [6]. □

Logical relations are useful because they interact very well with the semantics of the λ-calculus. In particular they are well suited to proofs by structural induction.

Definition 1.7 An indexed relation R over $\mathcal{I}_1, \ldots, \mathcal{I}_m$ is said to *admit structural induction* whenever it satisfies the following condition:

For every type environment $tenv = (v_1, t_1), \ldots, (v_n, t_n)$ and every well-typed expression e of type t, i.e. $tenv \vdash e : t$; if

$$R_{t_i}(w_i^1, \ldots, w_i^m) \quad \text{for all } i = 1, \ldots, n$$

$$R_{t'}(\mathcal{I}_1(c'), \ldots, \mathcal{I}_m(c')) \quad \text{for all constants } c' \text{ of type } t' \text{ occurring in } e$$

then

$$R_t(\mathcal{I}[\![e]\!]_{tenv}(w_1^1, \ldots, w_n^1), \ldots, \mathcal{I}_m[\![e]\!]_{tenv}(w_1^m, \ldots, w_n^m)).$$ □

Lemma 1.8 *Logical relations admit structural induction.* □

Proof. Using the notation of the definition this is a structural induction over e. For a variable v the result is immediate from the assumptions. This is also the case for a constant c. For an application $e_1\ e_2$ we use the induction hypothesis to obtain

$$R_{t' \to t}(\mathcal{I}_1[\![e_1]\!]_{tenv}(w_1^1, \ldots, w_n^1), \ldots, \mathcal{I}_m[\![e_1]\!]_{tenv}(w_1^m, \ldots, w_n^m))$$
$$R_{t'}(\mathcal{I}_1[\![e_2]\!]_{tenv}(w_1^1, \ldots, w_n^1), \ldots, \mathcal{I}_m[\![e_2]\!]_{tenv}(w_1^m, \ldots, w_n^m))$$

and then we use that R is logical; to be more specific we use the following proof rule

$$\frac{R_{t' \to t}(f_1, \ldots, f_m) \quad R_{t'}(w_1, \ldots, w_m)}{R_t(f_1(w_1), \ldots, f_m(w_m))}$$

whose validity is a direct consequence of R being logical. For a λ-abstraction $\lambda v : t'.\ e$ we must show

$$R_{t' \to t''}(\mathcal{I}_1[\![\lambda v : t'.\ e]\!]_{tenv}(w_1^1, \ldots, w_n^1), \ldots, \mathcal{I}_m[\![\lambda v : t'.\ e]\!]_{tenv}(w_1^m, \ldots, w_n^m))$$

By R being logical this amounts to assuming

$$R_{t'}(w_{n+1}^1, \ldots, w_{n+1}^m)$$

and showing

$$R_{t''}(\mathcal{I}_1[\![\lambda v : t'.\ e]\!]_{tenv}(w_1^1, \ldots, w_n^1)(w_{n+1}^1), \ldots, \mathcal{I}_m[\![\lambda v : t'.e]\!]_{tenv}(w_1^m, \ldots, w_n^m)(w_{n+1}^m)).$$

But since

$$\mathcal{I}_i[\![\lambda v : t'.\ e]\!]_{tenv}(w_1^i, \ldots, w_n^i)(w_{n+1}^i) = \mathcal{I}_i[\![e]\!]_{tenv,(v,t')}(w_1^i, \ldots, w_n^i, w_{n+1}^i)$$

this follows from the induction hypothesis. □

Taking $n = 0$ and $m = 1$ we get:

Corollary 1.9 If the closed expression e has type t, i.e. $(\,) \vdash e : t$, and $c' \models R[t']$ for all constants c' of type t' occurring in e, then $e \models R[t]$ provided that R is logical. □

Historical Remark The concept of logical relations, including the result on structural induction (our Lemma 1.8), is often attributed to [12]. Actually, [11] predated [12] and contained many of the ideas and one should also acknowledge the relational functors of [13]. That binary relations over a set, rather than just unary predicates, is sometimes needed for abstract interpretation was first realized in [6] in terms of a distinction between "first-order" and "second-order" analyses; the link to partial equivalence relations is due to [1]. □

2 Kripke-Logical Relations

The definitions of the predicates of the previous section were mostly rather natural. However, in Example 1.6 the use of partial equivalence relations accounted for a somewhat different flavour of the formulation. To motivate the development of the present section it is worthwhile to look closer at this difference.

All but one of the examples of the previous section were such that the formulation of the predicates was quite natural at level 0, i.e. for base types. The extension to higher levels, i.e. function types, was then accomplished using the general technique of logical relations. In Example 1.6 the predicate was quite natural to formulate at level 1, i.e. for functions in `num` $\rightarrow$ `num`. The formulation at level 0, i.e. for `num`, was not so straightforward and we found it necessary to use partial equivalence relations, or more precisely, to use the same interpretation more than once. Then the extension to higher levels could be accomplished using the general technique of logical relations.

In this section we shall consider an example that is more along the lines of Example 1.6 than the other examples. But it presents additional complications that we shall solve by parameterizing the predicates with elements drawn from a partially ordered set.

Example 2.1 As a variation of our `badge` example consider the following module for writing a letter of invitation:

```
spec letter:  charlist → charlist
with letter is a character list with hole(s) in it
impl letter = λx. "Dear Professor" ++ x ++", We hereby invite ..."
```

By mapping `letter` onto a list of names we will then obtain a list of letters. To ensure that all letters are materially the same, e.g. any discount is offered uniformly to all recipients, we request that `letter` is a character string with hole(s) in it; these holes will be filled with the names of recipients. To be more formal we may rephrase this as

$$\exists l_0, \ldots, l_n : \texttt{letter} = \lambda \texttt{x}.\ (l_0\texttt{++x++}l_1\texttt{++}\ldots\texttt{++x++}l_n)$$

Similar situations arise frequently in correctness proofs for code generation based on denotational semantics [9, 10].

The above formulation is given at level 1, i.e. on functions in **charlist** → **charlist**, and so we need to find a definition at level 0. Trying to adapt the use of partial equivalence relations we might search for a relation ~ and rephrase the interface condition as follows:

$$\mathtt{x} \sim \mathtt{y} \Rightarrow \mathtt{letter\ x} \sim \mathtt{letter\ y}$$

However, this approach does not seem to work because of difficulties in defining a relation like ~. The problem is that when analyzing the result of **letter x** it is not possible to distinguish between those substrings that are present because of the insertion of the parameter, and those substrings that just happened to be part of $l_0, \ldots, l_n$.

To overcome this problem we shall pretend that there are special characters called *holes* that may be used to indicate where substitutions should occur. We shall write $l = l_1[l_2/h]$ whenever l is obtained from l_1 by replacing each hole h by the substring l_2. (A formal definition will be given shortly.) The interface condition will then be formulated as follows:

$$SUBST(\{(h,w)\})([h],w) \Rightarrow SUBST(\{(h,w)\})(\mathtt{letter}[h], \mathtt{letter}\ w)$$

where the predicate is given by

$$SUBST(\{(h,l)\})(l_1,l_2) \equiv (l_1[l/h] = l_2)$$

and $[h]$ denotes a one-element list consisting of the character denoted by h. From this we shall see that we can infer $\mathtt{letter}\ w = (\mathtt{letter}[h])[w/h]$ and that the interface condition then holds. The formal details follow. □

Example 2.2 Before going into the formal development it is worthwhile to investigate the number of holes that will be necessary. So far we have only seen the need for one but consider the following module:

```
spec invite:  charlist → charlist → charlist
with invite is a character list with holes(s) in it
impl invite = λy. λx. "Dear Mr.  "++ x ++," You are hereby invited
                        to the "++ x ++" conference, ..."
```

(This might be suitable for a conference bureau.) To formulate the interface condition properly we will need two different holes and in general we will need an arbitrary finite number of holes. This means that the parameter to the *SUBST* relation will be a finite set and not just a singleton set; these parameters are naturally ordered by subset inclusion.— In terms of the motivating applications of code generation, this phenomenon arises whenever nested fixed points (e.g. nested while loops) are allowed. □

In the remainder of this section we develop the general theory of Kripke-logical relations and study some of their properties. We then go on to the rather more demanding task of applying Kripke-logical relations to Example 2.1.

Definition 2.3 A parameterized and indexed relation R over a non-empty partially ordered set Δ and interpretations $\mathcal{I}_1, \ldots, \mathcal{I}_m$ is a collection of parameterized m-ary relations $R_t[\delta] : \mathcal{I}_1[\![t]\!] \times \ldots \times \mathcal{I}_m[\![t]\!] \rightarrow \{true, false\}$ one for each type t and $\delta \in \Delta$. It is a *Kripke-indexed relation* iff

$$\forall \delta' \sqsupseteq \delta : R_t[\delta](w_1, \ldots, w_m) \Rightarrow R_t[\delta'](w_1, \ldots, w_m)$$

holds for all types t. It is a *Kripke-logical relation* iff it is a Kripke-indexed relation and

$$R_{t_1 \rightarrow t_2}[\delta](f_1, \ldots, f_m) \equiv \forall \delta' \sqsupseteq \delta : \forall (w_1, \ldots, w_m) : \quad R_{t_1}[\delta'](w_1, \ldots, w_m) \Downarrow R_{t_2}[\delta'](f_1(w_1), \ldots, f_m(w_m))$$

holds for all types t_1 and t_2. □

It is possible to weaken the assumptions on Δ, e.g. to be a quasi-ordered set, but for our purposes this is hardly worth the effort. Clearly a Kripke-logical relation is uniquely determined by its effect on the base types. A logical relation may be regarded as a Kripke-logical relation with Δ having only one element. The need for Δ to have more than one element was hinted at in Example 2.2. The need for the "$\forall \delta' \sqsupseteq \delta$:" will be illustrated in the proof of Lemma 2.13. To avoid excessive use of semantic brackets we shall write $e \models R[t, \delta]$ for $R_t[\delta](\mathcal{I}_1[\![e]\!]_{()}(\,), \ldots, \mathcal{I}_m[\![e]\!]_{()}(\,))$ and $e \models R[t]$ for $\forall \delta \in \Delta : e \models R[t, \delta]$ whenever R is a Kripke-indexed relation.

Fact 2.4 If R is a Kripke-indexed relation and Δ has a least element, $\perp_\Delta$, then $e \models R[t, \perp_\Delta]$ is equivalent to $e \models R[t]$. □

Luckily Kripke-logical relations share the good properties of logical relations, namely that they are well suited to proofs by structural induction.

Definition 2.5 A Kripke-indexed relation R over Δ and $\mathcal{I}_1, \ldots, \mathcal{I}_m$ is said to *admit structural induction* whenever it satisfies the following condition:

> For every type environment $tenv = (v_1, t_1), \ldots, (v_n, t_n)$, every element $\delta \in \Delta$ and every well-typed expression e of type t, i.e. $tenv \vdash e : t$; if
>
> $R_{t_i}[\delta](w_i^1, \ldots, w_i^m)$ for all $i = 1, \ldots, n$
>
> $R_{t'}[\delta](\mathcal{I}_1(c'), \ldots, \mathcal{I}_m(c'))$ for all constants c' of type t' occurring in e
>
> then
>
> $R_t[\delta](\mathcal{I}_1[\![e]\!]_{tenv}(w_1^1, \ldots, w_n^1), \ldots, \mathcal{I}_m[\![e]\!]_{tenv}(w_1^m, \ldots, w_n^m))$ □

Lemma 2.6 *Kripke-logical relations admit structural induction.* □

Proof. Using the notation of the definition this is a structural induction over e. For a variable v the result is immediate from the assumptions. This is also the case for a constant c. For an application $e_1\ e_2$ we use the induction hypothesis to obtain

$$R_{t'\to t}[\delta](\mathcal{I}_1[\![e_1]\!]_{tenv}(w_1^1,\ldots,w_n^1),\ldots,\mathcal{I}_m[\![e_1]\!]_{tenv}(w_1^m,\ldots,w_n^m))$$
$$R_{t'}[\delta](\mathcal{I}_1[\![e_2]\!]_{tenv}(w_1^1,\ldots,w_n^1),\ldots,\mathcal{I}_m[\![e_2]\!]_{tenv}(w_1^m,\ldots,w_n^m))$$

and then we use that R is Kripke-logical; to be more specific we use the following proof rule

$$\frac{R_{t'\to t}[\delta](f_1,\ldots,f_m)\quad R_{t'}[\delta](w_1,\ldots,w_m)}{R_t[\delta](f_1(w_1),\ldots,f_m(w_m))}$$

whose validity is a direct consequence of R being Kripke-logical (and $\delta \sqsupseteq \delta$). For a λ-abstraction $\lambda v : t'.\ e$ we must show

$$R_{t'\to t}[\delta](\mathcal{I}_1[\![\lambda v : t'.\ e]\!]_{tenv}(w_1^1,\ldots,w_n^1),\ldots,\mathcal{I}_m[\![\lambda v : t'.\ e]\!]_{tenv}(w_1^m,\ldots,w_n^m))$$

By R being Kripke-logical this amounts to choosing $\delta' \sqsupseteq \delta$ and assuming

$$R_{t'}[\delta'](w_{n+1}^1,\ldots,w_{n+1}^m)$$

and showing

$$R_t[\delta'](\mathcal{I}_1[\![\lambda v : t'.\ e]\!]_{tenv}(w_1^1,\ldots,w_n^1)(w_{n+1}^1),\ldots,\mathcal{I}_m[\![\lambda v : t'.\ e]\!]_{tenv}(w_1^m,\ldots,w_n^m)(w_{n+1}^m))$$

But by assumption we have

$$R_{t_i}[\delta](w_i^1,\ldots,w_i^m) \text{ for all } i = 1,\ldots,n$$

so using the proof rule

$$\frac{R_t[\delta](w_1,\ldots,w_m)}{R_t[\delta'](w_1,\ldots,w_m)}\ \delta' \sqsupseteq \delta$$

we obtain

$$R_{t_i}[\delta'](w_i^1,\ldots,w_i^m) \text{ for all } i = 1,\ldots,n$$

As we also have

$$R_{t_i}[\delta'](w_i^1,\ldots,w_i^m) \text{ for } i = n+1$$

it follows from the induction hypothesis that

$$R_t[\delta'](\mathcal{I}_1[\![e]\!]_{tenv,(v,t')}(w_1^1,\ldots,w_n^1,w_{n+1}^1),\ldots,\mathcal{I}_m[\![e]\!]_{tenv,(v,t')}(w_1^m,\ldots,w_n^m,w_{n+1}^m))$$

But since

$$\mathcal{I}_i[\![\lambda v : t'.\, e]\!]_{tenv}(w_1^i, \ldots, w_n^i)(w_{n+1}^i) = \mathcal{I}_i[\![e]\!]_{tenv,(v,t')}(w_1^i, \ldots, w_n^i, w_{n+1}^i)$$

this is the desired result. □

Taking $n = 0$ and $m = 1$ we get:

Corollary 2.7 If the closed expression e has type t, i.e. $(\,) \vdash e : t$, and $c' \models R[t']$ for all constants c' of type t' occurring in e, then $e \models R[t]$ whenever R is Kripke-logical. □

Extended Example: Establishing Substitution Properties

To apply the technique of Kripke-logical relations to our `letter` example we must take care of a few formalities before defining the *SUBST* relation. We begin by looking closer at the standard interpretation **S** and in particular the equation

$$\mathbf{S}(\texttt{charlist}) = \text{CHARLIST}$$

where CHARLIST is the flat domain of lists of characters. Henceforth we shall assume that

$$\text{CHARLIST} = ((\text{NORMAL} \cup \text{HOLE})^*)_\perp$$

where NORMAL is a (finite) set of characters, HOLE is a disjoint (and in general infinite) set of "hole characters", $(-)^*$ constructs lists and $(-)_\perp$ constructs flat domains. We shall assume that NORMAL includes all the usual ASCII characters and we shall write $h_1, h_2, \ldots$ for the elements of HOLE.

The partially ordered set Δ has as elements those sets of pairs of holes and lists of characters that are acceptable according to the definition given below. The partial order is subset inclusion and it will emerge that $\emptyset$, the empty set, is the least element. A set δ is *acceptable* iff

- $\delta \subseteq \text{HOLE} \times (\text{NORMAL} \cup \text{HOLE})^*$,
- δ is finite,
- δ is functional, i.e. $(h, l_1), (h, l_2) \in \delta \Rightarrow l_1 = l_2$,
- $(h, l) \in \delta \Rightarrow \text{FH}(l) \subseteq \text{DOM}(\delta)$

where FH(l) is the set of free holes in l, i.e.

$$\text{FH}([\,]) = \emptyset$$

$$\text{FH}([c]\text{++}l) = \begin{cases} \{c\} \cup \text{FH}(l) & \text{if } c \in \text{HOLE} \\ \text{FH}(l) & \text{if } c \in \text{NORMAL} \end{cases}$$

and DOM(δ) is the "domain" of δ, i.e.

$$\mathrm{DOM}(\delta) = \{h \mid \exists l : (h,l) \in \delta\}$$

The first three conditions for acceptability are rather straightforward; the fourth condition is of a more technical nature and is suitable for the subsequent development (see e.g. Fact 2.10). Whenever δ is acceptable and $h \in \mathrm{DOM}(\delta)$ we shall write $\delta(h)$ for the unique l such that $(h,l) \in \delta$.

We write $l[l_1/h_1,\ldots,l_m/h_m]$ for the result of substituting each list l_i for each hole h_i in l. More formally we have

$$\begin{aligned} [\,][l_1/h_1,\ldots,l_m/h_m] &= [\,] \\ ([c]{+}{+}l)[l_1/h_1,\ldots,l_m/h_m] &= \begin{cases} [c]{+}{+}(l[l_1/h_1,\ldots,l_m/h_m]) & \text{if } c \notin \{h_1,\ldots,h_m\} \\ l_i{+}{+}(l[l_1/h_1,\ldots,l_m/h_m]) & \text{if } c = h_i \end{cases} \end{aligned}$$

and it is convenient to write also $\bot[l_1/h_1,\ldots,l_m/h_m] = \bot$ as well as $\mathrm{FH}(\bot) = \emptyset$.

We may then attempt to define a Kripke-logical relation *SUBST* over Δ and S,S as follows:

$$\begin{aligned} &SUBST_{\mathbf{num}}[\delta](w^1,w^2) \equiv (w^1 = w^2) \\ &SUBST_{\mathbf{bool}}[\delta](w^1,w^2) \equiv (w^1 = w^2) \\ &SUBST_{\mathbf{charlist}}[\{(h_1,l_1),\ldots,(h_m,l_m)\}](w^1,w^2) \equiv \\ &\qquad (w^1[l_1/h_1,\ldots,l_m/h_m] = w^2) \wedge (\mathrm{FH}(w^1) \subseteq \{h_1,\ldots,h_m\}) \end{aligned}$$

Fact 2.8 For all base types t, if $SUBST_t[\delta](w^1,w^2)$ then $(w^1 = \bot) \vee (w^2 = \bot)$ is equivalent to $w^1 = \bot = w^2$. □

Proof. For t = num and t = `bool` the result is trivial. For t = `charlist` it follows because $\delta \in \Delta$ implies that any $(h,l) \in \delta$ has $l \neq \bot$. (It is unlikely that the result holds for function types.) □

Lemma 2.9 *SUBST as defined above is a Kripke-logical relation.* □

Proof. It suffices to prove that

$$\delta' \sqsupseteq \delta \wedge SUBST_t[\delta](w^1,w^2) \Rightarrow SUBST_t[\delta'](w^1,w^2)$$

for all base types $t \in \{$`num`, `bool`, `charlist`$\}$. This is immediate except for t = `charlist`. So assume that $\delta' \sqsupseteq \delta$ and that $SUBST_{\mathbf{charlist}}[\delta](w^1,w^2)$. If $w^1 = \bot$ or $w^2 = \bot$ then $w^1 = \bot = w^2$ and the result is immediate so we shall henceforth assume that $w^1 \neq \bot$ and $w^2 \neq \bot$. It is possible to find $m' \geq m$ and $h_1,l_1,\ldots,h_{m'},l_{m'}$ such that

$$\begin{aligned} \delta &= \{(h_1,l_1),\ldots,(h_m,l_m)\} \\ \delta' &= \{(h_1,l_1),\ldots,(h_{m'},l_{m'})\} \end{aligned}$$

Our assumption $SUBST_{\texttt{charlist}}[\delta](w^1, w^2)$ implies that $\mathrm{FH}(w^1) \subseteq \{h_1, \ldots, h_m\}$ and from this $\mathrm{FH}(w^1) \subseteq \{h_1, \ldots, h_{m'}\}$ immediately follows since $m' \geq m$. Next our assumption $SUBST_{\texttt{charlist}}[\delta](w^1, w^2)$ also implies that $w^1[l_1/h_1, \ldots, l_m/h_m] = w^2$ and from this $w^1[l_1/h_1, \ldots, l_{m'}/h_{m'}] = w^2$ follows because we also know that $\mathrm{FH}(w^1) \subseteq \{h_1, \ldots, h_m\}$. This establishes $SUBST_{\texttt{charlist}}[\delta'](w^1, w^2)$. □

It is convenient to note also

Fact 2.10 If $SUBST_{\texttt{charlist}}[\{(h_1, l_1), \ldots, (h_m, l_m)\}](w^1, w^2)$ then

$$\mathrm{FH}(w^1) \subseteq \{h_1, \ldots, h_m\}$$
$$\mathrm{FH}(w^2) \subseteq \textstyle\bigcup_{i=1}^{m} \mathrm{FH}(l_i) \subseteq \{h_1, \ldots, h_m\}$$ □

Proof. The first condition is immediate and then gives the first inclusion in the second condition because $w^1[l_1/h_1, \ldots, l_m/h_m] = w^2$. The second inclusion in the second condition then follows from acceptability of $\{(h_1, l_1), \ldots, (h_m, l_m)\}$. □

We now have two tasks ahead of us. One is to show that our *SUBST* relation is satisfied by `letter` and the other is to show that the *SUBST* relation does express the substitution property that we are interested in. We begin with the former.

Lemma 2.11 `letter` $\models$ *SUBST*[`charlist` $\rightarrow$ `charlist`]. □

For the proof we consider $\delta \in \Delta$. To show the result we must consider $\delta' \sqsupseteq \delta$ and assume that $SUBST_{\texttt{charlist}}[\delta'](w^1, w^2)$ and then show $SUBST_{\texttt{charlist}}[\delta'](\texttt{letter}\ w^1, \texttt{letter}\ w^2)$. Writing $\delta' = \{(h_1, l_1), \ldots, (h_m, l_m)\}$ our assumptions amount to $\mathrm{FH}(w^1) \subseteq \{h_1, \ldots, h_m\}$ and $w^1[l_1/h_1, \ldots, l_m/h_m] = w^2$. Since

`letter` = λx. `"Dear Professor "++ x ++", We hereby invite ..."`

and 'D', 'e', … ∈ NORMAL it follows that

$$\mathrm{FH}(\texttt{letter}\ w^1) = \mathrm{FH}(w^1) \subseteq \{h_1, \ldots, h_m\}$$
$$(\texttt{letter}\ w^1)[l_1/h_1, \ldots, l_m/h_m] = \texttt{letter}(w^1[l_1/h_1, \ldots, l_m/h_m]) = \texttt{letter}\ w^2$$

and this establishes the desired result.

Example 2.12 To show that the *SUBST* relation is not trivially true we shall show that

¬(`badge` $\models$ *SUBST*[`charlist` $\rightarrow$ `charlist`])

First define

l_1 = `"this is a name with 39 characters in it"`
$\delta = \{(h_1, l_1)\}$

and note that $\delta \in \Delta$ and clearly $SUBST_{\texttt{charlist}}[\delta]([h_1], l_1)$. But

$$\texttt{badge}\ [h_1] = \texttt{"Professor "++}\ [h_1]$$
$$\texttt{badge}\ l_1 = \texttt{"Prof.   "++}\ l_1$$

and clearly $SUBST_{\texttt{charlist}}[\delta](\texttt{badge}\ [h_1], \texttt{badge}\ l_1)$ fails. □

That $SUBST$ expresses the desired substitution property follows from

Lemma 2.13

$$SUBST_{\texttt{charlist}\to\texttt{charlist}}[\emptyset](f, f) \wedge f \neq \bot$$
$$\Updownarrow$$
$$\exists w_0, \ldots, w_n \in \text{CHARLIST} : \forall w \in \text{CHARLIST}\backslash\{\bot\} :$$
$$(f(w) = w_0\text{++}w\text{++}w_1\text{++}\ldots\text{++}w\text{++}w_n) \wedge$$
$$(\forall i : \text{FH}(w_i) = \emptyset \wedge w_i \neq \bot)$$

Proof. The downward implication is the more interesting one. The proof proceeds in three stages:

Stage 1 Choose some $h \in$ HOLE (e.g. the one with minimal index). Define $w_0, \ldots, w_n \in$ CHARLIST by the conditions that

$$f[h] = w_0\text{++}[h]\text{++}w_1\text{++}\ldots\text{++}[h]\text{++}w_n$$
$$\forall i : h \notin \text{FH}(w_i) \wedge w_i \neq \bot$$

This is possible if $f[h] \neq \bot$ and then uniquely defines $w_0, \ldots, w_n$ (subject to the choice of h).

To see that $f[h] \neq \bot$ suppose by way of contradiction that $f[h] = \bot$. Since $f \neq \bot$ there exists $w \in$ CHARLIST such that $f\ w \neq \bot$; we may without loss of generality assume that $w \neq \bot$. Now define

$$\delta = \{(h, w)\} \cup \bigcup\{(h', [h']) \mid h' \in \text{FH}(w) \wedge h' \neq h\}$$

and note that $\delta \in \Delta$. Clearly $SUBST_{\texttt{charlist}}[\delta]([h], w)$ and since $\delta \sqsupseteq \emptyset$, we get $SUBST_{\texttt{charlist}}[\delta](f[h], f\ w)$. But since $f[h] = \bot \neq f\ w$, this is a contradiction (Fact 2.8).

Stage 2 Let $w \in$ CHARLIST be given such that $w \neq \bot$. As in Stage 1 define

$$\delta = \{(h, w)\} \cup \bigcup\{(h', [h']) \mid h' \in \text{FH}(w) \wedge h' \neq h\}$$

and obtain that $SUBST_{\texttt{charlist}}[\delta](f[h], f\ w)$. This means that

$$\begin{aligned} f\ w &= (f[h])[w/h] \\ &= (w_0\text{++}[h]\text{++}w_1\text{++}\ldots\text{++}[h]\text{++}w_n)[w/h] \\ &= w_0\text{++}w\text{++}w_1\text{++}\ldots\text{++}w\text{++}w_n \end{aligned}$$

as was to be shown.

Stage 3 To show the remaining properties of $w_0, \ldots, w_n$ we first define

$$\delta = \{(h, [\,])\}$$

and note that $\delta \in \Delta$. Since $SUBST_{\texttt{charlist}}[\delta]([h], [\,])$, it follows from the assumptions that $SUBST_{\texttt{charlist}}[\delta](f[h], f[\,])$. Using Fact 2.10 we have $\mathrm{FH}(f[\,]) \subseteq \emptyset$ and by Stage 2 (with $w = [\,]$) this gives $\forall i: \ \mathrm{FH}(w_i) = \emptyset$ as desired.

The upward implication is along the lines of the proof of Lemma 2.11. We provide the details by means of:

Stage 4 Suppose that $w_0, \ldots, w_n$ are chosen such that

$$\forall w \neq \bot : f\ w = w_0\texttt{++}w\texttt{++}w_1\texttt{++}\ldots\texttt{++}w\texttt{++}w_n$$
$$\forall i: \ \mathrm{FH}(w_i) = \emptyset \wedge w_i \neq \bot$$

Then clearly $f \neq \bot$. To show $SUBST_{\texttt{charlist}\to\texttt{charlist}}[\emptyset](f, f)$ consider $\delta \in \Delta$ such that $SUBST_{\texttt{charlist}}[\delta](w^1, w^2)$ and show $SUBST_{\texttt{charlist}}[\delta](f\ w^1, f\ w^2)$. We may write δ in the form $\delta = \{(h_1, l_1), \ldots, (h_n, l_n)\}$. If $w^1 \neq \bot$ we have

$$\mathrm{FH}(f\ w^1) = \mathrm{FH}(w_0\texttt{++}w^1\texttt{++}w_1\texttt{++}\ldots\texttt{++}w^1\texttt{++}w_n) = \ \mathrm{FH}(w^1)$$
$$(f\ w^1)[l_1/h_1, \ldots, l_n/h_n] =$$
$$(w_0\texttt{++}w^1\texttt{++}w_1\texttt{++}\ldots\texttt{++}w^1\texttt{++}w_n)[l_1/h_1, \ldots, l_n/h_n] =$$
$$f(w^1[l_1/h_1, \ldots, l_n/h_n])$$

and then the desired result follows from the assumptions. If $w^1 = \bot$ we also have $w^2 = \bot$ so that $f\ w^1 = f\ w^2$. The result is then immediate if $f\ w^1 = f\ w^2 = \bot$ so assume that $f\ w^1 = f\ w^2 \neq \bot$. Then $f\ w^1 = f\ w^2 = f\ [\,]$ since $w^1 \sqsubseteq [\,]$ implies $f\ w^1 \sqsubseteq f\ [\,]$ and by flatness of CHARLIST equality follows. Next

$$\mathrm{FH}(f\ [\,]) = \ \mathrm{FH}(w_0\texttt{++}w_1\texttt{++}\ldots\texttt{++}w_n) = \emptyset$$
$$(f\ [\,])[l_1/h_1, \ldots, l_n/h_n] = f\ [\,]$$

and the result follows. □

In the examples we have given in this section the substitution property is something that may or may not be satisfied by the functions defined: it holds for `letter` but not for `badge`. In the applications to code generation [9, 10] that motivated the present development, the situation is slightly different. There the substitution property does hold for all functions defined (in the process of interpreting a metalanguage). The need to formulate the substitution property then arises because of the higher-order constant `fix`. It will be instructive to regard `fix` as having functionality

$$(\texttt{charlist} \rightarrow \texttt{charlist}) \rightarrow \texttt{charlist}$$

and to regard elements of `charlist` as pieces of code. Any function (of functionality `charlist → charlist`) that is passed as a parameter to `fix` will satisfy the substitution property because of the way it is defined. However, the domain for `charlist → charlist` contains many functions that do not and hence the definition of `fix` cannot make that assumption without formally defining a predicate like *SUBST* that expresses the substitution property.

This phenomenon has some connection to the question of full abstractness. Usually full abstractness means that equality of denotations is equivalent to equal behaviour in all program contexts. For our purposes it is more instructive to use the characterization of [Milner][1]: full abstractness holds provided all (compact) elements of the domains are denotable. The search for full abstractness then may be regarded as a search for models where there are no superfluous elements. Usually the superfluous elements express some features corresponding to parallel evaluation of arguments with the ability to retract a (possibly nonterminating) evaluation. For us the superfluous elements of `charlist → charlist` are those that do not satisfy the substitution property. The fact that no fully abstract models are known to exist for simple sequential languages suggests that techniques like our *SUBST* relation may be unavoidable.

Historical Remark The concept of Kripke-logical relations, including the result on structural induction (our Lemma 2.6) was already studied in [12]. Further studies along these lines may be found in [5] and a brief survey is contained in [4]. Independently of the latter works the authors used the concept in [9]. The use of Kripke-logical relations to achieve substitution properties (our Lemma 2.13) is due to [9] with preliminary ideas in [7]. (The main limitation of [7] is that all sets $\{(h_1, l_1), \ldots, (h_m, l_m)\}$ have $m = 1$ so that the development only allows the fixed point operator to occur once.)

3 Kripke-Layered Predicates

We now return to the challenge of producing well-structured proofs and for this to succeed our techniques must interact well with the concepts of logical and Kripke-logical relations. In Example 1.3 we managed to conduct a proof about an aggregate concept by conducting proofs about each constituent concept and then combining the results. However, we did indicate that this approach would not work in general and we shall give an example shortly. Furthermore we shall present an example showing that in general the constituent concepts must be allowed to depend on each other.

Example 3.1 As an extension of Examples 1.1 and 1.3 consider the following module:

```
spec compl:  (num → num) → (num → num)
with compl g maps nonnegative integers to nonnegative integers,
     provided that g does
impl compl = λg. λx. g(x)*g(x)/2 + g(x)/2
```

[1]The central result of [3] is the "Second Context Lemma".

Clearly comp1 satisfies its interface condition because comp1 g = sum1 ∘ g and we happen to know that sum1 $\models$ (*NONNEG* ∧ *INT*)[num → num] and we assume that g $\models$ (*NONNEG* ∧ *INT*)[num → num] and so may use the proof rule

$$\frac{R_{t_1\to t_2}(f_1) \quad R_{t_2\to t_3}(f_2)}{R_{t_1\to t_3}(f_2 \circ f_1)}$$

which holds for any logical relation *R*, in particular *NONNEG* ∧ *INT*.

However, this was not a simple proof by structural induction because it included algebraic transformations on comp1 g. To achieve a proof more along the lines of Example 1.3 we may begin by establishing that

$$\begin{array}{l}\texttt{comp1} \models NONNEG[(\texttt{num} \to \texttt{num}) \to (\texttt{num} \to \texttt{num})]\\ \texttt{comp1} \models INT[(\texttt{num} \to \texttt{num}) \to (\texttt{num} \to \texttt{num})]\end{array}$$

using the methods sketched in Example 1.3. Next we may aim at showing

$$\texttt{sum1} \models (NONNEG \wedge INT)[(\texttt{num} \to \texttt{num}) \to (\texttt{num} \to \texttt{num})]$$

using the proof rule

$$\frac{e \models R'[t] \quad e \models R''[t]}{e \models (R' \wedge R'')[t]} \text{ if } t \ldots$$

in the instance where $t = (\texttt{num} \to \texttt{num}) \to (\texttt{num} \to \texttt{num})$, $R' = NONNEG$, and $R'' = INT$.

Validation of this instance fails, intuitively because it relies on the validity of the rule instances

$$\frac{e \models (NONNEG \wedge INT)[\texttt{num} \to \texttt{num}]}{e \models NONNEG[\texttt{num} \to \texttt{num}]}$$

$$\frac{e \models (NONNEG \wedge INT)[\texttt{num} \to \texttt{num}]}{e \models INT[\texttt{num} \to \texttt{num}]}$$

$$\frac{e \models NONNEG[\texttt{num} \to \texttt{num}] \quad e \models INT[\texttt{num} \to \texttt{num}]}{e \models NONNEG \wedge INT[\texttt{num} \to \texttt{num}]}$$

The latter instance is valid (as seen in Example 1.3). For the first two instances note that taking *e* to be

$$\begin{array}{ll}\lambda x. & \text{if } x = -1 \text{ then } \tfrac{1}{2} \text{ else}\\ & \text{if } x = \tfrac{1}{2} \text{ then } -1 \text{ else}\\ & x\end{array}$$

invalidates both: the above function maps nonnegative integers to nonnegative integers but does not map nonnegative numbers to nonnegative numbers nor does it map integers to integers. □

Example 3.2 The previous example showed that a function might preserve an aggregation of properties but none of the constituent properties individually. Perhaps more "natural" are the settings where only one of the constituent properties is preserved individually. For an example of this consider the following slight variation on the module of Examples 1.1 and 1.3:

```
spec  sum0:  (num → num)
with  sum0 maps nonnegative integers to nonnegative integers,
      /* sum0 x = 0 + ...(x-1) */
impl  sum0 =  λg. λx. (x*x)/2 - x/2
```

Proceeding along the lines of Example 1.3 we might aim at first proving

$$\texttt{sum0} \models \mathit{NONNEG}[\texttt{num} \rightarrow \texttt{num}]$$

but this fails: sum0 maps $\frac{1}{3}$ to $-\frac{1}{9}$. On the other hand

$$\texttt{sum0} \models \mathit{INT}[\texttt{num} \rightarrow \texttt{num}]$$

succeeds. We can remedy our failure by showing that sum0 maps nonnegative integers to nonnegative numbers; this amounts to strengthening our assumptions without also strengthening our proof obligation. We shall allow to write this succinctly as

$$\texttt{sum0} \models (\mathit{INT} \wedge \mathit{NONNEG})[\texttt{num}] \Rightarrow \mathit{NONNEG}[\texttt{num}]$$

To prove the desired

$$\texttt{sum0} \models (\mathit{INT} \wedge \mathit{NONNEG})[\texttt{num} \rightarrow \texttt{num}]$$

we may then attempt to use the proof rule

$$\frac{e \models R'[t_1 \rightarrow t_2] \quad e \models (R' \wedge R'')[t_1] \Rightarrow R''[t_2]}{e \models (R' \wedge R'')[t_1 \rightarrow t_2]} \text{ if } t_1, t_2 \ldots$$

in the instance where $t_1 = t_2 =$ num, $R' = \mathit{INT}$, and $R'' = \mathit{NONNEG}$.
Validation of this instance succeeds because we have the following valid rule instances

$$\frac{e \models (\mathit{INT} \wedge \mathit{NONNEG})[\texttt{num}]}{e \models \mathit{INT}[\texttt{num}]}$$

$$\frac{e \models \mathit{INT}[\texttt{num}] \quad e \models \mathit{NONNEG}[\texttt{num}]}{e \models (\mathit{INT} \wedge \mathit{NONNEG})[\texttt{num}]}$$

and hence our proof is complete.

However, in general the above proof rule fails when t_1 or t_2 is a function type, intuitively because the analogues of the two rule instances above then may fail. □

These examples show that our problems are due to lack of introduction rules for proving $(R' \wedge R'')_t(w)$ given $R'_t(w)$ and $R''_t(w)$, and a lack of elimination rules for proving $R'_t(w)$ and $R''_t(w)$ given $(R' \wedge R'')_t(w)$. The latter example additionally suggests that it may be more appropriate to consider R'' as a way to extend R' rather than a predicate that should be preserved on its own; equivalently, to establish R'' of a result we need to know R' in addition to R'' of the argument. Our solution therefore will be to define a new notion of a layered combination of R' and R'' such that useful introduction and elimination rules do become valid.

Recall that a logical relation may be regarded as a Kripke-logical relation over a partially ordered set with just one element. For conciseness we therefore concentrate on the more general case.

Definition 3.3 Given Kripke-indexed relations P and Q over Δ and $\mathcal{I}_1,\ldots,\mathcal{I}_m$, we define a Kripke-indexed relation $P\&Q$ over Δ and $\mathcal{I}_1,\ldots,\mathcal{I}_m$ as follows:

$$\begin{aligned}
(P\&Q)_{\mathtt{num}}[\delta](w_1,\ldots,w_m) &\equiv P_{\mathtt{num}}[\delta](w_1,\ldots,w_m) \wedge Q_{\mathtt{num}}[\delta](w_1,\ldots,w_m)\\
(P\&Q)_{\mathtt{bool}}[\delta](w_1,\ldots,w_m) &\equiv P_{\mathtt{bool}}[\delta](w_1,\ldots,w_m) \wedge Q_{\mathtt{bool}}[\delta](w_1,\ldots,w_m)\\
(P\&Q)_{\mathtt{charlist}}[\delta](w_1,\ldots,w_m) &\equiv P_{\mathtt{charlist}}[\delta](w_1,\ldots,w_m) \wedge Q_{\mathtt{charlist}}[\delta](w_1,\ldots,w_m)\\
(P\&Q)_{t_1\to t_2}[\delta](f_1,\ldots,f_m) &\equiv P_{t_1\to t_2}[\delta](f_1,\ldots,f_m)\wedge\\
&\quad \forall\delta' \sqsupseteq \delta : \forall(w_1,\ldots,w_m)\!:\ (P\&Q)_{t_1}[\delta'](w_1,\ldots,w_m)\\
&\qquad\qquad\Downarrow\\
&\qquad (P\&Q)_{t_2}[\delta'](f_1\,w_1,\ldots,f_m\,w_m)
\end{aligned}$$

We shall say that $P\&Q$ is a Kripke-layered predicate over Δ and $\mathcal{I}_1,\ldots,\mathcal{I}_m$ and that it is the Kripke-layered combination of P and Q.

When P and Q are indexed relations (in the sense of Section 1) we shall say that $P\&Q$ is a layered predicate and that it is the layered combination of P and Q. □

Fact 3.4 With P and Q as above, $P\&Q$ is a Kripke-indexed relation over Δ and $\mathcal{I}_1,\ldots,\mathcal{I}_m$. However, $P\&Q$ need not be Kripke-logical even when P and Q both are. □

Proof. Only the latter claim is nontrivial. It suffices to find an instance where

$$\begin{aligned}
\forall\delta' \sqsupseteq \delta : \forall(w_1,\ldots,w_m) :\ & (P\&Q)_{t_1}[\delta'](w_1,\ldots,w_m)\\
&\Downarrow\\
&(P\&Q)_{t_2}[\delta'](f_1\,w_1,\ldots,f_m\,w_m)
\end{aligned}$$

does not imply $P_{t_1\to t_2}[\delta](f_1,\ldots,f_m)$. But this was established by the final part of Example 3.1. □

Fact 3.5 With P and Q as above, $(P\&Q)_t[\delta](w_1,\ldots,w_m) \Rightarrow P_t[\delta](w_1,\ldots,w_m)$ holds for all types t. □

Proof. This is a structural induction over t. In all cases the result follows because P_t is an explicit conjunct in $(P\&Q)_t$. □

Despite the negative statement in Fact 3.4, the concept of Kripke-layered predicates interacts well with the semantics of the λ-calculus. Recalling Definition 2.5 we have:

Lemma 3.6 *The Kripke-layered predicate P&Q admits structural induction provided P does.* □

Proof. Using the notation of Definition 2.5, this is a structural induction over e. For a variable v the result is immediate from the assumptions. This is also the case for a constant c. For an application $e_1\ e_2$ we use the induction hypothesis to obtain

$$(P\&Q)_{t'\to t}[\delta](\mathcal{I}_1[\![e_1]\!]_{tenv}(w_1^1,\ldots,w_n^1),\ldots,\mathcal{I}_m[\![e_1]\!]_{tenv}(w_1^m,\ldots,w_n^m))$$
$$(P\&Q)_{t'}[\delta](\mathcal{I}_1[\![e_2]\!]_{tenv}(w_1^1,\ldots,w_n^1),\ldots,\mathcal{I}_m[\![e_2]\!]_{tenv}(w_1^m,\ldots,w_n^m))$$

and then we use the definition of $P\&Q$; to be more specific we use the following proof rule

$$\frac{(P\&Q)_{t'\to t}[\delta](f_1,\ldots,f_m)\quad (P\&Q)_{t'}[\delta](w_1,\ldots,w_m)}{(P\&Q)_t[\delta](f_1(w_1),\ldots,f_m(w_m))}$$

that follows immediately from the definition of $P\&Q$. For a λ-abstraction $\lambda v : t'.e$ we must show two results. One is that

$$P_{t'\to t}[\delta](\mathcal{I}_1[\![\lambda v : t'.e]\!]_{tenv}(w_1^1,\ldots,w_n^1),\ldots,\mathcal{I}_m[\![\lambda v : t'.e]\!]_{tenv}(w_1^m,\ldots,w_n^m))$$

but this follows from the assumptions, Fact 3.5 and that P admits structural induction. The other amounts to choosing $\delta' \sqsupseteq \delta$ and assume that

$$(P\&Q)_{t'}[\delta'](w_{n+1}^1,\ldots,w_{n+1}^m)$$

and then show

$$(P\&Q)_t[\delta'](\mathcal{I}_1[\![\lambda v : t'.e]\!]_{tenv}(w_1^1,\ldots,w_n^1)(w_{n+1}^1),\ldots,\mathcal{I}_m[\![\lambda v : t'.e]\!]_{tenv}(w_1^m,\ldots,w_n^m)(w_{n+1}^m))$$

But by assumption we have

$$(P\&Q)_{t_i}[\delta](w_i^1,\ldots,w_i^m)\quad \text{for } i = 1,\ldots,n$$

so using the proof rule

$$\frac{(P\&Q)_t[\delta](w_1,\ldots,w_m)}{(P\&Q)_t[\delta'](w_1,\ldots,w_m)}\quad \delta' \sqsupseteq \delta$$

we obtain

$$(P\&Q)_{t_i}[\delta'](w_i^1,\ldots,w_i^m)\quad \text{for } i = n+1$$

It follows from the induction hypothesis that

$$(P\&Q)_t[\delta'](\mathcal{I}_1[\![e]\!]_{tenv,(v,t')}(w_1^1,\ldots,w_n^1,w_{n+1}^1),\ldots,\mathcal{I}_m[\![e]\!]_{tenv,(v,t')}(w_1^m,\ldots,w_n^m,w_{n+1}^m))$$

and since $\mathcal{I}_i[\![\lambda v : t'.e]\!]_{tenv}(w_1^i,\ldots,w_n^i)(w_{n+1}^i) = \mathcal{I}_i[\![e]\!]_{tenv,(v,t')}(w_1^i,\ldots,w_n^i,w_{n+1}^i)$ this is the desired result. □

Corollary 3.7 If P is Kripke-logical, then $P\&Q$ admits structural induction. □

Taking $n = 0$ and $m = 1$ we get:

Corollary 3.8 If the closed expression e has type t, i.e. $() \vdash e : t$, and $c' \models (P\&Q)[t']$ for all constants c' of type t' occurring in e, then $e \models (P\&Q)[t]$ provided that $P\&Q$ is the Kripke-layered combination of Kripke-logical relations P and Q. □

To complement Lemma 3.6 we also need to consider how to prove that $P\&Q$ holds for the constants. In the previous sections there was little to say because there the predicates had "no structure", but here the predicate are combinations of other predicates. This amounts to the study of introduction rules for $P\&Q$ and for the sake of completeness we shall give elimination rules and a few derived rules as well. We begin with the elimination rules:

$$[\text{E1}] \quad \frac{(P\&Q)_t[\delta](w_1,\ldots,w_m)}{P_t[\delta](w_1,\ldots,w_m)}$$

$$[\text{E2}] \quad \frac{(P\&Q)_t[\delta](w_1,\ldots,w_m)}{Q_t[\delta](w_1,\ldots,w_m)} \quad \text{if } t \text{ is a base type}$$

The validity of the first rule, for arbitrary t and δ, is a direct consequence of Fact 3.5. The validity of the second rule, for $t \in \{\texttt{num}, \texttt{bool}, \texttt{charlist}\}$, is a direct consequence of the definition of $P\&Q$; that the rule may fail for function types follows rather easily from Example 3.2. A derived rule that occasionally is useful is

$$[\text{E1}'] \quad \frac{\begin{array}{c}(P\&Q)_{t_n\to\ldots\to t_0}[\delta](f)\\ P_{t_n}[\delta](w_n)\\ \vdots\\ P_{t_1}[\delta](w_1)\end{array}}{P_{t_0}[\delta](f\ w_n\ldots w_1)} \quad \text{if } P \text{ is Kripke-logical}$$

(where for simplicity we took $m = 1$). Turning to the introduction rules it is helpful to say that t is an *iterated base type* (of order n) whenever

$$\exists\, t_n,\ldots,t_1,t_0 \in \{\texttt{num}, \texttt{bool}, \texttt{charlist}\} : t = t_n \to t_{n-1} \to \ldots \to t_1 \to t_0$$

We then have

$$[I] \quad \frac{P_t[\delta](w_1,\ldots,w_m) \quad Q_t[\delta](w_1,\ldots,w_m)}{(P\&Q)_t[\delta](w_1,\ldots,w_m)}$$

if t is an iterated base type and P and Q are Kripke-logical

Fact 3.9 The above rule is valid. □

Proof. Validity is proven by induction on the order n of the iterated base type t. The base case is trivial given the definition of $P\&Q$ on base types. For the inductive step we consider $t = t_{n+1} \to (t_n \to \ldots \to t_0)$ and assume

$$P_t[\delta](f_1,\ldots,f_m)$$
$$Q_t[\delta](f_1,\ldots,f_m)$$

and must show $(P\&Q)_t[\delta](f_1,\ldots,f_m)$. This amounts to showing $P_t[\delta](f_1,\ldots,f_m)$, which is trivial given the assumptions, and to consider $\delta' \sqsupseteq \delta$ and assume

$$(P\&Q)_{t_{n+1}}[\delta'](w_1,\ldots,w_m)$$

and show $(P\&Q)_{t_n\to\ldots\to t_0}[\delta'](f_1\ w_1,\ldots,f_m\ w_m)$. But from our two elimination rules we have $P_{t_{n+1}}[\delta'](w_1,\ldots,w_m)$ and $Q_{t_{n+1}}[\delta'](w_1,\ldots,w_m)$ so that our assumptions yield

$$P_{t_n\to\ldots\to t_0}[\delta'](f_1\ w_1,\ldots,f_m\ w_m)$$
$$Q_{t_n\to\ldots\to t_0}[\delta'](f_1\ w_1,\ldots,f_m\ w_m)$$

The desired result then follows from the induction hypothesis. □

It is possible to generalize this rule in various ways. One rule that may be useful is

$$[I'] \quad \frac{\begin{array}{l} P_{t_n\to\ldots\to t_0}[\delta](f) \\ (\forall i \in \{1,\ldots,n\} : (P\&Q)_{t_i}[\delta](w_i)) \Rightarrow Q_{t_0}[\delta](f\ w_n \cdots w_1) \end{array}}{(P\&Q)_{t_n\to\ldots\to t_0}[\delta](f)}$$

if t_0 is an iterated base type and P and Q are Kripke-logical

(where for simplicity we took $m = 1$); alternatively one could use a Gentzen-style presentation. Validity of this rule may be shown by numerical induction on n.

Example 3.10 We now briefly return to the successes and failures encountered in Examples 1.3, 3.1 and 3.2. In all three examples the predicate of interest is

INT&NONNEG

rather than *NONNEG* ∧ *INT*. Concerning Example 1.3 we were able to show

$$\mathtt{sum1} \models \mathit{INT}[\mathtt{num} \rightarrow \mathtt{num}]$$
$$\mathtt{sum1} \models \mathit{NONNEG}[\mathtt{num} \rightarrow \mathtt{num}]$$

and the desired

$$\mathtt{sum1} \models (\mathit{INT}\&\mathit{NONNEG})[\mathtt{num} \rightarrow \mathtt{num}]$$

then is a simple application of Introduction Rule $[I]$, since $\mathtt{num} \rightarrow \mathtt{num}$ is an iterated base type. This should hardly be surprising since this is the same approach that succeeded in Example 1.3 but for $\mathit{NONNEG} \wedge \mathit{INT}$, i.e. $\mathit{INT} \wedge \mathit{NONNEG}$, instead of $\mathit{INT}\&\mathit{NONNEG}$.

Concerning Example 3.1 we noted that the obvious approach is to begin by showing

$$\mathtt{comp1} \models \mathit{INT}[\mathtt{num} \rightarrow \mathtt{num}]$$
$$\mathtt{comp1} \models \mathit{NONNEG}[\mathtt{num} \rightarrow \mathtt{num}]$$

and this still succeeds. However, we still cannot achieve the desired result because Introduction Rule $[I]$ is not applicable as $(\mathtt{num} \rightarrow \mathtt{num}) \rightarrow (\mathtt{num} \rightarrow \mathtt{num})$ is not an iterated base type. Instead we aim at using the stronger rule $[I']$. For this we modify the second claim above to

$$\mathtt{comp1} \models (\mathit{INT}\&\mathit{NONNEG})[\mathtt{num} \rightarrow \mathtt{num}] \Rightarrow (\mathit{INT}\&\mathit{NONNEG})[\mathtt{num}] \Rightarrow \mathit{NONNEG}[\mathtt{num}]$$

where we have used "$\ldots \Rightarrow \ldots$" in the sense explained in Example 3.2. This succeeds and we may then used rule $[I']$ to obtain the desired result.

Finally Example 3.2 goes through in much the same way as above; first note that

$$\mathtt{sum0} \models \mathit{INT}[\mathtt{num} \rightarrow \mathtt{num}]$$
$$\mathtt{sum0} \models (\mathit{INT}\&\mathit{NONNEG})[\mathtt{num}] \Rightarrow \mathit{NONNEG}[\mathtt{num}]$$

and then use rule $[I']$ to obtain the desired result. □

Example 3.11 A "realistic example" is beyond the space available to us but we can give a very sketchy overview of the development of [10, Chapter 6]. The problem under study is that of translating a certain typed λ-calculus into an abstract machine somewhat similar to the categorical abstract machine. The λ-calculus allows arbitrary nesting of fixed point operators and this is the root of our first problem. The abstract machine works in a stack-like manner and this allows to separate the correctness proof into two parts. To be more specific the correctness predicate is of the form $(\mathcal{R}_1\&\mathcal{R}_2)\&\mathcal{R}_3$.

The first predicate, $\mathcal{R}_1$, aims at establishing a substitution property along the lines of the Extended Example of Section 2; thus $\mathcal{R}_1(w)$ roughly means $\mathit{SUBST}[\emptyset](w, w)$. This is necessary for the semantics of the abstract machine to behave as desired. This is because the code for the fixed point of a functional is the code resulting from supplying the functional with an appropriate call instruction that "points" to that code. The abstract machine then executes a call instruction by replacing it with yet another copy of that code. Having done this once the unfolded code, viewed in its original context, should desirably correspond to the result of applying the functional to that code. In symbols this amounts to

$$(F\ \texttt{call})[F\ \texttt{call}/\texttt{call}] = F(F\ \texttt{call})$$

where the functional is written as F. To achieve this we use the substitution property and we refer to [10, Section 6.2] for the details.

The second predicate, $\mathcal{R}_2$, aims at showing that the code generated from well-formed λ-expressions is well-behaved. Certainly the execution of a piece of code can result in errors as well as nontermination. However, there are several "structural properties" that will be fulfilled by the code generated although they may not hold for arbitrary code sequences. The typical example of this is that evaluation of an expression on a stack pushes an element upon the stack and leaves the remainder of the stack unchanged. In [10] the λ-calculus and the code generation is such that instead evaluation of an expression only modifies the top element of the stack and leaves the remaining elements and the height of the stack unchanged. There are several complications in the definition of the predicate because the elements on the stack may themselves contain code components. We refer to [10, Section 6.3] for the detailed definition and proofs.

The third predicate, $\mathcal{R}_3$, then finally expresses the correctness of the code generated with respect to the semantics of the λ-expression. The detailed development rather closely follows that of well-behavedness except that at each step the correctness considerations need to be added. We refer to [10, Section 6.4] for the details.

Overall the development of [10, Chapter 6] is almost 70 pages with about 50 pages devoted to establishing $(\mathcal{R}_1\&\mathcal{R}_2)\&\mathcal{R}_3$. We strongly believe that the "separation of concerns" facilitated by expressing the desired predicate as a combination of three simpler predicates, and by proving the desired predicate in three stages, is of immense help when developing the proof as well as when presenting it to others. □

Generalizations

It follows from Corollary 3.7 and Fact 3.4 that the Kripke-logical relations constitute a proper subset of those Kripke-indexed relations that admit structural induction. This suggests studying a notion of "benign" modifications of Kripke-logical relations so as to obtain a larger subset.

We have no formal definition of "benign" but the general idea is that the definition of the Kripke-indexed predicate P (over Δ and $\mathcal{I}_1, \ldots, \mathcal{I}_m$) is given by a formula

$$\begin{aligned} &P_t[\delta](w_1, \ldots, w_m) \equiv \forall \bar{\delta} \in \bar{\Delta} : \forall \bar{w} \in D_t : \\ &\quad P'_t[\partial(\delta, \bar{\delta})](\omega_1^t(w_1, \ldots, w_m, \bar{w}), \ldots, \omega_{m'}^t(w_1, \ldots, w_m, \bar{w})) \end{aligned}$$

where

$$\begin{aligned} &\partial : \Delta \times \bar{\Delta} \to \Delta' \\ &\omega_i^t : \mathcal{I}_1[t] \times \ldots \times \mathcal{I}_m[t] \times D_t \to \mathcal{I}'_i[t] \end{aligned}$$

and $\bar{\Delta}$ is a non-empty partially ordered set, D_t a (non-empty) domain that depends on t and P' is a Kripke-logical relation over Δ' and $\mathcal{I}'_1, \ldots, \mathcal{I}'_m$.

To simplify matters let us make the rather drastic assumption that each ω_i^t selects one of its first m arguments, i.e. $\omega_i^t(w_1, \ldots, w_m, \bar{w}) = w_{n_i}$ for $n_i \in \{1, \ldots, m\}$, and that the corresponding interpretations agree, i.e. $\mathcal{I}'_i = \mathcal{I}_{n_i}$. Then P admits structural induction. To see this, note that the assumptions

$$P_{t_i}[\delta](w_i^1, \cdots, w_i^m) \text{ for } \ldots$$
$$P_{t'}[\delta](\mathcal{I}_1(c'), \ldots, \mathcal{I}_m(c')) \text{ for } \ldots$$

amount to

$$P'_{t_i}[\partial(\delta, \bar{\delta})](\omega_i^{t_i}(w_i^1, \ldots, w_i^m), \ldots) \text{ for } \ldots$$
$$P'_{t'}[\partial(\delta, \bar{\delta})](\omega_i^{t'}(\mathcal{I}_1(c'), \ldots, \mathcal{I}_m(c')), \ldots) \text{ for } \ldots$$

for all choices of $\delta \in \Delta$ and where we have dropped the $\bar{w}$ argument. For each $\bar{\delta} \in \bar{\Delta}$, Lemma 2.6 (and Definition 2.5) then gives

$$P'_t[\partial(\delta, \bar{\delta})](\mathcal{I}'_1[\![e]\!]_{tenv}(\omega_1^{t_1}(w_1^1, \ldots, w_1^m), \ldots, \omega_1^{t_n}(w_n^1, \ldots, w_n^m)), \ldots)$$

and this amounts to

$$P'_t[\partial(\delta, \bar{\delta})](\omega_1^t(\mathcal{I}_1[\![e]\!]_{tenv}(w_1^1, \ldots, w_n^1), \ldots, \mathcal{I}_m[\![e]\!]_{tenv}(w_1^m, \ldots, w_n^m)), \ldots)$$

from which

$$P_t[\delta](\mathcal{I}_1[\![e]\!]_{tenv}(w_1^1, \ldots, w_n^1), \ldots, \mathcal{I}_m[\![e]\!]_{tenv}(w_1^m, \ldots, w_n^m))$$

follows.

We already used a result along these lines in Example 3.11 (and [10]): while *SUBST* is a Kripke-logical relation, the relation $\mathcal{R}_1$ is not although it is a "benign" modification of *SUBST*. Thus $\mathcal{R}_1$ does admit structural induction and by Lemma 3.6 so do $\mathcal{R}_1 \& \mathcal{R}_2$ and $(\mathcal{R}_1 \& \mathcal{R}_2) \& \mathcal{R}_3$.

In another direction we may generalize the number of P's and Q's considered. Specifically one may define

$$(P_1, \ldots, P_p) \& (Q_1, \ldots, Q_q)$$

for $p \geq 1$ and $q \geq 1$. For a base type $t_0 \in \{\texttt{num}, \texttt{bool}, \texttt{charlist}\}$ we set

$$((P_1, \ldots, P_p) \& (Q_1, \ldots, Q_q))_{t_0}[\delta](w_1, \ldots, w_m) \equiv$$
$$\bigwedge_{i=1}^p (P_i)_{t_0}[\delta](w_1, \ldots, w_m) \wedge \bigwedge_{j=1}^q (Q_j)_{t_0}[\delta](w_1, \ldots, w_m)$$

and for a function type $t_1 \rightarrow t_2$ we set

$$((P_1,\ldots,P_p)\&(Q_1,\ldots,Q_q))_{t_1\to t_2}[\delta](f_1,\ldots,f_m) \equiv$$
$$\bigwedge_{i=1}^{p}(P_i)_{t_1\to t_2}[\delta](f_1,\ldots,f_m)\wedge$$
$$\forall\delta'\sqsupseteq\delta:\forall(w_1,\ldots,w_m):\ ((P_1,\ldots,P_p)\&(Q_1,\ldots,Q_q))_{t_1}[\delta](w_1,\ldots,w_m)$$
$$\Downarrow$$
$$((P_1,\ldots,P_p)\&(Q_1,\ldots,Q_q))_{t_2}[\delta](f_1\,w_1,\ldots,f_m\,w_m)$$

Taking $p > 1$ defines a more general notion that may well be useful; taking $q > 1$ is useless as $(P_1,\ldots,P_p)\&(Q_1,\ldots,Q_q)$ is equivalent to $(P_1,\ldots,P_p)\&(Q_1\wedge\ldots\wedge Q_q)$ where $Q_1\wedge\ldots\wedge Q_q$ is defined as in Example 1.3.

Historical Remark The notion of (Kripke-) layered predicate is based on [10, Chapter 6] which is the only relevant reference that we know of. □

4 Conclusion

We have presented a number of techniques for the defining predicates so as to allow proofs by structural induction. All of these are based on the underlying concept of logical relations and have been applied to problems with substance; we refer to [10] and its bibliography for examples. Some of the main lessons learned may be summarized as follows:

- Some predicates have base cases that are most naturally expressed at level 1 (functions between base values) rather than at level 0 (base values). To adopt logical relations the notion of *partial equivalence relations* is useful or more generally using the same interpretation more than once. (Counting the levels from one rather than zero this also explains the distinction between "first-order" and "second-order" made in [6].)
- *Kripke-layered relations* have "local memory" consisting of the parameter (δ) drawn from the partially ordered set (Δ). This allows them to be used to describe a substitution property by means of a level 0 behaviour.
- *Kripke-layered predicates* are not simply Kripke-logical relations (Fact 3.4) but allow for more structured proofs that proceed in stages. The complexity of each stage is significantly smaller (but often still substantial) than a brute force proof.

The strengths of Kripke-layered predicates include the ability to reorder the parameters and to modify the partially ordered set over which the parameters are drawn. Comparing the proof of [10, Chapter 6] with that of [9], where only Kripke-logical relations were used, we believe that the advantages claimed for Kripke-layered predicates are indeed sustained.[2]

[2]The relative success of [9] also raises the question whether Kripke-layered predicates are more intimately connected to Kripke-logical relations than suggested by Fact 3.4.

The notions studied in this paper are fairly robust. One may add additional type constructors like sum, product and recursive types and still perform the development. Also one may restrict the attention to admissible predicates so as to support Scott-induction and the development still carries through. Finally, when no recursive types or fixed point constructs are present one may use ordinary sets instead of domains. This all calls for a more general categorical formulation of Kripke-layered predicates and this should also include a more general theory of "benign" modification.

Acknowledgement

This work was supported in part by The Danish Research Councils under grant 5.21.08.03 ("The DART-Project"). Torben Amtoft and Torben Lange provided useful comments and Karen Møller expert typing.

References

[1] S. Hunt: PERs Generalise Projections for Strictness Analysis, report DOC 90/14, Imperial College (1990).

[2] S. Hunt, D. Sands: Binding Time Analysis: A New PERspective, *Proc. ACM Symposium on Partial Evaluation and Semantics-Based Program Manipulation*, ACM Press (1991) 154-165.

[3] R. Milner: Fully abstract models of typed λ-calculi, *Theoretical Computer Science* **4** (1977) 1-22.

[4] J.C. Mitchell: Type Systems for Programming Languages, in: *Handbook of Theoretical Computer Science, vol. B: Formal Models and Semantics*, J. van Leeuwen (ed.), Elsevier (1990).

[5] J.C. Mitchell, E. Moggi: Kripke-style models for typed λ-calculus, *Proc. 2nd Ann. IEEE Symposium on Logic in Computer Science*, IEEE Press (1987) 303-314.

[6] F. Nielson: Program Transformations in a Denotational Setting, *ACM Transactions on Programming Languages and Systems* **7** (1985) 359-379.

[7] F. Nielson: Correctness of code generation from a two-level metalanguage, *Proc. ESOP 1986, Springer Lecture Notes in Computer Science* **213** (1986) 30-40.

[8] F. Nielson: Strictness Analysis and Denotational Abstract Interpretation, *Information and Computation* **76** 29-92.

[9] F. Nielson, H.R. Nielson: Two-Level Semantics and Code Generation, *Theoretical Computer Science* **56** (1988) 59-133.

[10] F. Nielson, H.R. Nielson: *Two-Level Functional Languages, Cambridge Tracts in Theoretical Computer Science* **34**, Cambridge University Press (1992).

[11] G.D. Plotkin: Lambda-definability and logical relations, Edinburgh AI memo, Edinburgh University (1973).

[12] G.D. Plotkin: Lambda-definability in the Full Type Hierarchy, in: To H.B. Curry: *Essays on Combinatory Logic, Lambda Calculus, and Formalism*, J.P. Seldin and J.R. Hindley (eds.), Academic Press (1980).

[13] J.C. Reynolds: On the relation between direct and continuation semantics, *Proc. 2nd ICALP, Springer Lecture Notes in Computer Science* **14** (1974).

A Hyperdoctrinal View of Concurrent Constraint Programming

Prakash Panangaden
School of Computer Science
McGill University
Montréal, Québec, Canada

Vijay Saraswat
Xerox PARC
Palo Alto, California, USA

P.J. Scott
University of Ottawa
Ottawa, Ontario, Canada

R.A.G. Seely
McGill University and John Abbott College
Montréal, Québec, Canada

Abstract: We study a relationship between logic and computation via concurrent constraint programming. In previous papers it has been shown that concurrent constraint programs can be modeled by closure operators. In the present paper we show that the programming interpretation via closure operators is intimately related to the logic of the constraints. More precisely, we show how the usual hyperdoctrinal description of first order logic can be functorially related to another hyperdoctrine built out of closure operators. The logical connectives map onto constructions on closure operators that turn out to model programming constructs, specifically conjunction becomes parallel composition and existential quantification becomes hiding of local variables.

Keywords: asynchronous systems, closure operators, constraint programs, fibrations, hyperdoctrines.

Contents

1 Introduction

In this paper we develop a category theoretic view of the relationship between concurrent constraint programming and logic. One may think of this as an explication of the relationship between logic and what is often called logic programming. More significantly, however, this is a semantical account of constraint programming in which concurrency fits naturally. Indeed parallel composition of processes is one of the easiest combinators to define. As far as the programmer is concerned the most important point of the concurrent constraint program paradigm is that *the programmer can work directly with the notion of partial information.*

The basic thesis is this: a computational account of (first-order) logic should spell out the computational significance of entailment in a minimal logical setting. Fascinating issues like "how does one efficiently decide whether an instance of entailment holds" or "what theorem-proving strategy is used" or "how do the other logical connectives fit in" come later. Thinking in terms of a weak logic with just conjunction and existential quantification led to the basic process calculus presented in [19] and studied extensively in [17]. In [20] a variety of denotational semantics, all based on closure operators, are introduced and studied.

In the present paper we show that the various constructions on closure operators, used in modeling the basic process combinators, arise as the functorial image of logical connectives. Thus from the computational point of view there is an intimate relation between the mathematical structures that arise in the study of closure operators and the logical connectives. From a certain point of view, this correspondence is as significant as the model theoretic semantics of logic programming languages [14, 1] because it shows how the notion of partial information enters naturally into the computational setting. Furthermore there is a tight correspondence between intersection of sets of fixed points of closure operators, parallel composition of processes and conjunction. Thus, the framework that we present can be seen as the starting point of a general study of asynchronous processes. The idea of using closure operators to model logic variables in a parallel functional language was originally thought of by Pingali and discussed in detail in [10].

The computational paradigm can be described in the following way. The crucial concept underlying this paradigm is to replace the notion of *store-as-valuation* behind imperative programming languages with the notion of *store-as-constraint*. By a constraint we mean a (possibly infinite) subset of the space of all possible valuations in the variables of interest. For the store to be a constraint rather than a valuation means that at any stage of the computation one may have only partial information about the possible values that the variables can take. We take as fundamental the possibility that the state of the computation may only be able to provide partial information about the variables of interest. This shift to partially specified values renders the usual notions of (imperative) "write" and "read" incoherent.

Instead, [17] proposes the replacement of read with the notion of *ask* and write with the notion of *tell*. An ask operation takes a constraint (say, c) and uses it to probe the structure of the store. It succeeds if the store contains enough information to entail c. Tell takes a constraint and conjoins it to the constraints already in place in the store. That is, the set of valuations describing the resultant store is the intersection of the set of valuations describing the original store and those describing the additional constraint. Thus, as computation progresses, more and more information is accumulated in the store—a basic step does not *change* the value of a variable but rules out certain values that were possible before; the store is *monotonically refined*.

The idea of monotonic update is central to the theoretical treatment of I-structures in Id Nouveau [10]. I-structures were introduced in order to have some of the benefits of in-place update without introducing the problems of interference. It is interesting that the concurrent constraint paradigm can be seen as arising as a purification of logic programming [17], an enhancement to functional programming and as a generalization of imperative programming. From the viewpoint of dataflow programming, the concurrent constraint paradigm is also a generalization in that the flow of information between two processes is *bidirectional*.

2 Concurrent Constraint Languages

In this section we give a brief summary of the theory of concurrent constraint languages [19, 20]. A detailed discussion of programming idioms within this paradigm is contained in the forthcoming book by Saraswat [17].

The basic picture is as follows. Consider a system of concurrent processes interacting via shared data. The shared data can be thought of as a collection of assertions in some first order language. Processes communicate by adding information to the common pool of data (a "tell" operation) or by asking whether an assertion is entailed by the existing pool of data (an "ask" operation). In a concurrent constraint language one has a language for describing processes or agents and a language for describing the assertions that one may make. Such a language equipped with an entailment relation is called a *constraint system*.

We have a constraint system given as a logical language using a very weak positive logic. This is used to state assertions about the data that are used in the programming language. There are some minimal logical connectives provided, *i.e.* conjunction and existential quantification, while on the programming side there are some process combinators, e.g. parallel composition and hiding of local variables. The point of the logic being so weak is that the constraint system itself is not forced to use a powerful theorem prover of some sort. It is the minimal structure needed to get a notion of concurrency and synchronization via the imposition of constraints and requires only a simple notion of answering entailment queries.

By previous work [20], we know that the denotational semantics is fully abstract with respect to a traditional operational semantics. We first describe what is meant by a constraint system and give some basic lemmas that we use later. In the next subsection we give an operational semantics in the style of the Chemical Abstract Machine [3] or CHAM. Finally we sketch the results that show that the program combinators are the functorial image of the logical connectives.

An Informal View of Constraint Systems

What do we have when we have a constraint system? First, of course, there must be a *vocabulary* of assertions that can be made about how things can be—each assertion will be a syntactically denotable object in the programming language. Postulate then a set D of *tokens*, each giving us partial information about certain states of affairs. At any finite state of the computation, the program will have deposited some finite set u of such tokens with the embedded constraint-solver and may demand to know whether some other token is *entailed* by u. Postulate then a *compact* entailment relation $\vdash \subseteq \mathcal{P}_{fin}(D) \times D$ ($\mathcal{P}_{fin}(D)$ is the set of finite subsets of D), which records the inter-dependencies between tokens. The intention is to have a set of tokens v entail a token P just in case for every state of affairs for which we can assert every token in v, we can also assert P. This leads us to:

Definition 2.1 *A simple constraint system is a structure $\langle D, \vdash\rangle$, where D is a non-empty (countable) set of* tokens *or* (primitive) constraints *and $\vdash \subseteq \mathcal{P}_{fin}(D) \times D$ is an* entailment relation *satisfying (where $\mathcal{P}_{fin}(D)$ is the set of* finite *subsets of D):*

C1 *$u \vdash P$ whenever $P \in u$, and,*

C2 *$u \vdash Q$ whenever $u \vdash P$ for all $P \in v$, and $v \vdash Q$.*

Extend $\vdash$ to be a relation on $\mathcal{P}_{fin}(D) \times \mathcal{P}_{fin}(D)$ by: $u \vdash v$ iff $u \vdash P$ for every $P \in v$. Define $u \approx v$ if $u \vdash v$ and $v \vdash u$.

Of course, in any implementable language, $\vdash$ must be decidable. Compactness of the entailment relation ensures that one has a semi-decidable entailment relation. If a token is entailed, it is entailed by a finite set and hence if entailment holds it can be checked in finite time. If the store does not entail the constraint it may not be possible for the constraint solver to say this at any finite stage of the computation.

Such a treatment of systems of partial information is, of course, well known, and underlies Dana Scott's information systems approach to domain theory [22]. A simple constraint system is just an information system with the consistency structure removed, since it is natural in our setting to conceive of the possibility that the execution of a program can give rise to an inconsistent state of affairs.

Following standard lines, states of affairs (at least those representable in the system) can be identified with the set of all those tokens that hold in them.

Definition 2.2 *The* elements *of a constraint system $\langle D, \vdash\rangle$ are those subsets c of D such that $P \in c$ whenever $u \subseteq_f c$ (*i.e. *u is a finite subset of c) and $u \vdash P$. The set of all such elements is denoted by $|D|$. For every $u \subseteq_f D$ define $\bar{u} \in |D|$ to be the set $\{P \in D \mid u \vdash P\}$.*

As is well known, $(|D|, \subseteq)$ is a complete algebraic lattice. The lub of chains is, however, just the union of the members in the chain. The finite elements of $|D|$ are just the elements generated by finite subsets of D; the set of such elements will be denoted $|D|_0$. We use a,b,c,d and e to stand for elements of $|D|$; $c \geq d$ means $c \vdash d$. Two common notations that we use when referring to the elements of $|D|$ or $|D|_0$ are $\uparrow c = \{d | c \leq d\}$ and $\downarrow c = \{d | d \leq c\}$.

The reader will have noticed that the constraint system need not generate a *finitary* lattice since, in general, Scott information systems do not generate finitary domains. Indeed many common constraint systems are not finitary even when the data type that they are defined over is finitary.

A concretely presented constraint system is basically a first order theory in the conjunctive calculus with only existential quantification. Unlike the case of simple constraint systems, it is not so obvious, a priori, to move from this to a structure that captures the notion of information in the way that one passes from an information system to a Scott domain or from a simple constraint system to a complete algebraic lattice. In particular we need to know how to carry over the structure described by the variables and the existential quantification. In previous work we used ideas from cylindric algebras [6] to define this algebraically. In the next section we give a presentation based on hyperdoctrines. We conclude this section with some semi formal examples.

Example 2.1 The Herbrand constraint system.
We describe this example quickly. There is an ordinary first-order language L with equality. The tokens of the constraint system are the atomic propositions. Entailment can vary depending on the intended use of the predicate symbols but it must include the usual entailment relations that one expects from equality. Thus, for example, $f(X,Y) = f(A, g(B,C))$ must entail $X = A$ and $Y = g(B,C)$. If equality is the only predicate symbol then the constraint system is finitary. With other predicates present the finitariness of the lattice will depend on the entailment relation.

Example 2.2 Rational intervals.
The underlying tokens are of the form $X \in [x,y]$ where x and y are rational numbers and the notation $[x,y]$ means the closed interval between x and y. We assume that every such membership assertion is a primitive token. The entailment relation is the one derived from the obvious interpretation of the tokens. Thus, $X \in [x_1,y_1] \vdash X \in [x_2,y_2]$ if and only if $[x_1,y_1] \subseteq [x_2,y_2]$. In the lattice generated by these assertions we will have lots of elements that we cannot think of in the usual set theoretic way. For example, since $\bigcap_{n>0}[0,1+1/n] = [0,1]$, we would normally have $\{X \in [0,1+1/n] | n > 0\} \vdash (X \in [0,1])$ but no finite subset of $\{X \in [0,1+1/n] | n > 0\}$ would entail $X \in [0,1]$. Instead there will be a new element of $|D|$ that sits below the intersection. Thus, for example, the join $\bigsqcup_{n>0} X \in [0,1+1/n]$ will not be $X \in [0,1]$ but rather a new element that sits below $X \in [0,1]$.

Semantics of Concurrent Constraint Languages

The discussion in this subsection is a condensation of the discussion in [20]. The syntax and operational semantics of the language are given in Table 1. We use the letter c to stand for an element of the constraint system. The basic combinators are the **ask** and **tell** written

Syntax.	$A ::= c \mid c \rightarrow A \mid A \| A \mid \text{new } x \text{ in } A$
Reaction Equations.	$c \rightharpoonup c, d \text{ if } c \geq d$ $c \rightarrow A, c \rightharpoonup A, c$ $(A \| B) \rightharpoonup A, B$ $(\text{new } x \text{ in } A) \rightharpoonup < A >_x$ $< A >_x, c \rightharpoonup < A, \exists x.c >_x$ $< c, d >_x \rightleftharpoons < c >_x, < d >_x$ $< c >_x \rightharpoonup \exists x.c$
Above, c and d range over constraints while A and B range over processes.	

Table 1: CHAM Operational semantics for the Ask-and-Tell cc languages

$c \rightarrow A$ and c respectively. Intuitively, $c \rightarrow A$ executes by asking the store whether c holds, if it does than A executes otherwise the process suspends; we also have an indeterminate generalization of the ask construct that simultaneously asks whether several constraints hold. The tell combinator c simply asserts the constraint c. The parallel composition of two agents is written $A_1 \| A_2$. Hiding is written new x in A. Finally we have procedure calls, including possibly recursive procedures but we exclude them from the present discussion.

The operational semantics is given as a set of reaction rules. We assume that the dynamics occurs in a "solution" in which one has all the assertions in the store and all the assertions entailed by those in the store. Furthermore one has processes in the solution as well. We use the following chemical imagery to describe existential quantification. A process may be shielded by a "membrane" that allows facts to enter but may filter out information in the process of letting facts enter and leave. We write $< P >_x$ for a process P shielded by an x-membrane. A reaction that can happen can also happen inside a membrane.

The first equation says that the solution is entailment closed. One can see that the interaction between the processes constraints does not destroy the constraints, thus the idempotence of the process behaviour is built into the operational semantics. The second rule says that if the solution contains enough information to satisfy an ask the process makes the transition to the body. If one has the parallel composition of two process they just dissociate and work independently. The last four rules describe how block structuring in the programming language interacts with existential quantification. The explanation uses the notion of membrane discussed above. The key points are that when a shielded process comes into contact with a constraint, the constraint must first penetrate the membrane in order to react with the process. In so doing all information about the variable(s) being shielded will be hidden, as is shown by the existential quantification of the constraint. Similarly when a constraint leaves a membrane it has its shielded variable quantified out.

The basic idea of the denotational semantics is to model processes as closure operators. Operationally, the important point is that in order to model a process *compositionally*, it suffices to record its resting points. Mathematically, this is mirrored by the fact that a closure operator is completely specified by its set of fixed points. Given this representation of closure operators, we can define some operations on sets of fixed points that are clumsy to

Syntax.

$$A ::= c \mid c \rightarrow A \mid A \parallel A \mid \mathsf{new}\ X\ \mathsf{in}\ A$$

Semantic Equations.

$$\mathcal{A}[\![c]\!] = \{d \in |D| \mid d \geq c\}$$
$$\mathcal{A}[\![c \rightarrow A]\!] = \{d \in |D| \mid d \geq c \Rightarrow d \in \mathcal{A}[\![A]\!]\}$$
$$\mathcal{A}[\![A \parallel B]\!] = \{d \in |D| \mid d \in \mathcal{A}[\![A]\!] \wedge d \in \mathcal{A}[\![B]\!]\}$$
$$\mathcal{A}[\![\mathsf{new}\ X\ \mathsf{in}\ A]\!] = \{d \in |D| \mid \exists c \in \mathcal{A}[\![A]\!].\exists_X d = \exists_X c\}$$

Above, c ranges over basic constraints, that is, finite sets of tokens.

Table 2: Denotational Semantics for the Ask-and-Tell cc languages

state in terms of closure operators as functions. Most notably, one can define intersection of sets of fixed points of closure operators; it is quite awkward to write down this combinator in terms of functions. It turns out that this operation is exactly what one needs to model parallel composition.

To be determinate, the process must define a function. This function maps each input c to a new store that corresponds to the result of the process augmenting the store. If the process, when initiated in c, engages in an infinite execution sequence we map c to the store that is the limit of the information added in this infinite process. Otherwise we map c to d if the process ultimately quiesces having upgraded the store to d. Intuitively the motivation for using closure operators is as follows. A closure operator is extensive (increasing), which reflects the fact that the processes add information. A closure operator is also idempotent. The fact that the processes are modeled by idempotent functions means that once they add the information that they are going to add the store is not going to be affected by adding the same information again. Finally we require monotonicity (and continuity) for the usual computability reason. The denotational semantics is given in Table 2. We have left out details like the definition of the environment mechanism and procedures. The closure operators are described by giving their set of fixed points.

3 Constraint Systems as Hyperdoctrines

In this section we review the connection, elucidated by Lawvere originally[15], between ordinary first-order logic and category theory through the use of hyperdoctrines. We will give a minimal and simplified account that only encompasses conjunction and existential quantification. These are the two connectives that any constraint system must have. Subsequent investigations will build on the present work to incorporate other logical connectives and their corresponding program combinators. Our main point in this section is to show that a constraint system is in fact a hyperdoctrine. The various axioms that we found necessary in our analysis of constraint programming languages [20] all follow from the adjunction between existential quantification and substitution. There is nothing original in this section; we follow the ideas in Seely's discussion [23] of the connection between natural deduction and hyperdoctrines.

Hyperdoctrines have, until recently, not received a great deal of attention, the main arena for categorical logic being elementary toposes. There has, however, been a surge of interest starting with the recent categorical description of models of the polymorphic lambda calculus [24]. There is also a recent trend to using more general fibred categories in describing dependent type systems, see for example the recent papers of Hyland and Pitts [7], Jacobs [8] and Pavlović [16].

Recall that constraint systems are given by a first order language interpreted over some structure and that they come equipped with a notion of entailment, conjunction and substitution. Our main task is to introduce existential quantification in terms of substitution. In order to facilitate the presentation, we do not use the most general definitions possible; for example, we assume that the constraint system is one sorted.

In the hyperdoctrinal presentation, one has a family of categories, called the *fibres*, indexed by the objects of a cartesian category called the *base* category. Corresponding to the arrows of the base category are functors between the fibres. Thus, in general, a hyperdoctrine over the base category is a contravariant functor[1] to **CAT**. For our purposes it will be sufficient to consider the fibres to be preordered sets.

We define a constraint system as a simplified hyperdoctrine.

Definition 3.1 *A constraint system is a contravariant functor* $\mathcal{P}() : \mathbf{B}^{op} \longrightarrow \wedge$**-Preord**, *where* $\wedge$**-Preord** *is the category of meet-preorders, and* $\mathbf{B}$ *is cartesian (*i.e. *has all finite products). We assume that for each arrow* f *in* $\mathbf{B}$, *the (monotone) function* $\mathcal{P}(f)$ *(often written* f^**) preserves meets and has a left adjoint, written* $\exists_f$. *We also require the following two conditions:*

1. **Beck condition** *If the following diagram is a pullback*

$$\begin{array}{ccc} A & \xrightarrow{f} & B \\ {\scriptstyle g}\downarrow & & \downarrow{\scriptstyle h} \\ A' & \xrightarrow[k]{} & B' \end{array}$$

and $\phi \in \mathcal{P}(B)$ *then* $\exists_g(f^*\phi) \sim k^*(\exists_h\phi)$, *where* $\sim$ *means that we have two way entailment.*

2. **Frobenius Reciprocity:** *For each* $f : A \longrightarrow B$ *in* $\mathbf{B}$ *and* $\phi \in \mathcal{P}(A)$ *and* $\psi \in \mathcal{P}(B)$ *we have* $\exists_f(f^*\psi \wedge \phi) \sim \psi \wedge \exists_f\phi$.

In the case where we have a constraint system syntactically presented as a concrete theory in first order conjunctive logic with existential quantification the hyperdoctrine conditions are easy to check [23]. In the next several paragraphs we describe the passage from a syntactically presented first order theory to a (hyperdoctrinal) constraint system.

At the least, the base category is generated by a set of basic data values V : the objects of B are all finite products of V, including the empty product 1, and the arrows are the smallest

[1] Generally these are pseudofunctors but in the posetal situation that we consider this does not make any difference.

set of arrows containing all the projections and identity arrows, and closed under composition and pairing. In general there may be other arrows between objects corresponding to terms. For example, if there is a function symbol f of arity two, this will appear as an arrow from V^2 to V. The role of the two conditions will be explained after we develop some elementary properties of the hyperdoctrine.

Convention 3.1 *Since the objects of* **B** *are indexed by nonnegative integers we will usually just write* n *when we mean the object* V^n *of* **B**.

The base category essentially contains information about "terms" that describe individuals.

Information about the formulas, the "predicates", lives in the fibres indexed by the objects of **B**. Rather than view the fibres as general categories we use the category **∧-Preord** of preorders equipped with binary meets.

Convention 3.2 *We will use greek letters like* ϕ, ψ *etc. to stand for formulas.*

Definition 3.2 *Given a concrete constraint system we define a functor* $\mathcal{P}()$ *from* $\mathbf{B}^{op}$ *to* **∧-Preord** *as follows. The functor* $\mathcal{P}()$ *takes an object* n *to the formulas with* n *free variables constructed out of terms, variables, predicate symbols, conjunction and existential quantification. The preorder describes the entailment relation. Thus, if* $\phi \vdash \psi$ *we define* $\phi \leq \psi$, *or, equivalently,* $\phi \to \psi$. *If* f *is an arrow from* m *to* n *in* **B**, *we define* $\mathcal{P}(f)$ *from* $\mathcal{P}(\mathrm{n})$ *to* $\mathcal{P}(\mathrm{m})$ *by* $\mathcal{P}(f)(\phi)[\vec{X}] = (\phi)[f(\vec{Y})]$, *where* $\vec{X}$ *and* $\vec{Y}$ *are vectors of variables.*

Note that the arrows $\mathcal{P}(f)$ are clearly meet preserving when f is one of the projection maps, because all this means in this case is that adjoining dummy variables is defined structurally. The entailment relation was originally defined between finite subsets of formulas and single formulas. One can easily redefine it in terms of pairs of formulas by introducing finitary conjunction.

Now we define existential quantification as the left adjoint to substitution and show how it corresponds to the usual definition in terms of variables. Consider, for definiteness, the fibres over **1** and **2**, *i.e.* $\mathcal{P}(\mathbf{1})$ and $\mathcal{P}(\mathbf{2})$. Recall that **2** is just $\mathbf{1} \times \mathbf{1}$; let p be the first projection from **2** to **1**. The functor (monotone function between preorders), $\mathcal{P}(p)$, written p^* by convention, from $\mathcal{P}(\mathbf{1})$ to $\mathcal{P}(\mathbf{2})$ is, according to the above, just $p^*(\phi)[X] = \phi[p(X,Y)]$. Because p^* preserves meets, it has a left adjoint[2], written $\exists_p$, a functor from $\mathcal{P}(\mathbf{2})$ to $\mathcal{P}(\mathbf{1})$. In fact,

$$\exists_p.\psi[X,Y] = \exists X'\exists Y'(p(X',Y') = X \wedge \psi[X',Y']).$$

By Tarski's trick, this equals $\exists Y'\psi[X,Y']$. It is easy to prove directly (for intuitionistic first order logic with equality) that $\exists_p$ is left adjoint to substitution p^*.

Slightly more generally, in the multisorted case, we may allow our base category **B** to be the cartesian category generated by a set of Sorts $U, V, \ldots$, in which any sorted function symbols $f : U \longrightarrow V$ become arrow-forming operations: *i.e.* the arrows of **B** are the smallest set of arrows containing the projections, identities, and the sorted function symbols f, closed under composition and pairing. We may then define *substitution and existential quantification along term* f , as follows (using lower case letters as variables): $f^*\Psi(v) =$

[2]This is easily proved for Galois connections between posets, see for example [5].

$\Psi[f(u)/v]$, and $\exists_f\Phi(u) = \exists u(f(u) = v \wedge \Phi(u))$. Again, rules of first-order intuitionistic logic with equality show that $\exists_f$ is left adjoint to f^*. It is easily verified that this definition includes the former, when f is a projection p.

Defined this way, the functor enjoys all the properties one normally expects of existential quantification. The only change that one needs to make is to insert p^* in appropriate places in order to take into account the stratification induced by the arities of formulas. For example, in the traditional presentations of first-order predicate calculus, one has $\phi \leq \exists_X.\phi$ where X is a variable. In the present framework, in order to make sense of $\phi \leq \exists_p\phi$ we really need to write $\phi \leq p^*(\exists_p\phi)$, since we need to make the formulas live in the same fibre before we can sensibly compare them. The fact that $\phi \leq p^*(\exists_p\phi)$, is of course just the unit of the adjunction. We collect together the basic facts about existential quantification in the present framework. For convenience, we write down the hyperdoctrinal version as well as the version with existential quantification defined in terms of free variables and without the stratification in terms of the number of free variables. Proofs are omitted here; in any case they are all trivial.

Fact 3.1 $\phi \leq p^*(\exists_p\phi)$ *[* $\phi \leq \exists_X.\phi$ *].*

The proof is immediate from the definition of $\exists_p$ as the left adjoint of p^*; this is the unit of the adjunction.

Fact 3.2 $\exists_p(p^*\phi) \leq \phi$ *[* $\exists_X.\phi \leq \phi$ *if* X *does not occur in* ϕ *].*

This is just the counit of the adjunction.

Fact 3.3 $\exists_p(p^*(\exists_p(\phi))) = \exists_p(\phi)$ *[* $\exists_X.\exists_X.\phi = \exists_X.\phi$ *], where the equality can mean either two way entailment or equality of subsets of* V^N.

This is just one of the two "triangle equalities" of adjunctions. (In the posetal context, this is an equality; generally one could only expect maps going each way, with equality of one composition.) This equation says that existential quantification is idempotent.

Fact 3.4 $p^*(\exists_p(p^*(\phi))) = p^*(\phi)$ *[* $\exists_X.\phi = \phi$ *if* X *does not occur in* ϕ *].*

This is the other triangle equality.

Fact 3.5 *If* $V \neq \emptyset$ (i.e. *if there is an arrow* $0 \to 1$ *in* **B***), then* $\exists_p(p^*(\phi)) = \phi$ *[* $\exists_X.\phi = \phi$ *if* X *does not occur in* ϕ *].*

The proof follows from applying f^* to the previous equation, for the map $f: 0 \to 1$ mentioned in the hypothesis. Thus, this says we have a reflection rather than just an adjunction. For the following we just use colimit preservation.

Fact 3.6 *Suppose that the fibres are equipped with a least element, generically written* $false_N$*. Then* $\exists_p.false_{N+1} = false_N$.

This is immediate because left adjoints preserve colimits, or initial objects in this case. In view of this we will skip the subscripts on $false$ henceforth.

Fact 3.7 *If joins, written* $\vee$, *exist then*

$$\exists_p(\phi \vee \psi) = \exists_p(\phi) \vee \exists_p(\psi)$$

$$[\ \exists_X.(\phi \vee \psi) = \exists_X.\phi \vee \exists_X.\psi\ ].$$

Again this is immediate because left adjoints preserve joins.

Fact 3.8 *If joins exist then,*

$$\exists_p(\phi \vee p^*(\exists_p(\psi))) = \exists_p(\phi) \vee \exists_p(\psi)$$

$$[\ \exists_X.(\phi \vee \exists_X.\psi) = \exists_X.\phi \vee \exists_X.\psi\ ].$$

This follows from facts 3.5 and 3.3.

The Beck condition that we discussed above needs to be checked for only a few simple classes of diagrams. Again when the constraint system is derived from syntax these are easily checkable formulas. Frobenius reciprocity, when one has implication, is equivalent to saying that the maps of the form f^* preserve implication. The following calculation demonstrates part of this claim.

$$\begin{array}{rcl} f^*(\psi) \wedge \phi & \vdash & f^*(\exists_f(f^*(\psi) \wedge \phi)) \\ \phi & \vdash & f^*(\psi) \Rightarrow f^*(\exists_f(f^*(\psi) \wedge \phi)) \\ \phi & \vdash & f^*(\psi \Rightarrow \exists_f(f^*(\psi) \wedge \phi)) \\ \exists_f \phi & \vdash & \psi \Rightarrow \exists_f(f^*(\psi) \wedge \phi) \\ \psi \wedge \exists_f \phi & \vdash & \exists_f(f^*(\psi) \wedge \phi) \end{array}$$

where the first line is the unit of the adjunction, the second is the adjunction between implication and conjunction, the third is preservation of implication and the last two are the same adjunctions used in the reverse direction. In the absence of an implication in the fibres we demand Frobenius reciprocity as a condition. When the hyperdoctrine arises from a concrete presentation of logic, we can easily prove Frobenius reciprocity. In fact Seely [23] shows how one can go back and forth between the hyperdoctrinal presentation and first order logic with equality.

We conclude this section with a discussion of equality. Suppose that we have equality in our syntax. Again, for simplicity, we consider the case where the relevant base objects are $\mathcal{P}(1)$ and $\mathcal{P}(2)$. In a cartesian category, we have, for any object A, an arrow, the diagonal arrow, Δ from A to $A \times A$ given by $\langle I_A, I_A \rangle$. Thus in the base category we have an arrow from $\mathcal{P}(1)$ to $\mathcal{P}(2)$. In the same way as we defined p^* we can define Δ^*, which now goes from $\mathcal{P}(2)$ to $\mathcal{P}(1)$. If our logic has equality then Δ^* has a left adjoint. The left adjoint to Δ^* is written $\exists_\Delta$. The definitions can be understood as follows. Let ϕ be a formula with one free variable, then $\exists_\Delta \phi$ is a formula with two free variables obeying $\exists_\Delta \phi[X, Y] \equiv (X = Y) \wedge \phi[X]$. In particular, if we choose ϕ to be $true_1$ we get $\exists_\Delta true_1$ is the same as $X = Y$. We can use a quick categorical argument to show that $\exists_X.X = Y$ is equal to $true_1$. We have that $\exists_X.X = Y$ is, in categorical form, $\exists_p \exists_\Delta true_1$. Since the existential quantifier acts functorially we can rewrite this as $\exists_{p \circ \Delta} true_1$ but $p \circ \Delta = Id$ so we have $\exists_{Id} true_1 = true_1$ where we have again used the functoriality of $\exists$ in the last step. Finally we remark that checking the Beck conditions is easy because one has to check them in the case that the hyperdoctrine expresses simple properties of first order logic or first order logic with equality as has already been done by Seely [23].

4 A Hyperdoctrine of Closure Operators

In this section we show how one can build a new hyperdoctrine, actually two new hyperdoctrines, by defining a suitable functor from $\wedge$-**Preord** to **CAL**, the category of complete algebraic lattices and then an endofunctor on **CAL**. Roughly speaking the first functor takes us from logic to "information structure" in a familiar way and the second takes us from an information structure to a collection of closure operators. The second construction is not familiar and, though, *in retrospect*, it is clear and easy to describe it makes precise an intuition for which it is not, a priori, clear that one can have a formalized statement.

The category $\wedge$-**Preord** has preordered sets equipped with binary meets as objects and monotone functions as the morphisms. The category we actually use is not quite **CAL** but instead $\mathbf{CAL}^{adj}$ which has complete algebraic lattices as objects and adjunction pairs as morphisms.

Definition 4.1 *The objects of the category* $\mathbf{CAL}^{adj}$ *are complete algebraic lattices. A morphism m from L to M is an* adjunction pair *between L and M. In more detail, a morphism m from L to M is a pair of monotone functions,* $\langle f : L \to M,\ g : M \to L\rangle$ *with f left adjoint to g* (i.e. $f \dashv g$)*. The composition of morphisms* $\langle f,\ g\rangle$ *and* $\langle h,\ k\rangle$ *is* $\langle h \circ f,\ g \circ k\rangle$.

Since it has a right adjoint, f preserves arbitrary sups.

The lattices in question are obtained by taking entailment closed sets of formulas or "theories". The programming significance of this is that these theories embody the information present in the store of a constraint programming system. The fact that we have a hyperdoctrine structure here means that one can pass from the logical concepts, conjunction and existential quantification, to the information theoretic concepts of combining information and hiding information. The fact that the hyperdoctrine is the functorial image of the previous hyperdoctrine under a very obvious functor means that there is a very small shift in viewpoint taking place here. Since we are getting this hyperdoctrine by composing the previous hyperdoctrine with a functor the Beck conditions and Frobenius reciprocity hold automatically. This is a great simplification over having to check these conditions explicitly.

We can define a functor, $\mathcal{F}()$, from $\wedge$-**Preord** to **CAL** as follows. In the next few paragraphs let A and B be meet preorders and $m : A \to B$ a monotone function between them.

Definition 4.2 *A* filter *in A is an upwards closed set that is also closed under the formation of binary (and hence all finitary) meets.*

Definition 4.3 *The lattice* $\mathcal{F}(A)$ *is defined to be the set of filters of A ordered by inclusion.*

It is easy to check that $\mathcal{F}(A)$ is a complete algebraic lattice. We could have equally well used the reverse inclusion order on filters. The present choice of order is the so called "information ordering", traditionally used in programming language semantics. It has the unfortunate effect of reversing the sense of a few adjunctions, but the intuitions associated with the notion of information are too useful to give up. The reason that we have meet closure in the definition of filters is because we want filters to be entailment closed with the notion of entailment introduced in our preliminary discussion of constraint systems. Our notion of entailment there was that a finite set of formulas could entail a formula. Thus if ϕ and ψ are in an entailment closed set and we have meets then $\phi \wedge \psi$ will have to be included as well.

Convention 4.1 *We use letters like u, v, w to stand for elements of the complete algebraic lattices generated in this way.*

Notation 4.1 *Given ϕ an element of A, we write $(\phi)\uparrow$ for the principal filter generated by ϕ. For any subset A' of A we write $(A')\uparrow$ for $\bigcup_{\phi \in A}(\phi)\uparrow$.*

Note that with our choice of ordering we have $\phi \leq \psi \Rightarrow (\psi)\uparrow \sqsubseteq (\phi)\uparrow$.

Notation 4.2 *Given any set X, a function f from X to X' and a subset Y of X we write $f(Y')$ for the direct image $\{f(y) | y \in Y\}$.*

Definition 4.4 *The arrow part of the functor $\mathcal{F}()$, is given by mapping the monotone function m to the pair, $\langle \mathbf{F}(m), m^{-1} \rangle$, where $\mathbf{F}(m)$ from $\mathcal{F}(A)$ to $\mathcal{F}(B)$ is given by $u \mapsto (m(u))\uparrow$ where $u \in \mathcal{F}(A)$ and m^{-1} is inverse image.*

It is easy to see that $\mathcal{F}()$ really is a functor between the categories defined above.

Proposition 4.5 *If A is a meet-preorder then $\mathcal{F}(A)$ is a complete algebraic lattice with joins given by upward closures of unions and meets given by intersections. If m is a monotone function from A to B then $\langle \mathbf{F}(m), m^{-1} \rangle$ is an adjunction pair from $\mathcal{F}(A)$ to $\mathcal{F}(B)$. $\mathcal{F}()$ defined in this way is a functor.*

Proof: The proof is straightforward. As an example we check that $\mathbf{F}(m) \dashv m^{-1}$. Suppose that $u \in \mathcal{F}(A)$ and $v \in \mathcal{F}(B)$. We want to show that $\mathbf{F}(m)(u) \subseteq v \iff u \subseteq m^{-1}(v)$. The forward direction is trivial. For the reverse direction, let $x \in \mathbf{F}(m)u$, then, for some $z \in u$, $m(z) \leq x$. Now by assumption, $m(z) \in v$ and, since v is upwards closed, $x \in v$. ∎

In fact we can think of $\mathcal{F}()$ as going from adjunction pairs to adjunction pairs. In view of this we have the following theorem.

Theorem 4.6 *The composition of the functors $\mathcal{F}()$ and $\mathcal{P}()$ produces another hyperdoctrinal structure on* **B** *with $(p^*)^{-1}$* right *adjoint to $\mathbf{F}(p^*)$.*

Note that if we had chosen the reverse ordering we would have had existential quantification as a left adjoint as before. The following calculation shows that $(p^*)^{-1}$ is in fact $\mathbf{F}(\exists_p)$. Suppose that $u \in \mathcal{F}(A)$, we show that $(p^*)^{-1}(u) = \mathbf{F}(\exists_p)(u)$. Suppose that $\phi \in (p^*)^{-1}(u)$, *i.e.* $p^*(\phi) \in u$ or, in other words, $\exists_p p^*(\phi) \in \exists_p(u)$. Now using the fact that $\exists_p p^*(\phi) \leq \phi$ we conclude that $\phi \in \mathbf{F}(\exists_p)(u)$. For the other direction, we note that if ϕ in $\mathbf{F}(\exists_p)(u)$ then, for some $\psi \in u$, $\exists_p \psi \leq \phi$. Using the adjunction, $\psi \leq p^*(\phi)$. Since u is a filter, and hence upwards closed, we have $p^*(\phi) \in u$ so $\phi \in (p^*)^{-1}(u)$. We will often write $\langle \mathbf{F}(p^*), \mathbf{F}(\exists_p)\rangle$ rather than $\langle \mathbf{F}(p^*), (p^*)^{-1}\rangle$, to emphasize the role of existential quantification.

Now we consider closure operators over the lattices produced in the last hyperdoctrine. We have already explained the significance of closure operators for constraint programming. The remarkable property of closure operators is that one can think of them either as functions or in terms of their sets of fixed points. We will pass back and forth between these two ways of viewing closure operators.

We recall the formal definition of closure operators and some basic facts about them [21, 5]. In order to avoid confusion in comparing our statements with those in the compendium we note that we say "left adjoint" where the compendium would say "lower adjoint" and similarly we say "right adjoint" where the compendium would say "upper adjoint".

Definition 4.7 *Given a lattice L a function c from L to L is a* closure operator *if c is monotone, idempotent,* i.e. $c = c \circ c$, *and increasing (extensive),* i.e. $\forall x \in L. x \leq c(x)$.

The following proposition, taken from pages 21 and 22 of [5], gives an equivalent characterization of closure operators.

Proposition 4.8 *Let f be a monotone function from L to L. Let f° be the corestriction to the image $f^\circ : L \to f(L)$ and let $f_\circ$ be the inclusion of the image of f in L, $f_\circ : f(L) \to L$. Then f is a closure operator iff f° is right adjoint to $f_\circ$.*

The next two propositions relate a closure operator with its set of fixed points.

Proposition 4.9 *The set of fixed points of a closure operator are closed under the formation of meets (infs) to the extent that they exist.*

Proposition 4.10 *Let L be a complete lattice. Let $\mathrm{Cl}(L)$ be the set of closure operators on L ordered extensionally. Let $C(L)$ be the set of meet-closed subsets of L ordered by* reverse inclusion. *Then the map $fix : \mathrm{Cl}(L) \to C(L)$ that takes a closure operator to its image (which is its set of fixed points) is an order isomorphism. The inverse of fix is the map $clo : C(L) \to \mathrm{Cl}(L)$ given by $clo(S)(x) = min((x)\uparrow \cap S) = inf((x)\uparrow \cap S)$.*

Proposition 4.11 *The collection of closure operators on a complete algebraic lattice ordered extensionally, form a complete algebraic lattice.*

The proof is sketched in Data Types as Lattices [21].

Notation 4.3 *We write $\mathrm{Cl}(L)$ for the closure operators on a lattice L.*

Now we define a hyperdoctrine of lattices by taking the closure operators on the lattices that form the fibres in the previous hyperdoctrine. Once again we will define the new hyperdoctrine as the functorial image of the preceding hyperdoctrine. It turns out, however, that in order to do this we need to use adjoint pairs in a fashion reminiscent of the use of embedding-projection pairs in the construction of D_∞. It does not seem possible to map directly the hyperdoctrinal structure above onto a hyperdoctrine of closure operators.

Now we note the following technique for lifting adjunctions between posets to adjunctions between their endofunction spaces.

Proposition 4.12 *Suppose that $\langle f,\ g\rangle$ is a morphism*[3] *in* $\mathbf{CAL}^{adj}$ *from L to M. Then $\langle f',\ g'\rangle$ is a morphism from $[L \to L]$ to $[M \to M]$, where $f' = \lambda h : [L \to L].f \circ h \circ g$, $g' = \lambda k : [M \to M].g \circ k \circ f$*

Proof: We need to establish that if $k \in [M \to M]$ and $h \in [L \to L]$ that $f \circ h \circ g \leq k$ iff $h \leq g \circ k \circ f$. Suppose that $f \circ h \circ g \leq k$, composing on the left with g and on the right with f we get $g \circ f \circ h \circ g \circ f \leq g \circ k \circ f$. The unit of the adjunction, $f \dashv g$, gives $g \circ f \geq Id_M$. Thus $h \leq g \circ f \circ h \circ g \circ f$ and hence $h \leq g \circ k \circ f$. Similarly for the other direction. ∎

The basic idea is to try to define an endofunctor from $\mathbf{CAL}^{adj}$ to $\mathbf{CAL}^{adj}$ as follows. We map an object L (a complete algebraic lattice) to the set of all closure operators on L ordered pointwise. For the arrow part of the functor, we define it by saying that it maps a morphism $\langle f,\ g\rangle$ from L to M to $\langle f',\ g'\rangle$ as defined in the last proposition. Since the closure operators on L are a sublattice of $[L \to L]$ we should have another adjoint pair and hence a morphism of $\mathbf{CAL}^{adj}$. Unfortunately, however, given h, a closure operator on L, $f \circ h \circ g$ need not be a closure operator on L.

In order to get around the above difficulty we use a remarkable function, V, discussed by Scott [21]. The function V maps functions on $[D \to D]$ to closure operators on D. It turns out that V is itself a closure operator on $[[D \to D] \to [D \to D]]$ whose fixed points are exactly the closure operators. In our discussion we use the characterization of closure operators in terms of their sets of fixed points.

Lemma 4.13 *If f is any monotone function in $[D \to D]$, where D is any poset, then $\{x \in D | f(x) \leq x\}$ is closed under the formation of meets insofar as they exist.*

Proof: Let S be any subset of $\{x \in D | f(x) \leq x\}$. Let u be $\sqcap S$. Note that $f(u)$ is a lower bound for S and hence $f(u) \leq u$. Thus $u = \sqcap S$ is in $\{x \in D | f(x) \leq x\}$. ∎

Definition 4.14 *Suppose that f is a function in $[D \to D]$ where D is any poset. We define the function V in $[[D \to D] \to [D \to D]]$ by $V(f) = clo(\{x \in D | f(x) \leq x\})$.*

The lemma tells us that this definition makes sense. In terms of functions, V is defined as $\lambda f.\lambda x.\mathbf{Y}(\lambda y.x \sqcup f(y))$. Intuitively this can be thought of as follows. In order to make f into a closure operator, extensionally greater than f, one has to guarantee that the result is bigger than the input; thus one is led to define it as $\lambda x.x \sqcup f(x))$ but now in order to guarantee idempotence one has to iterate this.

Thus, using V, we may take any monotone endofunction and convert it into a closure operator by applying V to it.

Notation 4.4 *Suppose that f is a monotone function in $[D \to D]$; we write $\overline{f}$ for $V(f)$.*

Comment 4.1 *Note that $\overline{f}$ is the least closure operator extensionally greater than f.*

Lemma 4.15 *If $\langle f,\ g\rangle$ is a morphism in* $\mathbf{CAL}^{adj}$ *from L to M then $\langle f',\ g'\rangle$ is a morphism in* $\mathbf{CAL}^{adj}$ *from $\mathrm{Cl}(L)$ to $\mathrm{Cl}(M)$ where $f' = \lambda h : \mathrm{Cl}(L).\overline{f \circ h \circ g}$ and $g' = \lambda k : \mathrm{Cl}(M).\overline{g \circ k \circ f}$.*

---
[3] We only use the fact that they form an adjunction.

Proof: This can be proved directly as follows. We need to show that for $h : \mathrm{Cl}(L)$ and $k : \mathrm{Cl}(M)$ we have $f'(h) \leq k$ iff $h \leq g'(k)$.
Suppose that $f'(h) \leq k$, *i.e.* $\overline{f \circ h \circ g} \leq k$. Since $\overline{(.)}$ is a closure operator itself, $f \circ h \circ g \leq k$. Now using the argument from the proposition above, we get $h \leq g \circ k \circ f$ and so $h \leq \overline{g \circ k \circ f}$.
Now suppose that $h \leq g'(k)$. We use the fact that closure operators can be represented by their sets of fixed points. In this paragraph, we will not notationally differentiate between the closure operator as a function and the closure operator as a set of fixed points; the resulting confusion is easily resolved by context. The payoff is that the proofs are easy to read (and invent!). In terms of sets of fixed points; $\overline{g \circ k \circ f} \subseteq h$. We will show that $k \subseteq \overline{f \circ h \circ g}$. Assume that $u \in k$, *i.e.* that $k(u) = u$. According to the counit of the adjunction $f \dashv g$, $f \circ g(u) \leq u$. Thus, since g is monotone $g \circ k \circ f \circ g(u) \leq g \circ k(u) = g(u)$. This means that $g(u) \in \overline{g \circ k \circ f} \subseteq h$. Thus $h(g(u)) = g(u)$, hence $h(g(u)) \leq g(u)$. Applying f to both sides and using the counit of $f \dashv g$, we get $f \circ h \circ g(u) \leq u$, *i.e.* $u \in \overline{f \circ h \circ g}$, in other words, $k \subseteq \overline{f \circ h \circ g}$. ∎

We can now define the promised endofunctor on $\mathbf{CAL}^{adj}$.

Definition 4.16 *The functor* $\mathrm{Cl}(-)$ *from* $\mathbf{CAL}^{adj}$ *to* $\mathbf{CAL}^{adj}$ *is defined as follows. It takes a complete algebraic lattice L to the complete algebraic lattice of closure operators on L ordered extensionally (reverse inclusion of the sets of fixed points). It takes a morphism* $\langle f, g\rangle$ *from L to M to the morphism* $\langle f', g'\rangle$ *where* $f' = \lambda h : [L \to L].\overline{f \circ h \circ g}$, $g' = \lambda k : [M \to M].\overline{g \circ k \circ f}$.

We need, of course, to check that we really have a functor, *i.e.* that identities and compositions are preserved. In order to do this, however, it is much easier to describe the arrow part of the functor in terms of the effects on sets of fixed points.

Lemma 4.17 *Suppose that* $\langle f, g\rangle$ *is a morphism from L to M with* $h \in \mathrm{Cl}(L)$ *and* $k \in \mathrm{Cl}(M)$. *Then* $\overline{g \circ k \circ f} = g(fix(k))$ *and* $\overline{f \circ h \circ g} = g^{-1}(fix(h))$.

Proof: We use the same ambiguity between a closure operator and its set of fixed points. Suppose that $u \in L$. Now $u \in \overline{g \circ k \circ f} \Leftrightarrow g \circ k \circ f(u) \leq u$ by definition. From the unit of $f \dashv g$ we have $u \leq g \circ f(u)$; now using monotonicity of g, the fact that k is a closure operator, and transitivity, we have $u \leq g \circ k \circ f(u)$ for any $u \in L$. Thus $u \in \overline{g \circ k \circ f} \Leftrightarrow u = g \circ k \circ f(u)$. The latter is of course in $g(k)$. The reverse inclusion is equally easy.
Suppose that $v \in M$. Now $v \in \overline{f \circ h \circ g} \Leftrightarrow (f \circ h \circ g(v) \leq v) \Leftrightarrow h \circ g(v) \leq g(v) \Leftrightarrow h(g(v)) = g(v) \Leftrightarrow v \in g^{-1}(h)$. ∎

With this in hand the proof of the following is trivial.

Lemma 4.18 $\mathrm{Cl}(\langle f_1, g_1\rangle) \circ \mathrm{Cl}(\langle f_2, g_2\rangle) = \mathrm{Cl}(\langle f_1 \circ f_2, g_1 \circ g_2\rangle)$.

This now completes the description of the endofunctor on $\mathbf{CAL}^{adj}$. Since we have defined it as acting on adjoint pairs it is evident that the hyperdoctrinal structure on $\mathbf{CAL}^{adj}$ is carried over to the closure operators.

One can now inspect the table for the denotational semantics of the concurrent constraint language and see that the definition of the construct new X in A uses the concrete version of the existential quantification operation in the last hyperdoctrine. Parallel composition is modeled by the sup operation in the lattices which of course comes ultimately from the meet operation in the first hyperdoctrine.

5 The Fibrational Version

It is often easier to study indexed structures in what is called the fibrational form. Instead of presenting an indexed structure as a functor F from a base category $\mathcal{B}$ to another category $\mathcal{C}$ one can present it as a "projection" functor P from $\mathcal{G}$ to $\mathcal{B}$, where $\mathcal{G}$ is a suitably constructed category. Roughly speaking, the category $\mathcal{G}$ "collects" all the fibres of the indexed structure into a single category.

It is well known that one can go from a hyperdoctrine to a fibration by a standard construction called the "Grothendieck" fibration. If the fibres are posets the Grothendieck construction still yields a non-posetal category. In this section we discuss the fibrational version of constraint systems. The main reason for doing this will be to develop a suitable notion of map between constraint systems. A good elementary reference for fibrations is the recent book by Barr and Wells [2]. Our discussion is taken from chapter 11 of that book, simplified where possible to take into account that our fibres are posets.

Suppose that we have a base category $\mathbf{B}$ and a functor $\mathcal{P}$ from $\mathbf{B}$ to a category of posets $\mathcal{C}$. For example, $\mathcal{C}$ could be $\wedge$-**Preord**. We construct a category $\mathcal{G}(\mathcal{P})$ and a functor $\mathbf{P}(\mathcal{P})$ from $\mathcal{G}(\mathcal{P})$ to $\mathbf{B}$. The inverse images of the functor $\mathbf{P}(\mathcal{P})$ are the fibres in the original indexed presentation. The construction is itself functorial in the sense that given arrows between indexed categories, *i.e.* natural transformations between functors from $\mathbf{B}$ to $\mathcal{C}$, one can define an arrow, *i.e.* a functor, between the corresponding fibrations.

The objects of $\mathcal{G}(\mathcal{P})$ are pairs $\langle \phi, n\rangle$ where n is an object of $\mathbf{B}$, which we are thinking of as an integer, and ϕ is an object in the fibre over n. Thus in our first hyperdoctrine the Grothendieck construction yields a category where the objects are formulas tagged by an integer which represents the number of free variables. The arrows of $\mathcal{G}(\mathcal{P})$ are pairs $\langle u, f\rangle : \langle \phi, n\rangle \longrightarrow \langle \phi', n'\rangle$ where f is an arrow in $\mathbf{B}$ from n' to n and u is an arrow over n' from $\mathcal{P}(f)(\phi)$ to ϕ'. An arrow like u is just an instance of the order relation. The definition of composition of arrows is more or less inevitable given the definition of arrows.

Note that the category $\mathcal{G}(\mathcal{P})$ is not posetal in general even when the fibres of the original indexed category are. In the case where the hyperdoctrine that we start with is just the one corresponding to a first order logic, the arrows in the resulting category are entailment instances between formulas and substitution instances of other formulas. Of course given two formulas with different numbers of free variables there may be several different substitution instances of one that entail the other.

6 Conclusions

We view the results of this paper as the start of a larger investigation in the same spirit. The most important direction is to formulate a notion of higher order constraint programming. Higher order process calculi are starting to be studied in earnest especially those related to the lambda calculus [4, 9]. In recent work, Jagadeesan and Pingali [11], and independently, Saraswat [18] have developed a higher order concurrent constraint process calculus. In order to understand models for these calculi we are using our framework to develop a category of constraint systems in analogy with the category of information systems. One can define such a category by applying the Grothendieck fibration construction to the hyperdoctrines that we have. The technical questions that we are studying are how one defines exponents in this category and how such exponential objects would be related to the models of higher order concurrent constraint calculi.

The other important direction to pursue is the study of other logical combinators and process combinators. For example, what happens when disjunction, negation, implication or universal quantification are added to the logic? One can also ask the reverse type of question: what is the logical significance of the meet operation on constraint systems? We have studied some of these issues already and are preparing additional investigations.

Acknowledgement

This research has been supported by research grants from the Natural Sciences and Engineering Research Council of Canada and team grants from Le Fonds pour la Formation de Chercheurs et l'Aide á la Recherche (Québec).

References

[1] K.R Apt and M.H. van Emden. Contributions to the theory of logic programming. *JACM*, 29(3):841–862, 1982.

[2] M. Barr and C. Wells. *Category Theory for Computing Science*. prentice-Hall, 1990.

[3] G. Berry and G. Boudol. The chemical abstract machine. In *Proceedings of the Seventeenth Annual ACM Symposium on Principles of Programming Languages*, pages 81–94. ACM, 1990.

[4] G. Boudol. Towards a lambda-calculus for concurrent and communicating systems. In J. Diaz, editor, *TAPSOFT 89, Lecture Notes in Computer Science 351*, pages 149–161. Springer-Verlag, 1989.

[5] G.Gierz, K.H.Hoffman, K.Keimel, J.D.Lawson, M.Mislove, and D.S.Scott, editors. *A compendium of continuous lattices*. Springer-Verlag Berlin Heidelberg New York, 1980.

[6] Leon Henkin, J. Donald Monk, and Alfred Tarski. *Cylindric Algebras (Part I)*. North Holland Publishing Company, 1971.

[7] J. M. E. Hyland and A. M. Pitts. The theory of constructions: Categorical semantics and topos-theoretic models. In *Categories in Computer Science and Logic*, pages 137–199. AMS, 1987. AMS Contemporory Mathematics Series 92.

[8] B. Jacobs. Fibrations. Submitted to Mathematical Structures in Computer Science, 1991.

[9] R. Jagadeesan and P. Panangaden. A domain-theoretic model of a higher-order process calculus. In M. Paterson, editor, *Proceedings of the 17th International Colloquium on Automata Languages and Programming*, pages 181–194. Springer-Verlag, 1990. Lecture Notes in Computer Science 443.

[10] R. Jagadeesan, P. Panangaden, and K. Pingali. A fully abstract semantics for a functional language with logic variables. In *Proceedings of IEEE Symposium on Logic in Computer Science*, pages 294–303, 1989.

[11] R. Jagadeesan and K. Pingali. A higher order functional language with logic variables. In *Proceedings of the Nineteenth Annual ACM Symposium on Principles of Programming Languages*, 1992.

[12] Peter Johnstone. *Stone Spaces*, volume 3 of *Cambridge Studies in Advanced Mathematics*. Cambridge University Press, 1982.

[13] G. Kahn. The semantics of a simple language for parallel programming. In *Information Processing 74*, pages 993–998. North-Holland, 1977.

[14] R.A. Kowalski and M.H. van Emden. The semantics of predicate logic as a programming language. *Journal of the ACM*, 23(4):733–742, 1976.

[15] F. W. Lawvere. Functorial semantics of algebraic theories. *Proc. Nat. Acad. Sci. U.S.A.*, 50:869–872, 1963.

[16] D. Pavlović. *Predicates and Fibrations*. PhD thesis, University of Amsterdam, 1991.

[17] V. Saraswat. *Concurrent Constraint Programming Languages*. PhD thesis, Carnegie-Mellon University, 1989. To appear Doctoral Dissertation Award and Logic Programming Series, MIT Press.

[18] V. Saraswat. The category of constraint systems is cartesian closed. In *Seventh Annual IEEE Symposium On Logic In Computer Science*, 1992.

[19] Vijay Saraswat and Martin Rinard. Concurrent constraint programming. In *Proceedings of the Seventeenth Annual ACM Symposium on Principles of Programming Languages*, pages 232–245, 1990.

[20] Vijay Saraswat, Martin Rinard, and Prakash Panangaden. Semantic foundations of concurrent constraint programming. In *Proceedings of the Eighteenth Annual ACM Symposium on Principles of Programming Languages*, 1991.

[21] D. Scott. Data types as lattices. *SIAM Journal of Computing*, 5(3):522–587, 1976.

[22] D. S. Scott. Domains for denotational semantics. In *Ninth International Colloquium On Automata Languages And Programming*. Springer-Verlag, 1982. Lecture Notes In Computer Science 140.

[23] R. A. G. Seely. Hyperdoctrines, natural deduction and the beck conditions. *Zeitschr. f. math. Logik und Grundlagen d. Math.*, 29:505–542, 1983.

[24] R. A. G. Seely. Categorical semantics for higher-order polymorphic lambda calculus. *J. Symb. Logic*, 52(4):969–989, 1987.

On the Foundations of Final Semantics: Non-Standard Sets, Metric Spaces, Partial Orders

Jan J.M.M. Rutten Daniele Turi

CWI
Kruislaan 413
NL – 1098 SJ Amsterdam

janr,turi@cwi.nl

Abstract. Canonical solutions of domain equations are shown to be *final coalgebras*, not only in a category of non-standard sets (as already known), but also in categories of metric spaces and partial orders. Coalgebras are simple categorical structures generalizing the notion of post-fixed point. They are also used here for giving a new comprehensive presentation of the (still) non-standard theory of *non-well-founded sets* (as non-standard sets are usually called).

This paper is meant to provide a basis to a more general project aiming at a full exploitation of the finality of the domains in the semantics of programming languages — concurrent ones among them. Such a *final semantics* enjoys uniformity and generality. For instance, semantic observational equivalences like bisimulation can be derived as instances of a single 'coalgebraic' definition (introduced elsewhere), which is parametric of the functor appearing in the domain equation. Some properties of this general form of equivalence are also studied in this paper.

Keywords: final semantics, category, functor, coalgebra, domain equation, fixed point, non-well-founded sets, non-standard set theory, metric spaces, partial orders, concurrency, (F-)bisimulation, ordered F-bisimulation.

Contents

The research of Daniele Turi was supported by the *Stichting Informatica Onderzoek in Nederland* within the context of the project "Non-well-founded sets and semantics of programming languages". (Project no. 612-316-034.)

0 Introduction

This work originates from an attempt to identify the common features of *partial orders*, *metric spaces*, and *non-standard sets*, that make these three different mathematical settings all suitable for defining semantic *domains* for concurrent programming languages. (To be precise, the distinctive feature of the domains under consideration is *non-determinism* rather than concurrency, the starting point being languages like *CCS* [Mil80] in which concurrency is reduced to sequentiality plus non-determinism.) It has resulted in a general semantic framework which could be called *final semantics*, as it is based on the observation that domains are final objects in a categorical sense.

This paper is a first account on this work, namely on its foundational part. It is shown that, regardless of the fact one is working with partial orders, metric spaces, or non-standard sets, domains are final objects in a suitable category of *coalgebras*. Moreover, some properties of final coalgebras are investigated in the abstract.

The categorical notion of coalgebra is quite elementary: given a category $\mathcal{C}$ (e.g., a category of complete metric spaces) and a functor $F : \mathcal{C} \to \mathcal{C}$, a coalgebra of F is a pair (A, α), with A an object in $\mathcal{C}$ and $\alpha : A \to F(A)$ an arrow in $\mathcal{C}$. Clearly, a solution to a domain equation $X \cong F(X)$ can be seen as a coalgebra (D, i), with i being an isomorphism between D and $F(D)$. The coalgebras of a given functor F over a category $\mathcal{C}$ form a category $\mathcal{C}_F$. Arrows are mappings of $\mathcal{C}$ which preserve the coalgebra structure (see the next section for a formal definition).

Semantic domains are usually obtained as solutions of recursive domain equations of the kind given above. There might be more than one such solution, but, for large classes of functors, a *canonical* one is taken. One of the starting points for the present work is a result in [Acz88], showing that, within a category of (classes over) non-standard sets, the canonical solution of a domain equation is a final coalgebra. (Non-standard sets are actually called *non-well-founded* sets in [Acz88], which is one of the standard references on the subject — but see also [FH83, FH92]. The word 'non-standard' has here a different meaning than in model theory.)

In this paper, it is shown that the canonical solutions of domain equations are final coalgebras, not only in that category of non-standard sets, but also in a category of complete metric spaces and in a category of complete partial orders. In other words, for these three different categories $\mathcal{C}$ and for large classes of functors F, the canonical solution to a domain equation $X \cong F(X)$ is a final object in the category $\mathcal{C}_F$.

0.1 Final Semantics

The finality of the domains is not only a unifying property. Final objects are the target of a unique arrow from any other object of the same category. This is a valuable property from a semantic point of view.

Recall that semantics can be given to a programming language by first defining a semantic domain and then associating a meaning to the programs of the language by mapping them onto elements of the chosen domain. The (by finality!) unique arrow from another coalgebra (of the same functor) into that domain is then a natural candidate for such an interpretation mapping. The problem is to give the class of programs of the language a coalgebra structure of the same functor used for the domain. Loosely speaking, syntax and semantics should live in the same category of coalgebras of this functor, the latter expressing the structure to be preserved under semantic mapping.

For instance, consider the language *CCS*. A semantic mapping should equate those programs which perform the same *computations* under a certain — informal — notion of *observation* (and keep the other distinct). As will become clear later, the choice of the functor for the domain amounts to making this notion of observation formal. Thus the functor defining the domain should be fixed according to the observation one has in mind. Further, computations are described by means of a transition system (induced by a set of structural rules) which is essentially a graph having programs as nodes and transitions as edges. Every program is the root of a tree obtained by unfolding the graph from that program. Such a tree gives the computations performable by the root program. Notice that there are many different ways of traversing a tree, each corresponding to a different notion of observation. The problem is thus, given a functor for a domain, to find a representation of the transition system as a coalgebra of that functor.

In general, the semantics shall depend on the observation one wants to perform on the computations or, more abstractly, on the functor one fixes. (Observations as functors!) For simplicity, it will be convenient that the functor be on some category of sets, possibly with some additional structure (e.g., metric or order), and leave to further developments generalizations to less concrete categories. More essentially, the existence of a final coalgebra for the functor will be needed, possibly to be shown via some limit construction. Then if one is able to find a representation of all the observable computations as a coalgebra of the same functor, the (final) semantics of the language will immediately follow. (Ideally, this scheme would include not only concurrent languages, but also applicative ones — see, e.g., [Abr90]). Alternatively, the observable computations of the class of programs of the language under study might be directly defined as a coalgebra of the chosen functor.

Of the general methodology sketched above at least one instance is to be found in the literature: it is the final semantics for *CCS* given in [Acz88]. There, the semantics is based on a (straightforward) coalgebra representation of transition systems for a specific functor (see Example 1.4). The existence of other representations (for different functors and, thus, domains) of transition systems (and, possibly, of observable computations in general) will be treated in a forthcoming paper (*Observations as Functors: final semantics for programming languages*), together with other issues (like compositionality) involving the languages. Instead here, as already mentioned, the attention is rather focussed on foundational issues, independent from the languages, like the general properties of functors ensuring the construction of final coalgebras. Moreover, there is a 'coalgebraic' notion which can be studied in the abstract and which is of major interest for semantics: the kind of equivalence induced by a functor and its coalgebras. Some properties of such an equivalence are useful in clarifying the relationship between final semantics and 'equivalence-based' semantics.

Consider again *CCS*. An alternative approach to its semantics is to formalize the notion of observation in terms of an (observational) equivalence. The semantic mapping associates to each program its equivalence class and the domain is then simply defined as the image of that mapping. A popular example of such an observational equivalence is (strong) bisimulation as defined in [Par81]. Now, the functor used for the final semantics in [Acz88] can be shown to induce bisimulation equivalence in the sense that two programs are mapped (via the final semantics) into the same process if and only if they are bisimilar.

One of the advantage of working with final semantics is that there is a single 'coalgebraic' notion of (possibly observational) equivalence which is parametric of the functor: it is the definition of F-bisimulation as given in [AM89]. For a particular choice of the functor F, namely the one used in [Acz88] (but see also [BZ82]), F-bisimulation coincides with bisimulation in the traditional sense, as was observed above. Also other equivalences, like for instance trace equivalence, can be obtained by instantiating F-bisimulation to a certain functor (as will be shown in the above mentioned *Observations as Functors*). And even for the existing observational equivalences which do not fall under this scheme, it might still be useful to understand why they fail to be described in this way.

0.2 Contribution of this Paper

It is now possible to be more precise about the technical results in this paper. First of all it is shown that final coalgebras are *strongly extensional* in the sense that two elements of a final F-coalgebra are equal if and only if they are F-bisimilar. Also other abstract properties concerning F-bisimulations are studied. Then a *final coalgebra theorem* is given for each of the three categories under study, stating that the canonical solution of a domain equation is a final coalgebra.

As already mentioned, the (so-called *special*) final coalgebra theorem for non-standard sets is not a new result ([Acz88]). However, the proof given here is somewhat more transparent than the original one because of a different formulation of the definition of *unifor-*

mity on maps, which occurs in the conditions of the theorem. An extensive description of non-standard set theory is included as well, both because this theory (still) is non-standard indeed, and because the way it is presented here has some interest on its own. A uniform characterization of *standard* and *non-standard* set theory is introduced, showing that the latter theory is as natural as the former: the foundation and anti-foundation axioms are stated in terms of initial algebras and final coalgebras, respectively. The use of final coalgebras is particularly helpful to have a concise and uniform presentation of equivalent forms of the anti-foundation axiom, like, e.g., the Solution Lemma used in the proof of the final coalgebra theorem.

For metric spaces the final coalgebra theorem is a new result. It is shown that locally contracting functors on the category of complete metric spaces (with non-expansive mappings as arrows) have a final coalgebra. The proof is based on a theorem stating that such functors have fixed points. The latter theorem extends earlier results of [AR89] along the lines of [SP82], and is proved in full detail.

For partial orders an initial algebra theorem and the so-called limit-colimit coincidence are well-known (see [SP82]), but, apparently, it was never proved in detail that (in $CPO_{\perp}$) initial algebras and final coalgebras coincide. (Actually, the proof given here of the 'order-theoretic' final coalgebra theorem does not make direct use of the limit-colimit coincidence.) It is shown that the fixed point of a locally continuous functor on the category of complete partial orders (with strict and continuous mappings) is a final coalgebra in that category.

The main result about the category of cpo's is the study of a new notion, called *ordered F-bisimulation*, which is a generalization of the definition of F-bisimulation. Both the notions of partial bisimulation from [Abr91] and that of simulation from [Pit92] (for the functorial case) can be seen to be examples of ordered F-bisimulations. Corresponding to the notion of ordered F-bisimulation is a generalized notion of strong extensionality. A proof is given of the fact that the final coalgebras of locally continuous functors are strongly extensional in such a generalized sense. It implies the internal full abstractness result from [Abr91], and the extensionality results (for the functorial case) from [Pit92].

0.3 Overview of the Paper

In Section 2 (algebras and) coalgebras of functors are introduced. Examples are given showing that the powerset functor can be used for coalgebra representations of graphs and (labelled) transition system. A third example consists of a metric variant of the final semantics given in [Acz88] (and mentioned above).

Section 3 is dedicated to the notion of F-bisimulation. It is first shown that for the same kind of functor as in Examples 1.4 and 1.8 it corresponds to strong bisimulation. Then abstract properties are proved like strong extensionality and preservation of F-bisimulation in the category of F-coalgebras.

In the next three sections, final coalgebras in the categories of non-standard sets, complete metric spaces, and complete partial orders are treated. These sections can be read independently from each other (but presuppose Sections 2 and 3).

In the last section, a comparative analysis is made between the three different final coalgebra constructions discussed in the paper. Related and future work, including the relationship between final coalgebras and *coinduction* (the dual of induction), are also discussed.

Although an extensive use of diagrams is made throughout the paper, no previous knowledge of category theory is required. Indeed, just a few (elementary) categorical notions are used.

1 Algebras and Coalgebras of Functors

Let $\mathcal{C}$ be a category and $F : \mathcal{C} \to \mathcal{C}$ be a functor from $\mathcal{C}$ to $\mathcal{C}$. (Such a functor is called an *endofunctor* on $\mathcal{C}$.)

Definition 1.1 An *F-coalgebra* is a pair (A, α), consisting of an object A and an arrow $\alpha : A \to F(A)$ in $\mathcal{C}$. It is dual to the notion of *F-algebra*: an *F-algebra* is a pair (A, α), consisting of an object A and an arrow $\alpha : F(A) \to A$ in $\mathcal{C}$. □

For instance, consider a preorder $(C, \leq)$. It can be interpreted as a category: the objects are the elements of C, and between any two elements $c, d \in C$ there is an arrow if and only if $c \leq d$. Any monotonic function $F : C \to C$ is then an endofunctor on C. Thus an F-coalgebra is a post-fixed point $x \in C$ with $x \leq F(x)$, and an F-algebra is a pre-fixed point $x \in C$ with $F(x) \leq x$.

Definition 1.2 *F-coalgebras* form a category, denoted by $\mathcal{C}_F$, by taking as arrows between coalgebras (A, α) and (A', α') those arrows $f : A \to A'$ in $\mathcal{C}$ such that $\alpha' \circ f = F(f) \circ \alpha$; that is, the following diagram commutes:

$$\begin{array}{ccc} A & \xrightarrow{\;f\;} & A' \\ {\scriptstyle\alpha}\downarrow & * & \downarrow{\scriptstyle\alpha'} \\ F(A) & \xrightarrow[F(f)]{} & F(A') \end{array}$$

Reversing the arrows one can easily define the category of F-algebras. □

Notice that in category theory the name F-(co)algebra is usually reserved for the case when F is the functor of a *(co)monad* (see, e.g, [Lan71]). F-(co)algebras have then some extra structure. They form a different category which, however, can be regarded as a subcategory of the above category of F-(co)algebras by simply forgetting the extra (co)monadic structure both in the objects and in the arrows.

As the name suggests, there is a relationship between algebras of functors and the more traditional Σ-algebras (sets with operations). For instance, the natural numbers together with the constant 0 and the successor function form a Σ-algebra (for any Σ consisting of a constant and a unary function symbol). Consider the functor $1 + -$ on the category *Set* of sets, where 1 is a one element set, and $+$ is the disjoint sum. An algebra of this functor is a pair (A, α), with $\alpha : 1 + A \to A$ defined as the sum of the functions

$$\begin{aligned} e:&\;\; 1 \to A \\ t:&\;\; A \to A. \end{aligned}$$

Now the natural numbers can be seen to be an algebra of the above functor by defining e and t as follows: e maps the only element of 1 to 0, and t is defined as the successor function.

Given this relationship between algebras of functors and algebras in the traditional sense, it is natural to look for a notion of coalgebra dual to the one of algebra. In other words, what is the dual of operations? An operation on a set A can be regarded as an action which, given some objects of A, *combines* them into a new object of A. Its dual is then an action which, given an object, *decomposes* it into several new components. A simple example is the following.

Example 1.3 *Graphs*
A graph is a pair $(N, \rightarrow)$ consisting of a set N of nodes and a collection $\rightarrow$ of (directed) arcs between nodes: $\rightarrow \subseteq N \times N$. A graph can be regarded as a coalgebra of the (covariant) powerset functor $\mathcal{P}$ on the category *Set* of sets as follows. Let $\mathit{child} : N \rightarrow \mathcal{P}(N)$ be defined by, for all $n \in N$,

$$\mathit{child}(n) \equiv \{m \mid n \rightarrow m\}.$$

□

A similar example is given by non-deterministic computations which can be said to be split at every state into a set of possible computations. To describe non-deterministic computations labelled transition systems in the style of [Plo81b] are often used:

Example 1.4 *Labelled Transition Systems*
A labelled transition system (LTS) is a triple $\mathcal{L} = (S, A, \rightarrow)$, consisting of a set S of states, a set A of labels, and a transition relation

$$\rightarrow \subseteq S \times A \times S$$

Often programs, given as closed terms over some signature, constitute the set S of states. Non-determinism is expressed by the fact that from a single state many different transitions are possible. Every LTS can be seen as a *labelled* graph: the nodes are the elements of S; there is an arc with label a between two nodes s and s' if and only if $(s, a, s') \in \rightarrow$ (also written as $s \xrightarrow{a} s'$). LTS's can be represented as coalgebras as follows. Let the functor

$$\mathcal{P}(A \times \text{-}) : \mathit{Set} \rightarrow \mathit{Set}$$

be defined, for any set X, by

$$\mathcal{P}(A \times X) \equiv \{U \mid U \subseteq A \times X\}.$$

A labelled transition system $(S, A, \rightarrow)$ can then be represented as a coalgebra (S, α) of the functor $\mathcal{P}(A \times \text{-})$ by defining $\alpha : S \rightarrow \mathcal{P}(A \times S)$, for all $s, s' \in S$, $a \in A$, by

$$< a, s' > \in \alpha(s) \iff s \xrightarrow{a} s'.$$

□

The above is the coalgebra representation of transition systems from [Acz88] (but see also [Hes88]) mentioned in the introduction. The LTS associated to a language like *CCS* has programs as states and atomic actions as labels. Transitions are given by the inductive closure of a set of structural rules. In Example 1.8, still along the lines of [Acz88], a final semantics based on this representation is illustrated. But first the definition of *final* objects in a category is needed:

Definition 1.5 An object A in C is called *final* if for any other object B in C there exists a unique arrow from B to A. It is the dual notion of initial object (unique arrow *from* the object). Final and initial objects are unique up to isomorphism. □

Consider again a preorder $(C, \leq)$ (viewed as a category) and a monotonic function $F : C \to C$. A final F-coalgebra is simply the greatest post-fixed point of F, which by a standard result is also the greatest fixed point. (Dually, an initial F-algebra is the least (pre-)fixed point of F.) Below, the notion of fixed point is generalized to functors and then a standard result is shown: final coalgebras are fixed points.

Definition 1.6 An F-coalgebra (A, α) is a *fixed point* for F (write $A \cong F(A)$) if α is an isomorphism between A and $F(A)$. That is, there exists an arrow $\alpha^{-1} : F(A) \to A$ such that

$$\alpha \circ \alpha^{-1} = \mathrm{id}_{F(A)} \text{ and } \alpha^{-1} \circ \alpha = \mathrm{id}_A.$$

□

Proposition 1.7 A final F-coalgebra is a fixed point of F.

Proof. Let (A, α) be a final F-coalgebra. Since $(F(A), F(\alpha))$ is also an F-coalgebra, there exists a unique $f : F(A) \to A$ such that the following diagram commutes:

$$
\begin{array}{ccc}
F(A) & \xrightarrow{\ f\ } & A \\
{\scriptstyle F(\alpha)}\downarrow & * & \downarrow{\scriptstyle \alpha} \\
F(F(A)) & \xrightarrow[F(f)]{} & F(A)
\end{array}
$$

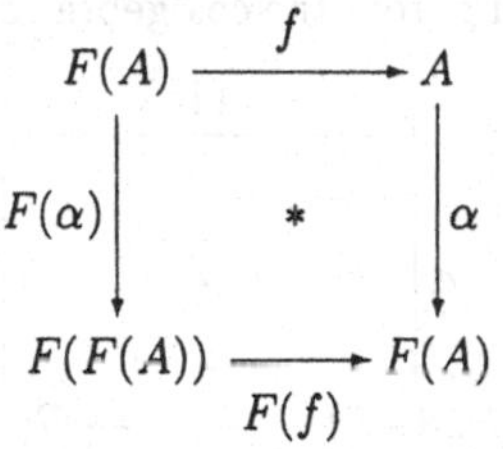

By finality, the only arrow from (A, α) into itself is the identity. Since both squares of the following diagram commute, $f \circ \alpha$ is the identity on A:

$$
\begin{array}{ccccc}
A & \xrightarrow{\ \alpha\ } & F(A) & \xrightarrow{\ f\ } & A \\
{\scriptstyle \alpha}\downarrow & * & {\scriptstyle F(\alpha)}\downarrow & * & \downarrow{\scriptstyle \alpha} \\
F(A) & \xrightarrow[F(\alpha)]{} & F(F(A)) & \xrightarrow[F(f)]{} & F(A)
\end{array}
$$

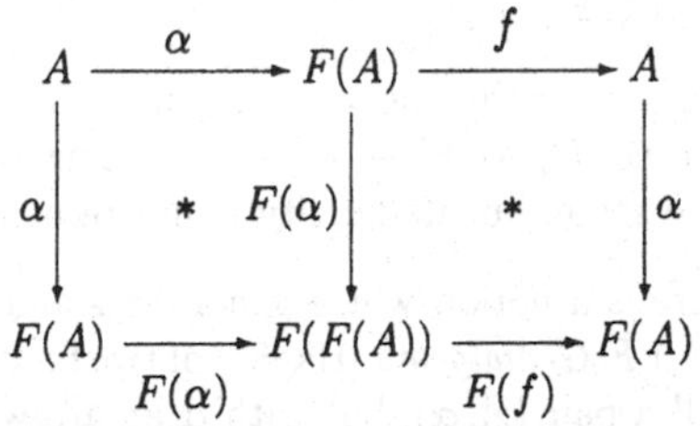

But then it also follows that $\alpha \circ f$ is the identity on $F(A)$:

$$\alpha \circ f = F(f) \circ F(\alpha) = F(f \circ \alpha) = F(\mathrm{id}_A) = \mathrm{id}_{F(A)}.$$

Therefore f is the inverse of α. □

Dually, an initial F-algebra is also a fixed point of F. Notice that a fixed point of a functor F can be regarded both as an F-coalgebra and as an F-algebra.

Example 1.8 *A Final Semantics*
Consider the category *CMS* of complete metric spaces (with non-expansive mappings as arrows). On this category, the usual constructions of disjoint sum and product are defined. Moreover, the powerset functor $\mathcal{P}_{comp}(\text{-})$, yielding all (metrically) compact subsets is well-defined on *CMS*. (Details on these constructions are omitted here; they are given in Section 4.) Similarly to Example 1.4, a LTS $(S, A, \rightarrow)$ can be represented as a coalgebra as follows. Let $\mathcal{P}_{comp}(A \times \text{-}) : CMS \rightarrow CMS$ be defined, for any metric space X, by

$$\mathcal{P}_{comp}(A \times X) \equiv \{U \subseteq A \times X \mid U \text{ is compact}\}.$$

The above LTS can be seen to be a coalgebra of this functor by supplying S with the discrete metric (any two different states in S have distance 1), and defining, for all $s, s' \in S$ and $a \in A$,

$$< a, s' > \in \alpha(s) \iff s \xrightarrow{a} s'.$$

(For $\alpha(s)$ to be well defined, the transition relation $\rightarrow$ should be finitely branching. For LTS's not having this property, other choices for the functor can be made.) As will be shown in Section 5, the functor $\mathcal{P}_{comp}(A \times \text{-})$ has a final coalgebra (P, i), which by Proposition 1.7 is a fixed point:

$$P \cong \mathcal{P}_{comp}(A \times P).$$

Let j be the inverse of the isomorphism i. A semantic mapping $[\![\cdot]\!]$ from S into P can now be defined as the unique mapping from the coalgebra (S, α) into the final coalgebra (P, i):

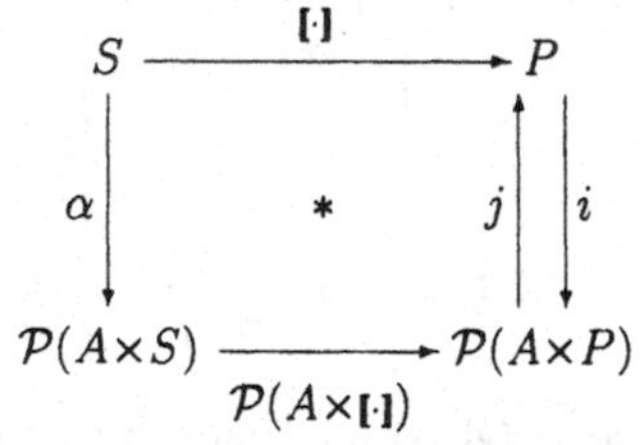

Thus $[\![\cdot]\!]$ satisfies the following recursive equation:

$$[\![s]\!] = j(\{< a, [\![s']\!] > \mid s \xrightarrow{a} s'\}).$$

This semantics mapping is precisely the same given in [BM88, Rut92] as the fixed point of a contracting function $\Phi : (S \rightarrow P) \rightarrow (S \rightarrow P)$, using Banach's fixed-point theorem. (There the domain is the same, but its finality is not recognized.) □

A final remark. There is a notion which generalizes and combines both algebras and coalgebras of functors: An F, G-*dialgebra* [Hag87] of two functors F and G from a category D to a category C is still a pair (A, α), but with α an arrow in C from $F(A)$ to $G(A)$. It is a notion useful in type theory.

2 F-Bisimulation

The final semantics example in the previous section has the property that it maps two states into the same process if and only if they are (strongly) ***bisimilar*** in the following sense: A relation $R \subseteq S \times S$ on the set of states S of a LTS $(S, A, \rightarrow)$ is called a ***(strong) bisimulation*** ([Par81]) if for all $a \in A$ and $s, t \in S$ with $sR\,t$,

$$s \xrightarrow{a} s' \Rightarrow \exists t' \in S,\ t \xrightarrow{a} t' \text{ and } s'R\,t'$$

and

$$t \xrightarrow{a} t' \Rightarrow \exists s' \in S,\ s \xrightarrow{a} s' \text{ and } s'R\,t'.$$

Next $\sim$ is defined as the union of all bisimulations and two states s and t are called *bisimilar* when $s \sim t$.

In [AM89] it was noticed that coalgebras can be used for a natural generalization of the above notion of bisimilarity: For every functor F on the category of classes, a relation on F-coalgebras is defined, called F-bisimulation. This definition is here (generalized to other categories and) repeated, and some of its properties are analyzed. It is shown that final coalgebras are strongly extensional, that is, any two elements of a final F-coalgebra are equivalent if and only if they are F-bisimilar. Moreover, arrows between F-coalgebras preserve F-bisimulation. Together, these facts imply that (F-)bisimilar states are semantically mapped into the same process by the final semantics given in 1.8. Also the converse is proved here, under the condition that F weakly preserve kernel pairs.

For sake of simplicity, the (F-bisimulation) relations considered here are of a set-theoretic nature. That is, relations are defined as subsets of a cartesian product. A more general categorical formulation would, on one hand, allow defining F-bisimulations for all categories of coalgebras, but, on the other hand, it would bring unnecessary complications, since the categorical product of the three categories under study here amounts to a cartesian product. In categorical words, for each of the categories C considered here, there exists a faithful forgetful functor U from C into a category of (possibly large) sets and, moreover, for every object A in C, $U(A \times A) = U(A) \times U(A)$. To be more specific, in the case of complete partial orders, the product $A \times A$ of a cpo $A = (|A|, \sqsubseteq_A)$ with itself is given by the cartesian (i.e., set-theoretic) product $|A| \times |A|$ together with the following order: for all $\langle x_1, y_1\rangle, \langle x_2, y_2\rangle \in |A| \times |A|$,

$$\langle x_1, y_1\rangle \sqsubseteq \langle x_2, y_2\rangle \equiv x_1 \sqsubseteq_A x_2 \text{ and } y_1 \sqsubseteq_A y_2.$$

Similarly, if $A = (|A|, d_A)$ is a complete metric space, the following metric is to be added to the cartesian product $|A| \times |A|$: for all $\langle x_1, y_1\rangle, \langle x_2, y_2\rangle \in |A| \times |A|$,

$$d(\langle x_1, y_1\rangle, \langle x_2, y_2\rangle) \equiv \max\{d_A(x_1, x_2), d_A(y_1, y_2)\}.$$

(All this can be more synthetically and generally rephrased as: C is a category for which the forgetful functor into *Set* exists and *creates products*.) The notation $|A|$ will be used also in the sequel to denote the set in a cpo or metric space A (i.e., $|A| \equiv U(A)$). If A is a (possibly large) set then $|A|$ will simply be A itself (U is the identity functor).

Definition 2.1 Let C, throughout the rest of this section, be a category of (possibly large) sets possibly with an additional metric or order-theoretic structure. For any object A in C, a *relation* R on A is an object R of C such that $|R| \subseteq |A| \times |A|$. If A is either a complete metric space or a cpo, then R inherits the metric or the order from $A \times A$. By abuse of notation, $R \subseteq A \times A$ will be used in the sequel to denote that R is a relation on A. □

Definition 2.2 Let $F : C \to C$ be a functor. Let (A, α) be an F-coalgebra. Let R be a relation on A. Then R is called an *F-bisimulation* on (A, α) if there exists an arrow $\beta : R \to F(R)$ such that the projections $\pi_1, \pi_2 : R \to A$ are arrows in C_F from (R, β) to (A, α). That is, both squares of the following diagram should commute:

$$\begin{array}{ccccc} R & \xrightarrow{\pi_1} & A & \xleftarrow{\pi_2} & R \\ \downarrow{\scriptstyle\beta} & * & \downarrow{\scriptstyle\alpha} & * & \downarrow{\scriptstyle\beta} \\ F(R) & \xrightarrow[F(\pi_1)]{} & F(A) & \xleftarrow[F(\pi_2)]{} & F(R) \end{array}$$

Two elements a and a' in A are called *F-bisimilar* (notation $a \overset{F}{\sim} a'$) if there exists a bisimulation relation R on (A, α) with aRa'; thus

$$\overset{F}{\sim} \; \equiv \bigcup\{R \subseteq A \times A \mid R \text{ is an } F\text{-bisimulation on } (A, \alpha)\ \}.$$

□

Definition 2.2 indeed generalizes the standard notion of strong bisimulation:

Example 2.3 *Bisimulation*
Recall from Example 1.4 that the functor

$$\mathcal{P}(A \times \text{-}) : \mathit{Set} \to \mathit{Set}$$

is used for representing LTS's. Consider a LTS $(S, A, \to)$ and let (S, α) be the corresponding $\mathcal{P}(A \times \text{-})$-coalgebra. It is shown that there is a one-to-one correspondence between the strong bisimulations and the $\mathcal{P}(A \times \text{-})$-bisimulations on S.

Let $R \subseteq S \times S$ be a strong bisimulation on S. Define $\beta : R \to \mathcal{P}(A \times R)$ by, for all $sR\,t$,

$$\beta((s,t)) \equiv \{< a, (s', t') > \mid s \xrightarrow{a} s' \wedge t \xrightarrow{a} t' \wedge s'R\,t'\}$$

It is straightforward to check that (R, β) satisfies the conditions of Definition 2.2.

Conversely, let R be an $\mathcal{P}(A \times \text{-})$-bisimulation, with corresponding coalgebra (R, β). Consider s and t such that $sR\,t$. By symmetry, it suffices to prove that, for all $s' \in S$, $a \in A$,

$$s \xrightarrow{a} s' \Rightarrow \exists t',\ s'R\,t' \text{ and } t \xrightarrow{a} t'.$$

That is, for all $s' \in S$, $a \in A$,

$$< a, s' >\in \alpha(s) \Rightarrow \exists t',\ s'R\,t' \text{ and } < a, t' >\in \alpha(t).$$

Suppose $< a, s' >\in \alpha(s)$. Since

$$\begin{aligned} \alpha(s) &= \alpha(\pi_1((s,t))) \\ &= \mathcal{P}(A \times \pi_1) \circ \beta((s,t)) \\ &= \{< a, u >|\ u \in S \text{ and } \exists v \in S,\ < a, (u,v) >\in \beta((s,t))\} \end{aligned}$$

there exists $t' \in S$ with $< a, (s', t') >\in \beta((s,t))$, and hence $s'Rt'$. Because

$$\begin{aligned} \alpha(t) &= \alpha(\pi_2((s,t))) \\ &= \mathcal{P}(A \times \pi_2) \circ \beta((s,t)) \end{aligned}$$

it follows that $< a, t' >\in \alpha(t)$. □

The above definition of F-bisimulation paves the way for a uniform treatment of different kinds of observational equivalence. Other observational equivalences can be described by choosing a different functor.

The rest of this section describes some semantically interesting properties of F-bisimulation, starting from strong extensionality:

Theorem 2.4 Any final F-coalgebra (A, α) is *strongly extensional*: for all $a_1, a_2 \in A$,

$$a_1 = a_2 \iff a_1 \overset{F}{\sim} a_2$$

(Recall that $\overset{F}{\sim}$ is the union of all F-bisimulations on (A, α).)

Proof. Let $=_A$ be the identity relation on A. The inclusion from left to right follows from the fact that $=_A$ can be seen to be an F-bisimulation on (A, α) as follows. Define $\Delta : A \rightarrow =_A$ by, for all $a \in A$, $\Delta(a) \equiv < a, a >$, and $\beta : =_A \rightarrow F(=_A)$ by $\beta \equiv F(\Delta) \circ \alpha \circ \pi_1$. Then $(=_A, \beta)$ is an F-bisimulation on (A, α):

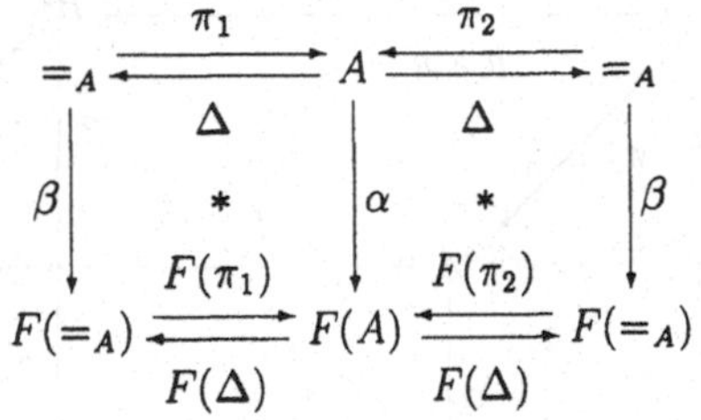

Conversely, let $R \subseteq A \times A$ be an F-bisimulation with (R, β) as in Definition 2.2. Since both π_1 and π_2 are arrows in $\mathcal{C}_F$ from (R, β) to the final F-coalgebra (A, α), it follows that $\pi_1 = \pi_2$. Thus $R \subseteq =_A$. □

Theorem 2.5 Let (B, β) be an F-coalgebra and (A, α) a final F-coalgebra. Let $[\![\cdot]\!] : (B, \beta) \rightarrow (A, \alpha)$ be the unique arrow from (B, β) to (A, α). For all b_1, b_2 in B,

$$b_1 \overset{F}{\sim} b_2 \Rightarrow [\![b_1]\!] = [\![b_2]\!].$$

Proof. Let (R, γ) be an F-bisimulation on B. Since both $[\cdot] \circ \pi_1$ and $[\cdot] \circ \pi_2$ are arrows between the F-coalgebras (R, γ) and (A, α), and since (A, α) is final it follows that $[\cdot] \circ \pi_1 = [\cdot] \circ \pi_2$. □

In general, in categories of (possibly large) sets one can prove that certain arrows between F-coalgebras preserve F-bisimulation. More precisely, this holds for arrows that have a right inverse (also called split epis). (In *Set* every surjective mapping has, by the axiom of choice, a right inverse.) The idea is that one would like to show that, given an arrow f between F-coalgebras (A, α) and (A', α'), and given an F-bisimulation (R, β) on (A, α), the following relation

$$R^f \equiv \{\langle f(a), f(a')\rangle \in |A'| \times |A'| \mid aRa'\}$$

is an F-bisimulation on (A', α'). If F is an endofunctor on a category either of complete partial orders or of complete metric spaces, one needs first of all to show that R^f is a complete partial order or a complete metric space, respectively. This can be shown under the assumption that f has a right inverse as follows. Let C be, for instance, $CPO_\perp$ (see Section 5 for the formal definition of $CPO_\perp$) and assume the existence of a right inverse h to f. Then one can show that R^f is a cpo: $\langle \perp_{A'}, \perp_{A'}\rangle$ is the minimal element, since f is (an arrow in $CPO_\perp$ and hence) strict, and $\langle \perp_A, \perp_A\rangle \in R$. Further suppose that $\langle f(a_n), f(a'_n)\rangle_n$ is an ω-chain in R^f. By monotonicity of h, $\langle h \circ f(a_n), h \circ f(a'_n)\rangle_n$ is a chain in R. Because R is a cpo this chain has a limit in R, say $\langle a, a'\rangle$. By continuity of f it follows that

$$\langle f \circ h \circ f(a_n), f \circ h \circ f(a'_n)\rangle_n = \langle f(a_n), f(a'_n)\rangle_n$$

converges to $\langle f(a), f(a')\rangle$, which is in R^f.

Now, the above right inverse can also be used to define the following arrow

$$\beta' \equiv F(f \times f) \circ \beta \circ (h \times h).$$

This β' turns R^f into an F-bisimulation. Indeed, consider the cube below:

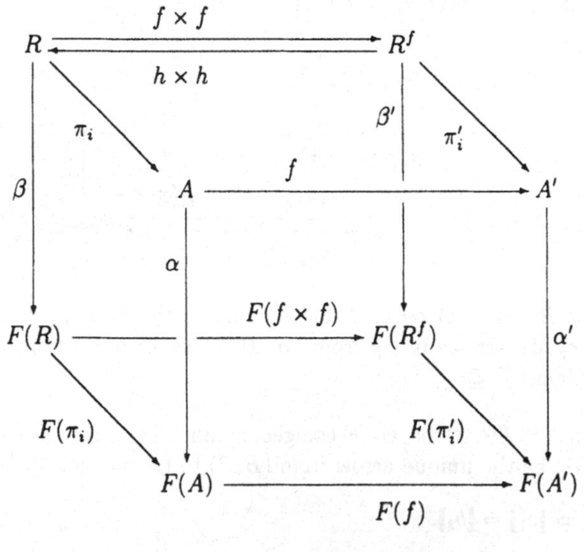

All sides commute but the back and the right one. One has to prove the commutativity of the latter. That is, $\alpha' \circ \pi_i' = F(\pi_i') \circ \beta'$, for $i = 1, 2$. Chasing the diagrams, it follows

$$\begin{aligned} \alpha' \circ \pi_i' &= \alpha' \circ \pi_i' \circ (f \times f) \circ (h \times h) \\ &= \alpha' \circ f \circ \pi_i \circ (h \times h) \\ &= F(f) \circ \alpha \circ \pi_i \circ (h \times h) \\ &= F(f) \circ F(\pi_i) \circ \beta \circ (h \times h) \\ &= F(\pi_i') \circ F(f \times f) \circ \beta \circ (h \times h) \\ &= F(\pi_i') \circ \beta'. \end{aligned}$$

All this proves the following:

Theorem 2.6 Let $f : (A, \alpha) \to (A', \alpha')$ be an arrow in $\mathcal{C}_F$ with a right inverse. For all $a, a' \in A$,

$$a \overset{F}{\sim} a' \Rightarrow f(a) \overset{F}{\sim} f(a').$$

For the converse of Theorem 2.5, it is sufficient to prove that for any arrow f between any two F-coalgebras (A, α) and (A', α'), the following relation

$$R_f \equiv \{(a, a') \in |A| \times |A| \mid f(a) = f(a')\}$$

is an F-bisimulation on (A, α). Again, it is not difficult to prove that R_f is an object of the category: E.g., if $\mathcal{C}$ is $CPO_\perp$ then the fact that R_f is closed (i.e., all ω-chains have a least upper bound) follows from the continuity of f and the observation that R_f is the inverse image of the diagonal in $|A'| \times |A'|$, which is trivially closed:

$$R_f = (f^{-1} \times f^{-1})\{\langle x, x \rangle \in |A'| \times |A'|\}.$$

Now for R_f to be an F-bisimulation, there should exist an arrow $\beta : R_f \to F(R_f)$ making both the back and the left side squares of the following cube commute:

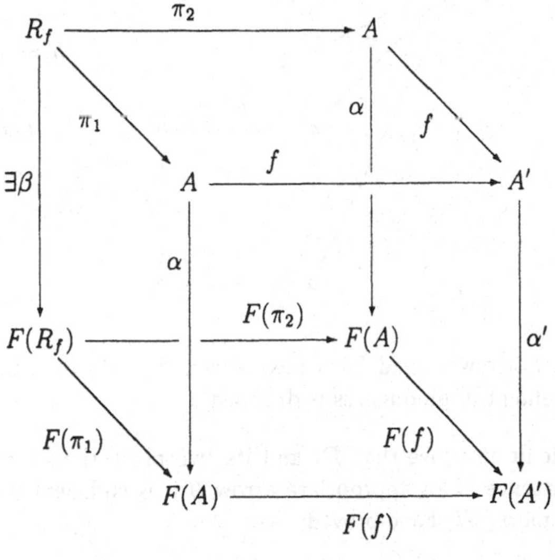

Note that the front and right squares are equal and commute, because f is an arrow between coalgebras. The top square also commutes; thus, by functoriality, the bottom one does as well. Further observe that

$$\begin{aligned} F(f) \circ \alpha \circ \pi_1 &= \alpha' \circ f \circ \pi_1 \\ &= \alpha' \circ f \circ \pi_2 \\ &= F(f) \circ \alpha \circ \pi_2 \end{aligned}$$

One needs the existence of an arrow β

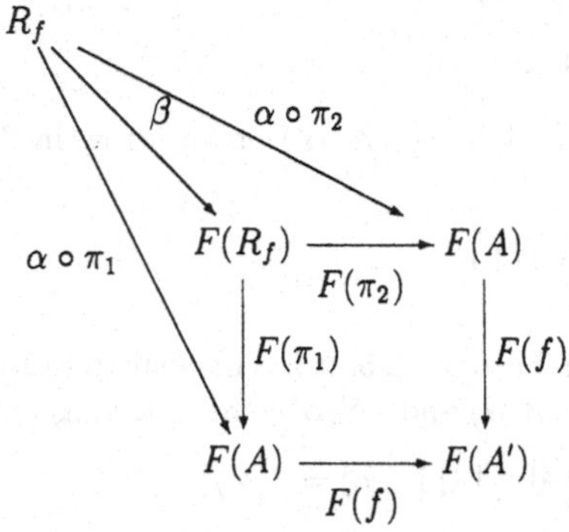

such that $\alpha \circ \pi_1 = F(\pi_1) \circ \beta$ and $\alpha \circ \pi_2 = F(\pi_2) \circ \beta$. It is sufficient for the existence of such an arrow that the inner square of the above diagram is a *weak kernel pair* for $F(f)$:

Definition 2.7 Consider an arrow $f : b \to c$ in a category C. A *kernel pair* for f is an object a and arrows $h : a \to b$ and $k : a \to b$ in C such that $f \circ h = f \circ k$, and such that for any other such triple (a', h', k') there exists a unique arrow e from a' to a such that

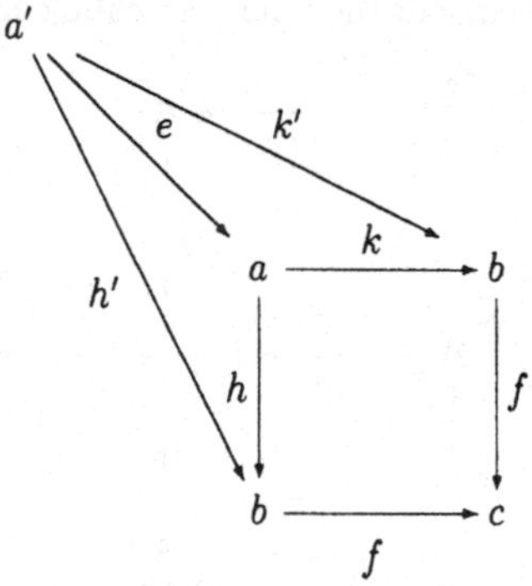

$$h' = h \circ e$$

and

$$k' = k \circ e.$$

The object a, with arrows h and k is called a *weak kernel pair* if in the preceding formulation the requirement of uniqueness is dropped. □

It is not difficult to prove that R_f and its two projections form a kernel pair for f. Thus for the existence of an appropriate arrow β it is sufficient if the functor F weakly preserves kernel pairs. We have proved:

Theorem 2.8 Let F be a functor weakly preserving kernel pairs. That is, the image under F of a kernel pair for an arrow f is a weak kernel pair for the arrow $F(f)$. For every arrow f between any two F-coalgebras (A, α) and (A', α'), the kernel pair R_f of f is an F-bisimulation on (A, α).

The above proof is motivated by [AM89], were it is shown that for functors F that preserve weak pullbacks, the notions of F-bisimulation and *congruence* coincide. Many standard functors (built from sum, product etc.) weakly preserve kernel pairs.

The following corollary generalizes the fact mentioned at the beginning of this section that two states are $(\mathcal{P}(A \times \text{-}))$bisimilar if and only if they are mapped into the same process:

Corollary 2.9 Let F be a functor weakly preserving kernel pairs. Let (B, β) be an F-coalgebra and (A, α) a final F-coalgebra. Let $[\![\cdot]\!] : (B, \beta) \to (A, \alpha)$ be the unique arrow from (B, β) to (A, α). For all b_1, b_2 in B,

$$b_1 \overset{F}{\sim} b_2 \iff [\![b_1]\!] = [\![b_2]\!].$$

The Rest of this Paper

In the rest of this paper, the categories *Class**, *CMS* and $CPO_\perp$ will be treated in great detail. For each of these, a family of functors having a final coalgebra will be identified. In other words, three final coalgebra theorems will be proved for functors satisfying certain conditions. The three next sections can be read independently from each other.

3 Non-Standard Set Theory

In this section, a first concrete category is presented in which a final coalgebra theorem holds. It is the category *Class**: objects are classes, possibly containing non-standard (or *non-well-founded*, [Acz88]) sets, and arrows are functions between classes. This (so-called special) final coalgebra theorem goes as follow: Consider an endofunctor F over *Class** which has a greatest fixed point $J_F = F(J_F)$. Then, if this functor preserves inclusions and is *uniform on maps*, the fixed point J_F, together with its identity mapping, is a final F-coalgebra.

The section is divided in four parts. The first recalls the basic set theory ZFC^- of which both standard and non-standard set theory are extensions (obtained by adding respectively foundation and anti-foundation axioms). For this, no previous knowledge of set-theory is required. This part also describes fixed points of class functors (needed in the main theorem).

The second part introduces a new formulation of foundation and anti-foundation axioms in terms of initial algebras and final coalgebras (of a powerset functor). A comparison with the standard formulations then follows. The anti-foundation axiom as formulated in [Acz88] is here called Decoration Lemma.

The third part recalls the Solution Lemma from [Acz88]. It is yet another formulation of the anti-foundation axiom. It is used in the proof of the main theorem. The Solution Lemma is stated using coalgebras and this makes its proof trivial.

In the last part, about the special final coalgebra theorem, a new definition of uniformity on maps is given and then the special final coalgebra theorem is proved.

3.1 Basic Set Theory

The intuitive idea of a set is that of a collection of objects which have a certain property φ. Moreover, two sets should be equal if and only if they have the same elements. A first step towards a formalization of such an idea is to fix a language to express these properties. A natural candidate is a first order predicate calculus with equality. The only primitive relation needed seems to be that of membership, which is a binary predicate usually denoted by "$\in$". For instance the usual notion of subset can be expressed as follows:

$$x \subseteq y \equiv \forall v\, (v \in x \Rightarrow v \in y).$$

Constant symbols for denoting the elements of a set will turn out not to be necessary, as every object of interest can be represented as a set.

Following this intuition, the only axioms would then be:

Extensionality:

$$x = y \Leftrightarrow x \subseteq y \wedge y \subseteq x.$$

Strong Comprehension:

$\forall$ property φ, $\{x \mid \varphi(x)\}$ is a set.

However, Russel's paradoxical set $\{x \mid x \notin x\}$ shows that such a strong comprehension axiom cannot be stated in its full generality. Strong comprehension is thus to be replaced by the following axiom:

Comprehension:

$\forall$ property φ, $\forall$ set v, $\{x \mid \varphi(x) \wedge x \in v\}$ is a set.

As comprehension can be applied only to members of already defined sets, it is necessary to postulate the existence of some sets, either primitive or derived by applying some basic operators:

Empty Set:

There exists a set $\emptyset$ with no elements.

Paring, Union, Power Set:

$\{x, y\}$, $\bigcup x$, $\mathcal{P}(x)$ are all sets.

(As usual, $\bigcup x$ and $\mathcal{P}(x)$ stand respectively for the collection of all members of members of x and the collection of all subsets of x.) By means of the union operator one can define an operator s acting as successor as follows: $s(x) = x \cup \{x\}$. Regarding the empty set as 0, the existence of an infinite set can be stated by postulating the existence of a set containing the natural numbers. That is:

Infinity:

There exists a set containing 0 and closed under the successor operator s.

(The axioms above, as well as those given in the sequel, are written for convenience in natural language but note that they can also be expressed in the language of set theory - see, e.g., [Lev79].)

Further useful notions can be derived from the above axioms, like, for instance, that of *ordered pair*:

$$< x, y > \equiv \{x, \{x, y\}\}.$$

A formal definition of function can then be given as a collection f of ordered pairs such that for every x there exists a unique y with $< x, y > \in f$. (This was also the first formal definition of function.) Two more axioms about functions are then usually added:

Replacement:

The image of a set under a function is a set.

Choice:

Every surjective function has a right inverse.

A *right inverse* of a function $f : a \to b$ is a function $g : b \to a$ such that $f \circ g$ is the identity on b. The above axiom of choice is equivalent to postulate that for every set a there exists a *choice function*, that is, a function f such that, for every $x \in a$, $f(x) \in x$.

Even though the collection $\{x \mid \varphi(x)\}$ of all sets x having a given property φ might not be a set it can still be of interest for set theory. Such 'specifiable' collections are called *classes*. Clearly, a set is a class, but the converse is not true, in which case one speaks of a *proper class*. For this reason classes are also called *large sets*. Extensionality can be applied also to classes, but the restriction has to be imposed that an element of a class is a set. Thus the classes specified by two properties φ and ψ are equal if and only if φ and ψ hold for the same sets. In the sequel, lower case letters will denote sets while capital letters will be used to denote classes.

An example of a proper class is the so-called *universe* of sets, namely the collection of all sets:

$$V \equiv \{x \mid x = x\}.$$

(V is indeed the collection of all sets as the property $x = x$ trivially holds for all sets!) Notice that different properties may specify the same class. For instance, any property other than '$x = x$' which holds for all sets can be used to specify the universe.

The theory associated with (i.e., the collection of all sentences derivable from) the above axioms (extensionality, comprehension, empty set, pairing, union, power set, infinity, replacement, choice) is usually denoted by ZFC^- in the literature (e.g., [Lev79, Lan86]). In the sequel it will be also called *basic set theory*.

From the axioms of basic set theory alone it is not possible to draw a canonical picture of how the universe looks like, a picture independent of the specific interpretation one might give to the theory. This was felt as a problem already in the early developments of set theory. The solution was found in the so-called *foundation axiom*, which was then added to basic set theory. This axiom restricts the universe to the 'smallest' of all possible ones. Then the picture arises of a universe in which sets are hereditarily constructed from the empty set, by iterative applications of the powerset operator. Every set has a *rank*, namely the stage at which it appears in such a *cumulative hierarchy*. This intuitive structure, together with the fact that all existing mathematics discovered at that time could still be carried out inside this restricted universe, made the axiom easily accepted. However, recent applications in computer science have raised interest in the dual choice, namely in postulating that the universe be the 'largest' possible one (*anti-foundation axiom*).

In the sequel, this duality between foundation and anti-foundation axiom will be expressed formally in terms of the categorical dualities between algebras and coalgebras and initiality and finality, the latter providing a formal definition of 'smallest' and 'greatest'. This makes the qualitative descriptive improvement in adding a foundational axiom to basic set theory quite transparent: the universe is described as a universal object in a suitable—that is, rich enough—category. Therefore, the above two extensions of basic set theory will be both called *categorical set theories*. The classical one (basic set theory with the foundation axiom) will be called *standard set theory*, while the other (basic set theory with the anti-foundation axiom) will be called *non-standard set theory*. Notice that here the use of the word 'non-standard' differs from the use of the same word in model theory: here non-standard is the postulated presence of non-well-founded sets in the universe, rather than a model of the universe.

Before introducing categorical set theories, it is useful to discuss some fixed point theory of functions within basic set theory. Notice that it is customary in set theory to consider strict equalities rather than isomorphisms as fixed points of functors:

Definition 3.1 A *fixed point* of an endofunctor F in a category of sets (or classes) is a set (or a class) X satisfying the equality $X = F(X)$. That is, X is a fixed point of F w.r.t. set-inclusion. □

The definitions and results in the rest of this subsection are from [Acz88].

Definition 3.2 Let F be a class function. Then:

F is *set-based* if

$$\forall \text{ class } A\, \forall x \in F(A) \Rightarrow \exists \text{ a set } a \subseteq A \text{ such that } x \in F(a).$$

F is *monotone* if

$$\forall A, B :\ A \subseteq B \Rightarrow F(A) \subseteq F(B).$$

F is *set-continuous* if it is both monotone and set-based. □

Theorem 3.3 If a class function F is set-continuous then:

1. There exists a class I_F which is the *least pre-fixed point* of F. As usual, it can be shown that I_F is also the *least fixed point* of F.
2. There exists a class J_F which is the *greatest post-fixed point* of F. It can be shown that J_F is also the *greatest fixed point* of F.

There is a characterization of least and greatest fixed points in terms of iterations. For this purpose the class *On* of all *ordinals* is needed. An ordinal is a *transitive set* (a set x is transitive if every element y of x is also a subset of x) x which is *well-ordered* by $\in$, that is, $\in$ totally orders x and every non-empty subset of x has a least element w.r.t. $\in$. If α and β are two ordinals such that $\beta \in \alpha$, one usually writes $\beta < \alpha$. The first ordinals are: $\emptyset$, $s(\emptyset)$, $s^2(\emptyset)$, etc. The first limit ordinal is $\omega \equiv \bigcup_{n \in N} s^n(\emptyset)$, which, by the infinity axiom, is indeed a set.

Corollary 3.4 If a class function F is set-continuous then the following definitions are sound:

$$F \uparrow \alpha \equiv F(\bigcup_{\beta<\alpha} F \uparrow \beta) \quad \text{and} \quad F \downarrow \alpha \equiv F(\bigcap_{\beta<\alpha} F \downarrow \beta).$$

Moreover,

$$I_F = \bigcup_{\alpha \in On} F \uparrow \alpha \quad \text{and} \quad J_F = \bigcap_{\alpha \in On} F \downarrow \alpha.$$

There is yet another characterization of J_F as union of sets (thus not arbitrary classes!) which are pre-fixed points of F:

$$J_F = \bigcup \{x \mid x \subseteq F(x)\}.$$

3.2 Categorical Set Theory: Standard vs Non-Standard

Classes form the objects of a category, having as arrows *class functions*, that is, mappings assigning to every class a class. Actually, to every set theory a different category of classes is associated.

Definition 3.5 The category of classes of (sets defined in terms of) basic set theory is denoted by *Class*. □

The powerset constructor can be turned into a (covariant) functor from *Class* to *Class* as follows: for every class A,

$$\mathcal{P}(A) \equiv \{x \mid x \text{ is a set} \wedge x \subseteq A\};$$

for every function $f : A \to B$ and every set $x \subseteq A$,

$$\mathcal{P}(f)(x) \equiv \{f(y) \mid y \in x\}.$$

Notice that only sub*sets* are taken into consideration. This makes possible that V be a fixed point of the powerset functor (which, by cardinality reasons, would not be the case if one would consider the collection of all sub*classes* of a given class):

Proposition 3.6 $\qquad V = \mathcal{P}(V)$.

Proof. V is the largest class. Thus, since $\mathcal{P}(V)$ is itself a class, $\mathcal{P}(V) \subseteq V$. For the converse it is sufficient to prove that every set x is a subset of V. That is, for every $y \in x$, y is also in V. This is immediate from the fact that y is a set. □

Since V is the largest class one also has:

Corollary 3.7 The universe V is the greatest fixed point of the powerset functor.

Notice that $\mathcal{P}$ is set-continuous, thus, by Corollary 3.4, $V = J_{\mathcal{P}}$.

Moreover, the identity mapping id_V of V can be seen both as a mapping from $\mathcal{P}(V)$ to V and as mapping from V to $\mathcal{P}(V)$:

Corollary 3.8 (V, id_V) is both a $\mathcal{P}$-algebra and a $\mathcal{P}$-coalgebra.

Notice that the categories of $\mathcal{P}$-algebras and a $\mathcal{P}$-coalgebras are very rich categories. For instance, every class function $f : A \to f(A)$ can be seen as an arrow between the $\mathcal{P}$-coalgebras $(A, sing_A)$ and $(f(A), sing_{f(A)})$, where the function *sing* maps every set x into $\{x\}$.

The notions of 'initial' and 'final' are the categorical abstraction of the notions of 'smallest' and 'largest'. Therefore, one could categorically express that the universe is the smallest or the largest possible one, respectively, as:

Foundation Axiom
(V, id_V) is an initial $\mathcal{P}$-algebra.

Anti-Foundation Axiom
(V, id_V) is a final $\mathcal{P}$-coalgebra.

A comparison of the above formulation of foundation and anti-foundation axioms with the standard one is made below, so that it will become clear that equivalent formulations of these axioms are expressible in the language of set theory. But first the answer is given to a question which might naturally arises here. Namely, whether initial $\mathcal{P}$-algebras and final $\mathcal{P}$-coalgebras exist at all in basic set theory. The following two theorems are from [AM89] and [Acz88], respectively:

Theorem 3.9 Every set-based functor $F : Class \to Class$ has a final coalgebra.

Proof. See [AM89], where the theorem is called *Final Coalgebra Theorem.* (The proof is actually based upon a definition of set-based functor which is even more liberal than the one given above.) □

From the above theorem one can (although not directly) prove that there exists a function α from V to $\mathcal{P}(V)$ such that (V, α) is a final $\mathcal{P}$-coalgebra. What cannot be proved is that the identity function is one such α which makes V final, which is in fact the content of the anti-foundation axiom as formulated above.

Set theory deals with strict equalities rather than just isomorphisms. If one postulates the anti-foundation axiom then one can prove that, under some rather liberal hyрotheses, the greatest fixed point of an endofunctor F, together with the identity mapping, is a final F-coalgebra (i.e., the special final coalgebra theorem). The dual theorem, instead, can be proved without further assumptions, that is, within basic set theory:

Theorem 3.10 The least fixed point $I_F = F(I_F)$ of a set-continuous functor $F : Class \to Class$ which preserves inclusion mappings (see definition below) is an initial F-algebra.

Proof. See [Acz88]. □

An inclusion mapping is a function associated with two classes A and B such that $A \subseteq B$. It has A as domain, B as codomain and maps every element a of A in the same a which, by inclusion, is also in B. It is denoted by $\iota_{A,B}$ and the subscript is dropped whenever clear from the context. An endofunctor F on *Class preserves inclusion mappings* when, for all classes A and B with $A \subseteq B$, if $F(A) \subseteq F(B)$ then $F(\iota_{A,B}) = \iota_{F(A),F(B)}$. The powerset functor is easily provable to preserve inclusion mappings, as well as being set-continuous. Thus its least fixed point is an initial algebra.

3.2.1 Well-Founded Sets

The formulation of the two axioms above is not quite standard. Usually, by *foundation axiom* the following is intended:

V is the least fixed point of $\mathcal{P}$. (1)

Since $\mathcal{P}$ is set-continuous, its least fixed point is, by Corollary 3.4, the so-called *cumulative hierarchy*

$$\bigcup_{\alpha \in On} \mathcal{P} \uparrow \alpha.$$

Thus, assuming V is such a class, a *rank* can be associated with every set, namely the stage α at which the set first appears in the hierarchy. This ranking function allows one to prove that (1) is equivalent to the following statement:

Every set is well-founded w.r.t. $\in$

which amounts to saying that every non empty set has an $\in$-least element. This can be easily expressed in the language of set theory as follows:

$$\forall x\,(x \neq \emptyset \Rightarrow \exists v\,(v \in x \wedge \neg\exists y\,(y \in x \wedge y \in v))).$$

In other words, there is no infinitely descending chain of sets w.r.t. $\in$. This explains why the universe of basic set theory together with the foundation axiom is called *universe of well-founded sets*.

Theorem 3.11 (V, id_V) is an initial $\mathcal{P}$-algebra $\Longleftrightarrow$ V is the least fixed point of $\mathcal{P}$.

Proof. Since $\mathcal{P}$ is set-continuous and preserves inclusion mappings, the implication from right to left follows from Theorem 3.10. For the implication from left to right consider an arbitrary fixed point $X = \mathcal{P}(X)$. Since:

1. $X \subseteq V$,
2. $\mathcal{P}$ preserves inclusion mappings,
3. (X, id_X) is a $\mathcal{P}$-algebra,
4. (V, id_V) is initial,

the unique arrow f from (V, id_V) to (X, id_X) is such that

$$\iota_{X,V} \circ f = \mathrm{id}_V.$$

From this, it easily follows that f itself is the identity on V and thus $V \subseteq X$. □

Basic set theory together with the foundation axiom is the ***standard set theory***. Virtually all known mathematics can be carried out inside such a theory and therefore for many decades only well-founded sets were considered to be sets. It was computer science that provided non-well-founded sets with one of the first significant applications: semantic processes are non-well-founded sets. (But see also [FH83] for a – previous – purely mathematical application.)

3.2.2 Decoration Lemma

In [Acz88] the *anti-foundation* axiom is formulated in terms of graphs and their "decorations". Corollary 3.8 shows that, already in basic set theory, the universe of sets is a $\mathcal{P}$-coalgebra. In Example 1.3 it is shown that graphs are $\mathcal{P}$-coalgebras as well. On the other hand every $\mathcal{P}$-coalgebra (A, α) can be seen as a (possibly large) graph, by interpreting A as a set (or class) of nodes and α as the *child* function. Therefore, the universe of sets can be interpreted as the class of nodes of a (large) graph. The childhood relation in such a graph is given by the membership relation between sets.

At a more local level one can observe that every set x can be "pictured" as a graph: nodes are the sets in the transitive closure w.r.t. $\in$ of x. The same membership relation gives also the childhood relation. For instance, the set $2 \equiv \{\emptyset, 1\}$, with $1 \equiv \{\emptyset\}$, can be pictured as:

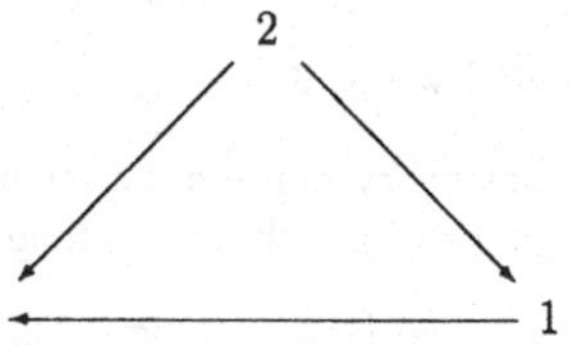

The converse of the notion of picture of a set by a graph is the "decoration" of a graph by a set:

Definition 3.12 Given a graph G, let $G_{\mathcal{P}}$ denote its $\mathcal{P}$-coalgebra representation (see Example 1.3). A *decoration* of a graph G is an arrow from the $\mathcal{P}$-coalgebra representation $G_{\mathcal{P}}$ of the graph into the $\mathcal{P}$-coalgebra (V, id_V). □

For instance the mapping

$$a \mapsto 2 \qquad b \mapsto \emptyset \qquad c \mapsto 1$$

is a decoration of the graph:

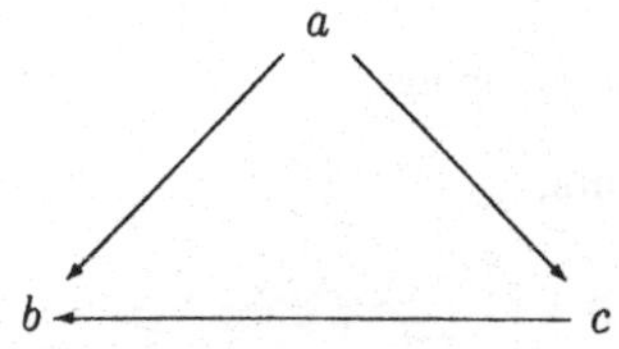

Moreover, it is the unique such decoration. In general, it can be proved within basic set theory that for every graph which contains no infinite path there exists a unique decoration. (Mostowski's Collapsing Lemma.) Notice that a graph has no infinite path if and only if its childhood relation is well-founded. Thus:

Proposition 3.13 For every well-founded graph there exists a unique decoration.

Clearly, every graph which is picture of a well-founded set is itself well-founded. And the (unique) decoration of a well-founded graph is a well-founded set.

Many graphs of interest, especially in computer science, are not well-founded, like, for instance, the cyclic graph with one node and one arc:

(2)

One might therefore consider a set theory in which the following generalization of the above proposition holds:

Decoration Lemma
For every graph there exists a unique decoration.

In fact, the above statement, expressible in the language of set theory is the formulation of the anti-foundation axiom as given in [Acz88]. It turns out to be equivalent to the anti-foundation axiom formulated in terms of finality:

Theorem 3.14 (V, id_V) is a final $\mathcal{P}$-coalgebra if and only if for every graph there exists a unique decoration.

Proof. The implication from left to right is immediate: if (V, id_V) is final, from any $\mathcal{P}$-coalgebra there exists a unique arrow into it; in particular this holds for coalgebras representing graphs. The implication from right to left follows by applying the Special Final Coalgebra Theorem (see below) to the powerset functor, as that theorem can be proved assuming the decoration lemma instead of the anti-foundation axiom in terms of finality (see [Acz88]). □

The unique decoration of the graph in (2) is thus then the unique arrow from the coalgebra $(\{\bullet\}, \alpha)$, with $\alpha(\bullet) = \{\bullet\}$, into (V, id_V):

$$\begin{array}{ccc} \{\bullet\} & \longrightarrow & V \\ \alpha \big\downarrow & * & \big\| \\ \mathcal{P}(\{\bullet\}) & \longrightarrow & \mathcal{P}(V) \end{array}$$

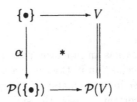

Chasing the diagram, the (only) node of the graph will be uniquely associated to a (non-well-founded) set, say Ω, such that $\Omega = \{\Omega\}$. (This example shows that non-well-founded sets can also be finite.)

Notice that, since the relation $\in$ is not any more well-founded, more than extensionality is needed in order to establish equality between sets. But a criterion for establishing equality of sets arises from the postulated finality of the universe and from Theorem 2.4, stating that final coalgebras are strongly extensional:

Theorem 3.15 Two sets are equal if and only if they are in a $\mathcal{P}$-bisimulation relation.

By applying Definition 2.2 to the powerset functor, one obtains:

Definition 3.16 A relation R on V is a *$\mathcal{P}$-bisimulation* if, for every set x and y such that xRy,

$$\forall x' \in x,\ \exists y' \in y,\ x' R\, y'$$

and

$$\forall y' \in y,\ \exists x' \in x,\ x' R\, y'.$$

□

Regarding sets as graphs, and thus edges going from sets into their members, this definition is just the standard definition of bisimulation as given in [Par81], abstracting from the fact that there graphs are labelled.

In the rest of this section only *non-standard set theory*, that is, basic set theory together with the anti-foundation axiom, will be considered. In particular:

Definition 3.17 The category denoted by *Class** is the category with objects the classes of non standard set theory and with arrows the functions between these classes. □

3.3 Solution Lemma

The finality of the universe V can be exploited not only to regard sets as decorations of graphs but also as *solutions of systems of set-equations*. This is the content of the *solution lemma*, illustrated in this subsection, which is yet another formulation of the anti-foundation axiom. This lemma is used in the special final coalgebra theorem.

Let x_1 and x_2 be two 'indeterminates'. Then the following is an example of a system of set-equations in $\{x_1, x_2\}$:

$$\begin{aligned} x_1 &= \{x_2, \{x_1, 0\}\}, \\ x_2 &= \{0, 2\}. \end{aligned}$$

In general, a set-equation has an indeterminate in its left hand side and a collection in its right hand side. The collection in the rhs is a set, apart from the fact that it might contain not only sets but also indeterminates as elements, and as elements of its elements, and so on. (It is thus important to keep the symbols used for indeterminates distinct from those used for 'pure' sets.) The collection of all these sets which might contain indeterminates in their transitive closure forms an 'expanded' universe:

Definition 3.18 Given a class X, the *expanded universe w.r.t. X* — denoted by V_X — is defined as the greatest fixed point of the (set-continuous) functor $\mathcal{P}(X + \text{-})$. Thus:

$$V_X = \mathcal{P}(X + V_X).$$

□

Clearly, the universe V is isomorphic to $V_\emptyset$ and can be embedded into any V_X.

The formal definition of a system of set-equations can now be given:

Definition 3.19 Given a class X, a *system of set-equations in* X is a function

$$\nu : X \to V_X.$$

That is, a collection of equations of the form

$$x = \nu_x,$$

with $x \in X$ and $\nu_x \in V_X$. □

Consider again the above example of a system of set-equations. A solution to that system would simply be a function $f : \{x_1, x_2\} \to V$ such that

$$f(x_1) = \{f(x_2), \{f(x_1), 0\}\}, \qquad f(x_2) = \{0, 2\}.$$

In general, a solution to a system $\{x = \nu_x\}_{x \in X}$ is a function $f : X \to V$ such that, for all $x \in X$,

$$f(x) = \hat{f}(\nu_x) \tag{3}$$

where, informally, $\hat{f}(\nu_x)$ is obtained by replacing every x_i in the transitive closure of ν_x by the corresponding $f(x_i)$. That is, if $x_0, x_1, \ldots$, are the variables appearing in the transitive closure of ν_x, and denoting ν_x by $\nu_x[x_0, x_1, \ldots]$, then

$$\hat{f}(\nu_x) = \nu_x[x_0/f(x_0),\ x_1/f(x_1), \ldots].$$

This intuitive idea has a formal definition:

Definition 3.20 A *solution to a system of set-equations* $\nu : X \to V_X$ is a composed arrow $\pi \circ \nu$, where $\pi : V_X \to V$ is any arrow making the square in the following diagram commute:

$$\begin{array}{ccccc}
X & \xrightarrow{\ \nu\ } & V_X & \xrightarrow{\ \pi\ } & V \\
 & & \Big\downarrow \Theta_\nu & * & \Big\| \\
 & & \mathcal{P}(V_X) & \xrightarrow[\ \mathcal{P}(\pi)\ ]{} & \mathcal{P}(V)
\end{array}$$

where, for every v in V_X, that is, for every $v \subseteq X + V_X$ (since $V_X = \mathcal{P}(X + V_X)$),

$$\Theta_\nu(v) \equiv \{\nu_x \mid x \in v \cap X\} \cup \{v' \mid v' \in v \cap V_X\}.$$

□

If one puts $f = \pi \circ \nu$ and $\hat{f} = \pi = \mathcal{P}(\pi) \circ \Theta_\nu$, then, for every v in V_X,

$$\hat{f}(v) = \{f(x) \mid x \in v \cap X\} \cup \{\hat{f}(v') \mid v' \in v \cap V_X\} \tag{4}$$

and, in particular, (3) holds.

Since solutions are defined in terms of $\mathcal{P}$-coalgebra arrows between (V_X, Θ_ν) and the universe, the finality of the latter immediately gives the following

Solution Lemma [Acz88]
For every system of set-equations there exists a unique solution.

This lemma provides thus sets with another representation, describing them as unique solutions of systems of equations; moreover, it is an important tool in proving properties of non-standard sets, as the next section will illustrate. Since its proof relies on the finality of the universe, the solution lemma holds only in non-standard set theory. In fact, it can be proved that the solution lemma is equivalent to the anti-foundation axiom.

Notice that the use of coalgebras makes the presentation of the solution lemma much simpler than in [Acz88]. In particular, its proof becomes here trivial, while the following is needed there:

Substitution Lemma [Acz88]
For every function $f : X \to V$ there exists a unique function $\hat{f} : V_X \to V$ such that, for every $v \in V_X$,

$$\hat{f}(v) = \{f(x) \mid x \in v \cap X\} \cup \{\hat{f}(v') \mid v' \in v \cap V_X\}.$$

Although the above lemma is not needed here for proving the solution lemma, the existence of such a unique extension of any function on X to a function on V_X is needed in the sequel (in the definition of *uniformity on maps*). Notice that it simply generalizes (4) to any function on X.

One final remark. Here, the definition of the expanded universe is carried out within the language of set theory, but, alternatively, indeterminates could also be added as new symbols in the language. For instance, in [BE88] indeterminates are indeed treated as primitive elements (*Urelemente*) of a set theory like the one in [Bar75]. But in order to carry out this extension of the language formally, an extension of the axioms of the theory is also required.

3.4 Special Final Coalgebra Theorem

The assumption that the universe (greatest fixed point of $\mathcal{P}$) be a final coalgebra of the powerset functor is strong enough to make the greatest fixed points of a large class of other functors be final coalgebras of the respective functors too. This is the content of the *special final coalgebra theorem* illustrated in this subsection.

The finality of the greatest fixed point of (certain) functors is proved here by means of the solution lemma. Arrows into such candidate final coalgebras are associated to solutions of systems of set equations (having the class in the source coalgebra as indeterminates). This is best illustrated by means of the powerset functor:

For any function $f : A \to V$ and any $\{a_0, a_1, \ldots\}$ in $\mathcal{P}(A)$,

$$\mathcal{P}(f)(\{a_0, a_1, \ldots\}) = \{f(a_0), f(a_1), \ldots\}.$$

Regard now A as a class of indeterminates and $\{a_0, a_1, \ldots\}$ as a set in V_A, that is, associate to A the obvious embedding function $\varphi_A : \mathcal{P}(A) \to V_A$. Then:

$$\{f(a_0), f(a_1), \ldots\} = \hat{f} \circ \varphi_A(\{a_0, a_1, \ldots\}).$$

Loosely speaking, this shows that the powerset functor behaves on maps as it behaves on objects (*uniform on maps*).

The mapping φ_A is described above as an embedding and this is indeed the case for most of functors of interest for semantics. In general, other mappings can be considered as well, so that what above generalizes to the following:

Definition 3.21 An endofunctor F : *Class** $\to$ *Class** is *uniform on maps* if for every class A there exists a *V_A-translation for F*, that is, a mapping $\varphi_A : F(A) \to V_A$ such that, for every function $f : A \to V$, the square in the following diagram commutes:

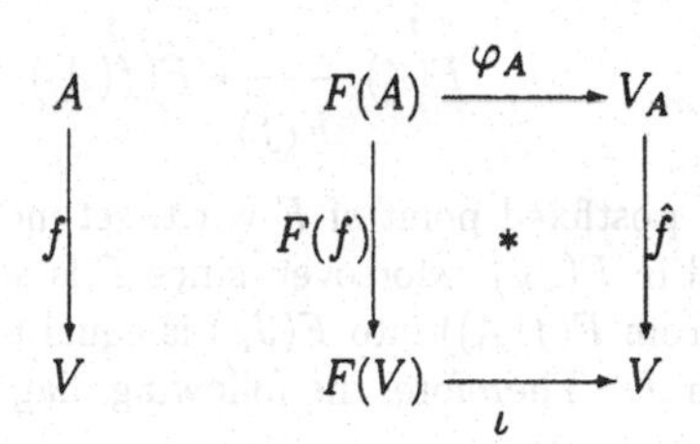

Briefly:

$$\forall A\, \exists \varphi_A : F(A) \to V_A \text{ such that } \forall f : A \to V \text{ and } \forall \sigma \in F(A)$$
$$F(f)(\sigma) = \hat{f} \circ \varphi_A(\sigma).$$

□

Theorem 3.22 (*Special Final Coalgebra Theorem*)
Let F : *Class** $\to$ *Class** be a functor uniform on maps and inclusion preserving. If, w.r.t. set-inclusion, F has a greatest fixed (as well as postfixed) point J_F, then (J_F, id) is a final F-coalgebra.

Proof. For every F-coalgebra (A, α) one needs to find a function $f : A \to J_F$ such that, for all a in A,

$$f(a) = F(f)(\alpha(a)) \tag{5}$$

and then show that it is unique. By uniformity on maps, there exists a V_A-translation for F. Since $\alpha(a)$ belongs to $F(A)$, one can rewrite (5) as

$$f(a) = \hat{f} \circ \varphi_A(\alpha(a)).$$

But then the unique solution of the system $\{a = \varphi_A(\alpha(a))\}_{a \in A}$ of set-equations in A is a function $f : A \to V$ for which (5) holds. Now it remains to be proved that the image of this function f is contained in J_F, that is, f is a function into J_F as well. From equation (5) one can derive that:

$$
\begin{aligned}
f(A) \ &= \ F(f)(\alpha(A)) \\
&\subseteq \ F(f)(F(A)) \\
&\subseteq \ F(f(A)),
\end{aligned}
$$

that is, $f(A)$ is a postfixed point of F. From all this follows that f is an arrow which makes the following diagram commute:

$$
\begin{array}{ccc}
A & \xrightarrow{\quad f \quad} & f(A) \\
{\scriptstyle\alpha}\downarrow & * & \downarrow{\scriptstyle\iota} \\
F(A) & \xrightarrow[\quad F(f) \quad]{} & F(f(A))
\end{array}
$$

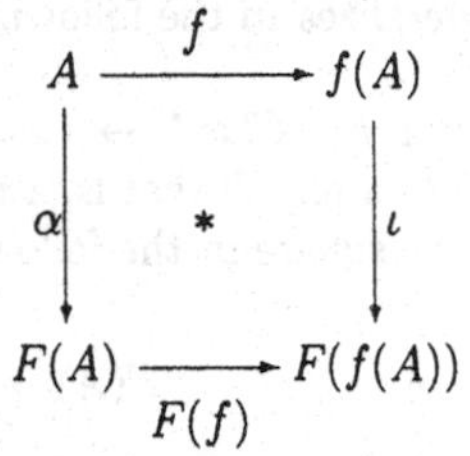

Since J_F is the greatest postfixed point of F w.r.t. set-inclusion, $f(A)$ is included in J_F and $F(f(A))$ is included in $F(J_F)$. Moreover, since F is an inclusion preserving functor, the inclusion mapping from $F(f(A))$ into $F(J_F)$ is equal to the F image of the inclusion mapping from $f(A)$ into J_F. Therefore, the following diagram commutes:

$$
\begin{array}{ccc}
f(A) & \xrightarrow{\quad \iota \quad} & J_F \\
{\scriptstyle\iota}\downarrow & * & \| \\
F(f(A)) & \xrightarrow[\quad F(\iota) \quad]{} & F(J_F)
\end{array}
$$

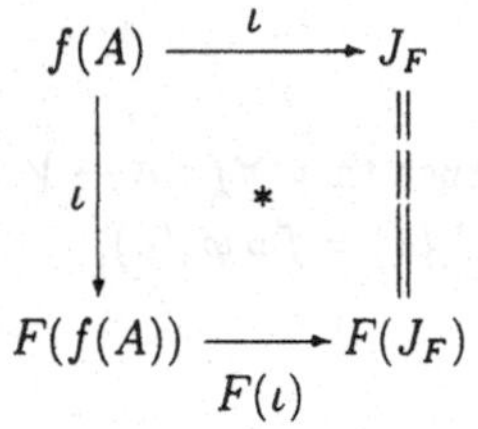

Combining the last two diagrams, f can be regarded as an arrow from A into J_F which makes the following diagram commute:

$$
\begin{array}{ccc}
A & \xrightarrow{\quad f \quad} & J_F \\
{\scriptstyle\alpha}\downarrow & * & \| \\
F(A) & \xrightarrow[\quad F(f) \quad]{} & F(J_F)
\end{array}
$$

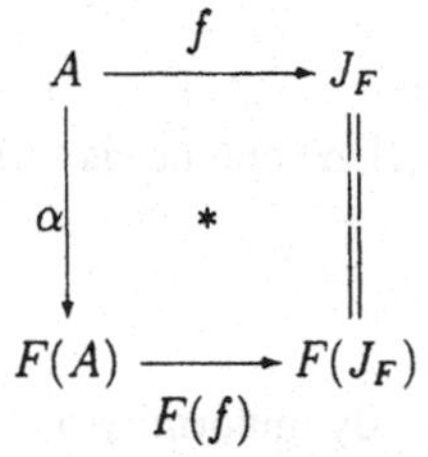

This shows the existence of an arrow from (A, α) into (J_F, id). Uniqueness follows from the fact that any such an arrow is also a solution of $\{a = \varphi_A(\alpha(a))\}_{a \in A}$, which by the solution lemma is unique. $\quad\square$

Corollary 3.23 The greatest fixed point of a set-continuous functor which is uniform on maps and inclusion preserving is, together with the identity mapping, a final coalgebra.

4 Complete Metric Spaces

Let *CMS* be the category with complete metric spaces (D, d_D) as objects and non-expansive (non-distance-increasing) functions as arrows. That is, functions $f : D \to E$ such that, for all $x, y \in D$,

$$d_E(f(x), (f(y)) \leq d_D(x, y).$$

(For basic facts on metric spaces see, e.g., [Dug66].) For any two complete metric spaces D and E, the set of arrows between D and E,

$$\hom(D, E) \equiv \{f : D \to E \mid f \text{ is non-expansive}\}$$

is itself a complete metric space, with metric, for all $f, g \in \hom(D, E)$,

$$d(f, g) \equiv \sup_{x \in D}\{d_E(f(x), g(x))\}.$$

In analogy to the so-called order-enriched (or **O**-) categories of [SP82], *CMS* is called a metric-enriched category.

Definition 4.1 A category C is called *metric-enriched* if every hom-set is a complete metric space and composition of arrows is continuous with respect to this metric. □

In the sequel, only metric-enriched categories like *CMS* will be considered, in which the objects themselves are metric spaces (from which the hom-sets inherit their metric structure). Nevertheless, it will turn out to be convenient to formulate some definitions and results about metric-enriched categories in general.

The fact that hom sets are metric spaces allows the following characterization of families of functors in terms of how they act on arrows.

Definition 4.2 Let $F : C \to C'$ be a functor on metric-enriched categories. It is called *locally continuous (non-expansive)* if, for any two objects $D, E \in C$, the mapping

$$F_{D,E} : \hom(D, E) \to \hom(F(D), F(E)) \qquad f \mapsto F(f)$$

is continuous (non-expansive). The functor F is called *locally contracting* (or hom-contracting) if there exists ϵ with $0 \leq \epsilon < 1$ such that, for all D, E, the mapping $F_{D,E}$ is a contraction with factor ϵ: for all $f, g \in \hom(D, E)$,

$$d_{\hom(F(D),F(E))}(F(f), F(g)) \leq \epsilon \cdot d_{\hom(D,E)}(f, g).$$

□

Example 4.3 Let $\mathcal{P}_{comp} : CMS \to CMS$ be the metric powerset functor defined on objects by, for all $(D, d_D) \in CMS$,

$$\mathcal{P}_{comp}(D) \equiv \{X \mid X \text{ is a compact (w.r.t. } d_D\text{) subset of } D\}.$$

The metric on $\mathcal{P}_{comp}(D)$ is the so-called Hausdorff metric d_H, given by, for $X, Y \in \mathcal{P}_{comp}(D)$,

$$d_H(X,Y) = \max\{\sup_{x\in X}\{d(x,Y)\}, \sup_{y\in Y}\{d(y,X)\}\},$$

where $d(x,Z) = \inf_{z\in Z}\{d_D(x,z)\}$ for every $Z \subseteq M$, $x \in M$. (by convention, $\sup\emptyset = 0$ and $\inf\emptyset = 1$.) One can show that if D is complete then $\mathcal{P}_{comp}(D)$ is complete as well. On arrows $f : D \to E$, we have

$$\mathcal{P}_{comp}(f) : \mathcal{P}_{comp}(D) \to \mathcal{P}_{comp}(E), \quad X \mapsto \{f(x) \mid x \in X\}.$$

It is not difficult to prove that $\mathcal{P}_{comp}$ is locally non-expansive. □

Example 4.4 For every ϵ with $0 \le \epsilon < 1$, the "shrinking" functor $id_\epsilon : CMS \to CMS$ is defined as the identity on arrows and, for any (D, d_D),

$$id_\epsilon((D,d_D)) \equiv (D, \epsilon \cdot d_D).$$

Clearly id_ϵ is locally contracting. □

4.1 A 'Metric' Final Coalgebra Theorem

The final coalgebra theorem below will be based on the following.

Theorem 4.5 Every fixed point of a locally contracting functor $F : CMS \to CMS$ is a final F-coalgebra.

Proof. Suppose that M is a fixed point for F, that is, $M \cong F(M)$. Let $i : M \to F(M)$ and $j : F(M) \to M$ be the two components of such an isomorphism. Thus $j \circ i = \mathrm{id}_M$ and $i \circ j = \mathrm{id}_{F(M)}$. Let (X, α) be an F-coalgebra. Define $\Phi : \hom(X,M) \to \hom(X,M)$ by, for all f,

$$\Phi(f) \equiv j \circ F(f) \circ \alpha$$

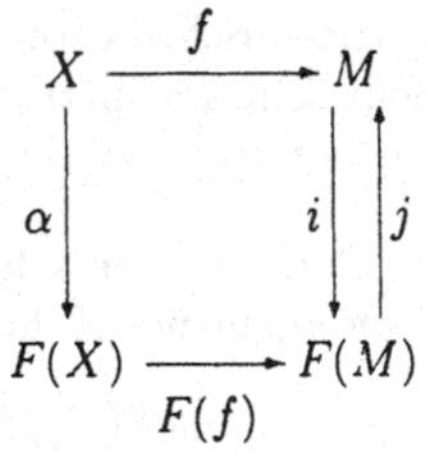

Let F be locally contracting with factor ϵ. Then Φ is a contraction with factor ϵ. That is, for all $f_1, f_2 \in \hom(X,M)$,

$$\begin{aligned}
d(\Phi(f_1),\Phi(f_2)) &= \sup_{x\in X}\{d_M(\Phi(f_1)(x), \Phi(f_2)(x))\} \\
&= \sup_{x\in X}\{d_M(j\circ F(f_1)\circ\alpha(x), j\circ F(f_2)\circ\alpha(x))\} \\
&\le \sup_{y\in F(X)}\{d_M(j\circ F(f_1)(y), j\circ F(f_2)(y))\} \\
&\le \sup_{y\in F(X)}\{d_{F(M)}(F(f_1)(y), F(f_2)(y))\} \ (j \text{ is non-expansive}) \\
&= d(F(f_1), F(f_2)) \\
&\le \epsilon\cdot d(f_1,f_2) \ (F \text{ is locally contracting}).
\end{aligned}$$

By Banach's theorem F has a unique fixed point $\pi : X \to M$. Moreover:

$$i \circ \pi = i \circ \Phi(\pi) = i \circ j \circ F(f) \circ \alpha = F(f) \circ \alpha,$$

which shows that π is the unique arrow from (X, α) into (M, i). □

The dual of this theorem can be proved similarly:

Theorem 4.6 Every fixed point of a locally contracting functor $F : CMS \rightarrow CMS$ is an initial F-algebra.

In subsection 4.3, the following theorem will be proved.

Theorem 4.7 Every locally contracting functor $F : CMS \rightarrow CMS$ has a fixed point.

From Theorem 4.5 and Theorem 4.7, the following final coalgebra theorem for *CMS* is immediate.

Theorem 4.8 Every locally contracting functor $F : CMS \rightarrow CMS$ has a final F-coalgebra.

Since final coalgebras are unique (up to isomorphism) the following is immediate.

Corollary 4.9 Every locally contracting functor $F : CMS \rightarrow CMS$ has a unique fixed point (which is at the same time a final F-coalgebra and an initial F-algebra).

4.2 F-Bisimulation in *CMS*

According to the definition of bisimulation (Definition 2.2), F-bisimulations have to be objects in the category under consideration. For the category *CMS* this implies that they have to be complete metric spaces: that is, an F-bisimulation on an F-coalgebra (A, α) in *CMS* is a closed subset of $A \times A$, satisfying the conditions of Definition 2.2.

The following theorem is an instantiation of Theorem 2.4 to the category *CMS*.

Theorem 4.10 The unique fixed point (M, i) of a locally contracting functor $F : CMS \rightarrow CMS$ is strongly extensional; that is, for all $x, y \in M$,

$$x = y \Leftrightarrow x \overset{F}{\sim} y.$$

(Recall that $\overset{F}{\sim} = \bigcup\{R \subseteq M \times M \mid R \text{ is an } F\text{-bisimulation on } (M, i)\}$.) □

Next the construction of a metric domain for strong bisimulation (as used in Example 1.8 and [BM88, Rut90]) will be described in detail.

Let A be an arbitrary set supplied with the discrete metric. The constant functor $F_A : CMS \rightarrow CMS$ assigns to all objects the complete metric space A, and to all arrows the identity arrow id_A. Let I be the identity functor on *CMS*. The product functor $\times : CMS \times CMS \rightarrow CMS$ gives for any two objects D and E in *CMS* the Cartesian product $D \times E$, with metric, for all $x_1, x_2 \in D$ and $y_1, y_2 \in E$,

$$d_{D \times E}(\langle x_1, y_1 \rangle, \langle x_2, y_2 \rangle) \equiv \max\{d_D(x_1, x_2), d_E(y_1, y_2)\}$$

On arrows $\times$ is defined as usual.

Let F_1 and F_2 be two functor from *CMS* to *CMS*. The functor $< F_1, F_2 >: CMS \rightarrow CMS \times CMS$ (the *tupling* of F_1 and F_2) is defined on objects D by

$$< F_1, F_2 > (D) \equiv < F_1(D), F_2(D) >$$

and on arrows $f : D \rightarrow E$ by

$$< F_1, F_2 > (f) \equiv < F_1(f), F_2(f) >$$

Let the functor $F : CMS \rightarrow CMS$ be defined as a composition of the above functors as follows:

$$F \equiv \mathcal{P}_{comp} \circ \times \circ < F_A, I > .$$

It has already been observed that $\mathcal{P}_{comp}$ is locally continuous, and the same applies to the other constructs. Composition of functors preserves local continuity, hence F is locally continuous. Next define, for some ϵ with $0 \leq \epsilon < 1$, a functor F_ϵ by

$$F_\epsilon \equiv id_\epsilon \circ F.$$

It is immediate that F_ϵ is locally contracting since id_ϵ is locally contracting and F is locally continuous. Finally we are ready for the following.

Definition 4.11 Let the metric domain for bisimulation P_M be the unique fixed point of the locally contracting functor F_ϵ. That is, P_M is the unique complete metric space satisfying

$$P_M \cong \mathcal{P}_{comp}(A \times P_M).$$

□

By Theorem 4.5 P_M is a final coalgebra. Recall that it is used in Example 1.8 for representing finitely branching labelled transition systems.

(For LTS's that are image finite (a weaker notion than finitely branching), one could replace in the above definition the functor $\mathcal{P}_{comp}$ by another powerset functor: $\mathcal{P}_{closed}$, which yields all metrically closed subsets. In [Bre92], domains are given suited for LTS's that satisfy even more general "branching" properties.)

4.3 Fixed Points in *CMS*

In this subsection, it will be shown that every locally contracting functor has a fixed point, thus proving Theorem 4.7. In [AR89], a similar theorem is proved: so-called contracting functors on a category of complete metric spaces (with double arrows) have a fixed point (see also below). Here the results of [AR89] are generalized; in summary, a reconstruction of that paper is given along the lines of [SP82] and [Plo81a].

A standard way of constructing fixed points of functors on a category of complete partial orders, as described in [SP82], can be seen as a category-theoretic generalization of the least fixed point construction of monotone functions on complete partial orders. In metric-enriched categories, the construction of fixed points of functors can be better compared to Banach's fixed point theorem: any contracting function f from a complete metric space to itself has a unique fixed point, which can be obtained as the limit of all finite iterations of f starting in an arbitrary element. (See also the remark following Theorem 4.23.)

As in [SP82], fixed points will be constructed in a category with so-called embedding-projection pairs as arrows. One of the reasons for this is that certain constructions, like the function space construction, are not functorial. However, such constructions can be turned into functors on this category with double arrows, which is introduced next.

Definition 4.12 Let $\mathcal{C}$ be a metric-enriched category. A subcategory $\mathcal{C}^E$ (of embeddings) can be defined by taking as objects the same objects as $\mathcal{C}$. Arrows $\alpha : D \to E$ in $\mathcal{C}^E$ are pairs $\alpha = \langle \alpha^e, \alpha^p \rangle$ such that

$$\alpha^e : D \to E, \ \ \alpha^p : E \to D$$

are arrows in $\mathcal{C}$ with

$$\alpha^p \circ \alpha^e = id_D.$$

The first component α^e is called an embedding and the second component α^p a projection. Identity arrows in $\mathcal{C}^E$ on objects D are $\langle id_D, id_D \rangle$, and composition of two arrows α and β is defined by

$$\beta \circ \alpha \equiv \langle \beta^e \circ \alpha^e, \alpha^p \circ \beta^p \rangle.$$

□

Note that for arrows $\alpha : D \to E$ in CMS^E the facts that α^e and α^p are non-expansive and $\alpha^p \circ \alpha^e = id_D$ imply that α^e is a distance-preserving embedding.

It is illustrative to compare the above definition to the standard example of an order-enriched category, namely the category $CPO_\perp$ of complete partial orders with strict continuous mappings. If D and E are cpo's and $i : D \to E$ and $j : E \to D$ are arrows in $CPO_\perp$ then $\langle i, j \rangle$ is called a projection pair from D to E provided that

$$j \circ i = id_D \text{ and } i \circ j \sqsubseteq_{\mathrm{hom}(E,E)} id_E.$$

Note that the one half of such projection pairs determines the other. For the metric case this does not hold. For instance, in CMS the trivial one point metric space can be embedded in different ways into any other metric space containing more than one element.

Though the latter condition of projection pairs ($i \circ j \sqsubseteq_{\mathrm{hom}(E,E)} id_E$) does not seem to have a direct corresponding metric counterpart, it is possible, due to the fact that hom-sets are complete metric spaces, to define a function on projection pairs that technically will play a similar role.

Definition 4.13 Let $\alpha : D \to E$ be an arrow in $\mathcal{C}^E$. Then

$$\delta(\alpha) \equiv d_{\mathrm{hom}(E,E)}(\alpha^e \circ \alpha^p, id_E).$$

More generally, let

$$< \alpha_1, \ldots, \alpha_n >:< D_1, \ldots, D_n > \rightarrow < E_1, \ldots, E_n >$$

be an arrow in $(\mathcal{C}^E)^n$. Then

$$\delta(< \alpha_1, \ldots, \alpha_n >) \equiv \max\{\delta(\alpha_1), \ldots, \delta(\alpha_n)\}.$$

□

The above $\delta(\alpha)$ is called the *approximation degree* of α: it can be understood as a measure of the quality with which E is approximated by D. (Note that $\delta(\alpha) = 0$ implies that D and E are isomorphic.) The approximation degree can be conveniently used in characterizing colimits in the category CMS^E. But let us first explain what a colimit is.

Definition 4.14 An ω-chain Δ in a category $\mathcal{C}$ is a sequence of objects and arrows like

$$\Delta = D_0 \rightarrow^{\alpha_0} D_1 \rightarrow^{\alpha_1} \cdots.$$

Given an object D in $\mathcal{C}$, a *cone* $\mu : \Delta \rightarrow D$ from Δ to D is a sequence of arrows $\mu_n : D_n \rightarrow D$ such that for all $n \geq 0$,

$$\mu_n = \mu_{n+1} \circ \alpha_n.$$

A *colimit* of Δ is an *initial* cone from Δ, that is, a cone $\mu : \Delta \rightarrow D$ such that for every other cone $\gamma : \Delta \rightarrow E$ there exists a unique arrow $\iota : D \rightarrow E$ satisfying, for all $n \geq 0$,

$$\iota \circ \mu_n = \gamma_n.$$

□

Theorem 4.15 Let $\mathcal{C}$ be a metric-enriched category and let Δ be an ω-chain in $\mathcal{C}$. Let $\mu : \Delta \rightarrow D$ be a cone from Δ. Then

$$\mu : \Delta \rightarrow D \text{ is initial (a colimit) for } \Delta \Leftrightarrow \lim_{n\rightarrow\infty} \delta(\mu_n) = 0.$$

Proof. The theorem generalizes the metric version of the 'initiality lemma' given in [AR89]. There the theorem is formulated for the category *CMS* and assumes, more importantly, Δ to be a so-called converging ω-chain. An inspection of the proof given there shows that this condition is superfluous. □

Observing that

$$\lim_{n\rightarrow\infty} \delta(\mu_n) = 0 \Leftrightarrow \lim_{n\rightarrow\infty} {\mu_n}^e \circ {\mu_n}^p = id_D$$

shows the correspondence with the order-theoretic version of the initiality lemma,

$$\mu : \Delta \rightarrow D \text{ is initial (a colimit) for } \Delta \Leftrightarrow \bigsqcup_n {\mu_n}^e \circ {\mu_n}^p = id_D,$$

interpreting Δ and μ over the category CPO^E.

In the sequel, also products of metric-enriched categories will be considered.

Definition 4.16 Let $\mathcal{C}$ and $\mathcal{C}'$ be two metric-enriched categories. The product category $\mathcal{C} \times \mathcal{C}'$ has as objects pairs $< D, E >$ of objects D in $\mathcal{C}$ and E in $\mathcal{C}'$. Arrows are pairs of arrows as usual: For any two pairs $< D, E >$ and $< D', E' >$,

$$\text{hom}(< D, E >, < D', E' >) =$$

$$\{< f, g > \mid f : D \to D' \text{ in } \mathcal{C} \text{ and } g : E \to E' \text{ in } \mathcal{C}'\}.$$

Clearly, $\mathcal{C} \times \mathcal{C}'$ is again a metric-enriched category, by putting for arrows $< f_1, g_1 >$ and $< f_2, g_2 >$ in the above hom-set,

$$d(< f_1, g_1 >, < f_2, g_2 >) \equiv \max\{d_{\text{hom}(D,D')}(f_1, f_2),\ d_{\text{hom}(E,E')}(g_1, g_2)\}.$$

□

Let $\mathcal{C}$ be a metric-enriched category. It is next shown how in general every functor $F : \mathcal{C}^{m+n} \to \mathcal{C}$, which is contravariant in its first m and covariant in its last n arguments (with $m + n \geq 1$) induces a functor

$$F^E : (\mathcal{C}^E)^{m+n} \to \mathcal{C}^E.$$

(Note that the general case includes, e.g., covariant functors of one argument.) A typical example of such a functor F is the function space constructor:

Example 4.17 The function space constructor $\to$: *CMS* $\times$ *CMS* $\to$ *CMS* gives for any two objects D and E the set $D \to E$ of non-expansive mappings from D to E: $D \to E \equiv \text{hom}(D, E)$. (The metric on $D \to E$ is as on $\text{hom}(D, E)$.) Consider the category *CMS* $\times$ *CMS* with arrows

$$< f, g >:< D, E > \to < D', E' >,$$

where $f : D' \to D$ and $g : E \to E'$ are arrows in *CMS*. Note the different directions: $\to$ is called contravariant in its first argument and covariant in its second. (Formally, $\to$ is a functor (covariant in both arguments) from $CMS^{op} \times CMS$ to *CMS*.) The image under $\to$ of such an arrow is given by

$$f \to g : (D \to E) \to (D' \to E'), \quad h \mapsto g \circ h \circ f.$$

□

Definition 4.18 Let $\mathcal{C}$ be a metric-enriched category and let $F : \mathcal{C}^{m+n} \to \mathcal{C}$ be contravariant in its first m arguments and covariant in its last n arguments. For convenience take $m = 1$ and $n = 1$. The functor

$$F^E : (\mathcal{C}^E)^{1+1} \to \mathcal{C}^E$$

is defined on objects by, for any $< D, E > \in (\mathcal{C}^E)^{1+1}$,

$$F^E(< D, E >) \equiv F(< D, E >).$$

On arrows $< \alpha, \beta >:< D, E > \to < D', E' >$ in $(\mathcal{C}^E)^{1+1}$ (with $\alpha : D \to D'$ and $\beta : E \to E'$ arrows in $\mathcal{C}^E$), F^E is defined by

$$F^E(<\alpha,\beta>) \equiv \langle F(<\alpha^p,\beta^e>), F(<\alpha^e,\beta^p>)\rangle.$$

Note that F^E is covariant in both arguments. If F and G are functors and $G \circ F$ is defined then $(G \circ F)^E = G^E \circ F^E$. □

It is easy to show that F^E is a functor. In particular,

$$\begin{aligned} F(<\alpha^e,\beta^p>) \circ F(<\alpha^p,\beta^e>) &= (F \text{ is contravariant in its first argument}) \\ & \quad F(<\alpha^p \circ \alpha^e, \beta^p \circ \beta^e>) \\ &= F(<id_D, id_E>) \\ &= F(id_{<D,E>}) \\ &= id_{F(<D,E>)}. \end{aligned}$$

Example 4.17 (continued) According to the above definition, the functor $\rightarrow: CMS \times CMS \rightarrow CMS$ induces a functor $\rightarrow^E$ defined on objects $<D,E>$ by

$$D \rightarrow^E E \equiv D \rightarrow E$$

and on arrows $<\alpha,\beta>:<D,E>\rightarrow<D',E'>$ by

$$\alpha \rightarrow^E \beta \equiv \langle \alpha^p \rightarrow \beta^e,\ \alpha^e \rightarrow \beta^p \rangle.$$

□

Starting with a locally continuous functor F will yield an ω-continuous functor F^E:

Definition 4.19 Let $\mathcal{C}$ be a metric-enriched category. A (covariant) functor $F : \mathcal{C}^E \rightarrow \mathcal{C}^E$ is *ω-continuous* if for every ω-chain Δ and every colimit (initial cone) $\mu : \Delta \rightarrow D$ of Δ the cone $F(\mu) : F(\Delta) \rightarrow F(D)$ is again initial. (This definition can be straightforwardly generalized to functors from $(\mathcal{C}^E)^n$ to $\mathcal{C}^E$.) □

In other words, F preserves colimits of ω-chains.

Theorem 4.20 Let $\mathcal{C}$ be a metric-enriched category and let $F : (\mathcal{C})^{m+n} \rightarrow \mathcal{C}$ be contravariant in its first m arguments and covariant in its last n arguments. If F is locally continuous then F^E is ω-continuous.

Proof. The proof mimics that of [Plo81a]. For simplicity let $m = 1 = n$. Consider $F : (\mathcal{C})^{1+1} \rightarrow \mathcal{C}$ and let $\mu : \Delta \rightarrow D$ and $\nu : \Gamma \rightarrow E$ be two initial cones. It has to be proved that $F^E(\mu,\nu) : F^E(\Delta,\Gamma) \rightarrow F^E(D,E)$ is again initial. Theorem 4.15 will be used:

$$\begin{aligned} & \lim_{n\to\infty} (F^E(<\mu,\nu>)_n)^e \circ (F^E(<\mu,\nu>)_n)^p \\ = \ & \lim_{n\to\infty} (F^E(<\mu_n,\nu_n>))^e \circ (F^E(<\mu_n,\nu_n>))^p \\ = \ & \lim_{n\to\infty} F(<\mu_n^p,\nu_n^e>) \circ F^E(<\mu_n^e,\nu_n^p>) \\ = \ & \lim_{n\to\infty} F(<\mu_n^e \circ \mu_n^p, \nu_n^e \circ \nu_n^p>) \\ = \ & (F \text{ is locally continuous}) \\ & F(<\lim_{n\to\infty} \mu_n^e \circ \mu_n^p, \lim_{n\to\infty} \nu_n^e \circ \nu_n^p>) \\ = \ & (\text{Theorem 4.15}) \\ & F(<id_D, id_E>) \\ = \ & F^E(<id_D, id_E>) \\ = \ & id_{F^E(<D,E>)}. \end{aligned}$$

Thus, again by Theorem 4.15, $F^E(\mu, \nu)$ is initial. □

There is also a property of functors on C^E that corresponds with the notion of local contractivity.

Definition 4.21 Let C be a metric-enriched category. A (covariant) functor $F : C^E \to C^E$ is *contracting* if there exists $0 \leq \epsilon < 1$ such that, for every arrow $\alpha : D \to E$ in C^E,

$$\delta(F(\alpha)) \leq \epsilon \cdot \delta(\alpha).$$

(Again the definition can be easily generalized to functors from $(C^E)^n$ to C^E.) □

The value of $\delta(\alpha)$ can be seen as a measure of the quality with which E is approximated, and hence contractivity of a functor amounts to the property that it strictly improves such approximations. Using the initiality lemma (Theorem 4.15), one can easily show that contractivity implies ω-continuity. There is also a relation between local contractivity and contractivity, as pointed out by Gordon Plotkin (personal communication):

Theorem 4.22 Let C be a metric-enriched category and let $F : (C)^{m+n} \to C$ be contravariant in its first m arguments and covariant in its last n arguments. If F is locally contracting then F^E is contracting.

Proof. Again restrict to the convenient case that $m = n = 1$. Let F be locally contracting with factor ϵ. Consider an arrow $< \alpha, \beta >$ from $< D, E >$ to $< D', E' >$ in $C^E \times C^E$. Then

$$\begin{aligned}
\delta(F^E(<\alpha,\beta>)) &= \text{(definition } F^E)\\
&\quad \delta(\langle F(<\alpha^p,\beta^e>), F(<\alpha^e,\beta^p>)\rangle)\\
&= \text{(definition } \delta)\\
&\quad d(F(<\alpha^p,\beta^e>) \circ F(<\alpha^e,\beta^p>), id_{F(<D',E'>)})\\
&= d(F(<\alpha^e \circ \alpha^p, \beta^e \circ \beta^p>), F(id_{<D',E'>}))\\
&\leq (F \text{ is locally contracting})\\
&\quad \epsilon \cdot d(<\alpha^e \circ \alpha^p, \beta^e \circ \beta^p>, id_{<D',E'>})\\
&= \epsilon \cdot d(<\alpha^e \circ \alpha^p, \beta^e \circ \beta^p>, <id_{D'}, id_{E'}>)\\
&= \epsilon \cdot \max\{d(\alpha^e \circ \alpha^p, id_{D'}), d(\beta^e \circ \beta^p, id_{E'})\}\\
&= \epsilon \cdot \max\{\delta(\alpha), \delta(\beta)\}\\
&= \epsilon \cdot \delta(<\alpha,\beta>).
\end{aligned}$$

□

Contracting functors on CMS^E are particularly interesting.

Theorem 4.23 Every contracting functor $F : CMS^E \to CMS^E$ has a fixed point.

Proof. The proof is given in [AR89]. It consists of a metric variant of the standard construction for cpo's. An important difference however is the use of the metric version of the 'initiality lemma', as formulated in Theorem 4.15. We give a sketch of the proof.

Let D_0 be the trivial one point metric space and let $\alpha_0 : D_0 \to F(D_0)$ be an arbitrary arrow embedding D_0 into $F(D_0)$. Define an ω-chain $\Delta \equiv (D_n, \alpha_n)_n$ by putting $D_{n+1} \equiv F(D_n)$ and $\alpha_{n+1} \equiv F(\alpha_n)$, for $n \geq 0$. The so-called direct (or projective) limit of Δ,

$$D \equiv \{(x_n)_n \mid \forall n \geq 0[x_n \in D_n \wedge \alpha_n^p(x_{n+1}) = x_n]\}$$

can be seen to be a complete metric space with metric d_D on D given by, for all $(x_n)_n, (y_n)_n$ in D,

$$d_D((x_n)_n, (y_m)_m) \equiv \sup_{n \geq 0}\{d_{D_n}(x_n, y_n)\}.$$

(It is assumed that the metrics d_{D_n} have a common upper bound.) Next D can be turned into a cone $\mu : \Delta \to D$ with arrows $\mu_n : D_n \to D$, for all $n \geq 0$, by defining for all $x \in D_n$, and $(x_m)_m \in D$,

$$\begin{aligned} \mu_n^e(x) &\equiv (\alpha_{n-1}^p \circ \cdots \circ \alpha_0^p(x),\ \alpha_{n-1}^p \circ \cdots \circ \alpha_1^p(x),\ \ldots, \\ &\qquad \alpha_{n-1}^p(x),\ x,\ \alpha_n^e(x),\ \alpha_{n+1}^e \circ \alpha_n^e(x),\ \ldots), \\ \mu_n^p((x_m)_m) &\equiv x_n. \end{aligned}$$

So far the fact that F is a contracting functor has not been used. An easy argument shows that the contractivity of F implies $\lim_{n\to\infty} \delta(\mu_n) = 0$, whence D is a colimit for Δ. Contractivity of F also implies that F preserves ω-chains and their colimits: $F(\mu) : F(\Delta) \to F(D)$ is again a colimit. Since Δ and $F(\Delta)$ are equal but for the first element and colimits are unique (up to isomorphism), it follows that $D \cong F(D)$. □

Remark: Contractivity of F implies $\lim_{n\to\infty} \delta(\mu_n) = 0$. Another way of describing this fact is to observe that the ω-chain Δ is *Cauchy* (in [AR89], it is called converging):

$$\forall \epsilon > 0\ \exists N > 0\ \forall m > n \geq N,\ \delta(\alpha_{m-1} \circ \cdots \circ \alpha_n) < \epsilon$$

Implicit in the above construction is the following fact: every ω-chain that is Cauchy has a colimit. (Thus the category CMS^E could be called Cauchy-ω-complete.) The parallel with Banach's fixed point theorem is now clear: iterating F from the one point metric space yields (by F's contractivity) an ω-chain that is Cauchy. By Cauchy-completeness of CMS^E, this chain has a colimit, which is a fixed point of F.

Combining the results of this subsection now yields a proof of Theorem 4.7.

Theorem 4.7 Every locally contracting functor $F : CMS \to CMS$ has a fixed point.

Proof. Let $F : CMS \to CMS$ be locally contracting. By Definition 4.18, it can be extended to a functor $F^E : CMS^E \to CMS^E$, which is by Theorem 4.22 contracting. Thus F^E has a fixed point, by Theorem 4.23, which is also a fixed point of F, since both functors act identically on objects. □

Example 4.24 Let $+ : (CMS)^2 \to CMS$ be defined, for D and E, by

$$D + E \equiv \{0\} \times D + \{1\} \times E,$$

the disjoint union of D and E (with the disjoint sum of their metrics); on arrows $+$ is defined as usual. Let $I = \{0\}$ be the one-point metric space. Let the functor $\Omega : CMS \to CMS$ be defined by, for objects D,

$$\Omega(D) \equiv I + D$$

Next define Ω_ϵ, for some ϵ with $0 \leq \epsilon < 1$, by $\Omega_\epsilon \equiv id_\epsilon \circ \Omega$. It is easy to see that $+$ is locally continuous and thus Ω_ϵ is locally contracting. Hence, by Theorem 4.22, Ω_ϵ^E is a contracting functor. Starting in I and embedding I into $\Omega_\epsilon^E(I)$ by α_0, the above construction yields a chain

$$I \rightarrow^{\alpha_0} I + I \rightarrow^{\alpha_1} I + (I + I) \rightarrow^{\alpha_2} \ldots$$

The n-th element $(\Omega_\epsilon^E)^n(I)$ in this chain contains from left to right $n-1$ copies of 0, which will be called $0, 1, 2, \ldots, n-1$, respectively. Note that for $i, j \in (\Omega_\epsilon^E)^n(I)$ their distance is given by $d(i,j) = \epsilon^{\min\{i,j\}}$, whenever $i \neq j$. Let ∞ denote the colimit as constructed above; it looks like

$$\infty = \{\mathbf{0}, \mathbf{1}, \mathbf{2}, \ldots, \omega\}$$

where, for all $n \geq 0$,

$$\mathbf{n} \equiv (0, 1, 2, \ldots, n-1, n, n, n, \ldots)$$

and

$$\omega \equiv (0, 1, 2, 3, \ldots)$$

From Corollary 4.9 it follows that ∞ is the unique fixed point of Ω_ϵ. □

5 Complete Partial Orders

Let $CPO_\perp$ be the category with complete partial orders $(D, \sqsubseteq_D)$ as objects and strict and continuous functions as arrows. For any two cpo's D and E, the set hom(D, E) of arrows between D and E is itself a cpo, with the usual order: for all $f, g \in$ hom(D, E),

$$f \sqsubseteq g \equiv \forall x \in D,\ f(x) \sqsubseteq_E g(x).$$

Moreover composition of arrows is continuous with respect to this ordering. Therefore the category $CPO_\perp$ is called an order-enriched (or **O**-) category ([SP82]).

As in the previous section, the structure on hom sets can be used to characterize a class of functors.

Definition 5.1 A functor $F : CPO_\perp \rightarrow CPO_\perp$ is called *locally continuous* if, for any two objects $D, E \in CPO_\perp$, the mapping

$$F_{D,E} : \text{hom}(D, E) \rightarrow \text{hom}(F(D), F(E)) \qquad f \mapsto F(f)$$

is continuous. □

Next the subcategory CPO^E of $CPO_\perp$ is introduced. If D and E are cpo's and $\mu^e : D \rightarrow E$ and $\mu^p : E \rightarrow D$ are arrows in $CPO_\perp$ then $\langle \mu^e, \mu^p \rangle$ is called an *embedding-projection* pair from D to E provided that

$$\mu^p \circ \mu^e = id_D \text{ and } \mu^e \circ \mu^p \sqsubseteq_{\text{hom}(E,E)} id_E.$$

Note that the one half of such projection pairs determines the other. Let CPO^E denote the subcategory of $CPO_\perp$ that has cpo's as objects and embedding-projection pairs as arrows. Note that also CPO^E is an order-enriched category. The following theorem is standard.

Theorem 5.2 Every $F : CPO_\perp \to CPO_\perp$ that is locally continuous can be extended to a functor $F^E : CPO^E \to CPO^E$ that is ω-continuous. A fixed point of F is obtained by constructing an initial F^E-algebra D in CPO^E.

The proof can be found in [SP82] and is similar to that for the metric case (since the latter mimics the original proof). Some parts of the proof are repeated next since they are needed later.

Let $D_0 \equiv \{\perp\}$ be the trivial one point cpo and let $\alpha_0 : D_0 \to F(D_0)$ be the unique arrow embedding D_0 into $F(D_0)$. Define an ω-chain $\Delta \equiv (D_n, \alpha_n)_n$ by putting $D_{n+1} \equiv F(D_n)$ and $\alpha_{n+1} \equiv F(\alpha_n)$, for $n \geq 0$. The direct (or projective) limit of Δ,

$$D \equiv \{(x_n)_n \mid \forall n \geq 0 [x_n \in D_n \wedge \alpha_n^p(x_{n+1}) = x_n]\}$$

can be seen to be a cpo with order $\sqsubseteq_D$ on D given by, for all $(x_n)_n, (y_n)_n \in D$,

$$(x_n)_n \sqsubseteq_D (y_m)_m \equiv \forall n \geq 0,\ x_n \sqsubseteq_{D_n} y_n.$$

Now D can be turned into a cone $\mu : \Delta \to D$ with arrows $\mu_n : D_n \to D$, for all $n \geq 0$, as usual. The fact that F is locally continuous implies $\bigsqcup_n \mu_n^e \circ \mu_n^p = id_D$. By the initiality lemma for cpo's (which is similar to the one for metric spaces—see the previous section), D is a colimit for Δ. It follows that $D \cong F(D)$, say with $i : D \to F(D)$ as the isomorphism. It satisfies the following fact (which will be used below): for all $n \geq 0$,

$$F(\mu_n^p) \circ i = \mu_{n+1}^p.$$

It is not difficult to prove that (D, i^{-1}) is an initial F^E-algebra in CPO^E.

5.1 An 'Order-Theoretic' Final Coalgebra Theorem

The fixed point D constructed above is an initial F-algebra (D, i^{-1}) in the category CPO^E. Moreover, it can also be seen to be initial in $CPO_\perp$: the fact that D is a colimit (of its defining chain) in CPO^E implies, by a small exercise, that it is a colimit in $CPO_\perp$ as well; then the 'Basic Lemma', from [SP82], immediately yields the result. For completeness, a direct proof is given below.

By the so-called "limit-colimit coincidence" for **O**-categories, which is extensively discussed in [SP82], the dual of these facts also holds. Thus (D, i) is a final F-coalgebra in CPO^P, which is defined as the opposite category of CPO^E: $CPO^P \equiv (CPO^E)^{op}$. (Thus arrows in CPO^P are projections μ^p for which there exists a (unique) μ^e such that $\langle \mu^e, \mu^p \rangle$ is an embedding-projection pair.) Again, (D, i) is a final coalgebra in $CPO_\perp$ as well, which can be shown by dualizing the little argument above. For completeness, and because we have never seen this fact stated explicitly in the literature, a direct proof is given next. A minor variation will also prove that (D, i^{-1}) is an initial F-algebra in the category $CPO_\perp$. (A direct proof of the latter can be found in [Plo81a].)

Theorem 5.3 Let $F : CPO_\perp \to CPO_\perp$ be a locally continuous functor and let (D, i^{-1}) be the (in CPO^E) initial F-algebra as described above. Then (D, i) is a final F-coalgebra in $CPO_\perp$ and (D, i^{-1}) is an initial F-algebra in $CPO_\perp$.

Proof. First it is shown that (D, i) is a final F-coalgebra in $CPO_\perp$. Let (A, α) be any F-coalgebra. The existence of an arrow in $(CPO_\perp)_F$ from (A, α) to (D, i) can be established similarly to the metric case (Theorem 4.5): Define a function $\Phi : \hom(A, D) \to \hom(A, D)$ by, for all $f \in \hom(A, D)$,

$$\Phi(f) \equiv i^{-1} \circ F(f) \circ \alpha.$$

Since F is locally continuous, it follows that Φ is a continuous function. The existence of a least fixed point for Φ provides an arrow from (A, α) to (D, i).

The uniqueness of such an arrow has still to be demonstrated. (Recall that in the metric case—for locally contracting functors—existence and uniqueness are established simultaneously.) Consider two arrows f_1 and f_2 from (A, α) to (D, i):

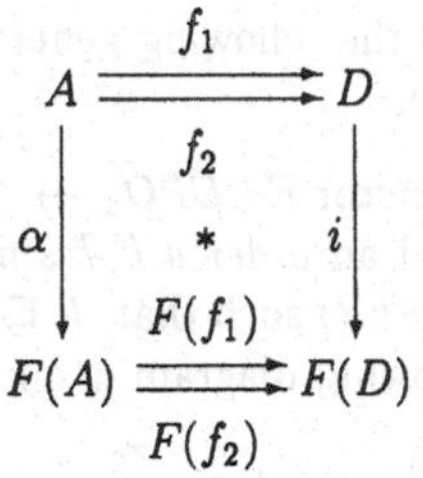

The equality of f_1 and f_2 is proved next. Let $(\mu_n : D_n \to D)_n$ be the cone used in the construction of D. It will be sufficient to prove, for all $n \geq 0$,

$$\mu_n^p \circ f_1 = \mu_n^p \circ f_2$$

because each of the following formulas implies the next one:

$$\mu_n^p \circ f_1 = \mu_n^p \circ f_2$$

$$\mu_n^e \circ \mu_n^p \circ f_1 = \mu_n^e \circ \mu_n^p \circ f_2$$

$$\bigsqcup_n \mu_n^e \circ \mu_n^p \circ f_1 = \bigsqcup_n \mu_n^e \circ \mu_n^p \circ f_2$$

$$f_1 = f_2$$

(The latter implication follows from the initiality lemma and the continuity of $\circ$.) Use induction on n. The case $n = 0$ is trivial because μ_0^p is the constant function $\lambda d.\ \perp$. Suppose next that $\mu_n^p \circ f_1 = \mu_n^p \circ f_2$. Then

$$\begin{aligned} \mu_{n+1}^p \circ f_1 &= \text{(by the fact stated at the end of Theorem 5.2)} \\ &\ F(\mu_n^p) \circ i \circ f_1 \\ &= F(\mu_n^p) \circ F(f_1) \circ \alpha \\ &= F(\mu_n^p \circ f_1) \circ \alpha \end{aligned}$$

$$
\begin{aligned}
&= \text{(by the induction hypothesis)}\\
&\quad F(\mu_n^p \circ f_2) \circ \alpha\\
&= F(\mu_n^p) \circ F(f_2) \circ \alpha\\
&= F(\mu_n^p) \circ i \circ f_2\\
&= \mu_{n+1}^p \circ f_2
\end{aligned}
$$

By a similar proof, (D, i^{-1}) can be shown to be an initial F-algebra in $CPO_\perp$. Existence of an arrow from (D, i^{-1}) to an arbitrary (A, α) is established by taking the least fixed point of a function $\Psi : \hom(D, A) \rightarrow \hom(D, A)$ defined by, for all $f \in \hom(D, A)$,

$$\Psi(f) \equiv \alpha \circ F(f) \circ i.$$

Uniqueness of such an arrow is proved as above, now using the fact that for all n, $\mu_{n+1}^e = i^{-1} \circ F(\mu_n^e)$.

5.2 Ordered F-Bisimulation

The order on hom sets makes the following generalization of the definition of F-bisimulation (Definition 2.2) possible.

Definition 5.4 Consider a functor $F : CPO_\perp \rightarrow CPO_\perp$ and let (A, α) be an F-coalgebra. A relation $R \subseteq A \times A$ is called an *ordered F-bisimulation* on (A, α) if there exist arrows $\beta_1 : R \rightarrow F(R)$ and $\beta_2 : R \rightarrow F(R)$ such that $\beta_1 \sqsubseteq \beta_2$, and the projections $\pi_1, \pi_2 : R \rightarrow A$ make both squares of the following diagram commute:

$$
\begin{array}{ccccc}
R & \xrightarrow{\ \pi_1\ } & A & \xleftarrow{\ \pi_2\ } & R\\
\Big\downarrow \beta_1 & * & \Big\downarrow \alpha & * & \Big\downarrow \beta_2\\
F(R) & \xrightarrow[F(\pi_1)]{} & F(A) & \xleftarrow[F(\pi_2)]{} & F(R)
\end{array}
\qquad \beta_1 \sqsubseteq \beta_2
$$

Note that the relation R should be an object in $CPO_\perp$. Thus it should be an ω-complete subset of $A \times A$ (that is, R should be closed under taking the least upper bound of ω-chains). The ordered F-bisimilarity relation is defined by

$$\sqsubseteq_F \equiv \bigcup\{R \subseteq A \times A \mid \ R \text{ is an ordered } F\text{-bisimulation on } (A, \alpha)\ \}.$$

□

Example 5.5 *Divergence and partial bisimulation*
In [Abr91] transition systems with divergence are considered (see also [Mil80]). A labelled transition system *with divergence* is a four tuple $< S, A, \rightarrow, \uparrow>$ consisting of a set S of states, a set A of actions (or action labels), a transition relation $\rightarrow \subseteq S \times A \times S$, and a divergence set $\uparrow \subseteq S$. The interpretation of $s \in \uparrow$ (notation: $s \uparrow$) is that in the state s there is the possibility of divergence. Similarly $s \downarrow$ is used to indicate that s converges, that is, $s \notin \uparrow$.

Also labelled transition systems with divergence can be represented in terms of coalgebras: let $\mathcal{P}^0(A \times \text{-}) : CPO_\perp \rightarrow CPO_\perp$ be defined by, for all $< D, \sqsubseteq_D > \in CPO_\perp$,

$$\mathcal{P}^0(A \times D) \equiv \{\emptyset\} \cup \{X \subseteq (A \times D)_\perp \mid X \text{ is both Lawson and convex closed}\}$$

(where the ordering on $A \times D$ is determined by taking the discrete ordering on A, and the ordering on D.) Though formulated slightly differently—using the lifted version of the Cartesian product rather than sum—this is Abramsky's version of the standard Plotkin powerdomain, to which the empty set has been added. The ordering is such that the empty set is greater than the bottom element $\{\perp\}$, and incomparable to all other elements; non-empty sets are ordered as usual by, for all sets $X, Y \in \mathcal{P}^0(A \times D)$,

$$X \sqsubseteq Y \equiv X = \{\perp\} \vee X \sqsubseteq_{EM} Y,$$

where $\sqsubseteq_{EM}$ is the Egli-Milner order. Now any labelled transition system with divergence $< S, A, \rightarrow, \uparrow>$ can be represented as a coalgebra of the above functor by supplying S with the discrete order (define $S_\perp \equiv S \cup \{\perp_S\}$) and defining

$$\alpha : S_\perp \rightarrow \mathcal{P}^0(A \times S_\perp)$$

by $\alpha(\perp_S) \equiv \{\perp\}$ and, for all $s \in S$,

$$\alpha(s) \equiv \{< a, s' > \mid s \xrightarrow{a} s'\} \cup \{\perp \mid s \uparrow\}.$$

Following [Abr91], a relation $R \subseteq S \times S$ is called a *partial bisimulation* if, for all states $s, t \in S$ with sRt, and actions $a \in A$,

$$s \xrightarrow{a} s' \Rightarrow \exists t', t \xrightarrow{a} t' \wedge s'Rt'$$

and

$$s \downarrow \Rightarrow t \downarrow \wedge (t \xrightarrow{a} t' \Rightarrow \exists s', s \xrightarrow{a} s' \wedge s'Rt').$$

Similar to Example 2.3, it is shown next that these partial bisimulations correspond precisely to the ordered bisimulations of Definition 5.4 for the functor $\mathcal{P}^0(A \times \text{-})$.

Let $R \subseteq S \times S$ be a partial bisimulation. It can be seen to be an ordered $\mathcal{P}^0(A \times \text{-})$-bisimulation as follows. Define $T \subseteq S_\perp \times S_\perp$ by

$$T \equiv R \cup (\{\perp_S\} \times S_\perp).$$

Next define, for $i = 1, 2$, $\beta_i : T \rightarrow \mathcal{P}^0(A \times T)$ as follows. For $t \in S$, define

$$\beta_1((\perp_S, t)) \equiv \{\perp\},$$

$$\beta_2((\perp_S, t)) \equiv \{< a, (\perp_S, t') > \mid < a, t' > \in \alpha(t)\} \cup \{\perp \mid \perp \in \alpha(t)\}.$$

For $(s, t) \in R$, put

$$\begin{aligned} \beta_1((s,t)) \;&\equiv\; \{< a, (s', t') > \mid < a, s' > \in \alpha(s) \wedge < a, t' > \in \alpha(t) \wedge s'Rt'\} \\ &\cup\; \{\perp \mid \perp \in \alpha(s)\}, \end{aligned}$$

$$\begin{aligned} \beta_2((s,t)) \;&\equiv\; \{< a, (s', t') > \mid < a, s' > \in \alpha(s) \wedge < a, t' > \in \alpha(t) \wedge s'Rt'\} \\ &\cup\; \{< a, (\perp_S, t') > \mid \perp \in \alpha(s) \wedge < a, t' > \in \alpha(t)\} \\ &\cup\; \{\perp \mid \perp \in \alpha(t)\} \end{aligned}$$

It is readily checked that β_1 and β_2 are (monotonic and thus) continuous and satisfy the conditions of Definition 5.4. In particular, $\alpha \circ \pi_2 = \mathcal{P}^0(A \times \pi_2) \circ \beta_2$ because for all pairs $(s,t) \in R$ with $\bot \in \alpha(s)$, the set $\beta_2((s,t))$ contains elements $< a, (\bot_S, t') >$, for every $< a, t' > \in \alpha(t)$. This will ensure the presence of $< a, t' >$ in $\mathcal{P}^0(A \times \pi_2) \circ \beta_2((s,t))$, even if there exist no $s' \in S$ with $< a, s' > \in \alpha(s)$. (Similarly for $(\bot_S, t) \in T$.)

Conversely, every ordered $\mathcal{P}^0(A \times \text{-})$-bisimulation can be seen to correspond to a partial bisimulation: Let $R \subseteq S_\bot \times S_\bot$ be an ordered $\mathcal{P}^0(A \times \text{-})$-bisimulation. Define

$$T \equiv R \cap (S \times S)$$

and let $(s,t) \in T$. Suppose $s \xrightarrow{a} s'$. Then there exists $t' \in S$ such that $< a, (s', t') > \in \beta_1((s,t))$. Since $\beta_1 \sqsubseteq \beta_2$, also $< a, (s', t') > \in \beta_2((s,t))$. Thus $t \xrightarrow{a} t'$ and $s'Tt'$.

Next suppose $s \downarrow$. It follows from $\beta_1 \sqsubseteq \beta_2$ that $t \downarrow$. Suppose moreover that $t \xrightarrow{a} t'$. Then there exists $s' \in S$ such that $< a, (s', t') > \in \beta_2((s,t))$. It follows from $s \downarrow$ and $\beta_1 \sqsubseteq \beta_2$ that $< a, (s', t') > \in \beta_1((s,t))$. Thus $s \xrightarrow{a} s'$ and $s'Tt'$. □

Example 5.6 *Simulation*
The above definition of ordered F-bisimulation was motivated by [Pit92]. Ordered F-bisimulations can be equivalently defined as follows: Let $F : CPO_\bot \to CPO_\bot$ be a functor and let (A, α) be an F-coalgebra. Consider a relation $R \subseteq A \times A$ with projections π_1 and π_2 as usual. A relation $R^F \subseteq F(A) \times F(A)$ is defined by

$$R^F \equiv \{< F(\pi_1)(x_1), F(\pi_2)(x_2) > \mid x_1, x_2 \in F(R) \ \wedge \ x_1 \sqsubseteq_{F(R)} x_2\}.$$

Then R is an ordered F-bisimulation on (A, α) if and only if, for all $(a, a') \in A \times A$,

$$aRa' \Rightarrow \ \alpha(a) R^F \alpha(a').$$

Now, in this shape, ordered F-bisimulations can be easily seen to generalize the *simulations* (for the functorial case) of [Pit92]. □

5.3 Strong Extensionality in $CPO_\bot$

Because the definition of F-bisimulation has been generalized to that of ordered F-bisimulation, the fact that final F-coalgebras are strongly extensional is not immediate from Theorem 2.4. In fact, a somewhat stronger property can be proved (again referred to as strong extensionality):

Theorem 5.7 The initial fixed point (D, i) of a locally continuous functor $F : CPO_\bot \to CPO_\bot$ is strongly extensional; that is, for all $d, e \in D$,

$$d \sqsubseteq_D e \Leftrightarrow d \sqsubseteq_F e$$

(where $\sqsubseteq_F \equiv \bigcup\{R \subseteq D \times D \mid \ R \text{ is an ordered } F\text{-bisimulation on } (D, i) \ \}$).

Proof. The inclusion from left to right follows from the observation that $\sqsubseteq_D$ is an ordered F-bisimulation on D: First observe that $\sqsubseteq_D$, with the inherited order from $D \times D$, is a cpo. Next define $\Delta : D \to \sqsubseteq_D$ by , for all $d \in D$,

$$\Delta(d) \equiv < d, d >$$

and $\beta_1, \beta_2 : \sqsubseteq_D \rightarrow F(\sqsubseteq_D)$ by

$$\beta_1 \equiv F(\Delta) \circ i \circ \pi_1$$

$$\beta_2 \equiv F(\Delta) \circ i \circ \pi_2.$$

Then $\sqsubseteq_D$ is an ordered F-bisimulation on D with β_1 and β_2:

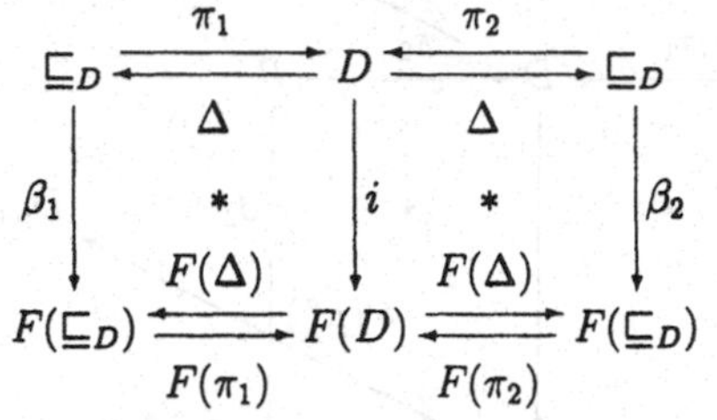

$\beta_1 \sqsubseteq \beta_2$

Conversely, let $R \subseteq D \times D$ be an ordered F-bisimulation with $\beta_1 \sqsubseteq \beta_2$. As usual, let π_1 and π_2 be the projections from R on D. We want to show $\pi_1 \sqsubseteq \pi_2$ (from which $R \subseteq \sqsubseteq_D$ follows). The proof is very similar to that of Theorem 5.3. Let $(\mu_n : D_n \rightarrow D)_n$ be the cone used in the construction of D. It will be sufficient to prove, for all $n \geq 0$,

$$\mu_n^p \circ \pi_1 \sqsubseteq \mu_n^p \circ \pi_2$$

because (as in Theorem 5.3) each of the following formulas implies the next one:

$$\mu_n^p \circ \pi_1 \sqsubseteq \mu_n^p \circ \pi_2$$

$$\mu_n^e \circ \mu_n^p \circ \pi_1 \sqsubseteq \mu_n^e \circ \mu_n^p \circ \pi_2$$

$$\bigsqcup_n \mu_n^e \circ \mu_n^p \circ \pi_1 \sqsubseteq \bigsqcup_n \mu_n^e \circ \mu_n^p \circ \pi_2$$

$$\pi_1 \sqsubseteq \pi_2$$

(The latter implication follows from the initiality lemma and the continuity of $\circ$.)

Use induction on n. The case $n = 0$ is trivial because μ_0^p is the constant function $\lambda d.\ \bot$. Suppose next that $\mu_n^p \circ \pi_1 \sqsubseteq \mu_n^p \circ \pi_2$. Then $\mu_{n+1}^p \circ \pi_1 \sqsubseteq \mu_{n+1}^p \circ \pi_2$ is proved as follows:

$$\mu_n^p \circ \pi_1 \sqsubseteq \mu_n^p \circ \pi_2$$

implies

$$F(\mu_n^p) \circ F(\pi_1) \sqsubseteq F(\mu_n^p) \circ F(\pi_2)$$

because F is a locally (continuous and thus) monotonic functor. Since $\beta_1 \sqsubseteq \beta_2$ this implies

$$F(\mu_n^p) \circ F(\pi_1) \circ \beta_1 \sqsubseteq F(\mu_n^p) \circ F(\pi_2) \circ \beta_2$$

Using the commutativity properties of β_1 and β_2, it follows that

$$F(\mu_n^p) \circ i \circ \pi_1 \sqsubseteq F(\mu_n^p) \circ i \circ \pi_2.$$

Finally the fact stated at the end of Theorem 5.2 yields

$$\mu_{n+1}^{p} \circ \pi_1 \sqsubseteq \mu_{n+1}^{p} \circ \pi_2.$$

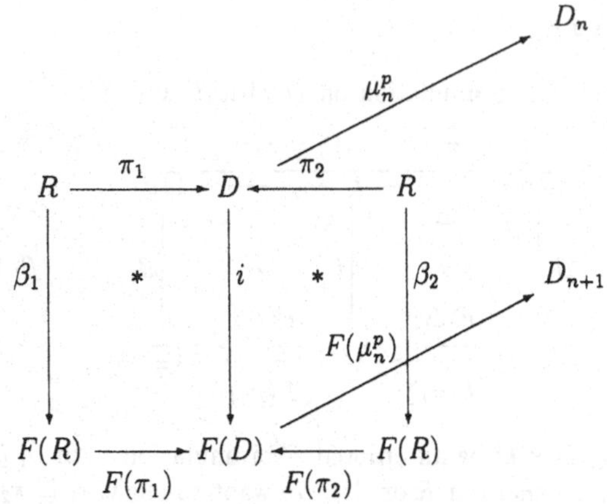

□

Corollary 5.8 Let us call an ordered F-bisimulation R on (D, i) *symmetric* if $\beta_1 = \beta_2$. Define $\overset{F}{\sim} \equiv \bigcup\{R \subseteq D \times D \mid R \text{ is a symmetric } F\text{-bisimulation on } (D,i)\}$. For all $d, e \in D$,

$$d \overset{F}{\sim} e \Leftrightarrow d = e.$$

Example 5.5 (continued) The fact that the initial fixed point of the functor $\mathcal{P}^0(A \times \text{-}) : CPO_\perp \to CPO_\perp$ is "internally fully abstract"—Proposition 3.10 of [Abr91]—follows from Theorem 5.7 and the observation that this functor is locally continuous.

Example 5.6 (continued) The extensionality results of [Pit92] (for the functorial case) can all be obtained as instantiations of Theorem 5.7.

6 Conclusion

The final coalgebra theorems discussed in this paper show that standard domain constructions are in fact final coalgebra constructions. A more categorical approach could be taken in the sense that only categorical properties, like the existence of colimits, would be taken into account in the construction of final coalgebras.

Recall that algebras and coalgebras can be regarded as abstractions of the notions of pre- and post-fixed points, respectively. It would then be natural to look for a generalization of the following standard fixed point theorems from lattice theory:

Let $\mathcal{L} = (L, \leq)$ be a complete lattice, with $\perp$ and $\top$ as bottom and top elements, and $\coprod$ and $\prod$ as join and meet operators. Let $f : \mathcal{L} \to \mathcal{L}$ be a monotone function and consider the following chains:

$$\perp \leq f(\perp) \equiv f{\uparrow}1 \leq f^2(\perp) \equiv f{\uparrow}2 \leq \cdots \leq \coprod_{n<\omega} f{\uparrow}n \equiv f{\uparrow}\omega \leq f{\uparrow}\omega + 1 \leq \cdots \qquad (6)$$

$$\top \geq f(\top) \equiv f{\downarrow}1 \geq f^2(\top) \equiv f{\downarrow}2 \geq \cdots \geq \prod_{n<\omega} f{\downarrow}n \equiv f{\downarrow}\omega \geq f{\downarrow}\omega+1 \geq \cdots \tag{7}$$

Then the least and the greatest fixed point (w.r.t. $\leq$) of f are

$$\coprod_{\alpha \in On} f{\uparrow}\alpha \qquad \text{and} \qquad \prod_{\alpha \in On} f{\downarrow}\alpha.$$

The generalization of the above theorem from least fixed points to initial algebras has already been worked out in [AK79]. Lattices (as pre-orders) generalize to categories, bottom elements to initial objects, monotone functions to endofunctors, least upper bounds to colimits. One has then the following diagram:

$$0 \xrightarrow{!} F(0) \xrightarrow{F(!)} F^2(0) \xrightarrow{F^2(!)} \cdots \xrightarrow{\cdot} \mathrm{Colim}_{n<\omega} F^n(0) = F^\omega \xrightarrow{!} F(F^\omega)) \longrightarrow \cdots \tag{8}$$

Here the fact is used that a unique arrow (denoted by '!') exists from the initial object to any other object of the category, and from a colimit of a diagram to any other cone over that diagram. In [AK79] conditions are given for the existence of an ordinal at which this construction stops and then shown that it yields an initial F-algebra.

A dual result would then be phrased in terms of final objects and limits, generalizing top elements and greatest lower bounds:

$$1 \xleftarrow{!} F(1) \xleftarrow{F(!)} F^2(1) \xleftarrow{F^2(!)} \cdots \xleftarrow{\cdot} \mathrm{Lim}_{n<\omega} F^n(1) = F^\omega \xleftarrow{!} F(F^\omega) \longleftarrow \cdots \tag{9}$$

This has not been fully investigated so far, although a 'schematological' approach to domain equations as in (9) is sketched in [Abr88].

A more abstract approach is taken in [Bar91] when dealing with the existence of final coalgebras in the category *Set* of sets (it is not immediately clear whether standard set theory or just basic set theory is assumed there). The existence of final coalgebras in such category is proved for a certain class of functors F (so-called *accessible*) by showing that the evident forgetful functor from the category of F-coalgebras Set_F to the category *Set* has a right adjoint. Moreover, if the functor F preserves limits of countable chains (i.e., it is *ω-continuous*) then this final coalgebra is the limit of the chain

$$1 \xleftarrow{!} F(1) \xleftarrow{F(!)} F^2(1) \xleftarrow{F^2(!)} \cdots \xleftarrow{F^n(!)} F^n(1) \xleftarrow{F^{n+1}(!)} F^{n+1}(1) \longleftarrow \cdots \tag{10}$$

where 1 is an arbitrary one element set (indeed final object in *Set*). In the same paper it is shown that, under the further assumption that $F(\emptyset) \neq \emptyset$, the final F-coalgebra is the Cauchy completion of the initial F-algebra.

As already mentioned in the section about non-standard set theory, the existence of final coalgebras in the category *Class* of classes over basic set theory has been proved in [AM89]. Also there the construction is of a categorical nature, but of a different character. It amounts to a "quotient construction": given a notion of F-congruence (of which F-bisimulation is a special case) the final F-coalgebra is obtained by taking the quotient under the (existing) maximal F-congruence of the (disjoint) union of all small F-coalgebras. A quotient construction is also carried out in [Bar91].

6.1 A Comparative Analysis

To come back to the constructions discussed in this paper, they can be regarded as instances of (9) and (10) (and even (8)). The construction in $CPO_\perp$ is the one which better fits into those schemata. By instantiating (10) in $CPO_\perp$, where the final object is $\{\perp\}$, and taking F to be a locally continuous endofunctor, one obtains a diagram which is both in $CPO_\perp$ and in CPO^P, the subcategory having projections as arrows. The latter category can be considered as a cpo itself and this structure can be used in order to find that the limit of that diagram is a final F-coalgebra in CPO^P. As indicated at the beginning of Section 4.1 a 'lifting lemma' can be proved which ensures that limits of ω-chains in CPO^P are limits in $CPO_\perp$ as well. By applying the dual of the Basic Lemma from [SP82] it follows that this limit is a final F-coalgebra in $CPO_\perp$.

Notice that the final object in $CPO_\perp$ is a final object in CPO^P as well. Moreover it is an initial object in both $CPO_\perp$ and CPO^E, the category of embeddings which is dual to CPO^P. This duality arises from an adjunction between the embedding and the projection in an embedding-projection pair. It implies that the dual of the diagram in CPO^P is a diagram in CPO^E with reversed arrows, which has as *colimit* the *limit* of the original diagram in CPO^P. A lifting lemma can be applied also to CPO^E so that initial and final coalgebras of a locally continuous endofunctor coincide. (See Theorem 5.3.)

For *CMS* there is a similar passage from the original category to a subcategory of embedding-projection pairs. However, the adjunction property between embeddings and projections which holds in $CPO_\perp$ is not available here. Therefore, the limit-colimit coincidence does not hold in this setting. The category CMS^P of projections can be defined as the subcategory of *CMS* with as arrows those non-expansive mappings which have a right inverse. This right inverse is an embedding (not unique!) making f part of an embedding-projection pair. Notice that singleton sets are final objects both in *CMS* and in CMS^P. Instantiating diagram (10) to *CMS* yields, for every locally contracting endofunctor F, a diagram in CMS^P whose limit is a limit in *CMS* as well. Although initial and final objects in *CMS* do not coincide and, more in general, the limit-colimit coincidence does not apply, in *CMS* final coalgebras are initial algebras as well.

For $Class^*$ the situation is rather different. The limit is still taken in a subcategory, but this is not a category of embedding-projection pairs. It is rather the subcategory, say $Class^I$, having inclusion mappings as arrows (and therefore with the extra structure of a lattice). The final object (top element) is the universe V, which is clearly not final in $Class^*$, while the initial object is the empty set, which is also initial in $Class^*$. Set-continuous functors have both a final coalgebra (greatest fixed point) and an initial algebra (least fixed point) in $Class^I$. These will in general be distinct (in contrast to what happens in $CPO_\perp$ and *CMS*). Set-continuous functors are not ω-continuous, hence these constructions cannot be seen as instances of (10) and its dual, but rather of (9) and (8) (as well as of (7) and (6)). Now, for functors which preserve inclusions, the initial algebra in $Class^I$ is also an initial algebra in $Class^*$. For final coalgebras an extra requirement is needed, namely that the functor be uniform on maps as well. This asymmetry has to be better understood.

6.2 Final Semantics (continued)

As suggested by the title and mentioned in the introduction, this paper is meant to provide a basis to a final coalgebra semantics. Two distinctive features of such semantics are the definition of *semantic mappings as final arrows* (which implies that the domain itself is final) and the use of coalgebras in order to express the *structure to be preserved* under (not necessarily semantic) transformations.

Semantic mappings as arrows into a final object are not an exclusive feature of final coalgebra semantics, apart from the fact that, as already mentioned, several semantics in the style of [BZ82] can be seen as final coalgebra semantics. For instance, in [Abr91] there is a 'Final algebra theorem' which says that the given semantic mapping associated to a specific domain for bisimulation is the unique morphism (in which category?) from a transition system into the domain, the latter regarded as a transition system itself. Here, 'algebra' presumably stands for the *Lindenbaum algebra* which is associated with a certain *domain logic* introduced in that paper. The definition of that semantic mapping makes use of the fact that that domain is the *Stone dual* of the finitary fragment of such logic. (By the way, the fact that the same (final) semantic construction in [Abr91] for *CCS*-like languages has been carried out in [Abr90] for the *lazy lambda-calculus* makes it plausible that final coalgebra semantics might be given to applicative languages as well.)

However, in the above as well as in other examples the recognized finality of the domain is not systematically exploited, except for the final coalgebra semantics for *CCS* given in [Acz88]. As mentioned in the introduction, in the forthcoming paper *Observations as Functors* other instances of final coalgebra semantics will be given, starting from the idea that observations can be formalized as functors. Other equivalences than bisimulation will be treated, like, for instance, trace equivalence. The coalgebraic approach will give a particular insight into the problem of *full abstraction* and other issues related to compositionality (see also below).

Notice that the specific domain defined in [Abr91] as an initial algebra not only is recognized there to be a final transition system, but also indicated to be a final coalgebra as a consequence of the limit-colimit duality. The latter has been used also in [Smy92] to prove that, for so-called *information categories* (general order-theoretic frameworks for solving domain equations) and suitable endofunctors over them, initial algebras and final coalgebras coincide. Finally, it should be mentioned that an early reference to finality as a definition method for semantic mappings can be found in [Ole82].

Consider now the other distinctive characteristic of final coalgebra semantics mentioned above. An extra coalgebraic structure is added to programs (as a function from programs to their observable computations) and arrows from the coalgebra associated with a program are transformations which preserve this extra structure — together with the information contained in it. Part of this information is, for instance, F-bisimilarity, which is indeed preserved by (certain) arrows between F-coalgebras. This addition of a categorical structure, together with its preservation under transformation, again is not exclusive of final coalgebra semantics. Another example of such an approach is the classical initial Σ-algebra semantics. The extra algebraic structure is used there in order to preserve the operators (of the signature Σ of the language) under transformation. The semantic mapping is again a unique arrow, only it is initial, instead of final: it is the unique arrow from the programs regarded as the (free and thus) initial Σ-algebra into the chosen domain. Since operators are preserved by transformations, the semantic will be by definition compositional. The problem there is to define suitable semantic operators, that is, to turn the domain into a suitable Σ-algebra.

The issue of defining semantic operators within the context of final coalgebra semantics has already been treated in [Acz88]. There, the finality of the domain is exploited for defining semantic operators for *CCS*, but by means of a rather ad hoc construction. Instead, in the forthcoming paper *Observations as functors*, a systematic method for deriving semantic operators from transition system specifications given in [Rut92] is rephrased in terms of final coalgebra semantics. This amounts to deriving a Σ-algebra for the domain by means of finality properties. It can be then proved that the original final semantics is compositional if and only if it coincides with the initial Σ-algebra semantics associated to that construction, which is also unique, but now w.r.t. a different category.

As already mentioned, the categories of F-coalgebras considered in this paper are not the standard ones in category theory. Usually, the endofunctor F is to be part of a *comonad* and the arrows between F-coalgebras have to preserve also this extra comonadic structure. Semantics by means of comonads has been investigated in [BG91]. (But see also [Mog89] for semantics in terms of the dual notion — *monads*.) It would be interesting to understand whether some connections can be established with that work.

6.3 Coinduction

For F-algebras the following induction principle can be easily proved: let (A, α) be an initial F-algebra and let (B, β) be any F-algebra. If $\pi : (A, \alpha) \to (B, \beta)$ is a mapping between F-algebras and π is monic (the category-theoretical generalization of injective), then π is an isomorphism. An immediate consequence is, for instance, the induction principle for natural numbers (viewed as initial algebra of a suitably chosen functor). (E.g., see [Plo81a] and [LS81].) The dualization of the induction principle yields what could be called a *coinduction* principle for final F-coalgebras: let (A, α) be a final F-coalgebra and let (B, β) be any F-coalgebra. If $\pi : (B, \beta) \to (A, \alpha)$ is a mapping between F-algebras and π is epic (the generalization of surjective), then π is an isomorphism. (See also [Smy92].) In [MT91], this principle is used in the basic case where the category under consideration is a lattice and the functor F a monotonic operation.

At the same time, the fact that an F-coalgebra (A, α) is final implies the principle of strong extensionality (stating that on (A, α) equality and F-bisimulation coincide—Theorem 2.4). (See also the remark about [Pit92] in Example 5.6.) And for many functors it is possible to deduce from the principle of strong extensionality the coinduction principle mentioned above. In a forthcoming paper, these different formulations of coinduction will be compared.

Acknowledgements

The members of the Amsterdam Concurrency Group, headed by Jaco de Bakker, made many constructive remarks during presentations of various drafts of this paper, which are gratefully acknowledged. Moreover, the following persons are thanked for discussions: Jaco de Bakker, Marcello Bonsangue, Franck van Breugel, Abbas Edalat, Tim Fernando,

Marco Forti, Wim Hesselink, Furio Honsell, Prakash Panangaden, Mike Smyth, and Fer-Jan de Vries.

References

[Abr88] S. Abramsky. A Cook's tour of the finitary non-well-founded sets. Department of Computing, Imperial College, London, 1988.

[Abr90] S. Abramsky. The lazy lambda calculus. In D.A. Turner, editor, *Research Topics in Functional Programming*, pages 65–116. Addison-Wesley, 1990.

[Abr91] S. Abramsky. A domain equation for bisimulation. *Information and Computation*, 92:161–218, 1991.

[Acz88] P. Aczel. *Non-well-founded sets.* Number 14 in Lecture Notes. CSLI, 1988.

[AK79] J. Adámek and V. Koubek. Least fixed point of a functor. *Jour. of Computer and System Sciences*, 19:163–178, 1979.

[AM89] P. Aczel and N. Mendler. A final coalgebra theorem. In D.H. Pitt, D.E. Rye-heard, P. Dybjer, A.M. Pitts, and A. Poigné, editors, *Proceedings category theory and computer science*, Lecture Notes in Computer Science, pages 357–365, 1989.

[AR89] P. America and J.J.M.M. Rutten. Solving reflexive domain equations in a category of complete metric spaces. *Journal of Computer and System Sciences*, 39(3):343–375, 1989.

[Bar75] J. Barwise. *Admisible Sets and Structures.* Perspectives in Mathematical Logic. Springer-Verlag, Berlin, 1975.

[Bar91] M. Barr. Terminal coalgebras in well-founded set theory. Department of Mathematics and Statistics, McGill University, 1991.

[BE88] J. Barwise and J. Etchemendy. *The Liar: An Essay in Truth and Circularity.* Oxford University Press, 1988.

[BG91] S. Brookes and S. Geva. Computational comonads and intensional semantics. Technical Report CMU-CS-91-190, Computer Science Department, Carnagie-Mellon University, 1991.

[BM88] J.W. de Bakker and J.-J.Ch. Meyer. Metric semantics for concurrency. *BIT*, 28:504–529, 1988.

[Bre92] F. van Breugel. Generalised finiteness conditions on labelled transition systems for operational semantics of programming languages. CWI, 1992.

[BZ82] J.W. de Bakker and J.I. Zucker. Processes and the denotational semantics of concurrency. *Information and Control*, 54:70–120, 1982.

[Dug66] J. Dugundji. *Topology.* Allyn and Bacon, inc., 1966.

[FH83] M. Forti and F. Honsell. Set theory with free construction principles. *Annali Scuola Normale Superiore, Pisa*, X(3):493–522, 1983.

[FH92] M. Forti and F. Honsell. A general construction of hyperuniverses. Technical Report 1992/9, Istituto di Matematiche Applicate U. Dini, Facoltà di Ingegneria, Università di Pisa, 1992.

[Hag87] T. Hagino. *A Categorical Programming Language*. PhD thesis, University of Edinburgh, September 1987.

[Hes88] W.H. Hesselink. Deadlock and fairness in morphisms of transition systems. *Theoretical Computer Science*, 59:235–257, 1988.

[Lan71] S. Mac Lane. *Categories for the Working Mathematician*, volume 5 of *Graduate Texts in Mathematics*. Springer-Verlag, Berlin, 1971.

[Lan86] S. Mac Lane. *Mathematics: Form and Function*. Springer-Verlag, Berlin, 1986.

[Lev79] A. Levy. *Basic Set Theory*. Perspectives in Mathematical Logic. Springer-Verlag, Berlin, 1979.

[LS81] D. Lehmann and M.B. Smyth. Algebraic specifications of data types: a synthetic approach. *Mathematical Systems Theory*, 14:97–139, 1981.

[Mil80] R. Milner. *A Calculus of Communicating Systems*, volume 92 of *Lecture Notes in Computer Science*. Springer-Verlag, Berlin, 1980.

[Mog89] E. Moggi. Computational lambda-calculus and monads. In *Proc. Fourth IEEE Symp. on Logic In Computer Science*, pages 14–23. IEEE Computer Society Press, 1989.

[MT91] R. Milner and M. Tofte. Co-induction in relational semantics. *Theoretical Computer Science*, 87:209–220, 1991.

[Ole82] F.J. Oles. *A category-theoretic approach to the semantics of programming languages*. PhD thesis, School of Computer and Information Science, Syracuse University, August 1982.

[Par81] D.M.R. Park. Concurrency and automata on infinite sequences. In P. Deussen, editor, *Proceedings 5th GI Conference*, volume 104 of *Lecture Notes in Computer Science*, pages 167–183. Springer-Verlag, Berlin, 1981.

[Pit92] A.M. Pitts. A co-induction principle for recursively defined domains. Technical Report 252, Computer Laboratory, University of Cambridge, 1992.

[Plo81a] G.D. Plotkin. Post-graduate lecture notes in advanced domain theory (incorporating the "Pisa Notes"). Department of Computer Science, Univ. of Edinburgh, 1981.

[Plo81b] G.D. Plotkin. A structured approach to operational semantics. Technical Report DAIMI FN-19, Computer Science Department, Aarhus University, 1981.

[Rut90] J.J.M.M. Rutten. Deriving denotational models for bisimulation from Structured Operational Semantics. In M. Broy and C.B. Jones, editors, *Programming concepts and methods, proceedings of the IFIP Working Group 2.2/2.3 Working Conference*, pages 155–177. North-Holland, 1990.

[Rut92] J.J.M.M. Rutten. Processes as terms: non-well-founded models for bisimulation. Technical Report CS-R9211, CWI (Centre for Mathematics and Computer Science), Amsterdam, 1992. To appear in Mathematical Structures in Computer Science.

[Smy92] M.B. Smyth. I-categories and duality. In M.P. Fourman, P.T. Johnstone, and A.M. Pitts, editors, *Applications of categories in computer science*, volume 177 of *London Mathematical Society Lecture Note Series*, pages 270–287. Cambridge University Press, 1992.

[SP82] M.B. Smyth and G.D. Plotkin. The category-theoretic solution of recursive domain equations. *SIAM J. Comput.*, 11:761–783, 1982.

Infinite Systems of Equations over Inverse Limits and Infinite Synchronous Concurrent Algorithms

V Stoltenberg-Hansen
Department of Mathematics, Uppsala University, P O Box 480,
S-75106 Uppsala, Sweden

J V Tucker
Department of Computer Science, University College of Swansea,
Swansea, SA2 8PP, Wales

ABSTRACT We consider the existence, uniqueness and effectiveness of solutions to infinite systems of equations in certain inverse limits of algebras. The notion of a guarded infinite system of equations is defined and used to establish existence and uniqueness results about the solutions. A domain structure associated with the inverse limit is used to prove the theorems. The use of infinite systems of equations is illustrated by the study of infinite synchronous concurrent algorithms (ISCAs). An ISCA is an infinite network of processors, operating in parallel, and synchronised by a global clock; the algorithm processes infinite streams of data. The algorithms are described by infinite systems of equations and, since the networks are deterministic, the equations are required to have unique solutions.

Keywords Inverse limits of algebras; ultrametric algebras; domains; infinite systems of equations; existence and uniqueness theorems; synchronous concurrent algorithms; streams; infinitely parallel deterministic systems.

CONTENTS

1. Introduction

Inverse limits of algebras occur widely in mathematics and computer science: For example, in constructing power series rings, the *p*-adic numbers, complete local rings, algebras of infinite trees and terms, infinite words, algebras of infinite streams, algebras of infinite processes in concurrent process theory, and nonwellfounded sets and processes. Loosely speaking, in computer science, the need to solve systems of equations in these algebras arises when giving a semantics to models of computing systems; in particular, finite and infinite systems of equations can be used to model finite and infinite computing systems, respectively.

We consider the solution of infinite systems of equations in certain inverse limits of algebras, and prove theorems about the existence of solutions, their uniqueness, their continuous dependence on parameters, and their effective computability.

In addition, we study an application of these general results in the theory of *infinite synchronous concurrent algorithms* (*ISCAs*). An infinite synchronous concurrent algorithm consists of a network of processors computing and communicating in parallel and synchronised by a global clock. The class of algorithms includes a wide variety of infinitely parallel deterministic computing systems (such as systolic arrays, dataflow systems, and neural networks), and of discrete space, discrete time dynamical systems (such as cellular automata, and coupled map lattices). To model mathematically such ISCAs we need to solve infinite systems of equations for functions on streams. Since the clock synchronisation makes the ISCA *deterministic*, we need to establish the *uniqueness* of the solutions that represent its behaviour. Since the ISCA is a computational model we need to know that the solution is *effective* and, in principle, implementable on a computer.

The mathematical starting point for the topic is that an inverse limit $\hat{A}$ of algebras has associated with it both a natural domain structure, in which $\hat{A}$ is contained in the space of maximal elements in the domain, and for many inverse limits an ultrametric structure, in which $\hat{A}$ is a complete ultrametric space. (In fact a wide class of complete ultrametric algebras are constructed in this way.) Thus equation solving in many inverse limits can be studied by using either of the fixed point theories of domains or metric spaces. The key point in the analysis is that to obtain unique solutions the equations must satisfy a property of being "guarded".

This paper is a sequel to Stoltenberg-Hansen and Tucker [91] which studied inverse limits, the solution of finite systems of equations in inverse limits, and applications to concurrent process theory (a comparison of ACP and CCS). In this paper we extend the previous theory by defining infinite guarded systems of equations and by an examination of continuity and computability aspects. Here the emphasis is on using elementary domain constructions to conduct the analysis of equation solving and effective computability in $\hat{A}$ with the objective of proving the following:

Theorem *Any guarded finite or infinite system of equations has a unique solution in $\hat{A}$ and the solution is obtained continuously from the parameters of the system. If the inverse system of computable algebras is effective and the parameters of the system of equations are computable then the solution is a computable element of $\hat{A}$.*

This and other results are applied to the study of the semantics of infinite synchronous concurrent algorithms. The mathematical analysis of equation solving explores rather fully the structural and computational properties of ISCAs. We derive new general classes of ISCAs based on notions of *finitely determined synchronisation, internal delay bounded by the present*, and *guardedness* with respect to a clock, and a new general class of *effective* ISCAs.

Theorem *Consider an* ISCA *with uniformly finitely determined synchronisation functions, whose internal delay functions are uniformly bounded by the present. If the* ISCA *equations are guarded then the behaviour of the* ISCA *is uniquely determined, continuously in the input data streams and initial state. If the* ISCA *is effective and the* ISCA *equations are effectively guarded then the behaviour of the* ISCA *is effective.*

The structure of the paper is as follows. In Section 2 we begin by giving a motivation for studying infinite systems of equations in the case of modelling infinite spatially distributed computer and discrete dynamical systems (such as cellular automata on the two dimensional plane). In Section 3 we summarise some concepts from domain theory and prove some basic results about solving systems of equations over domains. In Section 4 we prove results about our inverse limits using the ideas from Section 3. In Section 5 we revisit Section 2 and answer the questions left open.

JVT was partially supported by SERC Contract SO/103/91 and MRC Research Grant SPG 9017859.

2. Infinite Synchronous Concurrent Algorithms

2.1 SCA computation, hardware algebra and dynamical systems

A *synchronous concurrent algorithm* (SCA) is an algorithm consisting of a network of modules and channels, computing and communicating data in parallel, and synchronised by a global clock. Each module has finitely many input and output channels. Synchronous algorithms can process infinite streams of input data and return infinite streams of output data. Most importantly, an SCA is a *parallel deterministic algorithm*. The deterministic nature of these algorithms is established by the clock.

A *finite SCA* (FSCA) has finitely many modules in the network. An *infinite SCA* (ISCA) has infinitely many modules in the network. In the case of an ISCA we suppose that channels may be infinitely long and branch infinitely often.

The development of the theory of SCAs has been primarily concerned with giving a unified theory for the design and analysis of a wide range of apparently disparate parallel deterministic systems, for example: *systolic arrays, neural nets, cellular automata* (Fogelman Soulie et al [86]), *coupled map lattices* (Crutchfield and Kaneko [87], Kaneko [92]). A basic reference is Thompson and Tucker [91] and some general theory is in Meinke and Tucker [88]. Examples of work representing the two main application areas are:

Hardware: Hobley et al [88], Harman [88, 90], Eker and Tucker [88, 89], Eker, Stavridiou and Tucker [91], Martin and Tucker [88], and McConnell and Tucker [93].

Dynamical systems: Holden, Tucker and Thompson [90, 91], Holden, Tucker, Poole and Zhang [92].

Early research on finite SCAs and its connections with universal algebra and computability theory was surveyed in Tucker [91]; and its context in the theory of hardware described in McEvoy and Tucker [90].

In this paper we will focus on infinite SCAs, though mathematically all our results will apply to finite and infinite algorithms. The theory of ISCAs allows us to study

(i) infinite deterministic parallel systems;

(ii) finite parallel systems whose size is data dependent and unbounded;

(iii) uniformly defined families of finite parallel systems whose size $n \to \infty$.

Case studies in these areas are contained in McConnell and Tucker [92a, 93b].

2.2 A general model of synchronous concurrent computation

Consider any SCA that is based on a finite or infinite network of processors or modules $<m_i : i \in I>$. Suppose that the data processed by the network belongs to a single set A. To represent the algorithm, we first collect together the set A of data involved, and the functions f_i specifying the basic modules m_i of the network, to form an algebra $A = (A : f_i, i \in I)$. To this algebra we adjoin a clock $T = \{0, 1, \dots\}$ and the set $[T \to A]$ of *streams*, together with the operations of 0, $t+1$ and *eval*, defined by $eval(a,t) = a(t)$, to form a stream algebra $\underline{A}$. This stream algebra defines the components from which the SCA is built.

The network and algorithm is then represented by means of the following method.

Suppose for simplicity, that each module has finitely many input channels, but only *one* output channel. Each module may be connected to other modules, and be connected to the streams of data that form the input to the system from an external environment. Thus all modules may receive system input: suppose that the input streams to the system are indexed by J so that the set of all input streams to the SCA is $[T \to A]^J$. We suppose that some modules have their single output channels designated as output channels for the system; these we call *output modules*.

Finally, we suppose that our network of processors is deterministic in the following sense:

2.2.1 Assumption UT (for Unique Termination) Suppose that each module produces one, and only one, output from A at each clock cycle $t \in T$.

2.3 Equations for general model of an SCA

We formalise the informal description given in 2.2.

2.3.1 Representations of an SCA Thanks to the determinism of Assumption UT, to each module m_i we associate a total function

$$v_i : T \times [T \to A]^J \times A^I \to A$$

which defines the output value $v_i(t, a, x) \in A$ of the module m_i at time t, if the algorithm is processing input streams $a = (a_j : j \in J) \in [T \to A]^J$ from the initial state $x = (x_i : i \in I) \in A^I$ of the network. As a stream transformer, the algorithm is represented by its curried form

$$cv_i : [T \to A]^J \times A^I \to [T \to A]$$

defined by

$$(cv_i)(a, x)(t) = v_i(t, a, x).$$

From these local representations we construct corresponding global representations of the SCA: The parallel composition

$$v : T \times [T \to A]^J \times A^I \to A^I$$

of functions v_i defined by

$$v(t, a, x)\ (i) = v_i(t, a, x)$$

and its curried form

$$cv : [T \to A]^J \times A^I \to [T \to A^I].$$

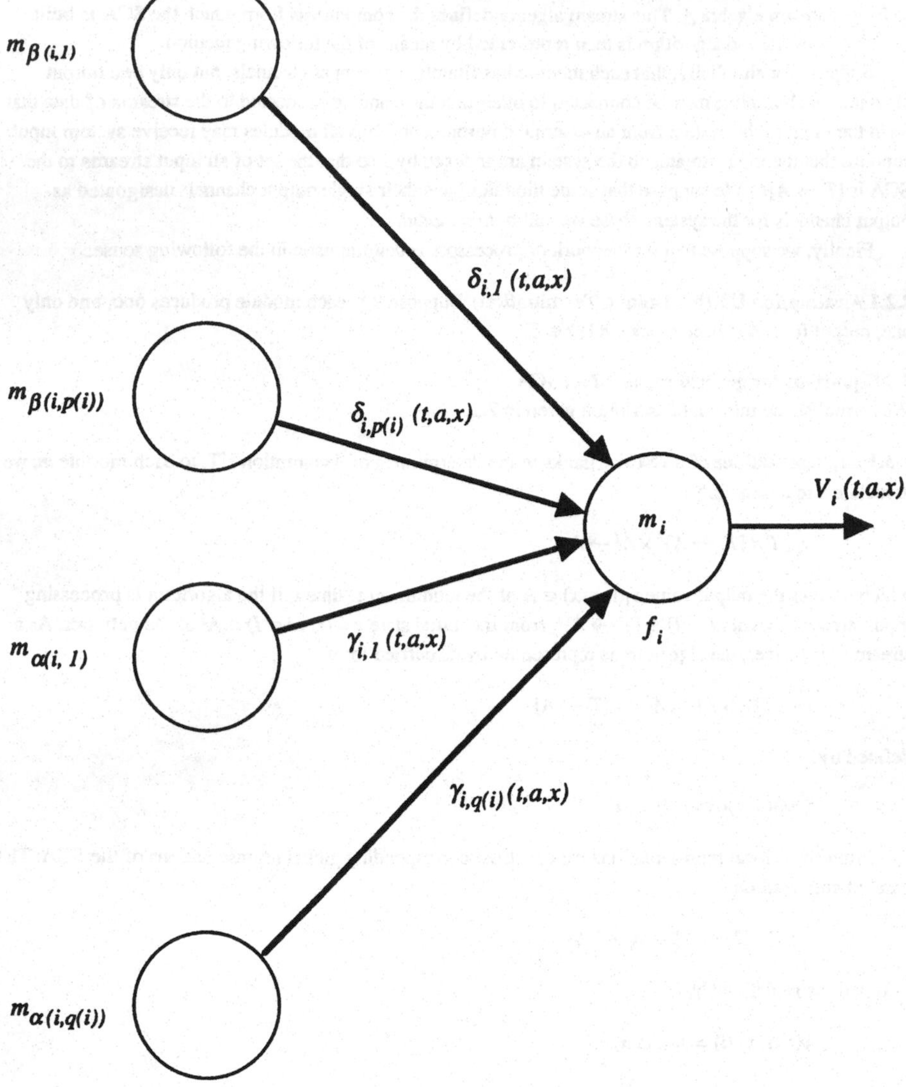

Figure 1: Value functions

2.3.2 Architecture More precisely, suppose that each module m_i has $p(i) + q(i)$ input channels, only 1 output channel, and is specified by a function

$$f_i : A^{p(i)+q(i)} \longrightarrow A.$$

Suppose that its $p(i)$ input channels are connected to the modules

$$m_{\beta(i,1)}, \ldots , m_{\beta(i,p(i))}$$

in the network and its $q(i)$ input channels are connected to input streams

$$a_{\alpha(i,1)}, \ldots , a_{\alpha(i,q(i))}$$

to the network from the external environment. Thus, the architecture of the network is represented by functions $\beta : I \times \omega \longrightarrow I$ and $\alpha : I \times \omega \longrightarrow J$ together with functions $p : I \longrightarrow \omega$ and $q : I \longrightarrow \omega$.

2.3.3 Assumption S (for Synchronisation) Suppose that the module m_i is connected by a channel to module m_j. There is a *synchronisation* or *scheduling of data* along this channel that is specified by the function

$$\delta_{ij} : T \times [T \longrightarrow A]^J \times A^I \longrightarrow T$$

such that $\delta_{ij}(t, a, x)$ is the time for which the output at module m_j is required on the channel at m_i in order to compute the output at m_i for each time $t > 0$ and all $a \in [T \longrightarrow A]^J, x \in A^I$.

Suppose that the module m_i is connected by a channel to the external environment and stream a_j. There is a *synchronisation* or *scheduling of data* that is specified by the function

$$\gamma_{ij} : T \times [T \longrightarrow A]^J \times A^I \longrightarrow T$$

such that $\gamma_{ij}(t, a, x)$ is the time for which the input from stream a_j is required on the channel at m_i to compute the output at m_i for each $t > 0$ and all $a \in [T \longrightarrow A]^J, x \in A^I$.

2.3.4 Equations The maps v_i for $i \in I$ are defined for all $t \in T$, $a \in [T \longrightarrow A]^J, x \in A^I$ as follows: For any module m_i,

$$v_i(0, a, x) = x_i$$

and at time $t > 0$,

$$v_i(t, a, x) = f_i(v_{\beta(i,1)}(\delta_{i1}(t, a, x), a, x), \ldots , v_{\beta(i,p(i))}(\delta_{ip(i)}(t, a, x), a, x), \\ a_{\alpha(i,1)}(\gamma_{i1}(t, a, x)), \ldots , a_{\alpha(i,q(i))}(\gamma_{iq(i)}(t, a, x))).$$

2.4 Equations of the general and unit delay model

There are several simple conditions we may impose on the δ_{ij} and γ_{ij} that reflect directly operational properties of the modules or channels, for instance:

2.4.1 Assumption D (for Delay) Suppose that the *delay* along the channel to module m_i from module m_j is specified by a function $\delta_{ij} : T \times [T \longrightarrow A]^J \times A^I \longrightarrow T$ such that

$$\delta_{ij}(t, a, x) < t$$

for all $t > 0$ and all $a \in [T \to A]^J$, $x \in A^I$. A similar delay property can be defined for the input channels in terms of the γ_{ij}.

In practice, the most important is the following special case of the general delay:

2.4.2 Assumption UD (for Unit Delay) Suppose there is a *unit delay* along the channel to module m_i from module m_j such that

$$\delta_{ij}(t, a, x) = t - 1$$

for all $t > 0$ and all $a \in [T \to A]^J$, $x \in A^I$. A similar unit delay property can be defined for the input channels in terms of the γ_{ij}.

For example, in the case that *every* channel has unit delay we can rewrite the equations for the maps v_i for $i \in I$ as follows: For any m_i,

$$v_i(0, a, x) = x_i$$
$$v_i(t+1, a, x) = f_i(v_{\beta(i,1)}(t, a, x), \ldots, v_{\beta(i,p(i))}(t, a, x), a_{\alpha(i,1)}(t), \ldots, a_{\alpha(i,q(i))}(t)).$$

In fact, recalling the stream algebra $\underline{A}$, from 2.2, the definition of the v_i in the case of Assumption D is a *simultaneous course-of-values recursion* on the stream algebra $\underline{A}$; and the definition of the v_i in the case of Assumption UD is a *simultaneous primitive recursion* over $\underline{A}$ (see Tucker and Zucker [92]).

2.5 Infinite systems of SCA equations

Let us consider the mathematical status of the equations for the SCA models in 2.3, involving general synchronisation, and 2.4, involving delay assumptions. We have a potentially infinite system of equations and the following tasks:

2.5.1 Existence To prove there exists a family

$$\langle v_i : i \in I \rangle$$

of total functions that satisfy the equations in 2.3.4. The existence of an output at every time cycle in Assumption UT requires that the functions be total.

2.5.2 Uniqueness To establish that the equations have unique solutions. The deterministic nature of the algorithms requires that the solutions are unique: This is contained in the statement of uniqueness of the output at every time cycle in Assumption UT.

2.5.3 Continuity To prove that each v_i and cv_i is continuous. The computation of module m_i at time t should only depend on finite parts of the input and on finite parts of streams computed by neighbouring modules.

2.5.4 Effectiveness To establish the sense in which the equations have computable solutions. If the data set A and module functions $\langle f_i : i \in I \rangle$ are computable, and if the synchronisation functions and architecture of the SCA is computable, then are the $\langle v_i : i \in I \rangle$ computable?

In many applications we find SCAs that are finite and, in particular, satisfy the Assumptions D or UD. These tasks arise whether or not I is finite or infinite, and in both cases Assumptions D and UD allow proofs of the existence, uniqueness and effectiveness of the functions to be based on induction, or course-of-values induction, on time.

We will use the equation solving methods of the next sections to analyse the general properties of the synchronisation functions and equations for the architecture that give rise to the desired existence, uniqueness, continuity and effectiveness of the SCA. The analysis highlights the special properties of the delay assumptions, and extends the range of synchronisation functions and architectures which constitute SCAs that are deterministic and effective. The central notion is that the SCA equations are guarded.

3. Preliminaries on domains and equation solving

3.1 Domains

We recall some concepts from domain theory; for a detailed introduction see Griffor, Lindström and Stoltenberg-Hansen [93]. Let $D = (D; \leq, \bot)$ be a partially ordered set with least element $\bot$. A set $A \subseteq D$ is *directed* if $A \neq \emptyset$ and if $x, y \in A$ then there is $z \in A$ such that $x \leq z$ and $y \leq z$. D is a *complete partial order* (*cpo*) if every directed set $A \subseteq D$ has a least upper bound in D, denoted $\bigvee A$. An element $a \in D$ is said to be *compact* or *finite* if whenever $a \leq \bigvee A$, where A is directed, then there is $x \in A$ such that $a \leq x$. Let $D_c = \{a \in D : a \text{ compact}\}$, and for each $x \in D$ let $approx(x) = \{a \in D_c : a \leq x\}$, the set of compact approximations of x. A cpo D is *algebraic* if, for each $x \in D$, $approx(x)$ is a directed set and $x = \bigvee approx(x)$. Furthermore, D is *consistently complete* if whenever $a, b \in D_c$ are consistent, i.e. a and b have an upper bound in D, then $\bigvee\{a, b\} = a \vee b$ exists in D, and hence in D_c. A *domain* is a consistently complete algebraic cpo.

A function $f: D \to E$ between domains is said to be *continuous* if f is monotone and $f(\bigvee A) = \bigvee f[A]$ for each directed set A. For the latter condition it suffices to show that for each $b \in approx(f(x))$ there is $a \in approx(x)$ such that $b \leq f(a)$. Furthermore, each monotone function $f: D_c \to E$ has a unique continuous extension $\overline{f} : D \to E$, namely $\overline{f}(x) = \bigvee\{f(a) : a \in approx(x)\}$. This concept of continuity corresponds to the topological notion with respect to the *Scott topology* generated by the topological base of sets $B_a = \{x \in D : a \leq x\}$ for $a \in D_c$.

For a domain D we denote by D_m the set of maximal elements in D. On giving D_m the subspace topology from the Scott topology on D, it is easily seen that D_m is a Hausdorff space. In fact, if $a \in D_c$ and $x \in D_m - B_a$ then there is $b \in approx(x)$ such that $B_a \cap B_b = \emptyset$. It follows that D_m has a clopen topological base.

A *conditional upper semilattice* or *cusl* is a partially ordered set $P = (P; \leq, \bot)$ with least element $\bot$ such that if $a, b \in P$ are consistent, that is have an upper bound in P, then $a \vee b$ exists in P. If D is a domain then D_c is a cusl. Each cusl P generates a domain $\overline{P}$, the *ideal completion* of P. The representation theorem for domains states that each domain D is the ideal completion of its compact elements D_c, that is $\overline{D_c} \cong D$.

Let $D_1, \ldots, D_n$ be domains. Then the cartesian product $D_1 \times \ldots \times D_n$ is a domain with the ordering defined coordinate-wise. It is easily verified that $(D_1 \times \ldots \times D_n)_c = (D_1)_c \times \ldots \times (D_n)_c$, that the projection functions are continuous and that $f: D_1 \times \ldots \times D_n \to E$ is continuous if and only if f is continuous in each argument.

For domains D and E we let $[D \to E]$ be the set of *continuous* functions from D into E. Then $[D \to E]$ is again a domain under the ordering $f \leq g \iff (\forall x \in D)(f(x) \leq g(x))$. The compact elements of $[D \to E]$ are the suprema of finite consistent sets of functions $<a; b>$ for $a \in D_c$ and $b \in E_c$, where

$$<a; b>(x) = \begin{cases} b & \text{if } a \le x \\ \bot & \text{otherwise.} \end{cases}$$

Furthermore the function *eval* : $[D \to E] \times D \to E$, defined by $eval(f, x) = f(x)$, is continuous.

Each continuous function $f: D \to D$ has a least fixed point denoted by $fix(f)$. Thus $fix : [D \to D] \to D$, and *fix* can easily be shown to be continuous.

For domains D, E and F the currying operation $c : [D \times E \to F] \to [D \to [E \to F]]$ defined by

$$c(f)(x)(y) = f(x, y)$$

is continuous and, in fact, an isomorphism.

3.2 Systems of equations and solutions

3.2.1 The system of equations We are going to be concerned with possibly infinite systems of equations over a domain D,

$$(E) \qquad X_i = \phi_i(X_{\beta(i,1)}, \dots, X_{\beta(i,p(i))}) \qquad i \in I$$

where $p : I \to \omega$, $\phi_i : D^{p(i)} \to D$ is continuous and $\beta(i, j) \in I$ for each $i \in I$ and $j = 1, \dots, p(i)$.

To study such systems of equations and to obtain a system of solutions $<x_i : i \in I>$ in D we consider the following domain.

3.2.2 Definition Let $D = (D; \le_D, \bot)$ be a partially ordered set with least element $\bot$ and let I be a non-empty set. Then define D^I by

$$D^I = \{f \mid f : I \to D\}$$

the set of all functions from I into D. Order D^I using the pointwise ordering

$$f \le g \Leftrightarrow (\forall i \in I)(f(i) \le_D g(i)).$$

Finally let $\lambda i.\bot \in D^I$ be the function whose value is $\bot \in D$ for all $i \in I$.

3.2.3 Theorem *Let $D = (D; \le, \bot)$ be a partially ordered set with least element $\bot$, let I be a non-empty set, and consider $D^I = (D^I, \le, \lambda i.\bot)$.*

(i) *D^I is a partially ordered set with least element.*

(ii) *If D is a cpo then D^I is a cpo.*

(iii) *If D is an algebraic cpo then D^I is an algebraic cpo. The compact elements are*

$$(D^I)_c = \{f \in D^I : (\forall i \in I)(f(i) \in D_c) \text{ and } f(i) = \bot \text{ a.e.}\},$$

where a.e. means almost everywhere, i.e. everywhere except at finitely many i.

(iv) *If D is a consistently complete cpo then D^I is a consistently complete cpo.*

(v) *In particular, if D is a domain then D^I is a domain.*

The trivial structure on I makes things much easier than in the usual function space construction: It is *not* true that if D and E are algebraic cpo's then the function space $[D \to E]$ is an algebraic cpo; this is a motivation for considering consistent completeness.

Proof. We leave (i) as a trivial exercise. Consider (ii) and assume that D is a cpo. Let $\mathcal{F} \subseteq D^I$ be a directed set. Then for each $i \in I$, $\{f(i) : f \in \mathcal{F}\}$ is directed so $\bigvee\{f(i) : f \in \mathcal{F}\}$ exists in D. Let $h \in D^I$ be defined by

$$h(i) = \bigvee\{f(i) : f \in \mathcal{F}\}.$$

Clearly h is an upper bound of $\mathcal{F}$. Suppose g is another upper bound of $\mathcal{F}$. Fix $i \in I$. Then for $f \in \mathcal{F}$, $f(i) \leq g(i)$, so $h(i) = \bigvee\{f(i) : f \in \mathcal{F}\} \leq g(i)$. It follows that $h \leq g$ so that $h = \bigvee\mathcal{F}$. This shows that D^I is a cpo.

Consider (iii). Let

$$C = \{h \in D^I : (\forall i \in I)(h(i) \in D_c \text{ and } h(i) = \bot \text{ a.e.})\}.$$

We claim that $(D^I)_c = C$. Let $h \in C$, and suppose $h \leq \bigvee\mathcal{F}$ where $\mathcal{F}$ is directed. Let $J = \{i \in I : h(i) \neq \bot\}$, so J is a finite set. For each $j \in J$,

$$h(j) \leq (\bigvee\mathcal{F})(j) = \bigvee\{f(j) : f \in \mathcal{F}\}.$$

By the compactness of $h(j)$ there is $f_j \in \mathcal{F}$ such that $h(j) \leq f_j(j)$. By the directedness of $\mathcal{F}$ and finiteness of J there is $g \in \mathcal{F}$ such that $f_j \leq g$ for $j \in J$. But then

$$h(j) \leq f_j(j) \leq g(j) \qquad \forall j \in J$$

and hence $h \leq g$ (since $h(i) = \bot$ for $i \notin J$.) Thus, h is compact in D^I and $C \subseteq (D^I)_c$.

For the converse, consider first more generally any $f \in D^I$. Let $A_f = \{h \in C : h \leq f\}$. We claim that $f = \bigvee A_f$ and that A_f is directed. Having proved this, it follows that if f is compact then $f = h$ for some $h \in C$, i.e. $f \in C$. Hence $(D^I)_c = C$. Furthermore, it follows that D^I is algebraic. We now show that A_f is directed. Let $h_1, h_2 \in A_f$. Fix $i \in I$. Then

$h_1(i) \leq f(i)$, i.e. $h_1(i) \in approx(f(i))$ and
$h_2(i) \leq f(i)$, i.e. $h_2(i) \in approx(f(i))$.

Let $J = \{i \in I : h_1(i) \neq \bot \text{ or } h_2(i) \neq \bot\}$. For $j \in J$, choose $a_j \in approx(f(j))$ such that

$$h_1(j) \leq a_j \text{ and } h_2(j) \leq a_j.$$

This is possible since $approx(f(j))$ is directed (under the assumption that D is algebraic). Define

$$k(i) = \begin{cases} a_i & \text{if } i \in J \\ \bot & \text{if } i \notin J. \end{cases}$$

Then $k \in C$ and $k \leq f$, i.e. $k \in A_f$. Clearly $h_1, h_2 \leq k$, so A_f is directed. To show that $f = \bigvee A_f$ we immediately have $\bigvee A_f \leq f$. For the converse we define for $i \in I$, $a \in D_c$, $<i, a> : I \to D$ by

$$<i, a>(j) = \begin{cases} a & \text{if } i = j \\ \bot & \text{otherwise.} \end{cases}$$

Then $<i, a> \in C$ for $i \in I$, $a \in D_c$. Fix $i \in I$. Then $f(i) = \bigvee approx(f(i))$ since D is algebraic. Suppose $a \in approx(f(i))$. Then $<i, a> \in A_f$. Let $k = \bigvee A_f$ (which exists since A_f is directed). Then

$$\begin{aligned} k(i) &= \bigvee\{h(i) : h \in \mathcal{C}, h \le f\} \\ &\ge \bigvee\{\langle i, a\rangle(i) : a \in approx(f(i))\} \\ &= \bigvee approx(f(i)) = f(i). \end{aligned}$$

We have shown that (iii) holds. It remains to show (iv). Suppose $h_1, h_2 \in \mathcal{C}$ are consistent in D^I. Then for each i, $h_1(i)$ and $h_2(i)$ are consistent in D. So, if D is consistently complete, then $h_1(i) \vee h_2(i)$ exists in D. Let $k \in D^I$ be defined by

$$k(i) = h_1(i) \vee h_2(i) \qquad i \in I.$$

Thus k is well-defined and $k = h_1 \vee h_2$.

Finally, (v) follows from (iii) and (iv). ◊

We should remark that the theorem easily generalizes to the cartesian product $\prod_{i\in I} D_i$ for families D_i, $i \in I$. In particular, if each D_i is an algebraic cpo then the Scott topology on $\prod_{i\in I} D_i$ is the Tychonoff topology obtained from the Scott topologies on each D_i.

3.2.4 Definition Let (E) be the system of equations in 3.2.1. Then $\Phi_E : D^I \to D^I$ is defined by

$$\Phi_E(f)(i) = \phi_i(f(\beta(i, 1)), \ldots, f(\beta(i, p(i))))$$

for $f \in D^I$ and $i \in I$.

3.2.5 Lemma $\Phi_E : D^I \to D^I$ *is continuous.*

Proof: To show monotonicity suppose $f \le g$ in D^I. We need to show that $\Phi_E(f) \le \Phi_E(g)$, that is $\Phi_E(f)(i) \le \Phi_E(g)(i)$ for each $i \in I$. This follows by the monotonicity of each ϕ_i. To show continuity, let $\mathcal{F} \subseteq D^I$ be a directed set. Then

$$\begin{aligned} \Phi_E(\bigvee\mathcal{F})(i) &= \phi_i((\bigvee\mathcal{F})(\beta(i, 1)), \ldots, (\bigvee\mathcal{F})(\beta(i, p(i)))) \\ &= \bigvee_{f_1\in\mathcal{F}} \cdots \bigvee_{f_{p(i)}\in\mathcal{F}} \phi_i(f_1(\beta(i, 1)), \ldots, f_{p(i)}(\beta(i, p(i)))). \end{aligned}$$

Given $f_1, \ldots, f_{p(i)} \in \mathcal{F}$ choose $f \in \mathcal{F}$ such that $f_1, \ldots, f_{p(i)} \le f$, which is possible since $\mathcal{F}$ is directed. Then, by the monotonicity of each ϕ_i,

$$\begin{aligned} \phi_i(f_1(\beta(i, 1)), \ldots, f_{p(i)}(\beta(i, p(i)))) &\le \phi_i(f(\beta(i, 1)), \ldots, f(\beta(i, p(i)))) \\ &\le \bigvee_{f\in\mathcal{F}} \phi_i(f(\beta(i, 1)), \ldots, f(\beta(i, p(i)))) \\ &= \bigvee_{f\in\mathcal{F}} \Phi_E(f)(i). \end{aligned}$$

It follows that $\Phi_E(\bigvee\mathcal{F}) \le \bigvee_{f\in\mathcal{F}} \Phi_E(f)$. ◊

3.2.6 Theorem *Each system of equations* (E) *as in* 3.2.1 *has a least (in* D^I*) solution over the domain D.*

Proof: Solutions to (E) correspond to fixed points of Φ_E. Thus by setting $X_i = fix(\Phi_E)(i)$ for each $i \in I$ we obtain a solution to (E). It is clearly the least solution in D^I since *fix* provides the least fixed point. ◊

3.3 Equations depending on parameters

3.3.1 The system of equations We shall now consider systems of equations ($E_{\mathbf{x}}$) depending on the finite sequence of parameters $\mathbf{x}$. Let $E_1, \ldots, E_m$ and D be domains and let I be a (possibly infinite) non-empty set. Let $\phi_i : E_1 \times \ldots \times E_m \to [D^{p(i)} \to D]$ be continuous for each $i \in I$. Then for every $x = (x_1, \ldots, x_m) \in E_1 \times \ldots \times E_m$ we consider the system of equations

$$(E_x) \qquad X_i = \phi_i(x)(X_{\beta(i,1)}, \ldots, X_{\beta(i,p(i))}) \qquad i \in I$$

where β and p are as in 3.2.1. For such an equation system we define $\Phi_{E_x} : D^I \to D^I$ by

$$\Phi_{E_x}(f)(i) = \phi_i(x)(f(\beta(i, 1)), \ldots, f(\beta(i, p(i)))).$$

3.3.2 Proposition *The function $\Xi : E_1 \times \ldots \times E_m \to [D^I \to D^I]$ defined by $\Xi(x) = \Phi_{E_x}$ is continuous.*

Proof: By Lemma 3.2.5, $\Xi(x) \in [D^I \to D^I]$ for each $x \in E_1 \times \ldots \times E_m$. To prove monotonicity for Ξ, let $x \leq y$ in $E_1 \times \ldots \times E_m$. Then, for $f \in D^I$ and $i \in I$,

$$\begin{aligned}\Phi_{E_x}(f)(i) &= \phi_i(x)(f(\beta(i, 1)), \ldots, f(\beta(i, p(i))))\\ &\leq \phi_i(y)(f(\beta(i, 1)), \ldots, f(\beta(i, p(i))))\\ &= \Phi_{E_y}(f)(i)\end{aligned}$$

by the monotonicity of ϕ_i. Thus $\Phi_{E_x} \leq \Phi_{E_y}$.

To show continuity it suffices to show for each $x \in E_1 \times \ldots \times E_m$ and each subbasic element $<f, g> \in [D^I \to D^I]_c$ such that $<f, g> \leq \Phi_{E_x}$, that there is $a \in (E_1 \times \ldots \times E_m)_c$, $a \leq x$, such that $<f, g> \leq \Phi_{E_a}$. Recall that $<f, g> \leq \Phi_{E_x}$ if and only if $g \leq \Phi_{E_x}(f)$. The latter means that, for each $i \in I$,

$$(*) \qquad g(i) \leq \Phi_{E_x}(f)(i) = \phi_i(x)(f(\beta(i, 1)), \ldots, f(\beta(i, p(i)))).$$

Let $J = \{i \in I : g(i) \neq \bot\}$, so J is a finite set. Note that the right hand side of (*) is continuous in x since the *eval* function is continuous. It follows that for each i there is $a_i \in (E_1 \times \ldots \times E_m)_c$, $a_i \leq x$, such that $g(i) \leq \phi_i(a_i)(f(\beta(i, 1)), \ldots, f(\beta(i, p(i))))$. Let

$$a = \bigvee_{i \in J} a_i.$$

Then a exists by the consistent completeness of $E_1 \times \ldots \times E_m$ and a is compact since J is finite.

If $i \notin J$ then $g(i) = \bot$, so (*) holds with a in place of x. If $i \in J$ then

$$\begin{aligned}g(i) &\leq \phi_i(a_i)(f(\beta(i, 1)), \ldots, f(\beta(i, p(i))))\\ &\leq \phi_i(a)(f(\beta(i, 1)), \ldots, f(\beta(i, p(i))))\end{aligned}$$

again by the monotonicity of ϕ_i. Thus we have shown that $g \leq \Phi_{E_a}(f)$, i.e. $<f, g> \leq \Phi_{E_a}$. ◊

3.3.3 Theorem *There is a continuous function $\Gamma : E_1 \times \ldots \times E_m \to D^I$ such that $\Gamma(x)$ is the least solution to the system of equations (E_x) of* 3.3.1.

Proof: Let $\Gamma(x) = fix(\Xi(x)) = fix(\Phi_{E_x})$. Then Γ is continuous since *fix* and Ξ are continuous and $\Gamma(x)$ clearly provides the least solution in D^I to (E_x). ◊

4. Inverse limits and equation solving

Our main concern in this section is systems of equations over an algebra or structure A, possibly depending on parameters, and their solutions. Of course, equations often do not have any solutions in the given algebra A. For example, the equation

$$X = X + 1$$

does not have a solution over the natural numbers $\mathbf{N}$. Nonetheless one may interpret the equation as the process of adding 1, that is the infinite sequence $(0, 1, 2, \ldots, n, \ldots)$ should be a solution. We want our solutions to be mathematical objects and hence they should live in some mathematical structure. The usual procedure is to "complete" the structure in some precise mathematical sense so as to incorporate the desired objects in the completion. The properties of the new objects depend on the chosen completion process. For example we may complete the natural numbers using the one point compactification, where the added point ∞ satisfies the equation $\infty = \infty + 1$. If we on the other hand completed $\mathbf{N}$ using an ultrapower construction then the equation would still not have a solution even though elements like $(0, 1, 2, \ldots, n, \ldots)$ do exist there.

The completion process we choose to consider here is that of the inverse limit. For ultrametric spaces this corresponds to the metric completion, up to topological equivalence (see Stoltenberg-Hansen and Tucker [91]).

4.1 Inverse limits

In this subsection we review how to construct certain inverse limits using a directed index set.

4.1.1 Definition Let $I = (I, \leq, 0)$ be a directed set with least element 0 and let A be a set. Then $\{\equiv_i\}_{i\in I}$ is a family of *separating equivalences on A over I* if

(i) each $\equiv_i$ is an equivalence relation on A,

(ii) $j \geq i$ and $a \equiv_j b \Rightarrow a \equiv_i b$, and

(iii) $\bigcap_{i\in I} \equiv_i = \{(a, a) : a \in A\}$.

For convenience we always assume $a \equiv_0 b$ for each $a, b \in A$. Often A will be an algebra and $\equiv_i$ a congruence relation on A. However there is no reason, at least initially, to restrict ourselves to that case.

4.1.2 Examples

(1) On the natural numbers $\mathbf{N}$, let $\equiv_n$ for $n \in \omega$ be the equivalence relation corresponding to the partition $\{0\}, \{1\}, \{2\}, \ldots, \{n-1\}, \{n, n+1, n+2, \ldots\}$.

(2) Let $T(\Sigma, X)$ be the term algebra over a signature Σ and a set of variables X. Then, for $t, t' \in T(\Sigma, X)$ let $t \equiv_n t'$ if t and t' are identical up to height $n - 1$, for $n \in \omega$.

(3) Let R be a local commutative ring whose unique maximal ideal is m. Define for $x, y \in R$ and $n \in \omega$, $x \equiv_n y \Leftrightarrow x - y \in m^n$. Then, by Krull's theorem, $\{\equiv_n\}_{n\in\omega}$ is a family of separating equivalences and, in fact, congruences with respect to the ring operations (see Stoltenberg-Hansen and Tucker [88]).

(4) Let $2^\omega = \{f \mid f : \omega \to \{0, 1\}\}$, the Cantor set. Define for $f, g \in 2^\omega$, $n \in \omega$,

$$f \equiv_n g \Leftrightarrow (\forall i < n)(f(i) = g(i)).$$

Then $\{\equiv_n\}_{n\in\omega}$ is a family of separating equivalences on 2^ω.

Suppose we are given a set A and a family of separating equivalences $\{\equiv_i\}_{i\in I}$ on A. Let J be a non-empty possibly infinite set. We will define a family of separating equivalences on $A^J = \{f \mid f : J \to A\}$ as follows. Let $I^{(J)} = \{s \mid s : J \to I \text{ and } s(j) = 0 \text{ a.e.}\}$. We order $I^{(J)}$ by

$$s \leq t \iff (\forall j \in J)(s(j) \leq t(j)).$$

Clearly $I^{(J)}$ is a directed set with least element the constant 0 function. For $a, b \in A^J$ and $s \in I^{(J)}$ define

$$a \equiv_s b \iff (\forall j \in J)(a(j) \equiv_{s(j)} b(j)).$$

4.1.3 Lemma *The family* $\{\equiv_s\}_{s\in I^{(J)}}$ *is a family of separating equivalences on* A^J *over* $I^{(J)}$.

Proof: Clearly $\equiv_s$ is an equivalence relation on A^J. Suppose $s \leq t$ and $a \equiv_t b$. For $j \in J$ we have $a(j) \equiv_{t(j)} b(j)$ and hence $a(j) \equiv_{s(j)} b(j)$ since $\{\equiv_i\}_{i\in I}$ is separating. Finally, if $a \neq b$ then for some $j \in J$, $a(j) \neq b(j)$. But then for some i, $a(j) \not\equiv_i b(j)$. Let s be defined by $s(j) = i$ and $s(k) = 0$ for each $k \neq j$. Then $a \not\equiv_s b$. ◊

Consider a fixed set A together with a family of separating equivalences $\{\equiv_i\}_{i\in I}$ on A over the directed set I. We shall complete A using the inverse limit construction. In case A is an algebra and each $\equiv_i$ is a congruence relation on A, then the completion of A is again an algebra.

For $a \in A$, let $[a]_i$ denote the equivalence class of $\equiv_i$ containing a, and let

$$A_i = A/\equiv_i = \{[a]_i : a \in A, i \in I\}.$$

For each $i \leq j \in I$ we define $\phi_i^j : A_j \to A_i$ by $\phi_i^j([a]_j) = [a]_i$. Then ϕ_i^j is well-defined by condition (ii) of 4.1.1. Furthermore $\phi_i^i = \mathrm{id}_{A_i}$ and $\phi_i^j \circ \phi_j^k = \phi_i^k$. These observations say that $\{A_i : i \in I\}$, $\{\phi_i^j : i \leq j \in I\}$ is an *inverse system* which is *surjective* in the sense that each ϕ_i^j is surjective. Let $\hat{A} = \varprojlim A_i$ be the projective or inverse limit with the associated maps $\hat{\phi}_i : \hat{A} \to A_i$. To be concrete, we may take $\hat{A}$ to consist of all I-sequences consistent with respect to the morphisms of the inverse system, that is

$$\hat{A} = \{(a_i)_i \in \prod_{i\in I} A_i : \phi_i^j(a_j) = a_i \text{ for } i \leq j\}.$$

The projections $\hat{\phi}_j : \hat{A} \to A_j$ are then defined by $\hat{\phi}_j((a_i)_i) = a_j$.

Let $\nu_i : A \to A_i$ be the canonical mapping defined by $\nu_i(a) = [a]_i$. Then for $i \leq j$, $\nu_i = \phi_i^j \circ \nu_j$, so there is a unique function $\theta : A \to \hat{A}$ commuting the following diagrams:

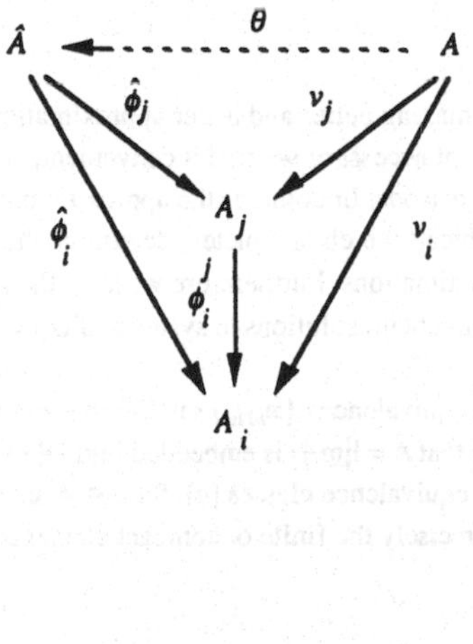

In fact, $\theta(a) = (v_i(a))_{i\in I} = ([a]_i)_{i\in I}$. By condition (iii) of 4.1.1, θ is injective so that θ embeds A into $\hat{A}$.

4.1.4 Topology In case $I = \omega$ with the usual ordering then a family of separating equivalences $\{\equiv_n\}_{n<\omega}$ induces an ultrametric on A by

$$d(a, b) = \begin{cases} 0 & \text{if } a = b, \\ r_n & \text{if } a \neq b \text{ and } n \text{ is least s.t. } a \not\equiv_n b \end{cases}$$

where (r_n) is some strictly decreasing sequence of real numbers approaching 0. If we define an ultrametric $\hat{d}$ on $\hat{A}$ by

$$\hat{d}(x, y) = \begin{cases} 0 & \text{if } x = y \\ r_n & \text{if } x \neq y, \text{ and } n \text{ is least s.t. } \hat{\phi}_n(x) \neq \hat{\phi}_n(y) \end{cases}$$

then the ultrametric space $(\hat{A}, \hat{d})$ is the *metric completion* of (A, d).

More generally, if I is a directed set and $\{\equiv_i\}_{i\in I}$ is a family of separating equivalences on A then we obtain a topology on A from the following family of basic open sets:

$$B(a, i) = \{b \in A : a \equiv_i b\} \qquad \text{for } a \in A \text{ and } i \in I.$$

These sets are easily shown to form a topological base. In case I is closed under finite suprema and $\{\equiv_i\}_{i\in I}$ is upward consistent (defined in 4.2.1) then the family is closed under finite intersections (when we include $\varnothing$).

Similarly we define a topological base on $\hat{A}$ by, for $a \in A$ and $i \in I$, the family of basic open sets $B(a, i) = \{y \in \hat{A} : \hat{\phi}_i(y) = [a]_i\}$.

Suppose $\{\equiv_i\}_{i\in I}$ is a family of separating equivalences on A and let J be a non-empty set. Then $I^{(J)}$ is a family of separating equivalences on A^J by Lemma 4.1.3. The topology on A^J obtained from $I^{(J)}$ is precisely the Tychonoff topology on A^J obtained from the topology on A. In particular, each projection function $\pi_j : A^J \to A$, defined by $\pi_j(f) = f(j)$, is continuous.

4.1.5 Examples Referring to Examples 4.1.2. we have that the completion of **N** as in (1) is the one point compactification with respect to the topology given by the ultrametric, where one element ∞ is added. The completion of $T(\Sigma, X)$ in (2) is the set $T^\infty(\Sigma, X)$ of all finite and infinite terms. The completion of a local ring R as in (3) is the standard construction of the completion for local rings. Finally, the completion of the Cantor space gives us the Cantor space back, i.e. θ is a bijection, since the Cantor space already is complete.

4.2 Inverse limits and domains

Our task is to solve systems of equations by making better and better approximations and then obtaining a solution as a limit of this process. Though not necessary we find it convenient, and interesting, to work with some simple domains for the following reasons. In domains the approximations are visible. The approximations in a domain are in fact the objects which completely determine the domain in the sense that the domain is the completion of its approximations. Furthermore we have the fixed point machinery available to us, which we already have used to obtain solutions to systems of equations in Theorems 3.2.6 and 3.3.3.

Given a set A and a family of separating equivalences $\{\equiv_i\}_{i\in I}$ satisfying some properties described below we will construct a domain $D(A)$ such that $\hat{A} = \varprojlim A_i$ is embedded into $D(A)$, in fact into $D(A)_m$, and such that $D(A)_c$ consists precisely of the equivalence classes $[a]_i$ for $a \in A$ and $i \in I$. In other words, the approximations of the inverse limit are precisely the finite or compact elements in $D(A)$.

4.2.1 Definition A family of separating equivalences $\{\equiv_i\}_{i\in I}$ on A is *upward consistent* if

$$a \equiv_i b \ \&\ a \equiv_j b \Rightarrow (\exists k \geq i, j)(a \equiv_k b).$$

In order to obtain consistent completeness for $D(A)$ we need in addition to the above assume that the index set I is closed under finite suprema. In that case upward consistency is characterized by

$$a \equiv_i b \ \&\ a \equiv_j b \Rightarrow (a \equiv_{i\vee j} b).$$

Clearly ω is closed under finite suprema and $\{\equiv_n\}_{n\in\omega}$ is upward consistent.

Let $\{\equiv_i\}_{i\in I}$ be a family of separating equivalences on A and let $\{\equiv_s\}_{s\in I^{(J)}}$ be the family of separating equivalences on A^J introduced in Section 4.1.

4.2.2 Lemma *If I is closed under finite suprema and $\{\equiv_i\}_{i\in I}$ is upward consistent then $I^{(J)}$ is closed under finite suprema and $\{\equiv_s\}_{s\in I^{(J)}}$ on A^J is upward consistent.*

Proof: For $s, t \in I^{(J)}$, define $u : J \to I$ by $u(j) = s(j) \vee t(j)$. Then $u(j) = 0$ a.e. so $u \in I^{(J)}$ and, clearly, $u = s \vee t$. Suppose for $a, b \in A^J$ that $a \equiv_s b$ and $a \equiv_t b$. Then, for each $j \in J$, $a(j) \equiv_{s(j)} b(j)$ and $a(j) \equiv_{t(j)} b(j)$. But then $a(j) \equiv_{(s\vee t)(j)} b(j)$ so $a \equiv_{s\vee t} b$. ◊

4.2.3 Construction of the domain $D(A)$ Let $\{\equiv_i\}_{i\in I}$ be a fixed family of separating equivalences on A which is upward consistent and let the index set I be closed under finite suprema. Let $A_i = A/\equiv_i$ be the set of equivalence classes of $\equiv_i$. Let $C = \dot\cup\{A_i : i \in I\}$, the disjoint union of the A_i. We denote an element of C by $[a]_i$ where $a \in A$ and $i \in I$, thus letting the i indicate that $[a]_i$ is taken from A_i in the disjoint union. We define a partial ordering on C by

$$[a]_i \leq [b]_j \Leftrightarrow i \leq j \text{ and } a \equiv_i b.$$

That is $[a]_i \leq [b]_j$ if and only if $i \leq j$ and $\phi_i^j([b]_j) = [a]_i$. We claim that C with this ordering is a cusl. Clearly $[a]_0$ is the least element in C by our standing assumption on $\equiv_0$ where 0 is the least element in I. Now suppose $[a]_i$ and $[b]_j$ are bounded in C by, say, $[c]_k$. Then $i, j \leq k$ and $a \equiv_i c$ and $b \equiv_j c$. Thus $[c]_{i\vee j}$ is an upper bound. To see that $[c]_{i\vee j}$ is the least upper bound let $[d]_m$ be another upper bound. This means that $i, j \leq m$ and $a \equiv_i d$ and $b \equiv_j d$. But then $c \equiv_i d$ and $c \equiv_j d$ and hence, by upward consistency, $c \equiv_{i\vee j} d$. It follows that $[c]_{i\vee j} \leq [d]_m$.

Having shown that C is a cusl we now define $D(A) = \overline{C}$, the ideal completion of the cusl C. Identifying the principal ideals in $D(A)$ with their generating elements in C, we have $D(A)_c = C$.

Let $(a_i)_i \in \hat{A}$. Then the consistency property of the sequence $(a_i)_i$, and the fact that I is directed, assures that the set $\{a_i : i \in I\} \subseteq C$ is directed. Thus we may define $\Psi : \hat{A} \to D(A)$ by

$$\Psi((a_i)_i) = \bigvee\{a_i : i \in I\}.$$

Furthermore, the set $\{a_i : i \in I\}$ is closed downwards in C so that $approx(\Psi((a_i)_i)) = \{a_i : i \in I\}$. It follows that Ψ is injective. It is easy to see that if $\mathcal{I} \subseteq C$ is an ideal such that $(\forall i \in I)(\exists a \in A)([a]_i \in \mathcal{I})$ then $\mathcal{I}$ is maximal in $D(A)$. It follows that $\Psi[\hat{A}] \subseteq D(A)_m$. We summarize our observations.

4.2.4 Theorem *Let I be a directed set closed under finite suprema. Suppose $\{\equiv_i\}_{i\in I}$ is a family of separating equivalences on A which is upward consistent. Then $D(A)$ is a domain with $D(A)_c = \{[a]_i : a \in A, i \in I\}$. Furthermore, there is an embedding $\Psi : \hat{A} \to D(A)$ such that* *approx*$(\Psi((a_i)_i)) = \{a_i : i \in I\}$ *and* $\Psi[\hat{A}] \subseteq D(A)_m$. *Finally,* Ψ *is a homeomorphism when* $\hat{A}$ *is given the topology in 4.1.4 and* $\Psi[\hat{A}]$ *is given the subspace topology of the Scott topology on* $D(A)$.

4.2.5 Definition Let $\{\equiv_i\}_{i\in I}$ be a family of separating equivalences on A. Define $\Theta : A \to D(A)$ by $\Theta(a) = \Psi(\theta(a))$, where $\theta : A \to \hat{A}$ is the unique embedding provided by the inverse limit construction, and $\Psi : \hat{A} \to D(A)$ is the embedding of Theorem 4.2.4.

4.2.6 Proposition *The embedding* $\Theta : A \to D(A)$ *is continuous.*

Proof: Recall the Scott topology on $D(A)$ and the topology on A given in 4.1.4. We have

$$\begin{aligned}\Theta(b) \geq [a]_i &\Leftrightarrow \bigvee\{[b]_j : j \in I\} \geq [a]_i\\ &\Leftrightarrow b \equiv_i a\\ &\Leftrightarrow b \in B(a, i). \quad \Diamond\end{aligned}$$

In this paper we will only consider the following situations.

4.2.7 Examples

(1) Let $I = \{0, 1\}$ with $0 < 1$. Let A be a set and define $a \equiv_1 b \Leftrightarrow a = b$. Then $\{\equiv_i\}_{i\in I}$ is a family of separating equivalences on A which is upward consistent. It is not hard to see that $D(A) \cong A_\bot$, the flat domain over A.

(2) Let $\{\equiv_n\}_{n\in\omega}$ be a family of separating equivalences on the set A. Then $D(A) \cong \hat{A} \,\dot{\cup}\, (\dot{\bigcup}\{A/\equiv_n : n < \omega\})$, the compact elements being $\dot{\bigcup}\{A/\equiv_n : n < \omega\}$. Note that $\dot{\bigcup}\{A/\equiv_n : n < \omega\}$ is an ω-tree and that the infinite branches correspond to the elements of $\hat{A}$, that is $D(A)_m = \hat{A}$.

(3) Let $\{\equiv_s\}_{s\in I(J)}$ be a family of separating equivalences on A^J as in Lemma 4.2.2. Then $D(A^J)_c$ is no longer a tree even in the case $I = \omega$. However we have the following equivalence:

4.2.8 Proposition $D(A^J) \cong D(A)^J$.

Proof: An order preserving bijection $F : D(A^J)_c \to (D(A)^J)_c$ is given by $F([a]_s) = f_{a,s}$ where $f_{a,s}$ is defined by $f_{a,s}(j) = [a(j)]_{s(j)}$. $\Diamond$

4.3 Representation of functions

Fix sets $A_1, \ldots, A_m$ and A with families of separating equivalences $\{\equiv^1_i\}_{i\in I_1}, \ldots, \{\equiv^m_i\}_{i\in I_m}$ and $\{\equiv_i\}_{i\in I}$, respectively, which are assumed to be upward consistent, and where all index sets are closed under finite suprema. Let $f : A_1 \times \ldots \times A_m \to A$ be a function. Then we want to *represent* f by a *continuous* function $\phi_f : D(A_1) \times \ldots \times D(A_m) \to D(A)$. Of course there is no hope to represent all functions but we should be able to represent those which are continuous with respect to the families of equivalences as described in 4.1.4. Even for such functions there is in general no unique representation since there may be many ways to approximate a given element in an inverse limit and these approximations appear as elements in the representing domain. A requirement we do have on our representation ϕ_f is that it should be *faithful* in the sense that

$$\Theta(f(a_1, \ldots, a_m)) = \phi_f(\Theta_1(a_1), \ldots, \Theta_m(a_m))$$

where $\Theta_i : A_i \to D(A_i)$ and $\Theta : A \to D(A)$ are the embeddings of 4.2.5.

4.3.1 Definition Let $\lambda : I_1 \times \ldots \times I_m \to I$ be a monotone function. Then a function $f : A_1 \times \ldots \times A_m \to A$ is *λ-congruent* if

$$a_1 \equiv^1_{i_1} b_1, \ldots, a_m \equiv^m_{i_m} b_m \Rightarrow f(a_1, \ldots, a_m) \equiv_{\lambda(i_1, \ldots, i_m)} f(b_1, \ldots, b_m).$$

To say that $\equiv_i$ is a *congruence relation* for each $i \in I$ with respect to an m-ary operation f on A is to say that f is λ-congruent where $\lambda(i, \ldots, i) = i$.

4.3.2 Definition Let $f : A_1 \times \ldots \times A_m \to A$ be λ-congruent. Define $\phi^\lambda_f : D(A_1)_c \times \ldots \times D(A_m)_c \to D(A)_c$ by

$$\phi^\lambda_f([a_1]_{i_1}, \ldots, [a_m]_{i_m}) = [f(a_1, \ldots, a_m)]_{\lambda(i_1, \ldots, i_m)}.$$

Note that ϕ^λ_f is well-defined by virtue of f being λ-congruent.

4.3.3 Lemma *ϕ^λ_f is monotone.*

Proof: It suffices to prove monotonicity in each argument so we assume for notational simplicity that f is unary. Suppose $[a]_i \leq [b]_j$, that is $i \leq j$ and $a \equiv_i b$. By the λ-congrunce of f we have $f(a) \equiv_{\lambda(i)} f(b)$, and by the monotonicity of λ we have $\lambda(i) \leq \lambda(j)$. Thus

$$\phi^\lambda_f([a]_i) = [f(a)]_{\lambda(i)} = [f(b)]_{\lambda(i)} \leq [f(b)]_{\lambda(j)} = \phi^\lambda_f([b]_j). \quad \Diamond$$

It follows that we can extend ϕ^λ_f uniquely to a continuous function

$$\phi^\lambda_f : D(A_1) \times \ldots \times D(A_m) \to D(A).$$

This is the representation of f with respect to λ.

4.3.4 Definition Let the function $f : A_1 \times \ldots \times A_m \to A$ be λ-congruent. Then f is *continuous with respect to* λ if λ is unbounded, that is for each $i \in I$ there is $i_1 \in I_1, \ldots, i_m \in I_m$ such that $i \leq \lambda(i_1, \ldots, i_m)$.

4.3.5 Lemma Let $f : A_1 \times \ldots \times A_m \to A$ *be continuous with respect to* λ. *Then* ϕ^λ_f *is a faithful representation of* f, *that is for each* $(a_1, \ldots, a_m) \in A_1 \times \ldots \times A_m$

$$\Theta(f(a_1, \ldots, a_m)) = \phi^\lambda_f(\Theta_1(a_1), \ldots, \Theta_m(a_m)).$$

Proof: For notational simplicity we assume that $m = 1$. First recall that $\theta(a) = ([a]_i)_{i \in I}$ for $a \in A$ and hence that $\Theta(a) = \bigvee\{[a]_i : i \in I\}$ and $approx(\Theta(a)) = \{[a]_i : i \in I\}$. Thus

$$\begin{aligned}
\phi^\lambda_f(\Theta_1(a)) &= \phi^\lambda_f(\bigvee\{[a]_i : i \in I\}) \\
&= \bigvee\{\phi^\lambda_f([a]_i) : i \in I\} \\
&= \bigvee\{[f(a)]_{\lambda(i)} : i \in I\} \\
&\leq \bigvee\{[f(a)]_j : j \in I\} \\
&= \Theta(f(a)).
\end{aligned}$$

The converse inequality follows from the continuity condition on λ. For given $j \in I$ choose $i \in I$ such that $\lambda(i) \geq j$. Then $\phi^\lambda_f(\Theta_1(a)) \geq [f(a)]_{\lambda(i)} \geq [f(a)]_j$ so $\phi^\lambda_f(\Theta_1(a)) \geq \Theta(f(a))$. $\Diamond$

In particular, if f is an m-ary operation on A which is continuous with respect to λ then Θ is a homomorphism with respect to f. Thus an algebra A with a family of separating equivalences, for which each operation is continuous with respect to some λ, can be represented by a (structured) domain $D(A)$ in such a way that the embedding of A into $D(A)$ is a homomorphism.

4.4 Systems of equations over A

4.4.1 The system of equations Let A be a set together with a family of separating equivalences $\{\equiv_n\}_{n<\omega}$. We are going to consider possibly infinite systems of equations over A,

$$(E) \qquad X_i = F_i(X_{\beta(i,1)}, \ldots, X_{\beta(i,p(i))}) \qquad i \in I$$

where $p : I \to \omega$, $\beta(i, j) \in I$ for each $i \in I$ and $j = 1, \ldots, p(i)$, and where $F_i : A^{p(i)} \to A$ is λ_i-congruent for some given monotone $\lambda_i : \omega^{p(i)} \to \omega$. The central notion for guaranteeing the existence and uniqueness of solutions to (E) is guardedness.

4.4.2 Definition Let $F : A^m \to A$ be λ-congruent.
(i) F is *guarded* with respect to λ if $\lambda(n, \ldots, n) > n$ for each $n \in \omega$.
(ii) F is *non-expansive* with respect to λ if $\lambda(n, \ldots, n) \geq n$ for each $n \in \omega$.

For example, the successor operation on the natural numbers is guarded while addition is non-expansive. In $T(\Sigma, X)$ each n-ary function symbol $f \in \Sigma$ defines a guarded operation F on $T(\Sigma, X)$ defined by $F(t_1, \ldots, t_n) = f(t_1, \ldots, t_n)$. Finally the operation of concatenation on the left by a non-trivial finite sequence is guarded on the Cantor space.

4.4.3 Definition Consider the system (E) of equations in 4.4.1.
(i) We define a binary relation on the set of variables $\{X_i : i \in I\}$ by $X_i \xrightarrow{u} X_{\beta(i,j)}$ if F_i is *not* guarded.
(ii) The system of equations (E) is a *guarded system of equations* if the relation $\xrightarrow{u}$ is well-founded.

Consider the relation $\xrightarrow{u}$. To each $i \in I$ we associate a tree T_i as follows: $T_i^0 = \{(0, i)\}$ and $T_i^{n+1} = \{(n+1, j) : (n, k) \in T_i^n \text{ and } X_k \xrightarrow{u} X_j\}$. Set $T_i = \cup\{T_i^n : n < \omega\}$ and order T_i by the transitive closure of

$$(n, k) < (n+1, j) \Leftrightarrow X_k \xrightarrow{u} X_j.$$

Note that each T_i is a finitely branching tree since each F_j has finite arity. Thus, by Kőnig's lemma, we obtain the following proposition.

4.4.4 Proposition *The system of equations (E) is guarded if and only if each T_i is finite.*

The system of equations (E) over A induces a system of equations $(\tilde{E})$ over $D(A)$ as follows:

$$(\tilde{E}) \qquad X_i = \phi_{F_i}^{\lambda_i}(X_{\beta(i,1)}, \ldots, X_{\beta(i,p(i))}) \qquad i \in I.$$

By Lemma 3.2.5, $\Phi_{\tilde{E}} : D(A)^I \to D(A)^I$ is a continuous function and, by Theorem 3.2.6, $fix(\Phi_{\tilde{E}})$ provides the least solution to the equation system $(\tilde{E})$ over $D(A)$. Under appropriate conditions this is also a solution of (E) over $\hat{A} = \varprojlim A/{\equiv_n}$.

4.4.5 Theorem *Let (E) be the system of equations over A in 4.4.1. Let λ_i be the congruence function associated with F_i. If (E) is guarded and each F_i is non-expansive then (E) has a unique solution over $\hat{A} = \varprojlim A/\equiv_n$.*

Proof: Let $\rho : D(A) \to \omega \cup \{\omega\}$ be a *rank function* defined by

$$\rho(x) = \begin{cases} n & \text{if } x = [a]_n \text{ for some } a \in A \\ \omega & \text{otherwise.} \end{cases}$$

It clearly suffices for both existence and uniqueness to show that $\rho(fix(\Phi_{\bar{E}})(i)) = \omega$ for each $i \in I$. By induction on n we therefore show that $\rho(fix(\Phi_{\bar{E}})(i)) > n$ for each i and n.

Recall that $fix(\Phi_{\bar{E}}) = \bigvee_{m<\omega}\Phi^m_{\bar{E}}(\lambda i.\bot)$, where $\Phi^m_{\bar{E}}$ is the m'th iterate of $\Phi_{\bar{E}}$. For readability we write $\Phi^m_{\bar{E}}$ for $\Phi^m_{\bar{E}}(\lambda i.\bot)$, and ϕ_i for $\phi_{F_i}^{\lambda_i}$. It suffices to show, for each n,

$$(*) \qquad (\forall i \in I)(\exists m)(\rho(\Phi^m_{\bar{E}}(i)) > n).$$

We use induction on n. First assume $n = 0$. Then (*) is proved by induction on $ht(T_i)$, the height of T_i. By Proposition 4.4.4 each T_i has finite height. Suppose $ht(T_i) = 0$. Then $T_i = \{0, i\}\}$ and F_i is guarded. Thus

$$\begin{aligned}\Phi^1_{\bar{E}}(i) &= \phi_i(\Phi^0_{\bar{E}}(\beta(i, 1)), \dots, \Phi^0_{\bar{E}}(\beta(i, p(i)))) \\ &= \phi_i(\bot, \dots, \bot).\end{aligned}$$

It follows that $\rho(\Phi^1_{\bar{E}}(i)) = \rho(\phi_i(\bot, \dots, \bot)) = \lambda_i(0, \dots, 0) > 0$ where the last inequality witnesses the guardedness of F_i.

Now suppose $(\exists m)(\rho(\Phi^m_{\bar{E}}(j)) > 0)$ is true for all j such that $ht(T_j) \le k$ and assume that $ht(T_i) = k + 1$. Then T_i is of the form

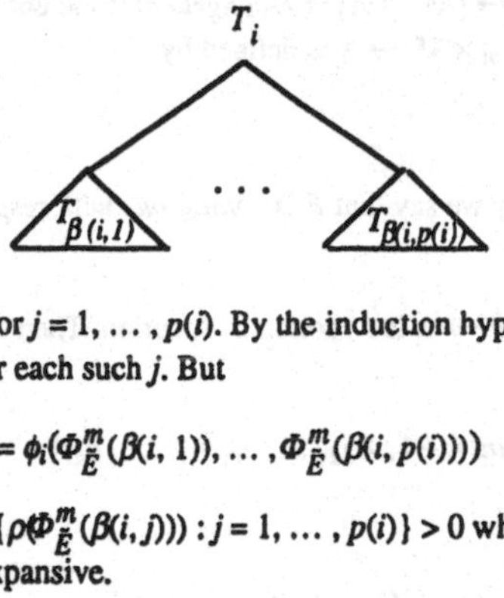

where $ht(T_{\beta(i,j)}) \le k$ for $j = 1, \dots, p(i)$. By the induction hypothesis there is m such that $\rho(\Phi^m_{\bar{E}}(\beta(i, j))) > 0$ for each such j. But

$$\Phi^{m+1}_{\bar{E}}(i) = \phi_i(\Phi^m_{\bar{E}}(\beta(i, 1)), \dots, \Phi^m_{\bar{E}}(\beta(i, p(i))))$$

so $\rho(\Phi^{m+1}_{\bar{E}}(i)) \ge min\{\rho(\Phi^m_{\bar{E}}(\beta(i, j))) : j = 1, \dots, p(i)\} > 0$ where the first inequality holds since F_i is assumed to be non-expansive.

Now we assume (*) holds for n in order to prove it for $n + 1$. Again we use induction on $ht(T_i)$. If $ht(T_i) = 0$ then F_i is guarded. Let m be such that $\rho(\Phi^m_{\bar{E}}(\beta(i, j))) > n$ for $j = 1, \dots, p(i)$. As above,

$$\Phi^{m+1}_{\bar{E}}(i) = \phi_i(\Phi^m_{\bar{E}}(\beta(i, 1)), \dots, \Phi^m_{\bar{E}}(\beta(i, p(i)))),$$

so $\rho(\Phi^{m+1}_{\bar{E}}(i)) > min\{\rho(\Phi^m_{\bar{E}}(\beta(i, j))) : j = 1, \dots, p(i)\} \ge n + 1$ by virtue of F_i being guarded. The case when $ht(T_i) = k + 1$ is entirely similar to the proof for $n = 0$. ◊

4.4.6 Example Consider the Cantor space 2^ω with the family of separating equivalences described in 4.1.2. Define operations $c_0, c_1 : 2^\omega \longrightarrow 2^\omega$ by

$$c_i(f)(n) = \begin{cases} i & \text{if } n = 0 \\ f(n-1) & \text{if } n > 0 \end{cases}$$

that is c_i concatinates f with i on the left. Clearly each c_i is a guarded operation. Let $f \in 2^\omega$ and consider the following guarded system of equations:

$$(E) \qquad X_n = c_{f(n)}(X_{n+1}) \qquad n \in \omega.$$

Thus (E) has a unique solution over 2^ω. It is easy to see that for this solution, $X_0 = f$. Thus, *each element in* 2^ω *is obtained from some guarded system of equations using only the operations* c_i.

4.5 Equations depending on parameters

4.5.1 The system of equations In this section we fix sets $A_1, \ldots, A_m$ and A together with families of separating equivalences $\{\equiv_i^1\}_{i \in I_1}, \ldots, \{\equiv_i^m\}_{i \in I_m}$ and $\{\equiv_n\}_{n \in \omega}$, respectively, which are upward consistent, and where all index sets are closed under finite suprema. Let I be a non-empty possibly infinite set and let $p : I \longrightarrow \omega$. Suppose we are given functions $F_i : A_1 \times \ldots \times A_m \longrightarrow [A^{p(i)} \longrightarrow A]$ for each $i \in I$. Let β be a function such that $\beta(i, j) \in I$ for each $i \in I$ and $j = 1, \ldots, p(i)$. Then for each $a = (a_1, \ldots, a_m) \in A_1 \times \ldots \times A_m$ we obtain a system of equations (E_a) by

$$(E_a) \qquad X_i = F_i(a)(X_{\beta(i,1)}, \ldots, X_{\beta(i,p(i))}) \qquad i \in I.$$

We shall give sufficient conditions for when (E_a) has a unique solution over $\hat{A}$ for each a and, in particular, when such a solution is obtained continuously from a.

We say that a function $F : A_1 \times \ldots \times A_m \longrightarrow [A^k \longrightarrow A]$ is *λ-congruent* if the uncurried version uF of F is λ-congruent. Recall that $uF : A_1 \times \ldots \times A_m \times A^k \longrightarrow A$ is defined by

$$uF(a, b) = F(a)(b)$$

where $a \in A_1 \times \ldots \times A_m$ and $b \in A^k$. Similarly we say that F is *continuous with respect to* λ if uF is continuous with respect to λ.

4.5.2 Definition Suppose $\lambda : I_1 \times \ldots \times I_m \times \omega^k \longrightarrow \omega$ is a monotone function. Then define $\tilde{\lambda} : \omega^k \longrightarrow \omega$ by

$$\tilde{\lambda}(n_1, \ldots, n_k) = \bigvee_{i_1 \in I_1} \cdots \bigvee_{i_m \in I_m} \min\{n+1, \lambda(i_1, \ldots, i_m, n_1, \ldots, n_k)\}$$

where $n = \min\{n_1, \ldots, n_k\}$.

4.5.3 Lemma *Let* $F : A_1 \times \ldots \times A_m \longrightarrow [A^k \longrightarrow A]$, *and let* $a \in A_1 \times \ldots \times A_m$.

(i) *If F is λ-congruent then $F(a)$ is $\tilde{\lambda}$-congruent.*

(ii) *If F is continuous with respect to λ then $F(a)$ is continuous with respect to $\tilde{\lambda}$.*

Proof: (i) Clearly $\tilde{\lambda}$ is monotone. Given $n_1, \ldots, n_k \in \omega^k$ let $n = \min\{n_1, \ldots, n_k\}$. From the definition of $\tilde{\lambda}$ we see that there is $i_1, \ldots, i_m$ such that

$$(*) \qquad \tilde{\lambda}(n_1, \ldots, n_k) \leq \lambda(i_1, \ldots, i_m, n_1, \ldots, n_k).$$

So suppose $b_1 \equiv_{n_1} b_1', \ldots, b_k \equiv_{n_k} b_k'$ and let $a \in A_1 \times \ldots \times A_m$. Choose $i_1, \ldots, i_m$ sufficiently large for (*) to hold. Thus, for $b = (b_1, \ldots, b_k)$ and $b' = (b_1', \ldots, b_k')$, we have

$$F(a)(b) = uF(a, b) \equiv_{\lambda(i_1,\ldots,i_m,n_1,\ldots,n_k)} uF(a, b') = F(a)(b').$$

But then, by (*), $F(a)(b) \equiv_{\tilde{\lambda}(n_1,\ldots,n_k)} F(a)(b')$.
(ii) Suppose F is continuous with respect to λ, that is λ is unbounded. Thus given $n \in \omega$ there is $i_1, \ldots, i_m$ and t such that $\lambda(i_1, \ldots, i_m, t, \ldots, t) \geq n$. But then, again from the definition, $\tilde{\lambda}(t, \ldots, t) \geq n$ so that $\tilde{\lambda}$ is unbounded. ◊

Let us again consider the family of systems of equations (E_a) of 4.5.1 for $a \in A_1 \times \ldots \times A_m$. We assume that each F_i is λ_i-congruent. Then, when we say that $F_i(a)$ or (E_a) has a certain property, for example $F_i(a)$ is non-expansive or (E_a) is guarded, we mean this with respect to the $\tilde{\lambda}_i$. Note that $F_i(a)$ being non-expansive or (E_a) being guarded depends only on the $\tilde{\lambda}_i$ and hence is *independent* of the choice of a.

4.5.4 Theorem *Let $A_1, \ldots, A_m$ and A be sets with families of separating equivalences $\{\equiv_i^1\}_{i \in I_1}, \ldots, \{\equiv_i^m\}_{i \in I_m}$ and $\{\equiv_n\}_{n \in \omega}$, respectively, which are upward consistent, and where all index sets are closed under finite suprema. Let I be a non-empty possibly infinite set and let $p : I \to \omega$. Suppose we are given functions $F_i : A_1 \times \ldots \times A_m \to [A^{p(i)} \to A]$ for each $i \in I$, which are continuous with respect to λ_i. If $F_i(a)$ is non-expansive for each i and (E_a) is guarded then there is a continuous function $G : A_1 \times \ldots \times A_m \to \hat{A}^I$ such that*

$$X_i = G(a)(i) \qquad\qquad i \in I$$

is the unique solution of (E_a) over $\hat{A}$.

Proof: Let $\phi_{uF_i}^{\lambda_i} : D(A_1) \times \ldots \times D(A_m) \times D(A)^{p(i)} \to D(A)$ be the continuous function representing uF_i with respect to λ_i. Then set $\phi_i = c(\phi_{uF_i}^{\lambda_i})$, where c is the curry operation. That is $\phi_i : D(A_1) \times \ldots \times D(A_m) \to [D(A)^{p(i)} \to D(A)]$ is defined by

$$\phi_i(x_1, \ldots, x_m)(y_1, \ldots, y_{p(i)}) = \phi_{uF_i}^{\lambda_i}(x_1, \ldots, x_m, y_1, \ldots, y_{p(i)}).$$

We know that each ϕ_i is continuous by the fact that currying is a continuous operation on domains. By Proposition 3.3.2, the function $\Xi : D(A_1) \times \ldots \times D(A_m) \to [D(A)^I \to D(A)^I]$ defined by $\Xi(x) = \Phi_{E_x}$ is continuous, where (E_x) is the system of equations obtained from the $\phi_i(x)$ as in 3.3.1. Furthermore, by Theorem 3.3.3, the function $\Gamma : D(A_1) \times \ldots \times D(A_m) \to D(A)^I$ defined by

$$\Gamma(x) = fix(\Xi(x)) = fix(\Phi_{E_x})$$

is continuous and provides the least solution of the system of equations (E_x) over $D(A)^I$.

It thus remains to prove that if $a = (a_1, \ldots, a_m) \in A_1 \times \ldots \times A_m$ then $\Gamma(\Theta_1(a_1), \ldots, \Theta_m(a_m)) \in \hat{A}^I$, where we for simplicity identify $D(A)_m$ with $\hat{A}$ as in 4.2.6. For this it suffices to show that $\Gamma(\Theta_1(a_1), \ldots, \Theta_m(a_m))(i)$ is maximal for each $i \in I$.

Let $a \in A_1 \times \ldots \times A_m$. Then

$$\begin{aligned}\phi_{F_i(a)}^{\tilde{\lambda}_i}([b_1]_{n_1}, \ldots, [b_k]_{n_k}) &= [F_i(a)(b_1, \ldots, b_k)]_{\tilde{\lambda}_i(n_1,\ldots,n_k)} \\ &= [uF_i(a, b_1, \ldots, b_k)]_{\tilde{\lambda}_i(n_1,\ldots,n_k)}\end{aligned}$$

$$\begin{aligned}&\le [uF_i(a, b_1, \ldots, b_k)]\lambda_i(i_1,\ldots,i_m,n_1,\ldots,n_k) \qquad \text{some } i_j\\ &= \phi^{\lambda_i}_{uF_i}([a_1]_{i_1}, \ldots, [a_m]_{i_m}, [b_1]_{n_1}, \ldots, [b_k]_{n_k})\\ &= \phi_i([a_1]_{i_1}, \ldots, [a_m]_{i_m})([b_1]_{n_1}, \ldots, [b_k]_{n_k})\\ &\le \phi_i(\Theta_1(a_1), \ldots, \Theta_m(a_m))([b_1]_{n_1}, \ldots, [b_k]_{n_k})\end{aligned}$$

where the last inequality is due to the monotonicity of ϕ_i. It follows that $\phi^{\tilde{\lambda}_i}_{F_i(a)} \le \phi_i(\Theta_1(a_1), \ldots, \Theta_m(a_m))$.

Let $\tilde{E}_a$ be the system of equations obtained from the functions $\phi^{\tilde{\lambda}_i}_{F_i(a)}$. Then, by the above, $\Phi_{\tilde{E}_a} \le \Phi_{E_{\Theta(a)}}$, where $\Theta(a) = (\Theta_1(a_1), \ldots, \Theta_m(a_m))$, and hence

$$fix(\Phi_{\tilde{E}_a}) \le fix(\Phi_{E_{\Theta(a)}}) = \Gamma(\Theta(a)).$$

But, by our hypothesis and (the proof of) Theorem 4.4.5, $fix(\Phi_{\tilde{E}_a})$ gives a unique solution and this solution lies in $\hat{A}^I$. Thus $\Gamma(\Theta(a)) \in \hat{A}^I$. Now we define $G : A_1 \times \ldots \times A_m \rightarrow \hat{A}^I$ by

$$G(a_1, \ldots, a_m) = \Gamma(\Theta_1(a_1), \ldots, \Theta_m(a_m)).$$

Note that G is continuous by virtue of Γ and Θ being continuous. ◊

5. Applications to synchronous concurrent algorithms

5.1 Overview

We now return to the tasks of 2.5 and address the question of the existence, uniqueness, continuity and effectivity of the family of functions

$$v_i : T \times [T \rightarrow A]^J \times A^I \rightarrow A \qquad i \in I,$$

which defines the output value $v_i(t, a, x) \in A$ of the module m_i at time t, if the SCA is processing input streams $a = (a_j : j \in J) \in [T \rightarrow A]^J$ from the initial state $x = (x_i : i \in I) \in A^I$ of the network. We require total functions that are unique solutions of the system (E) of equations in 2.3.4. Such functions depend on the synchronising functions δ_{ij} and γ_{ij} and on the equations that represent the architecture; in particular, the notion of guardedness will be used to imply the existence and uniqueness of the functions v_i.

To use the algebraic methods of this paper, we transform the problem of solving for the functions v_i into the problem of solving for their curried forms:

$$cv_i : [T \rightarrow A]^J \times A^I \rightarrow [T \rightarrow A],$$

defined for $a \in [T \rightarrow A]^J$, $x \in A^I$, and $t \in T$ by

$$(cv_i)(a, x)(t) = v_i(t, a, x).$$

We must construct a set of equations equivalent to (E) whose solutions lead to cv_i; this is done as follows:

For each $a \in [T \rightarrow A]^J$, $x \in A^I$, we define a system of equations

$$E_{a,x} = \{e_{a,x,i} : i \in I\}$$

over $[T \to A]$. The existence and uniqueness of solutions to $(E_{a,x})$ correspond to the existence and uniqueness of the streams $(cv_i)(a, x) \in [T \to A]$.

We are interested in the properties of the synchronising functions and architecture that guarantee the existence and uniqueness of these streams for all i, a, x. This process of assigning the new equations over $[T \to A]$ and obtaining their solutions involves a map

$$W : [T \to A]^J \times A^I \to [T \to A]^I$$

for which

$$W(a, x)(i) = (cv_i)(a, x).$$

We determine sufficient conditions for this map to be total, continuous and effective.

5.2 Algebraic methods

The methods used to solve the equations $(E_{a,x})$ in $[T \to A]$ are those of the last section. To define $(E_{a,x})$ we begin by defining an operation on $[T \to A]$ that is based on the module functions on A.

Fix any $a \in [T \to A]^J$, $x \in A^I$, and for all $i \in I$ define, from the functions f_i, δ_{ij} and γ_{ij}, the function $F_i(a, x) : [T \to A]^{p(i)} \to [T \to A]$ by

$$F_i(a, x)(b_1, \ldots, b_{p(i)})(0) = x_i$$

and for $t > 0$,

$$F_i(a, x)(b_1, \ldots, b_{p(i)})(t) = f_i(b_1(\delta_{i1}(t, a, x)), \ldots, b_{p(i)}(\delta_{ip(i)}(t, a, x)), a_{\alpha(i,1)}(\gamma_{i1}(t, a, x)), \ldots, a_{\alpha(i,q(i))}(\gamma_{iq(i)}(t, a, x))).$$

With this operation we define the equations of $(E_{a,x})$.

5.2.1 Lemma *Consider the following systems of equations: for all $i \in I$, $t \in T$, $a \in [T \to A]^J$, $x \in A^I$,*

(I) $v_i(t, a, x) = x_i$. if $t = 0$

$= f_i(v_{\beta(i,1)}(\delta_{i1}(t, a, x), a, x), \ldots, v_{\beta(i,p(i))}(\delta_{ip(i)}(t, a, x), a, x), a_{\alpha(i,1)}(\gamma_{i1}(t, a, x)), \ldots, a_{\alpha(i,q(i))}(\gamma_{iq(i)}(t, a, x)))$ if $t > 0$.

(II) $V_i(a,x) = F_i(a,x)(V_{\beta(i,1)}(a, x), \ldots, V_{\beta(i,p(i))}(a, x))$.

Suppose $v_i : T \times [T \to A]^J \times A^I \to A$, for $i \in I$, is a family of total functions that is a solution to the system of equations (I). Then the family in their curried form

$$cv_i : [T \to A]^J \times A^I \to [T \to A],$$

for $i \in I$, is a solution to the system of equations (II).

Conversely, suppose $V_i : [T \to A]^J \times A^I \to [T \to A]$ *for* $i \in I$ *is a family of total functions that is a solution to the system of equations* (II). *Then the family in their uncurried form*

$$uV_i : T \times [T \to A]^J \times A^I \to A$$

for $i \in I$ *is a solution to the system of equations* (I).

Proof. We prove the first statement. Suppose v_i satisfies the system (I). We show that cv_i satisfies the system (II). Consider the substitution of cv_i in the RHS of (II) at $t = 0$:

$$F_i(a, x)(cv_{\beta(i,1)}(a, x), \ldots, cv_{\beta(i,p(i))}(a, x))(0)$$
$$= x_i \qquad \text{by definition of } F_i(a,x);$$
$$= v_i(0, a, x) \qquad \text{by (I);}$$
$$= cv_i(a, x)(0) \qquad \text{by definition of } cv_i.$$

So the equation (II) is true at $t = 0$. Now consider the RHS of (II) at $t > 0$:

$$F_i(a, x)(cv_{\beta(i,1)}(a, x), \ldots, cv_{\beta(i,p(i))}(a, x))(t)$$
$$= f_i(cv_{\beta(i,1)}(a, x)(\delta_{i1}(t, a, x)), \ldots, cv_{\beta(i,p(i))}(a, x)(\delta_{ip(i)}(t, a, x)),$$
$$a_{\alpha(i,1)}(\gamma_{i1}(t, a, x)), \ldots, a_{\alpha(i,q(i))}(\gamma_{iq(i)}(t, a, x)))$$
$$= f_i(v_{\beta(i,1)}(\delta_{i1}(t, a, x), a, x), \ldots, v_{\beta(i,p(i))}(\delta_{ip(i)}(t, a, x), a, x),$$
$$a_{\alpha(i,1)}(\gamma_{i1}(t, a, x)), \ldots, a_{\alpha(i,q(i))}(\gamma_{iq(i)}(t, a, x)));$$
$$= v_i(t, a, x) \qquad \text{by (I)}$$
$$= cv_i(a, x)(t) \qquad \text{by definition of } cv_i.$$

So the equation is satisfied.

Conversely, we prove the second statement. Suppose V_i satisfies the system (II). We show that uV_i satisfies the system (I). We observe that $V_i(a, x)(0) = x_i$ and so, by definition of uV_i,

$$uV_i(0, a, x) = V_i(a, x)(0) = x_i;$$

and equation (I) is satisfied at $t = 0$. Now we consider the RHS of (I) in case $t > 0$:

$$f_i(uV_{\beta(i,1)}(\delta_{i1}(t, a, x), a, x), \ldots, uV_{\beta(i,p(i))}(\delta_{ip(i)}(t, a, x), a, x),$$
$$a_{\alpha(i,1)}(\gamma_{i1}(t, a, x)), \ldots, a_{\alpha(i,q(i))}(\gamma_{iq(i)}(t, a, x)))$$
$$= f_i(V_{\beta(i,1)}(a, x)(\delta_{i1}(t, a, x)), \ldots, V_{\beta(i,p(i))}(a, x)(\delta_{ip(i)}(t, a, x)),$$
$$a_{\alpha(i,1)}(\gamma_{i1}(t, a, x)), \ldots, a_{\alpha(i,q(i))}(\gamma_{iq(i)}(t, a, x)));$$
$$= F_i(a, x)(V_{\beta(i,1)}(a, x), \ldots, V_{\beta(i,p(i))}(a, x)(t)$$
$$= V_i(a, x)(t) \qquad \text{since equation (II) is satisfied;}$$
$$= uV_i(t, a, x) \qquad \text{by definition.}$$

So the equation (I) is satisfied. ◊

5.3 Equations

In the light of Lemma 5.2.1 it suffices to solve the system of equations

$$(E_{a,x}) \qquad X_i = F_i(a, x)(X_{\beta(i,1)}, \ldots, X_{\beta(i,p(i))}) \qquad i \in I,$$

over $[T \to A]$, where $a \in [T \to A]^J$ and $x \in A^I$. For this we intend to use Theorem 4.5.4. Therefore we need to introduce families of separating equivalences on these structures.

For $n \in \omega$ we define $\equiv_n$ on $[T \to A]$ by

$$f \equiv_n g \Leftrightarrow (\forall t < n)(f(t) = g(t)).$$

Clearly, $\{\equiv_n\}_{n \in \omega}$ is a family of separating equivalences on $[T \to A]$. In case A is finite then we essentially have the Cantor set as in Example 4.1.2 (4). For A we define a family of separating equivalences $\{\equiv_i\}_{i<2}$ by $a \equiv_0 b$ for all $a, b \in A$ and $a \equiv_1 b \Leftrightarrow a = b$. (Cf. Example 4.2.7 (1).) Now we obtain a family of separating equivalences $\{\equiv_u\}_{u \in \omega^{(J)}}$ on $[T \to A]^J$ and $\{\equiv_v\}_{v \in 2^{(I)}}$ on A^I as in Lemma 4.1.3. These are the ones we consider in the sequel.

5.3.1 Theorem *Let $F_i : [T \to A]^J \times A^I \to [[T \to A]^{p(i)} \to [T \to A]]$ be continuous with respect to λ_i for each $i \in I$. If $F_i(a, x)$ is non-expansive for each $i \in I$* and *$(E_{a,x})$ is guarded then there is a continuous function $W : [T \to A]^J \times A^I \to [T \to A]^I$ such that*

$$X_i = W(a, x)(i) \qquad i \in I$$

is the unique solution of $(E_{a,x})$ over $[T \to A]$.

Proof: This is Theorem 4.5.4, noting that $[T \to A] \equiv \widehat{[T \to A]}$. ◊

5.3.2 Corollary *Under the conditions of Theorem* 5.3.1, *the system of equations* 2.3.4 *has a unique solution.*

Proof: By Lemma 5.2.1. ◊

5.4 Solutions

The definition of the F_i's depend on the f_i's and, most important for continuity considerations, on the delay functions δ_{ij} and γ_{ij}. We shall now find conditions on the delay functions which are natural and also sufficient to guarantee that the hypotheses of Theorem 5.3.1 hold and hence that the equation systems of 2.3.4 have unique solutions and that these are obtained continuously from a and x.

5.4.1 Finitely determined synchronisation At each module m_i at each $t \in T$, $a \in [T \to A]^J$ and $x \in A^I$, the synchronisation times

$$\delta_{ij}(t, a, x) \text{ and } \gamma_{ij}(t, a, x)$$

for the $p(i)$ input modules and $q(i)$ input streams to m_i are determined from finite parts of a and x. Hence, the computation performed at m_i at time t is determined by finite parts of a and x. This is formalised as follows.

5.4.2 Definition The synchronisation map $\delta_{ij} : T \times [T \to A]^J \times A^I \to T$ (or $\gamma_{ij} : T \times [T \to A]^J \times A^I \to T$) is said to be *uniformly finitely determined* if for each $t \in T$ there is $u \in \omega^{(J)}$ and $v \in 2^{(I)}$ such that

$$a \equiv_u a' \text{ and } x \equiv_v x' \Rightarrow \delta_{ij}(t, a, x) = \delta_{ij}(t, a', x').$$

If δ_{ij} is uniformly finitely determined then there exists a function $\eta_{ij} : T \rightarrow \omega^{(J)} \times 2^{(I)}$ which calculates a required pair $\eta_{ij}(t) = (u, v)$; that is, (u, v) witnesses that δ_{ij} is uniformly finitely determined at time t. A function $\varepsilon_{ij} : T \rightarrow \omega^{(J)} \times 2^{(I)}$ is associated with γ_{ij} similarly.

Without loss of generality, since $\omega^{(J)} \times 2^{(I)}$ is closed under finite suprema, we can choose η_{ij} and ε_{ij} to be monotone, i.e. if $t \leq t'$ then $\eta_{ij}(t) \leq \eta_{ij}(t')$. Furthermore we set $\eta_{ij}(0) = \varepsilon_{ij}(0) =$ least element in $\omega^{(J)} \times 2^{(I)}$.

5.4.3 Bounded synchronisation The synchronisation map δ_{ij} (or γ_{ij}) is *uniformly bounded* if for each $t \in T, t > 0$, the set

$$\{\delta_{ij}(t, a, x) : a \in [T \rightarrow A]^J, x \in A^I\}$$

is bounded in T. That is, for each $t \in T$ there is $t' \in T$ such that for all a and x, $\delta_{ij}(t, a, x) \leq t'$. We say that the synchronisation function δ_{ij} (or γ_{ij}) is *uniformly bounded by the present* if $\delta_{ij}(t, a, x) \leq t$ for all t, a and x.

Under the assumption that each synchronisation map δ_{ij} is uniformly bounded there is for each i and j a monotone function $r_{ij} : \omega \rightarrow \omega$ such that

$$r_{ij}(n) \geq \sup\{\delta_{ij}(t, a, x) : 0 < t < n, a \in [T \rightarrow A]^J, x \in A^I\}$$

for $n > 1$. We always set $r_{ij}(1) = 0$. The map δ_{ij} is uniformly bounded by the present if and only if we can choose $r_{ij}(n) = n - 1$ for $n > 0$.

We think that finitely determined synchronisation is natural for an SCA. Bounded synchronisation, however, is a restriction. Nonetheless, in most natural situations the synchronisation functions will be bounded. In fact, most often we have all the synchronisation functions bounded by the present. *Observe that this does allow instantaneous transmission of data along all internal channels.*

Under the assumptions 5.4.1 and 5.4.3 we will define

$$\lambda_i : \omega^{(J)} \times 2^{(I)} \times \omega^{p(i)} \rightarrow \omega$$

such that F_i will be continuous with respect to λ_i.

5.4.4 Definition For $u \in \omega^{(J)}$, $v \in 2^{(I)}$ and $m_1, \dots, m_{p(i)} \in \omega$ define

$$\lambda_i(u, v, m_1, \dots, m_{p(i)}) = \begin{cases} 0 & \text{if } v(i) = 0 \\ 1 & \text{if } v(i) \neq 0 \text{ and } m = 0 \\ (\text{largest } n)\Phi(i, n) & \text{otherwise,} \end{cases}$$

where $m = min\{m_1, \dots, m_{p(i)}\}$, and $\Phi(i, n)$ is defined by

$$\Phi(i, n) \Leftrightarrow (1 \leq n \leq m + 1) \wedge [\textstyle\bigwedge_{j=1,\dots p(i)}(r_{ij}(n) < m \wedge \eta_{ij}(n - 1) \leq (u, v))] \\ \wedge [\textstyle\bigwedge_{j=1,\dots q(i)}(\varepsilon_{ij}(n - 1) \leq (u, v))],$$

and where r_{ij}, η_{ij} and ε_{ij} satisfy the assumptions made above.

5.4.5 Lemma *Suppose that each synchronisation function δ_{ij} and γ_{ij} is uniformly finitely determined and each δ_{ij} is uniformly bounded. Then each λ_i is monotone and unbounded.*

Proof: The monotonicity of λ_i follows immediately from its definition. To see that λ_i is unbounded let $n > 0$. Choose m large so that $m > n$ and $m > r_{ij}(n)$ for $j = 1, \dots, p(i)$. Then let

$$(u, v) = \eta_{ij}(n-1) \vee \varepsilon_{ij}(n-1) \vee (u_0, v_i)$$

where u_0 is some element in $\omega^{(J)}$ and $v_i(j) = 1$ if $j = i$ and $v_i(j) = 0$ otherwise. Then clearly $\lambda_i(u, v, m, \dots, m) \geq n$. ◊

5.4.6 Lemma *Each F_i is λ_i-congruent.*

Proof: Recalling 4.5.1, we need to show that $uF_i : [T \to A]^J \times A^I \times [T \to A]^{p(i)} \to [T \to A]$ is λ_i-congruent. So let $(u, v) \in \omega^{(J)} \times 2^{(I)}$ and let $m \in \omega$. Suppose $a \equiv_u a'$, $x \equiv_v x'$ and $b_i \equiv_m b_i'$ for $i = 1, \dots, p(i)$. We must show that

$$uF_i(a, x, b) \equiv_{\lambda_i(u,v,m)} uF_i(a', x', b')$$

where $m = (m, \dots, m) \in \omega^{p(i)}$, $b = (b_1, \dots, b_{p(i)})$ and $b' = (b_1', \dots, b_{p(i)}')$. Let $n = \lambda_i(u, v, m)$. Thus we must show that for each $t < n$, $uF_i(a, x, b)(t) = uF_i(a', x', b')(t)$.

If $n = 0$ then this is vacuously true. Suppose therefore $n > 0$. Then, by the definition of λ_i, $v(i) = 1$, and hence $x_i = x_i'$. That is, $uF_i(a, x, b)(0) = x_i = x_i' = uF_i(a', x', b')(0)$. For $t > 0$,

$$uF_i(a, x, b)(t) =$$
$$f_i(b_1(\delta_{i1}(t, a, x)), \dots, b_{p(i)}(\delta_{ip(i)}(t, a, x)), a_{\alpha(i,1)}(\gamma_{i1}(t, a, x)), \dots, a_{\alpha(i,q(i))}(\gamma_{iq(i)}(t, a, x))).$$

Since $\eta_{ij}(n-1) \leq (u, v)$ and $\gamma_{ij}(n-1) \leq (u, v)$ we have, for $t < n$,

$$\gamma_{ij}(t, a, x) = \gamma_{ij}(t, a', x')$$

and

$$\delta_{ij}(t, a, x) = \delta_{ij}(t, a', x') \leq r(n) < m.$$

But then $a_{\alpha(i,j)}(\gamma_{ij}(t, a, x)) = a_{\alpha(i,j)}(\gamma_{ij}(t, a', x'))$ and $b_j(\delta_{ij}(t, a, x) = b_j'(\delta_{ij}(t, a', x'))$. It follows that, for $t < n$, $uF_i(a, x, b)(t) = uF_i(a', x', b')(t)$, that is $uF_i(a, x, b) \equiv_n uF_i(a', x', b')$. ◊

5.4.7 Lemma *Suppose each synchronisation function δ_{ij} and γ_{ij} are uniformly finitely determined.*

(i) *If, for $j = 1, \dots, p(i)$,*

$$\delta_{ij}(t, a, x) < t$$

for each $a \in [T \to A]^J$, $x \in A^I$ and $t > 0$, then $F_i(a, x)$ is guarded.

(ii) *If, for $j = 1, \dots, p(i)$,*

$$\delta_{ij}(t, a, x) \leq t$$

for each $a \in [T \to A]^J$, $x \in A^I$ and $t > 0$, then *$F_i(a, x)$ is non-expansive.*

Proof: We need to show that $\tilde{\lambda}_i(m) = \bigvee_u \bigvee_v \lambda_i(u, v, m)$ has the required properties, as described in 4.5, where $m = (m_1, \dots, m_{p(i)})$. Let $m = min\{m_1, \dots, m_{p(i)}\}$.

(i) If $\delta_{ij}(t, a, x) < t$ then we can choose r_{ij} defined by $r_{ij}(n+1) = n - 1$, for $n > 0$, as a bounding function. In case $m = 0$ choose v such that $v(i) = 1$. Thus $\tilde{\lambda}_i(m) = 1$. If $m > 0$ choose (u, v) sufficiently

large so that $\eta_{ij}(m) \leq (u, v)$ and $\varepsilon_{ij}(m) \leq (u, v)$. But $r_{ij}(m+1) = m - 1 < m$, and hence $\tilde{\lambda}_i(m) = m + 1$.
(ii) In case $\delta_{ij}(t, a, x) \leq t$ then $r_{ij}(n) = n - 1, n > 0$, is a bounding function. Then, by an analogous argument, $\tilde{\lambda}_i(m) \geq m$. ◊

5.4.8 Definition Let us consider an SCA defined by the system of equations in 2.3.4. We define a relation $\xrightarrow{u}$ on the v_i's by

$$v_i \xrightarrow{u} v_j \Leftrightarrow (\exists t > 0)(\exists a)(\exists x)(\delta_{ij}(t, a, x) \geq t);$$

that is, $v_i \xrightarrow{u} v_j$ if δ_{ij} does not satisfy assumption D of 2.4.1. Then we say that the SCA is *guarded* if the relation $\xrightarrow{u}$ is well-founded.

5.4.9 Theorem *Consider an* SCA *whose synchronisation functions are uniformly finitely determined. Suppose that each internal synchronisation function* δ_{ij} *is uniformly bounded by the present. If the* SCA *is guarded then there is a continuous function* $W : [T \to A]^J \times A^I \to [T \to A]^I$ *such that*

$$W(a, x)(i) = (cv_i)(a, x) \qquad i \in I$$

is the unique solution of the system of equations $(E_{a,x})$, *for each a and x. Furthermore, the maps*

$$cv_i : [T \to A]^J \times A^I \to [T \to A] \quad \textit{and} \quad v_i : T \times [T \to A]^J \times A^I \to A \qquad i \in I$$

are continuous.

Proof: For each $i \in I$ and $j = 1, \dots, p(i)$ we choose as strict a bounding function r_{ij} as possible. Then we define λ_i as in 5.4.4, so that each F_i is λ_i-congruent by Lemma 5.4.6. By Lemma 5.4.7, each $F_i(a, x)$ is non-expansive and the system of equations $(E_{a,x})$ is guarded. Thus W exists and is continuous by Theorem 5.3.1.

It remains to show that cv_i is continuous for each $i \in I$. The projection function $\pi_i : [T \to A]^I \to [T \to A]$, defined by $\pi_i(a) = a(i)$, is continuous since the topology on $[T \to A]^I$ is the Tychonoff topology. But $cv_i = \pi_i \cdot W$, so cv_i is continuous. Also v_i is continuous when T is given the discrete topology since then the topology on $[T \to A]$ is conjoining. ◊

Observe that the synchronisation maps for the external input to the SCA need not be bounded by the present in order to establish unique behaviour.

5.5 Effectivity

We briefly consider conditions necessary for the solution function W of Theorem 5.4.9 to be effective. For this we consider the effectiveness of the definition of an SCA in 2.3 in the presence of some assumptions in 5.4.

5.5.1 Definition Consider an SCA that is uniformly finitely determined. Assuming the notations above, we say that the SCA is *effective* if the following hold:

(i) The architecture of the SCA defined by the index sets I and J and wiring functions

$$\beta : I \times \omega \to I \qquad \alpha : I \times \omega \to J$$
$$p : I \to \omega \qquad q : I \to \omega$$

are computable.

(ii) The data set A and module functions

$$f_i : A^{p(i)+q(i)} \to A$$

are computable uniformly in $i \in I$.
(iii) The synchronisation functions

$$\delta_{ij} : T \times [T \to A]^J \times A^I \to T \quad \text{and} \quad \gamma_{ij} : T \times [T \to A]^J \times A^I \to T$$

are effective.
(iv) There are functions, computable uniformly in $i \in I$ and $j \in J$,

$$\eta_{ij} : T \to \omega^{(J)} \times 2^{(I)} \quad \text{and} \quad \varepsilon_{ij} : T \to \omega^{(J)} \times 2^{(I)}$$

witnessing that the SCA is uniformly finitely determined.

Note that we do not require an effective SCA to be effectively bounded.

We say that an SCA is *effectively guarded* if the relation $\xrightarrow{u}$ on I is computable or, more generally, if there is a computable well-founded relation extending $\xrightarrow{u}$.

In the above the notion of *computable* is that of computable data type theory (see Bergstra and Tucker [87]) and the notion of *effective* is based on that of effective domain theory (see Griffor, Lindström and Stoltenberg-Hansen [93]). Here, because of lack of space, we omit the precise definitions and proof of the following main theorem

5.5.2 Theorem *Consider an effective* SCA. *If the* SCA *is uniformly bounded by the present and effectively guarded then the solution function W is effective and each solution* cv_i *and* v_i *is effective uniformly in i. In particular, if each input stream* $a_j \in [T \to A]$ *is computable uniformly in* $j \in J$ *and* $x \in A^I$ *is computable then the solution streams* $cv_i(a, x)$ *are computable uniformly in i, a and x.*

6. References

J P Crutchfield and K Kaneko, Phenomenology of spatio-temporal chaos, in H Bai-lin (ed.) *Directions in Chaos,* World Scientific, 1987.

H Ehrig and B Mahr, *Fundamentals of Algebraic Specifications 1 - Equations and initial semantics,* Springer-Verlag, 1985.

S M Eker, V Stavridou and J V Tucker, Verification of synchronous concurrent algorithms using OBJ3. A case study of the Pixel Planes architecture, In G Jones and M Sheeran (eds.) *Designing Correct Circuits,* Springer-Verlag, 1991, pp. 231-252.

S M Eker and J V Tucker, Specification, derivation and verification of concurrent line drawing algorithms and architectures, in R A Earnshaw (ed.), *Theoretical Foundations of Computer Graphics and CAD,* Springer-Verlag, 1988, pp. 449-516.

S M Eker and J V Tucker, Specification and verification of synchronous concurrent algorithms: a case study of the Pixel Planes architecture, in P M Dew, R A Earnshaw and T R Heywood (eds.), *Parallel Processing for Computer Vision and Display*, Addison Wesley, 1989, pp.16-49.

F Fogelman Soulie, Y Robert, M Tchuente (eds.), *Automata Networks in Computer Science*, Manchester University Press, 1986.

E Griffor, I Lindström and V Stoltenberg-Hansen, *Mathematical Theory of Domains*, Cambridge Tracts in Theoretical Compiuter Science, to appear 1993.

J A Goguen, J W Thatcher, E G Wagner, and J B Wright, An initial algebra approach to the specification, correctness and implementation of abstract data types, in R T Yeh (ed.), *Current Trends in Programming Methodology: IV Data Structuring*, Prentice Hall, 1978, pp. 80-149.

N A Harman and J V Tucker, Clocks, retimings, and the formal specification of a UART, in G Milne (ed.) *The Fusion of Hardware Design and Verification* (Proceedings of IFIP Working Group 10.2 Working Conference), North- Holland, 1988, pp. 375-396.

N A Harman and J V Tucker, The formal specification of a digital correlator I: User specification process, in K McEvoy and J V Tucker [90], pp. 161-262.

K M Hobley, B C Thompson, and J V Tucker, Specification and verification of synchronous concurrent algorithms: a case study of a convolution algorithm, in G Milne (ed.) *The Fusion of Hardware Design and Verification* (Proceedings of IFIP Working Group 10.2 Working Conference), North-Holland, 1988, pp. 347-374.

A V Holden, J V Tucker and B C Thompson, The computational structure of neural systems, in A V Holden and V I Kryukov (eds.) *Neurocomputers and Attention. I: Neurobiology, Synchronisation and Chaos*, Manchester University Press, 1990, pp. 223-240.

A V Holden, J V Tucker and B C Thompson, Can excitable media be considered as computational systems? *Physica D* 49 (1991) 240-246.

A V Holden, J V Tucker, M Poole and H Zhang, Coupled map lattices as computational systems, *American Institute of Physics Chaos* 2 (1992), 367-376.

K Kaneko (ed.), *Coupled Map Lattices - Theory and Applications*, J Wiley, in press.

A R Martin and J V Tucker, The concurrent assignment representation of synchronous systems, *Parallel Computing* 9 (1988/89) 227-256.

K McEvoy and J V Tucker (eds.), *Theoretical Foundations of VLSI Design*, Cambridge University Press, 1990.

B McConnell and J V Tucker, Infinite synchronous concurrent algorithms: the specifiation and verification of a hardware stack, in H Schwichtenberg (ed.) *Logic and Algebra for Specification*, Springer-Verlag, 1993.

B McConnell and J V Tucker, Direct limits of algebras and the parameterisation of synchronous concurrent algorithms, Department of Computer Science, University College of Swansea, Report, in preparation.

K Meinke and J V Tucker, Specification and representation of synchronous concurrent algorithms, in F H Vogt (ed.) *Concurrency '88*, Lecture Notes in Computer Science 335, Springer-Verlag, 1988, pp.163-180.

K Meinke and J V Tucker, Universal algebra, in S Abramsky, D Gabbay, T S E Maibaum (eds.) *Handbook of Logic in Computer Science*, Oxford University Press, pp. 189-411.

B C Thompson, A mathematical theory of synchronous concurrent algorithms. PhD Thesis, School of Computer Studies, University of Leeds, 1987.

B C Thompson and J V Tucker, Theoretical considerations in algorithm design, in R A Earnshaw (ed.), *Fundamental Algorithms for Computer Graphics*, Springer-Verlag, 1985, pp. 855-878.

B C Thompson and J V Tucker, Equational specification of synchronous concurrent algorithms and architectures, Computer Science Division Research Report, University College of Swansea, 1991.

V Stoltenberg-Hansen and J V Tucker, Complete local rings as domains, *J. Symbolic Logic* 53 (1988) 603-624.

V Stoltenberg-Hansen and J V Tucker, Algebraic and fixed point equations over inverse limits of algebras, *Theoretical Computer Science* 87 (1991) 1-24.

J V Tucker, Theory of computation and specification over abstract data types and its applications, in F L Bauer (ed), Proceedings of NATO Summer School 1989 at Marktoberdorf, in *Logic, algebra and computation*, Springer, 1991, pp 1-39.

J V Tucker and J I Zucker, Theory of computation over stream algebras and applications, in I M Havel and V Koubek (eds), *Mathematical Foundations of Computer Science 1992, 17th International Symposium, Prague*, Lecture Notes in Computer Science 629, Springer, Berlin, 1992, 62-80.

W Wechler, *Universal Algebra for Computer Scientists*, EATCS Monographs, Springer Verlag, Berlin, 1991.

M Wirsing, Algebraic specification, in J van Leeuwen (ed) *Handbook of Theoretical Computer Science. Volume B: Formal Models and Semantics*, Elsevier, 1990, pp. 675-788.

Some Issues in the Semantics of Facile Distributed Programming

Bent Thomsen
European Computer-Industry Research Centre
Arabellastrasse 17, D-8000 Munich 81, F.R.G.
Email: bt@ecrc.de

Lone Leth
European Computer-Industry Research Centre
Arabellastrasse 17, D-8000 Munich 81, F.R.G.
Email: lone@ecrc.de

Alessandro Giacalone
European Computer-Industry Research Centre
Arabellastrasse 17, D-8000 Munich 81, F.R.G.
Email: ag@ecrc.de

ABSTRACT Facile is an experimental programming language intended to support applications that require a combination of distribution and complex computation. The language originates from an integration of the typed call-by-value λ-calculus with a model of concurrency derived from Milner's CCS. At a theoretical level, an operational semantics has been developed in terms of labelled transition systems, and a notion of observability of programs has been defined by extending the notion of bisimulation. An experimental implementation currently supports distributed programming over networks of workstations. The implementation, obtained by extending the ML language, supports polymorphic types as well as mobility of functions, processes and communication channels across a distributed computing environment. A number of language constructs have been added or modified to handle certain issues that arise with real distribution. These include the need to control the locality of computation in a physically distributed environment, the potentially expensive implementation of certain operators and the need for a system to tolerate partial failures. In this paper we discuss a possible approach for the operational semantics of these constructs that follows the Facile philosophy and some recent results in concurrency theory.

Keywords Theory of Concurrency, Programming Languages, Functional Programming, Programming Language Semantics, Distributed Computing, Failure, Time

Contents

0 Introduction

The Facile project, in progress at ECRC, is concerned with the development of a high-level language and environment that can provide effective support for designing, implementing and managing the evolution of applications requiring a combination of complex computation and distributed/concurrent computing. The project originates mainly from research pursued at SUNY Stony Brook in 1989-1990 [12, 13] and has been greatly influenced by research on the semantics of higher-order processes [34] and mobile processes [20, 24].

The original work focused on establishing the formal foundations for an integration of the functional and the concurrent programming paradigms. To this purpose, an experimental programming language, Facile, was defined as an integration of the typed λ-calculus with a core set of constructs for programming with concurrent processes and communication derived from Milner's CCS [22, 23]. The concurrent component of the language includes constructs for: defining and dynamically creating concurrently executing processes and typed communication channels; specifying communication between processes over typed channels. The integration is symmetric. On one side, Facile provides a notion of processes as autonomous, sequentially executing agents with a local environment, whose internal execution may be specified in functional terms. Conversely, the evaluation of functions may involve dynamic activation of processes and communications. A key point is that programmers can always choose which paradigm to utilise at every point in the construction of a system; for example, they can choose the "granularity" of concurrency appropriate for any part of a given application. Functions, processes and channels are all first-class values which, in particular, can be communicated over channels. A brief and informal overview of the essential language constructs appears in section 1, by means of a few examples.

The semantics of Facile was developed in two phases. The first consists of a structural operational semantics defined in terms of labelled transition systems [12, 13]. The second consists of a notion of observability of programs defined by extending the notion of bisimulation [13]. We report and discuss this semantics in section 2, as it constitutes a (possible) basis for elaborating a number of issues in the semantics of (physically) distributed computing.

Since the beginning of the project's evolution at ECRC in 1991, a significant thrust has been placed on providing support for developing applications that need to operate in a physically distributed environment. An experimental implementation currently supports distributed programming over networks of workstations. The implementation, obtained by extending the ML language [25], supports polymorphic types as well as all the main features defined for Facile and outlined above. In particular, the system supports the communication over Facile channels of values of any type across a distributed environment. This includes functions, processes and channels, which remain thus available as first-class values in the implementation.

This paper focuses on a number of issues that arise in extending the semantics in the presence of real distribution. These include: the need to deal with multiple disjoint address spaces, and thus to control explicitly the locality of computation; the fact that communication of values between different address spaces is potentially expensive; the need to handle the potential for partial failures of a system's components. The basic idea is to offer high-level operators for specifying executions in distributed environments that enable programmers to work within a simple and well understood model. We are thus investigating the semantics of a number of language extensions, which are in good part already available in the current implementation.

Locality of processes – A typical Facile system executes as a collection of nodes situated on different networked processors. Within a node, Facile processes share the same address space and run with simulated concurrency under the control of a preemptive scheduler. In the current implementation a node is implemented by a modified SML/NJ system [2] running in a UNIX process or, in a partial implementation, in a Mach task. Transmission of data between nodes is implemented through a combination of inter-process communication facilities and network protocols. In the Facile context a node constitutes a notion of virtual processor, which could in principle coincide with a physical processor, and which can be implemented utilising whatever operating system construct supports the type of functionalities of a UNIX process or Mach task. In many applications (although not all) it is necessary to activate processes at specific nodes (e.g. because the remote transmission of large structures may have a high cost, or because of the location of physical resources such as graphics displays). The semantics needs to capture this notion, as well as that of observable communication between nodes.

Choice – Facile processes communicate over channels under a hand-shake discipline. This paradigm provides nice features for abstraction and reasoning; however, it does have a price at the implementation level. The scenario is further complicated by the presence of a "choice" operator which enables a process to select one out of several courses of action. The CCS-like semantics formulated for the original Facile [12, 13] (also see section 2) leads to severe implementation problems, especially in a distributed environment. We present a different version of the choice operator, which has a slightly more elaborate semantics but supports a more realistic implementation strategy.

Failures and exception handling – In this context we briefly discuss how the ML exception handling facilities are inherited by Facile and how we make sure that exceptions are handled locally by a process. This is still far from providing a complete solution, since at least two questions remain open; One is which failures ought to be made explicit at the programming language level vs. which ones ought to be handled automatically by the implementation. The question is a difficult one, since it is not always obvious when a failure has occurred (e.g. a network might by "down" temporarily). Another question concerns exceptions that do not interest one particular process but rather the system as a whole (e.g. "interrupts" generated by a user).

Delay and time-out operators – The hand-shaking communication discipline enforced by Facile may block processes when failures occur, e.g. in remote processors or physical networks. In a distributed application, on the other hand, one often wishes to avoid blocking an entire system when some component fails. A partial solution often adopted in distributed programming is to use time-out mechanisms. This requires the introduction of a notion of time. To define an operational semantics for the time constructs to be added to Facile we follow some recent developments in timed process algebra surveyed by Nicollin and Sifakis [29].

In sections 3, 4, 5 and 6 we present the language extensions that have been implemented so far and discuss possible approaches to the definition of an operational semantics. The formulations of semantics use in part results that are becoming available in semantics of concurrency. It should be noted that this area has proposed potentially interesting solutions for the single issues. However, these have been typically pursued in abstract settings, often under simplifying assumptions. And furthermore, the real value of the semantics in this context is determined by its ability to capture the presence of the combination of the issues outlined above. What we present here are quite preliminary, thus not stabilised, studies. We believe some of the approaches we discuss appear quite convincing, while for others the arguments may be still weak. In conclusion, this paper poses more problems than it proposes solutions.

Acknowledgement

The understanding of the issues discussed in this paper owes a great deal to the insight of F. Cosquer, F. Knabe, A. Kramer and T.-M. Kuo, as they have been working on the implementation of Facile. A special acknowledgement is owed to S. Prasad, from whose Ph. D. thesis [31] we extracted the overview material of sections 1 and 2.

1 A brief overview of Facile

We present a few simple examples to illustrate some of the key features of the original Facile, as presented in [12].

```
proc fib_server(a,b) = let fun fib(i) = if ( i = 0 ) or (i = 1) then 1
                                         else fib(i-1) + fib(i-2)
                       in
                         b ! ( fib( a ? ) )
                       end;
                       terminate
```

Figure 1: Processes use functions

The first example (Figure 1) shows the definition of a process which, provided with a non-negative integer i on input channel a, outputs the ith Fibonacci number on channel b and then terminates. The function fib is locally defined in the usual way as a recursive function. The function is applied to the integer received on a channel a. The result is then output on channel b. The syntax b ! e and a? stand for a send and receive operation over channels b and a. Note that a ? is an expression whose value is whatever value is received on channel a.

```
proc fib_server(a,b) =
     let fun fib(i) = if ( i = 0 ) or (i = 1) then 1
                      else
                        let val (in1, out1) = (channel(int), channel(int) );
                            val (in2, out2) = (channel(int), channel(int) )
                        in
                            spawn( out1 ! (fib(in1 ?)) ; terminate );
                            spawn( out2 ! (fib(in2 ?)) ; terminate );
                            ( in1 ! (i-1) ) ;
                            ( in2 ! (i-2) ) ;
                            ( (out1 ?) + (out2 ?) )
                        end
     in
        b ! ( fib( a ? ) )
    end;
    terminate
```

Figure 2: Functions use processes

The second example (Figure 2) illustrates how processes can be invoked by functions, by showing a process with the same external behaviour as the previous one, but where the Fibonacci function is implemented using a network of processes. `fib` is still a function, but recursive calls are not "stacked". Instead, for each recursive call to `fib`, a new process is created, by the **spawn** expression, and the integer argument passed to it on an input channel. The expression `channel(int)` yields a new channel on which integer values can be communicated. `spawn(`*be*`)` is an expression which returns a `triv` value locally, but has the effect of creating a new process whose behaviour is defined by *be*. Here new channels (e.g. `in1,out1` and `in2, out2`) are generated for each recursive call, and are used to communicate the arguments and results between processes representing recursive calls. The system of processes that compute the Fibonacci function evolves thus as a binary tree.

```
fun rsh(node_id, cmd)  =  node_id ! cmd

proc listener(mn)  =  activate ( let val x = mn ?
                                 in    code( activate x ||
                                             activate listener(mn) )
                                 end )
```

Figure 3: Remote shell

The third example (Figure 3) demonstrates a possible usage of processes as first-class values in Facile and introduces the concurrent composition operator "`||`". A kind of remote shell command is defined as a function `rsh`, which sends a given command `cmd` over a channel `node_id` identifying a given machine. At the receiving end, the process `listener` receives process `x` over channel `mn` and starts it locally. The constructor `code` "packages" a process behaviour definition into a value which can then be manipulated in the functional style. Both `node_id` and `mn` are channels on which `code` values can be transmitted. A `code` value can be activated by a process, which then takes on the specified behaviour. In our case, `activate x` creates a process running `x` in parallel with a reinvocation of `listener`.

The fourth example (Figure 4) demonstrates how references or memory cells can be implemented in Facile and introduces the % operator, an "exclusive or" similar to the CCS sum operator. Other abstract data types and persistent objects can also be implemented in a similar manner. The process `mem_cell` abstracts the behaviour of a memory location. The formal parameters **get** and **put** are channels for accessing and changing the contents of the location. `mem_cell` offers its contents to any reader on channel **get** (first alternative of %), and then reactivates itself. Or else it allows its contents to be updated (the second alternative) through the channel put. The first alternative is triggered by the evaluation of `get!contents`, the second by the evaluation of expression put?, which yields the new contents. Memory locations are manipulated via three functions: `ref`, `deref` and `assign`. A datatype **ref** is represented here by a pair of channels used to read and update the contents of a memory location. Function `ref` creates a memory cell process, by spawning an `activation` of an application of the `mem_cell` abstraction to the appropriate argument values. It then returns the pair of channels with which to access this memory cell process. Given the pair of access channels to a memory location, function `deref` returns the contents of that memory location. Finally, `assign`

```
proc mem_cell(get,put,contents) =
          ( get!contents ;
            activate mem_cell(get,put,contents) )
          %
            activate let val x = put ?
                     in mem_cell(get,put,x)
                     end

fun ref(x) = let val (get,put) = ( channel(int), channel(int) )
             in    spawn( activate mem_cell(get,put,x) );
                   (get,put)
             end

fun deref(loc) = let val (i,o) = loc  in    i ?  end

fun assign(loc,x) = let val (i,o) = loc  in   o ! x    end
```

Figure 4: Memory cells

changes the contents to the desired value.

2 Facile core syntax and operational semantics

In the previous section we have presented some examples given in the full Facile syntax. For brevity, the semantics is defined here in terms of a "core" syntax. Details of a translation from full to core syntax are shown in [13]. The core language consists of two parts: an expression part (the functions) and a behaviour expression part (the processes). Facile expressions are statically typed. The type system defined in [13] gives type judgements of the form $A \vdash e : t$ where A is a type environment and t is a type. We shall not review the type system, but we assume that all expressions are type correct and we only concern ourselves with the type-free language which has the following syntax:

Definition 2.1 Core Expressions

$$e ::= \; x \mid c \mid \lambda x.e \mid e_1 e_2 \mid \mathtt{code}(be) \mid \mathtt{spawn}(be) \mid \mathtt{channel}(t) \mid e_1!e_2 \mid e?$$

We denote by *exp* the set of expressions given by the above abstract syntax. The set of constants includes integers, booleans `true` and `false`, a distinguished value `triv`, and channel-valued constants. In addition, we assume that c also ranges over predefined operators such as the standard arithmetic operations and the `if-then-else` constructs. For convenience, we dispense with product types and tuples, and will assume that all the arithmetic and boolean operations are in a curried form, taking a single argument, in the core language. λ is a variable binder with the usual notion of free and bound variables. Substituting an expression for a variable with the usual avoidance of accidental binding is denoted by $e[x \mapsto e']$. For a formal definition of these concepts see [13].

The set of behaviour expressions *beh_exp* is given by the following grammar:

Definition 2.2 CORE BEHAVIOUR EXPRESSIONS

$$be \ ::= \ \texttt{terminate} \mid \texttt{activate}\ e \mid be_1 \parallel be_2 \mid be_1 \% be_2$$

The operational semantics of Facile programs follows a structural approach and is defined for closed well-formed or well-typed syntactic terms in the core syntax, i.e. those which have passed the static-semantics filter (for which we refer the reader to [13]). The definition consists of two labelled transition systems (LTS) respectively defining an "evaluates" relation for expression evaluation, and a "derives" relation, for process execution. The labels on transitions roughly correspond to the external effects of the computation performed by a process.

Facile has a call-by-value semantics. Values are a subclass of expressions that can be passed as parameters or communicated. The set *Val*, syntactic values, comprises expressions of the form:

$$v \ ::= \ x \mid c \mid \lambda x.e \mid \texttt{code}(be)$$

such that the static semantics can assign a type to these expressions without any type assumption. Values have no free variables and v is a typical value.

A *sort* is a set of typed channels. $\mathcal{S}$ denotes the universal set of all possible typed channels. $\mathcal{P}(\mathcal{S})$ denotes the powerset of $\mathcal{S}$. $\mathcal{P}^{finite}(\mathcal{S})$ denotes the set of finite subsets of $\mathcal{S}$. $\mathcal{S}_t$ denotes the subset of $\mathcal{S}$ consisting of channels on which values of type t can be communicated. K is a typical subset of $\mathcal{S}$, and k is a typical channel in $\mathcal{S}$. We say a value $v \in Val$ is transmittable on channel k if $\emptyset \vdash k : t\ chan\ \&\ \emptyset \vdash v : t$, that is v is a value of type t and k is a channel of type $t\ chan$.

We assume that whenever we talk of a sort (set of channels) other than $\mathcal{S}$ or $\mathcal{S}_t$, there are unboundedly many channels of each type outside that set. We may assume that these channels sets are finite.

Definition 2.3 LABELS
Comm, the set of communication labels is defined as :

$$Comm \ = \ \{k(v), \overline{k(v)} \mid \exists t.(k \in \mathcal{S}_t, v \in Val, \emptyset \vdash v : t)\}$$

$\mathcal{L}$, the set of labels is defined as :

$$\mathcal{L} \ = \ Comm \cup \{\tau\} \cup \{\Phi(be) \mid be \in beh\_exp\}$$

The labels $k(v)$ and $\overline{k(v)}$ represent, respectively, a potential input and output action of a value v over a channel k. The value v should be transmittable on channel k. $k(v)$ and $\overline{k(v)}$ are called complementary labels. The τ label, imported from CCS, represents a "hidden" or internal atomic action, such as a communication between two component processes in a system. The special $\Phi(be)$ label, generated by a spawn expression, is used to mark the creation of a process executing code *be*. This label enables us to provide a concise treatment of process creation in a symmetrically integrated language.

The LTS for behaviour expressions is $\langle Bcon, (Comm \cup \{\tau\}), \longrightarrow\!\!\!\!\!\rightarrow \rangle$ which is defined in terms of the LTS for expressions $\langle Econ, \mathcal{L}, \hookrightarrow \rangle$, where the configurations, labels and transition relations are described below. The transition relations are defined as the smallest relations closed under the rules given in Figure 5.

$Bcon \subseteq \mathcal{P}^{finite}(\mathcal{S}) \times beh\_exp$, is the set of behaviour configurations of the form (K, be) where K is a sort, which records channels already in existence, and *be* is a closed, well-formed behaviour expression. As mentioned before, we assume we can always find channels of every type not in the sort.

$Econ \subseteq (\mathcal{P}^{finite}(\mathcal{S}) \times exp)$, is the set of expression configurations of the form (K, e) where K is a sort and e is a closed and well-typed expression.

$\hookrightarrow \subseteq Econ \times \mathcal{L} \times Econ$ denotes the "evaluates" relation. $K, e \stackrel{\ell}{\hookrightarrow} K', e'$ is read as "a one-step evaluation of expression e, given the sort set K, results in expression e' and sort set K', on the occurrence of event ℓ".

$\longrightarrow\!\!\!\!\!\rightarrow \subseteq Bcon \times (Comm \cup \{\tau\}) \times Bcon$ is the "derives" relation. $K, be \stackrel{\ell}{\longrightarrow\!\!\!\!\!\rightarrow} K', be'$ is read as "Given the sort set K, behaviour expression *be* derives behaviour expression *be'* with sort set K', on the occurrence of event ℓ". Labels ℓ and ℓ' range over the set of labels $\mathcal{L}$. The letter e, possibly subscripted, stands for any expression, v for values, x for identifiers, k for channel values, and *be*, possibly subscripted, for behaviour expressions.

The "evaluates" and "derives" relations are defined inductively in terms of inference rules. They are the smallest relations closed under the inference rules of Figure 5 and the "δ-rules" for predefined operators.

In Figure 5, we present the rules for "core" Facile, omitting here the evaluation rules induced by the constants and primitive operators, and those for derived constructs. Below is a brief commentary. The rules are unordered, but we have numbered and grouped them for convenience when referring to them.

Evaluation Rules for Function Expressions

Rules (1a) and (1b) state that, in application $e_1 e_2$, first the operator e_1 is reduced to a value. Then the operator e_2 is reduced to a value v. Rule (1c) defines the binding between formal and actual parameters. The ℓ labelling the transitions in rules (1a) and (1b) represents the labels generated during one step in the reduction of e_1 and e_2. The τ label in rule (1c) says that parameter binding has no observable effect and that the initial and final configurations are related by substitution. We have omitted the δ-rules for predefined arithmetic and boolean operators.

Rules (2a-c) describe the evaluation of a send expression $e_1!e_2$. First e_1 is reduced to a channel value k using (2a), then e_2 is reduced to a value v by (2b). Finally, by rule (2c), the expression $k!v$ evaluates to value `triv` on the occurrence of the communication event labelled by $\overline{k(v)}$. The proviso ensures the existence of channel k.

Rule (3a) says that when evaluating a receive expression $e?$, the expression e is first reduced to a

1. Function Application

(a) $$\frac{K, e_1 \overset{\ell}{\hookrightarrow} K', e_1'}{K, e_1 e_2 \overset{\ell}{\hookrightarrow} K', e_1' e_2}$$

(b) $$\frac{K, e_2 \overset{\ell}{\hookrightarrow} K', e_2'}{K, v\ e_2 \overset{\ell}{\hookrightarrow} K', v\ e_2'}$$

(c) $$\frac{\square}{K, (\lambda x.e)v \overset{\tau}{\hookrightarrow} K, e[x \mapsto v]}$$

2. Send

(a) $$\frac{K, e_1 \overset{\ell}{\hookrightarrow} K', e_1'}{K, e_1!e_2 \overset{\ell}{\hookrightarrow} K', e_1'!e_2}$$

(b) $$\frac{K, e_2 \overset{\ell}{\hookrightarrow} K', e_2'}{K, k!e_2 \overset{\ell}{\hookrightarrow} K', k!e_2'}$$

(c) $$\frac{\square}{K, k!v \overset{\overline{k(v)}}{\hookrightarrow} K, \mathtt{triv}}$$

provided $k \in K$.

3. Receive

(a) $$\frac{K, e \overset{\ell}{\hookrightarrow} K', e'}{K, e? \overset{\ell}{\hookrightarrow} K', e'?}$$

(b) $$\frac{\square}{K, k? \overset{k(v)}{\hookrightarrow} K, v}$$

provided $k \in K$, value v transmittable on k.

4. Channel Creation

$$\frac{\square}{K, \mathtt{channel}(t) \overset{\tau}{\hookrightarrow} K \cup \{k\}, k}$$

where $k \notin K$ and $k \in \mathcal{S}_t$.

5. Process Creation

$$\frac{\square}{K, \mathtt{spawn}(be) \overset{\Phi(be)}{\hookrightarrow} K, \mathtt{triv}}$$

6. Activate

(a) $$\frac{K, e \overset{\ell}{\hookrightarrow} K', e'}{K, \mathtt{activate}\ e \overset{\ell}{\twoheadrightarrow} K', \mathtt{activate}\ e'}$$

provided $\ell \neq \Phi(be)$.

(b) $$\frac{K, e \overset{\Phi(be)}{\hookrightarrow} K', e'}{K, \mathtt{activate}\ e \overset{\tau}{\twoheadrightarrow} K', (\mathtt{activate}\ e' \parallel be)}$$

(c) $$\frac{\square}{K, \mathtt{activate}\ \mathtt{code}(be) \overset{\tau}{\twoheadrightarrow} K, be}$$

7. Concurrent Composition

(a) $$\frac{K, be_1 \overset{\ell}{\twoheadrightarrow} K', be_1'}{K, be_1 \parallel be_2 \overset{\ell}{\twoheadrightarrow} K', be_1' \parallel be_2}$$

(b) $$\frac{K, be_2 \overset{\ell}{\twoheadrightarrow} K', be_2'}{K, be_1 \parallel be_2 \overset{\ell}{\twoheadrightarrow} K', be_1 \parallel be_2'}$$

8. Complementary Communication

$$\frac{K, be_1 \overset{\ell}{\twoheadrightarrow} K', be_1' \qquad K, be_2 \overset{\ell'}{\twoheadrightarrow} K', be_2'}{K, be_1 \parallel be_2 \overset{\tau}{\twoheadrightarrow} K', be_1' \parallel be_2'}$$

where ℓ and ℓ' are complementary labels.

9. Alternative

(a) $$\frac{K, be_1 \overset{\ell}{\twoheadrightarrow} K', be_1'}{K, be_1 \% be_2 \overset{\ell}{\twoheadrightarrow} K', be_1'}$$

(b) $$\frac{K, be_2 \overset{\ell}{\twoheadrightarrow} K', be_2'}{K, be_1 \% be_2 \overset{\ell}{\twoheadrightarrow} K', be_2'}$$

Figure 5: Dynamic Semantics

channel value k. Rule (3b) says that $k?$ may evaluate to any permitted value v with observable effect $k(v)$. The proviso ensures that k is a valid existing channel and that value v can be received over k.

Rule (4), an axiom, describes channel creation. A new channel k, not already in the sort K, is generated and returned as the value of the channel expression. The τ label says that this evaluation does not have any externally visible effect.

Rule (5) says that a `spawn` expression evaluates to value `triv`. In doing so it generates a label that describes the process to be created. In Rule (6b), Φ labels are "discharged" resulting in the creation of the new process.

Rules Relating Function Expressions and Behaviour Expressions

Rule (6a) states: if label ℓ is produced in one evaluation step for expression e, then ℓ labels the derivation step for behaviour expression `activate` e. Rule (6b) states that whenever a behaviour expression `activate` e derives a behaviour expression `activate` e' through a label $\Phi(be)$, we interpret this as `activate` e silently deriving `activate` $e' \parallel be$, i.e., a composition of its own derivative and the new process be. Rule (6c) says that the activation of a `code` expression yields the corresponding behaviour expression, without any observable effect.

Derivation Rules for Behaviour Expressions

Rules (7a-b) define the observable behaviour of a concurrent composition of processes in terms of the transitions of component processes. Rule (7a) says that if a process be_1 can make a transition labelled ℓ, then when it is composed with another process be_2, it can still make the same transition. Rule (7b) is the symmetric case.

Rule (8) describes a synchronised communication discipline. For communication to occur, one process should attempt to send a value over a channel and another should attempt to receive over the same channel. This is expressed in the antecedent of rule (8). The τ label in Rule (8) indicates that a communication between two component processes of a system is not observable outside the system. Note that the sorts must match in both clauses of the antecedent.

Rules (9a-b) define the behaviour of a process that can either behave as be_1 or as be_2. Rule (9a) says that if a process be_1 can make a transition labelled ℓ to become be_1', then process $be_1\%be_2$, can also make the transition labelled ℓ to be_1'. Rule (9b) is the symmetric case.

Note that in the dynamic semantics we treat every aspect of evaluation operationally instead of axiomatically describing expression evaluation. For example, in the function application rule (1c) of Figure 5, we describe parameter binding as an operation with a τ effect rather than specifying call-by-value β-equivalence axiomatically, as in:

$$\frac{K, e[x \mapsto v] \overset{\ell}{\hookrightarrow} K', e'}{K, (\lambda x.e)v \overset{\ell}{\hookrightarrow} K', e'}$$

Similarly the "δ-rules" such as addition of integers etc., are also treated as labelled reductions. Intuitively, this is justified because these involve operations at the machine level. More significantly, by taking this approach we achieve a uniform framework in which we can relate internal computations and communication between internal components. This is very important in a symmetric integration, particularly in reasoning about the equivalence of functions implemented using local stacks and those using processes and communication. With this uniform treatment, notions of equivalence are formulated based on observational criteria [13], and properties such as the equivalence of $(\lambda x.e)v$ and $e[x \mapsto v]$ are stated and proven as theorems.

3 Locality and distribution

We discuss here the extensions to the core language presented in sections 1 and 2 which have to do with the locations where processes execute. As mentioned in the introduction, a Facile system executes in a collection of nodes, each supporting the (simulated) concurrent execution of Facile processes. Nodes can be dynamically created. Processes can be activated at specific nodes, and communication over channels may occur between different nodes.

The core Facile language is extended by introducing a **newnode** operator for creating nodes and by modifying the **spawn** operator to allow for spawning processes at specific nodes. These constructs appear at the expression level:

$$e ::= \ldots \mid \mathbf{newnode} \mid \mathbf{r\_spawn}(e, be)$$

and we add constants n of type **node** where **node** is a new constant type.

newnode returns a unique new node identifier. Behind the scene it creates a new virtual node. This node is conceptually empty until some computation is placed at the new virtual node.

r_spawn takes as argument a pair consisting of an expression which should evaluate to a node identifier and a behaviour. This behaviour is placed at the node to run concurrently with whatever is computing there.

To define an operational semantics for these constructs we follow some recent ideas described by Boudol et al. in [8]. There Milner's CCS is extended with an operator called location prefixing. In their notation a process P prefixed by a location u is denoted $u :: P$. Locations are made part of the notion of observation and initially a process under observation includes no location. These are introduced by the observer through transitions, e.g. $a.P \overset{a}{\underset{u}{\longrightarrow}} u :: P$ for any location name u. This transition is read as "$a.P$ may do an a-transition arising from location u and the resulting process P will be located at u". From then on actions of P will be observed as coming from location u. At least this is the case until P reaches a state where it splits itself into two concurrent processes (say $P' \mid Q$). To accommodate this situation Boudol et al. introduce a notion of sublocations. Thus if $P' \overset{a}{\underset{v}{\longrightarrow}} v :: P''$ then $u :: (P' \mid Q) \overset{a}{\underset{u.v}{\longrightarrow}} u :: (v :: P'' \mid Q)$.

Thus to give an operational semantics for computations at a virtual node we could adapt the behaviour expression part of Facile in a similar way. However, we have chosen to make our treatment slightly different, partly inspired by Aceto's work for finite state distributed processes [1]. Firstly, we want to separate the creation of locations/virtual nodes from the notion of observation (as in [1]), but we also leave the creation under user control at the expression level of Facile, since we allow dynamic creation of new virtual nodes. Secondly, we have chosen to keep the location space flat and thus avoid introducing a notion of sublocation. This fits the current implementation and our approach seems easy to adapt in case we decide to introduce a notion of sublocation. Thirdly, since we want to allow concurrent computations at each virtual node we add a new syntactic category for distributed behaviour expressions:

$$dbe ::= n :: be \mid dbe \;|||\; dbe$$

We denote by *dis_beh_exp* the set of distributed behaviour expressions defined by the grammar above. n is a virtual node identifier with $n \in \mathcal{N}$, the set of node identifiers. $n :: be$ stands for a behaviour expression be located at node n. This is the abstract syntax for a virtual node. Note that be can be a concurrent composition $be' \,||\, be''$, thus at each node we can have several Facile processes executing. A Facile system may comprise of several nodes, denoted by $dbe \;|||\; dbe$.

The operational semantics is defined by introducing a new LTS for distributed behaviours which we shall specify later in this section and by modifying the two LTS's defined in section 2 as follows: First the LTS for expressions $\langle Econ, \mathcal{L}, \hookrightarrow\rangle$ is modified by extending $Econ$ to $Econ \subseteq \mathcal{P}^{finite}(\mathcal{S}) \times \mathcal{P}^{finite}(\mathcal{N}) \times e$ and $\mathcal{L}$ is extended to $\mathcal{L} = Comm \cup \{\tau\} \cup \{\Phi(be) \mid be \in beh\_exp\} \cup \mathcal{N} \cup \{n(be) \mid be \in beh\_exp \;\&\; n \in \mathcal{N}\}$. The LTS for behaviour expressions $\langle Bcon, (Comm \cup \{\tau\}), \longrightarrow\!\!\!\!\!\!\gg\rangle$ is extended to $\langle Bcon, (Comm \cup \{\tau\} \cup \mathcal{N} \cup \{n(be) \mid be \in beh\_exp \;\&\; n \in \mathcal{N}\}), \longrightarrow\!\!\!\!\!\!\gg\rangle$ with $Bcon \subseteq \mathcal{P}^{finite}(\mathcal{S}) \times \mathcal{P}^{finite}(\mathcal{N}) \times be$. Thus expression configurations have the form (K, N, e) and behaviour expression configurations now have the form (K, N, be), that is both expression and behaviour expression configurations have an extra component $N \in \mathcal{P}^{finite}(\mathcal{N})$. This extra component is used for keeping track of generated locations and ensuring uniqueness of newly generated locations. The mechanism for creating and manipulating location identifiers resembles that for channel management as we shall see.

Furthermore we extend the transition relations $\hookrightarrow \subseteq Econ \times \mathcal{L} \times Econ$ and $\longrightarrow\!\!\!\!\!\!\gg \subseteq Bcon \times (Comm \cup \{\tau\} \cup \mathcal{N} \cup \{n(be) \mid be \in beh\_exp \;\&\; n \in \mathcal{N}\}) \times Bcon$ by adding transitions of the form $K, N, e \overset{n}{\hookrightarrow} K', N', e'$ and $K, N, e \overset{n(be)}{\hookrightarrow} K', N', e'$, respectively $K, N, be \overset{n}{\longrightarrow\!\!\!\!\!\!\gg} K', N', be'$ and $K, N, be \overset{n(be)}{\longrightarrow\!\!\!\!\!\!\gg} K', N', be'$ to the set of transitions for expressions, respectively behaviour expressions. The meaning of these new labels will be discussed below as they are introduced. The transition relations are the smallest relations closed under the inference rules of Figure 5 (modified as discussed later) and the rules introduced below. First we add the following rule:

$$K, N, \texttt{newnode} \overset{n}{\hookrightarrow} K, N \cup \{n\}, n \quad \text{provided } n \notin N$$

A **newnode** expression evaluates to a unique new node constant n. In doing so it also produces an n-label which will be a signal to create a new location as we shall see later. Note that the treatment of node creation is analogous to the creation of new channels.

$$K, N, \texttt{r\_spawn}(n, be) \overset{n(be)}{\hookrightarrow} K, N, \texttt{triv}$$

An $\texttt{r\_spawn}(n, be)$ expression evaluates locally to the trivial value. In doing so it produces an $n(be)$-label which will be a signal to place the behaviour expression be concurrently with whatever is computing at node n.

$$\frac{K, N, e \overset{l}{\hookrightarrow} K', N', e'}{K, N, \texttt{r\_spawn}(e, be) \overset{l}{\hookrightarrow} K', N', \texttt{r\_spawn}(e', be)}$$

This rule reflects the fact that the **r_spawn** function has a call-by-value semantics for the expression e.

We need to change all existing rules for Facile and add the component N which takes care of guaranteeing uniqueness of new node identifiers, e.g.:

$$\frac{K, N, e \overset{l}{\hookrightarrow} K', N', e'}{K, N, ee'' \overset{l}{\hookrightarrow} K', N', e'e''}$$

$$\frac{K, N, e \overset{l}{\hookrightarrow} K', N', e'}{K, N, \texttt{activate } e \overset{l}{\longrightarrow\!\!\!\gg} K', N', \texttt{activate } e'} \quad \text{provided } l \neq \Phi(be)$$

Thus n and $n(be)$ labels, as well as labels from $Comm \cup \{\tau\}$ are carried over from the expression level to the behaviour expression level.

Note that we may eliminate the $\Phi(be)$ labels by considering **spawn**(be) (the construct for spawning a behaviour expression concurrently on the same node) as a special case of **r_spawn(n,be)** with n identifying the local node.

To define an operational semantics for the distributed behaviour expression level we define a new LTS: $\langle DBcon, ((Comm \times \mathcal{N}) \cup \{\tau\}), \longrightarrow\!\!\!\ggg \rangle$ where $DBcon \subseteq \mathcal{P}^{finite}(S) \times \mathcal{P}^{finite}(S) \times dis\_beh\_exp$ is the set of distributed behaviour configurations of the form (K, N, dbe) and $\longrightarrow\!\!\!\ggg \; \subseteq DBcon \times ((Comm \times \mathcal{N}) \cup \{\tau\}) \times DBcon$. This transition relation is the smallest relation closed under the inference rules introduced below:

$$\frac{K, N, be \overset{n}{\longrightarrow\!\!\!\gg} K', N', be'}{K, N, n' :: be \overset{\tau}{\longrightarrow\!\!\!\ggg} K', N', n' :: be' \;|||\; n :: \texttt{terminate}}$$

This rule provides the interface between the concurrent part of Facile (the behaviour expressions) and the distributed part. It states that if a behaviour expression does an $\overset{n}{\longrightarrow\!\!\!\gg}$ -transition (a signal to create a new node) and this behaviour expression is located at node n' then a new node n is created. Note the analogy with the treatment of process creation at the behaviour expression level via the $\Phi(be)$ label. Initially the new node only contains the terminated behaviour expression. The following rule will allow some useful work to be done at location n:

$$\frac{K, N, be \overset{n(be'')}{\longrightarrow\!\!\!\gg} K', N', be'}{K, N, n' :: be \;|||\; n :: be''' \overset{\tau}{\longrightarrow\!\!\!\ggg} K', N', n' :: be' \;|||\; n :: (be''' \;||\; be'')}$$

This rule states that if a behaviour expression be produces an $n(be'')$ transition (a signal for spawning be'' at node n) then be'' is placed in concurrent composition with whatever is computing currently at node n (i.e. be''' becomes $be''' \parallel be''$).

The last set of rules is for observing distributed behaviour expressions.

$$\frac{K, N, be \overset{l}{\longrightarrow\!\!\!\!\gg} K', N', be'}{K, N, n :: be \underset{n}{\overset{l}{\twoheadrightarrow}} K', N', n :: be'} \quad \text{provided } l \neq n', n'(be), \Phi(be), \tau$$

This rule translates an external transition of a behaviour expression into an external transition for the distributed behaviour expression. Note that we have chosen to label the external transition with the node identifier. This will allow us to observe not only the communication capability of a system of distributed behaviours, but also which location distributed the communication. Later on we shall discuss how this can be used in an observational equivalence to express properties of distribution. It is worth mentioning that by letting external labels from the behaviour expression level go through to the distributed behaviour expression level we implicitly specify that we use the same communication mechanism between behaviours executing concurrently on one node and behaviours executing distributed on different nodes. Concretely, transmission of data between processes is implemented through a combination of inter-process communication facilities and network protocols making communication between local and non local processes transparent[1]. The following rule defines this:

$$\frac{K, N, dbe_1 \underset{n}{\overset{l}{\twoheadrightarrow}} K', N', dbe_1' \qquad K, N, dbe_2 \underset{n'}{\overset{\bar{l}}{\twoheadrightarrow}} K', N', dbe_2'}{K, N, dbe_1 \mid\mid\mid dbe_2 \overset{\tau}{\longrightarrow\!\!\!\!\ggg} K', N', dbe_1' \mid\mid\mid dbe_2'}$$

Since we later on want to consider internal transitions unobservable we adopt the following rule:

$$\frac{K, N, be \overset{\tau}{\longrightarrow\!\!\!\!\gg} K', N', be'}{K, N, n :: be \overset{\tau}{\longrightarrow\!\!\!\!\ggg} K', N', n :: be'}$$

Note that an interesting notion of observation of internal activity on and between nodes could be obtained by replacing the above two rules with the rules below:

$$\frac{K, N, dbe_1 \underset{n}{\overset{l}{\twoheadrightarrow}} K', N', dbe_1' \qquad K, N, dbe_2 \underset{n'}{\overset{\bar{l}}{\twoheadrightarrow}} K', N', dbe_2'}{K, N, dbe_1 \mid\mid\mid dbe_2 \underset{\{n, n'\}}{\overset{\tau}{\twoheadrightarrow}} K', N', dbe_1' \mid\mid\mid dbe_2'}$$

$$\frac{K, N, be \overset{\tau}{\longrightarrow\!\!\!\!\gg} K', N', be'}{K, N, n :: be \underset{n}{\overset{\tau}{\twoheadrightarrow}} K', N', n :: be'}$$

[1]modulo network failure as we shall discuss later

The first rule states that when a communication takes place between two nodes we can observe this through a τ-transition labelled with the two locations which participated in the communication. The second rule states that if internal activity takes place at node n then we can observe this via the $\xrightarrow[n]{\tau}$ transition.

It is worth remarking that Berry et al. in [5] have taken this approach though they have not used it to define a notion of observing distributed communication. Rather it has been used to solve some proof technical problems. However, we envision that this notion could be used to quantify "cost" of distribution in the sense that there would be an observable difference between a system solving a task locally and one that uses inter-node communication to solve a task. Under some notion of observation this may be relevant.

We allow interleaving between two locations and communication similar to the notion of concurrency and communication at the behaviour expression level:

$$\frac{K, N, dbe_1 \xrightarrow[n]{l} K', N', dbe_1'}{K, N, dbe_1 \;|||\; dbe_2 \xrightarrow[n]{l} K', N', dbe_1' \;|||\; dbe_2}$$

This rule maintains an interleaving semantics viewpoint also between physically distributed processes. A true concurrency model is probably more appropriate and will be the subject of future work.

In a physically distributed environment we may encounter a failure of a node. The semantics needs to reflect this and it can be specified by the following rule:

$$K, N, n :: be \;|||\; dbe \xrightarrow{\tau} K, N, dbe$$

This rule states that non-deterministically a node n may disappear. Note that n is not deleted from the set N of nodes currently in use. This ensures that we cannot recreate node n. We could specify a semantics for node failure where some information gets propagated when a node fails, i.e. a broadcast message that node n is going down. However, this would introduce a new communication paradigm in our model which is unfortunate. Furthermore there will be situations where such messages cannot be propagated i.e. in case of power failure. We feel that it is much more appropriate to enrich the language with constructs that will allow us to program system monitors and exception handlers and thus allow users of the language to build their own abstractions for these cases. Section 5 and 6 describe two such language constructs.

The operational semantics given above attempts to model the two implemented constructs **newnode** and **r_spawn** as directly as possible. However, it could be argued that the two-stage procedure of first creating (an empty) node and then placing a behaviour expression at this node is not the most primitive construct. We may obtain a more primitive solution by introducing the following construct:

$$e ::= \ldots \mid \mathbf{newnode}(be)$$

where **newnode** takes a behaviour expression as an argument which will be placed immediately at the new node.

The operational semantics could be given by the following rules:

$$K, N, \mathbf{newnode}(be) \overset{n(be)}{\hookrightarrow} K, N \cup \{n\}, n \quad \text{provided } n \notin N$$

$$\frac{K, N, be \overset{n(be'')}{\longrightarrow\!\!\!\gg} K', N', be'}{K, N, n' :: be \overset{\tau}{\longrightarrow\!\!\!\ggg} K', N', n' :: be' \;|||\; n :: be''}$$

Now a **newnode**(*be*) expression will return a new node identifier and at the same time send a signal containing the behaviour to be placed initially at this new node. The second rule shows how the new node is created with the specified behaviour.

r_spawn can then be implemented as a derived operator via communication by placing a remote shell process (as presented in Figure 3) at each node when they are created. As a matter of fact, this is exactly how these constructs have been implemented in the Facile system.

4 The choice operator

Facile, as described in [12, 13] and outlined in sections 1 and 2, offered an operator on behaviour expressions for selecting one out of several alternatives of execution, whose semantics was patterned after that of the "+" operator of CCS [22, 23]. While this semantics is possibly the simplest, most general and compact at the level of a formalism for specification [23, 11] it poses severe implementation problems once it is transferred into a programming language that allows the specification of distributed executions. The operational semantics specifies that the choice may be triggered by external communications as well as internal transitions in either branch. Since each branch is a behaviour expression, it may contain activations of concurrent processes and nested choices. It is therefore necessary to have a mechanism for keeping track of "child" processes until choices are resolved. In fact it may be necessary to freeze their computations until the choice is resolved. This is expensive and hard to implement, especially in a truly distributed implementation where processes may be spawned remotely. Furthermore, the fact that computations may have to be suspended until a choice is resolved will in general limit potential parallelism in a system.

At a different level, a source of complexity is that internal transitions in any of the alternatives may trigger the choice. Such internal transitions may be caused by β-reduction, channel creation and spawning of processes. In an implementation of Facile computational steps specified by the top-level semantics generally require the execution of several lower-level instructions (for example, environments rather than syntactical substitutions are used to bind variables to values). However, internal transitions generated by book keeping activities, such as environment look-ups, should not trigger the choice since these are not part of the top-level semantics. One is thus faced with a potentially subtle distinction between (at least) two types of internal transitions, one that can obfuscate the programmer's intuition about the construct.

These, and other considerations discussed in more detail in [21], have led to investigate and experiment with a choice operator which is easier and more efficient to implement in a distributed setting, while preserving as many of the "nice" mathematical properties as possible. Below we present the result so far. The operator has a deterministic evaluation strategy for evaluating its options. Non-determinism in the choice is based on the inherent non-determinism of the underlying system and on the availability of communication partners. To avoid unnecessary concurrent or distributed computations, the choice operator resides at the expression level which constitutes the sequential part of Facile. So far two different protocols for this choice operator have been implemented [19] and [18].

We introduce the following syntax:

$$e ::= \ldots \mid \mathtt{alternative}(e_1, e_2) \mid \mathtt{sendGuard}(e_1, e_2, e_3) \mid \mathtt{receiveGuard}(e_1, e_2)$$

We extend the values to include *guard_values*, given by the syntax below:

$$guard\_value ::= \mathtt{sendGuard}(k, v, \lambda x.e) \mid \mathtt{receiveGuard}(k, \lambda x.e)$$

The **alternative** construct takes as arguments two expressions evaluating to *guard_values* and chooses one of them based on the current state of the system and the availability of communication partners. A guard is either a **sendGuard** or a **receiveGuard**. A **sendGuard** takes three arguments: an expression evaluating to a channel constant; an expression evaluating to a value to be sent; a continuation to be invoked in case that branch of the **alternative** is chosen. Similarly, a **receiveGuard** takes as arguments: an expression which evaluates to a channel; an expression which evaluates to a continuation as its second argument. The continuations in the guards ensure the type safety of the construct and allow work to be done after the choice has been made.

```
proc mem_cell(get,put,contents) =
     alternative(
     sendGuard(get,contents,fn x => activate mem_cell(get,put,contents)),
     receiveGuard(put,fn x => activate mem_cell(get,put,x))
          )
```

Figure 6: Memory cell using the **alternative** construct

Figure 6 shows the memory cell from Figure 4 implemented using the **alternative** construct. Note that the continuation to the **sendGuard** takes a dummy argument, i.e. **x** is not in the body of the abstraction.

The operational semantics is defined by extending the LTS for expressions by adding the rules below. We start with a set of rules whose only function is to specify a deterministic, call-by-value, left-to-right evaluation of arguments for both the **alternative** and the *guard* constructs.

$$\frac{K, N, e_1 \overset{l}{\hookrightarrow} K', N', e_1'}{K, N, \mathtt{sendGuard}(e_1, e_2, e_3) \overset{l}{\hookrightarrow} K', N', \mathtt{sendGuard}(e_1', e_2, e_3)}$$

$$\frac{K, N, e_2 \stackrel{l}{\hookrightarrow} K', N', e_2'}{K, N, \texttt{sendGuard}(v, e_2, e_3) \stackrel{l}{\hookrightarrow} K', N', \texttt{sendGuard}(v, e_2', e_3)}$$

$$\frac{K, N, e_3 \stackrel{l}{\hookrightarrow} K', N', e_3'}{K, N, \texttt{sendGuard}(v_1, v_2, e_3) \stackrel{l}{\hookrightarrow} K', N', \texttt{sendGuard}(v_1, v_2, e_3')}$$

$$\frac{K, N, e_1 \stackrel{l}{\hookrightarrow} K', N', e_1'}{K, N, \texttt{receiveGuard}(e_1, e_2) \stackrel{l}{\hookrightarrow} K', N', \texttt{receiveGuard}(e_1', e_2)}$$

$$\frac{K, N, e_2 \stackrel{l}{\hookrightarrow} K', N', e_2'}{K, N, \texttt{receiveGuard}(v, e_2) \stackrel{l}{\hookrightarrow} K', N', \texttt{receiveGuard}(v, e_2')}$$

$$\frac{K, N, e_1 \stackrel{l}{\hookrightarrow} K', N', e_1'}{K, N, \texttt{alternative}(e_1, e_2) \stackrel{l}{\hookrightarrow} K', N', \texttt{alternative}(e_1', e_2)}$$

$$\frac{K, N, e_2 \stackrel{l}{\hookrightarrow} K', N', e_2'}{K, N, \texttt{alternative}(\mathit{guard\_value}, e_2) \stackrel{l}{\hookrightarrow} K', N', \texttt{alternative}(\mathit{guard\_value}, e_2')}$$

Note that external transitions produced during the evaluation of a guard will not trigger a choice. Only when each guard and all arguments to the guards have been evaluated to values an external transition which may trigger the choice will be produced. The core of the semantics is expressed by the following four rules.

The first two define the transitions (potentially) generated by *guard_values*: sendGuard's and receiveGuard's once their arguments have been reduced to values.

$$K, N, \texttt{sendGuard}(k, v, \lambda x.e) \stackrel{k!v}{\hookrightarrow} K, N, (\lambda x.e)\texttt{triv}$$

$$K, N, \texttt{receiveGuard}(k, \lambda x.e) \stackrel{k?v}{\hookrightarrow} K, N, (\lambda x.e)v$$

The second two specify that external transitions generated by *guard_values* trigger a choice.

$$\frac{K, N, \mathit{guard\_value}_1 \stackrel{l}{\hookrightarrow} K', N', e_1}{K, N, \texttt{alternative}(\mathit{guard\_value}_1, \mathit{guard\_value}_2) \stackrel{l}{\hookrightarrow} K', N', e_1}$$

$$\frac{K, N, guard\_value_2 \overset{l}{\hookrightarrow} K', N', e_2}{K, N, \mathtt{alternative}(guard\_value_1, guard\_value_2) \overset{l}{\hookrightarrow} K', N', e_2}$$

In its simplest, and perhaps safest usage, **alternative** can be viewed as a guarded choice operator. One can certainly argue that the semantics allows possibly undesirable "side-effects" during the evaluation of guards. However, there may be useful usages of such external communications. For example, these turned out to be useful in syntactically transforming an **alternative** construct in a program to send tracing information to a tracing tool. Since communications with the tracing tool occur during the evaluation of guards, they will not trigger the choice.

5 Exceptions

There seems to be an endless spectrum of potential failures in a distributed system, so trying to list them and propose solutions for each would be impossible. Instead we will try to provide language constructs that could allow the programmer to handle at least some foreseeable failures. In the Facile implementation there is already an exception mechanism inherited from ML. However, special care has been taken to ensure that raised exceptions stay local to the process in which they are raised. The syntax for exceptions and exception handling is:

$$e ::= \ldots \mid \mathtt{raise}\ e \mid e\ \mathtt{handle}\ eid\ \mathtt{with}\ e'$$

and we allow constants *eid* of type **exception**.

The **raise** *e* construct evaluates *e* until it becomes an exception identifier *eid*. In case an exception is not handled by the top-level expression **raise** *eid* may be the final result of a functional computation, thus we extend the value domain to allow raised exceptions to be returned as a final value:

$$v ::= \ldots \mid \mathtt{raise}\ eid$$

e **handle** *eid* **with** *e'* evaluates *e* until it either becomes a value *v* (different from **raise** *eid*) in which case the value *v* is returned, or *e* becomes a raised exception. If the raised exception equals *eid* then *e'* is computed, otherwise *e'* is discarded and the raised exception is the result. For simplicity we have restricted the **handle** construct to do matching on exception identifiers (*eid*'s) only. To mimic the general ML exception handling we have to extend the expression part with pattern matching. This is possible, but rather elaborate and has been left for future studies.

The operational semantics is based on an early version of exceptions in ML [14] and it is given by extending the LTS for expressions with the following rules which formalise the intuition stated above:

$$\frac{K, N, e \overset{l}{\hookrightarrow} K', N', e'}{K, N, e \texttt{ handle } eid \texttt{ with } e'' \overset{l}{\hookrightarrow} K', N', e' \texttt{ handle } eid \texttt{ with } e''}$$

$$\frac{K, N, e \overset{l}{\hookrightarrow} K', N', e'}{K, N, \texttt{raise } e \overset{l}{\hookrightarrow} K', N', \texttt{raise } e'}$$

$$K, N, \texttt{raise } eid \texttt{ handle } eid \texttt{ with } e \overset{\tau}{\hookrightarrow} K, N, e$$

$$K, N, \texttt{raise } eid \texttt{ handle } eid' \texttt{ with } e \overset{\tau}{\hookrightarrow} K, N, \texttt{raise } eid \quad \text{provided } eid \neq eid'$$

$$K, N, v \texttt{ handle } eid' \texttt{ with } e \overset{\tau}{\hookrightarrow} K, N, v \quad \text{provided } v \neq \texttt{raise } eid''$$

In addition we need a meta rule for propagating exceptions:

$$K, N, C[\texttt{raise } eid] \overset{\tau}{\hookrightarrow} K, N, \texttt{raise } eid \quad \text{provided } C \neq [\,] \texttt{ handle } eid \texttt{ with } e'$$

This meta rule prescribes that the context in which an exception is raised is discarded when the context is not a handler. A context is an expression with a hole to be filled. In the above rule the hole should only occur in redex position (see [21] for the formal definition of context and redex position). The following rule is an instance of the meta rule:

$$K, N, (\texttt{raise } eid)e \overset{\tau}{\hookrightarrow} K', N', \texttt{raise } eid$$

Having exceptions in the language would allow certain system exceptions to be raised and handled. For example we could allow a system dependent semantics for communication where an exception is raised in case no communication partners are willing to participate in a communication. This could be done by adding the rules below to the Facile semantics:

$$\texttt{send}(k, v) \overset{\tau}{\hookrightarrow} \texttt{raise } Send$$

$$\texttt{receive } k \overset{\tau}{\hookrightarrow} \texttt{raise } Receive$$

This would specify that we may non-deterministically raise an exception instead of (blocking on a) communication. The exception could then be handled by an exception handler which specifies what to do under exceptional circumstances.

This could be useful in the case of node failure, as discussed in the previous section, since if the only communication partner happened to be at a failed node then an exception could be raised. However, it would in general be up to the implementor of Facile to decide when and under which circumstances the exceptions should be raised. We feel that this is undesirable for several reasons. First it will mean very different behaviour of the same program on different implementations of the Facile system since arbitrary decisions for the raising of *Send*/*Receive* exceptions are allowed. Secondly it will make reasoning about Facile programs very tedious since for each communication we will have to reason about its exception(s) as well.

6 Time

In distributed computing systems it is a well-known problem that a computation may block because it needs to synchronise with its external environment (another process or system resources like I/O devices). In Facile communication constitutes the external synchronisation mechanism. We may view a transition $K, N, be_1 \xrightarrow{l}\!\!\!\!\!\!\gg K, N, be_1'$, where $l \neq \tau$, as a communication offer on l. However, if no matching communication $K, N, be_2 \xrightarrow{\bar{l}}\!\!\!\!\!\!\gg K, N, be_2'$ is offered by a process be_2 in the environment of be_1 then be_1 may be viewed as blocked on l. Most operating systems provide facilities for unblocking blocked processes or provide means for testing for availability of communication partners. In the previous section we discussed one approach based on raising exceptions. We found this approach unacceptable because of its potential ad hoc implementations. Thus we prefer to introduce some new primitive constructs which may provide means for breaking blocked communication(s) and at the same time are sufficiently general to address a whole class of systems issues not implementable through constructs introduced so far.

The most commonly used technique for breaking blocked communications is to introduce some time-out mechanism. Rather than introducing directly "time-out'able" send and receive constructs we introduce some more general/primitive constructs which will allow us, among other things, to implement the mentioned constructs.

To integrate time constructs in the Facile language we add the following expression:

$$e ::= \ldots \mid \texttt{delay}\ e$$

and we allow constants d of type `time`.

`delay` e first evaluates e until it becomes a time constant d. Then it will suspend itself for an amount of time no less than the time specified by d.

With this construct we may define a delay guard `delayGuard` which may be placed in a choice branch. Figure 7 shows a possible implementation as well as an example of its use in an abstraction for a send construct with "time-out".

To define an operational semantics for the `delay` construct we follow some recent developments in timed process algebra surveyed by Nicollin and Sifakis in [29]. This survey includes construct from ACP$_\rho$ [4, 17], ATP [27, 28, 30], TCSP [32, 9, 33], TeCCS [26], TiCCS [35, 36], TPL [15, 16], and U-LOTOS [7],

A timed system is viewed as a system with a global parameter D for time, ranged over by d, equipped with a binary operation $+$ which behaves like addition on non-negative numbers. This construction is analogous to the global sort K for channels management with "$\cup$" for adding new channels.

Definition 6.1 (Definition 2.1 in [29])
A time domain is a commutative monoid $(D, +, 0)$ satisfying the following requirements.

- $d + d' = d \Leftrightarrow d' = 0$

```
fun delayGuard (time, cont) =
    let val ch = channel(unit)
    in (spawn (delay (time); send (ch, triv);
        receiveGuard (ch, cont))
    end

fun time_out_send (ch, v, time_out) =
    alternative (
        sendGuard (ch, v, fn x => x),
        delayGuard (time_out, fn x => x)
            )
```

Figure 7: Implementation of **delayGuard** and time_out_send

- *the preorder $\leq$ defined by $d \leq d' \Leftrightarrow \exists d'' : d + d'' = d'$ is a total, well-founded order.*

We denote $D - \{0\}$ by D_*. We also write $d < d'$ instead of $d \leq d' \wedge d \neq d'$. D is called dense if $\forall d, d' : d < d' \Rightarrow \exists d'' : d < d'' < d'$. D is called discrete if $\forall d \exists d' : d < d' \wedge \forall d'' : d, d'' \Rightarrow d' \leq d''$.

Examples of time domains are $\mathcal{N}$ (discrete), $\mathcal{Q}^+$ and $\mathcal{R}^+$ (dense), or even the singleton $\{0\}$.

It is easy to prove that 0 is the least element of D and for any d, d', if $d \leq d'$, then the element d'' such that $d + d'' = d'$ is unique. It is denoted by $d' - d$.

Any execution sequence (i.e. transitions in the semantics) of the system is a sequence of two phase steps. In the first processes may execute independently or interact by communication, in the second all components coordinate to let time progress. In this approach, we assume that communication and internal (τ) actions take zero time, since this leads to relatively simple theories. This assumption is for example used in the ESTEREL language [6]. It has often been argued that models where actions take some non-zero time to execute allow more realistic descriptions. However, such an assumption destroys abstractions of time since it becomes dependent on specific implementation choices. The difference between ESTEREL and the context in which we are working is essentially that in ESTEREL it is feasible to assign delays to actions at some stage of reasoning (due to the restrictions in modeling power and to the range of applications), while it is not generally feasible in Facile, at least at the current state of technology. In conclusion, there are limits in our current treatment, to which we will return later in this section.

To give an operational semantics for the above time constructs we first modify the LTS for expressions $\langle Econ, \mathcal{L}, \hookrightarrow\rangle$ by defining $\mathcal{L} = Comm \cup \{\tau\} \cup \{\Phi(be) \mid be \in beh\_exp\} \cup \mathcal{N} \cup \{n(be) \mid be \in beh\_exp \;\&\; n \in \mathcal{N}\} \cup D_*$. The LTS for behaviour expressions is modified to $\langle Bcon, (Comm \cup \{\tau\} \cup \mathcal{N} \cup \{n(be) \mid be \in beh\_exp \;\&\; n \in \mathcal{N}\} \cup D_*), \longrightarrow\!\!\!\!\!\gg\rangle$.

Furthermore we extend the transition relations $\hookrightarrow \subseteq Econ \times \mathcal{L} \times Econ$ and $\longrightarrow\!\!\!\!\!\gg \subseteq Bcon \times (Comm \cup \{\tau\} \cup \mathcal{N} \cup \{n(be) \mid be \in beh\_exp \;\&\; n \in \mathcal{N}\}) \times Bcon$ by adding transitions of the form $K, N, e \stackrel{d}{\hookrightarrow}$

K', N', e' and $K, N, be \overset{d}{\twoheadrightarrow} K', N', be'$ to the set of transitions for expressions, respectively behaviour expressions. These transition relations are the smallest relations closed under the rules discussed so far and the rules presented below.

$$\frac{K, N, e \overset{l}{\hookrightarrow} K', N', e'}{K, N, \texttt{delay}\ e \overset{l}{\hookrightarrow} K', N', \texttt{delay}\ e'}$$

$$K, N, e \overset{d}{\hookrightarrow} K, N, e \quad \text{provided } e \neq \texttt{delay}\ e'$$

$$K, N, \texttt{delay}\ d \overset{d}{\hookrightarrow} K', N', \texttt{triv}$$

$$\frac{d' < d}{K, N, \texttt{delay}\ d \overset{d'}{\hookrightarrow} K, N, \texttt{delay}\ (d - d')}$$

$$K, N, \texttt{terminate} \overset{d}{\twoheadrightarrow} K, N, \texttt{terminate}$$

$$\frac{K, N, e \overset{d}{\hookrightarrow} K', N', e'}{K, N, \texttt{activate}\ e \overset{d}{\twoheadrightarrow} K', N', \texttt{activate}\ e'}$$

$$\frac{K, N, be_1 \overset{d}{\twoheadrightarrow} K', N', be_1' \quad K, N, be_2 \overset{d}{\twoheadrightarrow} K', N', be_2'}{K, N, be_1 \parallel be_2 \overset{d}{\twoheadrightarrow} K', N', be_1' \parallel be_2'}$$

The first rule says that **delay** is call-by-value. It means that **delay** has no effect before its argument expression is reduced to a time constant. The second rule is intended as a meta rule for all expressions which do not involve a delay construct. It states that such expressions can idle for an arbitrary amount of time. Rule number three describes the situation, where the **delay** is performed and rewrites to **triv** upon completion. The fourth rule simply describes that when the elapsed time d' is less than the delay time d the waiting process changes/updates the delay time to the difference in time values, i.e. $(d - d')$ instead of d. This is the "clock" advancing its time measurement. The fifth rule states that a terminated process does not change state when time progresses. On the other hand, it does not prevent time from progressing. This is a natural definition for a terminated process in a timed system since it allows time to progress even though it is deadlocked on other actions. Activated processes are covered by rule number six. It is this rule that gives the interplay between time actions at the expression level and time actions at the behaviour expression level ($\overset{d}{\hookrightarrow}$ above the line, $\overset{d}{\twoheadrightarrow}$ below). So if an expression progresses in time so does the activation of the expression. The final rule describes concurrent composition (on the same node), where the partners have to agree on an atomic action (producing labels) or a time progressing action. The concurrent rewrite only takes place when all partners involved perform a $\xrightarrow{d}\!\!\!\!\gg$ transition, where the d's are identical.

We have not defined the relationship between the time constructs and the distributed part of Facile discussed in section 3. We postpone this discussion to the latter part of this section.

The operational semantics given above satisfies several important properties which gives us confidence that the chosen model of time is appropriate:

Proposition 6.2 TIME DETERMINISM
If $K, N, e \overset{d}{\hookrightarrow} K', N', e'$ and $K, N, e \overset{d}{\hookrightarrow} K'', N'', e''$ then $e' = e''$ and $K = K' = K''$ and $N = N' = N''$. If $K, N, be \overset{d}{\twoheadrightarrow} K', N', be'$ and $K, N, be \overset{d}{\twoheadrightarrow} K'', N'', be''$ then $be' = be''$ and $K = K' = K''$ and $N = N' = N''$.

PROOF: By transition induction. □

This proposition states that when time progresses by some time d then the resulting behaviour is completely determined from e (respectively be) and d. In other words time progresses deterministically.

Proposition 6.3 TIME ADDITIVITY
$K, N, e \overset{d+d'}{\hookrightarrow} K', N', e'$ iff $K, N, e \overset{d}{\hookrightarrow} K'', N'', e''$ and $K'', N'', e'' \overset{d'}{\hookrightarrow} K', N', e'$ for some K'', N'', e''. $K, N, be \overset{d+d'}{\twoheadrightarrow} K', N', be'$ iff $K, N, be \overset{d}{\twoheadrightarrow} K'', N'', be''$ and $K'', N'', be'' \overset{d'}{\twoheadrightarrow} K', N', be'$ for some K'', N'', be''.

PROOF: By transition induction. □

This proposition states that if an expression (respectively a process) can idle for $d + d'$ time units, then it can idle for d time units and then idle for d' time units and vice versa and in both cases the resulting state is the same.

Proposition 6.4 TIME-LOCK FREENESS
*For all K, N, e there exists $l \in \mathcal{L}, K', N', e'$ such that $K, N, e \overset{l}{\hookrightarrow} K', N', e'$.
For all K, N, be there exists $l \in \mathcal{L}, K', N', be'$ such that $K, N, be \overset{l}{\twoheadrightarrow} K', N', be'$.*

PROOF: By transition induction. □

This proposition guarantees that time always can progress. This implies that there is no sink state for time in our model. It would be possible to add constructs for time-locks, but this would introduce unimplementable constructs. This may be useful in a calculus for specifying timed systems since such time-locked processes would express a flaw in the design. However, for a programming language it would be of little use.

Furthermore our model satisfies the property of time persistency:

Proposition 6.5 TIME PERSISTENCY
If $K, N, e \overset{l}{\hookrightarrow} K', N', e'$ and $K, N, e \overset{d}{\hookrightarrow} K'', N'', e''$ for some K', N', e' then $K'', N'', e'' \overset{l}{\hookrightarrow} K', N', e'$. If $K, N, be \overset{l}{\twoheadrightarrow} K', N', be'$ and $K, N, be \overset{d}{\twoheadrightarrow} K'', N'', be''$ for some K', N', be' then $K'', N'', be'' \overset{l}{\twoheadrightarrow} K', N', be'$.

PROOF: By transition induction. □

This proposition states that the progress of time cannot suppress the ability to perform an action. At first this can seem a bit contradictory to the desire of defining a time-out construct which will disable certain computation capabilities (which cannot be satisfied by the environment of a process). However, the disabling of an action in our model will not happen as a direct consequence of time progressing, but indirectly by time progressing and thus enabling certain attractive actions.

The semantics for **delay** d specifies that the expression suspends its evaluation for a time no less than d. Thus our notion of time only allows handling of minimum delay, but not of maximum delay where action has to take place before a specified time has elapsed. One way of enforcing maximum delay is to introduce the notion of action urgency.

Definition 6.6 Action urgency
If $K, N, e \overset{l}{\hookrightarrow} K', N', e'$ *then* $K, N, e \overset{d}{\not\hookrightarrow}$.
If $K, N, be \overset{l}{\twoheadrightarrow} K', N', be'$ *then* $K, N, be \overset{d}{\not\twoheadrightarrow}$.

which means that normal actions take priority over time. We have not enforced action urgency in the structural operational semantics defined above, since we still have to understand its implications. However, we could enforce action urgency by replacing the rule:

$$K, N, e \overset{d}{\hookrightarrow} K, N, e \quad \text{provided } e \neq \mathtt{delay}\ e'$$

by the rule:

$$\frac{K, N, e \overset{l}{\not\hookrightarrow}}{K, N, e \overset{d}{\hookrightarrow} K, N, e} \quad \text{provided } e \neq \mathtt{delay}\ e'$$

and the rule:

$$\frac{K, N, be_1 \overset{d}{\twoheadrightarrow} K', N', be_1' \quad K, N, be_2 \overset{d}{\twoheadrightarrow} K', N', be_2'}{K, N, be_1 \,||\, be_2 \overset{d}{\twoheadrightarrow} K', N', be_1' \,||\, be_2'}$$

by the rule:

$$\frac{K, N, be_1 \overset{d}{\twoheadrightarrow} K', N', be_1' \quad K, N, be_2 \overset{d}{\twoheadrightarrow} K', N', be_2' \quad K, N, be_1 \,||\, be_2 \overset{l}{\not\twoheadrightarrow}}{K, N, be_1 \,||\, be_2 \overset{d}{\twoheadrightarrow} K', N', be_1' \,||\, be_2'}$$

The two new rules have a negative premise to ensure that time actions only take place when no other actions can happen. However, this implies that a communication which cannot be satisfied can block the progress of time and thus leave the system deadlocked. This is actually what we tried to avoid in the first place by introducing a notion of time on which we can build constructs for time-outs.

A related concept that we may choose to enforce is τ urgency. This is obtained from action urgency by restricting the urgent actions l to be τ's only. If we enforce τ urgency we specify that communications (which produce τ-transitions) and internal transitions (such as function application, channel creation and spawning) are executed as soon as possible. This would ensure that a time-out happens exactly when the delay expires. However, it puts very strong requirements on any Facile implementation to ensure that this is obeyed. It is questionable if we can guarantee τ urgency in a distributed computing environment where arbitrary delays may arise from network latencies. Furthermore, τ urgency may be problematic in face of diverging computations, i.e. computations producing an infinite sequence of internal transitions without interacting with their environment. In effect such computations will prevent the progress of time since they will require all τ-transitions to happen before time can progress.

As mentioned earlier we have not defined the relationship between the time constructs and the distributed part of Facile. There are several options to pursue. One could be to assume a global clock for all agents in the distributed environment. Then we could specify the semantics straightforwardly as:

$$\frac{K, N, be \overset{d}{\twoheadrightarrow} K', N', be'}{K, N, n :: be \overset{d}{\ggg} K', N', n :: be'}$$

$$\frac{K, N, dbe_1 \overset{d}{\ggg} K', N', dbe'_1 \quad K, N, dbe_2 \overset{d}{\ggg} K', N', dbe'_2}{K, N, dbe_1 \mid\mid\mid dbe_2 \overset{d}{\ggg} K', N', dbe'_1 \mid\mid\mid dbe'_2}$$

That is we treat time in the distributed case analogously to concurrent composition on each node. We feel that this is an unreasonable assumption. It is fine for processes logically executing concurrently (by interleaving) at a single node since all processes will have access to the system clock at this node. But for a truly distributed environment this may be unrealistic, e.g. we may envision that each node has its own clock (potentially with its own time domain). However, the state of the art of timed process algebra does not seem to propose any solutions to this problem. A (temporary) solution could be to translate local time transitions into τ-transitions between distributed agents with the following rule:

$$\frac{K, N, be \overset{d}{\twoheadrightarrow} K', N', be'}{K, N, n :: be \overset{\tau}{\ggg} K', N', n :: be'}$$

Unfortunately this is problematic for dense time domains since this may introduce an uncountable number of τ-transitions before any external transition.

7 Conclusion

The objective of the work on the semantics of Facile is to reach a stage where the formulation of the semantics provides an effective basis for developing tools that aid system designers in two main types of activities: verification of properties of Facile programs, with a specific concern for properties of distributed systems; program transformation, e.g. to configure applications to execute in different distributed environments or to increase the reusability of designs and executable code. A quick conclusion of this paper might well be that a lot of work needs to be done to reach this rather ambitious objective. What we have presented are some preliminary steps which attempt to use some of the most interesting developments in the area of concurrency theory.

There are at least two major sources of difficulty in developing relatively comprehensive and effective formal foundations for Facile. One is that there is a big step in moving from the formulation of a theory in an abstract setting to the application of the theory to the reality of a complex programming language. For example, questions such as mobility of channels or higher-order processes have been studied in isolation. Here we are instead dealing with a programming environment that supports higher-order, timed, distributed, mobile processes. Another is that the objective of the work in semantics is to achieve a formulation of the semantics that captures as directly as possible the reality of programming with Facile. The introduction of any level of indirection or encoding of the notions present in the programming environment will inevitably introduce undesirable extra complexity, and thus ultimately hinder any practical usage of the semantics. In summary, it appears that what we can expect to import are certain ideas underlying some of the theoretical developments, but not the formalisms/calculi as such. Furthermore, many difficult decisions must be made because in a complex environment many "orthogonal" constructs must coexist in coherent way.

The next major goal will be to extend the notion of equivalence between Facile programs formulated in [13] and to establish an equational theory. We envision that parts of the formulation may benefit from results in generalising bisimulation-like techniques [3]. The extended theory should ideally be a conservative extension of the "old" one, in the sense of preserving the old properties. There are, however, several questions which remain open in the treatment we presented here, and which we believe need to be given an intuitively convincing operational treatment before we can formalise a useful notion of program observation. From this viewpoint, we find that the treatment of the semantic extensions we presented has reached varying levels of development, ranging from rather convincing (e.g. for locality or choice), to weakly convincing (e.g. for the time issue) and to incomplete as in the case of exception handling.

A question that the current treatment of locality and time leaves open could be characterised as one of "filtering" of information to achieve different levels of abstraction. As shown in sections 3 and 6, to account for computations at different nodes and for the passage of time we rendered the transition systems used for the operational definition more complex, through the introduction of new operators, new components in the transition configurations, new types of labels in the transition relations and new transition relations. It is clear that to obtain a usable operational formalisation a notion of mapping between different levels of abstractions in the same definition is needed. For example, to verify properties of a system that do not depend on the locality of components it would be desirable to collapse the transition system into one that essentially coincides with the old one, since the latter allows a simpler treatment of notions like communication and process creation. As for time, the abstraction could be achieved by assuming a zero time domain and showing that the resulting transition system is isomorphic to the original one. An interesting notion of different levels of observation is proposed in [10].

In section 6 we have introduced a notion of time which allows us to program certain constructs for breaking blocked communication. However, the approach applies only to the expression and behaviour expression level. We discussed a possible solution for distributed agents which translates local time transitions into global τ-transitions. However, this is problematic for dense time domains since an uncountable number of τ-transitions may be introduced before any external transition. We have considered treating time for distributed agents analogously to the treatment of time for concurrent composition on each node, i.e. with one global clock synchronising all components to let time progress. We feel that this is an unreasonable assumption in the distributed case. It is fine for processes that logically execute concurrently (by interleaving) at a single node since all processes will have access to the same system clock. For a truly distributed environment this may be unrealistic; e.g. we may envision that each node has its own clock, potentially with its own time domain. This is an instance where the state of the art of theoretical development (in this case in the area of timed process algebra) does not seem to propose solutions.

Finally, the treatment of exceptions and exception handling is still incomplete, mainly because of the absence of a notion of what we may call global exceptions. This is needed to model signals generated by the system (e.g. originated by users), which typically have both an asynchronous behaviour and a high priority. The question is still open and is of a practical nature: should signals be handled by the currently executing thread? should they be broadcast to all processes at a node? or should there be special "system processes" at each node in charge of global exception handling, which can be consulted by other processes? The last approach appears the most reasonable for various reasons: it is conceptually simple and reflects the way the mechanism would be implemented; it is the most primitive since it need not be dealt with in the semantics; it is the most platform independent since signals depend on the underlying operating system; it does not need to introduce another primitive communication mechanism such as broadcast.

References

[1] Aceto, L., *A Static View of Localities*, draft, INRIA-Sophia Antipolis, France, 1991.

[2] Andrew W. Appel and David B. MacQueen *Standard ML of New Jersey*, in Proceedings of the Third International Symposium on Programming Language Implementation and Logic Programming (PLILP), Lecture Notes in Computer Science 528, pp. 1-13, Springer Verlag, 1991.

[3] Astesiano, E., Giovini, A., Reggio, G., *Observational Structures and their Logics*, Theoretical Computer Science 94, North Holland, 1992.

[4] Baeten, J.C.M., Bergstra, J.A., *Real Time Process Algebra*, Technical Report CS-R9053, Centre for Mathematics and Computer Science, Amsterdam, The Netherlands, 1990.

[5] Berry, D., Milner, R., and Turner, D.N., *A semantics for ML concurrency primitives*, in Proceedings of 1992 POPL Conference.

[6] Berry, G., Cosserat, L., *The ESTEREL synchronous programming language and its mathematical semantics*, in Proceedings of CMU Seminar on Concurrency, LNCS 197, Springer-Verlag, 1985.

[7] Bolognesi, T., Lucidi, F., *LOTOS-like process algebra with urgent or timed interactions*, in Proceedings of REX Workshop "Real-Time: Theory in Practice", The Netherlands, 1991.

[8] Boudol, G., Castellani, I., Hennessy, M., Kiehn, A., *Observing Localities*, Report No. 4/91, University of Sussex, 1991.

[9] Davies, J., Schneider, S., *An Introduction to Timed CSP*, Technical Report PRG-75, Oxford University Computing Laboratory, 1989.

[10] Degano, P., Priami, C., *Observing Concurrency via Proved Trees*, in Proceedings of ICALP 92, LNCS 623, Springer-Verlag, 1992.

[11] DeNicola, R., Hennessy, M., *CCS without τs*, in Proceedings of 1987 TAPSOFT Conference, LNCS 250, Springer-Verlag, 1987.

[12] Giacalone, A., Mishra, P., Prasad, S., *Facile: A Symmetric Integration of Concurrent and Functional Programming*, International Journal of Parallel Programming, Vol. 18, No. 2, 1990.

[13] Giacalone, A., Mishra, P., Prasad, S., *Operational and Algebraic Semantics for Facile: A Symmetric Integration of Concurrent and Functional Programming*, in Proceedings of ICALP 90, LNCS 443, pp. 765-780, Springer-Verlag, 1990.

[14] Harper, R., MacQueen, D., Milner, R., *Standard ML*, Report ECS-LFCS 86-2, Laboratory for Foundations of Computer Science, Edinburgh University, 1987.

[15] Hennessy, M., Regan, T., *A Temporal Process Algebra*, Technical Report 2/90, University of Sussex, 1990.

[16] Hennessy, M., Regan, T., *A Process Algebra for Timed Systems*, Technical Report 5/91, University of Sussex, 1991.

[17] Klusener, A.S., *Completeness in Real Time Process Algebra*, Technical Report CS-R9106, Centre for Mathematics and Computer Science, Amsterdam, 1991.

[18] Knabe, F., *A Distributed Protocol for Channel-Based Communication with Choice*, in Proceedings of PARLE '92 (Parallel Architectures and Languages Europe), Poster in LNCS 605, Springer-Verlag, 1992.
Full version in tech. Report ECRC–92–16, European Computer-Industry Research Centre, 1992.

[19] Kramer, A., Cosquer, F., *Distributing Facile*, MAGIC Note[2], 1991.

[20] Leth, L., *Functional Programs as Reconfigurable Networks of Communicating Processes*, Ph.D. Thesis, Imperial College, 1991.

[21] Leth, L., Thomsen, B., *Some Facile Chemistry*, Tech. Report ECRC–92–14, European Computer-Industry Research Centre, 1992.

[22] Milner, R., *A Calculus of Communicating Systems*, Lecture Notes in Computer Science, vol. 92, Springer Verlag, 1980.

[23] Milner, R., *Communication and Concurrency*, Prentice Hall, 1989.

[2]MAGIC Notes are internal working documents from the MAGIC group at ECRC.

[24] Milner, R., Parrow, J. and Walker, D., *A calculus of mobile processes*, Tech. Reports ECS-LFCS-89-85 and -86, Laboratory for Foundations of Computer Science, Edinburgh University, 1989.

[25] Milner, R., Tofte, M., Harper, R., *Definition of Standard ML*, MIT Press, 1990.

[26] Moller, F., Tofts, C., *A Temporal Calculus of Communicating Processes*, in Proceedings of CONCUR'90, LNCS 458, Springer Verlag, pp. 401-415, 1990.

[27] Nicollin, X., Richier, J.-L., Sifakis, J., Voiron, J., *ATP: an Algebra for Timed Processes*, in Proceedings of the IFIP TC 2 Working Conference on Programming Concepts and Methods, Israel, 1990.

[28] Nicollin, X., Sifakis, J., *The algebra of timed processes ATP: theory and application*, Technical Report RT-C26, LGI-IMAG, France, 1990.

[29] Nicollin, X., Sifakis, J., *An Overview and Synthesis on Timed Process Algebras*, in Proceedings of CAV'91, LNCS 575, pp. 376-398, 1991.

[30] Nicollin, X., Sifakis, J., Yovine, S., *From ATP to Timed Graphs and Hybrid Systems*, in Proceedings of REX Workshop "Real-Time: Theory in Practice", The Netherlands, 1991.

[31] Prasad S., *Towards A Symmetric Integration of Concurrent and Functional Programming*, Ph. D. Thesis, State University of New York at Stony Brook, 1991.

[32] Reed, G.M., Roscoe, A.W., *A timed model for Communicating Sequential Processes*, Theoretical Computer Science vol 58, pp. 249-261, 1988.

[33] Schneider, S., *An Operational Semantics for Timed CSP*, Programming Research Group, Oxford University, 1991

[34] Thomsen, B., *A calculus of higher-order communicating systems*, in Proceedings of 1989 POPL Conference.

[35] Wang, Y., *Real-time behaviour of asynchronous agents*, in Proceedings of CONCUR'90, LNCS 458, Springer Verlag, pp. 502-520, 1990.

[36] Wang, Y., *CCS + Time = an Interleaving Model for Real Time Systems*, in Proceedings of ICALP 91, 1991.

On the Relation Between Unity Properties and Sequences of States

R.T. Udink*
Utrecht University, Department of Computer Science,
P.O. Box 80.089, 3508 TB Utrecht, the Netherlands

J.N. Kok
Utrecht University, Department of Computer Science,
P.O. Box 80.089, 3508 TB Utrecht, the Netherlands

ABSTRACT Stepwise refinement of programs has proven to be a suitable method for developing parallel and distributed programs. We examine and compare a number of different notions of program refinement for Unity. Two of these notions are based on execution sequences. Refinement corresponds to the reduction of the set of execution sequences, i.e. reducing the amount of nondeterminism. The other refinement notions are based on Unity properties as introduced by Chandy and Misra. The Unity approach is to refine specifications. Although it has proven a suitable formalism for deriving algorithms, it seems less suitable for handling implementation details. Following Sanders and Singh, we formalize program refinement in the Unity framework as the preservation of Unity properties. We show that Unity properties are not powerful enough to characterize execution sequences. As a consequence, the notion of property-preserving refinement differs from the notion of reducing the set of execution sequences.

Keywords Semantic models, Unity, program refinement.

CONTENTS

*This research has been supported by the Foundation for Computer Science in the Netherlands SION under project 612-317-044

0 Introduction

Developing correct parallel and distributed programs from specification to implementation is a difficult task. Stepwise refinement has proven to be a useful methodology for this task.

The Unity framework, as introduced by Chandy and Misra in [CM88], consists of a programming language and a programming logic. The logic is based on a set of temporal properties. These properties are used to give specifications. The Unity approach is to refine specifications toward a specific architecture until a program can be derived easily. A specification is refined by a stronger set of properties. As can be seen from the case studies in [CM88], this method is useful for deriving parallel and distributed algorithms. However, it is not easy to deal with low-level implementation details at the level of specification. So, the specification refinement seems less suitable for the final stage of program development. In this stage of the development process, program refinement is more useful. This consists of transforming programs toward a specific architecture in such a way that semantic properties of the program are preserved. There are different notions of what kind of properties are to be preserved. Because we are also interested in interactive programs, we need a semantic notion that takes into account some temporal behavior of the program, not only its pre- and postconditions. Sanders [San90] defines a syntactic notion of program refinement similar to reactive refinement as defined by Back in [Bac90]. For this kind of refinements, she is interested in the preservation of adjusted Unity properties. In [Sin91], Singh uses a similar approach for the original Unity properties. Lamport and Abadi [AL88] base their work on behaviors, sequences of states that can occur during program execution. Refinement of a program should reduce the set of behaviors, that is, it reduces the amount of nondeterminism.

In this paper the relation between these notions of program refinement is examined for Unity programs. Therefore, we define a number of semantic models for Unity programs. First, we define two models based on sequences of states. The first semantics of a program is the set of stutter-free sequences of states that can occur during program execution. An extension for compositionality results in the second model. Secondly, we define some models based on Unity properties. The semantics of a program is the set of properties (safety and progress properties) that it satisfies. We can choose for the semantics two notions of progress: either *leadsto* properties, or *ensures* properties. Since we can use properties defined by Chandy and Misra as well as those defined by Sanders, we define four different models. Each model yields a notion of refinement. At first sight one might think that the notion of refinement in terms of sequences and properties are equivalent. We will show that Unity properties are not powerful enough to characterize sequences. Consequently, the notion of property-preserving refinement differs from the notion of reducing the set of execution sequences.

This paper is organized as follows. In section 1, an introduction to Unity is given. It discusses the Unity programming language and the two Unity logics. Section 2 discusses some semantic models for Unity programs, which will be compared in section 3. Section 4 mentions some conclusions and further research.

1 Introduction to Unity

In this section a brief overview of Unity is given. Unity was introduced by Chandy and Misra in [CM88]. First, the Unity programming language is presented. Then, two logics for the language are discussed: a variation of the logic in [CM88] and a logic given by Sanders in [San91].

A Unity program has several parts that are called sections. (In the sequel Unity programs are denoted by F or G.) We will only consider a subset of Unity programs, namely, programs that are made up of the following sections.

- An *initially-section* defining the initial values of variables. We denote by *init*.F the set of possible states that satisfy the requirements of the *initially-section* of a program F.

- An *assign-section* containing a non-empty set of (possibly multiple and/or conditional) assignment statements (for a program F denoted by *assign*.F). Assignment statements are separated by the symbol $[\!]$. Assignment statements are deterministic and the execution of each statement always terminates.

When it is clear from the context we may use F to denote *init*.F or *assign*.F. Execution of a Unity program F starts in a state contained in *init*.F. In each step an assignment statement is chosen from the set *assign*.F and executed. Furthermore, an execution has to be fair, that is, each statement should be chosen infinitely often. If the guard of the statement evaluates to *false*, execution of that statement is a skip statement. The execution of a Unity program never terminates. However, there is the notion of fixed point: if after some moment the state cannot be changed by any statement of F, one can view this state as the result of the computation.

An example of a Unity program is given below.

Program F
  initially
    $x \geq 0$
  assign
    $x := x + 1$ **if** $x \geq 0$
  $[\!]$ $x := x - 1$ **if** $x < 0$
end$\{F\}$

Execution of this program starts in a state where $x = c$ for some $c \geq 0$ and repeatedly a statement is executed. Execution of the first statement increases x by one. This happens infinitely often. The second statement, which is also selected infinitely often, does not change the value of x. So, the execution results in an ever increasing value of x.

Two programs can be composed with the union operator $[\!]$:

Definition 1.1 *Let F and G be Unity programs. The union of F and G, denoted by $F[\!]G$, is defined as*

$$init.(F[\!]G) \triangleq init.F \cap init.G,$$

$$assign.(F[\!]G) \triangleq assign.F \cup assign.G.$$

For example, the program F, as given above, can be composed with program G. This results in program $F[\!]G$:

Program G
initially
$x > 0$
assign
$x := -x$
end$\{G\}$

Program $F \| G$
initially
$x > 0$
assign
$x := x + 1$ **if** $x \geq 0$
$\| \ x := x - 1$ **if** $x < 0$
$\| \ x := -x$
end$\{F \| G\}$

Before introducing two logics for Unity we need to introduce some predicate transformers. The semantics of a single assignment statement can be given by its weakest liberal precondition *wlp* or strongest postcondition *sp* predicate transformers, as shown in [DS90].

Definition 1.2 *Let* $(x := E)$ *be an assignment statement. The weakest liberal precondition and the strongest postcondition are defined as*

$$wlp.(x := E).p \triangleq p(E/x),$$

$$sp.(x := E).p \triangleq \langle \exists y : x = E(y/x) :: p(y/x) \rangle.$$

The predicate $p(E/x)$ *is the predicate* p *in which* x *is substituted by* E.

The definitions for multiple assignments are similar, using simultaneous substitution.

Because the execution of each assignment statement always terminates, the notions of weakest liberal precondition and weakest precondition are the same. In the next definition we lift the predicate transformers *wlp* and *sp* to Unity programs. (Note that we denote function application by a dot that associates to the left: $f.g.x = (f.g).x$.)

Definition 1.3 *Let* F *be a Unity program and* p *a predicate. The predicate transformers wlp and sp are lifted to Unity programs by*

$$wlp.F.p \triangleq \langle \forall s : s \in F.assign :: wlp.s.p \rangle,$$

$$sp.F.p \triangleq \langle \exists s : s \in F.assign :: sp.s.p \rangle.$$

Now we can give the Chandy and Misra logic for Unity. It is based on three temporal properties: *unless*, *ensures*, and *leadsto*. The properties are attached to an entire program. They are defined in terms of the statements of the program. Because we will introduce a second logic later we subscript the properties by *CM*. A state of a Unity programs is a function from program variables to values. Following Dijkstra and Scholten [DS90], we use square brackets to denote universal quantification over all states.

Definition 1.4 (Chandy-Misra Logic) *Let* p, q *be arbitrary predicates and* F *a Unity program. Define the following properties of* F *by*

1. *unless property:*

$$p \ unless_{CM} \ q \triangleq [(p \wedge \neg q) \Rightarrow wlp.F.(p \vee q)].$$

2. *ensures property:*

$$p \ ensures_{CM} \ q \triangleq p \ unless_{CM} \ q \ \wedge \ \langle \exists s : s \in F.assign :: [(p \wedge \neg q) \Rightarrow wlp.s.q] \rangle.$$

3. *leadsto property:* $\mapsto_{CM}$ *is defined as the smallest binary relation R between predicates satisfying the following conditions:*

   (a) $R \supseteq ensures_{CM}$,

   (b) *R is transitive,*

   (c) *for any set W, if* $\langle \forall m : m \in W :: p_m \; R \; q\rangle$ *then* $\langle \exists m : m \in W :: p_m\rangle \; R \; q$.

The $unless_{CM}$ property is a safety property. The operational interpretation of $p \; unless_{CM} \; q$ is that if p becomes *true* during the execution of the program it remains *true* as long as q is *false*. The $ensures_{CM}$ and $leadsto_{CM}$ properties are progress properties. The operational interpretation of $p \; ensures_{CM} \; q$ is that if p holds it remains to hold until q holds and q will hold within finite time, i.e., a finite number of execution steps. The operational interpretation of $p \mapsto_{CM} q$ is that whenever p is *true*, q will become *true* within finite time. The definition of the $leadsto_{CM}$ property is slightly different from the definition given in [CM88]. It is a definition of Pachl given in [Pac90]. We use this notion because of its correspondence to the operational intuition of the *leadsto* property. We will discuss this in section 3.

Using the three basic properties some "derived" properties can be defined. For example:

$stable_{CM} \; p = p \; unless_{CM} \; false$,

$invariant_{CM} \; p = (init.F \Rightarrow p) \wedge (stable_{CM} \; p)$,

$p \; until_{CM} \; q = (p \; unless_{CM} \; q) \wedge (p \mapsto_{CM} q)$.

If the program is not clear from the context we will mention the program explicitly using the connective **in**, e.g., *p unless q* **in** *F*.

In [CM88], Chandy and Misra give many theorems to combine Unity properties and derive new properties from them, e.g., the Simple Conjunction Theorem

$$\frac{\begin{array}{c} p \; unless_{CM} \; q \\ p' \; unless_{CM} \; q' \end{array}}{p \wedge p' \; unless_{CM} \; q \vee q'.}$$

They also propose a substitution axiom. This axiom says that

if $invariant_{CM} \; (a = b)$ *then we may substitute a for b in every property of the program.*

However, this gives an unsound proof system. For example, for program F, introduced before, we can derive the properties $(x = c \wedge x \geq 0) \; unless_{CM} \; x > c$ and $invariant_{CM} \; (x \geq 0) \equiv true$. The substitution axiom says that $(x = c) \; unless_{CM} \; (x \geq c)$ is a property of F. However, this is not true if c is negative. This is because Unity properties also say something about the behavior of the program in states that are never reached during any program execution, e.g., the states where $x < 0$ for program F.

Sanders introduced a new logic to eliminate this problem in [San91]. The properties are changed in such a way that unreachable states are disregarded. This results in weaker properties than the properties as defined by Chandy and Misra.

Before defining Sanders's properties we give predicate transformers *wst* and *sst* (weakest and strongest stable predicates) as given in [San91].

Definition 1.5 *1. The predicate wst.F.p is the weakest solution for q such that*

$$[q \Rightarrow wlp.F.q \wedge q \Rightarrow p].$$

2. The predicate sst.F.p is the strongest solution for q of

$$[q \Rightarrow wlp.F.q \land p \Rightarrow q].$$

Sanders has proven the following characterization of *wst* and *sst* that can be used to compute these predicate transformers.

Theorem 1.6 *Define functions* f, g *by* $f.y = (wlp.F.y) \land p$ *and* $g.y = (sp.F.y) \lor p$. *Then*

$wst.F.p = \langle \forall i : i \geq 0 :: f^i.true \rangle,$

$sst.F.p = \langle \exists i : i \geq 0 :: g^i.false \rangle,$

where $f^0 = identity$ *and* $f^i = f \circ f^{i-1}$ *if* $i > 0$.

Next, we give the definitions of Sanders's properties; the predicate *sst.F.(init.F)* is the strongest invariant of the program *F* and corresponds to the set of reachable states.

Definition 1.7 (Sanders Logic) *For any Unity program F define*

1. $invariant_S\, p \mathrel{\hat{=}} [sst.F.(init.F) \Rightarrow p]$,
2. $p\ unless_S\ q \mathrel{\hat{=}} [ss\,.F.(init.F) \;\Rightarrow\; (p \land \neg q \Rightarrow wlp.F.(p \lor q))]$,
3. $p\ ensures_S\ q \mathrel{\hat{=}} p\ unless_S\ q \;\land\; \langle \exists s \in F :: [sst.F(init.F) \;\Rightarrow\; (p \land \neg q \Rightarrow wlp.s.q)] \rangle$,
4. *The* $\mapsto_S$ *is defined in the same way as* $\mapsto_{CM}$ *but using* $ensures_S$ *instead of* $ensures_{CM}$.

Note that we have defined the property $invariant_S\, p$ separately because it is no longer a derived property. In this system the substitution axiom becomes a theorem. Note that the property $x = c\ unless_S\ x \geq c$ is indeed a property of *F*.

2 Models

In this section, we define semantic models for Unity programs. First, we define two models based on sequences. One consists of sequences of states, the other is an extension to make the model compositional. Next, we define models based on Unity properties. Using Chandy and Misra's properties or Sanders's properties, and *ensures* or *leadsto* properties to model progress results in four different models. Chandy and Misra have defined an execution model for Unity programs in terms of sequences of tuples. Each tuple consists of a state and a label of the statement that is executed. We use the operational view that only states can be observed. This means that it is not visible which statement is executed and no stutterings are observed. This corresponds with the idea of the Unity properties that also abstract from stutterings. In [Liu89], Liu gives the semantics of Unity programs in terms of fair execution sequences. This model resembles our first operational semantics.

We start with two operational semantics for Unity programs. The first model gives a set of stutter-free sequences of states that may occur during an execution of the program. We will first define some preliminaries. Let Σ be the set of states and $Seq = \mathcal{P}(\Sigma^*)$ be the domain of sets of state sequences. We use the $\langle\!\langle . \rangle\!\rangle$-brackets to denote sequences. For sequences an operator $\natural$ is defined by Abadi and Lamport in [AL88] that removes stutterings from a sequence, i.e., it replaces all maximal (finite or infinite) segments $\sigma\sigma\cdots\sigma$

of identical states with the single state σ. E.g., $\natural.\langle\langle\sigma_1\sigma_2\sigma_2\sigma_3\sigma_3\sigma_3\cdots\rangle\rangle = \langle\langle\sigma_1\sigma_2\sigma_3\cdots\rangle\rangle$, if σ_1,σ_2, and σ_3 are different states.

By $\sigma\ s\ \sigma'$ we denote that execution of statement s in state σ results in state σ'. For a deterministic statement s, this corresponds with $p_\sigma = wlp.s.p_{\sigma'}$ and $sp.s.p_\sigma = p_{\sigma'}$, where p_σ is the predicate that is *true* in σ and *false* otherwise, that is, $p_\sigma.\tau \triangleq (\tau = \sigma)$. We sometimes use σ to denote the predicate p_σ.

Now we define the first operational semantics of a Unity program.

Definition 2.1 *The operational semantics $\mathcal{O}_1$: Unity $\rightarrow$ Seq is defined for a Unity program F as the set of stutter-free sequences of states z for which there exists an infinite sequence*

$$z' = \langle\langle\sigma_0, \sigma_1, \sigma_2, \ldots\rangle\rangle$$

such that

- $\natural z' = z$,
- $\sigma_0 \in F.init$,
- $\langle\forall i :: \langle\exists s : s \in F.assign :: \sigma_i\ s\ \sigma_{i+1}\rangle\rangle$, *and*
- $\langle\forall s : s \in F ::$ *there are infinitely many indices i such that* $\sigma_i\ s\ \sigma_{i+1}\rangle$.

Note that $\mathcal{O}_1[\![F]\!]$ can contain both finite and infinite sequences. A finite sequence corresponds to an infinite computation in which the state does not change from some moment on, i.e., the execution has reached a fixed point.

The model $\mathcal{O}_1$ has the drawback that it is not compositional with respect to union of programs. This can be seen from the following example.

Program F	Program G
initially	**initially**
$x \geq 0$	$x \geq 0$
assign	**assign**
$x := x + 1$ **if** $x \geq 0$	$x := x + 1$ **if** $x \geq 0$
$[\!]\ x := x - 1$ **if** $x < 0$	**end**$\{G\}$
end$\{F\}$	

Both programs F and G do have the same stutter-free sequences of states, i.e., $\mathcal{O}_1[\![F]\!] = \mathcal{O}_1[\![G]\!]$. However, composition with the program consisting of the statement $x := -x$ will result in different sequences because x may become negative. If $x < 0$, x can be decreased by the second statement of F. No statement of G has the same effect.

Hence, for some compositional semantics it is not sufficient to have all execution sequences: we need a semantic model that allows for interleaving. Like [BKPR91], we use an extended notion of sequences to make the model compositional. Extended sequences have holes and the intuition is that the holes can be filled by the environment (that is, another Unity program). Extended sequences are sequences of pairs of states. The first state of each pair is arbitrary, reached by the program or its environment, the second is the result of the execution of any statement of the program. Because the first state of the first pair of an extended sequence can be any state, we have to take care of the initial states explicitly. So, we define the domain of extended sequences by $ESeq = (\mathcal{P}(\Sigma), \mathcal{P}((\Sigma \times \Sigma)^*))$.

We want to abstract from stuttering in the compositional model also. However, it is not possible to remove all stuttering from each extended sequence. Then, it would not be possible to derive the set of connected sequences. Like [BKPR91], we only remove connected stutterings, and to make the model more abstract it is allowed to add stutterings. To remove connected stutterings, we define the operator $\natural$. This operator removes all stuttering pairs (σ, σ) in an extended sequence for which the second element of the preceding pair, or the first element of the following pair is σ. For example: $\natural.\langle\!\langle(\sigma_0,\sigma_0),(\sigma_0,\sigma_1),(\sigma_1,\sigma_1),(\sigma_2,\sigma_2),(\sigma_3,\sigma_4),\cdots\rangle\!\rangle = \langle\!\langle(\sigma_0,\sigma_1),(\sigma_2,\sigma_2),(\sigma_3,\sigma_4),\cdots\rangle\!\rangle$, if $\sigma_0, \cdots, \sigma_4$ are different states. Then the compositional model is defined as follows.

Definition 2.2 *The operational semantics $\mathcal{O}_2$: Unity $\rightarrow$ ESeq is defined for a Unity program F as the pair (I, V) where $I = init.F$ and V is the set of all sequences of pairs of states v for which there exists an extended sequence*

$$v' = \langle\!\langle(\sigma_0,\sigma'_0),\cdots,(\sigma_n,\sigma'_n),\cdots\rangle\!\rangle$$

such that

- $\natural v' = v$,
- $\langle \forall i :: \langle \exists s : s \in F.assign :: \sigma_i \ s \ \sigma'_i \rangle \vee (\sigma = \sigma')\rangle$, *and*
- $\langle \forall s : s \in F ::$ *there are infinitely many indices i such that* $\sigma_i \ s \ \sigma'_i\rangle$.

To show that this model is compositional, we define the function $\tilde{[\!]}$, which is the semantic equivalent of program union.

Definition 2.3 *Let F, G be Unity programs and $\mathcal{O}_2[\![F]\!] = (I_F, V_F)$, and $\mathcal{O}_2[\![G]\!] = (I_G, V_G)$. Then*

$$\mathcal{O}_2[\![F]\!] \,\tilde{[\!]}\, \mathcal{O}_2[\![G]\!] \triangleq (I_F \cap I_G, \{\natural v \mid \text{there are subsequences } v_f, v_g \text{ of } v \text{ such that } v_f \in V_F,\ v_g \in V_G, \text{ and } v \in merge(V_f, V_g).\}$$

The operation merge is the standard fair interleaving on sequences.

Theorem 2.4 *For Unity programs F, G,*

$$(\mathcal{O}_2[\![F]\!] \,\tilde{[\!]}\, \mathcal{O}_2[\![G]\!]) = \mathcal{O}_2[\![F [\!] G]\!].$$

Proofs of the theorems can be found in [UK92].

Next, we define an abstraction function β that relates the two operational models. The idea is to take all the connected extended sequences.

Definition 2.5 *Let β : ESeq $\rightarrow$ Seq be defined by*

$$\beta.(I, V) \triangleq \{\natural cat.z \mid startin.(z, I) \wedge connected.z \wedge z \in V\},$$

where

$$startin.(\langle\!\langle(\sigma_0,\sigma'_0),(\sigma_1,\sigma'_1),\cdots\rangle\!\rangle, I) \triangleq (\sigma_0 \in I),$$

$$connected.\langle\!\langle(\sigma_0,\sigma'_0),\cdots,(\sigma_n,\sigma'_n),\cdots\rangle\!\rangle) \triangleq \langle \forall i :: \sigma'_i = \sigma_{i+1}\rangle,$$

and

$$cat.\langle\!\langle(\sigma_0,\sigma_1),(\sigma_1,\sigma_2),\cdots\rangle\!\rangle \triangleq \langle\!\langle \sigma_0,\sigma_1,\sigma_2,\cdots\rangle\!\rangle.$$

Theorem 2.6 $\quad \mathcal{O}_1 = \beta \circ \mathcal{O}_2$.

Now we define semantic models for Unity programs in terms of Unity properties. Therefore, we define a domain $U = (\mathcal{P}(\Sigma) \times \mathcal{P}(P) \times \mathcal{P}(P))$ as a triple containing a set of initial states, and two sets of properties. The domain P is the property domain, i.e., a pair of sets of states, $P = \mathcal{P}(\Sigma) \times \mathcal{P}(\Sigma)$ (we often switch between predicates and sets of states). We define in total four different models; two are based on the Unity logic of Chandy and Misra, and the others based on the logic of Sanders. For each logic one model is based on *ensures* properties and the other on *leadsto* properties.

Definition 2.7 *Define for* $* \in \{S, CM\}$ *and a Unity program* F

- $\mathcal{IUE}_*[\![F]\!] \triangleq (I, U, E)$,
  where $I = F.init$, $U = \{(p,q) |\ p\ unless_*\ q \textbf{ in } F\}$, *and*
  $E = \{(p,q) |\ p\ ensures_*\ q \textbf{ in } F\}$.
- $\mathcal{IUL}_*[\![F]\!] \triangleq (I, U, L)$,
  where $I = F.init$, $U = \{(p,q) |\ p\ unless_*\ q \textbf{ in } F\}$, *and* $L = \{(p,q) |\ p \mapsto_* q \textbf{ in } F\}$.

In contrast to Chandy and Misra's Logic, Sanders's logic is restricted to reachable states. It does not say anything about unreachable states, and hence, the models based on Sanders's logic are weaker than the ones based on Chandy and Misra's. Since the *leadsto* property is defined in terms of *ensures* properties for both Chandy and Misra's logic and Sanders's logic, $\mathcal{IUL}_*$ can be derived from $\mathcal{IUE}_*$. The *ensures* properties contain information about (atomicity of) statements of the programs that is not represented by *leadsto* properties. So, $\mathcal{IUE}_{CM}$ is the strongest model of the four.

The model $\mathcal{IUE}_{CM}$ is compositional. The semantical program composition is defined as follows.

Definition 2.8 *Let* F *and* G *be Unity programs and* $\mathcal{IUE}_{CM}[\![F]\!] = (I_F, U_F, E_F)$, *and* $\mathcal{IUE}_{CM}[\![G]\!] = (I_G, U_G, E_G)$. *Then*

$$\mathcal{IUE}_{CM}[\![F]\!] \,\tilde{[\!]}\, \mathcal{IUE}_{CM}[\![G]\!] = (I_F \cap I_G, U_F \cap U_G, (E_F \cap U_G) \cup (E_G \cap U_F)).$$

The following theorem follows directly from the properties of program union given in [CM88]:

Theorem 2.9 *For Unity programs* F *and* G

$$\mathcal{IUE}_{CM}[\![F]\!] \,\tilde{[\!]}\, \mathcal{IUE}_{CM}[\![G]\!] = \mathcal{IUE}_{CM}[\![F [\!] G]\!].$$

We have defined a number of semantic models for Unity programs. Each semantic model induces a notion of refinement of programs. Now we define these notions for all models. We use the connective **in** to indicate the model.

For $\mathcal{O}_1$, the sets of sequences, we use a notion that corresponds to the idea of implementation as defined by Abadi and Lamport in [AL88]; a specification S_1 is implemented by a specification S_2 if every behavior of S_2 is allowed by S_1. Going from specification to implementation, the set of execution sequences reduces. The number of choices that can be made decreases, in other words, the amount of nondeterminism decreases.

Definition 2.10 *Let* F, G *be Unity programs*

$$F \sqsubseteq G \textbf{ in } \mathcal{O}_1 \triangleq (\mathcal{O}_1[\![F]\!] \supseteq \mathcal{O}_1[\![G]\!]).$$

We can extend the notion of refinement to the domain of extended sequences as follows.

Definition 2.11 *For Unity programs F, G; $\mathcal{O}_2[\![F]\!] = (I_F, V_F)$, and $\mathcal{O}_2[\![G]\!] = (I_G, V_G)$,*

$F \sqsubseteq G$ **in** $\mathcal{O}_2 \triangleq (I_F \supseteq I_G \wedge V_F \supseteq V_G)$.

For the property-based models we define a notion of refinement that is based on the work of Sanders ([San90]) and Singh ([Sin91]): program F is refined by program G if every property of F is a property of G. In other words, refinement preserves properties.

Definition 2.12 *For $* \in \{S, CM\}$ and Unity programs F, G.*
Let $\mathcal{IUE}_*[\![F]\!] = (I_F, U_F, E_F)$ and $\mathcal{IUE}_*[\![G]\!] = (I_G, U_G, E_G)$. Then,

$F \sqsubseteq G$ **in** $\mathcal{IUE}_* \triangleq (I_F \supseteq I_G \wedge U_F \subseteq U_G \wedge E_F \subseteq E_G)$.

Let $\mathcal{IUL}_*[\![F]\!] = (I_F, U_F, L_F)$ and $\mathcal{IUL}_*[\![G]\!] = (I_G, U_G, L_G)$. Then,

$F \sqsubseteq G$ **in** $\mathcal{IUL}_* \triangleq (I_F \supseteq I_G \wedge U_F \subseteq U_G \wedge L_F \subseteq L_G)$.

In this section we have defined a number of semantic models for Unity programs. For each model, we have defined a notion of refinement. We are interested in the relation between the notions of refinement of the models, especially between those of the operational models and those of the models based on Unity properties. In the following section, we will examine these relations and we will show that all these notions of refinement are different.

3 Relation between the models

In the previous section we gave a number of semantic models for Unity programs and for each model we defined a refinement relation. In this section we examine the relations between the models. We want to know how the notions of refinement for the models are related. Therefore, we define the following relation on models.

Definition 3.1 *For two models $\mathcal{M}_1$ and $\mathcal{M}_2$,*

$$\mathcal{M}_1 \rightarrow \mathcal{M}_2 \triangleq \langle \forall F, G :: (F \sqsubseteq G \textbf{ in } \mathcal{M}_1) \Rightarrow (F \sqsubseteq G \textbf{ in } \mathcal{M}_2) \rangle,$$

$$\mathcal{M}_1 \not\rightarrow \mathcal{M}_2 \triangleq \neg(\mathcal{M}_1 \rightarrow \mathcal{M}_2).$$

If the arrow relation holds for two models, we can conclude that the equality of programs is related in the same way.

Lemma 3.2 *For two models $\mathcal{M}_1$ and $\mathcal{M}_2$,*

$$\mathcal{M}_1 \rightarrow \mathcal{M}_2 \Rightarrow \langle \forall F, G :: (\mathcal{M}_1[\![F]\!] = \mathcal{M}_1[\![G]\!]) \Rightarrow (\mathcal{M}_2[\![F]\!] = \mathcal{M}_2[\![G]\!]) \rangle.$$

In figure 1, the arrow relation is shown for all models given in the previous section. In this section, we establish the arrow relations. The relations between the property-based models are given in the previous section and will not be discussed here. We are especially interested in the relations between the operational semantics and the semantics based on Unity properties. Since the models $\mathcal{IUE}_{CM}$ and $\mathcal{O}_2$ are both compositional and contain some information about atomicity, one might think that these models are equivalent. Also, one might think that $\mathcal{O}_1$ and $\mathcal{IUL}_S$ are equivalent. In this section we will show that this is not true.

First, we are going to examine the relation between $\mathcal{O}_2$ and $\mathcal{IUE}_{CM}$. As can be seen from figure 1, there is a refinement-preserving abstraction relation from $\mathcal{O}_2$ to $\mathcal{IUE}_{CM}$, but not the other way around. We will start by proving the latter by counterexample.

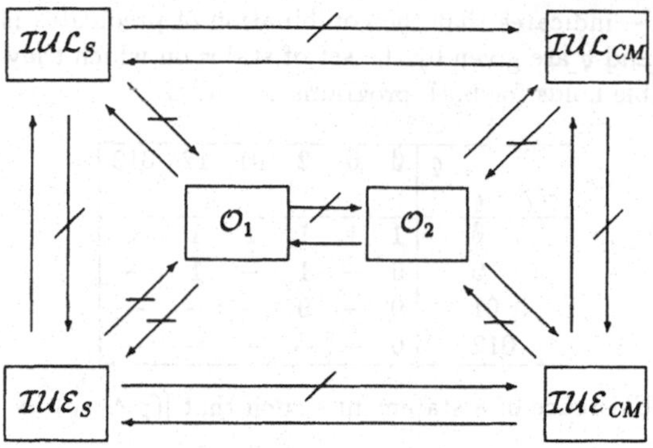

Figure 1: Relation of Refinements

Theorem 3.3 $\mathcal{IUE}_{CM} \not\rightarrow \mathcal{O}_2$.

Proof: Consider the following programs and their state transition diagrams.

Program F
  initially
    $x \in \{0,1,2\}$
  assign
    $x := x$
  $[]$ $x := (x+1) \bmod 3$
  $[]$ $x := (x+2) \bmod 3$
end$\{F\}$

Program G
  initially
    $x \in \{0,1,2\}$
  assign
    $x := -x \bmod 3$
  $[]$ $x := (1-x) \bmod 3$
  $[]$ $x := (2-x) \bmod 3$
end$\{G\}$

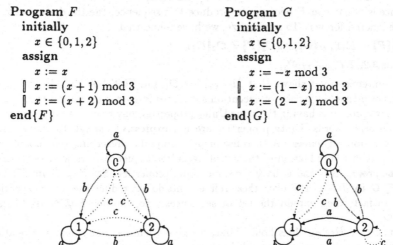

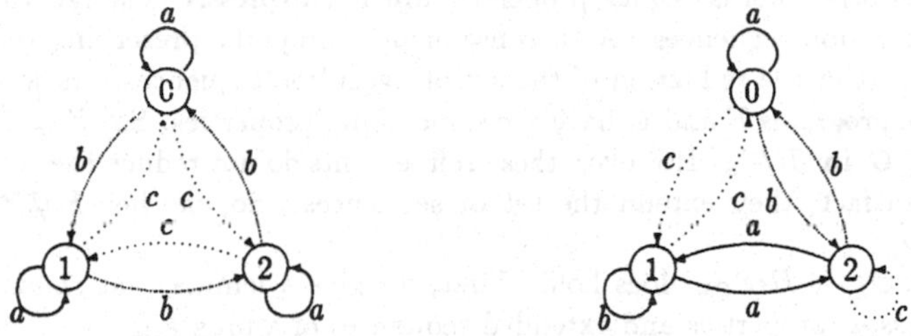

We start to show that $\mathcal{IUE}_{CM}[\![F]\!] = \mathcal{IUE}_{CM}[\![G]\!]$, in other words, that the properties of both programs are the same. Firstly, it is obvious that the initial sections of both programs are the same. Secondly, for *unless*$_{CM}$ properties: p *unless*$_{CM}$ q **in** $F \equiv p$ *unless*$_{CM}$ q **in** G, since both programs have the same state transition diagrams. So, F and G have the same *unless*$_{CM}$ properties.

Also, the *ensures*$_{CM}$ properties are the same: table 1 lists for all combinations of $(p \wedge \neg q)$ and q whether or not a statement exists such that $[(p \wedge \neg q) \Rightarrow wlp.s.q]$ holds. A one in the table indicates that there exists such a statement, a zero denotes that such a statement does not exist, and – indicates that the combination of predicates is not possible. The predicates $(p \wedge \neg q)$ and q are given by the set of states on which they are true. It is easy to check that the table holds for both programs F and G.

q / $p \wedge \neg q$	$\emptyset$	0	2	01	12	012
$\emptyset$	1	1	1	1	1	1
0	0	–	1	–	1	–
01	0	–	0	–	–	–
012	0	–	–	–	–	–

Table 1: Existence of a statement s such that $[(p \wedge \neg q) \Rightarrow wlp.s.q]$.

From this table and the fact that the $unless_{CM}$ properties of both programs are the same, it can be concluded that the $ensures_{CM}$ are the same for both programs. So, we proved that $\mathcal{IUE}_{CM}[\![F]\!] = \mathcal{IUE}_{CM}[\![G]\!]$.

However, the operational semantics $\mathcal{O}_2[\![F]\!]$ and $\mathcal{O}_2[\![G]\!]$ differ. The following extended sequence is an element of $\mathcal{O}_2[\![G]\!]$ but not of $\mathcal{O}_2[\![F]\!]$:

$$\langle\!\langle (0,1),(1,2),(2,0),(0,1),(1,2),\cdots \rangle\!\rangle.$$

This sequence is not fair in F because, to produce this sequence, the third statement of F should be ignored forever. To summarize, we have found that

$$\mathcal{IUE}_{CM}[\![F]\!] = \mathcal{IUE}_{CM}[\![G]\!]) \wedge (\mathcal{O}_2[\![F]\!] \neq \mathcal{O}_2[\![G]\!])$$

So, by lemma 3.2, $\mathcal{IUE}_{CM} \not\rightarrow \mathcal{O}_2$. □

The same counterexamples shows that $\mathcal{IUE}_{CM} \not\rightarrow \mathcal{O}_1$ and $\mathcal{IUE}_S \not\rightarrow \mathcal{O}_1$. In the proof above, it is shown that the notion of execution sequences is a stronger notion than Unity properties. Two programs having the same Unity properties may have different execution sequences. In other words, Unity properties are not expressive enough to characterize the set of execution sequences. As a consequence, property preserving refinement is a weaker notion than the reduction of the set of execution sequences. As we have seen in the proof, the programs F and G have the same Unity properties. So, $F \sqsubseteq G$ **in** $\mathcal{IUE}_{CM}$ and also $F \sqsubseteq G$ **in** $\mathcal{IUE}_S$. However, these refinements do not reduce the set of execution sequences. In fact, they extend the set of sequences. So, neither $F \not\sqsubseteq G$ **in** $\mathcal{O}_2$ nor $F \not\sqsubseteq G$ **in** $\mathcal{O}_1$.

The arrow $\mathcal{O}_2 \rightarrow \mathcal{IUE}_{CM}$ does hold. First, we give a lemma that shows the relation between $unless_{CM}$ properties and extended sequences of a program.

Lemma 3.4 *For a Unity program F and $\mathcal{O}_2[\![F]\!] = (I, V)$.*

$$p\ unless_{CM}\ q\ \textbf{in}\ F \equiv \langle \forall(\sigma,\sigma') : \langle\!\langle \cdots,(\sigma,\sigma'),\cdots \rangle\!\rangle \in V :: (p \wedge \neg q)(\sigma) \Rightarrow (p \vee q)(\sigma') \rangle.$$

Theorem 3.5 $\quad \mathcal{O}_2 \rightarrow \mathcal{IUE}_{CM}$.

Next, we examine the relation between sequences and Sanders's logic. There is a clear relation between the properties $unless_S$ and $\mapsto_S$, and sequences of states. This relation corresponds with the intuitive idea of Sanders's properties. The following lemmas show these relations. First, we write *sst.init* in terms of sequences.

Lemma 3.6 *For a unity program F*

$$sst.F.(init.F) \equiv \langle \exists z, i : z = \langle\langle \sigma_0, \sigma_1, \cdots \rangle\rangle \in \mathcal{O}_1[\![F]\!] :: \sigma_i \rangle.$$

Secondly, we characterize the *unless$_S$* property in terms of sequences.

Lemma 3.7 *For a Unity program F,*

$$p \text{ unless}_S\, q \textbf{ in } F \equiv \langle \forall z, i : z = \langle\langle \sigma_0, \sigma_1, \cdots \rangle\rangle \in \mathcal{O}_1[\![F]\!] :: (p \wedge \neg q)(\sigma_i) \Rightarrow (p \vee q)(\sigma_{i+1}) \rangle.$$

Also, the *leadsto* property can be characterized in terms of sequences, as shown by Pachl in [Pac92]:

Lemma 3.8 *For a Unity program F*

$$p \mapsto_S q \textbf{ in } F \equiv \langle \forall z, i : z = \langle\langle \sigma_0, \sigma_1, \cdots \rangle\rangle \in \mathcal{O}_1[\![F]\!] :: p(\sigma_i) \Rightarrow \langle \exists j : j \geq i :: q(\sigma_j) \rangle \rangle.$$

The arrow $\mathcal{O}_1 \rightarrow \mathcal{IUL}_S$ directly follows from these lemmas.

Theorem 3.9 $\mathcal{O}_1 \rightarrow \mathcal{IUL}_S$.

However, the reverse arrow does not hold.

Theorem 3.10 $\mathcal{IUL}_S \not\rightarrow \mathcal{O}_1$.

In fact, the counter-example of theorem 3.3 is a counter-example for this theorem also. However, this is not the only cause of trouble. In [Mis90], Misra shows that the notion of ensuring is essential when program composition is examined. The following theorem shows that the *ensures* also provides a really finer distinction of sequences than the *leadsto* when programs are examined in isolation.

Theorem 3.11 *There are Unity programs F, G for which*

$$\begin{aligned} \mathcal{O}_1[\![F]\!] &\neq \mathcal{O}_1[\![G]\!], \\ \mathcal{IUL}_S[\![F]\!] &= \mathcal{IUL}_S[\![G]\!], \\ \mathcal{IUE}_S[\![F]\!] &\neq \mathcal{IUE}_S[\![G]\!]. \end{aligned}$$

Proof: Consider the following programs

```
Program F
  assign
     x := x + 1
   [] x := x + 2 if even(x)
   [] x := x + 2 if odd(x)
   [] x := x + 2
end{F}
```

```
Program G
  assign
     x := x + 1
   [] x := x + 2 if even(x)
   [] x := x + 2 if odd(x)
end{G}
```

The programs F and G have the same state transitions, so the *unless$_S$* relations are the same. Using lemma 3.8 one can prove that both programs have the same $\mapsto_S$ properties. The programs F and G have different sequences, i.e. $\mathcal{O}_1[\![F]\!] \neq \mathcal{O}_1[\![G]\!]$. For example, the sequence $\langle\langle 0, 1, 2, 3, \cdots \rangle\rangle$ is an element of $\mathcal{O}_1[\![G]\!]$, but it is not an element of $\mathcal{O}_1[\![F]\!]$. This difference can be expressed with the *ensures$_S$* property

$$\textit{true ensures}_S\ ((x \bmod 4 = 0) \vee (x \bmod 4 = 1))$$

which is property a property of F but not of G. □

In this section we have shown that the notion of sequences is a stronger notion than Unity properties. Unity properties cannot characterize the (extended) sequences of programs completely. As a consequence, the notion of property preserving refinement is a weaker notion than the reduction of execution sequences or reduction of nondeterminism. It is also shown that the *ensures* property, although it is too strong ([Mis90]), is essentially stronger than $\mapsto$ in characterizing sequences.

4 Conclusions and Further Research

We have defined a number of semantic models to justify refinement of Unity programs and compared the notions of refinement induced by the different models. We have shown that the two notions of sequences are more expressive than Unity properties. Programs that have the same properties may have different execution sequences. Consequently, preservation of Unity properties, as used by Sanders ([San90]) and Singh ([Sin91]), differs from the usual notion of refinement, reducing the set of execution sequences. It is a weaker notion that may introduce new execution sequences.

Unity properties have proven to be insufficient to characterize sequences. The real expressive power of properties is not clear. We want to find a model of execution sequences that is equivalent to properties. It also might be of interest to find a Unity-like property model that is powerful enough to characterize sequences. As we have seen, $\mathcal{IUL}_S$ is not compositional, neither is $\mathcal{IUE}_S$. It is interesting to know whether $\mathcal{IUE}_{CM}$ is the fully abstract model above $\mathcal{IUL}_S$.

Acknowledgements

We like to thank the Calculi for Distributed Program Construction Club headed by Lambert Meertens and Doaitse Swierstra and the Formal Models Club at Utrecht University. We also want to acknowledge Patrick Lentfert, Frans Rietman, Beverly Sanders, David Meier, Kaisa Sere, Nissim Francez, Ted Herman, Jan van de Snepscheut, Harm Peter Hofstee and Robert Harley for their comments, discussions and carefully reading of preliminary versions, and Wim Hesselink for suggestions and references to the literature.

References

[AL88] M. Abadi and L. Lamport. The existence of refinement mappings. In *Proc. of the 3rd Annual IEEE Symp. on Logic in Computer Science*, pages 165–175, Washington D.C., July 1988. Computer Society Press.

[Bac90] R.-J.R. Back. Refinement calculus, part II: Parallel and reactive programs. In J.W. de Bakker, W.-P. de Roever, and G. Rozenberg, editors, *Stepwise Refinement of Distributed Systems: Models, Formalisms, Correctness*, pages 67–93. Springer-Verlag, 1990.

[BKPR91] F.S. de Boer, J.N. Kok, C Palamidessi, and J.J.M.M. Rutten. The failure of failures in a paradigm of asynchronous communication. In J.C.M. Baeten and J.F. Groote, editors, *CONCUR '91, Proceedings of the 2nd International*

Conference on Concurrency Theory, pages 111–126. Springer-Verlag, August 1991.

[CM88] K.M. Chandy and J. Misra. *Parallel Program Design – A Foundation.* Addison-Wesley Publishing Company, Inc., 1988.

[DS90] E.W. Dijkstra and C.S. Scholten. *Predicate Calculus and Program Semantics.* Texts and Monographs in Computer Science. Springer-Verlag, Berlin, 1990.

[Liu89] Z. Liu. A semantic model for UNITY. Technical Report Research report 144, Computer Science Department, University of Warwick, August 1989.

[Mis90] J. Misra. The importance of ensuring. *Notes on UNITY*, 11-90, January 1990.

[Pac90] J. Pachl. Three definitions of *leads-to* for UNITY. *Notes on UNITY*, 23-90, December 1990.

[Pac92] J. Pachl. A simple proof of a completeness result for *leads-to* in the UNITY logic. *Information Processing Letters*, 41:35–38, 1992.

[San90] B.A. Sanders. Stepwise refinement of mixed specifications of concurrent programs. In M. Broy and Jones C.B., editors, *Proc. IFIP Working Conf. on Programming and Methods*, pages 1–25. Elsevier Science Publishers B.V. (North Holland), May 1990.

[San91] B.A. Sanders. Eliminating the substitution axiom from UNITY logic. *Formal Aspects of Computing*, 3(2):189–205, 1991.

[Sin91] A.K. Singh. Parallel programming: Achieving portability through abstraction. In *11th International Conference on Distributed Computing Systems*, May 1991.

[UK92] R.T. Udink and J.N. Kok. On the relation between unity properties and sequences of states. Technical report, Utrecht University, 1992.

Expressiveness Results for Process Algebras

Frits W. Vaandrager*

CWI, Department of Software Technology

Kruislaan 413, 1098 SJ Amsterdam, The Netherlands

fritsv@cwi.nl

University of Amsterdam, Programming Research Group

Kruislaan 403, 1098 SJ Amsterdam, The Netherlands

ABSTRACT The expressive power of process algebras is investigated in a general setting of structural operational semantics. The notion of an *effective operational semantics* is introduced and it is observed that no effective operational semantics for an enumerable language can specify all effective process graphs up to trace equivalence. A natural class of Plotkin style SOS specifications is identified, containing the guarded versions of calculi like CCS, SCCS, MEIJE and ACP, and it is proved that any specification in this class induces an effective operational semantics. Using techniques introduced by Bloom, it is shown that for the guarded versions of CCS-like calculi, there is a double exponential bound on the speed with which the number of outgoing transitions in a state can grow. As a corollary of this result it follows that two expressiveness results of De Simone for MEIJE and SCCS depend in a fundamental way on the use of unguarded recursion. A final result of this paper is that all operators definable via a finite number of rules in a format due to De Simone, are derived operators in the simple process calculus PC.

Keywords process algebra, PC, labeled transition systems, process graphs, effective process graphs, effective operational semantics, structural operational semantics, expressiveness, bisimulation equivalence, trace equivalence, action transducers.

Contents

*Most of this work was carried out while the author was at the MIT Laboratory for Computer Science, supported by ONR contract N00014-85-K-0168. Part of this work took place in the context of the ESPRIT Basic Research Action 7166, CONCUR2.

0 Introduction

At this moment there are, besides numerous papers, four introductory textbooks on *process algebra* or, as some prefer to call it, *process theory* by resp. Milner [25], Hoare [21], Hennessy [20] and Baeten and Weijland [8]. Each of these books gives a thorough introduction into a *particular* approach to process theory. Milner focuses on operational semantics and bisimulation congruences in the setting of his Calculus of Communicating Systems (CCS). Hoare presents his theory of Communicating Sequential Processes (CSP) and concentrates on the denotational failures model. Hennessy elaborates in great detail the notion of testing equivalence for a language somewhere in between CCS and CSP. Baeten and Weijland, finally, advocate the algebraic perspective of the Algebra of Communicating Processes (ACP). A reader who takes the effort to read all the four books, will notice a lot of similarities between the approaches, but will also be puzzled by the differences, and consequently find it hard to make a choice between the available formalisms.

We think that the perspective of the general theory of structural operational semantics can be helpful at this point, because it suggests that the four books just happen to concentrate on different aspects of what can essentially be viewed as a single and homogeneous theory. It is becoming more and more clear that many of the key theorems in process theory are independent of the particular process language that is used. Using Plotkin's structural operational semantics (SOS), one can prove theorems for whole classes of languages at the same time. This is a much more efficient way to develop process theory, which in addition provides more insight. Examples of contributions along these lines are [33, 34, 14, 12, 10, 18, 11, 32, 13, 35, 2, 4, 19].

Milner had the idea that for a proper understanding of the basic issues concerning the behavior of concurrent systems it could be helpful to look for a simple language, with "as few operators or combinators as possible, each of which embodies some distinct and intuitive idea, and which together give completely general expressive power" [24, page 269]. The aim of this paper is to investigate expressiveness issues in a general setting of SOS.

There are at least three different ways in which a language can have "completely general expressive power":

1. Each Turing machine can be simulated in lock step.
2. Each "effective" process graph can be specified up to some notion of behavioral equivalence.

3. Each operation in a "natural" class of operations is realizable in terms of the operations in the language up to some notion of behavioral equivalence.

Most process calculi that have been proposed in the literature are Turing powerful, that is, universally expressive in the first sense.

A first result of this paper, which generalizes a result of Baeten, Bergstra and Klop [6], is that no enumerable language with an effective operational semantics can be universal in the second sense if, as behavioral equivalence, one chooses trace equivalence. Here, two process graphs are called trace equivalent if they have the same finite sequences of actions (so this notion of equivalence does not involve internal actions which can be deleted in a trace). This result implies that if one likes to have a language which is universal in the second sense, one either has to use a notion of behavioral equivalence that does not refine trace equivalence, or one has to give up the idea that the operational semantics should be effective.

A next result of this paper is the definition of a general format of Plotkin style transition system specifications (TSS's), containing the guarded versions of calculi like CCS, SCCS, MEIJE and ACP, and a proof that any TSS in this class induces an effective operational semantics. Since (the finitary versions of) process calculi like CCS are effective it follows that these calculi are not universally expressive in the second sense. Also, using techniques introduced by Bloom [10], it is shown that in the guarded versions of CCS-like calculi, there is a double exponential upper bound on the speed with which the fanout, *i.e.*, the number of outgoing transitions in a state, can grow. This implies that there exists a primitive recursive process graph that can not be denoted by CCS-like languages up to trace equivalence.

De Simone [33, 34] proved that any operation on process graphs that can be defined in some general format, can already be defined in SCCS and MEIJE up to bisimulation. As a corollary of the results concerning the growth rate of the fanout, it follows that also this result of De Simone depends in a crucial way on the use of unguarded recursion. The final result of this paper is that a simple calculus called PC is universal in the third sense, that is, each operation definable via a finite number of De Simone style rules, can already be defined in terms of the calculus PC.

Acknowledgements. The relational renaming operator of the language PC came up in a discussion with Rob van Glabbeek. Thanks to Jan Bergstra, Doeko Bosscher, Jan Friso Groote and Robert de Simone for useful comments on an earlier version of this paper.

1 A Basic Limitation of Operational Semantics

A *semantics* is a mapping that associates to each object in a syntactic domain a corresponding object in a semantic domain. More specifically, an *operational semantics* is a mapping that associates to each syntactic object a *machine* or *automaton*. These machines (which are mathematical objects) typically have an associated set of *states* and for each state there is a collection of *transitions* which give the possible ways in which the machine can evolve to a next state. This paper takes a rather abstract approach to operational semantics by only considering those aspects of machines and not features like real-time, true concurrency, distribution in space, etc. Thus our machines simply *are* process graphs in the sense defined below.

Definition 1.1 [Process graphs] A *labeled transition system (LTS)* over a given set A of labels is a pair $(S, \longrightarrow)$ where S is the set of *states* and $\longrightarrow \subseteq S \times A \times S$ is the *transition relation*. As usual $r \xrightarrow{a} s$ abbreviates $(r, a, s) \in \longrightarrow$. The *fanout fan(s)* of a state s is defined as the cardinality of the set of transitions starting in s. For $\sigma = a_1 \cdots a_n \in A^*$ a finite sequence over A, predicate $r \xrightarrow{\sigma} s$ is defined by

$$r \xrightarrow{\sigma} s \triangleq \exists r_0, \ldots, r_n \in S : r = r_0 \xrightarrow{a_1} r_1 \xrightarrow{a_2} \cdots \xrightarrow{a_n} r_n = s.$$

If $r \xrightarrow{\sigma} s$ for some $\sigma \in A^*$, then state s is called *reachable* from state r.

A *process graph* over A is a triple $g = (r, S, \longrightarrow)$ with $(S, \longrightarrow)$ a LTS over A and $r \in S$ the *root*, such that each state in S is reachable from the root. Sometimes r will be referred to as *root*(g), and the pair $(S, \longrightarrow)$ as *lts*(g). If $\mathcal{A}$ is a LTS and s is a state of $\mathcal{A}$, then *graph*$(s, \mathcal{A})$ is the process graph with root s and an underlying LTS that is obtained by restricting $\mathcal{A}$ to the part that is reachable from s.

Two process graphs g and h are *isomorphic*, notation $g \simeq h$, if there exists a bijective mapping between their sets of states that preserves the roots and the transition relation.

Definition 1.2 [Operational semantics] An *operational semantics* is a mapping that associates to each object in its domain a process graph.

Given our intuition of process graphs as machines that compute, it seems reasonable to focus attention to operational semantics that map expressions to *effective* process graphs, *i.e.*, graphs that have a countable number of states such that in each state the outgoing transitions can be computed. To formalize this notion of effectiveness, we need some simple coding functions known from recursion theory (see [31]). We first introduce a standard coding from ordered pairs of integers to integers:

$$\langle k, l \rangle \triangleq \frac{1}{2} \cdot (k^2 + 2kl + l^2 + 3k + l).$$

The function CI associates to each finite set of integers its *canonical index*, and provides a standard encoding of finite sets of integers into the integers.

$$CI(\{k_1, k_2, \ldots, k_n\}) \triangleq \textbf{if } n = 0 \textbf{ then } 0 \textbf{ else } 2^{k_1} + 2^{k_2} + \ldots + 2^{k_n}.$$

Finally, the function *Gödel* associates to each recursive function ϕ a corresponding Gödel number *Gödel*(ϕ).

Definition 1.3 Let $A = \{a_1, a_2, \ldots\}$ is a enumerable set of actions. A process graph $g = (r, S, \longrightarrow)$ over A is *effective* if

- $S = \{s_1, s_2, \ldots\}$ is an enumerable set of states;
- the transition relation is finitely branching, *i.e.*, for all $s \in S$, *fan*(s) is finite; and
- the transition relation is effective with respect to the enumerations of S and A. That is, the function $next(g) : \mathsf{N} \rightarrow \mathsf{N}$ defined by

$$next(g)(i) \triangleq CI(\{\langle k,l\rangle | s_i \xrightarrow{a_k} s_l\})$$

is recursive.

Graph g is *primitive recursive* if in addition the funtion $next(g)$ is primitive recursive.

Stated differently, a process graph is effective if there exists a Turing machine that, when provided with a (suitably coded) state as input, computes for a while and then first outputs the number of outgoing transitions from that state and then enumerates all these transitions (everything suitably coded). So in each state it is known what are the possibilities to proceed.

The notion of an effective graph we use here is essentially the same as the one proposed earlier by Baeten, Bergstra and Klop [6] and by Bloom, Istrail and Meyer [12]. A less restrictive definition has been put forward by Darondeau [15], who requires the transition relation, as a set, to be recursive. Boudol [14] and De Simone [34] employ an even less restrictive definition of effectiveness: they only require that the transition relation, as a set, is recursively enumerable.

If the machines, whose behavior is described by means of process graphs, are not in control of all their transitions, then one can argue that our notion of an effective process graph, and in particular the requirement of finite branching, is too restrictive.

Suppose that, like in the I/O automata model of Lynch and Tuttle [23], the set of actions (the labels of transitions) can be partitioned in a set of *input actions*, which are under control of the environment, and a set of *locally controlled actions*, which are under the control of the machine itself. Then it seems reasonable to allow for an infinite number of input transitions from a given state r, provided that, given an input action i, the set of states s which can be reached from r via an i-transition is finite and and can be effectively computed. In each state the machine should be able to decide what to do with a given input.

Also in the case of languages with unbounded nondeterminism due to *random assignment* (see Apt and Plotkin [3]), the requirement of finite branching seems too restrictive.

In this paper, just one particular definition of an effective process graph will be investigated, which certainly is not is the most general one possible.

Baeten, Bergstra and Klop [6] show that, modulo strong bisimulation equivalence, the calculus ACP with finite systems of guarded recursion equations is not universal. Below, we will show that the idea behind the proof of this result can be used to prove a much more general theorem: no effective operational semantics can be universal modulo trace equivalence.

Definition 1.4 An operational semantics $\mathcal{O}$ for an enumerable language L is *effective* with respect to an enumeration $\{p_1, p_2, \ldots\}$ of L if

- for all i, $\mathcal{O}(p_i)$ is effective;
- the function r defined by

  $$r(i) \triangleq index(root(\mathcal{O}(p_i)))$$

  is recursive, where *index* is the function that associates to each state s_i its index i;

- the function t defined by

$$t(i) \triangleq Gödel(next(\mathcal{O}(p_i)))$$

is recursive.

An effective operational semantics does not only associate an effective process graph to each expression, but also tells how one can compute the root and transitions of this graph. An example of an operational semantics that is not effective is a mapping that takes a natural number n and associates to it a graph with one state and no transitions if the n-th Turing machine halts, and a graph with one state and one transition otherwise. For each n, the associated graph is finite and hence effective, even though the operational semantics is not.

Let L be a programming language that one likes to implement in accordance with some operational semantics $\mathcal{O}$. If the machines of which $\mathcal{O}$ describes the behavior are in control of all their transitions, then it seems reasonable to require that $\mathcal{O}$ is in fact effective with respect to some enumeration of L. If $\mathcal{O}$ gives no clue about how to build effectively a machine that implements programs in L, then one may even argue that it does not deserve the predicate "operational". Theorem 1.6 says that, provided this very reasonable requirement is met, there is a limit on what operational semantics can do.

Definition 1.5 For $g = (r, S, \longrightarrow)$ a process graph over A, the set *traces*(g) is defined by

$$traces(g) = \{\sigma \in A^* \mid \exists s : r \xrightarrow{\sigma} s\}.$$

Process graphs h and h' are *trace equivalent*, notation $h \approx_T h'$, if $traces(h) = traces(h')$.

Theorem 1.6 *Suppose A is a set of labels containing at least two elements. Suppose $\mathcal{O}$ is an operational semantics that associates to each member of an enumerable language L a process graph over A, and suppose that $\mathcal{O}$ is effective with respect to some enumeration of L. Then there exists an effective graph over A that is not denoted by any member of L up to trace equivalence.*

Proof Via a diagonalization argument, as in the proof of Theorem 8.2 in [6]. Suppose $\mathcal{O}$ is effective with respect to an enumeration $\{p_1, p_2, \ldots\}$ of L. Let $a, b \in A$ with $a \neq b$. To each $n \in \mathsf{N}$, a function $f_n : \mathsf{N} \rightarrow \{0, 1\}$ is associated in the following way:

- $f_n(k) = 0$ if all traces of $\mathcal{O}(p_n)$ of length $k + 1$ end with an action a;
- $f_n(k) = 1$ otherwise.

From the fact that all process graphs $\mathcal{O}(p_n)$ are effective it follows that all f_n are recursive functions. Consequently, the following function $f_\omega : \mathsf{N} \rightarrow \{0, 1\}$ is also recursive:

- $f_\omega(n) = 0$ if $f_n(n) = 1$,
- $f_\omega(n) = 1$ if $f_n(n) = 0$.

Now consider the effective process graph Ω with states taken from $\mathbb{N}$, root 0, and transitions

$$n \xrightarrow{a} n+1 \quad \text{if} \quad f_\omega(n) = 0,$$
$$n \xrightarrow{b} n+1 \quad \text{if} \quad f_\omega(n) = 1.$$

We claim that, for all n, $\mathcal{O}(p_n) \not\approx_T \Omega$. The proof is by contradiction. Suppose that for some n, $\mathcal{O}(p_n) \approx_T \Omega$. The process graph Ω has exactly one trace of length $n+1$ which either ends with an a or with a b. If it ends with an a, then $f_n(n) = 1$. But this means that there is a trace of $\mathcal{O}(p_n)$ of length $n+1$ that does not end with an a. This contradicts the assumption that $\mathcal{O}(p_n) \approx_T \Omega$. If, in the other case, the unique trace of Ω ends with a b, then $f_n(n) = 0$. But this means that all traces of $\mathcal{O}(p_n)$ of length $n+1$ end with an a, so that again we have a contradiction. ■

Since trace equivalence is coarser than bisimulation equivalence, which in turn is coarser than graph isomorphism, the above theorem has as a trivial corollary that no effective operational semantics can denote all effective graphs modulo bisimulation equivalence or graph isomorphism. In this sense, the above result generalizes Theorem 8.2 of Baeten, Bergstra and Klop [6].

Various researchers have attempted to find universal expressiveness results for languages with an operational semantics in terms of process graphs. They all had to face the limitations imposed by Theorem 1.6, but came up with different solutions:

1. Baeten, Bergstra and Klop [6] prove that each effective process graph can be specified in the language ACP_τ with guarded recursion, modulo an equivalence called weak bisimulation congruence. This universality result is possible because weak bisimulation equivalence is incomparable with trace equivalence, due to the fact that it abstracts from internal actions.

2. De Simone [33, 34] shows that in MEIJE and SCCS, each process graph with r.e. sets of states and transitions can be finitely specified up to isomorphism. Each process graph that is effective in our sense clearly has r.e. sets of states and transitions, and can therefore be specified in MEIJE and SCCS. Since MEIJE and SCCS are clearly (recursively) enumerable, Theorem 1.6 tells us that the operational semantics for these languages is not effective. And in fact, it is easy to see that, due to the presence of unguarded recursion, these languages can specify process graphs with infinite branching. Boudol [14] points out that it is not even decidable whether a state has an outgoing transition.

3. Ponse [30] shows that in the calculus μCRL each effective process graph can be specified up to isomorphism. Here the twist is that the language μCRL, although enumerable, is not *recursively* enumerable. This makes that, even though for each individual μCRL program one can effectively compute the *root* and the Gödel number of the *next* function of the associated process graph, the operational semantics for the language as a whole is not effective with respect to any enumeration.

2 Structural Operational Semantics

Plotkin [28, 29], advocates a simple method for giving operational semantics to programming languages. The method, which is often referred to as *SOS* (for *Structural Operational Semantics*), is based on the notion of transition systems. The states of the transition systems are elements of some formal language that may extend the language for which one wants to give an operational semantics. The main idea of the method is to define the transitions between states by a set of conditional rules over the syntax of the language, using structural induction. Because of its power and simplicity, the SOS approach has been highly successful and has become the standard way to equip programming languages with an operational semantics.

In this section we will recall some basic definitions and results from the theory of SOS.

2.1 SOS Calculi and Their Operational Semantics

Definition 2.1 [Signatures and terms] To start with, we assume the presence of two disjoint countably infinite sets: a set $\mathcal{V}$ of *variables* with typical elements $x, y, \ldots$, and a set $\mathcal{N}$ of *names*. A *signature element* is a pair (f, n) consisting of a *function symbol* $f \in \mathcal{N}$ and an *arity* $n \in \mathsf{N}$. In a signature element $(c, 0)$, the c is often referred to as a *constant symbol*. A *signature* is a set of signature elements, *i.e.*, a subset of $\mathcal{N} \times \mathsf{N}$. The set of *terms* over a signature Σ is the smallest set $\mathbb{T}(\Sigma)$ with:

- $\mathcal{V} \subseteq \mathbb{T}(\Sigma)$,
- $(f, n) \in \Sigma$, $n \geq 0$, $t_1, \ldots, t_n \in \mathbb{T}(\Sigma)$ implies $f(t_1, \ldots, t_n) \in \mathbb{T}(\Sigma)$.

A term $c()$ is often abbreviated as c. $\mathrm{T}(\Sigma)$ is the set of *closed* terms over Σ, *i.e.*, terms in $\mathbb{T}(\Sigma)$ that do not contain variables. With $var(t)$ the set of variables occurring in t is denoted. For a term t, $|t|$ denotes the *size* of t, *i.e.*, the number of variables, and constant and function symbols occurring in t. A *substitution* ζ is a mapping from $\mathcal{V}$ to $\mathbb{T}(\Sigma)$. With $t[\zeta]$, we denote the result of the simultaneous substitution, for all x, of x by $\zeta(x)$:

- $x[\zeta] = \zeta(x)$,
- $f(t_1, \ldots, t_n)[\zeta] = f(t_1[\zeta], \ldots, t_n[\zeta])$.

The expression $t[t_1/x_1, \ldots, t_n/x_n]$ denotes the term obtained from t by simultaneous substitution of t_1 for x_1, t_2 for x_2, etc.

Definition 2.2 [Contexts] Let Σ be a signature. A *context of n holes* C over Σ is a term in $\mathbb{T}(\Sigma)$ in which n variables occur, each variable only once. If $t_1, \ldots, t_n$ are terms over Σ, then $C[t_1, \ldots, t_n]$ denotes the term obtained by substituting t_1 for the first variable occurring in C, t_2 for the second variable, etc. Thus, if $x_1, \ldots, x_n$ are all different variables, $C[x_1, \ldots, x_n]$, denotes a context of n holes in which x_i is the i-th variable that occurs. A context is *trivial* if it consists of a single variable only.

Let Σ be a signature. An equivalence $\equiv$ on $T(\Sigma)$ is *preserved under contexts*, and it is a *congruence*, if for all contexts $C[x]$, $t \equiv t' \Rightarrow C[t] \equiv C[t']$.

Lemma 2.3 *Let Σ be a signature and $\equiv$ an equivalence over $T(\Sigma)$. Then $\equiv$ is a congruence iff for all $(f,n) \in \Sigma$: $t_1 \equiv u_1 \wedge \cdots \wedge t_n \equiv u_n \Rightarrow f(t_1,\ldots,t_n) \equiv f(u_1,\ldots,u_n)$.*

Definition 2.4 [Calculi] Let A be a given set of *labels* and let Σ be a signature. The set $Tr(\Sigma, A)$ of *transitions* consists of all expressions of the form $t \xrightarrow{a} t'$ with $t, t' \in \mathbb{T}(\Sigma)$ and $a \in A$. The symbols $\phi, \psi, \ldots$ will be used to range over transitions. The set $Cf(\Sigma, A)$ of *inference rules* or *conditional formulas* over Σ and A consists of all expressions $\frac{\psi_1,\ldots,\psi_n}{\psi}$, where $\psi_1,\ldots,\psi_n,\psi$ in $Tr(\Sigma, A)$. The transitions ψ_i are called the *antecedents* and ψ is called the *conclusion* of the rule. If no confusion can arise, a rule $\frac{}{\psi}$ is also written ψ. The notions "substitution" and "closed" extend to transitions and rules in the obvious way. A *transition system specification* or *calculus* is a triple $P = (\Sigma, A, R)$ with Σ a signature, A a set of labels and $R \subseteq Cf(\Sigma, A)$ a set of rules. If P and P' are two calculi, then $P \cup P'$ is obtained by taking the componentwise union of the signatures and rules.

Definition 2.5 [Proofs] Let $P = (\Sigma, A, R)$ be a calculus. A *proof* of a transition ψ from P is a finite tree whose edges are ordered and whose vertices are labeled by transitions in $Tr(\Sigma, A)$, such that:

- the root is labeled with ψ,
- if ϕ is the label of some vertex and $\phi_1,\ldots,\phi_n$ are the labels of the children of this vertex, then there is a rule $\frac{\chi_1,\ldots,\chi_n}{\chi} \in R$ and a substitution ζ such that $\phi_i = \chi_i[\zeta]$ and $\phi = \chi[\zeta]$.

If a proof tree for ψ exists, then ψ is *provable* from P, notation $P \vdash \psi$.

Definition 2.6 [Operational semantics] Let $P = (\Sigma, A, R)$ be a calculus, The LTS $lts(P)$ is defined as $(T(\Sigma), \longrightarrow)$ where $(t, a, t') \in\ \longrightarrow$ iff $P \vdash t \xrightarrow{a} t'$. The operational semantics $\mathcal{O}_P$ is the mapping that associates to a closed term $t \in \mathrm{T}(\Sigma)$ the process graph $graph(t, lts(P))$.

The last definition in this subsection recalls the notion of a Σ-algebra.

Definition 2.7 Let Σ be a signature. A Σ-*algebra* $\mathcal{A}$ consists of a set $D_{\mathcal{A}}$, the *domain* of $\mathcal{A}$, and a mapping that associates to each signature element $(f,n) \in \Sigma$ an n-ary operation $f_{\mathcal{A}}$ on $D_{\mathcal{A}}$. A *valuation* in a Σ-algebra $\mathcal{A}$ is a function ξ that takes every variable x into an element of $D_{\mathcal{A}}$. The ξ-*evaluation* $[\![\cdot]\!]^{\xi}_{\mathcal{A}} : \mathbb{T}(\Sigma) \rightarrow D_{\mathcal{A}}$ is defined inductively by

$$[\![x]\!]^{\xi}_{\mathcal{A}} \triangleq \xi(x),$$

$$[\![f(t_1,\ldots,t_n)]\!]^{\xi}_{\mathcal{A}} \triangleq f_{\mathcal{A}}([\![t_1]\!]^{\xi}_{\mathcal{A}},\ldots,[\![t_n]\!]^{\xi}_{\mathcal{A}}).$$

The result of a ξ-evaluation of a term t depends only on the value assigned by ξ to the variables occurring in t. In particular, if t is a closed term, then $[\![t]\!]^{\xi}_{\mathcal{A}}$ does not depend on ξ at all. Thus we can write simply $[\![t]\!]_{\mathcal{A}}$ in such a situation.

$\mathbf{0}$	0	inaction
a	1	prefixing; for each $a \in A$
$+$	2	alternative composition, sum
$\|\|$	2	parallel composition, (free) merge
$\times$	2	synchronous composition, product
ρ_r	1	renaming; for each $r \subseteq A \times A$
X	0	process names; for each $X \in \mathcal{X}$

Table 1: The signature of PC.

A *congruence* on $\mathcal{A}$ is an equivalence relation $\equiv$ on $D_{\mathcal{A}}$ with the property that for all $(f,n) \in \Sigma$,

$$d_1 \equiv d_1' \wedge \cdots \wedge d_n \equiv d_n' \;\Rightarrow\; f_{\mathcal{A}}(d_1,\ldots,d_n) \equiv f_{\mathcal{A}}(d_1',\ldots,d_n').$$

For $\mathcal{A}$ a Σ-algebra and $\equiv$ a congruence on $\mathcal{A}$, the Σ-algebra $\mathcal{A}/\equiv$ is defined by

$$D_{\mathcal{A}/\equiv} \triangleq \{d/_{\equiv} \mid d \in D_{\mathcal{A}}\},$$

$$f_{\mathcal{A}/\equiv}(d_1/_{\equiv},\ldots,d_n/_{\equiv}) \triangleq (f_{\mathcal{A}}(d_1,\ldots,d_n))/_{\equiv},$$

where, of course, $e/_{\equiv} = \{e' \mid e' \equiv e\}$. Due to the congruence property this definition is independent of the choice of the representing $d_i \in d_i/_{\equiv}$.

2.2 The Calculus PC

As a running example in this paper, we will now present the calculus *PC* (for Process Calculus).

We assume the presence of a countable set A of *actions*, ranged over by $a, b, \ldots$, and of a countable set $\mathcal{X}$ of *process names*, ranged over by $X, Y, \ldots$. The set of *process terms*, which has typical elements $p, q, \ldots$, is defined via the signature Σ_{PC} displayed in Table 1.

Infix notation will be used for the binary function symbols, and we write $a{\cdot}p$ instead of $a{\cdot}(p)$. To avoid parentheses, it will be assumes that prefixing has most binding power, followed by product, which in turn is followed by free merge, which is followed by alternative composition (which has the weakest binding power). In the case of several sum, merge or product operations we will mostly omit brackets since semantically these operations are associative. (Readers who insist on complete parsing information may assume that missing brackets associate to the right.) For a finite index set $I = \{i_1,\ldots,i_n\}$ and process terms $p_{i_1},\ldots,p_{i_n}$, $\sum_{i\in I} p_i$ abbreviates $p_{i_1} + \ldots + p_{i_n}$. By convention $\sum_{i\in\emptyset}$ stands for $\mathbf{0}$. Trailing $\mathbf{0}$'s will often be dropped.

The constant 0 denotes *inaction*, a process that cannot do anything at all. The process $a{\cdot}p$ first performs an a-action and then behaves like p. Process $p+q$ will behave either like p or like q. It is not specified whether the choice between p and q is made by the process itself or by the environment. With $p||q$, we denote the parallel composition of p and q without any synchronization between the p and q. The product $p \times q$ denotes the parallel composition of p and q in which *all* actions have to synchronize. The operation ρ_r is a slight generalization of the renaming/relabeling operations in CCS, CSP, MEIJE and ACP. Process $\rho_r(p)$ behaves just like process p, except that if p has the possibility of doing an a, $\rho_r(p)$ can do any action b that is related to a via r. The recursive definitions of the process names are given by a *declaration* function $E : \mathcal{X} \rightarrow \mathrm{T}(\Sigma_{PC})$. The process expressions $E(X)$ may contain only guarded occurrences of process names. An occurrence of a process name is *guarded* if it occurs in a subexpression $a \cdot p$. The condition of guardedness is standard in process theory and excludes recursive declarations like $E(X) = X$ that give no clue about the specified behavior. Often we will write $X \Leftarrow t$ as abbreviation for $E(X) = t$.

Some references for those readers who are familiar with other work on process theory. The constant 0 also occurs in CCS and MEIJE, and plays the same role as δ in ACP. The $+$ is the same as in CCS and ACP. The $||$ operator occurs in ACP, CCS and TCSP, and the $\times$ operator is taken from TCSP. The ρ_r operator can be viewed as a *generalized state operator* in the sense of Baeten and Bergstra [5] if one assumes a state space that contains only a single element. It is also possible to view this operator as a special case of the *action refinement* operator as studied by Goltz and Van Glabbeek [17]: ρ_r refines an action a into the nondeterministic sum of the actions in $\{b \mid r(a,b)\}$.

The inference rules of PC are presented in Table 2. In the table a and b range over A, unless further restrictions are made. Further r ranges over $A \times A$, and variables x, x', y and y' are fixed and all different.

2.3 Power to Simulate 2-Counter Machines

The first (and weakest) form of universality that we consider is that a process calculus has the expressive power of 2-counter machines (or, equivalently, Turing machines) in the sense that, for each n, we can exhibit a term $U2CM_n$ whose process graph simulates in lock step a universal 2-counter machine on input n.

Calculi like CCS, CSP, ACP, and MEIJE are all universally expressive in this sense. Actually, trying to code a 2-counter or Turing machine in each of these languages is a nice way to get familiar with them. Via a rather tricky encoding, we prove below that also PC has the power of 2-counter machines.[1]

Theorem 2.8 *PC has the expressive power of 2-counter machines.*

Proof Suppose that a universal 2-counter machine has code of the form

l_1: `if I=0 goto` l_5
l_2: `inc I`
l_3: `dec J`

[1]In Section 4, it will be shown how many operations can be defined as derived opertions of PC. Using derived operations like sequential composition, much simpler encodings can be obtained.

$a:$	$a \cdot x \xrightarrow{a} x$	
$+:$	$\dfrac{x \xrightarrow{a} x'}{x+y \xrightarrow{a} x'}$	$\dfrac{y \xrightarrow{a} y'}{x+y \xrightarrow{a} y'}$
$\parallel:$	$\dfrac{x \xrightarrow{a} x'}{x \parallel y \xrightarrow{a} x' \parallel y}$	$\dfrac{y \xrightarrow{a} y'}{x \parallel y \xrightarrow{a} x \parallel y'}$
$\times:$	$\dfrac{x \xrightarrow{a} x',\ y \xrightarrow{a} y'}{x \times y \xrightarrow{a} x' \times y'}$	
$\rho_r:$	$\dfrac{x \xrightarrow{a} x'}{\rho_r(x) \xrightarrow{b} \rho_r(x')}$ if $r(a,b)$	
$X:$	$\dfrac{E(X) \xrightarrow{a} y}{X \xrightarrow{a} y}$	

Table 2: The inference rules for PC.

l_4: `goto` l_7

$\vdots$

l_k: `halt`

The finite control part of this machine can be modeled by the PC expression *Control*, defined recursively by:

$$
\begin{aligned}
Control &\Leftarrow X_1 \\
X_1 &\Leftarrow zero_I \cdot X_5 + non\_zero_I \cdot X_2 \\
X_2 &\Leftarrow inc_I \cdot X_3 \\
X_3 &\Leftarrow dec_J \cdot X_4 \\
X_4 &\Leftarrow skip \cdot X_7 \\
&\vdots \\
X_k &\Leftarrow halt \cdot 0
\end{aligned}
$$

The next step in the construction of a universal 2-counter machine is the following specification of a counter:

$$
\begin{aligned}
C &\Leftarrow inc \cdot \rho_r((Syn \| Full) \times C) + \overline{dec} \cdot C + zero \cdot C + \overline{non\_zero} \cdot C \\
Syn &\Leftarrow inc \cdot Syn + dec \cdot Syn + non\_zero \cdot Syn \\
Full &\Leftarrow \overline{dec} \cdot Empty + \overline{non\_zero} \cdot Full \\
Empty &\Leftarrow zero \cdot Empty
\end{aligned}
$$

where

$$r \triangleq \{(inc, inc), (dec, dec), (\overline{dec}, dec)(zero, zero), (non\_zero, non\_zero), \\ (zero, \overline{dec}), (zero, \overline{non\_zero}), (\overline{non\_zero}, non\_zero)\}$$

Using the above recursive definitions, we can define, for each n, a PC expression representing a counter with value n:

$$Counter_0 \triangleq C,$$
$$Counter_{n+1} \triangleq \rho_r((Syn \| Full) \times Counter_n).$$

Now the 2-counter machine with input n can be obtained by glueing together the finite control with 2 counters:

$$U2CM_n \triangleq Control \times (\rho_i(Counter_n) \| \rho_j(Counter_0)),$$

where

$$i \triangleq \{(inc, inc_I), (dec, dec_I), (\overline{dec}, dec_I), (zero, zero_I), (non\_zero, non\_zero_I)\}$$
$$j \triangleq \{(inc, inc_J), (dec, dec_J), (\overline{dec}, dec_J), (zero, zero_J), (non\_zero, non\_zero_J)\}$$

■

2.4 Bisimulation Equivalence

A serious problem with the isomorphism relation $\simeq$ on process graphs is that it is not a congruence for calculi like CCS and PC. For instance, $\mathbf{0} \simeq \mathbf{0} \| \mathbf{0}$ but $a\mathbf{0}+a\mathbf{0} \not\simeq a\mathbf{0}+a(\mathbf{0}\|\mathbf{0})$. Thus it is not allowed to replace a subexpression by an $\simeq$-equivalent expression if one likes to preserve $\simeq$.

In order to remedy this problem, we will introduce the notion of *bisimulation equivalence.* Bisimulation equivalence is somewhat coarser than isomorphism and is a congruence with respect to all the constructs in the language. Actually, most researchers who use bisimulations motivate them in a different way. In [25, 8], for instance, it is at least suggested that two process terms are bisimilar iff they cannot be distinguished by an observer. We consider the arguments for bisimulation as a testing equivalence (see [1]) not really convincing and prefer to motivate this important notion in a different way. The following definition is essentially due to Park [26].

Definition 2.9 [Bisimulation] Let $g_i = (r_i, S_i, \longrightarrow_i)$ $(i = 1, 2)$ be process graphs. A relation $R \subseteq S_1 \times S_2$ is a *(strong) bisimulation* between g_1 and g_2 if it satisfies:

1. $r_1 R r_2$;

2. if sRt and $s \xrightarrow{a}_1 s'$, then there exists a $t' \in S_2$ with $t \xrightarrow{a}_2 t'$ and $s'Rt'$;

3. if sRt and $t \xrightarrow{a}_2 t'$, then there exists an $s' \in S_1$ with $s \xrightarrow{a}_1 s'$ and $s'Rt'$.

Graphs g_1 and g_2 are *bisimilar*, notation $g_1 \leftrightarrow g_2$, if there exists a bisimulation between them. Note that bisimilarity is an equivalence relation.

Two states s and s' of a LTS $\mathcal{A}$ are bisimilar iff $graph(s, \mathcal{A})$ and $graph(s', \mathcal{A})$ are bisimilar.

Two closed terms t, t' are *bisimilar* with respect to a calculus P, notation $P : t \leftrightarrow t'$, if $\mathcal{O}_P(t) \leftrightarrow \mathcal{O}_P(t')$.

Since any isomorphism between two process graphs is also a bisimulation, it follows that $\simeq$ is contained in $\leftrightarrow$. It turns out that, just like isomorphism, bisimulation equivalence is not a congruence relative to all transition system specifications. For instance, if one adds to the calculus PC a rule $x + x \xrightarrow{b} \mathbf{0}$, then one can show that $\mathbf{0} \leftrightarrow \mathbf{0} \| \mathbf{0}$ but $\mathbf{0} + \mathbf{0} \not\leftrightarrow \mathbf{0} + \mathbf{0} \| \mathbf{0}$. In [19] the question under which conditions bisimulation is a congruence is considered in great depth. It turns out that if the rules in a calculus fit the very general *tyft/tyxt* format, bisimulation is a congruence. We will not discuss the *tyft/tyxt* format here, but instead present a more restricted format, essentially due to De Simone [33, 34], which is sufficiently general for our purposes. The reader may check that the transition system specification for the language PC fits this format.

Definition 2.10 [De Simone's format] Let $\{x_i \mid i \in \mathbb{N}\}$ and $\{y_j \mid j \in \mathbb{N}\}$ be two fixed sets of variables in $\mathcal{V}$ with all x_i and y_j different. Let Σ be a signature and let A be a set of labels.

A rule in $Cf(\Sigma, A)$ is a *De Simone* rule if it takes the form:

$$\frac{x_i \xrightarrow{a_i} y_i \quad (i \in I)}{f(x_1, \ldots, x_n) \xrightarrow{a} t}$$

where

- $(f, n) \in \Sigma$;
- $I \subseteq \{1, \ldots, n\}$;
- if, for $1 \leq i \leq n$, $z_i = y_i$ if $i \in I$ and $z_i = x_i$ otherwise, then $t \in \mathbb{T}(\Sigma)$ is a context with variables in $\{z_1, \ldots, z_n\}$ (so each variable occurs at most once).

In the above rule, (f, n) is the *type*, a the *action*, t the *target*, and the tuple $\langle l_1, \ldots, l_n \rangle$ with $l_i = a_i$ if $i \in I$ and $l_i = *$ otherwise, is the *trigger*. If $i \in I$, then the i-th position is *active* in the rule; otherwise it is *passive*. Each rule is characterized uniquely by its type, action, target and trigger. If r is a rule, these ingredients will be referred to as $type(r)$, $action(r)$, $target(r)$ and $trigger(r)$.

A calculus (Σ, A, R) is a *De Simone system* if Σ can be partitioned into Σ_1 and Σ_2, and R can be partitioned into R_1 and R_2 in such a way that:

- all the rules in R_1 are De Simone rules with a type in Σ_1;
- there exists a set $\mathcal{X} \subseteq \mathcal{N}$ and a mapping $E : \mathcal{X} \to \mathbb{T}(\Sigma)$ such that:

$$\Sigma_2 = \{(X, 0) \mid X \in \mathcal{X}\} \text{ and } R_2 = \{\frac{E(X) \xrightarrow{a} y_0}{X \xrightarrow{a} y_0} \mid X \in \mathcal{X} \text{ and } a \in A\}.$$

Elements of $\mathcal{X}$ are referred to as *process names* and E is called the *declaration mapping*. If a calculus P is a De Simone system, then both the set of process names and the declaration mapping are uniquely determined and will be referred to as $\mathcal{X}_P$ and E_P.

Theorem 2.11 *Let P be a De Simone system. Then bisimulation equivalence with respect to P is a congruence on the signature of P.*

Proof Standard. This theorem was first proved in [33] in a slightly different setting. The theorem is in fact a corollary of some of the other results in this paper (see remark at the end of Section 4.1). ■

3 Power to Specify Graphs

In this section we will present what one could call bad news: in the case of 'strong' equivalences the expressiveness of SOS languages is, in many cases, even less than suggested by Theorem 1.6. For a rather large class of languages we can give an upper bound on the speed with which the fanout can grow. This upper bound implies that, for each of these languages, there exists a primitive recursive process graph that cannot be denoted up to (strong) trace equivalence.

3.1 Effective De Simone Systems

In this subsection, we will identify a class of De Simone systems that induce an effective operational semantics. This result is a useful, because if one is able to define an operational semantics for a programming language by means of a calculus in this class, then one knows that (at least in principle) it is possible to implement the language.

Bloom, Istrail and Meyer [12] introduce a particular format of transition system specifications, which they call *GSOS rule system*'s, and show that for any specification in this format the associated operational semantics is effective and has some other desirable properties as well. The authors argue that it is not possible to generalize the GSOS format in any obvious way without loosing one of these desirable properties. However, one of the clauses in the definition of the GSOS format is that the number of rules must be finite. We think that this clause is unnecessarily restrictive and hinders application of the nice theory developed for this format. Calculi like CCS, SCCS and MEIJE all have an infinite number of actions and an infinite number of rules. Consequently it is not possible to view them as GSOS rule systems, even if one restricts attention to subcalculi with guarded recursion. Below, we introduce the increasingly restrictive notions of ***guarded***, ***bounded*** and *effective* De Simone systems. A bounded De Simone system associates to each term a finitely branching process graph. An effective De Simone system guarantees all the nice properties required in [12] and in particular that the induced operational semantics is effective. It will turn out that CCS-like calculi with guarded recursion can be viewed as effective De Simone systems. We claim that a similar restriction can replace the finiteness constraint in GSOS rule systems without any of the desired properties getting lost.

Definition 3.1 [Guardedness] Let $P = (\Sigma, A, R)$ be a De Simone system, let (f, n) be a signature element of Σ, and let $1 \leq i \leq n$. Then (f, n) ***tests*** its i-th argument and the

i-th argument is *awake* if there is a rule in R of type (f, n) in which the i-th position is active (*i.e.*, i occurs in the index set of the rule); otherwise the i-th position is *sleeping*. A term $t \in \mathbb{T}(\Sigma)$ is *guarded* if all process names in t occur in subterms that are on a sleeping position. P is *guarded* if all terms in the image of E_P are guarded.

The only signature elements of PC with a sleeping position are the prefixing operations. Thus, the above notion of guardedness generalizes the definition of guardedness for the language PC. The notion of an operator testing an argument is due to Bloom [11]. However, the use of this notion in a definition of guardedness is new in the present paper.

Definition 3.2 [Boundedness] A guarded De Simone system is *bounded* if for each type that is not a process name and for each trigger, the corresponding set of rules is finite.

The inference rules for the operations of CCS, SCCS and MEIJE, which are all in De Simone's format, have the property that for a given type and a given trigger there is only a single rule. If the action alphabet is infinite, then the De Simone system for PC is not bounded, due to the generalized renaming operator. In the case of PC it is easy to see that this unboundedness leads to infinite branching. Thus, if one prefers to have finite branching then one has to restrict attention to a subset of PC with renaming operations that relate each action to at most finitely many other actions.

Theorem 3.3 *Let P be a bounded De Simone system. Then the operational semantics $\mathcal{O}_P$ maps each term to a finitely branching process graph.*

Proof Routine and omitted. ■

Definition 3.4 A bounded De Simone system $P = (\Sigma, A, R)$ is *effective*, relative to enumerations $(f_1, n_1), (f_2, n_2), \ldots$ and $a_1, a_2, \ldots$ of Σ and A, respectively, if:

- the set of process names is recursive;
- for each type that is not a process name and for each argument, it is decidable whether this argument is tested or not;
- for a given type that is not a process name and a given trigger, the cardinality of the corresponding (finite) set of rules as well as the set itself are recursive;
- the function E_P is recursive.

If the action alphabet is infinite, then PC is not effective. Effective versions of PC can be obtained by allowing only renaming relations r which relate an action to at most finitely many other actions, in such a way that for each a_i the canonical index of $\{j \mid r(a_i, a_j)\}$ is recursive. Some additional restrictions will be needed to make the language recursively enumerable or recursive.

Theorem 3.5 *Each effective De Simone system induces an effective operational semantics.*

Proof Routine and omitted. ■

3.2 The Expressiveness of CCS-like Languages

In his Ph.D. thesis, Bloom [10] shows that no GSOS rule system can denote all effective process graphs up to strong bisimulation. This result is an immediate corollary of Theorem 1.6 of this paper and the basic result about the GSOS format of [12], which says that this format induces an effective operational semantics. A nice aspect of Bloom's proof however is that the counterexample which he produces (for any GSOS-language an effective graph that cannot be denoted up to bisimulation equivalence) is quite simple and provides additional insight in the expressive power of GSOS languages. Bloom's proof uses two lemma's. The first lemma provides, for a given set of rules, an upper bound on the *fanout* of a term (*i.e.*, the number of outgoing transitions) that only depends on the size of that term. The second lemma provides, given a set of rules and a transition $p \xrightarrow{a} q$, an upper bound on the size of successor q in terms of the size of p. The combination of the two lemma's implies that in any GSOS-specifiable process graph the rate at which the fanout can grow is bounded. Using this observation it is easy to construct a counterexample.

Below, we will adapt Bloom's idea to the setting of this paper. In the case of a De Simone system it is not possible to give upper bounds on the fanout and the size of successor states of p in terms of p. If p is a process name then, depending on the size of the recursive definition of this process name, fanout and successors of p can be arbitrarily big. Therefore, we will give upper bounds on the fanout and the size of successors in terms of the size of p and the supremum over all process names X that occur unguarded in p of the size of the recursive definition for X.

The different treatment of recursion and the different finiteness constraints make any comparison nontrivial but, due to the fact that De Simone rules are more restricted than GSOS-rules, it appears that the upper bounds which we derive are smaller than those of Bloom [10]. A closer investigation of these bounds will be interesting because it might lead to a proof that certain process graphs are GSOS definable but not definable using De Simone systems.

We start off by defining, for each De Simone system, some parameters which will determine the possible growth rate in the process graphs.

Definition 3.6 Let $P = (\Sigma, A, R)$ be a De Simone system.

- $\alpha_P \in \mathbb{N} \cup \{\infty\}$ is the supremum of 1 and, for each rule in R, the number of function symbols occurring in the target.
- $\beta_P \in \mathbb{N} \cup \{\infty\}$ is the supremum over all process names X of the size of $E_P(X)$.
- γ_P is the supremum over all types and triggers of the number of rules in R with that type and that trigger.

We write α, β and γ if P is clear from the context.

It is probably useful to illustrate this definition with some examples. In the De Simone system for PC, the α-parameter has value 1. In fact, and this is interesting to note, in most major process calculi proposed in the literature, the α-parameter is 1. One exception is the *desynchronising* operator Δ, present in an earlier version of SCCS and needed by

De Simone [34] in order to show equivalence of SCCS and MEIJE. The Δ operator has an α parameter of 2:

$$\frac{x \xrightarrow{a} x'}{\Delta x \xrightarrow{a} \delta \Delta x'} \quad \delta x \xrightarrow{a} \delta x \quad \frac{x \xrightarrow{a} x'}{\delta x \xrightarrow{a} x'}$$

Another example of an operator with an α-parameter of 2 is the is the p **watching** S construct from synchronous programming language Esterel [9].

It is possible to have an infinite number of recursive definitions in a De Simone system and still have the β-parameter finite for each expression. For instance, consider the following infinitary PC definition of a counter:

$$C_0 = zero{\cdot}C_0 + up{\cdot}C_1$$

$$C_{n+1} = down{\cdot}C_n + up{\cdot}C_{n+2}.$$

One can easily check that the β-parameter of this system is 5.

Due to the presence of the relational renaming operations, the γ-parameter for PC is $|A|$: if r is the universal relation, then for any trigger $\langle a\rangle$, ρ_r has $|A|$ rules. Process calculi like CCS, SCCS and MEIJE all have a γ of 1.

Below, we will show that for any guarded De Simone system P with α, β and γ finite, there are strong bounds on the speed with which branching can grow.

Lemma 3.7 *Let P be a guarded De Simone system with a transition $p \xrightarrow{a} q$. Suppose that α_P and β_P are finite. Then:*

$$|q| \leq \begin{cases} \alpha \cdot |p| & \textit{if } p \textit{ is guarded} \\ \alpha \cdot \beta \cdot |p| & \textit{otherwise} \end{cases}$$

Proof First, consider the case that p is guarded. By induction on the size of p, we prove that $|q| \leq \alpha \cdot |p|$.

Consider a proof of $p \xrightarrow{a} q$. Since p is guarded, it is not a process name. So the last inference rule used in the proof must be a De Simone rule. Let this rule be

$$\frac{x_i \xrightarrow{a_i} y_i \quad (i \in I)}{f(x_1, \ldots, x_n) \xrightarrow{a} t}$$

and let σ be the substitution by which this rule is instantiated. Then for all $i \in I$ the term $\sigma(x_i)$ is guarded and a proper subterm of p. Therefore the induction hypothesis can be used to conclude that for all $i \in I$, $|\sigma(y_i)| \leq \alpha \cdot |\sigma(x_i)|$. Because the rule is in De Simone's format, it follows that for all $1 \leq i \leq n$, t contains at most one occurrence of either x_i or y_i. This observation can be used to derive:

$$|q| = |\sigma(t)| \leq \alpha + \alpha \cdot |\sigma(x_1)| + \ldots + \alpha \cdot |\sigma(x_n)| =$$

$$= \alpha \cdot (1 + |\sigma(x_1)| + \ldots + |\sigma(x_n)|) = \alpha \cdot |\sigma(f(x_1, \ldots, x_n))| = \alpha \cdot |p|.$$

This completes the proof for the case p is guarded.

Next, we prove, by induction on the size of p, that $|q| \leq \alpha \cdot \beta \cdot |p|$ if p is not guarded.

If p is of the form X, with X a process name, then $E_P(X) \xrightarrow{a} q$. But since $E_P(X)$ is guarded, the statement proved in the above can be used to derive:

$|q| \leq \alpha \cdot |E_P(X)| \leq \alpha \cdot \beta = \alpha \cdot \beta \cdot |p|.$

So assume that p is not a process name. Consider a proof of $p \xrightarrow{a} q$. The last inference rule used in the proof must be a De Simone rule. By an inductive argument which is similar to the one used for the guarded case it follows that $|q| \leq \alpha \cdot \beta \cdot |p|$. ■

Lemma 3.8 *Let P be a guarded De Simone system and let p be a closed expression over the signature of P. Suppose that β_P and γ_P are finite. Then:*

$$fan(p) \leq \begin{cases} \gamma^{|p|} \cdot 2^{|p|-1} & \text{if } p \text{ is guarded} \\ \gamma^{\beta \cdot |p|} \cdot 2^{\beta \cdot |p|-1} & \text{otherwise} \end{cases}$$

Proof First, consider the case that p is guarded. By induction on the size of p, we prove $fan(p) \leq \gamma^{|p|} \cdot 2^{|p|-1}$.

Let $p = f(p_1, \ldots, p_n)$. Then (f, n) is not a process name, and for each argument i that is tested by (f, n) the term p_i is guarded. Consider the collection $\mathcal{I}$ of pairs $(r, ((u_1, q_1), \ldots, (u_n, q_n)))$ satisfying

- r is a rule with type (f, n) and trigger $\langle u_1, \ldots, u_n \rangle$, and
- for each i either $u_i = q_i = *$ or $p_i \xrightarrow{u_i} q_i$.

It is not hard to see that $\mathcal{I}$ has at most $\gamma \cdot \prod_{i \text{ tested}} (fan(p_i) + 1)$ elements. Since there is a straightforward surjective mapping from $\mathcal{I}$ to the transitions of p, it follows that

$$fan(p) \leq \gamma \cdot \prod_{i \text{ tested}} (fan(p_i) + 1).$$

By induction hypothesis we obtain, for each i that is tested, $fan(p_i) \leq \gamma^{|p_i|} \cdot 2^{|p_i|-1}$. Thus we can derive:

$$\begin{aligned} fan(p) &\leq \gamma \cdot \prod_{i \text{ tested}} (fan(p_i) + 1) \leq \\ &\leq \gamma \cdot \prod_{i \text{ tested}} (\gamma^{|p_i|} \cdot 2^{|p_i|-1} + 1) \leq \\ &\leq \gamma \cdot \prod_{i=1}^{n} (\gamma^{|p_i|} \cdot 2^{|p_i|-1} + 1) \leq \\ &\leq \gamma \cdot \prod_{i=1}^{n} (\gamma^{|p_i|} \cdot 2^{|p_i|}) \leq \\ &\leq \gamma^{|p|} \cdot 2^{|p|-1}. \end{aligned}$$

This completes the proof for the case p is guarded.

Next, we prove, by induction on the size of p, that $fan(p) \leq \gamma^{\beta \cdot |p|} \cdot 2^{\beta \cdot |p|-1}$ if p is not guarded. If p is of the form X for some process name X, then $E_P(X)$ is guarded and of size less or equal than β. Hence:

$1 \xrightarrow{1} 0$
$\dfrac{x \xrightarrow{n} x'}{succ(x) \xrightarrow{n+1} 0}$
$triple(x) \xrightarrow{0} triple(succ(x))$
$\dfrac{x \xrightarrow{n} x'}{triple(x) \xrightarrow{m} 0}$ if $0 < m < 2^{2^{2^n}}$

Table 3: Rules for process graph with triple exponential growth rate.

$$fan(p) = fan(E_P(X)) \leq \gamma^{\beta} \cdot 2^{\beta - 1} = \gamma^{\beta \cdot |p|} \cdot 2^{\beta \cdot |p| - 1}.$$

So assume that p is of the form $f(p_1, \ldots, p_n)$ with (f, n) not a process name. By an inductive argument very similar to that used for the guarded case one can show $fan(p) \leq \gamma^{\beta \cdot |p|} \cdot 2^{\beta \cdot |p| - 1}$. ■

Theorem 3.9 *Let A be a countably infinite set of actions. Then there exists a primitive recursive process graph g over A that cannot be denoted modulo trace equivalence by any guarded De Simone system over alphabet A with α_P, β_P and γ_P finite.*

Proof Without loss of generality assume $A = \mathbb{N}$. Let $P = (\Sigma, A, R)$ be a guurded De Simone system with α_P, β_P and γ_P finite. Suppose

$$p = p_0 \xrightarrow{a_1} p_1 \xrightarrow{a_2} \cdots \xrightarrow{a_n} p_n$$

is a sequence of transitions starting in p. Then, by Lemma 3.7, we have for all $i < n$: $|p_{i+1}| \leq \alpha \cdot \beta \cdot |p_i|$. Thus, for all i, $|p_i| \leq \alpha^i \cdot \beta^i \cdot |p|$. Combining this result with Lemma 3.8 yields:

$$fan(p_i) \leq \gamma^{\alpha^i \cdot \beta^{i+1} \cdot |p|} \cdot 2^{\alpha^i \cdot \beta^{i+1} \cdot |p| - 1}.$$

Thus, if $NT(n)$ is the number of different traces of length n in $\mathcal{O}_P(p)$, we have:

$$\begin{aligned} NT(n) &\leq \prod_{i=0}^{n-1} \gamma^{\alpha^i \cdot \beta^{i+1} \cdot |p|} \cdot 2^{\alpha^i \cdot \beta^{i+1} \cdot |p| - 1} \\ &< \gamma^{\alpha^{n-1} \cdot \beta^n \cdot n \cdot |p|} \cdot 2^{\alpha^{n-1} \cdot \beta^n \cdot n \cdot |p|} \end{aligned}$$

Even though $NT(n)$ can grow fast, its growth rate is still double exponential.

Let *Triple* be the calculus with a signature consisting of two constant symbols 1 and 0, two unary function symbols *succ* and *ack*, and rules as given in Table 3. Now define g to be the process graph $\mathcal{O}_{Triple}(triple(1))$. It is easy to see that graph g is primitive recursive, and also that, for each n, it has $2^{2^{2^n}}$ different traces of length n. Thus, if n is chosen sufficiently large, then there is some trace of length n in graph g, that is not a trace of the graph of p: a routine exercise tells us that, for big enough n, $NT(n) < 2^{2^{2^n}}$. Thus it cannot be the case that $\mathcal{O}_P(p) \approx_T g$. ■

A corollary of the above result is that graph g can not be specified in the guarded, finitary versions of calculi like CCS, SCCS, MEIJE and ACP.

Theorem 3.10 *The graph g can be specified in an effective version of PC.*

Proof Take as the alphabet of actions the set N of natural numbers. Define the relations *Succ* and *Triple* by:

$$\begin{array}{lcl} Succ & \triangleq & \{(0,0)\} \cup \{(n, n+1) \mid n > 0\}, \\ Triple & \triangleq & \{(0,0)\} \cup \{(n, m) \mid n, m > 0 \text{ and } m < 2^{2^{2^n}}\}. \end{array}$$

Let X be a process name with recursive definition $X \Leftarrow 0 \cdot \rho_{Succ}(X) + 1$. Then it is straightforward to check that the term $\rho_{Triple}(X)$ denotes g up to isomorphism. ■

4 Power to Specify Operations on Graphs

The third way in which a process calculus can be universal is that all operations in a given natural class can be defined in terms of the operations in the language modulo a given equivalence. The first result of this kind occurring in the literature is due to De Simone [33, 34], who shows that all operations that can be defined in a format similar to what we call De Simone's format in this paper, are definable in terms of both the languages MEIJE and SCCS up to (strong) bisimulation equivalence. Another result is due to Parrow [27], who shows that all *network* operators specifiable in a restricted De Simone format can be defined up to weak bisimulation equivalence in terms of only two operators: *disjoint parallelism* and *linking*.

4.1 From Calculi to Operations on Graphs

Strictly speaking, the above phrasing of De Simone's result is not correct. What he shows in fact is that for any calculus in a particular format, and for any n-ary function symbol f from that calculus, there exists a MEIJE-SCCS context which is "FH-bisimilar" with the expression $f(x_1, \ldots, x_n)$. Clearly, there is a close connection between the notion of FH-bisimilarity and the equality of certain operations on process graphs modulo bisimulation. However, this is left implicit in De Simone's work. It is not even made clear how a calculus determines operations on process graphs.

A first contribution of this section is a precise definition of the transformation from a calculus to operations on graphs. Although the result is the same, the definition of the transformation that we present here is quite different from the definition in Baeten and Vaandrager [7]. Our definition, which in spirit is very close to De Simone's notion of FH-bisimulation, turns out to be useful for proving that an operation from one calculus is a derived operation from another calculus.

Technically, a key role is played by the notion of an *action transducer*: to each function symbol in a given calculus a (rooted) action transducer is associated, which in turn determines an operation on process graphs. Action transducers were introduced by Larsen and Xinxin [22] as a technical tool for proving certain compositionality results. An action transducer is an object that consumes actions provided by its internal processes, in return produces an action for an external observer, and may change as a result of this transduction. The definition of an action transducer below differs from the corresponding definition of a context system in [22], and captures explicitly the possibility that in a dynamic situation a context may now and then lose some of its holes. The idea to associate an action transducer to a calculus using the notion of a *linear proof* is also new in this paper.

Definition 4.1 An *action transducer* over a set A of actions is a triple $T = (\mathcal{C}, h, \longrightarrow)$, where

- $\mathcal{C}$ is a countable set of *contexts*;
- h is a mapping from $\mathcal{C}$ to finite subsets of N, which associates *holes* to contexts;
- $\longrightarrow$ is a subset of $\mathcal{C} \times A \times Pow(\mathsf{N} \times A) \times \mathcal{C}$ with for each $(C, a, \eta, C') \in\longrightarrow$, $h(C') \subseteq h(C)$ and η a function with $domain(\eta) \subseteq h(C)$.

Elements of $\longrightarrow$ are called *transductions*, and we write $C \xrightarrow[\eta]{a} C'$ if $(C, a, \eta, C') \in\longrightarrow$.

A *rooted action transducer* or *operator graph* over A is a tuple $(C_0, \mathcal{C}, h, \rightarrow)$, where $(\mathcal{C}, h, \rightarrow)$ is an action transducer over A, $C_0 \in \mathcal{C}$ is the *root*, and each context in $\mathcal{C}$ is reachable via zero or more transductions from C_0. If T is an action transducer and C is a context of T, then $og(C, T)$ is the operator graph with root C and an underlying action transducer that is obtained by restricting T to the part that is reachable from C.

Definition 4.2 [Graph domain] $\mathcal{G}(A)$ is the set of process graphs with states taken from N and transition labels from A. For $g \in \mathcal{G}(A)$, $[g]$ denotes the isomorphism class of g. $\widehat{\mathcal{G}}(A)$ is the set of isomorphism classes of $\mathcal{G}(A)$.

Definition 4.3 [From action transducers to operations on graphs] Let $F = (C_0, \mathcal{C}, h, \longrightarrow)$ be an operator graph over A with $h(C_0) = \{i_1, \ldots, i_n\}$. To F an n-ary operator $op(F)$ on $\widehat{\mathcal{G}}(A)$ is associated as follows. Assume w.l.o.g. that $i_j < i_k$ for $1 \leq j < k \leq n$. Let, for $1 \leq j \leq n$, $g_j = (r_j, S_j, \longrightarrow_j) \in \mathcal{G}(A)$. Then $op(F)([g_1], \cdots, [g_n])$ is the isomorphism class in $\widehat{\mathcal{G}}(A)$ of graphs that are isomorphic to the process graph $graph(r, (S, \longrightarrow))$ where

- $r = (C_0, r_1, \ldots, r_n)$;
- $S = \mathcal{C} \times S_1 \times \cdots \times S_n$;
- $(C, s_1, \ldots, s_n) \xrightarrow{a} (C', s_1', \ldots, s_n')$ iff there is an η such that $C \xrightarrow[\eta]{a} C'$ and for $1 \leq j \leq n$, $i_j \notin domain(\eta) \Rightarrow s_j = s_j'$ and $\forall b \in A : (i_j, b) \in \eta \Rightarrow s_j \xrightarrow{b}_j s_j'$.

Lemma 4.4 *Let $F = (C_0, C, h, \longrightarrow)$ be an operator graph, with $op(F)$ an n-ary operator on $\hat{\mathcal{G}}(A)$. Let for $1 \le i \le n$, $g_i, g'_i \in \mathcal{G}(A)$. Then*

$$\forall i : g_i \leftrightarrows g'_i \quad \Rightarrow \quad op(F)([g_1], \ldots, [g_n]) \leftrightarrows op(F)([g'_1], \ldots, [g'_n]).$$

Proof Suppose that for all i, $g_i \leftrightarrows g'_i$. Let R_i be a bisimulation between g_i and g'_i. Define the relation R between states of $op(F)([g_1], \ldots, [g_n])$ and states of $op(F)([g'_1], \ldots, [g'_n])$ by

$$(C, s_1, \ldots, s_n) R (C, s'_1, \ldots, s'_n) \text{ iff } \forall i : s_i \leftrightarrows s'_i.$$

It is easy to check that R is a bisimulation, from which it follows that $op(F)([g_1], \ldots, [g_n]) \leftrightarrows op(F)([g'_1], \ldots, [g'_n])$. ■

We will now define how action transducers can be associated to De Simone calculi. The obvious choice for the contexts of the action transducer are the contexts of the De Simone calculi (open terms over the signature in which variables occur linearly). In an attempt to emphasize that an SOS calculus is essentially a logical theory, the transductions of the action transducer will be defined in terms of conditional formulas that are provable from the calculus.

Definition 4.5 [Linear proofs] Let $P = (\Sigma, A, R)$ be a calculus. A *linear proof* from P of a conditional formula $\rho = \frac{\psi_1, \ldots, \psi_n}{\psi} \in Cf(\Sigma, A)$ is a finite tree whose edges are ordered and whose vertices are labeled by transitions in $Tr(\Sigma, A)$, such that:

- the root is labeled with ψ;
- there are distinct vertices $v_1, \ldots, v_n$ in the tree, which occur as leaves and are labeled with $\psi_1, \ldots, \psi_n$, respectively;
- if ϕ is the label of a node $v \notin \{v_1, \ldots, v_n\}$ and $\phi_1, \ldots, \phi_m$ are the labels of the children of v, then there is a rule $\frac{\chi_1, \ldots, \chi_m}{\chi} \in R$ and a substitution ζ such that $\phi_i = \chi_i[\zeta]$ and $\phi = \chi[\zeta]$.

Write $P \vdash_L \rho$ if a linear proof of ρ from P exists.

The term "linear" is used because of the apparent connection with the Linear Logic of Girard [16]. In a linear proof of a conditional formula, each hypothesis is used exactly once. This "resource conciousness" should be contrasted with proofs in non-linear conditional logics, in which an hypothesis may be used several times, or not at all. The notion of linear provability generalizes the proof notion of Definition 2.5 in the sense that for closed terms t, t',

$$P \vdash t \xrightarrow{a} t' \text{ iff } P \vdash_L \frac{}{t \xrightarrow{a} t'}.$$

The following lemma is easily proved by induction on the structure of linear proofs.

Lemma 4.6 *Let P be a De Simone calculus with*

$$P \vdash_L \frac{x_i \xrightarrow{a_i} x_i \ \ (i \in I)}{C \xrightarrow{a} C'},$$

where C is a context with variables from $\{x_i \mid i \in \mathsf{N}\}$. Then C' is a context, $\{x_i \mid i \in I\} \subseteq var(C)$, and $var(C') \subseteq var(C)$.

Definition 4.7 [From calculi to transducers] To each De Simone system $P = (\Sigma, A, R)$, an action transducer $transducer(P) = (\mathcal{C}, h, \longrightarrow)$ is associated as follows.

- $\mathcal{C}$ consists of the contexts in $\mathbb{T}(\Sigma)$ with variables in $\{x_i \mid i \in \mathsf{N}\}$;
- h associates to each context the set of indices of its varables;
- Let $C, C' \in \mathcal{C}$, $a \in A$, and $\eta = \{(i, a_i) \mid i \in I\}$ a finite subset of $\mathsf{N} \times A$. Then

$$C \xrightarrow[\eta]{a} C' \quad \text{iff} \quad P \vdash_L \frac{x_i \xrightarrow{a_i} x_i \quad (i \in I)}{C \xrightarrow{a} C'}.$$

It follows using Lemma 4.6 that *transducer*(P) is indeed a transducer.

The use of premisses $x_i \xrightarrow{a_i} x_i$ in the above definition may appear strange at first sight: after performing a transition an agent does not in general evolves into itself and therefore the hypotheses seem too strong. However, this turns out not too be the case: one can prove by straightforward induction on the structure of proofs that

$$P \vdash_L \frac{x_i \xrightarrow{a_i} x_i \quad (i \in I)}{C \xrightarrow{a} C'} \quad \text{iff} \quad P \vdash_L \frac{x_i \xrightarrow{a_i} y_i \quad (i \in I)}{C \xrightarrow{a} C'[y_i/x_i(i \in I)]}.$$

Thus, modulo syntactic details, the transductions in *transducer*(P) are *exactly* the formulas that can be derived using a linear form of logical inference.

Definition 4.8 [From SOS contexts to operators] Let $P = (\Sigma, A, R)$ be a De Simone system and let C be an n-ary context over Σ and $\{x_i \mid i \in \mathsf{N}\}$. The n-ary operator $\langle\!\langle C \rangle\!\rangle_P$ on $\widehat{\mathcal{G}}(A)$ is given by

$$\langle\!\langle C \rangle\!\rangle_P = op(og(C, transducer(P))).$$

For $h(C) = \{i_1, \ldots, i_n\}$ with $j < k \Rightarrow i_j < i_k$, and $\xi : var(C) \to \widehat{\mathcal{G}}(A)$, the process graph $\langle\!\langle C \rangle\!\rangle_P^\xi$ is defined by

$$\langle\!\langle C \rangle\!\rangle_P^\xi = \langle\!\langle C \rangle\!\rangle_P(\xi(x_{i_1}), \ldots, \xi(x_{i_n})).$$

The following two technical lemmas play a key role in the further developments of this section.

Lemma 4.9 *Let P be a De Simone system and let t be a closed term over the signature of P. Then $\mathcal{O}_P(t) \simeq \langle\!\langle t \rangle\!\rangle_P()$.*

Proof Straightforward. ■

Lemma 4.10 *Let P be a De Simone system. Let $C, C_1, \ldots, C_n$ be contexts over the signature of P with $var(C) = \{x_1, \ldots, x_n\}$ and $var(C_i) \subseteq \{x_i \mid i \in \mathsf{N}\}$ such that $k \neq l \Rightarrow var(C_k) \cap var(C_l) = \emptyset$. Let ξ_i be mappings from $var(C_i)$ to $\widehat{\mathcal{G}}(A)$. Then*

$$\langle\!\langle C\rangle\!\rangle_P(\langle\!\langle C_1\rangle\!\rangle_P^{\xi_1},\ldots,\langle\!\langle C_n\rangle\!\rangle_P^{\xi_n}) \leftrightarrow \langle\!\langle C[C_1/x_1,\ldots,C_n/x_n]\rangle\!\rangle_P^{\xi_1\cup\cdots\cup\xi_n}.$$

Definition 4.11 [From calculi to process algebras] Let $P = (\Sigma, A, R)$ be a De Simone system. The Σ-algebra $\mathcal{A}(P)$ has as domain $\widehat{\mathcal{G}}(A)$; each signature element (f, n) is mapped to the n-ary operation $f_{\mathcal{A}(P)} = \langle\!\langle f(x_1,\ldots,x_n)\rangle\!\rangle_P$.

For a given De Simone system P, the evaluation function $[\![\cdot]\!]_{\mathcal{A}(P)}$ maps each closed term to an isomorphism class of process graphs. An obvious question is how this compositional semantics relates to the operational semantics $\mathcal{O}_P$. It turns out that the two mappings are different if we consider them up to isomorphism. The counterexample is similar to the one used in Section 2.4 to show that isomorphism is not a congruence for PC:

$$[\![a+a]\!]_{\mathcal{A}(PC)} \not\cong \mathcal{O}_{PC}(a+a).$$

However, as we will see, the two mapping are the same modulo bisimulation equivalence. Notice that, due to Lemma 4.4, strong bisimulation is a congruence on algebras $\mathcal{A}(P)$, and therefore the quotient algebra $\mathcal{A}(P)/\leftrightarrow$ is well-defined.

Theorem 4.12 *Let $P = (\Sigma, R)$ be a De Simone system over A, let C be a Σ-context with variables in $\{x_i \mid i \in \mathsf{N}\}$, and let ξ be an evaluation in $\mathcal{A}(P)$. Then*

$$[\![C]\!]^{\xi}_{\mathcal{A}(P)} \leftrightarrow \langle\!\langle C\rangle\!\rangle_P^{\xi\lceil var(C)}.$$

Proof By induction on the structure of C. If C is of the form x_i, then

$$\langle\!\langle C\rangle\!\rangle_P^{\xi\lceil var(C)} = \langle\!\langle x_i\rangle\!\rangle_P(\xi(x_i)) = op(og(x_i, transducer(P)))(\xi(x_i)).$$

The operator graph $og(x_i, transducer(P))$ has a single state x_i, and all its transductions are of the form

$$x_i \xrightarrow[(i,a)]{a} x_i$$

for a in A. It follows that $op(og(x_i, transducer(P)))$ is the identity operation on $\widehat{\mathcal{G}}(A)$. This implies

$$op(og(x_i, transducer(P)))(\xi(x_i)) = \xi(x_i) = [\![C]\!]^{\xi}_{\mathcal{B}}.$$

If C is of the form $f(C_1,\ldots,C_n)$, then we derive (with $\mathcal{B}$ short for $\mathcal{A}(P)$):

$$
\begin{aligned}
&[\![C]\!]^{\xi}_{\mathcal{B}} = \\
&= \langle\!\langle f(x_1,\ldots,x_n)\rangle\!\rangle_P([\![C_1]\!]^{\xi}_{\mathcal{B}},\ldots,[\![C_n]\!]^{\xi}_{\mathcal{B}}) && \text{\{by Definitions 2.7 and 4.11\}}\\
&\leftrightarrow \langle\!\langle f(x_1,\ldots,x_n)\rangle\!\rangle_P(\langle\!\langle C_1\rangle\!\rangle_P^{\xi\lceil var(C_1)},\ldots,\langle\!\langle C_n\rangle\!\rangle_P^{\xi\lceil var(C_n)}) && \text{\{by ind.hyp. and Lemma 4.4\}}\\
&\leftrightarrow \langle\!\langle C\rangle\!\rangle_P^{\xi\lceil var(C)} && \text{\{by Lemma 4.10\}}
\end{aligned}
$$

■

Corollary 4.13 (Compositional and operational semantics agree) *Let P be a De Simone system and let t be a closed term over the signature of P. Then $[\![t]\!]_{\mathcal{A}(P)} \leftrightarrow \mathcal{O}_P(t)$.*

Proof By combination of Lemma 4.9 and Theorem 4.12. ∎

One possible interpretation of Corollary 4.13 and the counterexample that a similar result does not hold up to isomorphism, is that there is some arbitrariness in the definitions of $[\![]\!]_{\mathcal{A}(P)}$ and $\mathcal{O}_P()$. This arbitrariness disappears if one considers the resulting graphs up to strong bisimulation congruence.

Lemma 4.10 and Lemma 4.4 can be used to give a short proof of Theorem 2.11, which says that bisimulation equivalence is a congruence for De Simone calculi. Because, suppose $P = (\Sigma, A, R)$ is a De Simone calculus, C is a unary context over Σ, and t and t' are closed terms over Σ with $\mathcal{O}_P(t) \leftrightarrows \mathcal{O}_P(t')$. Then

$$\begin{aligned}
&\mathcal{O}_P(C[t]) \leftrightarrows \\
&\leftrightarrows \langle\!\langle C[t] \rangle\!\rangle_P() && \{\text{by Lemma 4.9}\}\\
&\leftrightarrows \langle\!\langle C[x_1] \rangle\!\rangle_P(\langle\!\langle t \rangle\!\rangle_P()) && \{\text{by Lemma 4.10}\}\\
&\leftrightarrows \langle\!\langle C[x_1] \rangle\!\rangle_P(\mathcal{O}_P(t)) && \{\text{by Lemmas 4.4 and 4.9}\}\\
&\leftrightarrows \langle\!\langle C[x_1] \rangle\!\rangle_P(\mathcal{O}_P(t')) && \{\text{by Lemma 4.4}\}\\
&\leftrightarrows \cdots \leftrightarrows \mathcal{O}_P(C[t']).
\end{aligned}$$

Basically, what happens in the above derivation is that the question whether bisimulation is a congruence, is reduced via Lemma 4.10, from a problem in the *syntactic* world of SOS to a problem in the *semantic* world of action transducers. We claim that the same reduction can be used to give simple congruence proofs for a variety of behavioural equivalences which are coarser than bisimulation equivalence.

4.2 Realizing Operations in PC

Definition 4.14 [Realizability] Let $\mathcal{A}$ be a Σ-algebra and let f be an n-ary operation on a subset D of $D_{\mathcal{A}}$. We say that f is *realizable* (or *definable*) in terms of the operations of $\mathcal{A}$ if there exists a term t over signature Σ with $var(t) = \{x_1, \ldots, x_n\}$ such that for all valuations $\xi : \mathcal{V} \to D$, $f(\xi(x_1), \ldots, \xi(x_n)) = [\![t]\!]^{\xi}_{\mathcal{A}}$.

The following theorem gives a sufficient condition for realizability in the setting of De Simone systems:

Theorem 4.15 *Let P and Q be De Simone calculi over A, let f be an n-ary function symbol of P, and let C be a context over the signature of Q with variables $\{x_1, \ldots, x_n\}$, such that*

$$og(f(x_1, \ldots, x_n), transducer(P)) \leftrightarrows og(C, transducer(Q)).$$

Then $f_{\mathcal{A}(P)/\leftrightarrows}$ is realizable in $\mathcal{A}(Q)/\leftrightarrows$.

Once the notion of realizability has been defined, it is easy to see that also the other expressiveness result of De Simone [33, 34] depends in a crucial way on the use of unguarded recursion. First, we will state De Simone's theorem using the terminology of this paper.

As action alphabet De Simone considers an infinite commutative monoid M (The reader may just think of M as the set of natural numbers). In addition, a finite signature Σ is considered and a finite collection of rules of the form

$$\frac{\{x_i \xrightarrow{u_i} y_i \mid i \in I\}}{f(x_1, \ldots, x_n) \xrightarrow{u} t} \, Pr(u_{j_1}, \ldots, u_{j_l}, u)$$

where $I = \{j_1, \ldots, j_l\}$. These rules are De Simone rules in our sense, except that the $u_i, \ldots$ which occur above the arrows are variables ranging over actions and not actions. Moreover the rules have as an additional ingredient a recursively enumerable relation Pr on M. The reader may think of a rule in the above format as a way to define a *set* of rules in our sense of Definition 2.10, one for each instantiation of the action variables for which the predicate holds. In order to distinguish the above format from the De Simone format introduced earlier, we will refer to it as the *classic* De Simone format.

Phrased in the terminology of this paper, De Simone [33, 34] proved that any operation of the algebra induced by a specification in classic De Simone format (induced in the sense of Definition 4.11 with $\widehat{\mathcal{G}}(M)$ taken as domain) can be realized up to bisimulation equivalence in terms of the operations of the algebra induced by the calculi SCCS and MEIJE.

The question arises to what extent this result still holds if the guarded versions of SCCS and MEIJE are used. In guarded SCCS and MEIJE only finitely branching graphs can be specified. However, using the classic De Simone format it is easy to specify an infinitely branching graph that is not bisimilar with any finitely branching graph: just take a constant ω with the single rule

$$\frac{\emptyset}{\omega \xrightarrow{u} \omega} \, true.$$

Thus some restrictions have to be imposed on the classic De Simone format if we want to maintain the expressiveness result in a guarded setting. An obvious restriction is to allow only for predicates $Pr(u_1, \ldots, u_l, u)$ with for each $a_1, \ldots, a_l \in M$ the set $\{a \in M \mid Pr(a_1, \ldots, a_l, a)\}$ finite and recursive (together with its cardinality). However, this does not work. It is trivial to check that the rules of the calculus *Triple* in the proof of Theorem 3.9 fit the restricted format. Consider the result of applying the operation $triple_{\mathcal{A}(P)}$ on the graph $\mathcal{O}_{Triple}(1)$. Clearly, the resulting graph is isomorphic to the graph g defined in Theorem 3.9. However, as a corollary of Theorem 3.9, the graph g can not be specified up to trace equivalence in proces calculi like SCCS and MEIJE with guarded recursion. Thus the operation $triple_{\mathcal{A}(P)}$ is certainly not realizable up to bisimulation in terms of the operations of these calculi.

We can now state the following theorem, which asserts that the calculus PC is universally expressive for operations definable by finite De Simone systems.

Theorem 4.16 *Let f be an operation on the domain of finitely branching process graphs over some finite alphabet A that is specified via a De Simone system with a finite number of rules. Then f is realizable in terms of the operations of (a finite instantiation of) PC.*

Proof Similar to proof of the corresponding result in [34], using Theorem 4.15. ∎

References

[1] S. Abramsky. Observation equivalence as a testing equivalence. *Theoretical Computer Science*, 53:225–241, 1987.

[2] L. Aceto, B. Bloom, and F.W. Vaandrager. Turning SOS rules into equations. In *Proceedings 7th Annual Symposium on Logic in Computer Science*, Santa Cruz, California, pages 113–124. IEEE Computer Society Press, 1992. Full version available as CWI Report CS-R9218, June 1992, Amsterdam. Invited to the LICS 92 Special Issue of *Information and Computation.*

[3] K.R. Apt and G.D. Plotkin. Countable nondeterminism and random assignment. *Journal of the ACM*, 33(4):724–767, October 1986.

[4] E. Badouel and P. Darondeau. Structural operational specifications and trace automata. In W.R. Cleaveland, editor, *Proceedings CONCUR 92*, Stony Brook, NY, USA, volume 630 of *Lecture Notes in Computer Science*, pages 302–316. Springer-Verlag, 1992.

[5] J.C.M. Baeten and J.A. Bergstra. Global renaming operators in concrete process algebra. *Information and Computation*, 78(3):205–245, 1988.

[6] J.C.M. Baeten, J.A. Bergstra, and J.W. Klop. On the consistency of Koomen's fair abstraction rule. *Theoretical Computer Science*, 51(1/2):129–176, 1987.

[7] J.C.M. Baeten and F.W. Vaandrager. An algebra for process creation. *Acta Informatica*, 29(4):303–334, 1992.

[8] J.C.M. Baeten and W.P. Weijland. *Process Algebra.* Cambridge Tracts in Theoretical Computer Science 18. Cambridge University Press, 1990.

[9] G. Berry and G. Gonthier. The synchronous programming language **Esterel**: design, semantics, implementation. Report 842, INRIA, Centre Sophia-Antipolis, Valbonne Cedex, 1988. To appear in *Science of Computer Programming.*

[10] B. Bloom. *Ready Simulation, Bisimulation, and the Semantics of CCS-like Languages.* PhD thesis, Department of Electrical Engineering and Computer Science, Massachusetts Institute of Technology, August 1989.

[11] B. Bloom. Strong process equivalence in the presence of hidden moves. Preliminary report, October 1990.

[12] B. Bloom, S. Istrail, and A.R. Meyer. Bisimulation can't be traced: Preliminary report. In *Conference Record of the 15th ACM Symposium on Principles of Programming Languages,* San Diego, California, pages 229–239, 1988. Full version available as Technical Report 90-1150, Department of Computer Science, Cornell University, Ithaca, New York, August 1990. Accepted to appear in *Journal of the ACM.*

[13] R.N. Bol and J.F. Groote. The meaning of negative premises in transition system specifications (extended abstract). In J. Leach Albert, B. Monien, and M. Rodríguez, editors, *Proceedings* 18th *ICALP*, Madrid, volume 510 of *Lecture Notes in Computer Science*, pages 481–494. Springer-Verlag, 1991. Full version available as Report CS-R9054, CWI, Amsterdam, 1990.

[14] G. Boudol. Notes on algebraic calculi of processes. In K. Apt, editor, *Logics and Models of Concurrent Systems*, pages 261–303. Springer-Verlag, 1985. NATO ASI Series F13.

[15] P. Darondeau. Concurrency and computability. In I. Guessarian, editor, *Semantics of Systems of Concurrent Processes, Proceedings LITP Spring School on Theoretical Computer Science*, La Roche Posay, France, volume 469 of *Lecture Notes in Computer Science*, pages 223–238. Springer-Verlag, 1990.

[16] J.-Y. Girard. Linear logic. *Theoretical Computer Science*, 50(1):1–102, 1987.

[17] R.J. van Glabbeek and U. Goltz. Refinement of actions in causality based models. In J.W. de Bakker, W.P. de Roever, and G. Rozenberg, editors, *REX Workshop on Stepwise Refinement of Distributed Systems: Models, Formalism, Correctness*, Mook, The Netherlands 1989, volume 430 of *Lecture Notes in Computer Science*, pages 267–300. Springer-Verlag, 1990.

[18] J.F. Groote. Transition system specifications with negative premises. Report CS-R8950, CWI, Amsterdam, 1989. An extended abstract appeared in J.C.M. Baeten and J.W. Klop, editors, *Proceedings CONCUR 90*, Amsterdam, LNCS 458, pages 332–341. Springer-Verlag, 1990.

[19] J.F. Groote and F.W. Vaandrager. Structured operational semantics and bisimulation as a congruence. *Information and Computation*, 100(2):202–260, October 1992.

[20] M. Hennessy. *Algebraic Theory of Processes.* MIT Press, Cambridge, Massachusetts, 1988.

[21] C.A.R. Hoare. *Communicating Sequential Processes.* Prentice-Hall International, Englewood Cliffs, 1985.

[22] K.G. Larsen and L. Xinxin. Compositionality through an operational semantics of contexts. In M. Paterson, editor, *Proceedings* 17th *ICALP*, Warwick, volume 443 of *Lecture Notes in Computer Science*, pages 526–539. Springer-Verlag, July 1990. An extended version appeared as: Report R89-13, The University of Aalborg, Dept. of Mathematics and Computer Science, Aalborg, Denmark, May 1989.

[23] N.A. Lynch and M.R. Tuttle. Hierarchical correctness proofs for distributed algorithms. In *Proceedings of the* 6th *Annual ACM Symposium on Principles of Distributed Computing*, pages 137–151, August 1987. A full version is available as MIT Technical Report MIT/LCS/TR-387.

[24] R. Milner. Calculi for synchrony and asynchrony. *Theoretical Computer Science*, 25:267–310, 1983.

[25] R. Milner. *Communication and Concurrency.* Prentice-Hall International, Englewood Cliffs, 1989.

[26] D.M.R. Park. Concurrency and automata on infinite sequences. In P. Deussen, editor, 5th *GI Conference*, volume 104 of *Lecture Notes in Computer Science*, pages 167–183. Springer-Verlag, 1981.

[27] J. Parrow. The expressive power of parallelism. *Future Generation Computer Systems*, 6:271–285, 1990.

[28] G.D. Plotkin. A structural approach to operational semantics. Report DAIMI FN-19, Computer Science Department, Aarhus University, 1981.

[29] G.D. Plotkin. An operational semantics for CSP. In D. Bjørner, editor, *Proceedings IFIP TC2 Working Conference on Formal Description of Programming Concepts – II,* Garmisch, pages 199–225, Amsterdam, 1983. North-Holland.

[30] A. Ponse. Computable processes and bisimulation equivalence. Report CS-R9207, CWI, Amsterdam, January 1992. To appear in *Information and Computation.*

[31] H. Rogers. *Theory of Recursive Functions and Effective Computability.* McGraw-Hill Book Co., 1967.

[32] J.J.M.M. Rutten. Deriving denotational models for bisimulation from structured operational semantics. In M. Broy and C.B. Jones, editors, *Proceedings IFIP Working Conference on Programming Concepts and Methods,* Sea of Gallilea, Israel, pages 155–177. North-Holland, 1990.

[33] R. de Simone. *Calculabilité et Expressivité dans l'Algebra de Processus Parallèles* MEIJE. Thèse de 3e cycle, Univ. Paris 7, 1984.

[34] R. de Simone. Higher-level synchronising devices in MEIJE–SCCS. *Theoretical Computer Science*, 37:245–267, 1985.

[35] F.W. Vaandrager. On the relationship between process algebra and input/output automata (extended abstract). In *Proceedings* 6th *Annual Symposium on Logic in Computer Science,* Amsterdam, pages 387–398. IEEE Computer Society Press, 1991.

Compiling Joy Into Silicon: An Exercise in Applied Structural Operational Semantics.

Sam Weber*, Bard Bloom†, Geoffrey Brown‡

Cornell University

Abstract

We present the highlights of an algorithm and correctness proof for compiling programs written in Joy, a simple parallel language, into delay-insensitive circuits. The proof relies heavily on techniques of structural operational semantics, many of which should generalize to similar settings.

1 Introduction

Joy is a pared-down but complete concurrent programming language, with basic conditional, looping, and parallel control constructs, Boolean variables, and synchronization along communication channels. Most programs could be written in Joy, albeit clumsily, and we expect our methods to extend to a variety of other programming constructs: procedure and function calls, data-bearing channels, and so forth. We describe a scheme for compiling Joy programs to delay-insensitive circuits, present the highlights of the proof that the scheme is correct, and briefly discuss the implementation.

Our circuits are quite simple. A circuit consists of a set of primitive *components* connected by *wires* attached at *input* and *output* ports. A wire connects a single input port to a single output port. The unconnected ports of the constituent components of a circuit are the inputs and outputs of the circuit and connect to the outside environment. The components of a circuit communicate by initiating events on their output ports or by absorbing events on their input ports. One possible physical interpretation of an event is a voltage transition. For physical reasons, circuits cannot refuse input - even if that input may cause them to fail. Furthermore, input and output events on a wire must strictly alternate to prevent possible electrical interference. A wire connecting an

*`samuel@cs.cornell.edu`; Supported by NSF grants CCR-9003441 and CCR-9058180.

†`bard@cs.cornell.edu`; Supported by NSF grant CCR-9003441.

‡`gbrown@ee.cornell.edu`;Supported by a NSF grant CCR-9058180

output port to an input port is *active* if an event has been initiated on the output port but not yet absorbed on the input port.

We sketch the definition and verification of a compilation scheme from Joy programs to circuits. Our set of primitive components is quite small, and most of them are straightforward to implement. Indeed, most components turn out to be patterns of wires. For related work on implementing delay-insensitive circuits see [3, 6, 20, 24, 7, 12]. The resulting circuits are amenable to a simple low-level mathematical model of wires and impulses, which we use to verify the compilation scheme. The full correctness proof is too large to be presented in full here; it is available as a Cornell technical report. Indeed, any satisfactory proof of a silicon compiler must consider each kind of wire and component, and even our compiler has some fifty kinds of wire-component connections. We describe its mathematical foundations (based on structural operational semantics and bisimulation methodology), and sketch the main lemmas describing how programs and circuits execute. With these lemmas, the main proofs consist of fifty trivial cases each.

As the translation scheme is syntax-directed, we found it straightforward to implement with `lex` and `yacc`. Our Joy compiler produces netlists of basic components. The output of the compiler is suitable for input to any of the many place-and-route tools available for silicon compilation, given a VLSI cell-library of the basic components. The development of such a cell-library is fairly standard; see [3, 6, 8, 16]. As the implementation is routine compiler technology, we concentrate on the description of the compilation scheme and correctness proof.

1.1 Related Work

Previous efforts at verifying compilers for VLSI have been restricted to weaker languages than Joy. An early work by Milne verified the correctness of a compiler for NOR expressions. [13] A more recent work described a compiler for translating path expressions into self-timed circuits [22]. A related approach was taken by Straunstrup and Greenstreet. [21] They present a method for describing the behavior of a circuit in terms of a set of transition rules and define a set of "implementation conditions" which a circuit must meet in order to be delay-insensitive.

Martin's work, like that of Strauntrup and Greenstreet, provides a methodology for verifying delay-insensitive circuits with respect to an idealized model of hardware behavior [12]. Although Martin has developed a compiler from a process algebra to delay-insensitive circuits, he has not published a proof that his compilation algorithm is correct [7].

Van Berkel's thesis [25] verifies a quite similar compilation technique. His language Tangram is somewhat weaker than Joy; in particular, it does not seem to allow selective communication. A Tangram process cannot wait for a signal from either of two other processes.

Furthermore, the theorem that he gives is somewhat weaker in several ways. We show weak bisimulation, one of the more detailed notions of process equivalence; van Berkel shows only trace equivalence, which is one of the least detailed notions. Essentially, we show that our circuits and programs behave identically, to the point of making the same decisions at the same times; van Berkel's merely produce the same output in response to the same input. This difference is insignificant in the current setting, though it might be significant in a more powerful language; we suspect van Berkel's proof will not show his circuits correct with respect to the restriction operation of CCS and ACP.

The van Berkel meanings of programs are given as trace sets, which is a reasonable high-level semantics. The meaning of a circuit is the composition of the meanings of its primitive components as trace sets. Though we are confident that van Berkel's definition is correct, it is fairly high-level. The primitive components are quite reasonably described as simple trace structures. However, the parallel composition operation is far from trivial, requiring many pages of mathematics to describe. While we do not dispute that van Berkel's definition accurately models parallel composition, we prefer to use a simpler definition inspired by the physical behavior of the circuit. Our model is a state-transition model, where the state is the set of as-yet-unrecieved signals and the transition function is determined by the circuit.

The weaker theorem we regard as a minor matter, as (1) van Berkel's theorem is strong enough to show that Tangram programs behave correctly, and (2) we suspect that the Tangram compiler is actually correct up to bisimulation, for essentially the same reason that ours is; indeed, it should be routine to adapt our proof to cover Tangram. The difference in semantic model is a substantial matter of presentation – our model is designed in part to be easily checked by scientists with standard mathematical background; van Berkel's definitions are easy enough for experts to understand and check, but less obviously correct. Here and elsewhere in semantics, it is important for our intended audience to have confidence in our results. The difference in language is more significant, as selective communication is essential in many communication circuits.

2 Joy

In this section we present Joy. In the following BNF grammar, c is drawn from a set of channel identifiers *CID*, C is a set of channel identifiers, and v is drawn from a set of variable identifiers *VID*.

$$\begin{array}{llcl} & c & \in & CID \\ & v & \in & VID \\ \\ (expr) & E & ::= & v \mid \neg E \mid E_1 \wedge E_2 \mid E_1 \vee E_2 \mid \mathrm{tt} \mid \mathrm{ff} \\ (process) & P & ::= & \mathtt{skip} \mid v := E \mid c! \mid P_1 ; P_2 \\ & & \mid & \mathtt{if}\, G\, \mathtt{fi} \mid \mathtt{do}\, G\, \mathtt{od} \mid P_1 \parallel_C P_2 \\ (guard) & G & ::= & E \rightarrow P \mid c? \rightarrow P \mid E \,\&\, c? \rightarrow P \mid G_1 \,[\!]\, G_2 \end{array}$$

Informally, the process terms stand for the following processes:

skip: is a process which simply terminates.

$v := expr$: is a process which assigns *expr* to v.

$c!$ is a process which is ready to output along channel c. Send commands are blocking; that is, they will wait for the signal to be received before allowing the sender to continue. (Receives are done as part of guarded commands, and need not block.)

$P_1; P_2$: is the sequential composition of P_1 and P_2.

`if` G `fi`: attempts to execute the guarded command set G until it succeeds. A guarded command set consists of one or more guarded commands separated by $[\!]$ and is executed by executing one enabled command from the set. If no command is enabled, execution fails. A guarded command can be of the form $E \rightarrow P$, $c? \rightarrow P$, or $E\&c? \rightarrow P$. In the first case the command is enabled if E is true. In the second case the command is enabled if some process is prepared to output on channel c, and, in the third case the command is enabled if E is true and some process is prepared to output on c. The command is executed by inputting from channel c (for the second and third cases) and then executing P.

do G od: repeatedly executes the guarded command set G until execution fails.

$P_1 \parallel_C P_2$: is the concurrent composition of P_1 and P_2, communicating along the channels in C.

Legal Joy programs must satisfy some further syntactic restrictions. If $P_1 \parallel_C P_2$ appears in a Joy program, then

1. The input channels of P_1 and P_2 (except for those appearing in C) must be disjoint.
2. Similarly, the output channels not appearing in C must be disjoint.
3. Finally, no variable may appear in both P_1 and P_2.

These restrictions are not essential — for example, it is straightforward to allow parallel reading of variables — but we impose them for simplicity.

In particular, the set of input channels used by two concurrently executing processes must be disjoint; similarly for output channels. Furthermore, concurrently active processes may not share any variables; all communication must be done by communication commands. A shared variable may, of course, be realized by a shared process.

3 Compiling Joy Programs

We briefly sketch the compilation scheme. More details are given in [27]. The compilation method results in connection of primitive circuit components, which we specify by finite state machines. For circuit realizations of similar components see [3, 11, 20].

We construct our components out of building blocks. The implementations of our components can then be verified with respect to models of these building blocks using an automated tool such as that developed by Dill [9]. The next level of the proof, verifying the building blocks, is likely to be extremely difficult as any implementation of these is dependent upon analog transistor effects (e.g. transistor threshold voltages and gate capacitance); we thus make the fairly safe assumption that electrical engineers know how to built such primitive components as exclusive-or gates and wires correctly.

In order to ensure that these components are used in a manner which ensures the requirements on input and output events are met, we use a simple communication convention between components. Wires are always used in pairs or triples. This convention is illustrated in the following figure.

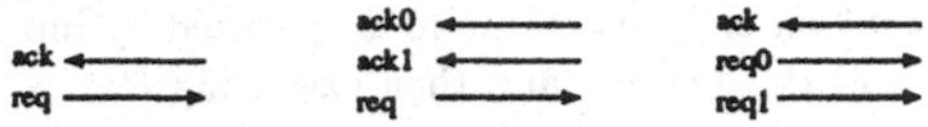

In the two-wire interface, every transition on the request wire `req` must be explicitly followed by a transition on the acknowledgement wire `ack`. There are two types of three wire interfaces. The read interface allows a binary value to be returned with an acknowledgment by allowing a transition on the request wire to be followed by a transition on either of the acknowledgement wires `ack0, ack1`. The write interface allows a value to be sent by allowing a transition on either of the request wires `req0, req1` followed by a transition of the `ack` wire.

The idea of rigidly following this communication convention was developed by the Philips group [24] who call the resulting components "handshake circuits." We illustrate the use of the handshake convention in our compilation scheme by describing a set of components to perform Boolean expression evaluation. A Boolean expression is implemented as a component with a three wire read interface.

We present each primitive component as a wiring diagram and a finite-state automaton. Input ports are pictured as arrows pointing into the component. Output ports are pictured as arrows pointing out of the component. The specification of a component consists of a finite-state machine with its initial state labeled `Init`. All legal state transitions are indicated by arcs in the specification, labeled by the input or output event associated with the state transition.

The simplest expressions are the Boolean constants `tt` and `ff` which return true and false respectively. `tt` is illustrated and specified in the following figure; `ff` is similar.

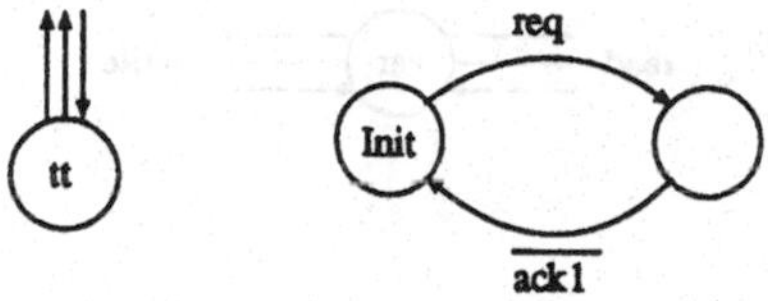

The simplest Boolean operator is negation (˜); the negation component simply switches the true and false reply lines.

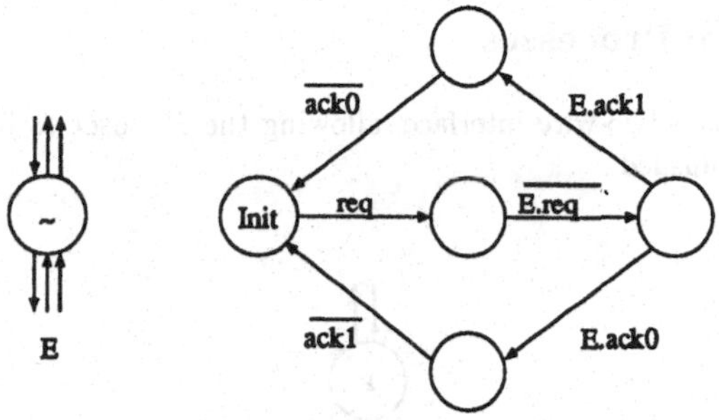

The binary operator ∧ is a short-circuiting and; it first evaluates the left expression and then, if necessary, the right expression. ∨ is similar. (For simplicity, we use sequential rather than parallel Boolean operations. Concurrent evaluation of Booleans would in general require concurrent read accesses to variables. Doing this should be routine; however, the details remain to be worked out.)

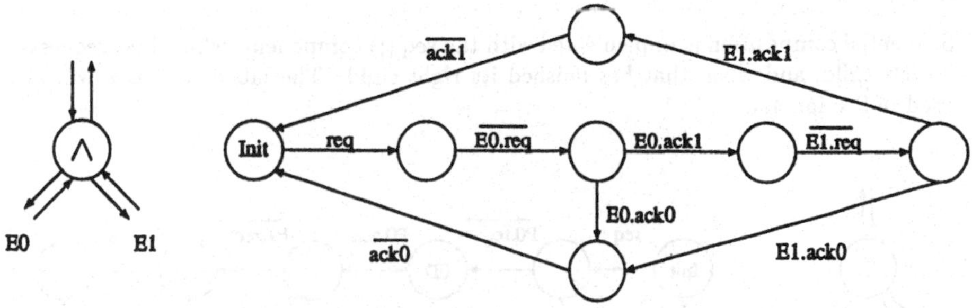

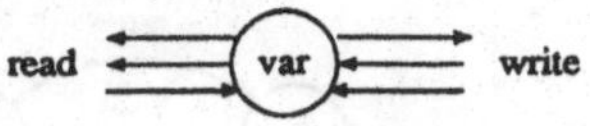

Boolean variables have two three-wire interfaces: a read interface for reading the variable, and a write interface for writing. More than one connection to each of these interfaces may be necessary (e.g. the process $v :=$ **expr1**; $v :=$ **expr2**); however, our rules for circuits prohibit multiple connections to a port. We solve this problem by introducing a set of components for sharing a single interface, corresponding to procedure call and return in sequential languages.

3.1 Primitive Processes

Each process P has a two-wire interface, allowing the P's user to invoke P and P to signal that it has finished.

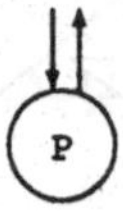

The simplest process is **skip**, which acknowledges each request immediately. It is implemented by a wire connecting request and acknowledgement channels. The assignment process **x** := e connects the result of e to the assignment ports of **x**, using the call process mentioned above.

3.2 Compound Processes

Sequential composition is implemented with the seq (;) component, which first requests its left child, and when that has finished its right child. The labels in states will be used in Section 4.4.

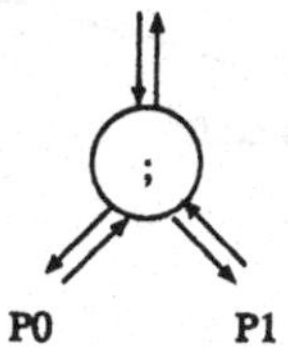

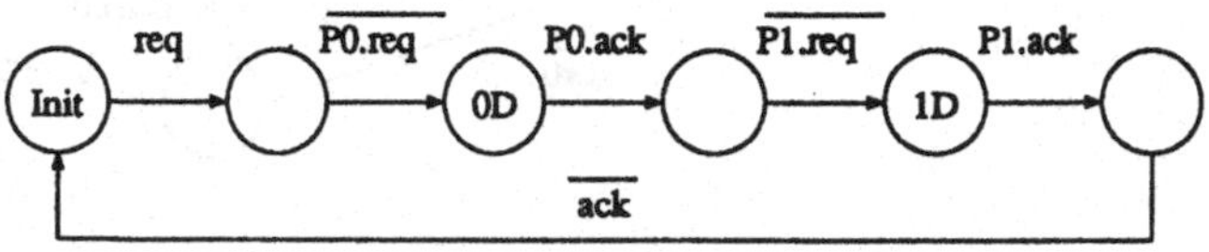

The par (||) component used for implementing parallel composition is similar, requesting both children in parallel and waiting for them both to acknowledge before proceeding.

The implementation of the iterative and conditional constructs is somewhat complex with expressions, and more complex with communication. Essentially, both commands are polling loops, evaluating the expressions and testing the availability of communications. It is clear why **do** loops are loops. **If** commands are loops as the **if** is defined to block until one of its guards becomes true; we implement this by polling the guards repeatedly. The details are unimportant for this study. Note however that the polling loop means that guards are tested in order, and so our semantics of Joy will reflect this.

4 Proof of Correctness

We verify our compilation scheme by a formal proof of correctness. We give a fairly abstract operational semantics of Joy, and a fairly concrete operational semantics of the circuits that the compilation scheme produces (at the level of basic components, which we have verified by more standard means). We then show that the two are equivalent. More specifically, we show that there is a precise correspondence between the possible actions of a program and the possible gate-firings of the circuit; as discussed below, we establish a *bisimulation* (one of the strongest forms of process equivalence, and hence a strong guarantee of correctness) between the two.

The semantics for Joy may appear unrealistically optimistic. For example, expressions and even lists of guards are evaluated instantaneously and atomically. This is not true in the compiled circuits; a complex expression requires many events to evaluate. This disparity is intentional. The semantics of Joy are designed to give a reasonable and useful model for programming, and have been successfully explained to electrical engineers untrained in formal semantics and logic. The compiler is charged with ensuring that the simple semantics of Joy correspond with what actually happens when the circuit is run - and the main theorem of this paper is that the two disparate kinds of semantics agree, and hence that the circuit behaves as it ought to.

4.1 Semantics of Joy

We sketch a structured operational semantics (SOS) for Joy, along the lines of [18]. This lets us conceptually execute Joy programs without compiling them; our main theorem will be that they execute the same before and after compilation.

The state of an executing Joy program consists of a *control state*, telling which parts of the program are executing — the program counter(s) — and a *variable state* telling what values variables have. It is convenient (and standard in the SOS methodology) to represent the control state of the circuit as a Joy program P, which is the code which remains to be executed. For example, if the original program is `x:=tt; y:=ff`, after executing the first command P will be roughly `y:=ff`. We extend the language slightly, to include a "command" **done** which represents a finished program. The variable state is simply a function η from variable names to their (Boolean) values. So, we represent the state of the circuit as a pairs, written $P+\eta$.

The ultimate purpose of a program is to perform *actions*: receives c? and sends c! on channels c, and a special action "-" for internal computation.[1] Processes will produce "-" actions when the results of their action are not visible outside the circuit; for example, a **skip** statement simply produces a "-" action.

The main operational semantic relation is $P+\eta \xrightarrow{\alpha} P'+\eta'$, which is intended to mean that a process in state $P+\eta$ can perform the action α and thereafter behave like $P'+\eta'$. For example, the rather silly program $(x := \mathrm{tt}\,;\, x := \mathrm{ff})$ started in state $\{x = \mathrm{ff}\}$ would evolve as follows:

$$(x := \mathrm{tt}\,;\, x := \mathrm{ff}) + \{x = \mathrm{ff}\} \xrightarrow{-} (\mathbf{done}\,;\, x := \mathrm{ff}) + \{x = \mathrm{tt}\} \xrightarrow{-} \mathbf{done} + \{x = \mathrm{ff}\} \qquad (1)$$

There are many cases in which we know that the variable state does not change over a transition, and one place where we need to know that a transition does not induce a state change. We thus have an auxiliary judgement $P \xrightarrow{\alpha} P'$, and the rules

$$\frac{P \xrightarrow{\alpha} P'}{P+\eta \xrightarrow{\alpha} P'+\eta} \qquad \frac{P+\eta \xrightarrow{\alpha} P'+\eta}{P \xrightarrow{\alpha} P'}$$

In the operational semantics, the program is gradually consumed as it executes. This is a standard technical convenience for the operational semantics – it allows us to avoid explicit program counters, or more accurately to use the program term itself as the program counters. In discussing these rules with people unfamiliar with the style, it is occasionally necessary to tell them that the rules simply describe behavior; they do not insist that pieces of the circuit flake off as it executes!

Processes without subprocesses are given behavior by axioms. For example, **skip** quietly evolves to a finished process in any state, giving the rule:

$$\mathbf{skip} \xrightarrow{-} \mathbf{done} \qquad (2)$$

Assignments behave in the obvious way:

$$(x := E) + \eta \xrightarrow{-} \mathbf{done} + \eta'$$

where η' is the same as η except that $\eta'(x)$ is the value of E in state η.

Sends, of course, send messages on their channel and then halt:

$$\mathrm{c!} \xrightarrow{\mathrm{c!}} \mathbf{done} \qquad (3)$$

Most composite processes are given behavior based on the behavior of their components. For example, a sequential composition executes the first process:

$$\frac{P_1+\eta \xrightarrow{\alpha} P_1'+\eta'}{(P_1\,;\,P_2)+\eta \xrightarrow{\alpha} (P_1'\,;\,P_2)+\eta'} \qquad (4)$$

[1] "-" is τ in [15], and does not appear explicitly in most models of CSP.

and when the first process finishes, the second one starts:

$$\mathbf{done}\,;P_2 \xrightarrow{\cdot} P_2 \tag{5}$$

Parallel composition is more complex. Either component may execute, or the two may coordinate on a send/receive pair. Note that in the communication rule we use transitions $P \xrightarrow{\alpha} P'$ which cannot involve variable state change; we therefore do not need to worry about the problem of merging two differently-changed variable states.

$$\frac{P_1 + \eta \xrightarrow{\alpha} P_1' + \eta', \alpha \notin C}{\begin{array}{c}(P_1 \parallel_C P_2) + \eta \xrightarrow{\alpha} (P_1' \parallel_C P_2) + \eta' \\ (P_2 \parallel_C P_1) + \eta \xrightarrow{\alpha} (P_2 \parallel_C P_1') + \eta'\end{array}} \qquad \frac{P_1 \xrightarrow{c?} P_1',\quad P_2 \xrightarrow{c!} P_2',\quad c \in C}{\begin{array}{c}P_1 \parallel_C P_2 \xrightarrow{\cdot} P_1' \parallel_C P_2' \\ P_2 \parallel_C P_1 \xrightarrow{\cdot} P_2' \parallel_C P_1'\end{array}} \tag{6}$$

A parallel composition finishes when both branches do:

$$(\mathbf{done} \parallel_C \mathbf{done}) \xrightarrow{\cdot} \mathbf{done}. \tag{7}$$

If and **do** statements require the evaluation of guarded commands. The semantics include a predicate GP **fails**. Basic guarded commands $(E\&\alpha \rightarrow P)$ evaluate E. If it is false, the guarded command fails. If it is true, then (nondeterministically) either the communication happens and P is executed or the guarded command fails. This rather peculiar behavior is required by delay-insensitivity for technical reasons: the signal saying that the communication is available may be delayed arbitrarily; the circuit cannot wait indefinitely for it, as that would make it wait indefinitely in the case when the communication is impossible; and so the circuit must be able to refuse a communication even when it is possible. (In the implementation, the probability that an available communication will be refused is extremely small.)

$$\frac{\eta(E) \Rightarrow \mathrm{tt}}{\begin{array}{c}(E\&\alpha \rightarrow P) + \eta \xrightarrow{\alpha} P \\ (E\&\alpha \rightarrow P)\ \mathbf{fails}\end{array}} \qquad \frac{\eta(E) \Rightarrow \mathrm{ff}}{(E\&\alpha \rightarrow P)\ \mathbf{fails}}$$

Executing a list of guarded commands $G_1 [\!] G_2 [\!] \cdots [\!] G_n$ tries G_1, then G_2, and so on; if one succeeds, then the list succeeds; if all fail, then the list fails.

$$\frac{GP_1 + \eta \xrightarrow{\alpha} P}{(GP_1 [\!] GP_2) + \eta \xrightarrow{\alpha} P}$$

$$\frac{\begin{array}{c}GP_1 + \eta\ \mathbf{fails} \\ GP_2 + \eta \xrightarrow{\cdot} P\end{array}}{(GP_1 [\!] GP_2) + \eta \xrightarrow{\cdot} P} \qquad \frac{\begin{array}{c}GP_1 + \eta\ \mathbf{fails} \\ GP_2 + \eta\ \mathbf{fails}\end{array}}{(GP_1 [\!] GP_2) + \eta\ \mathbf{fails}}$$

Finally, **if** and **do** do the natural things:

$$\frac{GP + \eta \xrightarrow{\alpha} P}{\textbf{if } GP \textbf{ fi} + \eta \xrightarrow{\alpha} P + \eta}$$

Note that there is no rule for the case where GP fails; when this happens, the **if** blocks and cannot fire.

A do-loop finishes when its body is finished, and otherwise executes its body and then runs itself again.

$$\frac{GP + \eta \text{ fails}}{\textbf{do } GP \textbf{ od} \xrightarrow{\cdot} \text{done} + \eta} \qquad \frac{GP + \eta \xrightarrow{\alpha} P}{\textbf{do } GP \textbf{ od} \xrightarrow{\alpha} (P\,; \textbf{do } GP \textbf{ od}) + \eta}$$

The rules for evaluating expressions are fairly straightforward. The basic notion here is that expression E in variable state η yields value b: $E + \eta \Rightarrow b$, where b is either $\mathbf{tt}$ or $\mathbf{ff}$. The rules are:

$$\begin{gathered} \eta(\mathbf{tt}) \Rightarrow \mathbf{tt} \\ \eta(\mathbf{ff}) \Rightarrow \mathbf{ff} \end{gathered} \tag{8}$$

$$\frac{\eta(v) = b}{\eta(v) \Rightarrow b} \tag{9}$$

$$\begin{gathered} \frac{\eta(E_1) \Rightarrow b_1 \text{ and } \eta(E_2) \Rightarrow b_2}{\eta(E_1 \wedge E_2) \Rightarrow b_1 \wedge b_2} \\ \eta(E_1 \vee E_2) \Rightarrow b_1 \vee b_2 \\ \eta(\neg E_1) \Rightarrow \neg b_1 \end{gathered} \tag{10}$$

4.2 Semantics of Circuits

We model delay-insensitive circuits as directed graphs. Processing components are nodes; wires are edges. Each node has a set of *port names*, generally including distinguished *request* and *acknowledge* ports; wires have a name at each end. The state of the circuit has two components: a set of wires W which currently have signals on them, and a function κ giving the states of state-bearing components.

We define the operational semantics of circuits in a quite obvious way. To determine the behavior of $W + \kappa$, we look for some patterns of active wires on the inputs to a processing component. If one of the patterns is found, then the processing component can fire, making other wires active. For example, we have a sequencing component with six ports, $\{r, r1, a1, r2, a2, a\}$, corresponding to the ";" connective in Joy programs. If its request wire (leading to r) is active, then it can fire and send a signal on its $r1$ port: this is the pair of transitions from Init to 0D in 8. It then waits for an impulse on $a1$, which is the acknowledgement that the first subterm has finished. It then sends an impulse on $r2$, awaits a signal on $a2$, and finally sends its acknowledgement on a. These behaviors correspond to the transition graphs given in Section 3.

Communication within the circuit is straightforward. Communication with the outside environment is similar; we must keep track of what the circuit could do if the environment would cooperate, assuming that the environment obeys the basic conventions of communication.

The formalization of the circuit as a graph is straightforward but tedious.

4.3 Bisimulation

Concurrent entities are often described in terms of *labeled transition systems* (lts's): tuples $L = \langle \Sigma, \xrightarrow{\cdot}, \sigma_0 \rangle$ where Σ is a set of states, $\xrightarrow{\cdot}$ is a family of transition relations $\xrightarrow{\alpha} \subseteq \Sigma \times \Sigma$ for each α, and $\sigma_0 \in \Sigma$ is the initial state. In our case, Joy programs and circuits (plus states) determine lts's, with Σ given by the set of $(P + \eta)$'s or $(W + \kappa)$'s.

Two labeled transition systems L and L' are *strongly bisimilar* iff there is a relation $\sim$ between their states which relates the initial states, such that, if $\sigma \sim \tau$, then any action which one of the two can take, the other can also take and the resulting states are still related. That is, if $\sigma \xrightarrow{\alpha} \sigma'$, then there is a τ' such that $\tau \xrightarrow{\alpha} \tau'$ and $\sigma' \sim \tau'$; and vice versa. This implies that (but is much stronger than) σ and τ have the same set of traces. Strong bisimulation is too detailed a notion for most purposes, as it insists that the processes have the same silent moves as well as visible ones.

We use a variant called *weak bisimulation*, which allows processes to take internal steps (- moves); the definition is the same, but processes are allowed to perform any number of silent actions before and after the a (or, when a = -, simply zero or more silent actions.) See [15] for the details of the theory. It is likely that our compilation technique actually is correct up to finer weak equivalences, such as branching bisimulation [1].

Bisimulation, strong or weak, is an extremely strong form of correctness. It has been shown [17, 14, 5] that bisimilar processes are indistinguishable in any reasonable setting, and in particular in Joy. Indeed, bisimulation is arguably too strong to be a good notion of specification of correctness, as in most settings there are non-bisimilar processes which are still indistinguishable. However, we are able to achieve bisimulation, and hence all weaker forms of correctness.

4.4 Highlights of the equivalence proof

We are now able to state the equivalence between Joy programs and their compilations. Let P_0 be any Joy program, and η_0 an initial state of its variables. Let C be the circuit into which P_0 is compiled, W_0 be its initial set of active wires (an impulse on the external request line and nothing else active), and κ_0 the initial state of variables corresponding to η_0. Then the lts's with initial state $P_0 + \eta_0$ and $W_0 + \kappa_0$ are bisimilar.

The major technical difficulty in the proof of correctness is that Joy programs and circuits execute in quite different ways. The operational semantics of Joy were designed to be understandable, to demonstrate that Joy is a reasonable programming language. We have tried to minimize the amount of unnecessary information kept by Joy programs. Consequently, as a Joy program executes, it loses information about the original program.

Conversely, circuits are physical entities, and our model of them is intended to be reasonably realistic. In particular, the wires and gates of a circuit continue to exist throughout and after the circuit's execution. This disparity between the two languages makes proving a correspondence directly rather challenging.

For example, consider the Joy program **skip** ; **skip**. This does nothing in three transitions:

$$\textbf{skip} \,;\, \textbf{skip} \xrightarrow{\cdot} \textbf{done} \,;\, \textbf{skip} \xrightarrow{\cdot} \textbf{skip} \xrightarrow{\cdot} \textbf{done} \tag{11}$$

However, as we have defined our circuits, the circuit does nothing in eight transitions:

1. The request line of **skip** ; **skip**
2. The request line of the first **skip**.
3. The first **skip** itself.
4. The acknowledge line of the first **skip**.
5. The request line of the second **skip**.
6. The second **skip** itself.
7. The acknowledge line of the second **skip**.
8. The acknowledge line of **skip** ; **skip**

Joy Prime To connect the two disparate models, we introduce an intermediate language Joy Prime which has aspects of both. Joy Prime programs resemble Joy programs augmented with additional labels and markers which keep track of the information that circuits retain and Joy programs lose. For example, the Joy Prime execution of the program corresponding to **skip** ; **skip** is:

$$
\begin{array}{ll}
1. & \left(\mathbf{skip}^{v2\mathbf{skip}}; \mathbf{skip}^{v3\mathbf{skip}}\right)^{v1;} \\
 & \downarrow - \\
2. & \left(\mathbf{skip}^{v2\mathbf{skip}}; \mathbf{skip}^{v3\mathbf{skip}}\right)^{1;} \\
 & \downarrow - \\
3. & \left(\mathbf{skip}^{2\mathbf{skip}}; \mathbf{skip}^{v3\mathbf{skip}}\right)^{1;} \\
 & \downarrow - \\
4. & \left(\mathbf{done}^{2\mathbf{skip}}; \mathbf{skip}^{v3\mathbf{skip}}\right)^{1;} \\
 & \downarrow - \\
5. & \left(\mathbf{skip}^{v3\mathbf{skip}}\right)^{1;} \\
 & \downarrow - \\
6. & \left(\mathbf{skip}^{3\mathbf{skip}}\right)^{1;} \\
 & \downarrow - \\
7. & \left(\mathbf{done}^{3\mathbf{skip}}\right)^{1;} \\
 & \downarrow - \\
8. & (\mathbf{done})^{1;}
\end{array}
$$

where the numbers in the first column correspond to the states on the previous page.

The similarity with Joy makes it straightforward to relate Joy and Joy Prime programs. However, Joy Prime programs execute in the same way as the corresponding circuits, making it possible (though not easy) to prove that the two are equivalent. We illustrate this construction for sequencing.

Each instance of each operation in Joy Prime is given a label, consisting of a unique identifier l and the operator symbol; for $P_1 ; P_2$, it will have the form "l;". This label will remain with the statement as long as it is active. We will have to identify *virgin programs*; that is, statements which have not been executed. We use a marker v. The Joy Prime statement corresponding to $P_1; P_2$ will be of the form $(P_1'; P_2')^{vl;}$ This corresponds to being in state Init of the diagram.

To start executing this, we use the Joy Prime rule

$$P^{vl*} \xrightarrow{-} P^{l*}$$

where $*$ is any operator; in our case, this gives us the transition $(P_1 ; P_2)^{vl;} \xrightarrow{-} (P_1 ; P_2)^{l;}$. This corresponds to a component processing a signal on its request line; in this case, to the transitions from Init to 0D of the diagram.

The Joy Prime rule for executing a sequence is identical to the Joy rule (4), except that it includes a label (which does not change):

$$\frac{P_1 + \eta \xrightarrow{\alpha} P_1' + \eta'}{(P_1 ; P_2)^{l;} + \eta \xrightarrow{\alpha} (P_1' ; P_2)^{l;} + \eta'}$$

When P_1 finishes executing, we use the rule corresponding to the Joy rule (5) and to the 0D transitions between states 0D and 1D: when the first child finishes, the ";" component starts the second.

$$(\mathbf{done}\,;P_2)^{l;} \xrightarrow{-} (P_2)^{l;} \tag{12}$$

Notice that the label of P_2 says that P_2 is part of a sequencing statement, even though the sequencing operator is gone. P_2 will execute ordinarily, but the "$l;$" label will remain:

$$\frac{P_2 \xrightarrow{\alpha} P_2'}{(P_2)^{l*} \xrightarrow{\alpha} (P_2')^{l*}}$$

When P_2 finishes, it will be in the state $\left(\mathbf{done}^{l'*}\right)^{l;}$ where "$l'*$" is the label of the main operator of P_2. The Joy Prime rule

$$\left(\mathbf{done}^{l'*}\right)^{l*} \xrightarrow{-} \mathbf{done}^{l*} \tag{13}$$

applies. This corresponds to the 1D to Init transitions: after the second child acknowledges that it is finished, the ";" component acknowledges as well.

Toward the Proof of Equivalence Once we have developed Joy Prime, it is possible to prove the main result: that the compilation scheme is correct.

Theorem 4.1 *Let P be a Joy program, P' the corresponding Joy Prime program, and C the corresponding circuit. Then:*

1. *P' behaves like P, except that it takes more silent moves. Formally P and P' are weakly bisimilar.*

2. *P' behaves just like C. Formally, P' and C are strongly bisimilar.*

As bisimulation is an equivalence relation, P and C are thus (weakly) bisimilar.

The first part of Prop. 4.1 is straightforward, as the rules for P' are essentially the same as those of P with a good deal of extra baggage added. The second part of Prop. 4.1 is proved by a detailed analysis of the behavior of programs and circuits, finishing with the precise correspondence demanded for strong bisimulation.

The proof of the second part starts with the *label sanity lemma*, which states that the structure of programs is not scrambled as they execute: e.g., if a term labelled l is a component of one labeled l', then if l is still present after executing, then l' is as well and l' is still a component of l.

The compilation scheme is a function compile(V) from virgin programs to circuits. We convert V to a Joy Prime program V' (by adding labels). Consider any possible state

$P' + \eta'$ which could arise in the execution of V' in some initial state η'_0. We define *wires*$(P' + \eta')$, a state of compile(V), which we hope corresponds to the execution of $V' + \eta'_0$ which gave $P' + \eta'$. So, the proof reduces to (1) defining *wires*$(\cdot)$, and (2) showing that it indeed maps executions to executions.

Defining *wires*$(\cdot)$ requires some auxiliary definitions. The hard part of the definition is to figure out which wires should have signals on them. However, wires which have signals correspond to *active* commands in the program, which, by no coincidence, are those which either are just ready to take a step, or have just finished taking one.

Active Components Thus, we define $act(P)$, the *active components* of P, by induction. Indeed, for many cases, $act(P) = \{P\}$ — the part of the program which takes a step is P itself. We call such P's *immediately active*. For example, c! and **done** ; P_2 are immediately active; the entire term is involved in the state transition.

The inductive cases involve composite statements. For example, when one of P_1 and P_2 is not done, then any activity in $P_1 \|_C P_2$ must take place within P_1 and P_2.

$$act(P_1 \|_C P_2) = act(P_1) \cup act(P_2) \text{ if } P_1 \neq \textbf{done} \vee P_2 \neq \textbf{done} \tag{14}$$

If both are done, the Joy Prime equivalent of (7) applies, so we have

$$act(P) = \{P\} \text{ if } P = \left(\textbf{done}^{l_1 *_1} \|_C \textbf{done}^{l_2 *_2}\right)^{l_3 *_3}. \tag{15}$$

We next prove two lemmas which show that the definition of $act(P)$ is correct; they are also the main tools we use to prove bisimulation. Together, they show that the subterms we have identified as being active are in fact the ones where activity occurs. The Activity Lemma states that, if a whole program can execute, then some active component enables it to do so; the Converse Activity Lemma states that if an active component could execute in isolation, then it can still do so in the whole program. Each lemma has a second case, in which two components act simultaneously by communicating along a channel.

Lemma 4.2 (Activity Lemma) *If $P + \eta \xrightarrow{\alpha} P' + \eta'$, then either:*

1. *There is some term $Q \in act(P)$ such that $Q + \eta \xrightarrow{\alpha} Q' + \eta'$ and P' is P with Q replaced by Q'.*[2]

2. *There are two terms $Q_1, Q_2 \in act(P)$ which communicate in the step giving P'. Specifically,*

[2]In general in algebra, substituting terms for terms is somewhat dangerous; when one turns c! into **done** in the program c! ; c!, one might intend the result to be either **done** ; c!, c! ; **done**, or **done** ; **done**. This is not a problem in Joy Prime. Each subprogram of a Joy Prime program has a unique label, and so substitution of terms for terms is meaningful.

- $Q_i + \eta \xrightarrow{\beta_i} Q'_i + \eta$ *for* $i = 1, 2$;
- β_1 *is a send along some channel* c *and* β_2 *is a receive from the same channel;*
- Q_1 *and* Q_2 *occur in parallel in* P;
- P' *is* P *with* Q_1, Q_2 *replaced by* Q'_1, Q'_2 *respectively;*

Lemma 4.3 (Converse Activity Lemma) *Suppose that* $Q \in act(P)$, *and* $Q + \eta \xrightarrow{\alpha} Q' + \eta'$, *where* α *is not a communication along a channel hidden by* P. *Let* P' *be* P *with* Q *replaced by* Q'. *Then* $P + \eta \xrightarrow{\alpha} P' + \eta'$.

Similarly, suppose $Q_1, Q_2 \in act(P)$, *and* $Q_i + \eta \xrightarrow{\beta_i} Q'_i + \eta$ *where* β_1 *and* β_2 *are send and receive along some internal channel* c *of* P. *Let* P' *be* P *with* Q_1,Q_2 *replaced by* Q'_1, Q'_2. *Then* $P + \eta \xrightarrow{-} P' + \eta$.

Activated Wires For any immediately active term R, we define the set of ***wires the term makes active***, ***activates***(R). This is one of the longer definitions of the proof, as there are three dozen kinds of wires in the circuit, and somehow each of them must be made active; hence the definition has three dozen cases. A typical case is $activates\left(Q^{\upsilon l*}\right) = \{l * .r\}$; that is, when a program is ready to be executed but its execution has not started, its request line is active.

Finally, we are in a position to define *wires*(P) for all P: the wires that should correspond to the circuit being in state P are simply the wires corresponding to each immediately active subterm:

$$wires(P) = \bigcup_{R \in act(P)} activates(R) \tag{16}$$

It is also necessary to calculate the expected states of calls, which can be done by a similar but simpler syntactic analysis of terms. From this definition, we can also show the *Communication Sanity Lemma*, stating that only one process is trying to use any call-box at any given time.

Proof of Bisimulation We are now ready to apply the bisimulation methodology. We define $P + \eta \sim W + \kappa$ if $W = wires(P')$ and η and κ give the same values to all state-bearing components. We must show that $\sim$ is a bisimulation relation; that is,

1. If $P + \eta \xrightarrow{\alpha} P' + \eta'$, then $W + \kappa \xrightarrow{\alpha} W' + \kappa'$ where $P' + \eta' \sim W' + \kappa'$, and
2. If $W + \kappa \xrightarrow{\alpha} W' + \kappa'$, then $P + \eta \xrightarrow{\alpha} P' + \eta'$ where $P' + \eta' \sim W' + \kappa'$

The labels and markers of Joy Prime were painstakingly chosen to give this exact correspondence between circuit and Joy Prime execution. Both proofs are long, simple case analyses, relying heavily on the Activity and Converse Activity Lemmas.

We need one Joy Prime rule for each input to each kind of component: some fifty rules.[3] Most of the subtlety of the proof of Theorem 4.1 is in the design of Joy Prime (which corresponds roughly to an induction hypothesis), and in careful choice of supporting lemmas such as the activity and converse activity lemmas. After much development of this mathematical machinery, the body of the proof consists of some eighty straightforward cases. This establishes Theorem 4.1.

5 Notes on the Method

Some aspects of this proof are specific to Joy and circuits; in particular, the main proof has no trace of generality. However, most of the infrastructure of the proof is applicable in more generality.

5.1 Labelling SOSses

In most detailed analyses of SOS systems of all kinds, one frequently wishes to trace the evolution of a subterm of a main program. This can frequently be done by adding labels and markers of various sorts. We were not the first researchers to use this technique; the first references we are aware of are [10, 26], who used labels to investigate the local theory of the models D_∞ and $P\omega$ of the untyped λ-calculus.

When one adds labels and markers to a language, one generally adds them in such a way as to preserve the behavior of terms, or at least to change it relatively little. For example, non-virgin labels in Joy Prime do not effect the behavior of programs at all. For most program constructs, the rules for Joy Prime are simply the rules for Joy, extended to preserve labels. Such labels are good for tracing terms as they execute; this technique was used in [4, 23].

Sometimes it is desirable to use markers to control the evaluation of terms. In Joy Prime, we need to add a transition corresponding to the request line to each subterm. In the theory of the untyped λ-calculus [2, Chapter 14], one wishes to control the number of times a term may be reduced. In this case, the rules for the modified system will be similar to those of the base system, but differ in minor ways.

5.2 Active Subterms

The technical key to the proof of strong bisimulation between Joy Prime and circuits were the Activity and Converse Activity lemmas, 4.2 and 4.3. Similar lemmas appear in many places in the operational theory of programming languages; e.g., the activity lemma of [19] proves a similar result about an applied simply-typed λ-calculus, and the

[3] This may seem excessive for as simple a language as Joy. However, it is probably impossible to avoid. A proof that a circuit is correct which does not at some point validate the behavior of each wire and component is too abstract at best, and unlikely to be fully satisfactory.

methodology of [28] (which they choose to distinguish from SOS) is based on this kind of lemma.

The activity lemma is true in general, for a wide variety of languages; indeed, the lemma may be deduced and proved entirely from the rule format. Indeed, the definition of $act(P)$ may be deduced entirely from the rules. The details are beyond the scope of this study, but in Joy-like SOSses, there are three kinds of rules:

1. Primitive operations, defined by axioms: $P \xrightarrow{a} Q$ where P is an operation without subprograms, like **skip** or c!. In this case, $act(P)$ is simply $\{P\}$; any activity involving P will involve all of P.
2. Composite operations $f(P_1, \ldots, P_n)$ have two kinds of rules.
   (a) Propagation rules, such as Rule 4 and Rule 6, which run one or more subterms one step and essentially preserve the operation symbol f. In such cases, activity must take place within one one of the components that is allowed to execute: $act(f(P_1, \ldots, P_n))$ is the union of the $act(P_i)$ for which P_i appears in the antecedent of a rule. For parallel composition, this is $act(P_1) \cup act(P_2)$; for sequential composition, it is simply $act(P_1)$. Note that Rule 5 is not a propagation rule, as executing that rule causes the body of the term to change form.
   (b) Completion rules, such as Rule 5 and Rule 7, which essentially mark the end of one state in a program's execution (*e.g.*, the completion of P_1 in $P_1 ; P_2$, or the completion of two parallel processes in $P_1 \|_C P_2$). Completion rules frequently look like axioms, and indeed are treated as axioms: computation changes the shape of the entire term, and thus $act(P) = \{P\}$.

6 Conclusion

We have presented Joy, a simple yet complete programming language for circuits. We have described the implementation of Joy programs in silicon, and stated and sketched the proof that the compilation scheme is correct.

Many extensions are desirable before this will be widely useful. Joy is a fairly sparse language. There are a number of obvious extensions: variables of types other than Boolean, procedures and functions, value-bearing communication channels, modules, and so forth. We have compilation techniques for many of these extensions, and expect our correctness proof to extend straightforwardly to cover them.

References

[1] J. C. M. Baeten and W. P. Weijland. *Process Algebra.* Cambridge Tracts in Theoretical Computer Science 18. Cambridge University Press, 1990.

[2] H. P. Barendregt. *The Lambda Calculus: Its Syntax and Semantics*, volume 103 of *Studies in Logic*. North-Holland, 1981. Revised Edition, 1984.

[3] H. Bisseling, H. Eemers, M. Kamps, and A. Peeters. Designing delay-insensitive circuits. Technical report, 1990.

[4] B. Bloom. Partial traces and the semantics and logic of ccs-like languages. Technical Report 89-1066, Cornell, 1989.

[5] B. Bloom. *Ready Simulation, Bisimulation, and the Semantics of CCS-Like Languages*. PhD thesis, Massachusetts Institute of Technology, Aug. 1989.

[6] E. Brunvand and R. F. Sproull. Translating concurrent communicating programs into delay-insensitive circuits. Technical Report CMU-CS-89-126, Carnegie-Mellon University, 1989.

[7] S. M. Burns and A. J. Martin. Syntax-directed translation of concurrent programs into self-timed circuits. In *Advanced Research in VLSI: Proceedings of the 5th MIT Conference*, pages 35–50, 1988.

[8] W. A. Clark and C. E. Molnar. Macromodular computer systems. In B. Waxman and R. Stacey, editors, *Biomedical Research Vol. IV*, pages 45–85. Academic, New York.

[9] D. L. Dill. *Trace Theory for Automatic Hierarchical Verification of Speed-Independent Circuits*. MIT Press, 1989.

[10] J. Hyland. A syntactic characterization of the equality in some models of the λ-calculus. *J. London Math. Soc.*, 2(12):361–370, 1976.

[11] R. M. Keller. Towards a theory of universal speed-independent modules. *IEEE Transactions on Computers*, C-23(1):21–33, January 1974.

[12] A. J. Martin. Compiling communicating processes into delay-insensitive VLSI circuits. *Distributed Computing*, 1:226–234, 1986.

[13] G. J. Milne. *The Correctness of a Simple Silicon Compiler.*, pages 1–12. North-Holland, 1983.

[14] R. Milner. A modal characterisation of observable machine-behaviour. In E. Astesiano and C. Böhm, editors, *CAAP '81: Trees in Algebra and Programming, 6th Colloquium*, volume 112 of *Lect. Notes in Computer Sci.*, pages 25–34. Springer-Verlag, 1981.

[15] R. Milner. *Communication and Concurrency*. Prentice Hall International Series in Computer Science. Prentice Hall, New York, 1989.

[16] C. E. Molnar, T.-P. Fang, and F. U. Rosenberger. Synthesis of delay-insensitive modules. In H. Fuchs, editor, *Chapel Hill Conference on VLSI*, pages 67–86, 1985.

[17] D. Park. Concurrency and automata on infinite sequences. In P. Deussen, editor, *Theoretical Computer Science*, Lect. Notes in Computer Sci., page 261. Springer-Verlag, 1981.

[18] G. Plotkin. A structural approach to operational semantics. Technical Report DAIMI FN-19, Aarhus University, Computer Science Department, Denmark, 1981.

[19] G. D. Plotkin. LCF considered as a programming language. *Theoretical Computer Sci.*, 5(3):223–255, 1977.

[20] R. Sproull and I. E. Sutherland. *Asynchronous Systems*. Sutherland, Sproull & Associates, 1986.

[21] J. Staunstrup and M. Greenstreet. Atomicity, programs, and hardware. Technical Report ID-TR 198-46, Technical University of Denmark, 1990.

[22] M. J. F. T. S. Anantharaman, E. M. Clarke and B. Mishra. Compiling path expressions into vlsi circuits. *Distributed Computing*, 1:150–166, 1986.

[23] F. Vaandrager. On the relationship between process algebra and input/output automata. In *Sixth annual IEEE symposium on Logic in Computer Science*, pages 387–389. IEEE Computer Society Press, 1991.

[24] C. H. K. van Berkel, C. Niessen, M. Rem, and R. W. Saeijs. VLSI programming and silicon compilation; a novel approach from philips research. In *ICCD*, 1988.

[25] K. van Berkel. *Handshake Circuits: an intermediary between communicating processes and VLSI*. PhD thesis, Technische Universiteit Eindhoven, 1992.

[26] C. Wadsworth. The relation between computational and denotational properties for Scott's D_∞-models of the λ-calculus. *SIAM J. Comput.*, 5:488–521, 1976.

[27] S. Weber, B. Bloom, and G. Brown. Compiling Joy to silicon: A verified silicon compilation scheme. In T. Knight and J. Savage, editors, *Proceedings of the Advanced Research in VLSI and Parallel Systems Conference*, pages 79–98. 1992.

[28] A. K. Wright and M. Felleisen. A syntactic approach to type soundness. Technical Report TR91-160, Rice University, 1991.

Springer-Verlag and the Environment

We at Springer-Verlag firmly believe that an international science publisher has a special obligation to the environment, and our corporate policies consistently reflect this conviction.

We also expect our business partners – paper mills, printers, packaging manufacturers, etc. – to commit themselves to using environmentally friendly materials and production processes.

The paper in this book is made from low- or no-chlorine pulp and is acid free, in conformance with international standards for paper permanency.

Printing: Weihert-Druck GmbH, Darmstadt
Binding: Buchbinderei Schäffer, Grünstadt

Lecture Notes in Computer Science

For information about Vols. 1–587
please contact your bookseller or Springer-Verlag

Vol. 588: G. Sandini (Ed.), Computer Vision – ECCV '92. Proceedings. XV, 909 pages. 1992.

Vol. 589: U. Banerjee, D. Gelernter, A. Nicolau, D. Padua (Eds.), Languages and Compilers for Parallel Computing. Proceedings, 1991. IX, 419 pages. 1992.

Vol. 590: B. Fronhöfer, G. Wrightson (Eds.), Parallelization in Inference Systems. Proceedings, 1990. VIII, 372 pages. 1992. (Subseries LNAI).

Vol. 591: H. P. Zima (Ed.), Parallel Computation. Proceedings, 1991. IX, 451 pages. 1992.

Vol. 592: A. Voronkov (Ed.), Logic Programming. Proceedings, 1991. IX, 514 pages. 1992. (Subseries LNAI).

Vol. 593: P. Loucopoulos (Ed.), Advanced Information Systems Engineering. Proceedings. XI, 650 pages. 1992.

Vol. 594: B. Monien, Th. Ottmann (Eds.), Data Structures and Efficient Algorithms. VIII, 389 pages. 1992.

Vol. 595: M. Levene, The Nested Universal Relation Database Model. X, 177 pages. 1992.

Vol. 596: L.-H. Eriksson, L. Hallnäs, P. Schroeder-Heister (Eds.), Extensions of Logic Programming. Proceedings, 1991. VII, 369 pages. 1992. (Subseries LNAI).

Vol. 597: H. W. Guesgen, J. Hertzberg, A Perspective of Constraint-Based Reasoning. VIII, 123 pages. 1992. (Subseries LNAI).

Vol. 598: S. Brookes, M. Main, A. Melton, M. Mislove, D. Schmidt (Eds.), Mathematical Foundations of Programming Semantics. Proceedings, 1991. VIII, 506 pages. 1992.

Vol. 599: Th. Wetter, K.-D. Althoff, J. Boose, B. R. Gaines, M. Linster, F. Schmalhofer (Eds.), Current Developments in Knowledge Acquisition - EKAW '92. Proceedings. XIII, 444 pages. 1992. (Subseries LNAI).

Vol. 600: J. W. de Bakker, C. Huizing, W. P. de Roever, G. Rozenberg (Eds.), Real-Time: Theory in Practice. Proceedings, 1991. VIII, 723 pages. 1992.

Vol. 601: D. Dolev, Z. Galil, M. Rodeh (Eds.), Theory of Computing and Systems. Proceedings, 1992. VIII, 220 pages. 1992.

Vol. 602: I. Tomek (Ed.), Computer Assisted Learning. Proceedings, 1992. X, 615 pages. 1992.

Vol. 603: J. van Katwijk (Ed.), Ada: Moving Towards 2000. Proceedings, 1992. VIII, 324 pages. 1992.

Vol. 604: F. Belli, F.-J. Radermacher (Eds.), Industrial and Engineering Applications of Artificial Intelligence and Expert Systems. Proceedings, 1992. XV, 702 pages. 1992. (Subseries LNAI).

Vol. 605: D. Etiemble, J.-C. Syre (Eds.), PARLE '92. Parallel Architectures and Languages Europe. Proceedings, 1992. XVII, 984 pages. 1992.

Vol. 606: D. E. Knuth, Axioms and Hulls. IX, 109 pages. 1992.

Vol. 607: D. Kapur (Ed.), Automated Deduction – CADE-11. Proceedings, 1992. XV, 793 pages. 1992. (Subseries LNAI).

Vol. 608: C. Frasson, G. Gauthier, G. I. McCalla (Eds.), Intelligent Tutoring Systems. Proceedings, 1992. XIV, 686 pages. 1992.

Vol. 609: G. Rozenberg (Ed.), Advances in Petri Nets 1992. VIII, 472 pages. 1992.

Vol. 610: F. von Martial, Coordinating Plans of Autonomous Agents. XII, 246 pages. 1992. (Subseries LNAI).

Vol. 611: M. P. Papazoglou, J. Zeleznikow (Eds.), The Next Generation of Information Systems: From Data to Knowledge. VIII, 310 pages. 1992. (Subseries LNAI).

Vol. 612: M. Tokoro, O. Nierstrasz, P. Wegner (Eds.), Object-Based Concurrent Computing. Proceedings, 1991. X, 265 pages. 1992.

Vol. 613: J. P. Myers, Jr., M. J. O'Donnell (Eds.), Constructivity in Computer Science. Proceedings, 1991. X, 247 pages. 1992.

Vol. 614: R. G. Herrtwich (Ed.), Network and Operating System Support for Digital Audio and Video. Proceedings, 1991. XII, 403 pages. 1992.

Vol. 615: O. Lehrmann Madsen (Ed.), ECOOP '92. European Conference on Object Oriented Programming. Proceedings. X, 426 pages. 1992.

Vol. 616: K. Jensen (Ed.), Application and Theory of Petri Nets 1992. Proceedings, 1992. VIII, 398 pages. 1992.

Vol. 617: V. Mařík, O. Štěpánková, R. Trappl (Eds.), Advanced Topics in Artificial Intelligence. Proceedings, 1992. IX, 484 pages. 1992. (Subseries LNAI).

Vol. 618: P. M. D. Gray, R. J. Lucas (Eds.), Advanced Database Systems. Proceedings, 1992. X, 260 pages. 1992.

Vol. 619: D. Pearce, H. Wansing (Eds.), Nonclassical Logics and Information Proceedings. Proceedings, 1990. VII, 171 pages. 1992. (Subseries LNAI).

Vol. 620: A. Nerode, M. Taitslin (Eds.), Logical Foundations of Computer Science – Tver '92. Proceedings. IX, 514 pages. 1992.

Vol. 621: O. Nurmi, E. Ukkonen (Eds.), Algorithm Theory – SWAT '92. Proceedings. VIII, 434 pages. 1992.

Vol. 622: F. Schmalhofer, G. Strube, Th. Wetter (Eds.), Contemporary Knowledge Engineering and Cognition. Proceedings, 1991. XII, 258 pages. 1992. (Subseries LNAI).

Vol. 623: W. Kuich (Ed.), Automata, Languages and Programming. Proceedings, 1992. XII, 721 pages. 1992.

Vol. 624: A. Voronkov (Ed.), Logic Programming and Automated Reasoning. Proceedings, 1992. XIV, 509 pages. 1992. (Subseries LNAI).

Vol. 625: W. Vogler, Modular Construction and Partial Order Semantics of Petri Nets. IX, 252 pages. 1992.

Vol. 626: E. Börger, G. Jäger, H. Kleine Büning, M. M. Richter (Eds.), Computer Science Logic. Proceedings, 1991. VIII, 428 pages. 1992.

Vol. 628: G. Vosselman, Relational Matching. IX, 190 pages. 1992.

Vol. 629: I. M. Havel, V. Koubek (Eds.), Mathematical Foundations of Computer Science 1992. Proceedings. IX, 521 pages. 1992.

Vol. 630: W. R. Cleaveland (Ed.), CONCUR '92. Proceedings. X, 580 pages. 1992.

Vol. 631: M. Bruynooghe, M. Wirsing (Eds.), Programming Language Implementation and Logic Programming. Proceedings, 1992. XI, 492 pages. 1992.

Vol. 632: H. Kirchner, G. Levi (Eds.), Algebraic and Logic Programming. Proceedings, 1992. IX, 457 pages. 1992.

Vol. 633: D. Pearce, G. Wagner (Eds.), Logics in AI. Proceedings. VIII, 410 pages. 1992. (Subseries LNAI).

Vol. 634: L. Bougé, M. Cosnard, Y. Robert, D. Trystram (Eds.), Parallel Processing: CONPAR 92 – VAPP V. Proceedings. XVII, 853 pages. 1992.

Vol. 635: J. C. Derniame (Ed.), Software Process Technology. Proceedings, 1992. VIII, 253 pages. 1992.

Vol. 636: G. Comyn, N. E. Fuchs, M. J. Ratcliffe (Eds.), Logic Programming in Action. Proceedings, 1992. X, 324 pages. 1992. (Subseries LNAI).

Vol. 637: Y. Bekkers, J. Cohen (Eds.), Memory Management. Proceedings, 1992. XI, 525 pages. 1992.

Vol. 639: A. U. Frank, I. Campari, U. Formentini (Eds.), Theories and Methods of Spatio-Temporal Reasoning in Geographic Space. Proceedings, 1992. XI, 431 pages. 1992.

Vol. 640: C. Sledge (Ed.), Software Engineering Education. Proceedings, 1992. X, 451 pages. 1992.

Vol. 641: U. Kastens, P. Pfahler (Eds.), Compiler Construction. Proceedings, 1992. VIII, 320 pages. 1992.

Vol. 642: K. P. Jantke (Ed.), Analogical and Inductive Inference. Proceedings, 1992. VIII, 319 pages. 1992. (Subseries LNAI).

Vol. 643: A. Habel, Hyperedge Replacement: Grammars and Languages. X, 214 pages. 1992.

Vol. 644: A. Apostolico, M. Crochemore, Z. Galil, U. Manber (Eds.), Combinatorial Pattern Matching. Proceedings, 1992. X, 287 pages. 1992.

Vol. 645: G. Pernul, A M. Tjoa (Eds.), Entity-Relationship Approach – ER '92. Proceedings, 1992. XI, 439 pages, 1992.

Vol. 646: J. Biskup, R. Hull (Eds.), Database Theory – ICDT '92. Proceedings, 1992. IX, 449 pages. 1992.

Vol. 647: A. Segall, S. Zaks (Eds.), Distributed Algorithms. X, 380 pages. 1992.

Vol. 648: Y. Deswarte, G. Eizenberg, J.-J. Quisquater (Eds.), Computer Security – ESORICS 92. Proceedings. XI, 451 pages. 1992.

Vol. 649: A. Pettorossi (Ed.), Meta-Programming in Logic. Proceedings, 1992. XII, 535 pages. 1992.

Vol. 650: T. Ibaraki, Y. Inagaki, K. Iwama, T. Nishizeki, M. Yamashita (Eds.), Algorithms and Computation. Proceedings, 1992. XI, 510 pages. 1992.

Vol. 651: R. Koymans, Specifying Message Passing and Time-Critical Systems with Temporal Logic. IX, 164 pages. 1992.

Vol. 652: R. Shyamasundar (Ed.), Foundations of Software Technology and Theoretical Computer Science. Proceedings, 1992. XIII, 405 pages. 1992.

Vol. 653: A. Bensoussan, J.-P. Verjus (Eds.), Future Tendencies in Computer Science, Control and Applied Mathematics. Proceedings, 1992. XV, 371 pages. 1992.

Vol. 654: A. Nakamura, M. Nivat, A. Saoudi, P. S. P. Wang, K. Inoue (Eds.), Prallel Image Analysis. Proceedings, 1992. VIII, 312 pages. 1992.

Vol. 655: M. Bidoit, C. Choppy (Eds.), Recent Trends in Data Type Specification. X, 344 pages. 1993.

Vol. 656: M. Rusinowitch, J. L. Rémy (Eds.), Conditional Term Rewriting Systems. Proceedings, 1992. XI, 501 pages. 1993.

Vol. 657: E. W. Mayr (Ed.), Graph-Theoretic Concepts in Computer Science. Proceedings, 1992. VIII, 350 pages. 1993.

Vol. 658: R. A. Rueppel (Ed.), Advances in Cryptology – EUROCRYPT '92. Proceedings, 1992. X, 493 pages. 1993.

Vol. 659: G. Brewka, K. P. Jantke, P. H. Schmitt (Eds.), Nonmonotonic and Inductive Logic. Proceedings, 1991. VIII, 332 pages. 1993. (Subseries LNAI).

Vol. 660: E. Lamma, P. Mello (Eds.), Extensions of Logic Programming. Proceedings, 1992. VIII, 417 pages. 1993. (Subseries LNAI).

Vol. 661: S. J. Hanson, W. Remmele, R. L. Rivest (Eds.), Machine Learning: From Theory to Applications. VIII, 271 pages. 1993.

Vol. 662: M. Nitzberg, D. Mumford, T. Shiota, Filtering, Segmentation and Depth. VIII, 143 pages. 1993.

Vol. 663: G. v. Bochmann, D. K. Probst (Eds.), Computer Aided Verification. Proceedings, 1992. IX, 422 pages. 1993.

Vol. 664: M. Bezem, J. F. Groote (Eds.), Typed Lambda Calculi and Applications. Proceedings, 1993. VIII, 433 pages. 1993.

Vol. 665: P. Enjalbert, A. Finkel, K. W. Wagner (Eds.), STACS 93. Proceedings, 1993. XIV, 724 pages. 1993.

Vol. 666: J. W. de Bakker, W. P. de Roever, G. Rozenberg (Eds.), Semantics: Foundations and Applications. Proceedings, 1992. VIII, 659 pages. 1993.

Vol. 667: P. B. Brazdil (Ed.), Machine Learning: ECML – 93. Proceedings, 1993. XII, 471 pages. 1993. (Subseries LNAI).